EDITION 9

CRIMINAL JUSTICE

IN AMERICA

GEORGE F. COLE

University of Connecticut

CHRISTOPHER E. SMITH

Michigan State University

CHRISTINA DEJONG

Michigan State University

CENGAGE
Learning·

Australia · Brazil · Mexico · Singapore · United Kingdom · United States

***Criminal Justice in America,* Ninth Edition**
George F. Cole, Christopher E. Smith, and
Christina DeJong

Senior Product Director: Marta Lee-Perriard

Senior Product Manager: Carolyn Henderson
    Meier

Senior Content Developer: Shelley Murphy

Product Assistant: Timothy Kappler

Marketing Director: Mark Linton

Senior Content Project Manager: Christy Frame

Senior Art Director: Helen Bruno

Senior Manufacturing Planner: Judy Inouye

Production Service: Greg Hubit Bookworks

Photo Development Editor: Sarah Evertson

Photo Researcher: Manojkiran Chander, Lumina
    Datamatics

Text Researcher: Ramya Selvaraj, Lumina
    Datamatics

Copy Editor: Carrie Crompton

Proofreader: Marne Evans

Indexer: Edwin Durbin

Text Designer: Diane Beasley

Cover Designer: Helen Bruno

Cover Image: Eagle: Steve Collender/Shutter-
    stock; Police officer: iStockPhoto.com/Jeff
    Griffin; Courthouse: iStockPhoto.com/Pierre
    Desrosiers; Inmate: iStockPhoto.com/ftwitty

Compositor: MPS Limited

For product information and technology assistance, contact us at
Cengage Learning Customer & Sales Support, 1-800-354-9706.

For permission to use material from this text or product,
submit all requests online at **www.cengage.com/permissions.**
Further permissions questions can be e-mailed to
permissionrequest@cengage.com.

Library of Congress Control Number: 2016941674

Student Edition:
ISBN: 978-1-305-96606-2

Loose-leaf Edition:
ISBN: 978-1-305-96617-8

Cengage Learning
20 Channel Center Street
Boston, MA 02210
USA

Cengage Learning is a leading provider of customized learning solutions with
employees residing in nearly 40 different countries and sales in more than 125
countries around the world. Find your local representative at
www.cengage.com.

Cengage Learning products are represented in Canada by Nelson Education, Ltd.

To learn more about Cengage Learning Solutions, visit **www.cengage.com.**
Purchase any of our products at your local college store or at our preferred
online store **www.cengagebrain.com.**

Printed in the United States of America
Print Number: 01   Print Year: 2016

Brief Contents

Contents

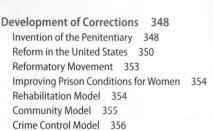

15 | Juvenile Justice   519

Features

CURRENT CONTROVERSIES IN CRIMINAL JUSTICE

THE CRIMINAL JUSTICE PROCESS

Cases Cited

Preface

Criminal Justice in America, Ninth Edition, is designed for instructors seeking a textbook that provides students a thorough introduction to the dynamics of the American system of criminal justice without overwhelming them. The text is an offspring of *The American System of Criminal Justice*, which has been used by more than half a million students over the course of its 15 editions. But much has changed in the 30 years since the first edition of *The American System of Criminal Justice* was published. And that is exactly why we created *Criminal Justice in America*— a briefer, more applied, student-centered introduction to the American system of criminal justice. In creating this text, we did not merely drop a few chapters, combine others, and limit the graphic elements to reduce page count, however. We started from scratch. So, while *Criminal Justice in America* relies on the research and conceptual framework of the larger text, it is not overly theoretical; throughout the book, examples from today's headlines are used to link the concepts and information to real-life criminal justice situations. And while the focus of *Criminal Justice in America* is just as interdisciplinary as the comprehensive book's focus is, it is less encyclopedic and benefits from added policy controversies and legal coverage; skill-building writing exercises; and up-to-the-minute coverage of technology, terrorism, homeland security, cybercrime, evidence-based practices, and other current topics.

The Approach of This Text

Three key assumptions about the nature of American criminal justice as a discipline and the way the introductory course should be taught run throughout the book.

1. *Criminal justice involves public policies* that are developed within the political framework of the democratic process.
2. *The concept of social system is an essential tool* for explaining and analyzing the way criminal justice is administered and practiced.
3. *American values provide the foundation on which criminal justice is based.*

With concerns about terrorism and civil liberties at the forefront of the national agenda, basic American values—individual liberty, equality, fairness, and the rule of law—need to be emphasized.

This book's approach has met with a high degree of acceptance and might be called the dominant paradigm in criminal justice education. Criminal justice is interdisciplinary, with criminology, sociology, law, history, psychology, and political science contributing to the field. The three themes of public policy, social system, and American values help place the research contributions of these disciplines in a context that allows students to better understand the dynamics of criminal justice.

Organization

The Ninth Edition is organized to introduce important fundamental concepts, use those concepts in presenting the important institutional segments of the justice system (police, courts, corrections), and then highlight important contemporary issues concerning reentry from prison, the use of technology, and juvenile justice. The organization of the book is designed to provide comprehensive coverage of the criminal justice system that follows an appropriate sequence, stimulates student interest, and illuminates contemporary issues and problems. The 15-chapter structure of the book creates an opportunity for instructors to move at a steady pace of approximately one chapter per week in the typical length of an academic semester.

Part One of the Ninth Edition presents three chapters that introduce core concepts of the criminal justice system, describe the nature and extent of crime, and supply a framework for understanding the role of law in defining crime and protecting individuals' rights.

Three chapters on police compose Part Two. Here the Ninth Edition builds upon the core concepts in Part One to describe and examine the history, functions, and organization of policing. One chapter examines contemporary issues affecting police, including choices about patrol strategies and delivery of services, the challenges of homeland security, and the increasing importance of private security. The legal issues surrounding police authority to conduct searches and question suspects are covered in a separate chapter. Part Two also examines issues concerning civic accountability and the abuse of police authority.

The focus of the chapters in Part Three is on the courts, plea bargaining, and adjudication. One chapter discusses the important roles of judges, prosecutors, and defense attorneys. Other chapters examine the bail process, plea bargaining, and trials. The final chapter in Part Three describes the sentencing process, including the forms and purposes of punishment.

Part Four concerns corrections, and includes material on corrections history and prisoners' rights. One chapter covers detailed aspects of incarceration and prison society. A separate chapter presents probation and intermediate sanctions.

Part Five covers special issues in criminal justice, and the chapter on reentry and parole completes the community corrections coverage introduced in the final chapter of Part Four. A separate chapter reveals the rapid changes in use of technology by all institutions within the criminal justice system. The final chapter examines juvenile justice and contemporary debates about appropriate punishment and treatment for youthful offenders.

New to the Ninth Edition

This edition encompasses important revisions in content and presentation. Users of the Ninth Edition will find many significant changes. In particular, we have expanded our coverage of contemporary controversies, especially those concerning police use of force, aggressive anticrime strategies, and renewed public attention to concerns about racial disparities and discrimination. There are now features in each chapter that challenge students to place themselves into the roles of justice system officials—police officers, prosecutors, and judges—and to make decisions about actual situations that have arisen in cities around the country. Topically, there is new coverage of racial profiling by police, gun control, police training, human trafficking, bail reform, the privatization of prisons, the use of technology, and solitary confinement. Amid significant budget cuts affecting criminal justice agencies at all levels of government, we have integrated discussions of the impacts of these budget reductions into topics concerning actors and agencies across the justice system. In addition, new topics are covered in the "Close Up," "The Policy Debate," and "Evidence-Based Practice and Policy" boxes, which focus on contemporary issues such as asset forfeiture, police body cameras, police training on implicit bias, police policies on use of force, and evidence-based practices in probation. The remainder of this section outlines the major content changes in the book and then examines the elements in each chapter that are new to this Ninth Edition.

Enhanced Coverage

Highly Publicized, Contemporary Issues Among the most significant developments affecting the justice system are contemporary controversies that have captured the public's attention through heavy news media coverage. In particular, key events in 2014 and 2015 included videotaped incidents of police officers' use of force, especially white officers' actions leading to the deaths of African American suspects. Incidents such as those in Ferguson, Missouri; New York City; Cleveland, Ohio; North Charleston, South Carolina; and Baltimore led to large-scale public protests, and the civil disorder in Ferguson and Baltimore resulted in extensive property damage and arrests. These incidents brought into sharp focus debates about use of force, police–community relations, and discrimination in the justice system. In order to highlight and examine these and other issues, we introduce a new feature, "Current Controversies in Criminal Justice." The focus on current controversies is used to illuminate aspects of each segment of the system, from policing to courts to corrections to juvenile justice. Several of these features concern police use of force and police–community relations. For example, one examines the consequences of aggressive, racially skewed stop-and-frisk practices. Others focus on issues elsewhere in the justice system, such as the "Ban the Box" movement to help ex-prisoners avoid having their job applications summarily rejected regardless of their qualifications.

Additional Opportunities to Develop Students' Analytical Skills A new feature in each chapter entitled "You Make the Decision" places students in the role of decision makers as they analyze how they would address specific problems and situations. These scenarios include the FBI Director dealing with armed people occupying federal property, a state legislator considering new laws, and a police officer deciding whether to make a stop-and-frisk search. The decision-making challenges also focus on issues in courts and corrections, such as a prosecutor considering plea agreement options and a warden addressing problems with corrections officers' use of force. After analyzing a given situation and arriving at their own decisions, students are directed to look online to learn what happened in the specific contemporary situation that provided the basis for the example in the feature.

Proposals for Reform of the Justice System In recent decades, the primary focus of the justice system has been on crime control and punishment. The past few years, however, have seen a shift toward concerns about the effectiveness and costs of policies and practices in criminal justice. There is greater recognition among policy makers about the high financial costs of incarceration and the significant societal costs of failing to prepare offenders for reintegration into society. In addition, social media and the proliferation of shared photos and videos have highlighted questions about police practices and fairness in the justice system in ways that have heightened public awareness and concern. Throughout the Ninth Edition, there are examples of reform initiatives and proposals intended to increase fairness, enhance effectiveness, and limit budgetary expenditures in criminal justice. Such initiatives include President Obama's task force on police reform, proposals for police officers to wear body cameras, and the U.S. Department of Justice's investigation of the city of Ferguson for using its justice system to increase revenue for its budget. Other contemporary reform issues include new training proposals to reduce police use of force, changes in asset forfeiture practices, and the debates over the use of solitary confinement.

Expanded Coverage of Technology and Cybercrime Rapidly expanding methods of cybercrime are imposing extraordinarily significant costs on governments, businesses, and individuals worldwide. To fully understand the ramifications of this misuse of technology, criminal justice students need to be aware of the challenges in addressing forms of criminal behavior that are continuously shifting and adapting with each technological innovation. In addition, law enforcement officials are incorporating new technologies to combat crime, including aerial drones, police departments' use of military equipment, and GPS monitoring of parolees. These developments also raise questions about people's rights and privacy interests as justice system agencies use new devices for surveillance and monitoring.

Chapter-by-Chapter Changes

- **Chapter 1,** "The Criminal Justice System," opens with a new vignette concerning the 2015 trial of former television actor Dustin Diamond, who was accused of using a knife to injure a man during an altercation at a bar. The case illustrates the steps in the criminal justice process, from police questioning of the suspect to bail to trial and sentencing. The new "You Make the Decision" feature places students in the position of an FBI director who must decide how to deal with armed people occupying federal property during a protest. The "Current Controversies in Criminal Justice" feature examines whether and when it is proper to criticize police officers amid many debates about whether police are being unfairly targeted by critics. There is expanded coverage of racial profiling, including a new "Close Up" with a first-person account of aggressive stop-and-frisk procedures from the perspective of a white father observing the experiences of his biracial son. A new "Question of Ethics" feature examines different sentences imposed on a husband and wife who were both involved in the same child sex-abuse crimes.

- **Chapter 2,** "Crime and Crime Causation," offers a new vignette concerning the shooting at Seattle Pacific University as well as a separate case of a wealthy man who embezzled money from a charitable foundation in Maine. These examples raise questions about the causes of crime and illuminate issues about how we define and treat victims of crime. The chapter contains expanded material on human trafficking, cybercrime, and sexual violence. The "You Make the Decision" feature casts students as state legislators who must consider whether it should be a crime to have sex with an underage teenager when the teen victim has misled the suspect about her age. The "Current Controversies in Criminal Justice" feature examines how terrorism—including domestic terrorism, unrelated to events in other countries—is characterized and defined in the United States. A new "Close Up" explores the polluted drinking water in Flint, Michigan, considering possible behavioral implications from children's exposure to lead in the water as well as possible criminal liability for decisions and errors that led to the toxic minerals coming into people's homes through their water pipes.

- **Chapter 3,** "Criminal Justice and the Rule of Law," presents a new chapter opener that highlights three different insanity-defense murder cases in Iowa in 2013 and 2014. Two of the individuals were found not guilty by reason of insanity and sent to mental institutions; it is uncertain whether they will ever be eventually released. The third, a teenager whose insanity defense failed, was convicted of second-degree murder and will probably eventually be released from custody. The "Policy Debate" presents updated information from 2015 and 2016 concerning executive action on gun control and the latest judicial decisions concerning the Second Amendment. Elsewhere in the chapter there is attention to the Supreme Court's recent decision limiting the use of trained drug-sniffing dogs during traffic stops (*Rodriguez v. United States*, 2015). The new "Current Controversies in Criminal Justice" focuses on racial disparities in police stops of pedestrians and drivers. A related "You Make the Decision" feature places students in the position of a police officer who must decide whether there is a sufficient factual basis for a stop-and-frisk search. The new "Question of Ethics" concerns the Supreme Court's decision in *Heien v. North Carolina*

(2014) that permits the acceptance of evidence from vehicle searches in cases where police have mistakenly stopped a driver who did not actually violate a state traffic law. The chapter also raises the issue of uncertainty about future decisions by the Supreme Court in light of the February 2016 death of Justice Antonin Scalia.

- **Chapter 4,** "Police," opens with the 2014 shooting of two Pennsylvania State Police troopers and the 48-day manhunt that followed to catch the survivalist, hiding in the woods, who was responsible for the shooting. This vignette effectively illustrates the unexpected dangers that law enforcement officers face every day. The chapter contains new material on evidence-based policing research that calls on police to prioritize crime prevention rather than arrests and to take more seriously the reactions of citizens, since officers depend on the cooperation and assistance of community members in order to succeed in their jobs. A new "Evidence-Based Practice and Policy" feature illuminates the use of psychology research for training officers about implicit bias as a means to reduce discriminatory law enforcement actions. The new "Close Up" discusses an emerging emphasis on de-escalation training for police officers in an effort to reduce the use lethal force. This emphasis emerged as a result of the Ferguson, Missouri, protests and other incidents involving the deaths of unarmed or mentally ill citizens at the hands of police officers. The "Current Controversies in Criminal Justice" feature describes the recommendations of President Obama's Task Force on 21st Century Policing that investigated police reform in the aftermath of police shootings and public protests around the country. The "You Make the Decision" feature places students in the role of a police chief who must consider ways to reform policy and practice in light of recent events that triggered protests.

- **Chapter 5,** "Policing: Contemporary Issues and Challenges," presents a new opening vignette concerning public demonstrations, property damage, and confrontations between protesters and police in Ferguson, Missouri, in the aftermath of the grand jury's decision in the Michael Brown shooting case. A new "Close Up" feature examines 30 proposed principles on police use of force issued by the Police Executive Research Forum. The "Current Controversies in Criminal Justice" discusses issues with a "police code of silence" that were revealed by police shootings in Chicago and South Carolina. The new "Policy Debate" discusses the use of police body cameras. There is additional new material on lawsuits against police and the movement away from aggressive stop-and-frisk practices. The "Question of Ethics" feature raises questions about how police supervisors should have handled situations in which officers were shown to have beaten suspects who were immobilized on the ground.

- **Chapter 6,** "Police and Law," opens with the Supreme Court decision in *Riley v. California* (2014) clarifying that police officers do not have the authority to conduct warrantless examinations of the contents of cell phones as part of searches incident to a lawful arrest. The new "Current Controversies in Criminal Justice" concerns the highly debated issue of whether the Apple computer company should help the FBI access the contents of a locked cell phone owned by a terrorism suspect killed after a shooting incident. The case raised issues about citizens' privacy and the risk that government officials would gain the means to access private information from innocent citizens as well as criminal suspects. There are new examples of legal issues, such as the debate over providing *Miranda* warnings to terrorism suspects and the use of the exclusionary rule in the case of the man who provided the heroin involved in the fatal overdose taken by actor Phillip Seymour Hoffman. "You Make the Decision" challenges students to decide whether a police officer should stop questioning when a suspect makes a vague response concerning his right to remain silent. The new "Question of Ethics" points to cases of police officers seizing drivers' cell phones in order to steal embarrassing photos of female drivers that are then shared among police officers.

- **Chapter 7,** "Courts and Adjudication," has a new opening vignette about the 2015 murder trial of former NFL football star Aaron Hernandez, highlighting the strategies of the prosecutor and the defense attorney. The prosecutor granted immunity to the defendant's fiancée so that she would testify, and the defense attorney raised issues about potentially sloppy police work in gathering evidence. "You Make Decision" places students in the role of a prosecutor advising police about whether they have enough evidence to constitute "probable cause" in order to seek a search warrant. There is new material on debates concerning the adequacy of voters' knowledge about judicial candidates. The new "Current Controversies in Criminal Justice" examines the dispute concerning whether the prosecutor in Ferguson, Missouri, properly handled the grand jury proceeding in the aftermath of the Michael Brown shooting. The new "Question of Ethics" concerns prosecutors' opposition to using newly developed DNA testing methods on preserved evidence from already-completed cases.
- **Chapter 8,** "Pretrial Procedures, Plea Bargaining, and the Criminal Trial," uses an opening scenario that focuses on the 2015 trial of a Harvard-bound senior at a prestigious New England prep school who was accused of sexual assault. He turned down the offer of a plea agreement and went to trial on the charges, thereby illustrating many aspects of pretrial procedures and trials. There is new material on the impact of bail on the poor, including examples of recent deaths of detainees who likely would be alive if not for their inability to make bail for minor offenses. In addition, there are examples of efforts to reform bail, including proposals to end the use of cash bail for minor offenses. "You Make the Decision" examines a prosecutor's decisions on charging and plea bargaining in a case of a high school senior who baked hashish into brownies and took them to school. "Current Controversies in Criminal Justice" discusses the use of vouchers to enable indigent criminal defendants to select and pay their own defense attorneys. The new "Question of Ethics" concerns a man who ended up with a 50-year sentence after his defense attorney advised him to refuse a plea agreement that offered a sentence of 30 years in prison.
- **Chapter 9,** "Punishment and Sentencing," begins with a comparison of recent sentences from various states imposed on teachers convicted of having sexual relationships with underage students. The sentences range from 10 days in jail to 20 years in prison. They illustrate differences in state laws, discretionary decisions, and local legal culture and courtroom workgroups. A new "Evidence-Based Practice and Policy" topic focuses on sentencing approaches that consider how to reduce the risk of reoffending. The "Close Up" focuses on the 2013 sentences imposed in the high-profile tax crime cases of singer Lauryn Hill and actor Stephen Baldwin. The significant differences in their sentences serve to illuminate several issues about severity and fairness in sentencing. The "Current Controversies in Criminal Justice" feature focuses on the U.S. Department of Justice's report on Ferguson, Missouri, where the city government used unfair and racially discriminatory practices to generate revenue for the city by making needless arrests and escalating fines on poor people. "You Make the Decision" concerns a U.S. Supreme Court decision examining whether a state judge can participate in a case after having been the head of the prosecutor's office when the case was at the trial stage. There is also new information on such topics as the "good time" policy in federal prisons and U.S. Supreme Court decisions concerning capital punishment.
- **Chapter 10,** "Corrections," presents a new "Evidence-Based Practice and Policy" topic that examines the challenges jails face in addressing the mental health needs of detainees. A new "Current Controversies in Criminal Justice" focuses on the issue of costs imposed on prisoners' loved ones for phone calls—an issue that creates a tension between states' desire for revenue and their objective of facilitating contact between prisoners and families for rehabilitation and reentry purposes. The "You Make the Decision" feature places students in the role of a federal judge examining a jail's restrictive policy on correspondence.

There is new material on the right of prisoners to practice their religion under the Religious Land Use and Institutionalized Persons Act, including a "Close Up" that features the 2015 Supreme Court decision (*Holt v. Hobbs*) unanimously endorsing a Muslim prisoner's right to grow a short beard.

- **Chapter 11,** "Incarceration and Prison Society," begins with a new chapter opener on the shocking news reports in 2015 about corrections officers' abuse of detainees and prisoners at New York City's Rikers Island jail, as well as the criminal charges against officers for viciously beating a prisoner at New York's Attica prison. There is new material on such topics as the escalating costs of incarcerating elderly prisoners, the smuggling of cell phones into prisons, the Prison Rape Elimination Act, and expanded discussion of educational and vocational programs. The new "Policy Debate" focuses on whether federal financial aid should support prisoners seeking college degrees while they are incarcerated. "You Make the Decision" places the student in the position of a warden considering how to reduce the risk of staff members using excessive force. "Current Controversies in Criminal Justice" examines the risks and problems of private contractors' employees providing services in prisons and interacting with prisoners in inappropriate ways.

- **Chapter 12,** "Probation and Intermediate Sanctions" presents a new chapter opener highlighting the 2014 arrest of singer Justin Bieber and questions whether his fame and fortune resulted in a more lenient punishment than would have been levied on other offenders. There is new material about ways to assess the risk of probationers committing new crimes and their specific needs for supervision and services. The "Evidence-Based Practice and Policy" feature concerns elements of California's probation practices, including targeted interventions for probationers, as featured in a report by the National Institute of Corrections. The "Close Up" illuminates problems with the use of profit-seeking private companies to administer county probation operations. "You Make the Decision" asks students to consider a probation revocation decision for a prominent local politician who traveled outside the geographic area permitted by his probation restrictions, and made excuses for flunking a drug test. The "Current Controversies in Criminal Justice" feature discusses debates about asset forfeiture and recent federal actions to reduce the national government's facilitation of property and cash seizures by local police. A new "Question of Ethics" example highlights the problem of probation officers accepting bribes and raises questions about the need for greater attention to the hiring and training of probation officers.

- **Chapter 13,** "Reentry into the Community" presents a new chapter opener that highlights increased interest in reentry as evidenced by the U.S. Department of Justice's designation of a week in April 2016 as "National Reentry Week." In "What Americans Think," a 2016 poll shows Americans' support for rehabilitation and the removal of barriers to employment by released prisoners. The "You Make the Decision" asks whether parole should be granted to a man who has served many decades in prison for a murder he committed while a teenager. "Current Controversies in Criminal Justice" discusses the expanding "Ban the Box" movement to remove questions about criminal records from job application forms. The new "Question of Ethics" highlights the desirability—and difficulties—of siting community corrections facilities in residential neighborhoods.

- **Chapter 14,** "Technology and Criminal Justice," presents a new opening vignette concerning the use of a police robot to examine and remove what appeared to be an explosive vest from a handcuffed robbery suspect. There is new information on such topics as counterfeit products, the kinds of information available to police through technology in patrol vehicles, the problem of untested rape kits, and biased testimony by crime laboratory scientists. There is a discussion of the Supreme Court's decision in *Riley v. California* (2014), which bars police officers from making warrantless examinations of digital content on cell phones after an arrest made during a traffic stop. "You Make the Decision" highlights privacy issues related to new handheld radar devices that police officers can use to "see" the presence of people through walls. The "Policy Debate" illuminates disagreements about police departments' use of aerial drones. "New Controversies in Criminal Justice" discusses the use of surplus military equipment by police departments, an issue brought to public attention by the weapons and gear used in response to protests in Ferguson, Missouri. The "Evidence-Based Practice and Policy" feature concerns the use of GPS technology to monitor parolees. A new "Question of Ethics" concerns individual police officers' efforts to turn off or damage cameras that might record improper actions by the officer.

- **Chapter 15,** "Juvenile Justice," provides a new opening vignette about a Massachusetts teen who faced manslaughter charges for allegedly encouraging her boyfriend to commit suicide. There is expanded discussion of the use of pepper spray in juvenile detention facilities, research on gang violence, and the Prison Rape Elimination Act. "You Make the Decision" addresses the decisions prosecutors must make about whether to try teens as adults for violent crimes. The "Evidence-Based Practice and Policy" feature highlights diversion programs for youthful offenders. The "Close Up" and "Policy Debate" features examine corrections issues, including the use of solitary confinement and the incarceration of juveniles in facilities for adult offenders. "Current Controversies in Criminal Justice" discusses cyberbullying and sexting, with questions about whether such behavior among teens should be addressed through the criminal justice system.

Study and Review Aids

To help students identify and master core concepts, *Criminal Justice in America* provides several study and review aids in each chapter:

- *Chapter outlines* preview the structure of each chapter.
- *Opening vignettes* introduce the chapter topic with a high-interest, real-life case or a discussion of a major contemporary policy issue, enhancing the book's relevancy for today's student.
- *Learning Objectives* highlight the chapter's key topics and themes and serve as a road map for readers.
- *Check Points* throughout each chapter allow students to test themselves on content and get immediate feedback to help them assess their understanding of concepts as they progress through the chapter.
- End-of-chapter *Summaries* and *Questions for Review* reinforce key concepts and provide further checks on learning.
- *Key Terms and Cases* are listed at the end of each chapter; these are defined throughout the text in the margins and included in the Glossary.

Promoting Understanding

Aided by the features just described, diligent students can master the essential content of the introductory course. While such mastery is no small achievement, most instructors aim higher. They want students to complete this course with the ability to take a more thoughtful and critical approach to issues of crime and justice. *Criminal Justice in America*, Ninth Edition, provides several features that help students learn how to think about the field.

- **Stop & Analyze** This feature follows each set of Check Point critical thinking questions and asks students to concretely articulate arguments and analytical conclusions about issues relevant to the preceding section of the text.

- **Close Ups and Other Real-Life Examples** Understanding criminal justice in a purely theoretical way does not give students a balanced understanding of the field. The wealth of examples in this book shows how theory plays out in practice and what the human implications of policies and procedures are. In addition to the many illustrations in the text, the "Close Up" features in each chapter draw on newspaper articles, court decisions, first-person accounts, and other current sources.

- **A Question of Ethics: Think, Discuss, Write** In the criminal justice system, decisions must be made within the framework of law but also be consistent with the ethical norms of American society. At the end of each chapter, completely revamped boxes entitled "A Question of Ethics: Think, Discuss, Write" use actual news reports on the justice system to place students in the context of decision makers faced with a problem involving ethics. Students become aware of the many ethical dilemmas that criminal justice personnel must deal with and the types of questions they may have to answer if they assume a role in the system. Moreover, they are challenged to offer solutions that administrators might employ in using training, supervision, or other approaches to reduce behavior problems by justice system employees.

- **Evidence-Based Practice and Policy** The most significant and expanding development in criminal justice today is the effort to identify and implement policies and practices that are based on the results of high-quality research. These new boxed features throughout the book highlight the opportunities and challenges of applying evidence-based approaches to policing, courts, and corrections. Each feature challenges students to consider the impediments to implementation, as practitioners may not wish to change their customary methods or they may adhere to beliefs about effective policies that are not supported by research studies.

- **What Americans Think** Public opinion plays an important role in the policy-making process in a democracy. Therefore, we present the opinions of Americans on controversial criminal justice issues, as collected through surveys.

- **The Policy Debate** In each chapter, we describe an issue such as aggressive policing or the death penalty, outline its pros and cons, and then ask students to decide which policy they think the United States should adopt. This teaching tool helps develop students' critical thinking skills.

- **Current Controversies in Criminal Justice** This new feature in each chapter highlights a contemporary issue that poses a challenge for the justice system. Topics include racial profiling, police officers' use of lethal force, police reform proposals, and solitary confinement for juvenile offenders. Students have the opportunity to analyze the difficult questions that arise from highly debated issues and events they have heard about through news reports. The features provide a basis for students to identify factual issues and apply analytical skills to topics that are often the focus of simplistic, ideological characterizations and debates.

- **Criminal Justice: Myth & Reality** Through the examination of widely held beliefs about criminal justice, students can look critically at the actual complexity or unexpected consequences of various policies and practices. Students are encouraged to question their own assumptions and seek information before drawing conclusions.

- **You Make the Decision** Drawing from actual recent events, these new features place students in the position of a specific decision maker in the criminal justice system. Students confront difficult decisions, such as whether to undertake a stop-and-frisk search, offer a particular plea agreement to a defendant, or change policies and training to reduce excessive use of force by corrections officers. These features are designed to engage and challenge students while building their knowledge about contemporary issues and enhancing their analytical skills.

- **Inside the Criminal Justice System & Beyond** Many students have limited first-hand knowledge of what it is like to be "processed" by the criminal justice system. A hallmark of *Criminal Justice in America* is this essay by Chuck Terry that is presented on the book's companion website. Terry, a college professor and criminal justice scholar, served time in prison for drug offenses as a young man. Terry's moving story provides a rare insider's look at the steps in the criminal justice process.

SUPPLEMENTS

MindTap® for *Introduction to Criminal Justice* The most applied learning experience available, MindTap is dedicated to preparing students to make the kinds of reasoned decisions required as criminal justice professionals faced with real-world challenges. Available for virtually every Criminal Justice course, MindTap offers customizable content, course analytics, an e-reader, and more—all within your current learning management system. With its rich array of assets—video cases, interactive visual summaries, decision-making scenarios, quizzes, and writing skill builders—MindTap is perfectly suited to today's Criminal Justice students, engaging them, guiding them toward mastery of basic concepts, and advancing their critical thinking abilities.

Instructor's Manual with Lesson Plans The manual includes learning objectives, key terms, a detailed chapter outline, a chapter summary, lesson plans, discussion topics, student activities, "what if" scenarios, media tools, and sample syllabi. The learning objectives are correlated with the discussion topics, student activities, and media tools.

Downloadable Word Test Bank The enhanced test bank includes a variety of questions per chapter—a combination of multiple-choice, true/false, completion, essay, and critical thinking formats, with a full answer key. The test bank is coded to the learning objectives that appear in the main text, and identifies where in the text (by section) the answer appears. Finally, each question in the test bank has been carefully reviewed by experienced criminal justice instructors for quality, accuracy, and content coverage so instructors can be sure they are working with an assessment and grading resource of the highest caliber.

Cengage Learning Testing Powered by Cognero, the accompanying assessment tool is a flexible, online system that allows you to:

- import, edit, and manipulate test bank content from the text's test bank or elsewhere, including your own favorite test questions
- create ideal assessments with your choice of 15 question types (including true/false, multiple choice, opinion scale/Likert, and essay)
- create multiple test versions using an instant using drop-down menus and familiar, intuitive tools that take you through content creation and management with ease
- deliver tests from your LMS, your classroom, or wherever you want, as well as import and export content into other systems as needed.

Online PowerPoint® Lectures Helping you make your lectures more engaging while effectively reaching your visually oriented students, these handy Microsoft PowerPoint slides outline the chapters of the main text in a classroom-ready presentation. The PowerPoint slides reflect the content and organization of the new edition of the text and feature some additional examples and real-world cases for application and discussion.

A GROUP EFFORT

No one can be an expert on every aspect of the criminal justice system. Authors need help in covering new developments and ensuring that research findings are correctly interpreted. The many criminal justice students and instructors who have used previous editions of *Criminal Justice in America* have contributed abundantly to this edition. Their comments provided crucial practical feedback. Others gave us their comments personally when we lectured in criminal justice classes around the country.

Many others have helped us, as well, and we are very grateful for their help and support. Chief among them was Senior Product Manager Carolyn Henderson Meier, who is very supportive of our efforts. Senior Content Developer Shelley Murphy contributed invaluable ideas and tremendous organizational skills as we revised the book. The project has benefited much from the attention of Senior Content Project Manager Christy Frame. Greg Hubit's managerial skills and oversight were essential to successfully moving the project from manuscript submission to the bound book. As copy editor, Carrie Crompton made valuable contributions to improving the effectiveness of our presentation, as did Marne Evans in her role as proofreader. Diane Beasley designed the interior of the book.

In addition, we owe our greatest debt to the late George F. Cole, the creator of the book whose recent passing has left a void that cannot be filled. He was our beloved leader, mentor, and guide who taught us how to draw from scholarly literature in order to present important concepts effectively to beginning criminal justice students. While we express our thanks to many people for their contributions, ultimately, the full responsibility for the book is ours alone. We hope you will benefit from it, and we welcome your comments.

Christopher E. Smith   smithc28@msu.edu

Christina DeJong   dejongc@msu.edu

About the Authors

The late **George F. Cole** (1935–2015) was Professor Emeritus of Political Science at the University of Connecticut. A specialist in the administration of criminal justice, he published extensively on such topics as prosecution, courts, and corrections. George Cole was also coauthor with Christopher Smith and Christina DeJong of *The American System of Criminal Justice*, coauthor with Todd Clear and Michael Reisig of *American Corrections*, and coauthor with Marc Gertz and Amy Bunger of *The Criminal Justice System: Politics and Policies*. He developed and directed the graduate corrections program at the University of Connecticut and was a Fellow at the National Institute of Justice (1988). Among his other accomplishments, he was granted two awards under the Fulbright-Hays Program to conduct criminal justice research in England and the former Yugoslavia. In 1995 he was named a Fellow of the Academy of Criminal Justice Sciences for distinguished teaching and research.

Trained as a lawyer and social scientist, **Christopher E. Smith**, JD, PhD, is Professor of Criminal Justice at Michigan State University, where he teaches courses on criminal justice policy, courts, corrections, and law. He holds degrees from several universities, including Harvard University and the University of Connecticut. He was named as the recipient of the Outstanding Teaching Award for the Michigan State University College of Social Science in 2012. In addition to writing more than 110 scholarly articles, he is the author of more than 25 books, including several other titles with Cengage Learning: *Criminal Procedure*; *Law and Contemporary Corrections*; *Courts, Politics, and the Judicial Process*; *The Changing Supreme Court: Constitutional Rights and Liberties* with Thomas R. Hensley and Joyce A. Baugh; *Courts and Public Policy*; *Politics in Constitutional Law*; and *Courts and the Poor*.

Christina DeJong, PhD, is Associate Professor of Criminal Justice at Michigan State University. She earned her degrees at the University of Texas and the University of Maryland. At Michigan State, she is a noted researcher and award-winning teacher for a variety of criminology topics, including recidivism, violence against women, police–community relations, and genocide. She is the coauthor of *The Supreme Court, Crime, and the Ideal of Equal Justice*, and numerous articles in such journals as *Justice Quarterly*, *Criminology*, *Women and Criminal Justice*, and *Violence and Victims*.

CRIMINAL
JUSTICE
IN AMERICA

1

The Criminal Justice System

LEARNING OBJECTIVES

1 Name the goals of the criminal justice system.

2 Identify the different responsibilities of federal and state criminal justice operations.

3 Analyze criminal justice from a systems perspective.

4 Identify the authority and relationships of the main criminal justice agencies, and list the steps in the decision-making process for criminal cases.

5 Explain the criminal justice "wedding cake" concept as well as the due process and crime control models.

6 Name the possible causes of racial disparities in criminal justice.

National news stories often focus on horrific, frightening crimes. In 2015, significant national attention focused on shootings that caused multiple deaths: the murders of nine African American church members by a young white supremacist in South Carolina; the killing of three people at a Planned Parenthood office in Colorado by a man opposed to abortion; the murders of fourteen people at a county health department in California by a couple who sympathized with radical militants in the Middle East; and the murders of nine people at a community college in Oregon by a student who seemed to be angry at a specific instructor as well as at religious classmates (CBS News, 2016). These examples are important for examining certain kinds of crimes as well as for illuminating policy debates about gun control, police emergency response procedures, hatred-motivated crimes, and other contemporary criminal justice issues. However, these crimes are not typical of the offenses and defendants whose cases fill the nation's courts day after day as they are processed in the criminal justice system. Yet, despite the unusual nature of the multiple-murder events, the defendants charged in these shocking crimes will go through the same stages in the justice system as other criminal defendants, from arrest to pretrial hearings to resolution of their cases through plea negotiations or trials.

In order to gain a more realistic sense of the criminal justice system, let's illustrate the system's processes through the example of a case that is more typical. It concerned one of the numerous less-serious offenses that occupy the time and attention of justice system officials. On Christmas evening in 2014, Dustin Diamond, a minor celebrity from his acting role in the early 1990s television series *Saved by the Bell*, went to a bar in Port Washington, Wisconsin, with his girlfriend. According to the police report filed when Diamond was arrested the following day, the girlfriend got into a fistfight with a woman whom she claimed was bothering her. Diamond stepped forward to assist his girlfriend when the other woman's male companion intervened. In the altercation between the two men, the other man suffered minor injuries from a knife that Diamond was holding. Diamond initially claimed that he had a pen in his hand and

Jeffrey Phelps/Getty Images

that the infliction of the injury was accidental as he swung his arm to break free from the man. Other witnesses at the bar told police that Diamond had a knife. The police officers who stopped Diamond's car as his girlfriend was driving them away from the bar found a knife in the car. The police charged Diamond with one felony—second-degree recklessly endangering safety—that, upon conviction, could produce a ten-year prison sentence. He was also charged with three misdemeanors: carrying a concealed weapon; use of a dangerous weapon; and disorderly conduct. Diamond was held in the county jail from his arrest on Friday, December 26 until Monday, December 29, when he made his initial court appearance with his lawyer. The judge set bail at $10,000, which created the opportunity for Diamond to be free as his case was processed, if he had enough money. He was released after posting $10,000 for bail (Sacks, 2014; Associated Press, 2016).

At a preliminary hearing on January 5, 2015, Ozaukee County Judge Paul Malloy heard testimony from the police officer who had interviewed Diamond and other witnesses and had written the report that led to Diamond's arrest. Judge Malloy ruled that there was sufficient evidence to proceed with the charges against Diamond (Vielmetti, 2015). Sometimes, the defendant's attorney may be able to successfully challenge the nature and sufficiency of the evidence and win a ruling to have charges dismissed. Not so in this case, as there were multiple eyewitnesses to the event. On January 22, Diamond appeared in court again to enter his plea to the charges. He pleaded "not guilty" to all charges. The judge reduced the bail amount for Diamond, releasing him on a $500 signature bond, meaning that he would face arrest and be charged $500 if he failed to appear for any scheduled court hearings or violated other conditions of bail release. Conditions of release typically include limitations on travel, prohibitions on communicating with victims and witnesses, and avoidance of arrest on any new charges.

As pretrial stages proceed, the prosecutor and defense attorney engage in discussions, called "plea bargaining," about whether there can be any agreement for the defendant to plead guilty on lesser charges or for a less-than-maximum sentence. In Diamond's case, there was no agreement on a guilty plea, and the case moved forward toward trial. In preparation for trial, Diamond's attorney sought unsuccessfully to help his client's case by requesting that security video of the altercation inside the bar be excluded from evidence because it was too murky to be helpful to a jury (Associated

Press, 2016). Defense attorneys often look for ways to have evidence excluded as unreliable or because it was obtained in violation of the defendant's constitutional rights against unreasonable searches and improper questioning.

A three-day trial took place at the end of May 2015. The first day, prosecutors selected jurors from the pool of citizens called to jury service that week at the county courthouse. Prosecutors also made their initial presentation of arguments and evidence about the events of Christmas evening. On the second day, jurors heard testimony from the stabbing victim as well as others at the bar about how the fight started and the exact actions that they claim to have seen Diamond undertake. The prosecutors showed jurors the bloodstained shirt worn by the victim.

On the third day, the defense presented its case, and Diamond took the witness stand. Because of the Fifth Amendment protection against compelled self-incrimination in the Constitution, criminal defendants are not required to testify. Many defendants do not testify at their own trials because of the fear that they may stumble and sound inconsistent under fierce questioning by the prosecutor. They may also want to avoid the risk that their presence on the witness stand will enable prosecutors to ask questions about any past criminal record. Diamond apparently decided to testify in order to make his best effort to convince the jury that the victim was injured accidentally and not "stabbed." On the witness stand, Diamond said he did not intentionally harm the victim. He believed that the man injured himself by grabbing Diamond and thereby running into Diamond's knife, causing the small, minor cut that produced blood on his shirt. Diamond's attorney emphasized the victim's admission that he did not even know that he had been injured until he saw blood on his clothing as he was being interviewed by police outside of the bar after the incident (Ferguson, 2015; Associated Press, 2016).

Jeffrey Phelps/Getty Images

After the lawyers for each side made their final arguments on the third day of the trial, the jury received instructions about the law and their decision-making responsibilities from the judge. The citizens on the jury were secluded in the jury room to discuss and decide the case without any outsiders, including the judge, observing their discussions. After several hours, they reached a verdict. They decided that Diamond was "not guilty" of the serious felony charge—recklessly endangering safety—that carried the prospect of a prison sentence. Apparently, the jury did not believe that the prosecution had proven "beyond a reasonable doubt" that Diamond intended to harm the victim. However, the jury convicted him on two misdemeanor charges: carrying a concealed weapon and disorderly conduct. The evidence about his guilt for these acts was apparently quite strong in the eyes of the jury. As described by multiple witnesses, Diamond pulled a knife from a coat pocket—a concealed weapon—and he was involved in a physical altercation—disorderly conduct (Associated Press, 2016).

Four weeks later, on June 25, Judge Malloy sentenced Diamond to four months in jail as his punishment for these crimes. Because his attorney filed an appeal in the Wisconsin court of appeals seeking to vacate the conviction and gain a new trial, Diamond was not required to report immediately to jail. In cases of more-serious offenses, defendants are typically taken straight to jail or prison from the courtroom as soon as their sentence is announced. If there is a fear that the defendant will flee or the conviction is based on a serious violent crime, defendants may be held in jail immediately upon conviction and kept in custody while they await the judge's decision on the sentence. In December 2015, Diamond dropped his appeal. He reported to the county jail in January 2016 to begin serving his sentence, with the expectation that good behavior would make him eligible for work release so that he would likely spend only nights in jail during the latter part of his sentence (Associated Press, 2016).

The case against Dustin Diamond illustrates many elements of the criminal justice system. As this chapter will discuss, cases are processed through a series of steps in which justice system officials make decisions about whether a case will move forward or leave the system. In the Diamond case, police officers interviewed witnesses and gathered physical evidence, including the bloody shirt and the knife from Diamond's car. They believed the witnesses' accounts of the incident and were skeptical of Diamond's statements. Undoubtedly, their skepticism about Diamond's truthfulness was affected by his inconsistency in twice saying while being interviewed, "I had the knife in my hand, or the, ah, pen in my hand," thus casting doubt on his original claim that he had held a pen rather than a knife (Sacks, 2014). The prosecutors relied on the police reports in preparing their case, and they evidently agreed with the officers' assessment of the facts. Sometimes, prosecutors disagree with police officers' conclusions or interpret events differently and use their discretion to drop charges. Not in Diamond's case.

Judge Malloy made an assessment of the facts and made the decision at the preliminary hearing that sufficient evidence existed to permit the prosecutor to proceed against Diamond with the criminal charges. Judge Malloy also made the decision to permit Diamond to be released on bail while his case proceeded and set the conditions for his release. In some cases, judges consider defendants to be too dangerous or too likely to flee to be eligible for pretrial release. In other situations, defendants must remain in jail because they do not have enough money to meet the bail amount set by the judge. Because the injuries to the victim were minor and the judge apparently believed that Diamond would appear at scheduled hearings, bail was set with conditions that Diamond was able to meet—initially, the $10,000 bail amount, which was later reduced to a signature bond, essentially a promise to show up and to obey rules. Yet Diamond actually spent several days in jail after his arrest because he had the bad luck to be arrested on a holiday weekend, so he could not appear before a judge for a bail hearing until the following Monday. Other defendants for lesser offenses may be released on bail the same day they are arrested or the following morning. Jails can be dangerous places. Thus, just being arrested, even if one is innocent and charges will be dropped within days, can raise risks. There is potential harm to one's health and physical safety as well as potential financial harm to one's family if one loses a job or misses a rent payment as a consequence of the arrest.

Ultimately, Diamond's fate rested on the discussions and final decisions of citizens drawn from the community to serve on the jury. Their decisions were based on their understanding of the witnesses' statements and the arguments by the prosecutors and defense attorneys. In the end, the jurors' understanding of what they heard in court determined the outcome of the case.

In this chapter, we examine how American criminal justice operates as a system. Accordingly, we shall see how that system's processes are shaped by its goals, scarce resources, individual decision makers, and other factors that can lead to divergent treatment for similar criminal cases. In cases that appear to be very similar, one defendant may be convicted and another defendant may be set free. Why do similar cases produce different results? Differences in the effectiveness of police and prosecutors in gathering evidence and in the persuasiveness of defense attorneys' arguments can be major factors. Another factor may be the attitudes and values of the decision makers in a case. For example, prosecutors in different counties may have varying attitudes about whether to seek maximum punishments for drug crimes or youthful defendants. Also, some jurors may make very close examinations of evidence while others may be swayed by their own emotional reactions to the crime or to the defendant.

Differences in the treatment of suspects, defendants, and offenders also may sometimes be related to issues of race, ethnicity, and social class, as these demographic factors interact with the criminal justice system's processes.

Anyone in the United States, including a law-abiding college student, can be drawn into the criminal justice system in a variety of roles: victim, witness, juror, defendant. Thus, all Americans need to gain an understanding of the system, how it operates, and how it affects people's lives.

The Goals of Criminal Justice

crimes Actions that violate laws defining which socially harmful behaviors will be subject to the government's power to impose punishments.

The criminal justice system focuses on the protection of the public both through the investigation and punishment of people who commit **crimes** and through efforts to prevent people from committing harmful acts. In a general sense, crimes are actions that violate laws defining which socially harmful behaviors will be subject to the government's power to impose punishments, including deprivation of liberty through imprisonment.

Why does the law label some types of behavior as criminal and not others? For example, why is it a crime to use marijuana in most states when it is legal to drink alcohol, another intoxicating, addictive substance with harmful health effects? The criminal law is defined by elected representatives in state legislatures and Congress. They make choices about the behaviors that the government will punish. Some of these choices reflect broad agreement in society that certain actions, such as rape and murder, are so harmful that they must be punished. Such crimes have traditionally been called *mala in se*—wrong in themselves.

mala in se Offenses that are wrong by their very nature.

However, legislatures may decide that certain actions are criminal even though many people in society disagree about the harmfulness of those actions. These crimes are called *mala prohibita*—they are crimes because they are prohibited by the government and not because they are necessarily wrong in themselves. Everyone does not agree, for example, that gambling, prostitution, and drug use should be punished.

mala prohibita Offenses prohibited by law but not necessarily wrong in themselves.

The definition of *crimes* in criminal law is the starting point for the criminal justice system. A good way to begin our study of that system is to look at its goals. Although these goals may seem straightforward when expressed as ideas, defining what they mean in practice can be difficult.

In 1967 the U.S. President's Commission on Law Enforcement and Administration of Justice described the criminal justice system as the means that society uses to "enforce the standards of conduct necessary to protect individuals and the community" (U.S. President's Commission, 1967:7). This statement provides the basis for our discussion of the goals of the system. Although there is much debate about the purposes of criminal justice, most people agree that the system has three goals: (1) doing justice, (2) controlling crime, and (3) preventing crime.

Periodically, people undertake public protests to call attention to social problems and crime in their communities. How can the interest and energy generated by such public events be translated into concrete actions to prevent crime?

John Moore/Staff/Getty Images

Doing Justice

Doing justice concerns fairness and equity in the treatment of people who are drawn into the criminal justice system. In the United States, doing justice forms the basis for the rules, procedures, and institutions of the criminal justice system. Without this primary goal, little difference would exist between the U.S. system and that of authoritarian countries where people lack legal rights.

Americans want to have fair laws, and they want to investigate, judge, and punish fairly. But doing justice requires upholding the rights of individuals as well as punishing those who violate the law. Thus, the goal of doing justice embodies three principles: (1) offenders will be held fully accountable for their actions; (2) the rights of persons who have contact with the system will be protected; and (3) like offenses will be treated alike, and officials will take into account relevant differences among offenders and offenses (DiIulio, 1993:10).

Doing justice successfully is a tall order. We can easily identify situations in which criminal justice agencies and processes fall short of this ideal. But unlike in authoritarian political systems, in which criminal justice primarily serves the interests of those in power, in a democracy, doing justice to serve the interests of the people is a key goal. By serving society's interests in fairness and justice, the American criminal justice system can gain the public support necessary for pursuing the additional goals of controlling and preventing crime.

Controlling Crime

The criminal justice system is designed to control crime by arresting, prosecuting, convicting, and punishing those who disobey the law. A major constraint on the system, however, is that efforts to control crime must be carried out within the framework of law. Thus, criminal law not only defines what is illegal but also outlines the rights of citizens and the procedures officials must use to achieve the system's goals. Police officers and prosecutors must follow the law when investigating crimes. They cannot use unrestrained methods of their own choosing in conducting searches and questioning suspects.

In every city and town, the goal of crime control is actively pursued: police officers walk a beat, patrol cars race down dark streets, lawyers speak before a judge, probation officers visit clients, and guards patrol the grounds of a prison. Taking action against wrongdoers helps control crime, but the system must also attempt to prevent crimes from happening.

Preventing Crime

Crime can be prevented in various ways, but perhaps most important is the deterrent effect of the actions of police, courts, and corrections. These actions not only punish those who violate the law but also provide examples that will likely keep others from committing wrongful acts. For example, a racing patrol car responding to a crime scene serves as a warning that law enforcement is at hand. Technological advances can deter crime as well, with new kinds of surveillance and searches, though sometimes at a cost to privacy and personal liberty.

Citizens do not have the authority to enforce the law; society has assigned that responsibility to the criminal justice system. Thus, citizens must rely on the police to stop criminals; they cannot take the law into their own hands. Still, they can and must be actively engaged in preventing crime by such commonsense measures as locking their homes and cars, installing alarm systems where appropriate, and refraining from walking in dangerous areas.

Advancing Goals: Evidence-Based Practices

Advancing the goals of criminal justice requires the development of specific policies to deal with a host of issues such as gun control, stalking, hate crimes, computer crime, child abuse, and global criminal organizations. Many of these issues are controversial. Policies concerning these and other issues must be hammered out in the political arenas of state legislatures and Congress. Any policy choice carries with it costs and consequences as well as potential benefits, yet predicting consequences can be difficult. In addition, legislators often enact laws based on their *beliefs* about the nature of a problem and the responses that will be effective in addressing the problem. These beliefs are not necessarily based on a thorough understanding of available research on the nature of problems in criminal justice. Similarly, police chiefs, prison wardens, and others who carry out laws and policies may rely on practices to which they have become accustomed rather than explore the full range of possible effective alternatives. Decision makers' reliance on unsupported beliefs or customary practices may result in missed opportunities to develop policies and practices with the potential to more effectively advance desired goals.

One emerging trend in creating policies within criminal justice is the use of **evidence-based practices**. These are practices that have proven effective in research studies. Social scientists examine many aspects of criminal justice, including the causes of crime, the effectiveness of crime control strategies, and the efficiency of police procedures, so as to discover which approaches are most useful and cost-effective in addressing problems. Research sometimes shows that certain approaches are unproven or ineffective. As described by Faye Taxman and Steven Belenko (2013:3), evidence-based practices are "practices that *should* be widely used because research indicates that they positively alter human behavior."

Legislators, police chiefs, prison wardens, and other decision makers are increasingly looking to scholars' research for guidance about which laws and policies to develop. However, even when evidence-based procedures are available, they are not always known or followed by decision makers. Legislators and other policymakers may resist adopting them because they conflict with their own strongly held beliefs or commitment to familiar, customary approaches. For an example, read the "Evidence-Based Practice and Policy" feature on a contemporary debate about drug policy that is influenced by evidence-based practices.

evidence-based practices
Policies developed through guidance from research studies that demonstrate which approaches are most useful and cost-effective for advancing desired goals.

EVIDENCE-BASED PRACTICE AND POLICY

Drug Policy

Research indicates that it is less expensive to provide drug-addicted offenders with treatment than it is to send them to prison. Moreover, although many people with substance-abuse problems will eventually fall into their old ways, treatment provides a greater likelihood that they will not, and therefore will avoid committing new crimes. In one New York program, it cost only $32,000 to send drug-addicted offenders to a two-year residential treatment program that included job training; it would have cost taxpayers twice as much to send them to prison for the same time period. It is even less expensive for those offenders who pose no danger to society to live at home and attend outpatient treatment programs. Treatment programs inside prisons can also improve offenders' likelihood of avoiding drugs upon release, an important consideration as states speed up early releases in order to reduce the costs of imprisonment.

Thus, evidence-based policies should lead Americans to consider the question of whether it would be best to treat the use of addictive and intoxicating substances as a public health problem instead of a crime problem. Indeed, why is the use of such substances criminal while the consumption of

alcoholic beverages is legal? Why not apply the education and treatment approaches used for nicotine addiction and alcoholism to marijuana and possibly to cocaine, methamphetamine, heroin, and prescription painkillers, as well?

Yet, as with other evidence-based approaches, there can be practical impediments to shifting criminal justice policies about substance abuse in an entirely new direction. Not only is it difficult to shift viewpoints about this behavior that has been loudly condemned as "illegal" and "wrong" for many years, it is all the more difficult to change approaches when millions of dollars have been spent on law enforcement efforts and correctional institutions to treat it.

In recent years, however, two factors have pushed legislators and other decision makers to reconsider American drug policy. First, the public's attitudes toward certain drug problems are changing. In an October 2015 poll, 58 percent of Americans supported legalizing the use of marijuana. Voters in several states have approved ballot issues that legalize the use of marijuana for medical purposes by people who have the approval of a doctor. In 2012, voters in Colorado and Washington went a step further and approved ballot issues that legalized individuals' possession and use of marijuana. These decisions may cause new problems; officials worry about such matters as driving under the influence of marijuana, medical harm to marijuana smokers' lungs, and a potential increase in marijuana use by young people. Despite these concerns, the slow spread of decriminalization efforts through ballot issues approved by voters clearly indicates that the public is becoming less supportive of treating marijuana use as a crime issue.

In addition, the sharp rise in prescription drug abuse, heroin use, and overdose deaths among young whites in suburbs and small towns has led many whites to increasingly view drug use as a public health problem rather than as a crime. Observers have noted that when drug use was associated with urban, minority communities, "political figures of both parties staunchly defended [severe punishment] policies as necessary to control violent crime... [but] with heroin ravaging largely white communities... the mood is more forgiving" (Seelye, 2015).

Second, government budget cuts throughout the country have led officials to look for ways to send fewer people to prison and to reduce the sentence lengths that helped to dramatically expand the country's prison population in the last three decades. In 1980, there were 320,000 offenders serving sentences in American prisons. By the beginning of 2015, that number had risen to more than 1.5 million, despite the fact that crime rates had fallen steadily since 1992 (Kaeble, Glaze, Tsoutis, & Minton, 2015; BJS, 2016). A tough-on-crime approach to sentencing led to hundreds of thousands of additional offenders being imprisoned. Many of these offenders were imprisoned on drug charges or for crimes such as thefts and robberies that were committed to support a drug habit. Their imprisonment has been enormously expensive, requiring the building and staffing of new prisons that supply food, shelter, medical care, and supervision. The increased rate of imprisonment has also created huge costs for the spouses and children of prisoners, because a parent and breadwinner can be sent away for years for committing the relatively minor crime of possessing illegal drugs. The desire to reduce financial costs and human consequences from severe drug offenses has led conservative Republicans and liberal Democrats to work together in Congress in the pursuit of reforms that might enjoy broad political support.

These two influences—changing public attitudes toward drugs and budgetary pressures to reduce prison populations—will not necessarily lead to the legalization of drugs. The U.S. Department of Justice maintains that marijuana and other drugs remain illegal under federal law no matter what voters in any state decide. However, the impetus for reform has pushed officials to look at research studies in considering how to cut costs by using evidence-based practices. For example, studies indicate that specific family counseling programs and school-based intervention programs can reduce alcohol and drug abuse by teenagers. Such early intervention programs may save society from long-term problems if these youths move away from a path that might have led them to engage in criminal acts that could eventually result in expensive periods of imprisonment.

Budgetary pressures and changes in public attitudes have combined to produce reconsideration of several aspects of drug policy, offering new opportunities to consider evidence-based practices. However, it remains to be seen whether states will devote significant resources to prevention and treatment. Governments could save resources merely by reducing enforcement of marijuana laws, shortening prison sentences, and moving prisoners out through early release. But in the long run, more money might be saved through investment in research-based treatment programs that reduce the problem of drug abuse.

Implementing New Practices

Legislators face difficult choices when evidence-based practices clash with long-standing policies that may be firmly fixed in the minds of officials and the public. How many legislators would risk political backlash by advocating that the consumption of marijuana be decriminalized and that drug use be treated as a public health problem that requires an investment in rehabilitation rather than an emphasis on imprisonment? Public attitudes are shifting in many regions, but significant numbers of American voters continue to hold punitive views about drug use. In addition, a shift to evidence-based policies may give rise to new, unanticipated problems, such as increased drug use or more robberies and thefts by drug users seeking to support their habits once the deterrent effect of criminal laws is removed.

Imagine that you are a legislator. Write a memo providing at least three arguments that present your position on whether the United States should treat substance abuse as a public health problem instead of a crime problem.

Researching the Internet

To listen to leading experts debate whether drugs should be legalized, go to http://www.npr.org/2012/ll/15/165211562/should-we-legalize-drugs.

Sources: G. H. Brody et al., "Family Centered Program Deters Substance Use, Conduct Problems, and Depressive Symptoms in Black Adolescents," *Pediatrics* 129 (2012): 108–15; F. Bruni, "Colorado's Marijuana Muddle," *New York Times,* January 14, 2013 (www.nytimes.com); J. Jones, "In U.S., 58% Back Legal Marijuana Use," Gallup Poll, October 21, 2015 (www.gallupcom); G. Kolata and S. Cohen, "Drug Overdoses Propel Rise in Mortality Rates of Whites," *New York Times,* January 17, 2016 (www.nytimes.com); D. McVay, V. Schiraldi, and J. Ziedenberg, "Treatment or Incarceration? National and State Findings on the Efficacy and Cost Savings of Drug Treatment versus Imprisonment," Washington, DC: Justice Policy Center, 2004; K. Seelye, "As Heroin Use by Whites Soars, Parents Urge Gentler Drug War," *New York Times*, October 30, 2015 (www.nytimes.com); J. Steinhauer, "Push to Scale Back Sentencing Laws Gains Momentum," *New York Times,* July 28, 2015 (www.nytimes.com); F. S. Taxman and S. Belenko, *Implementing Evidence–Based Practices in Community Corrections and Addiction Treatment* (New York: Springer, 2013); K. C. Winters et al., "Brief Intervention for Drug-Abusing Adolescents in a School Setting: Outcomes and Mediating Factors," *Journal of Substance Abuse Treatment* 42 (2012): 279–88.

1. **What is the difference between *mala in se* and *mala prohibita* crimes?**
   Legislatures define punishable, harmful behaviors that are wrongs in themselves, such as murder (*mala in se*), and other actions that they simply choose to prohibit as too harmful to be permitted (*mala prohibita*).

2. **What are the three goals of the criminal justice system?**
   Doing justice, controlling crime, preventing crime.

3. **What is meant by "evidence-based practices"?**
   The development of approaches to addressing problems in criminal justice and advancing the goals of criminal justice by using research studies to guide decisions about what will work effectively.

Criminal Justice in a Federal System

federalism A system of government in which power is divided between a central (national) government and regional (state) governments.

Criminal justice, like other aspects of American government, is based on the concept of **federalism**, in which power is divided between a central (national) government and regional (state) governments. States have a great deal of authority over their own affairs, but the federal government handles matters of national concern. Because of federalism, no single level of government is solely responsible for the administration of criminal justice.

The U.S. government's structure was created in 1789 with the ratification of the U.S. Constitution. The Constitution gave the national government certain powers, including raising an army, coining money, and making treaties with foreign countries. But the states retained all other powers, including police power. No national police force with broad powers may be established in the United States.

The Constitution does not include criminal justice among the federal government's specific powers. Yet the U.S. government is involved in criminal justice in many ways. For example, the Federal Bureau of Investigation (FBI) is a national law enforcement agency. Federal criminal cases are tried in U.S. district courts, which are federal courts, and there are federal prisons throughout the nation. Most criminal justice activity, however, occurs at the state level. The vast majority of crimes are defined by state laws rather than federal law. Thus, laws are enforced and offenders are brought to justice mainly in the states, counties, and cities. As a result, local traditions, values, and practices shape the way criminal justice agencies operate. For example, local leaders, whether members of the city council or influential citizens, can help set law enforcement priorities by putting pressure on the police. Will the city's police officers crack down on illegal gambling? Will juvenile offenders be turned over to their parents with stern warnings, or will they be sent to state institutions? The answers to these and other important questions vary from city to city.

Two Justice Systems

Both the national and the state systems of criminal justice enforce laws, try criminal cases, and punish offenders, but their activities differ in scope and purpose. Although most crimes are defined by state laws, various national criminal laws have been enacted by Congress and are enforced by the FBI, the Drug Enforcement Administration, the Secret Service, and other federal agencies.

Except in the case of federal drug offenses, relatively few offenders break federal criminal laws compared with the large numbers who break state criminal laws. For example, only small numbers of people violate the federal laws against counterfeiting and espionage, whereas large numbers violate state laws against assault, larceny, and drunken driving. With respect to drug offenses, there are debates about whether federal or state laws should control decisions on the definitions of crimes

THE POLICY DEBATE

Which Level of Government Should Control Marijuana Policy?

In March 2013, the Maryland legislature's House of Delegates voted to create a medical marijuana program that would permit doctors to approve patients to ingest the long-illegal substance for pain relief. In the same month, the Maryland Senate voted to decriminalize the possession of less than 10 grams of marijuana, thus potentially moving toward permissible use of the substance even by those who do not suffer from painful medical conditions. When the proposal stalled, it was reintroduced in the House of Delegates in February 2014.

In taking these actions in each house of its legislature, Maryland moved a step closer to joining the 17 other states that have approved the use of medical marijuana, often through ballot issues endorsed by the states' voters. In the states of Alaska, Oregon, Washington, and Colorado voters approved proposals in 2012 and 2014 to legalize the non-medical consumption of marijuana. Voters in a number of cities in recent years also approved measures to change possession of small amounts of marijuana from a criminal offense to a civil infraction warranting only a ticket and a fine.

These developments reflect changes in the public's attitude toward marijuana in many states. According to an October 2015 Gallup Poll, 58 percent of Americans believe that marijuana should be legal, a drastic change from just eight years earlier, when only one-third of Americans endorsed that view. Because 71 percent of Americans between ages 18 and 34 believe that marijuana should be legal, it seems likely that public support for legalization will continue to grow as the older generation that is less supportive of legalization gradually becomes smaller and the current younger generations become a larger proportion of the adult population.

Although the public has expressed clear support for either legalization of or access to medical marijuana in many states, the federal government continues to take a hard line on its production and use. In *Gonzales v. Raich* (2005), the U.S. Supreme Court endorsed the continuing authority of Congress to keep marijuana production criminalized and of the federal Drug Enforcement Administration to investigate and make arrests.

Under the Obama administration, the federal government has declined to prevent the introduction of legalized marijuana in Alaska, Oregon, Colorado, and Washington. Indeed, the administration even issued new guidelines to reassure banks in these states that they would not face federal prosecution for providing financial services to legal marijuana businesses. Future presidential administrations may change direction and assert federal authority over the law governing marijuana. Such a change would create legal clashes with states' efforts to decriminalize private consumption of the intoxicant. However, a December 2012 national poll indicated that 64 percent of Americans want the federal government to stay out of marijuana policy in the states. Who should control marijuana policy—the federal government or the states? Here is a summary of key arguments for each side in the debate.

For Federal Control

- The U.S. Supreme Court has said that the U.S. Constitution and statutes enacted by Congress give the federal government control over marijuana policy, including the ability to override state laws by initiating arrests and prosecutions for activities that state laws say are legal.
- International drug trafficking gangs are deeply involved in smuggling, distributing, and selling marijuana. Only the federal government has the resources, expertise, and nationwide law enforcement coverage to combat these organized crime groups.
- Legalized marijuana in specific states will lead to increased flow of marijuana over state borders and into states where it is not legal. The federal government has authority over crimes that cross state borders.
- Comprehensive policies concerning substance-abuse issues can come only from Congress, an institution that represents the views and interests of the entire nation.

For State Control

- States control most of their own criminal laws and policies. There is no reason to regard marijuana laws as concerning a matter of special national significance or posing especially dangerous threats to the nation.
- The decriminalization and legalization of marijuana in various states reflect the will of the people through the democratic processes of statewide ballot issues or statutes created by the people's elected representatives.
- In a democracy, the people in a state are entitled to have laws that reflect their own political values and priorities. Unpopular laws should not be imposed on them by the federal government, especially laws that infringe on individuals' liberty to engage in private activities that are no more harmful than legal activities such as drinking alcohol.
- Federalism is an important aspect of American government that emphasizes authority for both state and federal governments. This element of the design of the American system is intended to permit states to experiment with policy reforms and innovations so that examples of policy change, such as legalization of marijuana, if successful, can provide ideas that other states may wish to copy.

What Should U.S. Policy Be?

The debates about marijuana laws include a variety of elements, including aspects of the human and financial costs of punishment, individual liberty, and the development of laws through democratic processes that reflect the will of the people. The United States has spent an enormous amount of money over the years on punishing people for marijuana possession, pursuing those who grow or import marijuana, and launching public relations campaigns to teach children to say no to drugs. Despite spending this money and threatening people with criminal punishments, many Americans continue to use marijuana and increasingly regard

continued

The Policy Debate (*continued*)

existing criminal laws as misguided and outdated. Do current trends in public opinion and changes in state laws indicate that the legalization of marijuana is inevitable? If so, should the federal government step back and permit states to move ahead with their own policy priorities and decisions on this issue?

📶 Researching the Internet

For trends in public opinion concerning the legalization of marijuana, see http://www.gallup.com/poll/186260/back -legal-marijuana.aspx?g_source =marijuana&g_medium=search&g _campaign=tiles

Analyzing the Issue

Imagine that you and your classmates are advisors to the president of the United States. You have been asked to present a complete set of arguments on both sides of the marijuana issue and then make a recommendation about what the president's position should be. Suppose the president expresses concern about the harm of marijuana to young people and the risk that increased availability will spread its use among high school students. He is tempted to use federal power to block legalization in the states but is unsure whether this is the best course of action. What arguments and recommendations will you and your classmates produce? What reasons will you give for your recommendations?

and punishments. Read "The Policy Debate" feature about marijuana legalization to consider competing viewpoints on this controversial policy issue.

Expansion of Federal Involvement

Since the 1960s, the federal government has expanded its role in dealing with crime, a policy area that has traditionally been the responsibility of state and local governments. The report of the U.S. President's Commission on Law Enforcement and Administration of Justice (1967) emphasized the need for greater federal involvement in crime control at the local level and urged that federal grants be directed to the states to support criminal justice initiatives. Since then, Congress has allocated billions of dollars for crime control efforts and has passed legislation, national in scope, to deal with street crime, the "war on drugs," violent crime, terrorism, and juvenile delinquency.

Because many crimes span state borders, we no longer think of crime in general as being committed at a single location within a single state. For example, crime syndicates and gangs deal with drugs, pornography, and gambling on a national level. Therefore, over the course of the twentieth century Congress expanded the powers of

Federal law enforcement agencies bear special responsibility for certain crimes, such as antiterrorism investigations, bank robberies, and drug trafficking. Federal agencies also provide expert assistance for the investigation of crimes that rely on scientific evidence, such as arson. Also, local agencies may request assistance from federal experts. Would law enforcement nationwide be more effective if all police officers worked under a single federal agency rather than thousands of different state and local agencies?

AP Images/Laura Skelding

the FBI and other federal agencies to investigate criminal activities for which the states had formerly taken responsibility. As a national agency, the FBI can pursue criminal investigations across state borders better than any state agency can. Technology-based crimes, such as computer-fraud schemes and Internet-sourced child pornography, can also cross both state and international borders, and have spurred new national laws from Congress and enforcement actions by federal agencies (Hermann, 2014). Moreover, federal officials have become increasingly active in pursuing arms dealers, narcotics traffickers, and terrorists who operate in other countries but whose harmful activities violate the laws of the United States. For example, Russian arms dealer Viktor Bout was arrested in Thailand in 2008 and brought to the United States in 2010 where he was convicted and sentenced to 25 years in prison. In the same year, the reputed Jamaican drug kingpin Christopher Coke was brought to New York to face trial and an eventual sentence of two decades in prison (Weiser, 2011). In 2016, Mexican officials began working with American officials to send the leader of a major drug trafficking operation, Joaquín "El Chapo" Guzmán, to the United States for trial (BBC News, 2016).

Disputes over jurisdiction may occur when an offense violates both state and federal laws. If the FBI and local agencies do not cooperate, they might both seek to catch the same criminals; if information is not shared, one agency might miss an opportunity to make an arrest (Viser, 2013). These problems can have major implications if the agency that makes the arrest determines the court to which the case is brought. Usually, however, law enforcement officials at all levels of government seek to cooperate and coordinate their efforts.

After the September 11, 2001, attacks on the World Trade Center and the Pentagon, the FBI and other federal law enforcement agencies focused their resources and efforts on investigating and preventing terrorist threats against the United States. As a result, the role of the FBI as a law enforcement agency has changed. One month after the attacks, 4,000 of the agency's 11,500 agents were dedicating their efforts to the aftermath of September 11. The FBI has continued to increase its attention to terrorism and cybercrimes in the subsequent years of the twenty-first century and thereby diminished its involvement in aspects of traditional law enforcement. In testimony presented to Congress in December 2015, FBI Director James Comey emphasized that "counterterrorism remains the FBI's top priority" while also focusing attention on the FBI's increasing attention to cybercrimes (Comey, 2015). According to Comey, "an element of virtually every national security threat and crime problem the FBI faces is cyber-based or facilitated" (Comey, 2015).

The reorientation of the FBI's priorities is just one of many changes made in federal criminal justice agencies to address the issues of national security and terrorism. The most significant expansion of the federal government occurred with the creation of a new Department of Homeland Security (DHS) through the consolidation of border security, intelligence, and emergency-response agencies from other departments of government (see Table 1.1). Moreover, a new agency, the Transportation Security Administration (TSA), was created within DHS to assume responsibility for protecting travelers and interstate commerce by screening passengers and their luggage at airports throughout the country.

Because both state and federal systems operate in the United States, criminal justice here is highly decentralized. As Figure 1.1 shows, almost two-thirds of all criminal justice employees work for local governments. The majority of workers in all of the subunits of the system—except corrections—are tied to local government. Likewise, the costs of criminal justice are distributed among federal, state, and local governments (Kyckelhahn, 2015).

The nation's economic problems since 2007 have reduced government budgets for criminal justice in many cities, counties, and states. Federal agencies have been affected, too. When budget disagreements created a deadlock between Republicans and Democrats in Congress in 2013, automatic budget cuts were imposed through the federal government, resulting in a law enforcement hiring freeze, reduced training, and an inability to open new investigations by the FBI and other agencies (Horwitz, 2013). Depending on the outcome of the 2016 elections, there is a possibility of

TABLE 1.1 Department of Homeland Security

Congress approved legislation to create a new federal agency dedicated to protecting the United States from terrorism. The legislation merges 22 agencies and nearly 170,000 government workers.

	Agencies Moved to the Department of Homeland Security	Previous Department or Agency
Border and Transportation Security	Immigration and Naturalization Service enforcement functions Transportation Security Administration Customs Service Federal Protective Services Animal and Plant Health Inspection Service (parts)	Justice Department Transportation Department Treasury Department General Services Administration Agriculture Department
Emergency Preparedness and Response	Federal Emergency Management Agency Chemical, biological, radiological and nuclear response units Nuclear Incident Response Teams National Domestic Preparedness Office Office of Domestic Preparedness Domestic Emergency Support Teams	(Independent Agency) Health and Human Services Department Energy Department FBI Justice Department (From various departments and agencies)
Science and Technology	Civilian biodefense research program Plum Island Animal Disease Center Lawrence Livermore National Laboratory (parts)	Health and Human Services Department Agriculture Department Energy Department
Information Analysis and Infrastructure Protection	National Communications System National Infrastructure Protection Center Critical Infrastructure Assurance Office National Infrastructure Simulation and Analysis Center Federal Computer Incident Response Center	Defense Department FBI Commerce Department Energy Department General Services Administration
Secret Service	Secret Service including presidential protection units	Treasury Department
Coast Guard	Coast Guard	Transportation Department

Source: *New York Times*, November 20, 2002, p. A12.

FIGURE 1.1

Percentage (Rounded) of Criminal Justice Employees at Each Level of Government

The administration of criminal justice in the United States is very much a local affair, as these employment figures show. Only in corrections do states employ a greater percentage of workers than do cities and counties.

Source: T. Kyckelhahn, *Justice Expenditure and Employment Extracts, 2012–Preliminary*. U.S. Bureau of Justice Statistics, February 26, 2015. NCJ 248628 (www.bjs.gov).

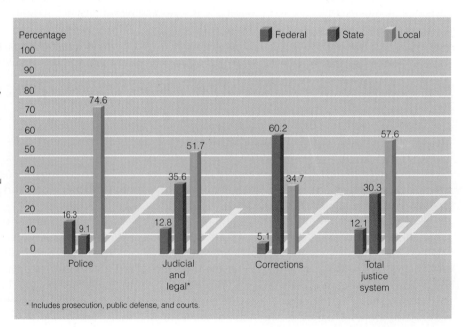

* Includes prosecution, public defense, and courts.

future budget freezes and automatic cuts if Congress and the president are locked in disagreements with each other. Similarly, as we shall see throughout the chapters of this book, budget problems during the last several years have forced criminal justice agencies at all levels of government to reduce law enforcement activities, release offenders early from prison, and take other measures to cope with a reduction in resources (Bluestein, 2011). These issues can have their greatest impact at the local level, especially when there are no longer enough police officers on duty to respond quickly to citizens' calls for assistance (Ingraham, 2015; LeDuff, 2011).

CHECK POINT

4. **What is the key feature of federalism?**
   A division of power between a central (national) government and regional (state) governments.

5. **What powers does the national government have in the area of criminal justice?**
   Enforcement of federal criminal laws.

6. **What factors have caused the expansion of federal laws and involvement in criminal justice?**
   The expansion of criminal activities across state borders; efforts to combat terrorism, cyberattacks, and international criminal activities.

STOP & ANALYZE

Is there a risk that the American system of criminal justice is too fragmented because authority is divided among three levels of government? List three problems that can arise because the United States lacks a single, specific authority to be in charge of running criminal justice agencies throughout the nation.

Criminal Justice as a Social System

To achieve the goals of criminal justice, many kinds of organizations—police, prosecutors' offices, courts, corrections—have been formed. Each has its own functions and personnel. We might assume that criminal justice is an orderly process in which a variety of professionals act on each case on behalf of society. To know the complexities involved, however, we must look beyond the formal organizational structures. In doing so, we can use the concept of a **system**: a complex whole made up of interdependent parts whose actions are directed toward goals and influenced by the environment in which they function.

Each of the subsystems of the criminal justice system—police, courts, corrections—has its own goals and needs, but they are also interdependent. When one unit changes its policies, practices, or resources, other units will be affected. An increase in the number of people arrested by the police, for example, will affect not only the judicial subsystem but also the probation and correctional subsystems. For criminal justice to achieve its goals, each part must make its own contribution but also have some contact with at least one other part of the system.

Although criminal justice agencies and actors can be described as functioning as a system, this description should not be understood to imply that they always cooperate fully, operate smoothly, or achieve efficiency in undertaking their responsibilities. It is a human system, with flawed decisions, imperfect communication, and uneven distribution of resources. Yet, the various agencies and actors are connected to and dependent on each other in order to fulfill their assigned tasks.

system A complex whole consisting of interdependent parts whose actions are directed toward goals and are influenced by the environment in which they function.

The system perspective emphasizes that criminal justice is made up of parts or subsystems, including police, courts, and corrections. Here, Judge Orlando Houston confers with prosecutors and defense attorneys during the Durham, North Carolina, trial of Michael Peterson, charged with murdering his wife, Kathleen. How do decisions by actors at each stage in the process determine the fates of individuals such as Peterson?

FIGURE 1.2

Exchange Relationships between Prosecutors and Others The prosecutor's decisions are influenced by relationships with other agencies and members of the community.

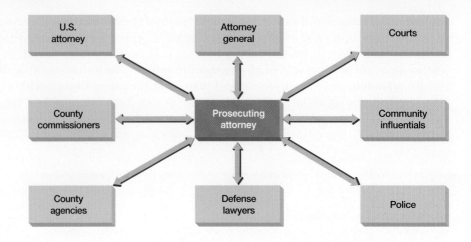

exchange A mutual transfer of resources; a balance of benefits and deficits that flow from behavior based on decisions about the values and costs of alternative courses of action.

plea bargain A defendant's plea of guilty to a criminal charge with the reasonable expectation of receiving some consideration from the state for doing so, usually a reduction of the charge. The defendant's ultimate goal is a penalty lighter than the one formally warranted by the charged offense.

In addition to understanding the nature of the criminal justice system and its subsystems, we also need to see how individual actors play their roles. This system is made up of a great many people doing specific jobs. Some, such as police officers and judges, are well known to the public. Others, such as bail agent and probation officers, are less well known. A key concept here is **exchange**, meaning the mutual transfer of resources among individual actors, each of whom has goals that she or he cannot accomplish alone. Each needs to gain the cooperation and assistance of other individuals by helping them achieve their own goals. The concept of exchange allows interpersonal behavior to be seen as the result of individual decisions about the costs and benefits of different courses of action.

Many kinds of exchange relationships exist in the criminal justice system, some more visible than others. Probably the most obvious example is the **plea bargain**, in which the defense attorney and the prosecutor reach an agreement: the defendant agrees to plead guilty in exchange for a reduction of charges or for a lighter sentence. As a result of this exchange, the prosecutor gains a quick, sure conviction; the defendant achieves a shorter sentence; and the defense attorney can move on to the next case. Thus, the cooperation underlying the exchange promotes the goals of each participant. See "A Question of Ethics" at the end of the chapter concerning the different sentences imposed in 2016 on a husband and wife in Nevada who both admitted to sexually abusing children. Consider whether prosecutors' use of discretion in plea bargaining should be guided by a concern for equal treatment of all similarly situated offenders.

The concept of exchange serves as a reminder that decisions are the products of interactions among individuals and that the subsystems of the criminal justice system are tied together by the actions of individual decision makers. Figure 1.2 presents selected exchange relationships between a prosecutor and other individuals and agencies involved in the criminal justice process.

▼ CHECK POINT

7. **What is a system?**
   A complex whole made up of interdependent parts whose actions are directed toward goals and influenced by the environment within which they function.

8. **What are the subsystems of the criminal justice system?**
   Police, courts, corrections.

9. **What is one example of an exchange relationship?**
   Plea bargaining.

STOP & ANALYZE

Is plea bargaining beneficial for society, or does it inappropriately permit lawbreakers to escape appropriate punishment? Give two arguments favoring each side in this debate. Which side has the stronger arguments?

Characteristics of the Criminal Justice System

The workings of the criminal justice system have four major characteristics: (1) discretion, (2) resource dependence, (3) sequential tasks, and (4) filtering.

Discretion

All levels of the justice process reflect a high degree of **discretion**. This term refers to officials' freedom to act according to their own judgment and conscience (O'Neal, Tellis, & Spohn, 2015). For example, police officers decide how to handle a crime situation, prosecutors decide which charges to file, judges decide how long a sentence will be, and parole boards decide when an offender may be released from prison (see Table 1.2).

The extent of such discretion may seem odd, given that the United States is ruled by law and has created procedures to ensure that decisions are made in accordance with law. However, criminal justice is not a mechanical system in which decisions are strictly dominated by law, but a dynamic system in which actors may take many factors into account and exercise many options as they dispose of a case.

Two arguments are often made to justify discretion in the criminal justice system. First, discretion is needed because the system lacks the resources to treat every case the same way. If every violation of the law were pursued from investigation through trial, the costs would be immense. Second, many officials believe that discretion permits them to achieve greater justice than rigid rules would produce. Within policing, discretion can also be important in individual situations to restore order or to reduce the risk of violence. As you read "You Make the Decision," consider the difficult discretionary choices that senior law enforcement officials can face as they try to enforce the nation's laws while simultaneously seeking to defuse situations with great potential for violence and conflict.

discretion The authority to make decisions without reference to specific rules or facts, using instead one's own judgment; allows for individualization and informality in the administration of justice.

TABLE 1.2	Who Exercises Discretion?
Discretion is exercised by various actors throughout the criminal justice system.	
These Criminal Justice Officials...	**Must Often Decide Whether or How to...**
Police	Enforce specific laws Investigate specific crimes Search people, vicinities, buildings Arrest or detain people
Prosecutors	File charges or petitions for adjudication Seek indictments Drop cases Reduce charges
Judges or Magistrates	Set bail or conditions for release Accept pleas Determine delinquency Dismiss charges Impose sentences Revoke probation
Correctional Officials	Assign to [which] type of correctional facility Award privileges Punish for infractions of rules Determine date and conditions of parole Revoke parole

Source: Bureau of Justice Statistics, *Report to the Nation on Crime and Justice*, 2nd ed. (Washington, DC: U.S. Government Printing Office, 1988), 59.

FBI Director

On January 2, 2016, a small group of armed individuals began occupying the office buildings at a remote federal wildlife refuge in Oregon. Their action was triggered by their opposition to the imprisonment of local ranchers who were convicted of arson for starting a fire on federal land—a fire that federal officials claimed was used to cover up evidence of poaching deer. When the convicted individuals disavowed the protesters' actions, the armed individuals shifted their focus to asserting that the federal government must return federal land to the state so that local ranchers and others could use the land more freely for grazing livestock and other activities currently regulated or prohibited by federal laws. As the FBI Director, you must decide what action to take in response to the armed occupation of the federal government's property.

In the actual event, law enforcement officials began to make arrests of individual protesters who left the site for supplies or meetings. However, for purposes of this exercise, imagine that they are staying on the site and refusing the leave at all.

One of your aides argues that the FBI should take strong action against these lawbreakers, because:

- a failure to act may encourage armed individuals elsewhere in the country to violate the law and occupy federal property with similar claims.
- a failure to act may serve to support the argument of critics who claim that law enforcement is racially biased in the United States: that officials tend to act more swiftly and strongly against African American protesters—as in the intervention of a massive force of heavily armed antiriot police when *unarmed* Black Lives Matter activists protested at the Mall of America in Minnesota—than against white protesters who are trespassing on federal lands.
- strong action does not require a direct confrontation or use of force: the FBI could cut off road access to the wildlife refuge to prevent anyone from bringing food supplies or reinforcements to the protesters, as well as cut off electricity and other utilities, while forcefully insisting that the protesters

must leave immediately if they wish to avoid prosecution.

Another aide argues against any provocative actions, because:

- violence must be avoided at all costs to protect the lives of law enforcement officials as well as the occupiers; if the occupiers do not cause any violence, then it is best to just wait them out.
- prior incidents when the FBI reacted with lethal force against armed antigovernment protesters barricaded at remote locations (e.g., Waco, Texas, 1993; Ruby Ridge, Idaho, 1992) led to needless loss of life and motivated antigovernment radical Timothy McVeigh to kill 168 people by bombing the Oklahoma City federal building in 1995.
- society's interests are better served by showing that the federal government can be patient and steering the news media toward publicizing the local community's opposition to the occupiers.

What will you decide to do? Provide three reasons for your decision.

Resource Dependence

Criminal justice agencies do not generate their own resources, but depend on other agencies for funding. Therefore, actors in the system must cultivate and maintain good relations with those who allocate resources—that is, political decision makers such as legislators, mayors, and city council members. Some police departments gain revenue through traffic fines and property forfeitures, but these sources cannot sustain their budgets.

Because budget decisions are made by elected officials who seek to please the public, criminal justice officials must also maintain a positive image and good relations with voters. If the police have strong public support, for example, the mayor will be reluctant to reduce the law enforcement budget. Criminal justice officials also seek positive coverage from the news media. Because the media often provide a crucial link between government agencies and the public, criminal justice officials may announce notable achievements while trying to limit publicity about controversial cases and decisions. In the second decade of the twenty-first century, resource issues have become especially difficult and important for criminal justice officials because of widespread and deep budget cuts in many cities, counties, and states (Gest, 2013).

Sequential Tasks

Decisions in the criminal justice system are made in a specific sequence. The police must arrest a person before the case is passed to the prosecutor to determine if charges should be brought. The prosecutor's decisions influence the nature of the court's workload. The accumulated decisions of police, prosecutors, and courts determine the number of offenders sent to corrections agencies. The sequential nature of the system is key to the exchange relationships among the justice system's decision makers, who depend on one another to achieve their goals. In other words, the system is highly interdependent partially because it is sequential.

Filtering

We can see the criminal justice system as a **filtering process**. At each stage, some defendants are sent on to the next stage while others are either released or processed under changed conditions. As shown in Figure 1.3, people who have been arrested

filtering process A screening operation; a process by which criminal justice officials screen out some cases while advancing others to the next level of decision making.

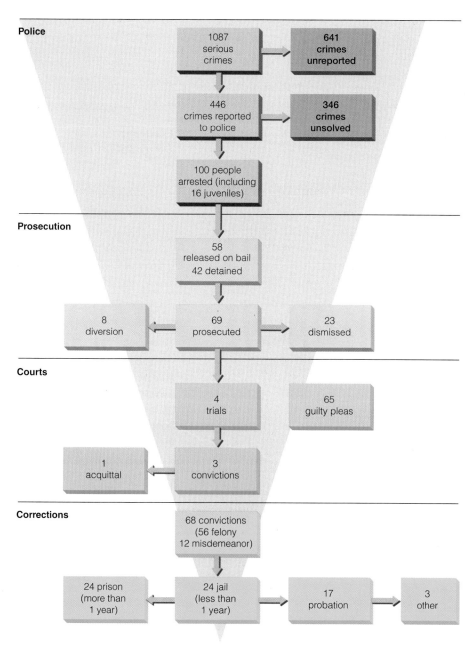

FIGURE 1.3

Criminal Justice as a Filtering Process
Decisions at each point in the system result in some cases being dropped while others are passed to the next point. Are you surprised by the small portion of cases that remain?

Sources: Estimates calculated from Thomas H. Cohen and Tracey Kyckelhahn, "Felony Defendants in Large Urban Counties, 2006," Bureau of Justice Statistics *Bulletin*, May 2010, Figure 1; FBI, *Crime in the United States, 2009* [Uniform Crime Reports], Tables 25 and 28; Jennifer L. Truman and Michael R. Rand, "Criminal Victimization, 2009," Bureau of Justice Statistics *Bulletin*, October 2010, Tables 1 and 11.

Police

1087 serious crimes → 641 crimes unreported

446 crimes reported to police → 346 crimes unsolved

100 people arrested (including 16 juveniles)

Prosecution

58 released on bail
42 detained

8 diversion ← 69 prosecuted → 23 dismissed

Courts

4 trials   65 guilty pleas

1 acquittal ← 3 convictions

Corrections

68 convictions (56 felony 12 misdemeanor)

24 prison (more than 1 year) ← 24 jail (less than 1 year) → 17 probation → 3 other

may be filtered out of the system at various points. Note that relatively few suspects are arrested in light of the number of crimes committed, and a portion of the arrestees will be released without being prosecuted or convicted.

Some go free because the police decide that a crime has not been committed or that the evidence is not sound. Or, in drug-related cases, the prosecutor may decide that justice would be better served by sending the suspect to a substance-abuse clinic than by imposing imprisonment. Many defendants will plead guilty and receive lesser punishments. Judges may dismiss charges against other defendants, and juries may acquit a few more. Most of the offenders who are actually prosecuted for serious charges will be convicted, however. Thus, the criminal justice system is often described as a funnel—only a portion of the cases that enter the system result in conviction and punishment. Some people look at how few people end up in prison and conclude that the system is not tough enough on criminal offenders. Consider this idea as you read the "Criminal Justice: Myth & Reality" feature.

To summarize, the criminal justice system is composed of a set of interdependent parts (subsystems). This system has four key attributes: (1) discretion, (2) resource dependence, (3) sequential tasks, and (4) filtering. Using this framework, we look next at the operations of criminal justice agencies, and then examine the flow of cases through the system.

Operations of Criminal Justice Agencies

The criminal justice system has been formed to deal with people who are accused of violating the criminal law. Its subsystems consist of more than 60,000 public and private agencies with an annual budget of more than $260 billion and more than 2.4 million employees (Kyckelhahn, 2015). Here we review the main parts of the criminal justice system and their functions.

As part of law enforcement responsibilities, the police must deal with a wide range of witnesses and victims in emotionally charged situations. What skills and personal qualities are required to respond to emergencies? What skills do officers need to deal one-on-one with traumatized victims and witnesses?

Police

We usually think of the police as being on the "front line" in controlling crime. The term *police*, however, does not refer to a single agency or type of agency, but to many agencies at each level of government. The complexity of the criminal justice system can be seen in the large number of organizations engaged in law enforcement. According to the most recent census of law enforcement agencies, there are only 50 federal law enforcement agencies in the United States, but there are 17,985 state and local law enforcement agencies in operation (Reaves, 2011). Fifty of these are state agencies. The remaining agencies are found in counties, cities, and towns, reflecting the fact that local governments dominate the police function. At the state and local levels, these agencies have more than 1 million full-time employees and a total annual budget that exceeds $80 billion (Reaves, 2011).

Police agencies have four major duties:

1. *Keeping the peace.* This broad and important mandate involves the protection of rights and persons in situations ranging from street-corner brawls to domestic quarrels.
2. *Apprehending violators and combating crime.* This is the task the public most often associates with police work, although it accounts for only a small portion of police time and resources.
3. *Preventing crime.* By educating the public about the threat of crime and by reducing the number of situations in which crimes are likely to be committed, the police can lower the rate of crime.
4. *Providing social services.* Police officers recover stolen property, direct traffic, give emergency medical aid, help people who have locked themselves out of their homes, and provide other social services.

Courts

The United States has a **dual court system** that consists of a separate judicial system for each state in addition to a national system. Each system has its own series of courts; the U.S. Supreme Court is responsible for correcting certain errors made in all other court systems. Although the Supreme Court can review cases from both the state and federal

dual court system A system consisting of a separate judicial system for each state in addition to a national system. Each case is tried in a court of the same jurisdiction as that of the law or laws broken.

Although prisons provide the most familiar image of corrections, two-thirds of offenders are actually in the community on probation, community-based sanctions, or parole. Do you ever notice the presence of convicted offenders serving their sentences in the community, or do they cause few problems that attract attention from the public?

AP Images/Elaine Thompson

courts, it will hear only cases involving federal law or constitutional rights. State supreme courts are the final authority for cases that solely concern issues of state law.

With a dual court system, laws may be interpreted differently in various states despite being worded similarly. To some extent, these variations in interpretation reflect different social and political conditions. The dominant values of citizens and judges often differ from one region to another. Differences in interpretation may also be due to attempts by state courts to solve similar problems by different means. For example, before the Supreme Court ruled that evidence obtained by the police in illegal ways should usually be excluded at trials, some states had already established rules barring the use of such evidence in their own courts.

adjudication The process of determining whether the defendant is guilty.

Courts are responsible for **adjudication**—determining whether or not a defendant is guilty. In so doing, they must use fair procedures that will produce just, reliable decisions. Courts must also impose sentences that are appropriate to the behavior being punished. For example, in some cases involving drugs or juveniles, offenders may be sent to specialized courts that focus on those types of cases.

Corrections

On any given day, nearly 7 million American adults (1 of every 36) are under the supervision of state and federal corrections systems (Kaeble, Glaze, et al., 2015). There is no "typical" correctional agency or official. Instead, a variety of agencies and programs are provided by private and public organizations—including federal, state, and local governments—and carried out in many different community and closed settings.

Although the average citizen may equate corrections with prisons, less than 30 percent of convicted offenders are in prisons and jails; the rest are being supervised in the community. Probation and parole have long been important aspects of corrections, as have community-based halfway houses, work release programs, and supervised activities.

The federal government, all the states, most counties, and all but the smallest cities engage in corrections. Nonprofit private organizations such as the Young Men's Christian Association (YMCA) have also contracted with governments to perform correctional services. And for-profit businesses have entered into contracts with governments to build and operate correctional institutions.

The police, courts, and corrections are the main agencies of criminal justice. Each is a part, or subsystem, of the criminal justice system. Each is linked to the other two subsystems, and the actions of each affect the others. These effects can be seen as we examine the flow of decision making within the criminal justice system.

11. What are the four main duties of police?

Keeping the peace, apprehending violators and combating crime, preventing crime, providing social services.

12. What is a dual court system?

A separate judicial system for each state in addition to a national system.

13. What are the major types of state and local correctional facilities and programs? What types of organizations operate them?

Prisons, jails, probation, parole, intermediate sanctions; public, nonprofit, and for-profit agencies carry out these programs.

The Flow of Decision Making in the Criminal Justice System

The processing of cases in the criminal justice system involves a series of decisions by police officers, prosecutors, judges, probation officers, wardens, and parole board members. At each stage in the process, they decide whether a case will move on to the next stage or be dropped from the system. Although the flowchart shown in Figure 1.4 appears streamlined, with cases entering at the top and moving swiftly toward the bottom, the actual route taken may be quite long and may involve many detours. At each step, officials have the discretion to decide what happens next. As a result, many cases are filtered out of the system, others are sent to the next decision maker, and still others are dealt with informally.

Moreover, the flowchart does not show the influences of social relations or of the political environment. In 2006, a retired FBI agent was charged with providing inside information to organized-crime figures so that informants could be murdered. It was then discovered that 30 years earlier, this agent had been caught illegally selling unlicensed handguns to undercover agents of the U.S. Bureau of Alcohol, Tobacco, and Firearms. If this FBI agent had been prosecuted for the handgun sales, his career in the FBI would have been over and he would never have achieved the high-level position that later allegedly allowed him to assist mobsters. However, according to one former federal prosecutor involved in the handgun case in 1976, a high official in the U.S. Justice Department used his discretion to drop the gun charges. According to the former prosecutor, the high official "expressed no other reason not to prosecute the guy except the guy was a cop—and he didn't want to embarrass the [FBI]" (Feuer, 2006). The flowchart does not take into account that someone in authority might exercise discretion unfairly in favor of certain people, such as those with wealth or political connections.

Thus, it is important to recognize that political influence, personal relationships, and specific circumstances may affect how officials' decisions shape the paths and outcomes of individual cases. In the next section, as we follow the 13 steps of the criminal justice process, bear in mind that the formal procedures do not hold in every case. Discretion, political pressure, and other factors can alter the outcome.

Steps in the Decision-Making Process

The criminal justice system consists of 13 steps that cover the stages of law enforcement, adjudication, and corrections. The system could be compared to a kind of assembly line, one where decisions are made about defendants. As these steps are described, recall the concepts discussed earlier: system, exchange, discretion, sequential tasks, and

FIGURE 1.4

The Flow of Decision Making in the Criminal Justice System Each agency is responsible for a part of the decision-making process. Thus the police, prosecution, courts, and corrections are bound together through a series of exchange relationships.

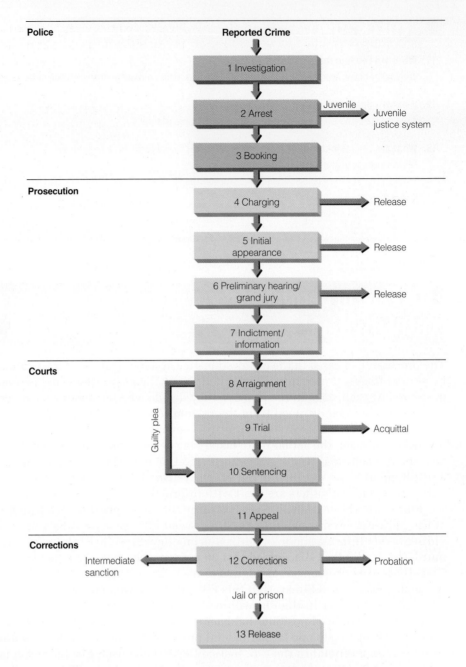

filtering. Be aware that the terms used for different stages in the process may differ from state to state and that the sequence of the steps differs in some parts of the country. Recall how Dustin Diamond's case, described in the chapter opener, moved through these stages toward trial. In general, the flow of decision making follows this pattern:

1. *Investigation.* The process begins when the police believe that a crime has been committed. At this point, an investigation is begun. The police typically depend on a member of the community to report the offense. Except for traffic and public-order offenses, it is unusual for the police to observe illegal behavior themselves. Most crimes have already been committed and offenders have left the scene before the police arrive, placing the police at a disadvantage in quickly finding and arresting the offenders.

2. *Arrest.* If the police find enough evidence showing that a particular person has committed a crime, an arrest may be made. An **arrest** involves physically taking a person into custody pending a court proceeding. This action not only restricts the suspect's freedom but also is the first step toward prosecution.

arrest The physical taking of a person into custody on the grounds that there is reason to believe that he or she has committed a criminal offense. Police are limited to using only reasonable physical force in making an arrest. The purpose of the arrest is to hold the accused for a court proceeding.

Under some conditions, arrests may be made on the basis of a **warrant**—a court order issued by a judge authorizing police officers to take certain actions, such as arresting suspects or searching premises. In practice, most arrests are made without warrants. In some states, police officers may issue a summons or citation that orders a person to appear in court on a certain date. This avoids the need to hold the suspect physically until decisions are made about the case.

3. *Booking.* After an arrest, the suspect is usually transported to a police station for booking, in which a record is made of the arrest. When booked, the suspect may be fingerprinted, photographed, questioned, and placed in a lineup to be identified by the victim or witnesses. Before being questioned, all suspects in custody must also be warned that they have the right to counsel, that they may remain silent, and that any statement they make may be used against them later. Bail may be set so that the suspect learns what amount of money must be paid or what other conditions must be met to gain release from custody until the case is processed.

4. *Charging.* Prosecuting attorneys are the key link between the police and the courts. They must consider the facts of the case and decide whether there is reasonable cause to believe that an offense was committed and that the suspect committed the offense. The decision to charge is crucial because it sets in motion the adjudication of the case.

5. *Initial appearance.* Within a reasonable time after arrest, the suspect must be brought before a judge. At this point, suspects are given formal notice of the charge(s) for which they are being held, advised of their rights, and, if approved by the judge, given a chance to post bail. At this stage, the judge decides whether there is enough evidence to hold the suspect for further criminal processing. If enough evidence has not been produced, the judge will dismiss the case. The purpose of bail is to permit the accused to be released while awaiting trial and to ensure that she or he will show up in court at the appointed time. Bail requires the accused to provide or arrange a surety (or pledge), usually in the form of money or a bond. The amount of bail is based mainly on the judge's view of the seriousness of the crime and the defendant's prior criminal record. Suspects may also be released on their own recognizance (also known as *ROR*, "release on own recognizance")—a promise to appear in court at a later date without the posting of bail. In a few cases, bail may be denied and the accused held because he or she is viewed as a threat to the community.

6. *Preliminary hearing/grand jury.* After suspects have been arrested, booked, and brought to court to be informed of the charges against them and advised of their rights, a decision must be made as to whether there is enough evidence to proceed. The preliminary hearing, used in about half the states, allows a judge to decide whether there is probable cause to believe that a crime has been committed and that the accused person committed it. If the judge does not find probable cause, the case is dismissed. If there is enough evidence, the accused is bound over for arraignment on an **information**—a document charging a person with a specific crime.

   In the federal system and in some states, the prosecutor appears before a grand jury, which decides whether there is enough evidence to file an **indictment** or "true bill" charging the suspect with a specific crime. The preliminary hearing and grand jury are designed to prevent hasty and malicious prosecutions, to protect people from mistakenly being humiliated in public, and to decide whether there are grounds for prosecution.

7. *Indictment/information.* If the preliminary hearing leads to an information or the grand jury vote leads to an indictment, the prosecutor prepares the formal charging document and presents it to the court.

8. *Arraignment.* The accused person appears in court to hear the indictment or information read by a judge and to enter a plea. Accused persons may plead guilty or not guilty or, in some states, stand mute. If the accused pleads guilty, the judge must decide whether the plea is made voluntarily and whether the

warrant A court order authorizing police officers to take certain actions—for example, to arrest suspects or to search premises.

information A document charging an individual with a specific crime. It is prepared by a prosecuting attorney and presented to a court at a preliminary hearing.

indictment A document returned by a grand jury as a "true bill" charging an individual with a specific crime on the basis of a determination of probable cause as presented by a prosecuting attorney.

person has full knowledge of the consequences. When a guilty plea is accepted as "knowing" and voluntary, there is no need for a trial—the judge imposes a sentence, either immediately, for a very minor offense or later, at a scheduled sentencing hearing, for a serious offense.

Plea bargaining may take place at any time in the criminal justice process, but it is likely to be completed just before or soon after arraignment. Very few criminal cases proceed to trial. Most move from the entry of the guilty plea to the sentencing phase.

9. *Trial.* For the small percentage of defendants who plead not guilty, the right to a trial by an impartial jury is guaranteed by the Sixth Amendment if the charges are serious enough to warrant incarceration for more than six months. In many jurisdictions, lesser charges do not entail the right to a jury trial. Most trials are summary, or bench, trials; that is, they are conducted without a jury. Because the defendant pleads guilty in most criminal cases, typically fewer than 10 percent of cases go to trial, and only about half of those are heard by juries. For example, among 33,000 felony defendants whose cases were concluded with either guilty pleas or trials in the nation's 75 largest counties in 2009, only 3 percent went through trials (Reaves, 2013). Whether a criminal trial is held before a judge alone or before a judge and jury, the procedures are similar and are set out by state law and U.S. Supreme Court rulings. A defendant shall be found guilty only if the evidence proves beyond a reasonable doubt that he or she committed the offense.

10. *Sentencing.* Judges are responsible for imposing sentences. The intent is to make the sentence suitable to the offender and to the offense within the limits set by the law. Although criminal codes place limits on sentences, the judge still typically has leeway. Among the judge's options are a suspended sentence, probation, imprisonment, or other sanctions such as fines and community service.

11. *Appeal.* Defendants who are found guilty may appeal convictions to a higher court. An appeal may be based on the claim that the trial court failed to follow the proper procedures or that constitutional rights were violated by the actions of police, prosecutors, defense attorneys, or judges. The number of appeals is small compared with the total number of convictions; further, in about 80 percent of appeals, trial judges and other officials are ruled to have acted properly. Even defendants who win appeals do not go free right away. Normally, the defendant is given a second trial, which may result in an acquittal, a second conviction, or a plea bargain to lesser charges.

12. *Corrections.* The court's sentence is carried out by the correctional subsystem. Probation, intermediate sanctions such as fines and community service, and incarceration are the corrections most often imposed. Probation allows offenders to serve their sentences in the community under supervision. Youthful offenders, first offenders, and those convicted of minor violations are most likely to be sentenced to probation rather than incarceration. The conditions of probation may require offenders to observe certain rules—to be employed, maintain an orderly life, or attend school—and to report to their supervising officer from time to time. If these requirements are not met, the judge may revoke the probation and impose a prison sentence.

Many new types of sanctions have been used in recent years. These intermediate sanctions are more restrictive than probation but less restrictive than incarceration. They include fines, intensive supervision probation, boot camp, home confinement, and community service.

Whatever the various reasons cited for having prisons, they exist mainly to separate criminals from the rest of society. Those convicted of misdemeanors usually serve their time in city or county jails, whereas felons serve time in state prisons. Isolation from the community is one of the most painful aspects of incarceration. Not only are letters and visits restricted, but supervision and censorship are ever present. Moreover, in order to maintain security, prison officials make unannounced searches of inmates and subject them to strict discipline.

13. *Release.* Release may occur when the offender has served the full sentence imposed by the court, but most offenders are returned to the community before that time, under the supervision of a parole officer. Parole continues for the duration of the sentence or for a period specified by law—unless it is revoked and the offender returned to prison because the parole conditions were not met or the parolee committed another crime.

To see the criminal justice process in action, read "The Criminal Justice Process" feature at the end of this chapter, which tells the story of Christopher Jones, who was arrested, charged, and convicted of serious crimes arising from the police investigation of a series of robberies.

The Criminal Justice Wedding Cake

Although the flowchart shown in Figure 1.4 is helpful, recall that not all cases are treated equally. The process applied to a given case, as well as its outcome, is shaped by many factors, including the importance of the case to decision makers, the seriousness of the charge, and the defendant's resources.

Some cases are highly visible, either because of the notoriety of the defendant or the victim or because of the shocking nature of the crime. At the other extreme are "run-of-the-mill cases" involving minor charges and no media attention.

As shown in Figure 1.5, the criminal justice process can be compared to a wedding cake in the sense that different layers show how different cases receive different kinds of treatment in the justice process.

Layer 1 of the "cake" consists of "celebrated" cases that are highly unusual, receive much public attention, result in a jury trial, and often drag on through many appeals. These cases embody the ideal of an adversarial system of justice in which each side actively fights against the other, either because the defendant faces a stiff sentence or because the defendant has the financial resources to pay for a strong defense. Not all cases in Layer 1 receive national attention, however. From time to time, local crimes, especially cases of murder and rape, are treated in this way.

These "Layer 1" cases serve as morality plays. The carefully crafted arguments of the prosecution and defense are seen as expressing key issues in our society or tragic flaws in individuals. Too often, however, the public concludes that all criminal cases follow the same pattern.

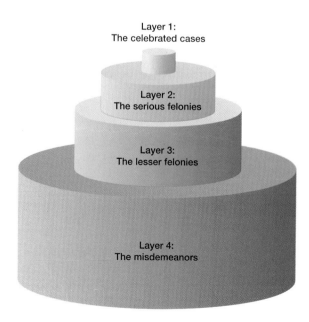

Layer 1:
The celebrated cases

Layer 2:
The serious felonies

Layer 3:
The lesser felonies

Layer 4:
The misdemeanors

FIGURE 1.5

The Criminal Justice Wedding Cake This figure shows that different cases are treated in different ways. Only a very few cases are played out as "high drama"; most are handled through plea bargaining and dismissals.

Source: Drawn from Samuel Walker, *Sense and Nonsense about Crime and Drugs*, 4th ed. (Belmont, CA: Wadsworth, 1998), 30–37.

In 2015, former Virginia governor Bob McDonnell was sentenced to two years in prison after a jury convicted him on corruption charges stemming from his acceptance of gifts from a businessman. The five-week trial had all of the earmarks of a Layer 1 case as a wealthy defendant refused to plead guilty and took his case to trial. Such cases embody the ideal of the due process model with attorneys for each side battling in front of the jury. Should society devote enough resources to the justice system to make it possible for all defendants—rich or poor—to have Layer 1, adversarial trials?

AP Images/Bob Brown

felonies Serious crimes usually carrying a penalty of death or of incarceration for more than one year.

misdemeanors Offenses less serious than felonies and usually punishable by incarceration of no more than one year in jail, or by probation or intermediate sanctions.

crime control model A model of the criminal justice system that assumes freedom for the public to live without fear is so important that every effort must be made to repress crime; it emphasizes efficiency, speed, finality, and the capacity to apprehend, try, convict, and dispose of a high proportion of offenders.

due process model A model of the criminal justice system that assumes freedom for individuals who are wrongly accused and risk unjust punishment is so important that every effort must be made to ensure that criminal justice decisions are based on reliable information; it emphasizes the adversarial process, the rights of defendants, and formal decision-making procedures.

Layer 2 consists of **felonies** that are considered serious by officials. Here we see violent crimes committed by persons with long criminal records against victims unknown to them. Police and prosecutors speak of serious felonies as "heavy" cases that should result in "tough" sentences. In such cases, the defendant has little reason to plead guilty and the defense attorney must prepare for trial.

Layer 3 also consists of felonies, but the crimes and the offenders are seen as less important than those in Layer 2. The offenses may be the same as in Layer 2, but the offender may have no record, and the victim may have had a prior relationship with the accused, for example. The main goal of criminal justice officials is to dispose of such cases quickly. For this reason, many are filtered out of the system, often through plea bargaining.

Layer 4 is made up of **misdemeanors**. About 90 percent of all cases fall into this category. They concern such offenses as public drunkenness, shoplifting, prostitution, disturbing the peace, and traffic violations. Looked on as the "garbage" of the system, these cases are handled by the lower courts, where speed is essential. Prosecutors use their discretion to reduce charges or recommend probation as a way to encourage defendants to plead guilty quickly. Trials are rare; processes are informal; and fines, probation, or short jail sentences result.

The wedding cake model is a useful way of viewing the criminal justice system. Cases are not treated equally. Some are seen as very important; others, as merely part of a large caseload that must be processed. When one knows the nature of a case, one can predict fairly well how it will be handled and what its outcome will be.

Crime Control versus Due Process

Models are simplified representations that illustrate important aspects of a system. As we saw in discussing the wedding cake model, they permit generalized statements and comparisons even though no one model necessarily portrays precisely the complex reality of specific situations. We now look at two more models to expand our picture of how the criminal justice system really operates.

In one of the most important contributions to systematic thought about the administration of justice, Herbert Packer (1968) described two competing models of the administration of criminal justice: the **crime control model** and the **due process model**. These are opposing ways of looking at the goals and procedures of the criminal justice system. The crime control model is much like an assembly line, whereas the due process model is like an obstacle course.

TABLE 1.3	Due Process and Crime Control Models Compared					

What other comparisons can be made between the two models?

	Goal	Value	Process	Major Decision Point	Basis of Decision Making
Due Process Model	Preserve individual liberties	Reliability	Adversarial	Courtroom	Law
Crime Control Model	Repress crime	Efficiency	Administrative	Police/pretrial processes	Discretion

In reality, no one official or agency functions according to one model or the other. Elements of both models are found throughout the system. However, the two models reveal key tensions within the criminal justice process, as well as the gap between how the system is described and the way most cases are actually processed. Table 1.3 presents the major elements of each model.

Crime Control: Order as a Value

The crime control model assumes that every effort must be made to repress crime. It emphasizes efficiency and the capacity to catch, try, convict, and punish a high proportion of offenders; it also stresses speed and finality. This model places the goal of controlling crime uppermost, putting less emphasis on protecting individuals' rights. As Packer points out, in order to achieve liberty for all citizens, the crime control model calls for efficiency in screening suspects, determining guilt, and applying sanctions to the convicted. Because of high rates of crime and the limited resources of law enforcement, speed and finality are necessary. All these elements depend on informality, uniformity, and few challenges by defense attorneys or defendants.

In this model, police and prosecutors decide early on how likely it is that the suspect will be found guilty. If a case is unlikely to end in conviction, the prosecutor may drop the charges. At each stage, from arrest to preliminary hearing, arraignment, and trial, established procedures are used to determine whether the accused should be passed on to the next stage. Instead of stressing the combative aspects of the courtroom, this model promotes bargaining between the state and the accused. Nearly all cases are disposed of through such bargaining, and they typically end with the defendant pleading guilty. Packer's description of this model as an assembly-line process conveys the idea of quick, efficient decisions by actors at fixed stations that turn out the intended product—guilty pleas and closed cases.

Due Process: Law as a Value

If the crime control model looks like an assembly line, the due process model looks more like an obstacle course. This model assumes that freedom is so important that every effort must be made to ensure that criminal justice decisions are based on reliable information. It stresses the adversarial process, the rights of defendants, and formal decision-making procedures. For example, because people are poor observers of disturbing events, police and prosecutors may be wrong in presuming a defendant to be guilty. Thus, people should be labeled as criminals only on the basis of conclusive evidence—that is, the government must be forced to prove beyond a reasonable doubt that the defendant is guilty of the crime. Therefore, the process must give the defense every opportunity to show that the evidence is not conclusive, and the outcome must be decided by an impartial judge and jury. According to Packer, the assumption that the defendant is innocent until proved guilty has a far-reaching impact on the criminal justice system.

Prosecutors must prove their cases while obeying rules dealing with such matters as the admissibility of evidence and respect for defendants' constitutional rights. Forcing the state to prove its case in a trial protects citizens from wrongful convictions. Thus, the due process model emphasizes particular aspects of the goal of doing justice by protecting the rights of individuals and reserving punishment for those who unquestionably deserve it. These values are stressed even though some guilty defendants may go free because the evidence against them is not conclusive enough. By contrast, the crime control model values efficient case processing and punishment over the possibility that innocent people might be swept up in the process.

▼ CHECK POINT

14. **What are the steps of the criminal justice process?**
    (1) Investigation, (2) arrest, (3) booking, (4) charging, (5) initial appearance, (6) preliminary hearing/grand jury, (7) indictment/information, (8) arraignment, (9) trial, (10) sentencing, (11) appeal, (12) corrections, (13) release.

15. **What is the purpose of the wedding cake model?**
    To show that not all cases are treated equally or processed in an identical fashion.

16. **What are the main features of the crime control model and the due process model?**
    Crime control: Every effort must be made to repress crime through efficiency, speed, and finality. Due process: Every effort must be made to ensure that criminal justice decisions are based on reliable information; it stresses the adversarial process, the rights of defendants, and formal decision-making procedures.

STOP & ANALYZE

Where in the wedding cake model is there a risk of incorrect or unjust outcomes? At the top—if effective defense lawyers persuade a judge or jury to acquit a guilty person? At the bottom— where quick administrative processing lacks the opportunity for defense attorneys to challenge the nature and quality of evidence? Make an argument for which layer of the wedding cake—and its related processes—carries the greatest risk of error.

Crime and Justice in a Multicultural Society

One of the most important American values is that of equal treatment. This value is prominently displayed in national documents such as the Declaration of Independence and the Fourteenth Amendment to the Constitution, which guarantees the right to "equal protection." Critics of the criminal justice system argue that this right is hampered by discretionary decisions and other factors that produce racial discrimination. Such discrimination calls into question the country's success in upholding the values that it claims to regard as supremely important. Consequently, it is instructive to look closely at whether or not discrimination exists in various criminal justice settings.

This issue exploded as a central controversy in American society after 2014 with the emergence of the "Black Lives Matter" Twitter hashtag and the related protest movement. Highly publicized deaths of African Americans at the hands of white police, including several videotapes released to the public, triggered protest marches, lawsuits, and a national commission to suggest reforms for police training and practices. In some cases, police officers were charged with crimes, but in other cases the officers' actions were labeled as "justifiable," leading to outrage from many critics. One key element of this debate is the question of whether an individual's race affects how that person is treated by criminal justice officials. An examination of that issue is presented in the text below. A second key element is the question of whether criticisms of police officers and other officials are fair and appropriate. Read the "Current Controversies in Criminal Justice" feature to consider this issue—an issue that will be at the center of controversies discussed in later chapters of this book.

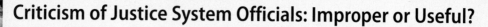

Criticism of Justice System Officials: Improper or Useful?

The year 2014 brought forth visible public controversies about unequal treatment of African Americans and whites by certain police officers as well as complaints about excessive use of force by police and the failure of police officers to be punished for such actions. Public protest marches emerged around the country in the aftermath of grand juries' decisions in Missouri and New York not to charge white police officers with crimes after those officers caused the deaths of African American men under questionable circumstances. Unarmed teenager Michael Brown was shot after he walked away from an altercation with a police officer in Ferguson, Missouri. An officer used a neckhold that contributed to the death of Eric Garner, a man accused of illegally selling individual cigarettes in New York. Amid debates about these cases, in late December 2014, two police officers in New York City were shot and killed as they sat in their patrol vehicle. The man who shot them subsequently committed suicide. The killer had shot in his girlfriend and then traveled from Baltimore to New York while indicating his intention to kill police officers in social media posts that referenced the deaths of Brown and Garner.

In the aftermath of the police officers' murders, New York City police union officials and Republican politicians claimed that Democratic New York City Mayor Bill de Blasio had "blood on his hands" and bore responsibility for the killings because he had previously expressed understanding of protesters' concerns about improper police actions. In fact, de Blasio had provoked the anger of police officers a year earlier in his successful election campaign when he opposed their stop-and-frisk practices targeting young minority men. At the same time, former New York City mayor and Republican political candidate Rudolph Giuliani publicly claimed that President Obama bore responsibility for the police officers' murders because, according to Giuliani, the president had spent months since the Brown and Garner deaths saying "that everybody should hate the police." It is notable that the *Washington Post* newspaper carefully examined all of Obama's statements in the preceding months, found nothing to support Giuliani's claim, and awarded Giuliani's statement a "Four Pinocchios" rating as being a complete falsehood.

The results of the newspaper's examination of Giuliani's statements as well as the New York police union's preexisting opposition to Mayor de Blasio for his previous criticisms of their stop-and-frisk tactics—tactics which a federal judge found to be unconstitutional—serve as reminders that criticisms voiced about officials can be politically motivated. Republican politicians consistently looked for ways to criticize Democratic President Obama through his time in office, and the New York police union was posturing to place the mayor at a disadvantage in negotiations over a new contract.

The risks of quickly condemning critics of police for purportedly causing serious harm were well illustrated when television commentator Bill O'Reilly blamed Black Lives Matter activists for "demoniz[ing]" police and creating "open season on police" in his comments on the September 2015 death-by-shooting of a police officer in Illinois (Perez-Pena, 2015). It turned out later that the officer committed suicide but staged his death to appear to be a murder as he was trying to deflect attention away from the increasing likelihood that he would soon be arrested for embezzling money from a youth program.

The condemnations of Mayor de Blasio, President Obama, and Black Lives Matter activists, among others, for purportedly improperly criticizing criminal justice officials raise a question that often causes discomfort in individual citizens: To what extent should citizens strongly support rather than criticize public employees who work to improve public safety, especially those like police officers who put their lives at risk in the process?

Professors who teach criminal justice courses will sometimes hear a student ask the question: "Why do you hate the police?" This formulation of the question makes clear that some people improperly equate criticism—something that professors often employ—with hatred.

How might one consider the question of whether it is proper to criticize the police or other criminal justice officials? The first step might be to pose the question: Do all of these officials act properly in all circumstances? Clearly not. It is easy to regularly find news stories about officers who engaged in improper conduct. From November 2015 to January 2016, for example, these stories appeared in the news:

- A Maryland police officer was sentenced to prison for pointing a gun at the head of man who had done nothing more than sit in a car legally parked in front of his own home while talking to his cousin;
- A Memphis police officer was convicted of using excessive force in striking a handcuffed arrestee twice in the head;
- An Oklahoma City police officer was convicted of sexually assaulting multiple women while on duty;
- A Houston police officer was convicted of helping a Mexican drug ring distribute illegal narcotics in the United States;
- A Florida police officer was convicted of stealing liquor from people that he investigated for shoplifting;
- A New York City police officer was sentenced for falsifying a police report in an attempt to avoid responsibility for the unjustified arrest of a newspaper photographer.

While it would be wrong to criticize all police based on the actions of a few officers, clearly there is good reason to criticize officers who behave improperly.

At times there are also good reasons to criticize police operations and procedures. In November 2014, a caller to 911 in Cleveland reported watching someone at a park who was pointing a gun at various people. The caller told the 911 operator that the

continued

Current Controversies in Criminal Justice (*continued*)

gun could likely be a toy. As later seen nationwide on a security video, when the Cleveland police patrol vehicle arrived at the scene, within seconds an officer immediately fatally shot a youngster, Tamir Rice, who turned out to be a 12-year-old holding a realistic-looking toy gun. It was soon revealed that the 911 operator neglected to tell the officers that the caller had said the gun might be a toy. In addition, the officers used poor tactics in driving the car right up to the boy on the playground rather than arriving at some distance to give themselves time to assess the situation and ask the boy to put down the toy gun. Moreover, the officer who fired the fatal shot had been found unfit for duty in his previous employment at a suburban police department because of dismal performance in shooting handguns, inability to follow orders, and inability to remain unemotional and think clearly. Yet the Cleveland Police Department never looked at his personnel file from his previous job before hiring him. Sadly, the police officers did not render any first aid to the bleeding boy. Four minutes passed after the shooting before an FBI agent arrived and began to attempt to save the boy with emergency first aid. No one knows if the boy might have survived if given immediate first aid for his wounds.

Might this tragedy have been averted with better hiring procedures and training for officers and 911 operators? Perhaps so. The Cleveland tragedy highlights the fact that critical analysis and criticism are necessary in order to identify flaws and design improvements for policing and every other aspect of criminal justice. One can only identify necessary and realistic plans for improving criminal justice agencies by honestly and critically identifying flaws. Thus

criticism is a necessary element for helping to improve the justice system for the benefit of society. If justice system officials or politicians try to portray criticism as inherently tearing down agencies that ought to be automatically praised, then they may be hindering opportunities to identify problems and seek improvements.

In a democratic society, it is necessary to criticize public officials, in criminal justice and elsewhere in government, in order to make those officials responsive to the citizens and aware of the need to make improvements. Sometimes criticisms will be misguided or unfair, but there will also be opportunities for other voices to provide information that will educate those critics about why their criticisms are not accurate or useful. At other times, there will be disagreements about whether criticisms are warranted, and thus we have a basis for policy debates—a hallmark of a democratic society in which citizens have a role in contributing to either preservation or reform of policies and practices. Fundamentally, criticism of public agencies and officials is an essential element in the exchange of ideas that can help improve government and society. Criticism of police practices should not automatically be equated with "hating" the police. In fact, criticism can actually reflect a strong belief in the possibility that police and other criminal justice actors can move ever closer to the ideal of consistently and ethically enforcing laws with effectiveness and fairness while respecting citizens' constitutional rights.

For Critical Thinking and Analysis

In light of the nation's need for and gratitude to police officers for their essential service to society, are there any criticisms that should never be directed at

police, either because they are inherently unfair or because citizens are not positioned to really know the reality of policing? How should police officials react and respond when they hear criticisms from politicians, community activists, and ordinary citizens? Write a memo in which you make at least two points about each of the foregoing questions.

Sources: Associated Press, "Ex-Houston Officer Convicted in Drug Cartel-Related Case," FoxNews.com, January 15, 2016 (www.foxnews.com); B. Blackwell, "Tamir Rice Killing Caused by Catastrophic Chain of Events: Analysis," Cleveland.com, December 10, 2014 (www.cleveland.com); L. Buhl, "Ex-Officer in Md. Gets 5 Years for Aiming Gun at Man's Head," *Washington Post*, January 8, 2016 (www.washingtonpost.com); "Police Unions, Others Blast de blasio after Shooting Deaths of Two NYPD Cops," CBS New York online, December 20, 2014 (newyork.cbslocal.com); B. Kochman, "Ex-Cop Sentenced to Community Service for Fabricating Facts in Arrest of *New York Times* Photographer," *New York Daily News*, December 2, 2015 (www.nydailynews.com); M. Lee, "Giuliani's Claim that Obama Launched Anti-Police 'Propaganda,'" *Washington Post*, December 23, 2014 (www.washingtonpost.com); C. Mai-Duc, "Cleveland Cop Who Killed Boy, 12, Was Deemed Unfit for Duty," *Los Angeles Times*, December 4, 2014 (www.latimes.com); M. Martinez and J. Mullen, "Victims Describe Assaults by Convicted Ex-Oklahoma City Cop Daniel Holtzclaw," CNN.com, December 11, 2015 (www.cnn.com); R. Perez-Pena, "Officer's Death Stuns Illinois Town a Second Time," *New York Times*, November 4, 2015 (www.nytimes.com); "Officer Convicted of Stealing Liquor from Theft Suspects," WFLX.com, January 14, 2016 (www.wflx.com); "Former Memphis Officer Convicted of Excessive Force," WSFA.com, November 25, 2015 (www.wsfa.com).

Disparity and Discrimination

African Americans, Hispanics, and other minorities are subjected to the criminal justice system at much higher rates than are the white majority (A. Baker, 2010; T. H. Cohen & Kyckelhahn, 2010; Collins, 2016; Epp, Maynard-Moody, & Haider-Markel, 2014; L. Glaze, 2011; McKinley, 2014; "New NYCLU Report," 2012; Poston,

2011; Rainville & Smith, 2003; B. Reaves, 2006; Spohn, 2011; Ulmer, Light, & Kramer, 2011). For example:

- African American men are sent to jails and prisons at a rate 6 times that of whites. The incarceration rate for Hispanic men is nearly 3 times that for whites. For women, the rates are 2.5 times as high (African American) and 1.5 times as high (Hispanics).

- In sentencing for federal crimes, African American male offenders on average received sentences more than 20 percent longer than those imposed on comparable white offenders, and sentences for Hispanic men were nearly 7 percent longer.

- A 2014 study in New York City found that African American and Hispanic defendants are more likely to be held in jail before trial and more likely to be offered plea bargains that include a prison sentence than are whites and Asians charged with the same crimes.

- Studies of traffic stops regularly find that police stop and search African American and Hispanic drivers more frequently than white drivers, even though they are no more likely than whites to be found with weapons or drugs. In 2011, in Milwaukee, for example, African American drivers were 7 times more likely to be stopped and Hispanic drivers were 5 times more likely to be stopped. African American drivers were twice as likely to be searched.

- A 2014 study of traffic stops in Kansas City found that African American and white drivers were equally likely to be stopped when there was a clear traffic violation and officers quickly issued tickets focused on that stop. However, African American drivers were 3 times more likely to be subjected to investigatory stops involving prolonged questioning and vehicle searches.

- Forty-five percent of felony defendants in the 75 largest, most-populous counties in the United States in 2009 were African American, although African Americans comprised only 14 percent of the population of those counties. Hispanics constituted 24 percent of felony defendants while only comprising 19 percent of the population.

- In the country's 40 most-populous counties, more than 60 percent of juvenile felony defendants were African Americans.

- A 2010 study in New York City concluded that African American and Hispanic pedestrians were 9 times more likely than whites to be stopped and searched by the police, although they were less frequently found to be carrying illegal weapons and were no more likely than whites to be arrested.

- A 2012 study found that of the 685,724 people stopped and questioned by New York City police in the preceding year, 87 percent were African American or Hispanic. Among those stopped, 90 percent were innocent and were neither ticketed nor arrested. Fifty-seven percent of these innocent people were also searched by police. Although young African American and Hispanic men in the 14-to-24 age group account for only 4.7 percent of the city's population, they were subjected to nearly 42 percent of police stops, and 90 percent of those stopped were innocent people about whom there was no evidence of wrongdoing.

- A 2016 report found that Connecticut police, when faced with a choice between giving a warning and using a stun gun, used electric stun guns disproportionately on minority group members, and gave warnings disproportionately to whites.

The experiences of minority group members with the criminal justice system may contribute to differences in their expressions of confidence about the fairness of institutions and individual actors in the criminal justice system (Epp, Maynard-Moody, & Haider-Markel, 2014; Lundman & Kaufman, 2003). Many young men, in particular, can describe multiple incidents when they were followed by officers, temporarily taken into custody, forced by police to hand over money or property, or subjected to physical force for no reason other than that they were walking down the sidewalk (Peart, 2011; Brunson, 2007). As an African American college

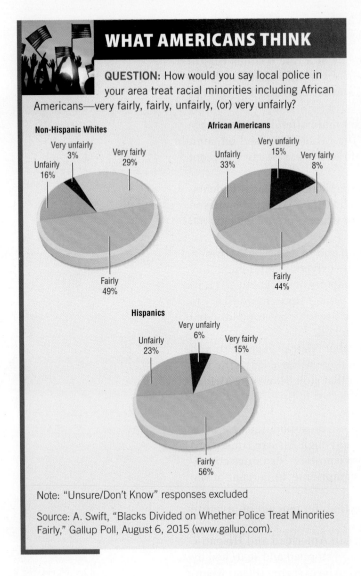

WHAT AMERICANS THINK

QUESTION: How would you say local police in your area treat racial minorities including African Americans—very fairly, fairly, unfairly, (or) very unfairly?

Non-Hispanic Whites

Very unfairly 3%
Unfairly 16%
Very fairly 29%
Fairly 49%

African Americans

Very unfairly 15%
Unfairly 33%
Very fairly 8%
Fairly 44%

Hispanics

Very unfairly 6%
Unfairly 23%
Very fairly 15%
Fairly 56%

Note: "Unsure/Don't Know" responses excluded

Source: A. Swift, "Blacks Divided on Whether Police Treat Minorities Fairly," Gallup Poll, August 6, 2015 (www.gallup.com).

---

student in New York City wrote after the fifth time he was searched for no reason and, in the last search, actually handcuffed while the officers took his keys and illegally entered his apartment, "The police should consider the consequences for a generation of young people who want nothing to do with them—distrust, alienation, and more crime" (Peart, 2011). See the "What Americans Think" feature for more on this subject.

A central question is whether racial and ethnic disparities like those just listed are the result of discrimination (S. Walker, Spohn, & DeLone, 2012). A **disparity** is simply a difference between groups. Such differences can often be explained by legitimate factors. For example, the fact that 18-to-24-year-old men are arrested out of proportion to their numbers in the general population is a disparity explained by the fact that this age group produces more crime. It is not thought to be the result of public policy of singling out young men for arrest. **Discrimination** occurs when groups are differentially treated without regard to their behavior or qualifications—for example, when people of color are routinely sentenced to prison regardless of their criminal history. In other words, disparities can result from either fair or unfair practices.

Explaining Disparities

Racial disparities in criminal justice are often explained in one of three ways: (1) people of color commit more crimes; (2) the criminal justice system is racially biased, with the result that people of color are treated more harshly; or (3) the criminal justice system expresses the racial bias found in society as a whole. We consider each of these views in turn.

disparity A difference between groups that may be explained either by legitimate factors or by discrimination.

discrimination Differential treatment of individuals or groups based on race, ethnicity, gender, sexual orientation, or economic status, instead of on their behavior or qualifications.

Explanation 1: People of Color Commit More Crimes   Nobody denies that the proportion of minorities arrested and placed under correctional supervision (probation, jail, prison, parole) is greater than their proportion in the general population. However, people disagree over whether racial bias is responsible for the disparity.

In theory, disparities in arrests and sentences might be due to legitimate factors. For example, prosecutors and judges are supposed to take into account differences between serious and petty offenses and between repeat and first-time offenders. It follows that more people of color will end up in the courts and prisons if they are more likely to commit serious crimes and have more-serious prior records than do whites (S. Walker, Spohn, & DeLone, 2012).

But why would minorities commit more crimes? The most extreme argument is that they are more predisposed to criminality. This assumes that people of color are a "criminal class." Research-based evidence does not support this view. Behavior that violates criminal laws is prevalent throughout all segments of society. For example, police made more than 6 million arrests of *whites* in 2014, including more than 183,000 arrests for aggravated assault, nearly 31,000 arrests for robbery, and 3,800 arrests for murder and manslaughter (FBI, 2015). Moreover, there are similar rates of illegal drug and marijuana use for whites, African Americans,

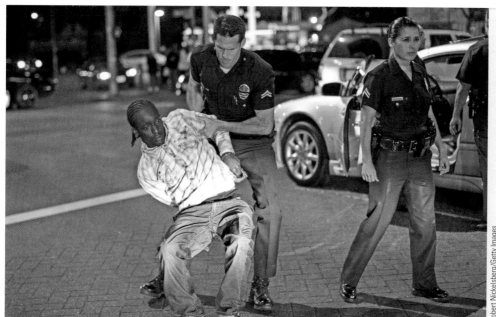

Many young African American and Hispanic men complain that police follow, stop, and search them without proper justification. In light of your own experience, do you see evidence that a person's race may play a role in arousing the suspicions of some police officers? What other factors may enhance police suspicions?

Robert Nickelsberg/Getty Images

and Hispanics (U.S. Department of Health and Human Services, 2014). Indeed, self-report studies show that nearly every adult American has committed an act for which she or he could be jailed. However, most are never caught for such common acts as using drugs, falsifying business-expense reports, driving drunk, cheating on taxes, or inflicting violence on an intimate partner.

Many of these kinds of crimes are difficult to detect or are low priorities for law enforcement agencies. In other instances, affluent perpetrators are better positioned to gain dismissals because of their status within the community, their social networks, or access to high-quality legal representation.

In evaluating theories about possible links between race and crime, we must be aware that many commentators may be focusing only on crimes that resulted in prosecutions. Such limitations can distort an accurate understanding of this important issue. Race itself is not a cause of criminal behavior. Instead, any apparent associations between crime and race relate only to subcategories of people within racial and ethnic groups, such as poor young men, as well as certain categories of crimes that are commonly investigated and prosecuted, such as open drug transactions in poor neighborhoods. Research links crime to social contexts, not to race (Bruce, 2003).

Crime problems evolve and change over time. Identity theft and computer crime, for example, cause economic losses in the billions of dollars, yet no one has claimed a link between these crimes and race. Even if we look at developments affecting only "street crimes," we can see that factors other than race appear to create the contexts for criminal behavior.

For example, one of the most significant crime problems to hit the United States at the dawn of the twenty-first century is the "meth crisis": the spread of highly addictive methamphetamine that can be "cooked" in homemade labs using over-the-counter medicines and readily available chemicals. Americans use this inexpensive, dangerous drug more often than crack cocaine or heroin. Yet, this drug's use has been most prevalent among poor whites in rural areas and has contributed to burglaries and robberies by white addicts seeking to support their drug habits (Harkin, 2005). In 2014, the death of actor Phillip Seymour Hoffman drew news media attention to the soaring rates for addiction and overdose deaths from heroin among white people in suburbs and small towns (Chen & Wilbur, 2014; Riddell, 2014). As with meth addiction, heroin use can lead to theft crimes and burglaries as addicts seek money to support their drug habits. Indeed, even the son of a U.S. senator was arrested for several thefts and car break-ins as he struggled with his heroin problem (Heil, 2014).

The link between crime and economic disadvantage is significant (Steffensmeier, Feldmeyer, Harris, & Ulmer, 2011; McNulty & Bellair, 2003). The meth crisis has spread among poor whites in rural areas and small towns. Other kinds of crime prevail among the poor in urban areas, where minority groups suffer greatly from poverty and unemployment. Less than 10 percent of whites live in poverty, compared with 26 percent of African Americans and 24 percent of Hispanics (U.S. Department of Health and Human Services, 2015). Unemployment rates are highest among people of color, and family income is lowest. In December 2015, white males over age 20 were unemployed at a rate of 4.2 percent, while the unemployment rate for African American men was 8.7 percent (Bureau of Labor Statistics, 2016). The gap may actually be even larger if minorities are overrepresented among the half-million people classified as "discouraged workers" who are not counted in government unemployment statistics because they have given up trying to find a job.

If poor people seek to steal, it is likely to be through available means, whether burglaries at farmhouses or carjacking and shoplifting in urban areas. These sorts of crimes receive more attention from police than do crimes such as tax cheating, employee theft, and illegal stock transactions, which are associated with economic advantage. In light of the associations between race and poverty and between economic status and criminal opportunities, it is not surprising to find Native Americans, Hispanics, and African Americans overrepresented among perpetrators of certain categories of crimes, especially those that are the focus of police attention (Beckett, Nyrop, & Pfingst, 2006).

Explanation 2: The Criminal Justice System Is Racially Biased

Racial disparities result if people who commit similar offenses are treated differently by decision makers in the criminal justice system because of their race or ethnicity. In this view, the fact that people of color are arrested more often than whites does not mean that they are more crime-prone. Critics point to *racial profiling* as an example of what many people believe is a racially biased activity by police (K. Johnson, 2010). Racial profiling involves police officers disproportionately targeting people from certain racial and ethnic groups for investigation without proper legal justification. In other words, instead of being based on the actual behavior of individuals, police actions are triggered by race-based assumptions about the criminality of members of a demographic group. For example, if law enforcement officials single out African Americans, Hispanics, Arabs, and others for traffic stops based on their skin color, critics regard the stops as discriminatory, and as evidence of racism. Evidence of racial profiling has led to new laws and policies that require many police departments to keep records about their traffic–law enforcement patterns (Diedrich & Barton, 2013; Engel, Calnon, & Bernard, 2002).

Despite efforts to monitor and prevent such activities, evidence that some police officers use race as the basis for stopping, searching, and arresting individuals persists (Diedrich & Barton, 2013; Rojek, Alpert, & Decker, 2012; Alpert, 2007). Obviously, racial profiling activities—or the lack thereof—can vary from officer to officer and from police department to police department (Warren et al., 2006). Recent studies showing that African American drivers are 7 times more likely than white drivers to be stopped in Milwaukee and African American pedestrians are 9 times more likely to be stopped and searched in New York City echo prior research that provides evidence of racial bias in many states (Poston, 2011; A. Baker, 2010). For example, a 2005 study of Texas law enforcement agencies reported that the Houston Police Department searched 12 percent of African American drivers and 9 percent of Hispanic drivers stopped by its officers, but searched only 3.7 percent of white drivers who were pulled over (Steward & Totman, 2005).

Finally, a nationwide study of traffic stops found that the odds of being searched were 50 percent higher for African American drivers and 42 percent higher for Hispanic drivers than for white drivers (Durose, Schmitt, & Langan, 2005; Engel & Calnon, 2004).

If minority group members are stopped, searched, subjected to rough use of force, and arrested at higher rates than whites, even if they do not have higher rates of committing offenses, then they will be overrepresented among those drawn into the criminal justice system. They are also at risk of being subjected more frequently to the use of force by police (Mullainathan, 2015). Moreover, there are risks of needless harm to police–community relations and the cooperation that criminal justice officials need from the public when innocent people feel targeted because of the color of their skin. Prominent people are not immune from being treated improperly in situations that raise concerns that officers' actions were motivated, at least in part, by the individual's race. In 2015, many people were shocked by the publicized release of a hotel security video showing a plainclothes police officer roughly tackling onto the sidewalk James Blake, a retired world-ranked tennis player and former Harvard University All-American, when he was mistaken for a suspect in a credit card fraud investigation (Goodman, 2015). Many people wondered: Would a white person who was standing perfectly still and not attempting to flee be treated in such a rough manner when suspected of a nonviolent theft offense? There have been many instances of prominent African Americans being stopped by police for what they believe was merely "driving while Black." For example, comedian Chris Rock documented on social media his experiences of being stopped by police three times in a seven-week period in 2015 while driving near his home in an affluent suburban community in New Jersey (Pearson, 2015).

The issue appears to be widespread. A study in 2015 that examined police records of traffic stops and vehicle searches in seven states found that African American drivers were stopped by police in numbers disproportionate to their percentage of the local population. They were also much more likely to be searched, even though the evidence indicated that white drivers were more likely to be found with criminal contraband such as drugs or illegal firearms (LaFraniere & Lehren, 2015). For example, in Greensboro, North Carolina, "officers were more likely to stop black drivers for no discernible reason. And they were more likely to use force if the driver was black, even when they did not encounter physical resistance" (LaFraniere & Lehren, 2015). In addition, officers arrested 4 times as many African American drivers "on the sole charge of resisting, obstructing, or delaying an officer," even though that offense is "so borderline that some North Carolina police chiefs discourage its use unless more serious crimes are involved" (LaFraniere & Lehren, 2015).

Evidence of racial profiling in the criminal justice system is not limited to traffic enforcement. A study by the U.S. Government Accountability Office (2000), the research agency that provides reports to Congress, discovered that African American women returning from abroad were 9 times as likely as white women to be held and subjected to X-ray searches of their bodies at airports, even though white women were found to be carrying illegal contraband into the country twice as often as African American women were.

For people who do not personally experience these situations and do not see such things happen to their friends and relatives, it can be difficult to feel certain that these problems really exist to the extent that critics claim. Read the "Close Up" feature to examine a personal perspective on this issue.

Is the criminal justice system racially biased? White Americans are less likely than African Americans to attribute the overrepresentation of minorities to biased decision making. A study published in 2008 found that 71 percent of African Americans believe that police bias is a "big reason" minorities are disproportionately convicted of crimes and imprisoned, but only 37 percent of whites share this

What I Learned about Stop-and-Frisk from Watching My Black Son

Note: One of the authors of this textbook, Dr. Christopher E. Smith, wrote this essay in 2014 as part of a series of perspectives on the New York City Police Department's stop-and-frisk practices. He wrote it based on his experiences as a white father of biracial children who are treated as African Americans by others in American society based on their skin color and physical appearance. New York City adopted a policy of stopping and frisking (i.e., a search of the outer clothing) hundreds of thousands of people, nearly 90 percent of whom were African American and Hispanic, although 90 percent of the individuals stopped were innocent of any offense. Among these stops, 42 percent were directed at young minority men, although they made up less than 5 percent of the city's population. This practice was the subject of a lawsuit in which a federal judge condemned the practice because, under American law, such stops are supposed to occur only when an individual has engaged in suspicious behavior that reasonably leads the officer to believe that the person is armed and involved in criminal activity (Terry v. Ohio, 1968). People are not supposed to be stopped based on their age, race, or gender. Such stops made without any justification based on individuals' specific, suspicious behaviors would violate their Fourth Amendment rights under the U.S. Constitution. In the evidence presented in the New York City lawsuit, a patrol officer secretly taped his supervisor instructing him to stop and frisk young African American men (Gearty & Siemaszko, 2013).

When I heard that my 21-year-old son, a student at Harvard, had been stopped by New York City police on more than one occasion during the brief summer he spent as a Wall Street intern, I was angry. On one occasion, while wearing his best business suit, he was forced to lie face-down on a filthy sidewalk because—well, let's be honest about it, because of the color of his skin.

Under New York law, a pedestrian can be stopped by police only when the officer "reasonably suspects that such person is committing, has committed, or is about to commit" a felony or misdemeanor. Such stops justify the officer in asking questions and requesting identification. The additional intrusion of a patdown search of the person's outer clothing is only justified when the officer "reasonably suspects that he is in danger of physical injury." How then does a well-dressed, unarmed person merely walking down the sidewalk end up face-down on the concrete? As an attorney and a college professor who teaches criminal justice classes, I knew that his constitutional rights had been violated. As a parent, I feared for his safety at the hands of the police.

Moreover, as the white father of an African American son, I am keenly aware that I never face the suspicion and indignities that my son continuously confronts. In fact, all of the men among my African American in-laws—and I literally mean every single one of them—can tell multiple stories of unjustified investigatory police stops of the sort that not a single one of my white male relatives has ever experienced.

Some commentators argue that such stop-and-frisk searches are merely a "special tax" that young minority men must endure in order to reduce crime. However, scholars disagree about whether crime rate data really substantiate the claim that such tactics make society safer. New York City saw crime rates decline while using its widespread stop-and-frisk tactics, but other cities also saw crime rate declines without using such tactics.

Proponents of stop-and-frisk often suggest that the imposition on their liberty and their equal right to walk unimpeded down city sidewalks would be tolerable for minority group members if officers were trained to be polite rather than aggressive and authoritarian. We need to remember, however, that with respect to African American men, we are talking about imposing an additional burden on a demographic that *already* experiences a set of alienating "taxes" not shared by the rest of society.

I can tell myriad stories about the ways my son is treated with suspicion and negative presumptions in nearly every arena of his life. I can describe the terrorized look on his face when, as a 7-year-old trying to learn how to ride a bicycle on the sidewalk in front of our suburban house, he was followed at 2-miles-per-hour from a few feet away by a police patrol car—a car that sped away when I came out of the front door to see what was going on. I can tell stories of teachers, coaches, and employers who have forced my son to overcome a presumption that he will cause behavior problems or that he lacks intellectual capacity. I can tell you about a U.S. Customs official inexplicably ordering both of us to exit our vehicle and enter a building at the Canadian border crossing so that a team of officers could search our car without our watching—an event that never occurs when I am driving back from Canada by myself.

If I had not witnessed all this so closely, I never would have fully recognized the extent of the indignities African American boys and men face. Moreover, as indicated by research recently published in the *American Journal of Preventive Medicine,* the cumulative physical toll this treatment takes on African American men can accelerate the aging process and cause early death. Thus, no "special tax" on this population can be understood without recognizing that it does not exist as a small, isolated element in people's lives.

It is equally important to recognize the more acute dangers posed by these encounters. When my son was walking home one night during his summer in New York City, two men jumped out of the shadows and grabbed him.

Any reasonable person would instantly have been jolted into wondering, "Am I being robbed?" That question demands quick decision making: "Do I defend myself? Do I break free and try to run away?"

However, because cautious African Americans learn that they are frequent targets of sudden and unexplained police stops, they must suppress their rational defensive reactions with self-imposed docility. What if these were plainclothes police officers? Any resistance could have led to my son's being tasered or even shot. And if the police were to shoot him in this context—all alone in the shadows on an empty street late at night—that act would likely be judged as a justifiable homicide. In my son's case, it turned out that they were plainclothes police officers who failed to identify themselves until the encounter was well underway.

This example is by no means unique. My African American brother-in-law, a white-collar professional who works for a major corporation, was driving to my house on Thanksgiving Day with his 20-something son when their car was stopped and surrounded by multiple police vehicles. The police officers immediately pointed guns at my relatives' heads. If my brother-in-law or nephew—or one of the officers—had sneezed, there could have been a terribly tragic police shooting. After the officers looked them over and told them that they could go, my relatives asked why they had been stopped. The officers hemmed and hawed before saying, "You fit the description of some robbery suspects—one was wearing a Houston Astros jersey just like the one your son is wearing."

In reality, if my in-laws had fit the description of the robbery suspect so well, there is no way the police could have ruled them out as the robbers without searching their car. Sadly, it seems likely that the police were stopping—and presumably pointing guns at—every African American male driver who happened by. I have heard similar stories from other African American friends—and never from any white friend or relative.

Many have noted that stop-and-frisk practices hinder important constitutional values: the liberty to walk freely down the sidewalk; the reasonable expectation of privacy against unjustified invasion of one's person by government officials; and the equal protection of the laws. But even the best-intentioned white writers often gloss over the actual human impacts of these encounters. Now and again, an individual white elite will have an experience that personalizes this principle of individualized suspicion.

For example, Linda Greenhouse, the Yale Law School Research Scholar and *New York Times* columnist, once wrote about the "unnerving" experience of being "unaccountably pulled over by a police officer" in a quiet, residential neighborhood in Washington, DC, at night. As Greenhouse wrote, "My blood pressure goes up as I recall it years later." Michael Powell, another white *New York Times* columnist, learned from his two 20-something sons that they had never been stopped by police despite traveling regularly all over New York City. By contrast, when he interviewed eight male African American students at a New York City college, they told him they had cumulatively been stopped a total of 92 times—in encounters that included rough physical treatment. Neither of these writers lacked knowledge about these issues, but their experiences obviously humanized and heightened their awareness.

My son's experiences aside, I can only call on one personal reference when the issue of stop-and-frisk is raised. As a graduate student in April 1981, I spent spring break traveling around Europe. When I visited Germany at this historical moment when the Berlin Wall was still in place and the Communist Party still ruled East Germany, I decided to spend one afternoon walking around Communist East Berlin. I quickly found myself being stopped at every single street corner by police officers whose suspicions were undoubtedly raised by my American clothing. Because of my limited knowledge of German, every encounter involved emphatic demands and raised voices, accompanied by threatening hand-slapping gestures. While Linda Greenhouse described her one-time experience with a police officer as "unnerving,"

my encounter with a Communist police state would be better described as "suffocating." I had the sense of being helplessly trapped, aware that no matter which direction I chose to walk, I would find more police waiting for me on the next block. I often wonder whether suspicionless stop-and-frisk searches regularly force African American males into an East Berlin–like sense of oppression—while the rest of us go our merry way without noticing.

I understand the necessity and inevitability of police discretion. I also understand the pressures we place on law enforcement agencies to prevent and control crime. However, stop-and-frisk practices frequently disregard the basic requirements laid out in the seminal 1968 Supreme Court case *Terry v. Ohio*. The Court ruled that an officer preforming a stop should note "unusual conduct which leads him reasonably to conclude in light of his experience that criminal activity may be afoot and that the persons with whom he is dealing may be armed and presently dangerous." By contrast, in their reports on stop-and-frisk encounters, contemporary New York City police officers can merely check a box that says "furtive movements" or one that implausibly just says "other."

If we truly believe that we must impose the "special tax" of setting aside Fourth Amendment constitutional rights against "unreasonable searches and seizures" by using suspicion-less searches to control crime, then shouldn't we all share the burden of that "special tax"? Is it fair to impose that burden on an already-overburdened demographic group (young African American males) because of their age, gender, and skin color? If we believe in this approach to crime control and think it is more important than constitutional rights, then wouldn't we control even more crime by also searching white men and women, the wealthy as well as the poor? Some might say, "Wait, it's a waste of the officers' time to impose these searches on innocent people instead of searching people who might actually be criminals." But the evidence shows that New York City police were already imposing stop-and-frisk searches on innocent people

continued

Close Up (continued)

nearly 90 percent of the time—it is just that the burden of those stops and searches was overwhelmingly imposed on innocent young minority men. If police start stopping and frisking hundreds of thousands of white women and men in the manner they have been searching young minority men, they will undoubtedly issue some citations and make some arrests. There are middle-class white people in possession of illegal guns—not to mention heroin, illegal prescription painkillers, and marijuana. The success rates of these searches may not be high. But low success rates have not stopped them from searching young men minority men for contraband and weapons.

If police were actually to apply this idea, even for a short while, it would test society's disregard for individualized suspicion and force us to think more deeply about what it means to impose unjustified stop-and-frisk on large numbers of innocent people. It is easy enough to accept and rationalize away a "special tax" when we apply it to "them." But how will we feel about that burden once it's shared by all of us?

Critical Thinking and Analysis

If you were the mayor of a city employing aggressive stop-and-frisk tactics that disproportionately affected young minority men, what would you do? Is there additional research about stop-and-frisk that you would seek to conduct in order to understand the consequences more fully? Would you feel obligated to defend the practice for fear that crime rates might increase if the practice were stopped? Are there specific changes to the practice—or to training for police officers—that would help the situation? Write a memo describing four things that you would say or do in addressing the controversial use of widespread stop-and-frisk searches.

Source: Adapted from Christopher E. Smith, "What I Learned about Stop-and-Frisk from Watching My Black Son," *The Atlantic* online, April 1, 2014 (http://www.theatlantic.com/national/archive/2014/04/what-i-learned-about-stop-and-frisk-from-watching-my-black-son/359962/). Copyright 2014 by Christopher E. Smith. Used by permission. *Other sources cited*: D. H. Chae et al., "Discrimination, Racial Bias, and Telomere Length among African American Men," *American Journal of Preventive Medicine* 46:103–11; J. Goldstein, "Judge Rejects New York's Stop-and-Frisk Policy," *New York Times,* August 12, 2013 (www.nytimes.com); L. Greenhouse, "Justice in Dreamland," *New York Times,* May 18, 2011 (www.nytimes.com); M. Powell, "Former Skeptic Now Embraces Divisive Tactic," *New York Times,* April 9, 2012 (www.nytimes.com).

view (Unnever, 2008). Yet the arrest rate of minority citizens is greater than their offense rates justify. According to data from the Bureau of Justice Statistics, victims of aggravated assaults identified their assailants as African Americans in 24 percent of cases, yet African Americans made up 34 percent of suspects arrested for aggravated assault. African Americans were 57 percent of the suspects arrested for robbery, but only 42 percent of the suspects described in government surveys of crime victims (Rand & Robinson, 2011). In sum, the odds of arrest are higher for African American suspects than for white suspects. These arrest rates raise the implication that greater police attention is devoted to investigating and arresting African Americans.

With respect to sentencing, research indicates that African American and Hispanic men are less likely than white men to receive the benefit of prosecutors' discretionary recommendations for charge reductions for federal weapons crimes and for lesser sentences in cocaine prosecutions (Shermer & Johnson, 2010; Hartley, Maddan, & Spohn, 2007). A similar finding of racial disparities emerged in a study of who benefits from Florida judges' discretionary authority to "withhold adjudication" for people sentenced to probation so that they can avoid having a felony record if they successfully complete the terms of their probation (Bontrager, Bales, & Chiricos, 2005). African Americans and Hispanics, especially young men, were less likely than whites to benefit from discretionary decisions and other factors so that, in the findings of one study, "young black and Hispanic males bear the disproportionate brunt of sentencing in the federal courts" (Doerner & Demuth, 2010:23).

Research findings indicating the existence of bias do not mean that every minority defendant is treated disadvantageously when compared with white defendants. The existence, nature, and extent of discrimination can vary from community to community (Britt, 2000). Thus, racial discrimination may be limited to specific types of cases, circumstances, and defendants (S. Walker, Spohn, & De Lone, 2012).

Explanation 3: America Is a Racially Biased Society   Some people claim that the criminal justice system is racially biased because it is embedded in a racially biased society. In fact, some accuse the system of being a tool of a racially biased society.

Evidence of racial bias exists in the way society asks the criminal justice system to operate. For example, even though Congress reduced the amount of crack cocaine needed for a specific mandatory sentence in 2010, federal sentencing guidelines still punish users of crack cocaine more harshly than they do users of powder cocaine, despite the drugs being virtually identical in their chemical composition and effect on users (Eckholm, 2010). The key difference is that whites tend to use powder, whereas people of color in the inner cities tend to use crack. Thus, the imposition of significantly harsher punishments for one form of the drug produces racial disparities in imprisonment rates. State and federal legislators pushed for lengthy prison sentences during the perceived "crack crisis" of the late twentieth century. By contrast, government responses to the meth crisis of the early twenty-first century placed greater emphasis on prevention, by means such as limiting sales of over-the-counter medications used to manufacture meth, and rehabilitation. For example, the state of Iowa's 2006 annual report entitled *Iowa's Drug Control Strategy* says, "More treatment and related resources need to be targeted to meth-addicted offenders.... It is only by reducing the demand for meth and other drugs that we can hope to break the cycle of addiction" (Governor's Office on Drug Control Policy, 2006:8). Some observers suspect that the less punitive orientation toward meth offenders, who are predominantly white, may reflect race-based attitudes that perceive crack cocaine offenders, many of whom have been African American, as more dangerous and less worthy of rehabilitation (M. Alexander, 2011). The same emphasis on treatment rather than punishment emerged in 2014 and 2015, as illegal heroin use expanded rapidly among whites in suburbs and small towns. As one newspaper headline expressed it, "In Heroin Crisis, White Families Seek Gentler War on Drugs" (Seelye, 2015).

Other evidence of racial bias in American society shows up in the stereotyping of offenders. For example, African American and Hispanic professionals have been stopped for no legitimate reason and even falsely arrested when the police were looking for a person of color and these individuals happened to be perceived as "out of place." For example, television news host T. J. Holmes was stopped by police officers near his suburban Atlanta home. When the officers recognized him, they became uncomfortable and claimed that they had only stopped him to make sure he had insurance for his car (Roberts, 2012).

If people of color are overrepresented in the justice system because of racial bias in society, the solution may seem a bit daunting. Nobody knows how to quickly rid a society of biased policies, practices, and attitudes.

▼ CHECK POINT

17. **What is meant by racial or ethnic disparities in criminal justice?**
    That racial and ethnic minorities are subjected to the criminal justice system at much higher rates than are the white majority.

18. **What explanation put forward to account for such disparities is most clearly not supported by evidence?**
    Available evidence fails to support the claim that racial disparities exist because minorities commit more crime; instead, evidence of unequal treatment raises questions about the existence of racial bias.

STOP & ANALYZE

If race is influential throughout the criminal justice system, what are three steps that might be taken to attempt to reduce disparities and biased decision making?

In March 2015, police in Elko, Nevada, arrested a Girl Scout volunteer leader who advertised babysitting services, and her husband, who worked as a babysitter for her business. They were arrested for sexually abusing and photographing four girls between the ages of 6 and 10. On the day of the arrest, one police officer told a news reporter after searching the couple's home, "We started viewing photos and learned that she's as involved as he is." They were both charged with the same crimes on the day of the arrests. Both defendants eventually entered guilty pleas through the plea bargaining process. The man pleaded guilty to two counts: lewdness with a child under 14 and abuse or neglect of a child through sexual exploitation. The woman pleaded guilty to four counts of the same abuse or neglect charge. The man was ordered to serve a prison sentence of 25 years to life. The woman's sentence was 9 to 24 years in prison. The woman's attorney argued at the sentencing hearing that she was obedient to and susceptible to manipulation by her husband. Is this justice? They were involved in the same criminal events that victimized and traumatized four young children. In offering to permit the woman to plead guilty to different charges, were the prosecutors influenced by different assumptions about the roles and relationships of men and women in a marriage? At the sentencing, the judge scolded the wife for her role in finding the children to exploit—two through Girl Scouts and two through her babysitting service. In light of that conclusion by the judge, should both defendants have received the same sentences?

Discussion/Writing Assignment

Do prosecutors have an ethical obligation to treat people the same if they are charged with the same crimes or have participated in the same criminal victimizations, no matter who they are? Imagine that you are a newly elected county prosecutor. How would you instruct your assistant prosecutors to handle cases? Could you avoid being influenced by the desire to gain quick convictions through pleas in order to preserve the limited resources of your office—scarce resources that would otherwise be stretched through an increase in time-consuming trials? Write a memo providing instructions for the assistant prosecutors. Be sure to address any ethical issues that influence your position. In a second brief memo, describe how the criminal justice system and the processing of cases in your county would be affected by your instructions.

Sources: F. Godwin-Butler, "Parkers Sentenced in Child Pornography Case," *Elko Daily Free Press*, January 9, 2016 (elkodaily.com); D. Harris, "Wife of Babysitter Also Arrested in Sexual Abuse Case," *Elko Daily Free Press*, March 27, 2015 (elkodaily.com).

SUMMARY

1 Name the goals of the criminal justice system.

- Criminal laws define punishable acts that are wrongs in themselves (*mala in se*) or acts that legislators believe deserve punishment (*mala prohibita*).
- The three goals of the criminal justice system are doing justice, controlling crime, and preventing crime.
- Doing justice forms the basis for the rules, procedures, and institutions of the criminal justice system.
- Controlling crime involves arresting, prosecuting, and punishing those who commit offenses.
- Preventing crime requires the efforts of citizens as well as justice system officials.
- Justice system officials increasingly rely on social science research in order to develop evidence-based policies that may increase their effectiveness in addressing problems and challenges.

2 Identify the different responsibilities of federal and state criminal justice operations.

- Both the national and state systems of criminal justice enforce laws, try cases, and punish offenders.
- Federal officials enforce laws defined by Congress.
- Federal agencies have shifted greater attention to antiterrorist efforts since 9/11.
- Most criminal laws and criminal cases are under the authority of state criminal justice systems.

3 Analyze criminal justice from a systems perspective.

- Criminal justice is composed of many organizations that are interdependent and therefore interact as they seek to achieve their goals.
- The primary subsystems of criminal justice are police, courts, and corrections.
- The key characteristics of the criminal justice system are discretion, resource dependence, sequential tasks, and filtering.

4 Identify the authority and relationships of the main criminal justice agencies, and list the steps in the decision-making process for criminal cases.

- The processing of cases in the criminal justice system involves a series of decisions by police officers, prosecutors, judges, probation officers, wardens, and parole board members.
- The criminal justice system consists of 13 steps that cover the stages of law enforcement, adjudication, and corrections: (1) investigation, (2) arrest, (3) booking, (4) charging, (5) initial appearance, (6) preliminary hearing/grand jury, (7) indictment/information, (8) arraignment, (9) trial, (10) sentencing, (11) appeal, (12) corrections, (13) release.

5 Explain the criminal justice "wedding cake" concept as well as the due process and crime control models.

- The four-layered criminal justice wedding cake model shows that not all cases are treated equally.
- The small top of the wedding cake represents the relatively small number of very serious cases that are processed through trials.
- The lower, larger portions of the wedding cake represent the increasing frequency of plea bargaining for larger numbers of cases as one moves down toward less serious offenses.
- The crime control model and the due process model are two ways of looking at the goals and procedures of the criminal justice system.
- The due process model focuses on careful, reliable decisions and the protection of rights, whereas the crime control model emphasizes efficient processing of cases in order to repress crime.

6 Name the possible causes of racial disparities in criminal justice.

- Analysts look to explain the disproportionate impact of the criminal justice system on minorities by examining the criminal behavior of different groups' members as well as how racial bias affects American society and the criminal justice system.
- Research does not support any theories about race causing criminal behavior.
- Evidence exists that there is differential treatment of members of various racial groups by criminal justice officials in some contexts.

Questions for Review

1. What are the goals of the criminal justice system?
2. What is a system? How is the administration of criminal justice a system?
3. Why is the criminal justice wedding cake model more realistic than a linear model depicting the criminal justice system?
4. What are the major elements of Packer's crime control model and the due process model?
5. What evidence exists concerning the impact of the criminal justice system on members of racial minority groups?

Key Terms

adjudication (p. 22)

arrest (p. 24)

crime control model (p. 28)

crimes (p. 6)

discretion (p. 17)

discrimination (p. 34)

disparity (p. 34)

dual court system (p. 21)

due process model (p. 28)

evidence-based practices (p. 8)

exchange (p. 16)

federalism (p. 10)

felonies (p. 28)

filtering process (p. 19)

indictment (p. 25)

information (p. 25)

mala in se (p. 6)

mala prohibita (p. 6)

misdemeanors (p. 28)

plea bargain (p. 16)

system (p. 15)

warrant (p. 25)

The State of Michigan versus Christopher Jones

In October 1998, police in Battle Creek, Michigan, investigated a string of six robberies that occurred in a 10-day period. People were assaulted during some of the robberies. One victim was beaten so badly with a power tool that he required extensive reconstructive surgery for his face and skull. The police received an anonymous tip on their Silent Observer hotline, which led them to put together a photo lineup—an array of photographs of local men who had criminal records. Based on the tip and photographs identified by the victims, the police began to search for two men who were well known to them, Christopher Jones and his cousin Fred Brown.

Arrest

Jones was a 31-year-old African American. A dozen years of struggling with cocaine addiction had cost him his marriage and several jobs. He had a criminal record stretching back several years, including attempted larceny and attempts at breaking and entering. Thus, he had a record of stealing to support his drug habit. He had spent time on probation and did a short stretch in a minimum-security prison and boot camp. But he had never been caught with drugs or been accused of an act of violence.

Fearing that Jones would be injured or killed by the police if he tried to run or resist arrest, his parents called the police and told them he was holed up in a bedroom at their home. As officers surrounded the house, the family opened the door and showed the officers the way to the bedroom. Jones surrendered peacefully and was led to the waiting police car in handcuffs.

At the police station, a detective with whom Jones was acquainted read him his *Miranda* rights and then informed him that he was looking at the possibility of a life sentence in prison unless he helped the police by providing information about Brown. Jones said he did not want to talk

to the police, and he asked for an attorney. The police thus ceased questioning Jones, and he was taken to the jail.

Booking

At the jail, Jones was strip-searched, given a bright orange jumpsuit to wear, and photographed and fingerprinted. He was told that he would be arraigned the next morning. That night he slept on the floor of the overcrowded *holding cell*—a large cell where people are placed immediately upon arrest.

Arraignment

The next morning, Jones was taken to a room for video arraignment. A two-way camera system permitted Jones to see the district courtroom in the neighboring courthouse. At the same time, the judge and others could view him on a television screen. The judge informed Jones that he was being charged with breaking and entering, armed robbery, and assault with intent to commit murder. The final charge alone could draw a life sentence. Under Michigan law, these charges can be filed directly by the prosecutor without being presented to a grand jury for indictment, as is required in federal courts and

some other states. The judge set bail at $200,000.

At a second video arraignment several days later, Jones was informed that he faced seven additional counts of assault with intent to commit murder, armed robbery, unarmed robbery, and home invasion for four other robberies. Bond was set at $200,000 for each alleged robbery. Thus, he faced 10 felony charges for the five robberies, and his total bail was $1 million.

Unable to make bail, Jones was held in the Calhoun County Jail to await his day in court. Eventually he would spend nine months in the jail before all of the charges against him were processed.

Defense Attorney

Under state court procedures, Jones was supposed to have a preliminary hearing within two weeks of his arraignment. At the preliminary hearing the district judge would determine whether enough evidence had been gathered to justify sending Jones's case up to the Calhoun County Circuit Court, which handled felony trials.

Jones received a letter informing him of the name of the private attorney appointed by the court to represent him, but he did not meet the attorney until he was taken to court for his preliminary hearing. Minutes before the hearing, the attorney, David Gilbert, introduced himself to Jones. Jones wanted to delay any preliminary hearing until a lineup could be held to test the victims' identifications of him as a robber. According to Jones, Gilbert said they must proceed with the preliminary hearing for the armed robbery case in which the victim was beaten with the power tool, because a witness had traveled from another state to testify. The testimony led the district judge to conclude that sufficient evidence existed to move that case to the circuit court on an armed robbery charge.

Lineup

Jones waited for weeks for the lineup to be scheduled. When he was taken to his rescheduled preliminary hearing, his attorney complained to the judge that the lineup had never been conducted. The judge ordered that the lineup be held as soon as possible.

At the lineup Jones and five other men stood in front of a one-way mirror. One by one, the victims of each of the six robberies looked at the men and attempted to determine if any were their assailant. At the end of each identification, one of the men was asked to step forward. Because he was asked to step forward only twice, Jones guessed that he was picked out by two of the victims.

Jones's defense attorney was unable to attend the lineup. Another attorney arrived and informed Jones that he would take Gilbert's place. Although Jones protested that the other men in the lineup were much shorter and older, he was disappointed that the substitute attorney was not more active in objecting that the other men looked too different from Jones to adequately test the victims' ability to make an accurate identification.

Preliminary Hearing

At the next preliminary hearing, the victims of the four additional robberies testified. Because they focused mainly on Brown as the perpetrator of the assaults and robberies, the defense attorney argued that many of the charges against Jones should be dropped. However, the judge determined that the victims' testimony provided enough evidence to send most of the charges against Jones to the circuit court.

Plea Bargaining

Jones waited for weeks in jail without hearing much from his attorney. Although he did not know it, the prosecutor was formulating a plea agreement and communicating to the defense attorney the terms under which some charges would be dropped in exchange for a guilty plea from Jones. A few minutes before a hearing on the proposed plea agreement, Gilbert told Jones that the prosecutor had offered to drop all of the other charges if Jones would

plead guilty to one count of unarmed robbery for the incident in which the victim was seriously injured by the power tool wielded by Brown and one count of home invasion for another robbery. Jones did not want to accept the deal, because he claimed he was not even present at the robbery for which he was being asked to plead guilty to home invasion. According to Jones, the attorney insisted that this was an excellent deal compared with all of the other charges that the prosecutor could pursue. Jones still resisted.

In the courtroom, Judge James Kingsley read aloud the offer, but Jones refused to enter a guilty plea. Like the defense attorney, the judge told Jones that this was a favorable offer compared with the other more serious charges that the prosecutor could still pursue. Jones again declined.

As he sat in the holding area outside the courtroom, Jones worried that he was making a mistake by turning down the plea offer. He wondered if he could end up with a life sentence if one of the victims identified him by mistake as having done a crime that was committed by Brown. When his attorney came to see him, he told Gilbert that he had changed his mind. They went right back into the courtroom and told the judge that he was ready to enter a guilty plea. As they prepared to plead guilty, the prosecutor said that as part of the agreement, Jones would be expected to provide information about the other robberies and to testify against Brown. The defense attorney protested that this was not part of the plea agreement. Jones told the judge that he could not provide information about the home invasion to which he was about to plead guilty because he was not present at that robbery and had no knowledge of what occurred. Judge Kingsley declared that he would not accept a guilty plea when the defendant claimed to have no knowledge of the crime.

After the hearing, discussions about a plea agreement were renewed. Jones agreed to take a polygraph test so that the

prosecutor could find out which robberies he knew about. Jones hoped to show prosecutors that his involvement with Brown was limited, but no polygraph test was ever administered.

Scheduled Trial and Plea Agreement

Jones waited in jail for several more weeks. According to Jones, when Gilbert came to visit him, he was informed that the armed robbery trial was scheduled for the following day. In addition, the prosecutor's plea offer had changed. Brown had pleaded guilty to armed robbery and assault with intent less than murder and was facing a sentence of 25 to 50 years in prison. Because of Brown's guilty plea, the prosecutor no longer needed Jones as a witness against Brown. Thus, the prosecutor no longer offered robbery and home invasion pleas. He now wanted Jones to plead to the same charges as Brown in exchange for dropping the other pending charges. According to Jones, Gilbert claimed that the prosecutor would be very angry if he did not take the plea, and the attorney encouraged Jones to accept the plea by arguing that the prosecutor would otherwise pursue all of the other charges, which could bring a life sentence if Jones refused to plead guilty.

The next day, Jones was given his personal clothes to wear instead of the orange jail jumpsuit, because he was going to court for trial rather than a hearing. Prior to entering court the next day, Jones says Gilbert again encouraged him to accept the plea agreement in order to avoid a possible life sentence after trial. According to Jones, his attorney said that the guilty plea could be withdrawn if the probation office's sentencing recommendation was too high. Because he did not want to risk a life sentence and believed he could later withdraw the plea, Jones decided to accept the offer.

With his attorney's advice, he entered a plea of "no contest" to the two charges. Before taking the plea, Judge Kingsley informed Jones that by entering the plea, he

continued

would be waiving his right to a trial, including his right to question witnesses and to have the prosecutor prove his guilt beyond a reasonable doubt. Judge Kingsley then read the charges of armed robbery and assault with intent to do great bodily harm and asked, "What do you plead?"

Jones replied, "No contest." A "no contest" plea is treated the same as a guilty plea for sentencing purposes. It indicates that the defendant is willing to accept the punishment while not openly admitting to committing the crime. Then the judge asked a series of questions.

Judge Kingsley: "Mr. Jones, has anyone promised you anything other than the plea bargain to get you to enter this plea?"

Jones: "No."

Judge Kingsley: "Has anyone threatened you or forced you or compelled you to enter the plea?"

Jones: "No."

Judge Kingsley: "Are you entering this plea of your own free will?"

Jones: "Yes."

The judge reminded Jones that there had been no final agreement on what the ultimate sentence would be and gave Jones one last opportunity to change his mind about pleading "no contest." Jones repeated his desire to enter the plea, so the plea was accepted.

Immediately after the hearing, Jones had second thoughts. According to Jones, "I was feeling uneasy about being pressured [by my attorney] to take the plea offer . . . [so I decided] to write to the judge and tell him about the pressures my attorney put upon me as well as [the attorney] telling me I had a right to withdraw my plea. So I wrote the judge that night." Jones knew he was guilty of stealing things in one robbery, but he had been unarmed. As it turned out, however, he was not allowed to withdraw his plea.

When Gilbert learned that Jones had written the letter, he asked the judge to permit him to withdraw as Jones's attorney. Judge Kingsley initially refused.

However, it became clear that the relationship between the lawyer and client had deteriorated when Jones spoke in open court, criticizing Gilbert, at his sentencing hearing. The judge decided to appoint a new defense attorney, Virginia Cairns, to handle sentencing at a rescheduled hearing.

Presentence Investigation

Probation officers are responsible for conducting presentence investigations, in which they review offenders' records and interview the offenders about their education, work history, drug use, and family background before making recommendations to the judge about an appropriate punishment. The presentence report prepared by the probation office ultimately recommended 5 to 25 years for armed robbery and 4 to 7 years for assault.

Sentencing

Although arrested in October 1998, Jones was not sentenced until July 1999. At the hearing, Judge Kingsley asked Jones if he would like to make a statement. Jones faced the judge as he spoke, glancing at his family and at the victim when he referred to them.

> First and foremost, I would like to say what happened to the victim was a tragedy. I showed great remorse for that. He is in my prayers along with his family. Even though, your Honor, I'm not making any excuses for what I'm saying here today, the injuries the victim sustained were not at the hands of myself nor did I actually rob this victim. I was present, your Honor, as I told you once before, yes, I was. And it's a wrong. Again I'm not making any kind of excuse whatsoever . . .
>
> Your Honor, I would just like to say that drugs has clouded my memory, and my choices in the past. I really made some wrong decisions. Only times I've gotten into trouble were because of my drug use. . . . One of the worst decisions I really made was my involvement of being around the codefendant Fred Brown. That bothers me to this day because actually we didn't even get along. Because of my drug use again I chose to be around him.

Jones also talked about his positive record as a high school student and athlete, his work with the jail minister, and his desire to talk to young people about his experiences to steer them away from drugs.

Attorney Cairns spoke next. She called the court's attention to several errors in the presentence report that recommended Jones serve 5–25 years for armed robbery and 4–7 years for assault. She emphasized letters of support from Jones's family, which she had encouraged them to write to the judge, describing his positive qualities and prospects for successful rehabilitation.

Next, the victim spoke about his injuries and how his $40,000 worth of medical bills had driven him to bankruptcy.

> I went from having perfect vision to not being able to read out of my left eye. I got steel plates in my head. . . . They left me to die that morning. He took the keys to my car. . . . So today it's true, I don't think Mr. Jones should be sentenced same as Brown. That's who I want—I want to see him sentenced to the maximum. He's the one that crushed my skull with a drill. But Jones did hit me several times while Mr. Brown held me there to begin with. It's true that I did hit him with a hammer to get them off me. But he still was there. He still had the chance of not leaving me without keys to my car so I could get to a hospital. He still had the choice to stop at least and phone on the way and say there's someone that could possibly be dead, but he didn't. . . . You don't treat a human being like that. And if you do you serve time and pretty much to the maximum. I don't ask the Court for twenty-five years. That's a pretty long time to serve. And I do ask the Court to look at fifteen to twenty. I'd be happy. Thank you.

Gary Brand, the assistant prosecutor, rose and recommended a 20-year sentence and noted that Jones should be responsible for $35,000 in restitution to the victim and to the state for the victim's medical expenses and lost income.

Judge Kingsley then addressed Jones. He acknowledged that Jones's drug problem had led to his criminal activity. He also noted that Jones's family support was much stronger than that of most defendants. He chastised Jones for falling into drugs when life was tougher after enjoying a successful high school career. Judge Kingsley then proceeded to announce his sentencing decision.

You are not in my view as culpable as Mr. Brown. I agree with [the victim] that you were there. When I read your letter, Mr. Jones, I was a bit disturbed by your unwillingness to confront the reality of where you found yourself with Mr. Brown. You were not a passive observer to everything that went on in my view. You were not as active a participant as Mr. Brown.... What I'm going to do, Mr. Jones, is as follows: Taking everything into consideration as it relates to the armed robbery count, it is the sentence of the Court that you spend a term of not less than twelve years nor more than twenty-five years with the Michigan Department of Corrections. I will give you credit for the [261 days] you have already served.

The judge also ordered payment of $35,000 in restitution as a condition of parole. He concluded the hearing by informing Jones of his right to file an application for a leave to appeal.

Prison

After spending a few more weeks in jail awaiting transfer, Christopher Jones was sent to the state correctional classification center at Jackson for evaluation to determine to which of Michigan's 40 prisons he would be sent.

Prison security classifications range from level I for minimum to level VI for "supermaximum," high security. Jones was initially assigned to a level IV prison. Because Jones was a high school graduate who had previously attended a community college, he was one of the most highly educated prisoners in his institution. After working as the head clerk of the prison

library in one prison, he was transferred to another prison, where he earned a certificate in substance-abuse counseling. He taught classes on substance abuse and addiction for other prisoners before he was transferred to several different lower-security institutions where he took classes, worked when prison jobs were available, and waited until he was eligible for parole.

Parole

After being incarcerated for more than nine and a half years, Jones came up for consideration for parole. He was interviewed by a parole board member through a closed-circuit television connection. The parole member had a favorable view of the record of Jones's behavior and self-improvement activities in prison. He warned Jones about the consequences if he were to resume taking drugs or commit any crimes after being released. Because Jones had suffered two heart attacks in prison, perhaps as the result of damage to his arteries from drug use, smoking, and other unhealthy habits prior to being incarcerated, Jones assured the parole board member: "Don't worry. I know that if I ever touch drugs again, it will kill me. And I don't want to die." Several months later, Jones received word that his parole had been granted, and he was released from prison after serving 10 years and 3 months of his 12-to-25-year sentence. He returned to his hometown facing the difficulties of finding a job in a depressed economy and attempting to reestablish relationships with his daughter and other family members.

A few months after his release, Jones was arrested and briefly placed in the county jail for violating his parole conditions by missing several appointments and drug tests with his parole officer. He was shaken by the thought of returning to prison. He became very conscientious about fulfilling his parole conditions. He volunteered to speak to churches and

youth groups about the dangers of drugs, and even police officials began to invite him to speak to troubled youths. By the end of his two-year parole period, he was hired to work in a program for high school dropouts to help them earn their diploma and gain work skills. When that program lost its funding, he took community college courses and was hired by a different program as a counselor for ex-offenders who struggled with substance-abuse problems and the challenges of reentering society successfully.

Researching the Internet

Examine closely the lineup procedure that was used to identify Jones as a suspect and then compare it with evidence-based lineup procedures later developed based on research about witnesses' perceptions and memories. Access the National Institute of Justice reports on lineup procedures at http://www.nij.gov/journals /258 /Pages/police-lineups.aspx.

For Critical Thinking and Analysis

Were any aspects of the processes and decisions in the Jones case unfair or improper? Did the outcome of the case achieve "justice"? List three possible issues concerning the processing of the case or the length and nature of the punishment. If you were the victim of the crime for which Jones was imprisoned, would you feel that justice had been achieved?

Sources: Calhoun County Circuit Court transcripts for plea hearing, May 20, 1999, and sentencing hearing, July 16, 1999; T. Christenson, "Two Charged in Violent Robberies," *Battle Creek Inquirer,* October 30, 1998, p. 1A; interview with Christopher Jones, St. Louis Correctional Facility, St. Louis, Michigan, October 19, 1999; letters to Christopher Smith from Christopher Jones, October and November 1999.

AP Images/Elaine Thompson

2 Crime and Crime Causation

LEARNING OBJECTIVES

1 Categorize crimes by their type.

2 Describe the different methods of measuring crime.

3 Explain why some people are at higher risk of victimization than others.

4 Summarize the negative consequences of victimization.

5 Name the theories put forward to explain criminal behavior.

6 Explain why there are gender differences in crime.

On the afternoon of June 5, 2014, Aaron Ybarra entered Otto Miller Hall on the campus of Seattle Pacific University and began shooting. He killed one student and injured two others before being subdued by students at SPU and held until the police arrived (Kang & Stokes, 2014; McLaughlin, 2014). In his journal, Ybarra wrote that he was seeking revenge on people who had humiliated him, and wanted to kill everyone in the world, except his family and friends. He also wrote that he chose Seattle Pacific University because he was unfamiliar with the campus, and thought that the University of Washington and Seattle University "represent Seattle more. I didn't want to have to attack my own city" (Cruz, 2014).

According to his attorney, Ybarra had been diagnosed with a mental illness, yet had not been taking his prescription medication for some time prior to the shootings (Cruz, 2014). The defense was expected to claim that Ybarra was "not guilty by reason of insanity" during his trial scheduled for 2016 ("January Trial Set," 2015). Psychological illness seems to be one possible explanation for his behavior, but are there others? At home, he lived with an alcoholic father and was himself treated for alcohol addiction, and his home life was described as "tumultuous" by reporters investigating his background (Cruz & Baker, 2014). How might these factors help explain his crimes? Could they also help explain other shootings, such as those that occurred in two tragic and highly publicized mass shootings in Colorado, at Columbine High School in 1999 and the Aurora movie theater in 2012?

Later in 2014, Russell "Rusty" Brace, an 81-year-old attorney in Maine, was accused of stealing $3.8 million from Midcoast Charities, an organization for which he had served as president from 2001 through August 2014 (Betts, 2014). The funds raised by Midcoast were meant to help people living in two counties on the coast of Maine; one recipient of funds from Midcoast ran a soup kitchen for residents facing hard times (Ramos, 2014).

Brace was born into a wealthy family and graduated from an Ivy League university. He ran large corporations, ran for state Senate in 1984 (and lost), and accrued significant wealth, including three separate homes. His main residence has been valuated at $774,800 (Ramos, 2014). Brace's assets have been frozen during the court process, and may be awarded to Midcoast Charities to make up for the funds he has stolen, but clearly, many people have been harmed by his actions. After pleading guilty in 2015, Brace was sentenced to serve four years in federal prison and ordered to pay more than $2 million (Betts, 2015).

Clearly, Brace was not lacking for money—so what was his motivation for stealing from a charity that helps those in need? Was it simply greed? Did he feel any guilt about defrauding the people he was tasked with helping? The crime left people in the community stunned and seeking answers to these questions. The victims in this crime include both the people (and organizations) that made sizable donations to Midcoast and the people who might have received important assistance from the charities. How does a crime like this differ from Ybarra's, which left one victim dead and two others injured?

The Seattle Pacific University shooting was highly publicized because it occurred on a peaceful college campus. It was the type of crime that raises the public's worst fears about becoming victims of random violence. The incident also raised significant questions about why anyone would commit such a terrible act. Yet as we consider the possible causes that led to this crime, we also recognize that this shooting is not a typical crime. Obviously, thefts, minor assaults, and credit card fraud are much more common than murders. Do the underlying motivations for all crimes have a common core? Or do different types of crime have distinctly different causes? These and other questions serve to illuminate the issues of victimization and crime causation, the topics of this chapter.

The Seattle Pacific University shooting provides a context in which we can examine a number of important questions. For example, who were the crime victims in this case? Clearly, the SPU students who were shot were victims. But what about their families? Are they also victims because they suffered psychological and emotional harm? Paul Lee, the only fatality in the shooting, used to help his father by working in the family restaurant (Brink, 2014). His death was a devastating loss not only to his family, but also to those who worked at the restaurant, as well as the surrounding community. Also, what about the city of Seattle? Has its reputation as a safe place to live been destroyed? Will fewer people decide to move to Seattle, or will potential students decide not to attend SPU? What financial losses might the campus experience if it is known as the location of a terrible crime? And how does a shooting

AP Images/Elaine Thompson

on a university campus affect college students, faculty, staff, and the community in general?

Brace's actions cost donors and community groups millions of dollars. The community of Camden, Maine, feels betrayed by one of their own, and poor people have not had access to services they need. Do incidents such as this cause people to rethink their decisions to donate to charity? How will this hurt people who benefit from charities such as Midcoast, which provides valuable services to the community?

These are important questions to consider, because how we answer them will define the scope of the subject of criminal victimization. In other words, when we talk about the victimizing consequences of crime, should we only talk about the individuals most directly harmed by a crime, or should we also consider people who suffer less direct, but equally real, consequences? These questions actually have practical consequences under circumstances in which we speak of "victims' rights," such as crime victims being entitled to compensation; and we must define what we mean by "victim" before we can implement any such policy.

A further question arises when we ask whether people bear any responsibility for their own victimization. If young women sit in parked cars in dark, out-of-the-way places, do they place themselves at risk of victimization? What about young men who walk alone late at night down empty, unfamiliar streets while wearing eye-catching expensive watches and rings? Is such a line of inquiry unfair and inhumane? Yet, as we study criminal events, we cannot help but notice that some crimes occur when victims make themselves more vulnerable or when they take actions that appear to trigger a violent response from the wrongdoer. Do such questions imply that victims are at fault for the crime directed at them? No. Clearly, people who commit criminal acts must be punished as the ones responsible for those acts. However, an understanding of criminal events and victim behavior may help us discover how to teach people to reduce their risk of criminal victimization.

An additional important question looms in the aftermath of the SPU shooting and the Midcoast embezzlement, and in that of every other criminal case: Why did the perpetrators do what they did? Criminal behavior is the main cause of criminal victimization. Research scholars, policy makers, and the public have long pondered questions such as "What causes crime?" and "Why do criminal offenders cause harm to other human beings?" These questions have significant implications for the subject of criminal victimization. Theories about crime causation often influence government policies with regard to violations of criminal laws.

In this chapter, we examine the many facets of crime victimization, including aspects that the general public does not usually recognize. In addition, we discuss the causes of crime. Many complex and controversial theories center on why people commit crimes. In considering this subject, we realize that no single theory can be expected to explain all crimes. Remember that "crimes" are whatever actions a legislature defines as deserving punishment at a particular moment in history. Thus, we should not assume that a man who steals money from a charitable organization has the same motives as the man who shoots innocent people on a college campus. The fact that crime has many causes, however, does not mean that all proposed theories about crime causation are equally useful or valid. We need to look closely at theories about crime and evaluate what evidence supports them.

In order to understand the criminal justice system, we must understand the nature of crime and recognize the range of people affected by it. Chapter 1 introduced you to decision makers in the system, such as police and prosecutors, as well as to the processes for handling criminal cases. Here you will consider other key individuals: criminal offenders and their victims. You will also examine the nature and extent of crime—how many offenders and victims will likely cause or be affected by what kinds of crime in a given year.

Types of Crime

Crimes can be classified in various ways, as you will recall from the description in Chapter 1 of *mala in se* and *mala prohibita* crimes, and from the distinction between felonies or misdemeanors. Crimes can also be categorized into seven types: visible crime, occupational crime, organized crime, transnational crime, victimless crime, political crime, and cybercrime. Each type has its own level of risk and reward; each arouses a characteristic degree of public disapproval; and each is committed by a certain kind of offender. New types of crime emerge as society changes. Cybercrime committed through the use of computers and the Internet is becoming a major global problem.

Visible Crime

Visible crime, often called "street crime" or "ordinary crime," ranges from shoplifting to homicide. For offenders, such crimes are the least profitable and, because they are visible, the hardest to hide. These are the acts that the public regards as the most "criminal." The majority of law enforcement resources are employed to deal with them. We can divide visible crimes into three categories: violent crimes, property crimes, and public-order crimes.

visible crime An offense against persons or property, committed primarily by members of the lower class. Often referred to as "street crime" or "ordinary crime," this type of offense is the one most upsetting to the public.

Violent Crimes   Acts against people in which death or physical injury results are *violent crimes.* These include criminal homicide, assault, rape, and robbery. The criminal justice system treats them as the most serious offenses and punishes them accordingly. Although the public is most fearful of violence by strangers, many of these offenses are committed by people known to their victims.

Property Crimes   *Property crimes* are acts that threaten property held by individuals or by the state. Many types of crimes fall under this category, including theft, larceny, shoplifting, embezzlement, and burglary. Some property offenders are amateurs who occasionally commit these crimes because of situational factors such as financial need or peer pressure. In contrast, professional criminals make a significant portion of their livelihood from committing property offenses.

Public-Order Crimes   Acts that threaten the general well-being of society and challenge accepted moral principles are defined as *public-order crimes.* They include public drunkenness, aggressive panhandling, vandalism, and disorderly conduct. Although the police tend to treat these behaviors as minor offenses, some scholars argue that stringent police enforcement of public-order crimes can result in significant reductions in violent crimes as well (Kane & Cronin, 2009).

Defining such behaviors as crimes and enforcing laws against them highlights the tensions between different interpretations of American values. Many people see such behavior as simply representing the liberty that adults enjoy in a free society to engage in offensive and self-destructive behavior that causes no concrete harm to other people. By contrast, other people see their own liberty limited by the need to be wary and fearful of actions by people who are drunk or out of control.

Those charged with visible crimes tend to be young men. Further, in many communities, members of minority groups tend to be overrepresented among those arrested and prosecuted for such offenses. Some argue that this is due to the class bias of a society that has singled out visible crimes for priority enforcement. They note that we do not focus as much police and prosecutorial attention on white-collar crimes, such as fraud and other acts committed by office workers and business owners, as we do on street crimes.

Occupational Crime

occupational crimes Criminal offenses committed through opportunities created in a legal business or occupation.

Occupational crimes are committed in the context of a legal business or profession. Often viewed as shrewd business practices rather than illegal acts, they are crimes that, if "done right," are never discovered. Such crimes are often committed by respectable, well-to-do people taking advantage of opportunities arising from business dealings. Such crimes impose huge costs on society. Although there are no precise figures on the cost of occupational crime to American society, some researchers estimate that losses due to occupational crime may be significantly higher than losses attributable to street crime. Some estimates indicate that for every $1 lost in street crime, about $60 is lost as a result of occupational crime (Friedrichs, 2010).

Organized Crime

organized crime A framework for the perpetration of criminal acts—usually in fields such as gambling, drugs, and prostitution—providing illegal services that are in great demand.

Rather than referring to criminal acts per se, the term **organized crime** refers to the framework within which such acts are committed. Organized crime "functions as a continuing enterprise that rationally works to make a profit through illicit activities and ... ensures its existence through the use of threats or force, and through corruption of public officials" (Albanese, 2010:3). Those active in organized crime provide goods and services to millions of people. They engage in any activity that provides a

Organized crime has changed significantly from the stereotyped images of Italian American mobsters portrayed in the movies. These motorcycle gang members charged with crimes show that organized crime groups are not necessarily based on ethnicity. Why do you believe that people become involved in organized-crime groups?

minimum of risk and a maximum of profit. Thus, organized crime involves a network of activities, usually cutting across state and national borders, which range from legitimate businesses to shady deals with labor unions and the provision of "goods"—such as drugs, sex, and pornography—that cannot be obtained legally. In recent years, organized crime has been involved in new services such as commercial arson, illegal disposal of toxic wastes, and **money laundering**. Some crime syndicates have also acquired significant funds through illegal recycling operations (K. Coleman, 2011). Few members of organized crime syndicates are arrested and prosecuted.

Although the American public often associates organized crime with Italian Americans—and, in fact, the federal government indicted 73 members of the Genovese New York crime "family" in 2001 (Worth, 2001), and another 11 in 2014 (Associated Press, 2014)—other ethnic groups have dominated at various times. Forty-five years ago, one scholar noted the strangeness of America's "ladder of social mobility," in which each new immigrant group uses organized crime as one of the first rungs of the climb (Bell, 1967:150). However, debate about this notion continues, because not all immigrant groups have engaged in organized crime (Kenney & Finckenauer, 1995), and some nonimmigrants have become involved in these crime syndicates (Mallory, 2012).

Over the last few decades, law enforcement efforts have greatly weakened the Italian American Mafia. An aging leadership, lack of interest by younger family members, and pressures from new immigrant groups have also contributed to its fall. However, other, somewhat similar groups have sprung up as the Italian American Mafia has declined. Organized crime has increased among "American" groups such as outlaw motorcycle groups and Hispanic and African American gangs. Drug dealing has brought Colombian and Mexican crime groups to U.S. shores, and groups led by Vietnamese, Chinese, and Japanese people have formed in California (Mallory, 2012).

Just as multinational corporations have emerged during the past 20 years, organized crime has also developed global networks. Increasingly transnational criminal groups "live and operate in a borderless world" (Zagaris, 1998:1402). In the aftermath of the events of September 11, American law enforcement and intelligence officials increased their efforts to monitor and thwart international organizations that seek to attack the United States and its citizens. Many of these organizations use criminal activities such as drug smuggling and stolen credit card numbers to fund their efforts. Others steal under the pretext of "terrorism" without embracing the ideals of terrorist groups; they are mostly interested in making money (Rosenthal, 2008). Policing organized crime on a global scale is a challenge for law enforcement, because the activities of these groups span different police jurisdictions. In addition, nongovernmental agencies must work with police in different countries to share information about organized crime groups that operate across borders (Harfield, 2008).

Transnational Crime

National borders define the boundaries of law enforcement agencies' authority and the definitions of particular crimes. Each country has its own police agencies that enforce its own laws. Borders do not, however, define or limit the nature of criminal activity (Bersin, 2012). The growth of global transportation systems, international trade, computerized financial transactions, and worldwide availability of information through the Internet has facilitated the expansion of the international economy. Simultaneously, these factors have provided the basis for **transnational crime**, a term that refers to crimes whose planning or execution crosses the borders of countries. Jay Albanese (2011) distinguishes profit-seeking transnational crimes—theft, fraud, counterfeiting, smuggling, and other violations of individual countries' criminal laws—from "international crimes"—acts of terrorism, genocide, human rights abuses, or other violations of international law.

Transnational crimes can be grouped into three categories (Albanese, 2011:3). The first category, provision of illicit goods, includes drug trafficking and moving stolen property, such as automobiles and artwork, from one country to another for sales that are difficult to trace back to the original theft (Alderman, 2012). It also

money laundering Moving the proceeds of criminal activities through a maze of businesses, banks, and brokerage accounts so as to disguise their origin.

transnational crime Profit-seeking criminal activities that involve planning or execution across national borders.

includes the transportation and sale of counterfeit goods, such as prescription medications and designer clothing. The second category, provision of illegal services, includes human trafficking, such as transporting sex workers or undocumented immigrants illegally into a country (Shamir, 2012). This category also includes various cybercrimes that often involve fraudulent financial investments, as well as child pornography. Bribery, extortion, and money-laundering activities define the third category, called "infiltration of business or government" (Albanese, 2011).

Organized crime groups are involved in all of the foregoing transnational crimes. Individual lawbreakers can victimize people in other countries through Internet scams or the theft of financial information. However, most of the harm from transnational crimes comes from the activities of formal criminal organizations or, alternatively, criminal networks that connect individuals with organizations to undertake specific criminal acts together. According to the United Nations, annual proceeds from transnational organized crime activities amount to more than $870 billion annually, with drug trafficking producing the largest portion of that total amount (UNODC, 2011).

Governments and international organizations are also very concerned about two forms of human trafficking—sexual slavery and forced labor (UNODC, 2011). Sex trafficking occurs when men, women, and children are lured or transported across international borders and held as prisoners while being forced to sell their bodies in the sex trade for the benefit of their captors (Lehti & Aromaa, 2006). Victims of forced labor trafficking are held prisoner and forced to work under deplorable conditions (Feingold, 2005).

The FBI has been tracking human trafficking data since 2013. In the United States, most arrests for trafficking have involved sex work, except in Texas, where involuntary servitude is more common (FBI, 2015b). The majority of individuals forced into sex work suffer serious mental and physical health consequences; they tend to have high rates of mental illness and physical disease, particularly HIV (Oram et al., 2012). Some have argued that sex trafficking could be fought by legalizing prostitution, thereby reducing the need for illegal sex trade (Reisenwitz, 2014). However, analysis of this issue indicates that legalizing prostitution might actually increase the demand for sex workers, and thus support continued trafficking across borders (Cho, Dreher, & Neumayer, 2013). In the Netherlands, for example, legalizing the sex trade has actually made it more difficult for the government to regulate and monitor health and safety, since brothels still operate in a culture of secrecy even when legal (Huisman & Kleemans, 2014).

Law enforcement officials face huge challenges in attempting to combat transnational crime. Because American police agencies cannot operate in other countries without permission, they must depend on assistance from officials abroad. It can be difficult to coordinate efforts with agencies in other countries that operate under different laws and have different priorities. There can be problems dealing with officials in countries that tolerate or protect transnational criminal organizations because of bribery and other forms of corruption. The United Nations Office on Drugs and Crime (UNODC) gathers and disseminates information about transnational crime. Working with other organizations, it seeks to facilitate communication and cooperation between countries so that there is an ongoing framework for international coordination rather than repeated requests for assistance from one country to another in response to specific criminal acts.

Victimless Crimes

victimless crimes Offenses involving a willing and private exchange of illegal goods or services that are in strong demand. Participants do not feel they are being harmed, but these crimes are prosecuted on the grounds that society as a whole is being injured.

Victimless crimes involve a willing and private exchange of goods or services that are in strong demand but illegal—in other words, offenses against morality. Examples include prostitution, gambling, and drug sales and use. These crimes are called "victimless" because those involved do not feel that they are being harmed. Prosecution for these offenses is justified on the grounds that society as a whole is harmed because the moral fabric of the community is threatened. However, using the law to enforce moral

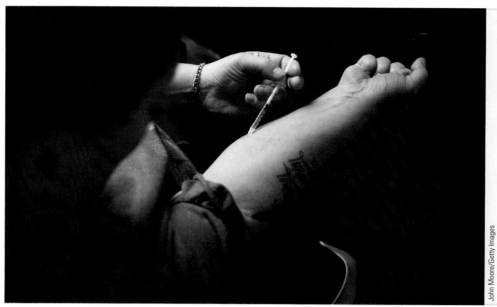

The sale and use of certain drugs are crimes. As states are beginning to make the personal use of marijuana legal, should adults' willing use of other mind-altering substances continue to lead to prosecution and imprisonment? Are these voluntary, private behaviors truly "victimless"? Why should this be considered a criminal activity?

John Moore/Getty Images

standards is costly. The system is swamped by these cases, which often require the use of police informers and thus open the door for payoffs and other kinds of corruption.

The "war on drugs" is the most obvious example of policies against one type of victimless crime. Possession and sale of drugs—marijuana, heroin, cocaine, opium, amphetamines—have been illegal in the United States for over a hundred years. Especially during the past 40 years, all levels of government have applied extensive resources to enforce these laws and punish offenders. However, laws about drug use have been changing in some states; medical marijuana is now legally available in 20 states and the District of Columbia. The state of Colorado legalized the sale of marijuana (for recreational use) in 2014 with the state recouping over $125 million in sales tax in 2015 on the sale of the drug (Keyes, 2015). The state of Washington also legalized personal use of marijuana. But despite changes to state laws, federal laws can emphasize different priorities. Even though possession of marijuana is still a federal crime, the U.S. Department of Justice has agreed not to challenge marijuana laws as long as they do not conflict with other priorities, such as convictions for selling marijuana to support terrorism (Johnson & Chebium, 2013).

The crime-fighting duties of police patrol officers typically focus on visible crimes and victimless crimes. But, as we shall see in later chapters, police officers also fulfill other functions, such as order maintenance and public service.

Political Crime

Political crime refers to criminal acts either by the government or against the government that are carried out for ideological purposes (F. E. Hagan, 1997:2). Political criminals believe they are following a morality that is above the law. Examples include James Kopp—arrested for murdering Dr. Barnett Slepian near Buffalo, New York, and for the murder of other doctors who performed abortions—and Eric Rudolph—convicted for the bombing of abortion clinics in Atlanta and Birmingham as well as for the pipe-bomb explosion at the Atlanta Olympics. Governments can commit political crime as well—for example, if one country attempted to change the outcome of an election in a neighboring country. Similarly, shocking acts of violence that are labeled as terrorism, such as the 1995 bombing of the federal building in Oklahoma City by Timothy McVeigh and the 2001 attacks on the World Trade Center and Pentagon, often spring from political motivations. Political crimes may also involve the release of classified documents, as when Edward Snowden and Chelsea Manning, both employees of the U.S. government, released classified documents in order to reveal government practices they felt were unethical or illegal. There is

political crime An act, usually done for ideological purposes, that constitutes a threat against the state (such as treason, sedition, or espionage); or a criminal act by the state.

Cybercrime is a growing problem that costs American businesses and individuals millions of dollars each year. Law enforcement officials work diligently to keep up with the criminals' computer expertise, technology, and methods of deception. How can American police effectively combat the evolving and spreading threat of cybercrime, especially when so many cybercriminals are located in other countries?

AP Images/Manuel Balce Ceneta

some difference of opinion on what constitutes terrorism in the United States, as discussed in the "Current Controversies" feature below.

In some authoritarian states, merely criticizing the government is a crime that can lead to prosecution and imprisonment. In Western democracies today, there are few actions deemed to be political crimes other than treason, which is rare. One rare example occurred in 2009, when a retired employee of the U.S. State Department and his wife were charged with being spies for Cuba. They reportedly stole government documents not because they were seeking financial payment from Cuba, but because of their ideological admiration for the Cuban government and their hostile feelings toward the U.S. government (G. Thompson, 2009). Many illegal acts, such as the World Trade Center and Oklahoma City bombings, can be traced to political motives, but they are usually prosecuted as visible crimes under laws against bombing, arson, and murder rather than as political crimes per se.

Cybercrime

cybercrimes Offenses that involve the use of one or more computers.

Cybercrimes involve the use of computers and the Internet to commit acts against people, property, public order, or morality. In 2014, the federal government's Internet Crime Complaint Center (IC3) received 269,422 complaints about cybercrime, with most offenses related to fraudulent online auto sales, e-mail impersonation scams, and intimidation/extortion scams (Internet Crime Complaint Center, 2015). Thus, cybercriminals have learned "new ways to do old tricks." Some use computers to steal

CURRENT CONTROVERSIES IN CRIMINAL JUSTICE

Differing Conceptions of Terrorism

The terrorist attacks on September 11, 2001, shocked the nation and brought a new awareness to the crime of terrorism. Even though Americans had experienced terrorist attacks at the World Trade Center in

1993 and in Oklahoma City in 1995, the scale of the 9/11 attacks changed law and government significantly as the United States attempted to increase its citizens' safety and hold offenders

accountable for their actions. People's fear of terrorism increased dramatically, and levels of fear exceeded the actual risk of being a victim of terror.

News media attention to terrorism, as well as statements from politicians and government officials, often treat this matter in a narrow way that obscures recognition of broader issues. The media play an important role in our perceptions, and 24-hour news coverage of shocking events can cause people to make inaccurate assessments about the risk of terrorism attacks. The media can also encourage biased perceptions of the "typical" terrorist, with many stories focused on people of Middle Eastern ancestry. But what is the reality of threats from terrorism, and who actually commits acts that fit the definition of terrorism?

The FBI's definition of terrorism, which covers people and action both in the United States and overseas, includes the following components:

- Acts dangerous to human life that violate federal or state law
- Acts intended (1) to intimidate or coerce a civilian population, (2) to influence the government by intimidation or coercion, or (3) to affect the conduct of a government by destruction, assassination, or kidnapping.

It is important to note that there is no mention of the characteristics of the offender in these definitions. In other words, race/ethnicity and nationality are not part of the definition.

Based on the official definition, what does terrorism actually look like in the United States? Since 9/11, researchers have been more focused on collecting and analyzing data on terrorist attacks to determine the extent and types of terrorist acts. An analysis of over 73,000 attacks by the National Consortium for the Study of Terrorism and Responses to Terrorism (START) indicates that North America has the lowest risk in the world for fatal terrorist attacks. Since 1970, only 0.41 percent of all fatal attacks have occurred in the United States, far fewer than in Latin America (28.5%), South Asia (24.2%), and Africa (13.2%).

Many Americans seem to believe that our sole or primary terrorism threat is from Islamic conspiracies that originate overseas. However, analyses by START indicate that most terrorist events in the United States were in fact acts of domestic terrorism, motivated by anti-abortion beliefs. Consider whether the following acts in 2015 and 2016 fit the definition of terrorism:

- In January 2016, Ammon Bundy led a group of armed people in the takeover of the Malheur National Wildlife Refuge, demanding that the government relinquish ownership of western lands that could be used for grazing by cattle ranchers. When he was arrested upon leaving the wildlife refuge, one of his companions drove past a police roadblock and then reportedly reached for a gun as he ran toward the police on foot. He was shot by the police. Bundy has been charged with felony conspiracy to use force and the use of intimidation or threats to impede federal officers from discharging their duties.
- Dylann Roof, a 21-year-old white man in South Carolina, shot and killed nine black members of a church in Charleston, South Carolina, on June 17, 2015. He actively followed several "pro-Confederacy" websites and owned flags and other symbols celebrating the apartheid era in South Africa (1948–1994), in which black people lacked citizenship rights and were subjected to violent treatment by the government.
- Robert Lewis Dear, 57, killed three people, including one police officer, at a Planned Parenthood Center in Colorado Springs, Colorado. He expressed strong opposition to the availability of abortion and other government policies.
- In December 2015 in San Bernadino, California, 14 people were killed by a married couple, Syed Farook and Tashfeen Malik, who had pledged allegiance to ISIS, the violent Middle Eastern group supported by a minority of Muslims that seeks to impose its religious vision on the majority of Muslims as well as people from other religions.

For Critical Thinking and Analysis

The language used in news articles and by government officials often reserves the use of the word "terrorist" for Muslims, such as the San Bernardino killers, who plan or carry out violent actions. By contrast, news reports referred to Dylan Roof and Robert Dear as "mentally troubled individuals" and the armed occupiers of the wildlife refuge as "political activists." Refer back to the FBI definition of terrorism. How many of the acts described above meet the definition of terrorism? All of these actions were undertaken by people carrying firearms. Were they all designed to invoke fear in the populace or change the behavior of government agencies? Is there a religious or ethnic bias that affects the image of "terrorism" in the United States? If we think of violent or otherwise armed and threatening non-Muslims as merely troubled individuals or political activists, is there a risk that our law enforcement officials will underestimate or fail to prepare adequately for other kinds of organized threats against American society? Write a memo as if you were a police chief and you needed to inform your department's officers about the meaning of "terrorism."

Sources: K. Conlon, G. Botelho, and P. Brown, "Source: Suspect Spoke of 'Baby Parts' after Planned Parenthood Shooting," CNN, November 29, 2015 (http://cnn.com); Federal Bureau of Investigation, "Definitions of Terrorism in the U.S. Code," (www.fbi.gov); P. Guasti and Z. Mansfeldova, "Perception of Terrorism and Security and the Role of Media," paper for the 7th ECPR General z, September 7, 2013); J. Harper, "9/11 'Misleads' Americans' View of Terrorism," Washington Times, May 28, 2009 (http://washingtontimes.com); L. Khalil, "Managing Public Perception of the Terrorist Threat," New York Times, April 16, 2014; G. LaFree and L. Dugan, "Introducing the Global Terrorism Database," Terrorism and Political Violence 19(2), 181–204 (2007); G. LaFree, N. A. Morris, and L. Dugan, "Cross-National Patterns of Terrorism," British Journal of Criminology 50, 622–49 (2010); R. Winton and J. Queally, "FBI Is Now Convinced that Couple Tried to Detonate Bomb in San Bernardino Terror Attack," Los Angeles Times, January 15, 2016 (http://latimes.com); G. Zoroya, "Oregon Standoff Grinds On as Bundy Brothers Denied Bail," USA Today, January 30, 2016 (http://usatoday.com).

information, resources, or funds, Others use the Internet to disseminate child pornography, advertise sexual services, or stalk the unsuspecting. Some sophisticated "hackers" create and distribute viruses designed to destroy computer programs or to gain control of computers from unsuspecting individuals. Others focus their attention on stealing funds or personal identities; in 2015, a man in Milwaukee was charged with stealing over $500,000 from Kohl's stores by writing a computer program to steal account numbers and buy merchandise illegally (Diedrich, 2016). You will read more about cybercrime in the discussion of criminal justice and technology in Chapter 14.

Cybercrime offenses do not only include hacking and online scams. These offenses can also occur on a smaller scale, as when individuals share sexual content without permission (content which breaches another person's "right to privacy") with others. This is especially troubling when the victims and offenders are juveniles. The increased use of technology by juveniles, who may not always understand the reach of social media, has also increased rates of cybercrime victimization and offending. In Connecticut, three juveniles were arrested and another 50 face charges for circulating nude pictures of classmates in their high school (Hanna, 2016). In New Jersey, a high school student threatened on social media to "shoot up" a school and was charged with making terroristic threats (Agnes, 2016). Because these activities used computers, they may be considered cybercrime by authorities.

Which of these main types of crime is of greatest concern to you? If you are like most people, it is visible crime. Thus, as a nation, we devote most of our criminal justice resources to dealing with such crimes. To develop policies to address these crimes, however, we need to know more about the amount of crime and all the types of crimes that occur in the United States.

CHECK POINT

1. **What are the seven main types of crime?**
   Visible crime, occupational crime, organized crime, transnational crime, victimless crimes, political crime, cybercrime.

2. **What is the function of organized crime?**
   Organized crime usually provides goods and services that are in high demand but are illegal.

3. **What is meant by the term *victimless crimes*?**
   These are crimes against morality in which the people involved do not believe that anyone has been victimized.

STOP & ANALYZE

Multiple states have legalized the use of medical marijuana in the past few years; however, marijuana is classified as a "Schedule I" narcotic. According to the U.S. Drug Enforcement Administration's (DEA) definition, "substances in this schedule have a high potential for abuse, have no currently accepted medical use in treatment in the United States, and there is a lack of accepted safety for use of the drug or other substance under medical supervision." Given this classification, does it make sense for states to be allowed to make marijuana use legal for medicinal purposes? Alternatively, should marijuana be removed from the list of Schedule I drugs? Provide a brief argument for the option you think that policy makers should adopt as this issue develops.

How Much Crime Is There?

Many Americans believe that the crime rate is rising, even though it has generally declined since the 1980s. For example, the rate of violent crime decreased from 747.1 violent crimes per 100,000 people in 1993 to 386.9 violent crimes per 100,000 by 2012, including a 19 percent drop from 2006 to 2012 (FBI, 2013a: Table 1). The Bureau of Justice Statistics reported that "rates of violent and property crime [measured by our survey] in 2009 were at the lowest overall levels recorded since 1973, the first year for which victimization estimates from the survey were produced" (Rand, 2010:1).

In December 2013, the FBI released preliminary crime statistics for the first half of 2013. The initial analysis showed a 5.4 percent decrease in violent crime. From January 2013 to June 2013, all types of violent crime decreased, with murder

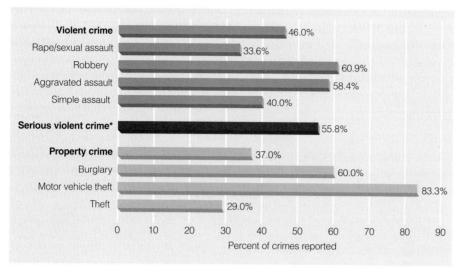

FIGURE 2.1

Violent and Property Victimizations Reported to Police, 2014 Why are some crimes less likely to be reported to the police than others? What can be done to increase the likelihood that victims will report crimes to the police?

*Includes rape or sexual assault, robbery, and aggravated assault.

Source: J. L. Truman and L. Langton, "Criminal Victimization, 2014," *Bureau of Justice Statistics Bulletin*, August 2015, Table 6.

and aggravated assault down by about 7 percent (FBI, 2013b: Table 1). The largest decrease in violent crime occurred in the Midwest (7.4 percent), while the Northeast demonstrated the greatest decrease in homicide rates (14.0 percent) (FBI, 2013b: Table 2). Some scholars and law enforcement professionals were concerned when crime rates increased modestly in 2006 and 2007; however, the increase was small, and crime rates still remain low compared with the rates from two decades ago.

One of the frustrations in studying criminal justice is the lack of accurate means of knowing the amount of crime. Surveys reveal that much more crime occurs than is reported to the police. This is referred to as the **dark figure of crime**. Rape is an example of this type of crime.

Most homicides and auto thefts are reported to the police. In the case of a homicide, a body must be accounted for, and in the case of auto theft, insurance companies require a police report before they will pay for a stolen car. But large numbers of rape victims do not report the attack. Figure 2.1 shows the percentage of different types of crimes that are reported to the police.

Until 1972 the only crimes counted by government were those that were known to the police and that made their way into the Uniform Crime Reports (UCR) compiled by the Federal Bureau of Investigation (FBI). Since then, the Department of Justice has sponsored the National Crime Victimization Surveys (NCVS), which survey the public to find out how much victimization has occurred. One might hope that the data from these two sources would give us a clear picture of the amount of crime, crime trends, and characteristics of offenders. However, the picture is blurred, perhaps even distorted, because of differences in the way crime is measured by the UCR and the NCVS.

dark figure of crime A metaphor that emphasizes the dangerous dimension of crimes that are never reported to the police.

The Uniform Crime Reports (UCR)

Issued each year by the FBI, the **Uniform Crime Reports (UCR)** publication is a statistical summary of crimes reported to the police. At the urging of the International Association of Chiefs of Police, Congress authorized this system in 1930 for compiling crime data (Rosen, 1995). The UCR data come from a voluntary national network of local, state, and federal law enforcement agencies policing 94.6 percent of the U.S. population (FBI, 2012b).

With the sharp drop in crime in recent years, new pressures have been placed on police executives to show that their cities are following the national trend. Some officials have even falsified their crime statistics as promotions, pay raises, and departmental budgets have become increasingly dependent on positive data. For example, an audit of police incident reports in Memphis in 2012 raised questions about whether the city's claims about reducing serious crimes were assisted

Uniform Crime Reports (UCR) An annually published statistical summary of crimes reported to the police, based on voluntary reports to the FBI by local, state, and federal law enforcement agencies.

by underreporting such crimes in official crime reports (Maki, 2012). The NYPD has been accused of undercounting shootings in New York City by using a very restrictive definition of what constitutes a "shooting" (Goodman, 2015). The Detroit Police Department was accused of misclassifying and undercounting homicides; newspaper reporters conducted their own count and alleged that the police undercount helped the city avoid acknowledging that it had the nation's worst homicide rate (LeDuff & Esparza, 2009). Because the FBI relies on reports from local police departments to compile the UCR, its accuracy is compromised when agencies underreport crime.

The UCR uses standard definitions to ensure uniform data on the 29 types of crimes listed in Table 2.1. For 8 major crimes—Part I (Index Offenses)—the data show factors such as age, race, and number of reported crimes solved. For the other 21 crimes—Part II (Other Offenses)—the data are less complete.

The UCR provides a useful but incomplete picture of crime levels. Because it covers only reported crimes, these reports do not include data on crimes for which people failed to call the police. Also, the UCR does not measure occupational crimes and other offenses that are not included in the 29 types covered. And because

TABLE 2.1 **Uniform Crime Report Offenses**

The UCR presents data on 8 index offenses and 21 other crimes for which there is less information. A limitation of the UCR is that it tabulates only crimes that are reported to the police.

Part I (Index Offenses)	Part II (Other Offenses)
1. Criminal homicide	9. Other assaults
2. Forcible rape	10. Forgery and counterfeiting
3. Robbery	11. Fraud
4. Aggravated assault	12. Embezzlement
5. Burglary	13. Stolen property: Buying, receiving, possessing
6. Larceny/theft	14. Vandalism
7. Auto theft	15. Weapons (carrying, possessing, etc.)
8. Arson	16. Prostitution and commercialized vice
	17. Sex offenses
	18. Drug abuse violations
	19. Gambling
	20. Offenses against the family and children
	21. Driving under the influence
	22. Liquor laws
	23. Drunkenness
	24. Disorderly conduct
	25. Vagrancy
	26. All other offenses
	27. Suspicion
	28. Curfew and loitering laws (juvenile)
	29. Runaways (juvenile)

Source: Federal Bureau of Investigation, 2004, *Uniform Crime Reporting Handbook* (Washington, DC: U.S. Government Printing Office).

reporting is voluntary, police departments may not take the time to make complete and careful reports.

In response to criticisms of the UCR, the FBI has made some changes in the program that are now being implemented nationwide. Some offenses have been redefined, and police agencies are being asked to report more details about crime events. Using the **National Incident-Based Reporting System (NIBRS)**, police agencies are to report all crimes committed during an incident, not just the most serious one, as well as all available data on offenders, victims, and the places where they interact. Whereas the UCR now counts incidents and arrests for the 8 index offenses and counts arrests for other crimes, the NIBRS provides detailed incident data on 46 offenses in 22 crime categories. The NIBRS distinguishes between attempted and completed crimes as well.

How is the NIBRS different from the UCR? In addition to including more types of crime than the UCR, NIBRS data are *disaggregated*—that is, rather than police departments reporting counts of crime to the FBI (as in the UCR), many jurisdictions now report information on individual crimes. Thanks to advances in technology and data transfer, police departments can now transfer data more easily than was possible when the UCR began collecting data from police departments in 1929. However, the reporting process is more difficult for NIBRS, and all agencies must adopt the same format for reporting data. These difficulties mean that not all states currently participate in the NIBRS system. For example, in 2013 only 15 states reported NIBRS data for all of their jurisdictions (Arkansas, Colorado, Delaware, Idaho, Iowa, Michigan, Montana, New Hampshire, North Dakota, South Carolina, South Dakota, Tennessee, Vermont, Virginia, and West Virginia). The remaining states report at least some crime through NIBRS or are in training to do so in the near future (FBI, 2013b).

National Incident-Based Reporting System (NIBRS) A reporting system in which the police describe each offense in a crime incident, together with data describing the offender, victim, and property.

The National Crime Victimization Surveys (NCVS)

As mentioned earlier, police agencies are aware that many crimes are not reported to them. In order to gain a better idea of the "dark figure of crime," the Census Bureau developed the **National Crime Victimization Surveys (NCVS)**. The NCVS is considered a "self-reported" measure of criminal behavior, because it uses survey research to ask people whether they've been victims of crime. Data have been gathered since 1972 on unreported as well as reported crimes. Interviews are conducted twice each year with a national probability sample of approximately 74,000 people in 41,000 households. The same people are interviewed twice a year for three years and asked if they have been victimized in the last six months (BJS, 2008).

National Crime Victimization Surveys (NCVS) Interviews of samples of the U.S. population conducted by the Bureau of Justice Statistics to determine the number and types of criminal victimizations and thus the extent of unreported as well as reported crime.

Each person is asked a set of "screening" questions (for example, "Did anyone beat you up, attack you, or hit you with something such as a rock or a bottle?") to determine whether he or she has been victimized. The person is then asked questions designed to elicit specific facts about the event, the offender, and any financial losses or physical injuries caused by the crime.

In the nation's 26 largest cities, additional studies are done to find out about the victimization of businesses. The combined data from the household and business surveys allow us to estimate how many crimes have occurred, learn more about the offenders, and note demographic patterns. The results show that for the violent crimes measured (rape, robbery, assault, domestic violence), there were 5.4 million victimizations in 2014, which was down from 7.7 million in 2003 (Truman & Langton, 2015). Interestingly, this number is much higher than the number of crimes actually reported to the police.

The NCVS data can also be used to track serial (or "repeat" victimizations). Those most likely to be repeated victims of crime tend to take risks—such as going to bars or clubs, taking public transit, or "hanging out" where teenagers congregate—and they tend to live in neighborhoods characterized by greater levels of disorganization (Outlaw, Ruback, & Britt, 2002). However, repeat sexual victimization is not always affected by the same risk factors. Living alone, drinking alcohol and using drugs, and spending time in places that are exclusively male are related to repeat victimization. Women who take actions to protect themselves from any sexual victimization may avoid both initial victimization and repeated victimizations (Fisher, Daigle, & Cullen, 2010).

Although the NCVS provides a more complete picture of the nature and extent of crime than the UCR does, it too has flaws (J. P. Lynch & Addington, 2009). Because government employees administer the surveys, the people interviewed are unlikely to report crimes in which they or members of their family took part. They also may not want to admit that a family member engages in crime, or they may be too embarrassed to admit that they have allowed themselves to be victimized more than once. In addition, the survey covers a limited range of crimes, and the relatively small sample of interviewees may lead to erroneous conclusions about crime trends for an entire country of over 300 million people (Mosher, Miethe, & Phillips, 2002).

The NCVS data are also imperfect because they depend on the victim's *perception* of an event. The theft of a child's lunch money by a bully may be reported as a crime by one person but not mentioned by another. People may say that their property was stolen when in fact they lost it. Moreover, people's memories of dates may fade, and they may misreport the year in which a crime occurred even though they remember the event itself clearly. The Bureau of Justice Statistics routinely evaluates how the NCS collects data and sporadically makes changes in the NCVS to improve its accuracy and detail.

The next time you hear or read about crime rates, take into account the source of the data and its possible limitations. Table 2.2 compares the UCR and the NCVS.

TABLE 2.2 The UCR and the NCVS

Compare the data sources. Remember that the UCR tabulates only crimes reported to the police, whereas the NCVS data are based on interviews with victims.

	UCR	NCVS
Offenses Measured	Homicide Rape Robbery (personal and commercial) Assault (aggravated) Burglary (commercial and household) Larceny (commercial and household) Motor vehicle theft Arson	Rape/sexual assault Robbery (personal) Assault (aggravated and simple) Household burglary Larceny (personal and household) Motor vehicle theft
Scope	Crimes reported to the police in most jurisdictions; in 2012, the data submitted represented 98.1% of the U.S. population.	Crimes both reported and not reported to police; all data are for the nation as a whole; some data are available for a few large geographic areas.
Collection Method	Police department reports to Federal Bureau of Investigation	Survey interviews: periodically measures the total number of crimes committed by asking a national sample of households about their experiences as victims of crime during a specific period. In 2012, 92,390 households were interviewed, representing 162,940 persons aged 12 or older.
Kinds of Information	In addition to offense counts, provides information on crime clearances, persons arrested, persons charged, law enforcement officers killed and assaulted, and characteristics of homicide victims	Provides details about victims (such as age, race, sex, education, income, and whether the victim and offender were related) and about crimes (such as time and place of occurrence, whether or not reported to police, use of weapons, occurrence of injury, and economic consequences)
Sponsor	Department of Justice's Federal Bureau of Investigation	Department of Justice's Bureau of Justice Statistics

Sources: J. L. Truman, L. Langton, and M. Planty (2003); FBI (2013a).

Trends in Crime

Experts agree that, contrary to public opinion and the claims of politicians, crime rates have not been steadily rising. The NCVS data—individual reports of victimization—show that the victimization rate has been dropping steadily over the past decade. These data show that from 2004 to 2014, most violent crimes decreased in number in the United States, with the greatest decreases seen in assaults (24% decrease) and domestic violence cases (22% decrease). The UCR data show similar results, with steady decreases in both violent and property crime reported to the police since 1995 (FBI, 2015a: Table 1).

Table 2.3 displays three measures of violent crime over a 30-year period. The first data column shows the results of NCVS surveys—individual reports of victimization. The second shows the number of victimizations recorded by the FBI from reports by police. The third column shows numbers of actual arrests. Remember that the differences in the trends indicated by the NCVS and the UCR are explained in part by the different data sources and the different populations on which their tabulations are based. Apparent inconsistencies in the two sources of data are likely to stem from a combination of problems with victims' memories, inaccuracies in crime records in individual police agencies, and inconsistencies in the data projections used to produce the NCVS and UCR. Even though the actual numbers of crimes reported did not decline significantly from 2010 to 2014, the population was steadily increasing, so that actually, there were fewer crimes recorded per 100,000 people in 2014 than in 1984; thus, the crime *rate* declined in that interval.

What explains the drop in both violent and property crime rates well below the 1984 levels? Among the reasons given by analysts are the aging of the baby-boom population, the increased use of security systems, aggressive police efforts to keep handguns off the streets, and the dramatic decline in the use of crack cocaine. Other factors may include the booming economy of the 1990s and the quadrupling of the number of people incarcerated since 1970. Let us look more closely at how age distribution in the United States can be used to predict future crime levels.

Age   Changes in the age makeup of the population are a key factor in the analysis of crime trends. It has long been known that men aged 16–24 are the most crime-prone

| TABLE 2.3 | Three Measures of Violent Crime |

The difficulty in accurately counting crimes and calculating crime rates stems from different sources of information, none of which capture the complete picture of crime. Because the crime rate is calculated as the number of recorded crimes per 100,000 population, a relatively constant number of crimes during a period of population increase represents a drop in the crime rate.

Year	Violent Victimizations (NCVS)	Violent Crimes Recorded by Police (UCR)	Arrests for Violent Crimes	UCR Crime Rate-Violent Crimes per 100,000 population
1984	5,954,000	1,273,282	493,960	540
1995	9,604,570	1,798,792	796,230	685
2004	6,726,060	1,360,088	586,558	466
2014	5,359,570	1,165,383	498,666	366

Sources: Bureau of Justice Statistics, *Sourcebook of Criminal Justice Statistics,* 2016 (www.albany.edu/sourcebook/); P. Kaus and C. Maston, *Criminal Victimization in the United States, 1995,* Bureau of Justice Statistics, May 2000, NCJ 171129; A. Timrots and M. DeBerry, "Criminal Victimization 1984," *Bureau of Justice Statistics Bulletin,* October 1985, NCJ 98904; H. N. Snyder and J. Mulako-Wangota, online *Arrest Data Analysis Tool,* Bureau of Justice Statistics website, 2014 (www.bjs.gov); J. L. Truman and L. Langton, "Criminal Victimization, 2014," *Bureau of Justice Statistics Bulletin,* September 2015, NCJ 248973; J. L. Truman and L. Langton, "Criminal Victimization, 2013," *Bureau of Justice Statistics Bulletin,* September 2014, NCJ 247068; FBI, *Crime in the United States, 2014* [Uniform Crime Reports] (www.fbi.gov).

Have Tough Crime-Control Policies Caused a Decline in Crime?

There's good news, and there's bad news. The good news is that the amount of crime in the United States has been decreasing in recent years. Significant reductions have been seen in every type of violent and property crime, and virtually every demographic group has experienced drops in violent victimization.

Any reduction in crime is welcome, but the bad news is that experts do not agree on the causes for the decline in crime. Have the tough crime-control policies of the past 20 years really reduced crime? Or have crime rates lessened because of factors unrelated to anything police, prosecution, courts, and corrections have done?

Some experts point out that there are more police officers on the streets, sentences are longer, and the probability upon conviction of going to prison is greater. They say the police have been more aggressive in dealing with public-order offenses, the waiting period for handgun purchases has been effective, and more than a million Americans are already in prison and off the streets. In other words, the police and other agencies of criminal justice have made the difference.

Other experts question the impact of tough policies. They point out that the number of men in the crime-prone age group is relatively low compared with that age group's percentage of the national population from the 1960s to the 1980s. Many also say that the tough crime policies, instead of reducing crime, have devastated minority communities and diverted resources that could be used to deal with the poverty that underlies crime. They urge policies that "put *justice* back in criminal justice."

Although crime rates have been falling, fear of crime is rising. Some opinion surveys find that Americans rank crime among the nation's most prominent problems after the economy, wars, and terrorism. Arguably, crime should rank much lower, given the decrease in victimizations. Because views of crime are shaped more by television news than by statistics, Americans have

an unrealistic picture of the crime problem. Grisly coverage of a murder scene on the evening news sticks in the mind in a way that the results of crime studies can never do.

Drugs and crime are perennially popular issues in U.S. politics. Legislators respond easily to pressures to "do something about crime." Who can argue with that? They usually act by coming up with new laws mandating stiffer sentences and allocating more money for police and corrections. But is this the best direction for public policy?

For Tough Crime Control

Supporters of tough crime-control policies say that crime, especially violent crime, is a serious problem. Even though rates have declined, they argue, violence is still many times higher here than in other developed democracies. We must continue to pursue criminals through strict law enforcement, aggressive prosecutions, and the sentencing of career criminals to long prison terms. They claim that taking the pressure off now will pave the way for problems in the future.

Here is a summary of the arguments for tough crime-control policies:

- The United States has a serious crime problem. Its laws must ensure that offenders receive strict and certain penalties.
- Crime is not caused by poverty, unemployment, and other socioeconomic factors. Instead, crime causes poverty.
- The expansion of the prison population has taken hardened criminals out of the community, thus contributing to the drop in crime.
- The police must have the resources and legal backing to pursue criminals.

Against Tough Crime Control

Opponents of the get-tough approach believe that better ways are available to deal with crime. They argue that crime is no more effectively controlled today than it was in the early 1970s

and that in many respects the problem has worsened, especially in the poorest neighborhoods. Neither the war on crime nor the war on drugs has stopped the downward spiral of livability in these neighborhoods. Another price of the tough crime-control policies has been an erosion of civil rights and liberties—especially for racial and ethnic minorities. What is needed is an infusion of justice into the system.

Here is a summary of the arguments against tough crime-control policies:

- The get-tough policies have not significantly reduced crime.
- Resources should be diverted from the criminal justice system to get to the underlying causes of criminal behavior—poor housing, unemployment, and racial injustice.
- Tough incarceration policies have devastated poor communities. With large numbers of young men in prison, families live in poverty, and children grow up without guidance from their fathers and older brothers.
- Crime policies emphasizing community policing, alternatives to incarceration, and community assistance programs will do more to promote justice than will the failed get-tough policies of the past.

What Should U.S. Policy Be?

The justice system costs about $200 billion a year. Advocates of tough crime-control policies say that the high cost is worth the price and that the aggressive and punitive policies of the past two decades have worked to reduce crime. Opponents of these policies respond that the police, courts, and corrections have had little impact on crime. Other factors, such as the booming economy of the 1990s and the smaller number of men in the crime-prone age cohort, have been responsible for the reduction. The recession that began in 2008 has caused many government agencies to rethink their spending.

group. The rise in crime in the 1970s has been blamed on the post–World War II baby boom. By the 1970s, the "boomers" had entered the high-risk crime group of 16- to 24-year-olds. They composed a much larger portion of the U.S. population than ever before, so between 40 and 50 percent of the total arrests during that decade could have been attributed to the growth in the total population and in the size of the crime-prone age group. Likewise, the decline in most crime rates that began during the 1980s has been attributed to the maturing of the post–World War II generation. During the 1990s, the 16- to 24-year age cohort was smaller than it had been at any time since the early 1960s, and many people believe that this contributed to the decline in crime.

In 1994, a small but influential group of criminologists predicted that by the year 2000, the number of young men in the 14- to 24-year-old cohort would greatly increase. It was argued that the decline in crime experienced in the 1990s was merely the "lull before the storm" (Steinberg, 1999:4WK). However, the predicted rise in violent crime has not occurred. In fact, after the homicide rate for young people peaked in 1993, it dropped to a new low in 2000 and continues to decline (Puzzanchera & Kang, 2011). The Office of Juvenile Justice and Delinquency Prevention found a 36 percent decrease in juvenile arrests for homicide between 2002 and 2011 (Puzzanchera, 2013).

There are many potential explanations for the continuing reductions in crime since the mid-1990s. Review the "The Policy Debate" feature to learn about the pros and cons of tough crime policy and whether this approach produced reductions in crime.

CHECK POINT

4. **What are the two main sources of crime data?**
   Uniform Crime Reports; National Crime Victimization Surveys.

5. **What are key factors in crime trends?**
   Age cohorts and social conditions.

STOP & ANALYZE

The state of Florida has experienced a 33 percent drop in crime since 1999, and many in the private and public sectors are looking for an explanation (K. Stanley, 2011). Some criminologists are examining the relationship between economics and crime. While many believe that worsening economic conditions will lead to more crime (people stealing food, for example), the trends show that the opposite seems to happen. Why would worsening economic conditions actually *decrease* the crime rate?

Crime Victimization

Until the mid-twentieth century, researchers paid little attention to crime victims. The field of **victimology**, which emerged in the 1950s, focuses attention on four questions: (1) Who is victimized? (2) What is the impact of crime? (3) What happens to victims in the criminal justice system? and (4) What role do victims play in causing the crimes they suffer?

victimology A field of criminology that examines the role the victim plays in precipitating a criminal incident and also examines the impact of crimes on victims.

Who Is Victimized?

Not everyone has an equal chance of being a crime victim. For example, people who are victimized by crime in one year are more likely to be victimized by crime in a subsequent year than nonvictims (Menard, 2000). Research also shows that members of certain demographic groups are more likely to be victimized than others. Puzzling over this fact, victimologists have come up with several answers (Karmen, 2001:87). One explanation is that demographic factors (age, gender, income) affect lifestyle—people's routine activities, such as work, home life, and recreation. Lifestyles, in turn, affect people's exposure to dangerous places, times, and people (Varano et al., 2004). Among contemporary Americans, the use of social media, dating apps, and Internet communications can increase visibility to and contact with strangers as a part of today's lifestyle. Read the "You Make the Decision" feature and consider how the use of social media can increase the opportunities for risky encounters with strangers while presenting legislators with new challenges about how to define crime and its consequences.

Routine activity explanations of crime posit that three factors converge to increase the likelihood of criminal behavior: (1) likely offenders, (2) suitable targets, and (3) the absence of capable guardians (Cohen & Felson, 1979). In other words, in order for a crime to occur, there must be people interested in committing crime, potential victims, and the lack of anyone "guarding" the victims. Thus, a man walking alone at night (having no guardian) who has just stopped at the ATM is a suitable target. All that is required is a likely offender looking to do harm.

Routine activity has been used to explain a number of different crimes, including cybercrimes: for instance, the presence of cybercriminals online combined with a suitable target (someone using an online credit card, for example) with a lack of capable guardians (no antivirus software installed) can increase the odds of cybercrime (Holt & Bossier, 2009). With respect to physical and sexual victimization, the homeless are at extremely high risk (Tyler & Beal, 2010). Thus, differences in lifestyles lead to varying degrees of exposure to risks (R. F. Meier & Miethe, 1993:466). Considering this theoretical perspective, think of people whose lifestyle includes going to nightclubs in a "shady" part of town. Such people run the risk of being robbed if they walk alone through a dark high-crime area to their car at two in the morning. By contrast, older individuals who watch television at

YOU MAKE THE DECISION

State Legislator

State legislators enact the laws that define crimes and punishments under state law. You are a state legislator considering whether to vote in support of a proposed law that would make having sex with an underage individual a "strict liability" offense—a crime even if the accused did not intend to have sex with an underage teenager and did not know the actual age of the teenager. As you consider this proposal, news reports surface about cases in other states in which sexual encounters were the result of underage teenagers meeting adults after using dating websites and hook-up apps that require users to be

age 18 or over. In other words, the underage teens lied about their ages in order to meet adult strangers through these apps and websites. The legislators who propose the law argue that it is so important to prevent the sexual victimization of underage teenagers that the burden should be placed on adults to make sure that they know the correct age of their sexual partners. Moreover, the severity of punishing such encounters as sex crimes with prison sentences and lifelong placement on sex-offender registries will make adults be extra cautious and careful about sexual encounters with strangers.

Opponents argue that it is unfair to impose criminal punishments on adults who have been deceived by underage teenagers who sought sexual encounters by using websites and apps that explicitly require users to be adults. Will you vote to support the "strict liability" criminal law? Give three reasons for your decision. Then conduct Internet searches to read about the Michigan Supreme Court's 2016 case concerning Kameron Leo Kilgo and the 2015 controversy concerning Zach Anderson, an Indiana resident.

night in their small-town home have a very low chance of being robbed. But these cases do not tell the entire story. What other factors make victims more vulnerable than nonvictims?

Crime rates also vary tremendously within locations over time, sometimes for reasons that are unclear to researchers. For example, Los Angeles has worked consistently to reduce gang activity in their city (see the "Stop & Analyze" at the end of this chapter), yet crime there has increased over the past two years (Poston, 2016). The city has also been struggling with a significant homelessness problem, which has resulted in a number of camps that may place those living there at higher risk of victimization (Anderson, 2016).

Women, Youths, Nonwhites The lifestyle-exposure model and survey data shed light on the links between personal characteristics and the chance that one will become a victim. Figure 2.2 shows the influence of gender, age, and race on the risk of being victimized by a violent crime such as rape, robbery, or assault. If we apply these findings to the lifestyle-exposure model, we might suggest that African American teenagers are most likely to be victimized because of where many live (urban, high-crime areas), how they may spend their leisure time (outside late at night), and the people with whom they may associate (violence-prone youths). Not surprisingly, juveniles who engage in a delinquent lifestyle are more likely to be victimized than those who do not (Melde, 2009). Lifestyle factors may also explain why elderly white men and women are least likely to be victimized by a violent crime. Perhaps it is because they do not go out at night, do not associate with people who are prone to crime, carry few valuables, and take precautions such as locking their doors. Thus, lifestyle choices directly affect the chances of victimization.

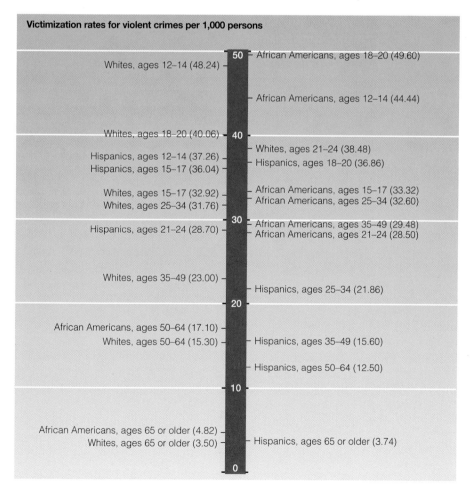

Victimization rates for violent crimes per 1,000 persons

Whites, ages 12–14 (48.24)
African Americans, ages 18–20 (49.60)
African Americans, ages 12–14 (44.44)
Whites, ages 18–20 (40.06) — 40
Whites, ages 21–24 (38.48)
Hispanics, ages 12–14 (37.26)
Hispanics, ages 18–20 (36.86)
Hispanics, ages 15–17 (36.04)
Whites, ages 15–17 (32.92)
African Americans, ages 15–17 (33.32)
Whites, ages 25–34 (31.76)
African Americans, ages 25–34 (32.60)
African Americans, ages 35–49 (29.48)
Hispanics, ages 21–24 (28.70)
African Americans, ages 21–24 (28.50)
Whites, ages 35–49 (23.00)
Hispanics, ages 25–34 (21.86)
African Americans, ages 50–64 (17.10)
Whites, ages 50–64 (15.30)
Hispanics, ages 35–49 (15.60)
Hispanics, ages 50–64 (12.50)
African Americans, ages 65 or older (4.82)
Whites, ages 65 or older (3.50)
Hispanics, ages 65 or older (3.74)

FIGURE 2.2

Victimization Rates for Violent Crime Young African Americans have the highest victimization rates. Why are younger people more likely to be violently assaulted than other age and race groups?

Note: Figures reflect average victimization rates for each demographic group for the time period 2010–2014.

Source: Bureau of Justice Statistics. (Rates of violent victimizations by race/Hispanic origin and age, 2010–2014). Generated using the NCVS Victimization Analysis Tool at www.bjs.gov .30-Jan-16.

Race is a key factor in exposure to crime. African Americans are more likely than whites to be raped, robbed, and assaulted—the rate of violent crime victimization for whites is 20.3 per 1,000 people, compared with 22.5 per 1,000 for African Americans and 23.0 for Hispanic/Latino individuals (Truman & Langton, 2015: Table 9). Although white Americans are fearful of being victimized by African American strangers (Skogan, 1995:59), most violent crime is intraracial. For both white and black victims, about two-thirds of victims are of the same race as the attacker (Harrell, 2007). These numbers simply reflect the fact that African Americans and whites often live in separate neighborhoods; most of their daily contacts are with people who share their demographic characteristics.

And, most importantly, African American neighborhoods are much more likely to experience what scholars call "high levels of socioeconomic disadvantage" with respect to unemployment, quality of schools, quality of housing, and other factors associated with income and wealth (Lauritsen & White, 2001). These factors are often associated with higher levels of street crime; other kinds of crime, such as occupational crime and computer crime, occur more frequently in other settings.

Low-Income City Dwellers   Income is also closely linked to exposure to crime. Americans with incomes below the poverty level experienced a victimization rate of 39.8 violent crimes per 1,000 people. By contrast, those with incomes at the "high" level experienced only 16.9 violent crimes per 1,000 people (Harrell et al., 2014). The reason is clear enough: economic factors largely determine where people live, work, and seek recreation. For low-income people, these choices are limited. Some have to live in crime-prone areas where housing is cheaper and they lack security devices for their homes, cannot avoid contact with people who are prone to crime, or cannot spend their leisure time in safe areas. Poor people and minorities have a greater risk of being victimized because they are likely to live in inner-city zones with high rates of street crime. People with higher incomes have more lifestyle-exposure choices open to them and can avoid risky situations (R. F. Meier & Miethe, 1993:468). Living in a city is, in fact, a key factor in victimization. For example, victimizations with firearms are much more common in urban areas (2.1 victimizations per 1,000 population) than in rural areas (0.9 victimizations per 1,000 people) (BJS, 2015b).

In the inner cities, where drug dealing and drug use pose significant and visible problems, murder rates are higher than elsewhere. Like their killers, most of the victims tend to be young African Americans. The national homicide-victimization rate among African American men aged 18–24 is 91 for every 100,000 of the same group, about eight times that for white men in the same age bracket (A. Cooper & Smith, 2011). But this does not tell the whole story, because homicide rates differ by city and state. In some cities and states, the gap between rates for African Americans and whites is even greater. Further, we cannot conclude that crime rates will be high in all poor urban areas. There is more crime in some poor areas than in others. Many factors besides poverty—such as the physical condition of the neighborhood, the residents' attitudes toward society and the law, the extent of opportunities for crime, and social control by families and government—can affect the crime rate of a given area.

According to the lifestyle-exposure model, demographic factors (age, gender, income) and exposure to dangerous places, times, and people influence the probability of being victimized. Based on this model, how would you assess your own risk of victimization?

Acquaintances and Strangers

The frightening image of crime in the minds of many Americans is the familiar scene played out in movies and television shows in which a dangerous stranger grabs a victim on a dark street or breaks into a home at night. It is true that many crimes are committed by strangers against people they have never seen before. However, most Americans do not realize the extent to which violent crimes occur among acquaintances, friends, and even relatives. In 2014, for example, female victims of violent crimes were victimized by strangers in only 27 percent of those crimes; acquaintances, spouses, boyfriends, or relatives committed 68 percent of the violent crimes against female victims. Although only 38 percent of male victims suffered violent crimes at the hands of acquaintances and relatives, that figure still constitutes a significant percentage of violent crimes (BJS, 2015a). As you read the following "Criminal Justice: Myth & Reality," consider how you evaluate your risk of victimization in different situations.

The kind of crime a victim suffers tends to depend on whether strangers or nonstrangers are the perpetrators. Most robberies are committed by strangers, but sexual-assault victims are more likely to be victimized by someone they know (Truman & Rand, 2010: Table 7). These differences reflect, in part, the contexts in which these crimes occur. In robberies, valuables are taken from an individual by force and then the robber typically runs away. Thus, the scenario fits situations in which the robber hopes to escape without being caught or identified. This result is much more difficult for a robber who is known to the victim. By contrast, sexual assaults often take place in isolated or private locations; and people are most likely to place themselves in isolated or private locations, such as inside a house or apartment, with someone they know.

Sexual assaults on college campuses have received increased attention since 2014, when the U.S. Department of Education opened an investigation into sexual assault on 55 college campuses (U.S. Department of Education, 2014). By December 2015, the list had grown to 159 colleges and universities (Kingkade, 2016). Due to the relationship between the victim and the offender in sexual assaults, it is sometimes difficult to determine whether a crime has been committed. Some colleges have been accused of sweeping these cases "under the rug" to avoid negative publicity, or tending to believe the accused rather than the victim. To combat issues regarding sexual assault on campus, the U.S. Department of Education is attempting to investigate how colleges handle sexual assaults in order to increase equality and help victims receive justice.

People may be reluctant to report crimes committed by relatives, such as the theft of their own valuables by a relative with a substance-abuse problem. They may be upset about losing their valuables, but they do not want to see

CRIMINAL JUSTICE

Myth&Reality

COMMON BELIEF: Women are more likely to be raped by a stranger than by someone they know.

- Most women take protective measures to avoid being attacked by strangers. They avoid walking alone at night, park their cars in well-lighted areas, or even carry weapons such as pepper spray.
- The "stranger-in-the-bushes" stereotype of rape certainly does occur, but women are significantly more likely to be raped by a friend or acquaintance than by a stranger.
- Approximately three-quarters of sexual assaults are perpetrated by someone the victim knows, whether an acquaintance, friend, or intimate partner (Truman, 2011).
- This misperception about the risk of sexual assault can lead women to take the wrong kinds of action to protect themselves from rape. For example, a college student drinking at a bar might fear walking alone at night and ask a male acquaintance from one of her classes to walk her home. While this action has reduced her risk of being raped by a stranger, it may actually increase her risk of victimization by placing her alone in the company of someone she does not know very well.

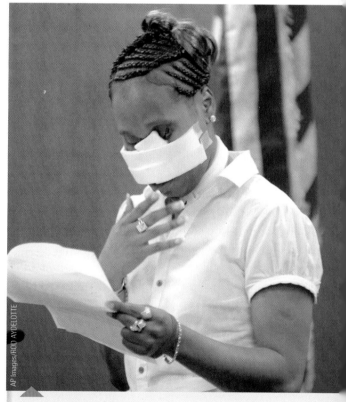

Although Americans often fear violent victimization at the hands of strangers, most violence against women is perpetrated by those with whom they are intimate—husbands, boyfriends, and former lovers. What policies could address this problem?

their son, daughter, or cousin arrested and sent to prison. If the perpetrators of such crimes know that their relatives will not report them, they may feel encouraged to victimize these people further in order to support a drug habit. Thus, the prior relationships among people may facilitate some crimes and keep victims from seeking police assistance.

Domestic violence is a crime that often is not reported to police due to the victim/offender relationship. Some victims may be reluctant to report their abuse when their victimizer is an intimate partner because they may fear retaliation, be financially dependent on their abuser, or just want their partner to cease the abuse (Burgess-Proctor, 2012). Historically, police were reluctant to become involved in domestic violence cases and viewed them as "personal matters," but this attitude changed with the advent of community policing (DeJong, 2012).

The lifestyle-exposure model helps us understand some of the factors that increase or decrease the risk of being victimized, but what is the impact of crime on the nation and on individuals? We turn to this question in the next section.

The Impact of Crime

Crime affects not only the victim but all members of society. We all pay for crime through fear, higher taxes, and higher prices. These factors impinge on key American values such as individual liberty and the protection of private property and personal wealth.

Costs of Crime Crime has many kinds of costs: (1) the economic costs—lost property, lower productivity, and medical expenses; (2) the psychological and emotional costs—pain, trauma, and diminished quality of life; and (3) the costs of operating the criminal justice system.

The costs of economic losses from crime in 2008 were estimated at $17.4 billion (BJS, 2010: Table 82); however, this value only includes the property lost through events such as theft or vandalism. Costs associated with damaged or lost property, lost work time, and medical expenses increase that value significantly. In addition, the intangible costs (pain, trauma, lost quality of life) to victims are difficult to estimate accurately. Adding the costs of operating the criminal justice system each year increases the total economic loss of criminal victimization. In the United States in 2007, approximately $228 billion was paid for police, courts, and corrections (Kyckelhahn, 2011). One study estimates the total cost of *each* homicide to be about $8.9 million, which includes victim costs, criminal justice system costs, crime career costs (the loss of income from a legitimate job by the offender due to incarceration), and other intangible costs (psychological suffering by victims, etc.) (McCollister, French, & Fang, 2010).

Government costs increased in the aftermath of the September 11 attacks, as more money was spent on airport security, border patrols, and counterterrorist activities. These increases do not include the costs to consumers stemming from occupational and organized crime. In 2014, complainants to the Internet Crime Complaint Center reported total losses exceeding $800 million—the majority of which occurred in California ($131M) (Internet Crime Complaint Center, 2015). It is difficult to estimate precise figures for economic losses, but clearly such losses are significant and appear to increase annually for crime such as Internet fraud and identity theft.

The costs of fighting crime came under increased scrutiny following the recession that began in late 2007. State agencies have begun to search for ways to save money, which frequently involve combining or sharing services with other agencies. In the state of Michigan, for example, several small police departments have been disbanded, and local law enforcement is increasingly provided by larger neighboring police agencies. Such consolidation can increase response times, especially in rural areas. In other areas, 911 services are being shared by several agencies in an attempt to reduce operating budgets. Some areas are even taking the more drastic step of combining police and fire services into a single agency. Only time (and research) will determine if these cost-cutting measures will also result in significant reductions in crime.

Fear of Crime   One impact of crime is fear. Fear limits freedom when people feel compelled to confine their activities to "safe" areas at "safe" times. Fear also creates anxieties that affect physiological and psychological well-being. Ironically, the very people who have the least chance of being victimized, such as women and the elderly, are often the most fearful (Miethe, 1995). Not all Americans experience the same fears, but some people do adjust their daily activities to prevent being victimized.

Since 1965, public-opinion polls have asked Americans whether they "feel more uneasy" or "fear to walk the streets at night." When people are afraid to walk near their homes, their freedom is severely limited. From 1972 to 1993, more than 40 percent of respondents indicated that fear of crime affected their nighttime activities in their neighborhoods. Coinciding with the declining crimes rates during the 1990s, the percentage of respondents who were fearful of walking near their homes dropped to 30 percent in 2001. However, as indicated in "What Americans Think," the percentage has remained around 37 percent since 2005—barely less than the percentages in some years with much higher national crime rates. Thus, a significant segment of the American public remains fearful despite the significant drop in crime rates over the past 20 years (Norman, 2015).

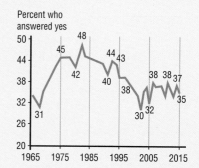

WHAT AMERICANS THINK

QUESTION: "Is there any area near where you live—that is, within a mile—where you would be afraid to walk alone at night?"

Percent who answered yes

50
48
45
44 44
44 43
42
40
38
38 38 37
38
35
32
32
31
30
26

20

1965   1975   1985   1995   2005   2015

CRITICAL THINKING: Should the government be more active in making the public aware about reduced crime rates and lessened risks of victimization? Or might increasing awareness about crime cause citizens to overreact to crime problems? In other words, might more information about crime lead to exaggerated fears rather than realistic ones?

Source: Gallup (2016). *In Depth Topics A to Z: Crime* (http://www.gallup.com).

Although crime rates are down, Americans' fears seem to exceed their actual risks of being victimized. They base their perceptions of the prevalence of crime on conversations at their workplace and from politicians' statements and campaign promises. Their views about crime also seem to be shaped more by what they see on television than by reality (Roche, Pickett, & Gertz, 2015). Although less than 8 percent of victimizations involve violent crime, such crimes are the ones most frequently reported by the media.

The Experience of Victims in the Criminal Justice System

After a crime has occurred, the victim is often forgotten. Victims may have suffered physical, psychological, and economic losses, yet the criminal justice system focuses on finding and prosecuting the offender and often is not sensitive to the needs of victims. For example, defense attorneys may ask them hostile questions and attempt to paint them, rather than the defendant, as having caused the crime to occur. Similarly, the police and prosecutors may question them closely—and in a hostile fashion—to find out if they are telling the truth. Often the victim never hears the outcome of a case. Worse yet, sometimes a victim comes face-to-face with the assailant who is out on bail or on probation. This can be quite a shock, especially if the victim assumed that the offender was in prison.

Victims may be forced to miss work and lose pay in order to appear at judicial proceedings. They may be summoned to court again and again, only to learn that the arraignment or trial has been postponed. Any recovered property may be held by the court for months as the case winds its way through the system. In short, after cases have been completed, victims may feel that they have been victimized twice, once by the offender and once by the criminal justice system.

During the past three decades, justice agencies have become more sensitive to the interests of crime victims. This has happened partly because victims often are the only witnesses to the crime, so their help is needed. Many victims are not willing to provide such help if it involves economic and emotional costs. Some research indicates that victims are more likely to cooperate with the prosecutor if victim-assistance workers meet with them to provide comfort as well as information about how the court system operates (Dawson & Dinovitzer, 2001).

Various laws adopted in recent years provide funds to counsel victims and give financial compensation for injuries, although victims often do not receive enough timely information to take advantage of these programs (Sims, Yost, & Abbott, 2005). In addition, victims' rights statutes in many states permit crime victims to speak at sentencing and parole hearings and to receive information about any impending release of the offender who victimized them. The Justice for All Act passed by Congress in 2004 mandates such rights for victims in those criminal cases processed in the federal courts.

Victims' assistance laws raise questions about which individuals or family members can receive benefits as "victims" (Trulson, 2005). Questions about fairness may arise if some individuals receive different benefits than others who have suffered the same type of loss. Read "A Question of Ethics" at the end of the chapter to consider whether the families of crime victims in general are treated fairly compared with the families of 9/11 victims.

The Role of Victims in Crime

Victimologists study the role victims play in certain crimes. Researchers have found that many victims behave in ways that facilitate the acts committed against them. This does not mean that it is the victim's fault that the crime occurred. It means instead that the victim's behavior may have led to the crime through consent, provocation, enticement, risk taking, or carelessness with property.

What do studies tell us about these situations? First, some people do not take proper precautions to protect themselves. For example, they leave keys in their cars or fail to lock their doors and windows at night; they seem to lack the "common sense" necessary for living safely in modern society. Second, some victims provoke or entice another person to commit a crime; arguing with a stranger at a bar can lead to a criminal assault. Third, some victims are reluctant to seek justice; when the offender is known to the victim, the victim may be unwilling to help with the investigation and prosecution. These behaviors do not excuse criminal acts, but they do force us to think about other aspects of the crime situation.

CHECK POINT

6. What are the main elements of the lifestyle-exposure model?
Demographic characteristics, adaptations, lifestyle, associations, exposure.

7. What are some of the impacts of crime?
Fear, financial costs, emotional costs, lifestyle restrictions.

8. Why do some crime victims feel mistreated by the criminal justice system?
The system focuses on finding and punishing the offender; police and lawyers often question victims closely, in an unsympathetic manner; victims do not always receive assistance that covers their medical expenses and other losses.

STOP & ANALYZE

Fear of crime among Americans has remained relatively stable since the mid-1990s; however, during this period, the crime rate has decreased significantly. List two factors that might explain this apparent "disconnect" between the perception and the reality of the prevalence of crime.

Causes of Crime

Whenever news of a crime hits the headlines, whether the crime is a grisly murder or a complex bank fraud, the first question is, "Why did he (or she) do it?" Do people commit crimes because they are poor, greedy, mentally ill, or just plain stupid? Do any of these explanations apply to Aaron Ybarra, who shot innocent people at Seattle Pacific University? Would any apply to Rusty Brace, who stole funds from a charitable organization and left people in need?

Various theories about the root causes of criminal behavior have been developed, and scholarly research regularly tests these theories. Using the scientific method, criminologists generate hypotheses, collect data, and derive findings about which theories best explain criminal behavior. When substantiated, these theories can provide the basis for new public policies aimed at preventing crime.

Criminology is concerned mainly with learning about criminal behavior, the nature of offenders, and how crime can be prevented. Research focuses mainly on the offender. Fewer questions are asked about how factors such as the economy, government policy, family, and education affect crime (Messner & Rosenfeld, 1994:45–47). In this section, we look at the two major schools of criminological thought—classical and positivist. We will review biological, psychological, sociological, life course, and integrated theories of the causes of criminal behavior. We then take a look at women's criminal behavior and conclude with an overall assessment of the theories discussed in this section.

Classical and Positivist Theories

Two major schools of criminological thought are the classical and positivist schools. Each was pioneered by scholars who were influenced by the dominant intellectual ideas of their times.

The Classical School
Until the eighteenth century, most Europeans explained criminal behavior in supernatural terms. Those who did wrong were "possessed" by the devil. Some Christians believed that all humanity had fallen with Adam and had remained in a state of total depravity ever since. Indictments often began: "[John Doe], not having the fear of God before his eyes but being moved and seduced by the instigation of the devil, did commit [a certain crime]." Before the eighteenth century, defendants had few rights. The accused had little chance to put forth a defense, confessions were obtained through torture, and the penalty for most offenses was physical punishment or death.

In 1764 Cesare Beccaria published *An Essay on Crimes and Punishment.* This was the first attempt to explain crime in secular, or worldly, terms, as opposed to religious terms. The book also pointed to injustices in the administration of criminal laws. Beccaria's ideas prompted reformers to try to make criminal law and procedures more rational and consistent. From this movement came **classical criminology,** whose main principles are as follows:

1. Criminal behavior is rational, and most people have the potential to engage in such behavior.
2. People may choose to commit a crime after weighing the costs and benefits of their actions.
3. Fear of punishment is what keeps most people in check. Therefore, the severity, certainty, and speed of punishment affect the level of crime.
4. The punishment should fit the crime rather than the person who committed it.
5. The criminal justice system must be predictable, with laws and punishments known to the public.

Classical ideas declined in the nineteenth century, partly because of the rise of science and partly because its principles did not take into account differences among individuals or the ways that crimes were committed.

Neoclassical Criminology
After remaining dormant for almost a hundred years, classical ideas took on new life in the 1980s, when America became more conservative. Some scholars argue that crimes may result from the rational choice of people who have weighed the benefits to be gained from the crime against the costs of being caught and punished. But they also recognize that criminal law must take into account the differences among individuals. To a large extent, sentencing reform, criticisms of rehabilitation, and greater use of incarceration stem from a renewed interest in classical ideas. However, the positivist school of

classical criminology A school of criminology that views behavior as stemming from free will, demands responsibility and accountability of all perpetrators, and stresses the need for punishments severe enough to deter others.

thought is what has dominated American criminology since the start of the twentieth century.

Positivist Criminology

By the middle of the nineteenth century, as the scientific method began to take hold, the ideas of the classical school seemed old-fashioned. Instead, **positivist criminology** used science to study the body, mind, and environment of the offender. Science could help reveal why offenders committed crimes and how they could be rehabilitated. Here are the key features of this approach:

1. Human behavior is controlled by physical, mental, and social factors, not by free will.
2. Criminals are different from noncriminals.
3. Science can be used to discover the causes of crime and to treat deviants.

Understanding the main theories of crime causation is important, because they affect how laws are enforced, guilt is determined, and crimes are punished. As we describe each of the theories, consider its implications for crime policies. For example, if biological theories are viewed as sound, then the authorities might try to identify potential offenders through genetic analysis and then segregate or supervise them. On the other hand, the acceptance of sociological theories might lead to efforts to end poverty, improve education, and provide job training.

Biological Explanations

The medical training of Cesare Lombroso (1835–1909) led him to suppose that physical traits distinguish criminals from law-abiding citizens. He believed that some people are at a more primitive state of evolution and hence are born criminal. These "throwbacks" have trouble adjusting to modern society. Lombroso's ideas can be summarized as follows (Lombroso, 1912/1968):

1. Certain people are **criminogenic**—that is, they are born criminals.
2. They have primitive physical traits such as strong canine teeth, huge jaws, and high cheekbones.
3. These traits are acquired through heredity or through alcoholism, epilepsy, or syphilis.

Early biological studies traced the generations of specific families to count how many people in each violated criminal laws. These early studies may no longer seem credible to us, but they were taken seriously in their time and affected criminal justice for decades. For example, many states passed laws that required repeat offenders to be sterilized. It was assumed that crime could be controlled if criminal traits were not passed from parents to children. Not until 1942 did the U.S. Supreme Court declare required sterilization unconstitutional (*Skinner v. Oklahoma*).

Although **biological explanations** of crime were ignored or condemned as racist after World War II, they have attracted renewed interest. *Crime and Human Nature,* by James Q. Wilson and Richard Herrnstein (1985), reviews the research on this subject. Unlike the early positivists, the authors do not claim that any one factor explains criminality. Instead, they argue that biological factors predispose some individuals to commit crimes. Genetic makeup, body type, and IQ may outweigh social factors as predictors of criminality. The findings of research on nutrition, neurology, genetics, and endocrinology give some support to the view that these factors may contribute to violent behavior in some people (Brennan, Mednick, & Volavka, 1995:65). Other researchers have identified physiological factors associated with antisocial behavior, an association they see as a step toward considering a possible link between biology and crime (Cauffman, Steinberg, & Piquero, 2005).

These new findings have given biological explanations a renewed influence and have reduced the dominance of sociological and psychological explanations. Scientists are doing further research to see if they can identify biological factors that make some people prone to violence and criminality (Fishbein, 1990:27). For example, a

positivist criminology A school of criminology that views behavior as stemming from social, biological, and psychological factors. It argues that punishment should be tailored to the individual needs of the offender.

criminogenic Having factors thought to bring about criminal behavior in an individual.

biological explanations Explanations of crime that emphasize physiological and neurological factors that may predispose a person to commit crimes.

psychological explanations Explanations of crime that emphasize mental processes and behavior.

single gene can help predict which abused children might become violent or antisocial adults—abused children with this gene were twice as likely as other abused children to commit acts of violence (Hathaway, 2002). Other studies examine the role of nutrition; in one study, the consumption of fish rich in omega-3 fatty acids was found to be associated with lower levels of hostility in young adults (Iribarren et al., 2004). Behavior may also be affected by head injuries, tumors in specific locations on the brain, and natural chemical imbalances within the body. Exposure to lead as a child can cause behavior problems, including criminal behavior by some teens and adults. (Reyes, 2015). In 2015, the main water source to the city of Flint, Michigan, was found to contain toxic levels of lead. The unfolding public health crisis has potential implications for the criminal justice system as the children in Flint grow older. See the "Close Up" on the Flint Water Crisis for more information and discussion of these issues. These findings linking biology and behavior do not purport to offer a single explanation for crime. They merely demonstrate that biological factors influence certain kinds of behavior in some offenders.

Psychological Explanations

People have often viewed criminal behavior as being caused by a mental condition, a personality disturbance, or limited intellect. **Psychological explanations** of crime center on these ideas.

Sigmund Freud (1856–1939), now seen as one of the foremost thinkers of the twentieth century, proposed a psychoanalytic theory that crime is caused by unconscious forces and drives. Freud also claimed that early childhood experiences greatly affect personality development. Freud's followers expanded his theory, saying that the personality is made up of three parts: id, ego, and superego. The id controls drives that are primarily sexual, the ego relates desires to behavior, and the superego (often referred to as the conscience) judges actions as either right or wrong. Psychoanalytic theory explains criminal behavior as resulting from either an undeveloped or an overdeveloped superego. For example, a person who commits a violent sex crime is

In 2015, Jessica Ewing, a Virginia Tech University student, was sentenced to 45 years in prison for the murder of a classmate. She strangled fellow student Samantha Shrestha in 2014. Does criminological theory help us understand what motivated a seemingly successful college student to commit such an act?

CLOSE UP

The Flint, Michigan, Water Crisis: Public Health and Criminal Justice

In April 2014, the City of Flint, Michigan, stopped using water supplied by the City of Detroit and switched to the Flint River as the source for the city water system. Shortly thereafter, residents started to complain that their water smelled and tasted bad, and in some cases had a brown color. The water was declared to be "safe" by the city's Mayor and Governor Rick Snyder's handpicked Emergency Manager, an individual appointed under state law to override locally elected decision makers in order to guide cities and school systems out of budget crises. They urged people to use tap water rather than bottled water. Four months after the

continued

Close Up (continued)

switch, harmful bacteria were found in Flint water, leading the city to add chlorine to the system. Citizens were instructed to boil tap water before drinking it. In early 2015, Detroit offered the opportunity to return to the prior water source and waive any fees for the move, but the Emergency Manager refused the offer in order to save money and continued insisting that Flint water was safe to drink. The Michigan Department of Environmental Quality (DEQ) agreed, stating that its tests had shown the water to be safe.

By September 2015, however, children in Flint were shown to have higher levels of lead in their bloodstream than in prior years of testing. After independent research by Virginia Tech professor Marc Edwards, the U.S. Environmental Protection Agency began additional testing. State DEQ officials were later found to have minimized the problem, even though their own tests demonstrated high levels of lead in Flint water due to incorrect treatment of the water, which led to the corrosion of lead pipes. Governor Rick Snyder declared a state of emergency for Flint and Genesee County in mid-January, 2016—nearly two years after the switch to the Flint River.

While boiling can help to remove harmful bacteria from water, it cannot remove lead. Thus, tests on Flint's children found damaging levels of lead in their bodies. The consequences of lead poisoning include lower intelligence, difficulty paying attention, and poor fine motor skills. These effects are irreversible and especially damaging to the developing brains of children, and can affect their future behavior (criminal and otherwise). It is not clear whether immediate government investments in special programs focused on nutrition, health care, education, and therapy for Flint's children have the potential to diminish the long-term risks for their behavior and overall well-being.

Flint already had significant economic problems, including high levels of poverty, prior to the water crisis; the water crisis added to them, affecting the ability of businesses to operate. Earlier in this chapter, we discussed how living in urban areas puts residents at higher risk of crime and victimization. In addition, poverty is associated with higher levels of criminal behavior by juveniles. Many residents of Flint live in economically depressed neighborhoods that pose higher-than-average risks of crime. The results of public health studies raise grave concerns that children growing up in Flint and affected by unhealthy levels of lead in their bodies will be more likely to manifest a lack of self-control and other behavior problems that may contribute to future law-breaking behavior. While some people presume that criminal behavior is always a matter of choice by individuals, the future risks presented by the Flint water crisis illustrate the potential for victims of environmental circumstances to experience undesirable behavioral impacts through no fault of their own.

There is an additional aspect of the Flint water crisis and its relationship to criminal justice that has become a source of debate. This debate has been intensified by the deaths of ten people in Flint from Legionnaires' Disease, a rare fatal illness caused by bacteria in inadequately treated water. When decision makers' carelessness and mistakes lead to widespread physical harms to people, should those decision makers be punished? Some Michigan residents called for the arrest and prosecution of government officials at the local and state levels—including Governor Rick Snyder. Others believe the crisis was caused by a series of miscommunications and errors that caused the population to suffer, but no one should be held criminally responsible and punished. In April 2016, Michigan's attorney general announced that criminal charges had been filed against two state officials and one city official for misconduct in office and tampering with evidence. The attorney general said other officials were likely to be charged as the investigation into the water crisis moved forward.

For Critical Thinking and Analysis

If lead exposure increases the risk of criminal behavior, the children suffering from lead poisoning may be more likely than other children to misbehave and later become juvenile or adult offenders. What types of social services need to be in place to prevent these children from eventually being arrested and incarcerated for law-breaking behavior? If there is a wave of juvenile arrests in Flint in the next several years, how will the juvenile justice system handle the victims of lead poisoning? What should happen to government officials who knowingly ignored or, even worse, covered up data indicating a serious lead problem in Flint? What responsibility—if any— do local, county, and state governments have if they put their residents at higher risk of crime and victimization? If it is demonstrated that officials could have, but did not, correctly provide proper water treatment in order to prevent the corrosion of lead water pipes, should they be convicted of a crime?

Sources: L. Bernstein and B. Dennis, "Flint's Water Crisis Reveals Government Failures at Every Level," *Washington Post*, January 21, 2016 (www.washingtonpost .com); J. Counts, "How Government Poisoned the People of Flint," *Michigan Live*, January 21, 2016 (www.mlive.com); B. Dennis and M. Berman, "'There Will Be More to Come,' Attorney General Vows after Criminal Charges Filed in Flint Water Crisis," *Washington Post*, April 20, 2016 (www.washingtonpost.com); P. Egan, "Snyder Declares Emergency as Feds Probe Flint," *Detroit Free Press*, January 15, 2016 (www.freep.com); "Michigan AG: Flint Water Not Even Safe to 'Bathe a Newborn,'" January 25, 2016 (foxnews .com); A. Goodnough and D. Parker, "The Facts about Lead Exposure and Its Irreversible Damage," *New York Times*, January 29, 2016 (www.nytimes.com); *Michigan Live*, January 21 (www.mlive.com); "How the Flint Water Crisis Emerged," *Michigan Live*, January 21, 2016 (www://mlive.com); J. Wisely, "Was Flint River Water Good Enough to Drink?" *Detroit Free Press*, January 30, 2016.

thought to have an undeveloped superego, because the urges cannot be controlled. Alternatively, a person with an overdeveloped superego may suffer from guilt and anxiety. To reduce the guilt, the person may commit a crime, knowing that punishment will follow. To ensure punishment, the offender will unconsciously leave clues at the crime scene. Psychoanalysts say this occurred in the famous Loeb and Leopold murder of Bobby Franks in 1924 (Regoli & Hewitt, 1994).

Psychiatrists have linked criminal behavior to such concepts as innate impulses, psychic conflict, and repression of personality. Such explanations propose that crime is a behavior that stems from abnormal urges and desires. Although the psychological approach takes many different forms, all are based on the idea that early personality development is a key factor in later behavior. The terms *psychopath, sociopath,* and *antisocial personality* refer to a person who is unable to control impulses, cannot learn from experience, and does not feel emotions such as love. This kind of person is viewed as psychologically abnormal, one who may become a crazed killer or sex fiend.

Psychological theories have been widely criticized. Some critics point to the fact that it is hard to measure emotional factors and to identify people thought to be prone to crime. Others note the wide range of sometimes contradictory theories that take a psychological approach to crime.

Sociological Explanations

In contrast to psychological approaches, **sociological explanations** focus on the way that belonging to social groups shapes people's behavior. Sociologists believe that criminality is not inborn but caused by external factors. Thus, sociological theories of crime assume that contact with the social world, as well as such factors as race, age, gender, and income, mold the offender's personality and actions.

In the 1920s, a group of researchers at the University of Chicago looked closely at aspects of urban life that seemed to be linked to crime: poverty, bad housing, broken families, and the problems faced by new immigrants. They found high levels of crime in those neighborhoods that had many opportunities for delinquent behavior but offered few legitimate means of earning a living. Since that time, researchers have found that the relationship between immigration and crime is actually negative—more immigration means less crime (Gladstone, 2016).

From a sociological perspective, criminals are made, not born. Among the many theories stressing the influence of societal forces on criminal behavior, three types deserve special mention: social structure theories, social process theories, and critical theories.

Social Structure Theories   **Social structure theories** suggest that criminal behavior is related to social class. People in various social classes have quite different amounts of wealth, status, and power. Those in the lower class suffer from poverty, poor education, bad housing, and lack of political power. Therefore, members of the lower class, especially the younger members, are the most likely to engage in crime. Thus, under these theories, crime is created by the structure of society.

In 1938 the sociologist Robert Merton, drawing from theories about the role of social change and urbanization on crime, concluded that social change often leads to a state of **anomie**, in which the rules or norms that guide behavior have weakened or disappeared. People may become anomic when the rules are unclear or they cannot achieve their goals. Under such conditions, antisocial or deviant behavior may result.

It is said, for example, that U.S. society highly values success but makes it impossible for some of its members to succeed. It follows that those who are caught in this trap may use crime as a way out. Theorists believe that this type of situation has led some ethnic groups into organized crime. Others argue that social disorganization brings about conditions in which, among other things, family structure breaks down, alcohol or drug abuse becomes more common, and criminal behavior increases. They assert that poverty must be ended and the social structure reformed if crime is to be reduced (R. J. Sampson & Wilson, 1995).

sociological explanations Explanations of crime that emphasize as causes of criminal behavior the social conditions that bear on the individual.

social structure theories Theories that blame crime on the existence of a powerless lower class that lives with poverty and deprivation and often turns to crime in response.

anomie A breakdown or disappearance of the rules of social behavior.

Contemporary theorists have drawn from social structure concepts and Merton's anomie theory to develop certain theories of crime causation. Prominent among modern approaches is the general theory of strain. According to this approach, negative relationships can lead to negative emotions. These emotions, particularly anger, are expressed through crime and delinquency. Strain is produced by the failure to achieve valued goals, which may particularly affect poor people in a society that values financial success. Strain is also produced by negative experiences, including unemployment, child abuse, criminal victimization, and family problems, which also tend to prevail in poor communities. Under this theory, those who cannot cope with negative experiences may be predisposed to criminal behavior (Liska & Messner, 1999:36–37).

As these ideas have become more refined, they have also been used to explain white-collar crime. To achieve even higher levels of success in a structure that values ever-increasing wealth, individuals may break rules and violate laws in order to enhance their personal success. White-collar criminals may commit crimes due to economic strain, but they may also be influenced by work-related strain or a perceived inability to reach a particular social status. These strains, combined with other factors, can increase the likelihood that they will engage in white-collar crime (Agnew, Piquero, & Cullen, 2009).

Social Process Theories   Despite such arguments, many criminologists believe that the social structure approach does not adequately explain criminality by middle-class and affluent people. More importantly, they fear that a focus on social structure erroneously emphasizes crime as primarily a problem of the poor. **Social process theories**, which date from the 1930s but did not gain recognition until the 1960s and 1970s, assume that any person, regardless of education, class, or upbringing, has the potential to become a criminal. However, some people are more likely to commit criminal acts because of the circumstances of their lives. Thus, these theories try to explain the processes by which certain people become criminals.

There are three main types of social process theories: learning theories, control theories, and labeling theories.

Learning theories hold that criminal activity is learned behavior. Through social relations, some people learn how to be a criminal and acquire the values associated with that way of life. This view assumes that people imitate and learn from one another. Thus, family members and peers are viewed as major influences on a person's development.

In 1939 Edwin Sutherland proposed a type of learning theory called the **theory of differential association**, which states that behavior is learned through interactions with others, especially family members (Sutherland, 1947). Therefore, criminal behavior is learned when a person encounters others who are favorably disposed toward crime rather than opposed to it. If a boy grows up in a family in which, say, an older brother is involved in crime, he is likely to learn criminal behavior. If people in the family, neighborhood, and gang believe that illegal activity is nothing to be ashamed of, this belief increases the chance that the young person will engage in crime.

Control theories hold that social links keep people in line with accepted norms (Gottfredson & Hirschi, 1990; Hirschi, 1969). In other words, all members of society have the potential to commit crime, but most are restrained by their ties to family, church, school, and peer groups. Thus, sensitivity to the opinion of others, commitment to a conventional lifestyle, and belief in the standards or values shared by friends all influence a person to abide by the law. A person who lacks one or more of these influences may be more likely to engage in crime.

Finally, **labeling theories** stress the social process through which certain acts and people are labeled as deviant. As Howard Becker noted, society creates deviance—and, hence, criminality—"by making the rules whose infraction constitutes deviance, and by applying those rules to particular people and labeling them outsiders" (1963:9). Decisions that result in the imposition of labels do not necessarily affect all individuals in the same way. Thus, researchers are exploring the

social process theories
Theories that see criminality as normal behavior. Everyone has the potential to become a criminal, depending on (1) the influences that impel one toward or away from crime and (2) how one is regarded by others.

learning theories Theories that see criminal behavior as learned, just as legal behavior is learned.

theory of differential association The theory that people become criminals because they encounter more influences that view criminal behavior as normal and acceptable than they do influences that are hostile to criminal behavior.

control theories Theories holding that criminal behavior occurs when the bonds that tie an individual to society are broken or weakened.

labeling theories Theories emphasizing that the causes of criminal behavior are found not in the individual but in the social process that labels certain acts as deviant or criminal.

association between labels and specific categories of people labeled as offenders (Chiricos et al., 2007).

According to labeling theories, social control agencies, such as the police, courts, and corrections, are created to label certain people as outside the normal, law-abiding community. When they have been labeled, those people come to believe that the label is true. They take on a deviant identity and start acting in deviant ways. Labeling theory suggests that the justice system creates criminals by labeling people in order to serve its own bureaucratic and political ends. Those who support this view call for decriminalization of drug use, gambling, and prostitution.

Critical Theories   In the mid-1960s, the reigning biological, psychological, and sociological explanations of criminal behavior were challenged by scholars who developed theories known as **critical criminology**. These theories assume that criminal law and the justice system are designed by those in power, whose purpose is to oppress those who are not in power (particularly, the poor, women, and minorities). The powerful commit as many crimes as the less powerful, it is argued, but unempowered individuals are more likely to be caught and punished. Those in power use the law to impose their version of morality on society in order to protect their property and safety. They also use their power to change the definitions of crime to cover acts they view as threatening.

Several different theories can be said to fall under the umbrella of critical criminology. **Social conflict theories** posit that crime is the result of conflict within societies. One type of social conflict theory has been proposed by critical, radical, and Marxist criminologists. It holds that the class structure causes certain groups to be labeled as deviant. In this view, "deviance is a status imputed to groups who share certain structural characteristics (e.g., powerlessness)" (Spitzer, 1975:639). Thus, the criminal law is aimed at the behavior of specific groups or classes. One result is that the poor are deeply hostile toward the social order, and this hostility is one factor in criminal behavior (Reiman & Leighton, 2012). Moreover, when the status quo is threatened, legal definitions of crime are changed in order to trap those who challenge the system. For example, vagrancy laws have been used to arrest labor union organizers, civil rights workers, and peace activists when those in power believed that their own interests were threatened by these groups.

Feminist theories of crime are based on the idea that traditional theory centers on male criminality and ignores the experiences of women. While this idea is adopted by all feminist theorists, some adopt less critical perspectives that integrate recognition of women's experiences into social process theories, psychological theories, and other existing approaches. Others, such as radical, Marxist, and socialist feminists, take a more critical view toward traditional, mainstream theories of crime. Recent feminist theorists underscore the need to integrate race and class issues with gender for a full understanding of crime (Burgess-Proctor, 2006).

Like other theories about the causes of criminal behavior, sociological theories have been criticized. Critics argue that these theories are imprecise, unsupported by evidence, and based on ideology. Even so, sociological theories have served as the basis for many attempts to prevent crime and rehabilitate offenders.

Life Course Theories

Life course theories seek to identify factors that shape criminal careers in order to explain when and why offenders begin to commit crimes and to see what factors lead individuals to stop their participation in crimes. Studies in this area often try to follow individuals from childhood through adulthood in order to identify the factors associated with beginning, avoiding, continuing, or ceasing criminal behavior. Criminal careers often begin at an early age; people who eventually become involved with crime often exhibit disruptive behavior, lack family support, and experiment with drinking and drugs as youths. Some theorists discuss *pathways* into crime, which may begin with minor habits of lying and stealing that lead to more-

critical criminology Theories that assume criminal law and the criminal justice system are primarily a means of controlling the lower classes, women, and minorities.

social conflict theories Theories that view crime as the result of conflict in society, such as conflict between economic classes caused by elites using law as a means to maintain power.

feminist theories Theories that criticize existing theories for ignoring or undervaluing women's experiences as offenders, victims, and people subjected to decision making by criminal justice officials. These theories seek to incorporate an understanding of differences between the experiences and treatment of men and women while also integrating consideration of other factors, such as race and social class.

life course theories Theories that identify factors affecting the start, duration, nature, and end of criminal behavior over the life of an offender.

serious offenses. However, pathways into crime are not identical for all kinds of offenders (S. R. Maxwell & Maxwell, 2000). For example, those youths who engage in bullying and fighting may begin a pathway toward different kinds of crimes than those who start out using drugs.

As identified by life course theorists, the factors that can impact criminal careers overlap with factors discussed in psychological, social structure, and social process theories, such as unemployment, failure in school, impulsiveness, and unstable families. In other words, life course theorists' ideas about factors associated with criminal behavior are consistent with factors identified in other theories. However, these theorists study criminal behavior from a broader perspective.

The research of Robert Sampson and John Laub is among the most influential in examining the life course in relation to criminal careers (Laub & Sampson, 2003; Sampson & Laub, 1993). This study reanalyzed and built on the famous studies of Sheldon and Eleanor Glueck that followed the lives of 1,000 Boston-area boys from 1940 through the 1960s (Glueck & Glueck, 1950). Sampson and Laub gathered data on the same men in the 1990s, by which time the surviving "boys" from the original study were senior citizens.

Using their research, Sampson and Laub discuss informal and formal social controls over the life course. Unlike some researchers, who see youthful criminality as setting behavior patterns that continue into adulthood, Sampson and Laub emphasize *turning points* in life that move individuals away from criminal careers. For example, their study showed that military service, employment, and marriage served as particularly important factors leading away from criminal careers. By contrast, incarceration and alcohol abuse were associated with continued lawbreaking. Researchers have also sought to test other factors, such as the development of religiosity, but further studies are needed to see if such factors generate turning points away from crime (Giordano et al., 2008).

Life course explanations do not seek to identify a single or primary factor as the cause of criminal behavior. Instead, they try to identify and evaluate the timing, interaction, and results of complex factors that affect people's lives.

Integrated Theories

integrated theories Theories that combine differing theoretical perspectives into a larger model.

As the number of theoretical perspectives has grown, researchers have called for the development of **integrated theories** drawn from different disciplines—that is, theories that merge several perspectives on crime. For example, in 1979 a group of researchers created a new theory from components of strain, social control, and social learning theories (D. S. Elliott, Ageton, & Cantor, 1979). From their data, they concluded that some juveniles enter delinquency through a combination of weak commitment to conventional norms (control theory) and vulnerability to delinquent peers (social learning theory). Others are more likely to become delinquent after forming strong commitments to conventional society (control theory), which are later weakened by their inability to achieve goals (strain theory). These weakened bonds lead to relationships with delinquent peers (social learning theory).

While the integration of theories makes sense, given the large array of factors that affect human behavior, there has been much debate about whether multiple theories can be integrated at all. For example, some theorists, such as Lombroso, postulate that humans are inherently criminal and that positive social forces are needed to keep people from offending, while other theorists believe that people are generally not prone to criminal behavior but that negative forces can lure them into committing crime (Henry & Lanier, 2006). These issues are currently being debated by modern criminologists in an attempt to construct valid, integrated theories of crime.

Women and Crime

As mentioned earlier in this section, theories about causes of crime are almost all based on observations of men. That women commit crime less often than do men (not to mention that most criminologists have historically been male) helps explain this fact (D. Klein, 1973). Traditionally, many people assumed that most women, because of their nurturing and dependent nature, could not commit serious crimes. Those who did commit crimes were labeled as "bad" or "fallen" women. Much more than male criminals, then, female criminals were viewed as moral offenders.

Most traditional theories of crime cannot explain two important facts about gender and offending. First, a theory must explain why women are less likely to commit crime than are men (the "gender gap"). Women accounted for approximately 23 percent of all arrests in 2014, with men responsible for the remaining 77 percent (FBI, 2015a: Table 33). Second, a theory must explain why women commit different kinds of crime than do men—women are less likely to be arrested for violent crimes than are men, and more likely to be arrested for crimes such as embezzlement and prostitution (FBI, 2015a: Table 33).

Female suspects are less likely than male suspects to be arrested for any type of offense. In 2014, for example, 89 percent of arrested murder suspects and 86 percent of arrested robbery suspects were men. At the same time, women were arrested more often for larceny/theft than for any other offense, although they constituted only 44 percent of all arrestees for this offense (FBI, 2015a: Table 33).

Two books published in 1975 attempted to explain these facts about female offending. Rita Simon's *Women and Crime* and Freda Adler's *Sisters in Crime* both hypothesized that women's liberation would result in increases in female offending. While Adler and Simon disagreed about how the *types* of crime committed by women would be affected by women's liberation, both predicted the gender gap would be reduced significantly. Although there are still significant differences in patterns of criminal behavior by men and women, these books helped alert scholars to societal changes that affect women's status, self-image, behavior, and opportunities to commit crimes.

Beginning in the 1990s, theorists recognized the importance of *social structure* in explaining female criminality. These theories are based upon three pillars: that our society is structured in such a way as to create different opportunities for men and women in the workforce; that power differentials exist between men and women; and that important differences in sexuality shape the behavior of men and women (Messerschmidt, 1993).

Recent developments related to women and crime include life course theories, which focus on the paths taken by individuals through life and identify important turning points in people's lives. Recall that these "transitions" can affect individual behavior and lead people either to or away from criminal activity (Sampson & Laub, 1990). To explain gender and crime, feminist "pathways" researchers focus on the impact of critical life events, such as victimization, to determine why some women engage in criminal behavior. Research shows, for example, that many women working as prostitutes were sexually abused as children (Widom, 1995).

In recent years, scholars have pointed out the need to incorporate race and class into theories explaining female criminality. Known as "multiracial feminism," this perspective advocates not only the inclusion of race and class but also an awareness that opportunities and transitions are shaped by our race, class, gender, sexuality, and many other relevant factors (Burgess-Proctor, 2006). Other research indicates that although the gender gap is growing

Although men commit offenses and go to prison at higher rates, there are concerns about increases in women's involvement in serious crimes. Should the government develop specific policies to attempt to steer young women away from crime and to provide special attention to women who are convicted of criminal offenses?

smaller, this is primarily due to a decrease in male offending rather than an increase in female offending, and the fact that police officers are more likely to arrest women today than in the past (Kruttschnitt, 2013).

Assessing Theories of Criminality

Scholars have presented evidence to support aspects of each theory of crime (see Table 2.4). This does not mean, however, that the strength of supporting evidence is the same for each theory. Also, some research may provide evidence for more than one theory. For example, research about the impact of neighborhoods may have implications for both social structure and social process theories (Kubrin & Stewart, 2006). When criminologists theorize that a recent rise in murders among young people in Boston is attributable, in part, to a "street culture" in which lethal violence

---

TABLE 2.4   Major Theories of Criminality and Their Policy Implications

Scholars and the public support various types of policies. We know little about the real causes of crime, but note how many people think they have the answers!

Theory	Major Premise	Policy Implications	Policy Implementation
Biological	Genetic, biochemical, or neurological defects cause some people to commit crime.	Identification and treatment or control of persons with crime-producing biological factors; selective incapacitation; intensive supervision.	1. Use of drugs to inhibit biological urges of sex offenders. 2. Use of controlled diet to reduce levels of antisocial behavior caused by biochemical imbalances. 3. Identification of neurological defects through CAT scans. Use of drugs to suppress violent impulses. 4. Special education for those with learning disabilities.
Psychological	Personality and learning factors cause some people to commit crime.	Treatment of those with personality disorders to achieve mental health; employment of punishment for those whose illegal behavior stems from learned behavior so that they realize crime is not rewarded.	1. Psychotherapy and counseling to treat personality disorders. 2. Behavior modification strategies, such as electric shock and other negative impulses, to change learned behavior. 3. Counseling to enhance moral development. 4. Intensive individual and group therapies.
Social Structure	Crime is the result of underlying social conditions such as poverty, inequality, and unemployment.	Actions taken to reform social conditions that breed crime.	1. Education and job-training programs. 2. Urban redevelopment to improve housing, education, and health care. 3. Community development to provide economic opportunities.
Social Process	Crime is normal learned behavior and is subject to either social control or labeling effects.	Treatment of individuals in groups, with emphasis on building conventional bonds and avoiding stigmatization.	1. Youth programs that emphasize positive role models. 2. Community organizing to establish neighborhood institutions and bonds that emphasize following society's norms. 3. Programs designed to promote family stability.
Critical	Criminal definitions and punishments are used by some groups to control other groups.	Fundamental changes in the political and social systems to reduce class conflict.	1. Development of programs to remove injustice in society. 2. Provision of resources to assist women, minorities, and the poor in dealing with the criminal justice system and other government agencies. 3. Modification of criminal justice to deal similarly with crimes committed by upper-class members and crimes committed by lower-class members.
Life Course	Offenders have criminal careers that often begin with pathways into youth crime but can change and end through turning points in life.	Fostering of positive turning points such as marriage and stable employment.	1. Policies to reduce entry pathways associated with youth incarceration and substance abuse. 2. Policies to promote educational success, full employment, successful marriages, and stable families.

is used to preserve reputations and respect (Liana, 2006), does that support social structure theory, social process theory, or some other theory? As yet, no theory is accurate enough to predict criminality or establish a specific cause for each offender's behavior.

The theories are limited in other ways, as well. They tend to focus on visible crimes and the poor. They have less to say about upper-class or organized crime. Most focus on male behavior. What is missing, and truly needed, is a theory that merges all the disparate ideas about the causes of crime. Once we have a complete and testable account of what causes crime, we can develop better policies to deal with it.

CHECK POINT

9. **What were the main assumptions of the classical school of criminology?**
   Criminal behavior is rational, and the fear of punishment keeps people from committing crimes.

10. **What are the different kinds of sociological theories?**
    Social structure theories; social process theories; critical theories, including social conflict theory.

11. **What are potential turning points for criminal careers in life course theories?**
    Military service, employment, marriage.

STOP & ANALYZE

The city of Los Angeles has instituted several social programs in an attempt to decrease gang violence. One of these programs, Summer Night Lights, keeps city parks open until midnight, providing meals, sporting events, and activities for local teens. Analysis has shown that gang violence is lower in L.A. neighborhoods with this program. Which theory might best explain this lower level of gang violence? Provide at least two reasons this theory accounts for the decrease.

Source: C. J. Lin, "Gang Violence Declines in Areas with Community Programs," *Los Angeles Daily News*, January 10, 2012 (http://dailynews.com).

A QUESTION OF ETHICS

Think, Discuss, Write

Imagine the following scenarios: Two women—one in New York City and one in Chicago—arise early one morning to prepare to leave for their jobs at different insurance companies. As single parents, they both bear the responsibility of providing financial support as well as parental guidance to their children. After the Chicago woman parks in the underground garage next to her office building, an unfamiliar man sneaks up behind her, places a handgun against her face, and demands her purse and the keys to her car. Because she is startled and frightened, she drops her keys and reflexively bends to retrieve them. When she moves, the gun goes off and she is killed. In New York City, the woman is sitting at her desk in her office tower when suddenly her entire office suite bursts into flames in an explosion. She is killed instantly. The date is September 11, 2001. One woman has been killed in a parking garage in Chicago, and the other has died in the hijackers' attack on the World Trade Center in New York City.

In the aftermath of the September 11 tragedy, Congress enacted legislation to compensate victims with financial awards that exceed those of standard victim compensation programs and instead match the kinds of significant awards that someone might win in a wrongful death lawsuit. Thus, the family of the woman killed at the World Trade Center would be eligible for significant financial support from the federal government to replace the income that she would have provided for her family. Reportedly, the average award to a family of someone killed at the World Trade Center was $2 million. By contrast, the family of the woman killed in the Chicago parking garage would be eligible for a maximum of only $27,000 under the Illinois Crime Victims Compensation Act. Both women were killed during sudden attacks by strangers. Both women left behind children who had relied on them for financial support as well as emotional support and parental guidance.

Discussion/Writing Assignment

Is it ethical for the federal government to provide financial support for one victim's family but not for the other? Are there any persuasive reasons to treat the two families differently? Imagine that you are the advisor to a commission that must propose a policy concerning compensation for future crime victims as well as future victims of terrorist attacks. Write a memo explaining how you would treat these two groups for

continued

A Question of Ethics (continued)

purposes of government compensation. Be sure to explain the reasons for your recommendation.

Sources: Illinois Attorney General's Office, "Crime Victim Compensation: Frequently Asked Questions by Relatives of Deceased Victims" (www.illinoisattorneygeneral.gov/victims/CV_FAQ _RelativesDeceased_0809.pdf); Ray Salazar, "How Does a Chicago

Public Schools Student Survive a Sibling's Violent Death—Twice?" *The White Rhino: A Chicago Latino English Teacher* (blog) *Chicago Now*, August 23, 2011 (www.chicagonow.com); Aaron Smith, "The 9/11 Fund: Putting a Price on Life," *CNN Money*, September 7, 2011 (http://money.cnn.com).

SUMMARY

1 Categorize crimes by their type.
- There are seven broad categories of crime: visible crime, occupational crime, organized crime, transnational crime, victimless crime, political crime, and cybercrime.
- Each type of crime has its own level of risk and profitability, each arouses varying degrees of public disapproval, and each has its own group of offenders with their own characteristics.

2 Describe the different methods of measuring crime.
- The amount of crime is difficult to measure. The National Incident-Based Reporting System (NIBRS), Uniform Crime Reports (UCR), and National Crime Victimization Surveys (NCVS) are the best sources of crime data.
- The complexity of crime statistics makes monitoring trends in crime a challenge.
- Crime rates are affected by changes in social conditions, including demographic trends and unemployment rates.

3 Explain why some people are at higher risk of victimization than others.
- Young male residents of lower-income communities are among those most likely to be victimized by crime.
- A person's routine activities may increase the likelihood of victimization.
- Because of the connection between race and social status in the United States, African Americans are more frequently victimized by crime than are whites.
- A significant percentage of crimes, especially those against women, are committed by acquaintances and relatives of victims.

4 Summarize the negative consequences of victimization.
- Crime significantly affects all of society through financial and other costs.

- Financial costs from white-collar crime, employee theft, and fraud lead to huge financial losses for businesses.
- Medical costs, psychological effects, and insensitive treatment by justice system officials are among the burdens on individual crime victims.
- Fear of crime may make everyone in society feel less free to go certain places or live their daily lives comfortably.

5 Name the theories put forward to explain criminal behavior.
- The classical school of criminology emphasized reform—of criminal law, procedures, and punishments.
- The rise of science led to the positivist school, which viewed behavior as stemming from social, biological, and psychological factors.
- Positivist criminology has dominated the study of criminal behavior since the beginning of the twentieth century.
- Biological theories of crime claim that physiological and neurological factors may predispose a person to commit crimes.
- Psychological theories of crime propose that mental processes and behavior hold the key to understanding the causes of crime.
- Sociological theories of crime emphasize as causes of criminal behavior the social conditions that bear on the individual. Three types of sociological theory are social structure theories; social process theories; and critical theories, including social conflict theories.
- Feminist theories call attention to scholars' neglect of women's criminal behavior. Such theories often take a conflict perspective, but some feminist theorists may draw from other theoretical approaches in examining women and crime.
- Life course theories consider pathways into crime and turning points, such as marriage,

employment, and military service, that move individuals away from criminal careers.

- Integrated theories combine components of theories from different disciplines. They attempt to provide a better explanation for crime than one single discipline can.

6 **Explain why there are gender differences in crime.**

- The criminality of women has only recently been studied. Some argue that as society increasingly treats women and men as equals, the number of crimes committed by women will increase.

- Theories of criminality are criticized for focusing too exclusively on lower-class and male perpetrators.

Questions for Review

1. What are the seven types of crimes?
2. What are the positive and negative attributes of the two major sources of crime data?
3. Who is most likely to be victimized by crime?
4. What are the costs of crime?

5. How does the criminal justice system treat victims?
6. What are the major theories of criminality?
7. What have scholars learned about the criminal behavior of women?

Key Terms

anomie (p. 77)

biological explanations (p. 74)

classical criminology (p. 73)

control theories (p. 78)

criminogenic (p. 74)

critical criminology (p. 79)

cybercrimes (p. 56)

dark figure of crime (p. 59)

feminist theories (p. 79)

integrated theories (p. 80)

labeling theories (p. 78)

learning theories (p. 78)

life course theories (p. 79)

money laundering (p. 53)

National Crime Victimization Surveys (NCVS) (p. 61)

National Incident-Based Reporting System (NIBRS) (p. 61)

occupational crimes (p. 52)

organized crime (p. 52)

political crime (p. 55)

positivist criminology (p. 74)

psychological explanations (p. 75)

social conflict theories (p. 79)

social process theories (p. 78)

social structure theories (p. 77)

sociological explanations (p. 77)

theory of differential association (p. 78)

transnational crime (p. 53)

Uniform Crime Reports (UCR) (p. 59)

victimless crimes (p. 54)

victimology (p. 65)

visible crime (p. 51)

3 Criminal Justice and the Rule of Law

LEARNING OBJECTIVES

1 Identify the bases and sources of American criminal law.

2 Discuss how substantive criminal law defines a crime and the legal responsibility of the accused.

3 Describe how procedural criminal law defines the rights of the accused and the processes for dealing with a case.

4 Explain the U.S. Supreme Court's role in interpreting the criminal justice amendments to the Constitution.

In July 2013, a woman returned home one evening to find her 43-year-old son in the garage covered with blood, claiming that he just killed Satan. Inside the house, she found her 73-year-old husband, a prominent restaurant owner in Mason City, Iowa, dead from stab wounds. The son, Thomas Barlas Jr., was charged with murder for killing his father ("Man Found," 2014).

As the defense attorney and the prosecutor began to prepare their cases for trial, Aaron Hamrock, the attorney for Barlas, announced that he would present an insanity defense. Under American law, if people are judged to be insane at the time they committed a crime, they are not guilty of the crime. As we will see later in this chapter, each state decides for itself what standard to use in evaluating whether or not someone should be declared not guilty by reason of insanity. Under Iowa law, it must be shown that the individual did not know right from wrong or did not understand the nature of his actions. The testimony provided by psychiatrists who evaluate the defendant typically have significant impact on the decision. Yet the decision is often difficult, because the defense and prosecution usually hire their own psychiatrists, and it is not unusual for the psychiatrists to disagree with each other in their conclusions (Senzarino, 2013a).

After the long trial preparation process, in August 2014 Judge Gregg Rosenbladt ruled that Barlas was not guilty by reason of insanity. He concluded that Barlas had suffered a psychotic episode on the night of killing and that he could not comprehend right from wrong or understand the nature and consequences of his actions (Senzarino, 2014a). Even though Barlas had clearly committed the crime, he was not sent to prison; instead, he went to a mental health institution where he would be periodically reevaluated to determine if he still posed a threat to himself or others. If the time ever comes when it is decided that he poses no threat, he may be released into the community.

A criminal defendant's claim of insanity raises difficult questions for the justice system. Critics question whether such a defense should be available to permit people to avoid **legal responsibility** and punishment for their criminal acts. Should an individual avoid imprisonment after committing a horrible act such as the one for which Barlas was responsible?

AP Images/Arian Schuessler

In the Barlas case, the psychiatrists for both the defense and the prosecution agreed that he was insane at the time of the killing. But in other cases, the psychiatrists disagree. In a 2013 case in Iowa, a 13-year-old boy was charged with attempting to sexually assault his mother and shooting her 22 times. The same year, in the same state, a 17-year-old was charged with beating his 5-year-old foster brother in the head with a brick and then drowning the youngster in a pond (Senzarino, 2013a; Nelson, 2014). Both cases presented insanity defenses with disputed testimony about the young killers' mental capacity. Without training in psychology or medicine, are judges or jury members the most appropriate decision makers to determine whether a defendant is legally insane? Although the decision is a difficult one, our justice system places this important responsibility in the hands of the community's representatives in the courtroom rather than deferring to experts' conclusions.

Because of the insanity-based "not guilty" verdict, Barlas could not be punished for the crime. A verdict of not guilty by reason of insanity does not, however, mean that a criminal defendant will be released from custody. Barlas could be released in the future if psychiatrists judge him fit for release, but there is no guarantee that this will ever happen. The 13-year-old who killed his mother, Noah Crooks, was found guilty of second-degree murder, but the prosecution did not successfully convince the jury that he had committed the sexual assault. Under Iowa law concerning juvenile offenders, he was to be held in a juvenile detention facility until his eighteenth birthday and then evaluated by the court to determine if he should serve a longer period of time in prison. In any event, he is likely to be released eventually (Senzarino, 2013b). By contrast, Cody

AP Images/Arian Schuessler

Metzker-Madsen, the older teen who killed his young foster brother, was found not guilty by reason of insanity. He was sent to a secure mental institution where he would be periodically evaluated. Commentators noted that the insanity verdict will likely keep him confined for life, while a murder conviction would have created a likelihood of eventual release (Wheater, 2014). A term of confinement to the psychiatric hospital is not considered *punishment* in the criminal justice system. Rather, it is mandatory *treatment* in a secure facility within the mental health system. Thus there is a loss of liberty as a result of the killing despite the lack of legal responsibility for the killing.

In this chapter, we shall examine the primary components of criminal law. *Substantive criminal law* is developed through statutes enacted by the American people's elected representatives in state legislatures and Congress. It addresses the specific acts for which people will be punished as well as the circumstances in which people may not be held fully responsible for their actions. We shall also introduce *procedural criminal law*, which defines the procedures used in legal processes and the rights possessed by criminal suspects and defendants. Even though Barlas, Crooks, and Metzker-Madsen all acknowledged that they committed the killings for which they were charged, they were still entitled to a trial and representation by an attorney as they attempted to show why they should not be held fully responsible for their actions. The right to counsel and the right to a fair trial are two of the elements provided by procedural criminal law. The precise nature of individuals' rights under procedural criminal law is determined by judges' interpretations of the U.S. Constitution, state constitutions, and relevant statutes enacted by Congress and state legislatures.

Foundations of Criminal Law

Like most Americans, you are no doubt aware that law and legal procedures are key elements of the criminal justice system. Americans are fond of saying that "we have a government of laws, not of men (and women)." According to our American values, we do not have a system based on the decisions of a king or dictator. In the United States, even our most powerful leaders have to make decisions within limits imposed by law. The government can seek to punish only people who violate defined laws, and their guilt has to be determined through procedures established by law.

Laws tell citizens what they can and cannot do. Laws also tell government officials when they can seek to punish citizens for violations and how they must go about it. Government officials, including the president of the United States, who take actions according to their own preferences run the risk that judges will order them to take different actions that comply with the law. In 2004, for example, the U.S. Supreme Court ordered then-President George W. Bush's administration to give a U.S. citizen being held as a suspected terrorist opportunities to meet with an attorney and to make arguments in court (*Hamdi v. Rumsfeld*). Government officials are expected to follow and enforce the law. Thus, in a democracy, laws are major tools for preventing government officials from seizing too much power or using power improperly.

Criminal law is only one category of law. Peoples' lives and actions are also affected by **civil law**, which governs business deals, contracts, real estate, and the like. For example, if you damage other people's property or harm them in an accident, they may sue you to pay for the damage or harm. By contrast, the key feature of criminal law is the government's power to punish people for damage they have done to society.

One of the two categories of criminal law, **substantive criminal law**, defines actions that the government can punish. It also defines the punishments for such offenses. Often called the *penal code* (discussed further in the next section), substantive law answers the question "What is illegal?" Elected officials in Congress, state legislatures, and city councils write the substantive criminal laws. These legislators decide which kinds of behaviors are so harmful that they deserve to be punished. They also decide whether the punishment should be imprisonment, a fine, probation, or another kind of punishment. When questions arise about the meaning of substantive criminal laws, judges interpret the laws by seeking to fulfill the legislators' intentions.

legal responsibility The accountability of an individual for a crime because of the perpetrator's characteristics and the circumstances of the illegal act.

civil law Law regulating the relationships between or among individuals, usually involving property, contracts, or business disputes.

substantive criminal law Law that defines acts that are subject to punishment and specifies the punishments for such offenses.

State legislatures create criminal laws for their states and Congress creates national criminal laws. These laws define acts that are illegal and specify punishments for each offense. Are there additional criminal laws that contemporary legislators should create for your state?

AP Images/Seth Perlman

procedural criminal law Law defining the procedures that criminal justice officials must follow in enforcement, adjudication, and corrections.

By contrast, **procedural criminal law** defines the rules that govern how the laws will be enforced. It protects the constitutional rights of defendants and provides the rules that officials must follow in all areas of the criminal justice system. Many aspects of procedural criminal law are defined by legislatures, such as how bail will be set and which kind of preliminary hearing will take place before a trial. However, the U.S. Supreme Court and state supreme courts also play a key role in defining procedural criminal law. These courts define the meaning of constitutional rights in the U.S. Constitution and in state constitutions. Their interpretations of constitutional provisions create rules on issues such as when and how police officers can question suspects and when defendants can receive advice from their attorneys.

▼ **CHECK POINT**

1. **What is contained in a state's penal code?**
   Penal codes contain substantive criminal law that defines crimes and also punishments for those crimes.

2. **What is the purpose of procedural criminal law?**
   Procedural criminal law specifies the defendant's rights and tells justice system officials how they can investigate and process cases.

STOP & ANALYZE

In 2011, the mayor of Baltimore proposed that the Maryland legislature enact a new law requiring a minimum 18-month prison sentence for anyone caught with an illegal, loaded firearm. Are legislators capable of predicting all the consequences of such a law? List three of your own predictions about the consequences of such a law. In light of your predictions, is the proposed law a good idea?

Substantive Criminal Law

Substantive criminal law defines acts that are subject to punishment and specifies the punishments. It is based on the doctrine that no one may be convicted of or punished for an offense unless the offense has been defined by the law. In short, people must know in advance what is required of them. Thus, no act can be regarded as illegal until it has been defined as punishable under the criminal law. While this sounds like a simple notion, the language of law is often confusing and ambiguous. As a result, judges must become involved in interpreting the law so that the meaning intended by the legislature can be understood.

Definitions and Classifications of Criminal Laws

In defining the behaviors deserving of punishment, legislatures also make decisions about the potential severity of punishments for various offenses. Typically, offenses are placed into specific categories according to the consequences that will follow. Crimes defined as **felonies** are those that can lead to incarceration for a year or more in state or federal prison as well as those subject to the death penalty. **Misdemeanors** are crimes for which the punishment may be a year or less in a county jail, but these are often punished with probation, fines, or community service instead. Some legislatures subdivide felonies and misdemeanors according to degrees of seriousness. For example, crimes classified as third-degree felonies lead to shorter sentences than those classified as first-degree felonies. Legislatures may also define a category of offenses as *petty offenses*—typically, behaviors for which the punishment is only a small fine. Similarly, legislatures may define the most minor offenses as **civil infractions** that are punishable only by fines, do not make the violator subject to arrest, and do not produce any criminal record for the individual. For example, such actions as crossing a street against a traffic light ("jaywalking") or possessing a small amount of marijuana for personal consumption can be defined as civil infractions if a legislature so chooses. Bear in mind that offenses within these classifications vary by state and that the terms (such as *petty offenses*) used to define classifications may also vary in their meaning in each jurisdiction.

felonies Serious crimes usually carrying a penalty of death or of incarceration for more than one year in prison.

misdemeanors Offenses less serious than felonies and usually punishable by incarceration of no more than one year in jail, or by probation or intermediate sanctions.

civil infractions Minor offenses that are typically punishable by small fines and produce no criminal record for the offender.

Legislatures do not necessarily define categories of crimes solely according to elected officials' ideal assessments of the seriousness of each offense. Due to budget crises affecting various states, several legislatures have redefined specific nonviolent felonies as misdemeanors in an effort to reduce the number of people sent to prison and thus lower the associated costs to the state. For example, Montana raised the threshold dollar amount for a charge of felony theft from $1,000 to $1,500 (K. Johnson, 2011). In 2014, the House of Representatives in the state of Washington considered a proposal to change certain drug possession offenses from felonies to misdemeanors ("Under the Dome," 2014). These changes in laws can have consequences beyond simply the goal of reducing the number of people subjected to expensive confinement in jails in prisons. After California converted many nonviolent felonies to misdemeanors, police in some cities complained of rising rates of theft offenses, because drug addicts who formerly would have been in jail for drug possession or theft were now on the street, stealing to support their drug habits without fear of going to jail (Kaste, 2016).

Legislatures do not act in isolation when developing definitions of crimes. Since the 1960s, they have been significantly influenced by the *Model Penal Code*. This suggested code came about when the American Law Institute, an organization of lawyers, judges, and law professors, produced model definitions of crimes to help states organize and standardize their many individual criminal statutes, which had developed over the course of the nation's first two centuries of existence. With guidance from legal scholars' commentaries explaining the reasons for the individual provisions within the *Model Penal Code*, as well as observation of actions and experiences in other states, many states revised their criminal statutes in the 1960s and 1970s (Robinson & Dubber, 2007).

Federal and state penal codes often define criminal acts somewhat differently. To find out how a state defines an offense, one must read its penal code; this will give a general idea of which acts are illegal. Then, to understand the court's interpretations of the code, one must analyze the judicial opinions that have sought to clarify the law.

The classification of criminal acts becomes complicated when statutes divide acts with the same end result, such as taking a person's life, into different offenses. For example, the definition of *criminal homicide* has been subdivided into degrees of murder and voluntary and involuntary manslaughter. In addition, some states have created new categories, such as reckless homicide, negligent homicide, and vehicular homicide. These distinctions involve slight variations in the action taken and the intention underlying the action. For example, did the individual plan in advance to kill someone, or was the death caused by the individual's careless action? Table 3.1 shows the definitions of offenses used in the Uniform Crime Reports (UCR), described in Chapter 2. The UCR is used as one means to track crime rates each year and is available on the FBI's website.

Beginning with the UCR issued in 2013, the FBI used a new, gender-neutral definition of forcible rape that focuses solely on sexual penetration without regard to whether the victim was female or male (U.S. Department of Justice, 2012). Under criminal homicide, there are important differences between intentional ("willful") homicides, which are labeled as murder and manslaughter deserving of severe punishment, and careless acts ("negligence") that lead to someone's death. These definitions are merely generic examples. Each state's actual statutes can have much more detailed wording to include various specific situations.

Criminal laws must be drafted carefully to define the specific actions and intentions that are regarded as deserving of punishment. Yet judgments must still be made by prosecutors, judges, and juries about whether specific actions occurred and what state of mind or intentions motivated the actions. In July 2015, for example, a teenager in North Dakota was injured when someone in a passing vehicle threw a firecracker through her open window as she drove (Sheeler, 2015). If the firecracker explosion has caused the victim to veer off the road into a tree and die, would this be have been considered a willful killing that should be classified as murder or manslaughter, or was this a careless act that should be classified as negligent homicide?

TABLE 3.1   Definitions of Offenses in the Uniform Crime Reports (UCR) (Part I)

The exact descriptions of offenses differ from one state to another, but these UCR definitions provide a national standard that helps us distinguish among criminal acts.

1. **Criminal homicide:**
   a. Murder and nonnegligent manslaughter: the willful (nonnegligent) killing of one human being by another. Deaths caused by negligence, attempts to kill, assaults to kill, suicides, accidental deaths and justifiable homicides are excluded. Justifiable homicides are limited to (1) the killing of a felon by a law enforcement officer in the line of duty and (2) the killing of a felon by a private citizen.
   b. Manslaughter by negligence: the killing of another person through gross negligence. Excludes traffic fatalities. While manslaughter by negligence is a Part I crime, it is not included in the crime index.

2. **Forcible rape:**
   The penetration, no matter how slight, of the vagina or anus with any body part or object, or oral penetration by a sex organ of another person, without the consent of the victim.

3. **Robbery:**
   The taking or attempting to take anything of value from the care, custody, or control of a person or persons by force or threat of force of violence and/or by putting the victim in fear.

4. **Aggravated assault:**
   An unlawful attack by one person upon another for the purpose of inflicting severe or aggravated bodily injury. This type of assault usually is accompanied by the use of a weapon or by means likely to produce death or great bodily harm. Simple assaults are excluded.

5. **Burglary—breaking or entering:**
   The unlawful entry of a structure to commit a felony or a theft. Attempted forcible entry is included.

6. **Larceny/theft (except motor vehicle theft):**
   The unlawful taking, carrying, leading, or riding away of property from the possession or constructive possession of another. Examples are thefts of bicycles or automobile accessories, shoplifting, pocket picking, or the stealing of any property or article that is not taken by force and violence or by fraud. Attempted larcenies are included. Embezzlement, "con" games, forgery, worthless checks, and so on, are excluded.

7. **Motor vehicle theft:**
   The theft or attempted theft of a motor vehicle. A motor vehicle is self-propelled and runs on the surface and not on rails. Specifically excluded from this category are motorboats, construction equipment, airplanes, and farming equipment.

8. **Arson:**
   Any willful or malicious burning or attempt to burn, with or without intent to defraud, a dwelling house, a public building, a motor vehicle or an aircraft, the personal property of another, and so on.

Sources: Federal Bureau of Investigation, *Crime in the United States, 2012*, Washington, DC: U.S. Government Printing Office, 2013; Federal Bureau of Investigation, *Preliminary Semiannual Uniform Crime Report, January–June 2013*, Washington, DC: U.S. Government Printing Office, 2014 (www.fbi.gov).

A close examination of statutes from different states helps to illuminate similarities and differences in statutes and to indicate legislatures' efforts to be precise in their definitions. Compare the statutes defining murder in Idaho and Delaware that follow. You will see that they both emphasize intentional killing as a fundamental characteristic of murder and that Idaho still uses the traditional phrase "malice aforethought" to mean specific intention. Look closely, however, and take note of the differences in the definitions and what the legislatures chose to emphasize in defining this crime for their states.

Idaho Statutes, Title 18, Chapter 40, 18–4001. Murder Defined.

Murder is the unlawful killing of a human being including, but not limited to, a human embryo or fetus, with malice aforethought or the intentional application of torture to a human being, which results in the death of a human being. Torture is the intentional infliction of extreme and prolonged pain with the intent to cause suffering. The death of a human being caused by such torture is murder irrespective of proof of specific intent to kill; torture causing death shall be deemed the equivalent of intent to kill.

As you examine the definition produced by the Idaho legislature, do you see any particular values or policy priorities reflected in the choice of language? Is it possible that highly publicized homicides that occurred in a certain manner may have influenced the legislature's emphasis and choice of words? Now examine the Delaware statute defining murder and ask yourself those same questions.

Delaware Statutes, Title 11, Chapter 5, section 636. Murder in the first degree; class A felony.

A person is guilty of murder in the first degree when:

(1) The person intentionally causes the death of another person; (2) While engaged in the commission of, or attempt to commit, or flight after committing or attempting to commit any felony, the person recklessly causes the death of another person; (3) The person intentionally causes another person to commit suicide by force or duress; (4) The person recklessly causes the death of a law-enforcement officer, corrections employee, fire fighter, paramedic, emergency medical technician, fire marshal or fire police officer while such officer is in the lawful performance of duties; (5) The person causes the death of another person by use of or detonation of any bomb or similar destructive device; (6) The person causes the death of another person in order to avoid or prevent the lawful arrest of any person, or in the course of and in furtherance of the commission or attempted commission of . . . escape after conviction.

Note that Delaware's legislature identified specific situations in which recklessly causing death would be punished as severely as intentionally causing the death of another person. Are there any homicide situations that would clearly be murder in one of these states but would be manslaughter or another lesser degree of homicide in the other state? The examples demonstrate the authority of legislatures in each state to develop the specific definitions of crimes for their own states, including emphasis on policy priorities that may not be evident in the statutes of other states.

Elements of a Crime

Legislatures define certain acts as crimes when they fulfill the seven principles under specific "attendant circumstances" while the offender is in a certain state of mind. These three factors—the act, the attendant circumstances, and the state of mind or intent—are together called the *elements* of a crime. They can be seen in the following section from a state penal code:

Section 3502. Burglary 1 Offense defined: A person is guilty of burglary if he enters a building or occupied structure, or separately secured or occupied portion thereof, with intent to commit a crime therein, unless the premises are at the time open to the public or the actor is licensed or privileged to enter.

Police officers must carefully gather evidence at crime scenes in order to identify the proper suspect and then prove that the suspect actually committed the crime. They seek evidence relevant to each element in the definition of the specific law that was broken. Here officers gather evidence at a crime scene in Missouri. When suspects are arrested for this crime, what will the prosecutor need to prove in order to gain a murder conviction?

Scott Olson/Getty Images

The elements of burglary are, therefore, entering a building or occupied structure (the act) with the intent to commit a crime therein (state of mind) at a time when the premises are not open to the public and the actor is not invited or otherwise entitled to enter (attendant circumstances). For an act to be a burglary, all three elements must be present.

Although most definitions of crimes focus on specific acts that produce harm to persons or property, some crimes involve specific intentions and plans for harm even if those plans are never carried out. Obviously, planning is a form of action, but even if the action itself never produces a specific harm, it can be the basis for a criminal conviction and punishment. Thus, the criminal law includes conspiracies and attempts, even when the lawbreaker does not complete the intended crime (Cahill, 2007a). These are called **inchoate or incomplete offenses**. For example, people can be prosecuted for planning to murder someone or hiring a "hit man" to kill someone. The potential for grave harm from such acts justifies the application of the government's power to punish.

inchoate or incomplete offenses Conduct that is criminal even though the harm that the law seeks to prevent has not been done, but merely planned or attempted.

Seven Principles of Criminal Law

In analyzing the definitions of crimes and the elements necessary to lead to conviction and punishment, legal scholar Jerome Hall (1947) summarized the major principles of Western criminal law that must be present. To convict a defendant of a crime, prosecutors must prove that all seven principles have been fulfilled (see Figure 3.1).

1. *Legality.* There must be a law that defines the specific action as a crime. Offensive and harmful behavior is not illegal unless it has been prohibited by law before it was committed. The U.S. Constitution forbids *ex post facto laws*, or laws written and applied "after the fact." Thus, when the legislature defines a new crime, people can be prosecuted only for violations that occur after the new law has been passed.

2. *Actus reus.* Criminal laws are aimed at human acts, including acts that a person failed to undertake. The U.S. Supreme Court has ruled that people may not be convicted of a crime simply because of their status. Under this *actus reus* requirement, for a crime to occur, there must be an act of either commission or omission by the accused. In *Robinson v. California* (1962), for example, the Supreme Court struck down a California law that made being addicted to drugs a crime. States can prosecute people for using, possessing, selling, or transporting drugs when they catch them performing these acts, but states cannot prosecute them for the mere status of being addicted to drugs.

3. *Causation.* For a crime to have been committed, there must be a causal relationship between an act and the harm suffered. In Ohio, for example, a prosecutor tried to convict a burglary suspect on a manslaughter charge when a victim, asleep in his house, was killed by a stray bullet as officers fired at the unarmed, fleeing suspect. The burglar was acquitted on the homicide charge because his actions in committing the burglary and running away from the police were not the direct cause of the victim's death (Bandy, 1991).

FIGURE 3.1

The Seven Principles of Criminal Law These principles of Western law provide the basis for defining acts as criminal and the conditions required for successful prosecution.

A crime is	
1 legally proscribed	(legality)
2 human conduct	(*actus reus*)
3 causative	(causation)
4 of a given harm	(harm)
5 which conduct coincides	(concurrence)
6 with a blameworthy frame of mind	(*mens rea*)
7 and is subject to punishment	(punishment)

4. *Harm.* To be a crime, an act (or failure to act) must cause harm to some legally protected value. The harm can be to a person, property, or some other object that a legislature deems valuable enough to deserve protection through the government's power to punish. This principle is often questioned by those who feel that they are not committing a crime because they are causing harm only to themselves. Laws that require motorcyclists to wear helmets have been challenged for this reason. Such laws, however, have been written because legislatures see enough forms of harm to individuals and society from such actions to require protective laws. In our motorcycle example, these forms of harm would include not only injuries to helmetless riders but also tragedy and loss for families of injured cyclists, plus the medical costs imposed on society for head injuries that could be prevented.

5. *Concurrence.* For an act to be considered a crime, the intent and the act must be present at the same time (J. Hall, 1947). Let us imagine that Joe is planning to murder his archenemy, Bill. He spends days planning how he will abduct Bill and carry out the murder. While driving home from work one day, Joe accidentally hits and kills a jogger who suddenly—and foolishly—runs across the busy street without looking. The jogger turns out to be Bill. Although Joe had planned to kill Bill, he is not guilty of murder, because the accidental killing was not connected to Joe's intent to carry out a killing.

6. *Mens rea.* The commission of an act is not a crime unless it is accompanied by a guilty state of mind. This concept is related to intent. It seeks to distinguish between harm-causing accidents, which generally are not subject to criminal punishment, and harm-causing crimes, in which some level of intent is present. As discussed previously, certain crimes require a specific level of intent; examples include first-degree murder, which is normally a planned, intentional killing, and larceny, which involves the intent to deprive an owner of his or her property permanently and unlawfully. Later in this chapter, we examine several defenses, such as necessity and insanity, that can be used to assert that a person did not have **mens rea**—"guilty mind," or blameworthy state of mind—and hence should not be held responsible for a criminal offense. The element of *mens rea* becomes problematic when there are questions about an offender's capacity to understand or plan harmful activities, as when the perpetrator is mentally ill or a child. The defense attorneys in the Thomas Barlas Jr. murder case, described at the beginning of the chapter, sought to attack the *mens rea* element by claiming that he was legally insane at the time the crime was committed.

   Exceptions to the concept of *mens rea* are strict liability offenses involving health and safety, in which it is not necessary to show intent. Legislatures have criminalized certain kinds of offenses in order to protect the public. For example, a business owner whose employees have been dumping pollutants into a river may be held responsible for violations of a toxic-waste law whether or not the owner was aware of the dumping. Other laws may apply strict liability to the sale of alcoholic beverages to minors. The purpose of such laws is to put pressure on business owners to make sure that their employees obey regulations designed to protect the health and safety of the public. Courts often limit the application of such laws to situations in which recklessness or indifference is present.

7. *Punishment.* There must be a provision in the law calling for punishment of those found guilty of violating the law. The punishment is enforced by the government and may carry with it social stigma, a criminal record, loss of freedom, and loss of rights.

mens rea "Guilty mind," or blameworthy state of mind, necessary for legal responsibility for a criminal offense; criminal intent, as distinguished from innocent intent.

The seven principles of substantive criminal law allow authorities to define certain acts as being against the law and provide the accused with a basis for mounting a defense against the charges. During a criminal trial, defense attorneys will often try to show that one of the seven elements either is unproved or can be explained in a way that is acceptable under the law.

Defenses against Criminal Charges

Defendants' attorneys can use several defenses to seek to avoid criminal convictions in cases for which defendants actually committed the acts proscribed by criminal law. These defenses are traditionally divided into justifications and excuses (Robinson et al., 2015). *Justifications* focus on the act and whether the act was socially acceptable under the circumstances. Justifications are invoked for actions based on self-defense or necessity in which the individual reasonably concluded that it was essential to cause harm for self-protection or survival under circumstances in which such actions are accepted by society. *Excuses* focus on the actor and whether the actor fulfilled the elements required for being held responsible under a criminal statute. Excuses are defenses that under specific circumstances either eliminate (e.g., insanity) or diminish (e.g., intoxication) criminal responsibility because the individual did not possess the knowledge, state of mind, or intent required for a criminal conviction (Milhizer, 2004).

As indicated by these general descriptions of justifications and excuses in regard to the seven principles of criminal law, *mens rea* is crucial in establishing responsibility for the act. To obtain a conviction, the prosecution must show that the offender not only committed the illegal act but also did so in a state of mind that makes it appropriate to hold her or him responsible for the act.

In 2011, two Indiana boys pleaded guilty in the shooting death of the older boy's stepfather. The 15-year-old received a 30-year prison sentence, and his 12-year-old accomplice was sentenced to 25 years (R. Green, 2011). In a case in Virginia in 2013, a teen was sentenced to 38 years in prison for a murder he committed when he was 15 years old (Adams, 2013). Were these youngsters old enough to plan their crimes and understand the consequences of their actions? Is a child capable of forming the same intent to commit a crime that an adult can form? The analysis of *mens rea* is difficult, because the court must inquire into the defendant's mental state at the time the offense was committed. It is not easy to know what someone was thinking when he or she performed an act. Moreover, as discussed in the "Close Up" box, factors such as age, specific medical conditions, and the effects of medications can complicate the task of deciding whether someone acted with the intent necessary to deserve criminal punishment.

Although many defendants admit that they committed the harmful act, they may still plead not guilty. They may do so not only because they know that the state must prove them guilty but also because they—or their attorneys—believe that *mens rea* was not present. Accidents are the clearest examples of such situations: the defendant argues that it was an accident that the pedestrian suddenly crossed into the path of the car.

The absence of *mens rea*, as we have seen, does not guarantee a verdict of not guilty in every case. In most cases, however, it relieves defendants of responsibility for acts that would be labeled criminal if they had been intentional. Besides the defense of accidents, there are eight defenses based on lack of criminal intent: self-defense, necessity, duress (coercion), entrapment, infancy, mistake of fact, intoxication, and insanity. These defenses are often divided into two categories, as mentioned earlier: justifications and excuses.

Justification Defenses

Justification defenses focus on whether the individual's action was socially acceptable under the circumstances despite causing a harm that the criminal law would otherwise seek to prevent.

Self-Defense   A person who feels that she or he is in immediate danger of being harmed by another person may ward off the attack in *self-defense*. The laws of most states also recognize the right to defend others from attack, to protect property, and to prevent a crime. For example, in August 2002, T. J. Duckett, an African

Criminal Intent and the Appropriateness of Punishment

The chapter opened with examples from Iowa in which people who killed their own family members used the insanity defense in an effort to avoid criminal convictions and punishment. Two of these cases involved teenagers and thereby heightened concerns about whether these individuals really understood what they were doing and met the legal requirements for criminal intent. Such issues arise with regularity in other difficult situations.

In 2009, an 18-year-old in Ohio was accused of beating his mother so badly that she died a few days later from internal injuries. Is this a clear-cut case of criminal responsibility? The suspect was an adult whose intentional violent actions caused a death. However, the suspect's autism gave him a limited ability to communicate by using specific words and phrases that only his mother understood. Jail officials, lawyers, and judges made accommodations to detain him safely in his jail cell: the deputies positioned a television set just outside the bars and played recordings of *The Price Is Right* over and over again, because watching his favorite show kept him calm; friends and relatives were permitted to bring barbecue potato chips, McDonald's Happy Meals, and items from his bedroom at home. In the days following his arrest, officials struggled to decide how best to handle his case, given their doubts about his ability to understand criminal charges and contribute to his lawyer's preparation of a defense.

In Arizona in 2008, an eight-year-old boy shot his father and another man at point-blank range with a hunting rifle that his father had given him for his birthday. He stopped and reloaded as he shot each victim at least four times. He was charged with premeditated murder. Some news reports indicated that the boy was tired of being spanked by his father. Was this an intentional act of homicide? Apparently, yes. But should a child so young be held criminally responsible in the same manner as an adult?

In South Carolina, a 12-year-old boy named Christopher Pittman walked into his grandparents' bedroom one night and killed them with two blasts of a shotgun as they slept. He was a troubled boy who lived with his grandparents because he

had been abandoned by his mother and had serious conflicts with his father. At the time, he was taking an antidepressant medication prescribed by doctors—but one that cannot be prescribed for teenagers in some countries because it is known to affect thinking and behavior, and carries a risk of suicide. Could the medication have affected his thinking so that he actually did not have the requisite intent to commit the crime? Did he really know what he was doing that night?

While being questioned by police in Michigan in 2013, a man confessed to a killing after he was misidentified by a witness as being involved in the crime. While he was in jail, two psychiatrists diagnosed him as suffering from schizophrenia. Police soon discovered that he was innocent, and they arrested the actual shooter. However, the prosecutor expressed the intention of charging the schizophrenic man with a felony for giving a false confession to the police.

All four of these examples raise serious questions about how we evaluate *mens rea* and determine whether someone is capable of forming criminal intent. Advances in modern science affect such situations. For example, the development and use of new medications may lead to unintended consequences for people's clarity of thought and control over their actions. In addition, greater understanding of mental conditions and neuroscience—the science of the brain and thinking—may help us analyze the capabilities of people with specific medical conditions. Yet, there will always be difficult decisions to be made.

In Ohio, a judge ordered that the autistic homicide suspect be moved from the jail to a state residential facility for developmentally disabled people while the court system decided whether he should stand trial. The boy in Arizona was eventually permitted to plead guilty to one count of negligent homicide instead of facing trial on two counts of first-degree murder. He was ordered to remain under the custody and supervision of the state until age 18, with further determinations to be made about whether he should live in a juvenile detention facility, be sent to a treatment facility, be placed with foster

parents, or be permitted to live with his mother. If he stayed out of trouble until age 18, his record would be expunged. By contrast, Christopher Pittman was unsuccessful in challenging the *mens rea* element of the crime by pointing to the effects of his medication. He was sentenced to 30 years in prison for murder. The U.S. Supreme Court declined to hear his appeal. In the Michigan case, the man was sent for an extended evaluation at the state mental hospital, and the prosecutor eventually decided not to pursue any criminal charges for the false confession.

Researching the Internet

To read about another case that raised issues concerning *mens rea*, visit http://www.apa.org/monitor/2013/02/jn.aspx

For Critical Thinking and Analysis

What rule could we formulate that would guide us in determining whether a person is capable of forming criminal intent and thus deserving of punishment? Alternatively, how could we use a case-by-case approach effectively to analyze the capability of each defendant? Would we advance the goal of justice by thinking about appropriate treatment instead of punishment when questions arise about the mental health or cognitive development of a defendant? What would you decide about each of the four defendants profiled here? Write a memo detailing how each of the four defendants should have been punished and/or given treatment.

Sources: "Son of Late KSU Professor Sent to State Facility," *Akron Beacon Journal*, March 27, 2009 (http://www.ohio.com); Associated Press, "Autistic Murder Defendant Poses Challenges," March 19, 2009 (http://www.msnbc.com); S. Dewan and B. Meier, "Boy Who Took Antidepressants Is Convicted in Killings," February 15, 2005; J. Dougherty and A. O'Connor, "Prosecutors Say Boy Methodically Shot His Father," November 11, 2008; K. Grasha, "Mentally Ill Man Who Falsely Confessed Could Be Hospitalized Up to 15 Months," *Lansing State Journal*, February 20, 2014 (www.lansingstatejournal.com); S. Moore, "Boy, 9, Enters a Guilty Plea in 2 Killings in Arizona," *New York Times*, February 19, 2009 (www.nytimes.com); articles from the *New York Times* (http://www.nytimes.com).

American football player for the NFL's Seattle Seahawks, was attacked by three white men who also yelled racial slurs at him as he walked toward his car after a concert. After he had lost a tooth and suffered a cut that would require four stitches when he was struck with a bottle, the 250-pound running back defended himself: he knocked one attacker unconscious and injured another seriously enough that he had to be hospitalized. The third attacker ran away. The attackers received the most serious injuries, yet they faced criminal charges, because Duckett was entitled to defend himself with reasonable force against an unprovoked criminal assault (Winkeljohn, 2002).

The level of force used in self-defense cannot exceed the person's reasonable perception of the threat (K. W. Simons, 2008). Thus, a person may be justified in shooting a robber who is holding a gun to her head and threatening to kill her, but a homeowner is usually not justified in shooting an unarmed burglar who has left the house and is running across the lawn. In a Florida case in 2014, the jury did not accept a man's claim that he fired 10 shots into a fleeing vehicle, one of which killed a teenager, because he believed a shotgun had been pointed out the vehicle's window at him. Because no gun was found in the bullet-ridden vehicle, the jury presumably did not accept as reasonable the man's claim of a perceived threat. In addition, none of the witnesses to the event in a store parking lot saw a shotgun pointed from the shooting victim's vehicle (DeJohn, 2014). Moreover, the shooter's decision to fire additional bullets at the vehicle as it drove away led at least one juror to conclude that any perceived threat had ended before the final shots were fired (Kuruvilla, 2014).

Necessity   Unlike self-defense, in which a defendant feels that he or she must harm an aggressor to ward off an attack, the *necessity* defense is used when people break the law in order to save themselves or prevent some greater harm (Cotton, 2015). A person who speeds through a red light to get an injured child to the hospital or breaks into a building to seek refuge from a hurricane could claim to be violating the law out of necessity.

In 2011, for example, a man in San Francisco was acquitted on charges of illegally carrying a concealed weapon when the jury heard that he borrowed the handgun in order to retrieve his niece's baby food from a car while visiting a housing project in a high-crime neighborhood where he had previously been robbed ("Man Acquitted," 2011). The jury accepted the necessity of his conduct, which under other circumstances would have provided the basis for a criminal conviction. By contrast in 2015, a woman with a permit to carry a concealed weapon fired several shots in a parking lot at a fleeing shoplifter and was convicted of "reckless use of a handgun." She accepted a plea agreement and received a sentence of probation and loss of her concealed-carry permit when it was clear that the prosecutor did not see any necessity in the action that she took over a store's loss of merchandise (Miller, 2015).

Excuse Defenses

Excuse defenses focus on the actor and whether she or he possessed the knowledge or intent needed for a criminal conviction.

Duress (Coercion)   The defense of *duress* arises when someone commits a crime because he or she has been coerced by another person. During a bank robbery, for instance, if an armed robber were to force one of the bank's customers at gunpoint to drive the getaway car, the customer would be able to claim duress. However, courts generally are not willing to accept this defense if the person does not try to escape from the situation if an opportunity arises.

entrapment The defense that the individual was induced by the police to commit the criminal act.

Entrapment   Entrapment is a defense that can be used to show lack of intent. The law excuses a defendant when it is shown that government agents have induced the person to commit the offense. That does not mean the police may not use undercover agents to set a trap for criminals, nor does it mean the police may not provide ordinary opportunities for the commission of a crime. But the entrapment defense may be used when the police have acted so as to induce the criminal act.

During the twentieth century, the defense of entrapment evolved through a series of court decisions (Costinett, 2011). In earlier times, judges were less concerned with whether the police had baited a citizen into committing an illegal act and were more concerned with whether or not the citizen had taken the bait. Today when the police implant an idea for a crime in the mind of a person who then commits the offense, judges are more likely to consider entrapment claims.

Entrapment raises tough questions for judges, who must decide whether the police went too far toward making a crime occur that otherwise would not have happened (Carlon, 2007). The key question is the predisposition of the defendant. The Supreme Court stressed that the prosecutor must show beyond a reasonable doubt that a defendant was predisposed to break the law before being approached by government agents. In recent years, controversies about entrapment have arisen concerning such law enforcement tactics as officers pretending to be teenagers in online conversations and attempting to generate interest in improper sexual activities among adults who are online specifically looking for relationships with other adults rather than looking for underage girls (Pransky, 2014). In Florida in 2014, a developmentally disabled man with the mental capacities of a second grader successfully used an entrapment defense to gain an acquittal from criminal charges after undercover federal law enforcement agents pretending to be store owners asked him multiple times to obtain guns for them (Diedrich, 2014).

Infancy Anglo-American law excuses criminal acts by children under age seven on the grounds of their *infancy* and lack of responsibility for their actions—in other words, *mens rea* is not present. Also called *immaturity*, this excuse is based on the recognition that young children do not yet have the capacity to think about and understand appropriate behavior and the consequences of their actions. Common law has presumed that children aged 7–14 are not liable for their criminal acts; however, prosecutors have on occasion been able to present evidence of a child's mental capacity to form *mens rea*. Juries can assume the presence of a guilty mind if it can be shown, for example, that the child hid evidence or tried to bribe a witness.

Of course, as a child grows older, the assumption of immaturity weakens. Since the development of juvenile courts in the 1890s, children generally have been tried using rules that are different from those applied to adults; but in some situations, they may be tried as adults—if, for example, they are repeat offenders or are charged with a particularly heinous crime. Because of the public's concerns about violent crimes by young people, in the 1990s, it became increasingly common to see prosecutors seek to hold children responsible for serious crimes in the same manner as adults (Henning, 2013). As mentioned in the "Close Up" feature, in 2008 the U.S. Supreme Court declined to hear an appeal from Christopher Pittman, the 12-year-old who had killed his grandparents. He was tried as an adult, and was sentenced to 30 years.

Mistake of Fact The courts have generally upheld the view that ignorance of the law is no excuse for committing an illegal act. But what if there is a *mistake of fact*? If an accused person has made a mistake on some crucial fact, that may serve as a defense. For example, suppose some teenagers ask your permission to grow sunflowers in a vacant lot behind your home. You help them weed the garden and water the plants. Then it turns out that they are growing marijuana. You were not aware of this because you have no idea what a marijuana plant looks like. Should you be convicted for growing an illegal drug on your property? The answer depends on the specific degree of knowledge and intent that the prosecution must prove for that offense. The success of such a defense may also depend on the extent to which jurors understand and sympathize with your mistake.

For example, in 2008 a college professor attending a professional baseball game bought his seven-year-old son a bottle of "lemonade." Because he and his family seldom watch television, however, he had no idea that "hard lemonade" even existed. Thus, he made a mistake of fact by purchasing an alcoholic beverage for his underage son. When police officers spotted the child drinking the beverage, the boy was taken from the custody of his parents for a few days until officials decided that it was an unintentional mistake. If prosecutors had pursued criminal charges against the professor, his fate would have depended on whether the jury believed his claim of making an ignorant mistake of fact in purchasing the alcoholic "lemonade" for a child (Dickerson, 2008).

Intoxication   The law does not relieve an individual of responsibility for acts performed while voluntarily intoxicated. There are, however, cases in which *intoxication* can be used as a defense, as when a person has been tricked into consuming a substance without knowing that it may cause intoxication (Piel, 2015). As described in the "Close Up," Christopher Pittman's attorney attempted unsuccessfully to use this defense by arguing that the boy's prescribed antidepressant drugs caused his violent behavior. Some complex cases arise in which the defendant must be shown to have had a specific intent to commit a crime. For example, people may claim that they were too drunk to realize that they had left a restaurant without paying the bill. Thus they lacked the specific criminal intent to "steal" from the restaurant by leaving without paying. Drunkenness can sometimes also be used as a mitigating factor to reduce the seriousness of a charge.

Insanity   The defense of *insanity* has been a subject of heated debate (Appelbaum, 2013). Four states—Idaho, Montana, Nevada, and Utah—no longer permit the insanity defense (Bennion, 2011). The public believes that many criminals "escape" punishment through the skillful use of psychiatric testimony. Yet less than 1 percent of criminal defendants are found "not guilty by reason of insanity" Typically, they do not go free but are sent to secure mental facilities as described in the chapter opener concerning the Iowa cases. The insanity defense is rare; it is generally used only in serious cases or where there is no other valid defense.

Over time, U.S. courts have used five tests of criminal responsibility involving insanity: the *M'Naghten* Rule, the Irresistible Impulse Test, the *Durham* Rule, the *Model Penal Code's* Substantial Capacity Test, and the test defined in the federal Comprehensive Crime Control Act of 1984. These tests are summarized in Table 3.2. One important feature of the insanity defense is the opportunity for state and federal laws to impose on defendants the burden of demonstrating their mental incapacity. The prosecution bears the burden of proving the defendant's guilt beyond a reasonable doubt, but the Supreme Court has said laws "may place the burden of persuasion on a defendant to prove insanity as the applicable law defines it, whether by a preponderance of the evidence or to some more convincing degree" (*Clark v. Arizona*, 2006). Thus, in an insanity defense, the law of the jurisdiction of the case will dictate whether it is the defendant's responsibility to present evidence to persuade the judge or jury about her or his insanity or the prosecutor's responsibility to prove that the defendant did not fit the legal definition of insanity at the time of the crime.

In 2011, a three-judge panel in Connecticut found Stephen Morgan to be "not guilty by reason of insanity" for first-degree murder charges after he stalked and shot a female student in the Wesleyan University bookstore. The judges ordered that he be committed to a secure psychiatric facility. Should severe mental problems enable people who kill others to avoid prison sentences?

TABLE 3.2 Insanity Defense Standards

The standards for the insanity defense have evolved over time.

Test	Legal Standard to Establish Insanity
M'Naghten (1843)	"Didn't know what he was doing or didn't know it was wrong."
Irresistible Impulse (1897)	"Could not control his conduct."
Durham (1954)	"The criminal act was caused by his mental illness."
Model Penal Code (1972)	"Lacks substantial capacity to appreciate the wrongfulness of his conduct or to control it."
Comprehensive Crime Control Act	"Lacks capacity to appreciate the wrongfulness of his conduct."

Source: National Institute of Justice, *Crime File*, "Insanity Defense," a film prepared by Norval Morris (Washington, DC: U.S. Government Printing Office, n.d.).

***M'Naghten* Rule** More than a dozen states use the *M'Naghten* Rule, which was developed in England in 1843. In that year, Daniel M'Naghten was acquitted of killing Edward Drummond, a man he had thought was Sir Robert Peel, the prime minister of Great Britain. M'Naghten claimed that he had been delusional at the time of the killing. The British court developed a standard for determining criminal responsibility known as the "right-from-wrong test." It asks whether "at the time of the committing of the act, the party accused was laboring under such a defect of reason, from disease of the mind, as not to know the nature and quality of the act he was doing, or if he did know it that he did not know he was doing what was wrong" (*M'Naghten's Case*, 1843). In Thomas Barlas's case, discussed in the opening of the chapter, Iowa law required the defense attorney to persuade the court that, in accordance with the *M'Naghten* Rule, Barlas was incapable of knowing the nature of his act and could not distinguish right from wrong in his own conduct (Senzarino, 2014b).

Irresistible Impulse Test Four states supplemented the *M'Naghten* Rule with the Irresistible Impulse Test. Because psychiatrists argued that some people can feel compelled by their mental illness to commit criminal actions even though they recognize the wrongfulness of their conduct, the Irresistible Impulse Test was designed to bring the *M'Naghten* Rule in line with modern psychiatry. This test excuses defendants when a mental disease was controlling their behavior even though they knew that what they were doing was wrong.

Durham Rule The *Durham* Rule, originally developed in New Hampshire in 1871, was adopted by the Circuit Court of Appeals for the District of Columbia in 1954 in the case of *Durham v. United States*. Under this rule, the accused is not criminally responsible "if an unlawful act is the product of mental disease or mental defect."

***Model Penal Code's* Substantial Capacity Test** Arguing that the *Durham* Rule offered no useful definition of "mental disease or defect," the case of *United States v. Brawner* led the federal courts to overturn the *Durham* Rule in 1972 in favor of a modified version of a test proposed in the *Model Penal Code*. (As explained earlier, the *Model Penal Code* was developed by the American Bar Association as a model of what "should" be.) By 1982 all federal courts and about half of the state courts had adopted the *Model Penal Code*'s Substantial Capacity Test, which states that a person is not responsible for criminal conduct "if at the time of such conduct as a result of mental disease or defect he lacks substantial capacity either to appreciate the criminality [wrongfulness] of his conduct or to conform his conduct to the requirements of law." The Substantial Capacity Test broadens and modifies the *M'Naghten* and Irresistible Impulse rules. By stressing "substantial capacity," the test does not require that a defendant be unable to distinguish right from wrong.

Comprehensive Crime Control Act   The Comprehensive Crime Control Act of 1984 changed the federal rules on the insanity defense by limiting it to those who are unable, as a result of severe mental disease or defect, to understand the nature or wrongfulness of their acts. This change means that the Irresistible Impulse Test cannot be used in the federal courts. It also shifts the burden of proof from the prosecutor to the defendant, who has to prove his or her insanity. Further, the act creates a new procedure whereby a person who is found not guilty only by reason of insanity must be committed to a mental hospital until she or he no longer poses a danger to society. These rules apply only in federal courts, but they are spreading to the states.

All of the insanity tests are difficult to apply. Moreover, deciding what to do with someone who has been found not guilty by reason of insanity poses significant difficulties. And jurors' fears about seeing the offender turned loose might affect their decisions about whether the person was legally insane at the time of the crime.

John Hinckley's attempt to assassinate President Ronald Reagan in 1981 reopened the debate on the insanity defense. Television news footage showed that Hinckley had shot the president. Yet with the help of psychiatrists, Hinckley's lawyers counteracted the prosecution's efforts to persuade the jury that Hinckley was sane. Hinckley did not go free, however. He has been confined to a mental hospital for nearly 35 years, although doctors and a federal judge have approved opportunities for him to leave the hospital to visit his mother in recent years (Marimow, 2013). When Hinckley was acquitted, the public was outraged, and several states acted to limit or abolish the insanity defense. Several states introduced the defense of "guilty but mentally ill." This defense allows a jury to find the accused guilty but requires that he or she be given psychiatric treatment while in prison (Johansen, 2015).

▼ CHECK POINT

3. **What are the seven principles of criminal law?**
   Legality, *actus reus*, causation, harm, concurrence, *mens rea*, and punishment.

4. **What are the defenses in substantive criminal law?**
   Self-defense, necessity, duress (coercion), entrapment, infancy, mistake of fact, intoxication, insanity.

5. **What are the tests of criminal responsibility used for the insanity defense?**
   M'Naghten Rule (right-from-wrong test), Irresistible Impulse Test, *Durham* Rule, *Model Penal Code*, Comprehensive Crime Control Act.

STOP & ANALYZE

Look through the list of justification and excuse defenses, and choose one that is the *least* important or necessary. Make three arguments for abolishing that defense. What would be the risks and consequences of abolishing the defense? What is the strongest argument in favor of keeping it?

Procedural Criminal Law

Procedural law defines how the state must process cases. According to procedural due process, accused persons must be tried in accordance with legal procedures, which include providing the rights granted by the Constitution to criminal defendants. As we saw in Chapter 1, the due process model is based on the premise that freedom is so valuable that efforts must be made to prevent erroneous decisions that would deprive an innocent person of her or his freedom. But rights are not only intended to prevent the innocent from being wrongly convicted. They also seek to prevent unfair police and prosecution practices aimed at guilty people, such as conducting improper searches, using violence to pressure people to confess, and denying defendants a fair trial.

The importance of procedural law has been evident throughout U.S. history, which contains many examples of police officers and prosecutors harassing and victimizing those who lack political power, such as poor people, racial and ethnic minorities, and unpopular religious groups. The development of procedural safeguards through the decisions of the U.S. Supreme Court has helped protect citizens from such actions. In these decisions, the Supreme Court may favor guilty people by ordering new trials or may even release them from custody because of the weight it places on protecting procedural rights and preventing police misconduct.

Individual rights and the protection against improper deprivations of liberty represent central elements of American values. Americans expect that their rights will be protected. At the same time, however, the protection of rights for the criminally accused can clash with competing American values that emphasize the control of crime as an important component of protecting all citizens' freedom of movement and sense of security. Because the rules of procedural criminal law can sometimes lead to the release of guilty people, some observers regard them as weighted too heavily in favor of American values emphasizing individual rights rather than equally valid American values that emphasize the protection of the community.

Public opinion does not always support the decisions by the Supreme Court and other courts that uphold the rights of criminal defendants and convicted offenders. Many Americans would like to see the goals of stopping crime and ensuring that guilty people are punished given priority over the protection of defendants' rights. Such opinions raise questions about Americans' commitment to the rights described in the Bill of Rights. Do you agree that there are too many rights for defendants?

Unlike substantive criminal law, which is defined by legislatures through statutes, procedural criminal law is defined by courts through judicial rulings. Judges interpret the provisions of the U.S. Constitution and state constitutions, and those interpretations establish the procedures that government officials must follow. Because it has the authority to review cases from state supreme courts as well as from federal courts, the U.S. Supreme Court has played a major role in defining procedural criminal law. The Supreme Court's influence stems from its power to define the meaning of the U.S. Constitution, especially the Bill of Rights—the first 10 amendments to the Constitution, which list legal protections against actions of the government. Although public opinion may clash with Supreme Court rulings, the Supreme Court can make independent decisions because its appointed members cannot be removed from office by the voters but only through impeachment for misconduct.

The Bill of Rights and the Fourteenth Amendment

The U.S. Constitution contained few references to criminal justice when it was ratified in 1788 and 1789. Because many people were concerned that the document did not set forth the rights of individuals in enough detail, 10 amendments were added in 1791. These first 10 amendments are known as the **Bill of Rights**.

American students typically gain exposure to the provisions of the Bill of Rights through required high school classes on civics and American government. Thus, many Americans know that rights concerning free speech and religion are contained in the First Amendment. Because of public debates about its meaning, many Americans also know that the Second Amendment contains this phrase: "the right of the people to keep and bear arms, shall not be infringed." The details of the other numbered amendments are not as familiar because they tend to receive less attention in

Bill of Rights The first 10 amendments added to the U.S. Constitution to provide specific rights for individuals, including criminal justice rights concerning searches, trials, and punishments.

The first Congress debated and approved the Bill of Rights, the first ten amendments to the U.S. Constitution. These amendments provided protections for suspects and defendants in the federal criminal justice process. Decisions by the U.S. Supreme Court later applied these protections to state court criminal cases, too. What might the American criminal justice system look like if it lacked the procedural rights provided by the Bill of Rights?

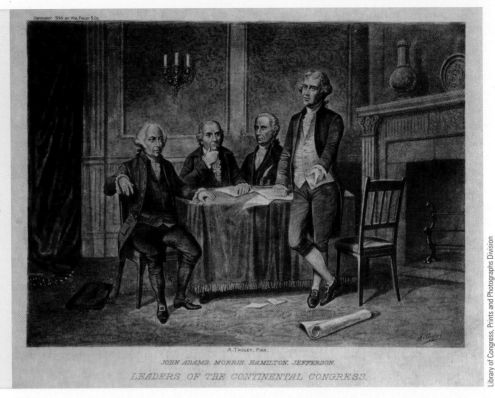

JOHN ADAMS. MORRIS. HAMILTON. JEFFERSON.
LEADERS OF THE CONTINENTAL CONGRESS.

Library of Congress, Prints and Photographs Division

politicians' speeches and news media articles. As described in "The Policy Debate" feature, the Second Amendment is one of several amendments in the Bill of Rights that has implications for criminal justice. However, the Second Amendment is not one of the four amendments that directly concern procedural criminal law. Instead, it is at the heart of debates about criminal justice policies that are shaped by judges' interpretations of the Constitution, scholars' studies of crime and violence, interest groups' beliefs about constitutional rights, and legislators' decisions about needed laws. As shown in "What Americans Think," public opinion polling in 2015 indicated that Americans are deeply divided about the issue of gun rights and the desirability of new laws to regulate aspects of firearms sales, ownership, and possession.

THE POLICY DEBATE

Should Ex-Felons' Gun-Ownership Rights Be Restored?

Shooting incidents that take multiple lives continually renew vigorous debates about appropriate gun control laws. Beginning with the mass shooting of school children at the elementary school in Newtown, Connecticut, in December 2012, and following each new event through the mass shooting that killed 49 people at an Orlando, Florida, nightclub in June 2016, President Obama unsuccessfully urged Congress to enact new gun restrictions into law. In January 2016, emotional debates erupted when President Obama took executive action to order new

resources devoted to federal background checks for gun purchasers, greater resources for attending to mental health issues and identifying people with mental problems seeking to buy guns, and new requirements for gun sellers. Critics argued that the president's actions violated the Second Amendment rights of Americans and would not stop mass shootings. Supporters argued that greater efforts must be made to keep guns out of the hands of people who might misuse firearms. In addition, supporters pointed to the fact that most gun

deaths are suicides, so greater attention to mental illness issues could potentially have beneficial effects for aspects of gun problems aside from crime prevention.

One aspect of debates about gun control concerns the meaning of the Second Amendment. While many people argue that the amendment should be regarded as broadly prohibiting government interference with citizens' ability to own and carry all types of firearms, in fact, the Supreme Court's interpretation of gun rights has specifically authorized governments to consider various types of regulations. In its decision in *District of*

Columbia v. Heller (2008) and reiterated in *McDonald v. City of Chicago* (2010), the Court declared that the Second Amendment protects a law-abiding citizen's fundamental right to keep a handgun in the home. The Court has not, as yet, expanded its interpretation of the right to cover other types of firearms or to the carrying of firearms outside of the home. Indeed, in 2015 the Court declined to expand this definition of the Second Amendment; the justices refused to consider people's lawsuits seeking to stop cities from having laws that required locking up handguns at home and prohibited the sale or possession of certain semiautomatic weapons (*Jackson v. San Francisco*, 2015; *Friedman v. Highland Heights*, 2015). The groundbreaking majority opinion by Justice Antonin Scalia in *Heller* that established the limited definition of the Second Amendment right explicitly said:

> Like most rights, the right secured by the Second Amendment is not unlimited.... [N]othing in our opinion should be taken to cast doubt on longstanding prohibitions on the possession of firearms by felons and the mentally ill, or laws forbidding the carrying of firearms in sensitive places such as schools and government buildings, or laws imposing conditions and qualifications on the commercial sale of arms.

Thus governments can legally enact laws placing various restrictions on the ownership and possession of guns, as long as law-abiding citizens can keep handguns in their homes for self-protection. As a result, there are debates about what regulations, if any, are appropriate and beneficial for society.

In 2014, nearly 640,000 people were released from prison. The number of ex-felons gaining release is increasing in many states as governments seek ways to reduce the expense of imprisonment. It is much less expensive to have offenders under parole supervision in the community than it is to incarcerate them. Because of attention to voting rights for ex-offenders, there has been a political push to restore all constitutional rights for ex-offenders after they successfully complete their prison sentences and parole supervision within the community. As a result, debates have emerged about whether gun-ownership rights should be restored for ex-felons.

For Restoring Gun-Ownership Rights for Ex-Felons

Supporters of the restoration of gun-ownership rights focus on the fact that ex-offenders who have completed their punishment should be reintegrated into the community, recognized as equal citizens, and permitted to rebuild their lives with full citizenship rights.

The arguments for restoring gun-ownership rights are these:

- Ex-offenders have completed their punishment and need to be regarded as full and equal citizens in order to be reintegrated into the society.
- Many ex-offenders live in high-crime neighborhoods, and they need to be able to protect their homes and families.
- Gun ownership is a basic right guaranteed for all Americans by the Second Amendment.
- States that have enacted laws to expand opportunities for citizens to possess and carry guns have not experienced increases in crime rates as a result.

Against Restoring Gun-Ownership Rights for Ex-Felons

Opponents of restoration of gun-ownership rights raise concerns about permitting the possession of firearms for people whose past behavior demonstrated that they lacked self-control, acted in a violent manner, or otherwise failed to obey society's rules. As a result, there would be grave risks of additional shootings and homicides that might have been prevented by barring ex-felons from owning guns or by approving gun ownership on an individual case-by-case basis.

The arguments against permitting ex-felons to own guns are these:

- The Second Amendment does not guarantee gun rights for all Americans; the Supreme Court's decision specifically said, "nothing in our opinion should be taken to cast doubt on longstanding prohibitions on the possession of firearms by felons and the mentally ill."
- Many ex-felons have psychological problems; indeed, a study by the Bureau of Justice Statistics found that 56 percent of state prisoners "have symptoms of serious mental illnesses."
- Congress and state legislatures can enact reasonable restrictions on gun ownership by specific categories of people as long as they do not prohibit handguns kept in the homes of people with established records of being law-abiding citizens.
- In states that require restoration of gun-ownership rights, there have been highly publicized shootings committed by mentally ill and otherwise troubled ex-felons.
- In addition to risks of shootings and homicides, gun ownership by ex-felons whose lives lack evidence of self-control, organizational skills, and concern for safety will also increase risks of gun accidents involving children, suicides, and the theft of unsecured firearms in burglaries and robberies.

What Should U.S. Policy Be?

What impact would the restoration of gun-ownership rights for ex-felons have on American society? Is it an essential element of reintegrating ex-offenders that all citizenship rights be restored? Would the availability of legal guns for ex-felons increase suicides, accidental shootings, and homicides or other crimes, and thereby harm society?

Researching the Internet

To read the Supreme Court's fundamental opinion on the definition of Second Amendment gun ownership rights, see *District of Columbia v. Heller* (2008) at http://www.law.cornell.edu/supct/pdf /07-290P.ZO.

Analyzing the Issues

Are gun-ownership rights essential to ex-felons' successful reintegration into American society, to the restoration of their status as equal citizens, and to the protection of their families? Alternatively, is society subject to increased danger and harm when ex-felons can readily own guns? What policy do you see as best for the United States? Give three reasons for your conclusion about this issue.

WHAT AMERICANS THINK

QUESTION: What is more important, gun rights or gun control?

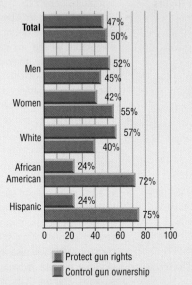

Total: 47% / 50%
Men: 52% / 45%
Women: 42% / 55%
White: 57% / 40%
African American: 24% / 72%
Hispanic: 24% / 75%

0 20 40 60 80 100

■ Protect gun rights
■ Control gun ownership

CRITICAL THINKING: What differences in beliefs, experiences, or information might explain the varying opinions among these demographic groups?

Source: "Race, Education, Gender Differences on Gun Control vs. Gun Rights," Pew Research Center, August 12, 2015 (www.people-press.org).

self-incrimination The act of exposing oneself to prosecution by being pressured to respond to questions when the answers may reveal that one has committed a crime. The Fifth Amendment protects defendants against compelled self-incrimination.

double jeopardy The subjecting of a person to prosecution more than once in the same jurisdiction for the same offense; prohibited by the Fifth Amendment.

Procedural criminal law is shaped by four specific amendments in the Bill of Rights, as well as by the Fourteenth Amendment, which was created in 1868 after the Civil War. The Fourth Amendment bars unreasonable searches and seizures. The Fifth Amendment outlines basic due process rights in criminal cases. For example, consistent with the assumption that the state must prove the defendant's guilt, protection against **self-incrimination** means that persons cannot be forced to respond to questions whose answers may reveal that they have committed a crime. The protection against **double jeopardy** means that a person may be subjected to only one prosecution or punishment for a single offense within the same jurisdiction. The Sixth Amendment provides for the right to a speedy, fair, and public trial by an impartial jury, as well as the right to counsel. The Eighth Amendment bars excessive bail, excessive fines, and cruel and unusual punishments. In practice, issues of racial disparity and discrimination, as introduced in Chapter 1, have arisen concerning several rights, including Fourth Amendment search and seizure situations, fair trials under the Sixth Amendment, and matters of bail and sentencing under the Eighth Amendment. Read the "Current Controversies" feature to consider a key problem affecting racial disparities and Fourth Amendment rights.

The texts of these four procedural criminal law amendments in the Bill of Rights are included here. Refer to these as you read the sections that follow. The first 10 amendments were ratified on December 15, 1791. The Fourteenth Amendment, which was ratified on July 28, 1868, also impacts procedural criminal law by providing rights to due process and equal protection of the laws. Unlike the four amendments that are primarily concerned with criminal justice, the Fourteenth Amendment also applies in a variety of other contexts, such as prohibiting racial discrimination in public schools and other government facilities and programs.

Fourth Amendment: The right of the people to be secure in their persons, houses, papers, and effects, against unreasonable searches and seizures, shall not be violated, and no Warrants shall issue, but upon probable cause, supported by Oath or affirmation, and particularly describing the place to be searched, and the persons or things to be seized.

Fifth Amendment: No person shall be held to answer for a capital or otherwise infamous crime, unless on a presentment or indictment of a Grand Jury, except in cases arising in the land or naval forces, or in the Militia, when in actual service in time of War or public danger; nor shall any person be subject for the same offence to be twice put in jeopardy of life or limb; nor shall be compelled in any criminal case to be a witness against himself, nor be deprived of life, liberty, or property, without due process of law; nor shall private property be taken for public use, without just compensation.

Sixth Amendment: In all criminal prosecutions, the accused shall enjoy the right to a speedy and public trial, by an impartial jury of the State and district wherein the crime shall have been committed, which district shall have been previously ascertained by law, and to be informed of the nature and cause of the accusation; to be confronted with the witnesses against him; to have compulsory process for obtaining witnesses in his favor, and to have the Assistance of Counsel for his defense.

Eighth Amendment: Excessive bail shall not be required, nor excessive fines imposed, nor cruel and unusual punishments inflicted.

Racial Disparities and Aggressive Policing Practices

As a means to reduce crime, many police departments adopted aggressive policing practices that involved making many stops of pedestrians and drivers in order to ask questions and conduct searches of people and vehicles. Under the Fourth Amendment, police officers are not supposed to stop people and vehicles just because they want investigate the possibility of criminal activity. They are supposed to rely on specific observations as the basis for the stop—either the observation of a pedestrian's behavior that leads to the reasonable conclusion that the individual potentially poses a danger through involvement in criminal activity or the observation of a specific traffic violation by a vehicle driver. In reality, police can, if they so choose, use their discretion to stop anyone and then claim that they saw the underlying justifiable basis in the pedestrian's behavior or the driver's traffic violation. There is usually no way for the stopped person to prove that the stop had no legal basis. If a police officer says that a driver failed to use a turn signal, how can the driver prove otherwise, even if the turn signal was actually used? Thus the protection of Fourth Amendment rights depends very much on the ethical behavior of police officers who voluntarily comply with the law, even when they have curiosity about a pedestrian or a driver.

Violations of the Fourth Amendment occur from individual officer's discretionary decisions as well as when police administrators order their officers to make many stops during each shift in order to demonstrate that the officers are working productively. Even worse, if officers' biases lead them to believe that members of minority groups are likely to commit crimes, these aggressive stops can fall most heavily on young men who are African American or Hispanic. The statistics demonstrating racial disparities in stops and searches are both eye-catching and disheartening.

In 2011, at the height of New York City's aggressive stop-and-frisk policy, before the city's practices were found to be unconstitutional in a lawsuit, officers reported that they stopped 685,000 people. Because 88 percent of these stopped and searched people were innocent of any wrongdoing, significant questions were raised about officers' actual compliance with the Fourth Amendment requirement of observing behavior that leads to the reasonable conclusion that criminal activity is afoot. Although African Americans make up only 23 percent of the city's population, they were subjected to 53 percent of the police stops. Hispanics endured 34 percent of police stops. Moreover, most stops were directed at a small segment of these demographic groups: young men between the ages of 14 and 24. Although non-Hispanic whites make up one-third of New York City's population, they were targeted for only 9 percent of the stop-and-frisk searches. Even when New York City was ordered to stop this aggressive practice and the number of recorded stops declined sharply, the court-appointed monitor of the police department found in 2015 that many police officers continued to make stops, but no longer kept records of the stops as required by their department. As a result, many members of minority groups felt unfairly targeted by the police. Surveys indicated a growing sense of dissatisfaction, and even hostility, directed at police from those who felt subjected to racial profiling and Fourth Amendment violations.

With respect to traffic stops, as noted in the discussion of disparities and discrimination in Chapter 1, parallel issues have been documented. A study published in 2015 found that African American drivers in Greensboro, North Carolina, were disproportionately stopped by police and were twice as likely as white drivers to have their cars searched, even though white drivers were significantly more likely to have illegal drugs or weapons in their vehicles (LaFraniere & Lehren, 2015). A report in 2016 highlighted disproportionate application of seat-belt enforcement to African American drivers who faced being stopped four times as frequently as whites in some Florida counties (Alvarez, 2016). Another study concerning Kansas City, published in 2014, found that young African American men were twice as likely as their white counterparts to be stopped for investigatory purposes not based on clear traffic violations. They were also five times more likely than whites to be subjected to searches (Epp, Maynard-Moody, & Haider-Markel, 2014).

Events since 2014 have demonstrated that this problem is not merely one of minor racial discrimination and hassles experienced by minority group members. Even seemingly small encounters between police and pedestrians or drivers can lead to tragic consequences. The 2014 police shooting of unarmed teenager Michael Brown, which resulted in protests and civil disorder in Ferguson, Missouri, began when an officer stopped Brown to tell him not to walk in the street. An officer in North Charleston, South Carolina, faced murder charges after a hidden bystander filmed him shooting an unarmed driver in the back when the driver attempted to flee on foot after a traffic stop. Motorist Sandra Bland died under controversial circumstances in a Texas jail after a traffic stop in which she was arrested for angering an officer by declining to extinguish her cigarette. In 2016, the officer who arrested Bland faced a criminal charge for allegedly lying in his police report about what happened during the traffic stop. The deceased citizens in all of these cases were African Americans. If African Americans are subjected to a disproportionate number of stops for racial reasons, they also face correspondingly greater risks of tragic escalations of events; many studies show that officers can be quicker to make arrests and use force against African Americans.

Many police departments have responded to the publicity surrounding racial disparities and police shootings

continued

Current Controversies in Criminal Justice (*continued*)

by increasing training for officers, teaching them about racial biases affecting decisions, and promoting techniques for keeping encounters with citizens from escalating into the lethal use of officers' weapons. Are these measures enough to address problems that appear to be widespread?

Many critics argue that police departments should stop measuring officers' productivity by the number of stops that they make on each shift. Such expectations about a minimum number of expected stops can pressure officers to make stops that are not legally justified. The authors of the Kansas City study argue that police officers should completely cease stopping pedestrians and drivers strictly for investigatory purposes. They see the harms of such stops—potential rights violations and the risk of alienating people against the police—as outweighing any benefits from

finding that some people are carrying drugs or weapons. They argue that traffic stops should be solely based on clear traffic violations that threaten public safety. In a parallel argument, Supreme Court Justice William O. Douglas claimed in *Terry v. Ohio* (1968) that police officers should not be able to stop pedestrians on "reasonable suspicion" of criminal activity; only when they have "probable cause" concerning the individual's involvement in crime—clear evidence that a crime has been committed—should police interfere with people's liberty to walk down the sidewalk.

For Critical Thinking and Analysis

If you were a police chief, what would you do? Would order a halt to investigatory stops of pedestrians and drivers? Describe three steps that you would take to address this controversy

through policies, training, or supervision of officers.

Sources: L. Alvarez, "Black Drivers in Florida Face Far Stricter Seatbelt Enforcement, Report Says," *New York Times*, January 27, 2016 (www.nytimes.com); C. Epp, S. Maynard-Moody, and D. Haider-Markel, *Pulled Over: How Police Stops Define Race and Citizenship* (University of Chicago Press, 2014); J. Goodman and A. Baker, "New York Police Department Is Undercounting Street Stops, Report Says," *New York Times*, July 9, 2015 (www.nytimes.com); S. LaFraniere and A. Lehren, "The Disproportionate Risks of Driving While Black," *New York Times*, October 24, 2015 (www.nytimes.com); D. Montgomery, "Texas Trooper Who Arrested Sandra Bland Is Charged with Perjury," *New York Times*, January 6, 2016 (www.nytimes.com); New York Civil Liberties Union, "Stop-and-Frisk Data," 2016 (www.nyclu.org/content/stop-and-frisk-data).

For most of American history, the Bill of Rights did not apply to most criminal cases, because it was designed to protect people from abusive actions by the federal government. It did not seek to protect people from state and local officials, who handled nearly all criminal cases. This view was upheld by the U.S. Supreme Court in the 1833 case of ***Barron v. Baltimore***. However, as we shall see shortly, this view gradually changed in the late nineteenth and early twentieth centuries.

Barron v. Baltimore (1833)
Case deciding that the protections of the Bill of Rights apply only to actions of the federal government.

The Fourteenth Amendment and Due Process

After the Civil War, three amendments were added to the Constitution. These amendments were designed to protect individuals' rights against infringement by state and local government officials. The Thirteenth Amendment abolished slavery, and the Fifteenth Amendment attempted to prohibit racial discrimination in voting; these amendments had little impact on criminal justice. However, the Fourteenth Amendment profoundly affected it by barring states from violating people's right to due process of law. Its key language says that "no State shall... deprive any person of life, liberty, or property, without due process of law; nor deny to any person within its jurisdiction the equal protection of the laws." These rights to due process and equal protection served as a basis for protecting individuals from abusive actions by local government officials. However, the terms *due process* and *equal protection* are so vague that it was left to the U.S. Supreme Court to decide if and how these new rights applied to the criminal justice process.

Powell v. Alabama (1932)
Case deciding that an attorney must be provided to a poor defendant facing the death penalty.

For example, in ***Powell v. Alabama*** (1932), the Supreme Court ruled that the due process clause required states to provide attorneys for poor defendants facing the death penalty. This decision stemmed from a notorious case in Alabama in which nine African American men, known as the "Scottsboro boys," were quickly convicted and condemned to death for allegedly raping two white women—but one of the alleged victims later admitted that she had lied about the rape (Goodman, 1994).

In these early cases, the justices had not developed clear rules for deciding which specific rights applied to state and local officials as components of the due process clause of the Fourteenth Amendment. They operated on the assumption that procedures must meet a standard of fundamental fairness. In essence, the justices simply reacted against brutal situations that shocked their consciences. In doing so, they showed the importance of procedural criminal law in protecting individuals from abusive and unjust actions by government officials.

The Due Process Revolution

From the 1930s to the 1960s, the fundamental fairness doctrine was supported by a majority of the Supreme Court justices. It was applied on a case-by-case basis, not always consistently. After Earl Warren became chief justice in 1953, he led the Supreme Court in a revolution that changed the meaning and scope of constitutional rights. Instead of requiring state and local officials merely to uphold fundamental fairness, the Court began to require them to abide by the specific provisions of the Bill of Rights (Marceau, 2008). Through the process of incorporation, the Supreme Court during the Warren Court era declared that elements of the Fourth, Fifth, Sixth, Eighth, and other amendments were part of the due process clause of the Fourteenth Amendment. Previously, states could design their own procedures so long as those procedures passed the fundamental fairness test. Under Warren's leadership, however, the Supreme Court's new approach imposed detailed procedural standards on the police and courts.

As the Court made more and more constitutional rights applicable against the states, it also made decisions that favored the interests of criminal defendants. Many had their convictions overturned and received new trials because the Court believed that it was more important to protect the values underlying criminal procedure than single-mindedly to seek convictions of criminal offenders. In the eyes of many legal scholars, the Warren Court's decisions made criminal justice processes consistent with the American values of liberty, rights, and limited government authority.

To critics, however, these decisions made the community more vulnerable to crime and thereby harmed American values by diminishing the overall sense of liberty and security in society (Nowlin, 2012). Warren and the other justices were strongly criticized by politicians, police chiefs, and members of the public. These critics believed that the Warren Court was rewriting constitutional law in a manner that gave too many legal protections to criminals who harm society. In addition, Warren and his colleagues were criticized for ignoring established precedents that defined rights in a limited fashion.

From 1962 to 1972, the Supreme Court, under Chief Justices Earl Warren (1953–1969) and Warren Burger (1969–1986), applied most criminal justice rights in the U.S. Constitution against actions by state and local officials. By the end of this period, the process of incorporation was nearly complete. Criminal justice officials at all levels—federal, state, and local—were obligated to respect the constitutional rights of suspects and defendants.

The Fourth Amendment: Protection against Unreasonable Searches and Seizures

The Fourth Amendment limits the ability of law enforcement officers to search a person or property in order to obtain evidence of criminal activity. It also limits the ability of the police to detain a person without proper justification (Taslitz, 2010). When police take an individual into custody or prevent an individual from leaving a location, such detentions are considered to be "seizures" under the Fourth Amendment. As we shall examine in greater detail in Chapter 6, the Fourth Amendment does not prevent the police from conducting searches or making arrests; it

fundamental fairness A legal doctrine supporting the idea that so long as a state's conduct maintains basic standards of fairness, the Constitution has not been violated.

incorporation The extension of the due process clause of the Fourteenth Amendment to make binding on state governments many of the rights guaranteed in the first 10 amendments to the U.S. Constitution (the Bill of Rights).

Police need to conduct searches and examine people's property as part of criminal investigations. They also need to search in order to prevent crimes by people who might conceal weapons, drugs, or other illegal items at airports, borders, nightclubs, and stadiums. All searches must either be done with warrants or be "reasonable" under judges' interpretations of the Fourth Amendment. Have you had your clothes or property examined by police or security guards? Is every examination of property a "search" under the Fourth Amendment? Is this dog "searching" the luggage?

merely protects people's privacy by barring "unreasonable" searches and arrests. It is up to the Supreme Court to define the situations in which a search or seizure is reasonable or unreasonable.

The justices also face challenges in defining such words as *searches* and *seizures.* For example, in 2005 the Supreme Court ruled that no issues concerning Fourth Amendment rights arose when a K-9 officer had a trained police dog sniff the exterior of a vehicle that was stopped for a traffic violation (Lunney, 2009). The dog indicated to the officer that the car's trunk contained marijuana, and that discovery led to a criminal conviction. However, unlike a *search,* for which officers must have proper justifications, the use of the dog did not require any justification, because the dog's scent-based examination of the vehicle's exterior did not invade the driver's right to privacy (*Illinois v. Caballes,* 2005). However, in 2015 the Supreme Court decided that police officers cannot extend the length of a traffic stop in order to wait for a K-9 unit to arrive (*Rodriguez v. United States,* 2015). To hold a driver in such circumstances would turn the traffic stop into an "unreasonable seizure" in violation of the Fourth Amendment.

The Court had previously placed another limitation in the use of trained police dogs. Officers can bring such dogs past objects sitting out in public, such as cars along a street or luggage at an airport, to detect the presence of drugs, explosives, or cash without a search warrant or other justification because such examinations are not "searches" under the Fourth Amendment. However, officers cannot bring trained dogs on the porch of a home without a warrant or other justification, because the presence of a police dog at the doorway to a house is a "search" that falls under the protective rules of the Fourth Amendment (*Florida v. Jardines,* 2013). The justices decided *Florida v. Jardines* (2013) by a five-to-four vote. Clearly the justices disagreed about whether the use of a drug-sniffing dog at a house constituted a "search" under the Fourth Amendment. Because Supreme Court justices do not always agree on the Constitution's meaning, the definitions of words such as *search, seizure,* and *unreasonable,* and hence the rules for police searches, can change as the makeup of the Court changes (Soree, 2013). Test your own sense of the Fourth Amendment's proper meaning by examining the "You Make the Decision" feature.

The wording of the Fourth Amendment makes clear that the authors of the Bill of Rights did not believe that law enforcement officials should have the power to pursue criminals at all costs. The Fourth Amendment's protections apply both to suspects and to law-abiding citizens. Police officers are supposed to follow the rules for obtaining search warrants, and they are not permitted to conduct unreasonable searches even when trying to catch dangerous criminals. As we shall see in Chapter 6, improper searches that lead to the discovery of criminal evidence can lead judges to bar police and prosecutors from using that evidence to prove the suspect's guilt. Thus, police officers need to be knowledgeable about the rules for searches and seizures and to follow those rules carefully when conducting criminal investigations.

Police face challenges in attempting to respect Fourth Amendment rights while also actively seeking to prevent crimes and catch offenders. Officers may be tempted to go too far in investigating crimes without an adequate basis for suspicion

The U.S. Supreme Court's landmark decision in *Terry v. Ohio* (1968) authorized officers to conduct stop-and-frisk, pat-down searches of pedestrians when the officers observe behavior by those pedestrians that leads to the reasonable conclusion that criminal activity is afoot and that they are armed and dangerous. According to the language in the New York law authorizing police action, "[A] police officer may stop a person in a public place . . . when he reasonably suspects that the person is committing, has committed, or is about to commit" a felony or misdemeanor.

You are a police officer on patrol in a high-crime neighborhood. As you ride in the passenger seat of a police patrol car at 11:00 p.m., you notice three young men walking down the street. They all turn to look at the passing patrol car. To you, they look nervous, and one of them touches his front pants pocket as if reflexively checking on something contained in the pocket. Do you have a sufficient basis to stop these individuals and conduct a stop-and-frisk, pat-down search of their outer clothing? Would this be an "unreasonable search"? Or should you simply let the patrol car drive on?

What will you do? Describe the reasons for your decision. Then search online for the decision of the Wisconsin Court of Appeals decision in *Wisconsin v. Gordon* (March 18, 2014).

and thereby violate Fourth Amendment rights. The discussion of racial profiling in Chapter 1 illustrates one aspect of the risk that officers will, by conducting stops and searches without an appropriate basis, use their authority in ways that collide with the Fourth Amendment (Harris, 2013). See "A Question of Ethics" at the end of this chapter to consider other ways that police officers might misuse their authority in violation of the Fourth Amendment.

The Fifth Amendment: Protection against Self-Incrimination and Double Jeopardy

The Fifth Amendment clearly states some key rights related to the investigation and prosecution of criminal suspects. For example, the protection against compelled *self-incrimination* seeks to prevent authorities from pressuring people into acting as witnesses against themselves. Presumably, this right also helps protect against torture or other rough treatment when police officers question criminal suspects. In Chapter 6, we shall discuss the Fifth Amendment rules that guide officers in questioning criminal suspects. Improper questioning can affect whether evidence obtained through that questioning can be used in court.

Because of the Fifth Amendment right that protects against *double jeopardy*, a person charged with a criminal act may be subjected to only one prosecution or punishment for that offense in the same jurisdiction. The purpose of the right is to prevent the government from trying someone over and over again until a conviction is obtained (Coffin, 2010). Generally, a person acquitted of a crime at trial cannot be tried again for that same crime.

As interpreted by the Supreme Court, however, the right against double jeopardy does not prevent a person from facing two trials or receiving two sanctions from the government for the same criminal acts (L. Griffin, 2010). Because a single criminal act may violate both state and federal laws, for example, a person may be tried in both courts. Consequently, when Los Angeles police officers were acquitted of assault charges in a state court after they had been videotaped beating motorist Rodney King, they were convicted in a federal court for violating King's civil rights. In yet another case, the Supreme Court permitted Alabama to pursue kidnapping and murder charges against a man who had already been convicted for the same murder in Georgia, because the victim was kidnapped in one state and killed in the other (*Heath v. Alabama,* 1985). Thus, the protection against double jeopardy does not prevent two different trials based on the same criminal acts as long as the trials are in different jurisdictions and based on different charges.

One of the rights in the Fifth Amendment, the entitlement to indictment by a grand jury before being prosecuted for a serious crime, applies only in federal courts. This is one of the few rights in the Bill of Rights that the Supreme Court has never applied to the states. A **grand jury** is a body of citizens drawn from the community to hear evidence from the prosecutor in order to determine whether there is a sufficient basis to move forward with a criminal prosecution (Washburn, 2008). Some states use grand juries by their own choice; they are not required to do so by the Fifth Amendment. Other states simply permit prosecutors to file charges directly against criminal suspects.

grand jury Body of citizens drawn from the community to hear evidence presented by the prosecutor in order to decide whether enough evidence exists to file charges against a defendant.

The Sixth Amendment: The Right to Counsel and a Fair Trial

The Sixth Amendment includes several provisions dealing with fairness in a criminal prosecution. These include the rights to counsel, to a speedy and public trial, and to an impartial jury.

The Right to Counsel

Gideon v. Wainwright (1963) Case deciding that indigent defendants have a right to counsel when charged with serious crimes for which they could face six or more months of incarceration.

Although the right to counsel in a criminal case had prevailed in federal courts since 1938, not until the Supreme Court's landmark decision in *Gideon v. Wainwright* (1963) was this requirement made binding on the states. Many states already provided attorneys, but in this ruling, the Court forced all of the states to meet Sixth Amendment standards. In previous cases, the Court, applying the doctrine of fundamental fairness, had ruled that states must provide poor people with counsel only when this was required by the special circumstances of the case. A defense attorney had to be provided when conviction could lead to the death penalty, when the issues were complex, or when a poor defendant was either very young or mentally handicapped.

Although the *Gideon* ruling directly affected only states that did not provide poor defendants with attorneys, it set in motion a series of cases that affected all the states by deciding how the right to counsel would be applied in various situations. Beginning in 1963, the Court extended the right to counsel to preliminary hearings, initial appeals, post-indictment identification lineups, and children in juvenile court proceedings. Later, however, the Burger Court declared that attorneys need not be provided for discretionary appeals or for trials in which the only punishment is a fine (*Ross v. Moffitt*, 1974; *Scott v. Illinois*, 1979). Even in recent years, the Supreme Court has continued to clarify the extent of the right to counsel (M. M. McCall, M. A. McCall, & Smith, 2013). In 2012, for example, the Court determined that defense attorneys must fulfill certain professional standards during the plea bargaining process by informing defendants of formal plea offers made by the prosecutor and by accurately providing advice on the consequences of turning down a plea offer (*Missouri v. Frye*, 2012; *Lafler v. Cooper*, 2012).

The Right to a Speedy and Public Trial

The nation's founders were aware that in other countries, accused people might often languish in jail for a very long time awaiting trial and often were convicted in secret proceedings. At the time of the American Revolution, the right to a speedy and public trial was recognized in the common law and included in the constitutions of six of the original states. But the word *speedy* is vague, and the Supreme Court recognizes that the interest of quick processes may conflict with other interests of society (such as the need to collect evidence) as well as with interests of the defendant (such as the need for time to prepare a defense). These factors create challenges for the Supreme Court in cases that raise claims about violations of the right to a speedy trial.

The right to a public trial is intended to protect the accused against arbitrary conviction. The Constitution assumes that judges and juries will act in accordance with the law if they must listen to evidence and announce their decisions in public. Again, the Supreme Court has recognized that there may be cases in which the need for a public trial must be balanced against other concerns. For example, the right to a public trial does not mean that *all* members of the public have the right to attend the trial. The courtroom's seating capacity and the interests of a fair trial, free of outbursts from the audience, may be considered. In hearings on sex crimes when the victim or witness is a minor, courts have barred the public in order to spare the child embarrassment. In some states, trials have become even more public than the authors of the Sixth Amendment ever imagined, because court proceedings are televised—some are even carried on national cable systems through CNN.com/CRIME and truTV (formerly known as COURT-TV).

The Right to an Impartial Jury The right to a jury trial was well established in the American colonies at the time of the Revolution. In their charters, most of the colonies guaranteed trial by jury, and it was referred to in the First Continental Congress's debates in 1774, the Declaration of Independence, the constitutions of the 13 original states, and the Sixth Amendment to the U.S. Constitution. Juries allow citizens to play a role in courts' decision making and to prevent prosecutions in cases in which there is not enough evidence. However, as discussed in "Criminal Justice: Myth & Reality," the right to trial by jury is not as widely available for criminal defendants as many Americans believe.

Several Supreme Court decisions have dealt with the composition of juries. The Court has held that the amendment requires selection procedures that create a jury pool made up of a cross section of the community (T. White & Baik, 2010). Most scholars believe that an impartial jury can best be achieved by drawing jurors at random from the broadest possible base (Vidmar & Hans, 2007). The jury is expected to represent the community, and the extent to which it does so is a central concern of jury administration.

CRIMINAL JUSTICE

Myth&Reality

COMMON BELIEF: Because the Sixth Amendment clearly says, "In all criminal prosecutions, the accused shall enjoy the right to a speedy and public trial, by an impartial jury," all criminal defendants who decline to plead guilty and choose to go to trial are entitled to a trial by jury.

- Despite the clear words of the Sixth Amendment, the U.S. Supreme Court has interpreted the constitutional right to trial by jury in a manner that limits the availability of jury trials.
- Although the justices did not specifically express concerns about the expense and time involved in jury trials, presumably such concerns were one unspoken aspect of their decision to limit the right to cases involving "serious" charges.
- In *Lewis v. United States* (1996), a majority of justices concluded that defendants charged with petty offenses, those punishable by sentences of six months or less of jail time, are entitled only to a bench trial before a judge and not a jury trial under the Sixth Amendment.
- Ironically, if a judge convicts a person of multiple petty offenses, each of which carries a six-month sentence, and the sentences are to be served consecutively, the offender will have no right to trial by jury prior to being sent to prison for several years.
- According to the Supreme Court, the right to trial by jury is triggered by the definition of each charge as "serious" (more than six months of imprisonment) rather than by the total sentence that could occur upon conviction of multiple petty offenses.
- A postal worker charged with 20 separate petty offenses of "obstructing the mail" for stealing 20 letters from the post office could end up with a cumulative sentence of 10 years in prison, yet have not have a right to trial by jury (C. E. Smith, 2004).

The Eighth Amendment: Protection against Excessive Bail, Excessive Fines, and Cruel and Unusual Punishments

Although it is the briefest of the criminal justice amendments, the Eighth Amendment deals with the rights of defendants during the pretrial (bail) and correctional (fines, punishment) phases of the criminal justice system.

Release on Bail The purpose of bail is to allow for the release of the accused while she or he is awaiting trial. The Eighth Amendment does not require that all defendants be released on bail, only that the amount of bail not be excessive. Many states do not allow bail for those charged with some offenses, such as murder, and there seem to be few limits on the bail amounts that can be required. In 1987, the Supreme Court, in *United States v. Salerno and Cafero*, upheld provisions of the Bail Reform Act of 1984 that allow federal judges to detain without bail suspects who are considered dangerous to the public.

Excessive Fines The Supreme Court ruled in 1993 that the forfeiture of property related to a criminal case can be analyzed for possible violation of the excessive fines clause (*Austin v. United States*). In 1998, the Court declared for the first time that forfeiture constituted an impermissible excessive fine. In that case, a man failed to comply with the federal law requiring that travelers report if they are taking $10,000 or more in cash outside the country (C. E. Smith, 1999). There is no law against transporting any amount of cash. The law only concerns filing a report to the government concerning the transport of money. When one traveler at a Los Angeles airport failed to report the money detected in his suitcase by a cash-sniffing dog trained to identify people who might be transporting money for drug dealers, he was forced to forfeit all $357,000 that he carried in his luggage. Because there was no evidence that the money was obtained illegally and because the usual punishment for the offense would only be a fine of $5,000, a slim five-member majority on the Supreme Court ruled that the forfeiture of all the traveler's money constituted an excessive fine (*United States v. Bajakajian*, 1998). It remains to be seen whether any future Supreme Court decisions will address the "excessive fines" clause and thereby limit law enforcement agencies' practices in forcing criminal defendants to forfeit cash and property.

Cruel and Unusual Punishments The nation's founders were concerned about the barbaric punishments that had been inflicted in seventeenth- and eighteenth-century Europe, where offenders were sometimes burned alive or stoned to death—hence the ban on "cruel and unusual punishments." The Warren Court set the standard for judging issues of cruel and unusual punishments in a case dealing with a former soldier who was deprived of U.S. citizenship for deserting his post during World War II (*Trop v. Dulles*, 1958). Chief Justice Earl Warren declared that judges must use the values of contemporary society to determine whether a specific punishment is cruel and unusual.

The Eighth Amendment protects offenders serving prison sentences. Under judges' interpretations of the Eighth Amendment, prisoners are entitled to food, shelter, sanitation facilities, and limited medical care. Is the maintenance of humane living conditions in prison an appropriate application of the protection against "cruel and unusual punishments"?

REUTERS/Lucy Nicholson

According to the test established by Chief Justice Warren, punishments may be declared unconstitutional for being either disproportionate to the offense or comparable to a form of torture through the infliction of physical or psychological pain. In recent years, the Supreme Court has seldom regarded punishments other than the death penalty as disproportionate to any crime for which a legislature chooses to mandate it. The Court reinforced this view in 2003 by endorsing California's sentences of 25 years to life for offenders convicted of three felonies, even in a case when the third offense was merely shoplifting some children's videos from Kmart (*Lockyer v. Andrade*, 2003). With respect to juvenile offenders, however, a majority of justices declared that life sentences without possibility of parole were unconstitutionally disproportionate for non-homicide offenses (*Graham v. Florida*, 2010). In 2012, the Supreme Court majority forbade the imposition of mandatory life without parole sentences for juveniles convicted of homicide offenses (*Miller v. Alabama*, 2012).

The Court's test has been used in death penalty cases, but the justices have strongly disagreed over the values of American society on this issue. These decisions in death penalty cases are extensively discussed in Chapter 9.

Since the 1950s, the rights of defendants in state criminal trials have greatly expanded. The Supreme Court has incorporated most portions of the Fourth, Fifth, Sixth, and Eighth Amendments. Figure 3.2 shows the amendments that protect defendants at various stages of the criminal justice process.

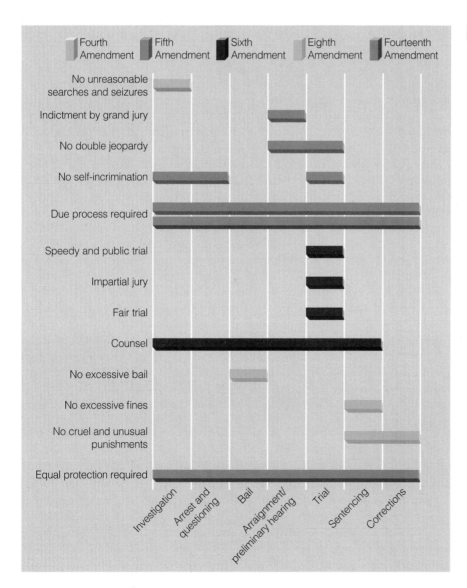

FIGURE 3.2

Protections of Constitutional Rights The Bill of Rights and the Fourteenth Amendment protect defendants during various phases of the criminal justice process.

6. What is incorporation?

Taking a right from the Bill of Rights and applying it to protect individuals against actions by state and local officials through the inclusion of that right as a component of the due process clause of the Fourteenth Amendment.

7. Which Supreme Court era made the most significant expansion in the definitions of constitutional rights for criminal defendants?

Warren Court era (1953–1969).

8. What are the main criminal justice rights set forth in the Fourth, Fifth, Sixth, and Eighth Amendments?

Fourth: the protection against unreasonable searches and seizures; Fifth: the right against compelled self-incrimination and against double jeopardy (also the right to due process); Sixth: the right to counsel, to a speedy and fair trial, to a jury trial (also to confrontation and compulsory process); Eighth: the right to protection against excessive bail, excessive fines, and cruel and unusual punishments.

If the phrase "cruel and unusual punishments" is to be interpreted according to contemporary values, what exactly does that mean? Consider the sentence of life in prison without possibility of parole for someone who drove the getaway car in a robbery in which the store owner was shot and killed by someone else involved in the robbery. Does that sentence violate the Eighth Amendment by being "cruel and unusual"? Make two arguments about whether that sentence violates contemporary values by being too severe and disproportionate to the driver's involvement in the crime.

Constitutional Rights and Criminal Justice Professionals

As a result of the Supreme Court's decisions, people in all states now enjoy the same minimum protections against illegal searches, improper police interrogations, and other violations of constitutional rights. In response to these decisions, police, prosecutors, and correctional officers have had to develop policies and guidelines to inform criminal justice professionals about what they are and are not permitted to do while investigating, prosecuting, and punishing criminal offenders.

If you were a police officer, prosecutor, or correctional officer, how would you feel about the Supreme Court's decisions defining rights that benefit criminal defendants? Although you would recognize the desirability of upholding constitutional rights in order to maintain democratic freedoms, you might also feel frustrated when court decisions limited your ability to conduct searches and question suspects. In addition, you would be concerned about whether the Supreme Court's decisions give you clear guidance about what to do. You would not want to make an unintentional error that prevents an offender from being properly convicted of a crime.

Many people question whether the Supreme Court has struck the proper balance between the protection of constitutional rights and the ability of criminal justice officials to punish offenders. Some people believe that criminal defendants' rights are too broad. Others believe that the Supreme Court favors law enforcement at the expense of constitutional rights. These debates are likely to continue even though the Supreme Court has moved consistently in one direction during the past two decades (C. E. Smith, DeJong, & McCall, 2011). In cases affecting criminal justice, the contemporary Supreme Court typically endorses the actions of police officers and prosecutors more frequently each year than it upholds constitutional rights' claims by suspects, defendants, and convicted offenders (M. M. McCall, McCall, & Smith, 2011).

In 2005 President George W. Bush appointed two new justices to the Supreme Court, Chief Justice John Roberts and Justice Samuel Alito. In their first terms on the Court, their decisions consistently reinforced the Court's support for broader police authority and more narrowly defined rights for criminal suspects and defendants (M. A. McCall, McCall, & Smith, 2008). In the aftermath of additional retirements from the Court, President Barack Obama subsequently had the opportunity to appoint Justices Sonia Sotomayor and Elena Kagan in 2009 and 2010, respectively.

These justices were more supportive of rights for criminal defendants than were President Bush's appointees. Neither the Bush appointees nor the Obama appointees significantly altered the Court's patterns of decisions on constitutional rights, because each new appointee replaced a justice with a similar orientation toward constitutional rights in criminal justice. For many issues, the Court remains deeply divided between those who seek to reduce the scope of constitutional rights in procedural criminal law and those who wish to retain the rights established during the Warren Court era and thereafter. If, however, one of the current justices retires and is replaced with a justice who has a very different viewpoint, the overall orientation of the Court may shift to strengthen one perspective or the other.

The sudden death of 79-year-old Justice Antonin Scalia during the middle of the Supreme Court's annual term in February 2016 served as a reminder that changes will occur in the Court's composition in the immediate future. Because Republican senators hope that their party's candidate will win the White House in the November 2016 election, they intend to stall or block any nominee put forward by President Obama to replace Justice Scalia, who was an appointee of a Republican president, Ronald Reagan, in 1986. Meanwhile, there are other elderly justices who could face health issues that might force them to leave the Court. Justice Ruth Bader Ginsburg celebrates her eighty-third birthday in 2016. Justice Anthony Kennedy turns 80, and Justice Stephen Breyer turns 78. Justice Clarence Thomas is also a senior citizen, as he turns 68. The future of the Supreme Court will be significantly affected by the timing of their retirements and the outcome of the 2016 presidential election. If a Democratic candidate wins the election and, due to the timing of retirements, is able to successfully appoint the replacement for Scalia—and other conservatives, such as Kennedy and Thomas, the future Supreme Court may be more protective of constitutional rights in criminal justice. If a Republican candidate wins the presidential election and selects the replacement for Scalia plus a liberal justice, such as Ginsburg or Breyer, more Supreme Court decisions are likely to favor the powers of police and prosecutors while limiting the definition of constitutional rights.

A QUESTION OF ETHICS

Think, Discuss, Write

A police officer stopped a vehicle for having only one working brake light. In the course of issuing a warning for a traffic violation to the driver and talking to the driver and passenger, the officer thought both men appeared to be nervous. The officer asked the men for permission to search the vehicle. Permission was granted, and the officer found a small amount of cocaine in the pocket of a duffel bag. The men's attorney sought to have the cocaine excluded from evidence as the product of an illegal search. Indeed, the North Carolina Court of Appeals ruled that the officer had been mistaken about state law in stopping the vehicle. Under state law, there is no traffic violation in having just one working brake light. In a later consideration of the case in 2014, the U.S. Supreme Court ruled that there is no Fourth Amendment violation when a search and seizure is the result of a police officer's mistaken understanding of state law that leads to the stop of a driver who has not violated any traffic laws (*Heien v. North Carolina*, 2014).

Does the Supreme Court's decision create a risk that police officers could intentionally be careless about learning the details of state traffic laws in an effort to maximize opportunities to make investigative traffic stops? Even worse, could the decision lead unethical officers to be dishonest in falsely claiming to believe that certain aspects of driving and vehicles violate state laws? Does it also expand possibilities for officers to make up after-the-fact excuses for traffic stops that had no basis at all except the officer's curiosity or improper racial profiling?

Discussion/Writing Assignment

Write a memo as if you are a police chief who is very concerned about properly respecting people's Fourth Amendment rights. How would you train your officers to diminish the possibility that officers would exploit this decision that forgives officers' mistakes in enforcing traffic laws? Give two examples of what you would teach your officers. In addition, how would you monitor or supervise officers to make sure that they were not engaging in actions without a proper legal basis? Give two examples of your approach to monitoring and supervision.

SUMMARY

1 **Identify the bases and sources of American criminal law.**

- Criminal law focuses on the prosecution and punishment of people who violate specific laws enacted by legislatures.
- Criminal law is divided into two parts: substantive law, which defines offenses and penalties, and procedural law, which defines individuals' rights and the processes that criminal justice officials must follow in handling cases.

2 **Discuss how substantive criminal law defines a crime and the legal responsibility of the accused.**

- Substantive criminal law involves seven important elements that must exist and be demonstrated by the prosecution in order to obtain a conviction: legality, *actus reus*, causation, harm, concurrence, *mens rea*, and punishment.
- The *mens rea* element, concerning intent, or state of mind, can vary with different offenses, such as various degrees of murder.
- Criminal law provides opportunities to present justification and excuse defenses, several of which focus on a lack of criminal intent: self-defense, necessity, duress (coercion), entrapment, infancy, mistake of fact, intoxication, and insanity.
- Standards for the insanity defense vary by jurisdiction, with various state and federal courts using several different tests: *M'Naghten* Rule, Irresistible Impulse Test, *Durham* Rule, *Model Penal Code*, and Comprehensive Crime Control Act.

3 **Describe how procedural criminal law defines the rights of the accused and the processes for dealing with a case.**

- The provisions of the Bill of Rights were not made applicable to state and local officials by the U.S.

Supreme Court until the mid-twentieth century, when the Court incorporated most of the Bill of Rights' specific provisions into the due process clause of the Fourteenth Amendment.
- The Fourth Amendment's prohibition on unreasonable searches and seizures seeks to impose limits on police authority to intrude on people's expectations of privacy with respect to their bodies, homes, and property.
- The Fifth Amendment provides protections against compelled self-incrimination and double jeopardy.
- The Sixth Amendment includes the right to counsel, the right to a speedy and public trial, and the right to an impartial jury.
- The Eighth Amendment includes protections against excessive bail, excessive fines, and cruel and unusual punishments. Supreme Court justices often disagree about whether certain sentences, including the death penalty, violate the prohibition on cruel and unusual punishments.
- The Fourteenth Amendment provides a right to due process of law as well as the right to equal protection of the laws.

4 **Explain the U.S. Supreme Court's role in interpreting the criminal justice amendments to the Constitution.**

- Changes in the Supreme Court's composition may affect decisions concerning specific legal issues. Such changes occur when presidents replace retiring justices with appointees who interpret constitutional rights in different ways than did prior justices.

Questions for Review

1. What are the two major divisions within criminal law?
2. What are the seven principles of criminal law theory?
3. What is meant by *mens rea*? Give examples of defenses that may be used by defendants to deny that *mens rea* existed when the crime was committed.
4. What is meant by the incorporation of rights into the Fourteenth Amendment of the U.S. Constitution?
5. What rights are contained in the Fourth Amendment?
6. What rights are contained in the Fifth Amendment?
7. What rights are contained in the Sixth Amendment?
8. What rights are contained in the Eighth Amendment?

Key Terms and Cases

Bill of Rights (p. 103)

civil infractions (p. 90)

civil law (p. 89)

double jeopardy (p. 106)

entrapment (p. 98)

felonies (p. 90)

fundamental fairness (p. 109)

grand jury (p. 112)

inchoate or incomplete
offenses (p. 94)

incorporation (p. 109)

legal responsibility (p. 87)

mens rea (p. 95)

misdemeanors (p. 90)

procedural criminal law (p. 90)

self-incrimination (p. 106)

substantive criminal law (p. 89)

Barron v. Baltimore (1833) (p. 108)

Gideon v. Wainwright (1963) (p. 112)

Powell v. Alabama (1932) (p. 108)

4 Police

1. Describe how policing evolved in the United States.
2. Name the main types of law enforcement agencies.
3. Analyze the recruitment of police officers and how they learn their job.
4. Describe the elements of the police officer's "working personality."
5. List the functions of the police.
6. Describe the organization of the police.
7. Identify influences on police policy and styles of policing.

On Friday, September 12, 2014, Corporal Byron Dickson, a 38-year-old trooper in the Pennsylvania State Police, was leaving the Blooming Grove state trooper barracks at the end of his workday. Suddenly, shots rang out and he fell with mortal wounds. Trooper Alex Douglass, who was just arriving to begin his shift, came to Dickson's aid. He, too, was shot but survived his wounds. Unbeknownst to the troopers, Eric Frein, a survivalist who liked to pretend that he was a Communist soldier from Cold War–era Eastern Europe, had hidden himself in the woods across from the entrance to the barracks. With the shooting, Frein had carried out his plan to kill a law enforcement officer. He then fled into the woods (Barry, 2014).

With the help of other law enforcement agencies, the state police organized a manhunt that involved searching many miles of thick woods. Within days, they identified Frein as the suspect when they found his vehicle abandoned in a pond two miles away; but because of his advance planning and his skill as a woodsman, Frein eluded capture for many weeks (Southall, 2014). The hundreds of law enforcement officers who participated in the search for him knew that he was armed and dangerous. Moreover, they knew that he wanted to kill police officers and that he could be hiding out of sight and pointing a gun at them in the dark woods without their realizing that he was nearby. In sum, they knew they were risking their lives in searching for him, yet they pressed ahead, determined to capture him. Eventually, after a 48-day-search, Frein was captured by U.S. marshals who spotted him at a small abandoned airport in the Poconos Mountains. Fortunately, no additional law enforcement officers were injured in the long manhunt that resulted in the Frein's arrest (McGraw and Gabriel, 2014).

What motivates a person to choose a career in policing—an occupation that carries with it the risk of being killed or injured in the course of serving the public? Sadly, police officers' deaths in the line of duty occur with troubling regularity. During 2015, gunfire killed 42 law enforcement officers in the United States, and another 52 died as a result of automobile collisions while on duty. These numbers reflect a substantial reduction in police deaths in the line of duty since the peak years of the early 1970s when, for example, 156 were killed by gunfire in 1973 (Chappell, 2015). Nevertheless, police officers still face significant potential risks in their jobs, and they never know when they may be called upon to courageously save a life—or put their own lives on the line while protecting society.

Who would choose a career that might entail life-threatening danger? What attracts people to a public-service career that brings them into situations of conflict? Further, how do the police, on an individual as well as an organizational level, carry out their duties in the face of such risks?

In this chapter, we examine several aspects of policing. A brief history of the police precedes discussion of the types of law enforcement agencies in the United States. We also examine the recruitment and training of contemporary police officers, the police subculture, and the functions, organization, and policies of policing.

AP Images/Butch Comegys

The Development of Police in the United States

Law and order is not a new concept; it has been a subject of debate since the first police force was formed in London in 1829. Looking back even earlier, we find that the Magna Carta of 1215 placed limits on constables and bailiffs. Reading between the lines of that historic document reveals that the modern problems of police abuse, maintenance of order, and the rule of law also existed in thirteenth-century England. Further, current remedies—recruiting better-qualified people to serve as police, stiffening the penalties for official misconduct, creating a civilian board of control—were suggested even then to ensure that order was kept in accordance with the rule of law.

The English Roots of the American Police

The roots of American policing lie in the English legal tradition. Three major aspects of American policing evolved from that tradition: (1) limited authority, (2) local control, and (3) fragmented organization. Like the British police, but unlike police in continental Europe, police officers in the United States have limited authority; their powers and duties are specifically defined by law. England, like the United States, has no national police force; instead, 43 regional authorities are headed by elected commissioners who appoint the chief constable. Above these local authorities is the home secretary of the national government, which provides funding and can intervene in cases of police corruption, mismanagement, and discipline. In the United States, policing is fragmented: there are many types of officers and agencies—constable, county sheriff, city police, FBI—all with their own special jurisdictions and responsibilities.

frankpledge A system in old English law in which members of a tithing (a group of 10 families) pledged to be responsible for keeping order and bringing violators of the law to court.

Systems for protecting citizens and property existed before the thirteenth century. The **frankpledge** system required that groups of 10 families, called *tithings,* agree to uphold the law, keep order, and bring violators to a court. By custom, every male person above the age of 12 was part of the system. When a man became aware that a crime had occurred, he was obliged to raise a "hue and cry" and to join others in his tithing to track down the offender. The tithing was fined if members did not perform their duties.

Over time, England developed a system in which individuals were chosen within each community to take charge of catching criminals. The Statute of Winchester, enacted in 1285, set up a parish constable system. Members of the community were still required to pursue criminals, just as they had been under the frankpledge system, but now a constable supervised those efforts. The constable was a man chosen from the parish to serve without pay as its law enforcement officer for one year. The constable had the power to call the entire community into action if a serious disturbance arose. Watchmen, who were appointed to help the constable, spent most of their time patrolling the town at night to ensure that "all's well" and to enforce the criminal law. They were also responsible for lighting street lamps and putting out fires.

Not until the eighteenth century did an organized police force evolve in England. With the growth of commerce and industry, cities expanded while farming declined as the main source of employment and the focus of community life. In the larger cities, these changes produced social disorder.

In the mid-eighteenth century, novelist Henry Fielding and his brother, Sir John Fielding, led efforts to improve law enforcement in London. They wrote newspaper articles to inform the public about crime, and they published flyers describing known offenders. After Henry Fielding became a magistrate in 1748, he organized a small group of "thief-takers" to pursue and arrest lawbreakers. The government was so impressed with Fielding's Bow Street Amateur Volunteer Force (known as the Bow Street Runners) that it paid the participants and attempted to form similar groups in other parts of London.

After Henry Fielding's death in 1754, these efforts declined. As time went by, however, many saw that the government needed to assert itself in enforcing laws and maintaining order. London, with its unruly mobs, had become an especially dangerous place. In the early 1800s, several attempts were made to create a centralized police force for London. While people saw the need for social order, some feared that a police force would threaten the freedom of citizens and lead to tyranny. Finally, in 1829 Sir Robert Peel, home secretary in the British Cabinet, pushed Parliament to pass the Metropolitan Police Act, which created the London police force.

This agency was organized like a military unit, with a thousand-man force commanded by two magistrates, later called "commissioners." The officers were called "bobbies" after Sir Robert Peel. In the British system, cabinet members who oversee government departments are chosen from the elected members of Parliament. Thus, because Peel supervised it, the first police force was under the control of democratically elected officials.

Under Peel's direction, the police had a four-part mandate:

1. To prevent crime without using repressive force and to avoid having to call on the military to control riots and other disturbances
2. To maintain public order by nonviolent means, using force only as a last resort to obtain compliance
3. To reduce conflict between the police and the public
4. To show efficiency through the absence of crime and disorder rather than through visible police actions (P. K. Manning, 1977).

In effect, this meant keeping a low profile while maintaining order. Because of fears that a national force would threaten civil liberties, political leaders made every effort to focus police activities at the local level. These concerns were transported to the United States.

Policing in the United States

As with other institutions and areas of public policy, the development of formal police organizations reflected the social conditions, politics, and problems of different eras of American history. The United States drew from England's experience but implemented policing in its own way.

The Colonial Era and the Early Republic As settlers arrived in North America from Europe and eventually moved westward from the East Coast, they relied on each other for assistance and protection in all matters, from weather disasters to conflicts with Native Americans. They also needed to protect themselves and their neighbors from those who might cause harm through theft or other crimes.

Along the East Coast, the colonists drew from their experiences in England by adopting the English offices of constable, sheriff, and night watchman as the first positions with law enforcement responsibilities. Boston's **watch system** began before 1640. Such systems served to warn of dangers ranging from fires to crime. Each male citizen was required to be a member of the watch, but paid watchmen could be hired as replacements. Although the watch system originally operated at night, cities eventually began to have daytime watches, too. Over time, cities began to hire paid, uniformed watchmen to deal with public danger and crime (S. Walker, 1999).

In the South, **slave patrols** developed as organized forces to prevent slave revolts and to catch runaway slaves. These patrols had full power to break into the homes of slaves who were suspected of keeping arms, to physically punish those who did not obey their orders, and to arrest runaways and return them to their owners. Under the watch system in Northern cities, watchmen reacted to calls for help. By contrast, the mobility of slave patrols positioned them to operate in a proactive manner by looking for African Americans whom whites feared would disrupt society, especially the economic system of slavery. Samuel Walker (1999) describes the slave patrols as a distinctly American form of law enforcement and the first modern police force in the United States.

Beginning in the 1830s and continuing periodically for several decades, many American cities experienced violent riots. Ethnic conflicts; election controversies; hostility toward free blacks and abolitionists; mob actions against banks during economic declines; and violence in settling questions of morality, such as the use of alcohol—all these factors contributed to fears that a stable democracy would not survive. The militia was called in to quell large-scale conflicts, because constables and watchmen proved ineffective in restoring order (Uchida, 2005). These disorders, along with perceptions of increased problems with serious crimes, helped push city governments to consider the creation of professional police forces.

American policing is often described in terms of three historical periods: the political era (1840–1920), the professional model era (1920–1970), and the community policing era (1970–present) (Kelling & Moore, 1988). This description has been criticized because it applies only to the urban areas of the Northeast and does not take into account the very different development of the police in rural areas of the South and West. Still, it remains a useful framework for exploring the organization of the police, the focus of police work, and the strategies employed by police (H. Williams & Murphy, 1990).

The Political Era: 1840–1920 The period from 1840 to 1920 is called the political era because of the close ties that were formed between the police and local political leaders at that time. In many cities, the police seemed to work for the mayor's political party rather than for the citizens. This relationship served both groups in that the political "machines" recruited and maintained the police while the police helped the machine leaders get out the vote for favored candidates. Ranks in the police force were often for sale to the highest bidder, and many officers took payoffs for not enforcing laws on drinking, gambling, and prostitution (S. Walker, 1999).

In the United States, as in England, the growth of cities led to pressures to modernize law enforcement. Around 1840 the large cities began to create police forces. In 1845 New York City established the first full-time, paid police force. Boston and Philadelphia were the first to add a daytime police force to supplement the night watchmen; other cities—Chicago, Cincinnati, New Orleans—quickly followed.

watch system Practice of assigning individuals to night observation duty to warn the public of fires and crime; first introduced to the American colonies in Boston and later evolved into a system of paid, uniformed police.

slave patrols Distinctively American form of law enforcement in Southern states that sought to catch and control slaves through patrol groups that stopped and questioned African Americans on the roads and elsewhere in public places.

During the political era, the officer on a neighborhood beat dealt with crime and disorder as it arose. Police also performed various social services, such as providing beds and food for the homeless. Should today's police officers devote more time to providing social services for the public?

Joseph Byron/The Granger Collection

By 1850 most major cities had created police departments organized on the English model. A chief, appointed by the mayor and city council, headed each department. The city was divided into precincts, with full-time, paid patrolmen assigned to each. Early police forces sought to prevent crimes and keep order through the use of foot patrols. The officer on the beat dealt with crime, disorder, and other problems as they arose.

In addition to foot patrols, the police performed service functions such as caring for derelicts, operating soup kitchens, regulating public health, and handling medical and social emergencies. In cities across the country, the police provided beds and food for homeless people. In station houses, overnight "lodgers" might sleep on the floor or sometimes in clean bunkrooms (Monkkonen, 1981). The police became general public servants as well as crime control officers.

Police developed differently in the South because of the existence of slavery and the agrarian nature of that region. As noted previously, the first organized police agencies with full-time officers developed in cities with large numbers of slaves (Charleston, New Orleans, Richmond, and Savannah), where white owners feared slave uprisings (Rousey, 1984).

Westward expansion in the United States produced conditions quite different from those in either the urban East or the agricultural South. The frontier was settled before order could be established. Thus, those who wanted to maintain law and order often had to take matters into their own hands by forming vigilante groups.

One of the first official positions created in rural areas was that of **sheriff**. Although the sheriff had duties similar to those of the "shire reeves" of seventeenth-century England, the American sheriff was elected and had broad powers to enforce the law. As elected officers, therefore, sheriffs had close ties to local politics. They also depended on the men of the community for assistance. This is how the *posse comitatus* (Latin for "power of the county"), borrowed from fifteenth-century Europe, came into being. Local men above age 15 were required to respond to the sheriff's call for assistance, forming a body known as a posse.

After the Civil War, the federal government appointed **U.S. marshals** to help enforce the law in the western territories. Some of the best-known folk heroes of American policing were U.S. Marshals Wyatt Earp, Bat Masterson, and Wild Bill Hickok, who tried to bring law and order to the "Wild West" (Calhoun, 1990). While some marshals did extensive law enforcement work, most had mainly

sheriff Top law enforcement official in county government who was an exceptionally important police official during the country's westward expansion and continues to bear primary responsibility for many local jails.

U.S. marshals Federal law enforcement officials originally appointed to handle duties in western territories; today they bear responsibility for providing federal court security and apprehending fugitives.

During the professional model era, the police saw themselves as crime fighters. Yet many inner-city residents saw them as a well-armed, occupying force that did not support efforts to advance civil rights and racial equality. If the police see themselves as crime fighters, how might that orientation interfere with efforts to gain citizens' cooperation and improve police–community relationships?

Spencer Platt/Staff/Getty Images

judicial duties, such as keeping order in the courtroom and holding prisoners for trial.

During the early twentieth century, much of the United States became more urban. This change toward urbanization blurred some of the regional differences that had helped define policing in the past. Other changes in policing came about as a result of growing criticism of the influence of politics on the police, which led to reform efforts aimed at making police officers more professional and reducing their ties to local politics.

The Professional Model Era: 1920–1970   American policing was greatly influenced by the Progressive movement. The Progressives were mainly upper-middle-class, educated Americans with two goals: more-efficient government and more government services to assist the less fortunate. A related goal was to reduce the influence of party politics and patronage (favoritism in handing out jobs) in government. The Progressives saw a need for professional law enforcement officials who would use modern technology to benefit the whole of society, not just local politicians.

The key to the Progressives' concept of professional law enforcement is found in their slogan, "The police have to get out of politics, and politics has to get out of the police." August Vollmer, the chief of police of Berkeley, California, from 1909 to 1932, was a leading advocate of professional policing. He initiated the use of motorcycle units, handwriting analysis, and fingerprinting. With other police reformers such as Leonhard Fuld, Raymond Fosdick, Bruce Smith, and O. W. Wilson, he urged that the police be made into a professional force, a nonpartisan agency of government committed to public service. This model of professional policing has six elements:

1. The force should stay out of politics.
2. Members should be well trained, well disciplined, and tightly organized.
3. Laws should be enforced equally.
4. The force should use new technology.
5. Personnel procedures should be based on merit.
6. The main task of the police should be fighting crime.

Refocusing attention on crime control and away from maintaining order probably did more than anything else to change the nature of American policing.

The narrow focus on crime fighting broke many of the ties that the police had formed with the communities they served. By the end of World War I, police departments had greatly reduced their involvement in social services. Instead, for the most part, cops became crime fighters.

O. W. Wilson, a student of Vollmer, was another leading advocate of professionalism. He earned a degree in criminology at the University of California in 1924 and became the chief of police of Wichita, Kansas, in 1928. By reorganizing the department and fighting police corruption, he came to national attention. He promoted the use of motorized patrols, efficient radio communication, and rapid response. He believed that one-officer patrols were the best way to use personnel and that the two-way radio, which allowed for supervision by commanders, made officers more efficient (Reiss, 1992:51). He rotated assignments so that officers on patrol would not become too familiar with people in the community (and thus prone to corruption). In 1960, Wilson became the superintendent of the Chicago Police Department with a mandate to end corruption there.

The new emphasis on professionalism had also spurred the formation of the International Association of Chiefs of Police (IACP) in 1902 and the Fraternal Order of Police (FOP) in 1915. Both organizations promoted training standards, the use of new technologies, and a code of ethics. By the 1930s, the police were using new technologies and methods to combat serious crimes. Officers became more effective against crimes such as murder, rape, and robbery—an important factor in gaining citizen support.

In the 1960s, the civil rights and antiwar movements, urban riots, and rising crime rates challenged many of the assumptions of the professional model. In their attempts to maintain order during public demonstrations, police officers found themselves enforcing laws that tended to discriminate against African Americans and the poor. The number of low-income racial minorities living in the inner cities was growing, and the professional style kept the police isolated from the communities they served. In the eyes of many inner-city residents, the police were an occupying army keeping them at the bottom of society, not public servants helping all citizens. Concurrently, although the police continued to portray themselves as crime fighters, as crime rates rose, citizens became aware that the police often were not effective in this role.

The Community Policing Era: 1970–Present
Beginning in the 1970s, calls were heard for a move away from the crime-fighting focus and toward greater emphasis on keeping order and providing services to the community. Research studies revealed the complex nature of police work and the extent to which day-to-day practices deviated from the professional ideal. The research also questioned the effectiveness of the police in catching and deterring criminals.

Three findings of this research are especially noteworthy:

1. Increasing the number of patrol officers in a neighborhood had little effect on the crime rate.
2. Rapid response to calls for service did not greatly increase the arrest rate.
3. Improving the percentage of crimes solved proved to be difficult.

Such findings undermined acceptance of the professional crime-fighter model. Critics argued that the professional style isolated the police from the community and reduced their knowledge about the neighborhoods they served, especially when police patrolled in cars. Instead, it was argued, police should get out of their cars and spend more time meeting and helping residents. Reformers hoped that closer contact with citizens would not only permit the police to help them in new ways but also make citizens feel safer, knowing that the police were available and interested in their problems.

In a provocative article titled "Broken Windows: The Police and Neighborhood Safety," James Q. Wilson and George L. Kelling argued that policing should work more on "little problems" such as maintaining order, providing services to those in

Community policing encourages personal contact between officers and citizens, especially interactions that facilitate citizens' cooperation with and support for the police. Is your own interest in criminal justice affected by your view of police officers and interactions with them?

need, and adopting strategies to reduce the fear of crime (1982:29). They based their approach on three assumptions:

1. Neighborhood disorder creates fear. Areas with street people, youth gangs, prostitutes, and drunks are high-crime areas.
2. Just as broken windows are a signal that nobody cares, and can lead to worse vandalism, untended disorderly behavior is a signal that the community does not care. This also leads to worse disorder and crime.
3. If the police are to deal with disorder and thus reduce fear and crime, they must rely on citizens for assistance.

community policing
Approach to policing that emphasizes close personal contact between police and citizens and the inclusion of citizens in efforts to solve problems, including vandalism, disorder, youth misbehavior, and crime.

problem-oriented policing
Community policing strategy that emphasizes solving problems of disorder in a neighborhood that may contribute to fear of crime and to crime itself.

Advocates of the **community policing** approach urge greater use of foot and bicycle patrols so that officers will become known to citizens, who in turn will cooperate with the police. They believe that through attention to little problems, the police may not only reduce disorder and fear but also improve public attitudes toward policing (Kelling, 1985).

Closely related to the community policing concept is **problem-oriented policing**. Herman Goldstein, the originator of this approach, argued that instead of focusing on crime and disorder, the police should identify the underlying causes of problems, such as rowdy teenagers, domestic violence, and abandoned buildings used as drug houses. In doing so, they could reduce disorder and fear of crime (Goldstein, 1979). Closer contacts between the police and the community might then reduce the hostility that has developed between officers and residents in many urban neighborhoods (Sparrow, Moore, & Kennedy, 1990). Research indicates that problem-oriented policing can have positive effects on the problems of crime and disorder (Weisburd et al., 2010).

In *Fixing Broken Windows,* written in response to the Wilson and Kelling article, George L. Kelling and Catherine Coles (1996) call for strategies to restore order and reduce crime in public spaces in U.S. communities. Many cities instructed police to pay greater attention to "quality-of-life crimes" by arresting subway fare-beaters; rousting loiterers and panhandlers from parks; and aggressively dealing with those who are obstructing sidewalks, harassing others, and soliciting. By handling these "little crimes," the police not only help restore order but also often prevent worse crimes. In New York, for example, searching fare-beaters often yielded weapons; questioning a street vendor selling hot merchandise led to a fence specializing in stolen weapons; and arresting a person for urinating in a park resulted in the discovery of a cache of weapons. This shift of emphasis therefore still retains police officers' crime-fighter role. Questions remain, however, about whether research can demonstrate that such strategies actually reduce citizens' fear of crime (Weisburd et al., 2015).

The federal government created the Office of Community Oriented Policing Services, more commonly known as the "COPS Office," which provides grants for hiring new officers and developing community policing programs. Between 1995 and 2003, the COPS Office supplied nearly $7 billion to 13,000 state and local agencies to hire 118,000 new officers and implement training and other programs (Uchida, 2005). In 2009, the Obama administration provided $1 billion additional dollars to the COPS Office to fund the hiring of police officers around the nation as part of the stimulus program to revive the national economy (Lewis, 2009). For 2013, the COPS Hiring Program was given $127 million by Congress to help police departments hire new officers or rehire officers laid off through budget cuts. In addition, the agency's key priority areas were (1) assisting in hiring officers who would work with children in schools, (2) hiring military veterans to become police officers, and (3) helping police departments add additional officers to combat problems of gun violence in communities (http://www.cops.usdoj.gov/).

In the 1980s, critics questioned whether the professional model really ever isolated police from community residents (Walker, 1984). Some wondered whether the opportunity to receive federal money and hire new officers led departments to use the language of community policing in portraying their activities even if they never fully adopted the new methods.

The Next Era: Homeland Security? Evidence-Based Policing?

Although many local police departments continue to emphasize community policing (Stein & Griffith, 2016), after the 9/11 attacks, homeland security and antiterrorist efforts became two of the highest priorities for the federal government. As we shall see in Chapter 5, this event shifted the federal government's funding priorities for law enforcement and led to a reorganization of federal agencies. The shift also affected state and local police (Hayes & Giblin, 2014; Stewart & Oliver, 2016). According to Craig Uchida, "Priorities for training, equipment, strategies, and funding have transformed policing once again—this time focusing on homeland security" (2005:38). Federal money for state and local police agencies moved toward supplying emergency preparedness training, hazardous-materials gear, equipment for detecting bombs and other weapons of mass destruction, and the collection of intelligence data.

In public comments, a few police officials have referred to "terrorist-oriented policing," but how such a concept or emphasis would be defined at the local level is not clear (Kerlikowske, 2004). Some observers believe that a shift toward homeland security may appeal to traditionalists in law enforcement who prefer to see themselves as heroically catching "bad guys." Yet a by-product of the increased emphasis on homeland security may be better-coordinated services for society in non-crime-fighting situations such as public emergencies. For example, in 2007, Minneapolis police officials credited their training in a course on Integrated Emergency Management, conducted by the federal government, as one of the reasons they could respond so quickly and effectively when the I-35W bridge collapsed, killing 13 people, injuring 145 others, and forcing quick rescues of drivers in sinking vehicles that fell from the bridge into the river below (Karnowski, 2008).

A factor in considering whether we have reached a new era in policing is that the emphasis on homeland security has grown in conjunction with the development of **intelligence-led policing** (Carter, Phillips, & Gayadeen, 2014). The concept of intelligence in regard to policing means an emphasis on gathering, analyzing, and sharing information while incorporating those elements into community policing plans (M. Peterson, 2005). Intelligence-led policing is based on cooperation and coordination among law enforcement agencies as well as between law enforcement officials and those in other sectors of government and business. Even though many police departments may not be directly affected by homeland security considerations in

intelligence-led policing An approach to policing, in conjunction with concerns about homeland security, that emphasizes gathering and analyzing information to be shared among agencies in order to identify, prevent, and solve problems.

all of their daily operations, departments throughout the country have been affected by the spread of data analysis techniques. Departments analyze crime trends, locations of events, informants' tips, surveillance observations and tapes, and other sources of information in order to distribute personnel and take action to prevent crimes from occurring (Kirby, Quinn, & Keay, 2010).

As discussed in previous chapters, when data on problems in local communities are combined with social science research on "what works" in crime prevention and crime control, departments are attempting to incorporate the principles of evidence-based practices into policing. An awareness of evidence-based practices has become a major emphasis in policing and could develop in ways that will define the next era in policing (L. Sherman, 2015). However, the dedicated use of evidence-based practices varies from department to department. Departments' ability to use evidence-based policing depends on their resources and their effectiveness in gathering and analyzing data about their communities as well as their openness and effectiveness in utilizing the results of scholars' research studies (Cave, Telep, & Grieco, 2015). Unfortunately, the contemporary era of budget cuts affecting personnel resources, training, and technology acquisition poses a significant barrier to the prospects of carrying out evidence-based policies and practices (Bueermann, 2012). It remains to be seen whether the establishment of priorities, the allocation of resources, and the implementation of practices will define a new era in policing.

Community policing will not disappear. Many police executives remain committed to its purposes and principles. However, budget issues may limit their ability to fulfill their ideal vision of policing. In addition, federal funding for local policing is more limited than in the past and currently reflects an emphasis on emergency preparedness and homeland security.

CHECK POINT

1. **What three main features of American policing were inherited from England?**
   Limited authority, local control, organizational fragmentation.

2. **What are the historical periods of American policing?**
   Colonial era and early republic; political era; professional model era; community policing era.

3. **What were the major recommendations of the Progressive reformers?**
   The police should be removed from politics, police should be well trained, the law should be enforced equally, technology should be used, merit should be the basis of personnel procedures, and the crime-fighting role should be prominent.

STOP & ANALYZE

If you were a police chief in a city plagued by difficult crime problems, how might your distribution and use of police officers differ if you emphasized the crime-fighter role instead of community policing? Would you do anything differently if you were equally committed to both goals?

Law Enforcement Agencies

As discussed in Chapter 1, the United States has a federal system of government with separate national and state structures, each with authority over certain functions. Police agencies at the national, state, county, and municipal levels are responsible for carrying out four functions: (1) enforcing the law, (2) maintaining order, (3) preventing crime, and (4) providing services to the community. They employ a total of more than 1 million sworn and unsworn personnel. Nearly 765,000 full-time sworn officers serve in state and local agencies, and an additional 120,000 sworn officers operate in federal agencies. Consider your own assumptions about the responsibilities of these agencies as you read the "Criminal Justice: Myth & Reality" feature.

Police agencies include the following (Reaves, 2012; Reaves, 2011):

- 12,501 municipal police departments
- 3,063 sheriff's departments
- 50 state police departments
- 135 Native American tribal police agencies
- 30 federal agencies that employ 100 or more full-time officers authorized to carry firearms and make arrests

In addition, there are 1,733 special police agencies (jurisdictions limited to transit systems, parks, schools, and so on) as well as additional federal agencies with fewer than 100 officers each.

This list shows both the fragmentation and the local orientation of American police. Seventy percent of expenditures for policing occur at the local level. Each level of the system has different responsibilities, either for different kinds of crimes, such as the federal authority over counterfeiting, or for different geographic areas, such as state police authority over major highways. Local units generally exercise the broadest authority.

Federal Agencies

Federal law enforcement agencies are part of the executive branch of the national government. They investigate a specific set of crimes defined by Congress. Recent federal efforts against drug trafficking, organized crime, insider stock trading, and terrorism have attracted attention to these agencies even though they handle relatively few crimes and employ only 120,000 full-time officers authorized to make arrests.

CRIMINAL JUSTICE

Myth&Reality

COMMON BELIEF: The FBI is the most important law enforcement agency in the United States.

REALITY

- The FBI handles many important responsibilities. However, it pursues only a limited number of crimes.
- As a federal agency, FBI agents are authorized to investigate federal crimes, including bank robbery, kidnapping, and a variety of terrorism and espionage matters.
- Whether or not the FBI is the "most important" agency is debatable, especially if one considers the impact of law enforcement on the daily lives of Americans.
- The vast majority of crimes are investigated by local police departments and county sheriff's departments. Officers from these departments also make the vast majority of arrests.
- When people experience medical emergencies, hear a window break during the night, or seek resolution of a dispute between neighbors, they call the local police. These are the kinds of police-related matters that most frequently affect the daily lives of Americans.
- Although local police officers do not receive as much attention from the news media as do special agents of the FBI, there are strong reasons to argue that local police are the most important law enforcement officials in terms of their daily impact on the quality of life and safety in neighborhoods and communities.

The FBI   The Federal Bureau of Investigation (FBI) is an investigative agency within the U.S. Department of Justice (DOJ). It has the power to investigate all federal crimes not placed under the jurisdiction of other agencies. Established as the Bureau of Investigation in 1908, it came to national prominence under J. Edgar Hoover, its director from 1924 until his death in 1972. Hoover made major changes in the bureau (renamed the Federal Bureau of Investigation in 1935) to increase its professionalism. He sought to remove political factors from the selection of agents, established the national fingerprint filing system, and oversaw the development of the Uniform Crime Reporting (UCR) system (discussed in Chapters 2 and 3). Although Hoover has been criticized for many things, including FBI spying on antiwar and civil rights activists during the 1960s, his role in improving police work and the FBI's effectiveness is widely recognized.

There are 13,913 **FBI special agents** and 22,231 support professionals (intelligence analysts, language translators, scientists, and computer experts) working out of 56 field offices and 381 additional satellite offices known as "resident agencies." The FBI lists its priorities as follows (FBI, 2016):

1. Protect the United States from terrorist attack.
2. Protect the United States against foreign intelligence operations and espionage.
3. Protect the United States against cyber-based attacks and high-technology crimes.
4. Combat public corruption at all levels.
5. Protect civil rights.
6. Combat transnational and national criminal organizations and enterprises.

FBI special agents The sworn law enforcement officers in the FBI who conduct investigations and make arrests.

7. Combat major white-collar crime.
8. Combat significant violent crime.
9. Support federal, state, county, municipal, and international partners.
10. Upgrade technology to successfully perform the FBI's mission.

As indicated by this list, the FBI has significant responsibilities for fighting terrorism and espionage against the United States. In addition, it continues its traditional mission of enforcing federal laws, including those aimed at organized crime, corporate crime, corrupt government officials, and violators of civil rights laws. The bureau also provides valuable assistance to state and local law enforcement through its crime laboratory; training programs; and databases of fingerprints, stolen vehicles, and missing persons. With the growth of cybercrime, the FBI has become a leader in using technology to counteract crime as well as to prevent terrorism and espionage. The antiterrorist activities of the FBI will be discussed in greater detail in Chapter 5. In addition, Chapter 14 contains additional coverage of the FBI's role in fighting cybercrime.

Specialization in Federal Law Enforcement The FBI is the federal government's general law enforcement agency. By contrast, other federal agencies enforce specific laws. Elsewhere within the Department of Justice is the semiautonomous Drug Enforcement Administration (DEA), which investigates the importation and sale of controlled drugs. The Internal Revenue Service (IRS) pursues violations of tax laws, and the Bureau of Alcohol, Tobacco, Firearms, and Explosives (ATF) deals with alcohol, tobacco, gun control, and bombings.

The Department of Justice also contains the U.S. Marshals Service. Federal marshals provide security at courthouses, transport federal prisoners, protect witnesses, and pursue fugitives within the United States who are wanted for domestic criminal charges or who are sought by police officials in other countries. Because of the FBI's increased emphasis on terrorism, its agents are now less involved in the pursuit of fugitives. This has increased the U.S. marshals' responsibilities for those duties. For example, marshals apprehended nearly 34,000 fugitives on federal warrants and assisted in the capture of 71,000 individuals wanted by local police departments in 2014 (U.S. Marshals Service, 2016).

Several federal law enforcement agencies were reorganized and relocated in conjunction with the creation of the Department of Homeland Security.

The FBI bears special responsibility for investigating federal crimes, such as those involving organized crime groups. The agency also provides assistance to state and local police. In the past decade, it has shifted its focus and resources to give greater emphasis to homeland security and counterterrorism efforts. Could the agency focus solely on these two important issues and leave other crimes entirely to state and local agencies? Why?

These agencies include those responsible for Customs and Border Protection (formerly the separate agencies Customs Service and Border Patrol), the Secret Service, and the Transportation Security Administration. The Secret Service was created in 1865 to combat counterfeit currency. After the assassination of President William McKinley in 1901, it received the additional duty of providing security for the president of the United States, other high officials, and their families. The Secret Service has 3,200 special agents in Washington, DC, and field offices throughout the United States. It also has 1,300 uniformed police officers who provide security at the White House, the vice president's residence, and foreign embassies in Washington.

Some other agencies of the executive branch, such as the National Parks Service, have police powers related to their specific duties. The park officers need to enforce law and maintain order to protect people and property at national parks. In addition, few people realize that some law enforcement officers investigate crimes while working in agencies with responsibility for policy issues that are not traditionally viewed as connected to the justice system. For example, special agents in the U.S. Department of Education investigate student loan fraud, and similar officers in the U.S. Department of Health and Human Services investigate fraud in Medicare and Medicaid programs.

State Agencies

Throughout the United States, the American reluctance to centralize police power has generally kept state police forces from replacing local ones. Each state has a police agency that patrols state highways; provides complete law enforcement services in rural areas; or, as in Hawaii, conducts statewide drug investigations and police services at state facilities and courts (Hawaii Department of Public Safety, 2012). All state forces regulate traffic on main highways, and two-thirds of the states have also given them general police powers. In only about a dozen populous states—such as Massachusetts, Michigan, New Jersey, New York, and Pennsylvania—can these forces perform law enforcement tasks across the state. For the most part, they operate only in areas where no other form of police protection exists or where local officers ask for their help. In many states, the crime lab is run by the state police as a means of assisting local law enforcement agencies.

County Agencies

Sheriffs are found in almost every one of the 3,063 U.S. counties except in Alaska and Connecticut. Sheriffs' departments employ 182,979 full-time sworn officers (Reaves, 2011). They are responsible for policing rural areas, but over time, especially in the Northeast, many of their criminal justice functions have been assumed by the state or local police. In parts of the South and West, however, the sheriff's department is a well-organized force. In more than 40 states, sheriffs are elected and hold the position of chief law enforcement officer in the county. Even when well organized, the sheriff's office may lack jurisdiction over cities and towns. In these situations, the sheriff and his or her deputies patrol unincorporated parts of the county or small towns that do not have police forces of their own.

In addition to performing law enforcement tasks, the sheriff often serves as an officer of the court; sheriffs may operate jails, serve court orders, and provide the bailiffs who maintain order in courtrooms.

Native American Tribal Police

Through treaties with the United States, Native American tribes are separate, sovereign nations and have a significant degree of legal autonomy. They have the power to enforce tribal criminal laws against everyone on their lands, including non-Native Americans (Mentzer, 1996). Traditionally, Native American reservations have been policed either by federal officers of the Bureau of Indian Affairs (BIA) or by their own tribal police. The Bureau of Justice Statistics identifies 178 tribal law enforcement agencies with a total of nearly 3,000 full-time sworn officers (BJS, 2016). Police on some reservations face especially daunting problems due to high rates of unemployment, poverty, and crime (T. Williams, 2012).

Municipal Agencies

The police departments of cities and towns have general law enforcement authority. City police forces range in size from nearly 34,500 full-time sworn officers in the New York City Police Department to fewer than 5 sworn officers in each of 5,400 small towns (New York Police Department, 2016). Sworn personnel are officers with the power to make arrests. There are 461,063 full-time sworn municipal police officers nationwide (Reaves, 2011). Nearly three-quarters of municipal police departments employ fewer than 25 sworn officers. The five largest city police departments—New York City, Chicago, Los Angeles, Philadelphia, and Houston—together employ 15 percent of all local police officers (Reaves, 2011).

In a metropolitan area composed of a central city and many suburbs, policing is usually divided among agencies at all levels of government, giving rise to conflicts between jurisdictions that may interfere with efficient use of police resources. The city and each suburb buy their own equipment and deploy their officers without coordinating with those of nearby jurisdictions. In some areas with large populations, agreements have been made to enhance cooperation among jurisdictions.

Special Jurisdiction Agencies

More than 1,700 law enforcement agencies serve a special geographic jurisdiction. Among them are 508 four-year college and university police forces along with 253 additional two-year college police departments with sworn officers who can make arrests. These agencies employ approximately 57,000 sworn officers. More than 10,000 of these officers serve on college campuses (Reaves, 2011). Another large group of special jurisdiction agencies enforce laws as conservation officers and police in parks and recreation settings. For example, they may be responsible for law enforcement and safety in county parks, including the enforcement of laws for safe boating on lakes. These settings account for 14,571 sworn officers working for 246 agencies. In addition, there are 167 special jurisdiction agencies that enforce law and protect safety at specific mass transit systems, airports, bridges, tunnels, and ports. These agencies employ 11,508 sworn officers (Reaves, 2011). These agencies must coordinate and communicate with state and local officials and agencies that have general law enforcement responsibilities in the immediate vicinity. For example, if there is a major criminal event or large public disturbance on a college campus, state and local police are often called to provide assistance or special technical expertise for the campus police department.

▼ **CHECK POINT**

4. **What is the jurisdiction of federal law enforcement agencies?**
   Enforcing the laws of the federal government.

5. **What are the functions of most state police agencies?**
   All state police agencies have traffic law enforcement responsibilities, and in two-thirds of the states, they exercise general police powers, especially in rural areas.

6. **Besides law enforcement, what functions do sheriffs perform?**
   Operate jails, move prisoners, and provide court bailiffs.

STOP & ANALYZE

What are the advantages and disadvantages of having a fragmented system of separate police agencies? List two advantages and two disadvantages.

Who Are the Police?

As they walk or drive on patrol, police officers never know what they might find around the next corner. What if they encounter an armed suspect who surprises them with gunfire as happened in the fatal Pennsylvania shooting described in the chapter opening? Who would want to face such risks? What motivates someone to choose such a career? These questions are important because they help determine which people will be granted the authority to carry firearms and make discretionary decisions about making arrests, conducting searches, and even ending the lives of other human beings by pulling the trigger during the stressful, fast-moving events that may confront police officers.

According to research, the biggest attractions of a career in policing are the opportunity to help people and job security. Other factors that attract people to a police career include the opportunity for excitement, a desire to fight crime, and job benefits such as early retirement (M. D. White et al., 2010; Raganella & White, 2004).

Because policing is such an important occupation, society would obviously benefit from recruiting its most thoughtful, athletic, and dedicated citizens as police officers. Happily, many such individuals are attracted to this field. Yet many other people who would make fine law enforcement officers turn to other occupations because policing is such a difficult job. The modest salaries, significant job stress, and moments of danger involved in police work can deter some individuals from choosing this public-service occupation.

Recruitment

How can departments recruit well-rounded, dedicated public servants who will represent the diversity of contemporary America? Moreover, how can law enforcement agencies make sure that each individual is qualified to handle the wide array of responsibilities facing police officers? When considering applications, all agencies refer to a list of requirements regarding education, physical abilities, and background. Some federal agencies, including the FBI and Drug Enforcement Administration, seek additional skills, such as expertise in computers and accounting or fluency in a foreign language. A typical list of basic requirements for a career in law enforcement includes the following (if you are

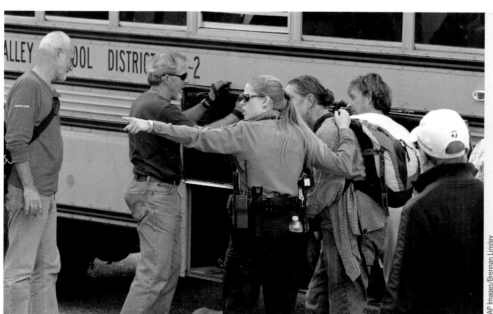

The police are no longer exclusively made up of white men. Women and minorities now represent an increasing portion of the force, especially in urban areas. Are women or minority group members visible among the police officers you see where you live?

interested in working for a particular agency, check for that agency's specific requirements):

- Be a U.S. citizen.
- Meet age requirements. The minimum age is normally 21, although some federal agencies place the minimum at 23. The maximum age for hiring in federal agencies ranges from 36 (FBI and DEA) to 39 (Border Patrol), depending on the agency.
- Have a high school diploma. Increasingly, state and local agencies require some college coursework (for instance, a four-year college degree is required for some federal agencies such as the FBI and DEA).
- Possess a valid driver's license.
- Have a healthy weight in proportion to height, body frame, and age.
- Pass a medical health examination, including a hearing test—reliance on a hearing aid can result in disqualification.
- Be in excellent physical condition. Recruits are typically required to pass a physical fitness exam administered by the agency or as part of a certification program in a police-training academy. For example, the U.S. Border Patrol requires 20 push-ups in one minute, 25 sit-ups in one minute, 30 steps-per-minute up and down a 1-foot step for 5 minutes, a 1.5-mile run in 13 minutes, a 220-yard dash in 46 seconds, and a timed obstacle course.
- Be able to lift and carry moderately heavy objects (45 to 60 pounds).
- Have vision correctable to 20/20 and uncorrected vision of at least 20/200; some agencies (the DEA, for example) require normal color vision.
- Pass a background investigation, including a clean arrest record and credit check. Prior felony or serious misdemeanor convictions can disqualify an applicant, as can a misdemeanor conviction for domestic violence.
- Pass a polygraph examination (lie detector test).
- Take a urinalysis drug test. Often recruits are also required to respond to written or interview questions about any prior use of illegal drugs.
- Take a written test to demonstrate literacy, basic math skills, and reasoning ability. Knowledge of the law and other subjects is also sometimes tested.

In addition, agencies increasingly require recruits to undergo psychological evaluations, because each officer will ultimately make important discretionary decisions, including those that determine life and death in stressful situations (Dantzker & McCoy, 2006).

Candidates for state and local enforcement positions must often obtain a certification for their state's law enforcement training agency, such as the Michigan Commission on Law Enforcement Standards. Many small towns and counties cannot afford to send their officer-applicants to a police academy program for this certification. Thus, they advertise job vacancies with the requirement that applicants have already obtained **law enforcement certification** by attending a police academy such as the 12- to 22-week nondegree classes offered through the criminal justice programs at many colleges.

However, the cost of attending police academy programs imposes a financial burden on many individuals who seek a career in law enforcement. Indeed, some police chiefs claim that they are limited in their ability to diversify their departments if working-class people cannot afford to pay for their own training (Apuzzo & Cohen, 2015). Some of these programs can fulfill several requirements for associate or bachelor's degrees in criminal justice, depending on the college offering the program, so college students receiving financial aid may be able to find a way to complete this training. Larger cities are more likely either to pay for their selected candidates to attend a police academy or to run their own academies to train their new hires. State police agencies also typically run their own training academies for newly hired officers. The U.S. Marine Corps base at Quantico, Virginia, is home to the training academies for new special agents in the DEA (16-week program) and the FBI (17-week program). New agents in the U.S. Secret Service, the ATF, and other federal law enforcement agencies attend 11-week training academies at the primary Federal Law Enforcement Training Center (FLETC) in Glynco, Georgia.

law enforcement certification Preservice training required for sworn officers in many states, which includes coursework on law, psychology, police procedures, and the use of weapons. Police departments for state and large cities often run training programs called *police academies* for their own recruits.

These agencies subsequently provide new agents with additional specialized training, sometimes at the other FLETC training centers in Artesia, New Mexico; Charleston, South Carolina; and Cheltenham, Maryland.

Which agencies are the most attractive to people seeking careers in law enforcement? According to the most recent federal government study, the average starting salary was $39,263 for local departments with collective bargaining (i.e., officers represented by unions or police officers' associations) but only $28,376 for departments without collective bargaining (Reaves, 2010). The foregoing figures are national averages, but salaries in different regions vary significantly. For example, starting salaries for new police officers in Seattle were more than $69,000 in 2014, with pay increases leading to salaries in excess of $90,000 after nine years of service (City of Seattle, 2016). High salaries often exist in areas with a high cost of living, thus making the salaries less lucrative than they might appear. The variation in pay among local police agencies can create incentives for officers, especially in departments that pay lower salaries, to seek ways to supplement their income through off-duty work.

Federal agencies, which offer higher salaries and better benefits than do many local departments, often attract large numbers of applicants. These positions also require higher levels of education and experience than do many local law enforcement agencies. Starting salaries for Border Patrol Agents are at least $39,858 per year, while those for FBI special agents who have graduated from the training academy begin at $51,298. FBI agents may actually receive much higher pay if assigned to a city with a high cost of living.

Federal agencies typically look for college graduates and often require special skills, such as foreign languages and knowledge of financial accounting, or graduate degrees. Most local law enforcement agencies, by contrast, require only a high school diploma, but they prefer to recruit new officers with at least some college education. In the largest cities, with populations greater than 500,000, about one-third of departments require at least some college, and a small percentage require either a two-year or four-year degree (Reaves, 2010). Some departments will accept years of military service as a replacement for an equal number of years of college education. The percentage of state and local law enforcement agencies that required education beyond high school tripled between 1990 and 2007 and is likely to continue to increase over time (Reaves, 2010). See Table 4.1 for examples of educational requirements and starting salaries in various law enforcement agencies.

TABLE 4.1   Educational Requirements and Starting Salaries in Law Enforcement Careers, 2016 (Selected Examples)

Position	Agency	Education Required	Starting Salary
Local			
Police Officer	New York City Police Dept.	2 years college or 2 years military service	$45,674
Police Officer	Alamogordo, NM, Police Dept.	HS diploma	$32,619
Deputy Sheriff	St. Mary's County, MD, Sheriff's Dept.	HS diploma	$40,307
Deputy Sheriff	Oneida County, NY, Sheriff's Dept.	HS diploma	$34,638
State			
Trooper	Tennessee Highway Patrol	HS diploma	$36,288
Highway Patrol Officer	California Highway Patrol	HS diploma	$74,700
Federal (minimum salaries listed; higher salaries come with more education and skills)			
Special Agent	Drug Enforcement Administration	4-year college degree or substantial work experience	$49,746
Special Agent	U.S. Secret Service	4-year college degree or substantial work experience	$43,964

Source: Websites of individual law enforcement agencies.

The Changing Profile of the Police

For most of the nation's history, almost all police officers were white men. Today, as illustrated in Figure 4.1, women and minorities represent a growing percentage of police departments in many areas. The Equal Employment Opportunity Act of 1972 bars state and local governments from discriminating in their hiring practices. Pressured by state and federal agencies as well as by lawsuits, most city police forces have mounted campaigns to recruit more minority and female officers (W. Jordan et al., 2009). Since the 1970s, the percentage of minority group members and women working in policing has doubled. Approximately 25 percent of local police officers nationwide belong to minority groups. The percentage is even larger—40 percent—in some police departments in large cities (*Governing*, 2015; Reaves, 2010). Scholars are currently monitoring whether budget cuts and downsizing of police departments will hamper efforts to recruit a more diverse police force (Guajardo, 2015).

Minority Police Officers   Before the 1970s, many police departments did not hire nonwhites. As this practice declined, the makeup of police departments changed, especially in large cities. The fact that minority officers now constitute 40 percent of the officers in certain large cities represents a dramatic change in staff composition over the past two decades. African Americans compose 12 percent of officers in local police departments. Hispanic officers constitute more than 10 percent of officers, and Asian, Pacific Islander, Native American, and multiracial officers account for an additional 3 percent of local police forces nationally. In cities with populations in excess of 1 million residents, 23 percent of officers are Hispanic and nearly 18 percent are African American (Reaves, 2010).

As minority populations increase in some U.S. cities and as minorities more frequently gain election to local political offices, the makeup of their police forces reflects this trend, too. The extent to which the police reflect the racial composition of a city is believed to affect police–community relations and thus the quality of law enforcement (*Governing,* 2015; Apuzzo & Cohen, 2015; Cochran & Warren, 2012).

Women on the Force   Women have been police officers since 1905, when Lola Baldwin became an officer in Portland, Oregon. Prior to that time, many cities had "police matrons" to assist in handling women and children in jails, but these police matrons did not have the power to arrest or engage in investigative and patrol activities (Horne, 2006). After Baldwin became the trailblazing first officer, the number of women officers remained small for most of the twentieth century

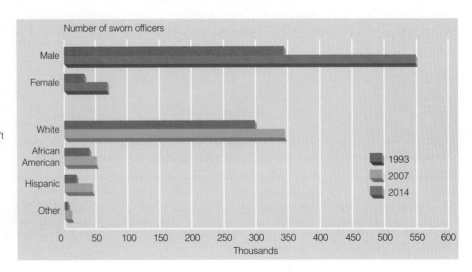

FIGURE 4.1

The Changing Profile of the American Police Officer Today about 1 in 8 officers is female and 1 in 4 belongs to a racial or ethnic minority.

Sources: FBI, *Crime in the United States, 2014* (www.fbi.gov., 2015); *Governing* Magazine Special Report, "Diversity on the Force: Where Police Don't Mirror Communities," September 2015 (www .governing.com); L. Langton, "Women in Law Enforcement, 1987–2008," Bureau of Justice Statistics Crime Data Brief (www.bjs.gov., 2010); B. Reaves, *Local Police Departments, 2007* (www.bjs.gov., 2010); B. Reaves, *Local Police Departments, 1993* (www.bjs.gov., 1996).

because of the prevailing belief that policing was "men's work." This attitude changed as the result of federal and state laws against employment discrimination as well as court decisions enforcing those laws. Court decisions opened up police work for women by prohibiting job assignments by gender; changing minimum height, weight, and physical fitness requirements; and insisting that departments develop job classification and promotion criteria that were nondiscriminatory (Kruger, 2007).

The percentage of female officers rose from 1.5 percent of sworn officers in 1970 to nearly 12 percent in 2014 (FBI, 2014 Langton, 2010; Reaves, 2010). Interestingly, the larger the department, the higher the proportion of women as sworn officers. In cities of more than 1 million inhabitants, women make up nearly 18 percent of officers, but in cities with fewer than 10,000 residents, women make up less than 8 percent of officers (Reaves, 2010). Yet in large police agencies, women hold less than 10 percent of the supervisory positions, and only 7 percent of the top command spots (rank of captain or higher) (Horne, 2006).

Many male officers were upset by the entry of women into what they viewed as a male world, and negative attitudes in some agencies have created barriers to women being promoted (Yu, 2015). Men have expressed concern that if their patrol partner were a woman, they could not be sure of her ability to provide necessary physical help in times of danger. Although some male police officers may still question whether women can handle dangerous situations and physical confrontations, most policewomen have easily met the expectations of their superiors. Studies done by the Police Foundation and other researchers have found that, in general, male and female officers perform in similar ways. Researchers are now examining how extra barriers faced by women officers may affect the stress that they experience in their jobs (Elliot et al., 2015).

Research has also found that most citizens have positive things to say about the work of policewomen (Haba et al., 2009; Worden, 1993). Moreover, some researchers believe that women have generally superior performance in avoiding excessive use of force (Rabe-Hemp, 2008) and in interviewing crime victims, especially in cases of sexual assault and domestic violence (Prussel & Lonsway, 2001). Rape victims sometimes specifically request to be interviewed by a female officer, so gender diversity on a police force may be valuable in investigating specific types of crimes or dealing with certain kinds of victims and witnesses (J. Jordan, 2002). Despite these findings, women still face challenges when entering police work (Hassell & Brandl, 2009). Cultural expectations of women often conflict with ideas about the proper behavior of officers (Morash & Haarr, 2012).

In a few cities such as Atlanta, Portland, Boston, and Detroit, a small number of women have risen to the top ranks of police departments. Elsewhere, employment discrimination lawsuits have helped open promotional opportunities for women. In many other departments, however, few women have gained supervisory jobs. Thus, male administrators are usually the ones who must identify and combat any remaining barriers to the recruitment, retention, and promotion of female officers (Archbold & Hassell, 2009; V. B. Lord & Friday, 2003).

Training

The performance of the police is not based solely on the types of people recruited; it is also shaped by their training. As mentioned previously, aspiring officers may have to pay for their own police academy training if they are not hired by departments that pay for or provide the training. Police academy training courses range from two-week sessions that stress the handling of weapons to academic four-month programs followed by fieldwork. Recruits hear lectures on social relations, receive foreign-language training, and learn emergency medical treatment. Read the "Close Up" to consider new areas of training being emphasized by many police departments in light of recent controversies concerning racial disparities and the use of force.

Training in an Era of Controversy: De-escalation and Use of Force

In 2014 and 2015, public demonstrations, including civil disorder, followed police use-of-force actions that killed unarmed citizens in a number of cities. In New York City, an unarmed man accused of selling individual cigarettes in violation of commercial laws died when a police officer placed him in a chokehold. In Ferguson, Missouri, an altercation between a police officer and a teenager after an exchange of words over the teen walking in the street led the officer to exit his vehicle and shoot the unarmed teenager. He later justified his action with the claim that the teen had made him fear for his life. In Albuquerque, New Mexico, a mentally ill homeless man on a barren mountainside was surrounded by dozens of heavily armed officers and then shot to death because he had two small camping knives in his hands. Critics claim that many police officers are too quick to use lethal force in situations that do not pose grave danger to themselves or the community. Officers are trained to react quickly and forcefully in the face of perceived danger. Is there a risk that traditional training has led officers to overestimate the risk of danger and reach for their firearms too quickly, resulting in needless and tragic deaths?

In the aftermath of public protests in Ferguson, New York City, Albuquerque, and other cities, police executives have given more attention to training officers about approaches to conflict situations that may reduce the risk of lethal violence. Too often, police officers have injured or killed people struggling with mental illness or hearing impairments, or people, including veterans, suffering from an episode of post-traumatic stress disorder (PTSD). Thus, they could not instantly and automatically obey commands quickly shouted by officers. In other situations, officers encounter citizens who are emotionally upset or angry. They may not be able to instantly calm down merely because an officer orders them to do so. The recognition of these issues has led to new, widespread initiatives to train officers in "de-escalation methods." Officers are trained to recognize that even in moments when individuals may seem aroused and angry, there is potential for patience and quiet communications to calm the situation. They also receive training on how to control their own anger or fear when people do not instantly obey their commands.

Officers need some ability to identify when people may need mental health services or when they did not understand the officers' commands due to language barriers or hearing impairment. They need to step back from presuming that failures to follow commands are motivated by dangerous disobedience. Officers may be able to influence the behavior of people behaving emotionally and irrationally through the way they stand as well as how they hold their hands, and by speaking calmly and listening to the individual to try to understand why the person is acting in a certain manner. If officers are taught to perceive danger everywhere and respond quickly with force according to their own fears, they may overlook information and ignore opportunities for calm resolutions of apparent conflicts.

In Seattle, Albuquerque, Cleveland, and other cities investigated by the U.S. Department of Justice for incidents of excessive use of force, new training methods have been introduced to emphasize de-escalation techniques. Reports from Seattle compared two different incidents. In 2010, a Native American woodcarver who was hearing-impaired walked across the street holding a knife and a piece of wood. When he did not respond to an officer's order to drop the knife, he was shot to death. By contrast, in 2015 a knife-wielding man upset about an argument with his wife was convinced to drop the knife after an officer, who kept himself at a distance from the man, talked to the man in an understanding manner for 30 minutes. De-escalation training will not prevent all lethal use of force by police officers. However, it is a step toward reducing the number of tragic situations in which officers use weapons too quickly in response to conflict.

Researching the Internet

Go to the website of the Office of Community Oriented Policing Services in the U.S. Department of Justice to see their newsletter about de-escalation training for police that is sensitive to situations involving veterans with PTSD. http://cops.usdoj.gov/html /dispatch/08-2014/LE_Instructors_and _DeEscalation.asp.

For Critical Thinking and Analysis

Imagine that you are the police chief in a department that has agreed to introduce de-escalation training as a response to an investigation by the U.S. Department of Justice of officers' use-of-force incidents. What arguments might you anticipate from officers who doubt that an outside trainer really understands the dangers that police officers face and the need to use force in many situations? List three things you would say or do to try to ensure that your officers undertake the de-escalation training without resisting the lessons that are being taught.

Sources: D. Fitzpatrick, "Officers Face Murder Charges in 2014 Albuquerque Homeless Man's Shooting," CNN.com, January 13, 2015 (www.cnn.com); G. Johnson and E. Tucker, "After Ferguson, a Push for More 'De-escalation' Training," *Boston Globe*, November 29, 2014 (www .bostonglobe.com); K. Johnson, "In Face of Criticism, Police Officials Preaching De-escalation Tactics," *USA Today*, October 7, 2015 (www.usatoday.com); S. Stoughton, "How Police Training Contributes to Avoidable Deaths," *The Atlantic,* December 12, 2014 (www .theatlantic.com); T. Williams, "Long Taught to Use Force, Police Warily Learn to De-escalate," *New York Times,* June 27, 2015 (www.nytimes.com).

Formal training is needed to gain an understanding of legal rules, weapons use, and other aspects of the job. However, the police officer's job also demands social skills that cannot be learned from a lecture or a book. Much of the most important training of police officers takes place during a probationary period when new officers work with and learn from experienced ones. When new officers finish their classroom training and arrive for their first day of patrol duty, experienced officers may say, "Now, I want you to forget all that stuff you learned at the academy. You really learn your job on the streets." Many departments require newcomers to ride with an experienced training officer for a certain number of weeks or months before they can patrol on their own.

The process of **socialization**—in which members learn the symbols, beliefs, and values of a group or subculture—includes learning the informal rather than the rulebook ways of law enforcement. New officers must learn how to look "productive," how to take shortcuts in filling out forms, how to keep themselves safe in dangerous situations, and how to analyze conflicts so as to maintain order; they also must learn a host of other bits of wisdom, norms, and folklore that define the subculture of a particular department. Recruits learn that loyalty to other officers, esprit de corps, and respect for police authority are highly valued.

In police work—perhaps more than many other types of groups—the success of the group depends on the cooperation of its members. All patrol officers are under direct supervision, and their performance is measured by their contribution to the group's work. Besides supervisors, the officers' colleagues also evaluate and influence them. Officers within a department may develop strong, shared views on the best way to "handle" various situations. How officers use their personal skills and judgment can mean the difference between defusing a conflict or making it worse so that it endangers citizens and other officers. In tackling their "impossible mandate," new recruits must learn the ways of the world from the other officers, who depend on them and on whom they depend.

socialization The process by which the rules, symbols, and values of a group or subculture are learned by its members.

CHECK POINT

7. What are the main requirements for becoming a police officer?
High school diploma, good physical condition, absence of a criminal record.

8. How has the profile of American police officers changed?
Better educated; more female and minority officers.

9. Where does socialization to police work take place?
On the job.

STOP & ANALYZE

Why might it be important for police department personnel to reflect the racial and ethnic composition of the community that they serve? List three potential benefits of a diverse police force.

The Police Subculture

A **subculture** is made up of the symbols, beliefs, values, and attitudes shared by members of a subgroup within the larger society. The subculture of the police helps define the "cops' world" and each officer's role in it. Like the subculture of any occupational group that sees itself as distinct, police develop shared values that affect their view of human behavior and their role in society. As we just saw, the recruit learns the norms and values of the police subculture through a process of socialization (Oberfield, 2012). This begins at the training academy but really takes hold on the job through interactions with experienced officers. The characteristics of a subculture are not static, though; they change as new members join the group and as the surrounding environment changes. For example, the composition of the police has changed dramatically during the past 30 years in terms of race, gender,

subculture The symbols, beliefs, values, and attitudes shared by members of a subgroup of the larger society.

and education. We should thus expect officers with varied life experiences and perspectives to bring different attitudes and cultural values to the police subculture (Paoline, 2003).

There are four key issues in our understanding of the police subculture: the concept of the "working personality" (discussed next), the role of police morality, the isolation of the police, and the stress involved in police work.

The Working Personality

Social scientists have demonstrated that there is a relationship between one's occupational environment and the way one interprets events. The police subculture produces a **working personality**—that is, a set of emotional and behavioral characteristics developed by members of an occupational group in response to the work situation and environmental influences. The working personality of the police thus influences the way officers view and interpret their occupational world.

Two elements of police work define the working personality of the police: (1) the threat of danger and (2) the need to establish and maintain one's authority (Skolnick, 1966:44).

working personality A set of emotional and behavioral characteristics developed by members of an occupational group in response to the work situation and environmental influences.

Danger   Because they often face dangerous situations, officers are keenly aware of clues in people's behavior and body language or in specific situations that indicate that violence and law-breaking may be imminent. As they patrol the streets, they notice things that seem amiss—a broken window, a person hiding something under a coat—anything that looks suspicious. As sworn officers, they are never off duty—and because they are known to be officers, they may be called on at any time, day or night, by neighbors or other acquaintances who need their help.

Throughout the socialization process, experienced officers warn recruits to be suspicious and cautious. Rookies are told about officers who were killed while writing a traffic ticket or trying to settle a family squabble. The message is clear: even minor offenses can escalate into extreme danger. Constantly pressured to recognize signs of crime and be alert to potential violence, officers may become suspicious of everyone, everywhere. Thus, police officers remain in a constant state of "high alert," always on the lookout and never letting down their guard. Read the "Evidence-Based Practice and Policy" feature to consider new efforts to reduce racial bias as a factor that leads officers to act too quickly by misperceiving suspiciousness and danger.

Being surrounded by risks creates tension in officers' lives. They may feel constantly on edge and worried about possible attack. This concern with danger may affect their interactions with citizens and suspects. Citizens who come into contact with them may see their caution and suspicion as hostile, and such suspicion may generate hostile reactions in turn from suspects. As a result, many on-the-street interrogations and arrests can lead to confrontations.

Authority   The second aspect of the working personality is the need to exert authority. Unlike doctors, psychiatrists, lawyers, and other professionals whose clients recognize and defer to their authority, police officers must establish authority through their actions. Their uniforms, badges, guns, and nightsticks symbolize their position and power, but their demeanor and behavior are what determine whether people will defer to them.

Victims are glad to see the police when they are performing their law enforcement function, but the order maintenance function puts pressure on officers' authority. If they try too hard to exert authority in the face of hostile reactions, they may cross the line and use excessive force (C. Cooper, 2009).

Researchers have studied expressions of disrespect by officers toward members of the public and vice versa. One finding indicates that police officers' own expressions of disrespect in encounters with citizens, such as name-calling and other kinds of derogatory statements, occur most often when those citizens have already shown disrespect to the officers (Mastrofski, Reisig, & McCluskey, 2002).

Police Officers and Implicit Bias

Evidence-based practices in policing are frequently discussed as if the primary goal of research to improve police training and practices is to enhance crime control. In other words, much of the attention to evidence-based policing concerns the effective use of police resources to prevent crime or apprehend criminal suspects. But research can also contribute to evidence-based practices that advance other goals, such as training police officers to reduce the risks of mistakes and conflicts, especially if those problems are associated with unrecognized racial biases that officers possess.

Psychological research has highlighted the problem of implicit bias. With explicit biases, people possess clear prejudices against members of different groups because of their open hostility to certain races, ethnic groups, or religions. By contrast, implicit bias operates at a subconscious level, even for people who see themselves as treating everyone as equals and who reject stereotyping of people by group membership. With police officers as well as others in society, research has demonstrated the existence of thinking and decision making that associates people from certain racial groups with crime or danger. Thus, for example, there are psychology experiments in which research subjects, both ordinary citizens and police officers, watching videos of specific situations are asked to decide when it is appropriate to fire a gun. These studies find that police officers and others tend to react more quickly if they perceive a sudden move by an African American man, even one who is innocently reaching for a cell phone. By contrast, they react more slowly to a white man who is actually pulling out a firearm to use against the police, perhaps because they do not have the same ingrained perception of whites as posing a danger (Sadler et al., 2012). The studies highlight risks that officers may reflexively use ingrained perceptions and assumptions to make decisions, especially when they act quickly. Having race incorporated in one's thinking in this way at a subconscious level can lead to disproportionate suspicion, stops, searches, and use of weapons against members of racial minority groups. Implicit bias can also affect police thinking and actions along dimensions other than race. For example, officers may believe the word of someone wearing a business suit over the word of someone wearing old clothing when sorting out what happened in a fistfight between drivers in the aftermath of an automobile collision.

Professor Lorie Fridell, faculty member at the University of South Florida and the former research director for the Police Executive Research Forum, leads training sessions on implicit bias at police departments across the nation. Many officers admit that they went to the first day of this training with a defensive attitude, assuming that they were going to be accused by outsiders of being "racists." However, the training uses the results of research to help officers understand that implicit biases affect all human beings, and the police are not being singled out for criticism. At the same time, training emphasizes the usefulness of recognizing and becoming highly aware of these unconscious biases. As a result, some police departments initiate community service and social contacts between officers and members of minority communities, because increased interactions in positive settings can help officers to reduce their own biases. Too often, police officers encounter individuals of a different race or ethnicity in unfamiliar neighborhoods only in situations of conflict, while investigating crimes, responding to calls about disorder, and angering drivers with traffic citations. According to one police captain involved in training about implicit biases, positive interactions between officers and community members in recreation and community service programs are very helpful. In the captain's words, they create "close-contact situations that allow officers to override their implicit biases and become better police officers... [and] allow the community to change their view of the police" (Raimondo, 2015).

Researching the Internet

You can read online about evidence-based training programs for police concerning implicit bias at http://www.fairimpartialpolicing.com/.

Implementing New Practices

Imagine that you are a police chief interested in hosting a training program on implicit bias for your officers. Many of your officers grumble that they have had plenty of "cultural sensitivity" training and they are tired of having people accuse them of being biased. What are three things that you would communicate to your officers to convince them to bring open minds to the implicit bias training?

Sources: L. Fridell and S. Brown, "Fair and Impartial Policing: A Science-Based Approach," *Police Chief* 82: 20–25 (June 2015) (www.policechiefmagazine.com); M. Kaste, "Police Officers Debate Effectiveness of Anti-Bias Training," *National Public Radio*, April 6, 2015 (www.npr.org); "Editorial: Anti-Bias Training for Police Is Just a Start," *Los Angeles Times*, May 11, 2015 (www.latimes.com); A. Raimondo, "The Sanford (Florida) Experience," *Police Chief* 82: 23–24 (June 2015) (www.policechiefmagazine.com); M. Sadler, J. Correll, B. Park, and C. Judd, 2012 "The World Is Not Black and White: Racial Bias in the Decision to Shoot in a Multiethnic Context." *Journal of Social Issues* 68(2): 286–313.

In sum, working personality and occupational environment are closely linked and constantly affect the daily work of the police. Procedural rules and the structure of policing are overshadowed by the need to exert authority in the face of potential danger in many contexts in which citizens are angry, disrespectful, or uncooperative.

Police Morality

In his field observations of Los Angeles patrol officers, Steve Herbert found a high sense of morality in the law enforcement subculture. He believes that three aspects of modern policing create dilemmas that officers' morality helps to overcome. These dilemmas include (1) the contradiction between the goal of preventing crime and the officers' inability to do so, (2) the fact that officers feel that they must use their discretion to "handle" situations in ways that do not strictly follow procedures, and (3) "the fact that they invariably act against at least one citizen's interest, often with recourse to coercive force that can maim or kill" (Herbert, 1996:799).

Herbert believes that justifying their actions in moral terms, such as upholding the law, protecting society, and chasing "bad guys," helps officers lessen the dilemmas of their work. Thus, they may condone use of force as necessary for ridding "evil from otherwise peaceable streets." It is the price we pay to cleanse society of the "punks," "crazies," or "terrorists." But police morality can also be applauded: officers work long hours and are genuinely motivated to help people and improve citizens' lives, often placing themselves at risk. Yet, to the extent that police morality crudely categorizes individuals and justifies insensitive treatment of some community members, it contributes to tension between police and citizens.

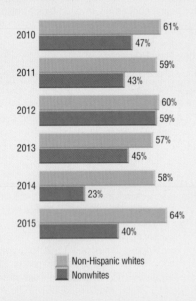

WHAT AMERICANS THINK

QUESTION: "Please tell me how you would rate the honesty and ethical standards of the police—very high, high, average, low, or very low?" Percentages indicate those who rated police honesty and ethics as "very high" or "high"

2010 — 61% / 47%
2011 — 59% / 43%
2012 — 60% / 59%
2013 — 57% / 45%
2014 — 58% / 23%
2015 — 64% / 40%

Non-Hispanic whites
Nonwhites

CRITICAL THINKING: There are persistent differences in views of the police expressed by whites and members of minority groups. Minority views became notably less positive during 2014, the year in which there were highly publicized police killings of unarmed African American men. If you were a police chief and you saw these poll results in your community, what are three steps that you would take to increase public confidence in the police, especially among minority residents?

Source: L. Saad, "Americans' Faith in the Honesty and Ethics of Police Rebounds," Gallup Poll, December 21, 2015 (www.gallup.org).

Police Isolation

Police officers' suspicion of and isolation from the public may increase when they believe that the public is hostile to them. Many officers feel that people regard them with suspicion, in part because they have the authority to use force to gain compliance. Some research scholars argue that this attitude increases officers' desire to use force on citizens (Regoli, Crank, & Culbertson, 1987). Public opinion polls have found that a majority of people have a high opinion of the police; however, as shown in "What Americans Think," various groups of people have different opinions regarding police officers' ethical standards (Wu, 2014). Research shows that young people in high-crime neighborhoods may develop negative attitudes based on their own experiences in being watched and questioned by the police (P. J. Carr, Napolitano, & Keating, 2007). In a single year, 2014, the percentage of nonwhites who rated police officers' honesty and ethical standards as "high" or "very high" dropped twenty points to 23 percent (Saad, 2015). Many observers believe that several highly publicized incidents of police officers killing unarmed African American men in 2014 contributed to this sudden drop in confidence in the police. These deaths and the resulting public protests in Ferguson, Missouri, New York City, and elsewhere contributed to President Obama's decision to form a national task force to make recommendations on how to strengthen trust between police and communities. As you read about the task force in the "Current Controversies" feature, bear in mind that these issues remain deeply troubling and triggered protests in such cities as Baltimore, Chicago, and North Charleston, South Carolina, in 2015 and 2016.

The President's Task Force on 21st Century Policing

During 2014, Americans witnessed widespread public protests, including civil disorder in Ferguson, Missouri, after grand juries declined to bring criminal charges against police officers in Missouri and New York whose actions caused the deaths of unarmed African American men. President Obama appealed for calm and thought about what, if anything, he could do to address the controversies. In December 2014, he announced that he would appoint a "Task Force on 21st Century Policing" to study problems and provide a report with recommendations. According to the White House announcement of the formation of the task force, its purpose was to "strengthen community policing and strengthen the trust among law enforcement officers and the communities they serve."

The task force had 11 members, including cochairpersons Charles Ramsey, the Commissioner of the Philadelphia Police Department, and Laurie Robinson, a criminal justice professor and former U.S. assistant attorney general responsible for providing federal advice and assistance to police departments. The other commission members included police chiefs, the leader of a police officers' association, executives from nonprofit organizations, and civil rights attorneys.

The task force was instructed to hold "listening sessions" in various cities in order to "hear testimony, including proposed recommendations for consideration, from invited witnesses and also receive comments and questions from the public." The process was intended to occur at a rapid pace so that the task force would produce a report less than three months after being formed.

At the task force's two-day session in Cincinnati in January 2015, the members heard from researchers, police union leaders, prosecutors, police chiefs, and activist citizens. Testimony from police emphasized how infrequently police officers use force with fatal results. Community activists emphasized that issues of police–community relations represented long-standing problems and not a new development. Researchers emphasized the need for greater training for police on how to de-escalate situations to avoid the use of violence. There was also discussion of using body cameras and other means to oversee police actions. A prosecutor advocated greater oversight by the U.S. Department of Justice, using independent audits of police departments, rather than investigating only after there was complaint about a troubling series of incidents. One police official raised the important question of who would provide the funds for additional training and equipment such as body cameras in an era in which many police departments were facing budget cuts.

The task force released its final report in May 2015. It included the following recommendations:

- Law enforcement culture should embrace a guardian—rather than a warrior—mindset, to build trust.
- By building a positive image and reputation with all segments of the public, the police will gain needed cooperation from the public.
- Police need to work with community groups and individuals in developing priorities and policies concerning crime.
- Training and policies must address racial profiling, de-escalation strategies to reduce use of force, and other contemporary issues of concern.
- Establish civilian oversight mechanisms over police.

- Incorporate new technology, such as body cameras and less-lethal weapons.
- Mandate Crisis Intervention Training (CIT) for police officers so that they are prepared to deal with a complete range of situations and people, including those with mental illness, drug abuse problems, and limited knowledge of the English language.

For Critical Thinking and Analysis

Police agencies and actions are primarily local matters. The decentralized nature of American policing means that the culture, organization, training, and practices of police vary from city to city and town to town. Can the president of the United States and a national task force influence policing throughout the country? Does the federal government need to offer money to local police departments—with strings attached—in order to induce them to adopt certain practices, training programs, and methods of supervision? Write a memo identifying three barriers to the introduction of the task force recommendations in local police departments around the country, as well as the best ways to overcome those barriers.

Sources: L. Cornwell, "President's Task Force on Policing Looks at Use of Force," *Springfield* (OH) *News-Sun*, January 30, 2015 (www.springfieldnewssun.com); Final Report of the President's Task Force on 21st Century Policing (Washington, DC: U.S. Department of Justice, 2015); C. Levingston, "Cincinnati's Community Policing Efforts Attract President's Task Force," *Springfield* (OH) *News-Sun*, January 31, 2015; (www.springfieldnewssun.com); Office of the Press Secretary, The White House, "Press Release: Fact Sheet: Task Force on 21st Century Policing," December 18, 2014 (www.whitehouse.gov).

Police officers' isolation from the public is made worse by the fact that many officers interact with the public mainly in moments of conflict, emotion, and crisis. Victims of crimes and accidents are often too hurt or distraught to thank the police. Citizens who are told to stop some activity when the police are trying to keep order may become angry; even something as minor as being told to turn down the volume on a stereo can make the police the "bad guy" in the eyes of people who believe that the officer's authority limits their personal freedom.

Ironically, these problems may be worst in poor neighborhoods, where effective policing is needed most. There, pervasive mistrust of the police may keep citizens from reporting crimes and cooperating with investigations. Because they believe that the public is hostile to them in those areas and that the nature of their work makes the situation worse, the police tend to separate themselves from the people there and to form strong in-group ties that tend to enhance that separation.

One result of the demands placed on the police is that officers often cannot separate their job from other aspects of their lives. From the time they receive badges and guns, they must always carry these symbols of the position—the "tools of the trade"—and be prepared to use them. Their obligation to remain vigilant even when off duty and to work at odd hours reinforces the values shared with other officers. Strengthening this bond is officers' tendency to socialize mainly with their families and other officers.

Job Stress

The work environment and police subculture contribute to the stress felt by officers (Dabney et al., 2013; Schaible & Gecas, 2010; Noblet, Rodwell, & Allisey, 2009). This stress can affect not only the way officers treat the citizens they encounter but also the officer's health (Gershon et al., 2009; G. Anderson, Litzenberger, & Plecas, 2002). Stress also affects how officers interact with each other (Haarr & Morash, 1999). Further, scholars have found that work environment, work–family conflict, and individual coping mechanisms are the most significant predictors of stress for individual officers (J. S. Zhao et al., 2003).

Police officers are always on alert, sometimes face grave danger, and feel unappreciated by a public they perceive to be hostile. That their physical and mental health suffers at times is not surprising. Analyses of job stress place police officers among the top 10 in most stressful occupations, along with military personnel, firefighters, and taxi drivers (S. Adams, 2013). The effects of stress are compounded by the long hours many officers work, including double shifts that deprive them of sleep and make them work under conditions of severe fatigue (Vila & Kenney, 2002). The stress of police work may help explain why officer suicide poses a problem for some law enforcement agencies (Hackett & Violanti, 2003).

Police officers often encounter citizens in moments of fear, anger, and trauma. As a result, people can lash out at the officer or otherwise become emotionally out of control. Do the danger and stress police officers face create a risk that they will overreact when citizens fail to cooperate with their requests and instructions?

Baltimore Sun/Tribune News Service/Getty Images

Only since the late 1970s have law enforcement officials become fully aware of the stress-related harms experienced by officers (Lumb & Breazeale, 2002). Psychologists have identified four kinds of stress that officers face and the factors that cause each (J. Shane, 2010; Cullen, Leming, et al., 1985):

1. *External stress.* This is produced by real threats and dangers encountered when entering a dark and unfamiliar building, responding to "man-with-a-gun" alarm, or chasing lawbreakers at high speeds.
2. *Organizational stress.* This is produced by the nature of work in a paramilitary structure: constant adjustment to changing schedules, irregular work hours, and detailed rules and procedures.
3. *Personal stress.* This can be caused by an officer's racial or gender status among peers, which can create problems in getting along with other officers and adjusting to group-held values that differ from one's own. Social isolation and perceptions of bias also contribute to personal stress.
4. *Operational stress.* This reflects the total effect of dealing with thieves, derelicts, and the mentally ill; being lied to so often that all citizens become suspect; being required to face danger to protect a public that seems hostile; and always knowing that one may be held legally liable for one's actions.

Some departments now have programs centering on stress prevention, group counseling, liability insurance, and family involvement. Although evidence-based practices in policing are generally discussed with respect to police strategies to prevent crime and catch lawbreakers, evidence-based practices could also be used to enhance the well-being of officers.

As we have seen, police officers face special pressures that can affect their interactions with the public and even harm their physical and mental health. How would you react to the prospect of facing danger and being on the lookout for crime at every moment, even when you were not actually working? It seems understandable that police officers become a close-knit group, yet their isolation from society may decrease their understanding of other people. It may also strengthen their belief that the public is ungrateful and hostile. As a result, officers' actions toward members of the public may be gruff or even violent.

CHECK POINT

10. **What are the two key influences on the police officer's working personality?**
    Danger; authority.

11. **What are the four types of stress felt by the police?**
    External stress, organizational stress, personal stress, operational stress.

STOP & ANALYZE

If you were a police chief, could you take steps to either reduce the stress experienced by officers or increase support for officers so that the effects of stress would be less harmful? List two approaches that you might use to counteract the causes or effects of stress on police officers.

Police Functions

The police are expected to maintain order, enforce the law, and prevent crime. However, they perform other tasks as well, many of them having little to do with crime and justice and more to do with community service. They direct traffic, handle accidents and illnesses, stop noisy parties, find missing persons, enforce licensing regulations, provide ambulance services, take disturbed people into protective custody, and so on. The list is long and varies from place to place. Some researchers have suggested that the police have more in common with social service agencies than with the criminal justice system.

How did the police gain such broad responsibilities? In many places, the police are the only public agency that is available 7 days a week, 24 hours a day to respond to calls for help. They are also best able to investigate many kinds of problems. Moreover, the power to use force when necessary allows them to intervene in problematic situations.

The functions of the police can be classified into three groups: (1) order maintenance, (2) law enforcement, and (3) service. Police agencies divide their resources among these functions on the basis of community need, citizen requests, and departmental policy.

Order Maintenance

order maintenance The police function of preventing behavior that disturbs or threatens to disturb the public peace or that involves face-to-face conflict between two or more people. In such situations, the police exercise discretion in deciding whether a law has been broken.

The **order maintenance** function is a broad mandate to prevent behavior that either disturbs or threatens to disturb the peace or involves face-to-face conflict between two or more people. A domestic quarrel, noisy drunken behavior, loud music in the night, panhandling on the street, a tavern brawl—all are forms of disorder that may require action by the police.

Unlike most laws that define specific acts as illegal, laws regulating disorderly conduct deal with ambiguous situations, which different police officers could view in different ways. For many crimes, determining when the law has been broken is easy. On the other hand, order maintenance requires officers to decide not only whether a law has been broken but also whether any action should be taken and, if so, who should be blamed. In a bar fight, for example, the officer must decide who started the fight, whether an arrest should be made for assault, and whether to arrest other people besides those who started the conflict.

Officers often must make judgments in order maintenance situations. They may be required to help people in trouble, manage crowds, supervise various kinds of services, and help people who are not fully accountable for what they do. The officers have a high degree of discretion and control over how such situations will develop. While undertaking their daily tasks, including order maintenance, patrol officers are not directly supervised and given instructions by superior officers. They have the power to arrest, but they may also decide not to make an arrest. The order maintenance function is made more complex by the fact that patrol officers are normally expected to "handle" a situation rather than to enforce the law, and this usually takes place in an emotionally charged atmosphere. In controlling a crowd outside a rock concert, for example, they may arrest an unruly person in order to restore order and also to give a warning to others that they could be arrested if they do not cooperate. However, such an arrest may cause the crowd to become hostile toward the officers, making things worse. Officers cannot always predict precisely how their discretionary decisions will promote or hinder order maintenance (Gau & Brunson, 2010).

Law Enforcement

law enforcement The police function of controlling crime by intervening in situations in which the law has clearly been violated and the police need to identify and apprehend the guilty person.

The **law enforcement** function applies to situations in which the law has been violated and the offender needs to be identified or located and then apprehended. Police officers who focus on law enforcement serve in specialized branches such as the vice squad and the burglary detail. Although the patrol officer may be the first officer at the scene of a crime, for serious offenses, a detective usually prepares the case for prosecution by bringing together all the evidence for the prosecuting attorney. When the offender is identified but not located, the detective conducts the search. If the offender is not identified, the detective must analyze clues to determine who committed the crime.

The police often portray themselves as enforcers of the law, but many factors interfere with how effectively they can do so. For example, when a property crime is committed, the perpetrator usually has some time to get away. This limits the ability of the police to identify, locate, and arrest the suspect. Burglaries, for instance, usually occur when people are away from home. The crime may not be discovered until

The crime fighter image of police affects both the public's view of officers' primary job and the image that may attract some new recruits to the job. In reality, police spend much of their time performing services for the public, including searching for lost children and rendering first aid. Which function—order maintenance, law enforcement, or service—do you believe officers can fulfill most effectively?

hours or days have passed. The effectiveness of the police is also reduced when assault or robbery victims cannot identify the offender. Victims often delay in calling the police, reducing the chances that a suspect will be apprehended.

Service

Police perform a broad range of services, especially for lower-income citizens, that are not related to crime. This kind of **service**—providing first aid, rescuing animals, helping the disoriented, and so on—has become a major police function. Crime prevention has also become a major component of police services to the community. Through education and community organizing, the police can help the public take steps to prevent crime.

It may appear that valuable resources are being inappropriately diverted from law enforcement to services. However, performing service functions can help police control crime. Through the service function, officers gain knowledge about the community and citizens come to trust the police. Checking the security of buildings clearly helps prevent crime, but other activities—dealing with runaways, people under the influence of drugs and alcohol, and public quarrels—may help solve problems before they lead to criminal behavior.

service The police function of providing assistance to the public for many matters unrelated to crime as well as for crime prevention education.

Implementing the Mandate

Although citizens depend most heavily on the order maintenance and service functions of the police, the citizenry acts as though law enforcement—the catching of lawbreakers—is the most important function of police. According to public opinion polls, the crime fighter image of the police is firmly rooted in citizens' minds and is the main function that attracts most recruits to policing careers.

The contemporary push for evidence-based policing has led scholars to assert that research shows a need to emphasize key principles in policing, including (1) crime prevention is more effective than arrests in law enforcement and the maintenance of order; and (2) the cooperation and assistance of community members is crucial to the effectiveness of police (Lum & Nagin, 2015). As with other aspects of evidence-based policies in criminal justice, significant challenges lie ahead in shifting police departments' orientation toward recognition and emphasis of these priorities.

Public support for police budgets is greatest when the crime-fighting function is stressed. This emphasis can be seen in the organization of big-city departments.

The officers who perform this function, such as detectives, enjoy high status. The focus on crime leads to the creation of special units to deal with homicide, burglary, and auto theft. All other tasks fall to the patrol division. In some departments, this pattern creates morale problems, because extra resources are allocated and prestige is devoted to a function that is concerned with a small percentage of the problems brought to the police. In essence, police are public servants who keep the peace, but their organization reinforces its own law enforcement image and the public's focus on crime fighting.

The severe budget cuts affecting many police agencies since the 2008 downturn in the nation's economy sometimes forces law enforcement administrators to make difficult choices about which functions will receive attention and resources (P. Wilson, 2010). When police agencies must reduce the number of officers and the number of patrols, there may not be personnel available to respond to nonemergency calls for service. Budget issues may have particularly powerful impacts on small communities and their police departments (K. Johnson, 2015). For example, in one Michigan county that saw its patrol force cut in half, a sheriff's department spokesman noted the harsh reality that "emergency calls come first and other problems might have to wait a day" (Hayden, 2011). Thus officers' actual attention to each of the three functions is also affected by the availability of personnel and resources.

▼ **CHECK POINT**

12. **What is the order maintenance function? What are officers expected to do in situations where they must maintain order?**
Police have a broad mandate to prevent behavior that either disturbs or threatens to disturb the peace or involves face-to-face conflict between two or more people. Officers are expected to "handle" the situation.

13. **How do law enforcement situations compare with order maintenance situations?**
The police in order maintenance situations must first determine if a law has been broken. In law enforcement situations, that fact is already known; thus, officers must only find and apprehend the offender.

STOP & ANALYZE

Which of the police functions do you see as most difficult to carry out? Give three reasons for your answer.

Organization of the Police

police bureaucracy The organizational description of police departments' design and operations that seek to achieve efficiency through division of labor, chain of command, and rules to guide staff.

Most police agencies follow a military model of organization, with a structure of ranks and responsibilities that mark a **police bureaucracy**. Police departments are bureaucracies designed to achieve objectives efficiently and, like most bureaucracies, are characterized by a division of labor, a chain of command with clear lines of authority, and rules to guide the activities of staff. Police organization differs somewhat from place to place depending on the size of jurisdiction, the characteristics of the population, and the nature of the local crime problems. However, all sizeable departments have the basic characteristics of a bureaucracy.

Bureaucratic Elements

The police department in Odessa, Texas, reveals the elements of bureaucracy in a typical urban police force. Figure 4.2 shows the Odessa Police Department's organizational chart, which we refer to in the following discussion.

Division of Labor   As indicated in Figure 4.2, the Odessa Police Department is divided into four divisions and bureaus: Administrative Division, Operations Bureau, Special Operations Bureau, and headquarters under the Chief of Police. In each of these divisions and bureaus, authority is further delegated to offices and

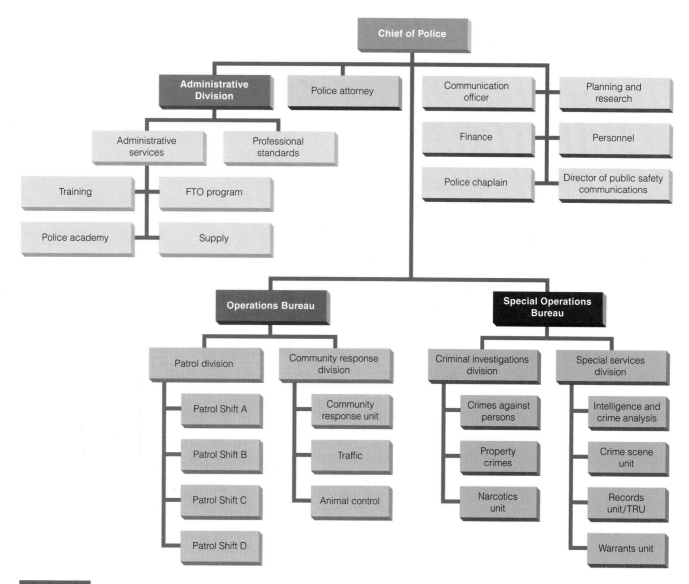

Organization of Odessa, Texas, Police Department This is a typical structure. Note the divisions between administrative services, operations, and special operations.

Source: Odessa, Texas, Police Department website 2013 (www.odessapd.com).

units that have special functions for such matters as training, finance, and communications. The Operations Bureau is divided into specific **patrol units**, designated by shift, and animal control. The Special Operations Bureau is divided according to various functions, including narcotics, crime scene investigations, and property crimes. Assignment to a unit in a Special Operations Bureau may give an officer higher status and greater freedom than that enjoyed by patrol officers. See "A Question of Ethics" at the end of the chapter to consider problems that may occur if officers violate rules in order to avoid being reassigned to regular street patrol units.

The bureaucratic organization of an urban police department such as Odessa's allows the allocation of resources and the supervision of personnel, taking into account the needs and problems that require the attention of specific units.

Chain and Unity of Command
The military character of police departments is illustrated by the **chain of command** according to ranks—officer, commander, sergeant, lieutenant, captain, major, and chief. Each person in the chain of command

patrol units The core operational units of local police departments that deploy uniformed officers to handle the full array of police functions for service, order maintenance, and law enforcement.

chain of command Organizational structure based on a military model with clear definition of ranks to indicate authority over subordinates and obligations to obey orders from superiors.

(except the chief) has an immediate supervisor who holds authority over—and is responsible for—the actions of the people in the rank below. Relationships between superiors and subordinates emphasize discipline, control, and accountability. These values help departments mobilize personnel resources in accordance with the priorities of the top commanders who often wish to employ certain patrol strategies or emphasize prevention of specific crimes. These values also help protect important legal rights; if police officers are accountable to their superiors, they are less likely to abuse their authority by needlessly interfering with the freedom and rights of citizens.

Operational Units

All but the smallest police departments assign officers to operational units that focus on specific functions: patrol, investigation, traffic, vice, and juvenile. These units perform the basic tasks of crime prevention and control. The patrol and investigation (detective) units form the core of the modern department. The patrol unit handles a wide range of functions, including preventing crime, catching suspects, mediating quarrels, helping the ill, and giving aid at accidents. The investigation unit identifies and apprehends suspects, and collects evidence against lawbreakers who commit serious crimes. Because their duties overlap in some ways, the patrol and investigation units can have disagreements about who is in charge of investigating specific crimes. In general, however, the investigation unit focuses on murder, rape, and major robberies. The patrol unit shares responsibility for investigating those crimes and is also solely responsible for investigating the more numerous lesser crimes.

special units Units within local police departments that deploy officers, often in plain clothes if not assigned to the traffic unit, who are dedicated to a specific task, such as investigation, or type of crime, such as narcotics enforcement.

The extent to which departments create **special units** may depend on the size of the city. Many departments have traffic units, but only those in midsize to large cities also have vice and juvenile units. As a result of the war on drugs, some cities have special units working only on this problem. Large departments usually have an internal affairs section to investigate charges of corruption against officers as well as other problems associated with the staff and officers. All special units depend on the patrol officers for information and assistance.

The Police Bureaucracy and the Criminal Justice System

The police play an important role as a bureaucracy within the broader criminal justice system. Four issues arise in the organizational context within which the police operate.

First, the police are the gateway through which information and individuals enter the justice system. Police have the discretion to determine which suspects will be arrested and moved into the system. Cases that are sent to the prosecutor for charging and then to the courts for adjudication begin with an officer's decision that there is probable cause for an arrest. The ultimate success of the prosecution depends on the care taken by the officer in making the arrest and collecting evidence. To a large extent, the outcome of the case hinges on the officer's judgment and evidence-gathering activities.

Second, police administration is influenced by the fact that the outcome of a case is largely in the hands of others. The police bring suspects into the criminal justice process, but they cannot control the decisions of prosecutors and judges. In some cases, the police officers feel that their efforts have been wasted (Stevens, 2014). For example, the prosecutor sometimes agrees to a plea bargain that does not, in the eyes of the officer, adequately punish the offender. The potential for conflict between police and other decision makers in the system is increased by the difference in social status between police officers, who often do not have college degrees, and lawyers and judges, who have graduate degrees.

Third, as part of a bureaucracy, police officers are expected to observe rules and follow the orders of superiors while at the same time making independent, discretionary judgments. They must stay within the chain of command yet also make their own choices about specific actions to take in response to events on the streets. They cannot await orders from headquarters when addressing fast-developing situations, so there are always risks that a superior officer may later second-guess their decisions.

Fourth, the organization and operation of police are affected by economic conditions and budgetary pressures. During the contemporary era of cutbacks in state and local budgets for law enforcement, the nature of a city's police bureaucracy can change as administrators make decisions about priorities. In 2016, for example, the police departments in Nashua and Manchester, New Hampshire, expected an impending budget cut to end the operation of their narcotics units (Marchocki, 2016).

CHECK POINT

14. **What are three characteristics of a bureaucracy?**
    Division of labor, chain and unity of command, rules and procedures.

15. **What are four operational units of all but the smallest police departments?**
    Patrol, investigation, traffic, vice.

STOP & ANALYZE

In light of budget cuts affecting contemporary police departments throughout the country, if you were a police chief, what would you cut and why? Describe and explain two possible budget cuts.

Police Policy

The police cannot enforce every law and catch every lawbreaker. Legal rules limit the ways officers can investigate and pursue offenders. For example, the constitutional ban on unreasonable searches and seizures prevents police from investigating many crimes without a search warrant.

Because the police have limited resources, they cannot have officers on every street at all times of the day and night. This means that police executives must develop policies regarding how the members of their department will implement their mandate. See the discussion in "The Policy Debate" to consider whether contemporary budget cuts should lead police executives to consider the use of volunteer officers as a means to carry out police functions. Policy choices by police executives guide officers as to which offenses will receive the most attention and which tactics will be used—for example, which neighborhoods to patrol and whether to patrol in cars or on foot. These policies also determine which people will be caught committing crimes and brought into the criminal justice system for prosecution and punishment. Changes in policy—such as increasing the size of the night patrol or tolerating prostitution and other public-order offenses—affect the amount of crime that gets official attention and thereby affect the system's ability to deal with offenders.

Police policies may reflect the preferences and values of police executives. However, choices about policies are also influenced by politics, public pressure, and social context. American cities differ in government, economic, and racial and ethnic characteristics, as well as in their degree of urbanization. These factors can affect the style of policing expected by the community. In a classic study, James Q. Wilson found that citizen expectations regarding police behavior affect departments through the political process; specifically, chiefs who run their departments in ways that antagonize the community are not likely to stay in office very long. Wilson's key finding was that a city's political culture, which reflects its socioeconomic characteristics and its government organization, had

The Use of Volunteers in Law Enforcement

Budget reductions since 2008 have caused many police departments to experience significant cuts in patrol personnel. In order to minimize the impact of these cuts on the fulfillment of police functions, some departments utilize citizen volunteers as auxiliary police officers. Many cities have police auxiliary units, composed of uniformed volunteers, who assist with police functions. In 2011, the Los Angeles Police Department had 700 unpaid citizens in its Reserve Corps. When these volunteers go through police academy training, they can be deployed on the streets as armed, uniformed officers who assist regular officers in order maintenance, crime investigation, and other police functions. Is the use of volunteer officers a wise approach to increasing police resources, especially in an era of government budget cuts?

In 2015, a national controversy erupted when a 73-year-old volunteer reserve deputy in Tulsa, Oklahoma, shot and killed a drug suspect who was on the ground struggling with other officers who were trying to apply handcuffs. The volunteer shot the suspect at close range, apparently by mistake; he claimed that he thought had grabbed his electric stun rather than his firearm. The volunteer was eventually convicted of manslaughter for his negligent action. Because the volunteer, a businessman who was a long-time friend of the sheriff's, had donate thousands of dollars in equipment to the sheriff's department, there were questions about whether selection and training of volunteer deputies was based on proper factors and not on friendship and financial contributions.

For the Use of Volunteer Officers

- The services provided by the use of volunteer officers save Los Angeles $5 million each year.
- In New York City, 4,500 volunteer auxiliary officers serve as unarmed, uniformed officers who are extra "eyes and ears" for the police department as they patrol the streets

on foot, observe subway platforms, and call regular officers via police radio when their suspicions are aroused.
- Volunteer officers can handle routine tasks such as directing traffic in order to free the time of sworn officers to handle more complex and dangerous tasks.
- The use of citizen-volunteers may help create closer connections and greater understanding between police departments and the citizens that they serve.

Against the Use of Volunteer Officers

- Even routine tasks such as directing traffic may involve dangerous situations, the discovery of criminal activity, or other matters that require quick decision making by highly trained sworn officers.
- Eight auxiliary officers in New York have been killed in the line of duty in the last 50 years. In a highly publicized tragedy in 2007, two auxiliary officers were killed by a shooting suspect whom they were following down the street. One victim was a 19-year-old sophomore at New York University who was intent on a career as a prosecutor, and the other was a 27-year-old aspiring novelist.
- The usefulness of such officers has been questioned, especially with respect to issues about training and judgment. In Tennessee, there is a traditional elective unpaid office called "constable," which gives citizens the authority to patrol, issue citations, and make arrests after only 40 hours of training. The constables' powers have been eliminated in four counties, and critics are seeking to abolish the office statewide, in part because of the misbehavior of several constables for wrongful arrests and sexual assaults.
- In 2011, the Illinois attorney general raised questions about the legality of employing auxiliary officers in her state because some departments used such officers in ways that

collided with state laws on carrying handguns and impersonating a police officer.

What Should the Policy Be?

While it may be tempting to use unpaid volunteers to handle specific police functions, there are risks involved. These risks include dangers to the volunteer officers and the community when incidents happen and someone other than a highly trained officer is making decisions. There are also risks of improper behavior by volunteer officers who may use their uniforms, badges, and inexperience in ways that violate laws, harm individual citizens, or create public relations issues for police departments. A key issue is whether departments that wish to use volunteers can adequately train and supervise those volunteers in order to avoid risks and problems. Because of the risk that police departments can be sued when someone is harmed as the result of an improper decision or action by a volunteer officer, many police chiefs and city attorneys will likely remain wary of relying on volunteers.

Researching the Internet

To learn more about the use of volunteers in policing, read the Los Angeles Police Department's description of the qualifications and duties for volunteers in its Reserve Corps. To view the report, visit http://www.lapdonline.org/join_the_team/content_basic_view/542.

Analyzing the Issue

Imagine that a mayor has appointed you and your classmates as members of a committee responsible for recommending a policy on the use of volunteer officers by the police department. After discussing the issue with your classmates, write a memo outlining how, if at all, you would permit volunteer officers to be used if you were a police chief. Provide reasons for your decision on whether or not to use volunteers. If you decide to use volunteers, give some examples of how they could be used.

Sources: N. Alund, "Value of Tennessee Constables Debated," *Knoxville News Sentinel,* December 11, 2011 (http://m.knoxnews.com); T. Andrews, "Jury Recommends 4-Year Sentence for Okla. Volunteer Deputy Who Mistook Gun for Taser and Killed Unarmed Black Man," *Washington Post,* April 28, 2016 (www.washingtonpost.com); J. Bacon and W. Welch, "Tulsa Reserve Deputy Charged with Manslaughter," *USA Today,* April 13, 2015 (www.usatoday.com); A. Feuer and A. Baker, "Greenwich Village Gun-Fight Leaves Four Dead," *New York Times,* March 15, 2007 (www.nytimes.com); G. Hillard, "In Tight Times, L.A. Relies on Volunteer Police," *National Public Radio,* May 19, 2011 (http://www.npr.org); E. McLaughlin, "Tulsa Shooting Casts Spotlight on Volunteer Police Programs," CNN.com, April 14, 2015 (www.cnn.com); L. Yellen, "Illinois Attorney General: Auxiliary Police Are Breaking Law," *Fox Chicago News,* March 1, 2011 (www.myfoxchicago.com).

a major impact on the style of policing found there. Wilson identified three different styles of policing—the *watchman, legalistic,* and *service* styles (J. Q. Wilson, 1968).

Departments with a **watchman style** stress order maintenance. Patrol officers may ignore minor violations of the law, especially those involving traffic and juveniles, as long as there is order. The police exercise discretion and deal with many infractions in an informal way. Officers make arrests only for flagrant violations and when order cannot be maintained. The broad discretion exercised by officers can produce discrimination when officers do not treat members of all racial and ethnic groups in the same way.

In departments with a **legalistic style**, police work is marked by professionalism and an emphasis on law enforcement. Officers are expected to detain a high proportion of juvenile offenders, act vigorously against illicit enterprises, issue traffic tickets, and make a large number of misdemeanor arrests. They act as if there is a single standard of community conduct—that prescribed by the law—rather than different standards for juveniles, minorities, people under the influence of drugs or alcohol, and other groups. Thus, although officers do not discriminate in making arrests and issuing citations, the strict enforcement of laws, including traffic laws, can seem overly harsh to some groups in the community.

watchman style Style of policing that emphasizes order maintenance and tolerates minor violations of law as officers use discretion to handle small infractions informally but make arrests for major violations.

legalistic style Style of policing that emphasizes strict enforcement of laws and reduces officers' authority to handle matters informally.

The styles of policing employed by police departments can vary by the characteristics of a community. Do you see evidence of the any of the three classic styles—watchman, legalistic, or service—in your hometown? Does the use of specific patrol methods, such as bicycles, tell you anything about the style of policing in a community?

A. Ramey/PhotoEdit

Police Chief

In recent years, highly publicized fatal shootings of African Americans by white police officers have led to protest marches, lawsuits, and, in a few cities, civil disorder. You are a police chief in a small, diverse city where there have been peaceful protests by people who want to show their support for protesters in other cities. Simultaneously, these citizens are urging you and other city officials to take actions to reduce police use of force and ensure equal treatment of all citizens in your city. You are concerned with ensuring that your officers are fair and effective while maintaining good relationships with people in all neighborhoods. At the same time, you do not want to harm the morale and attitudes of your officers if they feel that everyone portrays them as

"bad guys" who do not act properly. As you look around at other police chiefs, you see various reactions. At one end of the spectrum, Sheriff David Clarke of Milwaukee County, Wisconsin, defended police nationwide in October 2015 by saying on national television, "There is no police brutality in America.... There is no racism in the hearts of police officers." At the other end of the spectrum, Police Chief Chris Magnus of Richmond, California, joined a group of protesters and, while in uniform, was photographed holding a sign that said "#BlackLivesMatter." Clarke is African American and Magnus is white. What actions, if any, will you initiate regarding training, patrol operations, supervision, or aspects of your police

department's operations in light of these recent controversies? If you would initiate any actions, explain the justification for each action; if you see no need to change your department, explain why. Then search the Internet for information about the changes initiated in the Cleveland, Ohio, police department as part of a 2015 consent decree from a federal court.

Sources: D. Bice, "Sheriff David Clarke Says Police Brutality and Racism Have Ended," *Milwaukee Journal Sentinel*, October 28, 2015 (www.jsonline.com); R. Rogers, "Richmond Police Chief a Prominent Participant in Protest against Police Violence," *Contra Costa Times*, December 9, 2014 (www.contracostatimes.com).

---

service style Style of policing in which officers cater to citizens' desire for favorable treatment and sensitivity to individual situations by using discretion to handle minor matters in ways that seek to avoid embarrassment or punishment.

Suburban middle-class communities often experience a **service style**. Residents feel that they deserve individual treatment and expect the police to provide such service. Burglaries and assaults are taken seriously, whereas minor infractions tend to be dealt with by informal means such as stern warnings. The police are expected to deal with the misdeeds of local residents in a personal, nonpublic way so as to avoid embarrassment.

In all cases, before officers investigate crimes or make arrests, each police chief decides on policies that will govern the level and type of enforcement in the community. Given that the police are the entry point to the criminal justice system, the decisions made by police officials affect all segments of the system. Just as community expectations shape decisions about enforcement goals and the allocation of police resources, they also shape the cases that will be handled by prosecutors and correctional officials. Consider the recent controversies concerning police practices described in this chapter and Chapter 1 as you read "You Make the Decision" and consider what you would decide.

CHECK POINT

16. What are the characteristics of the watchman style of policing?
Emphasis on order maintenance, extensive use of discretion, and risk of differential treatment of racial and ethnic groups.

17. What are the key features of the legalistic style of policing?
Professionalism and the use of a single standard of law enforcement throughout the community.

18. Where are you likely to find the service style of policing?
Suburban middle-class communities.

STOP & ANALYZE

If you were a police chief, which style of policing would you seek to have your officers carry out? Would your choice depend on the type of city for which you have responsibility, or is there one style that is actually the ideal approach? Give three reasons for your choice of styles.

Think, Discuss, Write

In October 2011, former New York Police Department narcotics detective Stephen Anderson testified in court that a fellow undercover officer was worried about being sent back to uniformed street patrol for failing to meet his quota of drug arrests. Anderson, who had just made two buy-and-bust arrests in a bar, gave the other officer drugs, knowing that the officer was going to plant the drugs on innocent people and then arrest them on drug charges. The officers referred to this practice as "flaking." Anderson said he observed on multiple occasions that officers planted drugs on innocent people. "It was something I was seeing a lot of, whether it was from supervisors or undercovers and even investigators.... It's almost like you have no emotion with it, that they attach the bodies to it, they're going to be out of jail tomorrow anyway." Anderson also testified that officers made extra money by planting drugs on people because supervisors rewarded them with extra overtime pay for drug busts, even if the drug busts did not involve overtime work.

In 2015, New York City paid $155,000 to settle a lawsuit by a police officer who said he was punished by his superiors for speaking out against the arrest quotas imposed on the city's officers. Thus, as public concerns grow about police practices that may unjustly punish innocent people, police departments may be increasingly vulnerable to lawsuits and negative publicity from such policies.

Discussion/Writing Assignment

Imagine that you are the new police chief in New York City. What will you do to counteract illegal and unethical practices that go beyond simply improper actions by one bad cop and appear to be part of accepted practice? Should you modify the productivity measure of arrest quotas? Should you change supervisors' authority to approve overtime pay? What issues and problems might follow from any changes you propose? Also think about adjustments you could make in training and supervision. Write a memo detailing the actions you would propose and predicting the possible consequences of those actions.

Sources: B. Golding, "Cop Punished for Exposing Arrest Quotas to Get over $155K from NYC," *New York Post*, December 7, 2015 (www.nypost.com); J. Marzulli, "Cops Made Money by Fabricating Drug Charges against Innocent People, Stephen Anderson Testifies," *New York Daily News*, October 14, 2011 (www.nydailynews.com); J. Marzulli, "We Fabricated Drug Charges against Innocent People to Meet Arrest Quotas, Former Detective Testifies," *New York Daily News*, October 13, 2011 (www.nydailynews.com).

SUMMARY

1 Describe how policing evolved in the United States.

- The police in the United States owe their roots to early nineteenth-century developments in policing in England.
- Like their English counterparts, the American police have limited authority, are under local control, and are organizationally fragmented.
- The three distinctive eras of policing after the founding of the United States are the political era (1840–1920), the professional model era (1920–1970), and the community policing era (1970–present).

2 Name the main types of law enforcement agencies.

- In the U.S. federal system of government, police agencies are found at the national, state, county, and municipal levels.
- Federal agencies include the FBI, DEA, Secret Service, and sworn officers in dozens of other agencies.
- Most states have a state police force; at the county level, sheriffs' departments are the primary policing agencies.

3 Analyze the recruitment of police officers and how they learn their job.

- People seek to become police officers for a variety of reasons, including public service, a desire for varied tasks, and civil service pay and benefits.
- To meet current and future challenges, the police must recruit and train individuals who will uphold the law and receive citizen support.
- Improvements have been made during the past quarter-century in recruiting more women, racial and ethnic minorities, and well-educated people as police officers.

4 Describe the elements of the police officer's "working personality."

- Police work in an environment greatly influenced by their subculture.
- The concept of the working personality helps us understand the influence of the police subculture on how individual officers see their world.

- Police justify their work in moral terms to deal with dilemmas, but this can also increase tension with citizens.
- The isolation of the police strengthens bonds among officers but can also add to job stress.

5 **List the functions of the police.**
- The functions of the police are order maintenance, law enforcement, and service.
- Police have cultivated an image as crime fighters preoccupied with the law enforcement function.
- The service function is actually the basis for most calls to police departments.

6 **Describe the organization of the police.**
- The organization of police includes bureaucratic elements, such as division of labor, as well as military-style elements, such as chain and unity of command.

- Most police departments assign officers to operational units that focus on specific functions: patrol, investigation, traffic, vice, and juvenile.
- The police play an important role as a bureaucracy within the broader criminal justice system.

7 **Identify influences on police policy and styles of policing.**
- Police executives develop policies on how they will allocate their resources according to one of three styles: the watchman, legalistic, or service styles.
- The development of differing styles can be affected by the nature of the community and political context. Thus, for example, the service style is prevalent in suburban, middle-class communities.
- The service style aims to maintain order in a discreet fashion, the legalistic style emphasizes law enforcement, and the watchman style emphasizes order maintenance.

Questions for Review

1. What principles borrowed from England still underlie policing in the United States?
2. What have been the three eras of policing in the United States since the founding of the country, and what are the characteristics of each?
3. How do recruitment and training practices affect policing?

4. What is meant by the police subculture, and how does it influence an officer's work?
5. What are the functions of the police?
6. How are the police organized?
7. How do communities influence police policy and police styles?

Key Terms

chain of command (p. 151)

community policing (p. 128)

FBI special agents (p. 131)

frankpledge (p. 122)

intelligence-led policing (p. 129)

law enforcement (p. 148)

law enforcement certification (p. 136)

legalistic style (p. 155)

order maintenance (p. 148)

patrol units (p. 151)

police bureaucracy (p. 150)

problem-oriented policing (p. 128)

service (p. 149)

service style (p. 156)

sheriff (p. 125)

slave patrols (p. 124)

socialization (p. 141)

special units (p. 152)

subculture (p. 141)

U.S. marshals (p. 125)

watch system (p. 124)

watchman style (p. 155)

working personality (p. 142)

5 Policing: Contemporary Issues and Challenges

LEARNING OBJECTIVES

1 Describe the everyday actions of police.

2 Identify the ways police can abuse their power and the challenges of controlling this abuse.

3 List the methods that can be used to make police more accountable to citizens.

4 Describe the delivery of police services.

5 Name patrol strategies that departments employ.

6 Explain the importance of connections between the police and the community.

7 Identify issues and problems that emerge from law enforcement agencies' increased attention to homeland security.

8 Describe the policing and related activities undertaken by private-sector security management.

In the third week of November 2014, crowds of angry people gathered on consecutive nights in Ferguson, Missouri, and expressed their outrage about a local prosecutor's failure to convince a grand jury to issue criminal charges against a white police officer who shot and killed an unarmed African American teenager. There were reports of gunfire, arson, and property damage as businesses in the vicinity of the shooting site were burned to the ground, a police car was overturned, and protesters threw rocks and bricks that struck police officers' helmets and riot shields (M. Fernandez, 2014). Protesters and news reporters had traveled from across the nation to Ferguson to await the announcement of the grand jury's decision. Thus television reports and newspapers carried troubling images of burning buildings, angry crowds, and heavily armed police with military-style weapons and equipment confronting protesters (Davey & Bosman, 2014).

The public disorder in Ferguson served as a stark reminder of both public expectations about police behavior in a democratic society and the challenges facing police in fulfilling their role for society. Ferguson, Missouri, police officer Darren Wilson shot and killed an unarmed teenager, Michael Brown, in August 2014 after an altercation in which Wilson claimed that Brown had tried to grab Wilson's gun after the officer spoke to the young man about walking in the middle of the street. Witnesses then saw Wilson fire a dozen shots at Brown. It was not clear from witness accounts whether Brown was raising his hands in surrender as Wilson fired, or moving toward the officer in a threatening manner. Because Officer Wilson was white and Brown was African American, the incident reinforced concerns about unequal treatment of minorities by criminal justice officials. It rekindled anger at America's long history of police violence directed against the poor, minorities, and political protesters. The Ferguson protests triggered a social movement named after the Twitter hashtag "Black Lives Matter." This group of loosely affiliated organizations began by organizing protests in support of the people of Ferguson, and later, directed protests at police actions in other cities.

Confrontations between community members and police broke out in other cities after the deaths of other African American men at the hands of police. Some of these protests included property damage and disorder; others were generally peaceful, albeit with accompanying interference to traffic and retail businesses. For example, Baltimore experienced public disorder in April 2015, including broken windows, looting, and burned buildings, after a man died of a broken back after being transported in a police van (Swaine, Jacobs, & Lewis, 2015). Large crowds of protesters blocked access to the Mall of America and Minneapolis airport in December 2015 after a man was shot in the head by police who responded to a call about a domestic dispute (Smith, Chanen, & Reinan, 2015). Several witnesses claimed that the man was handcuffed and lying on the ground when he was shot. In December 2015 in Chicago, large crowds interfered with holiday

AP Images/Jeff Roberson

shopping at the city's retail district on Michigan Avenue to protest the city's belated release of video showing a police officer shooting a teenager multiple times (Martinez & Young, 2015). The video showed the youth walking up the street as if under the influence of drugs and appeared to refute the officer's claim that the youth was threatening the lives of the half-dozen officers who were observing him.

By the later decades of the twentieth century, rough treatment of citizens and criminal suspects, which had been widespread in the United States, was becoming less common due to the professionalization of police, improved hiring practices and training, and court decisions clarifying rules for police conduct. In a democracy, the public expects police to follow the law and emphasize equal treatment and fairness in their treatment of people. When these expectations are unfulfilled, Americans use their right to free speech as well as lawsuits against officers in order to pressure the police to follow the law. By contrast,

in authoritarian governing systems, the police are often permitted to use any means at their disposal to suppress dissent and preserve the power of dictatorial leaders and favoritism toward certain groups in society. Thus, people in these countries must keep quiet and silently endure the unlawful actions by the police., Despite increased professionalization of American police over history, there is evidence that some police officers, as well as other criminal justice officials, still engage in behaviors that produce unequal treatment and, at times, violate the laws and policies they have sworn to uphold.

The uniformed men and women who patrol American streets are the most visible presence of government in the United States. They are joined by thousands of plainclothes officers who share various law enforcement responsibilities. Whether they are members of the local or state police, sheriff's departments, or federal agencies, the more than 700,000 sworn officers in the country play key roles in U.S. society. Citizens look to them to perform a wide range of functions: crime prevention, law enforcement, order maintenance, and community services. Police officers are given a great deal of authority to perform these functions. Using their powers to arrest, search, detain, and use force, they can interfere with the freedom of any citizen. If they abuse such powers, they can threaten the basic values of a stable, democratic society.

Police officers have challenging jobs. They must respond to emergency calls, in ways that can range from rendering first aid to injured motorists to rescuing elderly people from rising flood waters to rushing into the potential dangers of a robbery in progress. They must make quick decisions about what actions they will take to restore order, protect citizens, or confront lawbreakers. There are risks that the police will face situations for which they are not fully trained or for which they lack needed resources to be completely effective. In their difficult jobs, they typically receive strong support from the general public. However, specific officers and police departments may, as in Ferguson, face strong criticism and opposition for decisions and actions that clash with high expectations about their performance and adherence to the rules of law. Moreover, because members of the public do not all share either identical expectations about the police or common experiences in interacting with the police, officers experience mixed reactions and differing levels of support from the people they encounter in their work.

In this chapter, we examine several aspects of the continuing challenges faced by American police in protecting lives and property. We focus on the actual work of the police as they pursue suspects, prevent crimes, and otherwise serve the public. The police must be organized so that patrol efforts are coordinated, investigations carried out, arrests made, evidence gathered, and violators prosecuted. Moreover, police responsibilities must be performed effectively in a variety of contexts, within an increasingly diverse society. Law enforcement officials must be prepared to tackle issues that might not be considered in the realm of typical crime prevention, including threats of civil disorder, public-safety emergencies, and natural disasters. Because each of these responsibilities must be executed while maintaining the highest principles and professional standards, we will examine the issues of police ethics, misconduct, and accountability.

This chapter also looks at the emerging challenges stemming from homeland security and antiterrorist efforts. We will conclude by discussing the role of private security officials in advancing society's interests in public safety and crime prevention. The topics explored in this chapter demonstrate the wide range of issues and problems handled by public police and private security officials in the twenty-first century as they work toward advancing society's goals of order, safety, and security.

Everyday Action of the Police

We saw in Chapter 4 how the police are organized to carry out their threefold mandate: law enforcement, order maintenance, and service. We have also recognized that police officers must be guided by policies developed by their superiors as to how policing is to be implemented. Moreover, police officers' actions and effectiveness depend on the resources available to them, as illustrated by the example of computers in patrol cars that will be discussed in greater detail in Chapter 14. In this section, we look at the everyday actions of the police as they deal with citizens in often highly discretionary ways. We then discuss domestic violence to show how the police respond to serious problems.

Encounters between Police and Citizens

To carry out their mission, the police must have the public's confidence, because they depend on the public to notify them about crimes and help them carry out investigations. Each year one in five Americans has a face-to-face contact with law enforcement officers. One-fifth of the contacts occur when police respond to calls for assistance or arrive at the scene of an automobile collision. Another fifth involve people reporting a crime. Still another fifth involve police investigating crimes or providing service and assistance. The remaining 40 percent of these contacts involve drivers and passengers stopped by a patrol officer. Overall, 90 percent of people who had contact with the police believed that the police acted properly. However, among drivers stopped by the police, African Americans were less likely than whites or Hispanics to believe that the police had stopped them for a legitimate reason (Eith & Durose, 2011). People's contacts with the police may shape their perceptions of the police and affect their willingness to cooperate.

Although most people are willing to help the police, factors such as fear and self-interest keep some from cooperating. Many people who avoid calling the police do so because they think it is not worth the effort and cost. They do not want to spend time filling out forms at the station, appearing as a witness, or confronting a neighbor or relative in court. In some low-income neighborhoods, citizens are reluctant to assist the police because their past experience has shown that contact with law enforcement "only brings trouble." Without information about a crime, the police may decide not to pursue an investigation. Clearly citizens have influence over the work of the police through their decisions to call or not call them. As a result, officers learn that developing and maintaining effective communication with people is essential to doing their job.

Citizens expect the police to act both effectively and fairly—in ways consistent with American values. Yet police departments have little direct control over the actions of individual officers. Departments have policies about when to conduct searches and other matters concerning officers' interactions with members of the public. However, officers possess the discretion to decide for themselves when to stop a driver, when to frisk a pedestrian, and when to make an arrest. Sometimes these individual decisions will violate policy or even ignore the legal rights of citizens. Thus, police officers' decisions about how to use their discretion have significant impact on how people are treated and how they feel about the criminal justice system.

Decisions by judges in the court system, including decisions by the U.S. Supreme Court, seek to give guidance to police officers about what they can and cannot do. In defining the constitutional rights of individuals, court decisions simultaneously define boundaries for police actions. These legal rules are not self-enforcing. Police officers need to know the rules of law and then respect those rules as a matter of their professionalism and commitment to ethics and law. Otherwise, they have many opportunities to violate rules because of their broad discretion. Read the "You Make the Decision" feature and consider how difficult it is to to create clear rules to guide the behavior of police officers in all possible situations.

Police Discretion

Police officers have the power to deprive people of their liberty, to arrest them, to take them into custody, and to use force to control them. In carrying out their professional responsibilities, officers are expected to exercise *discretion*—to make wise choices in often ambiguous situations as to how and when to apply the law. Discretion can involve ignoring minor violations of the law or holding some violators to rulebook standards. It can mean arresting a disorderly person or just taking that person safely home. In the final analysis, the officer on the scene must define the

YOU MAKE THE DECISION

U.S. Supreme Court Justice

Since the 1960s, the "exclusionary rule" developed by the Supreme Court has generally required that evidence obtained from an improper stop or search cannot be used to prove a suspect's guilt. In other words, when the evidence is the product of an improper police action, it cannot be used by the prosecution in the case. Although the Supreme Court has created a number of exceptions to the exclusionary rule over the years, the rule still requires the exclusion of evidence in many circumstances. For instance, imagine that an anonymous caller reports "narcotics activity" at a specific house. As a result of this call, a police

officer begins watching the house. He sees a man leave the house and walk to a nearby convenience store. The officer follows the man, orders him to stop, and asks to see the man's driver's license. The officer calls the department to inquire about any records and learns that there is an arrest warrant for this man based on failure to appear in court for a minor traffic ticket. The man is arrested and searched, and the officer finds illegal drugs in his pocket. Later, an appeals court rules that the officer violated the man's Fourth Amendment rights by stopping him without an adequate legal basis. Merely

seeing the man leave a house that an anonymous caller had described as the location of "narcotics activity" did not justify the stop. The officer's discovery of illegal drugs occurred only as a result of the improper stop, which led to the discovery of the arrest warrant and the subsequent search. Should the evidence found in the search be excluded from use against the suspect because its discovery originated with an improper stop? What would you decide? Give reasons for your decision. Then do an Internet search and read the Supreme Court's decision in *Utah v. Streiff* (2016).

situation, decide how to handle it, and determine whether and how the law should be applied. Five factors are especially important:

1. *The nature of the crime.* The less serious a crime is to the public, the more freedom officers have to ignore it.
2. *The relationship between the alleged criminal and the victim.* The closer the personal relationship, the more variable is the use of discretion. Family squabbles may not be as grave as they appear, and police are wary of making arrests, because a spouse may later decide not to press charges.
3. *The relationship between the police and the criminal or victim.* A polite complainant will be taken more seriously than a hostile one. Similarly, a suspect who shows respect to an officer is less likely to be arrested than one who does not.
4. *Race/ethnicity, age, gender, class.* Research studies show that some officers are more likely to investigate behavior (e.g., make stops and searches) and strictly enforce the law against young, minority, poor men while being more lenient to the elderly, to whites, and to affluent women.
5. *Departmental policy.* The policies of the police chief and city officials can authorize the exercise of either more or less discretion by officers.

Violence between spouses or intimate partners, typically called **domestic violence**, provides a good example of the role of police discretion. More than a quarter of violent victimizations experienced by women are at the hands of spouses or boyfriends (Truman & Rand, 2010; Truman & Planty, 2012). In 2014, intimate-partner violence remained a significant problem; more than 630,000 incidents were reported in the National Crime Victimization Survey, combining totals for both female and male victims (Truman & Langton, 2015). Until the 1970s and 1980s, many male officers treated such events as private matters for couples to handle themselves rather than as crimes, even when there was clear evidence of violence and injuries. In light of lawsuits and lobbying on behalf of injured women, nearly half of the states and the District of Columbia eventually developed policies that require the arrest of suspects in violent incidents, without a warrant, even if the officer did not witness the crime. In addition, most large departments and police academies have programs to educate officers about domestic violence and the victimization of women.

Even though we can point to policy changes imposed to deal with domestic violence, the fact remains that the officer in the field is the one who must handle these

domestic violence The term commonly used to refer to intimate partner violence or violent victimizations between spouses, boyfriends, and girlfriends or those formerly in intimate relationships. Such actions account for a significant percentage of the violent victimizations experienced by women.

Police officers use their discretion to make many decisions. Who should be stopped and questioned? When should an arrest be made? Who needs an encouraging word and who needs a stern warning? In making decisions, officers can significantly impact the lives of people who come into contact with the criminal justice system. Are there ways that supervisors could better monitor officers' use of discretion?

AP Images/Lynne Sladky

situations. Each context may differ, both in terms of the officer's perceptions about what occurred and with respect to the victim's desire to see the abuser arrested and punished (Hirschel & Hutchinson, 2003). As with most law enforcement situations, laws, guidelines, and training can help; however, as is often true in police work, in the end, the discretion of the officer inevitably determines what actions will be taken (R. C. Davis et al., 2008).

Police officers possess significant discretion because so much of their work is conducted independently, beyond the observation and supervision of superior officers. We count on them to be ethical and professional in all of their decisions and actions, but there is always the potential for improper police behavior and corruption, the topics we will examine in the next section.

Police Abuse of Power

Police officers can break the law and disobey departmental policies through corruption, favoritism, discrimination, and the failure to carry out their duties properly. Periodically, police corruption and abuse of power become major issues on the public agenda (Baker, 2016; Skolnick & Fyfe, 1993). In particular, the illegal use of violence by law enforcement officers, violations of constitutional rights, and the criminal activities associated with police corruption can gain news media attention and anger the public. As highlighted in the opening examples for this chapter, police shootings and the excessive use of force on unarmed people, especially in incidents for which videotapes have been released on social media, have drawn public attention to police actions and generated public protests since late 2014.

An additional aspect of this controversy is the fact that police officers are infrequently disciplined for their roles in events that produce injuries or questionable arrests (Williams, 2015). In 2014, newspapers highlighted New York City detectives sued multiple times for making false arrests, including one officer who was sued 28 times in an eight-year period at a cost of nearly $900,000 to the city for settling those lawsuits (Ryley & Gregorian, 2014). Although most officers do not engage in such misconduct, these problems deserve study because they raise questions about the extent to which the public can control and trust the police. The abuse of discretion by a few can affect the working lives of many officers, who must deal not only with public protests of those abuses but also with the loss of cooperation from citizens who no longer trust the police.

Use of Force

Although most people cooperate with the police, officers must at times use force to make arrests, control disturbances, and deal with the drunken or mentally ill. Thus, police may use *legitimate* force to do their job. It is when they use *excessive* force that they violate the law. But which situations and actions constitute **excessive use of force**? Both officers and experts debate this question.

Citizens use the term *police brutality* to describe a wide range of practices from the use of profane or abusive language to physical force and violence. Stories of police brutality are not new. However, unlike the untrained officers of the early 1900s, today's officers are supposed to be professionals who know the rules and understand the need for proper conduct (Wexler, 2015). Nevertheless, a 2011 report by the Los Angeles Sheriff's Department identified instances of improper conduct. In one case, a deputy shot at a driver who bumped into his vehicle in a fast-food restaurant parking lot; in another, an officer sought to cover up the fact that she had fired her gun at a burglary suspect (Faturechi, 2011).

Concerns are heightened by the fact that the public cannot know how often police engage in abusive behavior, even when it comes to light, because most violence remains hidden from public view (Weitzer, 2002). In 2015, an unseen bystander used his smartphone to film a police officer's confrontation with a driver after a traffic stop in North Charleston, South Carolina. In this video, the officer is shown firing eight shots at the back of a chunky, middle-aged man who is trying to run away (Shoichet, 2015). Before the video was released, news reports had advanced the officer's claim that he had fired the fatal shots in self-defense, because the driver had seized his police Taser and pointed it at him. After the video was released, the officer was charged with murder. If not for the video, how would the public know what the officer had done? In other situations, without direct proof, will the public believe criminal suspects who claim to have been beaten by police? How can we prevent such incidents, especially when they occur without witnesses?

The concept "use of force" takes many forms in practice. We can arrange the various types of force on a continuum ranging from most severe (civilians shot and killed) to least severe (being grasped by an officer). How often must force be used? Most research has shown that in police contacts with suspects, force is used infrequently, and the type of force used is usually at the low end of the continuum—toward the less severe. Resistance by a suspect can contribute to the officers' decision to use force (R. Johnson, 2011; J. H. Garner, Maxwell, & Heraux, 2002). Examinations of police use of force reveal that:

1. Police use force infrequently.
2. Police use of force typically occurs in the lower end of the force spectrum and involves grabbing, pushing, or shoving.
3. Use of force typically occurs when police are trying to make an arrest and the suspect is resisting.

Although more studies are needed, other research indicates that use of force is not necessarily linked to an officer's personal characteristics such as age, gender, or ethnicity (Klahm & Tillyer, 2010). However, a small percentage of officers may be disproportionately involved in use-of-force situations. The officer involved in the shooting that generated the December 2015 public protests in Chicago had faced 18 previous complaints from citizens, including improper use of force and use of racial slurs, but he was never punished. Another officer faced 68 citizen complaints without punishment, including complaints about improper use of force, but his only punishment came when he was ultimately convicted and sentenced to prison for robbing criminal suspects (Williams, 2015). In addition, use of force occurs more frequently when police are dealing with people affected by drugs, alcohol, or mental illness (Lord & Sloop, 2010). By law, the police have the authority to use force if necessary to make an arrest, keep the peace, or maintain public order. But the questions of just how much force is necessary and under what conditions force may be used are complex and open to debate.

When police kill a suspect or bystander while trying to make an arrest, their actions may produce public outrage and hostility. Chicago officials were on edge in early 2016 after a middle-aged woman was shot and killed by police officers who arrived at a house in response to a domestic violence call concerning the woman's

excessive use of force
Applications of force against individuals by police officers that violate either departmental policies or constitutional rights by exceeding the level of force permissible and necessary in a given situation.

Police grab a protester off his bike after he taunted them at a protest against free trade policies during a meeting of international leaders in Miami, Florida. Does this appear to be an appropriate use of force? Do police officers sometimes use force out of anger rather than out of necessity?

upstairs neighbors (Madhani, 2016). Such tragedies call into question the adequacy of police training and tactics regarding the use of force and police executives have reacted to highly publicized shootings by critically examining their own procedures (Baker, 2016). There are concerns about whether police use lethal force too quickly when there are opportunities to de-escalate potential conflicts, especially when dealing with mentally ill people or those holding weapons other than firearms (Wexler, 2015). In addition, there is evidence of racial disparities in the use of force by police. As indicated by the discussion of implicit bias in Chapter 4, evidence from psychology studies about unconscious perceptions of threat from members of minority groups may explain why unarmed African Americans are twice as likely as unarmed whites to be killed by the police (Swaine, Laughland, & Larty, 2015).

The risk of lawsuits by victims of improper police shootings and other injury-producing uses of force looms over police departments and creates an incentive for administrators to impose standards for the proper use of force (H. Lee & Vaughn, 2010). Police officers have caused deaths and injuries not only with firearms, but also with chokeholds and by striking people in the head with flashlights or batons (Klingler, 2012). Injuries can also result from seemingly routine procedures such as placing a suspect in handcuffs that are too tight.

As long as officers carry weapons, some improper uses of force, including shootings, will occur. Officers who are angry or guided by improper motives may use unnecessary force in situations beyond public view. See "A Question of Ethics" at the end of the chapter for examples of excessive force caught on video in 2015. Police administrators have limited tools available to restrain unethical officers. Training, internal review of incidents, and the disciplining or firing of quick-trigger officers may help reduce the use of unnecessary force. In 2016, the Police Executive Research Forum (PERF) developed 30 principles concerning policy and training that the organization urged local police departments to adopt in order to reduce citizens' deaths and injuries (Baker, 2016). Read the "Close Up" on the PERF principles and think about whether you believe they should be incorporated into American policing.

CLOSE UP

The Police Executive Research Forum's 2016 Proposed Principles on Use of Force

The Police Executive Research Forum, a nonprofit organization that sponsors research to improve policing and is governed by a board of directors composed of police chiefs from around the nation, responded to recent controversies by studying police use of force. The effort to develop and refine principles included sponsoring a trip to Scotland so American police executives could learn how their Scottish counterparts, who generally do not carry firearms, respond to

threatening people holding knives and people experiencing mental health crises without using lethal force. The principles put forth in the PERF report caused debate among police executives; some chiefs argued that they could not implement all of the principles in their departments, and others expressed concern that the principles did not focus enough on the safety of officers. What do you think of these proposed

principles? Below is a brief summary of the principles.

1. The sanctity of human life—as well as treating all persons with dignity and respect—should be at the heart of everything that a police agency does.
2. Departments should hold themselves to higher standards than the minimum standards set by courts

for reasonable use of force, developing policies and practices to prevent situations in which the use of force seems to be the only choice.

3. Police use of force must meet the test of proportionality. Officers must ask themselves whether members of the public would see a particular use of force as appropriate to the situation and severity of the threat.

4. Police departments should adopt de-escalation as a formal agency policy. Officers need more training in crisis intervention and de-escalation in order to avoid the use of force when possible.

5. Officers should use the Critical Decision-Making Model that PERF adapted from the National Decision Model used in England and Scotland. The Model includes collecting information, assessing threats, identifying options and the best course of action.

6. Duty to intervene: Officers need to prevent other officers from using excessive force.

7. Respect the sanctity of life by promptly rendering first aid to any injured by police use of force.

8. Shooting at moving vehicles is strictly prohibited unless the person in the vehicle is using or threatening use of a weapon.

9. Prohibit use of deadly force against individuals who pose a danger only to themselves.

10. Document use-of-force incidents and review data and enforcement practices to ensure that they are fair and nondiscriminatory. Review of video footage from body and vehicle cameras is important. Reports should be specific and clear and should avoid the use of generic language.

11. To build understanding and trust, agencies should issue regular reports to the public on use of force.

12. All critical incidents that result in death or serious bodily injury should be reviewed by specially trained personnel.

13. Agencies need to be transparent in providing information following use-of-force incidents.

14. Training academy content and culture must reflect agency values.

Field training must also reflect agency values.

15. Officers should be trained to use a Critical Decision-Making Model.

16. Officers should take advantage of distance, cover, and time—temporarily retreating and taking cover—in order to assess and de-escalate. This is a move away from traditional practices of using firearms against threatening individuals who approach within 21 feet of the officer.

17. De-escalation should be a core theme of an agency's training program.

18. De-escalation starts with effective communications. Officers should be trained in effectively communicating with enraged individuals and those suffering from crises due to mental health or substance abuse.

19. Mental illness: implement a comprehensive agency training program on dealing with mental health issues.

20. Tactical training and mental health training need to be interwoven to improve response to critical incidents.

21. Community-based outreach teams, including local mental health outreach personnel and social workers, can be a valuable component of agencies' mental health response.

22. Supervisors should immediately respond to the scene of a potentially dangerous situation where weapons or mental health issues have been reported. Supervisors can assist with assessment and de-escalation to prevent avoidable use of force.

23. Training as teams can improve performance in the field.

24. Scenario-based training should be prevalent, challenging, and realistic.

25. Officers need access to and training in less-lethal options, including the use of less-lethal weapons and physical techniques, to avoid the immediate resort to firearms.

26. Agencies should consider new options for chemical sprays.

27. If an electronic stun device is not effective, officers should not automatically move to use of firearms. Instead, there should be a reassessment about the prospect for de-escalation and less-lethal options.

28. Personal protection shields may support de-escalation efforts during critical incidents, including situations involving persons with knives, baseball bats, or other improvised weapons that are not firearms.

29. Well-trained call-takers and dispatchers are essential to police response to critical incidents.

30. Educate the families of persons with mental health problems on communicating effectively with call-takers so that police personnel can be fully informed when responding to a call about such persons.

Researching the Internet

Go to the website of the Police Executive Research Forum and read about how the new principles were developed: http://www.policeforum.org/how-perf-s-use-of-force-guiding-principles-were-developed

For Critical Thinking and Analysis

Notice how the principles focus repeatedly on various aspects of several specific elements—communication; de-escalation; understanding mental illness; careful decision making; emphasis on duty—to aid the injured and to prevent other officers from acting with excessive force. Will adoption of these elements result in a shift in some police departments' culture away from a group identity as tough, anti-crime warriors with loyalty to their colleagues and toward an orientation as crisis managers and soothing helpers of troubled individuals? What challenges will police chiefs face in considering whether and how to implement these principles? Choose the four principles that you believe will be the most difficult to implement and explain why they pose difficulties.

Sources: A. Baker, "Police Leaders Unveil Principles Intended to Shift Policing Practices Nationwide." *New York Times*, January 29, 2016 (www.nytimes.com); Police Executive Research Forum, "Use of Force: Taking Police to a Higher Standard," *Critical Issues in Policing Series*, January 29, 2016 (http://www.policeforum.org/assets/30%20guiding%20principles.pdf).

As a result of lawsuits by people injured at the hands of the police, departments have sought new means of applying force in ways that will not produce injuries. Some of the new methods center on specific holds and pressure points that officers can use to incapacitate people temporarily without causing permanent harm; officers can learn these techniques through training. In addition, police departments seek new weapons that use less-than-lethal force. In Chapter 14, when we discuss the impact of technology on police practices, we shall examine new weapons that use electric shocks, projectiles, and chemical sprays. These new weapons also pose serious risks, including the possibility that officers will resort too quickly to such weapons when situations could be solved through patience and persuasion (Adang & Mensink, 2004).

Corruption

police corruption Police officers' violations of law and departmental policy for personal gain or to help their families and friends.

Police corruption has a long history in America. Early in the twentieth century, city officials organized liquor and gambling businesses for their personal gain. In many cities, ties between politicians and police officials ensured that favored clients would be protected and competitors harassed. Much of the Progressive movement's efforts to reform the police were aimed at combating such corrupt arrangements.

Although such political ties have diminished in most cities, corruption still exists. A Georgia police chief was sentenced to prison in February 2015 for accepting money to protect an illegal gambling operation (Skutch, 2015). In December 2014, two San Francisco police officers were convicted of stealing property and cash from drug suspects, with evidence of their misdeeds caught on motel security cameras (Egelko, 2014). Earlier in 2014, a Kansas City police officer was convicted of corruption for accepting sexual favors from prostitutes in exchange for agreeing not to arrest them ("Kansas City Police Officer," 2014). Sadly, a number of such cases appear in the news each year.

Sometimes corruption is defined so broadly that it ranges from accepting a free cup of coffee to robbing businesses or beating suspects. Obviously, corruption is not easily defined, and people disagree about what it includes. As a useful starting point, we can focus on the distinction between corrupt officers who are "grass eaters" and those who are "meat eaters."

"Grass eaters" are officers who accept payoffs that the routines of police work bring their way. These officers may accept gifts from businesses or take a $20 bribe instead of writing a traffic ticket. "Meat eaters" are officers who actively use their power for personal gain. For example, several Chicago police officers were convicted of robbing drug dealers and conducting illegal searches in order to steal money and drugs (Williams, 2015; Meisner, 2011). Although meat eaters are few, their actions make headlines when discovered. By contrast, because grass eaters are numerous, they make corruption seem acceptable and promote a code of secrecy that brands any officer who exposes corruption as a traitor.

If police administrators judge success merely by the maintenance of order on the streets and a steady flow of arrests and traffic citations, they may not have any idea what their officers actually do while on patrol. Officers therefore may learn that they can engage in improper conduct without worrying about investigations by supervisors as long as there is order on the streets and they keep their activities out of the public spotlight.

Over time, illegal activity may become accepted as normal. Ellwyn Stoddard, who studied "blue-coat crime," has said that it can become part of an "identifiable informal 'code'" (Stoddard, 1968:205). He suggests that officers are socialized to the code early in their careers. Those who "snitch" on other officers may be ostracized. Recent research shows that officers risk retaliation from peers if they break the code (Cancino & Enriquez, 2004). When corruption comes to official attention, officers protect the code by distancing themselves from the known offender rather than stopping their own improper conduct (C. Cooper, 2009; Stoddard, 1968).

Officers are often placed in situations where they can be tempted to enrich themselves by stealing money, property or drugs, or by accepting favors, gifts, and bribes. If you were a police chief, how would you reduce the risks of police corruption?

AP Images/Paul Sancya

New police officers need to be instilled with a sense of ethics and professionalism in both their formal and informal training. This is necessary because of the significant discretion enjoyed by police and their independence in undertaking daily tasks, which makes it impossible for administrators to detect or prevent all misconduct. The public depends on officers to take seriously the responsibilities that come with the uniform and badge. When investigations reveal improper conduct by police, we must always wonder what impact that misconduct will have on the public's trust in and cooperation with law enforcement officers.

► CHECK POINT

3. **What kinds of problems arise with police use of force?**
   Risks that force will be used in ways that exceed what is needed for a specific situation; risks that force will be applied disproportionately to minority group members.

4. **What is the difference between "grass eaters" and "meat eaters"?**
   "Grass eaters" are officers who accept payoffs that police work brings their way. "Meat eaters" are officers who aggressively misuse their power for personal gain.

STOP & ANALYZE

If you were a police chief, what three actions might you take to better prepare your officers to make discretionary decisions that include respect for ethical standards and adherence to proper professional standards for conduct?

Civic Accountability

Making the police responsive to citizen complaints without burdening them with a flood of such grievances is difficult. The main challenge to improving police accountability is to use enough citizen input to force police to follow the law and departmental guidelines without restricting their ability to carry out their primary functions. At present, four less-than-perfect techniques are used in efforts to control the police: (1) internal affairs units, (2) civilian review boards, (3) standards and accreditation, and (4) civil liability lawsuits. We now look at each of these in turn.

Internal Affairs Units

The community must be confident that the department has procedures to ensure that officers will protect the rights of citizens. Yet department complaint procedures often seem designed to discourage citizen input. People with complaints cannot always be certain that the police department will take any meaningful action.

Depending on the size of the department, a single officer or an entire section can serve as an **internal affairs unit** that receives and investigates complaints against officers. An officer charged with misconduct can face criminal prosecution or disciplinary action leading to resignation, dismissal, or suspension. Officers assigned to the internal affairs unit have duties similar to those of the inspector general's staff in the military. They must investigate complaints against other officers. Hollywood films and television series depict dramatic investigations of drug dealing and murder, but investigations of sexual harassment, alcohol or drug problems, misuse of force, and violations of departmental policies are more common.

The internal affairs unit must receive enough resources to fulfill its mission. It must also have direct access to the chief. Internal affairs investigators find the work stressful because their status prevents them from maintaining close relationships with other officers. They may face a wall of silence from fellow officers as they investigate complaints of misconduct within a department. Read "Current Controversies in Criminal Justice" to consider the continuing problem of police officers who witness misconduct by their colleagues and then remain silent or, even worse, tell lies to protect other officers from punishment.

Civilian Review Boards

If a police department cannot show that it effectively combats corruption among officers, the public will likely demand that the department be investigated by a **civilian review board**. Such a board allows complaints to be channeled through a committee of people who are not sworn police officers. The organization and powers of civilian review boards vary, but all oversee and review how police departments handle citizen complaints. For instance, the Bay Area Regional Transit (BART) system in California created a citizens' board in the aftermath of a BART police officer's fatal shooting of an unarmed African American man under controversial circumstances (Melendez, 2011). Civilian review boards may also recommend remedial action. They do not have the power to investigate or discipline individual officers, however.

The main argument made by the police against civilian review boards is that people outside law enforcement do not understand the problems of policing. The police contend that civilian oversight lowers morale and hinders performance, and that officers will be less effective if they must worry about possible disciplinary actions. In reality, however, the boards have not been harsh.

The effectiveness of civilian review boards has not been tested, but their presence may improve police–citizen relations.

Standards and Accreditation

One way to increase police accountability is to require that police actions meet nationally recognized standards. The movement to accredit departments that meet these standards has gained momentum during the past decade. It has the support of the **Commission on Accreditation for Law Enforcement Agencies (CALEA)**, a private nonprofit corporation formed by four professional associations: the International Association of Chiefs of Police (IACP), the National Organization of Black Law Enforcement Executives (NOBLE), the National Sheriffs' Association (NSA), and the Police Executive Research Forum (PERF).

Police accreditation is voluntary. Departments contact CALEA to request assistance in their efforts to meet the standards. This process involves self-evaluation by departmental executives, the development of policies that meet the standards, and the training of officers. The CALEA representative acts like a military inspector general, visiting the department, examining its policies, and seeing if the standards are met in its daily operations. Departments that meet the standards receive certification. Administrators can use the standards as a management tool, training

internal affairs unit A branch of a police department that receives and investigates complaints alleging violation of rules and policies on the part of officers.

civilian review board Citizens' committee formed to investigate complaints against the police.

Commission on Accreditation for Law Enforcement Agencies (CALEA) Nonprofit organization formed by major law enforcement executives' associations to develop standards for police policies and practice; on request, will review police agencies and award accreditation upon meeting those standards.

CURRENT CONTROVERSIES IN CRIMINAL JUSTICE

Confronting the Police "Code of Silence"

In 2015, when Chicago officials, after pressure from a news reporter and a judge, released a police cruiser's dashboard video of the 2014 shooting of teenager Laquan McDonald, the public reacted strongly against officers' claims that the youth had lunged at officers with a knife. The video showed the youth walking down the street parallel to the officers watching him. When an additional police car arrived, Officer Jason Van Dyke stepped from the vehicle and almost immediately fired sixteen shots into the teenager. Van Dyke was charged with murder only after the video was released. Other officers were suspended because their reports on the events had supported Van Dyke's self-defense claim—a claim that was unsupported by the video. Other officers at the scene claimed that they were looking in another direction at the time of the shooting.

Earlier in 2015, a former Chicago police commander, Lorenzo Davis, who worked as a supervising investigator for the city's Independent Police Review Authority (IPRA)—the agency that investigates police officer's actions, including questionable use of force—was fired, allegedly for refusing orders to change his conclusions in investigations that found officers using force improperly. Since 2007, the IPRA had investigated 400 incidents of civilians being shot by the Chicago police and had cleared officers in every case except one. Davis, however, found that police acted improperly in six additional cases and said that he lost his job as an investigator when he refused administrators' orders to change his findings to favor the police.

When the officer in North Charleston, South Carolina, shot and killed the motorist in 2015 who was trying to run away on foot—without knowing that a witness was capturing the event on smartphone video—he must have known that the medical examiner and other officers would see that he had shot the man in the back. It would be difficult for him to claim that he fired in self-defense; he would need to claim that he needed to use lethal force to protect the public from danger. Presumably, that is why in the video, he appears to drop something—possibly his Taser—near the hand of the fallen motorist, with another officer close by. The police report said that officers performed CPR on the man while waiting for an ambulance, but the eyewitness who took the video said they did not render that aid to the man who was shot. Had the officer's years of experience taught him to believe that he could count on other officers as well as the medical examiner to help him cover up any use of violence, no matter how improper?

In 2015, two ex-Baltimore police officers gave interviews in which they described how the police targeted young African Americans for surveillance and arrest, conducted illegal searches, and used unjustified force in beating people. While on the job, one of the officers had reported misconduct by another officer who beat a suspect; but after his report, other officers would no longer provide backup for him and did not want to patrol with him. The report effectively ended his career. The other officer said that he never reported anything about other officers prior to his disability retirement because he had been part of the culture of backing up other officers no matter what they did.

For Critical Thinking and Analysis

These episodes from 2015 provide evidence of the continuing problem of a police "code of silence" in many police departments. Indeed, the firing of the Chicago investigator raises questions about the extent to which police commanders may pressure officers to remain silent even if they want to report misconduct. Officers depend on each other for backup when their lives are in danger. In such an occupational context, it may be difficult to avoid the pressure to conform and put loyalty ahead of all other values. If you were a police chief, how would you seek to prevent a "code of silence" inside your department? Write a memo with three ideas that you might pursue to address this issue.

Sources: V. Beckiempis, "Baltimore Police Whistleblower Michael Wood on Justice Reform: 'This Is a Revolution,'" *Newsweek*, September 7, 2015 (www.newsweek.com); N. Dillon, "Retired Cop Uses Twitter to Accuse Baltimore Police of Brutality and Corruption," *New York Daily News*, June 24, 2015 (www.nydaily.news); A. Grimm, "Despite Laquan Video, Reports from Cops Back Shooting," *Chicago Sun-Times*, December 15, 2015 (chicago.suntimes.com); M. Keneally, "Police Shooting Witness Says He Saw Officer Drop Something by Walter Scott's Body," April 9, 2015 (abcnews.go.com); C. Mitchell, "City Fires Investigator Who Found Cops at Fault in Shootings," WBEZ radio news, July 20, 2015 (www.wbez.org); S. St. Clair, J. Coen, and T. Lighty, "Officers in Laquan McDonald Shooting Taken Off Streets—14 Months Later," *Chicago Tribune*, January 22, 2016 (www.chicagotribune.com).

officers to know the standards and to be accountable for their actions. Obviously, the standards do not guarantee that police officers in an accredited department will not engage in misconduct. However, the guidelines serve as a major step toward providing clear guidance to officers about proper behavior. Accreditation can also show the public a department's commitment to making sure officers carry out their duties in an ethical, professional manner.

Civil Liability Lawsuits

Section 1983 lawsuits Civil lawsuits authorized by a federal statute against state and local officials and local agencies when citizens have evidence that these officials or agencies have violated their federal constitutional rights.

Civil lawsuits against departments for police misconduct can increase police accountability. In 1961, the U.S. Supreme Court ruled that Section 1983 of the Civil Rights Act of 1871 allows citizens to sue public officials for violations of their civil rights. The high court extended this opportunity for **Section 1983 lawsuits** in 1978 when it ruled that individual officials and local agencies may be sued when a person's civil rights are violated by an agency's "customs and usages." If an individual can show that harm was caused by employees whose wrongful acts were the result of these "customs, practices, and policies, including poor training and supervision," then he or she can sue a local agency (*Monell v. Department of Social Services of the City of New York*, 1978).

Lawsuits charging police officers with brutality, improper use of weapons, dangerous driving, and false arrest are brought in both state and federal courts. Often these lawsuits provide the basis for punishing officers who violate constitutional rights. Rights that are often the basis of such lawsuits are the Fourth Amendment right against unreasonable seizures (police using excessive force or making improper arrests) and the Fourth Amendment right against unreasonable searches (police wrongly searching a house without a warrant).

In many states, people have received damage awards of millions of dollars, and police departments have settled some lawsuits out of court. In 2013, for example, Chicago paid $4.1 million to the family of a man who was shot in the back multiple times by a police officer, even though he was unarmed and lying on the ground. (St. Clair & Gorner, 2013). In 2015, North Charleston, South Carolina, paid $6.5 million to the family of the motorist fleeing on foot who was shot in the back by a police officer, and Chicago paid $5 million to settle the case of Laquan McDonald, the teenager shot 16 times by an officer whose claims were not supported by the dashboard camera video of the incident ("Chicago Council Approves," 2015; Fausset, 2015). Civil liability rulings by the courts tend to be simple and severe: officials and municipalities are ordered to pay a sum of money, and the courts can enforce that judgment. The threat of significant financial awards gives police departments a strong incentive to improve the training and supervision of officers (Epp, 2009; Vaughn, 2001).

The use of body cameras by individual police officers is now a primary suggestion for making police officers think twice about acting improperly and for providing a mechanism to supervise police (Wexler, 2015). Read "The Policy Debate" feature to consider the potential advantages and drawbacks of police body cameras.

THE POLICY DEBATE

Should Police Officers Wear Individual Body Cameras?

During 2013, a highly publicized trial took place in New York City concerning allegations that police officers improperly performed hundreds of thousands of stop-and-frisk searches and that they engaged in racial discrimination in targeting young African American and Hispanic men. The trial judge's decision that the police had engaged in improper actions brought attention to an emerging technology. The judge ordered a one-year pilot program in which officers in precincts scattered throughout the city would wear individual body cameras that would record their interactions with citizens. The $900 cameras are small enough to attach to officers' sunglasses or collars. They record up to 12 hours of color video when are then downloaded into the department's central computer storage at the end of each shift.

In the aftermath of protest marches in 2014 concerning the controversial deaths of young, unarmed African Americans in encounters with police in

Missouri, New York, and Ohio, interest in body cameras grew. President Obama asked Congress to allocate $75 million in federal funds to help communities throughout the country obtain 50,000 more body cameras for police.

Many observers see this technology as beneficial to both police officers and citizens. The cameras can help police refute false claims that they used excessive force or engaged in improper searches. At the same time, the cameras can provide evidence if police officers violate citizens' rights. However, there are those who fear that the cameras may fail to fulfill expectations and create new problems. In the cities that have begun using the cameras, many police officers initially resist the requirement of using the cameras because, in effect, the devices put them under constant surveillance when the recording device is operating.

For the Use of Body Cameras:

- Cameras can provide evidence of police errors and wrongdoing in conducting searches and using force on people.
- The presence of the camera will force officers to be very conscious of following proper rules of police procedure and thereby reduce the risks of mistakes and misbehavior. Visible cameras may also make some citizens more self-conscious and careful about their own behavior and statements in interacting with officers.
- The cameras can help protect police officers against false claims of improper searches and excessive use of force.
- The cameras will allow supervisors to review officers' actions in order to identify errors, hold officers accountable, and identify needs for additional policies and training.
- In 2012, the first year the cameras were used in the city of Rialto, California, the police department experienced an 89 percent drop in complaints against officers.

Against the Use of Body Cameras:

- Equipping entire police departments with individual cameras is expensive and not necessarily the best use of scarce resources during a time of budget shortfalls.

- The limited field in the camera's view may not record a complete and accurate picture of the circumstances facing an officer at the moment when a decision is made to use force or conduct a search. Something that an officer sees but is not in the direct line of vision of the camera may be the basis for a statement or action, yet the video does not adequately portray everything that the officer observed. In addition, even events clearly recorded by the camera may be subject to interpretation in second-guessing officers' decisions and actions.
- Camera breakdowns or limited camera views may lead to assumptions that police have intentionally failed to use the equipment properly and then any dispute about events may weigh against the officer, even when the officer is telling the truth about what happened.
- A significant increase in the number of cameras used by a police department, in addition to the already-in-use patrol car cameras, will lead to enormous expenditures of time and money when reviewing footage in order to respond to requests for evidence or public information. Many cities are finding that they face costs of hundreds of thousands of dollars in computer storage costs and the paid time of technicians and officers in downloading and reviewing video footage.
- The costs of such programs are affected by whether departments require officers to run the cameras continuously while on duty or to turn on the cameras only during encounters with citizens. The latter policy may save video storage costs, but also creates risks that officers will neglect to turn on the cameras, either intentionally or unintentionally.
- There are risks to officers' privacy if they forget to turn the cameras off and the devices are running when they are on bathroom breaks or when they engage in private phone conversations with their own family members.

By 2015, roughly 3,000 law enforcement agencies had begun using the cameras with at least some of their

officers. In some departments, the use of the technology has gone smoothly, and officers come to view the device as protecting them against false allegations. In other departments, concerns have arisen about the development of appropriate policies and practices. If there is an allegation against the officer, should the officer be able to view the footage before answering questions about the incident? If the officer is not allowed to view the footage, will inconsistencies between the footage from the camera and the officer's statement be viewed with sensitivity to the fact that officers' honest perceptions and memories of the entire context are not fully captured in the recording? In the New York City case, the judge's order was presented in response to a specific problem. In such situations, the cameras have a very specific purpose: to ensure that officers properly follow the law in a city where evidence has shown that improper behavior has occurred. In places that have not been proven to have problems with police behavior, is there enough reason to undertake the expense and risks of using the cameras?

Analyzing the Issue

Imagine that you are an advisor to a city's mayor and police chief. Consider the competing arguments and issues surrounding the use of body cameras by police. Prepare a recommendation that includes the three most significant issues for them to address in implementing your recommendation.

Sources: Associated Press, "For Police Body Cameras, Big Costs Loom in Storing Footage," *New York Times*, February 6, 2015 (www.nytimes.com); Harry Bruinius, "Body Cams for NYC Police as a Check on 'Stop and Frisk': A Good Idea?" *Christian Science Monitor*, August 14, 2013 (www.csmonitor .com); Harry Bruinius, "New York Police Test Body Cameras: Effective Deterrent or Privacy Violation?" *Christian Science Monitor*, September 5, 2014 (www.csmonitor.com); Rory Carroll, "California Police Use of Body Cameras Cuts Violence and Complaints," *The Guardian*, November 4, 2013 (www .theguardian.com); J. T. Ready and J. T. N. Young, "Three Myths about Police Body Cams," Slate.com, September 1, 2014 (www.slate.com); D. Thompson, "Forcing America's Weaponized Police to Wear Cameras," *The Atlantic*, August 14, 2014 (www.theatlantic.com).

5. What are the four methods used to increase the civic accountability of the police?
Internal affairs units, civilian review boards, standards and accreditation, civil liability suits.

6. What is an internal affairs unit?
A unit within a police department designated to receive and investigate complaints alleging violation of rules and policies on the part of officers.

7. Why are civilian review boards criticized by police officers?
Police officers often fear that citizens do not understand the nature of law enforcement work and therefore will make inaccurate decisions about what constitutes improper behavior by officers.

What are two arguments in favor of using only professionals in investigating and deciding whether police have acted improperly? What are two arguments in favor of treating citizens as essential participants in these processes? Which set of arguments is more persuasive?

Delivery of Police Services

Law enforcement agencies attempt to structure their organization and processes to provide effective service to the public amid the reality of limited resources. In the contemporary era of significant budget cuts and reductions in personnel affecting agencies in various parts of the country, police departments must make difficult decisions about how to set priorities (Rudolph, 2012). These decisions include such matters as how to distribute officers on patrol and how to prioritize requests for assistance from the public.

Increasingly, police administrators are looking to evidence-based practices as tools for making decisions about deployment of personnel and officers' duties on patrol (Gross-Shader, 2011). With respect to crime prevention, for example, **evidence-based policing** practices draw from research studies that guide police to proactively employ specific strategies aimed at targeted locations within a city or town (Lum, Koper, & Telep, 2011). When they are engaged in specific activities at targeted trouble spots, officers can be more effective in preventing crime.

The effective use of evidence-based practices can be enhanced through cooperation and communication between law enforcement officials and criminal justice researchers. There are voices, however, that urge caution about an exclusive focus on evidence-based crime control research. As Jack Greene (2014:221) notes, "when we focus singularly on crime in geographic areas and [its] increase or reduction, we do not account for police–citizen interactions of a non-criminal nature, which nonetheless influence neighborhood dynamics in high and low crime areas."

evidence-based policing Police strategies and deployment of resources developed through examination of research on crime, social problems, and previously used strategies.

Police Response

In a free society, people do not want police to stand on every street corner and ask them what they are doing. Thus, the police are mainly **reactive** (responding to citizen calls for service) rather than **proactive** (initiating actions in the absence of citizen requests). Studies of police work show that 81 percent of actions result from citizen telephone calls, 5 percent are initiated by citizens who approach an officer, and only 14 percent are initiated in the field by an officer. These facts affect the way departments are organized and the way the police respond to incidents.

Because they are mainly reactive, the police usually arrive at the scene only after the crime has been committed and the perpetrator has fled. This means that the police are hampered by the time lapse and sometimes by inaccurate information given by witnesses. For example, a mugging may happen so quickly that victims and witnesses cannot accurately describe what occurred. In about a third of cases in which police are called, no one is present when the police arrive on the scene.

Citizens have come to expect that the police will respond quickly to every call, whether it requires immediate attention or can be handled in a more routine

reactive Acting in response to a notification about suspicious activity, a crime, a medical emergency, or other service need.

proactive Acting in anticipation; actively searching for potential offenders without waiting for a crime to be reported. Arrests for victimless crimes are usually proactive.

manner. This expectation has produced **incident-driven policing**, in which calls for service are the primary instigators of action. Studies have shown, though, that less than 30 percent of calls to the police involve criminal law enforcement—most calls concern order maintenance and service (S. Walker, 1999:80). To a large extent, then, reports by victims and observers define the boundaries of policing.

Most residents in urban and suburban areas can call 911 to report a crime or obtain help or information. The 911 system has brought a flood of calls to police departments—many not directly related to police responsibilities. In Baltimore, a "311 system" has been implemented to help reduce the number of nonemergency calls, estimated as 40 percent of the total calls. Residents have been urged to call 311 when they need assistance that does not require the immediate dispatch of an officer. Studies found that this innovation reduced calls to 911 and resulted in extremely high public support (Mazerolle et al., 2003).

To improve efficiency, police departments use a **differential response** system that assigns priorities to calls for service. This system assumes that it is not always necessary to rush a patrol car to the scene when a call is received. The appropriate response depends on several factors—such as whether the incident is in progress, has just occurred, or occurred some time ago, as well as whether anyone is or could be hurt.

The police do use proactive strategies such as surveillance and undercover work to combat some crimes. When addressing victimless crimes, for example, they must rely on informers, stakeouts, wiretapping, stings, and raids. Because of the current focus on drug offenses, police resources in many cities have been assigned to proactive efforts to apprehend people who use or sell illegal drugs. As you read "Criminal Justice: Myth & Reality," consider whether the use of proactive strategies will reduce crime.

Productivity

Following the lead of New York City's **CompStat** program, police departments in Baltimore, New Orleans, Indianapolis, and some smaller cities emphasized precinct-level accountability for crime reduction (Bass, 2012; Rosenfeld, Fornango, & Baumer, 2005). Through twice-weekly briefings before their peers and senior executives, precinct commanders must explain the results of their efforts to reduce crime. In the CompStat approach, they are held responsible for the success of crime control efforts in their precincts as indicated by crime statistics (Weisburd, Mastrofski et al., 2003). Essential to this management strategy is timely, accurate information. Accordingly, computer systems have been developed to put up-to-date crime data into the hands of managers at all levels (Willis, Mastrofski, & Weisburd, 2004). This allows discussion of department-wide strategies and puts pressure on low producers (Sherman, 1998:430; Silverman, 1999). However, the CompStat approach has raised questions as to how police work should be measured. It has also raised questions about how to integrate this centralized approach for measuring performance with community policing, a decentralized strategy for crime prevention, order maintenance, and fear reduction (Willis, Mastrofski, & Kochel, 2010).

Quantifying police work is difficult in part because of the wide range of duties and day-to-day tasks of officers. In the past, the crime rate and the clearance rate have been used as measures of "good" policing. A lower crime rate might be cited as evidence of an effective department, but critics note that factors other than policing affect this measure. Like other public agencies, the police departments

incident-driven policing Policing in which calls for service are the primary instigators of action.

differential response A patrol strategy that assigns priorities to calls for service and chooses the appropriate response.

CompStat Approach to crime prevention and police productivity measurement pioneered in New York City and then adopted in other cities that involves frequent meetings among police supervisors to examine detailed crime statistics for each precinct and develop immediate approaches and goals for problem solving and crime prevention.

CRIMINAL JUSTICE

Myth&Reality

COMMON BELIEF: If more police officers were actively patrolling the streets instead of sitting in offices at headquarters, crime rates in a city would certainly decline.

REALITY

- Crime rates are shaped by a complex variety of factors that seem unrelated to the number of officers in a city's police department.
- Some cities with the highest number of officers per capita on the streets also have the highest crime rates.
- In addition, patrols do not necessarily reduce crime. Officers cannot be everywhere at once.
- Cities that have attempted to flood neighborhoods with officers often simply see criminals move their activities to a different location.
- Research raises questions about whether more-numerous patrols impact crime rates.

clearance rate The percentage of crimes known to the police that they believe they have solved through an arrest; a statistic used to measure a police department's productivity.

and the citizens in a community have trouble gauging the quantity and quality of police officers' work.

The **clearance rate**—the percentage of crimes known to police that they believe they have solved through an arrest—is a basic measure of police performance. The clearance rate varies by type of offense. In reactive situations, this rate can be low. For example, the police may learn about a burglary hours or even days after it has occurred; the clearance rate for such crimes is only about 13 percent. Police have much more success in handling violent crimes, in which victims often know their assailants; the clearance rate for such cases is 47 percent (BJS, 2016).

These measures of police productivity are sometimes supplemented by other data, such as the number of traffic citations issued, illegally parked cars ticketed, and suspects stopped for questioning, as well as the value of stolen goods recovered. These additional ways of counting work done reflect the fact that an officer may work hard for many hours but have no arrests to show for his or her efforts. Some of these measures, however, may have adverse consequences for police–community relations. Citizens are usually not happy with the perception that officers may be expected to issue a specific number of traffic citations each day, since it leads residents to believe that officers will make unjustified traffic stops simply to impress superiors. State legislators have begun proposing and passing laws in various states to forbid police departments from imposing traffic ticket quotas on officers (Firozi, 2014). In New York City, during a 2013 lawsuit about racial profiling in stop-and-frisk searches of pedestrians that predominantly affected young African American and Hispanic men, a police chief testified about criticizing officers for not making enough frisks. His description about the pressure applied by supervisory officers raised questions about whether this productivity measure contributed to discriminatory treatment of citizens (Goldstein, 2013). How do we weigh the costs and benefits of using traffic and frisk stops as productivity measures, given that they may effectively encourage officers to employ these strategies too frequently or with a racial bias?

Society may benefit when officers spend their time in activities that are hard to measure, such as calming disputes, becoming acquainted with people in the neighborhood, and providing services to those in need. Some research as well as news stories indicate that officers who engage in activities that produce higher levels of measurable productivity, such as issuing citations or making arrests, also receive higher numbers of citizen complaints about alleged misconduct (Ryley & Gregorian, 2014; Lersch, 2002).

The use of crime statistics for Compstat discussions with precinct commanders is a way to measure productivity and a method of using evidence as the basis for police strategy. Should knowledge of statistics and research methods be required for officers who attain supervisory positions that involve decisions about personnel deployment and crime prevention strategies?

CHECK POINT

8. What is evidence-based policing?
Police strategies and deployment of resources developed through examination of research on crime, social problems, and previously used strategies.

9. What is differential response?
Policy that gives priority to calls according to whether an immediate or delayed response is warranted.

10. What are examples of measures of police productivity?
Crime statistics (CompStat), clearance rate, traffic citations.

STOP & ANALYZE

If you were a police chief, how would you measure your officers' productivity? Suggest two possible measures, and list the advantages and disadvantages of each.

Patrol Functions

Patrol is often called the backbone of police operations. The word *patrol* is derived from a French word, *patrouiller*, which once meant "to tramp about in the mud." This is an apt description of a function that one expert has described as "arduous, tiring, difficult, and performed in conditions other than ideal" (Chapman, 1970: ix). For most Americans, "policing" is the familiar sight of a uniformed and armed patrol officer on call 24 hours a day.

Every local police department has a patrol unit. Even in large departments, patrol officers account for up to two-thirds of all **sworn officers**—those who have taken an oath and received the powers to make arrests and to use necessary force in accordance with their duties. In small communities, police operations are not specialized, and the patrol force is the department. As we have seen, the patrol officer must be prepared for any imaginable situation and must perform many duties.

Television portrays patrol officers as always on the go—rushing from one incident to another and making several arrests in a single shift. A patrol officer may indeed be called to deal with a robbery in progress or to help rescue people from a burning building. However, the patrol officer's life is not always so exciting and often involves routine and even boring tasks such as directing traffic at accident scenes and road construction sites.

Most officers on most shifts do not make even one arrest. To better understand patrol work, examine the classic study illustrated in Figure 5.1 and note how the police of Wilmington, Delaware, allocate time to various activities.

The patrol function has three parts: answering calls for help, maintaining a police presence, and probing suspicious circumstances. Patrol officers are well suited to answering calls, because they usually are near the scene and can move quickly to provide help or catch a suspect. When not answering calls, they engage in **preventive patrol**—that is, making themselves visible and their presence known in an effort to deter crime. Officers are also prepared to respond quickly to any calls. Whether walking the streets or cruising in a car, the patrol officer is on the lookout for suspicious people and behavior. With experience, officers come to trust their own ability to spot signs of suspicious activity that merit stopping people on the street for questioning.

Patrol officers' duties sound fairly straightforward, yet these officers often find themselves in complex situations requiring sound judgment and careful actions.

sworn officers Police employees who have taken an oath and been given powers by the state to make arrests and to use necessary force in accordance with their duties.

preventive patrol Making the police presence known, to deter crime and to enable officers to respond quickly to calls.

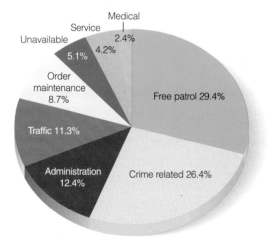

Free patrol: park and walk

Crime related: officer in trouble, suspicious person/vehicle, crime in progress, alarm, investigate crime not in progress, service warrant/subpoena, assist other police

Administration: meal break, report writing, firearms training, police vehicle maintenance, at headquarters, court related

Traffic: accident investigation, parking problems, motor vehicle driving problems, traffic control, fire emergency

Order maintenance: order maintenance in progress, animal complaint, noise complaint

Service: service related

Medical: medical emergency, at local hospital

FIGURE 5.1

Time Allocated to Patrol Activities by the Police of Wilmington, Delaware The time spent on each activity was calculated from records for each police car unit. Note the range of activities and the time spent on each.

Source: Based on J. R. Greene and C. B. Klockars, 1991, "What Police Do," in *Thinking about Police*, 2nd ed., ed. C. B. Klockars and S. D. Mastrofski (New York: McGraw-Hill, 1991), 279.

As the first to arrive at a crime scene, for example, the officer must comfort and give aid to victims, identify and question witnesses, control crowds, and gather evidence. These roles call for creativity and good communication skills.

Because the patrol officers have the most direct contact with the public, their actions in large part determine the image of the police and their relations with the community. Moreover, successful investigations and prosecutions often depend on patrol officers' actions in questioning witnesses and gathering evidence after a crime.

Investigation

detectives Police officers, typically working in plain clothes, who investigate crimes that have occurred by questioning witnesses and gathering evidence.

All cities with a population of more than 250,000 and 90 percent of smaller cities have officers called **detectives** who are assigned to investigative duties. Detectives make up 15 percent of police personnel. Compared with patrol officers, they enjoy a higher status in the department: their pay is higher, their hours are more flexible, and they are supervised less closely. Detectives do not wear uniforms, and their work is considered more interesting than that of patrol officers. In addition, they engage solely in law enforcement rather than in order maintenance or service work; hence, their activities conform more closely to the image of the police as crime fighters.

Within federal law enforcement agencies, the work of special agents is similar to that of detectives. In agencies such as the FBI, DEA, and Secret Service, special agents are plainclothes officers who focus on investigations. One key difference between federal special agents and detectives in local departments is that federal agents are more likely to be proactive in initiating investigations to prevent terrorism, drug trafficking, and other crimes. Local detectives are typically reactive, responding to crimes already discovered.

Detectives typically become involved after a crime has been reported and a patrol officer has done a preliminary investigation. The job of detectives is mainly to talk to people—victims, suspects, witnesses—to find out what happened. On the basis of this information, detectives develop theories about who committed the crime; they then set out to gather the evidence that will lead to arrest and prosecution.

In performing an investigation, detectives depend not only on their own experience but also on technical experts. Much of the information they need comes from criminal files, lab technicians, and forensic scientists. Many small departments turn to the state crime laboratory or the FBI for such information. Often depicted as working alone, detectives, in fact, operate as part of a team.

Apprehension   The discovery that a crime has been committed sets off a chain of events leading to the capture of a suspect and the gathering of the evidence needed to convict that person. It may also lead to several dead ends, such as a lack of clues pointing to a suspect or a lack of evidence to link the suspect to the crime.

The process of catching a suspect has three stages: detection of a crime, preliminary investigation, and follow-up investigation. Depending on the outcome of the investigation, these three steps may be followed by a fourth: clearance and arrest. As shown in Figure 5.2, these actions are designed to use criminal justice resources to arrest a suspect and assemble enough evidence to support a charge.

American police have long relied on science in gathering, identifying, and analyzing evidence. The public has become increasingly aware of the wide range of scientific testing techniques used for law enforcement purposes through the television drama *CSI: Crime Scene Investigation* and its spin-offs (S. Stephens, 2007). As we will examine in greater detail in Chapter 14, scientific analysis of fingerprints, blood, semen, hair, textiles, soil, weapons, and other materials has helped the police identify criminals.

Special Operations

Patrol and investigation are the two largest and most important units in a police department. In metropolitan areas, however, special units are set up to deal with specific types of problems. The most common of such units concern traffic, vice, juveniles, and SWAT (strategic weapons and tactics) teams. Some cities also have units to deal with

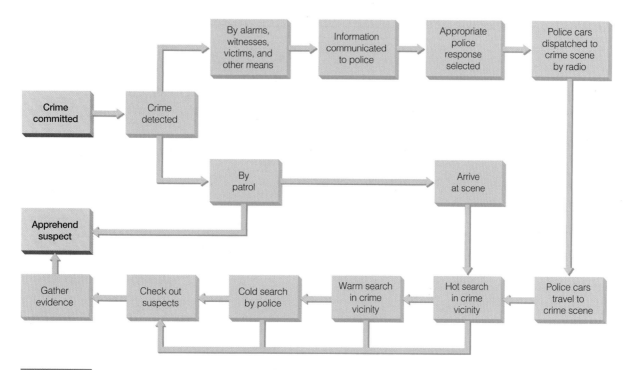

FIGURE 5.2

The Apprehension Process Apprehension of a felony suspect results from a sequence of actions by patrol officers and detectives. Coordination of these efforts is key to solving major crimes.

organized crime and drugs. Even with such special units in place, however, regular patrol officers and investigators continue to deal individually in their daily work with the drugs, juvenile delinquency, and other problems that are targeted by special units.

It is increasingly common for police agencies to cooperate with each other in multi-agency task forces to better address specialized problems that are not confined to a specific spot in one city. Such task-force participation is especially prevalent for the largest cities. For example, more than 80 percent of cities larger than 250,000 participate in antiterrorism task forces, and more than a third of such cities participate in human-trafficking task forces (Reaves, 2010).

As we examine the special units used by many departments, bear in mind that individual officers may receive special assignments, too. A good example is the development of **school resource officers (SROs)**, police officers assigned to high schools under contractual arrangements between public schools and local police departments. More than 85 percent of police departments in cities ranging in size from 25,000 to 500,000 have officers assigned to SRO duty (Reaves, 2010). School resource officers provide a visible presence that may deter misconduct, and they have full authority to enforce laws as well as school rules. They are expected to develop relationships with students, which will permit them to provide advice and guidance. These officers are positioned to help develop positive relationships between young people and police. In addition, they frequently give formal talks in classrooms to educate students about law and the criminal justice system (B. Finn et al., 2005).

However, there are concerns that teenage students may be unnecessarily routed into the criminal justice system as a result of SRO-issued misdemeanor citations for minor behavioral violations—incidents that would traditionally be handled by the high school principal's office (Na & Gottfredson, 2013; Eckholm, 2013). A controversial incident in 2015 recorded on smartphone cameras by students in a South Carolina high school showed a white police officer flipping an African American girl out of her chair to the floor, dragging her to the front of the room, and then handcuffing her (Fausset, Perez-Pena, & Blinder 2015). Her offense: refusing a teacher's instruction to leave the room because she had been caught using her smartphone in class.

school resource officers (SROs)
Police officers assigned for duty in schools to assist in order maintenance while also developing positive relationships with students, which may assist in delinquency prevention.

A police officer carefully dusts the window of a car in order to look for fingerprints that may identify an offender. Police departments use various forensic techniques to discover evidence. Some techniques are used at crime scenes, while others involve tests in scientific laboratories. Which techniques are likely to be most effective?

The incident highlighted evidence that there are racial disparities in the handling of disciplinary issues in schools. It also raised concerns that forceful police tactics are inappropriate in school classrooms.

When officers develop positive relationships with students and use their authority appropriately, there are potential benefits. The use of SROs represents a particularly important form of individualized special assignment, because it shows in one specific setting how police officers' functions and duties extend well beyond the crime-fighting image that is commonly associated with law enforcement.

Traffic Traffic regulation is a major job of the police in which they regulate the flow of vehicles, investigate accidents, and enforce traffic laws. This work may not seem to have much to do with crime fighting or order maintenance, but in fact it does. Besides helping to maintain order, enforcement of traffic laws educates the public by promoting safe driving habits and provides a visible service to the community.

Traffic work is mostly proactive and permits officers to use broad discretion about whom to stop and whether to issue a citation. Traffic duty can also help the police catch criminals, because in enforcing traffic laws, patrol officers can stop cars and question drivers. Stolen property and suspects linked to other criminal acts are often found this way. Most departments can now automatically check license numbers against lists of wanted vehicles and suspects.

Vice Enforcement of vice laws depends on proactive police work, which often involves the use of undercover agents and informers. Most big-city police departments have a vice unit. Strict enforcement of these laws requires that officers be given wide discretion. They often must engage in degrading and dangerous activities, such as posing as prostitutes or drug dealers, in order to catch lawbreakers. The special nature of vice work requires members of the unit to be well trained in the legal procedures required for arrests to lead to convictions.

The potential for corruption in this type of police work presents some administrative problems. Undercover officers are in a position to blackmail gamblers and drug dealers, and they may also be offered bribes. In addition, officers working undercover must be transferred when their identities become known.

Drug Law Enforcement Many large cities have a bureau to enforce drug laws. These agencies may include task forces that deal with organized crime or with gangs involved in drug dealing. Some groups may use sting operations to arrest drug sellers on the street; still others may provide drug education in the community.

Drug enforcement sometimes reflects the goal of *aggressive patrol*, or assigning resources so as to get the largest number of arrests and to stop street dealing. Police executives believe that they must show dealers and the community that drug laws are actively enforced. Streets on which drugs are dealt openly can be flooded with officers who engage in proactive stops and questionings. There are risks, however, that drug dealers will simply move their operations to new locations.

Many public officials argue that drugs should be viewed as a public-health problem rather than as a crime problem. Critics of current policies believe that society would benefit more from drug-treatment programs, which can help some people to stop using drugs, than from police actions that fill prisons without doing much to reduce drug use.

▼ **CHECK POINT**

11. **What are the three parts of the patrol function?**
Answering calls for assistance, maintaining a police presence, probing suspicious circumstances.

12. **What are the four steps in the apprehension process?**
(1) Detection of crime, (2) preliminary investigation, (3) follow-up investigation, (4) clearance and arrest.

13. **What are three kinds of special operations units that police departments often employ?**
Traffic, vice, narcotics.

STOP & ANALYZE

Think about the city or town where you live. Is there a need for a special operations unit in your police department? Why or why not? Give two reasons for your answer.

Issues in Patrolling

In the last 30 years, much research has been done on police methods of assigning tasks to patrol officers, deploying them, and communicating with them. Although the conclusions have been mixed, these studies have caused experts to rethink some aspects of patrolling.

Assignment of Patrol Personnel

In the past, it has been assumed that patrol officers should be assigned where and when they will be most effective in preventing crime, keeping order, and serving the public. For the police administrator, the question has been "Where should the officers be sent, when, and in what numbers?" There are no guidelines to answer this question, and most assignments seem to be based on the notion that patrols should be concentrated in "problem" neighborhoods or in areas where crime rates and calls for service are high. Thus, the assignment of officers is based on factors such as crime statistics, 911 calls, degree of urbanization, pressures from business and community groups, ethnic composition, and socioeconomic conditions. Experimentation with different strategies in various cities has led to numerous choices for police leaders. In addition, research on these strategies sheds light on the strengths and weaknesses of various options. We shall examine several options in greater detail: (1) preventive patrol, (2) hot spots, (3) foot versus motorized patrol, (4) aggressive patrol, and (5) community policing.

Preventive Patrol Preventive patrol has long been thought to help deter crime. Many have argued that a patrol officer's moving through an area will keep criminals from carrying out illegal acts. In 1974 this assumption was tested in Kansas City, Missouri. The surprising results shook the theoretical foundations of American policing (Sherman & Weisburd, 1995).

In the Kansas City Preventive Patrol Experiment, a 15-beat area was divided into three sections, each with similar crime rates, population characteristics, income levels, and numbers of calls to the police. In one area, labeled "reactive," all preventive patrol was withdrawn, and the police entered only in response to citizens' calls for service. In another section, labeled "proactive," preventive patrol was raised to as much as four times the normal level; all other services were provided at the same levels as before. The third section was used as a control, with the usual level of services, including preventive patrol, maintained. After observing events in the three sections for a year, the researchers concluded that the changes in patrol strategies had had no major effects on the amount of crime reported, the amount of crime as measured by citizen surveys, or citizens' fear of crime (Kelling et al., 1974). Neither a decrease nor an increase in patrol activity had any apparent effect on crime.

Despite contradictory findings of other studies using similar research methods, the Kansas City finding "remains the most influential test of the general deterrent effects of patrol on crime" (Sherman & Weisburd, 1995:626). Because of this study many departments have shifted their focus from law enforcement to maintaining order and serving the public. Some have argued that if the police cannot prevent crime by changing their patrol tactics, they may serve society better by focusing patrol activities on other functions while fighting crime as best they can.

Hot Spots   In the past, patrols were organized by "beats." It was assumed that crime can happen anywhere, and the entire beat must be patrolled at all times. Research shows, however, that crime is not spread evenly over all times and places. Instead, direct-contact predatory crimes such as muggings and robberies occur when three elements converge: motivated offenders, suitable targets, and the absence of anyone who could prevent the violation. This means that resources should be focused on *hot spots*, places where crimes are likely to occur.

Advocates of evidence-based policing argue that "place-based policing," such as focusing on hot spots, can prevent crime and also reduce arrests and costs of processing cases (Telep & Weisburd, 2012; Aden & Koper, 2011). According to David Weisburd, "If place-based policing were to become the central focus of police crime prevention, rather than arrest and apprehension of offenders, we would likely see at the same time a reduction in prison populations and an increase in crime prevention effectiveness of the police" (2011:16).

directed patrol A proactive form of patrolling that directs resources to known high-crime areas.

Administrators can assign officers to **directed patrol**—a proactive strategy designed to direct resources to known high-crime areas. Research indicates that directed-patrol activities focused on suspicious activities and locations can reduce violent gun crime (McGarrell et al., 2001). Observers fear, however, that the extra police pressure may simply cause lawbreakers to move to another area (Goldkamp & Vilcica, 2008). But one study found that increased activity in areas adjacent to the hot spots targeted by police was likely attributable to citizens in those areas increasing their willingness to call the police when they knew that police were nearby and eager to address community problems. Thus, there may have been an increase in reported crimes, but no actual increase in crime (B. Taylor, Koper, & Woods, 2010).

Foot versus Motorized Patrol   One of the most frequent citizen requests is for officers to be put back on the beat. This was the main form of police patrol until the 1930s, when motorized patrol came to be viewed as more effective. Foot patrol and bicycle patrol are used in the majority of cities larger than 10,000 residents, including approximately 90 percent of cities with 50,000 or more inhabitants (Hickman & Reaves, 2006). However, departments typically use these strategies only in selected neighborhoods or districts with a high business or population density. Most patrolling is still conducted in cars. Cars increase the amount of territory that officers can patrol; plus, with advances in communications technologies and onboard computers, patrol officers have direct links to headquarters and to criminal information databases. Now the police can be quickly sent where needed, with crucial information in their possession.

In contrast to police in vehicles, officers on foot stay close to the daily life of the neighborhood. They detect criminal activity and apprehend lawbreakers more easily than do car patrols. In addition, recent research indicates that foot patrols can be effective in reducing criminal activities at crime hot spots in neighborhoods (Ratcliffe et al., 2011).

Aggressive Patrol **Aggressive patrol** is a proactive strategy designed to maximize police activity in the community. It takes many forms, such as "sting" operations, firearms confiscation, raids on crack houses, programs that encourage citizens to list their valuables, and the tracking of high-risk parolees. Some have argued that the effect of the police on crime depends less on how many officers are deployed in an area than on what they do while they are there.

aggressive patrol A patrol strategy designed to maximize the number of police interventions and observations in the community.

The zero-tolerance policing of the 1990s in New York City is an example of aggressive patrol linked to the "broken windows" theory. As you will recall, this theory asserts that "if not firmly suppressed, disorderly behavior in public will frighten citizens and attract predatory criminals, thus leading to more serious crime problems" (Greene, 1999:172). Thus, the police should focus on minor public-order crimes such as aggressive panhandling, graffiti, prostitution, and urinating in public. By putting more police on the streets, decentralizing authority to the precinct level, and instituting officer accountability, the zero-tolerance policy was claimed to be a factor in reducing New York City's crime rate (Messner et al., 2007; Rosenfeld, Fornango, & Rengifo, 2007). However, the surge in police stop-and-frisk searches on New York City's streets in the early twenty-first century led to widespread complaints, a major lawsuit, and findings from a federal judge that police tactics were overly intrusive and discriminatory (J. Goldstein, 2013; A. Baker, 2008).

Aggressive policing has also been applied as part of the war on drugs, with police officers stopping many vehicles and frisking pedestrians on certain streets. In Detroit, aggressive zero-tolerance police practices reduced gang-related crime in targeted precincts (Bynum & Varano, 2002). Police departments also use aggressive patrol strategies to track high-risk parolees and apprehend them if they commit new offenses.

Research now raises questions about whether the "broken windows" approach actually reduces crime. Several studies present new analyses of data that challenge claims that it was aggressive policing that caused crime reduction during the 1990s (Harcourt & Ludwig, 2006). In some urban neighborhoods, there are rumblings that aggressive patrol has gone too far and is straining police relations with young African Americans and Hispanics. The new analyses of evidence-based policing argue that police should emphasize crime prevention rather than arrests and, moreover, link their crime prevention efforts to feedback from and communication with people in the community (Lum & Nagin, 2015). In 2016, New York City announced that it would alter its approach from its prior emphasis on aggressive patrol. Instead, certain offenses would be addressed with civil citations and reduced fines rather than the criminal proceedings that have clogged the courts with low-level offenders and alienated minority group members who were subject to disproportionate stops and searches (Goodman, 2016).

Community Policing To a great extent, community policing has been seen as the solution to problems with the crime-fighter stance that prevailed during the professional model era (P. V. Murphy, 1992). Community policing consists of attempts by the police to involve residents in making their own neighborhoods safer. Based on the belief that citizens are often concerned about local disorder as well as crime in general, this strategy emphasizes cooperation between the police and citizens in identifying community needs and determining the best ways to meet them (Reisig, 2010; M. Moore, 1992).

Many police chiefs credit aggressive take-back-the-streets tactics with reducing urban crime rates in the past two decades. In some cities, however, there are questions about whether such tactics have harmed police–community relations through searches and arrests that neighborhood residents view as unjustified. If you were a police chief, what patrol strategy would you choose and what specific goals would you seek to advance?

John Moore/Getty Images

Community policing has four components (Skolnick & Bayley, 1986):

1. Focusing on community-based crime prevention
2. Changing the focus of patrol activities to nonemergency services
3. Making the police more accountable to the public
4. Decentralizing decision making to include residents

As indicated by these four components, community policing requires a particular emphasis in the philosophy of policing. In essence, police officials must view citizens both as customers to be served and as partners in the pursuit of social goals, rather than as a population to be watched, controlled, and served reactively (Morash et al., 2002). Although crime control may remain a priority in community policing, the change in emphasis can strengthen police effectiveness for order maintenance and service (Zhao et al., 2003).

Departments that view themselves as emphasizing community policing do not necessarily share identical patrol strategies and initiatives (Thurman, Zhao, & Giacomazzi, 2001). Some departments emphasize identifying and solving problems related to disorder and crime. Other departments work mainly on strengthening local neighborhoods. A department's emphasis can affect which activities become the focus of officers' working hours. The common element in community-policing programs is a high level of interaction between officers and citizens and the involvement of citizens in identifying problems and solving them.

problem-oriented policing
An approach to policing in which officers routinely seek to identify, analyze, and respond to the circumstances underlying the incidents that prompt citizens to call the police.

A central feature of community policing for many departments is **problem-oriented policing**, a strategy that seeks to find out what is causing citizens to call for help (Weisburd et al. 2010; Goldstein, 1990). The police seek to identify, analyze, and respond to the conditions underlying the events that prompt people to call the police (Maguire, Uchida, & Hassell, 2012; Cordner & Biebel, 2005; DeJong, Mastrofski, & Parks, 2001). Knowing those conditions, officers can enlist community agencies and residents to help resolve them. Recent research indicates that problem-solving approaches can impact various crimes, including drug sales and homicides (Corsaro, Brunson, & McGarrell, 2012; Chermak & McGarrell, 2004). Police using this approach do not just fight crime (M. D. White et al., 2003); they address a broad array of other problems that affect the quality of life in the community.

Read the "Evidence-Based Practice and Policy" feature to examine examples of current research findings concerning police patrol. However, even when

Policing and Patrol

Police administrators make decisions about how to deploy their personnel. They must decide where their officers will patrol, when and how often officers will move down specific streets and sidewalks, and what officers will do at particular locations. Early research called into question the usefulness of having officers randomly patrol a city and wait for calls from citizens about crimes or other problems. Instead, research pointed to the benefits of officers devoting their attention to specific locations, typically referred to as "hot spots," where crimes or related issues of disorder repeatedly occur. Because crime and disorder are not randomly or evenly distributed around a city or town, there are benefits from targeting attention and resources to those places where trouble is known to occur. Evidence indicates that reductions in crime can occur when patrols give emphasis to known hot spots within a community.

In addition, research indicates that there are benefits from officers spending time at hot spots rather than just passing through the area. By spending 15 minutes at a hot spot, officers may create deterrent effects that lead potential lawbreakers to avoid the area or to be careful about their behavior. Moreover, there may be benefits from officers actively seeking to solve problems that they see in the vicinity of hot spots. This presents a merger of *problem-oriented policing (POP)* with a hot-spot focus of patrols. As a result, police may be able to identify physical vulnerabilities to crime for businesses or residences, interact with residents to learn their concerns, and speak to individuals whose behavior troubles other residents in a neighborhood.

Another form of police intervention that shows promising results in research involves direct interactions with offenders and potential offenders to provide clear communications about the consequences of criminal activity. For example, this may involve direct contact with gang members to let them know that they are being watched and that any use of guns or other illegal activities will be dealt with harshly in the criminal justice system.

These evidence-based patrol strategies are proactive in that they lead police officers to plan and carry out a set of activities at particular locations. As such, they differ from the traditional reactive approach to policing. However, the evidence-based approach can lead to the removal of regular patrols from neighborhoods that seldom experience problems, and this may cause unhappiness among citizens who had previously felt reassured by the regular presence of police patrols in their neighborhoods. Because of these and other changes that occur in a move toward evidence-based policing, there can be resistance among officers and members of the public to embrace new police patrol practices.

Researching the Internet

To read about a former police chief's assessment of evidence-based policing, read his views in a National Institute of Justice publication at http://www.nij.gov/journals/269/evidence.htm.

Implementing New Practices

If you were a police chief, how would you incorporate recent research into your plans for patrolling neighborhoods? How would you persuade your officers to adopt new approaches with enthusiasm? How would you reassure citizens who experience a reduction of patrols in their neighborhoods? Write a memo giving the reasoning behind each of your proposals.

Sources: A. Braga, A. Papachristos, and D. Hureau, "The Effects of Hot Spots Policing on Crime: An Updated Systematic Review and Meta-Analysis," *Justice Quarterly* 31(2014): 633–63; C. Lum, C. Koper, and C. Telep, "The Evidence-Based Policing Matrix," *Journal of Experimental Criminology* 7 (2011): 3–26; C. Lum, C. Telep, C. Koper, and J. Grieco, "Receptivity to Research in Policing," *Justice Research and Policy* 14 (2012): 61–95; D. Nagin and D. Weisburd, "Evidence and Public Policy: The Example of Evaluation Research in Policing," *Crimnology & Public Policy* 12: 651–79; B. Taylor, C. Koper, and D. Woods, "A Randomized Controlled Trial of Different Policing Strategies at Hot Spots of Violent Crime," *Journal of Experimental Criminology* 7 (2011): 149–81; C. Telep and D. Weiburd, "What Is Known about the Effectiveness of Police Practices in Reducing Crime and Disorder?" *Police Quarterly* 15 (2012): 331–57.

researchers agree on which patrol practices are the most effective, those practices often run counter to the desires of departmental personnel (Lum et al., 2012). For example, foot patrol may be a key component of community-policing strategies, but many officers would rather remain in squad cars than walk the pavement. Police administrators, therefore, must deal with many issues to successfully develop and implement effective patrol strategies.

The Future of Patrol

Preventive patrol and reactive response to calls for help have been the hallmarks of policing in the United States for the past half century. However, research done in the past 30 years has raised many questions about which patrol strategies police should employ. The rise of community policing has shifted law enforcement toward problems that affect residents' quality of life, and the continuing development of evidence-based policing is resulting in a focus on hot spots. Neighborhoods with crime hot spots may require different strategies than do neighborhoods where residents are concerned mainly with order maintenance. Many researchers believe that traditional patrol efforts have focused too narrowly on crime control, neglecting the order maintenance and service activities for which police departments were originally formed. Critics have urged the police to become more community oriented.

The current era of budget cuts and reductions in police-force personnel will constrict many police chiefs' flexibility in their use of officers. It remains to be seen whether financial problems will reduce various forms of patrol or if they will push departments toward either a purely reactive or a hot-spot emphasis. Some cities already face the worst-case scenario of having every patrol shift reduced to so few officers that they are unable to respond to all calls about felonies (LeDuff, 2011).

How the national effort to combat terrorism will affect local police patrol operations remains uncertain. Since the attacks of September 11, state and local police have assumed greater responsibility for investigating bank robberies and other federal crimes as the FBI and other federal agencies devote significant attention to catching people connected with terrorist organizations (Giblin, Burruss, & Schafer, 2014). In addition, even local police officers must be ready to spot suspicious activities that might relate to terrorist activity. They are the first responders in a bombing or other form of attack. Obviously, federal law enforcement officials must work closely with local police in order to be effective. The new concerns about terrorism do not alter the traditional police responsibilities—crime fighting, order maintenance, and service—but they do provide new challenges for police administrators in planning how to train and deploy their personnel.

▼ **CHECK POINT**

14. **What are the advantages of foot patrol? Of motorized patrol?**
Officers on foot patrol have greater contact with residents of a neighborhood, thus gaining their confidence and assistance. Officers on motorized patrol have a greater range of activity and can respond speedily to calls.

15. **What is aggressive patrol?**
Aggressive patrol is a proactive strategy designed to maximize the number of police interventions and observations in a community.

16. **What are the major elements of community policing?**
Community policing emphasizes order maintenance and service. It attempts to involve members of the community in making their neighborhoods safe. Foot patrol and decentralization of command are usually part of community-policing efforts.

STOP & ANALYZE

If you were a police chief, what approaches to patrol would you choose to implement? Give three reasons for your answer.

Police and the Community

The work of a police officer in a U.S. city can be very difficult, involving hours of boring, routine work interrupted by short spurts of dangerous crime fighting. Although police work has always been frustrating and dangerous, officers today must deal with situations ranging from helping the homeless to dealing with domestic violence to confronting shootouts at drug deals gone sour. Policing actions are sometimes mishandled by officers or misinterpreted by the public, making some people critical of the police in general.

Special Populations

Urban police forces must deal with a complex population. City streets contain growing numbers of people suffering from mental illness, homelessness, alcoholism, drug addiction, or serious medical conditions such as acquired immune deficiency syndrome (AIDS) (Reuland, 2010; Hails & Borum, 2003). In addition, they may find youthful runaways and children victimized by their parents' neglect. Several factors have contributed to increasing numbers of "problem" people on the streets. These factors include overcrowded jails; cutbacks in public assistance; and the closing of many psychiatric institutions, which must then release mental health patients into society. Most of these individuals do not commit crimes, but their presence disturbs many of their fellow citizens and thus may contribute to fear of crime and disorder (T. Coleman & Cotton, 2010).

Patrol officers cooperate with social-service agencies in helping individuals and responding to requests for order maintenance. Police departments have developed various techniques for dealing with special populations, such as the use of Crisis Intervention Teams (CIT) in conjunction with social service agencies (Morgan, 2013; Frantz & Borum, 2011). In some cities, mobile units are equipped with restraining devices and medical equipment to handle disturbed people.

Clearly, dealing with special populations is a major problem for police in most cities. Each community must develop policies so that officers will know when and how they are to intervene when a person may not have broken the law but is upsetting residents (Wexler, 2015). Inevitably, police officers will make mistakes in some situations. For instance, their interactions with troubled people sometimes lead to tragic consequences, such as using lethal force against deaf or mentally ill people whose actions are misperceived as threatening (Romney, 2012; Hubert, 2010).

Policing in a Multicultural Society

In the last half century, the racial and ethnic composition of the United States has changed. During the mid-twentieth century, many African Americans moved from rural areas of the South to northern cities. In recent years, immigrants from

In multicultural America, police must be sensitive to the perspectives and customs of many different groups. They must enforce the law while treating people equally and upholding civil liberties. These responsibilities can be difficult when people are angry or uncooperative. Have you heard about situations in which police officers' emotions, such as anger or frustration, affected their decisions or behavior?

WHAT AMERICANS THINK

QUESTION: "How would you say local police in your area treat racial minorities including African Americans—very fairly, fairly, unfairly (or) very unfairly?"

	very fairly	fairly	unfairly	very unfairly
Non-Hispanic whites	23%	50%	20%	5%
African Americans	8%	44%	33%	15%
Hispanics	15%	56%	23%	6%

CRITICAL THINKING: Can individual police officers take actions that will improve the perceptions and relationship between police and residents in a community? If so, what can officers do?

Based on Gallup Poll, June 15–July 10, 2015 (http://www.gallup .com).

Central and South America have become the fastest-growing minority group in many cities; Hispanics are now the largest minority population in the nation. Immigrants from Eastern Europe, Russia, the Middle East, and Asia have also entered the country in greater numbers than before.

Policing requires trust, understanding, and cooperation between officers and the public. People must be willing to call for help and provide information about wrongdoing. But in a multicultural society, relations between the police and minorities are complicated by stereotypes, cultural variations, and language differences. Most immigrants come from countries with cultural traditions and laws that may be unfamiliar to American police officers. Further, some immigrants cannot communicate easily in English. Lack of familiarity with immigrants' cultural background, difficulties in communicating, and excessive suspicion can increase the risk that officers will violate the American principle of equal treatment of all people (C. E. Smith et al., 2005).

Like other Americans who have limited personal experience or familiarity with people from different backgrounds, officers may attribute undesirable traits to members of minority groups (Miller, Zielaskowski, & Plant, 2012). Treating people according to stereotypes, rather than as individuals, creates tensions that harden negative attitudes. Public opinion surveys have shown that race and ethnicity play a key role in determining people's attitudes toward the police. As seen in the "What Americans Think" feature, questions of fair treatment by the police differ among racial groups (Stewart et al., 2009; Gabbidon & Higgins, 2009). Young, low-income, racial-minority men carry the most negative attitudes toward the police (Gabbidon, Higgins, & Potter, 2011; S. Walker, Spohn, & DeLeone, 2011). Residents of inner-city neighborhoods—the areas that need and want effective policing—often significantly distrust the police; citizens may therefore fail to report crimes and refuse to cooperate with the police (Carr, Napolitano, & Keating, 2007). Encounters between officers and members of these communities are often hostile and sometimes lead to large-scale disorders, as illustrated by this chapter's opening examples of protests in Ferguson, Missouri, and Baltimore. All aspects of officers' responsibilities, including service, order maintenance, and crime control, can suffer when police officers and the communities they serve lack cooperation and trust.

Why do some residents in predominantly minority neighborhoods resent the police? One likely factor is the differential treatment of Americans by police officers that leads Hispanics and African Americans to be disproportionately chosen for searches and other unwanted encounters with police (Rojek, Rosenfeld, & Decker, 2012). Many African Americans perceive themselves as targeted for suspicion when they are engaging in routine activities such as driving their cars or shopping. One recent study found that African American drivers were three times as likely as whites to be subject to investigatory traffic stops that were not based on actual traffic violations and five times as likely as whites to be searched in such stops. Such treatment led 64 percent of African Americans in the study but only 23 percent of the whites to say that you cannot always trust the police to do the right thing (Epp & Maynard-Moody, 2014). If both police and citizens view each other with suspicion or hostility, their encounters will be strained and the potential for conflict will increase.

Community Crime Prevention

There is a growing awareness that the police cannot control crime and disorder on their own. Social control requires involvement by all members of the community. **Community crime prevention** can be enhanced if government agencies and neighborhood organizations cooperate. Across the country, community programs to help the police have proliferated (Wehrman & DeAngelis, 2011; Arthur et al., 2010; Zhao et al., 2002). The federal government has funded and facilitated intergovernmental cooperation and citizen involvement through a variety of programs, including Project Safe Neighborhoods, an anticrime program with a significant focus on antigang efforts and the reduction in illegal firearms.

More than 6 million Americans belong to citizen crime-watch groups, which often have direct ties to police departments. Many communities also use the Crime Stoppers Program to enlist public help in solving crimes. Television and radio stations present the "unsolved crime of the week," sometimes with cash rewards given for information that leads to the conviction of the offender. Although these programs help solve some crimes, the number solved remains small compared with the total number of crimes committed.

community crime prevention Programs through which criminal justice officials cultivate relationships with and rely on assistance from citizens in preventing crime and apprehending offenders within neighborhoods.

CHECK POINT

17. What "special populations" pose challenges for policing?
Runaways and neglected children; people who suffer from homelessness, drug addiction, mental illness, or alcoholism.

18. What factors make policing in a multicultural society difficult?
Stereotyping, cultural differences, language differences.

19. How are citizen watch groups and similar programs helpful to the police?
They assist the police by reporting incidents and providing information.

STOP & ANALYZE

What innovative approaches to training police officers might help them be more effective in serving and working with people in contemporary American neighborhoods? Provide three ideas for training experiences that might help officers become more effective.

Homeland Security

The aftermath of 9/11 has brought expansion, redirection, and reorganization among law enforcement agencies, especially those at the federal level. For instance, the emphasis on counterterrorism has led to an increase in intelligence analysts at the FBI and an increase in the number of FBI special agents assigned to national security duties. The creation of the Department of Homeland Security, the reordering of crime control policies away from street crime and drugs to international and domestic terrorism, and the great increase in federal money directed against the war against terrorism are greatly affecting law enforcement at all levels of government.

This new thrust in policy has shifted the focus of the FBI from the investigation of local street crimes to cases of international and domestic terrorism. Former FBI Director Robert Mueller has acknowledged that following 9/11, many criminal investigations had to be set aside as more agents directed their attention toward al-Qaeda and related threats. Further, the bureau has come to rely on state and local law enforcement to fill the gaps that the FBI could not respond to, such as bank robberies, which are crimes under both federal and state laws.

To meet the challenges of terrorist threats and the increasingly international nature of criminal organizations, U.S. agencies have dramatically boosted the number of officers stationed in foreign countries. The FBI has 70 overseas offices known as Legal Attachés or Legats. These offices focus on coordination with law enforcement personnel in other countries. Their activities are limited by the formal agreements negotiated between the United States and each host country. In many other countries, American agents are authorized only to gather information and facilitate communications between countries. American agencies are especially active in working with other countries on counterterrorism, drug trafficking, and cybercrime (Mueller, 2011b).

Another vehicle for international antiterrorist and anticrime efforts is **Interpol**—the International Criminal Police Organization—created in 1946 to foster cooperation among the world's police forces. Based today in Lyon, France, Interpol maintains an intelligence database and serves as a clearinghouse for information gathered by agencies of its 186 member nations, including the United States. Interpol's six priority crime areas are (1) drugs and criminal organizations, (2) public safety and terrorism, (3) financial and high-tech crime, (4) trafficking in human beings, (5) fugitive apprehension, and (6) corruption (http://www.interpol.int).

Preparing for Threats

The events of September 11, 2001, altered the priorities of government agencies and pushed law enforcement agencies at the federal, state, and local levels to make plans for the possibility of future significant threats to homeland security. The FBI and DHS make concerted efforts to identify and combat risks in order to reduce the threat of additional attacks. The FBI switched a significant portion of its personnel away from traditional crime control activities in order to gather intelligence on people within the United States who may pose a threat to the nation. At the same time, the creation of the DHS reflected a desire to have better coordination between agencies that were previously scattered through the federal government. The DHS also instituted new security procedures at airports and borders as a means of identifying individuals and contraband that pose threats. Many critics believe that the federal government has not done enough to protect ports and critical infrastructure, including nuclear power plants, information systems, subway systems, and other elements essential for the functioning of U.S. society. Attacks with devastating consequences could range from computer hackers disabling key military information systems or computerized controls at energy companies to a suicide airline hijacker hitting a nuclear power or chemical plant. If an attack should target and disable any of these entities, it would fall to local police to maintain order and rescue victims.

Security at borders is an important component of homeland security. **U.S. Border Patrol** agents do not merely look for illegal immigrants and drug traffickers; they must also be aware that terrorists might try to sneak across the border, bringing with them weapons, explosives, and other dangerous materials.

Police agencies have traditionally gathered **law enforcement intelligence** about criminal activities and organizations, especially in their efforts to monitor motorcycle gangs, hate groups, drug traffickers, and organized crime. The new emphasis on homeland security broadens the scope of information that agencies need to gather (Kris, 2011). According to Jonathan White (2004), police must be trained to look for and gather information about such things as

- Emergence of radical groups, including religious groups
- Suspicious subjects observing infrastructure facilities
- Growth of phony charities that may steer money to terrorists
- Groups with links to foreign countries
- Unexpected terrorist information found during criminal searches
- Reports of bomb-making operations

Local police agencies need training that focuses on what to look for and whom to contact if any suspicious activities or materials are discovered. One effort to

---

Interpol The International Criminal Police Organization formed in 1946 and based in France with the mission of facilitating international cooperation in investigating transnational criminal activities and security threats.

U.S. Border Patrol Federal law enforcement agency with responsibility for border security by patrolling national land borders and coastal waters to prevent smuggling, drug trafficking, and illegal entry, including entry by potential terrorists.

law enforcement intelligence Information, collected and analyzed by law enforcement officials, concerning criminal activities and organizations such as gangs, drug traffickers, and organized crime.

Police officers throughout the nation have increased their training in emergency-response procedures in light of threats concerning terrorism and homeland security. In an environment of shrinking budgets, do local police have the time and resources to effectively add homeland security responsibilities to their traditional duties of law enforcement, service, and order maintenance?

J. Emilio Flores/Corbis via Getty Images

share information emerged in the form of **fusion centers** (Perrine, Speirs, & Horwitz, 2010). These are state and local intelligence operations that use law enforcement analysts and sophisticated computer systems to compile and analyze clues and then pass along refined information to various agencies (O'Harrow, 2008). The federal government has provided nearly $250 million for the development and operation of these centers.

The emphasis on information analysis and coordination among agencies at all levels of U.S. government, as well as coordination with foreign governments, also impacts law enforcement operations concerning other major problems, such as drug trafficking, money laundering, gun smuggling, and border security. For example, homeland security efforts overlap with initiatives to combat transnational street gangs. In one such case, the MS-13 gang from Central America has spread from Los Angeles to such places as Washington, DC, and Charlotte, North Carolina, bringing with it various criminal activities, including a series of gang-related homicides (Lineberger, 2011).

Within local police departments, the emphasis on homeland security has led to changes in training, equipment, and operations to prepare first responders to deal with the possibility of weapons of mass destruction and terrorist attacks (Magda, Canton, & Gershon, 2010). The police must also develop regional coordination with neighboring communities and state governments, because large-scale emergencies require the resources and assistance of multiple agencies. Communities need plans for conducting evacuations of buildings and neighborhoods. Police officials must work more closely with firefighters, public health officials, and emergency medical services to prepare for anything from a bomb to a bioterrorist attack using anthrax, smallpox, or other harmful agents. Some of these threats require the acquisition of new equipment, such as protective suits for suspected biological or chemical hazards, or communications equipment that can be used to contact multiple agencies. Many police departments are giving renewed attention to training specialized teams, such as bomb squads and SWAT teams, that will intervene in emergency situations. In addition, they must give all officers additional training on coordination with outside agencies, evacuation procedures for malls and hospitals, and containment of hazardous materials (Devaney, 2015; Perin, 2009).

fusion centers Centers run by states and large cities that analyze and facilitate sharing of information to assist law enforcement and homeland security agencies in preventing and responding to crime and terrorism threats.

20. What have law enforcement officials done to enhance the protection of homeland security?
Planning and coordinating with other agencies, gathering intelligence, acquiring new equipment, and providing training.

In light of the budget cuts affecting state and local government, imagine that you are a governor who must recommend choices about how to allocate shrinking resources. If faced with the following choices—reduce money for homeland security and law enforcement intelligence, reduce money for state police patrols and criminal investigation, or raise taxes— which would you choose and why? Give three reasons for your answer.

New Laws and Controversies

The hijackers' devastating attacks on September 11, 2001, spurred a variety of government actions intended to protect homeland security and combat terrorism. The George W. Bush administration asserted new presidential powers to arrest and detain indefinitely without trial Americans whom it accused of terrorist activities. In 2004, however, the U.S. Supreme Court ruled that the president does not possess unlimited authority and that American detainees are entitled to challenge their confinement through court procedures (*Hamdi v. Rumsfeld*, 2004). The Supreme Court's decision illustrates one aspect of the challenge facing the United States: how to provide government with sufficient power to fight terrorism while also protecting individuals' constitutional rights.

In 2011, the National Defense Authorization Act, which provides annual funding for the military, included provisions permitting terrorism suspects to be arrested and detained indefinitely and permitting the military to detain and question terrorism suspects on American soil. These provisions generated harsh criticism from civil libertarians who feared the expansion of governmental powers and the potential for Americans to be denied their rights. However, members of Congress claimed that the wording was carefully designed to balance individuals' rights with national security. President Obama expressed misgivings about the language but signed the bill into law in December 2011 (Klain, 2012; Nakamura, 2012).

Other controversies have developed concerning new state and federal statutes created since September 11. Both Congress and state legislatures have enacted new laws aimed at addressing various aspects of homeland security. More than 30 states have added new terrorism-related laws. These laws range from narrow to broad— from statutes addressing specific problems to authorizations of new powers for law enforcement officials and the definition of new crimes. At the narrow end of the spectrum, for example, Virginia passed a law to make it more difficult for foreign nationals to obtain a driver's license without possession of specific legal documents. This was in direct response to the discovery that several of the September 11 hijackers had obtained Virginia driver's licenses.

Because new laws provide tools for justice system officials, controversies can arise when those officials apparently stretch their authority beyond the intentions of the relevant statutes. For example, prosecutors in several cases have used new terrorism laws as a means to prosecute people for criminal acts that are not commonly understood to be related to terrorism. Thus, in New York, one of the first prosecutions under the state's antiterrorism laws enacted after September 11 arose when the Bronx district attorney charged street gang members with various crimes. There was no allegation that the gang members had connections to any foreign terrorist networks, but the prosecutor used the state's antiterrorism law to charge gang members with shootings committed with the intent to intimidate or coerce a civilian population (Garcia, 2005). In another example, a North Carolina prosecutor charged the operator of a small meth lab under a terrorism statute for manufacturing a nuclear or chemical weapon ("Charging Common Criminals," 2003). In 2014, a Michigan man who was diagnosed by psychiatrists with a delusional disorder was sentenced to fewer than 10 years on felonious assault charges for driving down the highway firing a gun at other cars. However, he received a sentence of 16 to 40 years for terrorism charges pursued by prosecutors for these actions (Abdilla & Kranz, 2014). These cases generated criticism in newspaper editorials and raised concerns that government officials would exploit terrorism laws for improper purposes.

The most controversial legislation came from Congress in the form of the "Uniting and Strengthening America by Providing Appropriate Tools Required to Intercept and Obstruct Terrorism Act." It is best known by its shorthand name, the **USA PATRIOT Act**. The PATRIOT Act moved quickly through Congress after the September 11 attacks and covered a wide range of topics, including the expansion of government authority for searches and surveillance and the expansion of definitions and penalties for crimes related to terrorism.

USA PATRIOT Act A federal statute passed in the aftermath of the terrorist attacks of September 11, 2001, that broadens government authority to conduct searches and wiretaps and expands the definitions of crimes involving terrorism.

Critics have raised concerns about many provisions because of fears that the government's assertions of excessive power will violate individuals' rights (Ahmadi, 2011; Lichtblau, 2008; Dority, 2005). The PATRIOT Act made it easier for law enforcement officials to monitor e-mail and obtain "sneak-and-peek" warrants in which they secretly conduct searches and do not inform the home or business owner that the premises have been searched until much later (K. M. Sullivan, 2003). The PATRIOT Act also authorized warrantless searches of third-party records such as those at libraries, financial institutions, phone companies, and medical facilities. This provision sparked an outcry from librarians and booksellers and was cited by many of the 150 communities across the country that passed resolutions protesting the excessive authority granted to government by the Act (J. Gordon, 2005). Despite the outcry, Congress approved extensions of the PATRIOT Act's key provisions in 2011 and 2015.

The PATRIOT Act defines domestic terrorism as criminal acts dangerous to human life that appear intended to intimidate civilians or influence public policy by intimidation. It also makes it a crime to provide material support for terrorism. Conservatives fear the law could be used against antiabortion protestors who block entrances at abortion clinics, as well as against their financial supporters. Liberals fear that it could be used against environmental activists and their financial supporters (Zerwas, 2011; Lithwick & Turner, 2003).

In 2013, new controversies arose when Edward Snowden, whom some view as a traitor and others view as a heroic whistleblower, revealed that the National Security Agency collected phone call information on virtually all Americans as well as calls involving foreign governments. One federal judge ruled that the agency's actions likely violated the U.S. Constitution. Yet even this judge acknowledged the difficulty in striking a proper balance between national security interests and individuals' privacy interests (Nakashima & Marimow, 2013).

The debates about new laws and policies as part of homeland security and counterterrorist efforts illustrate the struggle to maintain American values of personal liberty, privacy, and individual rights while simultaneously ensuring that law enforcement personnel have sufficient power to protect the nation from catastrophic harm.

Now that we have considered the government's role in homeland security, we turn our attention to the private sector. Corporations and other entities must safeguard their assets, personnel, and facilities. They, too, have heightened concerns about terrorism and other homeland security issues. For example, nuclear power plants, chemical factories, energy companies, and other private facilities make up part of the nation's critical infrastructure. Because terrorists might target such facilities, private-sector officials must address these concerns, just as they have long needed to address other security issues such as employee theft, fires, and trade secrets.

CHECK POINT	STOP & ANALYZE
21. What are the criticisms directed at the USA PATRIOT Act? Permits too much government authority for searches and wiretaps; defines domestic terrorism in ways that might include legitimate protest groups.	Are you willing to give up any of your rights and liberties in order to grant the government more power to take actions to strengthen homeland security? If so, which rights and liberties? If not, why not?

Security Management and Private Policing

Only a few years ago, the term *private security* called to mind the image of security guards, people with marginal qualifications for other occupations who ended up accepting minimal wages to stand guard outside factories and businesses. This image reflected a long history of private employment of individuals who served limited police patrol functions. In recent years, by contrast, private-sector activities related to policing functions have become more complex and important.

Many threats have spurred an expansion in security management and private policing; these include (1) an increase in crime in the workplace; (2) an increase in fear (real or perceived) of crime; (3) the fiscal crises of the states, which have limited public-police protection; and (4) increased public and business awareness and use of more cost-effective private security services (Steden & Sarre, 2007; Cunningham, Strauchs, & Van Meter, 1990). Today if one speaks of people employed in private security, it would be more accurate to envision them working in a variety of occupations—from traditional security guards to computer security experts to corporate vice presidents responsible for planning and overseeing safety and security at their companies' industrial plants and office complexes around the world.

Nationally, retail and industrial firms spend nearly as much for private protection as state and local governments spend for police protection. Many government entities hire private companies to provide security at specific office buildings or other facilities. In addition, private groups, such as residents of wealthy suburbs, have hired private police to patrol their neighborhoods. There are now more officers hired by private security companies than there are public police (Strom et al., 2010).

Contemporary security managers are well-educated professionals with administrative experience and backgrounds in management and law. They are responsible for evaluating security needs, acquiring technology, training personnel, complying with relevant laws and regulations, and cooperating with law enforcement officials. Are there any businesses or industries that do not need the services of security personnel in today's fast-changing world?

Juice Images/Alamy Stock photo

Functions of Security Management and Private Policing

Top-level corporate security managers have a wide range of responsibilities that in the public sector would cover several job descriptions: they simultaneously function as police chiefs, fire chiefs, emergency-management administrators, and computer-security experts. They hire, train, and supervise expert personnel to protect corporate computer systems that may contain credit card numbers, trade secrets, confidential corporate financial information, and other data sought by hackers intent on causing destruction or stealing money. This is an important issue for American consumers in light of the number of times that hackers have stolen social security numbers, credit card numbers, and other private information from the computer systems of major corporations (Constantin, 2016).

Frequently security managers combat cybercriminals who are attacking their computer resources from overseas and are therefore beyond the reach of U.S. law enforcement officials. They also plan security systems and emergency-response plans for fires and other disasters. Such plans include provisions for evacuating large buildings and coordinating their efforts with local police and fire departments in a variety of locales. In addition, they develop security systems to prevent employee theft that may involve sophisticated schemes to use company computer systems to transfer financial assets for illegal purposes. Because so many American companies own manufacturing plants and office buildings overseas, security companies must often implement their services in diverse countries around the globe.

At lower levels, specific occupations in private security compare more closely with those of police officers. Many security personnel are the equivalent of private-sector detectives. They must investigate attacks on company computer systems or activities that threaten company assets. Thus, for example, credit card companies have large security departments that use computers to monitor unusual activity on individual customers' credit cards, which may signal that a thief is using the card. Private-sector detectives must also investigate employee theft. Because this criminal activity extends beyond simple crimes such as stealing money from a store's cash register, investigations might examine whether people are making false reports on expense accounts, using company computers to run private businesses, or misspending company money.

Other activities compare more directly to those of police patrol officers, especially those of security officers who must guard specific buildings, apartments, or stores. The activities of these private security personnel vary greatly: some act merely as guards and call the police at the first sign of trouble, others have the power to carry out patrol and investigative duties similar to those of police officers, and still others rely on their own presence and the ability to make a citizen's arrest to deter lawbreakers.

Private Police and Homeland Security

Private-sector corporations control security for vital facilities in the United States, including nuclear power plants, oil refineries, military manufacturing facilities, and other important sites (Nalla, 2002). Fires, tornadoes, or earthquakes at such sites could release toxic materials into the air and water. Thus, emergency planning is essential for public safety (Simonoff et al., 2011). Moreover, because these sites are now recognized as potential targets of terrorist attacks, the role and effectiveness of security managers matter more than ever to society. They must work closely with law enforcement executives and other government officials to institute procedures that reduce known risks and to participate in emergency-preparedness planning.

Private Employment of Public Police

The officials responsible for asset protection, safety, and security at the top levels of major corporations are often retired police administrators or former military personnel. For example, recently retired New York City Police Commissioner

Raymond Kelly served as senior managing director of Global Corporate Security for a Wall Street financial firm after he left his position as director of the U.S. Customs Service and before he was appointed to serve as police commissioner.

The reliance on people with public-sector experience for important positions in private security management reflects the fact that asset protection and security management have only recently become emphasized as topics in college and university programs; relatively few professionals have yet gained specific educational credentials in this important area. As a result, the placement of retired law enforcement officials in high-level positions has often created opportunities for strategic communication and coordination between top-level security managers and public-sector police administrators.

At operational levels of security management, private security and local police often make frequent contact. Private firms are usually eager to hire public police officers on a part-time basis. Although police departments may forbid moonlighting by their officers, some departments simultaneously facilitate and control the hiring of their officers by creating specific rules and procedures for off-duty employment. For example, the New York City Police Department coordinates a program called the Paid Detail Unit. Event planners, corporations, and organizations can hire uniformed, off-duty officers for $37 per hour. The police department must approve all events at which the officers will work, and the department imposes an additional 10 percent administrative fee for the hiring of its officers. Thus, the department can safeguard against officers working for organizations and events that will cause legal, public relations, or other problems for the police department. The department can also monitor and control how many hours its officers work so that private, part-time employment does not lead them to be exhausted and ineffective during their regular shifts.

Several models have been designed to manage off-duty employment of officers. Some approaches can lead to controversy, as in New Orleans in 2011 when several high-ranking police officials were revealed to be earning six-figure incomes beyond their police salaries by imposing "coordination fees" as part of their authority over choosing which officers would perform security work at movie sets, football games, and other private settings (McCarthy, 2012).

The *department contract model* permits close control of off-duty work, because firms must apply to the department to have officers assigned to them. New York City's system fits this model. Officers chosen for off-duty work are paid by the police department, which is reimbursed by the private firm, along with an overhead fee. Departments usually screen employers to make sure that the proposed use of officers will not conflict with the department's needs.

The *officer contract model* allows each officer to find off-duty employment and to enter into a direct relationship with the private firm. Officers must apply to the department for permission, which is granted if the employment standards listed earlier are met. Problems can arise when an officer acts as an employment agent for other officers. This can lead to charges of favoritism and nepotism, with serious effects on discipline and morale.

In the *union brokerage model*, the police union or association finds off-duty employment for its members. The union sets the standards for the work and bargains with the department over the pay, status, and conditions of the off-duty employment.

The Public–Private Interface

The relationship between public and private law enforcement is a concern for police officials. Because private agents work for the people who employ them, their goals might not always serve the public interest. Questions have arisen about the power of private security agents to make arrests, conduct searches, and take part in undercover investigations. A key issue is the boundary between the work of the police and that of private agencies.

Criminal activity within a company is often considered a "private" issue. Many security managers in private firms tend to treat crimes by employees as internal matters that do not concern the police. They report UCR index crimes to the police, but employee theft, insurance fraud, industrial espionage, commercial bribery, and computer crime tend not to be reported to public authorities. In such cases, the chief concern of private firms is to prevent losses and protect assets. Most of these incidents are resolved through internal procedures (private justice). When such crimes are discovered, the offender may be convicted and punished within the firm by forced restitution, loss of the job, and the spreading of information about the incident throughout the industry. Private firms often bypass the criminal justice system so they do not have to deal with prosecution policies, administrative delays, rules that would open the firms' internal affairs to public scrutiny, and bad publicity. Thus, the question arises: to what extent does a parallel system of private justice exist with regard to some offenders and some crimes?

Recruitment and Training

Increasingly, higher-level security managers are college graduates with degrees in criminal justice who have taken additional coursework in such subjects as business management and computer science. These graduates are attracted to the growing private-sector employment market for security-related occupations, because the jobs often involve varied, complex tasks in a white-collar work environment. In addition, they often gain corporate benefits such as quick promotion, stock options, and other perks unavailable in public-sector policing.

By contrast, the recruitment and training of lower-level private security personnel present a major concern to law enforcement officials and civil libertarians (Enion, 2009; Strickland, 2011). These personnel carry the important responsibility of guarding factories, stores, apartments, and other buildings. Often on the scene when criminal activity occurs, they are the private security personnel most likely to interact with the public in emergency situations. Moreover, any failure to perform their duties could lead to a significant and damaging event, such as a robbery or a fire. Lack of coordination and communication between public and private agencies has led to botched investigations, destruction of evidence, and overzealousness.

Joe Raedle/Staff/Getty Images

Today's security personnel must be aware of numerous potential threats and have the necessary training and equipment to communicate with law enforcement officials. If security guards are minimum-wage employees, are they likely to have the qualifications and commitment to provide adequate security at important private enterprises such as chemical factories and nuclear power plants?

Growing awareness of this problem has led to efforts to have private security agents work more closely with the police. Current efforts to enhance coordination involve emergency planning, building security, and general crime prevention. However, effective coordination may be hampered if private firms lack standards for hiring and conduct little training for their employees.

In spite of these important responsibilities, which parallel those of police patrol officers, studies have shown that such personnel often have little education and training. A national study in 2008 found that 46 percent of private security officers had only a high school diploma or even less education and just 12 percent had bachelor's degrees. In addition, the median annual pay for private security officers is less than half that of police officers. Many private security officers are paid only minimum wage (Strom et al., 2010). Because the pay is low, the work often attracts people who cannot find other jobs or who seek temporary work. For example, private security firms in San Francisco reported annual staff turnover rates as high as 300 percent because their low pay and benefits led employees continually to seek higher-paying jobs, especially when better-paid public-sector security work opened up, such as jobs as airport screeners (Lynem, 2002).

The growth of private policing has brought calls for the screening and licensing of its personnel. However, there has been no systematic national effort to standardize training and licensing for private security personnel. As indicated in Figure 5.3, only eight states require all private security officers to be licensed. Other states require licensing only for contractual security officers or those carrying firearms. Remarkably, 16 states require no licensing at all (Strom et al., 2010).

The regulations that do exist tend to focus on contractual, as opposed to proprietary, private policing. Contractual security services are provided for a fee by locksmiths; alarm specialists; polygraph examiners; and firms such as Brink's, Burns, and Wackenhut, which provide guards and detectives. States and cities often

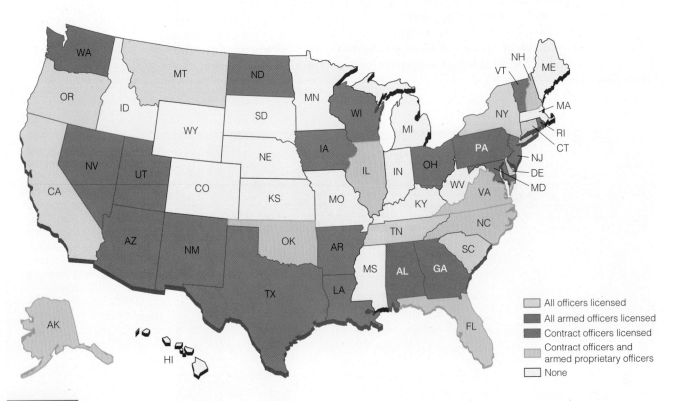

FIGURE 5.3

Licensing Requirements for Security Officers by State, 2009

Source: K. Strom, M. Berzofsky, B. Shook-Sa, K. Barrick, C. Daye, N. Horstmann, and S. Kinsey. *The Private Security Industry: A Review of the Definitions, Available Data Sources, and Paths Moving Forward.* Report prepared for Bureau of Justice Statistics, December 2010 (https://www.nqrs.gov/pdffiles1/bjs/grants/232781.pdf).

require contract personnel to be licensed and bonded. Similar services are sometimes provided by proprietary security personnel, who are employed directly by the organizations they protect—retail stores, industrial plants, hospitals, and so forth. Except for those who carry weapons, proprietary security personnel are not usually regulated by the state or city. Certainly the importance of private security and its relation to public policing demands further exploration of these and related issues in the years to come.

▼ CHECK POINT

22. What has caused the growth of security management and private policing?
Companies' recognition of the need to protect assets and to plan for emergencies, as well as problems with employee theft, computer crime, and other issues that require active prevention and investigation.

23. What are the three models for private employment of police officers?
Department contract model, officer contract model, and union brokerage model.

STOP & ANALYZE

To what extent can private security replace public police when police personnel and services are reduced due to state and city budget cuts? Give two examples of situations or places where private security can fill the gap and two situations where private security cannot effectively provide replacement services.

? A QUESTION OF ETHICS

Think, Discuss, Write

Go online to watch one of the videos of police officers in California beating suspects who were lying on the ground after being chased by officers. One, Francis Pusok, was an identity-theft suspect who also stole a horse; the other, Stanislav Petrov, allegedly stole a car. Visit http://www.cnn.com/2015/04/10/us/california-san-bernardino-police-beating/ OR http://www.theguardian.com/us-news/2015/nov/17/san-francisco-police-beating-captured-video.

In one incident, filmed from a TV news helicopter, multiple officers kicked and punched Pusok dozens of times after he was lying on the ground putting his hands behind his back. In the other incident, captured on video by a security camera in an alley, two officers beat Petrov repeatedly about the head with batons after tackling him and forcing him to the ground.

Discussion/Writing Assignment

Imagine that you are a police supervisor reviewing one of these videos. What, if anything, do you do after seeing the video? Write a memo analyzing whether the treatment of the suspect was appropriate and what actions, if any, you would take as a supervisor. Within the memo, provide rules for the circumstances in which officers can properly use this form of force.

Sources: R. Ellis and M. Pearson, "FBI Probing Possible Civil Rights Violations in California Videotaped Beating," CNN April 13, 2015 (http://www.cnn.com/2015/04/10/us/california-san-bernardino-police-beating/); J. Mayton, "San Francisco Police Beating Captured on Video Prompts Call for Charges," *The Guardian*, November 18 (http://www.theguardian.com/us-news/2015/nov/17/san-francisco-police-beating-captured-video).

SUMMARY

1 Describe the everyday actions of police.
- To carry out their mission, the police must have the public's cooperation and assistance because they depend on the public to help them identify crime and carry out investigations.
- Factors affect how police exercise discretion and make choices about actions, especially in ambiguous situations when it is not clear how to apply the law.

2 Identify the ways police can abuse their power and the challenges of controlling this abuse.
- Police corruption and excessive use of force erode community support.
- Studies of excessive use of force, especially the use of lethal force, raise questions about whether it is used in a biased manner.

- Police corruption includes officers who actively seek personal gain and others who simply accept the gifts and payoffs that come their way.

3 List the methods that can be used to make police more accountable to citizens.
- Internal affairs units, civil review boards, standards and accreditation, and civil liability lawsuits increase police accountability to citizens.

4 Describe the delivery of police services.
- The police are mainly reactive rather than proactive, which often leads to incident-driven policing.
- The productivity of a force can be measured in various ways, including clearance rate; however, measuring proactive approaches is more difficult.
- Police services are delivered through the work of the patrol, investigation, and specialized operations units.
- The patrol function has three components: answering calls for assistance, maintaining a police presence, and probing suspicious circumstances.
- The investigative function is the responsibility of detectives, who work in close cooperation with patrol officers.
- The felony apprehension process is a sequence of actions that includes crime detection, preliminary investigation, follow-up investigation, and clearance and arrest.
- Large departments usually have specialized units dealing with traffic, drugs, and vice.

5 Name patrol strategies that departments employ.
- Police administrators make choices about possible patrol strategies, which include preventive patrol, hot spots, foot versus motorized patrol, aggressive patrol, and community policing.
- Community policing seeks to involve citizens in identifying problems and working with police officers to prevent disorder and crime.

6 Explain the importance of connections between the police and the community.
- Police face challenges in dealing with special populations, such as the mentally ill and homeless, who need social services yet often disturb or offend other citizens as they walk the streets.
- Policing in a multicultural society requires an appreciation of the attitudes, customs, and languages of minority group members.
- To be effective, the police must maintain their connection with the community.

7 Identify issues and problems that emerge from law enforcement agencies' increased attention to homeland security.
- Homeland security has become an important priority for law enforcement agencies at all levels of government since September 11, 2001.
- Agencies need planning and coordination in order to gather intelligence and prepare for possible threats and public emergencies.
- The federal government provides funding for state and local fusion centers and emergency-preparedness equipment.
- New laws such as the USA PATRIOT Act have caused controversy about the proper balance between government authority and citizens' rights.

8 Describe the policing and related activities undertaken by private-sector security management.
- The expansion of security management and private policing reflects greater recognition of the need to protect private assets and to plan for emergencies.
- Security management produces new issues and problems, including concerns about the recruitment, training, and activities of lower-level private security personnel.
- Public–private interaction affects security through such means as joint planning for emergencies, hiring of private firms to guard government facilities, and hiring of police officers for off-duty private security work.

Questions for Review

1. What problems are posed by police corruption and excessive use of force?
2. What is the purpose of patrol? How is it carried out?
3. What responsibilities in large cities are handled by special operations units?
4. What problems do officers face in policing a diverse, multicultural society?
5. What have law enforcement agencies done to enhance homeland security?
6. What problems are associated with private policing?

Key Terms

aggressive patrol (p. 185)

civilian review board (p. 172)

clearance rate (p. 178)

Commission on Accreditation for Law Enforcement Agencies (CALEA) (p. 172)

community crime prevention (p. 191)

CompStat (p. 177)

detectives (p. 180)

differential response (p. 177)

directed patrol (p. 184)

domestic violence (p. 165)

evidence-based policing (p. 176)

excessive use of force (p. 167)

fusion centers (p. 193)

incident-driven policing (p. 177)

internal affairs units (p. 172)

Interpol (p. 192)

law enforcement intelligence (p. 192)

police corruption (p. 170)

preventive patrol (p. 179)

proactive (p. 176)

problem-oriented policing (p. 186)

reactive (p. 176)

school resource officers (SROs) (p. 181)

Section 1983 lawsuits (p. 174)

sworn officers (p. 179)

U.S. Border Patrol (p. 192)

USA PATRIOT Act (p. 195)

6 Police and Law

LEARNING OBJECTIVES

1 Describe the extent of police officers' authority to stop people and to conduct searches of people, their vehicles, and other property.

2 Explain how police officers seek warrants in order to conduct searches and make arrests.

3 Describe situations in which police officers can examine property and conduct searches without obtaining a warrant.

4 Explain the purpose of the privilege against compelled self-incrimination.

5 Define the exclusionary rule, and identify the situations in which it applies.

Police officers stopped David Riley's vehicle because they noticed that his license tags had expired. When they checked his driver's license, they discovered that it, too, had expired. Following departmental procedure in situations of drivers without valid licenses, they impounded his vehicle—that is, they seized it so that it would be in police possession. Impounded vehicles are typically released after the owner has complied with registration requirements and paid any fines for traffic violations, such as lapsed registrations. Such vehicles are subject to a warrantless inventory search so that officers can make a list of what is inside the vehicle and thereby avoid later claims that they lost or destroyed an individual's property after impounding and taking possession of the vehicle. Inventory searches also serve as a permissible way to look for criminal evidence when there is a basis for impounding a vehicle. In this case, they found two handguns, so they arrested Riley for illegal possession of concealed weapons.

Upon arrest, individuals are subject at the scene of arrest to a pat-down search of their clothing so officers can make sure that they are not concealing any weapons or evidence. The search revealed that Riley had a cell phone in his pants pocket as well as items associated with membership in a street gang. About two hours after the arrest, a detective specializing in gangs at the police station accessed photographs and information from Riley's cell phone. Among the photos on the phone was one of Riley standing in front of a vehicle that police believed had been involved in a shooting a few weeks earlier.

Riley was ultimately charged with several offenses related to the shooting, including attempted murder. He was also charged under a state statute that enhanced sentences for those convicted of felonies that were committed to advance the interests of a street gang. Riley's defense attorney asked the judge to exclude from consideration all evidence obtained from the cell phone, claiming that the examination of the cell phone's contents was an improper police search in violation of Riley's Fourth Amendment rights against "unreasonable searches." The judge rejected that argument; photos from the cell phone were introduced into evidence against Riley, and officers testified about photos and videos that they viewed on the cell phone. Riley was convicted and given a sentence of 15 years to life in prison.

Riley's attorney appealed, based on the Fourth Amendment claim originally rejected by the trial judge. The California Court of Appeals endorsed the trial judge's decision, based on an earlier California Supreme Court case, that police officers can make warrantless examinations of the contents of cell phones seized upon the arrest of criminal suspects. The California Supreme Court declined to hear the case, so the attorney took the case to the U.S. Supreme Court. Because cases typically move slowly through the various stages of the court system, the Supreme Court did not actually hear arguments in the case until nearly five years after the original arrest.

After hearing oral arguments from attorneys for both sides in the case on April 29, 2014, the Supreme Court issued a unanimous majority opinion written by Chief Justice John Roberts on June 25, 2014. The Court declared that Riley's attorney was correct. The warrantless search of Riley's cell phone to obtain information for use against him in a criminal trial violated his Fourth Amendment rights. Such successful claims in the appellate courts do not automatically declare that an individual is innocent and must be set free. Instead, they typically mean that an individual is entitled to a new trial in which the improperly obtained evidence is excluded from consideration. However, there is often other evidence, such as witness testimony, fingerprints on guns, and crime-scene evidence, that can be used to convict the individual again at a second trial.

The Supreme Court noted that police officers are entitled to search the clothing and immediate area around anyone that they arrest to make sure that there are no weapons that could harm the officers or others and that no nearby evidence can be destroyed by the arrestee. Thus the Court approved examining a cell phone found in such a search to make sure that no razor blades or other weapons are physically concealed in the cell phone. However, in order to examine the data contained inside a cell phone, officers must obtain a warrant from a judge. In order to obtain a warrant, officers would need to persuade the judge that there is a basis to conclude that the cell phone contains

AP Images/Mike Groll

criminal evidence. The Supreme Court opinion provided a clear acknowledgement that for people in contemporary society, cell phones can contain an extensive array of deeply personal information that government officials should not automatically be able to access and examine simply by making an arrest.

As you will see in "A Question of Ethics" at the end of this chapter, news reports have periodically surfaced indicating that some male officers in California, Texas, and presumably other places had been seizing cell phones from people at traffic stops and automobile collisions solely to look for nude or bathing-suit photos of female drivers in order to share those photos with other male officers for their personal entertainment (Friedersdorf, 2014). In one particularly outrageous case, an officer was caught not only stealing nude photos from a woman's phone after a traffic stop, but actually calling the woman later to invite her out to dinner (McVicker, 2005). The Supreme Court's opinion did not discuss this example of privacy invasions that can occur when police feel free to examine the contents of cell phones at their own discretion. Obviously, most Americans are likely to view such actions by police as serious and unjustified invasions of personal privacy. By clarifying the law concerning warrantless cell-phone searches, the Supreme Court's opinion provided a very clear basis for citizens to sue police officers for constitutional rights violations when such searches occur.

In *Riley v. California* (2014), the U.S. Supreme Court justices and lower court judges in California were interpreting the ambiguous words "unreasonable searches" from the Fourth Amendment. As we examine other Supreme Court decisions, think about the challenge presented by the necessity of applying brief phrases from the Bill of Rights to actual situations, thereby determining which people can be searched and questioned and, more importantly, whether certain individuals will spend many years in prison.

In this chapter, we examine individual rights and how those legal protections define the limits of police officers' powers of investigation and arrest. In particular, we look closely at two rights that were introduced in Chapter 3: the Fourth Amendment protection against unreasonable searches and seizures and the Fifth Amendment privilege against compelled self-incrimination.

Legal Limitations on Police Investigations

The provisions of the Bill of Rights embody very important American values regarding individual rights in society. They reflect the belief that we do not want to give government officials absolute power to pursue investigations and prosecutions, because that approach to crime control would impose excessive costs on the values of individual liberty, privacy, and due process. If police could do whatever they wanted to do, people would lack protections against arbitrary searches and arrests. On the other hand, crime control is an important policy goal; we do not want individuals' expectations about legal protections to restrict law enforcement officers' ability to protect citizens from crime or to punish wrongdoers. Judges must therefore seek to interpret the Constitution in ways that properly balance crime control and the protection of individual rights.

How does an officer know when her or his actions might violate laws protecting an individual's rights? Individual police officers do not have time to follow the details of the latest court decisions. That responsibility rests with those who train and supervise law enforcement officers. Officers depend on the information provided at the police academy and subsequent updates from city and state attorneys who monitor court decisions. Thus, police officers' compliance with the law depends on their own knowledge and decisions as well as those of their supervisors.

Search and Seizure Concepts

The Fourth Amendment prohibits police officers from undertaking "unreasonable searches and seizures." The Supreme Court defines a **search** as an action by law enforcement officials that intrudes on people's **reasonable expectation of privacy**. For example, someone who places a personal diary in a locked drawer within a bedroom of her home has demonstrated a reasonable expectation of privacy. Police officers cannot simply decide to enter her home in order to open the locked drawer and read the diary. But many situations raise questions about people's reasonable expectations. Should people reasonably expect a police officer not to reach into their pockets in order to see if they have guns? Should people reasonably expect an officer not to walk up to their houses and attempt to peer through small cracks in the window blinds? Should people expect that the text messages on their phones will not be examined by employers or police officers? (Wells & Keasler, 2011). Although judges do not always answer these questions in clear, consistent ways, people's reasonable expectations about their privacy play a key role in judges' determinations about legal guidelines for police investigations.

What if a police officer in a state where marijuana is still illegal sees a marijuana plant in the front window of a home as she walks down a public sidewalk? When police officers examine people's property without violating reasonable expectations of privacy, no search has occurred. In *Coolidge v. New Hampshire* (1971), the Court discussed the **plain view doctrine**, which permits officers to notice and use as evidence items that are visible to them when they are in a location where they are permitted to be, such as a public sidewalk. Similarly, police can see what is in open areas, including private property, either by walking through open fields or by flying a helicopter over people's houses and yards. Officers may not break into a home and then claim that the drugs found inside were in plain view on a table. However, if a homeowner invites officers into his home to file a report about a burglary, the officers do not need to obtain a warrant in order to seize drugs that they see lying on the kitchen table. Because the drugs are in plain view and the officers have a legal basis for their presence in the house, the owner has lost any reasonable expectation of privacy, and the officers are not required to obtain a search warrant.

If no search has occurred as a result of police actions, then the Fourth Amendment's protections do not apply, and police are free to take those actions. Thus, the Supreme Court is regularly faced with the challenge of deciding whether or

search Government officials' examination of and hunt for evidence on a person or in a place in a manner that intrudes on reasonable expectations of privacy.

reasonable expectation of privacy The objective standard developed by courts for determining whether a government intrusion into an individual's person or property constitutes a search because it interferes with the individual's interests that are normally protected from government examination.

plain view doctrine Officers may examine and use as evidence, without a warrant, contraband or evidence that is in open view at a location where they are legally permitted to be.

not a specific action by police constitutes a "search" in order to trigger the Fourth Amendment. In the case of *Florida v. Jardines* (2013), the Court faced just such a situation, and the majority decided that bringing a drug-sniffing dog to the front door of a house is, indeed, a search. Thus, the officers should have had a warrant or their actions should have fit with one of the warrantless search categories that we will discuss later in this chapter. Similarly, when police officers attached a Global Positioning System (GPS) tracking device on the outside of a suspected drug dealer's car in order to monitor his movements without a warrant, the Supreme Court decided that this action constituted a search and that the Fourth Amendment's protections applied to the situation (*United States v. Jones,* 2012). The GPS example is one of many emerging situations in which technological developments are creating clashes between the privacy interests protected by the Fourth Amendment and law enforcement officers' desire to pursue criminal investigations. Read the "Current Controversies" feature to consider difficult aspects of this continuing issue.

seizures Situations in which police officers use their authority to deprive people of their liberty or property and that must not be "unreasonable" according to the Fourth Amendment.

In defining **seizures**, the Supreme Court focuses on the nature and extent of officers' interference with people's liberty and freedom of movement. If an officer who is leaning against the wall of a building says to a passing pedestrian, "Where are you going?" and the person replies, "To the sandwich shop down the street," as she continues to

CURRENT CONTROVERSIES IN CRIMINAL JUSTICE

Mandating Corporations' Technological Assistance to Law Enforcement

In December 2015, a married couple in San Bernardino, California, who had sworn allegiance to a Middle Eastern terrorism group, entered a local government office building with firearms and killed 14 people at an office party. The couple was shot and killed by law enforcement officers later the same day, after they had escaped from the scene. The cell phone belonging to one of the shooters was recovered, but the FBI was unable to access the data due to security software. Later, in February 2016, a federal judge ordered the Apple computer company to produce software that would enable law enforcement officials to gain access to the Apple-made phone. Law enforcement officials in various cities applauded the court order because they faced the same difficulty in gaining access to information on criminal defendants' phones that might provide evidence regarding serious crimes such as rape and murder. However, Apple officials refused and promised to fight the order in court. Apple argued that even though the FBI claimed this would be a one-time use of such "backdoor" software, there would be grave risks that the software would eventually end up in the hands of terrorists or foreign governments that might

use it to access not just cell phones, but also to obtain national security information on our government's computers. Apple, supported by other computer companies, also worried that law enforcement officials would use such security-cracking software to improperly access the private information of innocent Americans.

Law enforcement officials had obtained search warrants to examine the contents of these cell phones, unlike in the chapter-opening example of police acting on their own to look at cell-phone photos without a warrant. But what happens if law enforcement officials are unable to gain access to technology-based information because of effective security software? Are private entities, such as computer and software companies, obligated to help the police obtain access to cell phones and computers? Is Apple correct in highlighting the risks of creating "backdoor" access software? On the other hand, what if the San Bernardino shooter's phone contacts and records might lead officials to others who are planning terrorist attacks? This situation goes beyond the usual Fourth Amendment problem of

balancing society's interests against the privacy interests of individuals. Two other interests are at stake here: (1) private corporations' interests in maintaining the integrity of their products and the promises of privacy and security that they have made to customers; and (2) the risks that "backdoor" software may subsequently be misused with potentially catastrophic results. What if terrorists or a foreign government could use it to gain access to sensitive information that controls the launch of American nuclear weapons?

For Critical Thinking and Analysis

If you were the president of Apple, would you comply with the court order? If so, why? If not, why not? Give three reasons for your decision.

Sources: M. Apuzzo, J. Goldstein, and E. Lichtblau, "Apple's Line in the Sand Was over a Year in the Making," *New York Times*, February 18, 2016 (www.nytimes.com); E. Lichtblau and K. Benner, "Apple Fights Order to Unlock San Bernardino Gunman's iPhone," *New York Times*, February 17, 2016. (www.nytimes.com).

walk without interference by the officer, there is virtually no intrusion on her liberty and freedom of movement. In cases like this, officers are free to speak to people on the street. If people voluntarily stop in order to speak with the officer, they have not been "seized," because they are free to move along their way whenever they choose. However, if officers assert their authority to halt that individual's movement, then a seizure has occurred; and the Fourth Amendment requires that the seizure be reasonable. One form of seizure is an arrest. This involves taking a suspect into custody. Property can also be subject to seizure, especially if it is evidence in a criminal case.

A **stop** is a brief interference with a person's freedom of movement for a duration that can be measured in minutes, usually under an hour. An interference with freedom of movement that lasts several hours risks being viewed as exceeding the proper duration of a stop and requires greater justification. When police require a driver to pull over in order to receive a traffic citation, that is a stop. Such stops can affect the rights of both drivers and passengers, especially if the stop leads to a search of the individuals or the vehicle. In *Rodriguez v. United States* (2015), the Supreme Court ruled that officers violate the Fourth Amendment if they prolong a driver's stay at a traffic stop for the purpose of waiting for a drug-sniffing dog to arrive at the scene. In order to be permissible under the Fourth Amendment, stops must be justified by **reasonable suspicion**—a situation in which specific articulable facts lead officers to conclude that the person may be engaging in criminal activity. Officers cannot legally make stops based on hunches; they must be able to describe specific aspects of the person's appearance, behavior, and circumstances that led them to conclude that the person should be stopped in order to investigate the occurrence of a crime. As we shall see, however, the courts permit police officers to make many kinds of stops without reasonable suspicion. Such stops can occur, for example, at border crossing points where it is especially important to prevent illegal activities such as smuggling and drug trafficking. Thus, everyone can be stopped in certain situations even if there is no specific basis to suspect them of wrongdoing.

Use of Force and the Fourth Amendment

In Chapter 5, we examined problems stemming from excessive use of force by police officers. Such actions reflect on the application of discretion, ethics, professionalism, and training of officers. When people sue police officers for violating constitutional rights through the excessive use of force, they claim that their Fourth Amendment right against "unreasonable seizures" has been violated. Although many people assume that an improper shooting or beating inflicted by a police officer might violate the Eighth Amendment prohibition on cruel and unusual punishments, the Supreme Court has interpreted this Eighth Amendment right to protect only individuals who are being "punished" by the justice system—namely, people who have been convicted of crimes. For people who have not been convicted of a crime, such as those encountered by the police in free society, the use of excessive force by government officials is a violation of the Fourth Amendment. Improper use of force can also violate the right to due process under the Fourteenth Amendment if used against unconvicted individuals being held in city or county jails while awaiting trial (*Kingsley v. Hendrickson*, 2015). According to the Supreme Court, when police officers victimize individuals through the use of excessive force, those individuals have suffered an "unreasonable seizure."

Until the 1980s, the police had broad authority to use deadly force in pursuing suspected felons. Police in about half the states were guided by the common-law principle that allowed the use of whatever force was necessary to arrest a fleeing felon. In 1985, the Supreme Court set a new standard in *Tennessee v. Garner*, ruling that the police may not use deadly force in apprehending fleeing felons "unless it is necessary to prevent the escape and the officer has probable cause to believe that the suspect poses a significant threat of death or serious physical injury to the officer or others."

The standard set by *Tennessee v. Garner* presents problems, because it can be difficult to judge how dangerous a suspect may be. Officers must make quick decisions

stop Government officials' interference with an individual's freedom of movement for a duration that typically lasts less than one hour and only rarely extends for as long as several hours.

reasonable suspicion A police officer's belief, based on articulable facts that would be recognized by others in a similar situation, that criminal activity is afoot and necessitates further investigation that will intrude on an individual's reasonable expectation of privacy.

Tennessee v. Garner (1985) Deadly force may not be used against an unarmed and fleeing suspect unless necessary to prevent the escape and unless the officer has probable cause to believe that the suspect poses a significant threat of death or serious injury to the officers or others.

in stressful situations, and for this reason, the Supreme Court and other courts cannot create clear rules that will guide police in every context that arises. However, to clarify the rules for police, the Supreme Court justices also established the standard of "objective reasonableness," saying that the officer's use of deadly force should be judged in terms of its reasonableness for the specific situation that confronts the officer (*Graham v. Connor*, 1989). This means that the use of the deadly force—or any form of force—should be judged from the point of view of the officer on the scene. The Court's decision recognized that "officers are often forced to make split-second judgments—in circumstances that are tense, uncertain, and rapidly evolving—about the amount of force that is necessary in a particular situation" (Georgiady, 2008).

In light of the police shootings and other uses of force that caused the deaths of unarmed African Americans in 2014 and 2015 and thereby generated protests by the Black Lives Matter movement, reforms have been suggested. As described in Chapter 5, the Police Executive Research Forum recommended 30 new principles concerning officers' responsibilities and training. For example, one principle is directed at officers adhering to a higher standard of conduct than that imposed by the Supreme Court decisions in *Tennessee v. Garner* (1984) and *Graham v. Connor* (1989):

> POLICY 2. Agencies should continue to develop best policies, practices, and training on use-of-force issues that go beyond the minimum requirements of *Graham v. Connor*. Departments should adopt policies that hold themselves to a higher standard than the legal requirements of *Graham v. Connor*. Agency use-of-force policies should go beyond the legal standard of "objective reasonableness" outlined in the 1989 U.S. Supreme Court decision *Graham v. Connor*. The landmark *Graham v. Connor* (1989) decision, which holds that the use of police force should judged by a standard of "objective reasonableness," should be seen as "necessary but not sufficient," because it does not provide police with sufficient guidance on use of force. As a result, prosecutors and grand juries often find that a fatal shooting by an officer is not a crime, even though they may not consider the use of force proportional or necessary. Agencies should adopt policies and training to hold themselves to a higher standard, based on sound tactics, consideration of whether the use of force was proportional to the threat, and the sanctity of human life. Many police agencies already have policies that go beyond legal requirements. For example, many police agencies have adopted pursuit policies, and rules barring officers from shooting at or from moving vehicles, that go beyond current legal precedents (Police Executive Research Forum, 2016).

It remains to be seen whether police agencies will adopt this higher standard and whether new standards will reduce the risk of fatal police shootings.

The Concept of Arrest

An arrest is a significant deprivation of liberty. In an arrest, a person is taken into police custody, transported to the police station or jail, and processed into the criminal justice system. Because arrests involve a more significant intrusion on liberty, they require a higher level of justification than stops. Unlike stops, which require only reasonable suspicion, all arrests must be supported by **probable cause**. Probable cause exists when sufficient evidence is available to support the reasonable conclusion that a person has committed a crime. To obtain an arrest warrant, the police must provide a judicial officer with sufficient evidence to support a finding of probable cause. Alternatively, police officers' on-the-street determinations of probable cause can produce discretionary warrantless arrests. A judge subsequently examines such arrests for probable cause in a hearing that must occur shortly after the arrest, typically within 48 hours. If the judge determines that the police officer was wrong in concluding that probable cause existed to justify the arrest, the suspect is released from custody.

Warrants and Probable Cause

Imagine that you are a judge. Two police officers come to your chambers to ask you to authorize a search warrant. They swear that they observed frequent foot traffic of

probable cause Reliable information indicating that it is more likely than not that evidence will be found in a specific location or that a specific person is guilty of a crime.

Arrest is the physical taking of a person into custody. What legal requirements must be met to make this a valid arrest? What limits are placed on the officers?

Bill Pugliano/Getty Images

suspicious people going in and out of a house. Moreover, they swear that a reliable informant told them that he was inside the house two days earlier and saw crack cocaine being sold. Does this information constitute probable cause, justifying issuance of a search warrant? Can you grant a warrant based purely on the word of police officers, or do you need more concrete evidence?

These questions are important not only for judges but for prosecutors, as well. Police and prosecutors must work closely together. If the police have made errors in seeking warrants or conducting searches, evidence could be excluded from use at trial, and as a result, prosecutors could lose their cases through no fault of their own.

The Fourth Amendment requires that "no Warrants shall issue, but upon probable cause, supported by Oath or affirmation, and particularly describing the place to be searched, and the persons or things to be seized." These particular elements of the Fourth Amendment must be fulfilled in order to issue a warrant. If they are not, then a defendant may later challenge the validity of the warrant.

The important elements are, first, the existence of probable cause. Second, evidence must be presented to the judicial officer and be supported by "oath or affirmation," which typically means that police officers must say "yes" when the judicial officer asks them if they swear or affirm that all information presented is true to the best of their knowledge. This requirement may be fulfilled by presenting an **affidavit**—a written statement confirmed by oath or affirmation—from the police officers. Third, the warrant must describe the specific place to be searched. A "general warrant" for searching many locations cannot be issued. Fourth, the warrant must describe the person or items to be seized. Thus, if the warrant authorizes a search for a person suspected of robbery, the officers should not open small dresser drawers or other places a person could not be hiding.

The U.S. Supreme Court has attempted to guide judicial officers in identifying the existence of *probable cause.* Mere suspicion cannot constitute probable cause, yet the level of evidence to establish probable cause need not fulfill the high level of proof "beyond a reasonable doubt" required to justify a criminal conviction. In essence, probable cause is a level of evidence sufficient to provide a reasonable conclusion that the proposed objects of a search will be found in a location that law enforcement officers request to search. For an arrest warrant, the essential issue is whether sufficient evidence is presented to lead to the reasonable conclusion that a specific person should be prosecuted for a criminal offense. There is no hard-and-fast definition of *probable*

affidavit Written statement of fact, supported by oath or affirmation, submitted to judicial officers to fulfill the requirements of probable cause for obtaining a warrant.

Illinois v. Gates (1983) U.S. Supreme Court decision that established the flexible "totality of circumstances" test for determining the existence of the probable cause needed for obtaining a search warrant.

totality of circumstances Flexible test established by the Supreme Court for identifying whether probable cause exists that permits the judge to determine whether the available evidence is both sufficient and reliable enough to issue a warrant.

cause that can be applied to every situation. It is a flexible concept that various judicial officers apply differently. In *Illinois v. Gates* (1983), the Supreme Court announced a flexible **totality of circumstances** test for determining the existence of probable cause. Judges are permitted to make a generalized determination about whether the evidence is both sufficient and reliable enough to justify a warrant.

Cases continue to arise concerning officers' need for and use of search warrants. In *Riley v. California* (2013), described in the opening of the chapter, the Supreme Court said that police could not examine the contents of a driver's cell phone without first obtaining a warrant from a judge to authorize such a search. With respect to residences, when conducting a search with a warrant, officers may detain people found on the premises in order to protect the safety of the officers and prevent any interference in the search. However, according to the Court's decision in *Bailey v. United States* (2013), officers may not follow people they observe leaving a residence that police are about to search and then detain those individuals a mile away, since there is no risk at that point that these people will interfere with the search.

This section's foregoing descriptions of the basic concepts of searches, arrests, and warrants generally apply to criminal justice cases. However, advancements in technology and the heightened concerns about terrorism threats have created contexts for new debates about the application of constitutional rights and proper balance between protecting individuals' liberty and safeguarding American society. As you read "The Policy Debate" feature concerning whether or how constitutional rights should apply to terrorism suspects, think about the role of an eighteenth-century document, the Bill of Rights (1791), in the twenty-first-century effort to prevent catastrophic, politically motivated attacks on innocent civilians.

THE POLICY DEBATE

Should Terrorism Suspects in the United States Enjoy the Protections of the Bill of Rights?

In the aftermath of the al-Qaeda organization's September 11, 2001, attacks on New York City's World Trade Center and the Pentagon in Washington, DC, the United States intervened militarily in Afghanistan. The administration of President George W. Bush decided to send captured terrorism suspects to the U.S. Naval base at Guantanamo Bay, Cuba, with the specific intention of avoiding the application of rights contained in the Bill of Rights. The U.S. Supreme Court had previously said that American officials are not obligated to adhere to the Bill of Rights in searching, seizing, and questioning foreign citizens overseas. This action generated debates about which aspects of international law and treaty obligations apply in such circumstances.

When the Bush administration asserted that American terrorism suspects detained on American soil could also be denied all constitutional rights, a divided Supreme Court rejected that argument. However, the Supreme Court justices

did not agree on whether or how the Bill of Rights applied in such circumstances (*Hamdi v. Rumsfeld,* 2004). At one extreme within the Supreme Court, Justice Clarence Thomas argued that the president, as commander in chief, had absolute authority to hold American suspects indefinitely without providing any access to court proceedings; without providing any Fourth or Fifth Amendment rights; and without providing any evidence that the individual had engaged in wrongdoing. At the other extreme, Justices Antonin Scalia and John Paul Stevens insisted that the Bill of Rights applies in its entirety to all Americans held by the government on American soil. Thus, they asserted that the government must either charge such individuals with crimes and provide them with the complete constitutional rights available to all criminal suspects or set the individuals free. This debate spurred Congress and the president to develop rules and practices

for terrorism investigations, detentions, and case processing that provided limited protections without granting the full rights promised by the Bill of Rights.

As discussed in Chapter 5, there have been several incidents that produced significant debates about the role of constitutional rights. The USA PATRIOT Act expanded government authority to undertake searches and engage in wiretapping without the knowledge of people suspected of supporting terrorist activities or organizations. These practices were initiated by the Bush administration and were continued by the administration of President Barack Obama. In 2011, President Obama signed into law a controversial provision that authorized indefinite detention of terrorism suspects in the United States (Hirshkorn, 2011). In another important event, many members of Congress criticized the FBI for reportedly informing the "underwear bomber" of his Fifth Amendment right against compelled self-incrimination after he attempted to ignite an explosive device in his clothing while a passenger on an airliner approaching the Detroit airport (Hunt, 2010). Some lawmakers argued that terrorism suspects should not be entitled to benefit from constitutional rights.

For Granting Bill of Rights Protections to Domestic Terrorism Suspects in the United States

Supporters of applying the Bill of Rights in all domestic cases focus on constitutional rights as a fundamental component of the American democracy. By failing to follow this country's laws of basic constitutional rights, the government violates America's most fundamental principles and, in effect, does just what the terrorists want—it surrenders these rights to the fear of terrorism.

The arguments for applying the protections of the Bill of Rights are these:

- The Bill of Rights embodies the fundamental values, principles, and rules of law for the nation.
- The country harms itself if it permits the threat of terrorism to scare it into rejecting its own most important principles.
- The nation's image in the world is harmed when it ignores its own rules and rights. There are also risks that other countries will be less willing to grant Americans legal rights when they are accused of wrongdoing abroad, and less willing to assist in antiterrorism efforts.

- Without constitutional rights, there are risks that suspects will be mistreated or that errors will be made that lead to innocent people being held in jail.
- Since 9/11 the U.S. government has successfully used regular criminal trials to convict more than 300 people for terrorism-related crimes while granting them the full rights under the Bill of Rights. These trials demonstrate that constitutional rights do not prevent the United States from protecting itself against terrorism.

Against Granting Bill of Rights Protections to Domestic Terrorism Suspects in the United States

- Taking the time necessary to establish probable cause and authorize searches, arrests, and questioning suspects may delay or impede terrorism investigations and hinder the acquisition of critical information. Suspected terrorists must be stopped with swift, decisive action to protect the lives of innocent people.
- People engaged in terrorism plots reject and seek to destroy the principles and institutions of American democracy. Therefore, they forfeit any claim to the benefits of American law.
- Law enforcement officials need broad authority to protect American society from terrorist threats.
- If suspected terrorists are processed through regular criminal trials and the rules of the legal system, terrorist organizations may endanger the American public by seeking to attack

jails and courthouses in an effort to free their associates. The public is safer if suspects are held secretly in isolation at military facilities.

What Should U.S. Policy Be?

Do Americans even notice if the government's investigatory and detention powers grow? What if we learned, hypothetically, that the government was intercepting e-mail messages from all Americans—is that something that would arouse public opposition? On the other hand, how would Americans react if there were another major attack within the borders of the country?

Researching the Internet

To read about the issues and arguments identified by a civil liberties organization concerning governmental violations of the Bill of Rights in the name of national security, see www.aclu.org/national-security.

Analyzing the Issue

What are the risks and benefits of permitting terrorism suspects in the United States to enjoy the protections of the Bill of Rights? Are there specific rights that pose fewer risks and other rights that pose greater risks? If you and your classmates were members of the president's cabinet, what would you say about the issue if the president sought your advice? After discussing the issue with your classmates, write a memo summarizing and explaining your conclusions.

CHECK POINT

1. **What is a search?**
   A government intrusion into an individual's reasonable expectation of privacy.

2. **What is the plain view doctrine?**
   The plain view doctrine permits officers to observe and seize illegal items that are visible to them when they are in a location in which they are legally permitted to be.

3. **What is the difference between an arrest and a stop?**
   An arrest requires probable cause and involves taking someone into custody for prosecution, whereas a stop is a brief deprivation of freedom of movement based on reasonable suspicion.

4. **What do police officers need to demonstrate in order to obtain a warrant?**
   The existence of probable cause by the totality of circumstances in the case.

STOP & ANALYZE

Give examples of two situations that you believe should be considered "unreasonable searches" in violation of the Fourth Amendment. What is it about those searches that makes them "unreasonable"?

Warrantless Searches

In day-to-day police work, the majority of searches take place without a warrant. It is in this area that the courts have been most active in defining the term *unreasonable*. Six kinds of searches may be legally conducted without a warrant, yet still comply with the Fourth Amendment: (1) search justified by special needs beyond the normal purposes of law enforcement, (2) stop and frisk on the streets, (3) search incident to a lawful arrest, (4) exigent circumstances, (5) search by consent, and (6) automobile searches. We examine these forms of warrantless searches in this section.

Special Needs beyond the Normal Purposes of Law Enforcement

In certain contexts, law enforcement officials have a justified need to conduct warrantless searches of every individual passing through. The use of metal detectors to examine airline passengers, for example, occurs in a specific context in which the need to prevent hijacking justifies a limited search of every passenger (Israelsen, 2013). Here the Supreme Court does not require officers to have any suspicions, reasonable or otherwise, about the illegal activities of any individual (Lum, Crafton, et al., 2015; Loewy, 2011).

Similarly, warrantless searches take place at the entry points into the United States—border crossings, ports, and airports (Chacon, 2010). The government's interests in guarding against the entry of people and items (weapons, drugs, toxic chemicals, and so forth) that are harmful to national interests outweigh the individuals' expectations of privacy (T. Miller, 2015). Typically, these border stops involve only a few moments as customs officers check required documents such as passports and visas, and ask where individuals have traveled and what they are bringing into the United States. The customs officers may have a trained dog sniff around people and their luggage, checking for drugs or large amounts of cash. At the Mexican and Canadian borders and at international airports, people may be chosen at random to have their cars and luggage searched. They may also be chosen for such searches because their behavior or their answers to questions arouse the suspicions of customs officers.

The Supreme Court has declared that police may set up sobriety checkpoints in which they establish roadblocks and stop all cars in an effort to detect drunk drivers. Do you think such roadblocks interfere with the rights of drivers who have done nothing to raise suspicions about improper behavior?

AP Images/Lenny Ignelzi

The Supreme Court has expanded the checkpoint concept by approving systematic stops to look for drunken drivers along highways. Michigan's state police implemented a sobriety checkpoint program. They set up a checkpoint at which they stopped every vehicle and briefly questioned each driver (*Michigan Department of State Police v. Sitz*, 1990). A group of citizens filed lawsuits alleging that checkpoints violated drivers' rights. However, the Court said that police can systematically stop drivers in order to seek information. The Court more recently approved checkpoints to ask drivers whether they had witnessed an accident (*Illinois v. Lidster*, 2004).

The U.S. Supreme Court has not given blanket approval for every kind of checkpoint or traffic stop that police might wish to use. For example, the Court forbids random stops of vehicles by officers on patrol (*Delaware v. Prouse,* 1979). Officers must have a basis for a vehicle stop, such as an observed violation of traffic laws. The Court has also ruled that a city cannot set up a checkpoint in order to check drivers and passengers for possible involvement in drugs or other crimes. The Court declared that a general search for criminal evidence does not justify the use of a checkpoint. Again, such stops must be narrowly focused on a specific objective, such as checking for drunken drivers (*City of Indianapolis v. Edmond,* 2000).

Stop and Frisk on the Streets

Police officers possess the authority to make stops and limited searches of individuals on the streets when specific circumstances justify such actions (Zeidman, 2012). In the landmark case of ***Terry v. Ohio*** (1968), the Court upheld the stop-and-frisk procedure when a police officer had good reasons to conclude that a person endangered the public by being involved in criminal activity. In the *Terry* case, a plainclothes detective in downtown Cleveland observed men walking back and forth to look in the window of a store and then conferring with each other. He suspected that they might be preparing to rob the store. He approached the men, identified himself as a police officer, patted down their clothing, and found unlicensed handguns on two individuals. Those individuals challenged the legality of the search.

The special needs of law enforcement at borders and airports provide authority for warrantless searches based on decisions of the officers looking for suspicious behavior. The need to protect public safety and national security justifies these searches. When you go to an airport, do you feel as if your privacy and rights are being violated when you are subjected to searches?

Terry v. Ohio **(1968)** Supreme Court decision endorsing police officers' authority to stop and frisk suspects on the streets when there is reasonable suspicion that they are armed and involved in criminal activity.

stop-and-frisk search Limited search approved by the Supreme Court in *Terry v. Ohio*, which permits police officers to pat down the clothing of people on the street if there is reasonable suspicion of dangerous criminal activity.

Although the justices supported the detective's authority to conduct the pat-down search based on his observations of the men's suspicious behavior, they struck a careful balance between police authority and individuals' rights by specifying the circumstances in which such a pat-down search—more commonly known as a **stop-and-frisk search**—can occur. In the *Terry* decision, the Court specifies the following criteria, all of which must be present, to define a legal stop and frisk:

We merely hold today that

1. where a police officer observes unusual conduct
2. which leads him reasonably to conclude in light of his experience
3. that criminal activity may be afoot and
4. that the persons with whom he is dealing may be armed and presently dangerous,
5. where in the course of investigating this behavior
6. he identifies himself as a policeman and makes reasonable inquiries,
7. and where nothing in the initial stages of the encounter serves to dispel his reasonable fear for his own or others' safety,
8. he is entitled for the protection of himself and others in the area to conduct a carefully limited search of the outer clothing of such persons in an attempt to discover weapons which might be used to assault him.

These factors impose an obligation on police officers to make observations, draw reasonable conclusions, identify themselves, and make inquiries before conducting the stop-and-frisk search. In addition, the search must be justified by a reasonable conclusion that a person is armed, thereby requiring the officer to act in order to protect him- or herself and the public.

As we discuss later with respect to the *exclusionary rule*, a suspect who, during a frisk search, is found to be carrying drugs or a weapon can seek to have the evidence excluded from use in court if the stop and frisk was not justified by proper observations and reasonable suspicion. Typically, a judge will believe the police officer's version of events rather than accept the claims of a person found to be carrying illegal items. Sometimes, however, the officer's version of events may not be persuasive. When an officer claims to have seen a lump under a suspect's jacket while the officer was standing 20 yards away on a busy street, judges may doubt whether an officer can reasonably draw such conclusions from such a distance. In New York City, for example, concerns arose that police officers were regularly searching anyone they saw on the streets, even though the officers did not have the proper justifications established in *Terry v. Ohio* and later cases (C. Smith, 2014). In response, federal judges closely examined officers' versions of events. In nearly two dozen cases, the judges concluded that the police officers either were not being truthful or were not carefully following the *Terry* rules (Weiser, 2008). Eventually, a federal judge ruled that the New York City police department's policy of disproportionately stopping young African American and Hispanic men violated constitutional rights under the Fourth Amendment (Weiser & Goldstein, 2014).

Court decisions have given officers significant discretion to decide when factors that justify a stop-and-frisk search exist. For example, if officers see someone running at the sight of police in a high-crime neighborhood, their observation can be one consideration in determining whether a stop-and-frisk search is justified (*Illinois v. Wardlow*, 2000). Thus, officers need not actually see evidence of a weapon or interact with the suspect prior to making the stop.

The Supreme Court also expanded police authority by permitting officers to rely on reports from reliable witnesses as the basis for conducting the stop and frisk (*Adams v. Williams*, 1972). However, an unverified anonymous tip does not serve as an adequate reason for a stop-and-frisk search (*Florida v. J. L.*, 2000).

Search Incident to a Lawful Arrest

The authority to undertake a warrantless search incident to a lawful arrest is not limited by the type of crime for which the arrestee has been taken into custody (Foley 2013). Even someone arrested for a traffic offense can be searched. Although there is no reason to suspect the person has a weapon or to believe that evidence related to the offense will be found in the person's pockets (*United States v. Robinson*, 1973), the arrestee is subject to the same arrest-scene search as someone taken into custody for murder. However, as emphasized in *Riley v. California* (2014), the search must focus on weapons and the potential destruction of evidence and cannot be a curiosity-based exploration of a driver's cell phone.

Chimel v. California (1969)
Supreme Court decision that endorsed warrantless searches for weapons and evidence in the immediate vicinity of people who are lawfully arrested.

The justification for searches of arrestees emerged in the Supreme Court's decision in **Chimel v. California (1969)**. This ruling stated that searches are lawful when the officers need to be sure that the arrestee does not have a weapon that could endanger the officers or others in the vicinity. They must also look for evidence that might be destroyed or damaged by the arrestee before or during the process of transporting the individual to jail. Hence, officers are permitted to search the arrestee and the immediate area around the arrestee.

Officers can also make a protective sweep through other rooms where the suspect may recently have been. However, the arrest would not justify opening drawers and conducting a thorough search of an entire house. If, after the arrest, officers have probable cause to conduct a more thorough search, they must obtain a warrant that specifies the items that they seek and the places where they will search.

In a traffic stop, because officers possess the authority to make arrests for minor offenses, including acts that would normally only be subject to traffic citations, officers have opportunities to use arrests of drivers as a basis for conducting warrantless searches of automobiles (*Virginia v. Moore*, 2008). However, the search of the passenger compartment must be limited to areas within reach of the arrestee (May, Duke, & Gueco, 2013). In *Arizona v. Gant* (2009), a majority of justices barred the search of an automobile after an arrest when the handcuffed driver posed no danger to the officers and could not reach into the car to destroy evidence.

Supreme Court decisions have clarified additional search implications that flow from arrests (Joh, 2015). In *Maryland v. King* (2013), the Supreme Court approved a state law that required taking a DNA sample using a cheek swab from those arrested for serious felonies in order to check databases to see if they might be guilty of other unsolved violent crimes, such as rape or murder, for which DNA evidence had been collected. According to the majority opinion, "When officers make an arrest supported by probable cause to hold for a serious offense and they bring the suspect to the station to be detained in custody, taking and analyzing a cheek swab of the arrestee's DNA is, like fingerprinting and photographing, a legitimate police booking procedure that is reasonable under the Fourth Amendment." Arrests, even for minor offenses, also lead those arrested to be subjected to intrusive strip searches and body cavity inspections when they are placed in jail (*Florence v. Board of Chosen Freeholders*, 2012).

Exigent Circumstances

Officers can make an arrest without a warrant when there are **exigent circumstances**. This means that officers are in the middle of an urgent situation in which they must act swiftly and do not have time to go to court to seek a warrant. With respect to arrests, for example, when officers are in hot pursuit of a fleeing suspected felon, they need not stop to seek a warrant and thereby risk permitting the suspect to get away (*Warden v. Hayden*, 1967). Similarly, exigent circumstances can justify the warrantless entry into a home or other building and an accompanying search that flows from the officers' response to the urgent situation. For example, the Supreme Court approved police officers' warrantless entry into a home when, on being called to the scene of a loud party, they observed through the home's window a violent altercation between a teenager and an adult (*Brigham City, Utah v. Stuart*, 2006). The unanimous decision written by Chief Justice John Roberts said that "law enforcement officers may enter a home without a warrant to render emergency assistance to an injured occupant or to protect an occupant from imminent injury." After the officers make the warrantless entry, the "plain view" doctrine permits them to examine and seize any criminal evidence that they can see in the course of actions taken to address the exigent circumstances.

In *Cupp v. Murphy* (1973), a man voluntarily complied with police officers' request that he come to the police station to answer questions concerning his wife's murder. At the station, officers noticed a substance on the man's fingernails that they thought might be dried blood. Over his objections, they took a sample of scrapings from his fingernails and ultimately used that tissue as evidence against him when he was convicted of murdering his wife. The Supreme Court said the search was properly undertaken under exigent circumstances. If officers had taken the time to seek a warrant, the suspect could have washed his hands and the evidence would have been lost.

Police officers can use the exigent circumstances justification for warrantless searches for the purpose of seeking evidence. To justify such searches, they do not need to show that there was a potential threat to public safety. As a practical matter, police officers make quick judgments about undertaking certain searches. If incriminating evidence is discovered, courts may be asked after the fact to determine whether the urgency of the situation justified a warrantless search and whether the nature and purpose of the search were reasonable. Judges are usually reluctant to second-guess a police officer's on-the-spot decision that the urgency of a situation required an immediate warrantless search. For example, in 2011, the Supreme Court decided a case concerning police officers who followed a drug suspect into an

exigent circumstances When there is an immediate threat to public safety or the risk that evidence will be destroyed, officers may search, arrest, or question suspects without obtaining a warrant or following other usual rules of criminal procedure.

apartment building and then smelled marijuana outside one apartment while hearing sounds that they believed could be the destruction of evidence. The Court ruled that the officers could legally kick in the door and enter the apartment, based on exigent circumstances, even though it turned out that it was not the apartment that their drug suspect had entered (*Kentucky v. King*).

Search by Consent

If people consent to a search, officers do not need probable cause or even any level of suspicion to justify the search. Consent effectively absolves law enforcement officers of any risk that evidence will be excluded from use at trial or that they will be found liable in a civil lawsuit alleging a violation of Fourth Amendment rights.

A **consent search** provides a valuable investigatory tool for officers who wish to conduct warrantless searches. Officers in many police departments are trained to ask people if they will consent to a search. Thus, some officers ask every motorist during a traffic stop, "May I search your car?" Or if called to the scene of a domestic dispute or a citizen complaint about noise, the officers may say, "Do you mind if I look around the downstairs area of your house?" Criminal evidence is often uncovered in such consent searches—a fact that may indicate that many citizens do not know they have the option to say no when officers ask for permission to search. Moreover, some citizens may fear that they will look more suspicious to the officer if they say no, so they agree to searches in order to act as if they have nothing to hide. In addition, in *United States v. Drayton* (2002), the Supreme Court said that police officers do not have to inform people of their right to say no when asked if they wish to consent to a search.

In deciding if a permissible consent search has occurred, one must address two key issues. First, the consent must be voluntary. Police officers may not use coercion or threats to obtain consent. Gaining consent by using certain tricks, such as dishonestly telling someone that there is a search warrant and thereby implying that the person has no choice but to consent, will result in the search being declared improper (*Bumper v. North Carolina*, 1968). Second, the consent must be given by someone who possesses the authority to give consent. Someone cannot, for example, consent to have a neighbor's house searched. The resident in a dwelling must be the one to consent to a search of that dwelling. A controversial Supreme Court decision said that the police may not search when one resident of a dwelling is present and objects, even if another resident consents to the search (*Georgia v. Randolph*, 2006). In some circumstances, a permissible search may occur if the officers reasonably believe that they have been given permission to search by someone who possesses such authority even if, for example, it later turns out that the person is a former rather than a current resident of the apartment searched (*Illinois v. Rodriguez*, 1990).

Automobile Searches

The U.S. Supreme Court first addressed automobile searches in *Carroll v. United States* (1925), a case in which federal agents searched a car for illegal alcohol. The *Carroll* case, in which the warrantless search was approved, provided an underlying justification for permitting such searches of automobiles: in essence, because cars are mobile, they differ greatly from houses and other buildings. Automobiles can be driven away and disappear in the time that it would take for police to ask a judicial officer for a search warrant.

Police officers have significant authority to search automobiles and to issue commands to people riding in vehicles. For example, during a traffic stop, officers can order passengers as well as the driver to exit the vehicle even if there is no basis for suspicion that the passengers engaged in any wrongdoing (*Maryland v. Wilson*, 1997).

Two key questions arise in automobile searches: (1) When can officers stop a car? and (2) How extensively can they search the vehicle? Many automobile searches arise as a result of traffic stops. A stop can occur when an officer observes a traffic violation, including defective safety equipment, or when there is a basis for reasonable suspicion concerning the involvement of the car, its driver, or its passengers in a crime. However, read the "Close Up" to consider the Supreme Court's approval of a

---

consent search A permissible warrantless search of a person, vehicle, home, or other location based on a person with proper authority or the reasonable appearance of proper authority voluntarily granting permission for the search to take place.

United States v. Drayton (2002) Judicial decision declaring that police officers are not required to inform people of their right to decline to be searched when police ask for consent to search.

Heien v. North Carolina, 135 S.Ct. 530 (2014)

Chief Justice John Roberts delivered the opinion of the Court on behalf of Justices Antonin Scalia, Anthony Kennedy, Clarence Thomas, Ruth Bader Ginsburg, Stephen Breyer, Samuel Alito, and Elena Kagan. Justice Kagan filed a concurring opinion that was joined by Justice Ginsburg. Justice Sonia Sotomayor wrote a dissenting opinion. Both the majority opinion and the dissenting opinion are presented here using excerpts from each one.

The Opinion of the Court

The Fourth Amendment prohibits "unreasonable searches and seizures." Under this standard, a search or seizure may be permissible even though the justification for the action includes a reasonable factual mistake. An officer might, for example, stop a motorist for traveling alone in a high-occupancy vehicle lane, only to discover upon approaching the car that two children are slumped over asleep in the back seat. The driver has not violated the law, but neither has the officer violated the Fourth Amendment.

But what if the police officer's reasonable mistake is not one of fact but of law? In this case, an officer stopped a vehicle because one of its two brake lights was out, but a court later determined that a single working brake light was all the law required. The question presented is whether such a mistake of law can nonetheless give rise to the reasonable suspicion necessary to uphold the seizure under the Fourth Amendment. We hold that it can. Because the officer's mistake about the brake-light law was reasonable, the stop in this case was lawful under the Fourth Amendment.

I

On the morning of April 29, 2009, Sergeant Matt Darisse of the Surry County Sheriff's Department sat in his patrol car near Dobson, North Carolina, observing northbound traffic on Interstate 77. Shortly before 8 a.m., a Ford Escort passed by. Darisse thought the driver looked "very stiff and nervous," so he pulled onto the interstate and began following the Escort. A few miles down the road, the Escort braked as it approached a slower vehicle, but only the left brake light came on. Noting the faulty right brake light, Darisse activated his vehicle's lights and pulled the Escort over.

Two men were in the car: Maynor Javier Vasquez sat behind the wheel, and petitioner Nicholas Brady Heien lay across the rear seat. Sergeant Darisse explained to Vasquez that as long as his license and registration checked out, he would receive only a warning ticket for the broken brake light. A records check revealed no problems with the documents, and Darisse gave Vasquez the warning ticket. But Darisse had become suspicious during the course of the stop— Vasquez appeared nervous, Heien remained lying down the entire time, and the two gave inconsistent answers about their destination. Darisse asked Vasquez if he would be willing to answer some questions. Vasquez assented, and Darisse asked whether the men were transporting various types of contraband. Told no, Darisse asked whether he could search the Escort. Vasquez said he had no objection, but told Darisse he should ask Heien, because Heien owned the car. Heien gave his consent, and Darisse, aided by a fellow officer who had since arrived, began a thorough search of the vehicle. In the side compartment of a duffle bag, Darisse found a sandwich bag containing cocaine. The officers arrested both men.

The State charged Heien with attempted trafficking in cocaine. Heien moved to suppress the evidence seized from the car, contending that the stop and search had violated the Fourth Amendment of the U.S. Constitution. After a hearing at which both officers testified and the State played a video recording of the stop, the trial court denied the suppression motion, concluding that the faulty brake light had given Sergeant Darisse reasonable suspicion to initiate the stop, and that Heien's subsequent consent to the search was valid. Heien pleaded guilty but reserved his right to appeal the suppression decision.

The North Carolina Court of Appeals reversed [another decision]. The initial stop was not valid, the court held, because driving with only one working brake light was not actually a violation of North Carolina law.

II

***

But reasonable men make mistakes of law, too, and such mistakes are no less compatible with the concept of reasonable suspicion. Reasonable suspicion arises from the combination of an officer's understanding of the facts and his understanding of the relevant law. The officer may be reasonably mistaken on either ground. Whether the facts turn out to be not what was thought, or the law turns out to be not what was thought, the result is the same: the facts are outside the scope of the law. There is no reason, under the text of the Fourth Amendment or our precedents, why this same result should be acceptable when reached by way of a reasonable mistake of fact, but not when reached by way of a similarly reasonable mistake of law.

***

Heien also contends that the reasons the Fourth Amendment allows some errors of fact do not

continued

extend to errors of law. Officers in the field must make factual assessments on the fly, Heien notes, and so deserve a margin of error. In Heien's view, no such margin is appropriate for questions of law: The statute here either requires one working brake light or two, and the answer does not turn on anything "an officer might suddenly confront in the field." But Heien's point does not consider the reality that an officer may "suddenly confront" a situation in the field as to which the application of a statute is unclear—however clear it may later become. A law prohibiting "vehicles" in the park either covers Segways or not,... but an officer will nevertheless have to make a quick decision on the law the first time one whizzes by.

Contrary to the suggestion of Heien and *amici*, our decision does not discourage officers from learning the law. The Fourth Amendment tolerates only *reasonable* mistakes, and those mistakes—whether of fact or of law—must be *objectively* reasonable.... And the inquiry is not as forgiving as the one employed in the distinct context of deciding whether an officer is entitled to qualified immunity for a constitutional or statutory violation. Thus, an officer can gain no Fourth Amendment advantage through a sloppy study of the laws he is duty-bound to enforce.

Finally, Heien and *amici* point to the well-known maxim, "Ignorance of the law is no excuse," and contend that it is fundamentally unfair to let police officers get away with mistakes of law when the citizenry is accorded no such leeway. Though this argument has a certain rhetorical appeal, it misconceives the implication of the maxim. The true symmetry is this: Just as an individual generally cannot escape criminal liability based on a mistaken understanding of the law, so too the government cannot impose criminal liability based on a mistaken understanding of the law. If the law required two working brake

lights, Heien could not escape a ticket by claiming he reasonably thought he needed only one; if the law required only one, Sergeant Darisse could not issue a valid ticket by claiming he reasonably thought drivers needed two. But just because mistakes of law cannot justify either the imposition or the avoidance of criminal liability, it does not follow that they cannot justify an investigatory stop. And Heien is not appealing a brake-light ticket; he is appealing a cocaine-trafficking conviction as to which there is no asserted mistake of fact or law.

Justice Sonia Sotomayor, Dissenting

***

It is common ground that Heien was seized within the meaning of the Fourth Amendment. Such a seizure comports with the Constitution only if the officers had articulable and reasonable suspicion that Heien was breaking the law. In *Ornelas v. United States* (1996), we explained that the "principal components" of that determination "will be the events which occurred leading up to the stop or search, and then the decision whether these historical facts, viewed from the standpoint of an objectively reasonable police officer, amount to reasonable suspicion or to probable cause." We described this kind of determination as "a mixed question of law and fact": "'[T]he issue is whether the facts satisfy the [relevant] statutory [or constitutional] standard, or to put it another way, whether the rule of law as applied to the established facts is or is not violated.'" What matters, we said, are the facts as viewed by an objectively reasonable officer, and the rule of law—not an officer's conception of the rule of law, and not even an officer's reasonable misunderstanding about the law, but the law.

As a result, when we have talked about the leeway that officers have in making probable-cause determinations, we have focused on their assessments of facts.

***

Both our enunciation of the reasonableness inquiry and our justification for it thus have always turned on an officer's factual conclusions and an officer's expertise with respect to those factual conclusions. Neither has hinted at taking into account an officer's understanding of the law, reasonable or otherwise.

II

Departing from this tradition means further eroding the Fourth Amendment's protection of civil liberties in a context where that protection has already been worn down. Traffic stops like those at issue here can be "annoying, frightening, and perhaps humiliating." We have nevertheless held that an officer's subjective motivations do not render a traffic stop unlawful. But we assumed in *Whren* [*Whren v. United States* (1996)] that when an officer acts on pretext, at least that pretext would be the violation of an actual law. Giving officers license to effect seizures so long as they can attach to their reasonable view of the facts some reasonable legal interpretation (or misinterpretation) that suggests a law has been violated significantly expands this authority.... One wonders how a citizen seeking to be law-abiding and to structure his or her behavior to avoid these invasive, frightening, and humiliating encounters could do so.

***

On the practical side, the Court primarily contends that an officer may confront "a situation in the field as to which the application of a statute is unclear." . . . One is left to wonder, however, why an innocent citizen should be made to shoulder the burden of being seized whenever the law may be susceptible to an interpretive question. . . .

***

To my mind, the more administrable approach—and the one more consistent with our precedents and principles—would be to hold that an officer's mistake of law, no matter how reasonable, cannot support the individualized suspicion necessary to justify a seizure under the Fourth Amendment. I respectfully dissent.

Researching the Internet

The North Carolina Justice Academy provides training and course materials for police officers to become certified in that state. Examine the subjects taught to police recruits as you consider whether the Supreme Court should have accepted officers' errors about traffic laws: http://ncja.ncdoj.gov/NCJAGeneral.aspx.

For Critical Thinking and Analysis

As you read the two perspectives in the opinion concerning stops based on officers' knowledge of the law, which perspective was most persuasive? Give three reasons why one opinion was more convincing than the other.

---

traffic stop even when police officers were mistaken in believing that a nonworking vehicle light violated state law (*Heien v. North Carolina*, 2014). Police officers are free to make a visible inspection of a car's interior by shining a flashlight inside and looking through the window. They can also look at the vehicle identification number on the dashboard and inside the door of a validly stopped vehicle (*New York v. Class*, 1986).

All sworn officers can make traffic stops, even if they are in unmarked vehicles and serving in special vice or detective bureaus that do not normally handle traffic offenses (*Whren v. United States,* 1996). A traffic violation by itself, however, does not provide an officer with the authority to search an entire vehicle (*Knowles v. Iowa*, 1998). Only specific factors creating reasonable suspicion or probable cause justify officers in doing anything more than looking inside the vehicle.

For example, the arrest of a driver justifies the search of a passenger's property or other locations in the vehicle if there is reason to believe that those locations could contain criminal evidence or weapons (*Wyoming v. Houghton*, 1999). In addition, the Court has expanded officers' authority to search automobiles even when no formal arrest has yet occurred. In *Michigan v. Long* (1983), the Court approved a search of the car's interior around the driver's seat after officers found the car in a ditch and the apparently intoxicated driver standing outside the car. The Supreme Court justified the search as an expansion of the *Terry* doctrine. In effect, the officers were permitted to "frisk" the car in order to protect themselves and others by making sure no weapon was available to the not-yet-arrested driver. Such a search requires that the officers have reasonable suspicion that the person stopped may be armed and may pose a threat to the officers. As described in "Criminal Justice: Myth & Reality," there are also opportunities for officers to search closed containers within a vehicle.

The Court permits thorough searches of vehicles without regard to probable cause when police officers inventory the contents of impounded vehicles (*South Dakota v. Opperman,* 1976). This means that

CRIMINAL JUSTICE

Myth&Reality

COMMON BELIEF: Under the Fourth Amendment's requirements for searches, only judges make determinations of "probable cause," and they do so in order to decide whether to issue a search warrant.

REALITY

- In *California v. Acevedo* (1991), the Supreme Court said that officers could search anywhere in the car for which they have probable cause to search. This includes a search of closed containers within the car.
- The officers themselves, rather than a judge, determine whether probable cause exists before conducting the warrantless search of the vehicle.
- If the defense attorney seeks to have evidence from such a search excluded as improperly obtained, it may be difficult for a judge to second-guess an officer's decisions.
- The judge must make an after-the-fact evaluation based on the officer's description of the facts and circumstances, and thus the officer's determination of probable cause is likely to stand as the basis for an automobile search.

inventory search Permissible warrantless search of a vehicle that has been "impounded"—meaning that it is in police custody—so that police can make a record of the items contained in the vehicle.

containers found within the course of the **inventory search** may also be opened and searched when the examination of such containers is consistent with a police department's inventory policies.

Table 6.1 reviews selected Supreme Court cases concerning those circumstances in which the police do not need a warrant to conduct a search or to seize evidence.

TABLE 6.1	Warrantless Searches
The Supreme Court has ruled that there are circumstances when a warrant is not required.	

Case	Decision
Special needs	
Michigan Department of State Police v. Sitz (1990)	Stopping motorists systematically at roadblocks designed for specific purposes, such as detecting drunken drivers, is permissible.
City of Indianapolis v. Edmond (2000)	Police traffic checkpoints cannot be justified as a generalized search for criminal evidence; they must be narrowly focused on a specific objective.
Stop and frisk	
Terry v. Ohio (1968)	Officers may stop and frisk suspects on the street when there is reasonable suspicion that they are armed and involved in criminal activity.
Adams v. Williams (1972)	Officers may rely on reports from reliable witnesses as the basis for conducting a stop and frisk.
Illinois v. Wardlow (2000)	When a person runs at the sight of police in a high-crime area, officers are justified in using the person's flight as a basis for forming reasonable suspicion to justify a stop and frisk.
Incident to an arrest	
Chimel v. California (1969)	To preserve evidence and protect the safety of the officer and the public after a lawful arrest, the arrestee and the immediate area around the arrestee may be searched for weapons and criminal evidence.
United States v. Robinson (1973)	A warrantless search incident to an arrest is not limited by the seriousness of the crime for which the arrestee has been taken into custody.
Exigent circumstances	
Warden v. Hayden (1967)	When officers are in hot pursuit of a fleeing suspect, they need not stop to seek a warrant and thereby risk permitting the suspect to get away.
Kentucky v. King (2011)	Officers may seize evidence to protect it if taking time to seek a warrant creates a risk of its destruction.
Search by Consent	
Bumper v. North Carolina (1968)	Officers may not tell falsehoods as a means of getting a suspect to consent to a search.
United States v. Drayton (2002)	An officer does not have to inform people of their right to refuse when he or she asks if they wish to consent to a search.
Automobiles	
Carroll v. United States (1925)	Because by their nature automobiles can be easily moved, warrantless searches are permissible when reasonable suspicion of illegal activity exists.
New York v. Class (1986)	An officer may enter a vehicle to see the vehicle identification number when a car has been validly stopped pursuant to a traffic violation or other permissible justification.
California v. Acevedo (1991)	Officers may search throughout a vehicle when they believe they have probable cause to do so.
Maryland v. Wilson (1997)	During traffic stops, officers may order passengers as well as the driver to exit the vehicle, even if there is no basis for suspicion that the passengers engaged in any wrongdoing.
Knowles v. Iowa (1998)	A traffic violation by itself does not provide an officer with the authority to search an entire vehicle. There must be reasonable suspicion or probable cause before officers can extend their search beyond merely looking inside the vehicle's passenger compartment.

5. **In what situations do law enforcement's special needs justify stopping an automobile without reasonable suspicion?**
   Warrantless stops of automobiles are permitted at international borders and sobriety checkpoints (unless barred within a specific state by its own supreme court) or when there is reasonable suspicion of a traffic violation or other wrongdoing.

6. **What is an exigent circumstance?**
   An urgent situation in which evidence might be destroyed, a suspect might escape, or the public would be endangered if police took the time to seek a warrant for a search or an arrest.

7. **What two elements must be present for a valid consent to permit a warrantless search?**
   Voluntary consent by a person with proper authority to consent.

Imagine that you were stopped for speeding while driving down a highway. If the officer gives you a warning rather than a ticket, how would you answer if the police officer then said to you, "Do you mind if I look in the trunk of your car?" What reasons would motivate your decision about how to answer? What concerns might you have about what the officer could do upon hearing the answer "no"?

Questioning Suspects

The Fifth Amendment contains various rights, including the one most relevant to police officers' actions in questioning suspects: "No person shall . . . be compelled in any criminal case to be a witness against himself." The privilege against compelled self-incrimination should not be viewed as simply a legal protection that seeks to assist individuals who may be guilty of crimes. By protecting individuals in this way, the Fifth Amendment discourages police officers from using violent or otherwise coercive means to push suspects to confess.

In addition to discouraging the physical abuse of suspects, the privilege against compelled self-incrimination can also diminish the risk of erroneous convictions. When police officers use coercive pressure to seek confessions, they create a significant risk that innocent people will confess to crimes they did not commit. The worst-case scenario took place in the film *In the Name of the Father* (1993), based on a true story in England, in which police officers gained a confession from a bombing suspect whom they knew to be innocent by placing a gun in the suspect's mouth and threatening to pull the trigger. This example from England took place at a time when people there were afraid of terrorist acts by militants who sought to force Great Britain to remove its soldiers and governing institutions from Northern Ireland. Since 9/11, many Americans feel similar fears about our own country's vulnerability to terrorists. See "What Americans Think" to assess how the threat of terrorism may have influenced the public's views on coercive questioning of terrorism suspects.

Miranda Rules

The decision by the Supreme Court in *Miranda v. Arizona* (1966) said that as soon as the investigation of a crime begins to focus on a particular suspect and that person is taken into custody, the so-called *Miranda* warnings must be read aloud before questioning can begin.

Suspects must be told that (1) they have the right to remain silent; (2) if they decide to make a statement, it can and will be used against them in court; (3) they have the right to consult with an attorney and have the attorney present during interrogation; and (4) if they cannot afford an attorney, the state will provide one.

Prior to the *Miranda* decision, police officers in some places solved crimes by picking up a poor person or an African American and torturing him or her until a confession was produced. In *Brown v. Mississippi* (1936), the Supreme Court ruled that statements produced after suspects were beaten by police were inadmissible, but it did not insist that counsel be available at the early stages of the criminal process.

Miranda v. Arizona (1966)
U.S. Supreme Court decision declaring that suspects in custody must be informed of their rights to remain silent and to be represented during questioning.

Two rulings in 1964 laid the foundation for the *Miranda* decision. In *Escobedo v. Illinois*, the Court made the link between the Fifth Amendment right against self-incrimination and the Sixth Amendment right to counsel. Danny Escobedo was questioned at the police station for 14 hours without counsel, even though he asked to see his attorney. He finally made incriminating statements that the police said were voluntary. The Court's ruling specified that defendants have a right to counsel

> when the investigation is no longer a general inquiry into an unsolved crime, but has begun to focus on a particular suspect, the suspect has been taken into police custody, [and] the police carry out a process of interrogations that lends itself to eliciting incriminating statements.

The Court effectively expanded the right to counsel to apply at an early point in the criminal justice process as a means to guard against law enforcement officers' actions that might violate the Fifth Amendment privilege against compelled self-incrimination. In *Massiah v. United States* (1964), the Supreme Court declared that the questioning of the defendant by a police agent outside of the presence of defense counsel violated the defendant's rights.

The *Miranda* warnings apply only to what are called custodial interrogations. If police officers walk up to someone on the street and begin asking questions, there is no need to inform the person of her or his rights. The justices say that people know they can walk away when an officer asks them questions in a public place. When police have taken someone into custody, however, the Supreme Court sees risks of excessive pressure. The loss of liberty and isolation experienced by detained suspects can make them vulnerable to abusive interrogation techniques, especially when interrogations take place out of view of anyone other than police officers. When a suspect is alone in a room with the police, will anyone believe the suspect if he or she later claims to have been beaten? If the police say that the suspect confessed, will anyone believe the suspect if she or he denies this? The *Miranda* warnings and presence of counsel during questioning are supposed to prevent such abuses (C. E. Smith, 2010b).

The Court has permitted police officers to forgo *Miranda* warnings when a threat to public safety would result if they took the time to provide the warnings (Wright, 2013). This exception is similar to the exigent circumstance justification for warrantless searches. The underlying premise is that some urgent, socially significant

A police officer questions a suspect in custody. In such a confined setting, are you confident that suspects will truly understand the nature of their rights before consenting to be questioned without an attorney present?

Marmaduke St. John/Alamy Stock Photo

situation outweighs the necessity of respecting individuals' rights. In the case that created this **"public safety" exception**, police officers chased an armed man into a supermarket after a reported assault and handcuffed him. When they found that he had an empty shoulder holster, they immediately asked, "Where's the gun?" (*New York v. Quarles*, 1984). Although he had not been informed of his *Miranda* rights, his statement in response to the question could be used against him in court because the public's safety might have been threatened if the police had taken the time to read him his rights before asking any questions.

Miranda warnings were created by the Supreme Court to combat law enforcement practices, including physical violence and psychological pressure, that had been used throughout most of American history to press criminal suspects into confessing. During the twenty-first century, debates have emerged about whether government officials should be permitted to return to pre-*Miranda* practices for a specific category of suspects: terrorism suspects. Indeed, FBI agents who questioned the man ultimately convicted for the 2013 Boston Marathon bombing used the "public safety exception" to avoid informing him of his rights (Heath & McCoy, 2013). During the presidential election campaign of 2016, several Republican candidates advocated going even further with terrorism suspects by using techniques of torture to extract information (Welna, 2016). How do such practices fit with Americans' claims about the country's commitment to the Bill of Rights? As you think about your own viewpoint, see "What Americans Think" for evidence about how this subject divides society.

The Supreme Court continues to refine and clarify the requirements of *Miranda* warnings (Kinports, 2011; Dery, 2011). In *Berghuis v. Thompkins* (2010), the Court concluded that a suspect being questioned cannot assert his right to remain silent simply by remaining silent in the face of continued questioning by an officer. Instead, he must actually tell the officer that he is asserting his right to remain silent in order to seek an end to the officer's questioning (Weisselberg, 2011). The Court permitted police to vary the precise words used to provide the warnings in *Florida v. Powell* (2010). The Court approved the officers' delivery of the warnings even though they failed to make clear that the suspect has a right to consult with an attorney throughout the entire questioning process and not just, as they stated it to the suspect, "before answering questions." And in *J. D. B. v. North Carolina* (2011), a case concerning police officers' questioning of a seventh-grader at school, the Court declared that juveniles may be entitled to *Miranda* warnings even in some situations in which an adult could freely walk away from the police and thus not be considered a detained suspect entitled to warnings.

Although some legal commentators and police officials have criticized the *Miranda* warnings and urged the Court to eliminate the rule, the Supreme Court strongly repeated its endorsement of the *Miranda* requirement in 2000 (*Dickerson v. United States*). In declaring that *Miranda* warnings are required by the Constitution, Chief Justice William Rehnquist's majority opinion stated that "*Miranda* has become embedded in routine police

"public safety" exception
Exception to *Miranda* requirements that permits police to immediately question a suspect in custody without providing any warnings, if public safety would be jeopardized by their taking the time to supply the warnings.

WHAT AMERICANS THINK

QUESTION: Is torture justified as a means to gain important information from suspected terrorists?

	Often	Sometimes	Rarely	Never	Don't Know
Total	20%	31%	20%	27%	3%
Men	24%	30%	19%	25%	3%
Women	16%	32%	21%	28%	3%
White	22%	32%	20%	24%	2%
African American	18%	30%	19%	31%	1%
Hispanic	13%	23%	21%	38%	5%
Postgraduate	13%	26%	21%	37%	2%
College grad	19%	30%	20%	28%	2%
Some college	21%	33%	21%	23%	2%
H.S. or less	21%	31%	19%	26%	2%

CRITICAL THINKING: Those respondents to the poll who believe that torture is justified in certain circumstances presumably also believe that torture is an effective way to obtain desired information. However, it is possible that the infliction of severe fear, pain, and discomfort will lead a tortured suspect to provide a false confession or inaccurate information out of sheer desperation—especially if the person really does not possess any pertinent information. How would you write a law that specifies when torture or coercive methods are allowed but that also ensures protection from excessive abuse or the infliction of pain? Is it possible to draft such a law in a workable manner?

Source: Pew Research Center, "Post-Grads Less Likely to Say Torture of Suspected Terrorists Can Be Justified." Survey conducted January 2015 (www.people-press.org).

practice to the point where the warnings have become part of our national culture." Rehnquist's conclusion was reinforced by a national survey of police chiefs in which more than three-quarters of respondents supported the Supreme Court's decision to keep the *Miranda* rule in place (Zalman & Smith, 2007).

The Consequences of *Miranda*

Miranda rights must be provided before questions are asked during custodial interrogations. However, police officers have adapted their techniques in various ways that enable them to question suspects without any impediment from the warnings. For example, officers may ask questions while standing on the suspect's doorstep before making an arrest. Even after arrest, the courts do not require that police inform suspects of their rights immediately. Thus, after taking a suspect into custody, some officers may delay providing *Miranda* warnings in case the suspect talks on his or her own. The suspect may be kept in the backseat of a car as officers drive around town, or the suspect may be left alone in a room at the police station. Some suspects will take the initiative to talk to officers because of feelings of guilt. Other suspects may start conversations with officers because they are so eager to convince the officers that they have an alibi or that they want to cooperate. This may lead the suspect to provide contradictory statements that will help build the case for the prosecution.

Officers are also trained in interrogation techniques that are intended to encourage suspects to talk despite *Miranda* warnings (Weisselberg, 2008). The words of the warnings are so familiar from their use in television police shows that many suspects never stop to think about the message being conveyed. In addition, officers may pretend to sympathize with the suspect (Leo, 1996). For example, they may say such things as, "We know that you had a good reason to go after that guy with a knife. Tell us how it happened." Police officers are not required to be truthful in speaking to suspects. They are permitted to use deception to induce suspects to talk. It is not uncommon for officers to say, untruthfully, "We have five witnesses that saw you do it. If you tell us everything right now, we may be able to get you a good deal." In reality, there were no witnesses and there will be no deal. Do such statements constitute improper pressure in violation of *Miranda*? Probably not—as long as the officers do not threaten suspects in ways that make them fear for their physical safety or the safety of their loved ones.

Many suspects talk to the police despite being informed of their right to remain silent and their right to have an attorney present during questioning. Some suspects do not fully understand their rights even after being read the *Miranda* warnings (R. Rogers et al., 2011). They may believe that they will look guilty if they remain silent or ask for an attorney, and therefore feel that they must talk to officers if they are to have any hope of claiming innocence. More importantly, many suspects believe (often accurately) that they will gain a more favorable charge or plea bargain if they cooperate with officers as fully and as early as possible. Read the "You Make the Decision" feature to consider your own views on how you might question a suspect.

Some commentators have argued that officers' efforts to get around the *Miranda* requirement could be prevented by requiring that all police interrogations be video recorded, to provide proof that suspects' statements are voluntary. Several states have introduced video-recording requirements, but they are often limited to certain categories of cases, such as murders or serious felonies (L. Lewis, 2007). In 2006, the FBI formally prohibited its agents from videotaping most interrogations for fear that the presence of cameras would discourage suspects from talking and that jurors might react unfavorably to seeing some of the techniques used by law enforcement officers to elicit incriminating statements. However, in 2014 the U.S. Department of Justice reversed that policy and required the videotaping of most interrogations. The new policy applies to the FBI as well as the Drug Enforcement Administration, (DEA), U.S. Marshals, and the Bureau of Alcohol, Tobacco, Firearms, and Explosives. Officials decided that it was more important for jurors to see and hear the actual incriminating statements in order to obtain convictions than to worry about the reactions of some suspects or jurors to the practice of videotaping in the

YOU MAKE THE DECISION

Police Officer

Before questioning a suspect in custody, police officers must give him or her the *Miranda* warnings, including the notification of the right to remain silent. At that point, if the suspect wishes to remain silent, he or she must make a statement to that effect. Officers must cease questioning at that point. If the suspect merely remains silent, officers may continue to ask questions until such time as the suspect asserts the desire to remain silent.

You are a police officer questioning a suspect in custody in a murder case. You inform the suspect of his right to remain silent. The exchange occurs as follows:

YOU: You watch TV shows, right? Do you see when the police walk up to somebody, and we want to ask you, we want to talk to you about something, we always read the person their rights? You've seen that on TV, right? They say you've got the right to remain silent. Anything you say can and will be used against you in court. You've heard that before, haven't you? Yeah. We have to go through that formality to get to what we want to talk about. That's—we have to go through that formality.

SUSPECT: I don't want to say nothing. I don't know—

YOU: But you don't have to say anything.

SUSPECT: Yeah.

YOU: You don't have to say anything. That's, you know, that's your right. But to get to one point, from point A to point B, we have to read you your rights. And the key word is, they're your rights. So we got to read them to you, so you understand.

In light of that exchange, do you continue questioning the suspect? If a court later decides that the suspect asserted the right to remain silent, any statements made after this point by the suspect cannot be used in evidence. If, however, this suspect is not regarded as having asserted the right to remain silent, subsequent statements obtained through questioning can be used in evidence. What will you do—continue questioning or leave the suspect alone? Explain your reasons. Then search the Internet and read the Maryland Court of Appeals decision in *Williams v. Maryland* (December 18, 2015).

interview rooms of federal law enforcement agencies (Schmidt, 2014). It remains to be seen whether such requirements will become more universal.

One of the concerns regarding *Miranda* warnings is the risk that innocent people, especially vulnerable people with developmental disabilities or little education, will be pressured into making self-incriminating statements. This is one cause of erroneous convictions. However, the leading cause of erroneous convictions is misidentifications made by witnesses and victims (Smalarz & Wells, 2015; Walsh, 2013). The "Evidence-Based Practice and Policy" feature discusses the use of research to reduce the risk of misidentifications.

CHECK POINT

8. What are *Miranda* rights?

Officers must inform suspects, *before* custodial interrogation, of their right to remain silent, the prosecution's authority to use any of the suspect's statements, the right to the presence of an attorney during questioning, and the right to have an attorney appointed if the suspect is too poor to hire one.

9. What is the "public safety" exception?

Officers can ask questions of suspects in custody without first providing *Miranda* warnings when public safety would be threatened by their taking the time to supply the warnings.

10. How have police officers adapted their practices in light of *Miranda*?

Officers ask questions before suspects are in custody; pretend to befriend or empathize with suspects being questioned; and misinform suspects about the existence of evidence demonstrating their guilt.

STOP & ANALYZE

Should police officers be permitted to lie to suspects during questioning, such as falsely claiming that they have eyewitnesses or other evidence of a suspect's guilt? Do such strategies create any risks, such as innocent people feeling hopelessly doomed and admitting guilt in order to seek a plea to a lesser charge? Write an argument in favor of giving police flexibility to use such strategies as well as an argument against permitting dishonest statements. Which argument do you support? Why?

Identification Procedures

One of the consequences of the development of DNA testing has been the discovery that many innocent people were convicted of crimes based on misidentifications by eyewitnesses. Men convicted of rape based on the victims' certain claims that they were the perpetrators have gained release, often after spending many years in prison, thanks to newly developed scientific tests of blood or semen from the crime scene that definitely exclude them as contributors of the biological material. These disappointing revelations about flaws and mistakes in the criminal investigation process helped to encourage research by psychologists and other social scientists about how and why eyewitnesses misidentify suspects.

Research studies indicate that risks of misidentification by eyewitnesses can be reduced simply by changing identification procedures. As portrayed in many movies and television dramas, lineups with people standing in a row as a victim or witness attempts to pick out the criminal offender have been very common in police work. However, research studies have identified a number of risks in lineups and other similar procedures as follows:

- *Showups*, in which a single suspect is brought before a victim or witness, create risks that the police will be regarded as signaling that this is indeed the guilty individual. Moreover, the victim or witness has no other individuals to consider or compare in a showup.

- In any procedure, victims or witnesses should be told that the guilty individual is not necessarily present in the lineup or array of photos. Otherwise there is a risk that an individual will be chosen, even if not well-remembered, simply because of an assumption that one of these people must be the guilty individual.

- Some research indicates that fewer errors occur when victims or witnesses are shown individuals one at a time, either in person or in photos. In this way, they are pushed to compare each individual with their own memories. Otherwise, they may believe that they are supposed to choose the individual who looks most like the perpetrator from among a lineup group or simultaneously viewed photos. Looking in sequences may increase the likelihood that they will honestly say, "I don't see the individual here," rather than make an inaccurate selection from among the choices.

- Errors may be reduced if the identification procedure is supervised by a police official who has nothing to do with the case and has no idea which individual the other police officers suspect of committing the crime. When active investigators run lineups or present photo arrays, there are risks that they will subtly or unconsciously signal through statements or body language that a specific individual is the actual person they believe to be the perpetrator. Such actions, even if subtle, can influence the identifications made by victims and witnesses.

- Many reformers also argue that identification procedures should be videotaped so that there are opportunities to see if the individuals supervising the procedures either intentionally or unintentionally provided cues about which individual to select. In addition, videotaping can help to show whether the victim or witness made a tentative, uncertain identification or if the identification was certain and confident.

In 2013, the Houston police department was criticized for continuing to use a photo lineup procedure in which a victim or witness is shown photos of all possible suspects at one time. At this time, many other Texas police departments, including Austin, Dallas, and San Antonio, had already switched to showing photos one at a time in order to reduce the risks of misidentification discussed in the research studies. These examples show that many police departments have adjusted their practices in light of evidence produced by research studies. However, other departments have yet to adopt evidence-based practices to reduce the risk of misidentifications.

Researching the Internet

Bearing in mind risks illuminated by research, read the identification procedure policy of the Seattle Police Department. Do you see any issues or problems with the specified procedures? http://www.seattle.gov/police-manual/title-15—primary -investigation/15170—conducting-identification-procedures

Implementing New Practices

Officers may prefer to continue practices with which they are familiar. There may be resistance to change, especially if officers are distrustful of the underlying research or if they believe that the new procedures needlessly permit guilty people to go free. Should the courts order police departments to conduct identification procedures in one specific way? Alternatively, would such an approach create risks that police could not adapt as new research is produced that refines understandings about the risks and benefits of different approaches? Write a memo that lists two reasons why you support either a specific, mandated set of procedures or opportunities for departments to develop their own methods. In addition, address the following question: If you were a police chief, how would you instruct your officers to conduct identification procedures, and how do you think you could convince them to cooperate in using the new methods?

Sources: M.D. Cicchini and J. G. Easton, "Reforming the Law on Show-Up Identifications," *Journal of Criminal Law and Criminology* 100 (2010): 381–413; M. McGuire, T. Kenny, and A. Grabic, "Eyewitness Identification for Prudent Police," *Policing: An International Journal of Police Strategies & Management* 38 (2015): 598–609; J. Pinkerton, "HPD, Sheriff Using Questioned Photo Lineups," *Houston Chronicle,* January 14, 2013 (www.houstonchronicle.com); B. Schuster, "Police Lineups: Making Eyewitness Identification More Reliable," *NIJ Journal,* 258 (October 2007): 2–9; L. Smalarz, and G. Wells, "Contamination of Eyewitness Self-Reports and the Mistaken-Identification Problem," *Current Directions in Psychological Science* 24 (2015): 120–24; *United States v. Ford,* 11-2034, U.S. Court of Appeals, 7th Circuit, June 6, 2012; G. L. Wells and D. S. Quinlivan, "Suggestive Eyewitness Identification Procedures and the Supreme Court's Reliability Test in Light of Eyewitness Science: 30 Years Later," *Law and Human Behavior* 33 (2009): 1–24.

The Exclusionary Rule

What happens when police commit rights violations? One primary remedy is the exclusion of evidence from court (Gray, 2013). In 1914, the U.S. Supreme Court declared in *Weeks v. United States* that federal courts must exclude any evidence that was obtained through an improper search by federal law enforcement agents. In *Weeks*, U.S. marshals searched a home without a warrant and found incriminating evidence. According to the Court,

> if letters and private documents can thus be seized and held and used in evidence against a citizen accused of an offense, the protection of the Fourth Amendment, declaring his right to be secure against such searches and seizures, is of no value, and, so far as those thus placed are concerned, might as well be stricken from the Constitution.

Thus, the Court required that the improperly obtained evidence be excluded from use in court, even if it meant that a guilty person might go free because of a lack of enough evidence to gain a conviction. As a result of this **exclusionary rule** created by the Court, it was assumed that law enforcement officers would obey the Fourth Amendment to avoid the loss of incriminating evidence. Later, the exclusionary rule was also applied to Fifth Amendment violations caused by improper questioning, such as a failure to inform arrested individuals of their *Miranda* rights.

exclusionary rule The principle that illegally obtained evidence must be excluded from trial.

Newspaper stories periodically report on cases in which prosecutors decide or judges rule that evidence must be excluded due to police errors or intentional actions that violate individuals' rights. For example, when Oscar-winning film actor Philip Seymour Hoffman died of a heroin overdose in New York City in 2014, the police arrested Robert Aaron, a friend of Hoffman's from whom he had reportedly purchased heroin. The prosecutor ended up dropping the most serious drug-selling charges against Aaron, because the police officers who first questioned him after his arrest had failed to inform him of his *Miranda* rights (Leland, 2014). Such decisions may come from prosecutors and judges at all levels of the state and federal court systems. One example is the U.S. Supreme Court's decision in *Arizona v. Gant* (2009) limiting police officers' ability to search vehicles based on the arrest of a driver who was handcuffed and moved away from the car. The Court's decision upheld the Arizona Supreme Court's 2007 decision that evidence from the search of the vehicle must be excluded from evidence in the prosecution of Gant

Police officers must take care to follow the rules for conducting proper searches that obey court rulings defining the Fourth Amendment protection against "unreasonable searches and seizures." Evidence will be excluded when the Fourth Amendment is violated, unless the police officers' actions fall within a specific exception to the exclusionary rule.

AP Images/Ted S. Warren

due to the improper search. In another example, New York's highest court, called the state Court of Appeals, ordered the exclusion of evidence from a vehicle search in *People v. Garcia* (2012) when officers did not have a proper basis for questioning the vehicle's driver. In 2013, a judge on Michigan's lowest level trial court ordered the exclusion of incriminating statements obtained from a homicide suspect when he had been held in custody too long without being formally charged with a crime (Misjak, 2013).

The exclusionary rule does not necessarily require that cases against defendants be dismissed when constitutional rights have been violated. The prosecution can continue, but improperly obtained evidence may not be used. In some cases, other valid evidence of guilt may exist in the form of witness testimony or confessions. As described by one scholar with experience as a prosecutor,

> during my seven years as a federal prosecutor,... I could see that the rule's mandatory nature forced police and federal agents to think about the rules before they acted. It caused both federal and local law-enforcement authorities to train their agents in the constitutional rules in order to [avoid] evidentiary exclusion.... Nor was it my impression that any significant number of cases were lost as a result of the rule, especially prosecutions of violent felonies (Bradley, 2010:212).

The Application of the Exclusionary Rule to the States

Wolf v. Colorado (1949) Supreme Court decision in which the Fourth Amendment was applied against searches by state and local police officers, but the exclusionary rule was not imposed as the remedy for violations of the Fourth Amendment by these officials.

Mapp v. Ohio (1961) Supreme Court decision that applied the exclusionary rule as the remedy for improper searches by state and local officials.

Weeks v. United States (1914) Supreme Court decision applying the exclusionary rule as the remedy for improper searches by federal law enforcement officials.

In *Wolf v. Colorado* (1949), the Supreme Court incorporated the Fourth Amendment. However, the justices declined to apply the exclusionary rule to the states because they believed states could develop their own remedies to handle improper searches by police. The situation changed during the Supreme Court tenure of Chief Justice Earl Warren (1953–1969), when the Court incorporated most of the criminal justice–related rights in a way that required state law enforcement officials to adhere to the same rules federal law enforcement officials had to follow. Not until *Mapp v. Ohio* (1961) did the Court apply the exclusionary rule to the states.

Why did the Supreme Court see the exclusionary rule as necessary? Several reasons emerge in *Weeks v. United States* (1914) and *Mapp*. First, *Weeks* declared that the exclusionary rule is essential to make the Fourth Amendment meaningful. In essence, the justices believed that constitutional rights are nullified if government officials are permitted to benefit by violating those rights. Second, *Mapp* indicated that the exclusionary rule is required by the Constitution. Third, the majority opinion in *Mapp* concluded that alternatives to the exclusionary rule do not work. The opinion noted that many states had found that nothing short of exclusion of evidence would work to correct constitutional rights violations and limit the number of violations that occur. Fourth, the *Mapp* opinion argued that the use of improperly obtained evidence by officials who are responsible for upholding the law serves only to diminish respect for the law. Fifth, the *Mapp* decision indicates that the absence of an exclusionary rule would diminish the protection of all rights because it would permit all constitutional rights "to be revocable at the whim of any police officer who, in the name of law enforcement itself, chooses to suspend... [the] enjoyment [of rights]." Sixth, the exclusionary rule is justified in *Mapp* as an effective means of deterring police and prosecutors from violating constitutional rights (Kainen, 2013).

The existence of the exclusionary rule demonstrates the Supreme Court's conclusion that it is sometimes necessary to risk setting a guilty criminal free to ensure that constitutional rights are protected.

Exceptions to the Exclusionary Rule

The exclusionary rule has many critics who claim that the Court's decision hampers police investigations and allows guilty criminals to go free. However, research has not clearly supported claims about the negative consequences of the exclusionary rule. Studies of the impact of the exclusionary rule have produced two consistent findings. First, only a small minority of defendants file a "motion to suppress," asking a judge to exclude evidence that has allegedly been obtained in violation of the defendant's rights. Second, only a very small fraction of motions to suppress evidence are granted (Uchida & Bynum, 1991; S. Walker, 2001). Despite continuing debates about the rule's impact and effectiveness (Dripps, 2010), the Supreme Court began creating exceptions to the exclusionary rule after Warren Burger became chief justice in 1969.

"Good Faith" Exception   The Supreme Court created a "good faith" exception to the exclusionary rule when officers use search warrants (*United States v. Leon,* **1984**). *Good faith* means that the officers acted with the honest belief that they were following the proper rules, but the judge issued the warrant improperly (Cox, 2015). In addition, the reliance on the warrant and the honest belief that they were acting correctly must be reasonable. If officers knew that a judge issued a warrant based on no evidence whatsoever, the officers could not claim that they reasonably and honestly relied on the warrant. But when officers present evidence of probable cause to the judge and the judge issues a warrant based on information that actually falls below the standard of probable cause, the officers may use evidence found in the resulting search, because it was the judge who made the error, not the police (Cammack, 2010). However, evidence can still be excluded if officers undertake a warrantless search based on their own discretionary decision, even if they honestly (but wrongly) believe that such a search is permitted in such circumstances.

"Inevitable Discovery" Rule   Another important exception to the exclusionary rule is the **"inevitable discovery" rule** (Grubman, 2011). This rule arose from a case involving the tragic abduction and murder of a young girl. The police sought an escapee from a psychiatric hospital who was seen carrying a large bundle. The man being sought contacted an attorney and arranged to surrender to police in a town 160 miles away from the scene of the abduction. The Supreme Court subsequently found that the police improperly questioned the suspect in the absence of his attorney while driving him back to the city where the abduction occurred (*Brewer v. Williams,* 1977). The Court declared that the girl's body and the suspect's statements had to be excluded from evidence because they were obtained in violation of his rights. Thus, his murder conviction was overturned and he was given a new trial. At the second trial, he was convicted again. However, at the second trial, the prosecution used the body in evidence against him based on the claim that search parties would have found the body eventually even without his confession. There was a search team within two and one-half miles of the body at the time that it was found. In *Nix v. Williams* (**1984**), the Supreme Court agreed that the improperly obtained evidence can be used when it would later have been inevitably discovered, without improper actions by the police. Table 6.2 summarizes selected Supreme Court decisions regarding the exclusionary rule as it applies to the Fourth and Fifth Amendments.

When the Court issued its decisions in *Weeks* and *Mapp*, it appeared that the exclusion of evidence would be guided by a trial judge's answer to the question: "Did police violate the suspect's rights?" Later, through the development of exceptions to the rule, the Court shifted its focus to the question: "Did the police make an error that was so serious that the exclusion of evidence is required?" For example, the "good faith" exception established in *United States v. Leon* (1984) emphasizes the fact that officers did what they thought they were supposed to do, not the fact that the suspect's Fourth Amendment rights were violated by a search conducted with an improper warrant. Thus, the Supreme Court's creation of exceptions to the exclusionary rule has given police officers the flexibility to make specific kinds of errors in an increasing variety of situations without jeopardizing the admissibility

"good faith" exception Exception to the exclusionary rule that permits the use of improperly obtained evidence when police officers acted in honest reliance on a defective statute, a warrant improperly issued by a magistrate, or a consent to search by someone who lacked authority to give such permission.

United States v. Leon (1984) Supreme Court decision announcing the "good faith" exception to the exclusionary rule.

"inevitable discovery" rule Supreme Court ruling that improperly obtained evidence can be used if it would inevitably have been discovered by the police.

Nix v. Williams (1984) Legal decision in which the Supreme Court created the "inevitable discovery" exception to the exclusionary rule.

TABLE 6.2   **Exclusionary Rule**

The Supreme Court has created the exclusionary rule as a means of ensuring that Fourth and Fifth Amendment rights are protected. It has also provided exceptions to this rule.

Case	Decision
Exclusionary rule *Mapp v. Ohio* (1961)	Because the Fourth Amendment protects people from unreasonable searches and seizures by all law enforcement officials, evidence found through improper searches or seizures must be excluded from use at state and federal trials.
"Good faith" exception *United States v. Leon* (1984)	When officers act in good faith reliance on a warrant, the evidence will not be excluded even if the warrant was issued improperly.
"Inevitable discovery" exception *Nix v. Williams* (1984)	Improperly obtained evidence can be used if it would later have inevitably been discovered without improper actions by the police.

of evidence that may help establish a defendant's guilt (Nolasco, del Carmen, & Vaughn, 2011).

In 2009 some commentators speculated that the Supreme Court was deeply divided on the issue of whether to eliminate the exclusionary rule (Liptak, 2009). For instance, when a man was wrongly arrested because sloppy records in a police database erroneously informed the officers that there was an arrest warrant for that man, five justices declined to apply the exclusionary rule to the resulting improper search based on the erroneous arrest (*Herring v. United States*, 2009).

Critics of the exclusionary rule hope that this decision moved the Court one step closer to abolishing the rule. In reality, the fate of the rule will be determined by new justices, who could go either way (C. E. Smith, McCall, & McCall, 2009). In the immediate future, it is unclear who will be appointed as the next Supreme Court justice by the new president elected in 2016 and what view of the exclusionary rule the next justice and subsequent new appointees will bring to the nation's highest court.

CHECK POINT

11. **Why was the exclusionary rule created and eventually applied to the states?**
   The exclusionary rule was created to deter officers from violating people's rights, and the Supreme Court considers it an essential component of the Fourth and Fifth Amendments.

12. **What are the criticisms of the exclusionary rule?**
   The rule is criticized for hampering police investigations and permitting some guilty people to go free.

13. **What are the main exceptions to the exclusionary rule?**
   "Good faith" exceptions in warrant situations; cases in which evidence would have been discovered by the police anyway ("inevitable discovery" rule).

STOP & ANALYZE

When you add up the pros and cons, does the exclusionary rule provide a needed benefit for our society and justice system? Describe three situations in which the exclusionary rule should definitely apply—*or* list three reasons why the exclusionary rule should be abolished. Give two reasons why you would treat *Miranda* cases differently from search cases *or* why you would treat them in the same manner with respect to the issue of excluding improperly obtained evidence.

Think, Discuss, Write

Recall that the chapter's initial discussion of cell-phone searches by police included the 2014 example of officers in California seizing motorists' cell phones in order to look for and steal revealing photos. In one case, an officer forwarded the image of a bikini-clad woman to a fellow officer as the woman whose cell phone contained the photo was being checked for injuries after an automobile collision. One writer described the incident by pointing sarcasm at the police: "The colleague upbraided him for violating a citizen's privacy, contacted the commanding officer, and arranged for [the fellow officer's] arrest on felony charges. I kid, of course. The colleague actually complained that the photo wasn't more explicit" (Friedersdorf, 2014). In actuality, the colleague complained that it was not a nude photo. Meanwhile, the officer who stole the photo requested that his colleague send him some photos from motorists' cell phones, too.

Discussion/Writing Assignment

If you were a police chief, what steps would you take to try to create a culture of ethics and professionalism among your officers? Ideally, officers with any thoughts of engaging in misconduct should believe that their colleagues will criticize and report them. Instead, too often certain officers automatically help to hide the misconduct of other officers. Write a memo that provides and explains three suggestions that a chief could initiate within a police department to tackle this issue.

Source: C. Friedersdorf, "California Can't Police Its Own Cops Stealing Nude Photos of Women," *The Atlantic*, October 29, 2014 (www.theatlantic.com).

SUMMARY

1 Describe the extent of police officers' authority to stop people and to conduct searches of people, their vehicles, and other property.

- The Supreme Court has defined rules for the circumstances and justifications for stops, searches, and arrests in light of the Fourth Amendment's prohibition on unreasonable searches and seizures.
- The "plain view" doctrine permits officers to visually examine and use as evidence, without a warrant, any contraband or criminal evidence that is in open sight when the officers are in a place where they are legally permitted to be.
- Most stops must be supported by reasonable suspicion; an arrest or a search warrant must be supported by enough information to constitute probable cause.
- Police use of deadly force occurs infrequently and can no longer be applied to unarmed fleeing felons.

2 Explain how police officers seek warrants in order to conduct searches and make arrests.

- To obtain a warrant, police officers present an affidavit (sworn statement) verifying the accuracy of the information that they present to the judge, which they hope the judge will regard as constituting probable cause to search or make an arrest.

3 Describe situations in which police officers can examine property and conduct searches without obtaining a warrant.

- Searches are considered "reasonable" and may be conducted without warrants in specific circumstances that present special needs beyond the normal purposes of law enforcement. For example, borders and airports always allow searches without warrants.
- Limited searches may be conducted without warrants when officers have reasonable suspicions to justify a stop and frisk for weapons on the streets, when officers make a lawful arrest, under exigent circumstances, when people voluntarily consent to searches of their persons or property, and in certain situations involving automobiles.

4 Explain the purpose of the privilege against compelled self-incrimination.

- The Fifth Amendment privilege against compelled self-incrimination helps protect citizens against violence and coercion by police and helps to maintain the legitimacy and integrity of the legal system.
- The Supreme Court's decision in *Miranda v. Arizona* requires officers to inform suspects of specific rights before custodial questioning, although officers have adapted their practices to accommodate this rule so that they can question people

without any impediment from the warning. Several exceptions to the warning have been created by the Supreme Court.

5 **Define the exclusionary rule, and identify the situations in which it applies.**

- By barring the use of illegally obtained evidence in court, the exclusionary rule is designed to deter police from violating citizens' rights during criminal investigations.
- The Supreme Court has created several exceptions to the exclusionary rule, including the "inevitable discovery" rule and the "good faith" exception in defective warrant situations.

Questions for Review

1. What are the requirements for police officers with respect to stops, searches, arrests, and warrants?
2. Under what circumstances are warrantless searches permissible?
3. How have police officers adapted to the requirements of *Miranda v. Arizona*?
4. What are the main exceptions to the exclusionary rule?

Key Terms and Cases

affidavit (p. 211)

consent search (p. 218)

exclusionary rule (p. 229)

exigent circumstances (p. 217)

"good faith" exception (p. 231)

"inevitable discovery" rule (p. 231)

inventory search (p. 222)

plain view doctrine (p. 207)

probable cause (p. 210)

"public safety" exception (p. 225)

reasonable expectation
of privacy (p. 207)

reasonable suspicion (p. 209)

search (p. 207)

seizures (p. 208)

stop (p. 209)

stop-and-frisk search (p. 215)

totality of circumstances (p. 212)

Chimel v. California (1969) (p. 216)

Illinois v. Gates (1983) (p. 212)

Mapp v. Ohio (1961) (p. 230)

Miranda v. Arizona (1966) (p. 223)

Nix v. Williams (1984) (p. 231)

Tennessee v. Garner (1985) (p. 209)

Terry v. Ohio (1968) (p. 215)

United States v. Drayton
(2002) (p. 218)

United States v. Leon (1984) (p. 231)

Weeks v. United States (1914) (p. 230)

Wolf v. Colorado (1949) (p. 230)

7 Courts and Adjudication

Reporters for both news and sports publications gathered in the courthouse in Fall River, Massachusetts, in early 2015 to provide coverage of a highly publicized murder trial. Aaron Hernandez, a star player for the National Football League's New England Patriots faced a trial on murder charges. He was accused of killing 27-year-old Odin Lloyd, the boyfriend of his fiancée's sister. A jogger found Lloyd's body in an industrial park less one mile from Hernandez's house in the town of North Attleborough. Lloyd had been shot with a .45 caliber handgun. Microscopic examinations of the five shell casings found near Lloyd's body by the Massachusetts State Police indicated they were likely fired by the same gun as the shell casing reportedly found in a car rented by Hernandez at the time of the shooting ("Shells Near Ex-NFL," 2015).

While Hernandez's fate would be determined by several factors, including the nature of the evidence against him and the jury's determinations about that evidence, the key actors who set the stage for that determination were the prosecutors and defense attorneys. In the adversarial setting of the trial, these attorneys bore responsibility for deciding which evidence to present and how to present it. For example, in order to gain additional evidence that might persuade the jury, Prosecutor William McCauley strongly pressed Judge E. Susan Garsh to admit into evidence text messages sent from the victim to his sister shortly before he was murdered (K. Armstrong, 2015). The attorneys also challenged their opponents' evidence and formulated arguments that sought to persuade the jury to understand the case in a certain way. The strategies and effectiveness of prosecutors and defense attorneys significantly affect whether or not defendants are convicted and punished.

For example, one strategy used by William McCauley and Patrick Bomberg was to meet with Hernandez's fiancée Shayanna Jenkins, presumably to talk about the potential for her to face criminal charges and imprisonment because there was reason to believe she may have helped cover up the crime by destroying evidence. After the meeting, the judge announced that Jenkins had been granted immunity from prosecution, and her name was placed on the prosecution's list of witnesses. If she and Hernandez had already been married at the time, she could not have been pressured to testify against him. The "spousal privilege" in American law protects spouses from being required to testify against each other in criminal cases. But since they were merely engaged to be married, the prosecutors were able to raise the threat of potential prosecution and offer the incentive of immunity—namely, freedom from prosecution—in exchange for her testimony (Candiotti, 2015).

By contrast, defense attorney James Sultan pursued a strategy of challenging the procedures used for gathering evidence, thereby raising questions about whether there had been sloppy police work. Sultan highlighted that the North Attleborough police department rarely handled murder investigations, only one every few years. He pressed Officer John Grim about why he failed to mention to the crime scene photographer that he saw footprints at the scene. He also challenged Grim about changing his statement about how far a towel was found from the body. He later pressed Sergeant Paul Baker of the Massachusetts State Police about the failure to put certain items immediately in evidence bags to avoid contamination rather than just putting them in the back of a truck. This approach seemed designed to cast doubts in the jurors' minds about whether they could trust the police officers' care in collecting evidence and the prosecutors' claims about the reliability of that evidence ("Aaron Hernandez Trial," 2015; "Hernandez Jurors," 2015). Ultimately, the defense attorney's efforts failed, and a jury found

Hernandez guilty of first-degree murder. He was sentenced to life in prison without possibility of parole (Belson & Mather, 2015).

Prosecutors and defense attorneys are key decision makers in the criminal justice process, whether or not cases actually proceed all the way to a trial. In most cases, the prosecutors and defense attorneys negotiate a plea agreement. Yet in both plea bargaining and trials, the attorneys' decisions, strategies, interactions, and effectiveness determine the fates of individuals facing criminal prosecution. Prosecutors make decisions about whom to charge and the list of charges to pursue. In some cases, they worry that the evidence is not strong enough, so they offer a plea agreement to the defendant. In other cases, the evidence is so strong that the defendant is eager to accept a plea and a specified sentence rather than risk a longer sentence by going through a trial. By contrast, defense attorneys must advise their clients and make strategic decisions about whether to plead guilty and what tactics to use during trial. Unfortunately, the system does not ensure that all defendants receive equally effective representation. Defendants who can afford to hire their own attorneys and pay for the services of expert witnesses have advantages over poor defendants who must rely on defense attorneys provided for them.

As illustrated by the Hernandez case, the American criminal justice system places great power and responsibility in the hands of attorneys for each side in a criminal case. The prosecutor and defense attorney are the most influential figures in determining the outcomes of criminal cases. Their discretionary decisions and negotiations determine people's fates. As we shall see in this chapter, the justice system's ability to handle cases and produce fair results depends on the dedication, skill, and enthusiasm of these lawyers. In addition, the lawyers who become judges assume important duties for overseeing court proceedings that decide whether accused defendants will be found guilty and punished.

AP Images/Ted Fitzgerald

The Functions and Structure of American Courts

The United States has a dual court system. Separate federal and state court systems handle matters throughout the nation. Other countries have a single national court system, but American rules and traditions permit states to create their own court systems to handle most legal matters, including most crimes.

In the United States, both state and federal courts use the **adversarial process** to protect the rights of defendants and examine evidence to determine whether a defendant is guilty. In the adversarial process, a professional attorney, trained in the rules of evidence and the strategies of advocacy, represents each side—the prosecution (government) and defense (defendant). These attorneys challenge each other's evidence and arguments while trying to persuade the judge or jury about the defendant's guilt or lack thereof. Even when the attorneys negotiate a guilty plea without going to trial, they are supposed to adopt an adversarial stance that represents the interests of their side. Although they may hold friendly and cooperative discussions, the content of these discussions often reflects probing, bluffing, compromising, and disagreeing.

In the adversarial context of American courts, judges often act like referees at a sporting event. They oversee the interactions and enforce the rules without imposing their will on the presentation of evidence by attorneys. The adversarial process is derived from British law and exists in the criminal justice systems of other former British colonies besides the United States. By contrast, other countries typically use an **inquisitorial process**, in which the judge takes an active role in questioning witnesses and asserts herself into the investigation of the case and the examination of evidence.

The federal courts oversee a limited range of criminal cases. For example, they deal with people accused of violating the criminal laws of the national government. Federal crimes include counterfeiting, kidnapping, smuggling, and drug trafficking, among others. But such cases account for only a small portion of the criminal cases that pass through U.S. courts each year. For every offender sentenced to incarceration by federal courts, more than 10 offenders are sent to prisons and jails by state courts, because most crimes are defined by state laws (BJS, 2016). This disparity may grow wider as federal law enforcement agencies increasingly emphasize antiterrorism activities rather than traditional crime control investigations. The gap is even greater for misdemeanors, because state courts bear the primary responsibility for processing the lesser offenses, such as disorderly conduct, that arise on a daily basis.

State supreme courts monitor the decisions of lower courts within their own states by interpreting state constitutions and statutes. Although most are named the "Supreme Court" of the state (for example, "Minnesota Supreme Court"), in a few states, they have different names. In New York, the top court is called the New York Court of Appeals, and "supreme courts" in that state are trial courts. The U.S. Supreme Court oversees both court systems by interpreting the U.S. Constitution, which protects the rights of defendants in federal and state criminal cases (Smith, DeJong, & McCall, 2011).

A third court system operates in several states; this adds to the issues of complexity and coordination that the country's decentralized courts face. Native Americans have tribal courts, whose authority is endorsed by congressional statutes and Supreme Court decisions, with **jurisdiction** over their own people on tribal land. The existence of tribal courts permits Native American judges to apply their people's cultural values in resolving civil lawsuits and processing certain criminal offenses (Nesper, 2015; Florey, 2013).

The Functions of Courts

Courts serve many important functions for society. We often picture courts as the settings for criminal trials, like those portrayed on television shows such as *Law and Order*. When courts focus on criminal matters, through bail hearings, preliminary hearings, plea bargaining, and trials, they are serving a *norm enforcement*

adversarial process Court process, employed in the United States and other former British colonies, in which lawyers for each side represent their clients' best interests in presenting evidence and formulating arguments as a means to discover the truth and protect the rights of defendants.

inquisitorial process Court process, employed in most countries of the world, in which the judge takes an active role in investigating the case and examining evidence by, for example, questioning witnesses.

jurisdiction The geographic territory or legal boundaries within which control may be exercised; the range of a court's authority.

function for society. A *norm* is a value, standard, or expectation concerning people's behavior. In other words, courts play a central role in enforcing society's rules and standards for behavior—a function that contributes to peace and stability in society. In addition, courts handle a wide variety of matters beyond criminal justice, matters that benefit society in ways that extend beyond merely determining the guilt of and punishments for criminal defendants.

Courts also handle *dispute processing* for society. When people disagree about contracts, money, property, and personal injuries in ways that they cannot resolve on their own, they file lawsuits seeking government intervention on their behalf. Presumably the availability of courts for dispute processing helps avoid the possibility that people will resort to violence when they become angry about disagreements with business partners, neighbors, and others. In criminal justice, the dispute-processing function plays a significant role when people file lawsuits against police officers or correctional officials for violating constitutional rights. As a result of such lawsuits, judges may order prisons to change their procedures or order police officers or their departments to pay thousands of dollars to compensate a citizen for an erroneous arrest, excessive use of force, or the improper search of a home.

Courts also engage in *policy making*, especially the highest courts, such as state supreme courts and the U.S. Supreme Court. When judges interpret the U.S. Constitution or other forms of law and thereby define the rights of individuals, they are simultaneously telling police officers, correctional officers, and other officials what they can and cannot do. Such judicial decisions determine how searches will be conducted, how suspects will be questioned, and how prisons will be managed. This function makes courts in the United States especially important and powerful, because judges in other countries usually do not have the authority to tell officials throughout all levels of government how to carry out their jobs.

The Structure of Courts

Both the federal and state court systems have trial and appellate courts. There are three levels of courts: trial courts of limited jurisdiction, trial courts of general jurisdiction, and appellate courts.

Cases begin in a trial court, which handles determinations of guilt and sentencing. **Trial courts of limited jurisdiction** handle only misdemeanors, lawsuits for small amounts of money, and other specific kinds of cases. The full range of felony cases and all other civil lawsuits are heard in **trial courts of general jurisdiction**. Trial courts are the arenas in which evidence is presented, witnesses give testimony and are questioned by attorneys, and lawyers make arguments about the guilt (or lack thereof) of criminal defendants. These are the courts in which jury trials take place and judges impose prison sentences. The federal system has no limited jurisdiction trial courts. All federal cases begin in the general jurisdiction trial courts, the U.S. district courts.

Cases move to intermediate **appellate courts** if defendants claim that errors by police or the trial court contributed to their convictions. Further appeals may be filed with a state supreme court or the U.S. Supreme Court, depending on which court system the case is in and what kind of legal argument is being made. Unlike trial courts, appellate courts do not have juries, nor do lawyers present evidence. Instead, lawyers for each side make arguments about specific alleged errors of law or procedure that the trial judge failed to correct during the proceeding that determined the defendant's guilt. Thus, the written and oral arguments presented in an entire appellate case may focus on a single question, such as: "Should the trial judge have excluded the defendant's confession because the police did not adequately inform her or him about *Miranda* rights?" Appellate judges often decide cases by issuing elaborate written opinions to explain why they answered the question at issue in a certain way (C. Jacobs & Smith, 2011).

All states have *courts of last resort* (usually called *state supreme courts*), and all but a few have an intermediate-level appellate court (usually called *courts of*

trial courts of limited jurisdiction Criminal courts with trial jurisdiction over misdemeanor cases and preliminary matters in felony cases. Sometimes these courts hold felony trials that may result in penalties below a specific limit.

trial courts of general jurisdiction Criminal courts with jurisdiction over all offenses, including felonies. In some states, these courts also hear appeals.

appellate courts Courts that do not try criminal cases, but hear appeals of decisions of lower courts.

The Supreme Court of the United States has the final word on questions concerning interpretations of the U.S. Constitution. Should a small group of appointed judges possess such power in a democracy?

The justices of the U.S. Supreme Court in 2012 (and year of appointment): front row (left to right): Clarence Thomas (1991); Antonin Scalia (1986); John Roberts (Chief Justice—2005); Anthony Kennedy (1988); Ruth Bader Ginsburg (1993); back row: Sonia Sotomayor (2009); Stephen Breyer (1994); Samuel Alito (2006); Elena Kagan (2010).

appeals). In the federal system, the U.S. Supreme Court is the court of last resort, and the U.S. circuit courts of appeals are the intermediate appellate courts. The U.S. Supreme Court, with its nine justices, controls its own caseload by choosing 75 to 85 cases to hear from among the 7,000 cases submitted annually. It takes the votes of four justices for the Supreme Court to decide to grant a request to hear a case. After the justices consider the written and oral arguments in the cases selected for hearing, a majority vote will determine the outcome and the rule of law to be expressed in the Court's majority opinion.

Many Supreme Court decisions are unanimous, but other cases are decided by a narrow 5-to-4 vote when the justices are deeply divided. For example, when the Court decided in 2010 that the Second Amendment's "right to bear arms" that gives law-abiding adults the constitutional right to own and keep handguns in their homes applies against city and state laws as well as federal law, the justices split five-to-four in reaching the decision (*McDonald v. City of Chicago*, 2010). Close decisions can be overturned in later years if the new justices appointed to replace retiring justices bring viewpoints to the Court that differ from those of their predecessors.

Although the basic three-tiered structure is found throughout the United States, the number of courts, their names, and their specific functions vary widely. For example, in state systems, 13,000 trial courts of limited jurisdiction typically handle traffic cases, small claims, misdemeanors, and other less serious matters. These courts handle 90 percent of all criminal matters. Some limited jurisdiction courts bear responsibility for a specific category of cases, sometimes including serious offenses. These courts were developed as part of a movement to create **problem-solving courts** that would directly address recurring problems or troubled individuals who appeared in court repeatedly (Kaiser & Holtfreter, 2016). Drug courts, for example, attempt to combine rehabilitation, close supervision, and the threat of punishment to push drug offenders to shake free from substance-abuse problems (Rempel et al., 2012; Rockwell, 2008). Mental health courts, which are expanding across the country, seek to handle cases of nonviolent offenders with mental disorders and to develop appropriate treatment, supervision, and assistance instead of incarceration (Dirks-Linhorst et al., 2013; Heaphy, 2010; Kimber, 2008). Some cities have developed domestic violence courts to give focused attention to recurring problems of violence within families and among those with intimate relationships (Boyd, 2011; Gover, MacDonald, & Alpert, 2003). Other cities have dedicated judges' time to addressing problems of veterans or the homeless (S. Burns, 2010).

The federal system begins with the U.S. district courts, its trial courts of general jurisdiction. In the states, these courts have a variety of names (circuit, district,

problem-solving courts
Lower-level local courts dedicated to addressing particular social problems or troubled populations. Examples of such courts include drug courts, domestic violence courts, and mental health courts.

FIGURE 7.1

The Dual Court System of the United States and Routes of Appeal Whether a case enters through the federal or state court system depends on which law has been broken. The right of appeal to a higher court exists in either system.

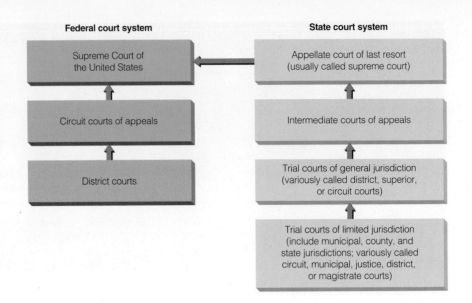

superior, and others) and are reserved for felony cases or substantial lawsuits. These are the courts in which trials take place, judges rule on evidence, and juries issue verdicts. Figure 7.1 shows the basic structure of the dual court system.

American trial courts are highly decentralized. Local political influences and community values affect the courts: local officials determine their budgets, residents make up the staff, and operations are managed so as to fit community needs. Only a few small states have a court system organized on a statewide basis, with a central administration and state funding. In most of the country, the criminal courts operate under the state penal code but are staffed, managed, and financed by county or city governments. Many of these courts have been significantly burdened by budget cuts since the onset of the nation's economic crisis in 2008 (Lagos, 2015). State courts in 42 states experienced budget cuts in 2011, and the New York state courts alone experienced a budget reduction of $170 million (Favate, 2012).

Lower courts, especially at the state level, do not always display the dignity and formal procedures of general jurisdiction trial courts and appellate courts. Instead, they may function informally. Decisions and processes in one judge's courtroom may differ from those in another courtroom. In most urban areas, local courts process seemingly endless numbers of people through the crime control model (see Chapter 1), and each defendant's "day in court" usually lasts only a few minutes. People expect their local courts to adhere to the standards that reflect American values of justice, and many are critical when the courts do not meet these ideals (Dyer, 2012).

CHECK POINT

1. **What is the dual court system?**
   Separate federal and state court systems handling cases in the United States.

2. **What different categories of courts exist within each court system?**
   The federal system is made up of the Supreme Court of the United States, circuit courts of appeals, and district courts. State court systems are made up of an appellate court of last resort, intermediate appellate courts (in most states), trial courts of general jurisdiction, and trial courts of limited jurisdiction.

3. **What does it mean for courts to be decentralized?**
   Operated, controlled, and funded by local communities, not a statewide administration; most state and county courts are decentralized.

STOP & ANALYZE

Could other institutions in society fulfill the functions currently handled by courts? For example, could a government agency handle dispute processing or norm enforcement without having courtrooms, trial, and judges? If institutions other than courts made decisions about disputes and criminal punishments, how would Americans react? Why do you think so?

To Be a Judge

People tend to see judges as the most powerful actors in the criminal justice process. Their rulings and sentencing decisions influence the actions of police, defense attorneys, and prosecutors. For example, if judges treat certain crimes lightly, police and prosecutors may be less inclined to arrest and prosecute people who commit those offenses. Although judges are thought of primarily in connection with trials, some of their work—signing warrants, setting bail, arraigning defendants, accepting guilty pleas, and scheduling cases—takes place outside the formal trial process.

More than any other person in the system, the judge is expected to embody justice, ensuring that the right to due process is upheld and that the defendant receives fair treatment. The prosecutor and the defense attorney each represent a "side" in a criminal case. By contrast, the judge's black robe and gavel symbolize impartiality. Both within and outside the courthouse, the judge is supposed to act according to a well-defined role. Judges are expected to make careful, consistent decisions that uphold the ideal of equal justice for all citizens (McKee, 2007; Dyer, 2012).

Who Becomes a Judge?

In U.S. society, the position of judge, even at the lowest level of the judicial hierarchy, brings high status. Public service, political power, and prestige in the community may matter more than a high-paying job to those who aspire to the judiciary. Indeed, many judges take a significant cut in pay to assume a position on the bench (Tillman, 2012). Private practice attorneys often work over 50 hours or more each week preparing cases and counseling clients. By contrast, judges can typically assert control over their own working hours and schedules. For example, although judges carry heavy caseloads, they frequently decide for themselves when to go home at the end of the workday. The ability to control one's own work schedule is therefore an additional attraction for lawyers interested in becoming judges.

Historically, the vast majority of judges have been white men with strong political connections. Women and members of minority groups had few opportunities to enter the legal profession prior to the 1960s and thus were seldom considered for judgeships. In 2016, women comprised 31 percent of state judiciaries, including

Judges bear important responsibilities for ensuring that both prosecutors and defense attorneys follow proper law and procedure. They must ensure that the rights of defendants are protected during court proceedings. Here, Judge Megan Shanahan presides over her courtroom in Cincinnati. What qualifications do you think someone should have in order to become a judge?

AP Images/John Minchillo

35 percent of judges on state appellate courts, 30 percent on general jurisdiction trial courts, and 33 percent on limited jurisdiction courts (National Association of Women Judges, 2016).

Contemporary political factors in many cities dictate that a portion of judges be drawn from specific demographic groups as political party leaders seek to gain the support of various segments of the voting public. In the federal courts, 12 percent of judges are African American, 8 percent are Hispanic, and 2 percent are Asian American. Overall, 7 percent of state trial judges are African American, 4 percent are Hispanic, 2 percent are Asian or Pacific Islander in ancestry, and less than one-half of 1 percent are Native American (Goldman, Slotnick, & Schiavoni, 2013; American Bar Association, 2010). These figures reflect great progress in advancing equal opportunity since the 1960s, but still demonstrate significant underrepresentation of every demographic group except white males. A majority of Americans are female, but women hold only one-quarter of judgeships. In addition, 2010 U.S. census figures show the country's population to be 12.6 percent African American, 16.3 percent Hispanic, 5.7 percent Asian or Pacific Islander, and 1 percent Native American (Humes, Jones, & Ramirez, 2011), whereas the percentages for diversity among judges are markedly lower.

Comparing the racial and ethnic makeup of the judiciary with that of the defendants in courts raises important questions (Nava, 2008). If middle-aged white men hold nearly all the power to make judgments about people from other segments of society, will people suspect that decisions about guilt and punishment are being made in an unfair manner? Will people think that punishment is being imposed on behalf of a privileged segment of society rather than on behalf of the entire, diverse U.S. society? Moreover, the political connections necessary to gain judgeships continue to disadvantage women and members of racial minority groups in many communities. Because judges both symbolize the law and make important decisions about law, the lack of diversity in the judiciary provides a visible contrast with American values related to equal opportunity (C. Stephens, 2015).

Functions of the Judge

Although people usually think that a judge's job is to preside at trials, in reality the work of most judges extends to all aspects of the judicial process. Defendants see a judge whenever decisions about their future are being made: when bail is set, pretrial motions are made, guilty pleas are accepted, a trial is conducted, a sentence is pronounced, and appeals are filed (see Figure 7.2). However, judges' duties are not limited to making such decisions about criminal defendants within the courtroom; judges also perform administrative tasks outside the courtroom. Judges have three major roles: adjudicator, negotiator, and administrator.

Adjudicator Judges must assume a neutral stance in overseeing the contest between the prosecution and the defense. They must apply the law in ways that uphold the rights of the accused in decisions about detention, plea, trial, and sentence. Judges receive a certain amount of discretion in performing these tasks—for example, in setting bail—but they must do so according to the law. They must avoid any conduct that could appear biased (Geyh, 2012).

Negotiator Many decisions that determine the fates of defendants take place outside of public view, in the judge's private chambers. These decisions come about through negotiations between prosecutors and defense attorneys about plea bargains, sentencing, and bail conditions. Judges spend much of their time in their chambers talking with prosecutors and defense attorneys. They often encourage the parties to work out a guilty plea or agree to proceed in a certain way. The judge may act as a referee, keeping both sides on track in accordance with the law. Sometimes the judge takes an even more active part in the negotiations,

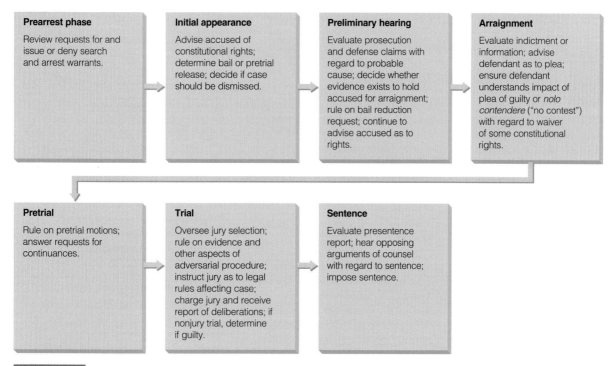

Prearrest phase	**Initial appearance**	**Preliminary hearing**	**Arraignment**
Review requests for and issue or deny search and arrest warrants.	Advise accused of constitutional rights; determine bail or pretrial release; decide if case should be dismissed.	Evaluate prosecution and defense claims with regard to probable cause; decide whether evidence exists to hold accused for arraignment; rule on bail reduction request; continue to advise accused as to rights.	Evaluate indictment or information; advise defendant as to plea; ensure defendant understands impact of plea of guilty or *nolo contendere* ("no contest") with regard to waiver of some constitutional rights.

Pretrial	**Trial**	**Sentence**
Rule on pretrial motions; answer requests for continuances.	Oversee jury selection; rule on evidence and other aspects of adversarial procedure; instruct jury as to legal rules affecting case; charge jury and receive report of deliberations; if nonjury trial, determine if guilty.	Evaluate presentence report; hear opposing arguments of counsel with regard to sentence; impose sentence.

FIGURE 7.2

Actions of a Trial Court Judge in Processing a Felony Case Throughout pretrial and trial processes, the judge ensures that legal standards are upheld; he or she maintains courtroom decorum, protects the rights of the accused, meets the requirement of a speedy trial, and makes certain that case records are maintained properly.

suggesting terms for an agreement or even pressuring one side to accept an agreement (Carodine, 2010).

Administrator A seldom-recognized function of most judges is managing the courthouse. In urban areas, a professional court administrator may direct the people who keep records, schedule cases, and do the many other jobs that keep a system functioning. But even in cities, judges are in charge of their own courtroom and staff. In rural areas, which do not usually employ professional court administrators, the judges' administrative tasks may expand to include managing labor relations, budgeting, as well as maintenance of the courthouse building. As administrator, the judge must deal with political actors such as county commissioners, legislators, and members of the state executive bureaucracy. Chief judges in large courts may also use their administrative powers to push other judges to cooperate in advancing the court's goals of processing cases in a timely manner (Jacob, 1973). For judges whose training as lawyers focused on learning law and courtroom advocacy skills, managing a complex organization with a sizeable budget and many employees can pose a major challenge (Levy, 2011; C. E. Smith & Feldman, 2001).

Many observers argue that a fourth role of judges is emerging in some court systems. They see judges acting as "problem solvers" in the newly developed problem-solving courts discussed earlier in this chapter, which seek to address the problems related to drugs, mental health, struggling veterans, and domestic violence (Melendez, 2014; S. Burns, 2010). These innovative courts steer people into treatment programs rather than into jail (Campbell, 2015). Because judges typically have no training in psychology or social work, critics worry that the development of the problem-solver role will lead judges to make decisions about matters in which they lack expertise. Read the "Close Up" feature on problem-solving courts to consider whether and how they can be effective.

Problem-Solving Courts

In 1989, a judge in Miami began to emphasize treatment and intensive monitoring of low-level substance abusers as an alternative to incarceration. From these beginnings emerged drug courts and other specialized courts aimed at diverting troubled offenders from traditional criminal sanctions while also seeking to help them with their problems. As these courts spread to other jurisdictions, the federal government provided funding to encourage new developments and to evaluate the success of such programs. In addition, several other countries have begun to copy the problem-solving courts that originated in the United States and adapt them to their own issues and objectives.

Similar efforts began to surface in regard to other problems. In the first years of the twenty-first century, many cities developed mental health courts (Redlich et al., 2012). In these courts, judges placed mentally ill people arrested for minor offenses into treatment programs and employment training (Staton & Lurigio, 2015). Anchorage, Alaska, experimented with a court dedicated to the problems of veterans, some of whom were arrested regularly for drunkenness, substance abuse, and disorderly conduct. In addition to these courts that address minor criminal offenses, New York City developed a parallel court for civil matters that focuses on homelessness and attempts to prevent evictions, encourage employment opportunities, and solve disputes between tenants and landlords. As described by two observers, in these courts, "judges are cheerleaders and social workers as much as jurists" (Eaton & Kaufman, 2005). Despite the positive intentions of such court programs, they raise questions about whether judges have sufficient training, knowledge, and resources to address individuals' significant personal problems.

Research shows that drug courts can have positive results in helping substance abusers and keeping them from going to jail. However, these programs do not always save money for the justice system, because they require funds to monitor, test, and provide services for troubled people. In addition, many substance abusers throughout society who could benefit from such programs do not gain access to the services and supervision that are available to only a small number of offenders in certain communities due to the limited resources and availability of drug courts (Sevigny et al., 2013). Some other kinds of courts are too new to have been fully evaluated.

As discussed elsewhere in this chapter, critics wonder whether specialized courts place judges in a role of problem solver, a position for which they are not fully prepared. In addition, questions have arisen about whether these courts advance the interests of justice. Domestic violence courts, in particular, cause controversy. Some critics believe that they are too lenient on batterers when they try to help them solve their problems rather than punishing them for committing acts of violence. Other critics contend that these courts favor alleged victims of domestic violence by pressuring the accused to accept anger-management treatment rather than letting the judicial processes take their course to determine whether the individual is actually guilty.

Veterans' courts, which first started in Buffalo, New York, in 2008 and subsequently are spreading across the nation, pose additional challenges about how to handle issues of violence. These courts can facilitate the provision of mentors and treatment for those veterans who commit minor offenses while struggling with issues of substance abuse, homelessness, unemployment, or psychological problems. There are debates, however, about whether such courts are appropriate settings to address issues of violence, such as intimate partner violence or other assaults that are regarded as connected to post-traumatic stress or substance abuse. Many people feel that veterans reentering society after combat experience need to be helped with their problems, rather than incarcerated for "acting out." On the other hand, does diversion into treatment programs under veterans' court supervision leave family members and others in society inadequately protected against the risk of subsequent episodes of violence if treatment is not effective for a particular troubled veteran?

As these new courts develop, research is needed to determine precisely how they impact the roles of judges, the resources of the justice system, and the lives of both accused offenders and victims.

Researching the Internet

You can find more information about drug courts at the combined website of the National Association of Drug Court Professionals and the National Drug Court Institute: http://www.ndci.org.

For Critical Thinking and Analysis

In a time of budget reductions for courts, should problem-solving courts be preserved and strengthened, or are they limited-purpose activities that draw needed resources away from the general court system? How do you view the value, importance, and potential of problem-solving courts? Write a memo that presents three reasons why you would either preserve them or subject them to budget cuts.

Sources: J. L. Burns, "The Future of Problem-Solving Courts: Inside the Courts and Beyond," *University of Maryland Journal of Race, Religion, Gender, and Class* 10 (2010): 73–87; L. Eaton and L. Kaufman, "In Problem-Solving Courts, Judges Turn Therapist," *New York Times*, April 26, 2005 (www.nytimes.com); D. C. Gottfredson, S. S. Najaka, and B. Kearley, "Effectiveness of Drug Treatment Courts: Evidence from a Randomized Trial," *Criminology & Public Policy* 2 (2003): 171–96; A. R. Gover, J. M. MacDonald, and G. P. Alpert, "Combating Domestic Violence: Findings from an Evaluation of a Local Domestic Violence Court," *Criminology and Public Policy* 3 (2003): 109–31; P. Kravetz, "Way Off Base: An Argument against Intimate Partner Violence Cases in Veterans Treatment Courts," *Veterans Law Review* A (2012): 162–205; A. J. Lurigio, "The First 20 Years of Drug Treatment Courts," *Federal Probation* 2008 (June): 13–17; C. McCoy, W. Heydebrand, and R. Mirchandani, "The Problem with Problem-Solving Justice: Coercion vs. Democratic Deliberation," *Restorative Justice: An International Journal* 3 (2015): 159–87; E. C. Moore, "A Mentor in Combat Veterans Court: Observations and Challenges," in *Future Trends in State Courts 2012*, Williamsburg, VA: National Center for State Courts, 2012, pp. 39–43; J. L. Nolan, "Redefining Criminal Courts: Problem-Solving and the Meaning of Justice," *American Criminal Law Review* 40(4):1541–65 (2003).

How to Become a Judge

The quality of justice depends to a great extent on the qualities of those who make decisions about guilt and punishment. Because judges have the power to deprive a citizen of his or her liberty through a prison sentence, judges should be thoughtful, fair, and impartial. When a judge is rude or hasty or allows the courtroom to become noisy and crowded, the public may lose confidence in the fairness and effectiveness of the criminal justice process.

Five methods are used to select state trial-court judges: **partisan election**, **nonpartisan election**, gubernatorial appointment, legislative selection, and merit selection. Some states use a combination of these methods.

Table 7.1 shows the method used in each of the states. All the methods bring up persistent concerns about the desired qualities of judges. By contrast, federal judges are nominated by the president and confirmed by a majority vote of the U.S. Senate. Federal judgeships also involve politics and questions about nominees' qualifications because presidents typically choose judges who are members of their own political party (Geyh, 2012). In addition, a judgeship can be a reward for loyal service to a political party's campaigns and fund-raising efforts.

partisan election An election in which candidates openly affiliated with political parties are presented to voters for selection.

nonpartisan election An election in which candidates' party affiliations are not listed on the ballot.

TABLE 7.1	Methods Used by States to Select Judges

States use different methods to select judges. Note that many judges are initially appointed to fill a vacancy, giving them an advantage if they must run for election at a later date.

Partisan Election	Nonpartisan Election	Gubernatorial Appointment	Legislative Selection	Merit Selection
Alabama	Arizona (some trial courts)	California (appellate)	South Carolina	Alaska
Illinois	Arkansas	Maine	Virginia	Arizona (appellate)
Indiana (trial)	California (trial)	Massachusetts (court of last resort)		Colorado
Louisiana	Florida (trial)	New Jersey		Connecticut
New Mexico	Georgia			Delaware
New York (trial)	Idaho			Florida (appellate)
Pennsylvania (initial)	Kentucky			Hawaii
Tennessee (trial)	Michigan			Indiana (appellate)
Texas	Minnesota			Iowa
West Virginia	Mississippi			Kansas
	Montana			Maryland
	Nevada			Massachusetts (trial, intermediate appellate)
	North Carolina			Missouri
	North Dakota			Nebraska
	Ohio			New Hampshire
	Oklahoma (trial)			New York (appellate)
	Oregon			Oklahoma (appellate)
	Pennsylvania (retention)			Rhode Island
	South Dakota (trial)			South Dakota (appellate)
	Washington			Tennessee (appellate)
	Wisconsin			Utah
				Vermont
				Wyoming

Source: American Judicature Society, 2012, "Judicial Selection in the States" (http://www.ajs.org).

Selection by public voting occurs in more than half the states and has long been part of this nation's tradition. This method of judicial selection embodies the underlying American value of democracy because it permits the citizens to control the choice of individuals who will receive the power to make decisions in civil and criminal cases (Lim & Snyder, 2015). This method also helps ensure that judges will remain connected to the community and demonstrate sensitivity to the community's priorities and concerns (Griffen, 2011). The American value of democracy may, however, have detrimental consequences if it pressures judges to follow a community's prejudices rather than make independent decisions using their best judgment in each case (Canes-Wrone, Clark, & Park, 2012; Pratt, 2011). Retired U.S. Supreme Court Justice Sandra Day O'Connor mounted a public campaign against selecting judges through elections because of her concerns about the impact on the appearance of justice, especially as judicial candidates must solicit campaign contributions and subsequently may make decisions affecting their contributors (Geyh, 2012).

When lawyers are first elected to serve as judges, they obviously have no prior experience in deciding cases or supervising courthouse operations. As a result, judges must learn on the job. This fact clashes with the belief that judges are trained to "find the law" and to apply neutral judgments. In Europe, by contrast, prospective judges are given special training in law school to become professional judges. These trained judges must serve as assistant judges and lower-court judges before they can become judges in general trial and appellate courts (Holvast & Doornbos, 2015).

Election campaigns for lower-court judgeships tend to be low-key contests marked by little controversy. Usually only a small portion of the voters participate, judgeships are not prominent on the ballot, and candidates do not discuss controversial issues because of ethical considerations. Most candidates run on the same two claims that reveal relatively little to the voters about how they will make specific decisions as judges: "I have the best prior experience" and "I'll be tough on crime." Read "What Americans Think" to see voters' assessment of the adequacy of information about judicial candidates. If voters do not know much about the candidates, then their ideal role as citizens in a democracy is diminished because elections presume that voters will choose the best candidates and hold those candidates accountable when subsequent elections occur.

Studies indicate that even lower-level judicial races have become more competitive as candidates raise money and seek connections with interest groups (Brandenburg & Berg, 2012; Abbe & Herrnson, 2002). Political parties typically want local judgeships to be elected posts, because they can use courthouse staff positions to reward party loyalists. When a party member wins a judgeship, courthouse jobs may become available for campaign workers, because the judge often chooses clerks, bailiffs, and secretaries.

In contrast, elections for seats on state supreme courts frequently receive statewide media attention (M. Hall & Bonneau, 2013). Because of the importance of state supreme courts as policy-making institutions, political parties and interest groups may devote substantial energy to organizing and funding the election campaigns of their preferred candidates. When organized interests contribute tens of thousands of dollars to judicial campaigns, questions sometimes arise about whether the successful candidates who received those contributions will favor the interests of their donors when they begin to decide court cases (Geyh, 2012).

WHAT AMERICANS THINK

QUESTION: "How often do you feel you have the information you need to make your mind up about who to vote for [among] judges?" [survey of Ohio voters, 2014]

Always	11%
Most of the time	29%
About half the time	28%
Not very often	20%
Rarely, never	12%

CRITICAL THINKING: What information do voters need about judicial candidates in order for judicial election systems to work well? Are there ways to provide this information to voters without relying solely on judicial candidates' campaign advertisements?

Source: Ray C. Bliss Institute of Applied Politics, University of Akron, "The 2014 Ohio Judicial Elections Survey" (https://www.uakron.edu /dotAsset/f119f1fd-14ed-45e6-95ac-5fc6636e8634.pdf).

Some states have tried to reduce the influence of political parties in the selection of judges while still allowing voters to select judges (Chertoff & Robinson, 2012). These states hold nonpartisan elections in which only the names of candidates, not their party affiliations, appear on the ballot. However, political parties are often strongly involved in such elections. In Ohio, for example, the Republican and Democratic political parties hold their own primary elections to choose the judicial candidates whose names will go on the nonpartisan ballot for the general election. In other states, party organizations raise and spend money on behalf of candidates in nonpartisan elections.

Public opinion data show that Americans express concern about the influence of politics on judges, especially with respect to elected judges. If so many Americans are concerned about judges' involvement in political campaigns, why do so many states still rely on elections to select judges?

Merit selection, which combines appointment and election, was first used in Missouri in 1940 and has since spread to other states. When a judgeship becomes vacant, a nominating committee made up of citizens and attorneys evaluates potential appointees and sends the governor the names of three candidates, from which the replacement is chosen. After one year, a referendum is held to decide whether the judge will stay on the bench. The ballot asks, "Shall Judge X remain in office?" A judge who wins support from voters serves out the full term, often eight years, before facing another retention election (Cady & Phelps, 2008).

Merit selection attempts to diminish the influence of politics on the selection of judges and supposedly allows the voters to unseat judges. However, interest groups sometimes mount publicity campaigns during retention elections in order to turn out judges with whom they disagree on a single issue or to open an important court seat so that a like-minded governor can appoint a sympathetic replacement. It may be difficult for judges to counteract a barrage of one-sided inflammatory television commercials focusing on a single issue such as capital punishment (T. V. Reid, 2000). If merit-selected judges feel intimidated by interest groups that might threaten their jobs at the next retention election, the independence of the judiciary will diminish (Breslin, 2010).

merit selection A reform plan by which judges are nominated by a committee and appointed by the governor for a given period. When the term expires, the voters approve or disapprove the judge for a succeeding term. If the judge is disapproved, the committee nominates a successor for the governor's appointment.

CHECK POINT

4. **What are judges' main functions?**
   Adjudicator, negotiator, administrator.

5. **Why do political parties often prefer that judges be elected?**
   To ensure that courthouse positions are allocated to party workers.

6. **What are the steps in the merit-selection process?**
   When a vacancy occurs, a nominating committee is appointed that sends the governor the names of approved candidates. The governor must fill the vacancy from the list. After a year's term, a referendum is held to ask the voters whether the judge should be retained.

STOP & ANALYZE

What is the best way to select judges? List three arguments for the method that you favor. List three arguments against a method that you do not prefer.

The Prosecutorial System

Prosecuting attorneys make discretionary decisions about whether to pursue criminal charges, which charges to make, and what sentence to recommend. They represent the government in pursuing criminal charges against the accused. Except in a few states, no higher authority second-guesses or changes these decisions. Thus, prosecutors are more independent than most other public officials. As with other aspects of American government, prosecution is mainly a task of state and local governments, because most crimes violate state laws. The vast majority of state criminal

prosecuting attorney A legal representative of the state with sole responsibility for bringing criminal charges. Depending on the state, this person is referred to as the district attorney, state's attorney, commonwealth attorney, or county attorney.

The U.S. Attorney in New York City, Preet Bharara, has handled a wide range of prosecutions, from financial crimes on Wall Street to international weapons trafficking to cybercrimes to political corruption in government. What kinds of political pressures can confront prosecutors?

cases are handled in the 2,341 county-level offices of the prosecuting attorney—known in various states as the district attorney, state's attorney, commonwealth attorney, or county attorney—who pursues cases that violate state law. Prosecutors have the power to make independent decisions about which cases to pursue and what charges to file. They can also drop charges and negotiate arrangements for guilty pleas. Since 2008, budget cuts have forced many prosecutors' offices to cut staff and, as a result, reduce defendants' charges and offer attractive plea deals more frequently in order to process cases efficiently (Simpson, 2015; Damron, Anderson, & Wisely, 2013; Singer, 2008).

Federal cases are prosecuted by **United States attorneys**. One U.S. attorney and a staff of assistant U.S. attorneys prosecute cases in each of the 94 U.S. district courts. Each state has an elected **state attorney general**, who usually has the power to bring prosecutions in certain cases. A state attorney general may, for example, handle a statewide consumer fraud case if a chain of auto repair shops is suspected of overcharging customers. In Alaska, Delaware, and Rhode Island, the state attorney general also directs all local prosecutions.

Politics and Prosecution

Except in a few states, such as Alaska, Connecticut, and New Jersey, prosecutors are elected, usually for a four-year term; local politics thus heavily influence the office. By seeking to please voters, many prosecutors have tried to use their local office as a springboard to a higher office—such as state legislator, governor, or member of Congress.

Prosecutors may choose certain cases for prosecution in order to gain the favor of voters or investigate charges against political opponents and public officials to get the public's attention. Political factors may also cause prosecutors to apply their powers unevenly within a community. Prosecutors' discretionary power can create the impression and reality of some groups or individuals receiving harsh treatment while others receive protection (M. Alexander, 2012; Podgor, 2010).

Discretion in decision making also creates the risk of discrimination. For example, some scholars see prosecutors' decisions as reflecting biases based on race, social class, and gender (M. Alexander, 2012; Frohmann, 1997), but other researchers

United States attorneys Officials responsible for the prosecution of crimes that violate the laws of the United States. Appointed by the president and assigned to a U.S. district court jurisdiction.

state attorney general Chief legal officer of a state, responsible for both civil and criminal matters.

believe that studies have not yet documented the full extent of discrimination by prosecutors (S. Walker, Spohn, & DeLeone, 2012). Several studies raise questions about discrimination in specific situations, such as prosecutors' decisions to seek the death penalty or make sentencing recommendations (J. Wu, 2016; Unah, 2010; Sorensen & Wallace, 1999). For the criminal justice system to fulfill American values concerning equality and fairness, prosecutors must use their decision-making authority carefully to avoid inequality and injustice (Butler, 2010; Kotch & Mosteller, 2010).

The Prosecutor's Influence

Most decision makers in the criminal justice system are involved in only one part of the process. However, prosecutors are involved at multiple stages and can therefore exert great influence through the use of their broad discretion in decision making (Krischke, 2010). From arrest to final disposition of a case, prosecutors can make choices that largely determine the defendant's fate. The prosecutor decides which cases to prosecute, selects the charges to be brought, recommends the bail amount, approves agreements with the defendant, and urges the judge to impose a particular sentence (Kenny, 2009).

Throughout the justice process, prosecutors' links with the other actors in the system—police, defense attorneys, judges—shape the prosecutors' decisions. Prosecutors may, for example, recommend bail amounts and sentences that match the preferences of particular judges. They may make "tough" recommendations in front of "tough" judges but tone down their arguments before judges who favor leniency or rehabilitation. Similarly, the other actors in the system may adjust their decisions and actions to match the preferences of the prosecutor. For example, police officers' investigation and arrest practices tend to reflect the prosecutor's priorities. Thus, prosecutors influence the decisions of others while also shaping their own actions in ways that reinforce their relationships with police, defense attorneys, and judges.

Prosecutors gain additional power from the fact that their decisions and actions take place away from public view. For example, a prosecutor and a defense attorney may strike a bargain whereby the prosecutor reduces a charge in exchange for a guilty plea or drops a charge if the defendant agrees to seek psychiatric help. In such instances, they reach a decision on a case in a way that is nearly invisible to the public.

The Prosecutor's Roles

As "lawyers for the state," prosecutors face conflicting pressures to press charges vigorously against lawbreakers while also upholding justice and the rights of the accused (O'Brien, 2009). These pressures are often called "the prosecutor's dilemma." In the adversarial system, prosecutors must do everything they can to win a conviction, but as members of the legal profession, they must see that justice is done even if it means that the accused is not convicted. Even so, they always face the risk of "prosecutor's bias," sometimes called a "prosecution complex." Although they are supposed to represent all the people, including the accused, prosecutors may view themselves as instruments of law enforcement. Thus, as advocates on behalf of the state, their strong desire to close each case with a conviction may keep them from recognizing unfair procedures or evidence of innocence. As discussed in the "Policy Debate" feature, it can be very difficult to hold prosecutors accountable if they ignore the interests of justice in their single-minded pursuit of a criminal conviction.

Although all prosecutors must uphold the law and pursue charges against lawbreakers, they may perform these tasks in different ways. Their personal values and professional goals, along with the political climate of their city or county, may cause them to define the prosecutor's role differently than do prosecutors in

The Accountability of Prosecutors

How can prosecutors be held accountable if they violate their responsibilities and the principles of justice? In theory, if the public hears about prosecutorial misconduct, the democratic selection process will enable voters to elect a new prosecutor in most states. However, because many prosecutors' discretionary decisions are not visible to the news media and public, voters may lack the information necessary to provide the accountability mechanism for improper conduct.

People can file lawsuits against police officers and corrections officers to hold them accountable for violating citizens' rights or improperly causing injuries and property damage. By contrast, the American legal system generally shields prosecutors and judges from the risk of lawsuits by granting them immunity, in much the same manner that the president and governors enjoy immunity in most circumstances. These are the officials who need to use their best judgment in making tough decisions, and the law is designed to protect them from being guided by fear of liability in making those decisions. However, this immunity from lawsuits effectively removes an important and useful accountability mechanism that might otherwise deter misconduct and provide remedies for citizens who are victimized by such misconduct.

In 2011, the U.S. Supreme Court decided the case of *Connick v. Thompson*, concerning a man who spent 18 years in prison and came within one month of being executed for a murder that he did not commit. Only a stroke of luck resulting from a private detective's discovery of a crime lab report in the New Orleans Police Crime Lab files saved Thompson from execution.

Prosecutors have a legal obligation to provide defense attorneys with all evidence that might indicate a defendant's innocence. In *Brady v. Maryland* (1963), the Supreme Court declared that in their efforts to get a conviction, prosecutors cannot hide evidence that is helpful to the defense. If they were to do so, prosecutors would greatly increase the

likelihood of innocent people being erroneously found guilty. In the *Thompson* case, New Orleans prosecutors hid evidence from the defendant's counsel. One prosecutor went so far as to remove a bloodstained piece of cloth from the evidence room, which, if tested by the defense and compared to the defendant's blood type, could have proved the defendant's innocence in one of the crimes for which he was convicted. Indeed, the prosecutor possessed a lab report indicating that the blood did not match Thompson's blood type, but that information did not become available to Thompson's attorneys until the investigator discovered it in the crime lab files 18 years later. When the prosecutor in question was dying of cancer, he confessed to another prosecutor that he had intentionally hidden evidence that would have been helpful to the defendant. In addition, other issues were raised concerning the failure of the prosecutors to accurately reveal the nature of witness statements taken during the investigation of the crime.

After he was found to be innocent and released from prison, Thompson sued the prosecutor's office for violating his rights by failing to train assistant prosecutors regarding their obligation to share relevant evidence. A jury awarded him $14 million in the lawsuit. Despite evidence that the assistant prosecutors—as well as the chief prosecutor—were not fully aware of the legal requirements of the *Brady* rule, a narrow five-member majority on the Supreme Court threw out the jury award and found that Thompson had not proved his case. Indeed, their ruling made clear that prosecutors seldom, if ever, should be subject to lawsuits, even when prosecutors acknowledge the intentional violation of a suspect's rights and when a wrongly convicted man spends many years on death row as a result.

Should we make prosecutors more susceptible to lawsuits as a means to hold them accountable and control the risk that they will engage in improper

conduct? Here is a summary of key arguments in the debate:

For Permitting Lawsuits against Prosecutors

- Voters do not know enough about prosecutors' errors to hold prosecutors accountable by using those errors as a basis for voting them out at the next election.
- Lawsuits have proven a very effective means to pressure police executives and corrections administrators to obey rules, supervise personnel, and develop effective training programs.
- Without the threat of lawsuits, prosecutors have little to fear other than having charges against a defendant dismissed if they violate rules, either intentionally or mistakenly. Thus, they feel little pressure, other than the pressure that they put on themselves, to be careful about following rules.
- People whose lives were ruined by prosecutors' misconduct, such as Thompson, the wrongly convicted man in the Supreme Court case, lack mechanisms to seek remedies for prosecutors' misdeed.

Opposing Lawsuits against Prosecutors

- If lawsuits were permitted, prosecutors would be flooded with groundless lawsuits from many people in prison who have little else to do with their time than read books in the prison law library in order to plan how to seek revenge against prosecutors.
- Society needs prosecutors to freely use their judgment to make the best possible decision in each criminal case without worrying about whether they will be sued for trying to do the right thing.
- Prosecutors have limited time, funds, and staff. Any time that is diverted to defending against lawsuits from unhappy defendants will come at the

expense of the prosecutors' important responsibility for protecting the public against crime and criminals.

- Qualified lawyers may avoid becoming prosecutors if they know that they will face a steady stream of lawsuits from unhappy defendants seeking revenge.

What Should U.S. Policy Be?

The U.S. Supreme Court's decision in *Connick v. Thompson* sent a clear message that the nation's highest court will not push changes in current policy. However, state legislatures and Congress have the authority to craft laws that could define the circumstances under which prosecutors would be subject to lawsuits. Those statutes would present an opportunity to find the right balance between the competing sets of arguments by permitting more lawsuits than currently allowed but for fewer types of actions than those directed at police and corrections officials. For example, the statutes could define limited categories such as intentional misconduct by prosecutors or inadvertent errors that result in innocent people being wrongly convicted of crimes. Should legislatures examine the issue and consider creating changes that would permit more lawsuits?

Researching the Internet

Read the Supreme Court's opinion in the *Thompson* case, including the strong objections voiced by the four dissenting justices who concluded that Thompson was entitled to the money that he was awarded by the jury in his lawsuit. http://scholar.google.com/scholar_case ?case=16887528200611439212&hl =en&as_sdt=6&as_vis=I&oi=scholarr.

Analyzing the Issue

Should citizens have the opportunity to sue prosecutors for violations of legal rights? If such lawsuits are not permitted, how will society make sure that prosecutors do their jobs properly? What would be the consequences if prosecutors could be sued for rights violations or wrongful convictions? Are there alternative mechanisms that could more effectively keep prosecutors accountable? Imagine that you and your classmates are legislators discussing the accountability of prosecutors as you consider whether to propose new laws. Do a majority in your class support more opportunities to file lawsuits? If so, would such lawsuits be limited to only certain kinds of cases? If not, are you relying on other mechanisms to reduce the risk of prosecutors' errors and misconduct?

other places. For example, a prosecutor who believes that young offenders can be rehabilitated may take different actions than one who believes that young offenders should receive the same punishments as adults. One might send juveniles to counseling programs, whereas the other would seek to process them though the adult system of courts and corrections. A prosecutor with no assistants and few resources for conducting jury trials may be forced to embrace effective plea bargaining, whereas a prosecutor in a wealthier county may have more options when deciding whether to take cases to trial. See the "Question of Ethics" feature at the end of the chapter to consider what priority should be foremost in the minds of prosecutors.

When prosecutors are asked about their roles in the criminal justice process, the following four functions are often mentioned:

1. *Trial counsel for the police*   Prosecutors who see their main function in this light believe that they should reflect the views of law enforcement in the courtroom and take a crime-fighter stance in public.
2. *House counsel for the police*   These prosecutors believe that their main function is to give legal advice so that arrests will stand up in court.
3. *Representative of the court*   Such prosecutors believe that their main function is to enforce the rules of due process to ensure that the police act according to the law and uphold the rights of defendants.
4. *Elected official*   These prosecutors may be most responsive to public opinion. The political impact of their decisions is one of their main concerns.

Each of these roles involves a different view of the prosecutor's "clients" as well as his or her own responsibilities. In the first two roles, prosecutors appear to believe that the police are the clients of their legal practice. Take a moment to think about who might be the clients of prosecutors who view themselves as representatives of the court or as elected officials. Read the "You Make the Decision" feature to place yourself in the position of a prosecutor who must provide legal advice to the police.

Prosecutor

In many jurisdictions, police officers work closely with prosecutors to determine priorities for law enforcement activities. Because local governments do not have unlimited resources, choices must be made about which crimes to emphasize and which specific suspects to pursue. Prosecutors often advise police agencies about when to seek search warrants, both as a matter of local law enforcement priorities and as a matter of ensuring that enough apparently incriminating information is available to persuade a judge that "probable cause" exists to justify issuing a search warrant under the requirements of the Fourth Amendment. You are a prosecutor, and police officers tell you that a few months ago, they observed a man accompanied by a small child coming out of a hydroponic supply store carrying a bag after making a purchase. It is widely recognized that hydroponic supplies are often used for the indoor cultivation of marijuana. Several months later, officers decided to go to the man's home and dig through the family's trash can that had been placed on the curb for weekly refuse collection. The officers discovered the remnants of dark, wet leaves. Rather than collecting the leaves for testing at a crime lab, the officers used a test kit to do a field test of the leaves on the spot. The leaves tested positive for marijuana. The police ask you if their observation of the man at the hydroponic supply store and the field test of the wet leaves provide enough apparently incriminating information to seek a search warrant from a judge.

The concept of "probable cause" is very vague. Prosecutors and judges make judgments about whether the available information leads to the reasonable conclusion that it is more likely than not that evidence of criminal activity will be found through a search of a specific location. You also know that a law-abiding citizen might purchase materials at a hydroponic supply store for the purpose of growing flowers and vegetables rather than marijuana and that field tests done by police officers sometimes inaccurately indicate the presence of marijuana when, in fact, no marijuana is present on the tested material. Field tests do not have the accuracy of tests done in crime labs. Is there enough evidence to constitute "probable cause" to justify a search? Do you recommend seeking a warrant to search the family's home? Give reasons for your decision. Then do an Internet search for the case of Robert Harte and the December 2015 decision in his case issued by the U.S. District Court in Kansas.

Discretion of the Prosecutor

Because they have such broad discretion, prosecutors can shape their decisions to fit different interests (K. Griffin, 2009). They might base their decisions on a desire to impress voters through tough "throw-the-book-at-them" charges in a highly publicized case (Maschke, 1995). Decisions may also be driven by changing events in society. For example, when American opinion held that the greed of business-people had helped to create the economic crisis of 2008, certain prosecutors placed new emphasis on pursuing criminal charges for fraudulent business transactions and mortgage loans (Segal, 2009). Decisions by prosecutors might also stem from their personal values and policy priorities, such as an emphasis on leniency and rehabilitation for young offenders or a desire to work with domestic violence victims to seek a specific result (Finn, 2013; Buzawa & Buzawa, 2013; Ferguson, 2009). They may also shape their decisions to please local judges by, for example, accepting plea agreements that will keep the judges from being burdened by too many time-consuming trials. Prosecutors who have doubts about whether available evidence actually proves the defendant's guilt may just shrug their shoulders and say, "I'll just let the jury decide" rather than face public criticism for dropping charges. Any or all of these motives may shape prosecutors' decisions, because there is generally no higher authority to tell prosecutors how they must do their jobs. From the time the police turn a case over to the prosecutor, the prosecutor has almost complete control over decisions about charges and plea agreements (M. Stephens, 2008).

Research has also shown that the staffing levels of individual prosecutors' offices may affect decisions to pursue felony charges. If offices lack sufficient resources to pursue all possible cases, prosecutors may establish priorities and then reduce or dismiss charges in cases deemed less important. This situation has increasingly affected decisions in many prosecutors' offices in light of budget cuts in state and local government (Stensland, 2011).

If you were a prosecutor, what would you consider to be the most important factors in deciding whether to pursue a case? Would you have any concerns about the possibility of prosecuting an innocent person? If a prosecutor pursues a case against someone she or he does not really believe is guilty of a crime, does this pose an ethical problem?

After deciding that a case should be prosecuted, the prosecutor has great freedom in deciding what charges to file. A single criminal incident may involve the violation of several laws, so the prosecutor can bring a single charge or more than one. Suppose that Smith, who is armed, breaks into a grocery store, assaults the proprietor, and robs the cash drawer. What charges can the prosecutor file? By virtue of having committed the robbery, the accused can be charged with at least four crimes: breaking and entering, assault, armed robbery, and carrying a dangerous weapon. Other charges, or **counts**, may be added, depending on the nature of the incident. A forger, for instance, may be charged with one count for each act of forgery committed. By filing as many charges as possible, the prosecutor strengthens his or her position in plea negotiations. In effect, the prosecutor can use discretion in deciding the number of charges and thus increase the prosecution's supply of "bargaining chips" (M. Simons, 2010).

> **count** Each separate offense of which a person is accused in an indictment or an information.

The discretionary power to set charges does not give the prosecutor complete control over plea bargaining, however. Defense attorneys strengthen their position in the **discovery** process, in which information from the prosecutor's case file must be made available to the defense. For example, the defense has the right to see any statements made by the accused during interrogation by the police, as well as the results of any physical or psychological tests. This information tells the defense attorney about the strengths and weaknesses of the prosecution's case. The defense attorney may use it to decide whether a case is hopeless or whether engaging in tough negotiations is worthwhile.

> **discovery** A prosecutor's pretrial disclosure to the defense of facts and evidence to be introduced at trial.

The prosecutor's discretion does not end with the decision to file a certain charge. After the charge has been made, the prosecutor may reduce it in exchange for a guilty plea or enter a notation of *nolle prosequi (nol. pros.)*. The latter is a freely made decision to drop the charge, either as a whole or as to one or more counts (Bowers, 2010). When a prosecutor decides to drop charges, no higher authorities can force her or him to reinstate them. When guilty pleas are entered, the prosecutor uses discretion in recommending a sentence.

> *nolle prosequi* An entry, made by a prosecutor on the record of a case and announced in court, indicating that the charges specified will not be prosecuted. In effect, the charges are thereby dismissed.

Key Relationships of the Prosecutor

Prosecutors do not base their decisions solely on formal policies and role conceptions (Fridell, 1990). Relationships with other actors in the justice system also influence their choices. Despite their independent authority, prosecutors must consider how police, judges, and others will react. They depend on these other officials in order to prosecute cases successfully. In turn, the success of police, judges, and correctional officials depends on prosecutors' effectiveness in identifying and convicting lawbreakers. Thus, these officials build exchange relationships in which they cooperate with each other.

Police Prosecutors depend on the police to provide both the suspects and the evidence needed to convict lawbreakers (Rowe, 2016). Because they cannot investigate crimes on their own, prosecutors are not in command of the types of cases brought to them. Thus, the police control the initiation of the criminal justice process by investigating crimes and arresting suspects. These actions may be influenced by various factors, such as pressure on police to establish an impressive crime-clearance record. As a result, police actions may create problems for prosecutors if, for example, the police make many arrests without gathering enough evidence to ensure conviction.

Prosecutors, Police, and the Ferguson, Missouri, Grand Jury in 2014

In prior chapters, we have seen examples of criminal justice issues that arose in 2014 related to public protests, after grand juries declined to bring criminal charges against police officers whose actions caused the deaths of unarmed African American men. As described in Chapters 4 and 5, for example, these significant events contributed to the development of suggestions for police reform put forward by President Obama's task force on policing and the Police Executive Research Forum. In light of the impact of these events, it is useful to take a closer look at the grand jury, especially the role of the prosecutor. Because the decision of the Ferguson, Missouri, grand jury triggered violence, the prosecutor released thousands of pages of documents about the information presented in the proceeding, information that would usually be kept secret, but is now available for study. The Ferguson proceeding provides a thought-provoking and controversial glimpse into potential abuses of the grand jury system.

A grand jury is a body of citizens called to hear the prosecutor's evidence in order to decide whether an individual should be charged with a crime. Grand juries are used in the federal system and some state systems to make charging decisions about serious crimes. In the typical grand jury proceeding, the citizens drawn from the community meet in secret and hear only information presented to them by the prosecutor. The prosecutor identifies and explains the relevant charges being sought and presents enough evidence to justify those charges. No defense attorneys are present to argue for alternative versions of events or to present counterevidence. The grand jury merely decides whether there is enough evidence to file criminal charges against an individual. Thus they do not need to be persuaded "beyond a reasonable doubt" that an individual has committed a crime. They merely need to conclude that, based on the evidence presented, it seems more likely than not that the individual committed a crime. If they conclude that enough evidence exists, they issue an indictment that serves to initiate charges against the targeted suspect. Afterward, the case moves to the plea bargaining and trial stages, where defense attorneys represent defendants. If the case moves to trial, the prosecutor faces a much higher burden of proof and an active battle with the defense attorney in trying to prove the defendant's guilt beyond a reasonable doubt.

The Ferguson, Missouri, grand jury proceeding in the aftermath of Officer Darren Wilson's fatal shooting of unarmed teenager Michael Brown was different from the typical proceeding in so many ways that it raised questions about the intentions of the prosecutor. Typically, grand juries may hear evidence and issue indictments against dozens of suspects in a single day. The Ferguson grand jury met for more than three weeks to focus on the possibility of bringing criminal charges against Officer Wilson. According to commentators who examined the documents released at the end of the grand jury proceeding, the length, structure, and content of the proceeding led critics to claim for various reasons that it was designed to help Officer Wilson avoid criminal charges. Among the unusual aspects of this grand jury process:

- Early in the proceeding, Officer Wilson testified at length about his version of events, and he did so without being closely questioned by the prosecutors. By contrast, the prosecutors asked pointed questions of the several witnesses who were critical of Officer Wilson. Thus Wilson, who had been advised by an attorney and presumably knew from that advice how to present his version in the most favorable light, had the opportunity to provide the initial story that established the baseline of the grand jurors' understanding of events. Moreover, he was permitted to present this version without questioning that could have highlighted inconsistencies and weaknesses between his initial statements after the shooting and his later prepared testimony to the grand jury. This was especially unusual because suspects rarely testify at all in grand jury proceedings.

- Prosecutors prepared the grand jurors to hear and understand testimony by telling them about an outdated Missouri law that permitted officers to shoot people in order to prevent them from escaping. In reality, that law's legal principle had been declared unconstitutional by the U.S. Supreme Court 30 years earlier in *Tennessee v. Garner* (1984). As described in Chapter 6, that case said the old "shoot-the-fleeing-felon" concept was invalid when officers did not see evidence that the individual was armed. Thus the grand jurors evaluated the testimony, including Wilson's, for several weeks through the lens of an erroneous understanding of permissible use of firearms by police officers against individuals who are unarmed. Prosecutors corrected their error near the end of the grand jury proceeding, but many observers concluded that the quick, vague way in which prosecutors presented the updated law to the grand jurors was likely to cause significant confusion.

- Prosecutors did not act in the usual manner to guide the grand jurors by specifying a charge and presenting evidence to provide a basis for issuing an indictment on that charge. Instead, they gave the grand jurors a list of charges to figure out for themselves and then presented all available evidence and testimony. Critics saw this approach as also likely to cause confusion by, in effect, overwhelming the grand jurors with excessive and contradictory evidence that would be difficult to sort and understand.

- Prosecutors permitted several witnesses to testify even though they knew these witnesses were not truthful and their testimony had already been discredited by investigators. One of these witnesses had reportedly been caught lying in other cases and had posted racist comments online against Michael Brown. Her claims of being at the site of the shooting had already been refuted by police investigators. Such discredited witnesses testified both for and against Office Wilson and, in the view of critics, enhanced the risk of confusion for the grand jurors who did not know which witnesses had already been discredited.

- Prosecutors moved forward with the grand jury proceeding before local police and the FBI had completed their investigations. Thus, in claiming to present all evidence to the grand jury, the prosecutors actually acted prematurely without waiting to see complete law enforcement reports on the events and evidence.

- Critics claimed that the lengthy proceeding created the illusion in the minds of many members of the public that the grand jury had thoroughly investigated the case

and produced a clear and evidence-supported determination that Wilson was "not guilty." In reality, however, the proceeding was not based on the adversarial process that would have occurred in a subsequent trial, and therefore the evidence in the case was not rigorously questioned and challenged by attorneys as it would be in a trial.

As indicated by these examples, public dissatisfaction with the Ferguson grand jury is not based merely on the disappointment of those who hoped to see Officer Wilson charged with a crime. The unusual manner in which the proceedings were conducted raised many questions for critics about whether prosecutors had decided in advance to keep Officer Wilson from facing criminal charges. Did the prosecutors design a confusing and arguably tilted proceeding to place responsibility for the failure to file charges on hopelessly confused grand jurors? Alternatively, did they feel pressured to have a lengthy proceeding that included as much information as possible in order to avoid potential accusations from critics that they were favoring Officer Wilson?

For Critical Thinking and Analysis

Prosecutors work closely with and depend on police in order to fulfill their

responsibilities. Does this relationship create a risk that prosecutors will not treat police officers suspected of wrongdoing in the same manner as other citizen-suspects? Should a prosecutor from outside the county handle grand jury proceedings concerning police officers? If prosecutors were correct in their conduct of the grand jury proceeding for Officer Wilson, does that mean that other criminal suspects are being denied equal rights when their cases are handled in brief proceedings through prosecutors' presentation of evidence about a specific charge and without any opportunity for the suspect to testify? Write a memo that describes how grand jury proceedings should operate when a police officer is suspected of committing a crime.

Sources: W. Freivogel, "Grand Jury Wrangled with Confusing Instructions," St. Louis Public Radio online, November 26, 2014 (http://news.stlpublicradio.org); W. Freivogel, "Was the Grand Jury Procedure in the Wilson Case Fair?" St. Louis Public Radio online, November 25, 2014 (http://news.stlpublicradio.org); K. Kindy and C. Leonnig, "In Atypical Approach, Grand Jury in Ferguson Shooting Receives Full Measure of Case," September 7, 2014 (www.washingtonpost.com); L. O'Donnell, "Missouri Attorney General: Change Deadly Force Law," MSNBC.com, December 3, 2014 (www.msnbc.com); C. Shalby, "St. Louis DA Says He Knew of Lying Witnesses in Ferguson Grand Jury Trial," PBS News online, December 19, 2014 (www.pbs.org).

Are there risks that prosecutors will give too much emphasis to maintaining a good relationship with the police, even at the cost of fair and proper decision making? Many critics believe that the prosecutor in Ferguson, Missouri, may have done just that in the way that he ran the grand jury proceeding that decided whether criminal charges should be filed against the police officer who shot unarmed teenager Michael Brown and thereby triggered national outrage and protests across the nation. Read "Current Controversies in Criminal Justice" to consider the unusual process that cleared the officer of potential criminal charges.

Victims and Witnesses   Prosecutors depend on the cooperation of victims and witnesses (Gaines & Wells, 2016; Rhodes et al., 2011). Although prosecutors can pursue a case whether or not a victim wishes to press charges, many prosecutors will not do so when the key testimony and other necessary evidence must come from a victim who is unwilling to cooperate (Dawson & Dinovitzer, 2001). In some cases, the decision to prosecute may be influenced by the victim's assertiveness in persuading the prosecutor to file charges (Stickels, Michelsen, & Del Carmen, 2007).

The decision to prosecute is often based on an assessment of the victim's role in his or her own victimization and the victim's credibility as a witness. If a victim has a criminal record, the prosecutor may choose not to pursue the case in the belief that a jury would not consider the victim a credible witness—despite the fact that the jury will never learn that the victim has a criminal record. If a victim is poorly dressed, uneducated, or somewhat inarticulate, the prosecutor may be inclined to dismiss charges out of fear that a jury would find the victim unpersuasive (Stanko, 1988). Research indicates that victim characteristics—such as moral character, behavior at the time of the incident, and age—influence decisions to prosecute sexual assault cases more than does the actual strength of the evidence against the suspect (Spears & Spohn, 1997). Studies have shown that prosecutions succeed most when aimed at defendants accused of committing crimes against strangers (Boland et al., 1983). When the victim is an acquaintance, a friend, or even a relative of the defendant, she or he may refuse to act as a witness, and prosecutors and juries may consequently view the offense as less serious (Beichner & Spohn, 2012).

Judges and Courts   Knowledge of and interactions with the judge can affect the prosecutors' recommendations about and influence over sentencing (Kim, Spohn, & Hedberg, 2015). The sentencing history of each judge gives prosecutors an idea of how a case might be treated in the courtroom. Prosecutors may decide to drop a case if they believe that the judge assigned to it will not impose a serious punishment. Because prosecutors' offices have limited resources, they cannot afford to waste time pursuing charges in front of a specific judge who shows a pattern of dismissing those types of charges. Interactions with defense attorneys also affect prosecutors' decisions, as in the case of plea bargains.

The Community   Public opinion and the media can play a crucial role in creating an environment that either supports or scrutinizes the prosecutor. Like police chiefs and school superintendents, county prosecutors will not remain in office long if they fall out of step with community values. They will likely lose the next election to an opponent who has a better sense of the community's priorities.

Many cities are experimenting with innovations designed to enhance communication and understanding between prosecutors and the community. One innovation called *community prosecution* gives specific assistant prosecutors continuing responsibilities for particular neighborhoods. These prosecutors may become known to people in the neighborhood, attend community meetings and social functions, and learn about residents' specific concerns. In so doing, they can build relationships that will help them gather information and identify witnesses when crimes occur (Porter, 2011).

Prosecutors' relationships and interactions with police, victims, defense attorneys, judges, and the community form the core of the exchange relations that shape decision making in criminal cases. Other relationships, such as those with news media, federal and state officials, legislators, and political-party officials, also influence prosecutors' decisions. This long list of actors illustrates that prosecutors do not base their decisions solely on whether a law has been broken. The occurrence of a crime is only the first step in a decision-making process that may vary from one case to the next. Sometimes charges are dropped or reduced. Sometimes plea bargains are negotiated quickly. Sometimes cases move through the system to a complete jury trial. In every instance, relationships and interactions with a variety of actors both within and outside the justice system shape prosecutors' discretionary decisions.

Decision-Making Policies

Prosecutors have the discretion to develop their own policies on how cases will be handled. Within the same state, prosecutors may pursue different goals in forming policies on which cases to pursue, which ones to drop, and which ones to plea bargain. For example, prosecutors who wish to maintain a high conviction rate will drop cases with weak evidence. Others, concerned about using limited resources effectively, will focus most of their time and energy on the most serious cases.

The policies they develop shape the decisions made by the assistant prosecutors and thus greatly affect the administration of justice (Holleran, Beichner, & Spohn, 2010).

Some prosecutors' offices make extensive use of screening and tend not to press charges in many cases. When charges are pursued, guilty pleas are typically their main method of processing cases. Because pleas of not guilty strain the prosecutors' and courts' trial resources, there are strong reasons to offer incentives to defendants to plead guilty. Some offices process cases and encourage guilty pleas soon after the police bring the cases to the prosecutor's attention. They may also divert or refer them to to social service agencies to address suspects' problems, rather than pursue punishment. Other prosecutors' offices delay finalizing plea bargain agreements, sometimes as late as the first day of trial. The period from the receipt of the police report to the start of the trial is thus a time of review in which the prosecutor uses her or his discretion to decide what actions should be taken.

The **accusatory process** is the series of activities that take place from the moment a suspect is arrested and booked by the police to the moment the formal charge—in the form of an indictment or information—is filed with the court. In an indictment, evidence is presented to a grand jury composed of citizens who determine whether to issue a formal charge. Grand juries are used in the federal system and in states where legislatures have mandated their use for serious charges. In jurisdictions that do not use grand juries, the prosecutor has full control of the charging decision when the filing of an information initiates prosecution. In other words, when an information is used to present formal charges, no body of citizens can protect a suspect from wrongful prosecution until the case goes to trial and a trial jury hears the case. However, earlier in the process, judges may decide at preliminary hearings that there is insufficient evidence to support the pursuit of the charges; in such circumstances, a judge can order that the charges be dismissed.

Clearly, the prosecutor's established policies and decisions play a key role in determining whether charges will be filed against a defendant. Keep in mind, though, that the prosecutor's decision-making power is not limited to decisions about charges. As shown in Figure 7.3, the prosecutor makes important decisions at each stage, both before and after a defendant's guilt is determined. Because the

accusatory process The series of events from the arrest of a suspect to the filing of a formal charge (through an indictment or information) with the court.

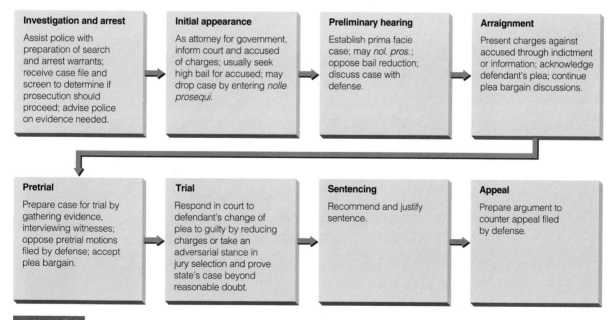

FIGURE 7.3

Typical Actions of a Prosecuting Attorney in Processing a Felony Case The prosecutor has certain responsibilities at various points in the process. At each point, the prosecutor is an advocate for the state's case against the accused.

prosecutor's involvement and influence span the justice process, from seeking search warrants during early investigations to arguing against postconviction appeals, the prosecutor is a highly influential actor in criminal cases. No other participant in the system is involved in so many different stages of the criminal process.

CHECK POINT

7. **What are the roles of the prosecutor?**
   Trial counsel for the police, house counsel for the police, representative of the court, elected official.

8. **How does the prosecutor use discretion to decide how to treat each defendant?**
   The prosecutor can determine the type and number of charges, reduce the charges in exchange for a guilty plea, or enter a *nolle prosequi* (thereby dropping some or all of the charges).

9. **What are the prosecutor's key exchange relationships?**
   Police, victims and witnesses, defense attorneys, judges, the community.

STOP & ANALYZE

Do prosecutors' exchange relationships contribute to or distract from the goal of achieving justice in each case? List two arguments in favor of exchange relationships, recognizing their benefits, and two arguments against them, citing negative consequences.

The Defense Attorney: Image and Reality

defense attorney The lawyer who represents accused offenders and convicted offenders in their dealings with criminal justice.

In an adversarial process, the **defense attorney** is the lawyer who represents accused and convicted persons in their dealings with the criminal justice system. Most Americans have seen defense attorneys in action on television dramas such as *The Good Wife* and *Law and Order*. In these dramas, defense attorneys vigorously battle the prosecution, and the jury often finds their clients innocent. The public also sees news stories mentioning prominent defense attorneys, such as Denver's Abraham Hutt, who represented famous writer Hunter Thompson and handled high-profile cases involving professional athletes (Nicholson, 2015; Steffen, 2014; Cardona, 2010). Neither the highly scripted television dramas nor the highly publicized news stories of cases that end in jury trials give a true picture of the work of the typical defense attorney, however. In reality, most cases find resolution through relatively quick plea bargaining, discretionary dismissals,

Abraham Hutt, a prominent defense attorney, has represented such clients as NFL stars Von Miller and T. J. Ward and the late celebrity-journalist Hunter Thompson. The defense attorney must be persuasive and knowledgeable as well as creative in identifying flaws in the prosecutor's evidence. Could you use your skills to enthusiastically represent criminal defendants?

AP Images/David Zalubowski

and similar decisions by actors in the justice system. In these cases, the defense attorney may seem less like the prosecutor's adversary and more like a partner in the effort to dispose of cases as quickly and efficiently as possible through negotiation (Edkins, 2011).

All the key courtroom actors discussed in this chapter—judges, prosecutors, and defense attorneys—are lawyers who have met the same educational requirements. After becoming lawyers, however, they have made different decisions about what career to pursue. Some people cannot understand why anyone would want to be a defense attorney and "work on behalf of criminals." Actually, defense attorneys work on behalf of people *accused* of crimes—and under the American system of criminal justice, defendants are presumed to be innocent until proven guilty. Indeed, many of them will have the charges against them reduced or dismissed. Others will be found not guilty. Thus, characterizing defense attorneys as only "representing criminals" is simply not accurate. Moreover, many lawyers who choose to work as defense attorneys see themselves as defending the Bill of Rights by ensuring that prosecutors actually respect the Constitution and provide proof beyond a reasonable doubt before defendants are convicted and punished.

The Role of the Defense Attorney

To be effective, defense attorneys must have knowledge of law and procedure, skill in investigation, experience in advocacy, and, in many cases, relationships with prosecutors and judges that will help a defendant obtain the best possible outcome. In the American legal system, the defense attorney performs the key function of ensuring that the prosecution proves its case in court or possesses substantial evidence of guilt before a guilty plea leads to conviction and punishment.

As shown in Figure 7.4, the defense attorney advises the defendant and protects his or her constitutional rights at each stage of the criminal justice process. The defense attorney advises the defendant during questioning by the police, represents her or him at each arraignment and hearing, and serves as advocate for the

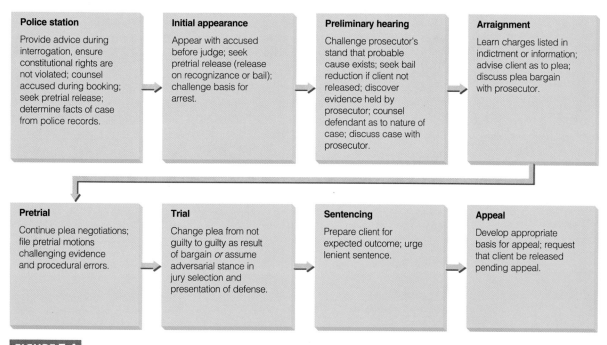

Police station
Provide advice during interrogation, ensure constitutional rights are not violated; counsel accused during booking; seek pretrial release; determine facts of case from police records.

Initial appearance
Appear with accused before judge; seek pretrial release (release on recognizance or bail); challenge basis for arrest.

Preliminary hearing
Challenge prosecutor's stand that probable cause exists; seek bail reduction if client not released; discover evidence held by prosecutor; counsel defendant as to nature of case; discuss case with prosecutor.

Arraignment
Learn charges listed in indictment or information; advise client as to plea; discuss plea bargain with prosecutor.

Pretrial
Continue plea negotiations; file pretrial motions challenging evidence and procedural errors.

Trial
Change plea from not guilty to guilty as result of bargain *or* assume adversarial stance in jury selection and presentation of defense.

Sentencing
Prepare client for expected outcome; urge lenient sentence.

Appeal
Develop appropriate basis for appeal; request that client be released pending appeal.

FIGURE 7.4

Typical Actions of a Defense Attorney Processing a Felony Case Defense attorneys are advocates for the accused. They have an obligation to challenge points made by the prosecution and to advise clients of their constitutional rights.

defendant during the appeal process. Without understanding the technical details of law and court procedures, defendants have little ability to effectively represent themselves in court. The defense attorney therefore ensures that prosecutors and judges understand and respect the defendant's rights.

While filling their roles in the criminal justice system, defense attorneys also psychologically support defendants and their families. Relatives are often bewildered, frightened, and confused. The defense attorney is the only legal actor available to answer the question, "What will happen next?" In short, the attorney's relationship with the client matters a great deal. An effective defense requires respect, openness, and trust between attorney and client. If the defendant refuses to follow the attorney's advice, the lawyer may feel obliged to withdraw from the case in order to protect his or her own professional reputation.

Realities of the Defense Attorney's Job

How well do defense attorneys represent their clients? Attorneys who are inexperienced, uncaring, or overburdened have trouble representing their clients effectively. They may quickly agree to a plea bargain and then work to persuade the defendant to accept the agreement. Their self-interest in disposing of cases quickly, receiving payment, and moving on to other cases may cause them to, in effect, work with the prosecutor to pressure the defendant to plead guilty. Skilled defense attorneys also consider plea bargaining in the earliest stages of a case; however, unlike their less experienced counterparts, these lawyers are guided by their role as advocate for the defendant, not by outside pressures. In many cases, a negotiated plea with a predictable sentence serves the defendant better than does a trial spent fending off more serious charges. An effective defense attorney does not try to take every case all the way to trial.

The defense attorney's job is all the more difficult because neither the public nor defendants fully understand a defense attorney's duties and goals. The public often views defense attorneys as protectors of criminals when, in fact, their basic duty is not to save criminals from punishment but to protect constitutional rights, keep the prosecution honest in preparing and presenting cases, and prevent innocent people from being convicted (Flowers, 2010). Surveys indicate that lawyers place much greater emphasis on the importance of right to counsel than does the public.

Three groups of private-practice lawyers can be called specialists in criminal defense because they handle criminal cases on a regular basis. The first group is composed of nationally known attorneys who charge large fees in highly publicized cases. The second group, found in every large city, is composed of the lawyers of choice for defendants who can afford to pay high fees. These attorneys make handsome incomes by representing white-collar criminals, drug dealers, and affluent people charged with crimes. The third and largest group of attorneys in full-time criminal practice is composed of courthouse regulars who accept many cases for small fees and who participate daily in the criminal justice system as either retained or assigned counsel. These attorneys handle a large volume of cases quickly. They negotiate guilty pleas and try to convince their clients that these agreements are beneficial. They depend on the cooperation of prosecutors, judges, and other courtroom actors, with whom they form exchange relationships in order to reach plea bargains quickly.

Many private attorneys who are neither defense specialists nor courthouse regulars sometimes take criminal cases. These attorneys often have little trial experience and lack well-developed relationships with other actors in the criminal justice system. In fact, their clients might be better served by a courthouse regular who has little interest in each case but whose relationships with prosecutors and judges will produce better plea bargains.

Government-salaried attorneys called *public defenders* handle criminal cases for defendants who are too poor to hire their own attorneys. These attorneys focus exclusively on criminal cases and usually develop significant expertise. They cannot always devote as much time as they want to each case, because they often have heavy caseloads.

The Environment of Criminal Practice

Defense attorneys have a difficult job. Much of their work involves preparing clients and their relatives for the likelihood of conviction and punishment. Even when they know that their clients are guilty, they may become emotionally involved because they are the only judicial actors who know the defendants as human beings and see them in the context of their family and social environment.

Most defense lawyers constantly interact with lower-income clients whose lives and problems are depressing. These attorneys might also visit the local jail at all hours of the day and night. Clearly, their work setting is far removed from the fancy offices and expensive restaurants of the world of corporate attorneys. As described by one defense attorney, "The days are long and stressful. I spend a good deal of time in jail, which reeks of stale food and body odor. My clients often think that because I'm court-appointed, I must be incompetent" (Lave, 1998:14).

Defense lawyers must also struggle with the fact that criminal practice does not pay well. Public defenders garner fairly low salaries, and attorneys appointed to represent poor defendants receive small sums. If private attorneys do not demand payment from their clients at the start of the case, they may find that they must persuade the defendants' relatives to pay—because many convicted offenders have no incentive to pay for legal services while sitting in a prison cell. To perform their jobs well and gain satisfaction from their careers, defense attorneys must focus on goals other than money, such as their key role in protecting people's constitutional rights. However, that they are usually on the losing side can make it hard for them to feel like professionals and enjoy the high self-esteem and satisfying work that is characteristic of the careers of other highly educated people. Because they work on behalf of criminal defendants, they may also face suspicion from the public.

Counsel for Indigents

Since the 1960s, the Supreme Court has interpreted the "right to counsel" in the Sixth Amendment to the Constitution as requiring that the government provide attorneys for indigent defendants who face the possibility of going to prison or jail. *Indigent defendants* are those who are too poor to afford their own lawyers. The Court has also required that attorneys be provided early in the criminal justice

A public defender represents indigent clients and carries a heavy caseload under difficult conditions. The quality of representation for poor defendants may vary from courthouse to courthouse, depending on the knowledge and efforts of the attorneys, caseloads, and administrative pressures to resolve cases quickly. How can we improve the quality of defense in criminal cases?

AP Images/Paul Sakuma

| TABLE 7.2 | The Right to Counsel: Major Supreme Court Rulings |

Case	Year	Ruling
Powell v. Alabama	1932	Indigents facing the death penalty who are not capable of representing themselves must be given attorneys.
Johnson v. Zerbst	1938	Indigent defendants must be provided with attorneys when facing serious charges in federal court.
Gideon v. Wainwright	1963	Indigent defendants must be provided with attorneys when facing serious charges in state court.
Douglas v. California	1963	Indigent defendants must be provided with attorneys for their first appeal.
Miranda v. Arizona	1966	Criminal suspects must be informed about their right to counsel before being questioned in custody.
United States v. Wade	1967	Defendants are entitled to counsel at "critical stages" in the process, including postindictment lineups.
Argersinger v. Hamlin	1972	Indigent defendants must be provided with attorneys when facing misdemeanor and petty charges that may result in incarceration.
Ross v. Moffitt	1974	Indigent defendants are not entitled to attorneys for discretionary appeals after their first appeal is unsuccessful.
Strickland v. Washington	1984	To show that ineffective assistance of counsel violated the right to counsel, defendants must prove that the attorney committed specific errors that affected the outcome of the case.
Rothgery v. Gillespie County, Texas	2008	The right to counsel attaches at the initial hearing before a magistrate when the defendant is informed of the charges and restrictions on liberty are imposed.
Missouri v. Frye	2012	Defense attorneys are obligated to inform their clients about plea agreement offers made by the prosecutor.

process, to protect suspects' rights during questioning and pretrial proceedings. See Table 7.2 for a summary of key rulings on the right to counsel.

The portion of defendants who are provided with counsel because they are indigent has increased greatly in the past three decades. For example, in the 22 states with public defender offices funded by state government rather than county or city governments, criminal caseloads increased by 20 percent from 1999 to 2007 (Langton & Farole, 2010). Government-salaried public defenders alone received 5.5 million cases of indigent criminal defendants in 2007, a figure that does not include thousands of indigents represented by private attorneys who are paid by the government on a case-by-case basis (Farole & Langton, 2010).

The quality of counsel given to indigent defendants has spurred debate. Ideally, experienced lawyers would be appointed soon after arrest to represent the defendant in each stage of the criminal justice process. Ideal conditions do not always exist, however. As we have seen, inexperienced and uncaring attorneys may be appointed. Some attorneys have little time to prepare their cases. Even conscientious attorneys may be unable to provide top-quality counsel if they have heavy caseloads or do not receive enough money to enable them to spend the time required to handle the case well. For example, in 15 of 22 states with state-funded public defender offices and three-quarters of the county-funded public defender offices in 27 other states, the defense attorneys had caseloads that exceeded the U.S. Department of Justice's recommended guidelines (Farole & Langton, 2010; Langton & Farole, 2010). If attorneys lack either the time or the desire to interview the client and prepare the case, they may simply persuade defendants to plead guilty right there in the courtroom during their first and only conversation. Of course, not all publicly financed lawyers who represent poor defendants ignore their clients' best interests. Even so, the quality of counsel received by the poor may vary from courthouse to courthouse, depending on the quality of the attorneys, conditions of defense practice, and administrative pressure to reduce the caseload.

Ways of Providing Indigents with Counsel   Each state determines for itself how indigent defendants will be provided with attorneys (Owens et al., 2015). There are three main ways of providing counsel to indigent defendants: (1) the **assigned counsel** system, also known as "appointed counsel" systems, in which a court appoints a private attorney to represent the accused; (2) the **contract counsel** system, in which an attorney, a nonprofit organization, or a private law firm contracts with a local government to provide legal services to indigent defendants for a specified dollar amount; and (3) **public defender** programs, which are public or private nonprofit organizations with full-time or part-time salaried staff. Figure 7.5 shows which states have statewide, centrally administered public defender systems and which have county-based systems for indigent defense. States that permit counties to choose their own methods for providing attorneys may have all three forms of counsel represented within their states.

The methods for providing defense attorneys and the quality of defense services may depend on the money available to pay attorneys. In the states where counties must fund their own defense services, resources—and the quality of indigent defense—may vary from county to county within a single state. As the chief state public defender in Ohio said with respect to the 88 counties in his state's county-run system, "When you have the state of Ohio law being enforced and defended in 88 different ways,... you end up with huge disparities in cost, quality and efficiency," (A. Manning, 2012).

Issues of resources and quality are complicated by budget cuts in the current era of economic recovery. In 2013, across-the-board cuts throughout the federal government forced public defenders who work in federal courts to take unpaid furloughs for several weeks. Such cuts affect the preparation of cases and timely representation of clients. They have also caused experienced public defenders to look for other jobs rather than deal with personal financial difficulties due to uncertainties regarding their future working hours and paychecks (C. Johnson, 2013).

assigned counsel An attorney in private practice assigned by a court to represent an indigent. The attorney's fee is paid by the government with jurisdiction over the case.

contract counsel An attorney in private practice who contracts with the government to represent all indigent defendants in a county during a set period of time and for a specified dollar amount.

public defender An attorney employed on a full-time, salaried basis by a public or private nonprofit organization to represent indigents.

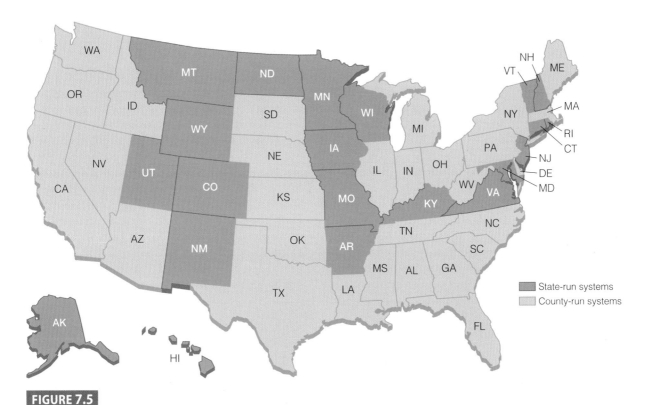

FIGURE 7.5

State-Run Public Defender Offices and County-Run Indigent Defense Systems   Note that county-run systems, in particular, may use different representation models (appointed, contract, or public defender) in counties within a given state or use more than one method within a county.

Source: Lynn Langton and Donald Farole Jr., "State Public Defender Programs, 2007," *Bureau of Justice Statistics Special Report*, September 2010, NCJ 228229.

Many states have been affected by budget problems, and some of these issues arose even earlier than the ones affecting the federal government. For example, in 2010, Gwinnett County, Georgia, cut the compensation for court-appointed defense attorneys from $75 to $65 per hour for serious felony cases, and instituted even lower pay rates for misdemeanor cases and out-of-court activities (Simmons & Rankin, 2010). In Oklahoma, the indigent defense system suffered a $1.5 million budget cut, resulting in its attorneys being assigned 400–500 cases per year (Bisbee, 2010). Public defender offices in Louisiana struggled with budget cuts in 2015 (Burris, 2015). Bear in mind that these discussions of dollar amounts impact not only working conditions for attorneys; they also impact the quality of representation for indigent defendants who are facing punishment if convicted of a crime.

Assigned Counsel In the assigned counsel system, the court appoints a lawyer in private practice to represent an indigent defendant. This system is widely used in small cities and in rural areas, but even some city public defender systems assign counsel in some cases, such as those with multiple defendants, where a conflict of interest might result if a public lawyer represented all of them.

Assigned counsel systems are organized on either an ad hoc or a coordinated basis. In ad hoc assignment systems, private attorneys tell the judge that they are willing to take the cases of indigent defendants. When an indigent requires counsel, the judge either assigns a lawyer from a prepared rotation list or chooses an attorney who is known and present in the courtroom. In coordinated assignment systems, a court administrator oversees the appointment of counsel.

Use of the ad hoc system raises questions about the loyalties of the assigned counsel. For example, Texas was criticized for giving judges free rein to assign lawyers to cases without any supervising authority to ensure that the attorneys actually do a good job (Flores, 2014). Are these attorneys trying to vigorously defend their clients, or are they trying to please the judges to ensure future appointments? In states where judges run for election, there are concerns about lawyers donating to judges' political campaigns: judges might return the favor by supplying their contributors with criminal defense assignments.

The fees paid to assigned defenders are often low compared with what a lawyer might otherwise charge. As described by one attorney, "The level of compensation impacts the level of representation.... If an attorney takes [an appointed criminal case], it means they lose the opportunity to take other cases at higher rates" (*Third Branch*, 2008a). Whereas a private practice attorney might charge clients at rates that exceed $200 per hour, hourly rates for appointed counsel in Cook County (Chicago), Illinois, are merely $40 per hour for in-court tasks and $30 per hour for out-of-court tasks (Gross, 2013). These same rates have been in place for more than 30 years. If their hourly fees fall short of their overhead costs for paying their own office expenses and staff, then attorneys actually lose money when spending time on these cases. Why would an experienced, successful attorney accept such cases under these circumstances? Is there a risk that such cases will go disproportionately to inexperienced or unsuccessful attorneys in courts with low rates of compensation? Look at Table 7.3 to see examples of fees paid to assigned defense counsel.

Contract System A few counties, mainly in western states that do not have large populations, use the contract system. The government contracts with an attorney, a nonprofit association, or a private law firm to handle all indigent cases. Some jurisdictions use public defenders for most cases but contract for services in multiple-defendant cases that might present conflicts of interest in extraordinarily complex cases or in cases that require more time than the government's salaried lawyers can provide.

This system has its problems (Clark, 2011). According to Robert Spangenberg and Marea Beeman (1995:49), "There are serious potential dangers with the contract model, such as expecting contract defenders to handle an unlimited caseload or

TABLE 7.3   Fees Paid to Assigned Counsel in Noncapital Felony Cases

State	Out-of-Court Hourly Rate	In-Court Hourly Rate	Per-Case Maximum
Alaska	$50	$60	$4,000 trial; $2,000 plea
Hawaii	$90	$90	$6,000
Illinois (Chicago)	$30	$40	$1,250
Maryland	$50	$50	$3,000
New York	$75	$75	$4,400
North Carolina	$65	$65	None
Ohio	$50	$60	$3,000
Wisconsin	$40	$40	None

Source: John P. Gross, "Rationing Justice: The Underfunding of Assigned Counsel Systems," *Part 1: Gideon at 50— A Three-Part Examination of Indigent Defense in America* (Washington, DC: National Association of Criminal Defense Lawyers), 2013, 20–32.

awarding contracts on a low-bid basis only, with no regard to the qualifications of contracting attorneys."

Public Defenders The position of public defender developed as a response to the legal needs of indigent defendants. The public defender system, which is growing fast, is used in 43 of the 50 most populous counties and in most large cities. There are about 22 statewide, state-funded systems; in other states, the counties organize and pay for indigent defense, and some counties choose to use full-time public defenders.

Experts and others often view the public defender system as better than the assigned counsel system, because public defenders are specialists in criminal law. As full-time government employees, public defenders, unlike appointed counsel and contract attorneys, do not sacrifice their clients' cases to protect their own financial interests. Public defenders do face certain special problems, however. They may have trouble gaining the trust and cooperation of their clients. Criminal defendants may assume that attorneys on the state payroll, even with the title "public defender," have no reason to protect the defendants' rights and interests. Lack of cooperation from the defendant may make it harder for the attorney to prepare the best possible arguments for use during hearings, plea bargaining, and trials (C. Campbell et al., 2015).

Public defenders may also face heavy caseloads. These burdens increase when government budget cuts affect the money devoted to indigent defense. Public defender programs are most effective when they have enough money to keep caseloads manageable. However, these programs do not control their own budgets, and state and local legislators usually do not see them as high priorities (Jaksic, 2007). Thus, these programs are increasingly underfunded, understaffed, and less able to give adequate attention to each defendant's case. Across New York state, for example, the average caseload was 680 cases for each public defender in 2014 (Virtanen, 2014). In addition, 40 percent of county-based public defender offices nationwide have no staff investigators at all, so the defense attorneys must handle all aspects of their own cases (Farole & Langton, 2010). By contrast, the prosecutors, whose presentations of evidence the public defenders must counteract, can rely on the police department to handle investigation.

Attorney Effectiveness and Competence Do defendants who can afford their own counsel receive better legal services than those who cannot? Many convicted offenders say, "You get what you pay for," meaning that they believe they would have received better counsel if they had been able to pay for their own attorneys. At one time, researchers thought public defenders entered more guilty pleas than did lawyers who had been either privately retained or assigned to cases. However, studies show little variation in case outcomes by various types of defense (Hanson & Chapper, 1991).

The right to counsel is of little value when the counsel is not competent and effective. Even in death penalty cases, attorneys with almost no knowledge of criminal law have made blunders that have needlessly sent their clients to death row (C. E. Smith, 1997). For example, lawyers have fallen asleep during their clients' death penalty trials, yet one Texas judge found no problem with such behavior. He wrote that everyone has a constitutional right to have a lawyer, but "the Constitution does not say that the lawyer has to be awake" (Shapiro, 1997:27). An appellate court later disagreed with this conclusion.

The U.S. Supreme Court has examined the question of what requirements must be met if defendants are to receive effective counsel. To prevail in claims that their counsel has been ineffective, defendants must identify specific errors made by their attorneys that affected the result of their case and made the proceedings unfair. By focusing on whether errors by an attorney were bad enough to make the trial result unreliable, thereby denying a fair trial, the Court has made it difficult for defendants to prove that they were denied effective counsel, even when defense attorneys perform very poorly. As a result, innocent people who were poorly represented have been convicted, even of the most serious crimes.

▼ CHECK POINT

10. **What special pressures do defense attorneys face?**
    Carrying heavy caseloads, receiving poor pay, enduring difficult working conditions, persuading clients to accept pleas, accepting the fact that they will lose most cases.

11. **What are the three main methods of providing attorneys for indigent defendants?**
    Assigned counsel, contract counsel, public defender.

STOP & ANALYZE

Which of the three methods of providing attorneys for indigent defendants works best? List the three strongest arguments in favor of each approach as well as two arguments against each approach. Which set of arguments is most persuasive?

The Courtroom: How It Functions

Criminal cases throughout the nation follow similar rules and procedures. However, courts differ in the precise ways they apply them. Social scientists are aware that the culture of a community greatly influences how its members behave. *Culture* implies shared beliefs about proper behavior. These beliefs can span entire nations or exist in smaller communities, including organizations such as corporations, churches, or neighborhoods. In any community, large or small, the culture can strongly affect people's decisions and behaviors.

local legal culture Norms shared by members of a court community as to how cases should be handled and how a participant should behave in the judicial process.

Researchers have identified a **local legal culture** of values and norms shared by members of a particular court community (judges, attorneys, clerks, bailiffs, and others) about how cases should be handled and the way court officials should behave (Church, 1985). The local legal culture influences court operations in three ways:

1. Norms (shared values and expectations) help participants distinguish between "our" court and other courts. Often a judge or prosecutor will proudly describe how "we" do the job differently and better than officials in a nearby county or city.

Criminal cases move through court processes as a result of discussions, interactions, and decisions involving judges, prosecutors, and defense attorneys. Even when the attorneys adopt strongly adversarial positions, courtroom participants interact, cooperate, and negotiate as they fulfill the responsibilities of their positions in the courtroom workgroup. How is the judge a key actor in this process?

2. Norms tell members of a court community how they should treat one another. For example, mounting a strong adversarial defense may be viewed as not in keeping with the norms of one court, but it may be expected in another.

3. Norms describe how cases should be processed. The best example of such a norm is the **going rate**, the local view of the proper sentence, which considers the offense, the defendant's prior record, and other factors. The local legal culture also includes attitudes on such issues as whether a judge should take part in plea negotiations, when **continuances**—lawyers' requests for delays in court proceedings—should be granted, and which defendants qualify for a public defender.

Differences among local legal cultures help explain why court decisions may differ even though the formal rules of criminal procedure are basically the same. For example, although judges play a key role in sentencing, sentences also stem from understandings of the going rate shared by the prosecutor, defense attorney, and judge. In one court, shared understandings may mean that a court imposes probation on a first-time thief; in another court, different shared values may send first offenders to jail or prison for the same offense.

Decision making in criminal cases is influenced by the fact that participants are organized in **work groups**. The judge, prosecutor, and defense attorney, along with the support staff (clerk, reporter, and bailiff), interact in the workplace on a continuing basis, share goals, develop norms regarding how activities should be carried out, and eventually establish a network of roles that differentiates the group from others and that facilitates cooperation. These relationships are necessary if the group is to carry out its task of disposing of cases. The work-group concept is especially important for urban courts that have heavy caseloads, many courtrooms, and large numbers of lawyers, judges, and other court personnel.

Work groups in various courthouses differ depending on the strength of the factors that define each of them in each setting. For example, a rotation system that moves judges among courtrooms in a large courthouse may limit the development of work-group norms and roles. Although the same prosecutors and defense attorneys may be present every day, the arrival of a new judge every week or month

going rate Local court officials' shared view of the appropriate sentence for a given offense, the defendant's prior record, and other case characteristics.

continuance An adjournment of a scheduled case until a later date.

work group A collection of individuals who interact in the workplace on a continuing basis, share goals, develop norms regarding how activities should be carried out, and eventually establish a network of roles, all of which differentiate the group from others and facilitate cooperation.

CRIMINAL JUSTICE

Myth&Reality

COMMON BELIEF: Plea bargaining defeats the purposes of the criminal justice system by permitting defense attorneys to arrange for offenders to avoid properly severe punishments for their crimes.

REALITY

- Actually, prosecutors maintain significant control over the outcomes of plea bargains. They often file charges despite knowing that they may not have enough evidence to prove a defendant's guilt. Such charges create pressure on the defendant to plead guilty to some lesser crime in order to avoid the worst penalties.
- The courtroom work group's shared understandings concerning the going rate of punishment for particular crimes permit the prosecutor, defense attorney, and judge to reach quick agreement on the appropriate charge and sentence without using the court's scarce resources on a trial.
- The plea bargain in these cases often represents the quick arrival at the same case outcome that would otherwise have been produced through the slower, more expensive trial process.
- In sum, the lesser charge is often for the most serious crime for which the prosecution could actually prove guilt at trial.

will require them to learn and adapt to new ideas about how cases should be negotiated or tried. When shared norms cannot develop, cases will tend to proceed in a more formal manner. The actors in such a courtroom have fewer chances to follow agreed-upon routines than would a work group with a well-developed pattern of interactions.

By contrast, when there are shared expectations and consistent relationships, the business of the courtroom proceeds in a regular but informal manner, with many shared understandings among members easing much of the work (Worden, 1995). Through cooperation, each member can achieve his or her goals as well as those of the group. The prosecutor wants to gain quick convictions, the defense attorney wants fair and prompt resolution of the defendant's case, and the judge wants cooperative agreements on guilt and sentencing. All of these actors want efficient processing of the steady flow of cases that burden their working lives. Through cooperative decision making, the courtroom work group can resist outside efforts to change case processing and sentencing through new laws and policies and thereby retain control of case outcomes (Kim, Spohn, & Hedberg, 2015; Gebo, Stracuzzi, & Hurst, 2006; Harris & Jesilow, 2000). Read "Criminal Justice: Myth & Reality" to see how an understanding of the courtroom work group can provide insight into the plea bargaining process.

Judges are the leaders of the courtroom team. They ensure that procedures are followed correctly. Even if prosecutors and defense attorneys appear to make the key decisions, the judge must approve them. Judges coordinate the processing of cases. Further, each judge may perform this role somewhat differently than another judge. For example, judges who run a loose administrative ship see themselves as somewhat above the battle. They give other members of the team a great deal of freedom in carrying out their duties and will usually approve group decisions, especially when the members of the group have shared beliefs about the court's goals and the community's values. Judges who exert tighter control over the process play a more active role. They anticipate problems; provide cues for other actors; and threaten, cajole, and move the group toward the efficient achievement of its goals. Such judges command respect and participate fully in the ongoing courtroom drama. Some judges' actions can, therefore, push defense attorneys to encourage their clients to plead guilty instead of insisting on a trial.

CHECK POINT

12. How does the local legal culture affect criminal cases?
The local legal culture consists of norms that distinguish a given court from other jurisdictions; stipulate how members should treat one another; and describe how cases should be processed.

13. What is the courtroom work group?
The courtroom work group is made up of the judge, prosecutor, defense counsel, and support staff assigned regularly to a specific courtroom. Through the interaction of these members, goals and norms are shared and a set of roles becomes stabilized.

STOP & ANALYZE

Should the fates of defendants be influenced by the relationships between judges and attorneys? Are case outcomes determined by the facts of the case and law when the courtroom work group operates? Does the courtroom work group advance or hinder the attainment of justice? List three arguments that either endorse the courtroom work group or criticize it.

A QUESTION OF ETHICS

Think, Discuss, Write

In 2015, a prosecutor in New Jersey opposed permitting DNA testing of preserved evidence from a rape case that had occurred in 1988. According to the prosecutor, although DNA testing was not available at the time of the crime, the tests should not be conducted because the man who was convicted of the crime had already served his prison sentence and been released many years earlier. Yet, as a result of the conviction, the man had had difficulty finding employment or a place to live and had been arrested twice for failing to register properly with police as a convicted sex offender. In light of the severe continuing burdens affecting the man's life from the rape conviction, lawyers for the man argued that the interests of justice required going forward with the laboratory test to see if his claims of innocence could be verified.

In a Michigan case in 2014, defense attorneys alleged that prosecutors and a local judge spent 12 years blocking newly developed DNA tests of preserved evidence from a rape-murder. Meanwhile, a man with mental illness problems confessed to the crime and gained release after serving more than 15 years in prison when DNA testing finally took place and provided

evidence that a different man, one of the original suspects under investigation in the case, was at the scene of the crime. No DNA evidence connected the imprisoned man to the crime.

Discussion/Writing Assignment

What is a prosecutor's highest obligation? To seek to convict people of crimes in the American adversary system? To make sure that justice is done? How do prosecutors' obligations translate into the decisions that they should make about supporting or opposing DNA testing? Write a memo describing the rules that you would create to guide prosecutors about what to do when asked to support or oppose DNA testing of evidence in old cases.

Sources: Kathleen Hopkins, "Prosecutors Block DNA Test That Could Clear Man's Name," *USA Today*, January 9, 2015 (www.usatoday.com); David Moran, "On DNA, Prosecutors Can't Handle the Truth," *Detroit News*, October 13, 2014 (www.detroitnews.com); Jim Schaefer, "DNA Evidence Frees Northern Michigan Man in Prison for 15 Years," *Detroit Free Press*, September 6, 2014 (www.freep.com).

SUMMARY

1 Describe the structure of the American court system.
- The United States has a dual court system consisting of state and federal courts that are organized into separate hierarchies.
- Trial courts and appellate courts have different jurisdictions and functions.

2 Name the qualities that the public desires in a judge.
- The judge is a key figure in the criminal justice process who assumes the roles of adjudicator, negotiator, and administrator. Effective performance in these roles requires knowledge of law, fairness, communication skills, and thoughtful decision making.
- The recent development of specialized courts, such as drug courts and mental health courts, places judges in the role of a problem solver.

3 Describe the process by which American judges are selected.
- State judges are selected through various methods, including partisan elections, nonpartisan elections, gubernatorial appointment, legislative selection, and merit selection.
- Merit-selection methods for choosing judges have gradually spread to many states. Such methods

typically use a screening committee to recommend potential appointees, who will, if placed on the bench by the governor, later go before the voters for approval or disapproval, based on their performance in office.

4 Identify some of the roles of the prosecuting attorney.
- American prosecutors, both state and federal, have significant discretion to determine how to handle criminal cases.
- The prosecutor can play various roles, including trial counsel for the police, house counsel for the police, representative of the court, and elected official.

5 Describe the role that the prosecutor's discretion plays in the process for filing criminal charges.
- Prosecutors possess significant authority to decide whether to pursue charges and which charges to pursue. Because most local prosecutors are elected officials who seek to please the voters, there are risks that political considerations may affect prosecutorial decisions.

- There is no higher authority over most prosecutors that can overrule a decision to pursue multiple counts against a defendant or to decline to prosecute (*nolle prosequi*).

6 **Identify those with whom the prosecutor interacts in decision making.**

- Prosecutors' decisions and actions are affected by their exchange relationships with many other important actors and groups, including police, judges, defense attorneys, victims and witnesses, and the public.

7 **Describe the day-to-day reality of criminal defense work in the United States.**

- The popular image of defense attorneys as courtroom advocates often differs from the reality of pressured, busy negotiators constantly involved in bargaining with the prosecutor over plea agreements.
- Relatively few private defense attorneys make significant incomes from criminal work, but larger numbers of private attorneys accept court appointments to handle indigent defendants' cases quickly for relatively low fees.

8 **List the methods for providing counsel for defendants who cannot afford a private attorney.**

- Three primary methods for providing attorneys to represent indigent defendants are assigned counsel, contract counsel, and public defenders.
- Overall, private and public attorneys appear to provide similar quality of counsel with respect to case outcomes.
- Indigent defense systems often face limited budgets, so that assigned counsel appointed to represent defendants are paid small amounts and public defenders are burdened by significant caseloads.
- The quality of representation provided to criminal defendants is a matter of significant concern, but U.S. Supreme Court rulings have made it difficult for convicted offenders to prove that their attorneys did not provide competent counsel.

9 **Describe the courtroom work group, and explain and how it functions.**

- The outcomes in criminal cases depend significantly on a court's local legal culture, which defines the going rates of punishment for various offenses.
- Courtroom work groups made up of judges, prosecutors, defense attorneys, and staff who work together can smoothly and efficiently handle cases through cooperative plea bargaining processes.

Questions for Review

1. The judge plays several roles. What are they? Do they conflict with one another?
2. What is the best method for selecting judges? Why? What are the flaws or risks of alternative selection methods?
3. What are the formal powers of the prosecuting attorney?
4. What considerations influence the prosecutor's decision about whether to bring charges and what to charge?
5. Why is the prosecuting attorney often cited as the most powerful office in the criminal justice system?

6. What are some of the problems faced by attorneys who engage in private defense practice?
7. What are the methods by which defense services are provided to indigents?
8. Why might it be argued that publicly financed counsel serves defendants better than does privately retained counsel?
9. What is the courtroom work group, and what does it do?

Key Terms

accusatory process (p. 259)

adversarial process (p. 239)

appellate courts (p. 240)

assigned counsel (p. 265)

continuance (p. 269)

contract counsel (p. 265)

count (p. 255)

defense attorney (p. 260)

discovery (p. 255)

going rate (p. 269)

inquisitorial process (p. 239)

jurisdiction (p. 239)

local legal culture (p. 268)

merit selection (p. 249)

nolle prosequi (p. 255)

nonpartisan election (p. 247)

partisan election (p. 247)

problem-solving courts (p. 241)

prosecuting attorney (p. 249)

public defender (p. 265)

state attorney general (p. 250)

trial courts of general jurisdiction (p. 240)

trial courts of limited jurisdiction (p. 240)

United States attorneys (p. 250)

work group (p. 269)

Pretrial Procedures, Plea Bargaining, and the Criminal Trial

1 Identify the elements in the pretrial process in criminal cases.

2 Explain how the bail system operates.

3 Describe the experience of pretrial detention.

4 Explain how and why plea bargaining occurs.

5 Give the reasons why cases go to trial, and describe the benefits of jurors' participation in trials.

6 Describe the stages of a criminal trial.

7 Explain the basis for an appeal of a conviction.

A recent high school graduate who had gained admission to Harvard after being a star student at an elite New Hampshire prep school stood trial in August 2015 on sexual-assault charges initiated by a 15-year-old female student. The case developed as a consequence of a tradition among the male seniors at St. Paul's School, called "senior salute," in which they proposition and reportedly seek to have an intimate encounter with a female student prior to graduation (Bidgood, 2015c). While much of the news media's attention to the case concerned the unfamiliar traditions and behavior of wealthy teens at an elite school, the case also served to remind people that crime and criminal prosecutions are not limited to poor people and urban areas. Less affluent people are certainly overrepresented among those in American society who are accused of crimes. Yet, any complete survey of the news can reveal arrests and prosecutions of people across the spectrum of society, such as the January 2016 arrests of a former Power Rangers television show actor for murder and a bank official for embezzling $20 million (Stedman, 2016; Turk, 2016). Although each case may have unique aspects, there are common elements in stages of the criminal justice process used to determine the outcomes in each case. The case of the New Hampshire prep school graduate can illustrate the steps in the criminal justice process.

As the school year was winding down, Owen Labrie, a senior, communicated with a freshman girl through Facebook and e-mail messages, inviting her to join him for "senior salute" which one report described as "when older students ask younger ones to join them for a walk, a kiss, or more" (Bidgood, 2015a). Eventually, she agreed to meet him, and on May 30, 2014, he led her to the roof of a building and then to a dark maintenance room. According to Labrie's testimony at the eventual trial, she willingly kissed him and permitted him to take off some of her clothes, but there was no sexual contact beneath her underwear. However, on June 3, the girl's mother reported to a school counselor that her daughter had been assaulted. The counselor notified the police, and the investigation of the alleged crime began (Doyle, 2014).

The girl was examined at a hospital and a sexual-assault nurse examiner found a laceration consistent with penetration. The girl told police that when Labrie moved to go beyond kissing, she resisted his efforts to remove her underwear and she said "no" to him (Doyle, 2014). Police officers presented the girl's account and the initial physical evidence to a judge. The presentations by the police led the judge to conclude that the evidence established probable cause that a crime had been committed and that Labrie's social media records probably contained evidence related to this crime. He issued a search warrant for Labrie's Facebook and e-mail records. One week later, police conducted a phone interview with Labrie, and the following day Labrie and his mother went to the police station to talk to detectives. He spoke to the police for two hours. One of Labrie's attorneys later claimed that all of his statements to the police should be excluded from evidence, because the police had not informed him of his *Miranda* rights—the right to remain silent and the right to have an attorney present during questioning. However, his statements were not excluded, because he was not under arrest when he spoke to the police, and therefore was free to leave at any time. *Miranda* warnings are required only when suspects are in custody, typically after they have been arrested, and are not free to leave (Blackmun, 2015). Thus considerations of suspects' constitutional rights—the need to gain a judge's approval to obtain a search warrant and the contexts in which *Miranda* warnings are required—affected both the actions of the police and the later claims by a defense attorney trying to protect his client's interests.

One month later, police officers informed Labrie that they had obtained an arrest warrant by presenting evidence to a judge that established probable cause concerning Labrie's likely responsibility for sexual-assault crimes. Labrie voluntarily turned himself in to the police and was charged with three felony sex crimes, three misdemeanor sex crimes, and an additional felony for using a computer to lure a minor (Doyle, 2014b). He was released on $15,000 personal recognizance bail that permitted him to remain free during the processing of his case, provided he obeyed the conditions of bail. Bail on personal recognizance means that Labrie did not have to provide any money or property to gain release. However, he faced the possibility of being placed in jail and

being charged $15,000 if he failed to appear at scheduled court dates or otherwise violated release conditions, which typically include avoiding contact with the victim, committing no further crimes, and abstaining from alcohol and drug use. In Labrie's case, one specific condition of bail release was a prohibition on contact with employees, students, and parents of students at St. Paul's School. In February 2015, Labrie was accused of violating this term of bail by sending a letter to St. Paul's School students and parents soliciting financial contributions to his legal defense fund. Violations of conditions can lead bail to be revoked and force defendants to sit in jail until their cases reach a conclusion. Labrie raised more than $100,000 in contributions from St. Paul's families that supported his side in the case. Although his sending of the letter violated his bail conditions, his bail was not revoked; prosecutors worked with defense attorneys to make his bail conditions more explicit, since it was agreed that Labrie had misunderstood the original rules (Blackmun, 2015; Cooper, 2015).

Labrie was originally scheduled to appear in court in September to enter his initial plea to the charges. His actual appearance in court was delayed while prosecutors negotiated a potential plea agreement with the attorney that Labrie had hired to represent him. News reports indicated that an agreement had been reached after hours of negotiation. It was later revealed that Labrie was offered the opportunity to plead guilty to a lesser charge that would require only a one-month jail sentence and no lifetime registration as a sex offender. Reportedly, the alleged victim hoped that he would plead guilty, because she did not want to experience the emotional trauma of testifying publicly in court about the specific details of her sexual victimization. Most criminal defendants prefer the certainty of a less-than-maximum sentence through a plea bargain, but Labrie turned down the plea deal, hired as his new lawyer a well-known attorney from Boston, and indicated that he would fight the charges in a jury trial. Labrie's decision to go to trial placed him at risk of receiving a sentence of many years in prison if the jury were to convict him of multiple felony charges (Blackmun, 2014; Blackmun, 2015; Cooper, 2015; Tuohy, 2015).

The American system regards the trial as the best method for determining a defendant's guilt. This is especially true when the defendant can afford to pay for an attorney to mount a vigorous defense. The Labrie case occupies the top layer of Samuel Walker's criminal justice wedding cake (see Chapter 1), as one of those relatively few cases that go to trial and command great public attention because a highly publicized defendant with resources from supporters could afford to hire an attorney to fight the case all the way to the end.

However, a trial is not a scientific process. Instead of calm, consistent evaluations of evidence, trials involve unpredictable human perceptions and reactions. Attorneys know that jury members—a mix of citizens drawn from society—may reach unexpected conclusions from the attorneys' presentations of evidence and the testimony of witnesses. Ultimately, in August 2015, the jury found Labrie guilty of one felony count of using a computer to lure a child and several misdemeanor sex charges, but acquitted him of the felony sex charges (Shapiro and Benitez, 2015). Apparently, the jury was not confident that either the victim or Labrie had presented an accurate version of events. They concluded that crimes had clearly been committed, but that the most serious charges were not proven "beyond a reasonable doubt." Two months later, after a sentencing hearing with arguments from the prosecution and defense, the judge imposed a sentence of one year in jail plus the lifetime consequence of registration as a sex offender because of the felony conviction (Bidgood, 2015b). While Labrie's attorney appealed the conviction, the jail sentence was delayed, so Labrie lived at his parents' home as a registered sex offender. He was not able to attend Harvard (Cooper, 2015).

Because of the high stakes and uncertainty that surround criminal trials, most defendants plead guilty as they get closer to the prospect of being judged by a random group of citizens drawn from the community. Even the cases of prominent defendants, who can afford to pay top-notch attorneys, are often determined by plea bargaining. For example, multimillionaire movie star Mel Gibson entered a plea in March 2011 to misdemeanor battery charges after he allegedly punched his girlfriend in 2010 (Cieply, 2011). In his plea deal, Gibson agreed to a sentence of 36 months of probation and 52 weeks of domestic violence counseling (McCartney, 2011). Gibson gained a specific sentence and spared his children from the embarrassment of a lengthy proceeding covered by newspapers and television. The prosecutor gained a quick conviction without expending time and other resources.

In this chapter, we examine the steps in the criminal justice process from arrest to dismissal or conviction. We give particular attention to bail, plea bargaining, and trials—the processes and decisions that most influence whether people will lose their liberty or otherwise receive punishment. As we shall see, interactions and decisions involving judges, prosecutors, and defense attorneys guide the outcomes from these important processes.

From Arrest to Trial or Plea

At each stage of the pretrial process, key decisions are made that move some defendants to the next stage of the process and filter others out of the system. An innocent person could be arrested on the basis of mistaken identification or misinterpreted evidence (Streib, 2010; Huff, 2002). However, pretrial processes ideally force prosecutors and judges to review the available evidence and dismiss unnecessary charges against people who should not face trial and punishment. These processes stem from the American value of due process. Americans believe that people should be entitled to a series of hearings and other procedural steps in which their guilt is proved before they are subjected to punishments such as the loss of liberty through incarceration.

After arrest, the accused is booked at the police station. This process includes taking photographs and fingerprints, which form the basis of the case record. Within 48 hours of a warrantless arrest, the defendant is usually taken to court for the initial appearance to hear which charges are being pursued, to be advised of her or his rights, and to receive the opportunity to post bail. At the initial appearance, the judge also must confirm that evidence exists to establish probable cause that the accused committed a crime and thereby is eligible to be prosecuted. If the police used an arrest warrant to take the suspect into custody, evidence has already been presented to a judge who believed that it was strong enough to support a finding of probable cause to proceed against the defendant.

Often the first formal meeting between the prosecutor and the defendant's attorney is the **arraignment**: the formal court appearance in which the charges

arraignment The court appearance of an accused person in which the charges are read and the accused, advised by a lawyer, pleads guilty or not guilty.

Criminal defendants typically make several court appearances as the judge makes decisions about evidence and the protection of each defendant's rights. Does the American system reduce the risk of errors by using a multistep process to examine evidence, protect rights, and determine guilt?

AP Images/Todd Davis

against the defendant are read and the defendant, advised by her or his lawyer, enters a plea of either guilty or not guilty. Most defendants will initially plead not guilty, even if they are likely to plead guilty at a later point. This is because, thus far, the prosecutor and defense attorney usually have had little chance to discuss a potential plea bargain. The more serious the charges, the more likely it is that the prosecutor and defense attorney will need time to assess the strength of the other side's case. Only then can plea bargaining begin.

At the time of arraignment, prosecutors begin to evaluate the evidence. This screening process greatly affects the lives of accused persons, whose fate rests largely on the prosecutor's discretion (Covey, 2011). If the prosecutor believes the case against the defendant is weak, the charges may be dropped. Prosecutors do not wish to waste their limited time and resources on cases that will not stand up in court. A prosecutor may also drop charges if the alleged crime is minor, if the defendant is a first offender, or if the prosecutor believes that the few days spent in jail before arraignment have provided enough punishment for the alleged offense. Jail overcrowding or the need to work on more-serious cases may also influence the decision to drop charges. In making these decisions, prosecutors at times may discriminate against the accused because of race, wealth, or some other factor, or they may discriminate against certain victims, such as women who have been sexually assaulted by an intimate partner or other acquaintance (Schlesinger, 2013; A. Davis, 2008; Spohn & Holleran, 2001).

Defense attorneys use pretrial proceedings to challenge the prosecution's evidence. They make **motions** to the court requesting that an order be issued to bring about a specific action. For example, the defense may seek an order for the prosecution to share certain evidence or for the exclusion of evidence that was allegedly obtained through improper questioning of the suspect or an improper search.

As Figure 8.1 shows, prosecutors use their decision-making power to filter many cases out of the system. The 101 cases illustrated are typical felony cases. The percentage of cases varies from city to city, depending on such factors as the effectiveness of police investigations and prosecutors' policies about which cases to pursue. In the figure, nearly half of those arrested did not ultimately face felony prosecutions. A small number of defendants were steered toward diversion programs (Alarid & Montemayor, 2010). A larger number had their cases dismissed for various reasons, including lack of evidence, the minor nature of the charges, or first-time offender status. Some of the 16 sentenced to probation may actually be imprisoned if the offenders commit a crime after release into the community. In these cases, the prosecutor simply chooses to pursue revocation of probation or parole, typically an easier and quicker process than proving guilt for a new crime (Weisberg, 2010;

motion An application to a court requesting that an order be issued to bring about a specific action.

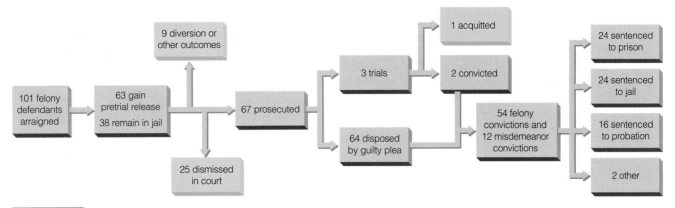

FIGURE 8.1

Typical Outcomes of 101 Urban Felony Cases Prosecutors and judges make crucial decisions during the period before trial or plea. Once cases are bound over for disposition, guilty pleas are many, trials are few, and acquittals are rare.

Approximations developed from B. Reaves, "Felony Defendants in Large Urban Counties, 2009—Statistical Tables," *Bureau of Justice Statistics Statistical Tables*, December 2013, NCJ 228944.

Kingsnorth, Macintosh, & Sutherland, 2002). Read the "You Make the Decision" feature to consider the kinds of decisions that you might make as a prosecutor.

During the pretrial process, defendants are exposed to the informal, "assembly-line" atmosphere of the lower criminal courts. Often decisions are quickly made about bail, arraignment, pleas, and the disposition of cases. Moving cases through court quickly seems to be the main goal of many judges and attorneys during the pretrial process. Courts throughout the nation face pressure to limit the number of cases going to trial. This pressure may affect the decisions of both judges and prosecutors, as well as the defense attorneys who seek to maintain good relationships with them. American courts often have too little funding, too few staff members, and too little time to give detailed attention to each case, let alone the time and resources needed for a full trial. Resource scarcity is a growing problem, due to the budget cuts experienced by many state and local court systems (Bluestein, 2011; Sullo, 2016).

YOU MAKE THE DECISION

Prosecutor

Prosecutors are key figures in the outcomes of criminal cases. They decide what charges to file initially against defendants. If they engage in the plea bargaining process for a case, they decide what reduction in charges they will offer or what reduced sentence recommendation they will make to the judge in exchange for the defendant's voluntary guilty plea. You are the prosecutor in a case in which a high school senior baked the illegal drug hashish into brownies, which he then gave to a teacher and classmates. The students ate the brownies without knowing that they were laced with drugs, but the teacher

was suspicious at first bite. You have charged the 19-year-old with three felonies—corrupting another with drugs; possession of hashish; and trafficking in hashish—in addition to three misdemeanor counts for contributing to the delinquency of a minor (for giving drugs to 17-year-old classmates). Conviction on all of these charges will lead the teenager to be sentenced to serve a term in state prison. The teen's defense attorney tells you that the youth baked the brownies as a joke and did not understand the seriousness of the action. The defense attorney urges you to drop most of the charges, permit the

teen to plead guilty to one misdemeanor charge of contributing to delinquency of a minor, and then recommend a sentence of probation, fine, and drug counseling classes. Will you accept the defense attorney's offer? Will you insist on a guilty plea to more serious charges and a more severe sentence? Will you refuse to plea bargain and insist that the teen go to trial on the original charges if he will not plead guilty to all of them? Describe how you would respond to the defense attorney and explain the reasons for your response. Then search the Internet to read about the January 2016 resolution of the case against Edward Goschinski in Springboro, Ohio.

1. **What are the purposes of the initial appearance, arraignment, and motions?**
   The initial appearance determines if there is probable cause to support the arrest. Arraignments involve the formal reading of charges and the entry of a plea. Motions seek information and the vindication of defendants' rights.

2. **Why and how are cases filtered out of the system?**
   Cases are filtered out through the discretionary decisions of prosecutors and judges when they believe that there is inadequate evidence to proceed or when prosecutors believe that their scarce resources are best directed at other cases.

Do prosecutors hold too much power in the pretrial process in light of their discretionary decisions about charging and plea bargaining? List two risks and two benefits from giving prosecutors significant authority over pretrial decisions.

Bail: Pretrial Release

It is often stated that defendants are presumed innocent until proved guilty or until they enter a guilty plea. However, people who are arrested are taken to jail. They are deprived of their freedom and, in many cases, subjected to miserable living conditions while they await the processing of their cases. The fact that people who are presumed innocent can lose their freedom—sometimes for many months—as their cases work their way toward trial is one that clashes with the American values of freedom and liberty. It is not clear how committed Americans are to preserving the ideal of freedom for people who have not yet been convicted of crimes. Concerns for such people may have further diminished in the aftermath of September 11, when the federal government began to hold persons suspected of connections to terrorism, labeling them as "material witnesses" or "enemy combatants" without providing any bail hearing, evidence of guilt, or access to defense attorneys. The outcry against such deprivations of liberty has come from civil rights groups and attorneys rather than from the general public (Tashima, 2008). Occasionally, prosecutors seek to have "material witnesses" held in other serious criminal cases if they fear the witnesses will disappear. Thus a man in Oregon was held for more than two years while waiting to testify at a murder trial in 2015 (E. Smith, 2015).

A conflict is bound to occur between the American value of individual liberty and the need to keep some criminal suspects in jail in order to protect society from violent people or from those who may try to escape prosecution. However, not every person charged with a criminal offense need be detained. Thus, bail and other release methods are used on the condition that the defendants will appear in court as required.

bail An amount of money, specified by a judge, to be paid as a condition of pretrial release to ensure that the accused will appear in court as required.

Bail is a sum of money or property, specified by the judge, that defendants present to the court as a condition of pretrial release. They forfeit the bail if they do not appear in court as scheduled. Although people are generally entitled to a bail hearing as part of their right to due process, there is no constitutional right to release on bail or even a right to have the court set an amount as the condition of release. The Eighth Amendment to the U.S. Constitution forbids excessive bail, and state bail laws are usually designed to prevent discrimination in setting bail. They do not guarantee, however, that all defendants will have a realistic chance of being released before trial. A study in New York City found that among 19,137 cases for which bail was set at $1,000 or less, 87 percent of those defendants could not post bail; they remained in jail for an average of 16 days while their cases were processed (Secret, 2010). Such statistics about the risk of pretrial detention for large numbers of poor people raise the possibility that such defendants may feel pressured to plead guilty whether or not they are in fact guilty, simply to obtain a sentence of probation for minor offenses and thereby more quickly gain their freedom from custody.

Because the accused is presumed to be innocent, bail should not be used as punishment. The amount of bail should therefore be high enough to ensure that the defendant appears in court for trial—but no higher. However, there must also be some assurance that the defendant will not commit more crimes while out on bail (Karnow, 2008). Congress and some of the states have passed laws that permit *preventive detention* of defendants when the judge concludes that they pose a threat to the community while awaiting trial (Wiseman, 2009).

The Reality of the Bail System

The reality of the bail system is far from the ideal. The question of bail may arise at the police station, at the initial court appearance in a misdemeanor case, or at the arraignment in most felony cases. For minor offenses, police officers may have a standard list of bail amounts. For serious offenses, a judge will set bail in court. In both cases, those setting bail may have discretion to set differing bail amounts for different suspects depending on the circumstances of each case. The speed of decision making and lack of information available at the moment of setting bail can enhance differential treatment. As described by the prosecutor in Staten Island, one of the boroughs of New York City, "We have an assistant prosecutor who in about 30 seconds has to come up with a dollar figure that that young person believes is adequate [an amount for bail].... We don't get to interview the defendant; we have to make a determination without substantiating any of the information before us" (Secret, 2010).

In almost all courts, the amount of bail is based mainly on the judge's view of the seriousness of the crime and of the defendant's record. As indicated by the foregoing statement from the New York prosecutor, this emphasis results, in part, from a lack of information about the accused. Because bail is typically determined 24 to 48 hours after an arrest, there is little time to conduct a more thorough assessment. As a result, judges in many communities have developed standard rates: so many dollars for such-and-such an offense. In some cases, a judge may set a high bail if the police or prosecutor wants a certain person to be kept off the streets.

Critics of the bail system argue that it operates to facilitate discrimination, especially against poor people (Wooldredge, 2012; Gerstein, 2013). Moreover, the overlap of racial minority status and poverty in American society can produce definite disparities in regard to who is actually subjected to pretrial detention (Robertson, 2014). Imagine that you have been arrested and have no money. Should you be denied a chance for freedom before trial just because you are poor? What if you have a little money, but if you use it to post bail, you will not have any funds left to hire an attorney? Professional criminals and the affluent have no trouble making bail; many drug dealers, for instance, can readily make bail and go on dealing while awaiting trial. In contrast, a poor person arrested for a minor violation may spend the pretrial period in jail (Secret, 2010). Should dangerous, wealthy offenders be allowed out on bail while nonviolent, poor suspects are locked up?

The consequences of failing to make bail are significant for poor people. The average period of time spent in jail awaiting case processing is 23 days. During that time unconvicted people can lose their jobs, have their families evicted for failing to pay rent, have their cars repossessed, and miss payments on other bills. Many observers fear that innocent people who cannot make bail for minor offenses will feel pressure to plead guilty in order to leave jail on probation rather than sit in a cell waiting for their day in court. Choosing to plead guilty may enable them to avoid missing work and keep making payments on rent and bills, but then they will have a criminal conviction that can impact their future employability, credit worthiness, and eligibility for new housing options in the future (Gass, 2015).

News media coverage in 2015 highlighted tragic stories of the deaths of people who were too poor to make bail for minor offenses. Sandra Bland was arrested after a minor traffic stop when the police officer became angry at her refusal to put out her cigarette. She was unable to come up with $500 to secure her release on bail (Pinto, 2015). After three days in jail, she was dead, amid controversy about whether she committed suicide, was injured by jail officers, or suffered a medical crisis. In New York City, 16-year-old Kalief Browder was arrested for stealing a backpack. He refused to plead guilty, and his family could not afford $3,000 for bail. He was held in jail for three years, including more than a year in solitary confinement. During that time he received beatings by corrections officers and other jailed detainees. Eventually, the charges against him were dropped. When he committed suicide after he was released, many observers blamed the psychological scars he carried from his lengthy, horrific experience in jail (Gass, 2015).

According to a study of felony defendants in the nation's most populous counties, 62 percent were released before disposition of their cases, 34 percent were unable to make bail, and 4 percent were detained without bail (Reaves, 2013). Figure 8.2 shows the amounts of bail set for various types of felony offenses. Those who cannot make bail must remain in jail awaiting trial, unless they can obtain enough money to pay a bail agent's fee. Given the length of time between arraignment and trial in most courts and the hardships of pretrial detention, bail agents are important to defendants in many cities. In 2009, there were 17,198 felony suspects in the 75 largest counties who could not make bail or use the services of a bail agent to gain release (Reaves, 2013). As indicated by the previously mentioned study in New York City, far larger numbers of people lose their liberty in the bail system when one adds the people detained for failing to produce small bail amounts after being arrested for misdemeanors.

Bail Agents

The bail agent, also known as a bail bondsman, is a key figure in the bail process. Bail agents are private businesspeople who are paid fees by defendants who lack the money to make bail. They are licensed by the state and can choose their own clients. In exchange for a fee, which may be 5 to 10 percent of the bail amount, the bail agent will put up the money (or property) to gain the defendant's release. Bail agents are not obliged to provide bail money for every defendant who seeks to use their services. Instead, they decide which defendants are likely to return for court appearances. If the defendant skips town, the bail money is forfeited, thus giving the bail agent a strong incentive to try to locate the missing defendant. Sometimes bail agents and

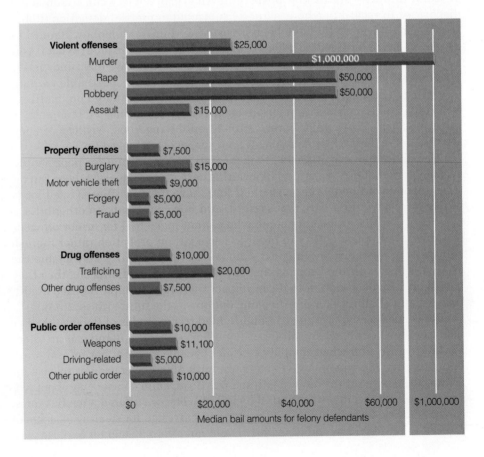

FIGURE 8.2

Median Bail Amounts for Felony Defendants by Offense Type The amount of bail varies according to the offense.

Source: Brian A. Reaves, "Felony Defendants in Large Urban Counties, 2009—Statistical Tables," *Bureau of Justice Statistics Statistical Tables,* December 2013, NCJ 228944.

their employees have used violence or otherwise gone outside the boundaries of the law in their efforts to capture missing defendants.

Bail agents may build relationships with police officers and jailers to obtain referrals. Many defendants may not know whom to call for help in making bail, and officers can steer them to a particular bail agent. This can lead to corruption if a bail agent pays a jailer or police officer to make such referrals. Moreover, these relationships may lead to improper cooperation, such as a bail agent refusing to help a particular defendant if the police would like to see that defendant remain in jail. Thus, the bail agent can pose ethical and practical problems for the system (Clisura, 2010).

The potential problems of using profit-seeking bail agents are widely recognized (M. Phillips, 2011). Only two countries in the world use commercial bail bond systems, the United States and the Philippines. Posting bail for a fee is illegal in many countries. In addition, four states—Illinois, Kentucky, Oregon, and Wisconsin—have abolished private bail bond systems and instead rely on deposits to courts instead of payments to private businesses (Liptak, 2008b).

There can be functional benefits from the activities of bail agents. One such benefit is that they can contribute to the smooth processing of cases. A major reason that defendants fail to appear for scheduled court appearances is forgetfulness and confusion about when and where they must appear. Courthouses in large cities are huge bureaucracies that do not always clearly communicate to a defendant a change in the time and location of a hearing. Bail agents can help by reminding defendants about court dates, calling defendants' relatives to make sure that the defendant will arrive on time, and warning defendants about the penalties for failing to appear. Such contributions, however, do not necessarily outweigh the risks and problems caused by bail agents. An agent in Brownsville, Texas, for example, was sentenced to serve time in federal prison in 2012 after bribing a state judge to reduce an accused drug trafficker's bail (Brezosky, 2012). Similarly, a bail agent in Portsmouth, Virginia, went to prison in 2012 for paying bribes to a judge and an employee of the sheriff's department for referring defendants to him as bail bond clients (FBI Press Release, 2012). In 2015, a multiyear investigation across three California counties resulted in the arrests of 30 bail agents when the inquiry revealed corrupt practices, such as paying people in jail to provide the bail agents with information about newly jailed arrestees, using unlicensed employees, and hiring an ex-felon as a bounty hunter (Larson, 2015). These examples show the continuing risks that exist from the use of bail agent in the criminal justice system.

Although the justice system may benefit from the activities of bail agents, court and law enforcement officials could handle the same functions as well or better if they had the resources, time, and interest to make sure that released defendants return to court. If all courts had pretrial services offices, such as those in the federal courts, defendants could be monitored and reminded to return to court but avoid the risks of discrimination and corruption associated with the use of bail agents (Cadigan, 2009).

Further, the problems caused by bail agents and bounty hunters in using their own means to find and capture fugitives could be avoided if pretrial services offices reduced the role of bail agents (M. Hirsch, 2007). The hunt for fugitives, such as defendants who skip bail, could remain the exclusive responsibility of trained law enforcement personnel. In the federal system, U.S. marshals are the main law enforcement officials in the court system and are responsible for handling court security, transporting prisoners, and tracking down fugitives.

Setting Bail

When the police set bail at the station house for minor offenses, they usually apply a standard amount for a particular charge. By contrast, when a judge sets bail, the amount of bail and conditions of release result from interactions among the judge, prosecutor, and defense attorney. These actors discuss the defendant's personal qualities and prior record. The prosecutor may stress the seriousness of the crime, the defendant's record, and negative personal characteristics. The defense attorney, if one

Each year, 20 percent of felony defendants out on bail fail to appear for scheduled court hearings. Some forget court dates or misunderstand instructions. Others intentionally skip town. Nearly all of them are eventually found, frequently by bail agents and their employees. Should such profit-seeking, private businesses be so deeply involved in the criminal justice process?

has been hired or appointed at this point in the process, may stress the defendant's good job, family responsibilities, and place in the community. Like other aspects of bail, these factors may favor affluent defendants over the poor, the unemployed, and people with unstable families. Yet, many of these factors provide no clear information about how dangerous a defendant is or whether he or she will appear in court. The amount of bail may also reflect the defendant's social class or even racial or ethnic discrimination by criminal justice officials (M. Johnson & Johnson, 2012).

Reforming the Bail System

The Black Lives Matter protests concerning the inappropriate use of force by police and inequality in the courts contributed to renewed efforts nationally to make the bail system fairer (Dewan, 2015; Hutchinson, 2015). Studies of pretrial detention in such cities as Philadelphia and New York have raised questions about the need to hold defendants in jail. Criticisms of the bail system focus on judges' discretion in setting bail amounts, the fact that the poor are deprived of their freedom while the affluent can afford bail, the negative aspects of bail agents, and jail conditions for those detained while awaiting trial.

In response to such criticisms, efforts to reform the bail system have arisen. Such efforts often focus on reducing the number of defendants held in jail. A key focus of many bail reform efforts is the elimination of cash bail, which has burdensome, life-altering consequences for poor people who find themselves stuck in jail for days or weeks because they cannot pay relatively small amounts of money to gain release (Pinto, 2015; Talbot, 2015). As a result of reform efforts, the percentage of defendants released on bail has increased in recent decades. This increase is due to the development of alternative mechanisms for pretrial release, which we now discuss.

citation A written order or summons, issued by a law enforcement officer, directing an alleged offender to appear in court at a specific time to answer a criminal charge.

Citation   A **citation**, or summons, to appear in court—a "ticket"—is often issued to a person accused of committing a traffic offense or some other minor violation. By issuing the citation, the officer avoids taking the accused person to the station house for booking and to court for arraignment and setting of bail. Citations are now being used for more-serious offenses, in part because the police want to reduce the amount of time they spend booking minor offenders and waiting in arraignment court for their cases to come up.

Release on Recognizance Pioneered in the 1960s by the Vera Institute of Justice in New York City, the **release on recognizance (ROR)** approach is based on the assumption that judges will grant releases if the defendant is reliable and has roots in the community. Soon after the arrest, court personnel talk to defendants about their job, family, prior record, and associations (Kim & Denver, 2011). They then decide whether to recommend release. In the first three years of the New York project, more than 10,000 defendants were interviewed, and about 3,500 were released. Only 1.5 percent failed to appear in court at the scheduled time. By contrast, the failure-to-appear rate was three times greater among those released on bail (Goldfarb, 1965). Programs in other cities have had similar results, although Sheila Royo Maxwell's research (1999) raises questions about whether women and property-crime defendants on ROR are less likely than other defendants to appear in court.

release on recognizance (ROR) Pretrial release granted on the defendant's promise to appear in court because the judge believes that the defendant's ties to the community guarantee that she or he will appear.

Washington, DC, prohibited cash bail years ago and switched to emphasizing ROR. Since then, 85 percent of criminal suspects have been released on ROR, and 88 percent of them have appeared in court as required. The other 15 percent of suspects have not been granted bail, because their violent crimes led to judicial determinations that they posed a danger to the community (Gass, 2015). Following Washington's lead, several states have enacted laws to limit the use of cash bail and give greater emphasis to ROR (Pinto, 2015).

Ten Percent Cash Bail Although ROR is a useful alternative to money bail, judges are unwilling to release some defendants on their own recognizance. Several states have **percentage bail** programs in which the defendants deposit with the court an amount of cash equal to 10 percent of their bail. When they appear in court as required, this amount is returned minus a 1 percent fee for administrative costs. Begun in Illinois in 1964, this plan is designed to release as many defendants as possible without using bail agents.

percentage bail Defendants may deposit a percentage (usually 10 percent) of the full bail with the court. The full amount of the bail is required if the defendant fails to appear. The percentage of bail is returned after disposition of the case, although the court often retains 1 percent for administrative costs.

Bail Fund An innovative program developed in New York City in 2009 was called the Bronx Freedom Fund. Poor people who were represented by the Bronx Defenders, a nonprofit organization that handles defense for indigent defendants, received loans from the fund in order to post bail and gain pretrial release (Clisura, 2010). The fund was created to prevent poor defendants from languishing in jail merely because they cannot pay a relatively small amount of money. Those freed on bail were monitored and assisted through the relationship between the fund and the defense attorneys. Ninety-six percent of defendants assisted by the fund returned for their court appearances and half of them had their charges dropped. By contrast, more than 90 percent of people in the Bronx whom the fund was unable to help due to limited resources and who were forced to stay in jail eventually entered guilty pleas in order to gain their freedom on probation. Presumably, many of them would have had earlier freedom, less disruption in their lives, and charges dropped instead of feeling pressure to plead guilty if they had been able to gain release (Pinto, 2015). Although a judge ordered the Bronx program to close in less than two years by deciding that it operated as an unlicensed bail agent, the idea took hold. In 2015, after the highly publicized death of Kalief Browder, New York City allocated money for a citywide fund to provide bail assistance to low-level offenders (Pinto, 2015).

In other locations, churches and other organizations have sometimes engaged in parallel activities by loaning money for bail. However, such programs are probably most effective when the loans are tied to contact, assistance, and supervision with people, such as counselors or defense attorneys, who remind defendants about court dates and otherwise help them to avoid violating conditions of bail.

Bail Guidelines To deal with the problem of unequal treatment, reformers have written guidelines for setting bail. The guidelines specify the standards judges should use in setting bail and also list appropriate bail amounts. Judges are expected to follow the guidelines but may deviate from them in special situations. The guidelines take into account the seriousness of the offense and the defendant's prior record in an effort to protect the community and ensure that released suspects will likely return for court appearances.

Preventive Detention   Reforms have been suggested by those concerned with unfairness in the bail system as well as by those concerned with stopping crime. Critics of the bail system point to a link between release on bail and the commission of crimes, arguing that the accused can commit other crimes while awaiting trial. A study of the nation's most populous counties found that 16 percent of felony defendants released on bail were rearrested for another crime (Reaves, 2013). To address this problem, legislatures have passed laws permitting detention of defendants without bail.

For federal criminal cases, Congress enacted the Bail Reform Act of 1984, which authorizes **preventive detention**. Under the act, if prosecutors recommend that defendants be kept in jail, a federal judge holds a hearing to determine (1) if there is a serious risk that the person will flee; (2) if the person will obstruct justice or threaten, injure, or intimidate a prospective witness or juror; or (3) if the offense is one of violence or one punishable by life imprisonment or death. On finding that any of these factors makes setting bail impossible without endangering the community, the judge can order the defendant be held in jail until the case is completed (C. E. Smith, 1990).

Critics of preventive detention argue that it violates the Constitution's due process clause because the accused is held in custody until a verdict is rendered (Wiseman, 2009). However, the Supreme Court has ruled that it is constitutional. The preventive detention provisions of the Bail Reform Act of 1984 were upheld in *United States v. Salerno and Cafero* (1987). The justices said that preventive detention was a legitimate use of government power because it was not designed to punish the accused. Instead, it deals with the problem of people who commit crimes while on bail. By upholding the federal law, the Court also upheld state laws dealing with preventive detention (M. Johnson & Johnson, 2012).

Supporters of preventive detention claim that it ensures that drug dealers, who often treat bail as a business expense, cannot flee before trial. Research has shown that the nature and seriousness of the charge, a history of prior arrests, and drug use all have a strong bearing on the likelihood that a defendant will commit a crime while on bail.

preventive detention Holding a defendant for trial, based on a judge's finding that if the defendant were released on bail, he or she would endanger the safety of any other person and the community or would flee.

United States v. Salerno and Cafero (1987) Preventive detention provisions of the Bail Reform Act of 1984 are upheld as a legitimate use of government power designed to prevent people from committing crimes while on bail.

▼ CHECK POINT

3. **What factors affect whether bail is set and how much money or property a defendant must provide to gain pretrial release?**
   Bail decisions are based primarily on the judge's evaluation of the seriousness of the offense and the defendant's prior record. The decisions are influenced by the prosecutor's recommendations and the defense attorney's counterarguments about the defendant's personal qualities and ties to the community.

4. **What methods are used to facilitate pretrial release for certain defendants?**
   Police citations, release on own recognizance (ROR), 10 percent cash bail, and bail fund.

STOP & ANALYZE

If you were the governor of a state that had never introduced reforms to reduce pretrial detention, which approach would you propose— 10 percent cash bail, bail fund, release on own recognizance, bail guidelines, or citation? Make two arguments in favor of the approach that you would choose.

Pretrial Detention

People who are not released before trial must remain in jail. Often called the "ultimate ghetto," American jails hold almost 600,000 people on any one day. Most of the people in jail are poor, half are in pretrial detention, and the rest are serving sentences (normally of less than one year) or are waiting to be moved to state prison or to another jurisdiction (Clear, Cole, & Reisig, 2012).

Urban jails also contain troubled people, many with mental health and drug-abuse problems, whom police have swept off the streets. Michael Welch calls this process, in which the police remove socially offensive people from certain areas, "social sanitation" (Welch, 1994:262). Conditions in jails are often much harsher than those in prisons. People awaiting trial are often held in barracks-like cells along with sentenced offenders. Thus, a "presumed innocent" pretrial detainee might spend weeks in the same confined space with troubled people or sentenced felons (Beck, Karberg, & Harrison, 2002). The problems of pretrial detention may be even worse in other countries where suspects languish in jail during the slow-moving processing of criminal cases.

The period just after arrest is the most frightening and difficult time for suspects. Imagine freely walking the streets one minute and being locked in a small space with a large number of troubled and potentially dangerous cellmates the next (Pinto, 2015). Suddenly, you have no privacy and must share an open toilet with hostile strangers. You have been fingerprinted, photographed, searched, and questioned—treated like the "criminal" that the police and the criminal justice system consider you to be (Schlanger, 2008). You are alone with people whose behavior you cannot predict and left to worry about what might happen. If you are female, you may be placed in a cell by yourself. Given the stressful nature of arrest and jailing, it is little wonder that most jail suicides and psychotic episodes occur during the first hours of detention.

Other factors can make the shock of arrest and detention even worse. Many people are arrested for offenses they committed while under the influence of drugs or alcohol. They may be less able than others to cope with their new situation. Young arrestees who face the risk of being victimized by older, stronger cellmates may sink into depression. Detainees also worry about losing their jobs while in jail, because they do not know if or when they will be released.

Although most Americans arrested for felonies have their cases adjudicated within six months, 15 percent of felony defendants wait more than a year (Reaves, 2013). Imagine the hardships for the arrestees who cannot gain pretrial release if they are among those who must wait months before the courts complete the processing of their cases. The median time for case processing for rape suspects who are detained in jail is nearly 250 days, and for robbery suspects, it is nearly 150 days (Reaves, 2013). For the detained suspects who eventually have their charges dropped or are acquitted of the crime, this is an especially harsh deprivation of liberty. The psychological and economic hardships faced by pretrial detainees and their families can be significant and prolonged.

Jails holding pretrial detainees may be crowded and lack education and counseling programs. Spending time in close quarters with strangers for weeks or months can be frightening and difficult as people worry about what will happen to them. What thoughts and feelings would you experience if you were arrested and detained in jail?

Pretrial detention not only imposes stresses and hardships that may reach a crisis level but also affects the outcomes of cases (McCoy, 2007). People in jail can give little help to their attorneys. They cannot help find witnesses and perform other useful tasks on their own behalf. In addition, they may feel pressured to plead guilty in order to end their indefinite stay in jail. Even if they believe that they should not be convicted of the crime charged, they may prefer to start serving a prison or jail sentence with a definite end point. Some may even gain quicker release on probation or in a community corrections program by pleading guilty, whereas they might stay in jail for a longer period by insisting on their innocence and awaiting a trial.

CHECK POINT

5. **What categories of people are found in jails?**
   Pretrial detainees for whom bail was not set or those who are too poor to pay the bail amount required; people serving short sentences for misdemeanors; people convicted of felonies awaiting transfer to prison; and people with psychological or substance-abuse problems who have been swept off the streets.

6. **What are the sources of stress for people in jail awaiting trial?**
   Living with difficult and potentially dangerous cellmates; feeling uncertain about what will happen to their case, family, and job; and not being able to contribute to the preparation of a defense.

STOP & ANALYZE

Some people in jail have been convicted of crimes and are serving short sentences or awaiting transfer to prison. Others are presumptively innocent pretrial detainees awaiting the processing of their cases. Make two arguments in favor of treating pretrial detainees differently and better than convicted offenders inside jails. Now make two arguments about why such differential treatment is either undesirable or too difficult to implement.

Plea Bargaining

For the vast majority of cases, plea bargaining—also known as negotiating a settlement, copping a plea, or copping out—is the most important step in the criminal justice process. Very few cases go to trial; instead, a negotiated guilty plea arrived at through the interactions of prosecutors, defense lawyers, and judges determines what will happen to most defendants. The courtroom work group, discussed in Chapter 7, uses plea bargaining to determine the outcomes of cases quickly and efficiently in those courthouses where the same actors work together repeatedly in processing cases.

Santobello v. New York (1971)
When a guilty plea rests on a promise of a prosecutor, the promise must be fulfilled.

The quick resolution of cases through negotiated guilty pleas became common and was upheld by the Supreme Court in the 1971 case of *Santobello v. New York*. In the decision, Chief Justice Warren Burger described plea bargaining in favorable terms in ruling that prosecutors were obliged to fulfill promises made during plea negotiations. Burger wrote, "'Plea bargaining' is an essential component of the administration of justice. Properly administered, it is to be encouraged" because it saves time and criminal justice resources while also protecting the community.

In 1976, Justice Potter Stewart revealed the heart and soul of plea bargaining when he wrote in *Blackledge v. Allison* that plea bargaining "can benefit all concerned" in a criminal case. There are advantages for defendants, prosecutors, defense attorneys, and judges. Defendants can have their cases completed more quickly and know what the punishment will be, instead of facing the uncertainty of a judge's sentencing decision. Moreover, the defendant is likely to receive less than the maximum punishment that might have been imposed after a trial. Prosecutors are not being "soft on crime" when they plea bargain. Instead, they gain an easy conviction, even in cases in which enough evidence may not have been gathered to convince a jury to find the defendant guilty; they also save time and resources by disposing of cases without having to prepare for a trial (Mongrain & Roberts, 2009). Plea bargaining also saves private defense attorneys the time that would be necessary to prepare for a trial. They earn their fee quickly and can move on to the next case.

In November 2015, a federal judge sentenced Jared Fogle to 15 years in prison and more than $1 million in fines. Fogle, who made millions of dollars as the spokesperson and star of commercials for the Subway sandwich chain, accepted a plea agreement on charges of having sex with underage girls and possession of child pornography. He had faced the possibility of up to 50 years in prison. Do reductions in charges and punishments produced by plea bargaining hurt the public's confidence in the justice system?

AP Images/Michael Conroy

Similarly, plea bargaining helps public defenders cope with large caseloads. Judges, too, avoid time-consuming trials and the prospect of having to decide what sentence to impose on the defendant. Instead, they often adopt the sentence recommended by the prosecutor in consultation with the defense attorney, provided that it is within the range of sentences that they deem appropriate for a given crime and offender.

Because the public often believes that plea bargaining permits offenders to avoid appropriate punishment for their crime, some jurisdictions, including Memphis, Tennessee, have attempted to prohibit it. Such prohibitions are usually aimed at preventing plea bargaining only in cases involving the most serious felony charges (McCoy, 1993). As discussed in "Criminal Justice: Myth & Reality," such bans on plea bargaining for serious crimes do not actually end negotiated case outcomes, because actors in the system find ways to influence cases in a manner that advances their interests in efficient case processing.

Exchange Relationships in Plea Bargaining

As we have seen, plea bargaining is a set of exchange relationships in which the prosecutor, the defense attorney, the defendant, and sometimes the judge participate. All have specific goals, all try to use the situation to their own advantage, and all are likely to see the exchange as a success.

Plea bargaining does not always occur in a single meeting between the prosecutor and the defense attorney. Plea bargaining is a process in which prosecutors and defense attorneys interact again and again as they move further along in the judicial process. As time passes, the discovery of more evidence or new information about the defendant's background may strengthen the prosecutor's hand (Emmelman, 1996). Often the prosecution rather than the defense is in the best position to obtain new evidence. However, the defense attorney's position may gain strength if the prosecutor does not wish to spend time preparing for a trial.

Tactics of Prosecutor and Defense

Plea bargaining between defense counsel and prosecutor is a serious game in which friendliness and joking can mask efforts to advance each side's cause. Both sides use various strategies and tactics (D. M. Brown, 2009). Each tries to impress the

CRIMINAL JUSTICE

Myth&Reality

COMMON BELIEF: Bans on plea bargaining for the most serious cases, such as murder, rape, and armed robbery, can ensure that society's most harmful offenders do not avoid the severe punishments that they deserve.

REALITY

- At different times in recent decades, there have been efforts—in such places as the states of Alaska and California and the cities of Memphis and Detroit—to abolish plea bargaining either completely or for serious offenses.

- Bans on plea bargaining do not end negotiated guilty pleas; they merely alter the form and timing of the negotiations.

- When California banned plea bargaining in the general-jurisdiction Superior Courts, guilty plea negotiations simply moved to a point earlier in the process, such as the pretrial stages in the limited-jurisdiction trial courts.

- In order to respect the ban on plea bargaining, some assistant prosecutors instead engage in "charge bargaining" (negotiating over charges rather than sentences), or judges get involved in discussing with defense attorneys what sentencing expectations might produce a quick guilty plea instead of a trial.

- The ban on plea bargaining in Memphis included a provision to make an exception for certain situations, and then significant numbers of serious cases were treated as if they fit the exceptions for which plea agreements were permitted.

- It appears that the shared sense of self-interest and mutual benefit in the plea bargaining process is so powerful that actors in the system will seek ways to control and settle outcomes rather than face the risk, time, and expense of trials in most cases.

other with its confidence in its own case while pointing out weaknesses in the other side's case. An unspoken rule of openness and candor usually keeps the relationship on good terms. Little effort is made to conceal information that could later be useful to the other side in the courtroom. Studies show that the outcomes of plea bargaining may depend on the relationships between prosecutors and individual attorneys, as well as the defense counsel's willingness to fight for the client (Champion, 1989).

A tactic that many prosecutors bring to plea bargaining sessions is the multiple-offense indictment. Multiple-offense charges are especially important to prosecutors in handling difficult cases—for instance, those in which the victim is reluctant to provide information, the value of the stolen item is unclear, or the evidence may not be reliable. Prosecutors often file charges of selling a drug when they know they can probably convict only for possession. Because the accused persons know that the penalty for selling is much greater, they are tempted to plead guilty to the lesser charge rather than risk a longer sentence, even if the probability of conviction on the more serious charge is uncertain. Such tactics can be especially powerful when the potential punishment upon conviction at trial would be severe (Erhard, 2008).

Defense attorneys may threaten to ask for a jury trial if concessions are not made (D. M. Bowen, 2009). To strengthen their hand further, they may also file pretrial motions that require a formal response by the prosecutor. Another tactic is to seek to reschedule pretrial activities in the hope that, with delay, witnesses will become unavailable, media attention will die down, and memories of the crime will grow weaker by the time of the trial. Rather than resort to such legal tactics, however, some attorneys prefer to bargain on the basis of friendship. Given the important role of defense attorneys in affecting the fates of their clients, there are concerns that inadequacies in the systems for providing attorneys for indigent defendants adversely affect clients in both the plea bargaining and the trial processes. In light of the overwhelming caseloads for many public defenders and inadequate pay for attracting private attorneys to take appointed cases, the "Current Controversies" feature examines a new idea for improving criminal defense.

Pleas without Bargaining

Classic studies have shown that in many courts give-and-take plea bargaining does not occur for certain types of cases, yet they have as many guilty pleas as do other courts (Eisenstein, Flemming, & Nardulli, 1988). The term *bargaining* may be misleading in that it implies haggling. Many scholars argue that guilty pleas emerge after the prosecutor, the defense attorney, and sometimes the judge have reached an agreement to "settle the facts" (Utz, 1978). In this view, the parties first study the facts of a case. What were the circumstances of the event? Was it really an assault, or was it more of a shoving match? Did the victim antagonize the accused? Each side hopes to persuade the other that its view of the defendant's actions is backed up by provable facts.

A Voucher System for Criminal Defense?

Indigent defense systems in many states face significant problems. Public defender systems are often underfunded. Therefore defendants face delays in having their cases processed and there are questions about whether attorneys can devote enough time and attention to each case. For example, the Missouri public defender's office said that it would need 125 more lawyers, 90 more secretaries, 109 more investigators, 130 more legal assistants, and more work space for these hoped-for new employees in order to fulfill their duties of timely and complete representation. In places that appoint private attorneys to represent indigent criminal defendants, the hourly pay rates may be too low to attract experienced attorneys, and there is often little supervision or evaluation of the actual effort and services provided by appointed counsel.

By 2013, efforts to call attention to these issues had moved beyond civil rights interest groups and defense attorneys. Opinions by judges increasingly demonstrated concern about the need for legislative action to provide more funding for indigent defense systems. In *Boyer v. Louisiana* (2013), the U.S. Supreme Court dismissed a case that was to address whether a seven-year delay from arrest to trial violated the defendant's Sixth Amendment right to a speedy trial. A majority of justices concluded that the defense attorney had been primarily responsible for the defendant's seven-year pretrial detention in jail by requesting delays for various reasons. In dissent, however, Justice Sonia Sotomayor, supported by Justices Ruth Bader Ginsburg, Stephen Breyer, and Elena Kagan, argued that the Court should examine the failings of the Louisiana indigent defense system. According to Sotomayor, the Court originally accepted the case to determine "whether a delay caused by a State's failure to fund counsel for an indigent's defense should be weighed against the State in determining whether there was a deprivation" of the right to a speedy trial. The four dissenting justices showed their interest in examining and possibly issuing orders concerning the failings of Louisiana's underfunded indigent defense system.

One suggestion for improving indigent defense systems relies on a different approach to attorney compensation. Under a voucher system, each defendant would be given a receipt, or "voucher," which would permit him to select his own attorney. In 2014, counties in Texas began to experiment with this new system. The attorney handles the case and then submits the voucher to the appropriate government agency in order to be paid, either for the number of hours worked or on a set fee per case. A fully implemented, universal voucher system might save money, as the disbanding of public defender offices would eliminate the obligation of states, counties, and cities to provide medical benefits and retirement funds for the now-departed defense attorney employees.

The system would be similar to current medical reimbursement programs such as Medicare and Medicaid, in which the client receives services from a private provider who is subsequently paid by the government agency. In other government services contexts, vouchers are also used to help low-income people rent apartments.

One of the purported strengths of the proposal is that defendants would be able to choose their own attorneys. Presumably, they would cooperate better and have less reason to complain about the case outcome than they do with an attorney who is assigned to them. In theory, the system could also permit indigent criminal defendants to fire their attorneys if they are dissatisfied with the attorneys' effort and performance. In addition, it would change the perception in some appointed counsel systems that defense attorneys are afraid to fight too vigorously for their clients because they fear that the judges will not appoint them in future cases if they do not cooperate in efficient plea bargaining processes that end in quick convictions.

Many attorneys might decide that the voucher system does not pay well enough to induce them to take indigent criminal cases. This same issue exists in the medical realm—some doctors do not accept Medicaid or Medicare patients. However, other attorneys, seeking to specialize in criminal defense and develop expertise, could implement efficient office procedures for a successful voucher-focused practice. Yet another group of attorneys would undoubtedly accept some voucher cases as part of a more general practice with paying clients for other kinds of cases.

On the other hand, a voucher system may simply encourage certain attorneys to take on a high volume of cases and process them quickly, without any guarantee about the quality of representation. The voucher system assumes that a "free market" approach would encourage attorneys to provide good service in order to keep attracting "customers." However, are criminal defendants really informed consumers who know whether one attorney puts forth more effort or is more effective than another? Might these consumers be affected by advertising rather than actual knowledge about the quality of service?

Critics of the voucher idea fear it may simply create opportunities for private practice attorneys to make money at the expense of clients who lack sufficient education and knowledge to make a consumer-driven system work effectively. Instead, these critics believe that the best approach is for state governments to fulfill their obligation to provide sufficient funding for highly trained and well-supervised public defenders who are dedicated, public-serving experts in criminal law.

For Critical Thinking and Analysis

What are the three strongest arguments in favor of a voucher system? What are the three strongest arguments against a voucher system? What is your viewpoint? Why?

Sources: M. Davey, "Budget Woes Hit Defense Lawyers for the Indigent," *New York Times,* September 9, 2010 (www.nytimes .com); V. Gupta and S. Hanlon, "Hitting Two Birds with One Stone: Strategies for Addressing the Indigent Defense Crisis and Overincarceration," *American Constitution Society* blog, September 4, 2012 (www .acslaw.org); A. Liptak, "Need-Blind Justice," *New York Times,* January 4, 2014 (www .nytimes.com); S. J. Schulhofer and D. D. Friedman, "Reforming Indigent Defense: How Free Market Principles Can Help to Fix a Broken System," *Policy Analysis,* No. 666, September 1, 2010 (Washington, DC: Cato Institute); J. Smith, "Stopping the Public Defender 'Wheel,'" *The Crime Report,* January 23, 2014 (www.thecrimereport.org).

The prosecution wants the defense to believe that strong evidence proves its version of the event. The defense attorney wants to convince the prosecution that the evidence is not solid and that there is a risk of acquittal if the case is heard by a jury.

In some cases, the evidence is strong and the defense attorney has little hope of persuading the prosecutor otherwise. Through their discussions, the prosecutor and the defense attorney seek to reach a shared view of the provable facts in the case. Once they agree on the facts, they will both know the appropriate charge, and they can agree on a sentence according to the locally defined going rate. At that point, a guilty plea can be entered without any formal bargaining, because both sides agree on what the case is worth in terms of the seriousness of the charge and the usual punishment. This process may be thought of as *implicit plea bargaining*, because shared understandings create the expectation that a guilty plea will lead to a less-than-maximum sentence, even without any exchange or bargaining.

As we saw in Chapter 7, the going rates for sentences for particular crimes and offenders depend on local values and sentencing patterns. Often both the prosecutor and the defense attorney belong to a particular local legal culture and thus share an understanding about how cases should be handled. Thus, they may both know right away what the sentence will be for a first-time burglar or second-time robber. The sentence may differ in another courthouse, because the local legal culture and going rates vary.

Legal Issues in Plea Bargaining

Boykin v. Alabama (1969)
Before a judge may accept a plea of guilty, defendants must state that they are making the plea voluntarily.

In *Boykin v. Alabama* (1969), the U.S. Supreme Court ruled that before a judge may accept a plea of guilty, defendants must state that the plea was made voluntarily. Judges have created standard forms with questions for the defendant to affirm in open court before the plea is accepted. Trial judges also must learn whether the defendant understands the consequences of pleading guilty and ensure that the plea was not obtained through pressure.

Missouri v. Frye (2012)
Criminal defendants' Sixth Amendment right to counsel includes protection against ineffective assistance of counsel in the plea bargaining process, such as defense attorneys' failures to inform their clients about plea bargain offers.

In 2012, the Supreme Court issued a pair of potentially far-reaching decisions confirming that defendants are entitled to effective assistance of counsel during the plea bargaining process. In *Missouri v. Frye* (2012), a lawyer failed to inform his client about a favorable plea bargain offer from the prosecutor. In *Lafler v. Cooper* (2012), the defense attorney gave the defendant bad advice about a potential plea agreement by being mistaken about the actual seriousness of the offense for which the defendant could be charged and convicted at trial (Liptak, 2012). It remains to be seen how these decisions will impact plea bargaining, but many observers predict that more plea offers will be placed in writing and that trial judges will provide closer supervision over the plea bargaining process to guard against attorney mistakes that disadvantage defendants (Covey, 2013; Goode, 2012). Read "A Question of Ethics" at the end of the chapter to consider the risks to defendants if defense attorneys' advice does not accurately predict the likely punishment upon conviction.

North Carolina v. Alford (1970)
A plea of guilty by a defendant who maintains his or her innocence may be accepted for the purpose of a lesser sentence.

Can a trial court accept a guilty plea if the defendant claims to be innocent? In *North Carolina v. Alford* (1970), the Court allowed a defendant to enter a guilty plea for the purpose of gaining a lesser sentence, even though he maintained that he was innocent. However, the Supreme Court also stated that trial judges should not accept such a plea unless a factual basis exists for believing that the defendant is in fact guilty.

Ricketts v. Adamson (1987)
Defendants must uphold the plea agreement or suffer the consequences.

Bordenkircher v. Hayes (1978)
A defendant's rights are not violated by a prosecutor who warns that refusing to enter a guilty plea may result in a harsher sentence.

Another issue is whether the plea agreement will be fulfilled (J. Cook, 2013). If the prosecutor has promised to recommend a lenient sentence, the promise must be kept (*Santobello v. New York*, 1971). As ruled in *Ricketts v. Adamson* (1987), defendants must also keep their side of the bargain, such as testifying against a codefendant. However, in *Bordenkircher v. Hayes* (1978), the justices ruled that prosecutors may threaten to seek more-serious charges, as long as such charges are supported by evidence, if defendants refuse to plead guilty. Some scholars criticize this decision as imposing pressures on a defendant that are not permitted elsewhere in the justice process (O'Hear, 2006).

Criticisms of Plea Bargaining

Critics express many concerns about plea bargaining (Sands, 2013). Two primary criticisms stand out. The first argues that plea bargaining is unfair because defendants give up some of their constitutional rights, especially the right to trial by jury (O'Keefe, 2010). The second stresses sentencing policy and points out that plea bargaining reduces society's interest in appropriate punishments for crimes. In urban areas with high caseloads, for example, harried judges and prosecutors are said to make concessions based on administrative needs, resulting in lighter sentences than those required by the penal code.

Plea bargaining also comes under fire because it is hidden from judicial scrutiny—as the agreement is most often made at an early stage when the judge has little information about the crime or the defendant and thus cannot adequately evaluate the case. Other critics believe that overuse of plea bargaining breeds disrespect and even contempt for the law. They say criminals look at the judicial process as a game or a sham, much like other "deals" made in life.

Critics further contend that it is unjust to penalize people who assert their right to a trial by giving them stiffer sentences than they would have received if they had pleaded guilty. Indeed, the threat of severe sentences is so great in the federal court system that the number of federal trials has dropped by two-thirds in the past 25 years—even as the number of defendants has nearly tripled (Fields & Emshwiller, 2012; "Thumb on the Scale," 2013). Research provides evidence that an extra penalty is often imposed on defendants who take up the court's time by asserting their right to trial (Devers, 2011; Ulmer, Eisenstein, & Johnson, 2010).

Finally, another concern about plea bargaining is that innocent people will plead guilty to acts that they did not commit. Although it is hard to know how often this happens, it is certain that some defendants have entered guilty pleas when they have not committed the offense (J. Bowen, 2008). It may be hard for middle-class people to understand how anyone could possibly plead guilty when innocent. However, people with little education and low social status may lack the confidence to say no to an attorney who strongly encourages them to plead guilty.

People may also lack confidence in court processes. What if you feared that a jury might convict you and send you to prison for 20 years based on circumstantial evidence (such as being in the vicinity of the crime and wearing the same color shirt as the robber that day)? Might you plead guilty and take a five-year sentence, even if you knew that you were innocent? How much confidence do you have that juries and judges will always reach the correct result? Poor people, in particular, may feel helpless in the stressful climate of the courthouse and jail. If they lack faith in the system's ability to protect their rights and find them not guilty, they may accept a lighter punishment rather than risk being convicted for a serious offense.

CHECK POINT

7. Why does plea bargaining occur?

It serves the self-interest of all relevant actors: defendants gain certain, less-than-maximum sentences; prosecutors gain swift, sure convictions; defense attorneys get prompt resolution of cases; and judges preside over fewer time-consuming trials.

8. What are the criticisms of plea bargaining?

Defendants might be pressured to surrender their rights; society's mandated criminal punishments are improperly reduced.

STOP & ANALYZE

The U.S. Supreme Court's decision in *North Carolina v. Alford* (1970) says that a judge can accept a guilty plea from someone who claims to be actually innocent. Does the acceptance of such pleas diminish the justice system's goal of punishing only those who are guilty of crimes? If you were a judge, would you accept such pleas? Write a brief statement explaining your position.

Trial: The Exceptional Case

If cases are not dismissed or terminated through plea bargaining, they move forward for trial. The seriousness of the charge is probably the most important factor influencing the decision to go to trial. Murder, felonious assault, or rape—all charges that bring long prison terms—may require judge and jury, unless the defendant fears a certain conviction and therefore seeks a negotiated plea deal. When the penalty is harsh, however, many defendants seem willing to risk the possibility of conviction at trial. Table 8.1 shows the differences in the percentages of defendants going to trial for offenses of varying severity. Notice that homicide offenses, which carry the most significant punishments, produce a higher percentage of trials than do other crimes.

Trials determine the fates of very few defendants. Although the right to trial by jury is ingrained in American ideology—it is mentioned in the Declaration of Independence, the U.S. Constitution and three of its amendments, and myriad opinions of the U.S. Supreme Court—year in and year out, fewer than 9 percent of felony cases go to trial. Of these, only about half are jury trials; the rest are **bench trials**, presided over by a judge without a **jury**. In 2009, trials produced only 3 percent of felony case outcomes in the nation's 75 most populous counties (Reaves, 2010). Defendants may choose a bench trial if they believe a judge will be more capable of making an objective decision, especially if the charges or evidence are likely to arouse emotional reactions in jurors.

The rates of trials also vary from city to city. This difference stems, in part, from the local legal culture. Think about how prosecutors' policies or sentencing practices in different cities may increase or decrease the incentives for a defendant to plead guilty. In addition, defense attorneys and prosecutors in different courthouses may have their own understandings about which cases should produce a plea bargain because of agreements (or disagreements) about the provable facts and the going rate of sentences for an offense.

Trials take considerable time and resources. Attorneys frequently spend weeks or months preparing for them—gathering evidence, responding to their opponents' motions, planning trial strategy, and setting aside a day to several weeks to present the case in court. From the perspective of judges, prosecutors, and defense attorneys, plea bargaining presents an attractive alternative for purposes of completing cases quickly.

Jury Trial

Trials are based on the idea that the prosecution and defense will compete as adversaries before a judge and jury so that the truth will emerge. As such, the rules of criminal law, procedure, and evidence govern the conduct of the trial. Above the battle, the judge ensures that the rules are followed and that the jury impartially evaluates the evidence and reflects the community's interests. In a jury trial, the

bench trials Trials conducted by a judge who acts as fact finder and determines issues of law. No jury participates.

jury A panel of citizens selected according to law and sworn to determine matters of fact in a criminal case and to deliver a verdict of guilty or not guilty.

TABLE 8.1	Percentage of Indicted Cases That Went to Trial, by Offense

The percentages of cases that went to trial differ both by offense and by jurisdiction. Typically, it seems that the stiffer the possible penalty, the greater the likelihood of a trial. However, a prosecutor may be able to gain guilty pleas even in the most serious cases.

Jurisdiction	Homicide	Rape/Sexual Assault	Robbery	Assault	Drug Offenses
State courts, 75 largest counties	30%	10%	3%	4%	1%
Federal courts	15	—	4	8	3
Mercer County, NJ (Trenton)	10	0	1	1	1

Sources: Adapted from Brian A. Reaves, "Felony Defendants in Large Urban Counties, 2009—Statistical Tables," *Bureau of Justice Statistics Statistical Tables,* December 2013, NCJ 228944; "Mercer County Prosecutor's Annual Report 2012" (2013); *Sourcebook of Criminal Justice Statistics 2014,* Table 5.24.2010 (for federal courts in the year 2010).

In 2015, a jury in Texas convicted Eddie Ray Routh, a former Marine, of killing Chris Kyle and another man at a shooting range. Kyle, a war veteran and author of the book *American Sniper*, had taken Routh to a shooting range as a recreational activity to help him deal with post-traumatic stress disorder problems. Routh was sentenced to life in prison. What other kinds of cases are likely to be processed through jury trials?

jury alone evaluates the facts in a case. The adversarial process and the inclusion of jurors in decision making often make trial outcomes difficult to predict. The verdict hinges not only on the nature of the evidence but also on the effectiveness of the prosecution and defense and on the jurors' attitudes. Does this adversarial and citizen-based process provide the best mechanism for finding the truth and doing justice in our most serious criminal cases?

However one assesses their effectiveness, juries perform six vital functions in the criminal justice system:

1. Prevent government oppression by safeguarding citizens against arbitrary law enforcement
2. Determine whether the accused is guilty on the basis of the evidence presented
3. Represent diverse community interests so that no one set of values or biases dominates decision making
4. Serve as a buffer between the accused and the accuser
5. Promote citizens' knowledge about the criminal justice system through the jury-duty process
6. Symbolize the rule of law and the community foundations that support the criminal justice system

As a symbol of law, juries demonstrate to the public, as well as to defendants, that decisions about depriving individuals of their liberty will be made carefully by a group of citizens who represent the community's values. In addition, juries provide the primary element of direct democracy in the judicial branch of government. Citizens have the opportunity to participate directly in decision making within the judicial branch of government. However, as indicated in "What Americans Think," even though most Americans have positive experiences with the jury process, they are not eager to serve.

In the United States, a jury in a criminal trial traditionally comprises 12 citizens, but some states now allow as few as 6 citizens to make up a jury. This reform was recommended to modernize court procedures and reduce expenses. It costs less for the court to contact, process, and pay a smaller number of jurors. The use of small juries was upheld by the Supreme Court in *Williams v. Florida* (1970). Six states use juries with fewer than 12 members in noncapital felony cases, and a larger number of states use small juries for misdemeanors. In *Burch v. Louisiana* (1979), the Supreme Court ruled that six-member juries must vote unanimously to convict a defendant, but unanimity is not required for larger juries. Some states permit juries to convict defendants

Williams v. Florida (1970) Juries of fewer than 12 members are constitutional.

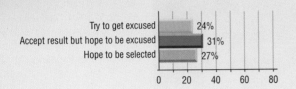
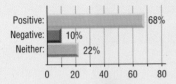
by votes of ten to two or nine to three. The change to six-person juries has its critics, who charge that the smaller group is less representative of the conflicting views in the community and too quick to bring in a verdict (Diamond et al., 2009; A. R. Amar, 1997).

The Trial Process

The trial process generally follows eight steps: (1) selection of the jury, (2) opening statements by prosecution and defense, (3) presentation of the prosecution's evidence and witnesses, (4) presentation of the defense's evidence and witnesses, (5) presentation of rebuttal witnesses, (6) closing arguments by each side, (7) instruction to the jury by the judge, and (8) decision by the jury. The details of each step may vary according to each state's rules. Although the proportion of trials may be small, understanding each step in the process and considering the broader impact of this institution are both important.

Jury Selection   The selection of the jury, outlined in Figure 8.3, is a crucial first step in the trial process. Because people always apply their experiences, values, and biases in their decision making, prosecutors and defense attorneys actively seek to identify potential jurors who may be automatically sympathetic or hostile to their side. When they believe they have identified such potential jurors, they try to find ways to exclude those who may sympathize with the other side, while striving to keep those who may favor their side. Lawyers do not necessarily achieve these goals, because the selection of jurors involves the decisions and interactions of prosecutors, defense attorneys, and judges, each of whom has different objectives in the selection process.

Jurors are selected from among the citizens whose names have been placed in the jury pool. The composition of the jury pool tremendously affects the ultimate composition of the trial jury. In most states, the jury pool is drawn from lists of registered voters, but research has shown that nonwhites, the poor, and young people register to vote at much lower rates than does the rest of the population. As a result, members of these groups are underrepresented on juries (Gau, 2016; Ali, 2013; Sommers, 2009).

In many cases, the presence or absence of these groups may make no difference in the ultimate verdict. In some situations, however, members of these groups may assert themselves in discussion and interpret evidence differently than do their older, white, middle-class counterparts who dominate the composition of juries (Cornwell & Hans, 2011). For example, the poor, nonwhites, and young people may be more likely to have had unpleasant experiences with police officers and therefore be less willing to believe automatically that police officers always tell the truth. Today, courts may supplement the lists of registered voters with other lists, such as those for driver's licenses, hunting licenses, and utility bills, in an effort to diversify the jury pool (Hannaford-Agor, 2011).

Several states are also considering increases in jurors' daily pay; Texas, for example, has gone from $6 per day to $40 per day in trials lasting more than one day. It is hoped that such efforts will make jury service more attractive for poor people who might otherwise avoid participating because they cannot afford to lose pay by missing work (Axtman, 2005). In addition, judges have increasing concerns about small-business owners as well as people worried about losing their jobs who seek to

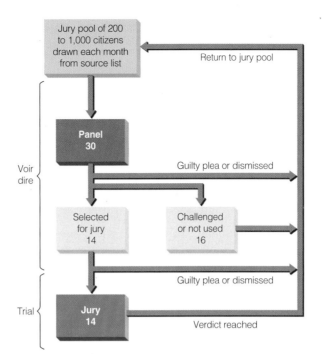

FIGURE 8.3

Jury Selection Process for a 12-Member Jury Potential jurors are drawn at random from a source list. From this pool, a panel is selected and presented for duty. The voir dire examination may remove some, whereas others will be seated. The 14 jurors selected include two alternates.

avoid jury duty for financial reasons (Weiss, 2009b; C. J. Williams, 2010). Unfortunately, the current era of budget cuts has hampered efforts to increase financial incentives for participation. Many jurisdictions, including Cleveland, Ohio, and Topeka, Kansas, have reduced jurors' pay to save money (Dubail, 2009; KTKA-TV, 2011).

Retired people and homemakers with grown children tend to be overrepresented on juries because they are less inconvenienced by serving and are often less likely to ask to be excused because of job responsibilities or child-care problems. To make jury duty less onerous, many states have moved to a system called "one-day-one-trial," in which jurors serve for either one day or for the duration of one trial.

The courtroom process of **voir dire** (which means "to speak the truth") is used to question prospective jurors in order to screen out those who might be biased or otherwise incapable of making a fair decision (C. Harrison, 2011). Attorneys for each side, as well as the judge, may question jurors about their background, knowledge of the case, and acquaintance with any participants in the case (Natoli, 2013). Jurors will also be asked whether they or their immediate family members have been crime victims or otherwise involved in a criminal case in a manner that may prevent them from making open-minded decisions about the evidence and the defendant. If a juror's responses indicate that she or he will not be able to make fair decisions, the juror may present a **challenge for cause**. The judge must rule on the challenge, but if the judge agrees with the attorney, then the juror is excused from that specific case (Arterton, 2008). There is usually no limit on the number of jurors that the attorneys may challenge for cause.

Although challenges for cause ultimately fall under the judge's control, the prosecution and defense can exert their own control over the jury's composition through the use of **peremptory challenges**. With these, the prosecution and defense can exclude prospective jurors without giving specific reasons. Attorneys use peremptory challenges to exclude jurors who they think will be unsympathetic to their arguments (Hoffman, 1999). Attorneys usually use hunches about which jurors to challenge; little evidence suggests that they can accurately identify which jurors will sympathize with their side or not (M. S. White, 1995). Normally the defense is allowed eight to ten peremptory challenges and the prosecution six to eight.

The use of peremptory challenges has raised concerns that attorneys can use them to exclude, for example, African American jurors when an African American is on trial or Hispanic jurors when there is a Hispanic defendant (Flanagan, 2015; Bagnato, 2010; Price, 2009; Enriquez & Clark, 2007). In a series of decisions in the

voir dire A questioning of prospective jurors to screen out people the attorneys think might be biased or otherwise incapable of delivering a fair verdict.

challenge for cause Removal of a prospective juror by showing that he or she has some bias or some other legal disability. The number of such challenges available to attorneys is unlimited.

peremptory challenge Removal of a prospective juror without giving a reason. Attorneys are allowed a limited number of such challenges.

Should the Peremptory Challenge Be Abolished?

Jimmy Elem faced trial on robbery charges in a Missouri state court. During jury selection, the prosecutor used peremptory challenges to exclude two African American men from the jury. Elem's attorney objected, claiming that the prosecutor appeared to be excluding potential jurors because of their race. Under the U.S. Supreme Court's decision in *Batson v. Kentucky* (1986), a trial judge is obligated to ask the prosecutor to provide a nonracial reason for removing jurors when a prosecutor's use of peremptory challenges seems based on racial exclusion. In response to the judge's question, the prosecutor replied,

> I struck [juror] number twenty-two because of his long hair. He had long curly hair. He had the longest hair of anybody on the panel by far. He appeared to me to not be a good juror for that fact, the fact that he had long hair hanging down shoulder length, curly unkempt hair. Also he had a mustache and a goatee type beard. And juror number twenty-four also has a mustache and goatee type beard. Those are the only two people on the jury... with the facial hair.... And I don't like the way they looked, with the way the hair is cut, both of them. And the mustaches and the beards look suspicious to me.

The trial judge accepted the prosecutor's explanation and the trial moved forward. Elem subsequently filed a habeas corpus action in the federal courts claiming that the prosecutor had used a flimsy, nonsensical excuse to cover the fact that the exclusions were really based on race. The U.S. court of appeals agreed with Elem and declared that peremptory challenges that appear to be based on race are valid only if actually based on reasons related to the individuals' qualifications to be a good juror. The court of appeals did not believe that having curly or long hair affected one's ability to be a good juror. Missouri carried the case forward to the U.S. Supreme Court (*Purkett v. Elem*, 1995). In a seven-to-two

decision, the Supreme Court reversed and said that prosecutors can put forward silly, superstitious, and implausible reasons as long as the trial judge accepts the exclusion as being based on something other than race or gender.

By contrast, the Supreme Court has looked more closely at other cases. For example, in *Snyder v. Louisiana* (2008), seven justices, including conservatives Chief Justice John Roberts and Justice Samuel Alito, called into question an African American man's conviction when prosecutors eliminated all of the African Americans from the jury pool. Unlike in *Purkett v. Elem*, the majority was not willing to automatically accept the prosecutor's and trial judge's reasons for excluding these jurors.

The use of peremptory challenges enables the attorneys in a case to influence the composition of a jury by permitting them to use their discretion to exclude potential jurors. The Supreme Court has declared that such challenges cannot be used to discriminate by race or sex, but it has not strictly enforced this rule. Trial judges continue to possess the authority to accept reasons for race- and sex-based exclusions that may merely cover up the actual discriminatory intent of the attorney.

Here is a summary of key arguments concerning the issue:

For Keeping the Peremptory Challenge

- Lawyers can use their discretion to exclude jurors who possess biases but whose biases are not obvious enough to convince a judge to exclude them for cause.
- Defendants will better accept the legitimacy of the jury and its ultimate verdict because their lawyers were able to play a role in shaping the jury's composition through the use of peremptory challenges.
- The peremptory challenge is a one of the long-standing traditions of trial practices in the American justice system.

- Because both sides in a case can use peremptory challenges, the exclusion of potential jurors by each side helps to create a fair jury with less doubt for either side that a biased juror will actually be one of the decision makers.

For Abolishing the Peremptory Challenge

- There is a long history of peremptory challenges being used by attorneys, especially prosecutors, to engage in racial discrimination and eliminate minority representation on the jury. The Supreme Court's decisions prohibiting this practice do not actually stop it from happening in individual cases.
- Lawyers merely act on hunches in excluding potential jurors through peremptory challenges. They do not actually know if they are excluding potential jurors with hidden biases.
- Lawyers use peremptory challenges in an attempt to slant the jury's composition in their own favor, not to create a fairer jury.
- Peremptory challenges are used to deny individuals the opportunity to participate in an important democratic element of the judicial process without any documentable reason for denying the chance to be jurors.

What Should U.S. Policy Be?

Although the U.S. Constitution does not say anything about peremptory challenges, the late Supreme Court Justice Antonin Scalia claimed that peremptory challenges should be retained because they are part of a long tradition in the jury-selection process. Others argue that peremptory challenges enhance the legitimacy of the trial process by letting defendants feel they have some influence over the composition of the jury. By contrast, the late Supreme Court Justice Thurgood Marshall indicated that peremptory challenges should be abolished because they were frequently used to late 1980s and early 1990s (such as *Batson v. Kentucky*, 1986), the Supreme Court prohibited using peremptory challenges to systematically exclude potential jurors because of their race or gender. In practice, however, the enforcement of this prohibition is up to the trial judge (C. E. Smith & Ochoa, 1996). If a trial judge is willing to accept flimsy excuses for race-based and gender-based exclusions, then the attorneys can ignore the ban on discrimination (Bray, 1992). Read "The Policy Debate" and consider whether you believe peremptory challenges should be eliminated.

Some lawyers believe that trials are won or lost in jury selection. If they succeed in seating a favorable jury, they may have a receptive audience that will readily support their arguments and evidence.

Opening Statements   After the jury has been selected, the trial begins. The clerk reads the complaint (indictment or information) detailing the charges, and the prosecutor and the defense attorney may, if they desire, make opening statements to the jury to summarize the position that each side intends to take. The statements are not evidence. The jury is not supposed to regard the attorneys' statements as proving or disproving anything about the case.

Presentation of the Prosecution's Evidence   One of the basic protections of the American criminal justice system is the presumption that the defendant is innocent until proved guilty. The prosecution carries the burden of proving beyond a reasonable doubt, within the demands of the court procedures and rules of evidence, that the individual named in the indictment committed the crime. This does not mean that absolute certainty is required, only that the evidence sufficiently excludes all reasonable doubt.

In presenting evidence to the jury, the prosecution must establish a case showing that the defendant is guilty. Evidence is classified as real evidence, demonstrative evidence, testimony, direct evidence, and circumstantial evidence. **Real evidence** might include such objects as a weapon, business records, fingerprints, or stolen property. These are real objects involved in the crime. **Demonstrative evidence** is presented for jurors to see and understand without testimony. Real evidence is one form of demonstrative evidence; other forms include maps, X-rays, photographs, models, and diagrams. Most evidence in a criminal trial, however, consists of the **testimony** of witnesses. Witnesses at a trial must be legally competent. Thus, the judge may be required to determine whether the witness whose testimony is challenged has the intelligence to tell the truth and the ability to recall what was seen. Witnesses with inadequate intelligence or mental problems might not be regarded as qualified to present testimony. **Direct evidence** refers to eyewitness accounts such as, "I saw John Smith fire the gun." **Circumstantial evidence** requires that the jury infer a fact from what the witness observed: "I saw John Smith walk behind his house with a gun. A few minutes later I heard a gun go off, and then Mr. Smith walked toward me holding

real evidence Physical evidence—such as a weapon, records, fingerprints, and stolen property—involved in the crime.

demonstrative evidence Evidence that is not based on witness testimony but that demonstrates information relevant to the crime, such as maps, X-rays, and photographs; includes real evidence involved in the crime.

testimony Oral evidence provided by a legally competent witness.

direct evidence Eyewitness accounts.

circumstantial evidence Evidence provided by a witness from which a jury must infer a fact.

a gun." The witness's observation that Smith had a gun and that the witness then heard a gun go off does not provide direct evidence that Smith fired his gun; however, the jury may link the described facts and infer that Smith fired his gun. After a witness has given testimony, counsel for the other side may cross-examine him or her.

Because many cases rely on scientific evidence, especially in the form of experts' testimony about DNA, blood spatters, bullet fragments and trajectories, and the nature of physical injuries, there are concerns that judges and juries might not fully understand the information presented (Cheng, 2005). Determinations of guilt may hinge on the effectiveness of the presentation of such evidence rather than the accuracy and verifiability of the scientific conclusions (McAuliff & Duckworth, 2010). Some prosecutors fear that the prevalence of definitive scientific evidence in television crime dramas may cause jurors to expect scientific evidence in each case, such as DNA, in order to issue a guilty verdict. As discussed in the "Close Up," there

CLOSE UP

The "CSI Effect" and Jurors' Expectations about Scientific Evidence

The CBS television network enjoys great success with three popular crime dramas, all entitled *CSI: Crime Scene Investigation* but distinguished by their settings: Las Vegas, Miami, and New York. Other networks have emulated the success of CBS by creating similar shows, including *Bones* (Fox network) and *Rosewood* (Fox network), which highlight the scientific techniques for the investigation of crimes and the development of criminal evidence. The public's fascination with the forensic science portrayed in these television shows has led some prosecutors to complain about an escalation in jurors' unrealistic expectations about the necessity of presenting DNA analysis or other scientific evidence in order to establish guilt in each criminal trial. In reality, many criminal investigations and prosecutions are not based on DNA, fingerprints, or other scientific evidence. Instead, prosecutors present witness testimony and circumstantial evidence about a suspect's presence in a certain location and relationship with the victim. However, some prosecutors have come to fear that jurors will not render a guilty verdict without the presentation of scientific evidence. Even if the purported "CSI effect" is a myth, if prosecutors are fearful of jurors' expectations, this might make them more reluctant to take cases to trial and thereby pressure them to offer more favorable plea agreements to defendants.

Research on the so-called "CSI effect" raises questions about whether jurors are actually less inclined to convict defendants in the absence of scientific evidence. Surveys indicate that jurors may indeed expect to see specific kinds of scientific evidence, but this expectation may be related to a more general "tech effect" of Americans using technology in their daily lives rather than watching specific television shows. Moreover, the increased expectation for scientific evidence does not necessarily mean that jurors will not vote to convict a defendant without it.

While the existence of a "CSI effect" continues to be debated by lawyers, judges, and scholars, prosecutors face a very real issue of deciding how, if at all, they will address the issue, just in case it affects jurors in a specific trial. One problem may be a lack of resources to actually gather and evaluate all potential scientific evidence for every case. For example, many crime labs have delays of several months due to backlogs for DNA evidence and other materials requiring scientific analysis. Although it may be necessary for a prosecutor to wait for definitive DNA testing on evidence in a murder case, should the same resources and time be devoted to analyzing all evidence in a burglary case? Prosecutors' options include educating jurors very directly about scientific evidence and why it may not exist in certain cases.

Researching the Internet
Read about the controversy of the "CSI effect" on the National Institute of Justice's website, http://www.nij.gov/journals/259/Pages/csi-effect.aspx.

For Critical Thinking and Analysis
Should society devote substantial additional resources to the collection, analysis, and storage of scientific evidence for all criminal cases? Give two reasons why or why not. If you feel that it should, what other departments and programs should be cut in order to devote more resources to the preservation of scientific evidence? If you feel that it should not, would educating jurors about the realistic use of scientific evidence (as compared to what they see on television) help them to make better decisions with the data available to them?

Sources: J. Alldredge, "The 'CSI Effect' and Its Potential Impact on Juror Decisions," *Themis: Research Journal of Justice Studies and Forensic Science* vol. 3, article 6 (http://scholarworks.sjsu.edu/themis/vol3/iss1/6); S. Cole and R.Dioso-Villa, "Investigating the 'CSI Effect': Media and Litigation Crisis in Criminal Law," *Stanford Law Review* 61: 1335–73 (2009); L. Huey, "'I've Seen This on CSI': Criminal Investigators' Perceptions about the Management of Public Expectations in the Field," *Crime, Media, Culture* 6 (1): 49–68 (April 2010); D. E. Shelton, "The 'CSI/Effect': Does It Really Exist?" *National Institute of Justice Journal* 259: March 2008 (www.nij.gov).

Prosecutors and defense attorneys present various forms of evidence during trials, including physical objects ("real evidence") as well as witness testimony. Do you think that the communication skills and persuasiveness of the attorneys could distract the jurors' attention from the actual evidence presented in the case?

are debates about whether a "*CSI* effect" (*Crime Scene Investigation*) has affected jurors' expectations and made it more difficult for prosecutors to gain convictions in cases for which there is only witness testimony and no scientific evidence.

The attorney for each side challenges the other side's presentation of evidence. If evidence presented by one attorney violates the rules, reflects untrustworthy hearsay, is a statement of opinion, or is not relevant to the issues in the case, the opposing attorney will object to its presentation. In effect, that attorney is asking the judge to rule that the jury cannot consider the opponent's questionable evidence.

After the prosecution has presented all of the state's evidence against the defendant, the court is informed that the people's case rests. It is common for the defense then to ask the court to direct the jury to bring forth a verdict of not guilty, based on the argument that the state has not presented enough evidence to prove its case. If the motion is sustained by the judge (it rarely is), the trial ends; if it is overruled, the defense presents its evidence.

Presentation of the Defense's Evidence The defense is not required to answer the case presented by the prosecution. As it is the state's responsibility to prove the case beyond a reasonable doubt, it is theoretically possible—and in fact sometimes happens—that the defense rests its case immediately, as we have seen. Usually, however, the accused's attorney employs one strategy or a combination of three strategies: (1) contrary evidence is introduced to rebut or cast doubt on the state's case, (2) an alibi is offered, or (3) an affirmative defense is presented. As discussed in Chapter 3, defenses include self-defense, insanity, duress, and necessity.

A key issue for the defense is whether the accused will take the stand. The Fifth Amendment protection against self-incrimination means that the defendant does not have to testify. The Supreme Court has ruled that the prosecutor may not comment on, nor can the jury draw inferences from, the defendant's decision not to appear in his or her own defense. The decision is not made lightly, because if the defendant does testify, the prosecution may cross-examine. *Cross-examination*—questioning by the opposing attorney—is broader than direct examination. The prosecutor may question the defendant not only about the crime but also about her or his past, including past criminal convictions. On the other hand, if the defendant does not testify, jurors might make assumptions about the defendant's guilt, even though they have been instructed not to do so.

When singer R. Kelly was acquitted of child pornography charges by a Chicago jury in 2008, the defense attorneys used every argument that they could, including arguments that were not consistent with each other (Streitfeld, 2008). Their objective was to cast doubt on the prosecution's case. The case hinged on whether a VHS tape showed Kelly having sex with a specific underage girl. The defense suggested that the tape showed another man who looked like Kelly; that computer manipulation had made the tape look like Kelly; or that the tape was made with models and prostitutes who looked like Kelly and the alleged victim. The defense attorneys did not need to prove Kelly's innocence; they just needed to raise questions in the jurors' minds about the accuracy of the prosecution's claims. R. Kelly never testified in court and thereby avoided cross-examination about any aspects of his private life and past behavior (St. Clair & Ataiyero, 2008).

Presentation of Rebuttal Witnesses

When the defense's case is complete, the prosecution may present witnesses whose testimony is designed to discredit or counteract testimony presented on behalf of the defendant. If the prosecution brings rebuttal witnesses, the defense has the opportunity to question them and to present new witnesses in rebuttal.

Closing Arguments by Each Side

When each side has completed its presentation of the evidence, the prosecution and defense make closing arguments to the jury. The attorneys review the evidence of the case for the jury, presenting interpretations of the evidence that favor their own side. The prosecutor may use the summation to connect the individual pieces of evidence in a way that forms a basis for concluding that the defendant is guilty. The defense may set forth the applicable law and try to show that the prosecution has not proved its case beyond a reasonable doubt. Each side may remind the jury of its duty to evaluate the evidence impartially and not to be swayed by emotion. Yet some attorneys may hope that the jurors react emotionally, especially if they think that those emotions will benefit their side.

Judge's Instructions to the Jury

The jury decides the facts of the case, but the judge determines the law. Before the jurors depart for the jury room to decide the defendant's fate, the judge instructs them on how the law should guide their decision. The judge may discuss basic legal principles such as proof beyond a reasonable doubt, the legal requirements necessary to show that all the elements have been proved by the prosecution, or the rights of the defendant. More specific aspects of the law bearing on the decision—such as complicated court rulings on the nature of the insanity defense or the ways certain types of evidence have been gathered—may be included in the judge's instructions. In complicated trials, the judge may spend an entire day instructing the jury.

reasonable doubt The standard used by a jury to decide if the prosecution has provided enough evidence for a conviction.

The concept of **reasonable doubt** forms the heart of the jury system. As we have seen, the prosecution is not required to prove the guilt of the defendant beyond all doubt. Instead, if a juror is

> satisfied to a moral certainty that this defendant... is guilty of any one of the crimes charged here, you may safely say that you have been convinced beyond a reasonable doubt. If your mind is wavering, or if you are uncertain... you have not been convinced beyond a reasonable doubt and must render a verdict of not guilty. (S. Phillips, 1977:214)

Listening to the judge may become an ordeal for the jurors, who must hear and understand perhaps two or three hours of instruction on the law and the evidence (Bradley, 1992). It is assumed that somehow jurors will fully absorb these details on first hearing them, so that they will thoroughly understand how they are supposed to decide the case in the jury room (Kramer & Koenig, 1990). In fact, the length, complexity, and legalistic content of jury instructions make them difficult for many jurors to comprehend (Gordon, 2013; Daftary-Kapur, Dumas, & Penrod, 2010). The jurors may be confused by the instructions and reach a decision through an inaccurate understanding of the law that applies to the case, such as the legal definitions of intent, premeditation, and other elements of the crime that must be proved in order

EVIDENCE-BASED PRACTICE AND POLICY

The Jury and Evidence-Based Practices

Within criminal justice, most of the attention to evidence-based practices has been directed toward police efforts to prevent crime and programs to reduce repeat offenses by prisoners, juveniles, and substance abusers. These are not, however, the only ways in which research by scholars has helped to shape policy and practice. For many years, a variety of scholars, especially in the field of psychology, have studied juries and jury processes. By gaining an understanding of how jurors receive and understand information, it is hoped that court procedures can be adjusted in ways that will increase jurors' understanding of evidence and legal concepts. As a result, it is presumed that the quality of juries' decision making will improve, and the risk of erroneous verdicts will decrease.

Jurors face challenges in remembering and understanding information presented as evidence, especially when it is a long trial that lasts for many days. In addition, studies show that jurors have difficulty understanding the jury instructions read to them at the end of the trial by the judge. As a result, many states have put effort into designing jury instructions that use plain language instead of confusing legal terms. Moreover, there is greater recognition that lengthy jury instructions can exceed the attention span of jurors. Thus, the extensive work on revising and delivering jury instructions seeks to address multiple concerns.

Although there is not universal agreement on exactly what jury practices to implement based on research evidence, specific states have moved forward with reforms that seek to address the problems identified by research. Not all of the reforms have been verified by research, and, indeed, some of the jury reform efforts are considered by the states to be experiments to see if they improve jury processes.

For example, Michigan's Supreme Court issued an order concerning jury reforms for courts to try during a three-year evaluation period. The reforms included

- Providing pretrial jury instructions to jurors so that they could begin understanding their role and the relevant law before hearing evidence
- Providing a copy of the jury instructions for each juror rather than the traditional method of giving only one copy to the entire jury

- Permitting jurors to write down questions during the trial and then request that the judge consider posing these questions to specific witnesses, thus perhaps filling information gaps if the attorneys do not realize what else the jurors would like to know
- Permitting jurors to ask questions about the final jury instructions delivered by the judge at the end of the trial

Jury trials determine the fates of accused individuals, with serious consequences in cases such as murder that are likely to draw severe punishments. It is important that the members of the jury understand both the relevant laws and the evidence presented. The implementation of evidence-based practices to enhance jury comprehension of the issues has the potential to reduce errors and improve the quality of jury decisions.

Researching the Internet

The Center for Jury Studies of the National Center for State Courts provides online information about proposed reforms for the jury system on its website, www.ncsc-jurystudies.org.

Implementing New Practices

If you were a trial judge, would you resent having the state supreme court or other authority impose new rules on your courtroom? Would it be preferable for a trial judge to simply use those methods that the judge believes from experience will be most effective? In the role of a trial judge, write a memo describing two things you would do to improve jurors' understanding of trials. Explain your reasons for each one.

Sources: D. Aaronson and S. Patterson, "Modernizing Jury Instructions in the Age of Social Media," *Criminal Justice* (American Bar Association), 27 (Winter 2013): 4–10; E. Chilton and P. Henley, *Improving the Jury System—Jury Instructions: Helping Jurors Understand the Evidence and the Law*, San Francisco: Public Law Research Institute (1996): S. Gordon, "Through the Eyes of Jurors: The Use of Schemas in the Application of 'Plain-Language' Jury Instructions," *Hastings Law Journal* 64 (2013): 643–77; P. Thomas, "Mississippi Should Consider Jury Reforms Similar to Those Adopted in Michigan," *MS Litigation Review and Commentary*, July 21, 2011 (www.mslitigationreview.com).

to justify a conviction (Bornstein & Green, 2011; Armour, 2008). Read the "Evidence-Based Practice and Policy" feature to consider how research findings might help to improve jury instructions.

Decision by the Jury   After they have heard the case and received the judge's instructions, the jurors retire to a room where they have complete privacy. They elect a foreperson to run the meeting, and deliberations begin. Until now, the jurors have been passive observers of the trial, unable to question witnesses or to discuss the case among themselves; now they can discuss the facts that have been presented. The jury may request that the judge reread to them portions of the instructions, ask for additional instructions, or hear portions of the transcript detailing what was said by specific witnesses.

Throughout their deliberations, the jurors may be *sequestered*—kept together day and night, away from the influences of newspapers and conversations with family and friends. If jurors are allowed to spend nights at home, they are ordered not to discuss the case with anyone. The proliferation of cell phones, personal computers, and social media presents new problems for judges seeking to focus the jury's attention solely on information presented in court (K. Brown, 2013).

If the jury becomes deadlocked and cannot reach a verdict, the trial ends with a hung jury, and the prosecutor must decide whether to try the case over again in front of a new jury. When a verdict is reached, the judge, prosecution, and defense reassemble in the courtroom to hear it. The prosecution or the defense may request that the jury be polled: each member individually tells her or his vote in open court. This procedure presumably ensures that no juror has felt pressured to agree with the other jurors.

Evaluating the Jury System

Individual jurors differ in their processing of information and interactions with others (Gunnell & Ceci, 2010). A classic study at the University of Chicago Law School found that, consistent with theories of group behavior, participation and influence in the jury process are related to social status. Men were found to be more active participants than were women, whites more active than minority members, and the better-educated more active than those less educated. Much of the discussion in the jury room was not directly concerned with the testimony but rather with trial procedures, opinions about the witnesses, and personal reminiscences (Strodtbeck, James, & Hawkins, 1957). Recent research has reinforced these results (Cornwell & Hans, 2011). Because of group pressure, only rarely did a single juror produce a hung jury (Sundby, 2010). Some jurors may doubt their own views or go along with the others if everyone else disagrees with them. Additional studies have upheld the importance of group pressure on decision making (Hastie, Penrod, & Pennington, 1983).

An examination of trials in the 75 largest counties found that 76 percent of jury trials ended in convictions, compared with 82 percent of bench trials (Kyckelhahn & Cohen, 2008). These numbers alone do not reveal whether judges and juries decide cases differently. However, research on trials provides clues about differences between these two decision makers.

Juries tend to take a more liberal view of such issues as self-defense than do judges and are likely to minimize the seriousness of an offense if they dislike some characteristic of the victim (S. J. Adler, 1994). For example, if the victim of an assault is a prostitute, the jury may minimize the assault. Perceived characteristics of the defendant may also influence jurors' assessments of guilt (Abwender & Hough, 2001). Judges have more experience with the justice process. They are more likely than juries to convict defendants based on evidence that researchers characterize as moderately strong (Eisenberg et al., 2005). As explained by the premier jury researchers Valerie Hans and Neil Vidmar (2008:227):

> [T]he jury's distinctive approach of common sense justice, and the judges' greater willingness to convict based on the same evidence, best explain why juries and judges sometimes reach different conclusions. These juror values affect the verdicts primarily in trials in which the evidence is relatively evenly balanced and a verdict for either side could be justified.

In recent years, the American Bar Association and other groups have worked to introduce reforms that might improve the quality of juries' decision making (Post, 2004). For example, some courts now permit jurors to take notes during trials and submit questions that they would like to see asked of witnesses (Bornstein & Greene, 2011). Other courts permit jurors to submit questions to the judge during the trial (Marder, 2010). There are also efforts to make judges' instructions to the jury more understandable through less reliance on legal terminology. It is hoped that jurors can make better decisions if they have more information and a better understanding of the law and the issues in a case.

9. What functions do juries serve in the criminal justice system?
    Safeguard citizens against arbitrary law enforcement, determine the guilt of the accused, represent diverse
    community interests and values, serve as buffer between accused and accuser, become educated about the
    justice system, and symbolize the law.

10. What is voir dire?
    The jury selection process in which lawyers and/or judges ask questions of prospective jurors and make
    decisions about using peremptory challenges and challenges for cause to shape the jury's composition.

11. What are the stages in the trial process?
    Jury selection, attorneys' opening statements, presentation of prosecution's evidence, presentation of
    defense's evidence, presentation of rebuttal witnesses, closing arguments by each side, judge's instructions
    to the jury, and jury's decision.

If you were charged with tax
evasion, would you prefer a trial
in front of a judge or a jury? Why?
Would you make a different choice
if you were charged with injuring
a small child when texting while
driving?

Appeals

Imposition of a sentence does not mean that the case is necessarily over; the defendant typically has the right to appeal the verdict to a higher court, and the right to counsel continues through the first appeal (Heise, 2009). Some states have limited the right to appeal when defendants plead guilty. An **appeal** is based on a claim that one or more errors of law or procedure were made during the investigation, arrest, or trial process (C. E. Smith, 2000b). Such claims usually assert that the trial judge made errors in courtroom rulings or by improperly admitting evidence that the police gathered in violation of some constitutional right. A defendant might base an appeal, for example, on the claim that the judge did not instruct the jury correctly or that a guilty plea was not made voluntarily.

Appeals are based on questions of procedure, not on issues of the defendant's guilt or innocence (Place, 2013). The appellate court will not normally second-guess a jury. Instead, it will check to make sure that the trial followed proper procedures

appeal A request to a higher court that it review actions taken in a trial court.

In appellate courts, several judges sit as a group to hear and decide cases. The appeals process provides an opportunity to correct errors that occurred in trial court proceedings. What are the advantages and disadvantages of having a group of appeals court judges decide a case together?

(Shay, 2009). If there were significant errors in the trial, then the conviction is set aside. The defendant may be tried again if the prosecutor decides to pursue the case again. Thus, a successful appeal may merely lead to reconviction on the charges in a second trial.

Most criminal defendants must file an appeal shortly after trial to have an appellate court review the case. By contrast, many states provide for an automatic appeal in death penalty cases (Alarcon, 2007). The quality of defense representation is important, because the appeal must usually meet short deadlines and carefully identify appropriate issues (Wasserman, 1990).

A case originating in a state court is first appealed through that state's judicial system. When a state case involves a federal constitutional question, however, a later appeal can go to the U.S. Supreme Court. State courts decide almost four-fifths of all appeals.

Most appeals do not succeed in gaining a new trial, a new sentence, or an outright acquittal. In almost 80 percent of the cases examined in one classic study, the decision of the trial courts was affirmed (Chapper & Hanson, 1989). Most of the other decisions produced new trials or resentencing; very few decisions (1.9 percent) produced acquittals on appeal.

Habeas Corpus

After people have used their avenues of appeal, they may pursue a writ of habeas corpus if they claim that their federal constitutional rights were violated during the lower-court processes (King & Hoffmann, 2011). Known as "the great writ," from its traditional role in English law and its enshrinement in the U.S. Constitution, **habeas corpus** is a judicial order requesting that a judge examine whether an individual is being properly detained in a jail, prison, or mental hospital (Wert, 2011). If there is no legal basis for the person to be held, then the judge may grant the writ and order the person to be released. In the context of criminal justice, convicted offenders may claim that their imprisonment is improper because one of their constitutional rights was violated during the investigation or adjudication of their case. Statutes permit offenders convicted in both state and federal courts to pursue habeas corpus actions in the federal courts. After first seeking favorable decisions by state appellate courts, convicted offenders can start their constitutional claims anew in the federal district courts and subsequently pursue their habeas cases in the federal circuit courts of appeal and the U.S. Supreme Court.

Overall, only about 1 percent of habeas petitions succeed (Flango, 1994). In one study, less than one-half of one percent of noncapital habeas petitioners gained a favorable judicial decision, but more than 12 percent of habeas petitioners in death penalty cases demonstrated a rights violation (King, Cheesman, & Ostrom, 2007). One reason for the overall low success rate may be that an individual has no right to be represented by counsel when pursuing a habeas corpus petition. Few offenders have sufficient knowledge of law and legal procedures to identify and present constitutional claims effectively in the federal courts (Shay, 2013). However, under state laws and court practices, attorneys are often provided to people sentenced to death during postconviction processes, thus increasing the likelihood of effective identification and presentation of errors in the habeas corpus process.

In 1996, the Antiterrorism and Effective Death Penalty Act placed additional restrictions on habeas corpus petitions. The statute was quickly approved by the U.S. Supreme Court. These reforms were based, in part, on a belief that prisoners' cases were clogging the federal courts (C. E. Smith, 1995). Ironically, habeas corpus petitions in the federal courts increased by 50 percent after the passage of the restrictive legislation (Scalia, 2002). By imposing strict filing deadlines for petitions, the legislation may have inadvertently focused more prisoners' attention on the existence of habeas corpus and thereby encouraged them to move forward with petitions in order to meet the deadlines.

habeas corpus A writ or judicial order requesting the release of a person being detained in a jail, prison, or mental hospital. If a judge finds the person is being held improperly, the writ may be granted and the person released.

Evaluating the Appellate Process

The public seems to believe that many offenders are being "let off" through the appellate process. Some critics have argued that opportunities for appeal should be limited. They claim that too many offenders delay imposition of their sentences and that others completely evade punishment by filing appeals endlessly. This practice not only increases the workload of the courts but also jeopardizes the concept of the finality of the justice process. However, given that 90 percent of accused persons plead guilty, the number of cases that might be appealed is relatively small.

The appeals process performs the important function of righting wrongs. It also helps ensure consistency in the application of law by judges in different courts. Beyond that, its presence constantly influences the daily operations of the criminal justice system, as prosecutors and trial judges must consider how a higher court might later evaluate their decisions and actions.

▼ CHECK POINT

12. **How does the appellate court's job differ from that of the trial court?**
Unlike trial courts, which have juries, hear evidence, and decide if the defendant is guilty or not guilty, appellate courts focus only on claimed errors of law or procedure in trial court proceedings. Victory for a defendant in a trial court means an acquittal and instant freedom. Victory in an appellate court may mean only a chance at a new trial—which often leads to a new conviction.

13. **What is a habeas corpus petition?**
The habeas corpus process may be started after all appeals have been filed and lost. Convicted offenders ask a federal court to review whether any constitutional rights were violated during the course of a case investigation and trial. If rights were violated, the person's continued detention in prison or jail may be improper.

STOP & ANALYZE

Do criminal offenders have too many opportunities to challenge convictions? List two benefits and two costs of having both an appeals process and a habeas corpus process.

? A QUESTION OF ETHICS

Think, Discuss, Write

Plea bargaining creates ethical challenges for defense attorneys. In a series of decisions, including *Padilla v. Kentucky* (2010) and *Missouri v. Frye* (2012), the U.S. Supreme Court made clear that defense attorneys are obligated to inform defendants of plea agreements offered by the prosecutor and to accurately inform defendants of the relevant law affecting those agreements, such as the prospect of deportation for noncitizens. In 2013, Tom Petters, a man serving a 50-year sentence in federal prison for stealing $3.6 billion from investors in a fraud scheme, claimed that his attorney had never informed him of a plea offer from prosecutors that would have given him a 30-year maximum sentence. His defense attorney, Jon Hopeman, responded by producing letters and notes to demonstrate that Petters knew about the offer and did not accept it. At the same time, Hopeman acknowledged that he had discouraged Petters from accepting the offer because he believed that a 30-year sentence would be too severe. Arguably, Hopeman either underestimated what the ultimate sentence could be or overestimated his client's prospects for acquittal.

Discussion/Writing Assignment

Defendants rely on their attorneys for expert advice. When the attorney advises against accepting a plea agreement and then the sentence turns out to be far more severe than what the defendant had expected, should the defendant be entitled to go back and accept the expired plea offer? How much good does it do for defendants to be informed of a plea offer if they lack knowledge and perspective on what the alternative sentence will be? Should the defense attorney, rather than the defendant, bear responsibility for inaccurate projections about the sentence that could be imposed after going to trial? Alternatively, if defendants maintain their innocence throughout the process, as Petters did, then isn't the defense attorney ethically obligated to advise against accepting a long sentence in a plea agreement? If you were a judge, would you rule that the defense attorney provided ineffective assistance of counsel and permit Petters to have the 30-year-sentence from the plea offer? Give three reasons for your answer.

Source: A. Simons, "Lawyer Says Petters Knew of Potential Plea Deal and Rejected It," *Minneapolis Star Tribune*, June 3, 2013 (www.startribune.com).

SUMMARY

1 **Identify the elements in the pretrial process in criminal cases.**

- Pretrial processes determine the fates of nearly all defendants through case dismissals, decisions defining charges, and plea bargains, all of which affect more than 90 percent of cases.
- Defense attorneys use motions to their advantage to gain information and delay proceedings to benefit their clients.

2 **Explain how the bail system operates.**

- The bail process provides opportunities for many defendants to gain pretrial release, but poor defendants may be disadvantaged by their inability to come up with the money or property needed to secure release. Some preventive detention statutes permit judges to hold defendants considered dangerous or likely to flee.
- Bail agents, also known as bail bondsmen, are private businesspeople who charge a fee to provide money for defendants' pretrial release. Their activities create risks of corruption and discrimination in the bail process, but bail agents may also help the system by reminding defendants about court dates.
- Although judges bear the primary responsibility for setting bail, prosecutors are especially influential in recommending amounts and conditions for pretrial release.
- Initiatives to reform the bail process include police-issued citations, release on own recognizance (ROR), percentage bail, bail guidelines, and preventive detention.

3 **Describe the experience of pretrial detention.**

- Despite the presumption of innocence, pretrial detainees endure difficult conditions in jails that often contain mixed populations of convicted offenders, detainees, and troubled people. The shock of being jailed creates risks of suicide and depression.

4 **Explain how and why plea bargaining occurs.**

- Most convictions are obtained through plea bargaining, a process that exists because it fulfills the self-interest of prosecutors, judges, defense attorneys, and defendants.
- Plea bargaining is facilitated by exchange relations between prosecutors and defense attorneys. In many courthouses, there is little actual bargaining, as outcomes are determined through the implicit bargaining process of settling the facts and assessing the going rate of punishment according to the standards of the local legal culture.

- Plea bargaining has been criticized both for pressuring defendants to surrender their rights and for reducing the sentences imposed on offenders.

5 **Give the reasons why cases go to trial, and describe the benefits of jurors' participation in trials.**

- Americans tend to presume that trials—dramatic courtroom battles of prosecutors and defense attorneys—are the best way to discover the truth about a criminal case.
- Less than 9 percent of cases go to trial, and half of those are typically bench trials in front of a judge, not jury trials.
- Typically, cases go to trial because they involve defendants who are wealthy enough to pay attorneys to fight to the very end, or because they involve charges that are too serious to create incentives for plea bargaining.
- Juries serve vital functions for society by preventing arbitrary action by prosecutors and judges, educating citizens about the justice system, symbolizing the rule of law, and involving citizens from diverse segments of the community in judicial decision making.
- The U.S. Supreme Court has ruled that juries need not be made up of 12 members, and 12-member juries can, if permitted by state law, convict defendants by a less-than-unanimous supermajority vote.

6 **Describe the stages of a criminal trial.**

- The trial process consists of a series of steps: jury selection, opening statements, presentation of prosecution's evidence, presentation of defense's evidence, presentation of rebuttal witnesses, closing arguments, judge's jury instructions, and jury's decision.
- The jury selection process, especially in the formation of the jury pool and the exercise of peremptory challenges, often creates juries that do not fully represent all segments of a community.
- Rules of evidence dictate what kinds of information may be presented in court for consideration by the jury. Types of evidence are real evidence, demonstrative evidence, testimony, direct evidence, and circumstantial evidence.

7 **Explain the basis for an appeal of a conviction.**

- Convicted offenders have the opportunity to appeal, although defendants who plead guilty, unlike those convicted through a trial, often have few grounds for an appeal.

- Appeals focus on claimed errors of law or procedure in the investigation by police and prosecutors or in the decisions by trial judges. Relatively few offenders win their appeals, and most who do gain only an opportunity for a new trial, not release from jail or prison.

- After convicted offenders have used all of their appeals, they may file a habeas corpus petition to seek federal judicial review of claimed constitutional rights violations in their cases. Very few of such petitions succeed.

Questions for Review

1. What is bail, and how has it been reformed to limit its traditionally harsh impact on poor defendants?
2. Why are some defendants held in pretrial detention?
3. Why does plea bargaining exist?
4. Given that there are so few jury trials, what types of cases would you expect to find adjudicated in this manner? Why?
5. What is the purpose of the appeals process?

Key Terms and Cases

appeal (p. 305)

arraignment (p. 277)

bail (p. 280)

bench trials (p. 294)

challenge for cause (p. 297)

circumstantial evidence (p. 299)

citation (p. 284)

demonstrative evidence (p. 299)

direct evidence (p. 299)

habeas corpus (p. 306)

jury (p. 294)

motion (p. 278)

percentage bail (p. 285)

peremptory challenge (p. 297)

preventive detention (p. 286)

real evidence (p. 299)

reasonable doubt (p. 302)

release on recognizance (ROR) (p. 285)

testimony (p. 299)

voir dire (p. 297)

Bordenkircher v. Hayes (1978) (p. 292)

Boykin v. Alabama (1969) (p. 292)

Missouri v. Frye (2012) (p. 292)

North Carolina v. Alford (1970) (p. 292)

Ricketts v. Adamson (1987) (p. 292)

Santobello v. New York (1971) (p. 288)

United States v. Salerno and Cafero (1987) (p. 286)

Williams v. Florida (1970) (p. 295)

AP Images/Melissa Phillip

9 Punishment and Sentencing

LEARNING OBJECTIVES

1 Name the goals of punishment.

2 Describe the types of sentences judges can impose.

3 Identify the influences on sentencing.

4 Explain how the system may treat wrongdoers unequally.

Among the many shocking crimes that occur with tragic regularity, one stands out as particularly disappointing. Americans are rightly shocked at murders and other violent crimes; but they cannot help but be both shocked and profoundly disappointed when teachers exploit underage students and manipulate these students into sexual relationships. These are crimes in which an adult who is trained for and entrusted with educational responsibilities for vulnerable young people engages in devastatingly harmful, self-interested behavior. Such crimes have the potential to psychologically scar young people for life.

What punishments do teachers deserve when they commit such harmful criminal acts against especially vulnerable victims? Does the American criminal justice system, with state-by-state differences in laws and legal culture, treat offenders in such cases fairly and equally? Are men and women teachers treated the same when they engage in these criminal acts? These are important questions that help to illuminate the complexities of sentencing and punishment in a large country with a fragmented justice system governed by the varied laws of fifty different states as well as differences in courtroom workgroups within individual courthouses inside each state.

In January 2015, Scott Tompkins, a 63-year-old high school teacher in rural northern Michigan, entered a guilty plea to one criminal charge for having a sexual relationship with a student in exchange for the prosecutor dropping two additional charges. Tompkins was given an indeterminate sentence requiring him to spend from 18 months to 10 years in prison (Wolcott, 2015). The actual time he ultimately serves in prison will depend on when he becomes eligible for parole release based on his behavior and his completion of treatment programs. A few months earlier, in July 2014, Torris Caston, a male ballet teacher in a suburb of St. Louis, Missouri, was sentenced to 10 years in prison for his sexual relationship with a 15-year-old student, a girl who had taken his classes for several years. Caston had entered a "not guilty" plea and taken his case to trial. A jury convicted him of statutory rape and two other sexual offenses (Mann, 2014). Both Tompkins and Caston faced additional charges related to claims by other victims.

In evaluating these two cases, one must begin with the difficult question of how much prison time is appropriate for this particular offense. Is a 10-year sentence too long, too short, or appropriate in severity? The two cases provide a clue to one important factor

311

affecting punishment in the American justice system: defendants who admit guilt typically get lesser sentences than those who take their cases all the way through expensive and time-consuming trials. Should asserting one's Sixth Amendment right to trial by jury produce harsher sentences? Or does this just reflect the reality that going to trial typically means missing the opportunity to accept fewer or less serious charges?

An interesting contrast is presented by two other cases in 2014, both involving female teachers. Katie Fazekas, a high school teacher in Ohio, admitted she had a sexual relationship with a 17-year-old female student. After pleading guilty, she was sentenced to 17 months in prison (Feehan, 2014). In Houston, Texas, Kathryn Murray, a middle school teacher, pleaded guilty to having a sexual relationship with a 15-year-old male student. She was sentenced to two years in county jail. These sentences were significantly less harsh than those imposed in the Michigan and Missouri cases on male teachers. The victim's father in the Texas case complained that the sentence reflected a double standard favoring women; he told news reporters that a male teacher with a female

AP Images/Melissa Phillip

student victim would have received a much longer sentence (Rogers, 2014). Was the father correct? Certainly, Texas has a reputation for handing out tough sentences for many offenses. In 2013, Brandon McDaniel, a male high school teacher in Arlington, was sentenced to 20 years in prison for sexual relationships with students. However, it is difficult to compare this case precisely with Kathryn Murray's case, because McDaniel had relationships with several students over the course of a decade and he took his case to trial (Crandall, 2013).

In considering the various factors that lead to significantly different sentences for the same type of shocking crime, consider one more case from 2014. In Annapolis, Maryland, Jason Webb, a 27-year-old martial arts teacher pleaded guilty to having a sexual relationship with one of his 14-year-old female students. His sentence: 10 *days* in jail ("Martial Arts Teacher," 2014). Was this sentence appropriate and fair? Can we explain why this sentence is so different from the others? It is not easy to know precisely why Webb received such a light sentence. As the foregoing examples illustrate, criminal behavior may produce a wide variety of punishments, which depend on the goals being pursued by officials who make laws and determine sentences. In essence, Webb's case highlights the fact that sentencing and punishment can vary drastically throughout the country as a result of different state laws, different local practices, and different discretionary decisions by judges and prosecutors.

The criminal justice system aims to solve three basic issues: (1) What conduct is criminal? (2) What determines guilt? and (3) What should be done with the guilty? Earlier chapters emphasized the first two questions. The answers given by the legal system to the first question compose the basic rules of society: do not murder, rob, sell drugs, commit treason, and so forth. The law also spells out the process for determining guilt or innocence; however, the administrative and interpersonal considerations of the actors in the criminal justice system greatly affect this process. In this chapter, we begin to examine the third problem: sanction and punishment. First, we consider the four goals of punishment: retribution, deterrence, incapacitation, and rehabilitation. We then explore the forms punishment takes to achieve its goals. These are incarceration, intermediate sanctions, probation, and death. Finally, we look at the sentencing process and how it affects punishment.

Criminal sanctions in the United States have four main goals: retribution (deserved punishment), deterrence, incapacitation, and rehabilitation. Ultimately, all criminal punishment aims at maintaining the social order, but the justifications for sentencing proceed from the American values of justice and fairness. There is no universal agreement, however, on how to make the severity of punishment just and fair. Further, the justice sought by crime victims often conflicts with fairness to offenders.

Punishments reflect the dominant values of a particular moment in history. By the end of the 1960s, for example, the number of Americans who were sentenced to imprisonment decreased because of a widespread commitment to rehabilitating offenders. By contrast, since the mid-1970s, an emphasis on imposing strong punishments for the purposes of retribution, deterrence, and incapacitation has resulted in record numbers of offenders being sentenced to prison. At the beginning of the twenty-first century, voices are calling for the addition of *restorative justice* as a fifth goal of the criminal sanction.

Retribution—Deserved Punishment

Retribution is punishment inflicted on a person who has harmed other people and so deserves to be penalized (Cahill, 2007b). The biblical expression "an eye for an eye, a tooth for a tooth" illustrates the philosophy underlying this kind of punishment. Retribution means that those who commit a particular crime should be punished alike, in proportion to the gravity of the offense or to the suffering their crime has caused others. Retribution is deserved punishment; offenders must "pay their debts."

Some scholars claim that the desire for retribution is a basic human emotion. They maintain, therefore, that if the state does not provide retributive sanctions to reflect community revulsion at offensive acts, citizens will take the law into their own hands to punish offenders. Under this view, the failure of government to satisfy the people's desire for retribution could produce social chaos.

This argument may not be valid for all crimes, however. If a rapist is inadequately punished, then the victim's family and other members of the community may be tempted to exact their own retribution. But what about a young adult smoking marijuana? If the government failed to impose retribution for this offense, would the community care? The same apathy may hold true for offenders who commit other nonviolent crimes that modestly impact society. Even in these seemingly trivial

retribution Punishment inflicted on a person who has harmed others and so deserves to be penalized.

In 2015, David Petraeus, former commander of the U.S. forces in Afghanistan and director of the Central Intelligence Agency, was sentenced to probation and a $100,000 fine for providing classified national security information to his biographer, a woman with whom he was having an extramarital affair. Was this an adequate punishment for failing to protect national secrets? Was his sentence lighter than what might have been imposed on a person of lesser prominence for a similar offense?

situations, however, retribution may serve as a necessary public reminder of the general rules of law and the important values they protect.

Since the late 1970s, retribution as a justification for the criminal sanction has aroused new interest, largely because of dissatisfaction with the philosophical basis and practical results of rehabilitation. Using the concept of "just deserts" or "deserved punishment" to define retribution, some theorists argue that one who infringes on the rights of others deserves to be punished; punishment is a moral response to harm inflicted on society (Bronsteen, 2010). In effect, these theorists believe that basic morality demands that wrongdoers be punished (von Hirsch, 1976). According to this view, punishment should be applied only for the wrong inflicted and not primarily to achieve other goals such as deterrence, incapacitation, or rehabilitation.

Deterrence

Many people see criminal punishment as a basis for affecting the future choices and behavior of individuals. Politicians frequently talk about being "tough on crime" to send a message to would-be criminals. The roots of this approach, called *deterrence,* lie in eighteenth-century England among the followers of social philosopher Jeremy Bentham.

Bentham was struck by what seemed to be the pointlessness of retribution. His fellow reformers adopted Bentham's theory of *utilitarianism,* which holds that human behavior is governed by the individual's calculation of the benefits versus the costs of his or her acts. Before stealing money or property, for example, potential offenders would consider the punishment that others have received for similar acts and be deterred from committing a theft.

general deterrence
Punishment of criminals that is intended to be an example to the general public and to discourage the commission of offenses.

There are two types of deterrence. **General deterrence** presumes that members of the general public, on observing the punishments of others, will conclude that the costs of crime outweigh the benefits. For general deterrence to be effective, the public must receive constant reminders of the likelihood and severity of punishment for various acts. They must believe that they will be caught, prosecuted, and given a specific punishment if they commit a particular crime. Moreover, the punishment must be severe enough to instill fear of the consequences of committing crimes.

For example, Jim Cramer, a close observer of Wall Street executives and the host of the CNBC show *Mad Money* commented on the reaction of corporate executives to the sentence of Wall Street business multimillionaire Raj Rajaratnam in 2011. For using illegal inside information from tipsters within a corporation as a basis for investment decisions, Rajaratnam was sentenced to 11 years in federal prison, a $10 million fine, and the forfeiture of $53.8 million (Lattman, 2011). According to Cramer, "It took their collective breaths away. . . . They are still reeling from the Raj sentence. . . . Nothing scares these guys more than jail time" (J. Warren, 2011). Whether or not Cramer is correct, there are some judges who believe that there is a general-deterrence benefit from stiff sentences for high-profile offenders. Yet not all judges share that view, as one news reporter noted when he asked two judges about whether high-profile sentences can deter people seeking to satisfy their own greed for money and power. According to the reporter, both judges laughed and one said, "Deter greed, eh? . . . Good luck!" (J. Warren, 2011).

specific deterrence
Punishment inflicted on criminals to discourage them from committing future crimes.

By contrast, **specific deterrence** targets the decisions and behavior of offenders who have already been convicted. Under this approach, the amount and kind of punishment are calculated to discourage that criminal from repeating the offense. The punishment must be severe enough to cause the criminal to say, "The consequences of my crime were too painful. I will not commit another crime, because I do not want to risk being punished again."

The concept of deterrence presents obvious difficulties (Stafford & Warr, 1993). Deterrence assumes that all people think before they act. As such, deterrence does not account for the many people who commit crimes while under the influence of drugs or alcohol or those whose harmful behavior stems from psychological problems or mental illness. Deterrence also does not account for people who act impulsively when stealing or damaging property. In other cases, the low probability of being caught defeats both general and specific deterrence. To be generally deterrent, punishment must be perceived as relatively fast, certain, and severe (Mannheimer, 2011). See "Criminal Justice: Myth & Reality" to explore the problems underlying fulfillment of the deterrence goal.

Knowledge of the effectiveness of deterrence is limited as well (Kleck et al., 2005). For example, social science cannot measure the effects of general deterrence, because only those who are not deterred come to the attention of researchers. A study of the deterrent effects of punishment would have to examine the impact of different forms of the criminal sanction on various potential lawbreakers. How can we truly determine how many people—or even if any people—stopped themselves from committing a crime for any reason, let alone because they were deterred by the prospect of prosecution and punishment? Therefore, although legislators often cite deterrence as a rationale for certain sanctions, no one really knows the extent to which sentencing policies based on deterrence achieve their objectives. Because contemporary U.S. society has shown little ability to reduce crime by imposing increasingly severe sanctions, the effectiveness of deterrence for many crimes and criminals should be questioned (Tonry, 2008).

Incapacitation

Incapacitation assumes that society can use detention in prison or execution to keep offenders from committing further crimes. Many people express such sentiments, urging officials to "lock 'em up and throw away the key!" In primitive societies, banishment from the community was the usual method of incapacitation. In earlier periods of American history, offenders often agreed to move away or to join the army as an alternative to some other form of punishment. In the United States today, imprisonment serves as the usual method of incapacitation. Offenders can be confined within secure institutions and thereby effectively prevented from committing additional harm against society for the duration of their sentence. Capital punishment is the ultimate method of incapacitation. Any sentence that physically restricts an offender may incapacitate the person, even when the underlying purpose of the sentence is retribution, deterrence, or rehabilitation.

Sentences based on incapacitation are future-oriented. Whereas retribution requires focusing on the harmful act of the offender, incapacitation looks at the offender's potential actions. If the offender is likely to commit future crimes, then the judge may impose a severe sentence—even for a relatively minor crime.

For example, under the incapacitation theory, a woman who kills her abusive husband as an emotional reaction to his verbal insults and physical assaults could receive a light sentence. As a one-time impulse killer who felt driven to kill by unique circumstances, she is not likely to commit additional crimes. By contrast, a woman who shoplifts merchandise and has been convicted of the offense on 10 previous occasions may receive a severe sentence. In a case like this, the criminal record and type of crime indicate that she will commit additional crimes if

incapacitation Depriving an offender of the ability to commit crimes against society, usually by detaining the offender in prison.

released. Thus, incapacitation focuses on characteristics of the offenders instead of aspects of their offenses.

Does it offend your sense of justice that a person could receive a severer sentence for shoplifting than for manslaughter? This question embodies one of the criticisms of incapacitation. Questions also arise about how to determine the length of sentence. Presumably, offenders will not be released until the state is reasonably sure that they will no longer commit crimes. However, can we accurately predict any person's behavior? Moreover, on what grounds can we punish people for anticipated behavior that we cannot accurately predict? In addition, there are questions about whether incapacitative policies will lead to an overall reduction in crime rates if there are other social forces that continue to foster criminal behavior among people living in various contexts in American society (Stahlkopf, Males, & Macallair, 2010).

In recent years, greater attention has been paid to the concept of **selective incapacitation**, whereby offenders who repeat certain kinds of crimes receive long prison terms. Research has suggested that a relatively small number of offenders commit a large number of violent and property crimes (Clear, 1994). Burglars, for example, tend to commit many offenses before they are caught. Thus, the reasoning goes, these "career criminals" should be locked up for long periods (Auerhahn, 1999). Such policies could be costly, however. Not only would correctional facilities have to be expanded, but the number of expensive, time-consuming trials also might increase if severer sentences caused more repeat offenders to plead not guilty. Another difficulty with this policy is that we cannot accurately predict which offenders will commit more crimes upon release (Vitiello, 2008).

Rehabilitation

Rehabilitation refers to the goal of restoring a convicted offender to a constructive place in society through some form of training or therapy. Americans want to believe that offenders can be treated and resocialized in ways that allow them to lead a crime-free, productive life upon release. Over the last hundred years, rehabilitation advocates have argued for techniques that they claim identify and treat the causes of criminal behavior. If the offender's criminal behavior is assumed to result from some social, psychological, or biological imperfection, the treatment of the disorder becomes the primary goal of corrections.

Rehabilitation focuses on the offender. Its objective does not imply any consistent relationship between the severity of the punishment and the gravity of the crime. People who commit lesser offenses can receive long prison sentences if experts believe effective rehabilitation requires it. By contrast, a murderer might win early release by showing signs that the psychological or emotional problems that led to the killing have been corrected.

According to the concept of rehabilitation, offenders are treated, not punished, and they will return to society when they are "cured." Consequently, adhering to this philosophy, judges would not set fixed sentences but rather ones with maximum and minimum terms so that parole boards can release inmates when they have been rehabilitated.

From the 1940s until the 1970s, the goal of rehabilitation was so widely accepted that treatment and reform of the offender were generally regarded as the only issues worth serious attention. Crime was assumed to be caused by problems affecting individuals, and modern social sciences were assumed to have the tools to address those problems. During the past 30 years, however, researchers and others have questioned the assumptions of the rehabilitation model. Studies of the results of rehabilitation programs have challenged the idea that criminal offenders can be cured (Martinson, 1974). Moreover, scholars no longer take for granted that crime is caused by identifiable, curable problems such as poverty, lack of job skills, low self-esteem, and hostility toward authority. Instead, some argue that we cannot identify the cause of criminal behavior for individual offenders.

selective incapacitation Making the best use of expensive and limited prison space by targeting for incarceration those individuals whose incapacitation will do the most to reduce crime in society.

rehabilitation The goal of restoring a convicted offender to a constructive place in society through some form of vocational or educational training or therapy.

During the first decade of the twenty-first century, rehabilitation reemerged as a goal of corrections. As we shall see in Chapter 13, it came to be discussed and applied through the concept of "reentry" rather than through a declaration that rehabilitation is a primary goal of the justice system (Butterfield, 2004a). States and the federal government endured significant financial costs through the expansion of prison systems and the growth of prison populations, caused by the imposition of severer prison sentences during the preceding two decades. Eventually, they confronted the reality that hundreds of thousands of prisoners were returning to society each year after serving long sentences. In addition, as governments at all levels experienced budget crises, officials sought ways to reduce prison populations. Thus, policies and programs emerged that were intended to prepare offenders for successful integration into society (Eckholm, 2008b). These programs are rehabilitative in nature, by providing education, counseling, skill training, and other services to help change offenders' behavior and prospects for success in society. Public opinion generally supports efforts to reform offenders through such rehabilitative efforts (Pew Charitable Trusts, 2012).

A New Approach to Punishment: Restorative Justice

In keeping with the focus on community justice for police, courts, and corrections, many people are calling for **restorative justice** to be added to the goals of the criminal sanction (Abid, 2012; J. Braithwaite, 2007). The restorative justice perspective views crime as more than a violation of penal law. The criminal act practically and symbolically denies community. It breaks trust among citizens and requires community members to determine how "to contradict the moral message of the crime that the offender is above the law and the victim beneath its reach" (Clear & Karp, 1999:85). Crime victims suffer losses involving damage to property and self. The primary aim of criminal justice should be to repair these losses (Waldman, 2007). Crime also challenges the heart of community, to the extent that community life depends on a shared sense of trust, fairness, and interdependence.

> **restorative justice** Punishment designed to repair the damage done to the victim and community by an offender's criminal act.

Shifting the focus to restorative justice requires a three-way approach that involves the offender, the victim, and the community. This approach may include mediation in which the three actors devise a punishment that all agree is fair and just, by which the offender can try to repair the harm done to victims and community. Communities in Vermont have well-established restorative justice programs through which alternative punishments, public apologies, restitution, and interaction between offenders and victims seek to advance both accountability and restoration (Dzur, 2011). This new approach to criminal justice means that losses suffered by the crime victim are restored, the threat to local safety is removed, and the offender again becomes a fully participating member of the community.

As yet, restorative justice represents a small minority of sanctions. To see how the four main punishment goals might be enacted in real life, consider again the sentencing of Torris Caston, the Missouri ballet teacher sentenced to 10 years in prison for his sexual relationship with an underage student. Table 9.1 shows various hypothetical sentencing statements that the judge might have given, depending on prevailing correctional goals.

As we next consider how such goals are expressed though the various forms of punishment, keep in mind the underlying goal— or mix of goals—that justifies each form of sanction.

Restorative justice seeks to repair the damage that an offender's criminal act has done to the victim and the community. Victims and their families can convey to the offender the severity and enduring nature of the pain and harm caused by his or her actions. How do such meetings advance the idea of justice?

TABLE 9.1 **The Goals of Punishment**

At sentencing, the judge usually gives reasons for the punishments imposed. Here are statements that Missouri Judge Jack Garvey might have given ballet teacher Torris Caston for the statutory rape of an underage girl, each promoting a different goal for the sanction.

Goal	Judge's Possible Statement
Retribution	I am imposing this 10-year sentence because you deserve to be punished for the harms caused to this young woman and to society by exploiting and harming this young woman. *What you did to this woman has cut such a path of destruction, of humiliation and pain. I don't know if it can ever be fixed.* [Note: italicized words were actually said by Judge Garvey at sentencing (Mann, 2014).] Your criminal behavior is the basis of the punishment. Justice requires that I impose a sanction at a level that illustrates the importance that the community places on respecting the law and contributing as a member of society.
Deterrence	I am imposing this 10-year sentence so that your punishment for statutory rape serves as an example and deters others who may contemplate similar actions. In addition, I hope that this sentence will deter you from ever again committing an illegal act, as the victim asked for strict punishment to make sure that others would not be victimized [Note: Judge Garvey actually made this last statement].
Incapacitation	I am imposing this 10-year sentence so that you will be incapacitated and hence unable to commit other sex offenses, in accordance with the victim's request for a sentence that would prevent you from victimizing other girls.
Rehabilitation	The trial testimony and information contained in the presentence report make me believe that there are aspects of your personality that contributed to your sex offenses. I am therefore imposing this 10-year sentence so that you will have time and opportunity to receive counseling treatment and correct your behavior in the future.

Source: Jeffrey Mann, "Webster Groves Ballet Teacher Sentenced to 10 Years for Sex with Student," *St. Louis Post Dispatch*, July 7, 2014 (www.stltoday.com).

CHECK POINT

1. **What are the four primary goals of the criminal sanction?**
   Retribution, deterrence, incapacitation, rehabilitation.

2. **What are the difficulties in showing that a punishment acts as a deterrent?**
   It is impossible to show who has been deterred from committing crimes; punishment isn't always certain; people act impulsively rather than rationally; people commit crimes while on drugs.

STOP & ANALYZE

What do you think should be the primary goal of the criminal sanction? List two problems or challenges to the achievement of that goal.

Forms of the Criminal Sanction

Incarceration, intermediate sanctions, probation, and death are the basic ways that the criminal sanction, or punishment, is applied. The United States does not have a single, uniform set of sentencing laws. The criminal codes of each of the states and of the federal government specify the punishments. Each code differs to some extent in the severity of the punishment for specific crimes and in the amount of discretion given judges to tailor the sanction to the individual offender.

As we examine the various forms of criminal sanction, bear in mind that applying these legally authorized punishments gives rise to complex problems. Judges often have wide discretion in determining the appropriate sentence within the parameters of the penal code.

Incarceration

Imprisonment is the most visible penalty imposed by U.S. courts. Although less than 30 percent of people under correctional supervision are in prisons and jails, incarceration remains the standard for punishing those who commit serious crimes. Imprisonment is thought to contribute significantly to deterring potential offenders. However, incarceration is expensive. It also creates the problem of reintegrating offenders into society upon release.

In penal codes, legislatures stipulate the types of sentences and the amount of prison time that can be imposed for each crime. Three basic sentencing structures are used: (1) indeterminate sentences; (2) determinate sentences; and (3) mandatory sentences. Each type of sentence makes certain assumptions about the goals of the criminal sanction, and each provides judges with varying degrees of discretion.

Indeterminate Sentences

When the goal of rehabilitation dominated corrections, legislatures enacted **indeterminate sentences** (often called *indefinite sentences*) (Fisher, 2007). In keeping with the goal of treatment, indeterminate sentencing gives correctional officials and parole boards significant control over the amount of time a prisoner serves. Penal codes with indeterminate sentences stipulate a minimum and a maximum amount of time to be served in prison (for example, 1 to 5 years, 10 to 15 years, or 1 year to life). At the time of sentencing, the judge informs the offender about the range of the sentence. The offender also learns that she or he will probably be eligible for parole at some point after the minimum term has been served. The parole board determines the actual release date. Recall in the chapter opener about teachers' sex offenses against students that the Michigan teacher, Tompkins, was given a sentence from 18 months to 10 years, a good example of an indeterminate sentence (Wolcott, 2015). Because it is based on the idea that the time necessary for treatment cannot be set, the indeterminate sentence is closely associated with rehabilitation (Zhang, Zhang, & Vaughn, 2014).

indeterminate sentence A period set by a judge that specifies a minimum and a maximum time to be served in prison. Sometime after the minimum, the offender may be eligible for parole.

Determinate Sentences

Dissatisfaction with the rehabilitation goal and support for the concept of deserved punishment led many legislatures in the 1970s to shift to **determinate sentences** (Dansky, 2008). With a determinate sentence, a convicted offender is imprisoned for a specific period (for example, 2 years, 5 years, 15 years). At the end of the term, minus credited *good time* (to be discussed shortly), the prisoner is automatically freed. The time of release depends neither on participation in treatment programs nor on a parole board's judgment concerning the offender's likelihood of returning to criminal activities.

determinate sentence A sentence that fixes the term of imprisonment at a specific period.

Of all correctional measures, incarceration represents the greatest restriction on freedom. These inmates are part of America's huge incarcerated population. Since 1980, the number of Americans held in prisons and jails has quadrupled. What are the costs to society from having such a large population of prisoners?

AP Images/David Goldman

presumptive sentence
A sentence for which the legislature or a commission sets a minimum and a maximum range of months or years. Judges are to fix the length of the sentence within that range, allowing for special circumstances.

Some determinate-sentencing states have adopted penal codes that stipulate a specific term for each crime category. Others allow the judge to choose a range of time to be served. Some states emphasize a determinate **presumptive sentence**: the legislature, or often a commission, specifies a term based on a time range (for example, 14–20 months) into which most cases should fall. Only in special circumstances are judges to deviate from the presumptive sentence. Whichever variation is used, however, the offender theoretically knows at sentencing the amount of time to be served. One objective of determinate sentencing is that by reducing the judge's discretion, legislatures can limit sentencing disparities and ensure that sentences correspond to those the elected lawmakers believe are appropriate (Engen, 2009).

Mandatory Sentences Reflecting the public's fear and anger about crime, politicians and the public periodically complain that offenders are released before serving sufficiently long terms, and legislatures have responded (Zimring, 2007). All states and the federal government now have some form of **mandatory sentences** (often called *mandatory minimum sentences*), stipulating some minimum period of incarceration that people convicted of selected crimes must serve. The judge is not permitted to consider either the circumstances of the offense or the background of the offender, and she or he cannot impose nonincarcerative sentences. Mandatory prison terms are most often specified for violent crimes, drug violations, repeat offenses, or crimes in which a firearm was used. However, opinion polls indicate that the public has become less supportive of this approach to criminal punishment (Pew Charitable Trusts, 2012).

mandatory sentence
A sentence determined by statutes and requiring that a certain penalty be imposed and carried out for convicted offenders who meet certain criteria.

The "three strikes and you're out" laws adopted in the 1990s by 26 states and the federal government provide an example of mandatory sentencing (Schultz, 2000). These laws require that judges sentence offenders with three felony convictions (in some states two or four convictions) to long prison terms, sometimes to life without parole. In some states, these laws have inadvertently clogged the courts, lowered the rates of plea bargaining, and have caused desperate offenders to violently resist arrest. Mandatory minimum sentences resulted in a great increase in the number of drug offenders serving very long terms in America's prisons, mostly for nonviolent offenses (Gezari, 2008).

In the past decade, state governments have been forced to cut their budgets as the nation's economic woes caused a decline in tax revenues; consequently, there has been increased attention to the high cost of long, mandatory sentences (Pew Center on the States, 2012). Some states initiated changes in sentencing in an effort to alleviate prison overcrowding and reduce their corrections budgets (Riccardi, 2009). Voters in California approved a ballot issue in 2012 to reduce the applicability of that state's three-strikes law by no longer applying life sentences to offenders whose third offense was nonviolent (Staples, 2012). The change in the law will save the state a significant amount of money as fewer offenders will receive life sentences and nearly 3,000 offenders imprisoned under the older version of the three-strikes law might seek eventual release.

In addition, mandatory sentences faced reexamination because of concerns that certain sentences are unfair. For example, in 2010 Congress reformed mandatory cocaine sentencing laws that, due to differential treatment of crack cocaine and powder cocaine, had led to lengthier sentences for many African American offenders who had been the primary users and sellers of crack cocaine. The change in the law still did not treat crack cocaine offenses identically with powder cocaine offenses, for which white offenders were heavily represented, but it did reduce the number of crack offenders subjected to the mandatory five-year sentence that previously applied (P. Baker, 2010).

The Sentence versus Actual Time Served Regardless of how much discretion judges have to fine-tune the sentences they give, the prison sentences that are imposed may bear little resemblance to the actual amount of time served. In reality, parole boards in indeterminate-sentencing states have broad discretion in release decisions once the offender has served a minimum portion of the sentence. In addition, offenders can have their prison sentence reduced by earning **good time** for good behavior, at the discretion of the prison administrator (O'Hear, 2014).

Most states have good-time policies. Days are subtracted from prisoners' minimum or maximum term for good behavior or for participation in various types of vocational, educational, or treatment programs. Correctional officials consider these policies necessary for maintaining institutional order and for reducing crowding. Good-time credit serves as an incentive for prisoners to follow institutional rules, because recently earned credits can be taken away for misbehavior (King & Sherry, 2008). Prosecutors and defense attorneys also take good time into consideration during plea bargaining. In other words, they think about the actual amount of time a particular offender will likely serve.

The amount of good time one can earn varies among the states, usually from 5 to 10 days a month. In some states, once 90 days of good time are earned, they are vested; that is, the credits cannot be taken away as a punishment for misbehavior. Prisoners who then violate the rules risk losing only days not vested.

Contemporary budget crises have led several states to increase good-time credits as a means to reduce prison populations through quicker release from custody (Homan, 2010). In 2010, for example, Louisiana made well-behaved prisoners eligible to receive a 35-day credit for every 30 days served. The change was expected to reduce the state's prison population by 2,386 prisoners in the first year and save the state $7 million in the first year alone (KATC-TV, 2010). In 2015, a member of Congress proposed legislation seeking to clarify that federal statutes intend to grant federal prisoners 54 days of good time for each year of good behavior rather than merely 47 days granted by the Bureau of Prisons through its interpretation of the laws (Marcos, 2015).

More than 30 states also grant **earned time** that may be offered in addition to good time. Unlike good time, which is based on good behavior, earned time is awarded for participation in education, vocational, substance-abuse, and other rehabilitation programs (Schinella, 2015). Earned time may also be awarded for work assignments, such as when low-security prisoners work on disaster relief or conservation projects or fight wildfires (Lawrence, 2009). Several states have expanded the use of earned time as part of their budget-reduction strategies for shrinking expensive prison populations.

Judges in the United States often prescribe long periods of incarceration for serious crimes, but good time, earned time, and parole reduce the amount of time spent in prison. Figure 9.1 shows the estimated time actually served by offenders in state prisons versus the average (mean) sentence.

This type of national data often hides the impact of variations in sentencing and releasing laws in individual states. In many states, because of prison crowding and release policies, offenders serve less than 20 percent of their sentences. In other states, where three-strikes and truth-in-sentencing laws are employed, the average time served is longer than the national average.

Truth in Sentencing   *Truth in sentencing* refers to laws that require offenders to serve a substantial proportion (usually 85 percent for violent crimes) of their prison sentence before being released on parole (Mayrack, 2008). In the 1990s, truth in sentencing became such a politically attractive idea that the federal government allocated almost $10 billion for prison construction to those states adopting truth in sentencing (Donziger, 1996). Critics maintain, however, that truth in sentencing increases prison populations at a tremendous cost. The concept is less attractive today to many states beset by budget problems as they try to reduce their prison populations through greater flexibility in sentencing and early release (Riccardi, 2009).

Intermediate Sanctions

Prison crowding and the low levels of probation supervision have spurred interest in the development of **intermediate sanctions**, punishments that are less severe and less costly than prison but more restrictive than traditional probation (R. Warren, 2007).

good time A reduction of an inmate's prison sentence, at the discretion of the prison administrator, for good behavior or participation in vocational, educational, or treatment programs.

earned time Reduction in a prisoner's sentence as a reward for participation in educational or other rehabilitation programs and for work assignments such as disaster relief and conservation projects.

intermediate sanction A variety of punishments that are more restrictive than traditional probation but less severe and less costly than incarceration.

FIGURE 9.1

Mean Time Served in State Prison Compared with Mean Length of Sentence (in months) Many offenders serve a half or less of the mean sentences. Why is there such a difference between the sentence and the actual time served?

Sources: T. Bonczar, *National Corrections Reporting Program, 2006*, U.S. Bureau of Justice Statistics, May 2010, Table 8); S. Rosenmerkel, M. R. Durose, and D. Farole, "Felony Sentences in State Courts, 2006—Statistical Tables," Bureau of Justice Statistics *Bulletin*, revised version, November 22, 2010.

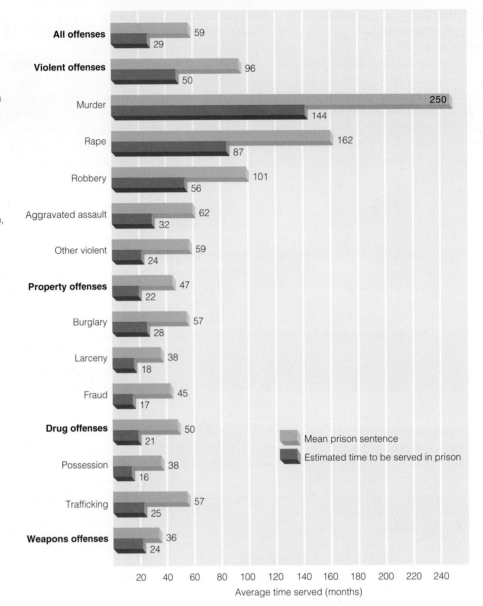

Intermediate sanctions provide a variety of restrictions on freedom, such as fines, home confinement, intensive probation supervision, restitution to victims, community service, boot camp, and forfeiture of possessions or stolen property. In 2010, Florida's Office of Program Policy Analysis and Government Accountability noted that more than 24,000 of the state's prison inmates were convicted of nonviolent offenses and had no prior convictions for violent offenses (Florida Office of Program Policy, 2010). As indicated in Table 9.2, the agency estimated that the state could enjoy substantial financial savings through the increased use of intermediate sanctions for such offenders, rather than imprisonment.

In advocating intermediate punishments, Norval Morris and Michael Tonry (1990) stipulate that these sanctions should be used not in isolation but rather in combination to reflect (1) the severity of the offense, (2) the characteristics of the offender, and (3) the needs of the community. In addition, intermediate punishments must be supported and enforced by mechanisms that take seriously any breach of the conditions of the sentence. If the law does not fulfill its promises, offenders may feel that they have "beaten" the system, which makes the punishment meaningless. Citizens who perceive any ineffectiveness in the system may develop the attitude that nothing but stiffer prison sentences will actually impose punishment.

TABLE 9.2 — Estimated Cost Savings for Florida from Increased Use of Intermediate Sanctions (based on 2009 costs)

Sanction	First–Year Cost per Offender	Total First-Year Cost for 100 Offenders[1]	Potential Savings per 100 Offenders[2]
Prison	$20,272	$2,027,200	—
Supervision with GPS monitoring	$5,121	$806,954	$1,220,246
Probation and restitution centers	$9,492	$1,639,211	$387,989
Day reporting	$4,191	$917,823	$1,109,377
Residential drug treatment	$10,539	$1,419,529	$607,671

Source: Florida Office of Program Policy Analysis and Government Accountability, *Intermediate Sanctions for Non-Violent Offenders Could Produce Savings*, Report No. 10-27, March 2010, p. 3.

[1]The first-year cost for 100 offenders is based on the actual program completion rates for 2008–2009. Offenders who do not complete the program are assumed to leave the program after 82 days and are sent to prison for the remaining 283 days of the year; the cost of prison for these offenders is included in the total first-year cost estimate.

[2]The savings for 100 offenders represents the difference between the cost of prison for one year based on $55.54 per day and the total first-year cost for intermediate sanctions.

Probation

The most frequently applied criminal sanction is **probation**, a sentence that an offender serves in the community under supervision. Nearly 60 percent of adults under correctional supervision are on probation. Ideally, under probation, offenders attempt to straighten out their lives. Probation is a judicial act granted by the grace of the state, not extended as a right. Conditions are imposed specifying how an offender will behave through the length of the sentence. Probationers may have to undergo regular drug tests, abide by curfews, enroll in educational programs or remain employed, stay away from certain people or parts of town, and meet regularly with probation officers. If probationers do not meet the required conditions, the supervising officer recommends to the court that the probation be revoked and that the remainder of the sentence be served in prison. Probation may also be revoked for commission of a new crime.

> **probation** A sentence that the offender is allowed to serve under supervision in the community.

Although probationers serve their sentences in the community, the sanction is often tied to incarceration. In some jurisdictions, the court is authorized to modify an offender's prison sentence, after a portion is served, by changing it to probation. This is often referred to as **shock probation** (or *split probation*): an offender is released after a period of incarceration (the "shock") and resentenced to probation. An offender on probation may be required to spend intermittent periods, such as weekends or nights, in jail. Whatever its specific terms, a probationary sentence will emphasize and require guidance and supervision in the community.

> **shock probation** A sentence in which the offender is released after a short incarceration and resentenced to probation.

Probation is generally advocated as a way of rehabilitating offenders whose crimes are not serious or whose past records are clean. It is viewed as less expensive yet more effective than imprisonment. For example, imprisonment may embitter youthful or first-time offenders while mixing them with hardened criminals from whom they learn more sophisticated criminal techniques.

Death

Although other Western democracies abolished the death penalty years ago, the United States continues to use it (C. E. Smith, 2010a). Capital punishment was imposed and carried out regularly prior to the late 1960s. Amid debates about the constitutionality of the death penalty and with public-opinion polls showing opposition to it, the U.S. Supreme Court suspended its use from 1968 to 1976. Eventually, however, the Court decided that capital punishment does not violate the Eighth Amendment's prohibition of cruel and unusual punishments. Executions resumed in 1977 as a majority of states began, once again, to sentence murderers to death.

During the 1980s, the number of people facing the death penalty increased steadily, with the number of people sentenced to death exceeding the number of actual executions, so that from the early 1990s onward, at any given time there have been more than 2,900 people on death rows awaiting execution. In January 2016, the total stood at 2,943 people awaiting execution in state prisons in 31 states (including two states, New Mexico and Nebraska, that have abolished capital punishment in recent years) and in federal prisons (62 offenders) and U.S. military prisons (6 offenders) (Death Penalty Information Center, 2016). Two-thirds of those on death row are in the South. The greatest numbers of death-row inmates are in California, Florida, Texas, and Alabama (see Figure 9.2).

One of the most striking contemporary developments affecting the death penalty is the decline both in the number of offenders sentenced to death each year and the number of executions actually carried out. The imposition of death sentences peaked during the period from 1994 through 1996: 312–315 offenders were sentenced to death during each of those years. Between 2006 and 2010, fewer than 126 offenders were sentenced to death annually; since 2010, the number of offenders sentenced per year has dropped to 80 or fewer. Only 49 convicted murderers were sentenced to death in 2015. Executions peaked at 98 in 1999 and then declined, so

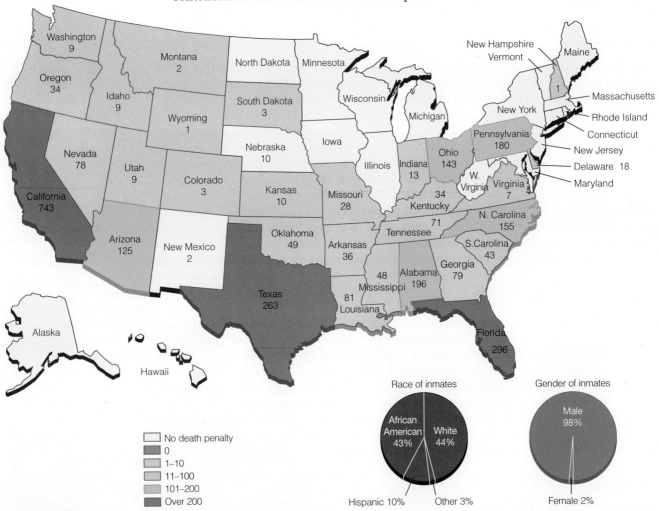

FIGURE 9.2

Death Row Census, 2016 Many of the inmates on death row are concentrated in certain states. African Americans make up about 13 percent of the U.S. population, but 43 percent of the death row population. How might you explain the higher percentage of death sentences in proportion to the population?

Note: The death penalty was abolished for future crimes in New Mexico in 2009 and in Nebraska in 2015, yet a small number of convicted murderers remain on death row in these states based on convictions prior to the elimination of capital punishment.

Source: Death Penalty Information Center, January 1, 2016, *Facts about the Death Penalty*, March 23, 2016 (www.deathpenalty.org).

there have not been more than 53 in any year since 2005. There were only 28 executions in 2015 (Death Penalty Information Center, 2016).

Many scholars attribute this trend to the heavy news media attention to the discovery and release of innocent people who had been sentenced to death (Baumgartner, Linn, & Boydstun, 2010). For example, in March 2014, Glen Ford was released after spending more than 30 years on death row in Louisiana after courts determined that prosecutors had hidden evidence and had excluded African Americans from the jury, local officials had testified falsely about evidence, and defense attorneys had failed to present expert witnesses to rebut the prosecution's case. The current prosecutor admitted that Ford had been victimized by an erroneous conviction (Cohen, 2014). Ford was the 144th person released from death row since 1973 after being found to be not guilty of the murder for which he had been sentenced to death. By the end of 2015, a total of 156 people had been exonerated after serving time on death row (Death Penalty Information Center, 2016).

Public-opinion polls indicate less support across American society for the death penalty in recent years. These statistics presumably include those Americans called for jury duty who are asked to decide whether to impose death sentences, as opposed to prison sentences, in murder cases. As you examine Figure 9.3 showing the decline in death sentences and executions since the Supreme Court's reactivation of capital punishment in 1977, bear in mind that there were more than 3,000 offenders on death row for most of this period since the early 1990s. The data merely show the trends in new sentences and executions.

Over this time period, nearly 8,000 convicted murderers were sent to death row, but only 1,431 executions occurred nationally. This gap reflects both the lengthy

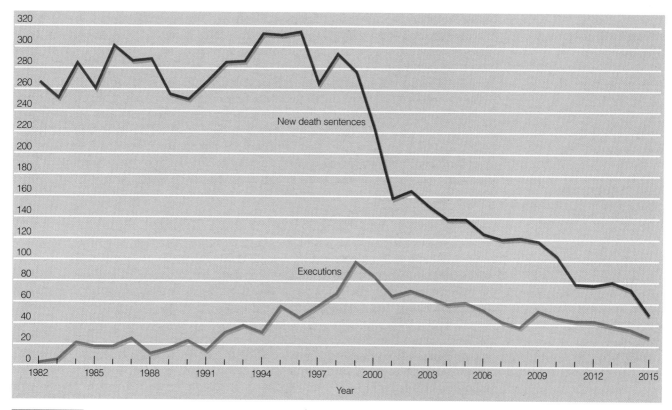

FIGURE 9.3

New Death Sentences and Executions, 1982–2015 The decline in death sentences and executions is attributed to shifts in public opinion affected by highly publicized cases of innocent people wrongly sent to death row. Does this trend indicate that the United States will eventually abolish the death penalty as the countries of Western Europe have done?

Sources: Bureau of Justice Statistics, *Sourcebook of Criminal Justice Statistics* (2016); Death Penalty Information Center, *Facts about the Death Penalty*, March 23, 2016 (www.deathpenalty.org).

appeals process that lasts many years for death penalty cases and individual states' varying commitments to actually carrying out executions. As indicated in Figure 9.2, for example, California leads the nation with 743 offenders sentenced to death, but the state has carried out only 13 executions since the resumption of the death penalty in 1977 (Death Penalty Information Center, 2016). Thus, the death penalty in California, as well as in a number of other states, is largely symbolic, as these states' governors and prosecutors have not uniformly pushed forward to see executions occur.

The states that carry out most executions are few in number. Five states—Texas, Virginia, Oklahoma, Florida, and Missouri—together account for nearly two-thirds of the total executions carried out in the United States since 1977 (Death Penalty Information Center, 2016). Texas has carried out 536 executions in that time period, demonstrating a commitment on the part of its public officials to put the punishment into practice. Indeed, in several cases, Texas has been accused of showing insufficient concern with careful reviews of cases, and there are accusations that the state may have executed one or more innocent people by failing to be careful about guarding against errors and by being unwilling to admit the possibility of errors (Mann, 2011). Thus, it appears that the political values and culture of a specific state affect not only whether the state's laws permit capital punishment but also the practical decisions that determine how frequently executions are carried out.

The Death Penalty and the Constitution

Death differs from other punishments in that it is final and irreversible. The Supreme Court has therefore examined the decision-making process in capital cases to ensure that it fulfills the Constitution's requirements regarding due process, equal protection, and cruel and unusual punishments. Because life is in the balance, capital cases must be conducted according to higher standards of fairness, using more-careful procedures than are used in other kinds of cases. Several important Supreme Court cases illustrate this concern.

In *Furman v. Georgia* (1972), the Supreme Court ruled that the death penalty, as administered, constitutes cruel and unusual punishment. The decision invalidated the death penalty laws of 39 states and the District of Columbia. A majority of justices found that the procedures used to impose death sentences were arbitrary and unfair. Over the next several years, more than three dozen states eventually enacted new capital punishment statutes that provided for different procedures in death penalty cases.

The new laws were tested before the Supreme Court in *Gregg v. Georgia* (1976). The Court upheld those laws that required the sentencing judge or jury to take into account specific aggravating and mitigating factors in deciding which convicted murderers should be sentenced to death. Further, the Court decided that, rather than having a single proceeding determine the defendant's guilt and whether the death sentence would be applied, states should use "bifurcated proceedings." In this two-part process, the defendant has first a trial that finds her or him guilty or not guilty and then a separate hearing that focuses exclusively on the issues of punishment. It seeks to ensure a thorough deliberation before someone receives the ultimate punishment.

Under the *Gregg* decision, the prosecution uses the punishment-phase hearing to focus attention on the existence of aggravating factors such as excessive cruelty or a defendant's prior record of violent crimes. The defense may focus on mitigating factors, such as the offender's youthfulness, mental condition, or lack of a criminal record. Before the judge or jury can decide to impose a death sentence, they must weigh these aggravating and mitigating factors. Because of the Court's emphasis on fair procedures and individualized decisions, state appellate courts review trial court procedures in virtually every capital case.

After *McCleskey v. Kemp* (1987), opponents of the death penalty felt disappointed that the U.S. Supreme Court failed to accept strong statistical evidence showing racial discrimination in the administration of the death penalty. In this case, the Court rejected an equal protection clause challenge to Georgia's death penalty law. Warren McCleskey, an African American, was sentenced to death for killing a white police officer. Before the U.S. Supreme Court, McCleskey's attorney cited

Furman v. Georgia (1972) The death penalty, as administered, constitutes cruel and unusual punishment.

Gregg v. Georgia (1976) Death penalty laws are constitutional if they require the judge and jury to consider certain mitigating and aggravating circumstances in deciding which convicted murderers should be sentenced to death. Proceedings must also be divided into a trial phase and a punishment phase, and there must be opportunities for appeal.

McCleskey v. Kemp (1987) The Supreme Court rejected a challenge of Georgia's death penalty on grounds of racial discrimination.

an elaborate research study that showed a disparity in the imposition of the death penalty in Georgia based on the race of the victim and, to a lesser extent, the race of the defendant (Baldus, Woodworth, & Pulaski, 1994). In particular, when African American men were murdered, there was little likelihood that the death penalty would be pursued. When an African American man was convicted of killing a white person, the likelihood of the death penalty increased dramatically (M. R. Williams, Demuth, & Holcomb, 2007).

By a five-to-four vote, the justices rejected McCleskey's assertion that Georgia's capital-sentencing practices produced racial discrimination that violated the equal protection clause of the Constitution. The slim majority of justices declared that McCleskey would have to prove that the decision makers acted with a discriminatory purpose in deciding his particular case. The Court also concluded that statistical evidence showing discrimination throughout the Georgia courts did not provide adequate proof. McCleskey was executed in 1991. The decision made it very difficult to prove the existence of racial discrimination in capital cases, because prosecutors and judges rarely make statements that openly indicate a discriminatory motive. Yet, when analyzed through the methods of social science, the patterns of decisions that determine which murderers receive the death penalty instead of imprisonment indicate that racial disparities are often present when looking at a state court system as whole. Thus, there are continuing concerns that death penalty cases can be infected with racial bias (R. N. Walker, 2006).

In June 2002, the Supreme Court broke new ground in a way that heartened opponents of the death penalty. First, in *Atkins v. Virginia* (2002), it ruled that execution of developmentally disabled individuals was unconstitutional. In the case, the Court used the older term "mentally retarded" to describe these individuals. Daryl Atkins, who has an IQ of 59, was sentenced to death for killing Eric Nesbitt in a 7-Eleven store parking lot. As the majority opinion noted, the characteristics of developmentally disabled offenders, people with IQs of less than 70, "undermine the strength of the procedural protections." This point is in keeping with the argument of mental health experts who say that their suggestibility and willingness to please leads developmentally disabled people to confess. At trial, they have problems remembering details, locating witnesses, and testifying credibly in their own behalf.

Atkins v. Virginia (2002) Execution of developmentally disabled offenders is unconstitutional.

The Supreme Court further reduced the scope of capital punishment in *Roper v. Simmons* (2005). A slim majority of justices decided that offenders cannot be sentenced to death for crimes that they committed before the age of 18. Prior to that decision, the United States was among only a half-dozen countries in the entire world with laws that permitted death sentences for juveniles. The same five-member majority also ruled that the death penalty cannot be imposed as a punishment for the crime of child rape (*Kennedy v. Louisiana,* 2008). Because the Court was deeply divided on these issues, some observers wonder if further changes in the Court's composition may lead to a reversal of these decisions.

Roper v. Simmons (2005) Execution of offenders for crimes committed while under the age of 18 is unconstitutional.

All states use lethal injection as the means to conduct executions, although a few states permit the condemned prisoners to choose the electric chair or another means that was in existence at the time of their conviction (Liptak, 2008a). Lethal injection remains a controversial method because of botched executions. In these cases, prolonged and painful deaths resulted from improperly inserted needles or malfunctioning tubes that carry the chemicals (Radelet, 2004). The constitutionality of lethal injection as a means of execution was examined by the U.S. Supreme Court in *Baze v. Rees* (2008) and *Glossip v. Gross* (2015). A majority of justices concluded that attorneys for the death row inmates had not proved that the use of lethal injection violates the Eighth Amendment. However, the death of Justice Antonin Scalia in 2016 creates the possibility that a new appointee with a critical view of the death penalty could tip the Court in a direction opposing the use of capital punishment.

New issues will arise concerning lethal injection, because the drugs used by most states for such executions are difficult to obtain and few companies manufacture them. European countries that produce a key drug and oppose the death penalty have threatened to prohibit sales of the drug in the United States. This development would have harmful effects on the American medical system, because the drug is used as anesthesia for many kinds of surgery. It remains to be seen if these drug shortages will affect the number of executions or whether states will simply change the combination of drugs used for their executions in order to use those that are more easily available. In 2014, for example, Oklahoma was forced to delay scheduled executions because it could not obtain the drugs needed for lethal injections (Bever, 2014).

The future of the death penalty's treatment by the Supreme Court will depend on such factors as who is elected president of the United States in 2016 and thereafter appoints new justices to the nation's highest court. The newest justices appointed by President Obama, Justice Sonia Sotomayor (confirmed in 2009) and Justice Elena Kagan (confirmed in 2010), were critical of lethal injection executions in *Glossip v. Gross* (2015). Two other justices, Justices Stephen Breyer and Justice Ruth Bader Ginsburg, raised questions about the constitutionality of capital punishment generally in their dissenting opinion in *Glossip*. Thus if a new appointee to replace Justice Scalia—or other appointees to replace future departing justices—adopts a similar stance, there is a possibility of Supreme Court decisions to either further limit or even eliminate capital punishment.

Continuing Legal Issues   The case law since *Furman* indicates that capital punishment is legal so long as it is imposed fairly. However, opponents continue to raise several issues in litigation and in arguments presented to legislatures and the public (Acker, 2007). Examine the "You Make the Decision" feature to consider an example of one of the many issues that can face a judge in the appellate process. As we will see, some people argue that mentally ill offenders should be ineligible for the death penalty, as are developmentally disabled and juvenile offenders.

Issues have arisen about the effectiveness of representation provided for capital defendants by defense attorneys. Many critics are concerned about the impact of jury selection processes that exclude citizens who are strongly opposed to capital punishment. Research raises questions about whether such "death-qualified" juries are more inclined to find defendants guilty and impose capital punishment (Summers, Hayward, & Miller, 2010). Other cases continue to raise issues about methods of execution and the lengthy periods that condemned offenders spend on death row because of appeals. We now look at several contemporary issues.

YOU MAKE THE DECISION

State Appellate Judge

Death penalty cases typically spend years going through the appeals process in intermediate appellate courts and courts of last resort, such as state supreme courts and the U.S. Supreme Court. You are a state supreme court justice. You previously served as the district attorney managing a large city's prosecutor's office that employs more than 200 assistant prosecutors who directly handle criminal cases. You served as the visible leader, administrator, public spokesperson, and policy maker for the prosecutor's office, but you rarely appeared in court for any cases. Now an appeal has been filed in the state supreme court from a murder case that was prosecuted more than 20 years earlier by the office that you then headed as district attorney. A lower appellate court ordered a new trial by finding that prosecutors failed to share with the defense attorney certain evidence that would have been useful to the defense at the trial. The prosecutor's office is asking the state supreme court to overrule that decision and deny a new trial. You had approved pursuing the death penalty in the case, as you had in other murder cases, but assistant prosecutors handled the actual case preparation and trial. The appeal includes a request that you recuse yourself— voluntarily withdraw from participating in deciding the appeal of the case— because of your previous role as district attorney in charge of the prosecutors who pursued the case. Given your very limited involvement in the original murder trial two decades earlier, will you recuse yourself and decline to participate with the other state supreme court justices in deciding the appeal? Give reasons for your decision. Then do an Internet search and read the U.S. Supreme Court's decision in *Williams v. Pennsylvania* (2016).

Execution of the Mentally Ill As we saw in Chapter 3, insanity is a recognized defense for commission of a crime. Moreover, the Supreme Court has said that people who become insane after entering prison cannot be executed (*Ford v. Wainwright*, 1986). But many people with mental illnesses do not meet the legal tests for insanity. They can be convicted of crimes and punished, and there is no guarantee that they will receive psychiatric treatment in prison. What happens if these people commit capital crimes? Is it appropriate to execute people whose mental illnesses may have affected their behavior? Opponents of the death penalty will undoubtedly seek to persuade the Supreme Court that mentally ill offenders should be excluded from capital punishment, following the rulings regarding developmentally disabled offenders and juveniles convicted of murder.

Effective Counsel In *Strickland v. Washington* (1984), the Supreme Court ruled that defendants in capital cases had the right to representation that meets an "objective standard of reasonableness." As noted by Justice Sandra Day O'Connor, the appellant must show that "there is a reasonable probability that, but for the counsel's unprofessional errors, the result of the proceeding would be different." Although it is possible to identify errors made by an attorney, it can be difficult to persuade judges that anything less than truly major errors actually affected the outcome of the case.

In recent decades, the public has learned of cases placing the defense attorney's competency in doubt, such as the case of a defense attorney sleeping during a murder trial. In 1999, the *Chicago Tribune* conducted an extensive investigation of capital punishment in Illinois. Reporters found that 33 defendants sentenced to death between 1977 and 1999 were represented by attorneys who had been, or were later, disbarred or suspended for conduct that was "incompetent, unethical or even criminal." These attorneys included David Landau, who was disbarred one year after representing a Will County defendant sentenced to death, and Robert McDonnell, a convicted felon and the only lawyer in Illinois to be disbarred twice. McDonnell represented four men who landed on death row (Armstrong & Mills, 1999). In subsequent decades, serious concerns have emerged about other cases in which defendants facing murder charges may have received inadequate representation (Armstrong, 2014). Such cases may affect the public's view on fairness, as indicated in "What Americans Think."

One highly publicized case highlighting the need for competent defense in capital cases caught the attention of the Supreme Court in 2003. In *Wiggins v. Smith* (2003), the Court found that the Sixth Amendment right to counsel was violated when a defense attorney failed to present mitigating evidence concerning the severe physical and sexual abuse suffered by the defendant during childhood. Whether the justices ever create clearer or stricter standards for defense attorneys remains to be seen.

Death-Qualified Juries Should people who are opposed to the death penalty be excluded from juries in capital cases? In *Witherspoon v. Illinois* (1968), the Supreme Court held that potential jurors who have general objections to the death penalty or who oppose it on the basis of religious conviction cannot be automatically excluded from jury service in capital cases. However, it upheld the practice of removing, during voir dire (preliminary examination), those people whose opposition is so strong as to

WHAT AMERICANS THINK

QUESTION: Do you favor or oppose the death penalty?

Group	Favor	Oppose
National	56%	38%
Men	64%	30%
Women	49%	45%
White	63%	33%
African American	34%	57%
Hispanic	45%	47%
Republican	77%	17%
Democrat	40%	56%

■ Favor death penalty
■ Oppose death penalty

CRITICAL THINKING: Why do you think opinions about the death penalty differ among demographic groups?

Source: "Less Support for Death Penalty, Especially among Democrats," Pew Research Center, April 16, 2015 (www.people-press.org).

Witherspoon v. Illinois (1968)
Potential jurors who object to the death penalty cannot be automatically excluded from service; however, during voir dire, those who feel so strongly about capital punishment that they could not give an impartial verdict may be excluded.

"prevent or substantially impair the performance of their duties." Such jurors have become known as "*Witherspoon* excludables." The decision was later reaffirmed in *Lockhart v. McCree* (1986).

Because society is divided on capital punishment, opponents argue that death-qualified juries do not represent a cross section of the community (Summers, Hayward, & Miller, 2010). Researchers have also found that "juries are likely to be nudged toward believing the defendant is guilty and toward an imposition of the death sentence by the very process of undergoing death qualification" (Luginbuhl & Burkhead, 1994:107).

Mark Costanzo (1997) points to research indicating that death qualification has several impacts. First, those who are selected for jury duty are more prone to convict and more receptive to aggravating factors presented during the penalty phase. A second, subtler impact is that jurors answering the questions about their willingness to vote for a death sentence often conclude that both defenders and prosecutors anticipate a conviction and a death sentence.

The Death Penalty: A Continuing Controversy Various developments in the twenty-first century appear to indicate a weakening of support for capital punishment in the United States. New York's capital punishment law was declared unconstitutional by its own state courts in 2004. The New Jersey state legislature and governor eliminated the death penalty in that state in 2007. Subsequently, the legislature of New Mexico voted to abolish capital punishment (Urbina, 2009). In March 2011, the governor of Illinois signed a law that eliminated capital punishment. He also commuted the sentences of the 15 offenders on death row so that they will now serve sentences of life without parole (Schwartz & Fitzsimmons, 2011). In 2012, Connecticut's legislature and governor abolished capital punishment for future crimes. Maryland's legislature and governor took the same step in 2013 (Witte, 2013). In March 2014, the New Hampshire House of Representatives voted to abolish capital punishment as the first step toward the possible end of the death penalty in that state, but the repeal of capital punishment narrowly failed to gain approval in the Senate (Tuohy, 2014). In Nebraska, Democratic and Republican senators joined to override the governor's veto of a bill to abolish capital punishment in 2015 (Bosman, 2015).

Concerns about the conviction of innocent people may lead some other states to reconsider the use of capital punishment. In addition, the extraordinary costs of capital trials and appeals are likely to deter many states from seeking to use the punishment widely in murder cases. Small counties are typically responsible for the costs of trials in their jurisdictions, and they frequently cannot afford to seek the death penalty in murder cases, as these trials can last for weeks and require the services of expensive scientific testing and expert witnesses. On the other hand, a future terrorism attack on the United States may intensify public support for capital punishment and spur efforts to expand the penalty. Thus, it remains to be seen whether the nation will continue to see diminishing use of the death penalty.

Although public-opinion polls still reflect significant support for the death penalty, the number of executions remains low. A Gallup Poll in October 2013 found that support for sentencing convicted murderers to death had

Prisoners sentenced to death typically must wait several years as their cases move through the appeals process. Randy Halprin was among a group of Texas prison escapees who killed a police officer during a robbery in 2000. His final unsuccessful appeal in the Texas Court of Criminal Appeals was decided in 2013. As of early 2016, he had not been executed. Should appeals in death penalty cases be accelerated in order to speed up executions, or would speedy appeals increase the risk of executing an innocent person?

AP Images/Brett Coomer

dropped from a high of 80 percent of Americans in the mid-1990s to only 60 percent in 2013 (J. Jones, 2013). Recent surveys show that the public is split when asked to choose between life imprisonment (without parole) and death. When poll respondents know that a sentence of life without parole is available to apply to convicted murderers, then only 49 percent support death penalty sentences (Newport, 2010). Does this mean that Americans are ambivalent about carrying out the punishment? What might it say about capital punishment in the next decade? Debate on this important public-policy issue has gone on for more than two hundred years, yet there is still no consensus (see "The Policy Debate" for more).

The criminal sanction takes many forms, with offenders punished in various ways to serve various purposes. Table 9.3 summarizes how these sanctions operate and how they reflect the underlying philosophies of punishment.

TABLE 9.3	The Punishment of Offenders

The goals of the criminal sanction are carried out in a variety of ways, depending upon the provisions of the law, the characteristics of the offender, and the discretion of the judge. Judges may impose sentences that combine several forms to achieve punishment objectives.

Form of Sanction	Description	Purposes
Incarceration	Imprisonment	
Indeterminate sentence	Specifies a maximum and minimum length of time to be served	Incapacitation, deterrence, rehabilitation
Determinate sentence	Specifies a certain length of time to be served	Retribution, deterrence, incapacitation
Mandatory sentence	Specifies a minimum amount of time that must be served for given crimes	Incapacitation, deterrence
Good time	Subtracts days from an inmate's sentence to reward good behavior or participation in prison programs	Rewards behavior, relieves prison crowding, helps maintain prison discipline
Intermediate sanctions	Punishment for those requiring sanctions more restrictive than probation but less restrictive than prison	Retribution, deterrence
Administered by the judiciary		
Fine	Money paid to state by offender	Retribution, deterrence
Restitution	Money paid to victim by offender	Retribution, deterrence
Forfeiture	Seizure by the state of property illegally obtained or acquired with resources illegally obtained	Retribution, deterrence
Administered in the community		
Community service	Requires offender to perform work for the community	Retribution, deterrence
Home confinement	Requires offender to stay in home during certain times	Retribution, deterrence, incapacitation
Intensive probation supervision	Requires strict and frequent reporting to probation officer	Retribution, deterrence, incapacitation
Administered institutionally		
Boot camp/shock incarceration	Short-term institutional sentence emphasizing physical development and discipline, followed by probation	Retribution, deterrence, rehabilitation
Probation	Allows offender to serve a sentence in the community under supervision	Retribution, incapacitation, rehabilitation
Death	Execution	Incapacitation, deterrence, retribution

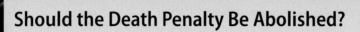

THE POLICY DEBATE

Should the Death Penalty Be Abolished?

The applicability of the death penalty has diminished in the twenty-first century. The U.S. Supreme Court reduced the applicability of capital punishment by excluding the developmentally disabled and juveniles from executions. In 2011, the Illinois legislature and Governor Pat Quinn approved legislation to end capital punishment in that state, just as New Jersey did in 2007 and New Mexico in 2009. Connecticut did the same in 2012, as did Maryland in 2013 and Nebraska in 2015.

Opponents of capital punishment continue the fight to abolish it. They argue that poor people and minorities receive a disproportionate number of death sentences. They also believe that executing people who are teenage, insane, or developmentally disabled is barbaric.

Even the proponents of capital punishment remain dissatisfied with how it is applied. They point to the fact that although more than 2,900 convicted murderers wait on death row, the number of executions since 1976 has never exceeded 98 per year and has declined through the first years of the twenty-first century. The appeals process is a major factor halting this pace, given that it can delay executions for years.

For the Death Penalty

Supporters argue that society should apply swift, severe punishments to killers to address the continuing problems of crime and violence. Execution should occur quite soon after conviction to maximize its value as a deterrent. Justice requires that we execute one person who murders another; to do less is to denigrate the value of human life.

The arguments for the death penalty include the following:

- The death penalty deters criminals from committing violent acts.
- The death penalty achieves justice by paying killers back for their horrible crimes.
- The death penalty prevents criminals from doing further harm while on parole.
- The death penalty is less expensive than holding murderers in prison for life.

Against the Death Penalty

Opponents believe that the death penalty lingers as a barbaric practice from a less civilized age. They point out that most other developed democracies in the world have ceased to execute criminals. Opponents challenge the death penalty's claims for effectiveness in reducing crime. They also raise concerns about whether the punishment can be applied without errors and discrimination.

The arguments against the death penalty include the following:

- No hard evidence proves that the death penalty is a deterrent.
- It is wrong for a government to participate in the intentional killing of citizens.

- The death penalty is applied in a discriminatory fashion.
- Innocent people have been sentenced to death.
- Some methods of execution are inhumane, causing painful, lingering deaths.

What Should U.S. Policy Be?

With people every year still being sentenced to death, but fewer than 50 individuals executed, death penalty policy is at a significant crossroads. Will the United States increase the pace of executions; allow the number of capital offenders in prison to keep growing; or take a middle ground that satisfies neither side completely, such as life imprisonment without parole for convicted murderers?

Researching the Internet

Compare the perspectives presented at the websites of Pro-Death Penalty and the Death Penalty Information Center. You can access them both by going to http://www.prodeathpenalty.com/ and http://www.deathpenaltyinfo.org/.

Analyzing the Issue

Evaluate the pros and cons of the death penalty debate. What political factors might influence your state's legislators to abolish, modify, or retain the death penalty?

CHECK POINT

3. What are the three types of sentences used in the United States?
Determinate, indeterminate, and mandatory sentences.

4. What are thought to be the advantages of intermediate sanctions?
Intermediate sanctions give judges a greater range of sentencing alternatives, reduce prison populations, cost less than prison, and increase community security.

5. What requirements specified in *Gregg v. Georgia* must exist before a death sentence can be imposed?
Judge and jury must be able to consider mitigating and aggravating circumstances, proceedings must be divided into a trial phase and a punishment phase, and there must be opportunities for appeal.

STOP & ANALYZE

Which goals of punishment are advanced by intermediate sanctions? Do intermediate sanctions adequately advance those goals? Imagine that you are a state legislator. For which crimes would you vote to authorize the use of intermediate sanctions? Which goals would you be seeking to advance with those punishments?

The Sentencing Process

Regardless of how and where guilt has been determined—misdemeanor court or felony court, plea bargain or adversarial context, bench or jury trial—judges hold the responsibility for imposing sentences. Often difficult, sentencing usually involves more than applying clear-cut principles to individual cases. In one case, a judge may decide to sentence a forger to prison as an example to others, even though the offender poses no threat to community safety and probably does not need rehabilitative treatment. In another case, the judge may impose a light sentence on a youthful offender who has committed a serious crime but may be a candidate for rehabilitation if moved quickly back into society.

Legislatures establish the penal codes that set forth the sentences judges can impose. These laws generally give judges discretion in sentencing. However, there may be specific requirements that can tie the hands of judges for specific crimes or offenders. As mentioned previously concerning mandatory minimums, legislatures may specify required sentences for certain crimes. In particular, some legislatures, including Congress, have mandated specific added time periods in prison for crimes committed with firearms (P. J. Cook, 2013). In effect, these sentencing laws appear to have both deterrent and incapacitative objectives with respect to the use of guns for criminal purposes. Such laws seek to impose the legislature's sentencing expectations in specific cases. What would happen if sentencing practices were guided by research findings rather than by legislature's commands or judges' personal discretion? Read the "Evidence-Based Practice and Policy" feature to consider this question.

Judges may combine various forms of punishment in order to tailor the sanction to the offender. The judge may specify, for example, that the prison terms for two charges are to run either concurrently (at the same time) or consecutively (one after the other) or that all or part of the period of imprisonment may be suspended. In other situations, the offender may receive a combination of a suspended prison term, a fine, and probation. Judges may suspend a sentence as long as the offender stays out of trouble, makes restitution, or seeks medical treatment. They may also delay imposing any sentence but retain the power to set penalties at a later date if the offender misbehaves.

In misdemeanor cases, judges' sentencing decisions may be influenced by many factors, including the defendant's remorse, the availability of space for new offenders in the county jail, and the defendant's prior record. Is it important for judges to impose comparable sentences on offenders who are convicted of similar crimes?

Within the discretion allowed by the code, various elements influence the decisions of judges (B. D. Johnson, 2006). Social scientists believe that several factors influence the sentencing process: (1) the administrative context of the courts, (2) the attitudes and values of judges, (3) the presentence report, and (4) sentencing guidelines.

EVIDENCE-BASED PRACTICE AND POLICY

Evidence-Based Sentencing

The Center for Sentencing Initiatives of the National Center for State Courts advocates that states consider implementing evidence-based sentencing practices. The purpose of evidence-based sentencing (EBS) is to reduce recidivism. When criminal punishments are designed with consideration for the goal of reducing reoffending, states may benefit from both a reduction in crime and a potential reduction in the costs associated with sending convicted offenders to prison. The use of EBS is not intended to determine the appropriate severity of punishments for specific offenses. Instead, it is an approach designed to provide useful information to judges so that they can evaluate potential supervision and treatment conditions that may reduce the risk that the offender will commit future crimes.

As described by the Center for Sentencing Initiatives, evidence-based sentencing relies on the Risk-Need-Responsivity (RNR) model for the identification of important principles to reduce recidivism. The first principle, Risk, posits that treatment and supervision should be tailored to the risk posed by the offenders, with higher-risk offenders requiring more significant supervision and services. The second principle, Need, holds that treatments should be designed to address the specific factors that may contribute to the risk that a specific individual will reoffend. The third principle, Responsivity, recognizes that individuals will have differing characteristics, education levels, and abilities; therefore specific teaching, learning, and treatment approaches need to be considered for each individual.

The risk element is evaluated through assessment tools, including interview questions and the evaluation of documents on the "static factors" associated with individual offenders' lives, such as their criminal history and age at first offense, that cannot be changed through treatment. In addition, information is compiled about "dynamic risk factors," such as antisocial attitudes, that can potentially be changed through appropriate treatment and services. Judges can use this information to incorporate into punishment decisions considerations about reducing the risk of recidivism as determinations are made about available intermediate sanctions and services for those offenders who do not require incarceration based on severity of offense or threat to public safety.

Advocates of EBS note that additional elements and practices must be in place when risk-related information is used at sentencing in an attempt to reduce reoffending.

For example, judges, probation officers, prosecutors, and defense attorneys need to cooperate and coordinate their focus on the likelihood that the offender will change his or her behavior. In addition, EBS needs to integrate services and sanctions with a recognition that supervision alone, without treatment and services, will have only limited prospects for successfully altering behavior beyond the period of the sanction. Judges also need to be role models who use court hearings to encourage offenders to develop personal motivation to change. When judges are perceived by offenders to be caring, polite, and encouraging, as opposed to threatening and shaming, it is less likely that offenders will respond to sentencing and supervision with resistance and hostile attitudes.

Researching the Internet

Read about the recommendations made by the Center for Sentencing Initiatives at the website of the National Center for State Courts, http://www.ncsc.org/~/media/Microsites/Files/CSI/EBS%20Fact%20Sheet%208-27-14.ashx.

Implementing New Practices

Evidence-based sentencing reflects an effort to incorporate a rehabilitative focus into the design of criminal sanctions. Is this an appropriate job for judges? Do judges know enough about the causes of criminal behavior to accurately apply information from the EBS process to their attempts to tailor an appropriate sanction that will simultaneously punish and reduce the risk of reoffending? If you were the governor of a state, would you recommend that new laws require judges to use EBS? Give three reasons for the decision you would make as a governor.

Sources: P. M. Casey, R. K. Warren, and J. K. Elek, *Using Offender Risk and Needs Assessment Information at Sentencing: Guidance for Courts from a National Working Group*, National Center for State Courts, 2011; Center for Sentencing Initiatives, *NCSC Fact Sheet: Evidence-Based Sentencing*, National Center for State Courts, August 2014; Pew Center on the States, *Arming the Courts with Research: 10 Evidence-Based Sentencing Initiatives to Control Crime and Reduce Costs*, Public Safety Policy Brief No. 8, May 2009; R. K. Warren, "Evidence-Based Sentencing: The Application of Principles of Evidence-Based Practice to State Sentencing Practice and Policy," *University of San Francisco Law Review* 43 (2009): 585–634.

The Administrative Context of the Courts

Judges are strongly influenced by the administrative context within which they impose sentences. As a result, differences are found, for example, between the assembly-line style of justice in misdemeanor courts and the more formal proceedings in felony courts.

Misdemeanor Courts: Assembly-Line Justice

Misdemeanor or lower courts have limited jurisdiction because typically they can impose no greater punishment than jail sentences of less than one year. These courts hear about 90 percent of criminal cases. Whereas felony cases are processed in lower courts only for arraignments and preliminary hearings, misdemeanor cases are processed completely in the lower courts. Only a minority of cases adjudicated in lower courts end in jail sentences. Most cases result in fines, probation, community service, restitution, or a combination of these.

Most lower courts are overloaded and therefore allot minimal time to each case. Judicial decisions are mass-produced because actors in the system share three assumptions: First, any person appearing before the court is guilty, because the police and prosecution have presumably filtered out doubtful cases. Second, the vast majority of defendants will plead guilty. Third, those charged with minor offenses will be processed in volume, with dozens of cases being decided in rapid succession within a single hour. The citation will be read by the clerk, a guilty plea entered, and the sentence pronounced by the judge for one defendant after another.

Defendants whose cases are processed through the lower court's assembly line may appear to receive little or no punishment. However, a person who is arrested but eventually released still incurs various tangible and intangible costs. Time spent in jail awaiting trial, the cost of a bail bond, and days of work lost create an immediate and concrete impact. Poor people may lose their jobs or be evicted from their homes if they fail to work and pay their bills for even a few days. For most people, simply being arrested is a devastating experience. It is impossible to measure the psychological and social price of being stigmatized, separated from family, and deprived of freedom.

The sentencing practices of misdemeanor courts drew national attention when the U.S. Department of Justice issued a report in 2015 on practices in Ferguson, Missouri, that reflected racial bias and favoritism. Read the "Current Controversies" feature to evaluate the problems illuminated by the Justice Department report.

CURRENT CONTROVERSIES IN CRIMINAL JUSTICE

Improperly Running a Local Justice System to Make Money for a City

The public anger and protests in Ferguson, Missouri, after the fatal shooting of unarmed teenager Michael Brown by Officer Darren Wilson in 2014 did not merely reflect objections to the specific incident and the failure to charge with Wilson with a crime; they also flowed from long-standing complaints about unfair treatment of African Americans in Ferguson by police officers and the municipal court. In response to the national attention to civil disorder in Ferguson, the U.S. Department of Justice launched two investigations. One investigation found that federal prosecutors lacked a basis to charge Wilson with a federal crime for any provable racial motive or clear denial of Brown's rights. The other investigation looked more broadly at police and court practices in Ferguson. The second investigation resulted in a scathing report that documented frequently used police practices that violated citizens' rights with unjustified stops, searches, arrests, and applications of force. This second investigation also found that the municipal court worked with the police department to intentionally use municipal code citations, fines, and jailing as mechanisms to improperly produce revenue to fund city government. While Americans typically expect judges and courts to be guardians of the law in order to advance equal justice, the Justice Department report painted a picture of a court operation that appeared to disregard principles of law in order to advance the interests of city officials.

continued

Current Controversies in Criminal Justice (*continued*)

- Statistics showed that Ferguson police officers primarily targeted African American residents for traffic and other citations, often with the intent of writing as many tickets as possible in a single traffic stop. African Americans comprise 67 percent of the population but received 90 percent of the citations and were subject to 93 percent of the arrests. Burdensome fines imposed by the court multiplied and increased as poor people, in particular, had difficulty paying on time. For example, one woman "received two parking tickets for a single violation in 2007 that totaled $151 plus fees. Over seven years later, she still owed Ferguson $541—after already paying $550 in fines and fees, having multiple arrest warrants issued against her, and being arrested and jailed on several occasions" (U.S. Department of Justice, 2015).
- City officials specifically communicated to the police department their desire to increase city revenue through issuing more citations.
- While the municipal court lacked the legal authority to impose a fine over $1,000 for any offense, it was not uncommon for individuals who were unable to pay their fines on time to end up paying for more than $1,000 to the city in additional court fees, additional citations for failure to appear in court, and forfeited bail payments.
- The federal report found that the municipal court failed to give individuals adequate notice of allegations against them and an opportunity to be heard. When citizens and their attorneys attempted to present arguments in court against the basis for their treatment by the police and the citations issued, they reportedly faced retaliation from the judge and prosecutor. In one example, an attorney was repeatedly interrupted by the judge during trial and was threatened with being jailed for contempt of court for daring to object to the judge's interruptions, thus stopping the attorney from thoroughly questioning a police officer who had been found to be untruthful in a prior case.
- There were reportedly needlessly complicated court processes that provided opportunities for court officials to increase the number of fines imposed on individuals: "We have heard repeated reports, and found evidence in court records, of people appearing in court many times—in some instances on more than ten occasions—to try to resolve a case but being unable to do so and subsequently having additional fines, fees, and arrest warrants issued against them" (U.S. Department of Justice, 2015). Moreover, police officers frequently gave people incorrect dates and times for their court appearances, thus leading to the risk of additional fines even when the citizens followed the officers' instructions.
- Ferguson imposed exceptionally high fines for offenses as compared to the fines imposed for the same offenses in nearby St. Louis suburbs. For example, Ferguson fined people $375 for failing to show proof of auto insurance while the median fine for this offense in nearby communities was $175.
- The Ferguson court issued an extraordinary number of arrest warrants as a means to secure payment for fines rather than to protect public safety: over 9,000 warrants issued in fiscal year 2013 in a community with a population of 21,000 people. In addition, bail amounts set for people to gain release from jail were haphazard and inconsistent with the city's own policies. People arrested for failure to pay minor municipal fines were routinely held in jail for three days and could be rearrested and held again when they were unable to pay.
- A city council member complained that a part-time municipal judge "does not listen to testimony, does not review the reports or the criminal history of defendants, and doesn't let all the pertinent witnesses testify before rendering a verdict." However, the city manager retained the judge by emphasizing his role in collecting money for the city. According to the city manager, "the city cannot afford to lose any efficiency in our courts, nor experience any decrease in fines and forfeitures" (Yokley & Eligon, 2015).
- As the courts were imposing unfair hardships on poor African Americans in order to fund city government, court officials fixed tickets for city officials so that they would not have to pay the fines being imposed on other members of the community. In addition, a newspaper investigation found that the part-time judge deeply involved in fining and jailing the defendants, who were overwhelmingly African Americans, for their failure to pay accumulating fines for municipal offenses, was himself behind in paying his federal income taxes. He owed the federal government a reported $170,000—but unlike the poor people who owed a few hundred dollars to Ferguson, he was not subject to the arrest and jailing that he helped to impose on others.

For Critical Thinking and Analysis

Critics argued that Ferguson, Missouri, created a "debtors' prison" environment that punished poor people for their inability to pay and constantly increased their financial burdens for minor offenses solely to generate money for city government. Write a memo that describes specific steps you would recommend to achieve fairness and equal justice by reforming the approach to policing and punishment taken by Ferguson, Missouri, police, prosecutors, and court officials.

Sources: H. Bruinius, "Does Ferguson Run 'Debtor's Prison'? Lawsuit Targets a Source of Unrest," *Christian Science Monitor*, February 9, 2014 (www.csmonitor.com); J. Eligon, "Ferguson City Manager Cited in Justice Department Report Resigns," *New York Times*, March 10, 2015 (www.nytimes .com); C. Robertson, "A City Where Policing, Discrimination and Raising Revenue Went Hand in Hand," *New York Times*, March 4, 2015 (www.nytimes.com); J. Swaine, "Ferguson Judge behind Aggressive Fines Policy Resigns as City's Court System Seized," *The Guardian*, March 9, 2015 (www.theguardian.com); U.S. Department of Justice, *Investigation of Ferguson Police Department*, Civil Rights Division, U.S. Department of Justice, March 4, 2015; E. Yokley and J. Eligon, "Missouri Court Assigns a State Judge to Handle Ferguson Cases," *New York Times*, March 9, 2015 (www.nytimes.com).

Felony Courts   Felony cases are processed and felony offenders are sentenced in courts of general jurisdiction. Because of the seriousness of the crimes, the atmosphere is more formal and generally lacks the chaotic, assembly-line environment of misdemeanor courts. Caseload burdens can affect how much time individual cases receive. Exchange relationships among courtroom actors can facilitate plea bargains and shape the content of prosecutors' sentencing recommendations. Sentencing decisions are ultimately shaped, in part, by the relationships, negotiations, and agreements among the prosecutor, defense attorney, and judge. Table 9.4 shows the types of felony sentences imposed for conviction on different charges.

Attitudes and Values of Judges

All lawyers recognize that judges differ from one another in their sentencing decisions. Administrative pressures, the conflicting goals of criminal justice, and the influence of community values partly explain these differences. Sentencing decisions also depend on judges' attitudes concerning the offender's blameworthiness, the protection of the community, and the practical implications of the sentence (Steffensmeier & Demuth, 2001).

Blameworthiness concerns such factors as offense severity (such as violent crime or property crime), the offender's criminal history (such as recidivist or first-timer), and role in commission of the crime (such as leader or follower). For example, a judge might impose a harsh sentence on a repeat offender who organized others to commit a serious crime.

Protection of the community hinges on similar factors, such as dangerousness, recidivism, and offense severity. However, it centers mostly on the need to incapacitate the offender or to deter would-be offenders.

Finally, the practical implications of a sentence can affect judges' decisions. For example, judges may take into account the offender's diminished ability to "do time," as in the case of an elderly person. They may also consider the impact on the offender's family; a mother with children may receive a different sentence than

TABLE 9.4	Types of Felony Sentences Imposed by State Courts

Although a felony conviction is often equated with a prison sentence, almost a third of felony offenders receive probation.

Most Serious Conviction Offense	Percentage of Felons Sentenced to		
	Prison	Jail	Probation
All offenses	41	28	27
Murder	93	2	3
Rape	72	15	10
Robbery	71	14	13
Burglary	49	24	24
Larceny	34	34	28
Drug possession	33	31	30
Drug trafficking	41	26	29
Weapons offenses	45	28	25

Note: For persons receiving a combination of sanctions, the sentence designation came from the most severe penalty imposed—prison being the most severe, followed by jail, and then probation. Rows do not add up to 100% because a small percentage of offenders for each crime were sentenced to other nonincarceration sanctions.

Source: S. Rosenmerkel, M. R. Durose, and D. Farole Jr., "Felony Sentences in State Courts, 2006—Statistical Tables," *Bureau of Justice Statistics Statistical Tables*, December 2009, p. 4.

Judges and Sentencing

Grammy award-winning singer Lauryn Hill went to the Newark, New Jersey, federal courthouse in May 2013 to learn what punishment she would receive after pleading guilty for the crime of failing to file tax returns for three years. She faced the possibility of 24 to 36 months in prison for failing to pay taxes on $1.8 million in income (Wood, 2013). Her attorney had argued that she should be sentenced to probation, because she had paid all of her back taxes and penalties prior to the sentencing hearing. However, U.S. Magistrate Judge Madeline Cox Arleo sentenced Hill to three months in prison to be followed by three months of house arrest (McKinley, 2013). Did she receive an appropriate sentence for her crime? Was it too harsh, considering that she had already paid what she owed? Alternatively, was it too lenient because she is an affluent celebrity who could afford to pay what she owed quickly after admitting guilt? Would others facing the same charges be treated the same way?

One way to evaluate Hill's sentence is to compare it with sentences received by offenders convicted of the same crimes. For example, also in 2013, actor Stephen Baldwin pleaded guilty to failing to pay taxes for three years. However, Baldwin admitted to violating New York state laws rather than federal tax laws, as Hill had done. Although Baldwin paid only $100,000 of the $400,000 that he owed to New York prior to his sentencing hearing, he received a sentence of probation with the promise that his criminal record would be erased if he paid the entire amount within one year (Martinez, 2013). However, failure to pay within one year would extend his period of probation to five years and keep his criminal record intact (D'Zurilla, 2013a). His crime was virtually the same as Hill's, yet Baldwin would face no time behind bars and could get his record erased because he was convicted under a different set of laws—state instead of federal—and he also was sentenced in a different court by a different judge.

By contrast, in the same spring months in which Hill and Baldwin faced their sentencing hearings in 2013, movie actor Wesley Snipes was released to a supervised residential facility after spending three years in prison for the very same charge: failure to file tax returns for three years (D'Zurilla, 2013b; Wood, 2013). Why did Snipes receive such a severe sentence? Many observers believe that there is a trial penalty in the form of harsher sentences for defendants who insist on going to trial rather than entering a guilty plea. Unlike Hill and Baldwin, who entered guilty pleas, Snipes was convicted after a highly publicized jury trial. He claimed that he was not guilty because he had relied on bad advice from financial advisors. In addition, Snipes failed to file a tax return and pay federal taxes during a period in which he earned an estimated $40 million, an amount far larger than the incomes of Hill and Baldwin during their periods of nonpayment (D'Zurilla, 2013b). Are the three celebrity tax offenders' differing sentences understandable, appropriate, and fair? Such questions are often the subject of debate.

Researching the Internet

Look at the website of the U.S. Sentencing Commission to see what percentage of convicted tax offenders are sentenced to probation and the average sentence for tax offenders sentenced to prison: http://www.ussc.gov/.

For Critical Thinking and Analysis

Write down the sentences that you would have given Hill, Baldwin, and Snipes in order to achieve justice. Write a brief explanation for each sentence. What punishment goals are advanced by the sentences that you designed?

a single woman would. Finally, costs to the corrections system may play a role in sentencing, as judges consider probation officers' caseloads or prison crowding (Steffensmeier, Kramer, & Streifel, 1993). The "Close Up" gives examples of judges' sentencing decisions in prominent cases.

Presentence Report

presentence report A report, prepared by a probation officer, that presents a convicted offender's background and is used by the judge in selecting an appropriate sentence.

Even though sentencing is the judge's responsibility, the **presentence report** has become an important ingredient in the judicial mix. Usually a probation officer investigates the convicted person's background, criminal record, job status, and mental condition to suggest a sentence that is in the interests of both the offender and society. Although the presentence report serves primarily to help the judge select the sentence, it also assists in the classification of probationers, prisoners, and parolees for treatment planning and risk assessment. In the report, the probation officer makes judgments about what information to include and what conclusions to draw from that information. In some states, however, probation officers present only factual material to the judge and make no sentencing recommendations. Because the probation officers do not necessarily follow evidentiary rules, they may include hearsay statements as well as firsthand information.

In the federal court system, the presentence report is supplemented by an additional report written by a *pretrial services officer* (*PSO*). This report focuses on the defendant's behavior and compliance with conditions while out on bail—prior to trial or plea or between the date of conviction and the date of sentencing.

The presentence report is one means by which judges ease the strain of decision making. Because a substantial number of sentencing alternatives are open to judges, they often rely on the report for guidance. The report lets judges shift partial responsibility to the probation department.

Sentencing Guidelines

Since the 1980s, **sentencing guidelines** have been established in the federal courts and in more than two dozen states. Such guidelines indicate to judges the expected sanction for particular types of offenses. They are intended to limit the sentencing discretion of judges and to reduce disparity among sentences given for similar offenses. Although statutes provide a variety of sentencing options for particular crimes, guidelines attempt to direct the judge to more specific actions that should be taken. The range of sentencing options provided for most offenses centers on the seriousness of the crime and on the criminal history of an offender.

Legislatures—and in some states and in the federal government, commissions—construct sentencing guidelines as a grid of two scores (Tonry, 1993). As shown in the Minnesota Guidelines portrayed in Table 9.5, one dimension relates to the seriousness of the offense, the other to the likelihood of offender recidivism. The offender score is obtained by totaling the points allocated to such factors as the number of juvenile offenses, adult misdemeanors, and adult felony convictions; the number of times incarcerated; the status of the accused at the time of the last offense, whether on probation or parole or escaped from confinement; and employment status or educational achievement. Judges look at the grid to see what sentence should be imposed on a particular offender who has committed a specific offense. Judges may go outside the guidelines if aggravating or mitigating circumstances exist; however, they must provide a written explanation of their reasons for doing so (Fischman & Schanzenbach, 2011).

Sentencing guidelines are to be reviewed and modified periodically so that recent decisions will be included. Given that guidelines are constructed on the basis of past sentences, some critics argue that they do not reform sentencing. Others question the choice of characteristics included in the offender scale and charge that some are used to mask racial criteria. Although guidelines make sentences more uniform, many judges object to having their discretion limited in this manner (Zimmerman, 2011). However, Peter Rossi and Richard Berk (1997) found a fair amount of agreement between the sentences prescribed in the federal guidelines and those desired by the general public.

The future of sentencing guidelines is uncertain. In 2004, the U.S. Supreme Court decided that aspects of Washington State sentencing guidelines violated the Sixth Amendment right to trial by jury by giving judges too much authority to enhance sentences based on unproved factual determinations (*Blakely v. Washington*). One year later the Supreme Court applied the *Blakely* precedent to the federal sentencing guidelines and found a similar violation of the Sixth Amendment when judges enhance sentences based on their own determinations (*United States v. Booker,* 2005). In effect, federal judges are expected to consult the guidelines, but they are not mandatory, and federal judges can make reasonable deviations (Wu & Spohn, 2010). In 2008, the Supreme Court ruled that federal judges are not required to give advance notice to defendants prior to imposing a sentence that

sentencing guideline A mechanism to indicate to judges the expected sanction for certain offenses, in order to reduce disparities in sentencing.

TABLE 9.5   Minnesota Sentencing Guidelines Grid (presumptive sentence length in months)

The italicized numbers in the grid are the range within which a judge may sentence without the sentence being considered a departure. The criminal-history score is computed by adding one point for each prior felony conviction, one-half point for each prior gross-misdemeanor conviction, and one-quarter point for each prior misdemeanor conviction.

Severity of Offense (Illustrative Offenses)		Less Serious ⟵ Criminal-History Score ⟶ More Serious						
		0	1	2	3	4	5	6 or more
Murder, second degree (intentional murder, drive-by shootings)	XI	306 *261–367*	326 *278–391*	346 *295–415*	366 *312–439*	386 *329–463*	406 *346–480*	426 *363–480*
Murder, third degree Murder, second degree (unintentional murder)	X	150 *128–180*	165 *141–198*	180 *153–216*	195 *166–234*	210 *179–252*	225 *192–270*	240 *204–288*
Assault, first degree Controlled substance crime, first degree	IX	86 *74–103*	98 *84–117*	110 *94–132*	122 *104–146*	134 *114–160*	146 *125–175*	158 *135–189*
Aggravated robbery, first degree Controlled substance crime, second degree	VIII	48 *41–57*	58 *50–69*	68 *58–81*	78 *67–93*	88 *75–105*	98 *84–117*	108 *92–129*
Felony DWI	VII	36	42	48	54 *46–64*	60 *51–72*	66 *57–79*	72 *62–84*
Controlled substance crime, third degree	VI	21	27	33	39 *34–46*	45 *39–54*	51 *44–61*	57 *49–68*
Residential burglary Simple robbery	V	18	23	28	33 *29–39*	38 *33–45*	43 *37–51*	48 *41–57*
Nonresidential burglary	IV	12	15	18	21	24 *21–28*	27 *23–32*	30 *26–36*
Theft crimes (over $5,000)	III	12	13	15	17	19 *17–22*	21 *18–25*	23 *20–27*
Theft crimes ($5,000 or less) Check forgery ($251–$2,500)	II	12	12	13	15	17	19	21 *18–25*
Sale of simulated controlled substance	I	12	12	12	13	15	17	19 *17–22*

▮ At the discretion of the judge, up to a year in jail and/or other nonjail sanctions can be imposed instead of prison sentences as conditions of probation for most of these offenses. If prison is imposed, the presumptive sentence is the number of months shown.

▯ Presumptive commitment to state prison for all offenses.

Note: First-degree murder has a mandatory life sentence and is excluded from the guidelines by law.

Source: Minnesota Sentencing Guidelines Commission, *Minnesota Sentencing Guidelines and Commentary*, effective August 1, 2013.

varies from the guidelines (*Irizarry v. United States,* 2008); yet most sentences in federal courts remain in conformity with the guidelines (U.S. Sentencing Commission, 2006). Observers anticipate that the U.S. Supreme Court will need to revisit this issue in order to provide guidance about how sentencing guidelines can be properly designed and applied. For example, in 2011, the Court determined that federal judges can consider evidence of an offender's rehabilitation in imposing a sentence that is below those specified in sentencing guidelines (*Pepper v. United States*, 2011).

Judges' decisions have profound impacts on the lives of people drawn into the criminal justice system. Would you want to make sentencing decisions that determine the fates of people convicted of crimes? In addition, bear these considerations in mind as you assume the role of a judge and design a sentence for a controversial 2014 case as described at the end of the chapter in "A Question of Ethics."

Who Gets the Harshest Punishment?

Harsh, unjust punishments can occur because of sentencing disparities and wrongful convictions. The prison population in most states contains a higher proportion of African American and Hispanic men than occurs in the general population. Are these disparities caused by racial prejudices and discrimination, or are other factors at work? Wrongful conviction takes place when people who are in fact innocent are nonetheless found guilty by plea or verdict. It also occurs in those cases in which the conviction of a truly guilty person is overturned on appeal because of due process errors.

Racial Disparities Studies of racial disparities in sentencing are inconclusive. Because some studies show disparities in specific states or cities, though, there are grave concerns about the possibility of racial discrimination. Studies of sentencing in Pennsylvania, for example, found that there is a "high cost of being black, young (21–29 years), and male." Sentences given these offenders resulted in a higher proportion going to prison and incurring longer terms (Steffensmeier, Ulmer, & Kramer, 1998). While supporting the Pennsylvania results, research in Chicago, Miami, and Kansas City, Missouri, found variation among the jurisdictions as to sentence length (Spohn & Holleran, 2000). Other research shows disproportionate effects on African American men being sent to prison through mandatory punishments and sentence enhancements (Schlesinger, 2011).

Do these disparities stem from the prejudicial attitudes of judges, police officers, and prosecutors? Are African Americans and Hispanics viewed as a "racial threat" when they commit crimes of violence and drug selling, which are thought to be spreading from the urban ghetto to the "previously safe places of the suburbs" (Crawford, Chiricos, & Kleck, 1998:484)? Are enforcement resources distributed so that certain groups are subject to closer scrutiny than are other groups?

Scholars have pointed out that the relationship between race and sentencing is complex. For example, recent research on federal court sentencing found racial disparities largely caused by prosecutors' decisions to charge minority defendants with more-serious crimes rather than by the sentencing decisions of judges (Starr & Rehavi, 2013). These findings cannot be applied to state courts because the sentencing laws and courthouse contexts vary greatly from city to city and state to state. Judges as well as prosecutors are important decision makers in the process.

The analysis of these issues is complex, because judges consider many defendant and case characteristics. According to analyses that focus on the complexity and interaction of factors used in sentencing decisions, judges assess not only the legally relevant factors of blameworthiness, dangerousness, and recidivism risk but also race, gender, and age characteristics (Steen, Engen, & Gainey, 2005). The interconnectedness of these variables, not judges' negative attitudes, is what culminates in the disproportionately severe sentences given young black men.

Federal sentencing guidelines were adjusted in 2007 and 2008 to reduce the impact of a highly criticized source of racial disparities in prison sentences for offenders convicted of cocaine-related offenses. The federal sentencing guidelines for crack cocaine offenses—which disproportionately affected African American defendants—were adjusted to be more closely aligned with shorter sentences for

In recent years, the development of DNA evidence has contributed to the reinvestigation of cases and the release of people sent to prison for crimes that they did not commit. Here, Joseph Sledge gained release from prison in 2015 after serving 37 years for a double-murder that he did not commit. His innocence was discovered when DNA tests were performed on newly discovered evidence that had been saved from the crime scene. How could criminal justice processes be changed to reduce the risks of erroneous convictions?

possessing and selling similar amounts of powder cocaine, crimes more commonly associated with white offenders. The U.S. Sentencing Commission voted to apply these new guidelines retroactively, meaning that offenders currently serving long sentences for crack cocaine offenses were eligible to be resentenced to shorter terms in prison. In many cases, this adjustment led to the release in 2008 of offenders who had already served longer periods than those required under the new sentencing guidelines (Gezari, 2008; *Third Branch,* 2008b). As mentioned earlier, President Obama signed into law a new federal statute that reduced, but did not eliminate, the disparities in mandatory sentences for crack and powder cocaine offenders (Eckholm, 2010).

Wrongful Convictions
A serious dilemma for the criminal justice system concerns people who are wrongly convicted and sentenced. Whereas the public expresses much concern over those who "beat the system" and go free, they pay comparatively little attention to those who are innocent yet convicted. Many of these people are wrongly convicted because victims and witnesses make mistakes in identifying alleged criminals from photographs and lineups. Other wrongful convictions occur due to misconduct by police and prosecutors or ineffective performance by defense attorneys (Covey, 2013).

The development of DNA technology has increased the number of people exonerated after being convicted. However, many cases do not have DNA evidence available. C. Ronald Huff notes that "because the great majority of cases do not produce biological material to be tested, one can only speculate about the error rate in those cases" (2002:2). Even when DNA evidence is available, the U.S. Supreme Court has ruled that convicted offenders do not have a constitutional right to have the stored evidence tested. According to a five-member majority on the Court, state legislatures and Congress should develop their own rules concerning opportunities to have old evidence tested (*District Attorney's Office v. Osborne,* 2009). Every year national attention focuses on several cases in which innocent people have been erroneously convicted, yet there is no way to know how many more innocent people may be wrongly confined in prisons today.

Whether they stem from racial discrimination or wrongful convictions, unjust punishments do not serve the ideals of justice. Such punishments raise fundamental questions about the criminal justice system and its links to the society it serves.

CHECK POINT

6. **What are the four factors thought to influence the sentencing behavior of judges?**
The administrative context of the courts, the attitudes and values of judges, the presentence report, and sentencing guidelines.

STOP & ANALYZE

If your son were arrested for a crime and you believed his claim that he was innocent, are there any steps you could take to reduce the likelihood that he would be subject to an erroneous conviction? Make a list of what you might do to help your son.

A QUESTION OF ETHICS

Think, Discuss, Write

In February 2014, a national controversy arose when Judge Jean Boyd, a state court judge in Texas, imposed a sentence of 10 years of probation on teenager Eric Couch, who as a 16-year-old, killed four people and seriously injured two others when driving while drunk. Couch pleaded guilty to charges of intoxication manslaughter. Prosecutors said Couch drove 70 miles per hour in a zone with a speed limit of 40. His blood alcohol level was three times the state limit of 0.08 when he lost control of his speeding truck and hit people changing a flat tire on the side of the road. One passenger in Couch's truck suffered severe brain injuries and can longer move or talk.

Boyd sentenced Couch to a long period of probation, and his family committed to paying for him to go to an in-patient facility for treatment and counseling. National news reporters focused on the case because a psychologist for the defense supported the case for a lenient sentence by saying that Couch suffered from "affluenza," a shorthand term for someone who is so wealthy and spoiled that he does not connect his actions with the likelihood of bad consequences. The victims' families were outraged at the sentence, which was, in their view, too light. They believed that he should be incarcerated for the loss of life caused by his irresponsible actions.

By contrast, two years earlier Judge Boyd had imposed a 10-year sentence on a 14-year-old boy who killed another youth with one punch. The death occurred when the victim fell and hit his head on the pavement. In that case, the defendant could be paroled after five years or be sent to an adult prison at age 19 to serve the final five years. Critics expressed concern that Boyd had imposed a more severe sentence on the 14-year-old, an African American youth who killed one person, than she did on a wealthy white teen who killed four people and seriously injured others.

Does this provide evidence of racial discrimination? Some observers noted that Boyd had sought to emphasize rehabilitation for both boys, but no treatment program would accept the boy who threw the punch. Thus, he ended up in juvenile prison. By contrast, Couch's parents were so wealthy that they could afford to send him to a treatment facility in California that cost $450,000 per year per patient. In addition, Couch's bad behavior continued; later, he violated his probation conditions by drinking alcohol, and fled to Mexico with his mother. He was eventually caught and returned to the United States in January 2016.

Wealth discrimination? Racial discrimination? Excessive leniency? Excessive emphasis on rehabilitation without proper concern for other objectives of punishment? These cases raise challenging questions about a judge's responsibilities in sentencing.

Discussion/Writing Assignment

Imagine that you were the judge in these two cases. Write a memo describing the sentence that you would impose in each case and the punishment objectives that you would pursue with these sentences. To what extent do your sentences reflect a concern or prediction about the teenagers' future lives after they complete their periods of confinement or probation?

Sources: L. Bever, "'Affluenza' Teen Flown Back to U.S., Turned Over to Juvenile Authorities," *Washington Post*, January 28, 2016 (www.washingtonpost.com); M. Hennessey-Fiske, "Judge in 'Affluenza' Case Rules Out Jail Time for Teen Driver," *Los Angeles Times*, February 5, 2014 (www.latimes.com); C. Kim, "Families of Affluenza' Teen's Victims Reach Settlements," MSNBC online, March 18, 2014 (www.msnbc.com); C. Sterbenz, "Judge in 'Affluenza' Case Sentenced Black Teen to 10 Years for Killing a Guy with a Single Punch," *Business Insider*, December 20, 2013 (www.businessinsider.com); G. Strauss, "No Jail for 'Affluenza' Teen in Fatal Crash Draws Outrage," *USA Today*, February 6, 2014 (www.usatoday.com).

SUMMARY

1 Name the goals of punishment.
- In the United States, the four main goals of the criminal sanction are retribution, deterrence, incapacitation, and rehabilitation.
- Restoration, a new approach to punishment, has not become mainstream yet.
- The goals of the criminal sanction are carried out through incarceration, intermediate sanctions, probation, and death.

2 Describe the types of sentences judges can impose.
- Penal codes vary as to whether the permitted sentences are indeterminate, determinate, or mandatory. Each type of sentence makes certain assumptions about the goals of the criminal sanction.
- "Good time" allows correctional administrators to reduce the sentence of prisoners who live according to the rules and participate in various vocational, educational, and treatment programs.
- The U.S. Supreme Court allows capital punishment only when the judge and jury are allowed to take into account mitigating and aggravating circumstances.
- Judges often have considerable discretion in fashioning sentences to account for factors such as the seriousness of the crime, the offender's prior record, and mitigating and aggravating circumstances.

3 Identify the influences on sentencing.
- The sentencing process is influenced by the administrative context of the courts, the attitudes and values of the judges, the presentence report, and sentencing guidelines.

4 Explain how the system may treat wrongdoers unequally.
- Many states have formulated sentencing guidelines as a way of reducing disparity among the sentences given offenders in similar situations.
- Harsh, unjust punishments may result from racial discrimination or wrongful convictions.

Questions for Review

1. What are the major differences between retribution, deterrence, incapacitation, and rehabilitation?
2. What is the main purpose of restoration (restorative justice)?
3. What are the forms of the criminal sanction?
4. What purposes do intermediate sanctions serve?
5. What has been the Supreme Court's position on the constitutionality of the death penalty?
6. Is there a link between sentences and race?

Key Terms and Cases

determinate sentence (p. 319)

earned time (p. 321)

general deterrence (p. 314)

good time (p. 321)

incapacitation (p. 315)

indeterminate sentence (p. 319)

intermediate sanctions (p. 321)

mandatory sentence (p. 320)

presentence report (p. 338)

presumptive sentence (p. 320)

probation (p. 323)

rehabilitation (p. 316)

restorative justice (p. 317)

retribution (p. 313)

selective incapacitation (p. 316)

sentencing guidelines (p. 339)

shock probation (p. 323)

specific deterrence (p. 314)

Atkins v. Virginia (2002) (p. 327)

Furman v. Georgia (1972) (p. 326)

Gregg v. Georgia (1976) (p. 326)

McCleskey v. Kemp (1987) (p. 326)

Roper v. Simmons (2005) (p. 327)

Witherspoon v. Illinois (1968) (p. 329)

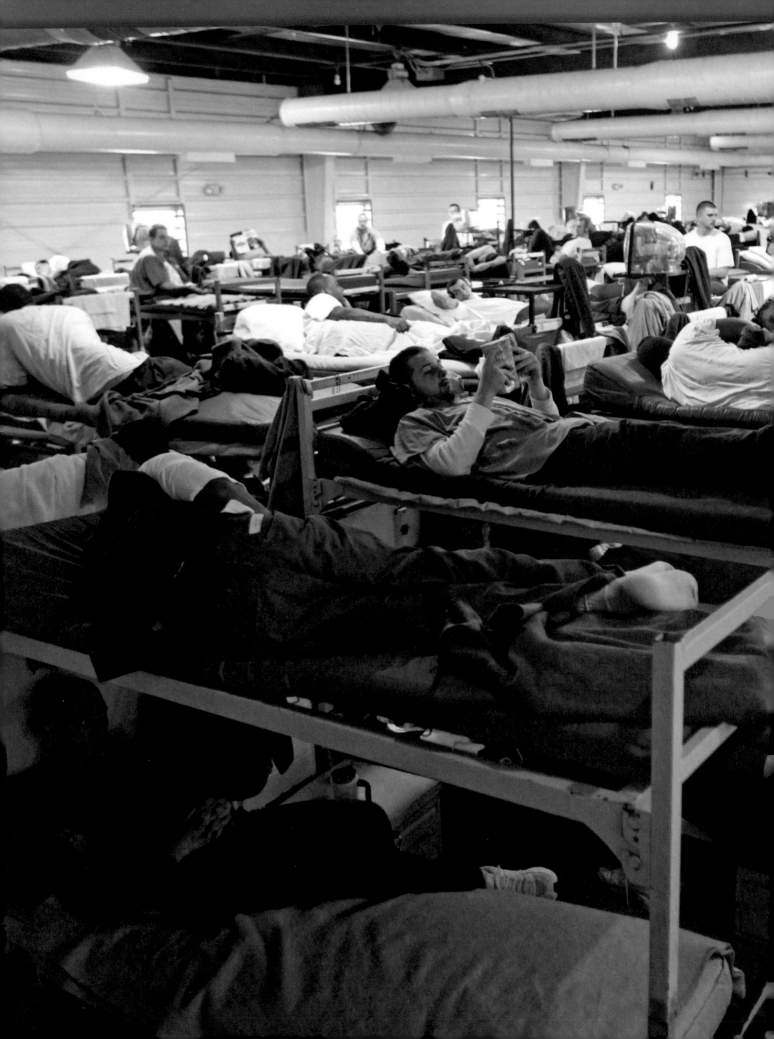

AP Images/Kiichiro Sato

10 Corrections

LEARNING OBJECTIVES

1 Describe how the American system of corrections has developed.

2 Describe the roles that the federal, state, and local governments play in corrections.

3 Explain the law of corrections and how it is applied to offenders and correctional professionals.

4 Explain why the prison population has nearly quadrupled in the past 30 years.

A report issued in March 2013 revealed an important development in American corrections: the prison population had declined for two years in a row (Pew Center, 2013). This was extraordinary news, because prison populations had increased steadily in dramatic fashion for the preceding 30 years. These statistics were especially significant because the size and expense of corrections systems had reached levels few people had imagined possible. By the end of 2014, American prison populations had declined an additional 1 percent (Carson, 2015). Just a few years earlier, in February 2008, a report released by the Pew Center on the States showed that for the first time in history, 1 in 100 American adults was behind bars in prisons (1,596,127) and jails (723,000). For policy makers and the socially conscious public, the "1 in 100" report brought to the forefront the fact of the country's tremendously large and, at that time, expanding prison population. The 2008 report also noted that the United States incarcerates more of its residents than any other country. China is second, with 1.5 million behind bars—a comparable number of prisoners, but a much lower incarceration rate because China's population is four times that of the United States (J. Warren, 2008). The United States has less than 5 percent of the world's population, but almost a quarter of the world's prisoners. Even with the recent decrease in prison population, the United States has approximately 35 times as many prisoners as Canada, while having only 10 times its population.

The foregoing developments raise two important questions. First, why does this gap exist between American justice and that of the rest of the world? Second, will the recent decrease in the American prison population make the U.S. incarceration rate less striking compared with rates elsewhere in the rest of the world? With respect to the first question, we know certain things. Over the past 30 years, the incarceration rate quadrupled, even though crime in the United States has been declining for two decades (Liptak, 2008c). The prison populations increased due to the imposition of longer sentences on offenders, including nonviolent drug offenders who were imprisoned in large numbers. Some states imposed decades-long sentences on repeat offenders, even if they had not committed the most serious crimes. The increase in prison populations had significant financial consequences. The larger number of convicted offenders increased the need for new prisons, resulting in a construction boom and a surge in the hiring of corrections officers. Correctional budgets climbed an average of 10 percent annually, and many states diverted money from education, welfare, and health programs to meet the soaring needs of corrections.

With respect to the second question, it is possible that imprisonment trends will continue to move in this new direction. Many states are taking specific actions to change sentencing practices in ways that would send fewer people to prison and thereby reduce the national incarceration rate that is so starkly different from that of other countries (Carson, 2015; A. Johnson, 2011; "Indiana's Answer," 2011). The high financial cost of imprisonment and its impact on limited state budgets is a significant factor in the reconsideration of lengthy prison sentences for drug offenders and other non-homicide offenses. Thus, states are increasingly investing their corrections funds in initiatives that provide alternatives to incarceration, such as community programs, as well as programs to help offenders succeed in society after they are released from prison (Martin and Grattet, 2015; Pew Center, 2013).

AP Images/Kiichiro Sato

The public usually thinks of prisons when it thinks of corrections; however, about 70 percent of persons under supervision are not in prisons or jails, but are instead living in the community on probation or parole. The percentage of offenders in these less-expensive correctional settings is likely to increase as states adjust their sentencing and release practices in the effort to save money.

Corrections refers to the great number of programs, services, facilities, and organizations responsible for the management of people accused or convicted of criminal offenses. In addition to prisons and jails, corrections includes probation, halfway houses, education and work release programs, parole supervision, counseling, and community service. Correctional programs operate in Salvation Army hostels, forest camps, medical clinics, and urban storefronts. Corrections is authorized by all levels of government, is administered by both public and private organizations, and costs more than $60 billion a year. A total of 6.8 million adults and juveniles receive correctional supervision by 750,000 administrators, psychologists, officers, counselors, social workers, and other professionals (Kaeble et al., 2015; BJS, 2016). This chapter will examine (1) the history of corrections, (2) the organization of corrections, (3) the law of corrections, and (4) the policy trends in community corrections and incarceration.

Development of Corrections

corrections The variety of programs, services, facilities, and organizations responsible for the management of people who have been accused or convicted of criminal offenses.

How did corrections get to where it is today? Why are offenders now placed on probation or incarcerated instead of whipped or burned as in colonial times? Over the past 200 years, ideas about punishment have moved like a pendulum from one extreme to another (see Table 10.1). As we review the development of present-day policies, think about how future changes in society may lead to new forms of corrections.

Invention of the Penitentiary

The late eighteenth century stands out as a remarkable period. At that time, scholars and social reformers in Europe and America were rethinking the nature of society

TABLE 10.1   History of Corrections in America

Note the extent to which correctional policies have shifted from one era to the next and are influenced by societal factors.

Correctional Era						
Colonial (1600s–1790s)	**Penitentiary (1790s–1860s)**	**Reformatory (1870s–1890s)**	**Progressive (1890s–1930s)**	**Medical (1930s–1960s)**	**Community (1960s–1970s)**	**Crime Control (1970s–2000s)**
Features						
Anglican Code Capital and corporal punishment, fines	Separate confinement Reform of individual Power of isolation and labor Penance Disciplined routine Punishment according to severity of crime	Indeterminate sentences Parole Classification by degree of individual reform Rehabilitative programs Separate treatment for juveniles	Individual case approach Administrative discretion Broader probation and parole Juvenile courts	Rehabilitation as primary focus of incarceration Psychological testing and classification Various types of treatment programs and institutions	Reintegration into community Avoidance of incarceration Vocational and educational program	Determinate sentences Mandatory sentences Sentencing guidelines Risk management
Philosophical Basis						
Religious law Doctrine of predestination	Enlightenment Declaration of Independence Human perfectibility and powers of reason Religious penitence Power of reformation Focus on the act Healing power of suffering	National Prison Association Declaration of Principles Crime as moral disease Criminals as "victims of social disorder"	The Age of Reform Positivist school Punishment according to needs of offender Focus on the offender Crime as an urban, immigrant ghetto problem	Biomedical science Psychiatry and psychology Social work practice Crime as signal of personal "distress" or "failure"	Civil rights movement Critique of prisons Small is better	Crime control Rising crime rates Political shift to the right New punitive agenda

and the place of the individual in it. During the **Enlightenment**, as this period is known, philosophers and reformers challenged tradition with new ideas about the individual, about limitations on government, and about rationalism. Such thinking was the main intellectual force behind the American Revolution and laid the foundation of American values. The Enlightenment also affected the new nation's views on law and criminal justice. Reformers began to raise questions about the nature of criminal behavior and the methods of punishment.

Prior to 1800, Americans copied Europeans in using physical punishments such as flogging, branding, and maiming as the main criminal sanctions, and criminals were regularly sentenced to death for pickpocketing, burglary, robbery, and horse stealing (Rothman, 1971). Jails existed throughout the country, but they served only to hold people awaiting trial or to punish people unable to pay their debts. As in England, the American colonies maintained houses of correction, where offenders were sentenced to terms of "hard labor" as a means of turning them from crime (A. J. Hirsch, 1992).

Enlightenment A movement during the eighteenth century in England and France in which concepts of liberalism, rationalism, equality, and individualism dominated social and political thinking.

Until the early 1800s, Americans followed the European practice of relying on punishment that was physically painful, such as death, flogging, and branding. Would such punishments be appropriate today?

With the spread of Enlightenment ideas during the late eighteenth century, the use of physical punishment began to wane. Gradually, "modern" penal systems emerged that emphasized fitting the punishment to the individual offender. The new goal was not to inflict pain on the offender's body (corporal punishment) but to change the individual and set him or her on the right path.

Many people promoted the reform of corrections, but John Howard (1726–1790), sheriff of Bedfordshire, England, was especially influential. His book *The State of Prisons in England and Wales*, published in 1777, described the horrible conditions he observed in the prisons he visited (Howard, 1777/1929). Public response to the book resulted in Parliament's passing the Penitentiary Act of 1779, which called for the creation of a house of hard labor where offenders would be imprisoned for up to two years. The institution would be based on four principles:

1. A secure and sanitary building
2. Inspection to ensure that offenders followed the rules
3. Abolition of the fees charged offenders for their food
4. A reformatory regime

At night, prisoners were to be confined to individual cells. During the day, they were to work silently in common rooms. Prison life was to be strict and ordered. Influenced by his Quaker friends, Howard believed that the new institution should be a place of industry. More important, it should be a place that offered criminals opportunities for penitence (sorrow and shame for their wrongs) and repentance (willingness to change their ways). In short, the **penitentiary** served to punish and to reform.

Howard's idea of the penitentiary was not implemented in England until 1842, some 50 years after his death. Although England was slow to act, the United States applied Howard's ideas much more quickly.

penitentiary An institution intended to punish criminals by isolating them from society and from one another so they can reflect on their past misdeeds, repent, and reform.

Reform in the United States

From 1776 to around 1830, a new revolution occurred in the American idea of criminal punishment. Although based on the work of English reformers, the new correctional philosophy reflected many ideas expressed in the Declaration of Independence, including an optimistic view of human nature and of individual perfectibility. Emphasis shifted from the assumption that deviance was part of human nature to a belief that crime resulted from environmental forces. The new nation's humane and optimistic ideas focused on reforming the criminal.

In the first decades of the nineteenth century, the creation of penitentiaries in Pennsylvania and New York attracted the attention of legislators in other states, as well as investigators from Europe. By the mid-1800s, the U.S. penitentiary had become world famous.

The Pennsylvania System
Several groups in the United States dedicated themselves to reforming the institutions and practices of criminal punishment. One of these groups was the Philadelphia Society for Alleviating the Miseries of Public Prisons, formed in 1787. This group, which included many Quakers, was inspired by Howard's ideas. They argued that criminals could best be reformed if they were placed in penitentiaries—isolated from one another and from society to consider their crimes, repent, and reform.

Eastern State Penitentiary, located outside Philadelphia, became the model for the Pennsylvania system of separate confinement. The building was designed to ensure that each offender was separated from all human contact so that he could reflect on his misdeeds. If you designed a prison, what details would it contain?

In 1790, the Pennsylvania legislature authorized the construction of two penitentiaries for the solitary confinement of "hardened and atrocious offenders." The first, created out of an existing three-story stone structure in Philadelphia, was the Walnut Street Jail. This 25-by-40-foot building had eight dark cells, each measuring 6 by 8 by 9 feet, on each floor. A yard was attached to the building. Only one inmate occupied each cell, and no communications of any kind were allowed. From a small, grated window high on the outside wall, prisoners "could perceive neither heaven nor earth."

From this limited beginning, the Pennsylvania system of **separate confinement** evolved. It was based on five principles:

1. Prisoners would not be treated vengefully but should be convinced, through hard and selective forms of suffering, that they could change their lives.
2. Solitary confinement would prevent further corruption inside prison.
3. In isolation, offenders would reflect on their transgressions and repent.
4. Solitary confinement would be punishment, because humans are by nature social animals.
5. Solitary confinement would be economical, because prisoners would not need a long time to repent, and so fewer keepers would be needed and the cost of clothing would be lower.

separate confinement
A penitentiary system, developed in Pennsylvania, in which each inmate was held in isolation from other inmates. All activities, including craftwork, took place in the cells.

The opening of the Eastern Penitentiary near Philadelphia in 1829 culminated 42 years of reform activity by the Philadelphia Society. On October 25, 1829, the first prisoner, Charles Williams, arrived. He was an 18-year-old African American sentenced to two years for larceny. He was assigned to a 12-by-8-by-10-foot cell with an individual exercise yard 18 feet long. In the cell was a fold-up steel bed, a simple toilet, a wooden stool, a workbench, and eating utensils. Light came from an 8-inch window in the ceiling. Solitary labor, Bible reading, and reflection were the keys to the moral rehabilitation that was supposed to occur within the penitentiary. Although the cell was larger than most in use today, it was the only world the prisoner would see throughout the entire sentence. The only other human voice heard would be that of a clergyman who would visit on Sundays. Nothing was to distract the penitent prisoner from the path toward reform.

Within five years of its opening, Eastern endured the first of several outside investigations. The reports detailed the extent to which the goal of separate confinement was not fully observed, physical punishments were used to maintain discipline, and prisoners suffered mental breakdowns from isolation. Separate confinement had declined at Eastern by the 1860s, when crowding required doubling up in each cell, yet it was not abolished in Pennsylvania until 1913 (Teeters & Shearer, 1957:ch. 4).

The New York System In 1819, New York opened a penitentiary in Auburn that evolved as a rival to Pennsylvania's concept of separate confinement. Under New York's **congregate system**, prisoners were held in isolation at night but worked with other prisoners in shops during the day. Working under a rule of silence, they were forbidden even to exchange glances while on the job or at meals.

Auburn's warden, Elam Lynds, was convinced that convicts were incorrigible and that industrial efficiency should be the overriding purpose of the prison. He instituted a reign of discipline and obedience that included the lockstep and the wearing of prison stripes. He also started a **contract labor system**. By the 1840s, Auburn was producing footwear, barrels, carpets, harnesses, furniture, and clothing. American reformers, seeing the New York approach as a great advance, copied it throughout the Northeast. Because the inmates produced goods for sale, advocates said operating costs would be covered.

During this period, advocates of the Pennsylvania and New York plans debated on public platforms and in the nation's periodicals. Advocates of both systems agreed that the prisoner must stay isolated from society and follow a disciplined routine. In their view, criminality resulted from pervasive corruption that the family and the church did not sufficiently counterbalance. Only when offenders were removed from the temptations and influences of society and kept in a silent, disciplined environment could they reflect on their sins and offenses and become useful citizens. The convicts were not inherently depraved; rather, they were victims of a society that had not protected them from vice. While offenders were being punished, they would become penitent and motivated to place themselves on the right path. See Table 10.2 for a comparison of the Pennsylvania and New York systems.

Prisons in the South and West Scholars tend to emphasize the nineteenth-century reforms in the populous Northeast, neglecting penal developments in the South and the West. Before 1817, four Southern states—Georgia, Kentucky, Maryland, and Virginia—had built prisons, some following the penitentiary model. Later prisons, such as the ones in Jackson, Mississippi (1842), and Huntsville, Texas (1848), followed the Auburn model. Further expansion ended with the advent of the Civil War, however. In the sparsely populated western states, only one prison—San Quentin (1852)—was built before the latter part of the nineteenth century.

After the Civil War, Southerners began to rebuild their communities and largely agricultural-based economy. They lacked funds to build prisons and instead developed a "plantation model" of corrections that exploited prisoners as slave labor (Feeley & Rubin, 1998). To address their governments' need for revenue, Southern states developed

congregate system
A penitentiary system, developed in Auburn, New York, in which each inmate was held in isolation during the night but worked and ate with other prisoners during the day under a rule of silence.

contract labor system
A system under which inmates' labor was sold on a contractual basis to private employers who provided the machinery and raw materials with which inmates made salable products in the institution.

TABLE 10.2	Comparison of Pennsylvania and New York (Auburn) Penitentiary Systems			
	Goal	Implementation	Method	Activity
Pennsylvania (separate system)	Redemption of the offender through the well-ordered routine of the prison	Isolation, penance, contemplation, labor, silence	Inmates kept in their cells for eating, sleeping, and working	Bible reading, work on crafts in cell
New York (Auburn) (congregate system)	Redemption of the offender through the well-ordered routine of the prison	Strict discipline, obedience, labor, silence	Inmates sleep in their cells but come together to eat and work	Work together in shops making goods to be sold by the state

the **lease system**. Businesses in need of workers negotiated with the state for the custody of prisoners and exploitation of their labor (logging, agriculture, mining, railroad construction.) As described in Douglas Blackmon's Pulitzer Prize-winning book, *Slavery by Another Name: The Re-Enslavement of Black Americans from the Civil War to World War II* (2008), the corrections system was used, in effect, to perpetuate slavery on many African Americans for nearly 80 years after slavery had been prohibited by the Constitution's Thirteenth Amendment in 1865. In some ways, this slavery was arguably worse than the original form. Unlike slaveholders before the Civil War, the business owners had no financial investments in their involuntary laborers. Prior to 1865, slave owners would lose their investments if their slaves died; but the business owners relying on the lease system did not care how many African Americans prisoners were worked to death under the most dangerous and inhumane conditions. They could always rely on criminal justice officials to provide more slaves by convicting innocent African Americans of imaginary crimes. The prisoner death rate soared. For example, among the 285 prisoners sent to work on the Greenwood and Augusta Railroad between 1877 and 1880, a full 45 percent lost their lives under the brutal working conditions (Friedman, 1993). As described by historian Lawrence Friedman, "these were young black men in the prime of their lives. You can imagine what it would take, what cruelty, what conditions of work, to kill off almost half of them" (Friedman, 1993:95).

Settlement in the West did not take off until the California gold rush of 1849. The prison ideologies of the East did not greatly influence corrections in the West, except in California. Prior to statehood, Western prisoners were held in territorial facilities or in federal military posts and prisons. Until Congress passed the Anti-Contract Law of 1887, restricting the employment of federal prisoners, leasing programs existed in California, Montana, Oregon, and Wyoming. In 1852, a lessee chose Point San Quentin and, using convict labor, built two prison buildings. In 1858, after reports of deaths, escapes, and brutal discipline, the state of California took over the facility. The Oregon territory had erected a log prison in the 1850s but soon leased it to a private company. On joining the Union in 1859, however, the state discontinued the lease system. In 1877, Oregon built a state prison on the Auburn plan, but with labor difficulties and an economic depression in the 1890s, the state turned it over to a lessee in 1895 (McKelvey, 1977:228).

Reformatory Movement

By the middle of the nineteenth century, reformers had become disillusioned with the penitentiary. Within 40 years of being built, penitentiaries had become overcrowded, understaffed, and minimally financed. Discipline was lax, brutality was common, and administrators were viewed as corrupt.

Cincinnati, 1870   The National Prison Association (the predecessor of today's American Correctional Association), at its 1870 meeting in Cincinnati, embodied a new spirit of reform. In its famous Declaration of Principles, the association advocated a new design for penology: that prisons should operate according to a philosophy of inmate change, with reformation rewarded by release. Sentences of indeterminate length would replace fixed sentences, and proof of reformation—rather than mere lapse of time—would be required for a prisoner's release. Classification of prisoners on the basis of character and improvement would encourage the reformation program.

Elmira Reformatory   The first **reformatory** took shape in 1876 at Elmira, New York, when Zebulon Brockway was appointed superintendent. Brockway believed that diagnosis and treatment were the keys to reform and rehabilitation. An interview with each new inmate resulted in an individualized work and education treatment program. Inmates followed a rigid schedule of work during the day, followed by courses in academic, vocational, and moral subjects during the evening. Inmates who did well achieved early release.

lease system A system under which inmates were leased to contractors who provided prisoners with food and clothing in exchange for their labor.

reformatory An institution that emphasizes training, a mark system of classification, indeterminate sentences, and parole.

mark system A point system in which prisoners can reduce their term of imprisonment and gain release by earning "marks," or points, through labor, good behavior, and educational achievement.

Designed for first-time felons aged 16–30, Elmira incorporated a **mark system** of classification, indeterminate sentences, and parole. Each offender entered the institution at grade 2, and if he earned nine marks a month for six months by working hard, completing school assignments, and causing no problems, he could be moved up to grade 1—necessary for release. If he failed to cooperate and violated the rules, he would be demoted to grade 3. Only after three months of satisfactory behavior could he re-embark on the path toward eventual release. In sum, this system placed "the prisoner's fate, as far as possible, in his own hands" (Pisciotta, 1994:20).

By 1900, the reformatory movement had spread throughout the nation, yet by the outbreak of World War I in 1914, it was already in decline. In most institutions, the architecture, the attitudes of the guards, and the emphasis on discipline differed little from those of the past. Too often, the educational and rehabilitative efforts took a backseat to the traditional emphasis on punishment. Yet, the reformatory movement contributed the indeterminate sentence, rehabilitative programs, and parole. The Cincinnati Declaration of Principles and the reformatory movement set goals that inspired prison activists well into the twentieth century.

Improving Prison Conditions for Women

Until the beginning of the nineteenth century, female offenders in Europe and North America were treated no differently than men and were not separated from men when they were incarcerated. Only with John Howard's 1777 exposé of prison conditions in England and the development of the penitentiary in Philadelphia did attention begin to focus on the plight of the female offender. Among the English reformers, Elizabeth Gurney Fry, a middle-class Quaker, was the first person to press for changes. When she and other Quakers visited London's Newgate Prison in 1813, they were shocked by the conditions in which the female prisoners and their children were living (Zedner, 1995).

News of Fry's efforts spread to the United States. The Women's Prison Association was formed in New York in 1844 with the goal of improving the treatment of female prisoners and separating them from men. Elizabeth Farnham, head matron of the women's wing at Sing Sing from 1844 to 1848, implemented Fry's ideas until male overseers and legislators thwarted her, forcing her to resign.

The Cincinnati Declaration of Principles did not address the problems of female offenders. It only endorsed the creation of separate treatment-oriented prisons for women. Although the House of Shelter, a reformatory for women, was created in Detroit following the Civil War, not until 1873 did the first independent female-run prison open in Indiana. Within 50 years, 13 other states had followed this lead.

Three principles guided female prison reform during this period: (1) the separation of female prisoners from men, (2) the provision of care in keeping with the needs of women, and (3) the management of women's prisons by female staff. "Operated by and for women, female reformatories were decidedly 'feminine' institutions" (Rafter, 1983:147).

As time passed, the original ideas of the reformers faltered. In 1927, the first federal prison for women opened in Alderson, West Virginia, with Mary Belle Harris as warden. Yet, by 1935 the women's reformatory movement had "run its course, having largely achieved its objective (establishment of separate prisons run by women)" (Heffernan, 1972; Rafter, 1983:165).

Rehabilitation Model

In the first two decades of the twentieth century, reformers known as the Progressives attacked the excesses of big business and urban society and advocated government actions against the problems of slums, vice, and crime. The Progressives urged that knowledge from the social and behavioral sciences should replace religious and traditional moral wisdom as the guiding ideas of criminal rehabilitation. They pursued two main strategies: (1) improving conditions in social environments that seemed to be the breeding grounds of crime, and (2) rehabilitating individual offenders. By the 1920s, probation, indeterminate sentences, presentence reports, parole, and treatment programs were being promoted as a more scientific approach to criminality.

Although the Progressives were instrumental in advancing the new penal ideas, not until the 1930s did reformers attempt to implement fully what became known as the **rehabilitation model** of corrections. Taking advantage of the new prestige of the social sciences, penologists helped shift the emphasis of corrections. The new approach saw the social, intellectual, or biological deficiencies of criminals as causing their crimes. Because the essential elements of parole, probation, and the indeterminate sentence were already in place in most states, incorporating the rehabilitation model meant adding classification systems to diagnose offenders and treatment programs to rehabilitate them.

Because penologists likened the new correctional methods to those used by physicians in hospitals, this approach was often referred to as the **medical model**. Correctional institutions were to be staffed with people who could diagnose the causes of an individual's criminal behavior, prescribe a treatment program, and determine when the offender was cured and could be safely released to the community.

Following World War II, rehabilitation won new followers. Group therapy, behavior modification, counseling, and several other approaches became part of the "new penology." Yet even during the 1950s, when the medical model reached its height, only a small proportion of state correctional budgets went to rehabilitation. What frustrated many reformers was that even though states adopted the rhetoric of the rehabilitation model, the institutions were still run with custody as the overriding goal.

Because the rehabilitation model failed to achieve its goals, it became discredited in the 1970s. According to critics of rehabilitation, reportedly high recidivism rates proved its ineffectiveness. Robert Martinson undertook what was probably the most thorough analysis of research data from treatment programs; using rigorous standards, he surveyed 231 studies of rehabilitation programs. Martinson summarized his findings by saying, "With few and isolated exceptions, the rehabilitative efforts that have been reported so far have had no appreciable effect on recidivism" (Martinson, 1974:25). The report had an immediate impact on legislators and policy makers, who took up the cry, "Nothing works!" As a result of dissatisfaction with the rehabilitation model, new reforms emerged.

Community Model

The social and political values of particular periods have long influenced correctional goals. During the 1960s and early 1970s, U.S. society experienced the civil rights movement, the war on poverty, and resistance to the war in Vietnam. People challenged the conventional ways of government. In 1967, the U.S. President's Commission on Law Enforcement and Administration of Justice (1967:7) argued for a model of **community corrections**, which claimed that the purpose of corrections should be to reintegrate the offender into the community.

Proponents of this model viewed prisons as artificial institutions that hindered offenders from finding a crime-free lifestyle. They argued that corrections should focus on providing psychological treatment and on increasing opportunities for offenders to succeed as citizens. Programs were supposed to help offenders find jobs and remain connected to their families and the community. Imprisonment was to be avoided, if possible, in favor of probation, so that offenders could seek education and vocational training that would help their adjustment. The small proportion of offenders who had to be incarcerated would spend a minimal amount of time in prison before release on parole. To promote reintegration, correctional workers were to serve as advocates for offenders in dealing with government agencies providing employment counseling, medical treatment, and financial assistance.

rehabilitation model
A model of corrections that emphasizes the need to restore a convicted offender to a constructive place in society through some form of vocational or educational training or therapy.

medical model A model of corrections based on the assumption that criminal behavior is caused by biological or psychological conditions that require treatment.

community corrections
A model of corrections based on the goal of reintegrating the offender into the community.

The community model dominated corrections until the late 1970s, when it gave way to a new punitiveness in criminal justice, in conjunction with the rebirth of the determinate sentence. Advocates of reintegration claimed, as did advocates of previous reforms, that the idea was never adequately tested. Nevertheless, community corrections remains one of the significant ideas and practices in the recent history of corrections.

Crime Control Model

As the political climate changed in the 1970s and 1980s, legislators, judges, and officials responded with an emphasis on crime control through incarceration and risk containment. The critique of rehabilitation led to changes in the sentencing structures in more than half of the states and the abolition of parole release in many. Compared with the community model, this **crime control model of corrections** is more punitive and makes greater use of incarceration (especially for violent offenders and career criminals), longer sentences, mandatory sentences, and strict supervision of probationers and parolees.

The effect of these get-tough policies shows in the record numbers of people incarcerated, the long terms being served, the great number of parolees returned to prison, and the huge size of the probation population. In some states, the political fervor to be tough on criminals has resulted in the reinstitution of chain gangs and the removal of television sets, body-building equipment, and college courses from prisons. Some advocates point to the crime control policies as the reason for the fall of the crime rate. Others ask whether these policies are in fact the reason for the difference, considering the smaller number of men in the crime-prone age group and other changes in U.S. society.

The history of corrections in the United States reflects a series of swings from one model to another. The time may now be ripe for another look at correctional policy. The rhetoric used in criminal justice journals today differs markedly from that found in their pages 40 years ago. For example, the optimism that once suffused corrections has waned. Researchers are now scrutinizing the financial and human costs of the harsh crime control policies of recent decades. Are the costs of incarceration and surveillance justified? Has crime been reduced? Is society safer today than it was 25 years ago? Many researchers think not. Will corrections, then, find a new direction? If so, what will it be?

crime control model of corrections A model of corrections based on the assumption that criminal behavior can be controlled by more use of incarceration and other forms of strict supervision.

CHECK POINT

1. **What was the Enlightenment, and how did it influence corrections?**
   A period in the late eighteenth century when philosophers rethought the nature of society and the place of the individual in the world. The Enlightenment affected views on law and criminal justice; reformers began to raise questions about the nature of criminal behavior and the methods of punishment.

2. **How did the Pennsylvania and New York systems differ?**
   The Pennsylvania system of separate confinement held inmates in isolation from one another. The New York congregate system kept inmates in their cells at night, but they worked together in shops during the day.

3. **What are the underlying assumptions of the rehabilitation, community, and crime control models of corrections?**
   Rehabilitation model: Criminal behavior is the result of a biological, psychological, or social deficiency; clinicians should diagnose the problem and prescribe treatment; when cured, the offender may be released. *Community model:* The goal of corrections is to reintegrate the offender into the community, so rehabilitation should be carried out in the community rather than in prison if possible; correctional workers should serve as advocates for offenders in their dealings with government agencies. *Crime control model:* Criminal behavior can be controlled by greater use of incarceration and other forms of strict supervision.

STOP & ANALYZE

Do you foresee the current state budget crises affecting the states' future approach to corrections? Which approach is most likely to be emphasized in the future? Give two reasons for your answer.

Organization of Corrections in the United States

The organization of corrections in the United States is fragmented, with each level of government holding some responsibility. The federal government, the 50 states, the District of Columbia, the 3,047 counties, and most cities all have at least one correctional facility and many correctional programs. State and local governments pay about 95 percent of the cost of all correctional activities in the nation (BJS, 2014).

Federal Corrections System

The correctional responsibilities of the federal government are divided between the Department of Justice, which operates prisons through the Federal Bureau of Prisons, and the Administrative Office of the United States Courts, which covers probation and parole supervision.

Federal Bureau of Prisons   The Federal Bureau of Prisons, created by Congress in 1930, now operates a system of prisons located throughout the nation and housing over 196,000 inmates, supervised by a staff of more than 38,000. Approximately 80 percent of federal offenders are in facilities run by the Bureau of Prisons, but others are in privately run or community-based facilities (U.S. Bureau of Prisons, 2016). Facilities and inmates are classified by security level, ranging from Level 1 (the least secure, camp-type settings such as the Federal Prison Camp in Pensacola, Florida) through Level 5 (the most secure, such as the "supermax" penitentiary in Florence, Colorado). Between these extremes are Levels 2 through 4 federal correctional institutions—other U.S. penitentiaries, administrative institutions, medical facilities, and specialized institutions for women and juveniles. The Bureau of Prisons enters into contractual agreements with states, cities, and private agencies to provide community services such as halfway houses, prerelease programs, and electronic monitoring.

Federal Probation and Parole Supervision   Probation and parole supervision for federal offenders are provided by the Federal Probation and Pretrial Services System, a branch of the Administrative Office of the U.S. Courts. The federal judiciary appoints probation officers, who serve the court. The first full-time federal probation officer was appointed in 1927; today nearly 4,000 are assigned to the judicial districts across the country. They assist with presentence investigations but focus primarily on supervising offenders on probation and those released either on parole or by mandatory release.

State Corrections Systems

In all states, the administration of prisons falls under the executive branch of state government. However, states vary in how they organize corrections: the judiciary often controls probation; parole may be separate from corrections; and in most states, the county governments run the jails.

Community Corrections   States vary in how they carry out the community punishments of probation, intermediate sanctions, and parole. In many states, probation and intermediate sanctions are administered by the judiciary, often by county and municipal governments. By contrast, parole is a function of state government. The decision to release an offender from prison is made by the state parole board in those states with discretionary release. Parole boards are a part of either the department of corrections or an independent agency. In states with a mandatory system, the department of corrections makes the release. In all states, a state agency supervises the parolees.

State Prison Systems   A wide range of state correctional institutions, facilities, and programs exists for adult male felons—from prisons, reformatories, prison farms, and forestry camps to halfway houses. Because the female prisoner population is so much smaller, this variety does not exist for women.

States vary considerably in the number, size, type, and location of correctional facilities they have. Louisiana's state prison at Angola, for example, can hold 5,100 prisoners, whereas specialized institutions hold one hundred or fewer inmates. Some states (such as New Hampshire) have centralized incarceration in a few institutions, and other states (such as California, New York, and Texas) have a wide mix of sizes and styles—secure institutions, diagnostic units, work camps, forestry centers, and prerelease centers. For example, the website of the Pennsylvania Department of Corrections (2014) describes the state corrections system as follows:

> [T]he department—with a budget of $1.9 billion—oversees 25 state correctional institutions, one motivational boot camp, 14 community corrections centers, nearly 40 contract facilities, a training academy, approximately 15,000 employees and more than 51,300 inmates.

Correctional institutions for men are usually classified by level of security: maximum, medium, and minimum. For example, the website of the Minnesota Department of Corrections (2016) characterizes its prisons' security levels as "Level 2-Minimum," "Level-3 Medium," "Level-4 Close," and "Level 5-Maximum." Only one Minnesota prison is classified as Level 5. Three institutions hold Level 4 prisoners and three prisons hold Level 3 prisoners. One of the Level 4 facilities and two of the Level 3 facilities also each contain a section housing Level 2 prisoners. Three other facilities solely hold Level 2 inmates.

Forty states have created prisons that exceed maximum security. An estimated 20,000 inmates are currently kept in these "supermax" prisons. These institutions, such as California's Pelican Bay and Connecticut's Northern Correctional Facility, hold the most disruptive, violent, and incorrigible offenders—the "toughest of the tough." In such institutions, inmates spend up to 23 hours a day in their cells. They are shackled whenever they are out of their cells—during recreation, showers, and telephone calls. All of these measures are designed to send a message to other inmates (Reiter, 2012).

The maximum-security prison (holding about 21 percent of state inmates) is built like a fortress, usually surrounded by stone walls with guard towers. It is designed to prevent escape. New facilities are surrounded by double rows of chain-link fences with rolls of razor wire in between and along the tops of the fences. Inmates live in cells that include plumbing and sanitary facilities. Some facilities' barred doors operate electronically so that an officer can confine all prisoners to their cells with the flick of a switch. The purposes of the maximum-security facility are custody and

Prisoners in California live under crowded conditions. Offenders in other states' prisons live under similarly crowded conditions. How should society address the issue of prison overcrowding?

REUTERS/Lucy Nicholson

discipline. It maintains a military-style approach to order, with prisoners following a strict routine. Some of the most famous prisons, such as Attica (New York), Folsom (California), Stateville (Illinois), and Yuma (Arizona), are maximum-security facilities.

The medium-security prison (holding 40 percent of state inmates) externally resembles the maximum-security prison, but it is organized somewhat differently and its atmosphere is less rigid. Prisoners have more privileges and contact with the outside world through visitors, mail, and access to radio and television. The medium-security prison usually places greater emphasis than maximum-security prisons do on work and rehabilitative programs. Although the inmates may have committed serious crimes, they are not perceived as hardened criminals.

The minimum-security prison (with 33 percent of state inmates) houses the least-violent offenders, long-term felons with clean disciplinary records, and inmates who have nearly completed their terms. The minimum-security prison lacks the guard towers and stone walls associated with correctional institutions. Often chain-link fencing surrounds the buildings. Prisoners usually live in dormitories or even in small private rooms rather than in barred cells. There is more personal freedom: inmates may have television sets, choose their own clothes, and move about casually within the buildings. The system relies on rehabilitation programs and offers opportunities for education and work release. It also provides reintegration programs and support to inmates preparing for release.

A small percentage of state inmates are held in other settings, such as work camps and county jails. Sentenced offenders may remain in local jails while they await transfer to a state prison or when there are agreements between state correctional officials and county sheriffs in response to overcrowding in state prisons. For example, beginning in October 2011, newly sentenced California offenders serving time for nonviolent, nonserious, nonsexual crimes were sentenced to three years or less in county jails; this was a change from the previous practice of sending all offenders serving more than one year to state prison (Santos, 2013; "California's Prison Realignment," 2011).

State Institutions for Women   Just less than 8 percent of incarcerated people are women (Carson, 2015). Although the ratio of arrests is approximately 6 men to 1 woman, the ratio in state and federal prisons is 14 men to 1 woman. A higher proportion of female defendants are sentenced to probation and intermediate punishments, partly because, as compared to men, women less frequently commit crimes involving violence. However, the growth rate in the number of incarcerated women has exceeded that for men in recent decades; from 2004 to 2014, the male

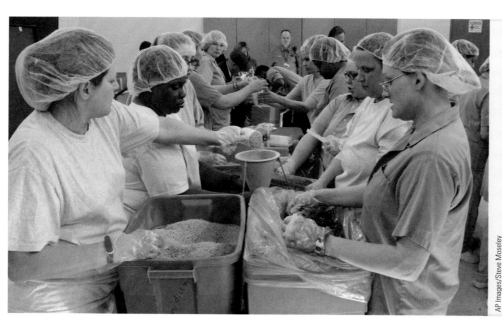

Traditionally, women's prisons lacked the education and technical job-training programs offered inside men's prisons. Instead, women were trained for sewing, typing, cooking, and other skills reflecting a limited view of women's roles in society. Should prisons for men and women be identical, or are there reasons to have differences in facilities and programs?

AP Images/Steve Moseley

population in state and federal prisons increased 4 percent while the female population increased by nearly 8 percent (Carson, 2015).

The increase in the number of women prisoners seems driven by the war on drugs. It varies by state—for example, Oklahoma incarcerates 10 times as many women per capita as Massachusetts and Rhode Island, largely due to punitive sentencing policies in drug cases (B. Palmer, 2011). This increase has significantly affected program delivery, housing conditions, medical care, staffing, and security (A. Wolf, Bloom, & Krisberg, 2008).

Conditions in correctional facilities for women are often more pleasant than those in similar institutions for men. Usually the buildings have no gun towers or barbed wire. Because of the small population, however, most states have only one facility, which is often located in a rural setting far removed from urban centers. Thus, women prisoners may be more isolated from their families and communities than male prisoners are.

Private Prisons

Corrections is a multibillion-dollar government-funded enterprise that purchases supplies and services from the private sector. Many jurisdictions have long contracted with private vendors to furnish food and medical services, educational and vocational training, maintenance, security, and the operation of aftercare facilities (Antonuccio, 2008). All of this has been referred to as the "prison-commercial complex," reflecting the close connections between private corporations that provide services to corrections and the legislators whose political campaigns they support with financial contributions.

One response to prison and jail crowding and rising staff costs has come from private entrepreneurs who argue that they can build and run prisons at least as effectively, safely, and humanely as any level of government can—and at a profit and a lower cost to taxpayers. The management of entire institutions for adult felons under private contract is a relatively new approach in corrections that was launched in the 1980s. Such privately run entities pose serious challenges for supervision and accountability as the government seeks to make sure that they are being run properly (Fathi, 2010).

By the end of 2014, the federal system and 30 states reported a total of 131,300 prisoners held in privately operated facilities. This figure reflected a decline of 2,100 from the prior year (Carson, 2015). By contrast, the number of prisoners in private facilities had increased steadily in the first decade of the twenty-first century. States' budget cuts reduced opportunities for private prisons to make money by filling their cells with prisoners paid for by the government. The Corrections Corporation of America, for example, had 11,600 unoccupied beds in its facilities (N. Cook, 2010).

In 2014, private facilities held 6 percent of all state prisoners and 19 percent of all federal prisoners (Carson, 2015). Texas (14,368) and Florida (12,395) had the largest numbers of offenders in private facilities, but other states had higher percentages of offenders held in corporate-managed prisons and jails. Seven states housed 20 percent or more of their offender population in private prisons and jails—New Mexico (44 percent), Montana (39 percent), Oklahoma (26 percent), and Hawaii (24 percent) (Carson, 2015).

In addition to inmates held for criminal offenses, 17 percent of the estimated 34,000 individuals detained by the Immigration and Customs Enforcement (ICE) agency of the U.S. Department of Homeland Security are held in private facilities. The federal government contracts with private companies that run 13 facilities used to detain people being processed for possible deportation as violators of immigration laws (Childress, 2015; Childress, 2013).

The $3 billion-a-year private prison business is dominated by two companies—Corrections Corporation of America (CCA) and the GEO Group (formerly known as the Wackenhut Corrections Corporation) (Palmer, 2015). CCA now operates the fifth-largest correctional system in the United States. It currently manages 80,000 beds in 71 facilities in 19 states and the District of Columbia. This makes up more than half of all beds under contract. Today, because prison population reductions left many states with excess capacity in their own prisons, the growth of the private prison industry has leveled off. However, the federal government will continue to rely on private facilities to detain people who entered the country in violation of immigration laws and are awaiting hearings and deportation.

Advocates of privately operated prisons claim that they provide the same level of care as the states but do it more cheaply and flexibly (Antonuccio, 2008). Research on private prison, however, points to the difficulties of measuring the costs and quality of these institutions (Oppel, 2011). Many of the "true costs" (fringe benefits, contracting supervision, federal grants) are often not taken into consideration. A study of 48 juvenile correctional facilities found little difference between private and public institutions in terms of environmental quality (G. S. Armstrong & MacKenzie, 2003). The Bureau of Justice Statistics found that, compared with private prisons, a greater proportion of state facilities provide access to work, educational, and counseling programs (BJS, 2003). More recent studies continue to raise questions about whether private prisons actually provide the benefits that supporters claim (Kish & Lipton, 2013; Genter, Hooks, & Mosher, 2013).

Before corrections becomes too heavily committed to the private ownership and operation of prisons, it is hoped that researchers will examine many political, fiscal, ethical, and administrative issues. The political issues, including questions concerning the delegation of social-control functions to people other than state employees, may be the most difficult to overcome. Some people believe that the administration of justice is a basic function of government that should not be delegated. They fear that private operations would skew correctional policy, because contractors would use their political influence to continue programs not in the public interest. For example, in 2015 a newspaper's analysis of campaign contributions in Oklahoma found that private-prison interests had contributed a total of more than $200,000 in campaign dollars and gifts to dozens of members of the state legislature (Palmer, 2015).

Some experts also fear that the private corporations will press to maintain high occupancy and will be interested only in skimming off the best inmates, leaving the most troublesome ones to the public corrections system. The profit incentive may also lead to corruption. In 2009, for example, two Pennsylvania juvenile court judges pleaded guilty to federal wire fraud and income tax fraud for taking more than $2.6 million in kickbacks to send teenagers to privately run youth detention centers (Urbina & Hamill, 2009). See the "Question of Ethics" feature at the end of the chapter to consider ethical issues that can arise when judges' sentences may be connected to their own interests.

Although some states have shown evidence of cost savings (J. F. Blumstein, Cohen, & Seth, 2008), the fiscal value of private corrections has not yet been fully demonstrated. However, labor unions have opposed these incursions into the public sector, pointing out that the salaries, benefits, and pensions of workers in spheres such as private security are lower than in their public counterparts. Finally, questions have arisen about quality of services, accountability of service providers to correctional officials, and problems related to contract supervision. Opponents cite the many instances in which privately contracted services in group homes, daycare centers, hospitals, and schools have been terminated because of reports of corruption, brutality, or substandard services. Research and publicized incidents show that staff turnover, escapes, and drug use are problems in many private prisons (Childress, 2015; S. D. Camp & Gales, 2002). Similar issues can also arise when prisons privatize certain aspects of their operations, such as hiring private companies to provide food services (Egan, 2014). Read the "Current Controversies" feature to consider one context, prisoners' phone calls, in which both private companies and state institutions gain profits through operations that raise questions about fairness.

The idea of privately run correctional facilities has stimulated much interest among the general public and within the criminal justice community, but the future of this approach is quite uncertain. Ironically, despite the questions about the true costs and consequences of private prisons, budget-cutting governors who have a strong belief in the benefits of privatization continue to push for private prisons even without clear evidence of savings (Oppel, 2011).

Profits from Prisoners' Phone Calls

Experts on rehabilitation and the successful reentry of prisoners into society point to contact between prisoners and their families and friends as a key element that can facilitate an individual's move into a crime-free, productive life in society. Without support from family and friends, prisoners reenter society with risks of isolation and a lack of family resources that can contribute to homelessness, lack of contacts for finding work, and an absence of emotional and material support. Visits from family members are important, but visits are often limited to fewer than a half-dozen per month. Moreover, prisoners are often placed at facilities that are at a great distance from where their family and friends reside, especially in geographically large states. Thus telephone contact between prisoners and their families and friends are both necessary and important for maintaining relationships and sources of support.

As we will see in Chapter 11, prisoners are forbidden to have cell phones in prisons, yet some obtain them through smuggling by corrections officers and other sources. These cell phones are a source of major problems, as prisoners have used them to continue with criminal activities, such as arranging gang activity outside the prison or committing fraud crimes via telephone. Prison officials constantly search and punish prisoners to make sure that they do not illegally possess cell phones.

States do not own telephone networks and therefore they must develop contracts with private communication companies to provide controlled and supervised phone service to prison inmates. Typically, prisons have a bank of phones in an open area that prisoners can use to make calls to family and friends. Depending on the system, the prisoners must either deposit money into their prison accounts to pay for the calls or rely on traditional collect calls in which the outside person receiving the call is charged. Controversies exist because private phone companies charge high rates for these calls and then pay a portion of that money to prison systems in the form of fees or commissions. Because states gain direct financial benefits from this system, there is little stopping private companies from charging as much as they can for calls. As a result, the profit-seeking of companies and states can collide with prisoners' need to maintain contact with family and friends. Moreover, there is an issue of fairness. Why should prisoners and their families pay so much more than everyone else in the country to speak to family members by phone?

Most Americans take for granted the ability to make long-distance calls without paying a fee per call, because such calls are included in their monthly cell-phone charges. By contrast, prisoners and their families have been forced to pay as much as $14 per minute for calls. In one example, a prisoner had to pay an additional transaction fee of nearly $14 for making a $1.80 call. One system charged prisoners a fee of $6.95 in order to add $5 to a phone account, meaning that it cost $11.95 to purchase 20 minutes of talk time. Many families of prisoners pay $250 per month or more just to stay in regular contact with their loved ones. Some families have been driven into debt or had their phone service shut off when the costs of receiving these calls goes beyond their means to keep up with the bills. While some people may argue that prisoners have harmed society and therefore should not complain about this "tax" on phone calls, in reality the cost is really imposed on their families. Is this a form of "punishment" on the families of people convicted of crimes? Is this system counterproductive to the current emphasis on finding ways to facilitate reentry and rehabilitation?

In 2015, the Federal Communication Commission (FCC) took action to cap charges on prisoners' phone calls. The commission bears responsibility for regulating many aspects of communications in the United States but had not previously taken action on this issue. The FCC decision was intended to reduce costs imposed on prisoners, but it did not eliminate opportunities for company profits and commissions paid to states. Clearly, this action would have the effect of reducing profits for the $1.2 billion prison phone industry. Reportedly, state corrections systems received more than $460 million in payments from prison phone service companies in 2014. One of the phone service companies reportedly made nearly $115 million in profit beyond the cost of providing services in 2014. Obviously, states and corporations continue to have an interest in charging as much as they are permitted to charge. Thus prison phone companies and several states challenged the FCC's decision in court, and a federal court of appeals put the FCC action on hold in 2016. It remains to be seen whether the courts will ultimately uphold the FCC's authority to limit the cost of prisoners' phone calls.

For Critical Thinking and Analysis

If you were the head of a state department of corrections that charges higher-than-average fees for inmate phone service, how would you view this matter? This issue affects two potentially conflicting goals for a state official: advancing rehabilitation and gaining revenue for operations. Write a memo on your position and recommendations to your governor. Give three reasons for your position.

Sources: C. Bozelko, "The Prison-Commercial Complex," *New York Times*, March 21, 2016 (www.nytimes.com); Campaign for Prison Phone Justice, *Prison Phone Fact Sheet*, n.d. (centerformediajustice.org); Tracy Connor, "'Huge Step': FCC Slashes Costs of Prison Phone Calls," NBC News, October 22, 2015 (www.nbcnews.com); J. Gershman, "Appeals Court Puts on Hold FCC Caps on Prison Phone-Call Charges," *Wall Street Journal*, March 7, 2016 (www.wsj.com); T. Williams, "High Cost of Inmates' Phone Calls May End," *New York Times*, September 30, 2015 (www.nytimes.com).

Jails: Detention and Short-Term Incarceration

Most Americans do not distinguish between jails and prisons. A **prison** is a federal or state correctional institution that holds offenders who are sentenced to terms of more than one year. A **jail** is a local facility for the detention of people awaiting trial (about 50 percent of inmates) and sentenced misdemeanants. Jail also serves as a holding facility for social misfits—derelicts, drug addicts, prostitutes, those with mental illness, and disturbers of public order.

Of the 3,376 jails in the United States, 2,700 operate at the county level, with most administered by an elected sheriff. About 600 fall under municipal jurisdiction. Only in six states—Alaska, Connecticut, Delaware, Hawaii, Rhode Island, and Vermont—does the state administer jails for adults. There are also 13,500 police lockups and similar holding facilities authorized to detain people for up to 48 hours. The Federal Bureau of Prisons operates 12 jails that hold nearly 10,000 inmates. More than 15,000 pretrial detainees and offenders are held in 37 private jails that operate under contract to state or local governments (BJS, 2016). On any given day during 2014, nearly 732,000 people were held in jails throughout the United States (Minton & Zeng, 2015).

Increasingly, jails are being used to detain undocumented immigrants prior to the processing of charges or prior to deportation by U.S. Immigration and Customs Enforcement (ICE) of the Department of Homeland Security. In recent years, the federal crackdown on undocumented immigrants has escalated sharply. Holding ICE detainees not only adds to the overcrowding problems of some jails but is also costly to local governments, even with partial reimbursement by the federal government (Chanen, 2014; Miroff, 2008).

Who Is in Jail? With an estimated 13 million jail admissions per year, more people directly experience jails than experience prisons, mental hospitals, and halfway houses combined. Even if we consider that some of the people represented in this total are admitted more than once, probably at least 6 to 7 million people are detained at some time during the year. Nationally, nearly 732,000 people, both the convicted and the unconvicted, sit in jail on any one day (Minton & Zeng, 2015). However, the number of people held at any one time in jail does not tell the complete story. Many are held for less than 24 hours. A few may await their trial for more than a year. Others may reside in jail as sentenced offenders, typically for up to one year, but some states are now using jails to hold convicted offenders for as long as five years.

prison An institution for the incarceration of people convicted of serious crimes, usually felonies.

jail An institution authorized to hold pretrial detainees and sentenced misdemeanants for periods longer than 48 hours.

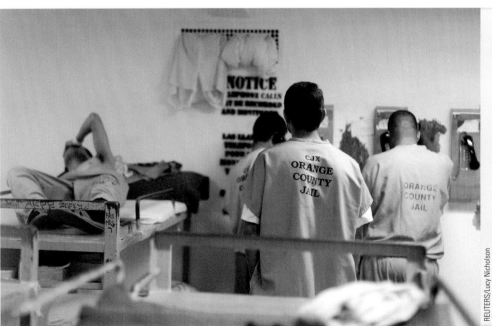

Jails contain both pretrial detainees, who are presumptively innocent until proved guilty, and convicted offenders awaiting transfer to prison or serving short sentences. Should as-yet-unconvicted detainees, some of whom may eventually be found not guilty, experience the same conditions and deprivations as convicted offenders inside jails? Or should pretrial detainees be kept in separate areas and given more-extensive privileges? What if the jail lacks the space and resources to treat the groups differently?

REUTERS/Lucy Nicholson

The National Jail Census reports show that about 85 percent of inmates are men, most are younger than 30 years old, less than half are white, and most have limited education and low incomes (Minton & Zeng, 2015; Minton, 2011). A significant percentage of jail inmates have mental health problems (Petteruti & Walsh, 2008). During the twenty-first century, as the country has become more anxious about immigrants, the jailing of people for immigration violations grew by 100 percent (Minton, 2011). The demographic characteristics of the jail population differ greatly from those of the national population (Figure 10.1).

Managing Jails   Jail administrators face several problems that good management practices cannot always overcome. These problems include (1) the perceived role of the jail in the local criminal justice system, (2) the characteristics of the inmate population, and (3) fiscal problems.

Role of the Jail   As facilities to detain accused people awaiting trial, jails customarily have been run by law enforcement agencies. Most of the 150,000 correctional officers in the jail system work under the direction of county sheriffs. We might reasonably expect that the agency that arrests and transports defendants to court should also administer the facility that holds them. Typically, however, neither sheriffs nor deputies have much interest in corrections. Further, almost half the jail inmates are sentenced offenders under correctional authority. Thus, many experts argue that jails have outgrown police administration.

Inmate Characteristics   The mixture of offenders of widely diverse ages and criminal histories in U.S. jails is an oft-cited problem. Because criminal justice professionals view most inmates as temporary residents, they make little attempt to classify them for either security or treatment purposes. Horror stories of the mistreatment of young offenders by older, stronger, and more violent inmates occasionally come to public attention. The physical condition of most jails aggravates this situation, because most are old, overcrowded, and lacking in basic facilities. Many sentenced felons prefer to move on to state prison, where the conditions tend to be better.

FIGURE 10.1

Characteristics of Jail Inmates in U.S. Jails Compared with the American population as a whole, jails are disproportionately inhabited by men, minorities, the poorly educated, and those with low income.

Sources: C. W. Harlow, "Education and Correctional Populations," *Bureau of Justice Statistics Bulletin Special Report*, January 2003; T. D. Minton and Z. Zeng, "Jail Inmates at Midyear 2014," *Bureau of Justice Statistics Bulletin*, June 2015, NCJ 248629.

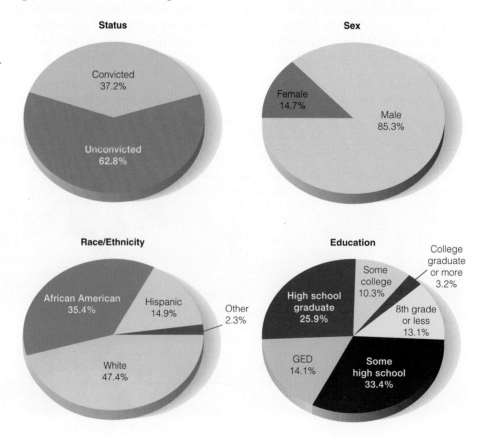

Because inmate turnover is high and because local control provides an incentive to keep costs down, jails usually lack correctional services. They do not typically offer recreational facilities or treatment programs, and medical services are generally minimal. Such conditions add to the idleness and tensions of the inmates. Suicides and high levels of violence are hallmarks of many jails. In any one year, almost half the people who die while in jail have committed suicide. People with mental illnesses are among those with the greatest risk of suicide while in jail. They present significant challenges for jail officials who run institutions designed for custody but that typically are not prepared to provide treatment. Read the "Evidence-Based Practice and Policy" feature to consider research-based practices for addressing the needs of detainees struggling with mental illness.

EVIDENCE-BASED PRACTICE AND POLICY

Jails and Mental Illness

A report in 2014 by the Treatment Advocacy Center, a nonprofit organization focused on expanding the availability of treatment for mental illnesses, reported the striking statistic that there were 10 times as many people with severe mental illnesses in jails and prisons as in psychiatric hospitals—356,000 in prisons and jails and only 35,000 in state psychiatric hospitals. Because of the deinstitutionalization movement of the past 40 years that replaced treatment in mental hospitals with less-expensive treatment within the community, jails have found themselves on the frontlines of mental illness issues. People with mental illnesses often end up in jails for behaving in unusual ways that upset their fellow citizens, even if their behavior does not clearly constitute a crime.

In light of the challenges facing jails with respect to this issue, many mental health professionals have worked with criminal justice officials to try to develop evidence-based practices that will benefit people needing treatment and also protect safety and security in society. These efforts have produced a number of important recommendations:

- Criminal justice officials, including police, jail officials, and other corrections officials, must collaborate and coordinate with mental health professionals and local health service providers.
- Efforts must be made to evaluate and classify people who enter the jail to better determine who requires mental health services and the nature of their needs. Those identified should be assigned to safe housing settings that minimize opportunities for suicide or conflict with others and that provide adequate supervision if there is a need for crisis intervention.
- Efforts must be made to develop jail diversion programs that can place eligible people with mental illnesses into alternative living and treatment settings that do not contain the relatively harsh conditions of jail and avoid their being mixed with the diverse populations within jails. Diversion efforts may include the use of Crisis Intervention Teams, in which police officers and social workers respond together when there are calls about the behavior of people exhibiting signs of mental illness.

- Alternative programs, such as mental health courts, can often provide more effective treatment and supervision than that provided in jail.
- Jails need to work with service providers to bring mental health professionals into jails to train jail staff and provide treatment programs for detainees and offenders who are confined within these institutions. Larger jails may be able to establish separate housing units for those who are receiving mental health treatment.
- Jails must develop procedures within applicable federal and state guidelines for providing medications, with or without the consent of the detainee, when medically necessary and permitted by law.
- Jails, and other correctional institutions, must have special planning for the transition of detainees with mental illness and offenders from confinement to society, facilitating access to housing assistance and other social services as well as mental health aftercare plans.

Researching the Internet
Look at the research and recommendations provided by the Treatment Advocacy Center concerning mental illness issues in corrections at **http://www.tacreports.org/treatment-behind-bars**.

Implementing New Practices
If you were a sheriff who had just received a substantial grant from a private foundation for the purpose of adopting evidence-based practices, what would be your priorities? What agencies and organizations would you contact in order to create a well-planned program for dealing with people with mental illness who are brought to your jail by the police?

Sources: California Corrections Standards Authority, *Jails and the Mentally Ill: Issues and Analysis* (2014); (http://www.cdcr.ca.gov /Comio/docs/MENTALLY_ILL_IN_JAILS_PAPER%20.pdf); Treatment Advocacy Center, *The Treatment of Persons with Mental Illness in Prisons and Jails: A State Survey (abridged)*, April 8, 2014 (http://www.tacreports.org/treatment-behind-bars).

Fiscal Problems   Jails help control crime but also drain local revenues. The tension between these two public interests often surfaces in debates over expenditures for jail construction and operation. Because revenues often fall short, many jails are overcrowded, lack programs, and do not have enough officers for effective supervision. In some areas, multicounty jails serve an entire region as a means of operating facilities in a cost-efficient way.

As criminal justice policy has become more punitive, jails, like prisons, have become crowded. Even with new construction and with alternatives such as release on recognizance (ROR) programs, diversion, intensive probation supervision, and house arrest with electronic monitoring, the jail population continues to rise. The annual cost of operating jails heavily burdens local governments, and this burden has become more difficult in an era of budget cuts and layoffs of sheriff's deputies and other jail officers. In February 2016, for example, Mercer County, New Jersey, announced that it would lay off two-thirds of its 280 jail employees and move 600 detainees to a neighboring county. The county could afford neither to maintain its aging jail nor to build a new one (Shea, 2016).

▼ **CHECK POINT**

4. **What agencies of the U.S. government are responsible for prisons and probation?**
   The Federal Bureau of Prisons, which handles prisons, and the Administrative Office of the U.S. Courts, which handles probation.

5. **What agencies of state government are responsible for prisons, probation, intermediate sanctions, and parole?**
   Prisons: department of corrections (executive branch); *probation:* judiciary or executive department; *intermediate sanctions:* judiciary, probation department, department of corrections; *parole:* executive agency.

6. **What are the functions of jails?**
   Holding of offenders before trial and incarceration of offenders sentenced to short terms.

STOP & ANALYZE

Does a philosophical problem arise when convicted offenders are sent to privately operated prisons and jails? In criminal law, the government imposes punishment on people for breaking the laws made by the government. Does this mean that only the government should administer the punishment? List two arguments either supporting or opposing the idea that all criminal punishment should be administered by government.

The Law of Corrections

hands-off policy Judges should not interfere with the administration of correctional institutions.

Prior to the 1960s, most courts maintained a **hands-off policy** with respect to corrections. Only a few state courts had recognized rights for offenders. Most judges felt that prisoners and probationers did not have protected rights and that courts should not interfere with the operational agencies dealing with probation, prisons, and parole.

Since the 1960s, however, offenders have gained access to the courts to contest correctional officers' decisions and challenge aspects of their punishment that they believe violate basic rights. Judicial decisions have defined and recognized the constitutional rights of probationers, prisoners, and parolees, as well as the need for policies and procedures that respect those rights. As you read "Criminal Justice: Myth & Reality," consider your own views about the recognition of constitutional rights for convicted criminal offenders.

Constitutional Rights of Prisoners

Cooper v. Pate (1964) Prisoners are entitled to the protection of the Civil Rights Act of 1871 and may challenge in federal courts the conditions of their confinement.

The U.S. Supreme Court decision in *Cooper v. Pate* (1964) signaled the end of the hands-off policy. The court said that through the Civil Rights Act of 1871 (referred to here as Section 1983), state prisoners were *persons* whose rights are protected by the Constitution. The act imposes *civil liability* on any official who violates someone's constitutional rights. It allows suits against state officials to be heard in the federal courts. Because of *Cooper v. Pate*, the federal courts now recognize that prisoners may sue state officials over such things as brutality by guards, inadequate nutrition or medical care, theft of personal property, and the denial of basic rights.

The first successful prisoners' rights cases involved the most excessive of prison abuses: brutality and inhumane physical conditions. Gradually, however, prison litigation has focused more directly on the daily activities of the institution, especially on the administrative rules that regulate inmates' conduct (C. E. Smith, 2007). This focus has resulted in a series of court decisions concerning the First, Fourth, Eighth, and Fourteenth Amendments to the Constitution. (See Chapter 3 for the full text of these amendments.)

First Amendment The First Amendment guarantees freedom of speech, press, assembly, petition, and religion. In the courts, prisoners have successfully challenged many of the restrictions of prison life—access to reading materials, censorship of mail, and rules affecting some religious practices (A. C. Burns, 2007). However, the Supreme Court has also approved restrictions on access to written materials, including Pennsylvania's denial of access to newspapers and magazines for prisoners housed in a disciplinary segregation unit (*Beard v. Banks*, 2006).

Since 1970 courts have extended the rights of freedom of speech and expression to prisoners. They have required correctional administrators to show why restrictions on these rights must be imposed. For example, in 1974 the Supreme Court ruled that censorship of mail was permissible only when officials could demonstrate a compelling government interest in maintaining security (*Procunier v. Martinez*). Communication between inmates and the outside world has since increased markedly. However, in *Turner v. Safley* (1987), the Court upheld a Missouri ban on correspondence between inmates in different institutions, as a means of combating gang violence and the communication of escape plans. See "You Make the Decision" to consider how you might evaluate policies about communications if you were a federal judge considering a case about correspondence at a county jail.

The First Amendment prevents Congress from making laws respecting the establishment of religion or prohibiting its free exercise. Cases concerning the free exercise of religion have caused the judiciary some problems, especially when the religious practice may interfere with prison routine and the maintenance of order.

The growth of the Black Muslim religion in prisons set the stage for suits demanding that this group be granted the same privileges as other faiths (special diets, access to clergy and religious publications, opportunities for group worship). Attorneys for the Muslims succeeded in winning several important cases that helped establish for prisoners the First Amendment right to free exercise of religion. These decisions also helped Native Americans, Orthodox Jews, and other

CRIMINAL JUSTICE

Myth&Reality

COMMON BELIEF: People convicted of crimes should forfeit all constitutional rights, because they have violated laws and harmed people. They have broken their "social contract" with our country, through which they receive the benefits of rights and the opportunity for economic success in exchange for their commitment to follow the country's rules.

REALITY

- The U.S. Constitution does not make the possession of rights contingent on specific behavior. In fact, many provisions of the Bill of Rights are clearly written as specific limitations on what the government can do to people, including people who commit crimes.

- The Eighth Amendment's prohibition on "cruel and unusual punishments" implies that there are limits on what the government may do to criminal offenders. If offenders literally had no rights, they could be tortured, starved, and killed without any legal intervention to save them.

- Punishment for incarcerated offenders is the loss of their liberty for a period of time under strict conditions. Such punishment is not supposed to include a potentially deadly environment in which they have no entitlement to food, shelter, protection from violence, or treatment for serious illnesses.

- Is the American value of justice upheld if an 18-year-old who is sentenced to two years in prison for stealing is beaten, starved, deprived of medical care, or even killed in prison? In other words, should a short prison sentence ever be a potential death sentence?

- Is there widespread agreement about exactly which rights prisoners should possess? No. However, American history itself demonstrates that an absence of rights creates risks of abuses that are contrary to our country's conceptions of justice.

- As you shall see, prisoners have very limited rights that are defined in light of the institution's needs to maintain safety and security. Nevertheless, these include the right to humane treatment while they are imprisoned.

Federal Trial Judge

Sheriffs who manage county jails throughout the country have increasingly imposed "postcard only" rules for mail sent by and to their inmates—both presumptively innocent detainees and convicted offenders. Jail officials claim that the rule is necessary because it takes staff too much time to make sure that envelopes do not contain communications to or from outside accomplices about escape plans, drugs, pornography, or other harmful items. In many jails, the only exception to the "postcard only" rule is the right of jailed individuals to correspond with their attorneys using envelopes, as part of the constitutional right to representation by counsel. A group that advocates rehabilitation programs for criminal offenders has helped a jailed offender file a lawsuit against the county in which he is jailed. The lawsuit claims that such "postcard only" rules violate First Amendment rights to free speech by limiting not only jailed individuals' rights to communicate with others but also their right to receive books, magazines, and other publications, including publications that educate offenders about their constitutional rights. As a federal trial judge, you must decide whether or not the "postcard only" rule violates the First Amendment rights of offenders and detainees in jails. Give reasons for your decision. Then conduct an Internet search to read articles about such policies in San Diego, California, and Knoxville, Tennessee, that were challenged in 2015.

prisoners to practice their religions. Court decisions have upheld prisoners' rights to be served meals consistent with religious dietary laws, to correspond with religious leaders, to possess religious literature, to wear a beard if their belief requires it, and to assemble for services. In sum, members of religious minorities have broken new legal ground on First Amendment issues.

Members of Congress have demonstrated a protective orientation toward prisoners' right to free exercise of religion. Two statutes enacted by Congress, the Religious Freedom Restoration Act (RFRA) and the Religious Land Use and Institutionalized Persons Act (RLUIPA), require that corrections officials provide a "compelling" justification for any policies and practices that interfere with the exercise of religion. The RFRA applies to federal correctional institutions and the RLUIPA applies to state and local facilities. These laws enable judges to look especially closely at issues that arise concerning this particular right of prisoners.

Issues concerning freedom of religion continue to be raised with regularity by contemporary prisoners. For example, in 2013 John Walker Lindh, widely labeled by the news media as "the American Taliban," won a court order permitting him to join with other Muslim prisoners in daily group prayers within a federal prison in Indiana (*Lindh v. Warden*, 2013). Lindh was a middle-class American from California who converted to Islam as a teenager and moved to the Middle and Near East to study languages and religion. He ended up joining an al-Qaeda group defending the Taliban government of Afghanistan in 2001 and was captured by American-backed military forces when the Taliban government was overthrown after 9/11. Lindh is serving a 20-year sentence after pleading guilty to providing services for the Taliban government and carrying weapons in opposition to U.S.-backed forces. Although Lindh was labeled as a "traitor" by many Americans, our legal system recognizes that he has a constitutional right to practice his religion. In another example, the Supreme Court unanimously endorsed the right of a Muslim prisoner in Arkansas in 2015 to grow the short beard required by his religious beliefs despite the objections of corrections officials (*Holt v. Hobbs*). Read the "Close Up" feature to see the Supreme Court's analysis of the issue in *Holt v. Hobbs* (2015).

Fourth Amendment The Fourth Amendment prohibits *unreasonable* searches and seizures, but courts have extended only very limited protections to prisoners. Thus, prison regulations viewed as reasonable to maintain security and order in an institution may justify searches that would not be permitted in other contexts.

The Supreme Court's Decision in *Holt v. Hobbs* (2015)

Justice Samuel Alito delivered the opinion of the Court.

Petitioner Gregory Holt, also known as Abdul Maalik Muhammad, is an Arkansas inmate and a devout Muslim who wishes to grow a ½-inch beard in accordance with his religious beliefs. [The prisoner's] objection to shaving his beard clashes with the Arkansas Department of Correction's grooming policy, which prohibits inmates from growing beards unless they have a particular dermatological condition. We hold that the Department's policy, as applied in this case, violates the Religious Land Use and Institutionalized Persons Act of 2000 (RLUIPA), 114 Stat. 803, 42 U.S.C. § 2000cc *et seq.*, which prohibits a state or local government from taking any action that substantially burdens the religious exercise of an institutionalized person unless the government demonstrates that the action constitutes the least restrictive means of furthering a compelling governmental interest.

We conclude in this case that the Department's policy substantially burdens petitioner's religious exercise. Although we do not question the importance of the Department's interests in stopping the flow of contraband and facilitating prisoner identification, we do doubt whether the prohibition against petitioner's beard furthers its compelling interest about contraband. And we conclude that the Department has failed to show that its policy is the least restrictive means of furthering its compelling interests. We thus reverse the decision of the United States Court of Appeals for the Eighth Circuit.

Congress enacted RLUIPA and its sister statute, the Religious Freedom Restoration Act of 1993 (RFRA), 107 Stat. 1488, 42 U.S.C. § 2000bb *et seq.*, "in order to provide very broad protection for religious liberty."

***

Petitioner, as noted, is in the custody of the Arkansas Department of Correction and he objects on religious grounds to the Department's grooming policy, which provides that "[n]o inmates will be permitted to wear facial hair other than a neatly trimmed mustache that does not extend beyond the corner of the mouth or over the lip" ... The policy makes no exception for inmates who object on religious grounds, but it does contain an exemption for prisoners with medical needs: "Medical staff may prescribe that inmates with a diagnosed dermatological problem may wear facial hair no longer than one quarter of an inch." *Ibid.* The policy provides that "[f]ailure to abide by [the Department's] grooming standards is grounds for disciplinary action."

Petitioner sought permission to grow a beard and, although he believes that his faith requires him not to trim his beard at all, he proposed a "compromise" under which he would grow only a ½-inch beard. Prison officials denied his request, and the warden told him: "[Y]ou will abide by [Arkansas Department of Correction] policies and if you choose to disobey, you can suffer the consequences."

Petitioner filed a *pro se* complaint in Federal District Court challenging the grooming policy under RLUIPA. We refer to the respondent prison officials collectively as the Department. In October 2011, the District Court granted petitioner a preliminary injunction and remanded to a Magistrate Judge for an evidentiary hearing. At the hearing, the Department called two witnesses. Both expressed the belief that inmates could hide contraband in even a ½-inch beard, but neither pointed to any instances in which this had been done in Arkansas or elsewhere. Both witnesses also acknowledged that inmates could hide items in many other places, such as in the hair on their heads or their clothing. In addition, one of the witnesses—Gaylon Lay, the warden of petitioner's prison—testified that a prisoner who escaped could change his appearance by shaving his beard, and that a prisoner could shave his beard to disguise himself and enter a restricted area of the prison. Neither witness, however, was able to explain why these problems could not be addressed by taking a photograph of an inmate without a beard, a practice followed in other prison systems. Lay voiced concern that the Department would be unable to monitor the length of a prisoner's beard to ensure that it did not exceed one-half inch, but he acknowledged that the Department kept track of the length of the beards of those inmates who are allowed to wear a ¼-inch beard for medical reasons.

As a result of the preliminary injunction, petitioner had a short beard at the time of the hearing, and the Magistrate Judge commented: "I look at your particular circumstance and I say, you know, it's almost preposterous to think that you could hide contraband in your beard." Nevertheless, the Magistrate Judge recommended that the preliminary injunction be vacated and that petitioner's complaint be dismissed for failure to state a claim on which relief can be granted. The Magistrate Judge emphasized that "the prison officials are entitled to deference," and that the grooming policy allowed petitioner to exercise his religion in other ways, such as by praying on a prayer rug, maintaining the diet required by his faith, and observing religious holidays.

***

Since petitioner met his burden of showing that the Department's grooming policy substantially burdened his exercise of religion, the burden shifted to the Department to show that its refusal to allow petitioner to grow a ½-inch beard "(1) [was] in furtherance of a compelling governmental interest; and (2) [was] the least restrictive means of furthering that compelling governmental interest."

The Department argues that its grooming policy represents the least restrictive means of furthering a "'broadly formulated interes[t],'" namely, the Department's compelling interest in prison safety and security.

***

continued

Close Up (continued)

The Department contends that enforcing this prohibition is the least restrictive means of furthering prison safety and security in two specific ways.

A

The Department first claims that the no-beard policy prevents prisoners from hiding contraband. The Department worries that prisoners may use their beards to conceal all manner of prohibited items, including razors, needles, drugs, and cellular phone subscriber identity module (SIM) cards.

We readily agree that the Department has a compelling interest in staunching the flow of contraband into and within its facilities, but the argument that this interest would be seriously compromised by allowing an inmate to grow a ½-inch beard is hard to take seriously. As noted, the Magistrate Judge observed that it was "almost preposterous to think that [petitioner] could hide contraband" in the short beard he had grown at the time of the evidentiary hearing. An item of contraband would have to be very small indeed to be concealed by a ½-inch beard, and a prisoner seeking to hide an item in such a short beard would have to find a way to prevent the item from falling out. Since the Department does not demand that inmates have shaved heads or short crew cuts, it is hard to see why an inmate would seek to hide contraband in a ½-inch beard rather than in the longer hair on his head.

***

The Department failed to establish that it could not satisfy its security concerns by simply searching petitioner's beard. The Department already searches prisoners' hair and clothing, and it presumably examines the ¼-inch beards of inmates with dermatological conditions. It has offered no sound reason why hair, clothing, and ¼-inch beards can be searched but ½-inch beards cannot. The Department suggests that requiring guards to search a prisoner's beard would pose a risk to the physical safety of a guard if a razor or needle was concealed in the beard. But that is no less true for searches of hair, clothing, and ¼-inch beards. And the Department has failed to prove that it could not adopt the less restrictive alternative of having the prisoner run a comb through his beard. For all these reasons, the Department's interest in eliminating contraband cannot sustain its refusal to allow petitioner to grow a ½-inch beard.

B

The Department contends that its grooming policy is necessary to further an additional compelling interest, *i.e.*, preventing prisoners from disguising their identities. The Department tells us that the no-beard policy allows security officers to identify prisoners quickly and accurately. It claims that bearded inmates could shave their beards and change their appearance in order to enter restricted areas within the prison, to escape, and to evade apprehension after escaping.

We agree that prisons have a compelling interest in the quick and reliable identification of prisoners, and we acknowledge that any alteration in a prisoner's appearance, such as by shaving a beard, might, in the absence of effective countermeasures, have at least some effect on the ability of guards or others to make a quick identification. But even if we assume for present purposes that the Department's grooming policy sufficiently furthers its interest in the identification of prisoners, that policy still violates RLUIPA as applied in the circumstances present here. The Department contends that a prisoner who has a beard when he is photographed for identification purposes might confuse guards by shaving his beard. But as petitioner has argued, the Department could largely solve this problem by requiring that all inmates be photographed without beards when first admitted to the facility and, if necessary, periodically thereafter. Once that is done, an inmate like petitioner could be allowed to grow a short beard and could be photographed again when the beard reached the ½-inch limit. Prison guards would then have a bearded and clean-shaven photo to use in making identifications.

C

[The] Department failed to show, in the face of petitioner's evidence, why the vast majority of States and the Federal Government permit inmates to grow ½-inch beards, either for any reason or for religious reasons, but it cannot.... That so many other prisons allow inmates to grow beards while ensuring prison safety and security suggests that the Department could satisfy its security concerns through a means less restrictive than denying petitioner the exemption he seeks.

In sum, we hold that the Department's grooming policy violates RLUIPA insofar as it prevents petitioner from growing a ½-inch beard in accordance with his religious beliefs.

It is so ordered.

Researching the Internet

To read the Supreme Court's complete opinion visit http://www.supremecourt.gov/opinions/14pdf/13-6827_5h26.pdf.

For Critical Thinking and Analysis

Are there any other arguments that prison officials might have made to advance their view that giving in to the prisoner's demand to grow a beard would affect safety and security at the prison? Create and explain two additional arguments you might have presented if you were the lawyer for the prison.

Hudson v. Palmer (1984)
Prison officials have the authority to search cells and confiscate any materials found.

For example, *Hudson v. Palmer* (1984) upheld the authority of officials to search cells and confiscate any materials found without any suspicion of wrongdoing by the prisoner or other justification for the search.

The Supreme Court's opinions with regard to the Fourth Amendment reveal the balance between institutional need and the right to privacy. Body searches have been harder for administrators to justify than cell searches, for example. But body searches have been upheld when they advance policies clearly related to identifiable and legitimate institutional needs and when they are not intended to humiliate or degrade (*Bell v. Wolfish*, 1979). In a recent decision, the U.S. Supreme Court cleared up disagreements in lower courts by declaring that people who are arrested can be strip-searched upon entering a jail, even if they are only charged with very minor offenses and there is no specific reason to believe that they are hiding drugs or weapons on their bodies (*Florence v. Board of Chosen Freeholders*, 2012). The Supreme Court declared that jails' security needs outweighed the intrusion on the privacy of people arrested for minor offenses.

Eighth Amendment   The Constitution's prohibition of cruel and unusual punishments has been tied to prisoners' needs for decent treatment and minimum health standards. The courts have traditionally applied three principal tests under the Eighth Amendment to determine whether conditions are unconstitutional: (1) whether the punishment shocks the conscience of a civilized society, (2) whether the punishment is unnecessarily cruel, and (3) whether the punishment goes beyond legitimate penal aims. In the past two decades, however, courts have coupled their concerns about these issues with a focus on the intentions of correctional administrators, especially the question of whether officials intentionally ignored problems within their institutions.

Federal courts have ruled that although some aspects of prison life may be acceptable, the combination of various factors—the *totality of conditions*—may be such that life in the institution constitutes cruel and unusual punishment. When courts have found brutality, unsanitary facilities, overcrowding, and inadequate food, judges have used the Eighth Amendment to order sweeping changes and even, in some cases, to take over administration of entire prisons or corrections systems. In these cases, judges have ordered wardens to follow specific internal procedures and to spend money on certain improvements. The U.S. Supreme Court has instructed lower court judges to focus findings of Eighth Amendment violations on those situations in which correctional officials showed "deliberate indifference" to substandard living conditions (*Wilson v. Seiter*, 1991).

A correctional officer leads a "sniffer" dog through a cell at Big Muddy Correctional Center in Ina, Illinois. A 150-member tactical team conducted this search without giving the prisoners any prior warning. Is there anything that officers might do during such a search that would violate a prisoner's Fourth Amendment right against unreasonable searches and seizures?

In 2011, a closely divided U.S. Supreme Court upheld lower court decisions ordering California to reduce its prison population because overcrowded conditions had overwhelmed the prison system's ability to provide proper health care and mental health treatment for prisoners (*Brown v. Plata*, 2011). The competing opinions issued in the case illustrated continuing divisions among the justices about forcing prisons to uphold certain standards for living conditions as opposed to permitting states to handle their own issues and avoid the risk that public safety would be threatened by early releases (C. E. Smith, 2013). In actuality, rather than use the mass releases that some justices feared, the state reduced prison populations by shifting nonviolent, nonserious, and nonsex offenders to serve shorter sentences in county jails rather than in state prisons (Carson & Golinelli, 2013b). Initial research shows that crime has generally declined in California even as the prison population has been reduced, and a portion of those who would previously have been sent to prisons are placed in county jails (Males, 2015).

Fourteenth Amendment   One word and two clauses of the Fourteenth Amendment are key to the question of prisoners' rights. The relevant word is *state*, which is found in several clauses of the Fourteenth Amendment. It was not until the 1960s that the Supreme Court ruled that through the Fourteenth Amendment, portions of the Bill of Rights limit actions by state criminal justice officials.

The first important clause concerns procedural due process, which requires that government officials treat all people fairly and justly and that official decisions be made according to procedures prescribed by law. The second important clause is the equal protection clause. Assertions that prisoners have been denied equal protection of the law are based on claims of racial, gender, or religious discrimination.

Wolff v. McDonnell (1974) Basic elements of procedural due process must be present when decisions are made about imposing significant punishments on prisoners for violating institutional rules.

Due Process in Prison Discipline

In *Wolff v. McDonnell* (1974), the Supreme Court ruled that basic procedural rights must be present when decisions are made about the disciplining of inmates for serious infractions of prison rules. Specifically, prisoners have the right to receive notice of the complaint, to have a fair hearing, to confront witnesses, to get help in preparing for the hearing, and to be given a written statement of the decision. However, the Court also recognized special conditions of incarceration in that prisoners do not have the right to cross-examine witnesses and that the evidence presented by the offender shall not be unduly hazardous to institutional safety or correctional goals.

As a result of these Supreme Court decisions, prison officials have established rules that provide elements of due process in disciplinary and other proceedings. In many institutions, a disciplinary committee receives the charges, conducts hearings, and decides guilt and punishment. Even with these protections, prisoners remain powerless and may risk further punishment if they challenge the warden's decisions too vigorously.

Equal Protection

In 1968, the Supreme Court firmly established that racial discrimination cannot be official policy within prison walls (*Lee v. Washington*). Segregation can be justified only in rare instances by compelling circumstances, such as a temporary expedient during periods when violence between races is demonstrably imminent (*Johnson v. California*, 2005). In recent decades, some cases have concerned equal protection issues affecting female offenders. Judges in state courts and lower federal courts have addressed these issues. For example, in a series of decisions spanning nearly two decades, female inmates in Michigan successfully argued that their equal protection rights were violated because programs and services for them were not as good as those provided to male inmates (*Glover v. Johnson*, 1991). Critics who believe that prisons neglect the needs of women prisoners argue that judges have generally permitted too many differences in facilities and programs for women without providing sufficient attention to issues of equality (Carroll-Ferrary, 2006).

Impact of the Prisoners' Rights Movement

The Supreme Court in recent years has reduced its support of the expansion of prisoners' rights (C. E. Smith, 2011). Nonetheless, the prisoners' rights movement has spurred some positive changes in American corrections since the late 1970s. The most obvious are improvements in institutional living conditions and administrative practices. Law libraries and legal assistance are now generally available, communication with the outside is easier, religious practices are protected, inmate complaint procedures have been developed, and due process requirements are emphasized. Prisoners in solitary confinement undoubtedly suffer less neglect than they did in the past. Although overcrowding remains a major problem, many conditions have greatly improved, and the most brutalizing elements of prison life have diminished.

These changes did not entirely result from court orders, however. They also coincided with the growing influence of college-educated correctional professionals who sought on their own to improve prisons (C. E. Smith, 2000a). There are, however, lingering debates about whether judges have intruded improperly. Read "The Policy Debate" to consider the long-running dispute about whether judges should avoid telling prison officials how corrections institutions should be run.

Should Judges Defer to Decisions of Prison Officials?

As mentioned concerning Supreme Court justices' competing opinions in *Brown v. Plata* (2011), there are significant disagreements about whether and when it is proper for judges to order changes in prison policies and practices. Everyone agrees that judges bear responsibility for identifying constitutional rights violations in prisons. However, judges and commentators express strong disagreements about the rights to which convicted offenders are entitled and how broadly those rights should be defined.

Moreover, heated controversies arise when judges do not merely identify rights violations, but actually issue detailed orders about needed changes in prisons in order to remedy rights violations. Some of these remedies, such as constructing new facilities or hiring more staff, could impose significant financial expenses. Other orders were viewed by critics as threatening order and security in prisons. Prison officials argue that judges should leave it to them to figure out how to fix problems while also maintaining safety and security. After all, it is prison officials rather than judges who have training and experience in prison administration. Thus, state officials resisted court orders to reduce prison populations in *Brown v. Plata* (2011). In *Johnson v. California* (2005) concerning Fourteenth Amendment equal protection issues, prison officials argued unsuccessfully that they needed to separate prisoners by race and ethnicity during initial processing in order to avoid violence between race-based gangs.

Governors whose prisons were affected by court orders lobbied Congress to enact laws that would limit the authority of judges. Congress passed the Prison Litigation Reform Act in 1996 that limited the authority of individual federal judges to order reductions in prison populations. It also required that judges' orders expire after two years unless new hearings took place to prove that there were continuing rights violations. In addition, the law limited the ability of prisoners to file repeated lawsuits over rights violations if they could not pay their own court fees. Three unsuccessful lawsuits that were deemed to be "frivolous" forfeited future opportunities for individual prisoners to ask the courts to waive filing fees for subsequent rights-violation lawsuits, even for matters related to such issues as sexual assaults or violations of religious rights.

For Judges' Deference to Prison Officials

- Prison officials rather than judges are the actual experts on what policies and procedures need to be imposed to maintain safety and security in prisons.
- Judges, who lack training and experience in corrections, may impose orders that cause difficult problems in prisons.
- Judges' orders may impose needless expenses, whereas prison officials, if left to handle their own problems, can develop effective, less costly solutions.
- Judges' orders that include expensive remedies, such as the construction of new facilities or the hiring of staff, improperly affect state government budgets and taxes by forcing money to be shifted away from other priorities such as schools and road construction.
- Judges' orders can make prisoners bolder in filing additional lawsuits, resisting prison rules and regulations, and assuming that they can use the courts to force changes in aspects of prison operations that they do not like.

For Judges' Independence in Upholding Constitutional Rights

- Judges swear an oath to uphold the Constitution, which includes the responsibility to make absolutely sure that constitutional rights are respected in prison.
- There is a long history in the United States of officials in many prisons failing to respect the constitutional rights of prisoners.
- Without strong orders from judges, prison officials will not receive the money from state legislatures that is needed to genuinely fix problems related to certain constitutional-rights problems, such as inadequate medical care.
- Prison officials often use the claim of safety and security issues too broadly as a means to deny access to nonthreatening reading materials or requests to engage in certain kinds of religious worship.
- Because prisons are closed institutions that cannot be scrutinized by the news media or the public, judges must have the authority to look closely at what happens inside in order to identify and fix problems as well as ensure that relevant laws are being followed.

What Should U.S. Policy Be?

The debates about judges' roles illustrate the risks and benefits of strong court actions to supervise and correct problems in prisons. Perspectives on this debate are often driven by very different viewpoints about whether prisoners have too many rights or, alternatively, inadequate protection under the Constitution. Do you think prisoners have too many rights or too few? Does your perspective on this issue affect how you evaluate the proper role of judges in prison litigation?

Researching the Internet

To read about criticisms of the Prison Litigation Reform Act and its limitations on opportunities to protect convicted offenders' rights, visit https://www.acslaw.org/files/Schlanger%20Shay%20PLRA%20Paper%203-28-07.pdf.

Analyzing the Issue

Imagine that you and your classmates are on a panel of federal appellate court judges considering a claim that convicted offenders in a women's

continued

The Policy Debate (continued)

prison have been denied equal protection of the law under the Fourteenth Amendment. Assume that you all agree that rights violations have occurred under the Fourteenth Amendment because, unlike in men's prisons, there is no gymnasium for prisoners to have indoor exercise during bad weather and there is no vocational program to

teach women prisoners job skills in electronics and computer repair. In addition, no one on the medical staff specializes in women's issues, a matter that is not relevant in men's prisons. What do you say in your decision about the case? Do you order specific remedies for these problems? Do you

leave it to prison officials to come up with solutions, even though they say that they will have to develop solutions without spending any additional money due to budget cuts? Can you and your fellow "judges" agree on what the court's decision should say?

Law and Community Corrections

Although most correctional law concerns prisons and jails, two-thirds of adults under supervision live in the community on probation and parole. However, as with prisoners, offenders in the community have certain rights, and courts have addressed issues concerning due process and searches and seizures.

Probationers and parolees must live according to conditions specified at the time of their sentencing or parole release. These conditions may interfere with their constitutional rights in that they typically limit the right of free association by restricting offenders from contact with their crime partners or victims. However, courts have struck down conditions that prevented parolees from exercising their First Amendment rights to give public speeches and receive publications.

The case of *Griffin v. Wisconsin* (1987) presents a good example of the clash between the Fourth Amendment and community corrections. Learning that Griffin might have a gun, probation officers searched his apartment without a warrant. Noting the practical problems of obtaining a search warrant while a probationer was under supervision, the Supreme Court said that the probation agency must be able to act before the offender damages himself or society. In Griffin's case, the Court felt that the agency had satisfied the Fourth Amendment's reasonableness requirement. Similarly, in *Samson v. California* (2006), the Supreme Court approved a California statute that requires every parolee to agree to be subject to warrantless searches, even in the absence of any suspicion of wrongdoing.

When parole is revoked, prisoners are returned to prison to complete their sentences. Before that happens, a revocation hearing takes place. In a 1998 case, *Pennsylvania Board of Pardons and Parole v. Scott*, a closely divided Court ruled that evidence that would be barred from use in a criminal trial can be used in parole revocation hearings. Operating without a search warrant, officers found guns in the home of a paroled murderer who was barred from owning weapons. Although the Pennsylvania courts decided that an improper search had been conducted, the U.S. Supreme Court concluded that the weapons could be used as evidence at a parole revocation hearing despite any Fourth Amendment violations that may have occurred. The exclusionary rule does not apply to parole revocation proceedings.

Morrissey v. Brewer (1972) Due process rights require a prompt, informal, two-stage inquiry handled by an impartial hearing officer before parole may be revoked. The parolee may present relevant information and confront witnesses.

The Supreme Court has also addressed the question of due process when revocation is being considered. In *Morrissey v. Brewer* (1972), the court ruled that parolees facing revocation must be given a two-stage hearing process. In the first stage, a hearing officer determines whether there is probable cause that a violation has occurred. Parolees have the right to be notified of the charges against them, to know the evidence against them, to be allowed to speak on their own behalf, to present witnesses, and to confront the witnesses against them. In the second stage, the revocation hearing, the parolee must receive a notice of charges, the evidence of a violation is disclosed, and he or she may cross-examine witnesses. The hearing body determines if the violation is sufficiently severe to warrant revocation. It must give the parolee a written statement outlining the evidence, with reasons for the decision.

In the following year, the Supreme Court applied the *Morrissey* procedures to probation revocation proceedings in *Gagnon v. Scarpelli* (1973). In this case, however, the Court also looked at the question of the right to counsel. It ruled that there was no absolute requirement but that in some cases probationers and parolees might request counsel, to be allowed on a case-by-case basis depending on the complexity of the issues, mitigating circumstances, and the competence of the offender.

Law and Correctional Personnel

Gagnon v. Scarpelli (1973) Before probation can be revoked, a two-stage hearing must be held and the offender must be provided with specific elements of due process. Requested counsel will be allowed on a case-by-case basis.

Just as law governs relationships among inmates, probationers, and parolees, laws and regulations also define the relationships between correctional administrators and their staff. With the exception of those working for private, nonprofit organizations, correctional personnel are public employees. Here we consider two important aspects of correctional work. First, as public employees, all correctional employees are governed by civil service rules and regulations. Second, correctional clients may sue state employees using Section 1983 of the United States Code.

Civil Service Laws

Civil service laws set the procedures for hiring, promoting, assigning, disciplining, and firing public employees. These laws protect public employees from arbitrary actions by their supervisors. Workplace rules also come to be developed through collective-bargaining agreements between correctional-employee unions and the government. These agreements have the force of law and contain rules concerning assignments, working conditions, and grievance procedures.

Like their counterparts in the private sector, government employees are protected from discrimination. With the Civil Rights Act of 1964, Congress prohibited employment discrimination based on race, gender, national origin, and religion. Subsequent federal legislation prohibits some forms of age discrimination (Age Discrimination in Employment Act) and discrimination against people with disabilities (Americans with Disabilities Act). States have their own antidiscrimination laws. All these laws have increased the number of minorities and women who work in corrections.

Unlike many public employees, those who work in corrections operate from a difficult position. They must assert authority over persons who have shown that they lack self-control or have little regard for society's rules. Whether in prison, in a probationer's home, or on the street, this responsibility creates pressures and difficult—sometimes dangerous—situations.

Liability of Correctional Personnel

In *Cooper v. Pate* (1964), the Supreme Court said that Section 1983 provides a means for prisoners, but also probationers and parolees, to bring lawsuits against correctional officials. *Monell v. Department of Social Services of the City of New York* (1978) clarified the meaning of Section 1983. Individual public employees and their agency may be sued when a person's civil rights are violated by the agency's "customs and usages." Specifically, if an individual can show that harm was caused by employees whose wrongful acts were the result of these "customs, practices, and policies, including poor training and supervision," then the employees and the local agency that employs them may be sued.

The Supreme Court has identified other kinds of legal actions that may be filed against corrections officials. For example, the Supreme Court has said that federal corrections officials can be sued under the Federal Tort Claims Act for intentional harms inflicted on prisoners (*Millbrook v. United States*, 2013). In the case decided by the high court, the prisoner claimed that he had been sexually assaulted by corrections officials. The Court's decision permitted him to proceed with his opportunity to prove the case after corrections officials had sought to have the case dismissed for using the wrong kind of legal action.

Although huge financial settlements make headlines and the number of Section 1983 filings is large, few cases come to trial and very few correctional employees must personally pay financial awards to plaintiffs. However, no correctional employee wants to be involved in such legal situations.

7. **Why is the case of *Cooper v. Pate* important to the expansion of prisoners' rights?**
   It allows state prisoners to challenge, in federal courts, rights violations conditions of their confinement.

8. **Which two clauses of the Fourteenth Amendment have been interpreted by the Supreme Court to apply to prisoners' rights?**
   Due process and equal protection clauses.

Can judges accurately anticipate the consequences of their decisions that shape policies and practices in prisons? Do judges really understand what goes on inside prisons and the problems that corrections officials face in running these institutions? List two possible undesirable consequences that could result from judges' rulings that instruct administrators to run their correctional institutions in a manner that respects prisoners' constitutional rights.

Correctional Policy Trends

The United States has a large and expanding population under correctional supervision. Since the middle of the 1970s, the United States has fought a war on crime mainly by increasing the severity of sanctions against offenders. This has led to a 500 percent increase in correctional budgets, nearly 4 million people on probation, over 2 million incarcerated in prisons and jails, and more than 850,000 under parole supervision. These are staggering figures, especially considering that crime has been decreasing for the past decade. Figure 10.2 shows the tremendous growth in the correctional population since 1985.

Correctional costs are mainly borne by the states and are now outpacing budget growth in education, transportation, and public assistance. Only Medicaid spending grew faster than that of corrections in recent years. Correctional costs

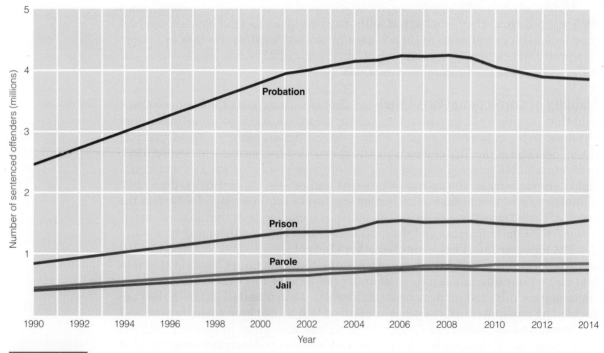

FIGURE 10.2

Correctional Populations in the United States 1990–2014 Although the increase in prison populations receives the most publicity, a greater proportion of correctional growth has occurred in probation and parole.

Source: D. Kaeble et al., "Correctional Populations in the United States, 2014," *Bureau of Justice Statistics Bulletin*, December 2015, NCJ249513, Figure 1 and Table 1.

have quadrupled during the past two decades. Even as states face huge budget short-falls, prison costs are driving spending increases. Some states spend more than 10 percent of all tax dollars on corrections, and nearly 90 percent of corrections allocations are for prisons. A survey of states found that they spent an average of $31,000 a year on each prisoner (Henrichson & Delaney, 2012). By contrast, costs for probationers and parolees were much lower, only $1,250 per probationer and $2,750 per parolee (S. Moore, 2009). California faces one of the most difficult budgetary situations, because of the size of the prison population and the relatively high compensation paid to its corrections officers. In 2011, the state spent $9.6 billion on prisons but only $5.7 billion on state colleges and universities. As critics have noted, California has built only one university since 1980 yet has built 20 new prisons in that time period (Flock, 2012).

Some observers believe that the drop in crime has resulted from harsher arrest and sentencing policies. Critics, however, say that the "lock 'em up" policies have had little impact, as drops in crime rates have been seen in states with different imprisonment rates. Moreover, critics claim that the financial and human costs of current policies severely damage families and communities. In the rest of the chapter, we examine community corrections and incarceration policies in order to understand current practices and future trends.

Community Corrections

Although escalating prison growth has captured the public's attention, the number of people on probation and parole has actually risen at a faster rate than the number of people incarcerated. Many factors may explain this growth, including more arrests and successful prosecutions, the lower costs of probation compared with incarceration, prison and jail crowding, and the large numbers of felons now being released from prison.

Probation   People on probation now make up nearly 60 percent of the correctional population, yet budgets and staffing have not risen accordingly. In many urban areas, probation caseloads are growing well beyond reasonable management levels: 200- and even 300-person caseloads are no longer unusual for individual probation officers. This has led to a deterioration in the quality of supervision. Yet, the importance of probation for public safety has never been greater. As a result, a renewed emphasis on public safety has arisen. Many agencies have seen a resurgence of intensive and structured supervision for selected offenders.

In many respects, then, probation finds itself at a crossroads. Its workload is growing dramatically and, in view of the crowding in prison and jails, will probably continue to do so. Under the strain of this workload and on-again, off-again public support, probation faces a serious challenge. Can its methods of supervision and service be adapted successfully to high-risk offenders?

Parole   With the incarcerated population nearly quadrupling during the past 30 years, the number of parolees has, not surprisingly, also grown. Currently, over 635,000 felons gain release from prison each year (Carson & Golinelli, 2013b). In 2014, there were 856,900 parolees under supervision in the community, a threefold increase since 1980 (Glaze & Herberman, 2013; Kaeble et al., 2015). The number on parole will likely reach 1 million in the next few years, because several states have been increasing parole releases as a way to cut expensive prison budgets (Lambert, 2011).

Compared with parolees in 1990, today's parolees are older, are more likely to have been sentenced for drug violations, have served longer prison sentences, and have higher levels of substance abuse and mental illness. These characteristics increase reentry problems related to renewing family ties, obtaining a job, and living according to parole rules. Most parolees cannot obtain the assistance necessary to reenter the community successfully. (The reentry problem is extensively discussed in Chapter 13.)

Further, increased numbers of offenders are being returned to prison as parole violators. In 2014, an estimated 164,000 parole violators were returned to prison, constituting more than 25 percent of offenders entering prison that year (Carson, 2015). Thus a significant portion of admissions to state prison each year can be attributed to the return of parolees for committing new crimes or violating conditions of release. Many states are devoting new efforts to more effectively transition parolees for reentry into society. We discuss this trend in Chapter 13.

Incarceration

From 1940 until 1973, the number of people incarcerated in the United States remained fairly stable, ranging from 250,000 to 330,000. However, since 1973, when the overall crime rate started to fall, the incarceration rate has quadrupled: 2.2 million were in prisons and jails by 2014. The United States has the highest incarceration rate in the developed world. The ongoing influence of budget issues and new approaches to sentencing are projected to produce continued decreases in prison populations in various states.

Keep in mind that the size and growth of the prison population varies across the country. Some states have had recent declines in prison populations while others have continued to see their corrections populations grow. As Figure 10.3 shows, 8 of the 10 states with the highest incarceration rates are in the South.

Crime rates have dropped throughout the country in recent years, even in states that did not have high incarceration rates. If little relationship exists between the crime rate and the incarceration rate, what factors explain the growth in imprisonment since 1980? Five reasons are often cited for the rise: (1) increased arrests and more likely incarceration, (2) tougher sentencing, (3) prison construction, (4) the war on drugs, and (5) state politics. None of these

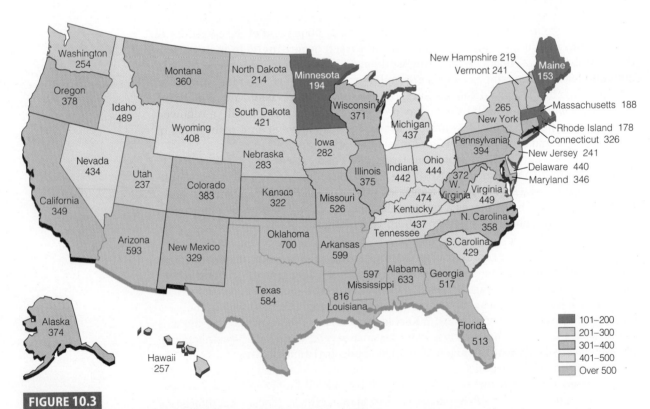

FIGURE 10.3

Sentenced Prisoners in State Institutions per 100,000 Population, December 31, 2014 What can be said about the differences in incarceration rates among the states? There are not only regional differences but also differences between adjacent states that seem to have similar socioeconomic and crime characteristics.

Source: E. A. Carson, "Prisoners in 2014," *Bureau of Justice Statistics Bulletin*, September 2015, NCJ 248955. Table 2.

reasons should be viewed as being the only explanation or as having more demonstrated impact than the others.

Increased Arrests and More Likely Incarceration
Some analysts argue that the billions of dollars spent on the crime problem may be paying off. Not only have arrest rates increased, particularly for some offenses such as drug violations, aggravated assaults, and sexual assaults, but the probability of being sent to prison has also dramatically increased. In 2009, the U.S. Sentencing Guidelines Commission reported that the percentage of federal offenders sent to prison had increased over the past 10 years from 75.4 percent to 85.3 percent, while the use of alternatives to incarceration such as probation and intermediate sanctions decreased over the same period (Coyle, 2009).

In addition, the number of offenders returned to prison for parole violations also increased. In 2014, one-quarter of the 626,000 people admitted into American prisons were parolees who had either committed new crimes or violated the conditions of parole.

Tougher Sentencing Practices
Some observers think that a hardening of public attitudes toward criminals resulted in longer sentences, in a smaller proportion of those convicted getting probation, and in fewer being released at the time of the first parole hearing. Yet, in the past few years, budget pressures have led some states to emphasize probation and parole to reduce the costs of prisons.

An important element affecting the size of prison populations is the actual length of time served in prison for specific crimes, notwithstanding the formal length of the announced sentence. Between 1980 and the early twenty-first century, the states and the federal government passed laws that increased sentences for most crimes. However, due to reductions in time for good behavior and parole releases, tougher sentences do not necessarily keep each offender in prison for the full length of these longer sentences. Yet over time, these tougher sentences have effectively resulted in a 13-percent increase in the actual amount of time served by many offenders even if they eventually gained early releases on parole, because they have had to wait longer to be eligible for parole release. Recent budget-driven developments may diminish the prior effects of tougher sentencing and contribute to further declines in prison growth.

Prison Construction
As the public in the 1970s began to favor harsher sentencing policies, the rate of incarceration grew. Prison crowding eventually reached crisis proportions, creating health and security issues. Many states attempted to build their way out of this problem—literally.

Large state budget surpluses during the booming economy of the 1990s made many legislatures willing to advance the huge sums required for prison expansion. Between 1975 and 2000, more than 400 prisons were built across the country, at least doubling the number of facilities in each state. The new facilities increased the capacity of state prisons by 81 percent. Pressures from contractors, building material providers, and correctional-officer unions also spurred expansion in many states. Often, states that tried to build their way out of their crowded facilities found that as soon as a new prison came on line, it was quickly filled. The increased rate of incarceration may thus be related to the creation of additional space in the nation's prisons. As Joseph Davey notes,

During the 1990s, many new, expensive correctional facilities were built throughout the country by both state governments and private corporations. As economic problems affected state budgets in the first decade of the twenty-first century, many states found it difficult to justify additional construction. Instead, states began to rethink their sentencing policies and look for ways to assist increasing numbers of parolees to reenter society successfully. Will shorter sentences and the faster release of offenders pose any problems for society?

WHAT AMERICANS THINK

QUESTION: "Do you think the use of marijuana should be made legal or not?"

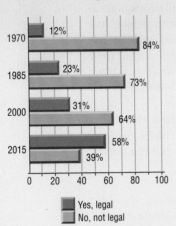

- 1970: 12%, 84%
- 1985: 23%, 73%
- 2000: 31%, 64%
- 2015: 58%, 39%

(scale: 0, 20, 40, 60, 80, 100)

■ Yes, legal
■ No, not legal

CRITICAL THINKING: How can changing public attitudes toward the permissibility of using certain drugs affect laws and policies in the criminal justice system? Make a prediction about what laws and policies will exist 25 years from now concerning drug use in the United States.

Source: J. Jones, "In U.S., 58% Back Legal Marijuana Use," Gallup Poll website, October 21, 2015 (www.gallup.com).

"The presence of empty state-of-the-art prison facilities can encourage a criminal court judge to incarcerate a defendant who may otherwise get probation" (J. D. Davey, 1998:84).

The War on Drugs Crusades against the use of drugs have recurred in U.S. politics since the late 1800s. The latest manifestation began in 1982, when President Ronald Reagan declared another "war on drugs" and asked Congress to set aside more money for drug-enforcement personnel and for prison space. This came at a time when the country faced the frightening advent of crack cocaine, which ravaged many communities and increased the murder rate. In 1987, Congress imposed stiff mandatory minimum sentences for federal drug law violations, and many states copied these sentencing laws. The war continues today, with recent presidents urging Congress to appropriate billions more for an all-out law enforcement campaign against drugs. The war on drugs succeeded on one front by packing the nation's prisons with drug-law offenders, but many scholars think this is about all it has achieved. With additional resources and pressures for enforcement, the number of people sentenced to prison for drug offenses increased steadily. In 1980, only 19,000, or about 6 percent of state prisoners, had been convicted of drug offenses; by 2003, the number had risen to 250,000. More than 18 percent of state prisoners were incarcerated for drug offenses in 2010, and the percentage in federal prisons was even higher, at 51 percent (Guerino, Harrison, & Sabol, 2011). Furthermore, the average state drug sentence increased during the 1980s and 1990s.

Changes in the public opinion about drugs may help to lessen the steady increase in prison populations attributable to stiff sentences for drug offenses in recent decades. In 2011, for the first time a national public opinion poll found that half of Americans favor the legalization of marijuana, and the support increased to 58 percent in favor of legalization in 2013 and, as illustrated by "What Americans Think," stood at the same level in 2015. The convergence of the budget crisis affecting the criminal justice system and a softening of punitive attitudes toward certain drugs is likely to affect future sentencing policies.

State Politics Incarceration rates vary among the regions and states, but why do states with similar characteristics differ in their use of prisons? How much do local political factors influence correctional policies?

One might think that each state would show an association between crime rates and incarceration rates—the more crime, the more prisoners. However, even when states have similar socioeconomic and demographic characteristics—poverty, unemployment, racial composition, drug arrests—unaccountable variations among their incarceration rates exist. For example, North Dakota and South Dakota share similar social characteristics and crime rates, yet in 2014, the incarceration rate in South Dakota was 421 per 100,000 population; North Dakota's rate was 214 per 100,000 population (Carson, 2015). One can find other pairs of similar and contiguous states such as Connecticut and Massachusetts, Arizona and New Mexico, and Minnesota and Wisconsin, where, at times, the state with the *higher* crime rate has the *lower* incarceration rate.

Scholars have shown that local officials often promote the siting of prisons in their towns as a means of economic development. A good example of the impact of prison siting is found in the state of New York, which in the 1970s passed tough drug-sentencing laws. New prisons had to be built to handle the resulting increase in the incarcerated population. Most of the new prisons were located in the northern, rural, economically impoverished region of the state. The influx of prisoners brought jobs to the region. Legislative districts with local employment rates tied to prison payrolls soon found their politics dominated by the union representing correctional officers (F. Santos, 2008). Across the nation, 221 counties have been found in which at least 21 percent of the residents were inmates (Butterfield, 2004a).

No one factor stands out as the primary cause of the doubling of the incarceration rate in recent decades. Several plausible hypotheses exist. However, now that the costs of this form of punishment impinge more on the pockets of taxpayers and affect funding for other priorities, such as education, we are seeing a shift to greater consideration of alternatives to incarceration in many states. As described in the chapter opener, several states have taken steps to reduce prison populations. Yet serious challenges remain because of the monumental growth in prison populations that preceded the very recent slight declines. Prison systems across the United States still remain very large and very expensive.

CHECK POINT

9. **What are five explanations for the great increase in the incarcerated population?**

   Increased arrests and more likely incarceration, tougher sentencing, prison construction, the war on drugs, state politics.

STOP & ANALYZE

In light of what you have read about the factors that led to the increase in incarceration, if you were hired as a governor's consultant and were tasked with finding ways to reduce the cost of a state's prison system, what would you recommend? List three recommendations that you would make, and state your reasons for each one.

A QUESTION OF ETHICS

Think, Discuss, Write

One of the concerns about the existence of private, profit-seeking organizations handling corrections functions is the political influence private companies may exert to convince public officials to send them offenders to treat or hold. A newspaper investigation in 2014 revealed that a Detroit-area judge regularly subjected misdemeanor offenders to months of daily drug and alcohol testing as well as the use of interlock devices that prevent cars from starting if the driver has alcohol on her or his breath. At the same time, the judge's son was employed for 16 months as a case manager for the largest Detroit-area private drug and alcohol testing company where many of the offenders ended up. These offenders must each pay $9 per day to the company for many months of daily testing. In addition, the judge's wife worked from home in a part-time position, which paid her $40,000 per year plus overtime bonuses as the executive director of the Michigan Association of Drug Court Professionals—an organization that receives thousands of dollars annually in contributions from private drug- and alcohol-testing companies. Judicial ethics rules forbid judges from having any financial interests that could affect their

decisions. The judge in question claims that there is no conflict of interests because he receives no benefits from these private companies.

Discussion/Writing Assignment

Imagine that you are a member of Michigan's Judicial Tenure Commission that examines allegations of misconduct by judges. Would you regard this situation as violating ethical rules against judges having any self-interest in decisions? Is there actual self-interest here, or if not, should the activity be prohibited anyway because of the possible appearance of self-interest in the eyes of the public? Write a memo describing your analysis of the case and any recommendations you would make, including any sanctions against the judge if you believe they would be appropriate.

Sources: L. L. Braiser and J. Wisely, "Oakland Prosecutor Says Novi District Judge Brian MacKenzie Continues to Mishandle Cases," *Detroit Free Press*, January 16, 2014 (www.freep.com); J. Wisely and L. L. Brasier, "Novi Judge Denies Conflict over Ties to Testing Firms," *Detroit Free Press*, February 13, 2014 (www.freep.com).

SUMMARY

1 **Describe how the American system of corrections has developed.**

- From colonial days to the present, the methods of criminal sanctions that are considered appropriate have varied.
- The development of the penitentiary brought a shift away from corporal punishment.
- The Declaration of Principles of 1870 contained the key elements for the reformatory and rehabilitation models of corrections.
- Although based on the social sciences, the rehabilitation/medical model failed to reduce recidivism.
- The community model of corrections tried to increase opportunities for offenders to be successful citizens and receive psychological treatment.
- The crime control model emphasized incarceration, long and mandatory sentencing, and strict supervision.

2 **Describe the roles that the federal, state, and local governments play in corrections.**

- The administration of corrections in the United States is fragmented, in that various levels of government are involved.
- The correctional responsibilities of the federal government are divided between the Federal Bureau of Prisons (of the U.S. Department of Justice) and the Administrative Office of the U.S. Courts.
- In all states, the administration of prisons falls under the executive branch of state government.

- Jails, which are administered by local government, hold people waiting trial and hold sentenced offenders.

3 **Explain the law of corrections and how it is applied to offenders and correctional professionals.**

- Until the 1960, the courts held a hands-off policy with respect to corrections.
- The rights of offenders are found in the First, Fourth, Eighth, and Fourteenth Amendments to the U.S. Constitution.
- Through lawsuits in the federal courts, the prisoners' rights movement has brought many changes to the administration and conditions of U.S. prisons.
- Decisions of the Supreme Court have affected community corrections through rules governing probation and parole revocation.
- Civil service laws set the procedures for hiring, promoting, and firing correctional professionals. Individual public employees and their agency may be sued when a person's civil rights are violated.

4 **Explain why the prison population has nearly quadrupled in the past 30 years.**

- Scholars trying to explain the great increase in the prison population have advanced the following explanations: increased arrests and more likely incarceration, tougher sentencing practices, prison construction, the war on drugs, state politics. No factor stands alone as the primary cause of the increase.

Questions for Review

1. What were the major differences between the New York and Pennsylvania systems in the nineteenth century?
2. What pressures do administrators of local jails face?
3. What types of correctional programs does your state support? What government agencies run them?
4. Why do some state officials see private prisons as an attractive correctional option?

5. What Supreme Court decisions are the most significant to corrections today? What effect has each had on correctional institutions? On probation and parole?
6. What explanations might be given for the increased use of incarceration during the past few decades?

Key Terms and Cases

community corrections (p. 355)

congregate system (p. 352)

contract labor system (p. 352)

corrections (p. 348)

crime control model of corrections (p. 356)

Enlightenment (p. 349)

hands-off policy (p. 366)

jail (p. 363)

lease system (p. 353)

mark system (p. 354)

medical model (p. 355)

penitentiary (p. 350)

prison (p. 363)

reformatory (p. 353)

rehabilitation model (p. 355)

separate confinement (p. 351)

Cooper v. Pate (1964) (p. 366)

Gagnon v. Scarpelli (1973) (p. 375)

Hudson v. Palmer (1984) (p. 370)

Morrissey v. Brewer (1972) (p. 374)

Wolff v. McDonnell (1974) (p. 372)

AP Images/Bebeto Matthews

11 Incarceration and Prison Society

Throughout 2014 and 2015, horrifying stories appeared in newspapers about abusive practices at Rikers Island, New York City's massive jail for holding pretrial detainees and offenders serving short sentences. In January 2015, for example, six corrections officers were fired because, three years earlier, they had hog-tied and savagely beaten an inmate being held in a cellblock for offenders who were mentally ill. Critics complained about a culture of silence among corrections officers, in which officers looked the other way when their colleagues committed acts of misconduct (Winerip, 2015). Previously, Rikers Island officers proven to have used excessive force seldom received any punishment worse than a brief suspension. However, by 2015, Rikers Island was under intense scrutiny because the U.S. Department of Justice had issued a report in August 2014 detailing what it called "a culture of violence" in which teenage inmates, as well as adult offenders, were beaten by staff members. The report documented officers using radios, batons, broomsticks, and pepper spray, and slamming teens' heads into walls, resulting in skull fractures and other injuries. A *New York Times* investigation corroborated 129 cases of detainees and convicted offenders at Rikers Island suffering serious injuries at the hands of staff members (Weiser and Schwirtz, 2014; Winerip and Schwirtz, 2015).

Another case of New York state prison officer misconduct emerged in 2015, when three officers faced criminal charges for a nonsexual assault on a prisoner at Attica Correctional Facility. As reported in news stories, they apparently mistook the prisoner for someone who had yelled an obscenity at officers. Witnesses described the prisoner as drenched in blood after absorbing fifty kicks and a dozen blows from a baton, while prisoners two floors away could hear him scream and beg for his life (Robbins, 2015). Ultimately, as their trial was about to begin, the officers were permitted to resign from their jobs and plead guilty to a single misdemeanor count, thereby avoiding the risk of prison sentences if they were convicted at trial (Robbins & D'Avolio, 2015).

These examples from New York are not representative of the actions of corrections officers throughout the country. Large numbers of corrections officers do difficult jobs with a high degree of professionalism and a strong commitment to following proper rules and procedures. However, by bringing these shocking examples to the forefront of public attention, these cases highlighted important aspects of corrections.

AP Images/Bebeto Matthews

First and foremost, corrections is, in many respects, a world usually hidden away from public scrutiny and attention. Prisons and jails are typically closed institutions whose operations are not visible to outsiders. Similarly, most members of the public are unaware of the nature and number of corrections programs in their communities and of the large population on probation who walk the streets with them every day. A result of these "blinders" is the risk that improper actions can occur when correctional institutions employ officers and administrators who lack a complete commitment to professionalism. Thus, even in the second decade of the twenty-first century, abuses that many people associate with the first decades of the twentieth century and earlier, when people held in prisons and jails were unprotected by law and constitutional rights, appear with disappointing regularity.

Second, these cases help to remind us that corrections can be a difficult environment for offenders and employees alike. Officials have limited resources for securely holding or supervising a wide array of defendants and offenders in a safe and appropriate manner. The challenges in corrections are compounded by the need to deal with people suffering from mental illness and drug abuse as well as those who can be angry and violent in reaction to close supervision and confinement under difficult conditions. Both offenders and corrections officers may tend to "snap" in tense or overcrowded conditions.

What goes on inside U.S. prisons? What does incarceration mean to the inmates, the guards, the administrators, and the public? Are the officers in charge, or do the prisoners "rule the joint"? In the "Close Up" feature, Michael Santos describes the anxiety he felt as a 24-year-old first-time offender entering the U.S. Federal Penitentiary in Atlanta.

In this chapter, we focus on the goals of incarceration, the challenges of management, and the inmates' experience. Discussion also centers on violence in prison and the policies and programs intended to keep that violence from boiling over.

The Modern Prison: Legacy of the Past

American correctional institutions have always been more varied than the way movies or novels portray them. Fictional depictions of prison life are typically set in a fortress, the "big house"—the maximum-security prisons where the inmates are tough and the guards are just as tough or tougher. Although so-called big houses predominated in much of the country during the first half of the twentieth century, many prisons were based on other models. In the South, for instance, prisoners worked outside at farm labor, and the massive walled structures were not so common.

The typical big house of the 1940s and 1950s held about 2,500 prisoners. It was a walled prison with large, tiered cellblocks, a yard, shops, and industrial workshops. The prisoners came from both urban and rural areas; were usually poor; and outside the South, were predominantly white. The prison society was essentially isolated, with restricted access to visitors, mail, and other communication. Prisoners' days were strictly structured, with rules enforced by the guards. Rank was observed and discipline maintained. In the big house, few treatment programs existed; custody was the primary goal.

During the 1960s and early 1970s, when the rehabilitation model prevailed, many states built new prisons and converted others into "correctional institutions."

Treatment programs administered by counselors and teachers became a major part of prison life, although the institutions continued to give priority to the custody goals of security, discipline, and order.

During the past 40 years, as the population of the United States has changed, so has the prison population. The number of African American and Hispanic inmates has greatly increased. More inmates come from urban areas, and more have been convicted of drug-related and violent offenses. Former street gangs, often organized along racial lines, today regroup inside prisons; such gangs have raised the level of violence in many institutions.

Further, the focus of corrections has shifted to crime control, which emphasizes the importance of incarceration. Not only has the number of people in prison greatly increased, but many states have removed educational and recreational amenities from institutions.

Today, prisoners are less isolated from the outside world than they were before. As we have seen, the Supreme Court has ruled on issues of communication and access to information for prisoners, weighing their constitutional rights against the need for order and safety within the prison walls. Another difference from the past is that correctional officers have used collective bargaining to improve their working conditions.

Although today's correctional administrators seek to provide humane incarceration, they must struggle with limited resources and shortages of cell space. Thus, the modern prison faces many of the difficult problems that confront other parts of the criminal justice system: racial conflicts, legal issues, limited resources, and growing populations. Despite these challenges, can prisons still achieve their objectives? The answer to this question depends, in part, on how we define the goals of incarceration.

▼ CHECK POINT

1. **How does today's prison differ from the big house of the past?**
   The characteristics of the inmate population have changed; more inmates are from urban areas and have been convicted for drug-related or violent offenses; the inmate population is fragmented along racial and ethnic lines; prisoners are less isolated from the outside world; and correctional officers have used collective bargaining to improve their working conditions.

STOP & ANALYZE

With access to television, telephones, and, in an increasing number of prison systems, e-mail communications (F. Green, 2011), prisoners are not as isolated from the outside world as they once were. What are some possible negative and positive consequences of this increased contact? How might this affect life inside prisons?

Goals of Incarceration

Citing the nature of inmates and the need to protect staff and the community, most people consider security the dominant purpose of a prison. High walls, barbed-wire fences, searches, checkpoints, and regular counts of inmates serve the security function: few inmates escape. More importantly, the features set the tone for the daily operations. Prisons stand as impersonal, quasi-military places where strict discipline, minimal amenities, and restrictions on freedom serve to punish criminals.

Three models of incarceration have predominated since the early 1940s: the custodial, rehabilitation, and reintegration models. Each is associated with one style of institutional organization.

1. The **custodial model** assumes that prisoners have been incarcerated for the purpose of incapacitation, deterrence, or retribution. It emphasizes security, discipline, and order in subordinating the prisoner to the authority of the warden. Discipline is strict, and most aspects of behavior are regulated. Having prevailed in corrections before World War II, this model dominates most maximum-security institutions today.

2. The **rehabilitation model**, developed during the 1950s, emphasizes treatment programs designed to reform the offender. According to this model, security and housekeeping activities are viewed primarily as preconditions for rehabilitative

custodial model A model of incarceration that emphasizes security, discipline, and order.

rehabilitation model A model of incarceration that emphasizes treatment programs to help prisoners address the personal problems and issues that led them to commit crimes.

One Man's Walk through Atlanta's Jungle
Michael G. Santos

I was not expecting to receive the Southern hospitality for which Atlanta is famous when the bus turned into the penitentiary's large, circular drive, but neither did I expect to see a dozen uniformed prison guards—all carrying machine guns—surround the bus when it stopped. A month in transit already had passed by the time we made it to the U.S. Penitentiary (USP) in Atlanta, the institution that would hold me (along with over 2,000 other felons) until we were transferred to other prisons, we were released, or we were dead.

I left the jail in Tacoma, Washington, on the first of August, but I didn't see the huge gray walls that surround USP Atlanta until the first of September. That month was spent in a bus operated by the U.S. Marshal Service as it moved across the country, picking up federal prisoners in local jails and dropping them off at various Bureau of Prison facilities.

As I crossed the country, I listened to tales from numerous prisoners who sat beside me on the bus. There wasn't much to discuss except what was to come. Each of us was chained at the hands and feet. There were neither magazines to read nor music playing. Mostly people spoke about a riot that had taken

place behind USP Atlanta's walls a few months earlier. A lot of the men had been to prison before, and Atlanta would be nothing new. Those prisoners only talked about reuniting with old friends, explaining prison routine, or sat like stone-cold statues waiting for what was to come. I'd never been confined before, so it was hard to tune out the stories that others were telling. While I was listening, though, I remember telling myself that I would survive this sentence. No matter what it took, I would survive.

I was in my early 20s, younger than perhaps every other prisoner on the bus. Pimples spotted my face as I began my term, but I was certain my black hair would be white by the time I finished. I had been sentenced to 45 years by a U.S. district court judge in Tacoma on charges related to cocaine trafficking. I was expected to serve close to 30 years before release. It was hard then—just as it is hard now—to believe the sentence was real. The best thing I could do, I reasoned, was to stay to myself. I'd heard the same rumors that every suburban kid hears about prison. I was anxious about what was to come, but I was determined to make it

out alive and with my mind intact. Now it was all to begin!

After the bus stopped, the guards began calling us off by last name and prison number. It is not easy to walk with a twelve-inch chain connected to each ankle, and wrists bound to a chain that runs around the waist, but when my name was called, I managed to wobble through the bus's aisle, hop down the steps, and then begin the long march up the stairs leading to the fortress. As I was moving to the prison's doors, I remember glancing over my shoulder, knowing it would be the last time I'd see the world from the outside of prison walls for a long time.

Once I was inside the institution, the guards began unlocking my chains. About 50 other prisoners arrived with me that day, so the guards had plenty of chains to unlock, but their work didn't stop there. They also had to squeeze us through the dehumanizing admissions machine. The machine begins with photographs, fingerprints, and interrogations. Then comes the worst part, the strip search, where each prisoner stands before a prison official, naked, and responds to the scream: "Lift up your arms in the air! Let me see the back of your hands! Run your fingers through your hair! Open your mouth!

---

efforts. Because all aspects of the organization should center on rehabilitation, professional treatment specialists carry a higher status than do other employees. Since the rethinking of the rehabilitation goal in the 1970s, treatment programs still exist in most institutions, but few prisons conform to this model today.

reintegration model A correctional model that emphasizes maintaining the offender's ties to family and community as a method of reform, recognizing that the offender will be returning to society.

3. The **reintegration model** is linked to the structures and goals of community corrections. Recognizing that prisoners will be returning to society, this model emphasizes maintaining the offenders' ties to family and community as a method of reform. Prisons following this model gradually give inmates greater freedom and responsibility during their confinement, moving them to halfway houses or work release programs before giving them community supervision.

Although one can find correctional institutions that conform to each of these models, most prisons are mainly custodial. Nevertheless, treatment programs do exist, and because almost all inmates return to society at some point, even the most custodial institutions must prepare them for reintegration. See "What Americans Think" for a look at how the public views the goals of incarceration.

Much is asked of prisons. As Charles Logan notes, "We ask them to correct the incorrigible, rehabilitate the wretched, deter the determined, restrain the dangerous, and punish the wicked" (Logan, 1993:19). Because prisons are expected to pursue

Stick your tongue out! Lift your balls! Turn around! Bend over! Spread your ass! Wider! Lift the bottom of your feet! Move on!" The strip search, I later learned, is a ritual Atlanta's officers inflict on prisoners every time they have contact with anyone from outside the walls, and sometimes randomly as prisoners walk down the corridor.

There was a lot of hatred behind those walls. Walking through the prison must be something like walking through a jungle, I imagined, not knowing whether others perceive you as predator or prey, knowing that you must remain always alert, watching every step, knowing that the wrong step may be the one that sucks you into the quicksand. The tension is ever present; I felt it wrapped all over, under and around me. I remember it bothering me that I didn't have enough hatred, because not hating in the jungle is a weakness. As the serpents slither, they spot that lack of hatred and salivate over a potential target.

Every prisoner despises confinement, but each must decide how he or she is going to do the time. Most of the men run in packs. They want the other prisoners either to run with them or run away from them. I wasn't interested in doing either. Instead of scheming on how I could become king of the jungle, I thought about ways that I could advance my release date. Earning academic credentials, keeping a clean record, and initiating projects that would benefit the communities both inside and outside

of prison walls seemed the most promising goals for me to achieve. Yet working toward such goals was more dangerous than running with the pack; it didn't take me long to learn that prisoners running in herds will put forth more energy to cause others to lose than they will to win themselves. Prison is a twisted world, a menagerie.

I found that a highly structured schedule would not only move me closer to my goals, but also would limit potential conflicts inside the prison. There is a pecking order in every prison, and prisoners vying for attention don't want to see others who are cutting their own path. I saw that bullies generally look for weaker targets, so I began an exercise routine that would keep me physically strong. If I were strong, I figured, others would be more reluctant to try me. Through discipline, I found, I could develop physical strength. Yet I've never figured out how to develop the look of a killer, or the hatred off which that look feeds.

I don't know whether the strategies I have developed for doing time are right for everyone. But they are working for me. Still, I know that I may spend many more years in prison. The only fear I have—and as I'm working on my eighth year, it's still here—is that someone will try me and drag me into an altercation that may jeopardize my spotless disciplinary record. I've been successful in avoiding the ever-present quicksand on my walk through the jungle so far, but I

know that on any given day, something may throw me off balance, or I may take a wrong step. And one wrong step in this jungle can drown me in quicksand, sucking me into the abysmal world of prison forever. That wrong step also could mean the loss of life, mine or someone else's.

In prison, more than anywhere else I know, understanding that some things are beyond an individual's sphere of control is vital. No matter how much preparation is made, the steel and concrete jungle is a dangerous place in which to live.

Researching the Internet

Michael Santos was incarcerated at the Federal Prison Camp in Taft, California. While in prison, he completed his bachelor's and master's degrees. He is the author of *About Prison* (Belmont, CA: Wadsworth, 2004); *Inside: Life behind Bars in America* (New York: St. Martin's Press, 2006); and four other books. He was released from prison on August 12, 2013, after serving 26 years. He now works as a life coach and teaches a course at San Francisco State University entitled "The Architecture of Imprisonment." He married his wife in 2003 (while still incarcerated), and they now live in Northern California. You can contact Santos through his website at http://michaelsantos.com/.

Source: Written for this book by Michael G. Santos. In 1987, he was sentenced to 45 years in prison for drug trafficking.

many different and often incompatible goals, they are almost doomed to fail as institutions. Logan believes that the mission of prisons is confinement. He argues that imprisonment serves primarily to punish offenders fairly and justly through lengths of confinement proportionate to the seriousness of their crimes. He summarizes the mission of prison as follows: "to keep prisoners—to keep them in, keep them safe, keep them in line, keep them healthy, and keep them busy—and to do it with fairness, without undue suffering, and as efficiently as possible" (Logan, 1993:21). If the purpose of prisons is punishment through confinement under fair and just conditions, what are the implications of this purpose for correctional managers?

CHECK POINT

2. What three models of incarceration have predominated since the 1940s?
The custodial, rehabilitation, and reintegration models.

STOP & ANALYZE

Given the complex challenges facing today's prisons—including increased racial diversity within prisons, the greater likelihood of gang membership, and states' need to reduce corrections budgets—which model of incarceration seems best suited to addressing these challenges?

QUESTION: "State prison systems could offer the following four alternative prison policies for people who have committed nonviolent crime. What would you prefer the state implement?"

Policy 1: Treat prison as punishment and do not offer rehabilitation services to people either during their time in prison or after their release.

Policy 2: Make state-funded rehabilitation services available to incarcerated people while they are serving time in prison.

Policy 3: Make state-funded rehabilitation services available to incarcerated people only after they have been released from prison.

Policy 4: Make state-funded rehabilitation services available to incarcerated people both while they are in prison and after they have been released from prison.

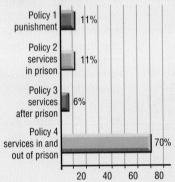

Percentage who prefer:

Policy 1 punishment — 11%
Policy 2 services in prison — 11%
Policy 3 services after prison — 6%
Policy 4 services in and out of prison — 70%

CRITICAL THINKING: A study of public attitudes on punishment found that women tend to be more supportive of rehabilitation than men are. List two reasons why this gender difference in attitudes might exist.

Note: May not add to 100% due to rounding and missing responses.

Source: Barry Krisberg and Susan Marchionna. "Attitudes of U.S. Voters toward Prison Rehabilitation and Reentry Policies," *Focus: Views from the National Council on Crime and Delinquency* (April) (Oakland, CA: National Council on Crime and Delinquency, 2006).

The prison's physical features and function set it apart from almost every other institution and organization in modern society. It is a place where a group of employees manage a group of captives. Prisoners must live according to the rules of their keepers, and their movements remain sharply restricted. Unlike managers of other government agencies, prison managers

- cannot select their clients.
- have little or no control over the release of their clients.
- must deal with clients who are there against their will.
- must rely on clients to do most of the work in the daily operation of the institution—work they are forced to do and for which they are not always paid.
- need to maintain satisfactory relationships between clients and staff.

Given these unique characteristics, how should a prison be run? What rules should guide administrators? As the description just given indicates, wardens and other key personnel are asked to perform a difficult job, one that requires skilled and dedicated managers (Vickovic & Griffin, 2013).

Most prisons are expected to fulfill goals related to keeping (custody), using (working), and serving (treating) inmates. Because individual staff members are not equipped to perform all functions, separate lines of command organize the groups of employees that carry out these different tasks. One group is charged with maintaining custody over the prisoners, another group supervises them in their work activities, and a third group attempts to treat them.

The custodial employees are the most numerous. They are typically organized along military lines, from warden to captain to officer, with accompanying pay differentials down the chain of command. The professional personnel associated with the using and serving functions, such as industry supervisors, clinicians, and teachers, are not part of the custodial structure and have little in common with its staff. All employees are responsible to the warden, but the treatment personnel and the civilian supervisors of the workshops have their own salary scales and titles. Figure 11.1 presents the formal organization of staff responsibilities in a typical prison.

The multiple goals and separate lines of command often cause ambiguity and conflict in the administration of prisons. For example, the goals imposed on prisons are often contradictory and unclear. Conflicts between different groups of staff (custodial versus treatment, for instance), as well as between staff and inmates, present significant challenges for administrators.

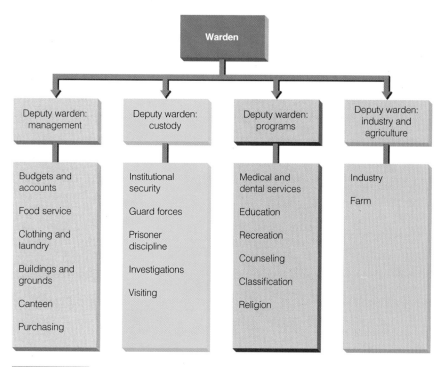

FIGURE 11.1

Formal Organization of a Prison for Adult Felons Prison staff are divided into various sections consistent with the goals of the organization. Custodial employees are the most numerous.

How, then, do prisons function? How do prisoners and staff try to meet their own goals? Although the U.S. prison may not conform to the ideal goals of corrections, and the formal organization may bear little resemblance to the ongoing reality of the informal relations, order *is* kept and a routine *is* followed.

CHECK POINT

3. **How do prisons differ from other organizations in society?**
   Prisons are the only organizations in which a group of workers manages a group of captives.

STOP & ANALYZE

How might the multiple goals of prisons collide with each other? Select two of the goals, and describe how the pursuit of one goal may make the effective attainment of the other goal more difficult.

Governing a Society of Captives

Much of the public believes that prisons are operated in an authoritarian manner: correctional officers give orders and inmates follow orders. Strictly enforced rules specify what the captives may and may not do. Staff members have the right to grant rewards and to inflict punishment. In theory, any inmate who does not follow the rules can be placed in solitary confinement. Because the officers have the legal justification and the means to enforce rules and can call in the state police and the National Guard if necessary, many people believe that prison discipline is not difficult to maintain. Read "Criminal Justice: Myth & Reality" to test your perceptions about the power of correctional officials.

CRIMINAL JUSTICE

Myth&Reality

COMMON BELIEF: Because correctional officers have access to guns, clubs, tear gas, and other weapons, they can readily control the behavior of prisoners through the threat of force and, if necessary, the use of force, including lethal force.

REALITY

- Although prison officials typically have firearms locked in an accessible area for emergencies, and the correctional officers standing guard in towers or walking outside the prison's perimeter carry guns, most correctional officers cannot carry weapons.
- These officers must supervise, question, and frisk prisoners close at hand and in a context in which they are heavily outnumbered by the prisoners. If they carried weapons, they might easily be overpowered and have their weapons taken by the prisoners.
- Thus, effective officers cannot rely on the threat of force to accomplish their daily tasks smoothly. Instead, they must encourage the cooperation and obedience of the prisoners by communicating effectively, establishing their own reputations for toughness and fairness, and showing some understanding and flexibility in the enforcement of minor rules.
- If a violent event or uprising occurs, prison staff members will use force to restore order. However, the use of force throughout the day is not an efficient way to keep the institution running smoothly.
- Moreover, there are now legal rules that limit when and how force may be used, and prisoners may file lawsuits for rights violations and personal injuries suffered through the improper use of force.

What quality of life should be maintained in prison? According to John Dilulio, a good prison is one that "provides as much order, amenity, and service as possible given the human and financial resources" (1987:12). *Order* is here defined as the absence of individual or group misconduct that threatens the safety of others—for example, assault, rape, and other forms of violence or threat. *Amenities* include anything that enhances the comfort of the inmates, such as good food, clean cells, and recreational opportunities. *Service* includes programs designed to improve the lives of inmates: vocational training, remedial education, and work opportunities. Here, too, we expect inmates to be engaged in activities during incarceration that will make them better people and enhance their ability to lead crime-free lives upon release.

If we accept the premise that inmates, staff, and society need well-run prisons, what problems must correctional administrators address? The correctional literature points to four factors that make governing prisons different from administering other public institutions: (1) the defects of total power, (2) the limitation on the rewards and punishments officials can use, (3) the co-optation of correctional officers by inmates through exchange relationships, and (4) the strength of inmate leadership. After reviewing each of these research findings, we consider which types of administrative systems and leadership styles best ensure that prisons are safe and humane and serve inmates' needs.

The Defects of Total Power

Imagine a prison society in which officers could use force to rule hostile and uncooperative inmates. Prisoners could legally be isolated from one another, physically abused until they cooperate, and put under continuous surveillance. Although all of these things are possible, such practices would probably not be countenanced for long, because the public expects correctional institutions to be run humanely.

In reality, the power of officers to force compliance with prison rules is limited. Many prisoners have little to lose by misbehaving, and when officers are unarmed, they must find means other than force to maintain order. Perhaps more important is the fact that the use of force on a regular basis disrupts the very order that the officers wish to maintain; efficiency further diminishes because of the ratio of inmates to officers (typically 40 to 1) and the consequent potential danger of inmates overpowering officers.

Rewards and Punishments

Correctional officers often rely on rewards and punishments to gain cooperation. To maintain security and order among a large population in a confined space, they impose extensive rules of conduct. Instead of using force to ensure obedience, however, they reward compliance by granting privileges and punish rule violators by denying these same privileges.

Officers face significant challenges in maintaining order and safety, given the small number of officers and the large number of inmates. What qualities and skills do correctional officers need in order to be effective?

Bryan Chan/Getty Images

To promote control, officers may follow any of several policies. One is to offer cooperative prisoners rewards such as choice job assignments, residence in the honor unit, and favorable parole reports. Inmates who do not break rules receive "good time." Informers may also be rewarded, and administrators may ignore conflict among inmates on the assumption that it keeps prisoners from uniting against authorities.

The system of rewards and punishments has some deficiencies. One is that the punishments for rule breaking do not represent a great departure from the prisoners' usual circumstances. Because inmates already lack many freedoms and valued goods—heterosexual relations, money, choice of clothing, and so on—not being allowed to attend, say, a recreational period does not carry much weight. Further, inmates receive authorized privileges at the start of the sentence and lose them if rules are broken, but officials authorize few rewards for progress or exceptional behavior. However, as an inmate approaches release, opportunities for furloughs, work release, or transfer to a halfway house can serve as incentives to obey rules.

Gaining Cooperation: Exchange Relationships

One way that correctional officers obtain inmate cooperation is by tolerating minor rule infractions in exchange for compliance with major aspects of the custodial regime. The correctional officer plays the key role in these exchange relationships. Officers and prisoners remain in close proximity both day and night—in the cellblock, workshop, dining hall, recreation area, and so on. Although the formal rules require a social distance between officers and inmates, the physical closeness makes them aware that each relies on the other. The officers need the cooperation of the prisoners so that they will look good to their superiors, and the inmates count on the officers to relax the rules or occasionally look the other way. For example, officers in a Midwestern prison told researcher Stan Stojkovic that flexibility in rule enforcement especially mattered as it related to the ability of prisoners to cope with their environment. As one officer said, "Phone calls are really important to guys in this place. You cut off their calls and they get pissed. So what I do is give them a little extra and they are good to me." Yet the officers also told Stojkovic that prison personnel would be crazy to intervene to stop illicit sex or drug use (Stojkovic, 1990:214).

Correctional officers must take care not to pay too high a price for the cooperation of their charges. Under pressure to work effectively with prisoners, officers may be blackmailed into doing illegitimate favors in return for cooperation. Officers who establish *sub-rosa*, or secret, relationships can be manipulated by prisoners into smuggling contraband or committing other illegal acts. Corrections officers are caught each year smuggling drugs and cell phones to prisoners. In addition, bans on cigarettes inside some prisons have created a lucrative and tempting market for corrections officers to smuggle tobacco into institutions and receive payments from the prisoners' relatives. Because scarce tobacco can be worth hundreds of dollars per bag, unethical officers can significantly enhance their incomes through such smuggling—at the same time that they risk being arrested and sent to prison themselves for such illegal activity (Goldschmidt & Shoichet, 2013; Ingold, 2011). At the end of the chapter, "A Question of Ethics" presents a recent example of such risks of co-optation for corrections officers.

Inmate Leadership

In the traditional prison of the big-house era, administrators enlisted the inmate leaders to help maintain order. Inmate leaders had been "tested" over time, so they were neither pushed around by other inmates nor distrusted as "snitches." Because the staff could rely on them, they served as the essential communications link between staff and inmates. Their ability to acquire inside information and gain access to higher officials brought inmate leaders the respect of other prisoners and special privileges from officials. In turn, they distributed these benefits to other prisoners, thus bolstering their own influence within the prison society.

Prisons seem to function more effectively now than they did in the recent past. Although prisons are more crowded, riots and reports of violence have declined. In many prisons, the inmate social system may have reorganized, so that correctional officers again can work through prisoners respected by fellow inmates. Yet some observers contend that when wardens maintain order in this way, they enhance the positions of some prisoners at the expense of others. The leaders profit by receiving illicit privileges and favors, and they influence other prisoners by distributing benefits.

Further, descriptions of the contemporary maximum-security prison raise questions about administrators' ability to run these institutions using inmate leadership. In most of today's prisons, inmates are divided by race, ethnicity, age, and gang affiliation, so that no single leadership structure exists.

The Challenge of Governing Prisons

The factors of total power, rewards and punishments, exchange relationships, and inmate leadership exist in every prison and must be managed. How they are managed greatly influences the quality of prison life (Griffin & Hepburn, 2013). John Dilulio's research (1987) challenged the common assumption of many correctional administrators that "the cons run the joint." Instead, successful wardens have made their prisons function well by applying management principles within the context of their own style of leadership. Prisons can be governed, violence minimized, and services provided to the inmates if correctional executives and wardens exhibit leadership. Although governing prisons poses an extraordinary challenge, it can be and has been effectively accomplished.

▼ **CHECK POINT**

4. **What four factors make governing prisons different from administering other public institutions?**
The defects of total power, a limited system of rewards and punishments, exchange relations between correctional officers and inmates, and the strength of inmate leadership.

STOP & ANALYZE

Think about the type of rewards that correctional officers can use to recognize and encourage good behavior among prisoners. What types of rewards would you expect to be most effective, and why?

Correctional Officers: The Linchpins of Management

A prison is simultaneously supposed to keep, use, and serve its inmates. The achievement of these goals depends heavily on the performance of its correctional officers. Their job is not easy. Not only do they work long and difficult hours with a hostile client population, but their superiors expect them to do so with few resources or punishments at their disposal. Most of what they are expected to do must be accomplished by gaining and keeping the cooperation of the prisoners.

The Officer's Role

Over the past 30 years, the correctional officer's role has changed greatly. No longer responsible merely for "guarding," the correctional officer now stands as a crucial professional who has the closest contact with the prisoners and performs a variety of tasks. Officers are expected to counsel, supervise, protect, and process the inmates under their care. But the officer also works as a member of a complex bureaucratic organization and is expected to deal with clients impersonally and to follow formal procedures. Fulfilling these contradictory role expectations is difficult in itself, and the physical closeness of the officer and inmates over long periods exacerbates this difficulty.

Recruitment of Officers

Employment as a correctional officer is neither glamorous nor popular. The work is thought to be boring, the pay is low, and career advancement is minimal. Studies have shown that one of the primary incentives for becoming involved in correctional work is the financial security that civil service status provides (Schlosser, Safran, & Sbaratta, 2010). In addition, because most correctional facilities are located in rural areas, prison work often is better than other available employment. Because correctional officers are recruited locally, many of them are rural and white (see Figure 11.2), unlike the majority of prisoners, who come from urban areas and are often either African American or Hispanic (see Figure 11.3). Yet some correctional officers see their work as a way of helping people, often the people most in need in U.S. society.

Much of the work of correctional officers involves searches and counting. Officers have a saying: "We're all doing time together, except guards are doing it in eight-hour shifts." What are the professional rewards—if any—of working as a correctional officer?

AP Images/Elaine Thompson

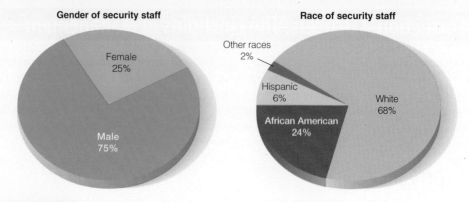

Gender of security staff

Female
25%

Male
75%

Race of security staff

Other races
2%

Hispanic
6%

African American
24%

White
68%

FIGURE 11.2

Characteristics of Correctional Officers Compare these pie charts with the data found in Figure 11.3. How do correctional officers differ from those incarcerated in terms of sex and race/ethnicity?

Source: United States Department of Justice, Office of Justice Programs, Bureau of Justice Statistics, *Census of State and Federal Adult Correctional Facilities*, 2005 (http://doi.org/10.3886/ICPSR24542.V2).

Today, because they need well-qualified, effective correctional officers, states seek to recruit quality personnel. Salaries have been raised so that the median annual pay nationally is $39,700, although states vary in their pay rates for corrections personnel. Thus, the lowest-paid 10 percent of corrections officers nationally have salaries below $27,280 while the highest-paid 10 percent earns more than $72,790 (Bureau of Labor Statistics, 2015). For example, the starting salary for corrections officers in Texas is about $32,000; with step increases over time, Texas officers reach a top salary of $43,000 after seven years of service (Texas Department of Criminal Justice, 2015). By contrast, after graduating from the state training academy, corrections officers in California begin their careers making $45,000 with the prospect of earning nearly $76,000 when they reach the top pay grade (California Department of Corrections and Rehabilitation, 2016). Because of attractive pay and retirement benefits, California can receive as many as 120,000 applications for 900 places in a training academy class (Finley, 2011). In other states, however, factors such as low salaries, crowded prisons, and a more violent class of prisoners have all probably contributed to a shortage of correctional officers when other job opportunities are available in the local area.

Correctional administrators have made special efforts to recruit women and minorities. Today approximately 30 percent of correctional officers belong to minority groups, and 25 percent of officers are women (see Figure 11.2). Female officers are no longer restricted to working with female offenders. For example, in Maryland, approximately 60 percent of correctional officers are women (Goldman, 2013). In the Federal Bureau of Prisons, only 27 percent of staff were women in 2015 (Federal Bureau of Prisons, 2016).

The diversification of the corrections workforce can create issues for corrections administrators concerned with the performance, effectiveness, job satisfaction, and stress levels among corrections officers (Cheeseman & Downey, 2012). For example, female officers often have greater perceptions of the risk of victimization on the job than do their male counterparts (J. A. Gordon, Proulx, & Grant, 2013). There are also issues about corrections officers' attitudes toward prisoners and whether prisoners' attitudes and behavior with respect to officers varies according to the demographic composition of the workforce.

States generally require cadets, or new recruits, to complete a preservice training program. The length of preservice training varies from state to state. For example, cadets in California receive 12 weeks, or about 480 hours, of full-time training (California Department of Corrections and Rehabilitation, 2016). In contrast, new recruits in Ohio receive 120 hours of classroom training and 40 hours of firearms,

CPR, and transportation/restraint training prior to supervised work (Ohio Department of Rehabilitation and Correction, 2016). In most states, new cadets receive at least a rudimentary knowledge of the job and correctional rules. Classroom work includes learning about report writing, communicable diseases, inmate classification, self-defense, and the use of force. The classroom work, however, often bears little resemblance to problems confronted on the cellblock or in the yard. On completing the course, the new officer is placed under the supervision of an experienced officer. On the job, the new officer experiences real-life situations and learns the necessary techniques and procedures. Through encounters with inmates and officers, the recruit becomes socialized to life behind the walls and gradually becomes part of that subculture.

While these practical skills are essential to managing inmate populations, other skills are essential to success—skills that are not easily taught in a classroom. For example, effective correctional officers tend to have high integrity, empathy, and confidence (Arnold, 2016).

For most correctional workers, being a custodial officer is a dead-end job. Although officers who perform well may be promoted to higher ranks, such as correctional counselor, few ever move into administrative positions. However, in some states and in the Federal Bureau of Prisons, people with college degrees can move up the career ladder to management positions without having to rise through the ranks of the custodial force.

Use of Force

The use of force by correctional officers, like that by the police, generates much controversy. Although corporal punishment and the excessive use of force are not permitted, correctional officers use force in many situations. They often confront inmates who challenge their authority or are attacking other inmates. Though unarmed and outnumbered, officers must maintain order and uphold institutional rules. Under these conditions, they feel justified in using force.

All correctional agencies now have policies regarding the legitimate use of force. Officers violating these policies may face an inmate lawsuit and dismissal (M. Miller, 2014). There are five situations in which the use of force is legally acceptable:

1. *Self-defense* If officers are threatened with physical attack, they may use a level of force that is reasonable to protect themselves from harm.
2. *Defense of third persons* As in self-defense, an officer may use force to protect an inmate or another officer. Again, only reasonably necessary force may be used.
3. *Upholding prison rules* If prisoners refuse to obey prison rules, officers may need to use force to maintain safety and security. For example, if an inmate refuses to return to his or her cell, using handcuffs and forcefully transferring the prisoner may be necessary.
4. *Prevention of a crime* Force may be used to stop a crime, such as theft or destruction of property, from being committed.
5. *Prevention of escapes* Officers may use force to prevent escapes, because they threaten the well-being of society and order within correctional institutions. Some agencies limit the use of deadly force to prisoners thought to be dangerous, whereas others require warning shots.

Correctional officers face challenges to self-control and professional decision making. Inmates often "push" officers in subtle ways such as moving slowly, or they use verbal abuse to provoke officers. Correctional officers are expected to run a "tight ship" and maintain order, often in situations where they are outnumbered and dealing with troubled people. In confrontational situations, they must defuse hostility yet uphold the rules—a difficult task at best. Read the "You Make the Decision" feature to consider how you might plan to reduce the risk of excessive force if you were a warden.

Prison Warden

You have just been hired to reduce allegations of misconduct against corrections officers in one prison. As an outsider who is new to the prison, you have read many reports from lawyers and seen grievances filed by prisoners, but you are not personally acquainted with the staff at your new prison. In particular, there are claims of excessive use of force, including the fatal beating of a prisoner with mental illness, allegedly at the hands of corrections officers. Other prisoners who witnessed the event claim that they were threatened by corrections officers and

placed in solitary confinement when they tried to provide information about what they had seen. In the reports that you have read, you see that the state has paid out tens of thousands of dollars to settle lawsuits filed against corrections officers concerning injuries to prisoners when officers used force against them, yet no officer has ever been punished for misconduct or fired. You were hired because top state officials believe there is a serious problem with staff behavior at this prison. What actions will you take to address these reported problems?

What policies and procedures will you recommend? Make a list of ideas and explain what each proposal would seek to accomplish. Then search the Internet and read about the problems identified in 2015 by journalists examining events at New York's prisons, including the deaths of prisoners Samuel Harrell and Leonard Strickland (at Fishkill Correctional Facility and Clinton Correctional Facility, respectively), as well as the prosecution of corrections officers at New York's Attica prison.

CHECK POINT

5. **Name three of the five legally acceptable reasons for the use of force.**
   Self-defense, defense of third persons, upholding prison rules, prevention of crime, prevention of escapes.

STOP & ANALYZE

What should happen when a corrections officer uses force in an inappropriate situation or uses too much force in an approved situation? If you were a warden, what procedures would you put in place to hear excessive-force complaints from prisoners? What would you do if you were persuaded that excessive force had been used by one of your officers?

Who Is in Prison?

The average age, education, and criminal history of the inmate population influence how correctional institutions function. What are the characteristics of inmates in our nation's prisons? Do most offenders have long records of serious offenses, or are many of them first-time offenders who have committed minor crimes? Do some inmates have special needs that dictate their place in prison? These questions are crucial to understanding the work of wardens and correctional officers.

The federal government routinely collects information on all people incarcerated in the United States. The Bureau of Justice Statistics reports that a majority of prisoners are men aged 25 to 44 and members of minority groups. Approximately 40 percent of state prisoners have not completed high school (see Figure 11.3).

Recidivists and those convicted of violent crimes make up an overwhelming portion of the prison population. It is time-consuming to collect data on recidivism, because sufficient time has to lapse (usually several years) in order to collect reliable data on re-offending. In 2014, for example, out of 626,644 admissions to prison, 164,225 were parole violators being returned to prison for committing new crimes or violating parole conditions while living under supervision in the community (Carson, 2015). The rate of return for parolees varies by state. For example, in Vermont, Washington, Idaho, and Arkansas, a majority of admissions to prison in 2014 were based on parole violations. By contrast, parole violators accounted

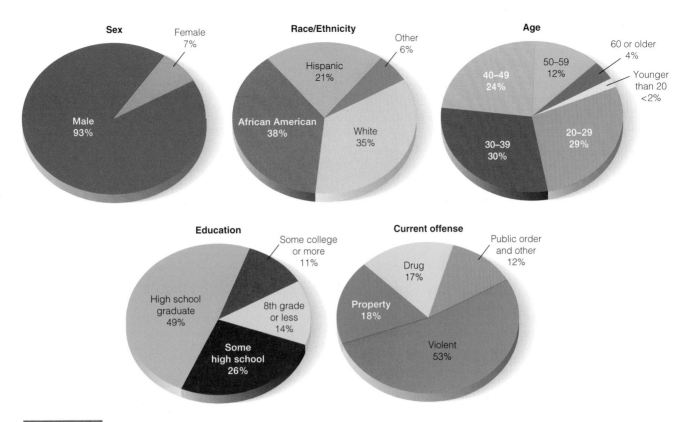

Sex
Male 93%
Female 7%

Race/Ethnicity
Hispanic 21%
Other 6%
African American 38%
White 35%

Age
40–49 24%
50–59 12%
60 or older 4%
Younger than 20 <2%
20–29 29%
30–39 30%

Education
High school graduate 49%
Some college or more 11%
8th grade or less 14%
Some high school 26%

Current offense
Drug 17%
Public order and other 12%
Property 18%
Violent 53%

FIGURE 11.3

Characteristics of Male and Female Inmates in State Prisons These data reflect the types of people held in state prisons. Are any of the percentages surprising? Do these numbers provide any clues about whether too many people are held in prison or the specific challenges faced by corrections administrators?

Note: Totals may not equal 100% due to rounding.

Sources: E. A. Carson and W. J. Sabol, "Prisoners in 2011," *Bureau of Justice Statistics Bulletin* (Washington, DC: U.S. Department of Justice, 2012); E. A. Carson and D. Golinelli, "Prisoners in 2012—Advance Counts," *Bureau of Justice Statistics Bulletin* (Washington, DC: U.S. Department of Justice, 2013); E. A. Carson and D. Golinelli, "Prisoners in 2012: Trends in Admissions and Releases, 1991–2012," *Bureau of Justice Statistics Bulletin* (Washington, DC: U.S. Department of Justice, 2013); C. W. Harlow, "Education and Correctional Populations," *Bureau of Justice Statistics Special Report* (Washington, DC: U.S. Department of Justice, 2003).

for relatively small percentages of admissions to prison in Florida (3 percent) and California (14 percent). Obviously, states differ in the policies and practices that they use regarding the reimprisonment of parole violators (Carson, 2015). Many of today's prisoners have a history of persistent criminality. Four additional factors affect correctional operations: the increased number of elderly prisoners, the many prisoners with HIV/AIDS, the thousands of prisoners who are mentally ill, and the increase in long-term prisoners.

Elderly Prisoners

Correctional officials face difficult and costly problems from the growing number of inmates over age 55. In 2000, approximately 42,300 inmates in U.S. prisons were 55 years or older (A. J. Beck & Harrison, 2001). By 2014, this number had increased to over 151,500 (Bureau of Justice Statistics, 2015). In Florida, 8 percent of inmates in 2000 were over age 50; by 2014, 20 percent fell in that same range. As of 2014, Florida prisons contained 1,091 inmates at least 70 years old, 130 at least 80, and 10 inmates in their 90s (Florida Tax Watch, 2014). Prisoners over the age of 50 accounted for 30 percent of all sick-call visits and half of all emergency calls (State of Florida Correctional Medical Authority, 2014). A number of states have created "geriatric prisons" designed to hold older inmates classified according to need: wheelchair users and prisoners needing long-term (nursing home) care. The "True Grit" Senior Structured Living Program in Nevada is one example of a program created

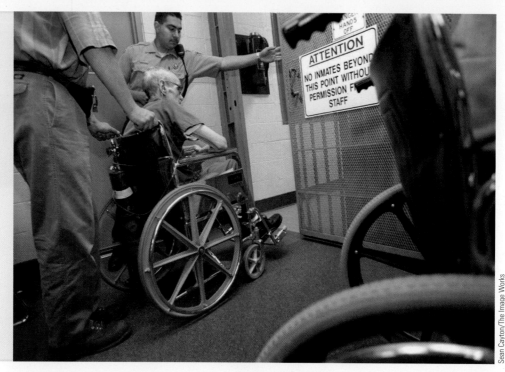

The imposition of long mandatory sentences increased the population of elderly prisoners and also prolonged the confinement of many prisoners who need medical care. These prisoners create extra financial burdens on correctional budgets. Are there less expensive ways to punish elderly and chronically ill prisoners?

specifically for elderly prisoners. In this program, inmates benefit from programs designed to enhance their physical, mental, and spiritual health (Vogel, 2014).

To some extent, the aging of the prison population reflects the aging of the overall citizenry, but to a greater extent, it reflects the fact that sentencing practices have changed. Consecutive lengthy sentences for heinous crimes, long mandatory minimum sentences, and life sentences without parole mean that more people who enter prison will spend most or all of the rest of their lives behind bars.

Elderly prisoners have medical and security needs that differ from those of the average inmate (Habes, 2011). For example, they cannot climb into top bunks. In many states, special sections of the institution have been designated for this older population so they will not have to mix with the younger, tougher inmates. Elderly prisoners are more likely to develop chronic illnesses such as heart disease, stroke, and cancer; thus, the cost for maintaining an elderly inmate averages about $69,000 per year, triple the average cost for a younger inmate. Ironically, while in prison, the offender will benefit from much better medical care and live a longer life than if she or he were discharged and living in poverty in free society.

Prisoners with HIV/AIDS

For several decades, AIDS was a leading cause of death for inmates aged 35 and younger. With 52 percent of the adult inmate population under age 35, correctional officials must cope with the problem of HIV as well as AIDS and related health issues. By the end of 2008, there were more than 20,000 HIV-positive inmates in state facilities (1.6 percent of the prison population) and 1,538 federal inmates (0.8 percent of the federal population) with AIDS or HIV-positive status (Maruschak, 2009). The number of HIV-positive inmates is undoubtedly low because not all states conduct mandatory testing of inmates. Further, the rate of confirmed AIDS cases in state and federal prisons is two and a half times higher than in the total U.S. population. Because many inmates who are HIV infected remain undiagnosed, these numbers underestimate the scope of the problem. However, advances in treatment and improved reporting have reduced the number of AIDS-related deaths in prison significantly, from over 1,000 deaths in 1995 to 52 in 2013 (Maruschak, 2012; Noonan, Rohloff, & Ginder, 2015).

To deal with offenders who have AIDS symptoms or who test positive for the virus, prison officials can develop policies on methods to prevent transmission of the disease, including housing arrangements for those infected and medical care for inmates with the full range of symptoms. However, administrators face a host of competing pressures as they decide what actions the institution should take (Westergaard, Spaulding, & Flanigan, 2013).

Prisoners Who Are Mentally Ill

Mass closings of public hospitals for the mentally ill began in the 1960s. At the time, new antipsychotic drugs made treating patients in the community seem a humane and relatively inexpensive alternative to long-term hospitalization. It soon became apparent, however, that community treatment works only if the drugs are taken and if clinics and halfway houses actually exist to help the mentally ill. Inmates who are mentally ill tend to follow a revolving door from homelessness to incarceration and then back to the streets, with little treatment. In Miami, for example, 97 people diagnosed with a mental illness were arrested 2,200 times and spent a combined 27,000 days in jail over a five-year period, costing taxpayers $13 million. Other people with mental illness commit crimes that lead them to serve sentences in prison. Thus, there are an estimated 350,000 offenders with mental illness currently in custody in corrections institutions, and the three largest inpatient psychiatric facilities in the country are inside jails in Los Angeles, New York City, and Chicago (*National Public Radio*, 2011).

Correctional workers are usually unprepared to deal with the mentally ill (Galanek, 2013). Cellblock officers, for instance, often do not know how to respond to disturbed inmates. Although most corrections systems have mental health units that segregate the ill, many inmates with psychiatric disorders live among other prisoners in the general population, where they are teased and otherwise exploited. Prisoners with mental illness often suffer, as the stress of confinement deepens their depression, intensifies delusions, or leads to mental breakdown. Some commit suicide.

Long-Term Prisoners

Prisoners in the United States serve longer sentences than do prisoners in other Western nations. A recent survey shows that nearly 310,000 prisoners are currently serving at least 20-year sentences. Of all inmates, about 10 percent are serving "natural life," which means there is no possibility that they will be paroled, a tripling since 1992. These long-term prisoners are often the same people who will become elderly offenders, with all their attendant problems. Each life sentence costs the taxpayers over $1 million.

Severe depression, feelings of hopelessness, and other health problems are common among long-termers. Such emotional stress tends to take place early in the sentence as these inmates lose contact with their families. Addressing the mental health needs of this special population is critical to preventing suicide attempts.

Long-term prisoners are generally not seen as control problems. They receive disciplinary infractions about half as often as do short-term inmates. Rather, administrators must find ways to make long terms bearable. Experts suggest that administrators follow three main principles: (1) maximize opportunities for inmates to exercise choice in their living circumstances, (2) create opportunities for meaningful living, and (3) help inmates maintain contact with the outside world (Flanagan, 1995). Many long-term inmates will eventually be released after spending their prime years incarcerated. Will offenders be able to support themselves when they return to the community at age 50, 60, or 70?

The contemporary inmate population presents several challenges to correctional workers. Resources may not be available to provide rehabilitative programs for most inmates. Even if the resources exist, the goal of maintaining a safe and healthy environment may tax the staff's abilities. These difficulties are compounded by AIDS and the increasing numbers of elderly and long-term prisoners.

6. What are the major characteristics of today's prisoners?
Today's prisoners are largely men in their late twenties to early thirties with less than a high school education. They are disproportionately members of minority groups.

Draft a solution to alleviate the institutional difficulties presented by one of the four groups discussed above: elderly prisoners, prisoners with HIV/AIDS, prisoners with mental illness, or prisoners serving long sentences. In light of the budget difficulties faced by states, are there any solutions that can save money?

The Convict World

Inmates of a maximum-security prison do not serve their time in isolation. Rather, prisoners form a society with its own traditions, norms, and leadership structure. Some choose to associate with only a few close friends; others form cliques along racial or "professional" lines. Still others serve as the politicians of the convict society; they attempt to represent convict interests and distribute valued goods in return for support. Just as the free world has a social culture, the "inside" has a prisoner subculture. Membership in a group provides mutual protection from theft and physical assault, the basis of wheeling and dealing, and a source of cultural identity.

inmate code The values and norms of the prison social system that define the inmates' idea of the model prisoner.

As in any society, the convict world has certain norms and values. Often described as the **inmate code**, these norms and values develop within the prison social system and help define the inmate's image of the model prisoner. As Robert Johnson notes, "The public culture of the prison has norms that dictate behavior 'on the yard' and in other public areas of the prison such as mess halls, gyms, and the larger program and work sites" (2002:100). Prison is an ultra-masculine world. The culture breathes masculine toughness and insensitivity, impugns softness, and emphasizes the use of hostility and manipulation in one's relations with fellow inmates and staff. Maintaining a "tough" reputation can limit the probability of being victimized while one is incarcerated (Copes, Brookman, & Brown, 2013). It makes caring and friendly behavior, especially with respect to the staff, look servile and silly (Sabo, Kupers, & London, 2001:7).

The code also emphasizes the solidarity of all inmates against the staff. For example, according to the code, inmates should never inform on one another, pry into one another's affairs, "run off at the mouth," or put another inmate on the spot. They must be tough and trust neither the officers nor the principles for which they stand. Guards, who are called "hacks" or "screws," are to be considered always wrong and the prisoners always right.

Some sociologists believe that the code emerges within the institution as a way to lessen the pain of imprisonment (Sykes, 1958); others believe that it is part of the criminal subculture that prisoners bring with them (Irwin & Cressey, 1962). The inmate who follows the code enjoys a certain amount of admiration from other inmates as a "right guy" or a "real man." Those who break the code are labeled "rat" or "punk" and will probably spend their prison life at the bottom of the convict social structure, alienated from the rest of the population and targeted for abuse (Sykes, 1958:84).

AP Images/Ben Margot

Contemporary prison society is divided along social, ethnic, and gang subgroups. There is no longer a single inmate code to which all prisoners subscribe. As a correctional officer, how would you deal with white supremacists and other gangs based on racial and ethnic divisions within the prison population?

Survival Tips for Beginners
TJ Granack

Okay, so you just lost your case. Maybe you took a plea bargain. Whatever. The point is you've been sentenced. You've turned yourself over to the authorities and you're in the county jail waiting to catch the next chain to the R Unit (receiving) where you'll be stripped and shaved and photographed and processed and sent to one of the various prisons in your state.

So what's a felon to do? Here are some survival tips that may make your stay less hellish:

1. *Commit an honorable crime.* Commit a crime that's considered, among convicts, to be worthy of respect. I was lucky. I went down for first-degree attempted murder, so my crime fell in the "honorable" category. Oh, goodie. So I just had to endure the everyday sort of danger and abuse that comes with prison life.

2. *Don't gamble.* Not cards, not chess, not the Super Bowl, and if you do, don't bet too much. If you lose too much and pay up (don't even think of doing otherwise), then you'll be known as a rich guy who'll be very popular with the vultures.

3. *Never loan anyone anything.* Because if you do, you'll be expected to collect one way or another. If you don't collect you will be known as a mark, as someone without enough heart to take back his own.

4. *Make no eye contact.* Don't look anyone in the eye. Ever. Locking eyes with another man, be he a convict or a guard, is considered a challenge, a threat, and should therefore be avoided.

5. *Pick your friends carefully.* When you choose a friend, you've got to be prepared to deal with anything that person may have done. Their reputation is yours, and the consequences can be enormous.

6. *Fight and fight dirty.* You have to fight, and not according to the Marquis of Queensbury Rules, either. If you do it right, you'll only have to do it once or twice. If you don't, expect regular whooping and loss of possessions.

7. *Mind your own business.* Never get in the middle of anyone else's discussion/argument/confrontation/fight. Never offer unsolicited knowledge or advice.

8. *Keep a good porn collection.* If you don't have one, the boys will think you're funny.

9. *Don't talk to staff, especially guards.* Any prolonged discussion or associations with staff make you susceptible to rumor and suspicion of being a snitch.

10. *Never snitch.* Or even appear to snitch. And above all, avoid the real thing. And if you do, you'd better not get caught.

Researching the Internet
Compare this set of rules with the official information given to North Carolina prisoners to convey the rules and regulations of prison. To link to this document, go to http://www.doc.state.nc.us/Publications/inmate%20rule%20book.pdf.

For Critical Thinking and Analysis
If you were sent to prison, how would you seek to learn the code that prisoners enforce among themselves?

Source: From TJ Granack "Welcome to the Steel Hotel: Survival Tips for Beginners" in *The Funhouse Mirror: Reflections on Prison* (pp. 6–10), edited by R. E, Gordon. Copyright © 2000 by Washington State University Press. Reprinted by permission of Washington State University Press (http://wsupress.wsu.edu/recenttitles/).

Elements of the core code described by Sykes over 50 years ago are probably found in every prison today, but a single, overriding inmate code probably no longer exists in American prisons. Today, convict society tends to divide along racial lines (Carroll, 1974; Irwin, 1980), with the greatest division found in maximum-security prisons. When no single code of behavior is accepted by the entire population, the tasks of administrators become much more difficult. They must be aware of the different groups, recognize the norms and rules that members hold in each, and deal with the leaders of many cliques rather than with a few inmates who have risen to top positions in the inmate society. In the "Close Up" feature, TJ Granack provides "Survival Tips for Beginners."

Adaptive Roles

On entering prison, a newcomer ("fish") is confronted by the question: "How am I going to do my time?" Some decide to withdraw and isolate themselves. Others decide to become full participants in the convict social system. The choice, influenced by prisoners' values and experiences, helps determine strategies for survival and success.

Most male inmates use one of four basic role orientations to adapt to prison: "doing time," "gleaning," "jailing," and functioning as a "disorganized criminal" (Irwin, 1970:67).

Doing Time Men "doing time" view their prison term as a brief, inevitable break in their criminal careers, a cost of doing business. They try to serve their terms with the least amount of suffering and the greatest amount of comfort. They avoid trouble by living by the inmate code, finding activities to fill their days, forming friendships with a few other convicts, and generally doing what they think is necessary to survive and to get out as soon as possible.

Gleaning Inmates who are "gleaning" try to take advantage of prison programs to better themselves and improve their prospects for success after release. They use the resources at hand: libraries, correspondence courses, vocational training, schools. Some make a radical conversion away from a life of crime.

Jailing "Jailing" is the choice of those who cut themselves off from the outside and try to construct a life within the prison. These are often "state-raised" youths who have spent much of their lives in institutional settings and who identify little with the values of free society. These are the inmates who seek power and influence in the prison society, often becoming key figures in the politics and economy of prison life.

Disorganized Criminal A fourth role orientation—the "disorganized criminal"—describes inmates who cannot develop any of the other three orientations. They may be of low intelligence or afflicted with psychological or physical disabilities, and they find functioning in prison society difficult. They are "human putty" to be manipulated by others. These are also the inmates who cannot adjust to prison life and who develop emotional disorders, attempt suicide, and violate prison rules (K. Adams, 1992).

As these roles suggest, prisoners are not members of an undifferentiated mass. Individual convicts choose to play specific roles in prison society. The roles they choose reflect the physical and social environment they have experienced and also influence their relationships and interactions in prison. How do most prisoners serve their time? Although the media generally portray prisons as violent, chaotic places, research shows that most inmates want to get through their sentence without trouble. As journalist Pete Earley found in his study of Leavenworth, roughly 80 percent of inmates try to avoid trouble and do their time as easily as possible (1992:44).

The Prison Economy

In prison, as outside, individuals want goods and services. Although the state feeds, clothes, and houses all prisoners, amenities are sparse. Prisoners lack everything but bare necessities. Their diet and routine are monotonous and their recreational opportunities scarce. They experience a loss of identity (due to uniformity of treatment) and a lack of responsibility. In short, prison is relatively unique in having been deliberately designed as "an island of poverty in the midst of a society of relative abundance" (V. Williams & Fish, 1974:40).

The number of items that a prisoner can purchase or receive through legitimate channels differs from state to state and from facility to facility. For example, prisoners in some state institutions may have televisions, civilian clothing, and hot plates. Not all prisoners enjoy these luxuries, nor do these amenities satisfy the lingering desire for a variety of other goods. Some state legislatures have decreed that amenities will be prohibited and that prisoners should return to the spartan living conditions that existed before amenities were introduced.

Recognizing that prisoners do have some basic needs that are not met, prisons have a commissary, or "store," from which inmates may, on a scheduled basis, purchase a limited number of items—toilet articles, tobacco, snacks, and other food products—in exchange for credits drawn on their "bank accounts." The size of a bank account depends on the amount of money deposited at the time of the inmate's entrance, gifts sent by relatives, and amounts earned in the low-paying prison industries.

However, the peanut butter, soap, and cigarettes of the typical prison store in no way satisfy the consumer needs and desires of most prisoners. Many items taken for granted on the outside are inordinately valued on the inside, and are traded in an informal, underground economy. For example, talcum powder and deodorant become more important because of the limited bathing facilities. Goods and services that a prisoner would not have consumed at all outside prison can take on an exaggerated importance inside prison. For example, unable to get alcohol, offenders may seek a similar effect by sniffing glue. Or, to distinguish themselves from others, offenders may pay laundry workers to iron distinctive creases or designs into a shirt, a modest version of conspicuous consumption.

Many studies point to the pervasiveness of this economy. The research shows that a market economy provides the goods (contraband) and services not available or not allowed by prison authorities. In many prisons, inmates run private "stores." Food stolen from the kitchen for late-night snacks, homemade wine, and drugs such as marijuana are available in these stores.

This informal economy reinforces the norms and roles of the prison social system and influences the nature of interpersonal relationships. The extent of the underground economy and its ability to produce desired goods and services—food, drugs, alcohol, sex, preferred living conditions—vary according to the scope of official surveillance, the demands of the consumers, and the opportunities for entrepreneurship. Inmates' success as "hustlers" determines the luxuries and power they can enjoy.

Because real money is always prohibited, a traditional currency of the prison economy is cigarettes—even when prison officials try to ban smoking. Cigarettes are easily transferable, have a stable and well-known standard of value, and come in "denominations" of singles, packs, and cartons. Furthermore, they are in demand by smokers. Even those who do not smoke keep cigarettes for prison currency. As more prisons become smoke free, however, institutions that ban cigarettes have seen new forms of currency emerge, such as cans of tuna fish, postage stamps, and coffee (Paynter, 2011). At the same time, tobacco becomes more valuable because of its scarcity in the smoke-free facilities, with prisoners making efforts to persuade corrections officers to smuggle in tobacco. Officers have been convicted and incarcerated for smuggling cigarettes into correctional institutions (Pratt, 2015). Forty-six corrections officers in the Georgia prison system were arrested in February 2016 for smuggling cigarettes and other items into the state's prisons (Brown & Ryan, 2016).

Certain positions in the prison society enhance opportunities for entrepreneurs. For example, inmates assigned to work in the kitchen, warehouse, and administrative office steal food, clothing, building materials, and even information to sell or trade to other prisoners. The goods may then become part of other market transactions. Thus, the exchange of a dozen eggs for two packs of cigarettes may result in the reselling of the eggs in the form of egg sandwiches made on a hot plate for five cigarettes each. Meanwhile, the kitchen worker who stole the eggs may use the income to get a laundry worker to starch his shirts, to get drugs from a hospital orderly, or to pay another prisoner for sex.

Participation in the prison economy can put inmates at greater risk for victimization while incarcerated (Copes et al., 2010). Economic transactions can lead to violence when goods are stolen, debts are not paid, or agreements are violated. Disruptions of the economy can occur when officials conduct periodic "lockdowns" and inspections. Confiscation of contraband can result in temporary shortages and price readjustments, but gradually, profits result. The prison economy, like that of the outside world, allocates goods and services, rewards and sanctions, and it is closely linked to the society it serves.

7. **Why is it unlikely that a single, overriding inmate code exists in today's prisons?**
   The prison society is fragmented by racial and ethnic divisions.

8. **What are the four role orientations found in adult male prisons?**
   Doing time, gleaning, jailing, and functioning as a disorganized criminal.

9. **Why does an underground economy exist in prison?**
   To provide goods and services not available through regular channels.

Is it possible to stop the underground economy in prisons? If you were a warden, what are two steps you would take to reduce the problems associated with the underground economy? (For this discussion, disregard whether you believe that you—or anyone—can completely stop it.)

Women in Prison

Most studies of prisons have focused on institutions for men. How do prisons for women differ, and what special problems do female inmates face?

Women constitute only about 8 percent (about 112,000) of the entire U.S. prison population (Carson & Mulako-Wangota, 2016). However, the growth rate in the number of incarcerated women has exceeded that of men since 1981. In fact, from 2000 to 2010, the male population increased by 16 percent while that of women increased by 25 percent (Guerino, Harrison, & Sabol, 2011). The increased number of women in prison has significantly affected the delivery of programs, housing conditions, medical care, staffing, and security.

Female offenders are incarcerated in 98 confinement facilities for women and 93 facilities that house men and women separately. Life in these facilities both differs from and resembles life in institutions for men alone. Women's prisons are smaller, with looser security and less structured relationships; the underground economy is not as well developed; and female prisoners seem less committed to the inmate code. Women also serve shorter sentences than do men, so their prison society is more fluid as new members join and others leave.

Many women's prisons have the outward appearance of a college campus, often seen as a group of "cottages" around a central administration/dining/program building. Generally these facilities lack the high walls, guard towers, and cyclone

Women's experiences in prison can differ markedly from those of men. Although there is less violence between prisoners in women's institutions, women often have fewer options for educational and vocational programs. In addition, many prisons have discovered problems with male correctional officers sexually abusing women prisoners. How would you organize the selection of staff, staff training, and the development of programs to properly run a prison for women?

REUTERS/Carlo Allegri

fences found at most prisons for men. In recent years, however, the trend has been to upgrade security for women's prisons by adding barbed wire, higher fences, and other devices to prevent escapes.

The characteristics of correctional facilities for women also include geographic remoteness and inmate heterogeneity. Few states operate more than one institution for women, so inmates generally live far from their children, families, friends, and attorneys. In many institutions, the small numbers of inmates limit the extent to which the needs of individual offenders can be recognized and treated. Housing classifications are often so broad that dangerous prisoners or inmates who have mental illness are mixed with women who have committed minor offenses and have no psychological problems. Similarly, available rehabilitative programs are often not used to their full extent, because correctional departments fail to recognize women's problems and needs.

In most respects, we can see incarcerated women, like male prisoners, as disadvantaged losers in this complex and competitive society. However, the two groups differ with regard to types of offenses and length of sentences, patterns of drug use, and criminal history. Thirty-seven percent of female prisoners are sentenced for violent offenses, compared with 54 percent of male prisoners, and 24 percent for drug-related offenses, versus 15 percent of the men (Carson, 2015). Overall, women serve shorter prison sentences than do men. The typical female in prison spends about 18 months behind bars, whereas the typical male spends about 29 months incarcerated (Bonczar, 2011).

The Subculture of Women's Prisons

Studies of the subculture of women's prisons have been less extensive than those of male-convict society. Further, just as few ethnographic studies of men's prisons have taken place during the past two decades, even fewer exist for women's prisons.

Much early investigation of women's prisons focused on types of social relationships among female offenders. As in all types of penal institutions, same-sex relationships were found, but unlike in male prisons, such relationships among women appeared more voluntary than coerced. Perhaps more importantly, scholars reported that female inmates tended to form pseudofamilies in which they adopted various roles—father, mother, daughter, sister—and interacted as a unit, rather than identifying with the larger prisoner subculture (Girshick, 1999; Propper, 1982). Esther Heffernan views these "play" families as a "direct, conscious substitution for the family relationships broken by imprisonment, or . . . the development of roles that perhaps were not fulfilled in the actual home environment" (1972:41–42). She also notes the economic aspect of the play families and the extent to which they are formed to provide for their members. Such cooperative relationships help relieve the tensions of prison life, assist the socialization of new inmates, and permit individuals to act according to clearly defined roles and rules.

In discussing the available research on women in prison, we need to consider the most recent shifts in prison life. Just as the subculture of male prisons has changed since the pioneering research of the 1950s, the climate of female prisons has undoubtedly changed. Kimberly Greer (2000) found support for the idea that, compared with male prisons, prisons for women are less violent, involve less gang activity, and lack racial tension; however, the respondents indicated that their interpersonal relationships may be less stable and less familial than in the past. They reported higher levels of mistrust among women and greater economic manipulation.

In one notable study of women's prison culture, Barbara Owen (1998) found that the inmates at the Central California Women's Facility developed various styles of doing time. She observed that the vast majority wanted to avoid "the mix"—"behavior that can bring trouble and conflict with staff and other prisoners." A primary feature of "the mix" is anything for which one can lose "good time" or can result in being sent to administrative segregation. Being in "the mix" was related to "'homo-secting,' involvement in drugs, fights, and 'being messy,' that is, being involved in conflict and trouble." Owen found that most women want to do their time and go home, but some "are more at home in prison and do not seem to care if they 'lost time'" (Owen, 1998:179).

Male versus Female Subcultures

Comparisons of male and female prisons are complicated by the nature of the research: most studies have been conducted in single-sex institutions, and most follow theories and concepts first developed in male prisons. However, it is important to recognize the differences between men and women who are incarcerated. Figure 11.3 contains descriptive information on the characteristics of incarcerated men and women in the United States. Based on what we know about women's prisons, the following facts may explain the differences in subculture:

- Over half of male inmates but only a third of female inmates are serving time for violent offenses.
- There is less violence in prisons for women than in prisons for men.
- Women show greater responsiveness to prison programs.
- Men's prison populations are divided by security level, but most women serve time in facilities where the entire population is mixed.
- Men tend to segregate themselves by race; this is less true of women.
- Men rarely become intimate with their keepers, but many women share their lives with officers.

A major difference between the two types of prisons relates to interpersonal relationships. Male prisoners act for themselves and are evaluated by others according to how they adhere to subcultural norms. An early comparative study of one women's prison and four men's prisons found that men believe they must demonstrate physical strength and consciously avoid any mannerisms that might imply homosexuality (Fox, 1982). To gain recognition and status within the convict community, the male prisoner must strictly adhere to these values. Men form cliques, but not the family networks found in prisons for women. Male norms stress autonomy, self-sufficiency, and the ability to cope with one's own problems, and men are expected to "do their own time." Fox found little sharing in the men's prisons.

Women, on the other hand, place less emphasis on achieving status or recognition within the prisoner community. Women are also less likely "to impose severe restrictions on the sexual (or emotional) conduct of other members" (Fox, 1982:100). As noted previously, in prisons for women, close ties seem to exist among small groups akin to extended families. These family groups provide emotional support and share resources.

The differences between male and female prisoner subcultures have been ascribed to the nurturing, maternal qualities of women. Some critics charge that such an analysis stereotypes female behavior and imputes a biological basis to personality where none exists. Of importance as well is the issue of inmate–inmate violence in male and female institutions. Physical violence between female inmates occurs less often than between male inmates, but it is important to note that the violence that does exist is shaped by the different culture in women's prisons (Owen et al., 2008).

Issues in the Incarceration of Women

Under pressures for equal opportunity, states seem to believe that they should run women's prisons as they do prisons for men, with the same policies and procedures. However, advocates for female prisoners have urged governments to keep in mind that women inmates have different needs than their male counterparts (Bartels & Gaffney, 2011). Understanding the pathways by which women end up incarcerated can also help prison and jail administrators manage their facilities. Many incarcerated women have been victims of physical and sexual abuse, and that history can affect their behavior while incarcerated (McCampbell, 2005).

Although correctional departments have been playing "catch up" to meet the unique needs of women offenders, sexual misconduct by officers persists, along with women prisoners' demands for education and training, medical services, and methods for dealing with the problems of mothers and their children. We next examine each of these issues and the policy implications they pose for the future.

Sexual Misconduct   When the number of female prisoners increased in the late 1990s, cases of sexual misconduct by male correctional officers escalated. After an investigation of sexual misconduct of officers in the women's prisons of five states—California, Georgia, Illinois, Michigan, and New York—Human Rights Watch reported that male officers had raped, sexually assaulted, and abused female inmates. In 2009, the state of Michigan paid over $100 million to 500 female prisoners who were raped in Michigan prisons (McFarlane, 2009).

Congress approved the federal Prison Rape Elimination act as a national law in 2003 (Struckman-Johnson & Struckman-Johnson, 2013). This law requires that all state correctional systems develop standards in an effort to collect data on rape in prisons and reduce its incidence; the act also provides funding to state agencies to meet these national standards (Prison Rape Elimination Act, 117 STAT. 972). Research funded by this initiative has determined that prison inmates do not view rape in the same way that people outside prisons do. Even with protections against rape, women in prison frequently report their knowledge of "consensual" sexual relationships between inmates and guards (Fleischer & Krienert, 2006). However, because prison guards exert power and control over inmates in prisons, it is difficult to argue that sex between the two can be considered consensual. In fact, guards who have sex with inmates under their care can be charged criminally for such behavior.

Illicit relationships can also occur between inmates and civilian employees. Private contractors are sometimes used by prisons to provide services such as food, laundry, and janitorial services. Read the issues discussed in the "Current Controversies" feature to learn more about problems that correctional administrators have faced with private contractors.

Educational and Vocational Training Programs   A major criticism of women's prisons is that they lack the variety of vocational and educational programs available in male institutions. Critics also charge that programs tend to offer training only in stereotypically "female" occupations—cosmetology, food service, housekeeping, and sewing (Morash, Haarr, & Rucker, 1994). Such training does not correspond to the wider employment opportunities available to women in today's world. However, both men's and women's facilities usually offer educational programs so inmates can become literate and earn general equivalency diplomas (GEDs).

Such programs matter a great deal, considering that, upon release, most women must support themselves, and many must support their children, as well (Kruttschnitt, 2010). In addition, vocational training programs have been shown to reduce the likelihood that inmates will return to prison after being released. Female offenders in prison have different needs than male offenders, and vocational training should be designed around the specific needs of women (Holtfreter & Morash, 2003).

Medical Services   Because of their socioeconomic status and limited access to preventive medical care, women prisoners usually have more-serious health problems than do men; they have a higher incidence of asthma, drug abuse, diabetes, and heart disorders (T. L. Anderson, 2003). Yet women's prisons often lack the medical personnel, equipment, and pharmaceutical supplies to deal with these diseases. In addition, prison officials often dismiss the gynecological needs of female inmates as "unimportant" (L. Braithwaite, Treadwell, & Arriola, 2005). Although a higher percentage of women than men report receiving medical services in prison, women's institutions are less likely than men's to have a full-time medical staff or hospital facilities.

Privatization of Services in Public Prisons and the Risk of Misconduct

In December 2013, the State of Michigan awarded the state's prison food service responsibility to Aramark Corporation, which also provides food service to schools and other institutional entities. This was controversial, because in the past, prison food service had been supplied by state employees. Hiring Aramark resulted in the loss of 370 state jobs; however, state officials assured taxpayers that using Aramark would result in significant cost savings for the state.

Within months of Aramark taking over the food contract, prison officials began receiving reports that inmates were receiving insufficient food portions, and that some of the food being served was rotten, moldy, and even contained maggots. Even worse, the private company's employees were accused of engaging in criminal acts with—and for—inmates. Aramark employees were accused of smuggling contraband such as tobacco and drugs into prisons, and engaging in sexual relationships with prisoners. Eventually, a total of 186 Aramark employees were barred from entering prisons due to their misconduct. Michigan has not been the only state in which Aramark employees have been accused of inappropriate conduct in prison—from 2014 to 2016, several employees were arrested in Michigan, Indiana, and Texas.

Some have suggested that employees of private corporations are more likely to engage in illicit behavior because they are paid significantly less than state employees and may have less training. Exacerbating the problems occurring in Michigan prisons was the state's failure to act when reports of problems started coming in.

Aramark was fined by the state on two separate occasions for their failures, but at least one fine was never paid to the state. Eventually, the contract with Aramark was terminated early and a new private company was brought in, but some believe problems will continue until state workers are rehired to provide meals to prisoners. In 2016, at least two prisons in Michigan have reported that inmates have staged peaceful protests over the quality of the food provided by the new vendor, Trinity Services. In addition, 59 Trinity employees were fired and barred from the prisons for misbehavior within the first six months of the initiation of the new food service.

The food and other services provided to inmates can have a significant impact on prison culture. Prisoners need to eat, and we assume that the food they are served is edible and provides appropriate nutrition. Failing to provide this basic service could be viewed as "cruel and unusual punishment" under the Eighth Amendment protections provided to prisoners by the Constitution. In addition, managing inmate populations can be very difficult when prisoners feel that they are treated unfairly, as they would if their food contains insects. Finally, the smuggling of illegal drugs, other contraband, and inappropriate sexual relationships with prisoners poses a serious problem for prison security and safety.

For Critical Thinking and Analysis

When states contract with private companies to run prisons or probation operations, philosophical questions arise about whether it is proper to permit private actors to impose criminal punishments on the state's behalf. These philosophical questions do not arise when private contractors merely provide a specific service within a state prison, such as food service or education programs. However, as indicated by the Michigan example, there are questions about the risks that arise when prisons seek to provide services as cheaply as possible rather than relying on employees selected, trained, compensated, and supervised by the state government. If you were the Director of the Department of Corrections in Michigan, what would you do? Would you recommend to the governor that the prisons return to the use of state employees? Alternatively, are there ways you could supervise or pressure private contractors to provide better service while still saving money for the state? Give three reasons for your decision.

Sources: "Aramark Employee Arrested for Trafficking Drugs to Inmates," February 3, 2016 (http://wishtv.com); Associated Press, "Inmates Protest Food Quality at Second Northern Michigan Prison," *Oakland Press*, March 31, 2016 (http://theoaklandpress .com); B. Devereaux, "Report: Aramark Worker Arrested for Smuggling at Gratiot County Prison," September 16, 2014 (http://www.mlive.com); P. Egan, "Michigan to End Prison Food Deal with Aramark." *Detroit Free Press*, July 13, 2015 (http:// freep.com); P. Egan, "Prisoners Protest Food under New Contractor Trinity," *Detroit Free Press*, March 22, 2016 (www.freep .com); P. Egan, "Report: Michigan Failed to Hold Aramark Accountable." *Detroit Free Press*, August 18, 2015 (http://freep.com); D. Ibanez, "Aramark Employee Arrested in Jail Sting Operation," KSAT News, July 15, 2014 (http://www.ksat.com).

Saying that corrections must "defuse the time bomb," Leslie Acoca argues that failure to provide female inmates with basic preventive and medical treatments such as immunizations, breast cancer screenings, and management of chronic diseases "is resulting in the development of more serious health problems that are exponentially more expensive to treat" (1997:67). She says that poor medical care for the incarcerated merely shifts costs to overburdened community health care systems after the women are released.

Mothers and Their Children   Of greatest concern to incarcerated women is the fate of their children. Over 60 percent of women inmates are mothers, with 25 percent having children aged four or younger. Especially troubling is the increase in the number of children younger than 18 with an incarcerated parent—the number of children with a mother in prison more than doubled between 1991 and 2007 (Glaze & Maruschak, 2008).

Because about 65 percent of incarcerated mothers were single caretakers of minor children before they entered prison, they do not always have partners to take care of their children. In about one-third of these cases, children are cared for by their fathers. In most cases, though, they live with grandparents or other relatives. If neither the father nor other relatives take them, they live with friends of the family or are placed in foster care (Glaze & Maruschak, 2008). Due to high incarceration rates in black communities, locking up parents differentially affects black children and harms communities (Roberts, 2004). Children with incarcerated mothers are more likely to have contact with the criminal justice system as adults and are more likely to be convicted of crimes as adults (Huebner & Gustafson, 2007).

Imprisoned mothers have difficulty maintaining contact with their children. Because most states have only one or two prisons for women, mothers may be incarcerated 150 miles or more away. This makes transportation difficult, visits short and infrequent, and phone calls uncertain and irregular. When the children do visit the prison, they face strange and intimidating surroundings. In some institutions, children must conform to the rules governing adult visitations: strict time limits and no physical contact.

Other correctional facilities, however, seek ways to help mothers maintain links to their children. For example, at Logan Correctional Center, the prison to which all women prisoners in Illinois were moved in 2013, there are a variety of programs (Fak, 2013). The "Mom and Me" camp brings children ages 7 through 12 together with their imprisoned mothers for three days of activities in the summer. Through the "Family Connections Visitation" program, an outside social services agency transports 30 children and their caregivers, usually their grandmothers, to visit imprisoned mothers each month. The assistance of the outside agency with transportation and arrangements creates visitation opportunities that would otherwise not occur. In the prison's "Operation Storybook" program, incarcerated mothers and grandmothers have the opportunity to read children's books aloud that are recorded and copied on CDs to be sent to their children and grandchildren. The Illinois prison also cooperates with the national Angel Tree program through which volunteers provide Christmas gifts, summer camp experiences, and mentors for the children of incarcerated mothers.

In some states, children can meet with their mothers at almost any time, for extended periods, and in playrooms or nurseries where contact is possible. Some states even transport children to visit their mothers; some institutions let children stay overnight with their mothers. A few prisons have family visitation programs that let the inmate, her legal husband, and her children be together, often in a mobile home or apartment, for up to 72 hours (DAlessio, Flexon, & Stolzenberg, 2013).

The future of women's correctional institutions is hard to predict. More women are being sent to prison now, and more have committed the violent crimes and drug offenses that used to be more typical of male offenders. Will these changes continue to affect the adaptive roles and social relationships that differentiate women's prisons from men's? Will women's prisons need to become more security conscious and to enforce rules through more-formal relationships between inmates and staff? These important issues need further study.

10. **What accounts for the neglect of facilities and programs in women's prisons?**
The small number of female inmates compared with the number of male inmates.

11. **How do the social relationships among female prisoners differ from those among their male counterparts?**
Men are more individualistic, and their norms stress autonomy, self-sufficiency, and the ability to cope with one's own problems. Women are more sharing with one another.

12. **What problems do female prisoners face in maintaining contact with their children?**
The distance of prisons from homes, intermittent telephone privileges, and an unnatural visiting environment.

To what extent should society worry about, pay attention to, and spend money on programs for children whose parents are in prison? Give two arguments supporting each side of this debate.

Prison Programs

Modern correctional institutions differ from those of the past in the number and variety of programs they provide for inmates. Early penitentiaries included prison industries, but educational, vocational, and treatment programs were added when rehabilitation goals became prevalent. During the last 35 years, as the public called for harsher punishment of criminals, legislators have gutted prison educational and treatment programs as "frills" that only "coddled" inmates. In addition, the great increase in the number of prisoners has limited access to those programs that are still available.

Administrators argue that programs help them deal with the problem of time on the prisoners' hands. They know that the more programs prisons offer, the less likely that inmate idleness will turn into hostility; less cell time means fewer tensions. Evidence suggests that inmate education and jobs may positively affect the running of prisons, as well as reduce recidivism. However, in an era of government budget cuts, prison vocational training and education programs are often targeted for reduction because they are less essential than preserving resources for safety and security. In 2015, Oklahoma cut several programs and services for inmates after the private prison contractor proved more costly than expected (Palmer, 2015). Connecticut's budget cuts have resulted in the termination of a program that helps juvenile offenders catch up in school (Kovner, 2016); West Virgnia was on the verge of laying off all instructions in their correctional system, until the governor threatened to veto the budget bill containing those cuts (Quinn, 2016).

There is also the first indication of a potential countertrend in support of prison programs. As governors and legislators become more aware of the need to prepare convicted offenders for reentry into society, they may become more willing to devote resources to vocational and educational programs. In 2014, for example, New York Governor Andrew Cuomo proposed spending state money to provide college classes for incarcerated offenders, a practice that had ended 2 years earlier. The proposal did not move forward, so Cuomo proposed it again in 2016—this time with funding specifically coming from money the state acquired from asset forfeiture by criminal offenders (McKinley & McKinley, 2016). However, many people oppose providing free programs for criminal offenders that law-abiding citizens must struggle to pay for on their own. Thus, it remains to be seen whether Cuomo's proposal will become a reality or if other states might make similar moves. The New York proposal reflects the idea that programs can be used to cut recidivism. There are also other research-based programs and treatments that can be used to cut recidivism, as discussed in the "Evidence-Based Practice and Policy" feature.

Classification of Prisoners

classification The process of assigning an inmate to a category based on his or her risk to security, educational level, ability to work, and readiness for release.

Determining the appropriate program for an individual prisoner usually involves a process called **classification**. A committee—often comprising the heads of the security, treatment, education, and industry departments—evaluates the inmate's

EVIDENCE-BASED PRACTICE AND POLICY

Prison Practices to Reduce Recidivism

The National Institute of Corrections promotes evidence-based practices in prisons by holding training sessions and distributing research-based materials on effective practices, procedures, and programs. A central element of evidence-based programming to reduce recidivism is the assessment and classification of prisoners to identify their individual problems and needs. One prominent assessment tool is the Level of Service Inventory-Revised instrument that is used in structured interviews with individual prisoners to gather information about 54 items, including criminal history, educational background, family relationships, substance-abuse problems, emotional and personal issues, and social attitudes.

Other principles of evidence-based practices in prisons include focusing resources on prisoners with the greatest needs and ensuring that programs and treatments are of sufficient duration and appropriate timing to help with successful reentry and avoidance of recidivism. Studies indicate that high-risk offenders should spend 40–70 percent of their time in highly structured activities and programs in the months preceding their release from prison into community supervision. In addition, there should be extended continuity of treatment during community supervision for those with specific, difficult problems, such as drug addicts and sex offenders. As one state's description of evidence-based practices described the approach and goal, "treatment should be delivered as a life-long plan for changing entrenched negative lifestyle behaviors."

Evidence-based practices also rely on positive reinforcement approaches to helping offenders change their attitudes and behavior and learn new ways to think about values, choice of friends, intoxicating substances, and interactions with others. Obviously, the use of effective evidence-based practices requires extensive training for staff members, as well as the time and resources spent in the actual teaching and counseling of offenders.

Researching the Internet

Learn more about classification of prisoners through the many publications available online from the National Institute of Corrections. To link to this website, go to http://nicic.gov/library/topic/440-prison-classification.

Implementing New Practices

Prisons face challenges in considering whether and how to implement evidence-based practices aimed at reducing recidivism. They must always place a priority on safety and security. In addition, these institutions may not have staff members with appropriate expertise and training to implement evidence-based programs. How much time, money, and staff should be devoted to programs for offenders in prison? In an era of budget cuts, can states afford to provide extensive programs when they must reduce prison populations and staffing in order to save money? If you were a governor, would you see the greatest benefit to society resulting from cutting budgets for corrections programs in an effort to reduce burdens on taxpayers, or from increasing corrections program budgets to reduce recidivism? Write a memo that explains two reasons that support your position.

Sources: "Evidence Based Correctional Practices," report prepared by the Colorado Division of Criminal Justice based on materials from the National Institute of Corrections, August 2007 (https://cdpsdocs.state.co.us/ors/docs/reports/2007_CCJJ_EBP.pdf); D. Hooley, "6 Evidence-Based Practices Proven to Lower Recidivism," CorrectionsOne website, March 30, 2010 (www.correctionsone.com); F. Osher, D. D'Amora, M. Plotkin, N. Jarrett, and A. Eggleston, *Adults with Behavioral Health Needs under Correctional Supervision*, Council of State Governments Justice Center, 2012 (http://cjgjusticecenter.org).

---

security level, treatment and educational needs, work assignment, and eventually, readiness for release.

Classification decisions are often based on the institution's needs rather than on those of the inmates. For example, inmates from the city may be assigned to farm work because that is where they are needed. Further, certain programs may remain limited even though the demand for them is great. Thus, inmates may find that the few open seats in, for example, a computer course are filled and that there is a long waiting list. Prisoners often become angered and frustrated by the classification process and the limited availability of programs. Although release on parole can depend on a good record of participation in these programs, entrance for some inmates is blocked.

Educational Programs

Offenders constitute one of the most undereducated groups in the U.S. population. In many systems, all inmates who have not completed eighth grade are assigned full-time to prison school. Many programs provide remedial help in reading,

English, and math. Nearly 80 percent of prisons offer courses to enable prisoners to earn their GED, but only 35 percent offer courses in cooperation with a college or university (Stephan, 2008). There is scientific evidence, however, that prison education programs can reduce recidivism and improve the chances that former inmates can find employment after release (Davis et al., 2013). Based on those findings, President Obama reinstated prisoners' eligibility to receive Pell Grants while incarcerated as encouragement for them to improve their education (U.S. Department of Education, 2015).

Even though there is empirical support for college education programs in prison, some people are opposed to prisoners having access to college courses. Read "The Policy Debate" feature to learn more about the pros and cons of offering college courses to prisoners.

THE POLICY DEBATE

Should Prisoners Have Access to the Pell Grant Program?

Educational and vocational programs for prisoners were severely reduced during the "get tough" period of crime control. Recently, however, government and industry leaders have recognized that offering these programs to inmates can benefit prisoners, families, and their communities upon release. President Obama's recent actions to open Pell Grants to prisoners on a limited basis has raised issues surrounding eligibility for federal education funds. There are opinions on both sides of this issue:

In Favor of Pell Grants:

- The pilot program is a test case that will also collect data to determine whether inmates who receive the grants are more likely to find jobs after release, and are less likely to recidivate.
- There is substantial research indicating that prisoners with college educations fare better in the community—they are less likely to return to prison, and those who do return stay crime-free for longer periods of time.
- Prisoners who participate in college programs while incarcerated are more likely to find jobs upon release, which also helps reduce the risk of recidivism.
- Investing in prisoners' education programs can save money in the long run if they do not return to prison. Each $1 invested by the government in an inmate's education may save $5 in future costs that would have been spent incarcerating that individual.

Opposed to Pell Grants:

- Introduced in 2015, the "Kids Before Cons Act" argues that federal taxpayer funds should not be used to provide college educational programs to inmates.
- Students currently in college outside of prison are amassing loans to complete their degrees. It is not fair that prisoners have access to free education.
- Others argue that inmates receiving Pell Grants are taking funds that otherwise would have gone to deserving students outside of prison; however, the funds set aside for the prisoner Pell Grant Program are separate from those slated for others.

What Should U.S. Policy Be?

There is significant evidence from research that access to college education helps keep inmates from returning to crime after release. However, some struggle with the issue of equality, and whether it is fair for inmates to receive Pell Grants while law-abiding students incur significant debt to pay for college. While the debate goes on, over 200 colleges and universities have indicated that they are interested in participating in this program and may provide educational opportunities to inmates. Research on the lives of inmates who receive grants under this test program may help to improve our understanding of how college education can keep people from participating in a life of crime.

Researching the Internet

To read a summary of the findings of a study entitled "Evaluating the Effectiveness of Correctional Education," go to http://www.rand.org/content/dam/rand/pubs/research_reports/RR200/RR266/RAND_RR266.sum.pdf.

Analyzing the Issue

Imagine that you and your classmates are state legislators considering a proposal to implement college classes in prisons. What information would you want to have before making the decision? What arguments could be made on each side of the proposal? Choose one side, and justify your position.

Sources: "Colleges Embrace Pell Grants for Prisoners" *Inside Higher Ed*, October 20, 2015 (http://www.insidehighered.com); G. Druwc and V. Clark (2014), "The Effects of Prison-Based Educational Programming on Recidivism and Employment," *The Prison Journal*, 94(4), 454–78; A. Grasgreen. "Kids before Cons Act Aims to Fight Pell Grants for Prisoners." *Politico*, July 31, 2015 (http://www.politico.com); R. H. Kim and D. Clark (2013) "The Effect of Prison-Based College Education Programs on Recidivism: Propensity Score Matching Approach," *Journal of Criminal Justice*, 41(3), 196–204; J. Palazzolo, "Congressman moves to block Pell Grants for prisoners," *Wall Street Journal*, July 30, 2015 (http://blogs.wsj.com); The Rand Corporation, *How Effective is Correctional Education and Where Do We Go from Here?* Rand Corporation: Santa Monica, CA (2014).

Vocational Education

Vocational education programs attempt to teach offenders a marketable job skill. Unfortunately, too many programs train inmates for trades that already have an adequate labor supply or in which new methods have made the skills taught obsolete.

Inmates often lack the attributes necessary to obtain and keep a job—punctuality, accountability, deference to supervisors, cordiality to coworkers. Therefore, most prisoners need to learn not only a skill but also how to act in the work world. For example, Minnesota's "Affordable Homes Program" teaches prisoners construction skills as they build or remodel homes for low-income families. An evaluation of this program determined that prisoners who participated were more likely to be hired in construction jobs after release, and the state saved over $13 million by using inmate labor; however, graduates of this program did not have reduced rates of criminal behavior after release (Bohmert & Duwe, 2012).

Yet another problem is perhaps the toughest of all. In one state or another, the law bars ex-felons from practicing certain occupations, including nurse, beautician, barber, real estate salesperson, chauffeur, worker where alcoholic beverages are sold, cashier, and insurance salesperson. Unfortunately, some prison vocational programs actually train inmates for jobs they can never hold.

Prison Industries

Prison industries, which trace their roots to the early workshops of New York's Auburn Penitentiary, are intended to teach work habits and skills that will assist prisoners' reentry into the outside workforce. In practice, institutions rely on prison labor to provide basic food, maintenance, clerical, and other services they themselves require. Many prisons contain manufacturing facilities that produce goods, such as office furniture and clothing, used in correctional and other state institutions.

The prison industries system has a checkered career. During the nineteenth century, factories were established in many prisons, and inmates manufactured items that were sold on the open market. With the rise of the labor movement, however, state legislatures and Congress passed laws restricting the sale of prison-made goods so that they would not compete with those made by free workers. In 1979, Congress lifted restrictions on the interstate sale of prison-made products and urged correctional administrators to explore with the private sector possible improvements for prison industry programs. Industrial programs would relieve idleness, allow inmates to earn wages that they could save until release, and reduce the costs of incarceration. The Federal Bureau of Prisons and some states have developed industries, but generally their products are not sold on the free market, and the percentage of prisoners employed varies greatly. Nonetheless, about 3.5 percent of the prisoners in the United States produced goods and services worth $1.5 billion (Swarz, 2004).

Although the idea of employing inmates sounds attractive, the inefficiencies of prison work may

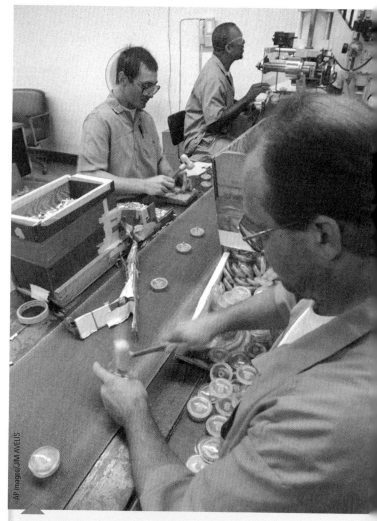

Companies are finding that using prison labor can be more efficient than outsourcing to low-wage countries elsewhere in the world. Prisoners at the Wabash Valley Correctional Facility assemble yo-yos as part of a joint venture between the Indiana Department of Corrections' prison industry program and the Flambeau Products Corporation. Are these prisoners doing jobs that would otherwise provide wages for law-abiding citizens?

offset its economic value. Turnover is great, because many inmates are transferred among several institutions or released over a two-year period. Many prisoners have little education and lack steady work habits, making it difficult for them to perform many of the tasks of modern production. An additional cost to efficiency is the need to stop production periodically to count heads and to check that tools and materials have not been stolen. Also, participation in prison industry programs does not reduce recidivism after release for many inmates (Richmond, 2012).

Rehabilitative Programs

Rehabilitative programs seek to treat the personal defects thought to have brought about the inmate's criminality. Most people agree that rehabilitating offenders is a desirable goal, but they disagree a great deal on the amount of emphasis that these programs should receive. Counseling and special programs are offered in 97 percent of public prisons but in only 74 percent of private institutions (Stephan, 2008).

Reports in the 1970s cast doubt on the ability of treatment programs to stem recidivism. They also questioned the ethics of requiring inmates to participate in rehabilitative programs in exchange for the promise of parole (Martinson, 1974). Supporters of treatment programs argue that certain programs, if properly run, work well for certain types of offenders (Andrews et al., 1990; T. Palmer, 1992). Others argue that the idea of "rehabilitation" has changed from in-prison programming to a greater focus on reentry and transitioning inmates back into communities (Phelps, 2011).

Most corrections systems still offer a range of psychological, behavioral, and social services programs. How much they are used seems to vary according to the goals of the institution and the attitudes of the administrators. Researcher Michelle Phelps (2011) argues that while public opinion supported the "nothing works" perspective that decried rehabilitative efforts, there was no significant change in prison programming until the 1990s. At that point, efforts to rehabilitate inmates focused more on preparing inmates to reenter society (to be discussed in Chapter 13) than on providing them with educational programming. Incarceration's current goal of humane custody implies no effort to change inmates.

Medical Services

Most prisons offer medical services through a full-time staff of nurses, augmented by part-time physicians under contract to the corrections system. Nurses take care of routine health care and dispense medicines from a secure in-prison pharmacy; regularly scheduled visits to the prison by doctors can enable prisoners to obtain checkups and diagnoses. For cases needing a specialist, surgery, or emergency medical assistance, prisoners must be transported to local hospitals, under close supervision by correctional staff. The aim is for the prison system to provide a range of medical assistance to meet the various needs of the population as a whole. In 2008, most states spent about $5,000 annually per inmate for health care, but some spend up to $12,000 (California) and a few under $3,000 (Louisiana, South Carolina, Illinois) (Pew Charitable Trusts, 2013). Costs are also dependent on inmate age—health care costs in Oregon prisons range from $299 per inmate for those under age 30 up to $6,527 per inmate for those older than 70 (Zaitz, 2011).

Medical services in some states have not kept up with the increase in the incarcerated population. In 1976, the U.S. Supreme Court ruled that prisoners have a constitutional right to health care. In 2011, the Supreme Court's decision in *Brown v. Plata* ordered California to reduce its incarcerated population significantly to reduce overcrowding and create a healthier prison environment. The decision supported earlier findings by lower court judges that the state's failure to provide medical and mental health care was needlessly causing the death of at least one inmate every month and was subjecting prisoners to cruel and unusual punishment, which is prohibited by the Constitution (Liptak, 2011).

13. **Why are prison programs important from the standpoint of prison administrators?**
    Programs keep prisoners busy and reduce security problems.

14. **Why have legislators and the general public been so critical of educational and rehabilitative programs in prisons?**
    Such programs are thought to "coddle" prisoners and may not reduce future criminal behavior.

If budget cuts led to the elimination of all vocational training and education programs in prisons, how would that impact daily life for prisoners and corrections officers? List three possible effects from the elimination of programs.

Violence in Prison

Prisons for men provide a perfect recipe for violence. They confine in cramped quarters a thousand men, some with histories of violent behavior. While incarcerated, these men are not allowed contact with women and live under highly restrictive conditions. Sometimes these conditions spark collective violence, as in the riots at Attica, New York (1971); Santa Fe, New Mexico (1980); Atlanta, Georgia (1987); Lucasville, Ohio (1993); Florence, Colorado (2008); and Folsom, California (2012); and Atmore, Alabama (2016).

Although prison riots are widely reported in the news, few people have witnessed the level of everyday interpersonal violence that takes place in U.S. prisons. For example, each year about 34,000 inmates are physically attacked by other inmates. In 2002, 48 assault victims died. An additional 168 prisoners committed suicide (Mumola, 2005). Great numbers of prisoners live in a state of constant uneasiness, always on the lookout for people who might demand sex, steal their few possessions, or otherwise hurt them. Some researchers suggest that the level of violence varies by offender age, institutional security designation, and administrative effectiveness (Maitland & Sluder, 1998). Others point out that inmates' own behavior affects their likelihood of victimization; those who have violent prior offenses and those who participate in the prison economy are more likely to be victimized in prison (Copes et al., 2010; Kerley, Hochstetler, & Copes, 2009).

Assaultive Behavior and Inmate Characteristics

For the person entering prison for the first time, the anxiety level and fear of violence run especially high. Gary, an inmate at Leavenworth, told Pete Earley, "Every convict has three choices, but only three. He can fight (kill someone), he can hit the fence (escape), or he can fuck (submit)" (1992:55). Even if a prisoner is not assaulted, the potential for violence permeates the environments of many prisons, adding to the stress and pains of incarceration.

Violence in correctional institutions raises serious questions for administrators, criminal justice specialists, and the general public. What causes prison

Mikael Karlsson/Alamy Stock Photo

To remove an uncooperative or violent prisoner from a cell, trained cell extraction teams must overwhelm the prisoner through the use of force while also limiting the risk of injury to themselves. Such events are often filmed to prevent false claims by prisoners that officers used excessive force. Are there additional precautions that these officers should take in order to avoid injuries to themselves and to the prisoner?

violence? What can be done about it? We consider these questions by examining three main categories of prison violence: prisoner–prisoner, prisoner–officer, and officer–prisoner. First, we discuss three characteristics of prisoners that underlie these behavioral factors: age, race, and mental illness.

Age   Studies have shown that young men aged 16–24, both inside and outside prison, are more prone to violence than are older men. As prisoners age, they are less likely to be violent toward other inmates as well as staff (Morris & Worrall, 2014). Not surprisingly, 93 percent of adult prisoners are men, with an average age of 27 at time of admission.

Besides having greater physical strength than their elders, young men lack the commitments to career and family that can restrict antisocial behavior. In addition, many have difficulty defining their position in society. Thus, they interpret many things as challenges to their status. Studies also show that younger prisoners face a greater risk of being victimized than do older inmates.

Machismo, the concept of male honor and the sacredness of one's reputation as a man, requires physical retaliation against those who insult one's honor. Some inmates adopt a preventive strategy of trying to impress others with their bravado, which may result in counter-challenges and violence. The potential for violence among such prisoners is clear.

Race   Race has become a major divisive factor in today's prisons. Racist attitudes, common in the larger society, have become part of the convict code. Forced association—having to live with people one would not likely associate with on the outside—exaggerates and amplifies racial conflict. Violence against members of another race may be how some inmates deal with the frustrations of their lives. The presence of gangs organized along racial lines contributes to violence in prison.

Mental Illness   Inmates with diagnosed mental illnesses are significantly more likely to be victims of violence in prison than those not mentally ill (Blitz, Wolff, & Shi, 2008), and are also more likely to be abused sexually during incarceration (Cristanti & Frueh, 2011). Prison is a traumatic experience and can cause mental illness to develop in individuals who were not suffering from illness when they arrived. Incarceration can also exacerbate preexisting mental conditions to the point where psychological treatment is required (Rich, Wakeman, & Dickman, 2011). If these inmates are more likely to be victimized, their mental condition can worsen, causing even greater problems for them during their incarceration (Listwan et al., 2010).

Prisoner–Prisoner Violence

Although prison folklore may attribute violence to sadistic guards, most prison violence occurs between inmates. As Hans Toch has observed, the climate of violence in prisons has no free-world counterpart: "Inmates are terrorized by other inmates, and spend years in fear of harm. Some inmates request protective custody segregation, others lock themselves in, and some are hermits by choice" (1976:47–48). The Bureau of Justice Statistics reports that the rate of prisoner–prisoner assaults between inmates is 26 attacks per 1,000 inmates (Stephan & Karberg, 2003). But official statistics likely do not reflect the true amount of prisoner–prisoner violence, because many inmates who are assaulted do not make their victimization known to prison officials.

Prison Gangs   Racial or ethnic gangs (also referred to as "security threat groups") are now linked to acts of violence in most prison systems. Gangs make it difficult for wardens to maintain control. By continuing their street wars inside prison, gangs make some prisons more dangerous than even the worst American neighborhoods. Gangs are organized primarily to control an institution's drug, gambling, loan-sharking, prostitution, extortion, and debt-collection rackets. In addition, gangs protect their members from other gangs and instill a sense of macho camaraderie.

Prison gangs exist in the institutions of most states and the federal system, but it is sometimes difficult for management to determine the percentage of their inmates with gang affiliations. A survey of prisons in the United States found that wardens reported between 2 percent and 50 percent of their inmates were gang members, with a mean of 19 percent (Winterdyk & Ruddell, 2010). In Illinois, as many as 60 percent of the population are gang members (Hallinan, 2001:95), and the Florida Department of Corrections has identified 240 street gangs operating in their prisons (Davitz, 1998).

Many facilities segregate rival gangs by housing them in separate units of the same prison or by moving members to other prisons (sometimes even in different states), which wardens believe is an effective means of reducing gang-related violence (Winterdyk & Ruddell, 2010). Administrators have also set up intelligence units to gather information on gangs, particularly about illegal acts both inside and outside the prison. In some prisons, however, these policies create a power vacuum within the convict society that newer groups with new codes of behavior soon fill.

Prison Rape   Much of the mythology of prison life revolves around sexual assaults. Perpetrators are typically strong, experienced cons, either African American or white, who are serving sentences for violent offenses. Victims are portrayed as young, white, physically weak, mentally challenged, effeminate first-time nonviolent offenders.

Prison rape is a crime hidden by a curtain of silence. Inmate–inmate and inmate–staff sexual contact is prohibited in all prisons, yet it exists, and much of it remains hidden from authorities. Sexual violence ranges from unwanted touching to nonconsensual sex. When incidents are reported, correctional officers say that it is difficult to distinguish between rapes and consensual sex. Most officers do not catch the inmates in the act; when they do observe sexual activity, only a few officers report that they ignored the inmates' violations of prison rules (Eigenberg, 2000).

The 2004 Prison Rape Elimination Act (PREA) established a zero-tolerance standard for the incidence of rape in prison. This law requires the Bureau of Justice Statistics to conduct annual surveys in the nation's prisons and jails to measure the incidence of rape. The law also requires the attorney general to provide a list of the incidence of prison rape in each institution.

A survey of 91,177 inmates in the United States indicated that 4% of prison inmates and 3.2% of jail inmates reported one or more incident of sexual victimization in 2011–2012. Victims of inmate-on-inmate assault were most likely to be female, aged 25–34, but similar percentages of men and women reported assaults by staff, and victims of staff assaults tended to be younger (20–24 years of age). There is some evidence that inmates who identify as being gay, lesbian, or bisexual report higher rates of assault than heterosexual inmates, and victims who were assaulted by staff or other inmates also reported experiencing sexual victimization prior to their incarceration (Beck et al., 2013).

Guerino and Beck (2011) also assessed the characteristics of victims and offenders in incidents of staff-on-inmate sexual violence. Unlike inmate-on-inmate violence, a greater percentage of staff-on-inmate violence was directed at male prisoners (37 percent), and female guards committed a majority of substantiated sexual assaults (56 percent of such assaults were by female corrections officers, compared with only 44 percent by male guards). Most of these types of incidents were committed in program service areas, such as the commissary, kitchen, storage areas, laundry, cafeteria, workshop, and hallways between the hours of noon and 6 p.m.

Victims of prisoner–prisoner sexual victimization have few options. According to the inmate code, prisoners should "stand and fight" their own battles. For many, this is not feasible. Alternatively, some may seek the protection of a gang or a stronger inmate to whom the victim is then indebted. Others may try to fade into the shadows. Still others may seek protective custody. Each option has its pluses and minuses, but none provides victims with the ability to serve their time without constantly looking over their shoulders.

Protective Custody   For many victims of prison violence, protective custody offers the only way to escape further abuse. About 5,000 state prisoners are in protective custody. Life is not pleasant for these inmates (Browne, Cambier, & Agha, 2011). Often they are let out of their cells only briefly to exercise and shower. Inmates who ask for "lock up" have little chance of returning to the general prison population without being viewed as a weakling—a "snitch" or a "punk"—to be preyed on. Even when they are transferred to another institution, their reputations follow them through the grapevine.

Prisoner–Officer Violence

The mass media have focused on riots in which guards are taken hostage, injured, and killed. However, violence against officers typically occurs in specific situations and against certain individuals. Yearly, inmates assault approximately 18,000 staff members (Stephan & Karberg, 2003). Correctional officers do not carry weapons within the institution, because a prisoner might seize them. However, prisoners do manage to obtain lethal weapons and can use the element of surprise to injure an officer. In the course of a workday, an officer may encounter situations that require the use of physical force against an inmate—for instance, breaking up a fight or moving a prisoner to segregation. Because such situations are especially dangerous, officers may enlist others to help them minimize the risk of violence. The officer's greatest fear is an unexpected attack, such as a "missile" thrown from an upper tier or an "accidental" push down a flight of stairs. The need to watch constantly against personal attacks adds stress and keeps many officers at a distance from the inmates.

Officer–Prisoner Violence

A fact of life in many institutions is unauthorized physical violence by officers against inmates. Stories abound of guards giving individual prisoners "the treatment" when supervisors are not looking. Many guards view physical force as an everyday, legitimate procedure. In some institutions, authorized "goon squads" composed of physically powerful officers use their muscle to maintain order.

Correctional officers are expected to follow departmental rules in their dealings with prisoners, yet supervisors generally cannot observe staff–prisoner confrontations directly. Further, prisoner complaints about officer brutality are often not believed until the officer involved gains a reputation for harshness. Even in this case, wardens may feel they must support their officers in order to retain their support in return. Research indicates that officers are more likely to victimize inmates who are male and nonwhite and who are confined in maximum-security institutions. Inmates with a paid work assignment are less likely to be victimized by staff (Perez et al., 2009).

Decreasing Prison Violence

Five factors contribute to prison violence: (1) inadequate supervision by staff members, (2) architectural design that promotes rather than inhibits victimization, (3) the easy availability of deadly weapons, (4) the housing of violence-prone prisoners near relatively defenseless people, and (5) a general high level of tension produced by close quarters (Bowker, 1982:64). The physical size and condition of the prison and the relations between inmates and staff also affect violence.

The Effect of Architecture and Size   The fortress-like prison certainly does not create an atmosphere conducive to normal interpersonal relationships, and the size of the larger institutions can create management problems. The massive scale of the megaprison, which may hold up to 3,000 inmates, provides opportunities for aggressive inmates to hide weapons, dispense private "justice," and engage more or less freely in other illicit activities. The size of the population in a large prison may also result in some inmates "falling through the cracks"—being misclassified and, though not violent themselves, forced to live among violent offenders.

Much of the emphasis on "new generation prisons"—small housing units, clear sight lines, security corridors linking housing units—is designed to limit such opportunities and thus prevent violence. However, a study of rape in Texas prisons found that cellblocks with solid doors may contribute to sexual assault (Austin et al., 2006).

The Role of Management   The degree to which inmate leaders are allowed to take matters into their own hands can affect the level of violence among inmates. When administrators run a tight ship, security measures prevent sexual attacks in dark corners, the making of "shivs" and "shanks" (knives) in the metal shop, and open conflict among inmate groups. A prison must afford each inmate defensible space, and administrators should ensure that every inmate remains secure from physical attack.

Effective management can decrease the level of assaultive behavior by limiting opportunities for attacks. Wardens and correctional officers must therefore recognize the types of people with whom they are dealing, the role of prison gangs, and the structure of institutions. John DiIulio argued that no group of inmates is "unmanageable [and] no combination of political, social, budgetary, architectural, or other factors makes good management impossible" (1991:12). At the time of his study more than two decades ago, he pointed to individual correctional institutions in California and New York; the Federal Bureau of Prisons; and the Texas Department of Corrections under the leadership of George Beto as examples of good management. According to DiIulio, good management practices have resulted in prisons and jails where inmates can "do time" without fearing for their personal safety. Wardens who exert leadership can manage their prisons effectively, so that problems do not fester and erupt into violent confrontations. Prisons must also be managed transparently—that is, incidents of violence in prisons must be dealt with openly and investigated by management. In addition, the public should be made aware of the nature of prison violence to better understand the challenges faced by inmates during incarceration and upon release (Byrne & Hummer, 2007).

Budget cuts in the area of corrections increasingly affect the management and organization of prisons. Reductions in the crime rate mean that fewer prisons are needed, but states are also looking to solutions that are both economical and successful in rehabilitating prisoners (Pew Center on the States, 2009). In addition, there has been increasing public concern that most states spend more on corrections than on public education. For example, in 2007 Michigan spent $1.19 on corrections for every $1.00 spent on education. Compare this to Minnesota, which spent $.17 on corrections for every $1.00 spent on education (Pew Center on the States, 2009). Which of these institutions is more important in terms of state funding? How can states balance funding for public safety with adequate support for education?

In sum, prisons must be made safe. Because the state uses its authority to incarcerate inmates, it has a responsibility to prevent violence and maintain order. To exclude violence from prisons, officials may have to limit movement within institutions, contacts with the outside, and the right of inmates to choose their associates. Yet these measures may run counter to the goal of producing men and women who will be accountable when they return to society.

▼ **CHECK POINT**

15. What five factors are thought to contribute to prison violence?
Inadequate supervision, architectural design, availability of weapons, housing of violence-prone inmates with the defenseless, and the high level of tension among people living in close quarters.

STOP & ANALYZE

Think about the role of architectural design in facilitating or preventing prison violence. Draw a design of a prison that would reduce the risks of and opportunities for violence. List three aspects of your design that are intended to reduce opportunities for violence.

Think, Discuss, Write

A significant problem for corrections officials in many states is the smuggling of cell phones into prisons for use by prisoners. The use of secret phones by prisoners creates many difficult problems, including harassment of crime victims, planning of crimes and escapes, and communication between prisoners in different prisons. In 2014, a prisoner in North Carolina used a smuggled cell phone to arrange the kidnapping of the father of the prosecutor who had put the prisoner behind bars. Prisoners in Indiana used cell phones smuggled by guards to run a drug trafficking operation while sitting behind bars. Most recently, 46 corrections officers in Georgia were arrested for a number of violations, including smuggling drugs and cell phones to prisoners.

How do prisoners obtain cell phones, an item that they are not allowed to have? Sadly, one primary source of cell phones is corrections officers who smuggle them into prisons and sell them to convicted offenders. A prisoner on death row in Texas told a state legislator that he obtained a cell phone and charger after paying $2,100. In March 2106, a prisoner used a smuggled cell phone to record video of a prison riot at Holman Correctional Facility in Alabama in protest of the new warden, who some claim uses harsh tactics to control inmates.

Discussion/Writing Assignment

If you were the warden of a prison, what steps would you take to prevent unethical activity by corrections officers, monitor the actions of officers, and create an environment in which you could stop improper conduct from taking place? Create a list of actions that you would take, and explain your reasoning for each.

Sources: M. Biesecker and A. G. Breed, "FBI: Inmate Orchestrates Kidnapping of Lawyer's Father Using Smuggled Cellphone," Associated Press, April 11, 2014 (www.thespec.com); P. Brown and M. Ryan, "'Staggering Corruption': 46 Officers Charged in Years-Long Trafficking Sting," CNN Politics, February 12, 2016 (www.cnn.com); B. Farrington, "Smuggled Cellphones in Prisons Run Rampant," *Huffington Post*, February 17, 2014 (www.huffingtonpost.com); "Final 4 of 29 Inmates and Guards Convicted in Operation Prison Cell in Southeast Texas," U.S. Immigration and Customs Enforcement News Release, November 26, 2013 (www.ice.gov); K. Lipp, "Alabama Prisoners Use Secret Cellphones to Protest—and Riot," *The Daily Beast*, March 20, 2016 (http://thedailybeast.com).

SUMMARY

1 Describe how contemporary institutions differ from the old-style "big house" prisons.

- The typical "big house" was a walled prison with large, tiered cellblocks, a yard, and workshops.
- Prisoners came from both rural and urban areas; were poor; and outside of the South, were mainly white.
- The prison society in the past was isolated, with restrictions on visitors, mail, and other communications. The inmates' days were highly structured, with rules enforced by the guards.

2 Identify the three models of incarceration that have predominated since the 1940s.

- The custodial model emphasizes the maintenance of security.
- The rehabilitation model views security and housekeeping activities as a framework for treatment efforts.
- The reintegration model recognizes that prisoners must be prepared for their return to society.

3 Describe the organization of prisons and their staffs.

- Most prisons are expected to fulfill goals related to keeping (custody), using (working), and serving (treating) inmates. They are organized to fulfill these goals.

4 Explain how a prison is governed.

- The public's belief that the warden and officers have total power over the inmates is outdated.
- Good management through effective leadership can maintain the quality of prison life as measured by levels of order, amenities, and services.
- Four factors make managing prisons different from administering other public institutions: the defects of total power, limited use of rewards and punishments, exchange relationships, and the strength of inmate leadership.

5 Summarize the roles of correctional officers in a prison.

- Because they remain in close contact with the prisoners, correctional officers are the linchpins of the prison system. The effectiveness of the institution rests on their shoulders.

6 List the characteristics of the incarcerated population.

- Most prisoners are male, young, members of minority groups, with low education levels.

- Prison administrators must deal with the special needs of some groups, including elderly prisoners, prisoners with HIV/AIDS, prisoners with mental illness, and long-term prisoners.

7 **Describe the world of the convict.**
- Inmates do not serve their time in isolation, but are members of a subculture with its own traditions, norms, and leadership structure. Such norms are often described as the inmate code.
- Today's prisons, unlike those of the past, do not have a uniform inmate code but several, in part because of the influence of gangs.
- Inmates deal with the pain of incarceration by assuming an adaptive role and lifestyle.

8 **Discuss what prison is like for men and for women.**
- Male inmates are individualistic, and their norms stress autonomy, self-sufficiency, and the ability to cope with one's own problems. Female inmates share with one another and place less emphasis

on achieving status or recognition within the prisoner community. There is less violence in female prisons than in male ones.

9 **List some of the programs and services available to prisoners.**
- Educational, vocational, industrial, and rehabilitative programs are available in prisons. Administrators believe that these programs are important for maintaining order.
- Medical services are provided to all inmates.

10 **Describe the nature of prison violence.**
- Violence occurs between prisoners and between prisoners and guards.
- Violence in prison depends on such things as administrative effectiveness; the architecture and size of prisons; and inmate characteristics such as age, attitudes, and race. Prison gangs play an increasing role in causing prison violence.

Questions for Review

1. How do modern prisons differ from those in the past?
2. What characteristics of prisons distinguish them from other institutions?
3. What must a prison administrator do to ensure successful management?
4. What is meant by an adaptive role? Which roles are found in male prison society? In female prison society?
5. How does the convict society in institutions for women differ from that in institutions for men?
6. What are the main forms of prison programs, and what purposes do they serve?
7. What are forms and causes of prison violence?

Key Terms

classification (p. 412)
custodial model (p. 387)

inmate code (p. 402)
rehabilitation model (p. 387)

reintegration model (p. 388)

Joe Raedle/Getty Images

12 Probation and Intermediate Sanctions

LEARNING OBJECTIVES

1 Name the philosophical assumptions that underlie community corrections.

2 Describe how probation evolved and how probation sentences are implemented today.

3 Describe intermediate sanctions, and give examples of how they are administered.

4 Identify the key issues faced by community corrections at the beginning of the twenty-first century.

P op star Justin Bieber was arrested twice in January 2014—first in Florida for careless driving, and then later in California for throwing eggs at his neighbor's house. After his arrest in Florida, Bieber pleaded guilty to careless driving and resisting arrest and agreed to donate $50,000 to a local charity rather than serve probation.

As punishment for his egg-throwing vandalism in California, he was ordered to serve two years of probation, five days of community service, complete an anger management program, and pay his neighbor $80,900 in restitution (Reuters, 2014). However, Bieber was not able to complete his required community service—his attorney explained that due to an ankle injury, time spent in the recording studio, and the taping of several television programs, he would need extra time to complete the terms of his probation. The judge agreed (Brown, 2015).

Does the fact that Bieber is a celebrity affect the type of punishment he has received? Did he receive probation rather than jail due to his fame? Does his celebrity also allow him to extend the deadline for completing his requirements? Would the average person receive such leniency from a judge if he or she had work conflicts or minor injuries? The average person cannot afford to make $50,000 donations to avoid punishment. Does this mean that Bieber was able to buy his freedom? These are serious and important questions. Moreover, Bieber's case stands in stark contrast with the U.S. Department of Justice's report on the local court system in Ferguson, Missouri, where poor people faced jailing and additional fines for failing to pay *parking tickets* in a timely manner (Robertson, 2015). Community corrections are an important aspect of criminal punishment, but we must be concerned about whether they are applied appropriately and fairly.

Since the early nineteenth century, supervision in the community has been recognized as an appropriate punishment for some offenders. Probation was developed in the 1840s, and parole followed in the 1870s. By the 1930s, every state and the federal government used these forms of community corrections either to punish offenders without

425

incarceration (probation) or to supervise offenders in the community after leaving prison (parole). Intermediate sanctions were developed in the 1980s when people saw the need for punishments that were less restrictive than prison but more restrictive than probation.

Two-thirds of offenders who are under correctional supervision are in the community, not behind bars (see Figure 12.1). One in 52 adults was on probation or parole in 2014, while 1 in 111 was in prison or jail (Kaeble, Glaze, et al., 2015). In 2009, the Pew Center on the States released a major report emphasizing the major role played by community corrections in the criminal justice system. A key finding was that strong community supervision programs for lower-risk, nonviolent offenders not only cost significantly less than incarceration but, when appropriately resourced and managed, could cut recidivism by as much as 30 percent. Diverting these offenders to community supervision programs also frees up prison beds needed to house violent offenders and can free up money for other pressing public priorities (Pew Center on the States, 2009).

In years to come, community corrections can be expected to play a much greater role in the criminal justice system. This role will likely increase as states try to reduce the high costs of imprisoning large populations of offenders. Formal programs are emerging across the nation to give increased emphasis to community options. For example, the Justice Reinvestment Initiative, funded by the federal government's U.S. Bureau of Justice Assistance, provides financial incentives and

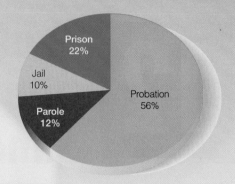

FIGURE 12.1

Percentage of People in Each Category of Correctional Supervision

Source: D. Kaeble, L. Glaze, A. Tsoutis, and T. Minton. "Correctional Populations in the United States, 2014," *Bureau of Justice Statistics Bulletin*, December 2015, NCJ249513.

Joe Raedle/Getty Images

technical assistance for states to find ways to reduce their prison populations and then reinvest those savings in community-oriented alternatives to imprisonment (Keller, 2014). One of the biggest drivers of increased costs in corrections stems from the number of people sent from community supervision into expensive prisons and jails as a result of violating conditions of probation and parole. Thus, a major emphasis of the Justice Reinvestment Initiative is to develop evidence-based approaches to community supervision as well as effective diversion programs, such as drug courts, to efficiently encourage and monitor appropriate behavior through incentives and sanctions other than incarceration (LaVigne et al., 2014).

Community Corrections: Assumptions

Probation and intermediate sanctions are important components of community corrections. As discussed in Chapter 10, community corrections seeks to keep offenders in the community by building ties to family, employment, and other normal sources of stability and success. This model of corrections assumes that the offender must change, but it also recognizes that factors within the community that might encourage criminal behavior (unemployment, for example) must also change.

Probation and intermediate sanctions are sentences imposed for lesser offenses in an effort to avoid the expense and consequences of imprisonment.

Parole, another component of community corrections, to be discussed in Chapter 13, involves completing a sentence in the community after serving a term in prison. Parolees, who have often served time in prison for violent offenses or a lengthy list of other crimes, face especially significant challenges in seeking to reintegrate into the community.

Proponents usually cite four factors in support of community corrections:

1. Many offenders' criminal records and current offenses are not serious enough to warrant incarceration.
2. Community supervision is cheaper than incarceration.
3. Rates of **recidivism**, or returning to crime, for those under community supervision are no higher than for those who go to prison.
4. Ex-inmates require both support and supervision as they try to remake their lives in the community.

Community corrections is based on the goal of finding the "least restrictive alternative"— punishing the offender only as severely as needed to protect the community and to satisfy the public. Advocates call for programs to assist offenders in the community so they will have opportunities to succeed in law-abiding activities and to reduce their contact with the criminal world. Surveys have found that the public supports community placement for some offenders currently in prison. The increasing severity of prison sentences for drug offenders was a significant driver of expensive increases in prison populations. Thus, new trends in opinions by the public, as well as by politicians from both political parties, seem to indicate that community corrections will continue to receive significant emphasis in the immediate future (See "What Americans Think.")

WHAT AMERICANS THINK

QUESTION: "On drug policy, government should focus more on..."

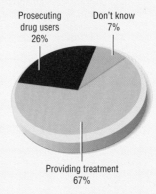

Prosecuting drug users 26%

Don't know 7%

Providing treatment 67%

QUESTION: "Some states have moved away from mandatory prison sentences for nonviolent drug crimes. Is this a..."

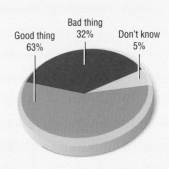

Good thing 63%

Bad thing 32%

Don't know 5%

CRITICAL THINKING: If a governor directed you to be in charge of developing alternatives to imprisonment for nonviolent drug users, what approaches to treatment and/or punishment would you suggest? What factors or considerations would guide your thinking?

Note: Survey conducted February 14–23, 2014.

Source: Pew Research Center for the People and the Press, "America's New Drug Policy Landscape," Pew Center website, April 2, 2014 (http://www.people-press.org/2014/04/02 /americas-new-drug-policy-landscape/).

Probation: Correction without Incarceration

recidivism A return to criminal behavior.

As we have seen, probation is the conditional release of the offender into the community under the supervision of correctional officials. Although probationers live at home and have regular jobs, they must report regularly to their probation officers. They must also abide by specific conditions, such as submitting to drug tests, obeying curfews, and staying away from certain people or parts of town. Although probation is used mainly for lesser offenses, states are increasingly using probation for more-serious felonies, as shown in Figure 12.2.

Probation is significantly less expensive than imprisonment, a fact that has become increasingly important as state budget cuts force justice system officials to consider how to expand the use of lower-cost punishments for criminal offenders.

FIGURE 12.2

Most Serious Offenses Committed by Offenders Sentenced to Probation Most probationers are serving their sentence because they committed property or drug offenses, but almost 20 percent of probationers have been convicted of violent offenses. Sex offenders comprise only a small portion of people sentenced to probation.

Source: D. Kaeble, L. Maruschak, and T. Bonczar, "Probation and Parole in the United States, 2014," *Bureau of Justice Statistics Bulletin*, November 2015, NCJ 249057.

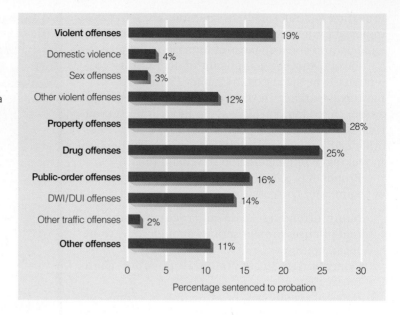

The federal court system calculates that the cost of incarcerating a federal prisoner in a Bureau of Prisons facility is $28,948 per year. By contrast, the cost of supervising that individual in the community is $3,347 per year—a savings of $25,601 per offender per year (U.S. Courts, 2013). In a state-level example, Pennsylvania officials calculated that it costs the state more than $32,000 per year for each offender held in prison, but less than $3,000 per year for each offender supervised in the community on probation (Couglin, 2012). When one multiplies the amount saved by the hundreds or thousands of offenders placed on probation rather than sent to prison, it represents a significant reduction in the corrections system's burden on the state budget. Thus, there is consideration for using probation for a larger number of offenders, including even those who have committed crimes that led to imprisonment in the past.

Probation can be combined with other sanctions, such as fines, restitution, and community service. Fulfillment of these other sanctions may, in effect, become a condition for successful completion of probation. The sentencing court retains authority over the probationer, and if she or he violates the conditions or commits another crime, the judge can order the entire sentence to be served in prison. Although probation offers many benefits over incarceration, the public often sees it as merely a "slap on the wrist" for offenders (Public Opinion Strategies, 2010).

Today, although nearly 4 million offenders are on probation, probation budgets in many states have been cut and caseloads increased as lawmakers struggle with shrinking resources. In 2012, for example, the Florida Department of Corrections attempted to address a $79 million budget deficit in part by cutting funds for probation (Campbell, 2012). Given that caseloads in some urban areas reach 300 offenders per officer, probation officers often cannot provide the level of supervision necessary (Edgemon, 2013).

Origins and Evolution of Probation

Probation first developed in the United States when John Augustus, a Boston boot maker, persuaded a judge in the Boston Police Court in 1841 to give him custody of a convicted offender for a brief period and then helped the man appear rehabilitated by the time of sentencing.

Massachusetts developed the first statewide probation system in 1880; by 1920 another 21 states had followed suit. The federal courts were authorized to hire probation officers in 1925. By the beginning of World War II, probation systems had been established in 44 states.

Probation began as a humanitarian effort to allow first-time and minor offenders a second chance. Early probationers were expected not only to obey the law but also to behave in a morally acceptable fashion. Officers sought to provide moral leadership to help shape probationers' attitudes and behavior with respect to family, religion, employment, and free time.

By the 1940s, the development of psychology as a field of social science research led probation officers to shift their emphasis from moral leadership to therapeutic counseling. This shift brought three important changes. First, the officer no longer acted primarily as a community supervisor charged with enforcing a particular morality. Second, the officer became more of a clinical social worker who aimed at helping the offender solve psychological and social problems. Third, the offender was expected to become actively involved in the treatment. The pursuit of rehabilitation as the primary goal of probation gave the officer extensive discretion in defining and treating the offender's problems. Officers used their judgment to evaluate each offender and develop a treatment approach to the personal problems that presumably had led to crime.

During the 1960s, probation moved in another direction. Rather than counseling offenders, probation officers provided them with concrete social services such as assistance with employment, housing, finances, and education. This emphasis on reintegrating offenders and remedying the social problems they faced fit with federal efforts to wage a war on poverty. Instead of being a counselor or therapist, the probation officer served as an advocate, dealing with private and public institutions on the offender's behalf.

In the late 1970s, the orientation of probation changed as the goals of rehabilitation and reintegration gave way to "risk management." This approach, still dominant today, seeks to minimize the probability that an offender will commit a new offense (Cadigan, Johnson, & Lowenkamp, 2012). Risk management reflects two basic goals. First, in accord with the deserved-punishment ideal, the punishment should fit the offense, and correctional intervention should neither raise nor lower the level of punishment. Second, according to the community protection criterion, the amount and type of supervision are determined according to the risk that the probationer will return to crime. This is measured using "risk assessment instruments," which use characteristics of the offender to determine the risk of rearrest for that person. For example, the Post-Conviction Risk Assessment Tool (PCRA) includes such items as a history of violent offending, alcohol problems, educational attainment, and mental health issues to calculate the probability that an offender will be rearrested during their term of probation (Lowenkamp et al., 2012).

During the past decade, probation officials have developed methods of classifying clients according to their service needs, the element of risk they pose to the community, and the chance that they will commit another offense (Cadigan, Johnson, & Lowenkamp, 2012). Risk classification fits the deserved-punishment model of the criminal sanction in that the most serious cases receive the greatest restrictions and supervision. If probationers live according to the conditions of their sentence, the level of supervision is gradually reduced.

Today there is a growing interest in probation's role as part of **community justice**, a philosophy that emphasizes restorative justice (see Chapter 9), reparation to the victim and the community, problem-solving strategies instead of adversarial procedures, and increased citizen involvement in crime prevention. By breaking away from traditional bureaucratic practices, community justice advocates hope to develop a more flexible and responsive form of local justice initiatives—and many see probation leading the way (Hudson, 2012).

community justice A model of justice that emphasizes reparation to the victim and the community, a problem-solving perspective with regard to crime, and citizen involvement in crime prevention.

Organization of Probation

As a form of corrections, probation falls under the executive branch, and people usually see it as a concern of state government. However, in about 25 percent of the states, probation falls to county and local governments. Further, in many states, the judiciary administers it locally. The state sets the standards and provides financial support and training courses, but locally administered programs handle about two-thirds of all people under probation supervision.

In many jurisdictions, although the state is formally responsible for all probation services, the locally elected county judges are in charge. This seemingly odd arrangement produces benefits as well as problems. On the positive side, having probationers under the supervision of the court permits judges to keep closer tabs on them and to order incarceration if the conditions of probation are violated. On the negative side, some judges know little about the goals and methods of corrections, and the probation responsibility adds to the administrative duties of already overworked courts.

Judicially enforced probation seems to work best when the judges and the supervising officers have close relationships. Proponents of this system say that judges need to work with probation officers whom they can trust, whose presentence reports they can accurately evaluate, and on whom they can rely to report the success or failure of individual cases.

For the sake of their clients and the goals of the system, probation officers need direct access to corrections and other human services agencies. However, whereas probation is often part of the judicial branch, human services agencies are located within the executive branch of government, and coordination between the branches can be complicated. Several states have combined probation and parole services in the same agency to coordinate resources and services that might otherwise be split between judicial (probation) and corrections (parole) agencies. Others point out, however, that probationers differ from parolees. Parolees have served prison terms, frequently have been involved in more-serious crimes, and often have been disconnected from mainstream society. By contrast, most probationers have not developed criminal lifestyles to the same degree and do not have the same problems of reintegration into the community. Thus probation and parole operations may need different resources and services.

Probation Services

Probation officers play roles similar to both the police and social workers. In addition to assisting the judiciary with presentence investigations (see Chapter 9), probation officers supervise clients to keep them out of trouble and enforce the conditions of their sentences. This law enforcement role involves discretionary decisions about whether to report violations of probation conditions. Probation officers are also expected to act like social workers by helping clients obtain the housing, employment, and treatment services they need (Bourgon, Gutierrez, & Ashton, 2012). The potential conflict between the roles is great. Not surprisingly, individual officers sometimes emphasize one role over the other. Advocates of evidence-based practices argue that probation officers must find "balanced roles" in which they are "neither indulgent of anti-social attitudes and noncompliance nor authoritative and heavy-handed" (Whetzel et al., 2011).

A continuing issue for probation officers is the size of their caseloads. How many clients can one officer effectively handle? In the 1930s, the National Probation Association recommended a 50-unit caseload; in 1967, the U.S. President's Commission on Law Enforcement and Administration of Justice reduced it to 35. However, today the national average for adult supervision is about 150, with some urban caseloads exceeding 300. The oversized caseload is usually cited as one of the main obstacles to successful probation. In Sacramento, California, $12 million in budget cuts over five years left over 90 percent of the county's 22,000 probationers without any supervision, drug testing, or services because probation officers simply could not handle the average caseload of 124 that resulted from staff reductions (Branan, 2013). In such situations, it is difficult to see how any goal of punishment is being advanced.

In some cities, budget cuts have led to the expanded use of volunteers to assist in probation functions. These programs operate according to at least two different models. In one model, the volunteers actually act as unpaid probation officers. After receiving training, they carry out the duties of professionals, enabling their cities and counties to administer probation programs less expensively. For example,

Frequent alcohol and drug testing are a condition of probation for many offenders. Administering these tests has become part of the officer's supervisory role. How difficult is it to monitor the behavior of offenders in the community?

the website of the city of Westminster, Colorado, insists that "volunteers do not do 'social' type activities with the clients" and describes the responsibilities carried out by volunteers: enforce court orders, provide mentoring, monitor compliance with probation terms, write monthly reports on each offender, attend probation court hearings, and attend monthly training sessions (City of Westminster website, 2016). In the second model, volunteers conduct a wider array of activities in support of the probation office. For example, in San Diego, the "Volunteers in Probation" program carries out fund-raising activities and clothing drives to provide clothing, eye exams, scholarships, emergency funds, and bus passes for probationers who are fulfilling the conditions of probation (Volunteers in Probation, 2016).

Another development produced by budget cuts is the administration of probation by private companies. Read the "Close Up" to consider the debate about how private companies have used probation operations as a way to make profits.

Revocation and Termination of Probation

Probation ends in one of two ways: (1) the person successfully completes the period of probation, or (2) the probationary status is revoked because of misbehavior. Revocation of probation typically occurs for either a **technical violation** or a new arrest.

Technical violations occur when a probationer fails to meet the conditions of a sentence by, for instance, violating curfew, failing a drug test, or using alcohol. Officers have discretion as to whether or not they bring this fact to the attention of the judge. In making these discretionary decisions, they must be professional, ethical, and fair. Read the "You Make the Decision" feature to consider what recommendations you would make if you were a probation officer. Also read the Question of Ethics feature at the end of the chapter to consider the potential for unethical behavior by these officials.

Probation officers and judges have widely varying notions of what constitutes grounds for revoking probation. When encountering technical violations, probation officers may first try to impose stricter rules, sternly lecture the probationer, and increase

technical violation The probationer's failure to abide by the rules and conditions of probation (specified by the judge), resulting in revocation of probation.

Private Probation

A woman in Alabama received a $179 fine for speeding. When she failed to appear in court, her driver's license was revoked. She claimed that the ticket bore the wrong court date. The next time she was stopped, she was arrested for driving without a license. She was fined again and could not afford to pay the fine. She was placed under the supervision of a private probation company, which charged extra fees of its own every time she was jailed for failure to pay the fines she owed. Over the next three years, she spent 40 days in jail, and eventually owed more than $3,000—most of it to the private probation company—because she was too poor to pay the original fines.

A 64-year-old veteran living solely on a monthly Social Security check of $600 was sentenced to two years of probation and a $4,500 fine for driving under the influence. He was placed under a private company's probation supervision. As he made monthly payments on his fine, he also had to pay $40 per month to the private probation company. More than a third of his monthly income went to the fine. If he had been living in a county that ran its own probation operations, he would not have been required to pay the

extra fee. Private probation companies are attractive to many counties, because the county bears no direct expense for probation administration. There are actual expenses for the county, however. Because the probation companies are given the authority to request that arrest warrants be issued when probationers fall behind on payments, counties end up paying jail expenses for the time periods when probationers are locked up for failure to pay. In addition, probation companies are able to extend the period of probation when their fees are not paid, so poor people can be sent to jail for failure to pay over a longer period of time.

At least a dozen states permit counties to contract with private companies for probation administration and services. In Kentucky, no central entity oversees the administration of private probation. Some counties sign contracts with companies, while others handle their own probation. Individuals placed on probation in counties that utilize private companies pay extra fees and experience the risk that private decision makers—possibly relying on self-interested profit motives—will extend probation or seek to have them jailed.

The use of private probation has been profitable and widespread in certain states. One company that operated in several Georgia counties was reported to have made $5.58 million in a single month from the extra fees that it charged to the thousands of probationers under its supervision. Private probation companies claim that they are providing a valuable service that saves money for the counties that sign contracts. Critics, however, raise many issues about how these companies operate.

Many critics see the probation companies profiting from the misfortune of poor people convicted of minor offenses. In several lawsuits against these companies, people claim that they went without food or sold their blood plasma in desperate efforts to pay ever-increasing fines, because the private companies kept threatening them with jail. The private companies have also been sued for imposing and charging fees for drug tests that were never ordered by any court. The Supreme Court has said that people should not be jailed for being unable to pay fines—only for being unwilling to pay when they do have the money. Yet private probation companies have been accused of refusing to let

the frequency of contacts with the probationer. Yet, the probation officer may face special challenges if the probationer does not take seriously the likelihood of consequences for technical violations. Indeed, a study in Wisconsin found that 68 percent of probationers failed on at least one occasion to report as required to the probation officer, while only 42 percent of parolees committing the same technical violation (Van Stelle & Goodrich, 2009). Unlike parolees, who, as we will see in Chapter 13, have already been to prison and therefore may be more likely to fear being sent back, many probationers are young and less experienced with the system. This failure to fulfill probation conditions may demonstrate their greater immaturity as well as their failure to recognize that technical violations could actually lead to incarceration if their probation officer seeks revocation. Nationally, in 2012, among offenders who exited from probation supervision, 68 percent completed their probation sentence successfully and only 15 percent were incarcerated. The remainder left probation supervision for a variety of other reasons—absconding, gaining early release from probation, and being deported from the country for immigration law violations (Maruschak & Bonczar, 2013).

Once the officer calls a violation to the attention of the court, the probationer may be arrested or summoned for a revocation hearing. The Legislative Analyst's Office for the State of California calculates that it costs taxpayers an extra $50,000, on average, each time an offender is sent to prison for a probation revocation. That probationers do the alternative of community service—as many courts would do—unless and until the probationers pay additional community service fees to the companies. The companies can maintain arrest warrants on court and police computer systems for all missed payments. Thus a person risks arrest months and years after his or her original probation sentence has been completed, as long as he or she is behind in payments to the probation company.

In February 2016, a jury in Georgia awarded a probationer $175,000 for false imprisonment in a lawsuit against a private probation company. She was jailed when she was unable to pay the company. She spent three weeks in jail before she saw a judge who then ordered her released because her probation sentence had expired four years earlier.

Civil rights organizations have filed lawsuits against private probation companies and lobbied state and local officials to stop enabling private companies to profit by controlling the lives and resources of poor people convicted of misdemeanors. This system raises serious questions about governments taking responsibility for the punishments that they impose. More importantly,

there are disturbing issues about the risk that profit-seeking companies will unfairly deprive people of liberty, extend their length of probation, and continually increase fees simply in order to make money—well beyond the time period of the actual probation sentence.

Researching the Internet

The 2014 report by Human Rights Watch was highly critical of private probation. Read the report at https://www.hrw.org/report/2014/02/05/profiting-probation/americas-offender-funded-probation-industry.

Also read the presentation by Sentinel Supervision, a leading provider of private probation services, at http://sentinelsupervision.net/?page_id=255.

For Critical Thinking and Analysis

If you were a state legislator asked to support a new law to prohibit the private administration of probation, how would you respond to the request? Counties would lobby you to help them save costs by permitting private companies to handle probation. Civil rights groups would point out the alleged abuses that

have occurred in other states. Do you have any philosophical disagreement with the idea of a profit-seeking company having power over the punishment of criminal offenders? Should private actors be able to make decisions about issuing arrest warrants, requiring drug tests, and sending people to jail for being unable to pay? Give three reasons for your position on this issue.

Sources: C. Albin-Lackey, "'You Got to Come Up with that Money or You Are Going to Jail': How Privatizing Probation Hurts the Poor," *Slate*, February 10, 2014 (www.slate.com); E. Bronner, "Poor Land in Jail as Companies Add Huge Fees for Probation," *New York Times*, July 2, 2012 (www.nytimes.com); T. Carter, "Jury Awards $175K in False Imprisonment Case against Private Probation Company," *American Bar Association Journal*, February 29, 2016 (www.abajournal.com); S. Dewan, "Private Probation Company Accused of Abuses in Tennessee," *New York Times*, October 1, 2015 (www.nytimes.com); W. C. Jones, "Top Georgia Court Rules for Private Probation Company," *Athens Banner-Herald*, March 29, 2016 (http://onlineathens.com); J. McNair, "Inside Kentucky's Unregulated Private Probation Industry," Kentucky Center for Investigative Reporting website, January 20, 2016 (http://kycir.org).

amount includes not only the marginal cost of sending an offender to prison but also the average length of the probationer's sentence (17 months), the subsequent cost of parole supervision, and the likelihood that some percentage of these offenders will be sent to prison again for parole violations (Taylor, 2009). Because of the contemporary emphasis on avoiding the expense of incarceration except for flagrant and continual violations of the conditions of probation, revocations increasingly rest on a new arrest or multiple violations of rules rather than on a small number of technical violations.

As discussed in Chapter 10, the U.S. Supreme Court extended due process rights to probationers by ruling that before probation can be revoked, the offender is entitled to both a preliminary and a final hearing, and in some cases, a right to counsel. When a probationer is taken into custody for violating the conditions of probation, a preliminary hearing must be held to determine whether probable cause exists to believe that the incident occurred. If there is a finding of probable cause, a final hearing, where the revocation decision is made, is mandatory. At these hearings, the probationer has the right to cross-examine witnesses and to receive notice of the alleged violations and receive a written report of the proceedings. The Court ruled, though, that the probationer does not have an automatic right to counsel; this decision is to be made on a case-by-case basis. At the final hearing, the judge decides whether to continue probation or to impose tougher restrictions, such as incarceration.

Probation Officer

Probation and parole officers must make discretionary decisions about when violations of conditions of probation and parole should trigger a request to ask a judge to send the probationer to jail or prison. You are the probation officer supervising an offender who was previously a prominent local politician and is serving three years on probation after serving two years in prison for perjury (making false statements in court). In some states, any supervised release after imprisonment would be called "parole" and require the supervision of a parole officer. In this state, this offender was given a separate sentence of probation after serving the first portion of his sentence in prison. The probationer failed a drug test and spent more days than permitted by the probation office at an out-of-state professional football game where there were unproven reports that he was seen at bars. The probationer claims that the failed drug test may be due to his unknowing consumption of a marijuana-laced brownie at a Halloween party and his use of a cough syrup with codeine to treat coughing symptoms from an illness. He noted that he had spoken to his probation officer prior to his trip and claimed a misunderstanding from "a lack of communication" had led him to believe that his out-of-state travel was fully approved by his probation officer. At the same time, he also stated: "I take full responsibility...and apologize to the judge."

Are these two violations and the circumstances surrounding them sufficient to lead you to request that a judge make the probationer spend time in jail or be returned to prison? What would you decide? Would it influence your decision if you were to learn that the probationer had been charged with murdering a woman with whom he had had an extramarital affair? Medical experts who testified in the case could not determine with certainty whether she died from a self-inflicted gunshot wound or whether someone else shot her at close range. The jury was deadlocked. Because prosecutors were unsure if they could obtain a murder conviction at a second trial, they offered him the opportunity to plead guilty to perjury—lying about his eligibility for representation by a state-provided public defender—in exchange for dropping the murder charge. Is this additional information even relevant to your decision about whether to request that he be jailed for probation violations? Give reasons for your decision. Then search the Internet and read about the 2016 case of Stephen Nodine, a former county commissioner in Mobile, Alabama.

For those who successfully complete probation, the sentence ends. Ordinarily, the probationer is then a free citizen again, without obligations to either the court or the probation department.

Assessing Probation

Critics see probation as nothing more than a slap on the wrist—certainly not as an appropriate punishment for a serious crime. Yet studies indicate that 56 percent of those sentenced to probation in 2014 were assigned that punishment upon conviction for a felony, a slight increase over the 52 percent figure back in 2000 (Kaeble, Maruschak, & Bonczar, 2015). This statistic is striking: many people assume that probationers have typically committed only misdemeanors. But as states deal with continuing budget difficulties, the use of probation is certain to expand, and the potential for accompanying challenges to public safety will likely grow as a concern for both the public and probation officials.

Despite the fact that many probationers have been convicted of serious crimes, caseload burdens and limited resources lead many probation officers to meet with individual offenders little more than once a month. Such limited contact raises questions about whether convicted felons receive adequate supervision and monitoring in the community. Yet, as budget cuts aimed at the expense of imprisonment increase the number of offenders assigned to community sanctions, contact between officers and probationers may be further reduced in many jurisdictions that cannot afford to simultaneously increase the number of probation officers.

Although the recidivism rate for probationers is lower than the rate for those who have been incarcerated, researchers question whether this is a direct result of supervision or an indirect result of the maturing of the offenders. Most offenders placed on probation do not become career criminals—their criminal activity is

Probation officers make decisions about whether probationers should be taken into custody for violating the terms of probation. After the decision is made, they often require police assistance for this task. Do probation officers need the same training as police officers, or should they receive a different kind of training in order to do their jobs effectively?

AP Images/Damian Dovarganes

short-lived, and they become stable citizens as they obtain jobs and get married. Most of those who are arrested a second time do not repeat their mistake.

To offer a viable alternative to incarceration, probation services need the resources to supervise and assist their clients appropriately. The new demands on probation have brought calls for increased electronic monitoring and for risk-management systems that provide different levels of supervision for different kinds of offenders. Because of the growing importance of probation and other forms of community corrections, it is important for criminal justice officials to use evidence-based practices in order to enhance the effectiveness of these approaches to punishment and treatment. Read the "Evidence-Based Practice and Policy" feature concerning community corrections, and consider whether there are any impediments to the implementation of these practices.

EVIDENCE-BASED PRACTICE AND POLICY

Probation and Community Corrections

Significant efforts are being undertaken to identify and verify the effectiveness of programs and then publicize and provide training about effective programs for agencies interested in implementing reforms. In 2009, the Administrative Office of the U.S. Courts formed the Evidence-Based Practice Working Group, chaired by experienced federal probation officers, to advise the federal Office of Probation and Pretrial Services about evidence-based principles and effective approaches. This working group identified important priorities, including the nationwide use of proven, evidence-based risk assessment tools to determine the supervisory and programmatic needs of offenders. In addition, the working group emphasized the need to train probation personnel in evidence-based practices as well as particular skills that have proven to have the greatest effect on reducing recidivism.

One important approach for advancing the use of evidence-based practices is the STARR program—"Staff Training Aimed at Reducing Rearrest." The training program is provided for federal probation officers, but its principles are also useful for community corrections officials at the state and local levels of government. The program teaches active listening, effective use of reinforcement and punishment, and techniques for addressing offenders' thought processes that may not appropriately connect their thinking to their behavior.

The program recognizes that high-risk offenders need more intensive services. It also is based on the idea that counseling and other services should target those factors that are actually associated with criminal behavior, such as substance abuse, contact with those who commit criminal acts, and attitudes that endorse criminal behavior, rather

continued

Evidence-Based Practice and Policy (*continued*)

than such matters as self-esteem or emotional distress. Research indicates that these elements, as well as others, such as involving families in the treatment process and providing treatment for at least 90 days, can be effective in reducing the number of offenders in community corrections who commit subsequent crimes.

The 2009 report of the Pew Center on the States presented research-based recommendations designed to strengthen community corrections systems, saving money and reducing crime. These recommendations included the following:

- Sort offenders by risk to public safety to determine appropriate levels of supervision.
- Base intervention programs on sound research about what works to reduce recidivism.
- Harness advances in supervision technology, such as electronic monitoring and rapid-result alcohol and drug tests.
- Impose swift and certain sanctions for offenders who break the rules of their release but who do not commit new crimes.
- Create incentives for offenders and supervision agencies to succeed, and monitor their performance.

In the past few years, additional research and field experience has illuminated the elements most likely to produce successful change in probationers' attitudes and behavior. The California courts' webpage on evidence-based practices describes the sequences of elements and actions needed to utilize evidence-based programs in community corrections, such as probation:

1. Assess the actuarial risk/needs of the individual offender.
2. Enhance the offender's intrinsic motivation—cultivate and encourage the offender's interest in changing his or her own behavior.
3. Target interventions—design programs to address needs and tap motivation

   a. *Risk Principle*: Prioritize supervision and treatment resources for higher-risk offenders.
   b. *Need Principle*: Target interventions to criminogenic needs.
   c. *Responsivity Principle*: Be responsive to temperament, learning style, motivation, culture, and gender when assigning programs.
   d. *Dosage*: Structure 40–70 percent of high-risk offenders' time for 3–9 months.
   e. *Treatment*: Integrate treatment into the full sentence/sanction requirements.

4. Skill train with directed practice (use cognitive behavioral treatment methods).
5. Increase positive reinforcement.
6. Engage ongoing support in natural communities.
7. Measure relevant processes/practices.
8. Provide measurement feedback.

Within this evidence-based practice is the concept of "dosage"—designing treatment and activities to address the probationer's needs while bearing in mind the level of risk posed by the offender. This concept was highlighted in a 2014 report for the National Institute of Corrections. Central to this element is the creation of incentives for the probationer to reduce and change risk-enhancing behaviors as well as carefully tracking the number of "dosage" hours for treatment and activities while monitoring evidence of change.

The literature on evidence-based practices in community corrections makes clear that important challenges extend beyond identifying effective practices and providing training to justice system officials who have face-to-face contact and supervisory responsibility with offenders. It can be challenging to convince individual officers and agencies to actually incorporate evidence-based practices into their standard routines. When people have been doing their jobs and operating their offices in a certain way over a long period of time, it can be difficult to get them to change their customary practices, even when there is evidence that new approaches will be more effective. In addition, budget cuts can complicate the implementation of new practices, as there may be insufficient time or personnel to carry out evidence-based practices in the manner that is most effective.

Researching the Internet

Read a brief report entitled *Dosage Probation: Rethinking the Structure of Probation Sentences* (2014) at the National Institute of Corrections website.

Implementing New Practices

Are you optimistic that probation officers and other community corrections officials can be trained to effectively help offenders become less likely to commit new crimes? Given the number of people on probation and in other community corrections programs and the limited number of officials who must supervise these offenders, the limitations on available time and resources may make the actual implementation of evidence-based practices an impossible dream. If you are optimistic about the possibility of progress, describe what you see as the two biggest priorities for those seeking to implement evidence-based practices. If you are not optimistic, would you steer time, attention, and resources to other aspects of probation and community corrections? Briefly describe what you would do if you were the head of a local probation office.

Sources: California Courts webpage, "Evidence-Based Practice," (http://www.courts.ca.gov/5285.htm. Accessed April 2016); M. Carter and R. Sankovitz, *Dosage Probation: Rethinking the Structure of Probation Sentences*, National Institute of Corrections, January 2014; J. Hurtig and L. M. Lenart, "The Development of the Evidence-Based Practice Blue Print and Where We Are Now," *Federal Probation* 75 (2011): 35–36; Pew Center on the States, *One in 31: The Long Reach of American Corrections*, Washington, DC: Pew Charitable Trusts, 2009; "Program Profile: Staff Training Aimed at Reducing Rearrest (STARR)," U.S. Office of Justice Programs website, 2013 (http://www.crimesolutions.gov); C. R. Robinson, S. VanBenschoten, M. Alexander, and C. T. Lowenkamp, "A Random (Almost) Study of Staff Training Aimed at Reducing Re-arrest (STARR): Reducing Recidivism through Intentional Design," *Federal Probation* 75 (2011): 57–63; F. S. Taxman and S. Belenko, *Implementing Evidence-Based Practices in Community Corrections and Addiction Treatment*, New York: Springer, 2013.

CHECK POINT

1. **What are the four main assumptions underlying community corrections?**
   Many offenders' crimes and records do not warrant incarceration; community supervision is cheaper; recidivism rates for those supervised in the community are no higher than for those who serve prison time; incarceration is more destructive to the offender and society.

2. **What are the main tasks of the probation officer?**
   To assist judges by preparing presentence reports and to provide assistance and supervision to offenders in the community.

3. **What are the grounds for revocation of probation?**
   An arrest for a new offense or a technical violation of the conditions of probation that were set by the judge.

STOP & ANALYZE

Why would a probation officer decline to seek revocation for every technical violation? Does the criminal justice system benefit from such decisions? Give two arguments for each side of this question.

Intermediate Sanctions in the Community

Dissatisfaction with the traditional means of probation supervision, coupled with the crowding and high cost of prisons, has resulted in the expansion of intermediate sanctions. These sanctions are more restricting than simple probation and therefore constitute a greater degree of actual punishment, especially for those who have committed more-serious offenses.

Many experts support the case for intermediate sanctions. For example, Norval Morris and Michael Tonry observed, "Prison is used excessively; probation is used even more excessively; between the two is a near vacuum of purposive and enforced punishments" (1990:3). Sixty-nine percent of convicted felons are incarcerated, incarceration being the severest sentence, whereas 27 percent receive probation, the least severe. Hence, nearly all convicted felons receive either the severest or the most lenient of possible penalties (Rosenmerkel, Durose, & Farole, 2009). Morris and Tonry have urged that punishments be created that are more restrictive than probation yet match the severity of the offense and the characteristics of the offender and that can be carried out while still protecting the community. In addition, they emphasize that intermediate punishments must be supported and enforced by mechanisms that take any breach of the conditions of the sentence seriously.

We can view intermediate sanctions as a continuum—a range of punishments that vary in levels of intrusiveness and control, as shown in Figure 12.3. Corrections employs many types of intermediate sanctions. They can be divided into (1) those administered primarily by the judiciary (fines, restitution, and forfeiture), (2) those administered primarily in the community with a supervision component (home

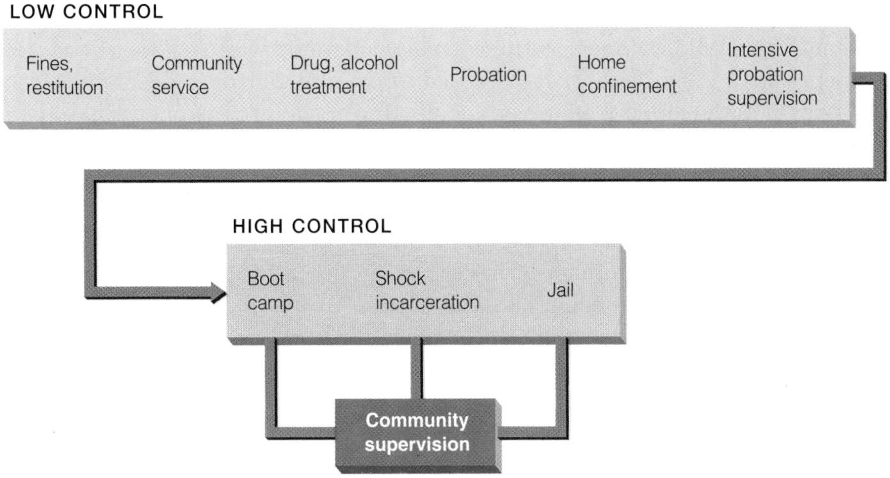

FIGURE 12.3
Continuum of Intermediate Sanctions
Judges may use a range of intermediate sanctions, from those imposing a low level of control to those imposing a high level.

confinement, community service, day reporting centers, and intensive probation supervision), and (3) those administered inside institutions and followed by community supervision. Furthermore, sanctions may be imposed in combination—for example, a fine and probation, or boot camp with community service and probation.

Intermediate Sanctions Administered Primarily by the Judiciary

The judiciary administers many kinds of intermediate sanctions. Here we discuss three of them—fines, restitution, and forfeiture. Because all three involve the transfer of money or property from the offender to the government or crime victim, the judiciary is considered the proper body not only to impose the sanction but also to collect what is due.

fine A sum of money to be paid to the state by a convicted person, as punishment for an offense.

Fines Fines are routinely imposed for offenses ranging from traffic violations to felonies. Studies have shown that the fine is used widely as a criminal sanction and that nationally, well over $1 billion in fines has been collected annually. Yet, judges in the United States make little use of fines as the *sole* punishment for crimes more serious than motor vehicle violations. Instead, they typically use fines in conjunction with other sanctions, such as probation and incarceration: for example, two years of probation and a $500 fine.

Many judges cite the difficulty of collecting fines as the reason they do not make greater use of this punishment. They note that offenders tend to be poor, and many judges fear that fines will be paid from the proceeds of additional illegal acts. Other judges are concerned that relying on fines as an alternative to incarceration will let affluent offenders "buy" their way out of jail while forcing the poor to serve time.

Fines are used extensively in Europe. There they are enforced and are normally the sole sanction for a wide range of crimes. To deal with the concern that fines exact a heavier toll on the poor than on the wealthy, Finland, Sweden, and Germany have developed the "day fine," which bases the penalty on offenders' daily income and the gravity of the offense. Although a millionaire would pay much more than a minimum-wage worker if punished with a day fine for five days' worth of pay as a criminal sanction, in theory they would be equivalent burdens. Thus wealthy people can be forced to view fines as a genuine punishment rather than a nearly unnoticed annoyance. In 2015, for example, Finland imposed a fine of $58,000 on a multimillionaire for a speeding ticket when he drove 64 mph in a 50 mph zone (Thornhill, 2015). Such significant fines raise questions in the minds of critics about the fairness of day fines for minor offenses. Experiments in the use of day fines have been conducted by courts in several American states, including Arizona, Connecticut, Iowa, New York, and Washington (Zedlewski, 2010).

restitution Repayment—in the form of money or service—by an offender to a victim who has suffered some loss from the offense.

Restitution Restitution is repayment by an offender to a victim who has suffered some form of financial loss from the crime. It is *reparative* in that it seeks to repair the harm done. In the Middle Ages, restitution was a common way to settle a criminal case (Karmen, 2001). The offender was ordered to pay the victim or do the victim's work. The growth of the modern state saw the decline of such punishments based on "private" arrangements between offender and victim. Instead, the state prosecuted offenders, and punishments focused on the wrong the offender had done to society.

Though largely unpublicized, victim restitution has remained a part of the U.S. criminal justice system. In many instances, restitution derives from informal agreements between the police and offenders at the station during plea bargaining or it is stated in the prosecutor's sentence recommendation. Only since the late 1970s has restitution been institutionalized, usually as one of the conditions of probation.

As with fines, convicted offenders differ in their ability to pay restitution, and the conditions inevitably fall more harshly on less affluent offenders. Someone who has the "good fortune" to be victimized by an affluent criminal might receive full compensation, whereas someone victimized by a poor offender might never receive a penny. In 2016, Dzhokhar Tsarnaev, the convicted Boston Marathon bomber, was ordered to pay $101 million in restitution to the many people injured in the bombing and the families of those who were killed. Because Tsarnaev had no money and was sitting in a maximum-security prison waiting for the appeals process to move forward concerning his death sentence, there was never any chance that any victims would receive restitution through this court order (Fortier, 2016).

In Colorado, a corps of investigators work with probation officers to monitor cases, collecting restitution and working out payment plans if necessary. As a result, collections in Colorado counties have increased by 25–50 percent since the late 1980s. However, even in a well-organized system, it can be difficult to collect from many offenders. In 2009, offenders in Colorado still owed an uncollected $563 million in restitution and $215 million in court fines and costs. Pennsylvania, which was less active and organized in collecting from offenders, was owed $1.5 billion by criminal offenders (Crummy, 2009).

Restitution is more easily imposed when the "damage" inflicted can be easily measured—the value of property destroyed or stolen or medical costs, for instance. Thus, restitution is most frequently ordered for property crimes.

Forfeiture With the passage of two laws in 1970—the Racketeer Influenced and Corrupt Organizations Act (RICO) and the Continuing Criminal Enterprise Act (CCE)—Congress resurrected forfeiture, a criminal sanction that had lain dormant since the American Revolution. Through amendments in 1984 and 1986, Congress improved ways to implement the law. Most states now have similar laws, particularly to deal with organized crime and with trafficking in controlled substances.

Forfeiture is government seizure of property and other assets derived from or used in criminal activity. Assets seized by federal and state agencies through forfeiture can be quite considerable and have increased significantly in the past 30 years. For example, in 1989, U.S. attorneys seized $285 million in assets—by 2010, that amount had increased to $1.8 billion (BJS, 2014).

forfeiture Government seizure of property and other assets derived from or used in criminal activity.

Forfeiture is controversial. Critics argue that confiscating property without a court hearing violates citizens' constitutional rights. They have also raised concerns about the excessive use of this sanction, because forfeited assets often go into the budget of the law enforcement agency taking the action (Witt, 2009).

Those in opposition further argue that ownership of the seized property is often unclear. For example, in Hartford, Connecticut, a woman's home was seized

A potential buyer examines property seized by federal officials from Congressman Randy "Duke" Cunningham after his conviction for taking bribes. Presumably obtained through illegal funds, the property items were to be sold at auction. Should law enforcement agencies be permitted to keep or sell the property that they seize from criminal offenders?

Asset Forfeiture and the Risk of Law Enforcement Self-Interest

There has been growing concern over the power of police agencies to seize property, including cash, from people, even when they have not been convicted of a crime. Civil forfeiture laws allow police to seize property from individuals suspected of committing a crime, and then require the property owner to prove that their possessions were acquired legally. Newspaper reports provide numerous accounts of people carrying cash as they head to a casino for a recreational weekend and having their money seized by police when they are stopped for traffic violations. Similarly, small business owners, including immigrants who are accustomed to doing business in cash, have had money seized during traffic stops; in some cases, they were carrying thousands of dollars to pay for new restaurant equipment or other legitimate business transactions.

Civil forfeiture laws are controversial because police officers, in practice, typically make discretionary decisions about seizures based on their own suspicions and justifications, and without having to prove that people whose property they have seized were involved in wrongdoing. People subjected to asset forfeitures often face long, expensive legal battles to seek the return of money and property. In effect, rather than being presumed innocent until proved guilty of a crime, they may be required to prove their innocence.

Originally developed to target high-level drug distributors, the practice of seizure has been expanded by some police departments to target those accused of committing minor infractions. Police often assume that anyone driving with large amounts of cash is involved in drug trafficking.

From the 1980s until recently, local police agencies used civil forfeiture laws to seize property under the U.S. Department of Justice's "Equitable Sharing" program, which permitted local police departments to keep up to 80 percent of the proceeds seized for potential—though unproven—federal law violations. Under California state law, by contrast, police were allowed to keep only two-thirds of assets seized. Thus California agencies preferred to use the more generous federal law. In 2013, California police used state forfeiture law to acquire $28 million in cash and property while using the federal forfeiture program to acquire $98 million.

In light of news media attention to seizures of cash from innocent people, Attorney General Eric Holder ended aspects of that program in January 2015, and subsequently limited the authority of local police to seize property under federal law. In December 2015, the U.S. Department of Justice completely suspended the program.

Major law enforcement organizations complained bitterly about the suspension of the program. They argued that asset forfeiture was an essential tool for law enforcement officers. But the change in the federal practice did not prevent police from seizing evidence of criminal activity; it merely limited their ability to profit from seizures, especially seizures from people who were never charged or never convicted of crimes. Were the law enforcement organizations' concerned about losing the ability to stop crime, or were they concerned about losing a source of revenue for their police departments?

Police officers may still enjoy broad authority to make such seizures under their own states' laws. Obviously a significant problem with these practices concerns the apparent self-interest of police departments that use seized assets to enhance their own annual budgets. As a result, many members of Congress, both Republicans and Democrats, are concerned that the law enforcement authority to seize assets from unconvicted people has gone too far.

Proponents of civil forfeiture laws claim that many high-level drug distribution networks have been disrupted due to their use. Victims of economic crime can also benefit from civil forfeiture laws. High-profile offenders like Bernie Madoff and his associates (who defrauded investment clients of over $20 billion) were subjected to civil forfeiture laws in order to pay back their victims. Their money, homes, cars, and other assets were seized and sold to reimburse victims for their losses. However, these forfeitures were imposed only after the offenders had been convicted, and the proceeds were not used to enhance police agencies' budgets.

For Critical Thinking and Analysis
Many believe that forfeiture laws create an unreasonable intrusion of the government into citizens' lives. Others believe that these laws serve to cripple drug-trafficking organizations, provide restitution to victims, and help police departments financially. Imagine you are a defense attorney who is counseling a client whose home was seized by police after her son was arrested for dealing drugs out of the house without her knowledge. After the arrest, police confiscated the house and planned to sell it at auction. As her attorney, what three points would you make to the judge to argue that the seizure was inappropriate? Next, imagine you are the district attorney handling the same case. What three points would you make to the judge to justify the seizure of the home?

Sources: C. Ingraham, "The Justice Department Just Shut Down a Huge Asset Forfeiture Program," Washington Post, December 23, 2015 (www.washingtonpost .com); C. Ingraham, "What Life Is Like after Police Ransack Your House and Take 'Every Belonging'—Then the Charges Are Dropped, Washington Post, March 30, 2016 (www.washingtonpost.com); L. Neyfakh, "Helicopters Don't Pay for Themselves," Slate, January 16, 2015 (http://www.slate .com); R. O'Harrow Jr. and S. Rich, "Justice Clarifies New Limits on Asset Forfeiture Involving Local, State Police." Washington Post, February 11, 2015 (http://washingtonpost.com); M. Sallah, R. O'Hallow Jr., and S. Rich, "Stop and Seize," Washington Post, September 6, 2014 (http://washingtonpost.com): S. Stillman, "Taken," New Yorker, August 12, 2013 (http://newyorker.com).

because her grandson, unbeknownst to her, was using it as a base for selling drugs. Under a federal law passed by Congress in 2000, owners' property cannot be seized if they can demonstrate their innocence by a preponderance of evidence. However, this places a burden on innocent people to prove they were not involved in any crime. Laws vary from state to state regarding forfeiture and how law enforcement agencies may gain resources from seizing property. Read the "Current Controversies in Criminal Justice" feature to consider debates about this issue.

Intermediate Sanctions Administered in the Community

One argument for intermediate sanctions is that probation, as traditionally practiced, cannot accommodate the large numbers of offenders whom probation officers must supervise today. Probation leaders have responded to this criticism by developing new intermediate sanction programs and expanding old ones. Four of these are home confinement, community service, day reporting centers, and intensive supervision probation.

Home Confinement With technological innovations that provide for electronic monitoring, **home confinement**, in which offenders must remain at home during specific periods, has gained attention. Offenders under home confinement (often called "house arrest") may face other restrictions, such as the usual probation rules against the use of alcohol and drugs, as well as strictly monitored curfews and check-in times. As you read the "Close Up," consider whether home confinement is an appropriate and effective intermediate sanction for people who have been convicted of crimes.

home confinement A sentence requiring the offender to remain inside his or her home during specified periods.

Some offenders are allowed to go to a place of employment, education, or treatment during the day but must return to their homes by a specified hour. Those supervising home confinement may telephone offenders' homes at various times of the day or night to speak personally with offenders to make sure they are complying.

Home confinement offers a great deal of flexibility for judges and corrections officials. It can be used as a sole sanction or in combination with other penalties. It can be imposed at almost any point in the criminal justice process: during the pretrial period, after a short term in jail or prison, or as a condition of probation or parole. In addition, home confinement relieves the government of the responsibility for providing the offender with food, clothing, and housing, as it must do in prisons. For these reasons, home confinement programs have grown and proliferated.

The development of electronic monitoring equipment has made home confinement an enforceable sentencing option. Two basic types of electronic monitoring devices exist. Passive monitors respond only to inquiries; most commonly, the offender receives an automated telephone call from the probation office and is told to place the device on a receiver attached to the phone. Active monitors send continuous signals that a receiver picks up; a computer notes any break in the signal.

Despite favorable publicity, home confinement with electronic monitoring poses certain legal, technical, and correctional issues that must be addressed before it can become a standard punishment. First, some criminal justice scholars question its constitutionality. Monitoring may violate the Fourth Amendment's protection against unreasonable searches and seizures. At issue is a clash between the constitutionally protected reasonable expectation of privacy and the invasion of one's home by surveillance devices. Second, the monitoring devices still have extensive technical problems, such as frequently giving erroneous

AP Images/Wilfredo Lee

Probation officers are responsible for offenders who are subject to home confinement and other forms of electronic monitoring, such as GPS (global positioning systems), to keep track of a probationer's movements. Does home confinement and monitoring actually impose punishment on offenders?

reports that the offender is home. Third, offender failure rates may prove to be high. There is little evidence that electronic monitoring reduces recidivism rates (Renzema & Mayo-Wilson, 2005). Being one's own warden is difficult, and visits by former criminal associates and other negative enticements may become problematic for many offenders. Anecdotal evidence suggests that four months of full-time monitoring is about the limit before a violation will occur. Fourth, an additional issue is that some crimes—such as child abuse, drug sales, and assaults—can be committed while the offender is at home. Finally, observers point out that the only offenders eligible for this type of program are those who own telephones and can afford the weekly rental rates of $35–$120 for the electronic system and components.

Washington County, Oregon, says its "Electronic Home Detention Program is an alternative custody program that allows low-risk inmates to serve the last portion of a jail sentence at home, making more space available in our jail for inmates who pose a greater threat to our community" (Washington County Sheriff's Office, 2016). Participants must consent in writing to random home visits and searches. They must also pay a $30 processing fee, a $150 deposit for the ankle monitor and related equipment, and a $15 per day charge during the home confinement period. The program admits only low-risk offenders. It excludes certain categories of offenders, including sex offenders, those convicted of domestic violence and other violent crimes, and repeat drug offenders (Washington County Sheriff's Office, 2016).

Whatever the potential benefits of home confinement, they cannot be achieved unless monitoring programs operate appropriately. Newspaper investigations in 2013 found that Florida judges were ordering home confinement for some people who were supposed to be ineligible for such sanctions due to the violent crimes for which they had been convicted. In one county, more than 50 people on home confinement disappeared. Nearly all were eventually caught, but not before some committed crimes and used drugs. In the worst instance, a defendant on home confinement—as part of conditions of bail prior to trial—murdered one of the witnesses against him in his upcoming home invasion trial. County officials noted that the escapees represented only 6 percent of the 900 people assigned to home confinement in Orange County, Florida. However, that small percentage still represented a large number of people who caused harm in the community and raised questions about the effectiveness of the entire home confinement program (Weiner, 2013a; Weiner, 2013b). These problems highlighted the need for judges to be careful about which individuals are assigned to home confinement and the need for equipment to work properly and officials to respond quickly and effectively when people violate their assignment to home confinement.

Community Service

community service A sentence requiring the offender to perform a certain amount of unpaid labor in the community.

A **community service** sentence requires the offender to perform a certain amount of unpaid labor in the community. When singer Chris Brown was convicted of assaulting his girlfriend, singer Rihanna, he was required to perform community labor as part of his sentence. His service included shoveling at the police horse stables and working along local roads. Community service can take a variety of forms, including assisting in social-service agencies, cleaning parks and roadsides, or helping the poor. The sentence specifies the number of hours to be worked and usually requires supervision by a probation officer. Judges can tailor community service to the skills and abilities of offenders. For example, less-educated offenders might pick up litter along the highway, whereas those with schooling might teach reading in evening literacy classes. Many judges order community service when an offender cannot pay a fine. The offender's effort to make reparation to the community harmed by the crime also serves a symbolic function.

Ricardo Aratanha/Getty Images

Many offenders pick up trash, shovel snow, and do other tasks in fulfillment of a community service sentence. Such sanctions can provide benefits to the community. There may also be a "shaming" effect if offenders are embarrassed to be seen in public fulfilling a criminal punishment. Can you think of creative and effective ways to expand the use of community service sanctions?

Although community service has many supporters, some labor unions and workers criticize it for possibly taking jobs away from law-abiding citizens. In addition, some experts believe that if community service is the only sanction, it may be too mild a punishment, especially for upper-class and white-collar criminals. Examine your own views about community service as a punishment when you read "Criminal Justice: Myth & Reality."

Day Reporting Centers Another intermediate sanction is the **day reporting center**—a community correctional center to which the offender must report each day to carry out elements of the sentence. Designed to ensure that probationers follow the employment and treatment stipulations attached to their sentence, day reporting centers also increase the likelihood that offenders and the general public will consider probation supervision to be credible.

Most day reporting centers incorporate multiple correctional methods. For example, in some centers, offenders must remain in the facility for eight hours or report for drug-related urine checks before going to work. Centers with a rehabilitation component carry out drug and alcohol treatment, literacy programs, and job searches. Others provide staff–offender contact levels equal to or greater than those in intensive supervision programs.

As with many newly established criminal justice programs, strict eligibility requirements result in small numbers of cases actually entering the program; but even with the limited number of participants under day reporting center supervision, there is evidence that recidivism rates can be reduced (Riely, 2014; Ostermann, 2009). Evaluations of jail-run day reporting centers find that the participants have lower levels of drug use and absconding. However, because participants were carefully screened for acceptance, applicability may be limited to low-risk cases (Porter, Lee, & Lutz, 2002).

One additional problem often faces day reporting centers and other community corrections facilities: opposition from citizens about the placement of such facilities in or near their neighborhoods. Even when people recognize the value of community corrections facilities, they may be very nervous about the thought of convicted offenders congregating each day near their homes or their children's schools. Read "The Policy Debate" to consider the controversy about deciding where to place community corrections facilities.

CRIMINAL JUSTICE
Myth&Reality

COMMON BELIEF: Community service does not punish those who receive the sanction.

REALITY

- There are elements of punishment in the community service sanction.
- Individuals suffer a partial loss of liberty as they must report to specific locations, surrender their time and freedom of movement, and obey authorities' orders to complete tasks they would otherwise not do.
- They also risk feeling the shame and embarrassment of being seen doing tasks, such as collecting trash along a highway, that indicate to other people that they have gotten into trouble with the law.
- Does this mean that community service is sufficiently severe to serve as a punishment for all kinds of nonviolent offenses? No. Society may legitimately conclude that greater restrictions on liberty and behavior, such as those associated with home confinement, may be appropriate for some offenses and repeat offenders.
- We should recognize, however, that community service carries sanctioning elements while simultaneously avoiding the high costs of more expensive sanctions and permitting minor offenders to stay connected to their families and communities by retaining their jobs or continuing in school.

day reporting center A community correctional center where an offender reports each day to comply with elements of a sentence.

Intensive Supervision Probation (ISP) Intensive supervision probation (ISP) is a means of dealing with offenders who need greater restrictions than traditional community-based programs can provide. Jurisdictions in every state have programs to intensively supervise such offenders. ISP uses probation as an intermediate form of punishment by imposing conditions of strict reporting to a probation officer who has a limited caseload.

There are two general types of ISP programs. *Probation diversion* puts under intensive surveillance those offenders thought to be too risky for routine supervision. *Institutional diversion* selects low-risk offenders already sentenced to prison and provides supervision for them in the community. Daily contact between the probationer and the probation officer may cut rearrest rates. Such contact also gives the probationer greater access to the resources the officer can provide, such as treatment services in the community. Offenders have incentives to obey rules, knowing that they must meet

intensive supervision probation (ISP) Probation granted under conditions of strict reporting to a probation officer with a limited caseload.

Should Community Corrections Facilities Be Dispersed throughout a City?

Newspapers regularly report about citizens' efforts to prevent the placement of community corrections facilities near their neighborhoods. People sign petitions and gather groups to attend city council or local zoning commission meetings. The attitude that many people have about the siting of community corrections is referred to as "NIMBY"—Not In My Back Yard. Similar citizen activism can arise when cities discuss the placement of waste disposal facilities, power plants, and other needed public facilities that are perceived as being noisy or unpleasant or as reducing housing values and the quality of life for people who live nearby. In efforts to influence where facilities are placed, middle-class and affluent people typically possess more political power than poor people do. As a result, there can be risks that community corrections facilities will be concentrated in poor neighborhoods or commercial areas, even if the buildings at those locations are less suitable for providing needed space and services than buildings located closer to middle-class neighborhoods.

For Dispersing Community Corrections Facilities

- Community corrections programs should be housed in the most suitable building without regard to the opposition and political influence of middle-class and affluent people.
- Everyone benefits from effective programs to reduce crime; therefore, everyone in a city should bear equal risks and burdens in the placement of facilities, which means they should not be concentrated in poor neighborhoods.

- Placement of community corrections centers in poor neighborhoods or commercial areas may place offenders, especially those with substance-abuse issues, closer to the associates and locations that may tempt them to relapse and reoffend.

Against Dispersing Community Corrections Facilities

- Placing offenders in residential neighborhoods creates needless risks for citizens and their homes, especially if offenders travel to the area every day during the hours when many homes are empty because the homeowners are at work.
- Many offenders under community supervision are drug users who relapse during their period of supervision, thus creating risks that drug transactions will begin occurring near homes and schools.
- Many offenders live in poor neighborhoods. Thus, it is easier for them to travel to nearby locations or take public transportation to commercial areas rather than try to find their way to far-flung residential areas that are not necessarily served by frequent public bus service.

What Should U.S. Policy Be?

The siting of community corrections facilities is controversial, because there is no escaping the fact that the administrators of such facilities cannot guarantee that the offender-clients will never misbehave. Opposition is often especially intense with regard to residential facilities for substance-abuse treatment or for transitional reentry into society by parolees just released from prison. In such cases, local residents are very

aware that offenders will be nearby 24 hours a day, including the nighttime hours. They are not easily reassured by the reminder that offenders in community corrections programs have a strong motivation to obey the rules in order to avoid jail or a return to prison.

At the heart of the controversy is the question of who should decide where community corrections facilities will be located. Should state officials have the authority to place such facilities in the most appropriate building, wherever it happens to be located? Should city councils and local zoning commissions, comprised of and influenced by local residents, make such decisions about their own communities?

Researching the Internet

To read the policy position of the International Community Corrections Association on siting facilities, visit http://iccalive.org/icca/index.php?option=com _content&view=article&id=95& Itemid=554.

Analyzing the Issue

Imagine that you and your classmates are staff members of the community corrections unit of your state department of corrections. You must select the best site for the state to build a new day reporting center in the town where your college is located. What factors would you consider in deciding where to place the building? In anticipation of public opposition, what arguments would you use to educate the public about the necessity and desirability of placing a day reporting center in the community? Can you and your classmates agree on the best location for the center?

with their probation officers daily and, in some cases, must speak with them even more frequently. Offenders often face additional restrictions as well, such as electronic monitoring, alcohol and drug testing, community service, and restitution.

ISP programs have been called "old style" probation because each officer has only 20 clients and requires frequent face-to-face contact (Jalbert & Rhodes, 2012). Nonetheless, some people question how much of a difference constant surveillance can make to probationers with numerous problems. Such offenders frequently need help to get a job, counseling to deal with emotional and family situations, and a variety of supports to avoid drug or alcohol problems that may have contributed to their criminality. Nevertheless, ISP may be a way of getting the large number of drug-addicted felons into treatment.

Because it presents a "tough" image of community supervision and addresses the problem of prison crowding, ISP has become popular among probation administrators, judges, and prosecutors. Most ISP programs require a specific number of monthly contacts with officers; performance of community service; curfews; drug and alcohol testing; and referral to appropriate job-training, education, or treatment programs.

Some observers warn that ISP is not a "cure" for the rising costs and other problems facing corrections systems. Ironically, ISP can increase the number of probationers sent to prison. All evaluations of ISP find that probably because of the closer contact with clients, probation officers uncover more violations of rules than they do in regular probation. Therefore, ISP programs often have higher failure rates than do regular probation programs, even though their clients produce fewer arrests. But recent analyses of recidivism post-ISP indicate that it can be successful, particularly if combined with rewards for noncriminal behavior (Wodahl et al., 2011).

One surprising finding is that when given the option of serving prison terms or participating in ISP, many offenders choose prison. In New Jersey, 15 percent of offenders withdrew their applications for ISP once they learned the conditions and requirements. Similarly, when offenders in Marion County, Oregon, were asked if they would participate in ISP, one-third chose prison instead (Petersilia, 1990). Apparently, some offenders would rather spend a short time in prison, where tough conditions may differ little from their accustomed life, than a longer period under demanding conditions in the community. To these offenders, ISP does not represent freedom, because it is so intrusive and the risk of revocation seems high.

Despite problems and continuing questions about its effectiveness, ISP has rejuvenated probation. Many of these programs have demonstrated especially effective supervision of offenders. As with regular probation, the size of a probation officer's caseload, within reasonable limits, often matters less in preventing recidivism than does the quality of supervision and assistance provided to probationers. If properly implemented, ISP may improve the quality of supervision and services that foster success for many offenders.

Intermediate Sanctions Administered in Institutions and the Community

Among the most publicized intermediate sanctions are **boot camps**. Often referred to as *shock incarceration*, these programs vary; however, all stem from the belief that young offenders (usually 14- to 21-year-olds) can be "shocked" out of their criminal ways. Boot camps put offenders through a 30- to 90-day physical regimen designed to develop discipline and respect for authority. Like the Marine Corps, most programs emphasize a spit-and-polish environment and restrict the offenders to a disciplined and demanding routine that seeks ultimately to build self-esteem. Most camps also include education, job-training programs, and other rehabilitation services. On successful completion of the program, offenders are released to the community. At this point, probation officers take over, and the conditions of the sentence are imposed.

Boot camps proliferated in the 1980s. By 1995, some states and the Federal Bureau of Prisons operated 93 camps for adults and 30 for juveniles. At their peak, boot camps held more than 7,000 offenders. By 2000, however, about one-third of the camps had closed, and the decline in boot camp operations has continued. Further, the public uproar following the death of teenager Martin Anderson caused Florida to scrap its system of juvenile boot camps. Anderson died after being pummeled by a group of guards at a Panama City boot camp. He had been sent to the camp for joyriding in his grandmother's automobile (Caputo & Miller, 2006).

Evaluations of boot camp programs have reduced the initial optimism about such approaches. Critics suggest that the emphasis on physical training ignores

boot camp A short-term institutional sentence, usually followed by probation, that puts the offender through a physical regimen designed to develop discipline and respect for authority. Also referred to as *shock incarceration*.

Military-type drills and physical workouts are part of the regimen at most boot camps, such as this one in Massachusetts. Evaluations of boot camps have reduced the initial optimism about the effectiveness this approach. Boot camps have been closed in many states. What are the potential shortcomings of using boot camps as punishment?

AP Images/Mike Groll

young offenders' real problems. Other critics point out that, like the military, boot camp builds esprit de corps and solidarity, characteristics that can improve the leadership qualities of the young offender and therefore enhance a criminal career. In fact, follow-up studies of boot camp graduates do show evidence of changes in attitudes (Kurlychek, 2010), but not necessarily changed behavior in avoiding subsequent criminal acts (Meade & Steiner, 2010).

Research has also found that, like intensive supervision probation, boot camps do not automatically reduce prison crowding. A National Institute of Justice summary of the boot-camp experiment notes that they fail to reduce recidivism or prison populations (Parent, 2003). Yet because boot camps have been popular with the public, which imagines that strict discipline and harsh conditions will instill positive attitudes in young offenders, such camps will probably continue operating whether or not they are more effective than probation or prison.

Although there are fewer boot camps run by the criminal justice agencies, the concept has spread as a means of instilling discipline in troubled youths who have not yet entered the criminal justice system. With federal funding, the National Guard (NG) runs three dozen "ChalleNGe" programs throughout the United States, including the Michigan Youth ChalleNGe Academy. At no cost to teens and their families, high school dropouts can enroll in military-style programs that include tough discipline, uniforms, marching, full days of academic classes, and rigorous physical exercise. As with the use of boot camps as punishment, these programs are intended to instill discipline in troubled teens while helping them to earn high school diplomas (Estep, 2009; National Guard Youth Foundation, 2016).

Implementing Intermediate Sanctions

Although the use of intermediate sanctions has spread rapidly, three major questions have emerged about their implementation: (1) Which agencies should implement the sanctions? (2) Which offenders should be admitted to these programs? (3) Will the "community corrections net" widen as a result of these policies so that more people will come under correctional supervision?

As in any public-service organization, administrative politics play an ongoing role in corrections. In many states, agencies compete for the additional funding needed to run the programs. The traditional agencies of community corrections,

446 **PART FOUR** • CORRECTIONS

such as probation offices, could receive the funding, or the new programs could be contracted out to nonprofit organizations. Probation organizations argue that they know the field, have the experienced staff, and—given the additional resources—could do an excellent job. They correctly point out that a great many offenders sentenced to intermediate sanctions are also on probation. Those critical of giving this role to probation services argue that the established agencies are not receptive to innovation. They say that probation agencies place a high priority on the traditional supervision function and would not actively help clients solve their problems.

The different types of offenders who receive intermediate sanctions prompt a second issue in the implementation debate. One school of thought emphasizes the seriousness of the offense; the other focuses on the problems of the offender.

If categorized by the seriousness of their offense, offenders may receive such close supervision that they will not be able to abide by the sentence. Sanctions for serious offenders may accumulate to include, for example, probation, drug testing, addiction treatment, and home confinement. As the number of sentencing conditions increases, even the most willing probationers find fulfilling every one of them difficult.

Some agencies want to accept into their intermediate sanctions program only those offenders who *will* succeed. These agencies are concerned about their success rate, especially because of threats to future funding if the program does not reduce recidivism. Critics point out that this strategy leads to "creaming"—taking the most promising offenders and leaving those with worse problems to traditional sanctions.

The third issue concerns **net widening**, a process in which the new sanction increases the control over offenders' lives, rather than reducing it. This can occur when a judge imposes a more intrusive sentence than is usual. For example, rather than merely giving an offender probation, the judge might also require that he or she perform community service. Critics of intermediate sanctions in this regard argue that they have created the following:

net widening Process in which new sentencing options increase rather than reduce control over offenders' lives.

- *Wider nets* Reforms increase the proportion of individuals in society whose behavior is regulated or controlled by the state.
- *Stronger nets* By intensifying the state's intervention powers, reforms augment the state's capacity to control individuals.
- *Different nets* Reforms transfer jurisdictional authority from one agency or control system to another.

Some have advocated intermediate sanctions as a less costly alternative to incarceration and a more effective alternative to probation. But how have such sanctions been working in that regard? Significant questions still remain to be answered about whether such programs reduce recidivism, especially as states vary in their enforcement of rule violations (Tonry & Lynch, 1996; Pew Center on the States, 2011). With incarceration rates still at record highs and probation caseloads increasing, intermediate sanctions will probably play a major role in corrections through the next decade of this century.

CHECK POINT

4. **What is the main argument for intermediate sanctions?**
   Judges need a range of sentencing options that are less restrictive than prison and more restrictive than simple probation.

5. **How does intensive supervision probation differ from traditional probation?**
   In ISP, the offender is required to make stricter and more-frequent reporting to an officer who carries a much smaller caseload than is typical.

6. **What are three problems in the implementation of intermediate sanctions?**
   Deciding which agencies should implement the sanctions, deciding which offenders should be admitted to these programs, and possibly widening the "community corrections net."

STOP & ANALYZE

If the contemporary government budget crisis leads states and counties to make a genuine commitment to expanding intermediate sanctions, what will be the consequences for society? List three likely outcomes.

The Future of Community Corrections

In 1995, there were 3.7 million Americans under community supervision; by 2014, this figure stood at 4.7 million (Kaeble, Maruschak, & Bonczar, 2015). Despite this growth, community corrections does not always enjoy firm public support. Community corrections can suffer from the image of being "soft on crime." Moreover, news stories about probationers and offenders on home confinement committing serious crimes can reduce public support when community corrections is perceived to threaten public safety (Weiner, 2013a).

Community corrections also faces the challenge that many offenders today require close supervision. The crimes, criminal records, and drug problems of many offenders are worse than those of lawbreakers of earlier eras. Fifty-six percent of the offenders on probation in 2014 had been convicted of felonies, and 19 percent were guilty of violent felonies (Kaeble, Maruschak, & Bonczar, 2015). Those people are supervised by probation officers whose caseloads can number in the hundreds. Such officers, and their counterparts in parole who will be discussed in Chapter 13, cannot readily provide effective supervision and services to all their clients.

Community corrections is burdened by even greater caseload pressures than in the past. With responsibility for about three-fourths of all offenders under correctional supervision, community corrections needs an infusion of resources. For community corrections to succeed, the public must support it. However, such support will come only if citizens believe that offenders are receiving appropriate punishments.

Citizens must realize that policies designed to punish offenders in the community yield not mere "slaps on the wrists" but meaningful sanctions, even while these policies allow offenders to retain ties to their families and reconnect with society. Joan Petersilia argues that long-term investments in community corrections will pay off for the offender and the community. While acknowledging the need for prisons to house violent offenders with no inclination to change, she says, "we need to invest heavily in helping offenders who are not yet steeped in criminal behavior and wish to chart a different path. Sending someone to prison should be our last resort—it is expensive, it is stigmatizing, and it can increase risk for future criminal behavior" (Pew Center on the States, 2007).

A QUESTION OF ETHICS

Think, Discuss, Write

During the first two months of 2016, there were disheartening news reports about probation officers in states such as Ohio, Arkansas, Connecticut, and Louisiana being arrested or convicted for taking bribes. The Ohio probation officer admitted accepting money to falsify repots on probationers. In Connecticut, the probation officer asked for money in exchange for recommending to judges that offenders' periods of probation be shortened. In late 2015, a Massachusetts probation officer was convicted of lying to law enforcement officers who were investigating whether probationers were being treated properly. Probation officers elsewhere have also been convicted of falsifying drug test results, providing information to drug traffickers, and overlooking probation violations.

Like other officials in the criminal justice system, probation officers work independently on a wide range of tasks. They use their discretion to make decisions, including those that can have significant impact on others' lives, such as recommending the revocation of probation. Thus, probation officers,

like police officers and corrections officers, need to be professional, ethical, and educated as they make discretionary decisions and perform important tasks without anyone directly supervising each moment of their day. Obviously, probation officers need to act professionally and treat probationers fairly, taking care to avoid any improper discrimination when making decisions. They must also avoid the temptation to accept money or favors from people who want to avoid fulfilling all of the requirements of a community corrections sentence.

Discussion/Writing Assignment

Even if we cannot prevent unlawful behavior by all probation officers, what can be done to reduce the problems illustrated by the foregoing cases? Better selection of candidates for probation officer positions? Better training? Better supervision? Develop four recommendations to help guard against unethical behavior by probation officers.

SUMMARY

1 **Name the philosophical assumptions that underlie community corrections.**

- Community corrections is based on four assumptions: (1) Many offenders' crimes do not warrant incarceration. (2) Community supervision is cheaper than incarceration. (3) Recidivism is no greater for those under community supervision than for those who go to prison. (4) Ex-inmates require both support and supervision when they return to the community.
- Community supervision through probation, intermediate sanctions, and parole is a growing part of the criminal justice system.

2 **Describe how probation evolved and how probation sentences are implemented today.**

- Probation evolved as a humanitarian effort to allow first-time and minor offenders a second chance.
- Probation is imposed on more than half of offenders. People with this sentence live in the community according to conditions set by the judge and under the supervision of a probation officer.

3 **Describe intermediate sanctions, and give examples of how they are administered.**

- Intermediate sanctions are designed as punishments that are more restrictive than probation and less restrictive than prison.

- The range of intermediate sanctions allows judges to design sentences that incorporate one or more of these punishments.
- Some intermediate sanctions are implemented by courts (fines, restitution, forfeiture), others in the community (home confinement, community service, day reporting centers, intensive supervision probation), and others in institutions and the community (boot camps).

4 **Identify the key issues faced by community corrections at the beginning of the twenty-first century.**

- Despite its growth and the necessity amid budget cuts and efforts to reduce the high costs of imprisonment, community sanctions often lack public support.
- Many offenders today require closer supervision with attendant higher costs.
- The use of community corrections is expected to grow in the twenty-first century in spite of the problems of implementing these sanctions.

Questions for Review

1. What is the aim of community corrections?
2. What is the nature of probation, and how is it organized?
3. What is the purpose of intermediate sanctions?
4. What are the primary forms of intermediate sanctions?
5. Why is net widening a concern?

Key Terms

boot camp (p. 445)

community justice (p. 429)

community service (p. 442)

day reporting center (p. 443)

fine (p. 438)

forfeiture (p. 439)

home confinement (p. 441)

intensive supervision probation (ISP) (p. 443)

net widening (p. 447)

recidivism (p. 427)

restitution (p. 438)

technical violation (p. 431)

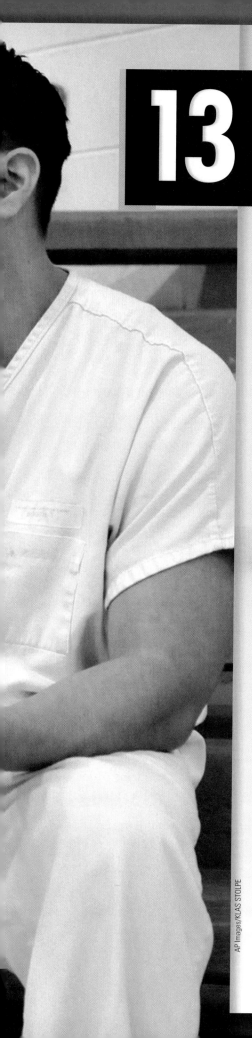

13 Reentry into the Community

LEARNING OBJECTIVES

1 Describe the nature of the "reentry problem."

2 Explain the origins of parole and how it operates today.

3 Name and define the mechanisms for the release of felons to the community.

4 Describe how ex-offenders are supervised in the community.

5 Identify the problems that parolees face during their reentry.

The excited looks on the men's faces highlighted the special quality of the occasion. As a group, with their tattoos, scars, and lined faces, they did not call to mind the image of a graduating class. However, with hugs from family members and congratulatory handshakes from corrections officials, they had reason to bask in a moment of accomplishment and optimism—despite the harsh and uncertain reality of the difficulties they would face in finding jobs and reentering society. Through an initiative at the Orleans Parish Prison in New Orleans, these offenders had completed a 10-week course on job skills, self-development, and behavior, intended to help them succeed as they neared release from incarceration. Fifty-two-year-old J. C. Alford, who had been in and out of prison since 1977, noted that it was the first time that anyone cared about whether or not he would succeed in society after being released (Chang, 2012).

The New Orleans program is just one example of the rapidly expanding effort to address the fact that many offenders released from prison will simply end up right back in the criminal justice system if they do not have any preparation and support in their effort to reenter society successfully (Ferner, 2015). Reentry initiatives do not stop with prerelease education programs; they can also involve community corrections centers where released offenders can go to seek clothing, assistance in finding jobs and housing, and access to counseling, as at the Partners Reentry Center in Anchorage, Alaska. The Anchorage center is a joint project of several nonprofit organizations that receive government grants and private contributions (Boots, 2013).

Newspaper headlines regularly remind us about the risks posed by offenders who are released from prison: "Parolee Arrested Again on Drug Trafficking Charges" (*Central Kentucky News*, 2015); "Police: Parolee Arrested after 1 Adult, 2 Kids Stabbed" (Greenwood & Fournier, 2015); "Parolee Arrested for Attempted Murder of Acquaintance Made while in Prison" (*Salt Lake Tribune*, 2015). With more than 600,000 people released from state and federal prisons each year, such events can make people understandably fearful about the return of convicted offenders to society. Yet society must become ready for the return of these offenders and, more importantly, have developed programs to prepare these offenders for successful reentry into the community. Only a small percentage of imprisoned offenders are serving life sentences, as illustrated by a description of the Montana Women's Prison: "Only one inmate . . . is currently serving a life sentence. That means at some point roughly 265 offenders will be released back into society" (Wooley, 2011). Reentry issues are an inevitable component of the corrections process, and they have become more pressing as budget crises push states to reduce prison populations by moving offenders back into society more quickly.

Offenders who leave prison, either under parole supervision or after the completion of their sentences, face serious difficulties. Many of them were never successful in mainstream society prior to incarceration, so they are in great need of education and job training, as well as reorientation about values and proper behavior. Moreover, many offenders will be returning to the community environment in which their problems with drugs and alcohol began, and may be renewed. These newly released individuals will seek jobs in a slowly recovering economy that makes finding jobs difficult even for those who do not have criminal records. If their criminal record does not stop employers from considering them as employees, their limited education and employment experience will still make it hard for them to compete with other job applicants.

AP Images/KLAS STOLPE

Many offenders stumble when they initially reenter society by failing to obey their conditions of parole, returning to drug use, or quitting education and job-training programs. Some of these offenders overcome these missteps, perhaps after a stint in jail awakens them to the looming prospect of a return to prison, but many fail, and are returned to prison for parole violations or the commission of new crimes. Given the expense of incarceration—$32,000 per year for each imprisoned offender in Pennsylvania, for example—it is in society's interest to find ways to reduce the number returned to prison. Yet reentry programs are not available for all offenders as they near their release dates.

The resurgence in interest on reentry is highlighted by the fact that the U.S. Department of Justice announced that it was designating a week during April 2016 as "National Reentry Week" (Lynch, 2016). Apparently, the purpose of the designation was to increase public awareness about the new emphasis on reentry and to encourage corrections officials to devote additional time and attention to the effort. According to U.S. Attorney General Loretta Lynch, "we are asking the Bureau of Prisons to coordinate reentry events at their facilities across the country—from job fairs, to practice interviews, to mentorship programs, to events for children of incarcerated parents—designed to help prepare inmates for release" (Lynch, 2016). Federal prosecutors were also instructed to coordinate events to emphasize the importance of creating job opportunities and support systems for ex-prisoners reentering society.

In this chapter, we discuss the many problems facing parolees as they reenter society. In addition, we examine the mechanisms by which prisoners are released from incarceration as well as their supervision in the community.

Prisoner Reentry

Reentry has been described as a "transient state between liberty and recommitment" (A. Blumstein & Beck, 2005:50). It is a limited period of supervision during which an inmate either moves to full liberty in the community or returns to prison for committing a new crime or for violating the terms of parole. Prisoner reentry has become an important public issue. As indicated in "What Americans Think," surveys indicate support for a greater emphasis on rehabilitation and the removal of barriers that hinder released prisoners from finding employment.

In 2011, in response to the increasing recognition of the importance of the issue, then U.S. Attorney General Eric Holder established the Federal Interagency Reentry Council, made up of the leaders of 20 federal agencies, to create a comprehensive plan to address the full range of issues and problems related to prisoner reentry. In the words of Attorney General Holder (2013),

> After all, we know reentry is not just a matter of public safety—it's also an issue of housing and health care policy; a question of education and employment; and a fatherhood and family challenge that affects millions across the country every year.

Holder described the work of the Federal Interagency Reentry Council by saying, "We're calling attention to successful programs, striving to dispel myths about reentry, strengthening our policies, and engaging with an expanding group of allies to advance this comprehensive work." As indicated by the attorney general's statements, there are now increased efforts to address a wide range of issues that may affect successful reentry and to coordinate efforts among agencies at different levels of government. As mentioned previously, this effort continued with Holder's successor, Attorney General Loretta Lynch, who was a key figure in initiating National Reentry Week in 2016 (Lynch, 2016).

The sudden flood of offenders leaving prison—of whom more than 40 percent may return to prison, because of either a new crime or a parole violation—raises serious questions as to how the criminal justice system should deal with the reentry of ex-felons (Carson & Golinelli, 2013b). Moreover, the ones who avoid a return to prison need significant initial help with respect to housing, employment, and other factors that affect their ability to support themselves and live successfully in a free society. What is the crux of the problem?

Jeremy Travis and Joan Petersilia (2001) point to several factors contributing to the reentry problem. They argue that, beginning in the 1970s, the power of parole boards to make release decisions was abolished in mandatory release states and severely restricted in discretionary release states. This means that more inmates are automatically leaving prison, ready or not, when they meet the requirements of their sentence. It also means that there has been little or no prerelease planning to ensure that the new parolee has a job, housing, and a supportive family when he or she hits the streets.

A second factor they believe contributes to the reentry problem is the uneven commitment of resources for prison education, job training, and other rehabilitation programs designed to prepare inmates for their return to the community. States

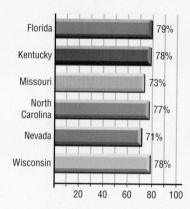

WHAT AMERICANS THINK

QUESTION: Should the main goal of our criminal justice system be to rehabilitate criminals so they can become productive, law-abiding citizens? (percent of those polled who say yes, by state)

State	Percent
Florida	79%
Kentucky	78%
Missouri	73%
North Carolina	77%
Nevada	71%
Wisconsin	78%

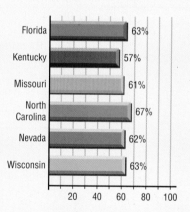

QUESTION: Should the federal government remove barriers that make it more difficult for released prisoners to find jobs? (percent of those polled who say yes, by state)

State	Percent
Florida	63%
Kentucky	57%
Missouri	61%
North Carolina	67%
Nevada	62%
Wisconsin	63%

Source: U.S. Justice Action Network, "Surveys of Voter Attitudes on Criminal Justice Reform in FL, NC, NV, KY, MO & WI," January 2016 (www.justiceactionnetwork.org).

developed programs in an effort to reduce expensive prison populations, but across-the-board budget cuts since the national financial crisis of 2008 often created pressure to cut funding for all aspects of corrections, including reentry programs (Bousequet, 2012a).

Finally, Travis and Petersilia note that the profile of returning prisoners has changed in ways that pose new challenges to successful reentry. In particular, the conviction offense and time served differ from what they were 20 years ago. Now, more than a third of prisoners released to parole are incarcerated for a drug offense—up from 12 percent in 1985. The average time served has also increased by almost six months since 1990. Further, some drug and violent offenders are exiting prison after very long terms, perhaps 20 or more years—a long time to have lived apart from family and friends.

Many have expressed concern regarding how the corrections system prepares prisoners to live as law-abiding citizens. Successful prisoner reentry requires that parole and post-release services focus on linking offenders with community institutions—

churches, families, self-help groups, and nonprofit programs. Research indicates that the prisoners most likely to succeed in the job market are those who had work experience prior to prison, were connected to employers prior to release, and had conventional family relationships (Visher, Debus-Sherill, & Yahner, 2011). Many prisoners do not have these assets as they exit prison. Thus, efforts must be made to improve their chances for success in free society. According to Joan Petersilia (2003), because public safety and neighborhood stability depend on successful reentry, communities must share with corrections officials the responsibility for transitioning offenders to the community.

Contemporary Budget Cuts and Prisoner Release

The economic recession of 2008 and its lingering aftermath produced a drop in employment rates and created difficulties for many American businesses and families. When the incomes of families fall and businesses are less profitable, the government receives less tax revenue to fund needed programs, including corrections. Because incarceration is such an expensive form of punishment, with states and counties paying $25,000 or more annually to cover the costs of holding each prisoner in a secure facility, government officials began to rethink sentencing policies that had caused prison populations to skyrocket since the 1980s. In particular, they gave consideration to greater utilization of probation and community corrections for nonviolent and drug offenders. In addition, many states sought ways to reduce their prison populations by accelerating the release into the community of nondangerous offenders and those nearing the completion of their sentences. For example, Michigan, a state with budget problems stemming from one of the nation's highest unemployment rates, reduced its prison population from a peak of 51,554 in March 2007 to 43,359 in December 2014 (Carson, 2015; Deng, 2012). The reductions enabled the state to save money by closing several prisons. These developments were facilitated in part by Michigan's effort to develop reentry programs that would help prisoners become prepared to move back into the community (Pew Center, 2011).

Such efforts to reduce prison populations can be affected by continuing budget difficulties that lead to cuts in reentry programs, thereby diminishing the state's ability to prepare offenders for effective reentry. In 2014, Michigan cut its budget for reentry programs by 37 percent (Ruiter, 2014). Kansas cut funding for its reentry programs by nearly 50 percent between 2009 and 2013, raising concerns from officials at the state's department of corrections that short-sighted cuts would increase overall expenses as released offenders ended up back in prison (Marso, 2014). Those state budget cuts often terminate programs and reduce services that help to prepare early release prisoners for reentry into society. Congress has sought to counteract funding problems through the federal Second Chance Act that provides grants to states and localities for the development of reentry programs since 2008. For example, when annual awards were announced under this law in October 2015, 45 jurisdictions around the country received grants totaling $53 million (U.S. Department of Justice, 2015).

Institutional Reentry Preparation Programs

Most of this chapter discusses post-release community corrections, especially issues involving parole. However, states are increasingly developing programs within prisons as the first step to begin offenders' preparation for reentry. States have also experimented with the creation of specific correctional institutions dedicated to preparing offenders for reentering society so that they can spend the last portion of their sentences in a special prison among other prisoners who are also focused on taking classes to prepare for release. Some correctional officials argue that preparation for reentry should begin at an even earlier point in the prison sentence. As one prison warden said,

> Instead of waiting until the last few months, or when we know they had parole, to start this re-entry, we're trying to start the day they come in [to the prison]. I want you to start looking at what do you need to do here to prepare yourself when you go. We try to get that into their minds immediately. (Wooley, 2011)

In 2011, the Pew Center on the States issued a report entitled *State of Recidivism: The Revolving Door of America's Prisons*, which noted that nationwide, a consistent percentage of offenders—40 percent—was reimprisoned within three years of release. This percentage remained steady throughout the study period of 1999–2007 (Pew Center, 2011). The Pew Center report pointed out that the recidivism rate actually varied by state and that some states had seen declines in recidivism even as the national rate hovered at the same level. After examining the various approaches taken by the states, one of the Pew Center report's recommendations was to "begin preparation for release at time of prison admission" (Pew Center, 2011).

The report highlighted the need to see the period of imprisonment as a time in which efforts can be made to address offenders' problems and needs. This is contrary to the traditional practice of using prisons for custody, a practice that typically gives little attention to preparing inmates for reentry into the community at the time of release. The recommendation does not advocate treating offenders as "victims of society" who deserve attention and care; rather, it reflects the practical recognition that society benefits from thinking in advance about the reality that most offenders will eventually be released back into the community. Critics of the prison system have raised this question: If we treat offenders as "monsters" while they are in prison, shouldn't we expect that they will inevitably affect society by acting as "monsters" when they again live among us?

South Carolina, Florida, Indiana, and other states have developed reentry preparation programs within prisons to assist offenders with the transition back to society. These programs are often in special facilities and involve individuals spending a specific period of months in the programs just prior to release. At Michigan's Detroit Reentry Center, for example, many prerelease offenders spend time preparing for parole at a low-security facility only a few minutes from downtown Detroit. In a building once used by Daimler Chrysler to store automobiles, they attend sessions that include reading skills and training for jobs. About 200 volunteers assist by providing faith-based programming to inmates (Michigan Department of Corrections, 2015). By establishing these programs, criminal justice officials are acknowledging that successful reentry depends not only on gaining employment but also on having sufficient knowledge about finances and asset management to use money wisely for expenses and family responsibilities (Martin, 2011).

The concept of prerelease facilities and programs has gained the support of those people, including legislators, who recognize that society benefits in many ways, including cost savings, when it helps offenders avoid a return to the expensive environment of prison. In 2012, the Florida Department of Corrections announced that it would close two reentry facilities as part of an effort to solve a $79 million budget deficit. Closing the centers would result in cutting 300 prisoners from job-training and life-skills courses and returning them to the general inmate population at other prisons. State legislators and newspaper editorial writers complained that it was shortsighted to target reentry programs for cuts. They argued that in closing the two centers, the short-term budget savings would amount to only $1 million, which would barely affect the overall corrections budget deficit. Ultimately, the political pressure and public outcry led Florida's corrections officials to decide to keep the reentry facilities in operation (Bousquet, 2012a, 2012b).

CHECK POINT

1. **How have government budget problems contributed to challenges in prisoner reentry?**

   States seek to reduce expensive prison populations, yet continuing budget difficulties can hamper efforts to develop and sustain programs to facilitate offenders' successful return to society.

STOP & ANALYZE

Take note of Professor Petersilia's argument that communities must share with corrections officials the responsibility for transitioning offenders into society. What are two things that community members can do to help parolees stay away from criminal activities and succeed in reentry?

Release and Supervision

parole The conditional release of an inmate from incarceration, under supervision, after part of the prison sentence has been served.

On average, fewer than 7 percent of inmates die in prison; the rest are eventually released to live in the community. Currently about 77 percent of felons will be released on parole and will remain under correctional supervision for a specific period. About 19 percent will be released at the expiration of their sentence, having "maxed out" and earned the freedom to live in the community without supervision.

Parole is the *conditional* release of an offender from incarceration but not from the legal custody of the state. Thus, offenders who comply with parole conditions and do not have further conflict with the law receive an absolute discharge from supervision at the end of their sentences. If a parolee breaks a rule, parole can be revoked and the person can be returned to a correctional facility. Parole rests on three concepts:

1. *Grace* The prisoner could be kept incarcerated, but the government extends the privilege of release.
2. *Contract* The government enters into an agreement with the prisoner whereby the prisoner promises to abide by certain conditions in exchange for being released.
3. *Custody* Even though the offender is released from prison, she or he remains a responsibility of the government. Parole is an extension of correctional programs into the community.

Only felons are released on parole; adult misdemeanants are usually released immediately after they have finished serving their sentences. Today about 857,000 people are under parole supervision, a fourfold increase since 1980 (Kaeble, Glaze, et al., 2015).

The Origins of Parole

Parole in the United States evolved during the nineteenth century from the English, Australian, and Irish practices of conditional pardon, apprenticeship by indenture, transportation of criminals from one country to another, and issuance of "tickets of leave." These were all methods of moving criminals out of prison as a response to overcrowding, unemployment, and the cost of incarceration.

A key figure in developing the concept of parole in the nineteenth century was Captain Alexander Maconochie, an administrator of British penal colonies in Tasmania and elsewhere in the South Pacific. A critic of definite prison terms, Maconochie devised a system of rewards for good conduct, labor, and study. Under his classification procedure, prisoners could pass through stages of increasing responsibility and freedom: (1) strict imprisonment, (2) labor on government chain gangs, (3) freedom within a limited area, (4) a ticket of leave or parole resulting in a conditional pardon, and (5) full restoration of liberty. Like modern correctional practices, this procedure assumed that prisoners should be prepared gradually for release. The roots of the American system of parole lie in the transition from imprisonment to conditional release to full freedom.

Maconochie's idea of requiring prisoners to earn their early release caught on first in Ireland. There Sir Walter Crofton built on Maconochie's idea to link an offender's progress in prison to a "ticket of leave." Prisoners who graduated through Crofton's three successive levels of treatment were released on parole under a series of conditions. Most significant was the requirement that parolees submit monthly reports to the police. In Dublin, a special civilian inspector helped releasees find jobs, visited them periodically, and supervised their activities.

The Development of Parole in the United States

In the United States, parole developed during the prison reform movement of the latter half of the nineteenth century. Relying on the ideas of Maconochie and Crofton,

American reformers such as Zebulon Brockway of the Elmira State Reformatory in New York began to experiment with the concept of parole. After New York adopted indeterminate sentences in 1876, Brockway started to release prisoners on parole. Under the new sentencing law, prisoners could be released when their conduct showed they were ready to return to society. This idea spread, so that 20 states had parole systems by 1900, and 44 states and the federal government had them by 1932 (Friedman, 1993). Today every state has some procedure for the release of offenders before the end of their sentences.

Although it has been used in the United States for more than a century, parole remains controversial. To many people, parole allows convicted offenders to avoid serving the full sentence they deserve. The public hue and cry following commission of a particularly heinous act by a parolee creates pressure for authorities to limit release. For example, when two parolees in Michigan were accused of committing home invasions and murdering a senior citizen, media attention and public outcry contributed to an audit of prisoner release programs, a report criticizing aspects of parole supervision, and the suspensions of two parole officials (Martindale, 2012). On the other hand, public officials are obligated to balance shrinking corrections budgets, so they feel countervailing pressures to find ways to reduce the number of offenders in prison through increased parole releases.

CHECK POINT

2. **In what countries did the concept of parole first develop?**
   England, Australia, Ireland.

STOP & ANALYZE

If you were placed in charge of a state's parole system, what are three steps that you would take to diminish the likelihood that parolees would commit crimes?

Release Mechanisms

From 1920 to 1973, there was a nationwide sentencing and release policy. During this period, all states and the federal government used indeterminate sentencing, authorized discretionary release by parole boards, and supervised prisoners after release—and they did this all in the interest of the rehabilitation of offenders.

With the 1970s came critiques of rehabilitation along with a move to determinate sentencing and the public's view that the system was "soft" on criminals. By 2002, the federal government and 16 states had abolished discretionary release by parole boards. Another 5 states had abolished discretionary parole for certain offenses (Petersilia, 2003). Further, in some of the states that kept discretionary release, parole boards were reluctant to grant it.

There are now four basic mechanisms for people to be released from prison: (1) expiration release, (2) mandatory release, (3) other conditional release, and (4) discretionary release. Figure 13.1 shows the percentage of felons released by the various mechanisms.

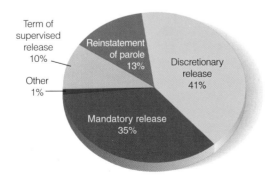

Term of supervised release 10%
Reinstatement of parole 13%
Other 1%
Discretionary release 41%
Mandatory release 35%

FIGURE 13.1

Methods of Release from State Prison
Felons are released from prison to the community, usually under parole supervision, through various means depending on the law.

Source: L. Maruschak and T. Bonczar, "Probation and Parole in the United States, 2012," *Bureau of Justice Statistics Bulletin,* December 2013, p. 8.

Expiration Release

expiration release The release of an inmate from incarceration, without further correctional supervision; the inmate cannot be returned to prison for any remaining portion of the sentence for the current offense.

An increasing percentage of prisoners receive an **expiration release**. As noted earlier, such offenders have served the maximum court sentence, minus good time—in other words, they have "maxed out." These inmates are released from any further correctional supervision, and cannot be returned to prison for their current offense, because they are not on parole and therefore not subject to parole restrictions.

Mandatory Release

mandatory release The required release of an inmate from incarceration to community supervision upon the expiration of a certain period, as specified by a determinate sentencing law or parole guidelines.

Mandatory release occurs after an inmate has served time equal to the total sentence minus good time, if any, or to a certain percentage of the total sentence as specified by law. Mandatory release is found in federal jurisdictions and states with determinate sentences and "good time" provisions (see Chapter 9). Without a parole board to make discretionary decisions, mandatory release is a matter of bookkeeping to check the correct amount of good time and other credits and make sure the sentence has been accurately interpreted. The prisoner is conditionally released to parole supervision for the rest of the sentence.

Other Conditional Release

other conditional release A term used in some states to avoid the rigidity of mandatory release by placing convicts in various community settings, under supervision.

Because of the growth of prison populations, many states have devised ways to get around the rigidity of mandatory release by placing inmates in the community through furloughs, home supervision, halfway houses, emergency release, and other programs (Linke & Ritchie, 2004). These types of other conditional release also avoid the appearance of the politically sensitive label "discretionary parole."

Circumstances may also arise in which prison officials use their discretion to release offenders early instead of going through the usual parole process. In order to close a budget deficit in 2002, Montana corrections officials released nonviolent offenders early from prison and placed them under the supervision of community corrections authorities. An important study of the results of that release showed that those offenders who received this conditional release from prison, instead of going through the usual parole decision process, had higher levels of recidivism (Wright & Rosky, 2011). As in other states, a significant portion of admissions to prison in Montana are composed of offenders returning to prison for violating conditions of release or for committing new crimes while under the supervision of community corrections. According to Wright and Rosky (2011:901), "Montana, in particular, experienced a significant increase in the annual 3-year recidivism rate as a result of the early release program."

Thus, when undertaking conditional releases, states need to be aware of preparing prisoners for release and of the supervision capabilities of community corrections officials. Inadequate preparation and oversight may result in returning many offenders to the expensive environment of imprisonment, thereby undercutting the intended financial benefits of reducing prison populations through this mechanism.

The situation faced by Montana is reflected in larger debates about the proper course of action, just as it reflected specific debates within Montana itself. As the authors of the study observed, "Not surprisingly, a public battle among [the Montana Department of Corrections] and legislators, judges, and prosecutors ensued over the appropriateness of the early release program in Montana" (Wright & Rosky, 2011:887). Although there has been a growing consensus among liberal and conservative politicians alike about rethinking the costs of using incarceration to punish nonviolent offenders (Savage, 2011b), there are debates about the wisdom of releasing prisoners as opposed to a more gradual approach of simply changing sentencing policies as they affect certain offenders ("Our View," 2011; Mauer, 2011). As you read "The Policy Debate" on this issue, consider which side has the more compelling argument.

Litigation can create pressure on states with overcrowded prisons to step up releases outside the usual parole process, on the grounds that the overcrowding causes constitutional violations. In the provisions of the Prison Litigation Reform Act of 1996, Congress attempted to limit the ability of judges to order the release

THE POLICY DEBATE

Should Prison Populations Be Reduced through the Accelerated Release of Offenders?

States throughout the country currently face budget pressures, and their tax revenues remain uncertain while the national economy is slowly recovering from the recession of 2008. Because incarceration is an especially expensive form of punishment, with each imprisoned offender costing the state tens of thousands of dollars each year, many state governments have sought to reduce their prison populations through accelerated releases.

For Accelerated Release of Offenders

Those who support the accelerated release of offenders find fault in the overuse of expensive incarceration during the past three decades. They point to the many nonviolent and drug offenders who, through needlessly long prison sentences, have had no hope of being rehabilitated or of regaining a productive place in the community. As a result of these long incarcerations, families and specific neighborhoods suffered financial declines and devastation that affected children, as well as the quality of life in those communities. Moreover, taxpayers paid needlessly high bills for expensive punishments when cheaper approaches within the community would have been a more effective mechanism to simultaneously punish offenders as well as to support and guide their reentry into the community.

The arguments for accelerating the release of offenders from prison include these:

- Imprisonment has been overused as a punishment for thousands of nonviolent offenders.
- State budget difficulties require the immediate reduction of prison populations in favor of less expensive approaches to punishment within the community.
- Moving offenders from prison to community settings or granting them early release will assist in their

successful reentry into the community and permit them to reestablish relationships with family members, thereby providing support to children and needed contributions to their families' financial support.
- Community-based programs are more effective than prison-based programs in rehabilitating offenders.

Against Accelerated Release of Offenders

Opponents of accelerated release worry that offenders released early from prison are likely to commit new crimes or otherwise violate the conditions of their release. They also worry that the focus on saving money through releases often outweighs careful examination of which offenders should be released, and that many of those released will not be ready for life in the community.

The arguments against accelerated release of offenders include these:

- Excessive focus on saving money through accelerated prison releases can lead to inadequate evaluation of early release candidates and insufficient supervision of these offenders once they are in the community.
- Because studies present evidence of troubling recidivism rates in many states, the release of offenders places citizens under unnecessary risk of crime victimization from these offenders who would otherwise be behind bars.
- Early releases mean that some offenders do not receive appropriately severe punishments for their crimes.
- Community-based programs have not proven their effectiveness in lowering the recidivism rates of those offenders released early from prison.

What Should U.S. Policy Be?

The massive increase in incarceration since the 1980s has been very costly

in both financial and human terms. Because of budget pressures, states have accelerated efforts to reduce their prison populations, including the use of early release for many offenders. Have enough resources been devoted to community programs for us to feel confident that society is prepared to assist in the reentry of increasing numbers of released offenders? Do persistent recidivism rates in many states indicate that the releases pose risks to society? Alternatively, do recidivism rates merely show that some states have not prepared adequate programs for education and supervision of offenders released from prison? Does the weight of budget pressures lead policy makers to engage in wishful thinking about the effectiveness of less expensive community corrections?

Researching the Internet

To see the 2011 report *State of Recidivism: The Revolving Door of America's Prisons* issued by the Pew Center on the States, visit the Center's website at http://www .pewtrusts.org/en/research-and -analysis/reports/2011/04/12/state -of-recidivism-the-revolving-door-of -americas-prisons.

Analyzing the Issue

Imagine that you and your classmates are advisors to a governor who wishes to reduce costs associated with the state's large prison population. You must develop recommendations to advise the governor on the following questions: What are the consequences of choosing not to accelerate the release of offenders? What steps could be taken to reduce the concerns expressed by the opponents of accelerated release? Provide a list of recommendations for the governor.

of prisoners by mandating that any such decisions be made by three-judge panels rather than by a single judge. However, as the Supreme Court decided with respect to overcrowding and the lack of medical services in California's prisons in *Brown v. Plata* (2011), circumstances can arise in which states may be forced to quickly and creatively find ways to reduce prison populations. Because most states are currently seeking ways to save money by reducing prison populations, the prospect for more litigation affecting releases seems unlikely during the current era.

Discretionary Release

discretionary release The release of an inmate from prison to conditional supervision at the discretion of the parole board, within the boundaries set by the sentence and the penal law.

States retaining indeterminate sentences allow **discretionary release** by the parole board within the boundaries set by the sentence and the penal law. This is a conditional release to parole supervision. This approach, as discussed in the next section, lets the board members assess the prisoner's readiness for release within the minimum and maximum terms of the sentence. In reviewing the prisoner's file and asking questions, the parole board focuses on the nature of the offense, the inmate's behavior, and his or her participation in rehabilitative programs. This process places great faith in the ability of parole board members to predict the future behavior of offenders.

The Parole Board Process

State parole boards are typically composed of citizens who are appointed for fixed terms in office by the governor. For example, the Vermont Parole Board consists of five regular members and two alternates who are appointed for three-year terms by the governor. The Texas Board of Pardons and Paroles consists of seven members who receive appointments by the governor for renewable six-year terms. The people on the Texas board include a former government official, a former probation and parole official, a former county sheriff, two former police officers, a former member of a victims' services board, and an individual with experience in education and criminal justice—who is also the spouse of a former top official in the Texas corrections system (Texas Board of Pardons and Parole, 2015).

Obviously, the members bring with them values, perspectives, and experiences that inform their judgments about whether offenders should be released on parole. It is possible that the governor's decision to appoint board members with prior connections to the criminal justice system may be an effort to ensure there is caution and skepticism about prisoners' claims of self-improvement during incarceration. The Texas structure also includes 11 commissioners, all of whom are experienced criminal justice professionals, who join with the parole board members in making decisions about parole.

Parole hearings are often brief proceedings in which board members ask questions of the prisoner who is eligible for parole. In many places, the crime victim or the victim's family are permitted to communicate with the board, in writing or in person, to express their views about the prospect of the offender's early release from prison. How much influence should crime victims have over parole decisions?

AP Images/Jessica Prokop

Parole boards are often described as if the governors' appointees sit together as they question and listen to the parole-eligible prisoner and also hear arguments from the prisoner's attorney. In fact, there are differences in the parole processes in various states. For example, parole-eligible prisoners in California, all of whom are serving life sentences, have attorneys at parole hearings, either one they have hired or one who is appointed for them. In other states, parole board members simply interview the prisoner. Elsewhere, the parole board may simply review the written file on the prisoner's progress in prison. There is no single model for what "the parole board process" looks like.

As indicated by the great increase in prison populations in the last few decades, large numbers of prisoners become parole eligible each year—too many to have hearings in front of a state's full parole board. Thus, parole processes involve hearings or interviews conducted by only a portion of a parole board, often with other members of the board making decisions based on the report written by their colleague. In some circumstances, if a panel of a board is divided on a decision, the full board may examine the records in the case and make a decision.

In California, for example, each parole hearing is conducted by a two-member panel. At least one of the two members is a "commissioner," the title used in that state for the 12 parole board members appointed by the governor. The other member is either a second commissioner or a "deputy commissioner," a state employee who works in the parole process. Immediately after the hearing, the two decision makers leave the hearing room and finalize their decision. If they disagree about whether to recommend parole, then there will be a second hearing in front of the full 12-member California Board of Parole Hearings. After a unanimous decision by the two-member panel or a vote by the full board, the decision goes to the staff of the board to make sure that there were no errors of law or fact in the process. The decision is then submitted to the governor, who can approve the parole, add a condition to the parole release, refer a panel decision to the full board, or reverse the decision to grant parole in cases of convicted murderers (California Department of Corrections and Rehabilitation, 2016).

By using only a portion of the parole board for interviews and hearings, states can conduct many interviews and hearings simultaneously. This is the only way that they can handle the large volume of cases. Texas uses a different procedure to process the 77,300 prisoners who were considered for parole in 2014. The Texas Board of Pardons and Paroles operates out of six different offices around the state, each with three-member panels composed of one board member and two "commissioners." For each parole-eligible prisoner, a parole official interviews the prisoner and writes a report before panel members review that report and the written file. If two of the three members approve, then the prisoner gains release under parole supervision (Texas Board of Pardons and Paroles, 2015).

Even small states divide their parole boards for hearings. In Wyoming, the least populous state in the country, a seven-member board sits in three-member hearing panels and conducts some hearings by telephone and video conference (Wyoming Board of Parole, 2016). In Vermont, another of the least populous states, hearings and interviews are conducted by a minimum of three of the parole board's five members and two alternates (Vermont Department of Corrections, 2016).

Parole board hearings and interviews are much less formal than court proceedings. Board members want the opportunity to ask prisoners about their crimes, their remorse, their attitudes, their disciplinary records, their participation in programs in prison, and their concrete plans for where they will live and work if they are granted parole. Prisoners are typically nervous because they do not know exactly what will be asked. They may quickly discover that the board members seem very skeptical about what they say. They may also find that board members lecture them about what they have done wrong in life and issue stern warnings to them about what will happen if they are released and then violate conditions of parole. Because board panels must necessarily schedule back-to-back-to-back interviews or hearings with numerous parole-eligible prisoners on any given day, prisoners may leave the brief encounter feeling very dissatisfied and disappointed—as if they did not have

Parole Board Member

You are a parole board member (called a "commissioner" in this state) interviewing a prisoner who was convicted of second-degree murder. As a 16-year-old, when his 14-year-old girlfriend broke up with him, he killed her and hid her body in a barrel. He was given a sentence of 22 years to life in prison. He is now in his late fifties and has been in prison for more than 37 years. He is believed to be the state's longest-serving offender convicted of second-degree murder; prisoners with good behavior convicted of the same offense typically are released on parole after 24 years. He has been denied parole on seven occasions. Each time he faced the parole board, members asked him about the details of his crime. Their questions indicated that they were troubled that, after killing his girlfriend, he pretended to help her family look for her body,

and he did not actually admit to the committing the crime until after he was convicted and had served several years in prison. After his previous unsuccessful appearance before the parole board, he appealed to a state court to ask whether the parole board members were reviewing the details of his crime rather than focusing on his admission of responsibility and good behavior in prison. The state judge ruled in his favor by saying, "A parole interview is not supposed to be a retrial. . . . This parole board based its denial of parole on commissioners' personal opinions regarding the nature of the offense, and their personal opinions regarding petitioner's behavior after he murdered the victim." The judge ordered a new hearing and barred one particular parole commissioner from participating because she had asked specific

questions about the crime at the last hearing. Now you have been appointed as the new commissioner to replace the excluded parole board member. Given that the details of the crime are known to you and contained in the offender's file, do you believe that you can make a decision about parole that excludes consideration of the details of the killing? Make a list of the questions you would ask the offender and describe what answers, if any, would lead you to support parole release. Then search the Internet to read about the case of Dempsey Hawkins in New York.

Source: Michael Wilson, "A Crime's Details Are Rehashed and Parole Is Denied, Again and Again," *New York Times*, July 3, 2015 (http://www.nytimes.com/2015/07/04 /nyregion/a-crime-rehashed-and-parole -denied-again-and-again.html?_r=0).

---

a full opportunity to explain how much their attitudes and behavior had changed since they entered prison. When a prisoner feels as if there was no complete opportunity to make a good, persuasive presentation about being reformed, he or she is likely to be highly anxious about whether the long-awaited opportunity to speak to a parole board member or panel will actually lead to release. Read "You Make the Decision" to consider the difficulty involved in making decisions on parole applications.

Crime victims have become much more important participants in the parole decision process in recent decades. Many states have victims' rights laws that require officials to keep victims informed of offenders' upcoming parole evaluations and to invite victims to provide input in the process. In California, crime victims and their families are invited to parole hearings where they are permitted to speak, or they can bring a representative to speak for them about the impact of the crime and their concerns about the offender being granted parole. Alternatively, they can submit written statements or audio or video statements for consideration by the board members. At the hearing, the victim is accompanied by a victim services representative from the state's Office of Victim and Survivor Rights and Services. A prosecutor also attends the hearing and may speak about the offender who is being considered for parole. In addition, news reporters may be permitted to attend California parole hearings (California Department of Corrections and Rehabilitation, 2016).

In Wyoming, crime victims are invited to meet with the board separately from the prisoner's hearing. Similarly, in Vermont the victim can testify prior to the scheduled appearance of the prisoner before the board. In both of these states, the interviews or hearings are held in private, and the policies about victims' participation are designed to prevent the victim from having a face-to-face encounter with the offender. By contrast, Connecticut is more like California in that the victim is invited to speak at hearings that, while not open to the public, are more available to the public in the sense that they can be recorded and broadcast on public television, just as California's hearings may be covered by the news media in some cases. In all of these states, victims have the option of submitting written statements to be added to the file that is reviewed by the board members. Read the "Close Up" on pages 464–465 for a personal account of the parole process in Michigan.

Impact of Release Mechanisms

Parole release mechanisms do more than simply determine the date at which a particular prisoner will be sent back into the community. Parole release also greatly affects other parts of the system, including sentencing, plea bargaining, and the size of prison populations.

One important effect of discretionary release is that an administrative body—the parole board—can shorten a sentence imposed by a judge. Even in states that have mandatory release, various potential reductions built into the sentence mean that the full sentence is rarely served. Good time, for example, can reduce punishment even if there is no eligibility for parole.

To understand the impact of release mechanisms on criminal punishment, we must compare the amount of time actually served in prison with the sentence specified by the judge. In most states, good time and jail time are the main factors that reduce the time actually served. On a national basis, felony inmates serve an average of two and a half years before release. Figure 13.2 shows the average time served for selected offenses.

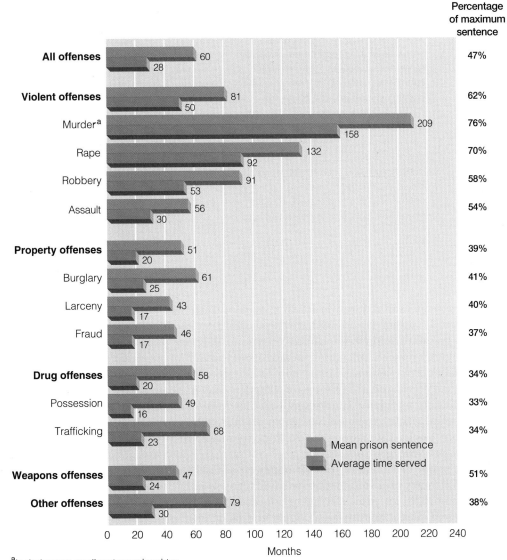

Percentage of maximum sentence

Offense	Mean prison sentence	Average time served	Percentage of maximum sentence
All offenses	60	28	47%
Violent offenses	81	50	62%
Murder[a]	209	158	76%
Rape	132	92	70%
Robbery	91	53	58%
Assault	56	30	54%
Property offenses	51	20	39%
Burglary	61	25	41%
Larceny	43	17	40%
Fraud	46	17	37%
Drug offenses	58	20	34%
Possession	49	16	33%
Trafficking	68	23	34%
Weapons offenses	47	24	51%
Other offenses	79	30	38%

Months: 0 20 40 60 80 100 120 140 160 180 200 220 240

[a]Includes non-negligent manslaughter

FIGURE 13.2

Estimated Time to Be Served by Adults Convicted of Selected Crimes The data indicate that the average felony offender going to prison for the first time spends about two years in prison. How would you expect the public to react to that fact?

Source: Thomas P. Bonczar, *National Corrections Reporting Program—Statistical Tables*, May 5, 2011, Table 9 (http://bjs.ojp.usdoj.gov/index. cfm?ty=pbdetail&iid=2174).

A Personal Encounter with the Parole Process in Michigan

Note: *Dr. Christopher Smith, one of the coauthors of this textbook, served as the "representative" for Christopher Jones (whose story of arrest and imprisonment appears in Chapter 1) at the parole board interview that ultimately led to Jones's release on parole. This is a first-person account of that process.*

I agreed to serve as the "representative" for Christopher Jones at the parole interview because I had known him and his family since he was a teenager. As an outside observer, I had seen his self-destruction through drugs and theft crimes as well as his gradual self-rehabilitation, as I corresponded with him and occasionally visited him during his 10 years behind bars. Moreover, I was grateful for his eagerness to present his story in this book so that college students could learn about the justice process through his mistakes and experiences. In Michigan, a parole interview representative is typically a family member or someone else who can vouch for the prisoner's progress and good qualities. (Unlike in California, prisoners are not represented by lawyers at these interviews.) In speaking with a former parole board member prior to

the interview, I knew that prisoners often had their mothers appear as their representatives. However, this was often counterproductive, because mothers too often made excuses for their children or displayed emotion rather than providing information that would be useful in the parole decision. Although I am trained as a lawyer, I agreed to vouch for Christopher Jones simply as person who knew him and could provide personal endorsement and information.

After spending nearly an hour in the prison's visitor waiting room, I was searched and led through several sets of locked doors to a small office. Outside of the office, I came upon a dozen or more prisoners fidgeting nervously in a long line of chairs as they waited to be called one by one into the interview room. Mr. Jones was in the first chair. He rose to greet me, and we were immediately ushered into the office together.

I had driven nearly 250 miles from Lansing, in the middle of Michigan's Lower Peninsula, to a low-security prison in the Upper Peninsula to be present for the interview. Ironically, the interview was conducted via video conference by one of the 10 members of the Michigan parole board who was

physically back in Lansing—the very place I had left the day before and to which I would return later that day. We saw him live on a television screen in the prison up north while he saw us on a screen in his office in Lansing. Video technology permits Michigan to save a substantial amount of money that previously would have been spent for the parole board members to travel to prisons throughout the state to conduct interviews.

After Mr. Jones introduced me as his representative, the parole board member introduced himself and informed me that he had many questions for Mr. Jones and that I should refrain from speaking until questions were directed to me. The parole board member noted that Mr. Jones had participated in many prison programs and that the file contained an impressive number of letters of support from family members and a minister. The board member asked Mr. Jones about his plan to live with his parents and work for his father's home inspection business. Mr. Jones was asked about how he had changed from when he committed his crimes. The board member pressed Mr. Jones about how he would

Supporters of discretion for the paroling authority argue that parole benefits the overall system. Discretionary release mitigates the harshness of the penal code. If the legislature must establish exceptionally strict punishments as a means of conveying a "tough on crime" image to frustrated and angry voters, parole can effectively permit sentence adjustments that make the punishment fit the crime. Not everyone convicted of larceny, for example, has done equivalent harm, yet some legislatively mandated sentencing schemes impose equally strict sentences. Early release on parole can be granted to an offender who is less deserving of strict punishment, such as someone who voluntarily makes restitution, cooperates with the police, or shows genuine regret.

A major criticism of discretionary release is that it shifts responsibility for many primary criminal justice decisions from a judge, who holds legal procedures uppermost, to an administrative board, where discretion rules. Judges know a great deal about constitutional rights and basic legal protections, but parole board members may not have such knowledge. Moreover, in most states with discretionary release, parole hearings are secret, with only board members, the inmate, and respond to the availability of drugs and alcohol if he was on parole back in his hometown. Predictably, Mr. Jones, who had spent years looking forward to the chance to have a parole interview, provided reassuring responses and pledged to stay away from the people, places, and substances that had been his downfall in the past. The board member spoke sternly to him about the consequences of violating the conditions of parole or committing new crimes. During this lecture, Mr. Jones nodded his head and repeatedly said, "Yes, sir, yes, sir."

Throughout the interview with Mr. Jones, I restrained myself from speaking, though I thought of many helpful things to say. When the board member turned to me to ask what information I wished to add for the board's consideration, I gave a brief endorsement of the changes that I had observed in Mr. Jones over the years he had been in prison and described his participation in education and substance-abuse recovery programs. And then the interview was over. It was obvious that the board member had many other interviews that he needed to do, so he could not spend more than 15 minutes or so on any individual interview.

I came away from the brief experience without any strong sense about what the decision would be. The interview seemed to go as well as it could have gone, but it was so short that there was not much information exchanged. Moreover, I wondered whether a parole board member could really trust reassurances from a parole-eligible prisoner, especially a former drug user, when the board member obviously knew that a notable percentage of such offenders return to drugs, violate parole conditions, or commit new crimes once back in the community. Obviously, the most significant information for the decision came from the reports and prison disciplinary records in the file. The quick interview gave the board member an opportunity to gain a brief impression of the prisoner's attitude and demeanor. Moreover, it was an opportunity to issue stern warnings to the prisoner about returning to prison for any failure to behave properly on parole. This board member's recommendation and report would be significant factors in determining whether at least two of the three board members

(including himself) assigned to the case would vote to grant parole.

Ultimately, the parole decision is shaped by impressions and judgments, not just those of the board members, but also those of the prison counselors who write evaluative reports for the file and thereby shape the impressions of the board members. No one can make an absolutely certain prediction about whether a specific prisoner will commit future violations or crimes on parole—not even the prisoner himself. The prisoner may feel determined to succeed, but he does not yet know the practical challenges of parole that await—being offered drugs, feeling frustrated by unemployment, or having conflicts with friends and family who have become, in some sense, strangers after years of separation.

For Critical Thinking and Analysis

Does this parole interview process, as described, provide enough information to make a decision about whether or not to grant parole? Should the process be changed in any way? Provide three arguments either supporting the interview process as adequate or supporting specific changes in the process.

correctional officers present. Often, no published criteria guide decisions, and prisoners receive no reason for denial or granting of parole. However, an increasing number of states permit oral or written testimony by victims and by members of the offender's family.

CHECK POINT

3. **What are the four release mechanisms for prisoners?**
Discretionary release, mandatory release, other conditional release, and expiration release.

STOP & ANALYZE

In light of the differences in parole processes used in different states, how do you see the importance (or lack thereof) of involvement by defense attorneys and crime victims in parole hearings? Do they provide helpful information about whether an offender is reformed enough for release? Provide two advantages and two risks in permitting attorneys to represent prisoners at parole hearings. Provide two advantages and two risks in allowing victims to provide input.

conditions of release Conduct restrictions that parolees must follow as a legally binding requirement of being released.

Parolees are released from prison on condition that they abide by laws and follow rules, known as **conditions of release**, designed to aid their readjustment to society and control their movement. As in probation, the parolee may be required to abstain from alcohol, keep away from undesirable associates, maintain good work habits, and not leave the state without permission. If they violate any of these conditions, they could be returned to prison to serve out the rest of their sentence. Nearly 80 percent of released prisoners are subject to some form of community supervision. Only those who have served their full sentence minus good time ("maxed out") are free from supervision.

The restrictions are justified on the grounds that people who have been incarcerated must readjust to the community so that they will not fall back into preconviction habits and associations. The strict enforcement of these rules may create problems for parolees who cannot fulfill all the demands placed on them. For example, a parolee may find it impossible to be tested for drugs, attend an Alcoholics Anonymous meeting, and work full-time while also meeting family obligations.

The day they come out of prison, parolees face a staggering array of challenges. In most states, they receive only clothes, a token amount of money, a list of rules governing their conditional release, and the name and address of the parole officer to whom they must report within 24 hours. Although a promised job is often required for release, an actual job may be another matter. Most former convicts are unskilled or semiskilled, and the conditions of release may prevent them from moving to areas where they could find work. If the parolee is African American, male, and under 30, he joins the largest demographic group of unemployed people in the country. Figure 13.3 shows the personal characteristics of parolees.

Parolees bear the added handicap of former-convict status. In most states, laws prevent former prisoners from working in certain types of establishments—where alcohol is sold, for example—thus ruling out many jobs. In some states, those who have served time are assumed to have "a lack of good moral character and trustworthiness," a condition required to acquire a license to be a barber, for example. Finally, ex-convicts face a significant dilemma. If they are truthful about their backgrounds, many employers will not hire them. If they are not truthful, they can be fired for lying if the employer ever learns about their conviction.

As they prepare for release, prisoners at this Alaska correctional facility participate in the Success Inside and Out program in which community volunteers teach them about financial, legal, and other matters that they will encounter in society. In your view, what do prisoners need to be taught in order to prepare them for a successful transition back to society?

AP Images/Juneau Empire, Klas Stolpe

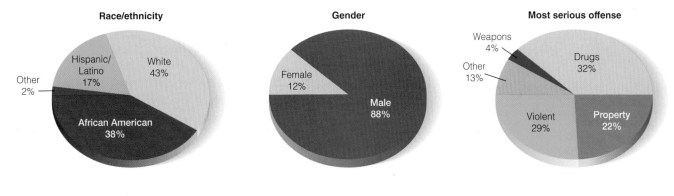

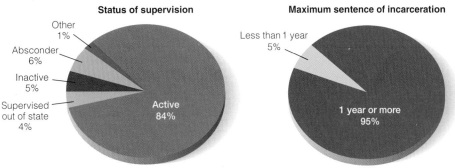

FIGURE 13.3

Personal Characteristics of Parolees Prison releasees tend to be men in their thirties who have an inadequate education and were incarcerated for a nonviolent offense.

Source: E. J. Herberman and T. P. Bonczar, "Probation and Parole in the United States, 2013," *Bureau of Justice Statistics Bulletin*, October 2014, NCJ 248029.

Other reentry problems plague parolees. For many, the transition from the highly structured life in prison to open society is too difficult to manage. Many just do not have the social, psychological, and material resources to cope with the temptations and complications of modern life. For these parolees, freedom may be short-lived, as they fall back into forbidden activities such as drinking, using drugs, and stealing.

Community Programs following Release

There are various programs to assist parolees. Some help prepare offenders for release while they are still in prison; others provide employment and housing assistance after release. Together, the programs are intended to help the offender progress steadily toward reintegration into the community. Almost all penologists agree that there should be pre- and post-release programs to assist reentry, yet many prisoners do not now participate in such programs. Although all states offer reentry programs, relatively few prisoners have access to them.

Among the many programs developed to help offenders return to the community, three are especially important: work and educational release, furloughs, and halfway houses. Although similar in many ways, each offers a specific approach to helping formerly incarcerated individuals reenter the community.

Work and Educational Release   Programs of **work and educational release**, in which inmates are released from correctional institutions during the day to work or attend school, were first established in Vermont in 1906. However, the

work and educational release
The daytime release of inmates from correctional institutions so they can work or attend school.

Many states have programs that permit offenders to participate in work release. They work at jobs in the community while living in a lower-security correctional setting, such as a halfway house. These programs ease reentry into the community. Should the government assist offenders in finding jobs?

Huber Act, passed by the Wisconsin legislature in 1913, is usually cited as the model on which such programs are based. By 1972, most states and the federal government had instituted these programs. Nonetheless, by 2002, only about one-third of prisons operated them, for fewer than 3 percent of U.S. inmates (Petersilia, 2009).

Although most work and educational release programs are justifiable in terms of rehabilitation, many correctional administrators and legislators also like them because they cost relatively little. In some states, a portion of the inmate's earnings from work outside may be deducted for room and board. One problem with these programs is that they allegedly take jobs from free citizens, a complaint often made by organized labor.

Furloughs Isolation from loved ones is one of the pains of imprisonment. Although correctional programs in many countries include conjugal visits, only a few U.S. corrections systems have used them. Many penologists view the **furlough**—the temporary release of an inmate from a correctional institution for a visit home—as a meaningful approach to inmate reintegration.

Furloughs are thought to offer an excellent means of testing an inmate's ability to cope with the larger society. Through home visits, the inmate can renew family ties and relieve the tensions of confinement. Most administrators also feel that furloughs increase prisoners' morale. The general public, however, does not always support the concept. Public outrage is inevitable if an offender on furlough commits another crime or fails to return. Correctional authorities are often nervous about using furloughs, because they fear being blamed for such incidents.

furlough The temporary release of an inmate from a correctional institution for a brief period, usually one to three days, for a visit home. Such programs help maintain family ties and prepare inmates for release on parole.

halfway house A correctional facility housing convicted felons who spend a portion of their day at work in the community but reside in the halfway house during nonworking hours.

Halfway Houses As its name implies, the **halfway house** is a transitional facility for soon-to-be-released inmates that connects them to community services, resources, and support. Usually, felons work in the community but reside in the halfway house during nonworking hours. Halfway houses range from secure institutions in the community, with programs designed to assist inmates who are preparing for release on parole, to group homes where parolees, probationers, or others diverted from the system live with minimal supervision and direction. Some halfway houses deliver special treatment services, such as programs designed to deal with alcohol, drug, or mental problems.

Residential programs face specific problems. Few neighborhoods want to host halfway houses or treatment centers for convicts. Community resistance has significantly impeded the development of community-based correctional facilities and has even forced some successful facilities to close. Many communities, often wealthier ones, have blocked the placement of halfway houses or treatment centers within their boundaries. For example, a suburban city council near Grand Rapids, Michigan, considered a new ordinance in 2012 that would limit future housing facilities for parolees to locations in the industrial area of the city

(L. Smith, 2012). Such opposition does not arise in every community, but it is a common issue ("Re-entry Services Center," 2015). One result of the NIMBY ("not in my backyard") attitude is that many centers are established in deteriorating neighborhoods inhabited by poor people, who lack the political power and resources to block unpopular programs. Think about this problem as you read "A Question of Ethics" at the end of the chapter.

Nonetheless, a survey found a striking increase in the number of community-based residential corrections facilities. Such facilities were defined as those in which 50 percent or more of residents regularly leave unaccompanied for work or study in the community, thus including halfway houses and similar programs that provide substance-abuse treatment. What was most striking about the survey was the decrease in the number of public facilities—from 297 to 221—between 2000 and 2005, at the same time that private facilities increased from 163 to 308 (Stephan, 2008). These private facilities undoubtedly rely on contracts from state governments to provide services that the state believes are less expensive in the private sector. The interesting question for contemporary times is whether, in an atmosphere of budget cuts, state governments will find money for the use of such facilities to assist in the reentry of prisoners. Budget reductions can eliminate the availability of funds for outside contracts but, alternatively, such cuts can also lead to increased reliance on private facilities if their use is viewed as means of saving money (S. Davis, 2012).

Parole Officer: Cop or Social Worker?

After release, a parolee's principal contact with the criminal justice system is the parole officer, who must provide both surveillance and assistance. Thus, parole officers are asked to play two different, some might say incompatible, roles: cop and social worker. Whereas parole was originally designed to help offenders make the transition from prison to the community, supervision has shifted ever more toward conducting surveillance, testing for drugs, monitoring curfews, and collecting restitution. Safety and security have become major issues in parole services.

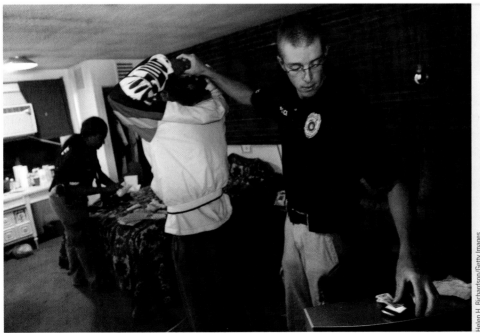

Parole officers have dual responsibilities for protecting the public from lawbreaking activities of parolees and also helping the parolee transition successfully into society. Depending on their caseloads, they may have limited ability to supervise or help each individual parolee. What training and experience would best prepare a person to become a parole officer?

Helen H. Richardson/Getty Images

The Parole Officer As Cop In their role as cop, parole officers have the power to restrict many aspects of the parolee's life, to enforce the conditions of release, and to initiate revocation proceedings if parole conditions are violated. Like other officials in the criminal justice system, the parole officer has extensive discretion in low-visibility situations. In many states, parole officers have the authority to search the parolee's house without warning; to arrest him or her, without the possibility of bail, for suspected violations; and to suspend parole pending a hearing before the board. This authoritarian component of the parole officer's role can give the ex-offender a sense of insecurity and hamper the development of mutual trust. Research has shown that a supportive orientation and style by officers can help produce positive outcomes (Morash et al., 2015).

The parole officer is responsible for seeing that the parolee follows the conditions imposed by the parole board or department of corrections. Typically, the conditions require the parolee to follow the parole officer's instructions; to permit the officer to visit the home and place of employment; to maintain employment; not to leave the state without permission; not to marry without permission; not to own a firearm; not to possess, use, or traffic in narcotics; not to consume alcohol to excess; and to comply with all laws and be a good citizen.

Parole officers are granted law enforcement powers in order to protect the community from offenders coming out of prison. However, because these powers diminish the possibility for the officer to develop a close relationship with the client, they can weaken the officer's ability to help the parolee adjust to the community.

The Parole Officer As Social Worker Parole officers must act as social workers by helping the parolee to find a job and to restore family ties. Officers channel parolees to social agencies, such as psychiatric, drug, and alcohol clinics, where they can obtain help. As caseworkers, officers try to develop a relationship that allows parolees to confide their frustrations and concerns (Blasko et al., 2015).

Because parolees may not talk honestly if they are constantly aware of the parole officer's ability to send them back to prison, some researchers have suggested that parole officers' conflicting responsibilities of cop and social worker should be separated. Parole officers could maintain the supervisory aspects of the position, and other personnel—perhaps a separate parole counselor—could perform the casework functions. Another option would be for parole officers to be charged solely with social work duties, while local police check for violations.

Because of the new emphasis on decreasing prison populations and strengthening efforts to help parolees succeed with reentry, some states have shifted the focus of their parole officers' priorities. While protection of public safety will always be a concern, there is a renewed emphasis in some places on assisting parolees with reentry rather than just monitoring them to watch for parole violations. This emphasis can result in hiring as parole officers people, such as trained social workers, who do not necessarily see law enforcement as the sole priority in their work with parolees. The increased emphasis on assisting parolees with successful reentry also leads to implementing new training programs and evaluation criteria for parole officers (Justice Policy Institute, 2010; Eckholm, 2008). The attitude of parole and law enforcement officials toward the desirability of assisting with reentry can make a big difference in the prospects for success of individual parolees (Valley, 2012).

The Parole Bureaucracy

Although parole officers have smaller caseloads than do probation officers, parolees require more-extensive services. One reason is that parolees, by the very fact of their incarceration, generally have committed more-serious crimes than those perpetrated by probationers. Another reason is that parolees must make a difficult transition from the highly structured prison environment to a society in which they have previously failed to live as law-abiding citizens. It is exceptionally difficult for a parole officer to monitor, control, and assist clients who may have little knowledge of or experience with living successfully within society's rules.

The parole officer works within a bureaucratic environment. Like most other human services organizations, parole agencies are short on resources and expertise. Because the difficulties faced by many parolees are so complex, the officer's job is almost impossible. As a result, parole officers frequently must classify parolees and give priority to those most in need. For example, most parole officers spend extra time with the newly released. As the officers gain greater confidence in the parolees, they can adjust their level of supervision to "active" or even "reduced" surveillance. Depending on how the parolees have functioned in the community, they may eventually be allowed to check in with their officers periodically instead of submitting to regular home visits, searches, and other intrusive monitoring.

Adjustment to Life outside Prison

With little preparation, the ex-offender moves from the highly structured, authoritarian life of the institution into a world filled with temptations and complicated problems. Suddenly, ex-convicts who are unaccustomed to undertaking even simple tasks, such as going to the store for groceries, are expected to assume pressing, complex responsibilities. Finding a job and a place to live are not the only problems the newly released person faces (Arditti & Parkman, 2011). Parolees no longer receive medical care from the department of corrections (Sung, Mahoney, & Mellow, 2011). Also, the parolee must make significant social and psychological role adjustments. A male ex-convict, for example, must suddenly become not only a parolee but also an employee, a neighbor, and possibly a father, husband, and son. The expectations, norms, and social relations in the free world differ greatly from those learned in prison. The relatively predictable inmate code gives way to society's often unclear rules of behavior—rules that the offender had failed to cope with during his or her previous life in free society.

In terms of living a crime-free life, today's parolees face even greater obstacles than did those released prior to 1990 (Bender, Cobbina, & McGarrell, 2016). Since that time, Congress and many state legislatures have imposed new restrictions on ex-felons. These include denial of many things, including welfare benefits such as food stamps, for those convicted of even minor drug crimes; access to public housing; receipt of student loans; and in some states, voting rights. Studies have found that returning inmates often face so many restrictions after long periods of incarceration that the conditions amount to years of "invisible punishment" (Mauer & Chesney-Lind, 2002:1). The effects of these policies impact not only individual parolees but also their families and communities (Travis, 2002). Read the "Current Controversies in Criminal Justice" feature to consider the difficulties faced by ex-prisoners seeking to succeed in society.

News accounts of brutal crimes committed by ex-offenders on parole fuel a public perception that parolees pose a threat to the community. The murder of 12-year-old Polly Klaas by a parolee and the rape and murder of 7-year-old Megan Kanka by a paroled sex offender spurred legislators across the nation to enact "sexual offender notification" laws. These laws require that the public be notified of the whereabouts of "potentially dangerous" sex offenders. In some states, paroled sex offenders must register with the police, whereas in others, the immediate neighbors must be informed. Many states now have publicly accessible sex-offender websites listing the names and addresses of those registered. The state of Washington created a statewide online database that not only lets you see which sex predators are in your midst but also can alert you by email if an offender moves close by (J. Sullivan, 2009).

The Movement to "Ban the Box"

One of the biggest challenges faced by ex-prisoners returning to life in society is the difficulty in finding employment. Often they lack the education, skills, and experience to compete with others for jobs. In addition, they risk facing automatic exclusion from consideration for jobs when employers discover their criminal records. Prisoners often ask in anticipation of release, "Should I tell potential employers that I was in prison and face automatic exclusion from consideration, or should I lie about my criminal record and risk getting fired if the employer ever discovers the truth about my past?"

In recent years, several advocacy groups have pushed a campaign called "Ban the Box" to reduce barriers to employment for ex-prisoners. The "box" this campaign opposes is the box on employment applications that asks people if they have been convicted of a crime. Checking that box has often prevented ex-prisoners from being considered. The point of "ban the box" is not to hide the criminal backgrounds from potential employers; rather, it is an effort to permit ex-prisoners to get to the interview stage, where they can impress employers with their personal qualities, sincerity, and enthusiasm, before being asked about their criminal records. The applicants can be asked about their past records either in interviews or in other evaluations after the initial application stage.

The problem of automatic exclusion from consideration hits minority group members especially hard. Some groups that have studied the issue found that minority ex-prisoners were twice as likely as white ex-offenders to be automatically excluded from jobs when checking the box on an application form. Moreover, discrimination in policing, such as studies indicating officers in Chicago arrested African Americans and Hispanics by falsely claiming these individuals possessed drugs, create lifelong consequences for innocent people.

The campaign to "Ban the Box" enjoys increasing success around the country. By April 2016, more than 100 cities and counties as well as 22 states decided to "ban the box" for government employment. Seven states have imposed the same requirement on private employers. In November 2015, President Obama directed federal agencies to delay examining job applicants' criminal records until after the initial application stage. Advocates of "ban the box" hope that all employers will eventually use what they call "fair chance" principles by taking into consideration how long ago a criminal conviction occurred, whether the crime was related to the type of job being advertised, and whether there is evidence of rehabilitation or mitigating circumstances, such as a crime that was an impulsive act by a teenager.

Those who oppose "ban the box" do not want employers to be forced to waste time and resources considering ex-prisoners that they might never hire anyway when they learn about the criminal record later in the process. They also worry that such policies simply add to the number of rules and regulations that employers must follow and thereby add to the time and expense of running a business.

For Critical Thinking and Analysis

Do you support or oppose the "ban the box" movement? If you were an employer, what, if anything, would you specifically fear as you considered the possibility of hiring an ex-prisoner? Give three reasons for the position on this issue that you would adopt if you were an employer.

Sources: J. Aloe, "Lawmakers Attempt to 'Ban the Box,'" *Burlington Free Press*, March 7, 2016 (www.burlingtonfreepress .com); A. Melber, "Obama Bans the Box," MSNBC News, November 2, 2015 (www .msnbc.com); M. Rodriguez and B. Avery, "Ban the Box: U.S. Cities, Counties, and States Adopt Fair Hiring Policies," National Employment Law Project, April 11, 2016 (www.nelp.org); B. Strohl, "'Ban the Box' Movement Could Remove Criminal Questions on Job Applications," KTTS News, April 16, 2016 (www.ktts.com); N. Van Cleve, "Chicago's Racist Cops and Racist Courts," *New York Times*, April 14, 2016 (www.nytimes.com).

These laws have generated several unintended consequences. For example, parolees have been "hounded" from communities, the media have televised the parolees' homecomings, homes have been burned, parolees have been killed, and neighbors have assaulted parolees they erroneously thought were sex offenders. In some states, legislators wrote laws so broadly that consensual sex between teenagers and third-degree assault that might constitute inappropriate touching or sexual contact are included in the notification mandate. In 2006, two Maine parolees were shot by a man intent on killing registered sex offenders. One of those killed was on the list because, at age 19, he had been convicted of having consensual sex with his underage girlfriend. His murder heightened national debate as to whether the online registries put those who are listed at risk (G. Adams, 2006).

The fact of repeat violence fuels a public perception that parolees represent a continuing threat to the community. Although the new laws primarily focus on people who have committed sex offenses against children, some fear that the community will eventually target all parolees. This preoccupation with potential parolee criminality makes successful reentry even more difficult for ex-offenders. Read "Criminal Justice: Myth & Reality," and consider your views on the policies adopted by some states to control the offenders whom they fear most.

Revocation of Parole

The potential revocation of parole, for committing a new crime or violating the conditions of release, hangs constantly over the ex-inmate's head. The public tends to view the high number of revocations as a failure of parole. Correctional officials point to the great number of parolees who are required to be drug free, be employed, and pay restitution—conditions that many parolees find difficult to fulfill.

As discussed in Chapter 10, the Supreme Court ruled in *Morrissey v. Brewer* (1972) that if the parole officer alleges a technical violation, a two-step revocation proceeding is required. In the first stage, a hearing determines whether there is probable cause to believe the conditions have been violated. The parolee has the right to be notified of the charges, to be informed of the evidence, to present witnesses, and to confront the witnesses. In the second stage, the parole authority decides if the violation is severe enough to warrant the return to prison.

CRIMINAL JUSTICE

Myth&Reality

COMMON BELIEF: Offenders who never qualify for parole will still inevitably be returned to society upon completion of their sentences.

REALITY

- The foregoing statement is generally true for those offenders who are not serving life sentences. However, some states, such as Kansas and Washington, enacted laws to prolong the detention of offenders whom officials regard as especially dangerous: predatory sex offenders.
- Under these laws, offenders who are diagnosed with mental conditions that make them highly likely to commit further sex crimes are transported to secure mental facilities upon the completion of their prison sentences. In other words, even after serving their full prison sentences, they remain locked up in state facilities.
- The U.S. Supreme Court ruled that such indefinite detention statutes are permissible as long as the purpose of the laws is treatment rather than punishment (*Kansas v. Hendricks*, 1997).
- In theory, these individuals will be released when psychiatrists conclude that they can safely reenter society. In practice, they may never receive such approval.
- One of the most significant risks of such laws is that they will be applied to people who actually do not pose a significant risk of re-offending. This is especially true because the psychiatric conditions that justify post-sentence detentions are vaguely defined and difficult to diagnose accurately.

Because of the effort to reduce prison populations, a recent trend in many states is to increase the number of prisoners released on parole and avoid revoking parole unless there is serious misconduct. The emphasis on successful reentry can lead to using alternative incentives and sanctions regarding compliance with conditions of parole. Thus, there is decreased emphasis on technical violations of parole conditions. On the other hand, arrest and conviction for a new crime are still likely to lead to a return to prison.

In Texas, for example, the Board of Pardons and Paroles approved only 25 percent of parole applications in 2001. By contrast, the board approved 36 percent of the 77,300 parole applications in 2014 (Battson, 2012; Texas Board of Pardons and Paroles, 2015). An additional factor in the increase in parole approval is a recognition that keeping offenders in prison until they have served their complete sentences means that they will be freed without parole supervision. Thus, a greater awareness of the importance of reentry preparation may lead to more approvals of parole releases late in a sentence for those who might have previously served their complete terms (Ward, 2012).

At the same time that the number of parolees is growing in Texas, there has also been a reduction in the number of parole revocations. In 2003, the board revoked parole for 10,554 parolees out of the 30,598 called before hearings to face the possibility of revocation. By contrast, in 2012, the board revoked parole for only 6,455 parolees out of the 37,134 called before hearings (Texas Board of Pardons and Paroles, 2015).

4. **What are three programs designed to ease the reentry of offenders into the community?**
Work and educational release programs, furlough programs, and halfway houses.

5. **What are the main tasks of parole officers?**
Surveillance and assistance.

6. **What two conditions can result in the revocation of parole?**
Arrest for a new crime or a technical violation of one or more of the conditions of parole.

Should criminal justice officials be able to revoke parole without a hearing? Alternatively, should parolees be entitled to a full trial and representation by counsel before parole is revoked, since the revocation decision has such a huge impact on their personal liberty? Give three reasons for your response to each of these two questions.

The Future of Prisoner Reentry

The rising number of offenders returning to the community has new importance to policy makers. Large numbers of offenders are gaining release each year as a natural consequence of the nation's significant expansion of its prison population in the past few decades. Moreover, many states are attempting to increase the number of offenders released from prison as a means to cut costs amid the contemporary budget crisis affecting all levels of government. These factors increase the necessity of looking closely at ways to make reentry effective for offenders and society.

The likelihood of rules violations by released offenders is affected not only by the kinds of crimes for which they were convicted but also by the intensity and duration of their supervision (Grattet, Lin, & Petersilia, 2011). The longer the period of time a released offender must live under a strict set of rules, the greater is the likelihood that he or she will violate some rules; if any conditions of release are broken, the state is faced with the question of whether to send the offender back to prison, even if the offender has not committed a new crime.

The 2011 report by the Pew Center on the States highlighted Oregon as a place where great efforts are made to respond to violations by parolees without sending them back to the expensive and unproductive environment of prison. For example, research has shown that using community-based sanctions for parole violations can be an effective and less costly approach to combatting recidivism (Steiner, Makarios, et al., 2012). States can also benefit from proactively reaching out to employers and, in cooperation with employers, developing transitional job programs that provide financial and personal support as well as the necessary training and supervision for parolees and ex-offenders (Rosenberg, 2012). Successful entry into the workforce can have substantial beneficial effects for offenders, although this important step can contain numerous obstacles for the many offenders who lack meaningful prior work experience or the commitment to fulfill the responsibilities of a job.

An additional challenge facing reentry is the maintenance of budgets for programs that facilitate reintegration into the community even as states are cutting funds elsewhere in corrections. For example, some cities have used reentry courts with judges dedicated to overseeing the progress of parolees (Hamilton, 2010). Yet in San Francisco in 2011, budget cuts eliminated the Parole Reentry Court despite its record of helping parolees avoid recidivism, leading Judge Jeffrey Tauber to apologize to parolees in the courtroom by saying, "I'm truly apologizing that I've not been able to fulfill my commitment and promise to you" (Bundy, 2011). Elsewhere in the country, other parole and reentry programs have shared the burden of budget cuts. The need to facilitate the successful reentry of a large number of parolees and ex-offenders will lead to hard questions and difficult choices about how to allocate resources in the justice system.

The recognition of the important need to reduce prison populations and facilitate successful reentry at the same time that states are dealing with budget

Parole and Reentry

The Justice Policy Institute has highlighted a number of approaches to help states reduce prison populations and increase success rates for parolees reentering society. Although many of these recommendations require creation of programs and the expenditure of money, evidence that these strategies can work may serve to convince legislators and corrections officials that these approaches are worthwhile endeavors for spending limited financial resources. Examine the list of recommendations, and ask yourself if any can be followed without significant commitments of new funds.

- *Utilize risk assessments.* By analyzing specific characteristics of offenders (mental health, education level, criminal record, support from family, etc.) in light of prior research, states can predict more effectively which offenders are likely to succeed on parole and which may need special services or extra supervision.
- *Reduce administrative delays in parole hearings and decisions.* Efficiency can help reduce the costs associated with time spent in prison awaiting parole processing.
- *Increase access to in-prison programming.* Prerelease education can help begin the process of eventual transition to society.
- *Use medical parole and parole for aging prisoners.* Elderly prisoners and those with chronic medical conditions are especially expensive to house in prisons and often pose much lower risks of reoffending.
- *Allow offenders to earn "good time" credits while on parole and not just while in prison.* The opportunity to shorten the sentence and period of supervision can be an effective incentive to encourage proper behavior and compliance with parole conditions.
- *Expand work release and community corrections.* These programs can provide important mechanisms to assist offenders in reestablishing connections with society.
- *Match the intensity of parole supervision with the level of risk posed by the offender's record and characteristics.* Resources are wasted when all parolees receive the same level of supervision despite presenting differing levels of risk.
- *Increase access to treatment in the community.* Many offenders have substance-abuse or mental health problems for which they need treatment in order to assist with their transition to society.

Researching the Internet

To read about Kentucky's efforts to reduce prison populations and enhance reentry, including strengthening the effectiveness of parole, go to http://www.pewstates.org/uploadedFiles/2011_Kentucky_Reforms_Cut_Recidivism.pdf.

Implementing New Practices

Legislators and corrections officials face difficult choices. They are responsible for protecting public safety and, indeed, can lose their positions if they are blamed for an unfortunate incident such as a parolee committing a horrific crime. Although they are likely to be cautious about new initiatives that place offenders in the community, they also increasingly recognize that states are spending more money than they need to spend on prisons in order to keep the public safe. Thus, more and more decision makers in criminal justice recognize that they must devote more attention and resources to parole and reentry.

As you look through the list of recommendations, which ones do you think are likely to encounter resistance? Are there recommendations that actually will not cost much extra money but simply require more effectiveness in organizing how the criminal justice system carries out its responsibilities? Which recommendations do you see as most important and beneficial to society? Write a memo that addresses these three questions.

Source: Justice Policy Institute. 2010, "How to Safely Reduce Prison Populations and Support People Returning to Their Communities," June (Press Release) (http://www.justicepolicy.org).

problems makes a focus on evidence-based practices especially important. When there are limited resources to devote to parole and reentry, then they should be used efficiently with great awareness of approaches that have been proven to enhance success. Read the "Evidence-Based Practice and Policy" feature to consider recommended approaches for reducing prison populations and facilitating reentry.

Legislators and correctional officials increasingly recognize that government lacks the money and facilities to incarcerate all offenders for the sentence lengths that had been imposed in recent decades. Alternative approaches will affect not only sentencing decisions for nonviolent and drug offenders but also efforts to increasingly reduce prison populations through various release mechanisms. Parole and other community programs represent an effort to address the inevitability of prison reentry. Even if such programs do not prevent all offenders from returning to crime, they do help some to turn their lives around.

A QUESTION OF ETHICS

Neighborhood Resistance to Placement of Community Corrections Programs and Facilities

Community corrections programs and aftercare are vital components of a releasee's transition out of prison; however, there are always public debates over the best location for these centers. Given that many parolees have limited access to personal transportation, it can be difficult for them to travel long distances to visit their parole officer, or attend important rehabilitative programs. Placing community corrections programs in neighborhoods would give parolees easy access to these centers, but many neighborhood residents have a "Not In My Backyard" (NIMBY) attitude toward placement of these offices in their area. Expressing concerns over safety and increased crime, these residents fear that increased foot traffic from parolees will make their neighborhoods more dangerous.

For example, in Amelia Island, Florida, a halfway house where 12 men live, has faced opposition by residents. As part of the private nonprofit American Recovery Program, these men are working to become sober, gain employment, and reconnect with their families. Neighborhood residents, however, are fearful. One (anonymous) resident says,

> "I believe that everybody should have a second chance. We should help those people with whatever, but not in my neighborhood" (McKee, 2015).

Discussion/Writing Assignment

Is there any way to meet the competing demands of (1) providing parolees with easy access to valuable services while (2) keeping neighborhoods safe and crime free? If you were the spokesperson for the Florida Department of Corrections, how would you respond to the statement by the resident above?

SUMMARY

1 Describe the nature of the "reentry problem."

- Prisoner reentry to the community has become an important public issue because of the large number of offenders who gain parole eligibility or complete their sentences each year.
- Preventing recidivism by assisting parolees to become law-abiding citizens requires government resources and the development of helpful programs to prepare offenders for release.
- During the contemporary period of state government budget problems, there is an effort to reduce prison populations, yet funding cuts for reentry programs can hamper efforts to prepare offenders to rejoin society.

2 Explain the origins of parole and how it operates today.

- Parole is the conditional release from prison and is the primary method by which inmates return to society. While on parole, they remain under correctional supervision.
- Parole in the United States evolved during the nineteenth century from the English, Australian, and Irish practices of conditional pardon, apprenticeship by indenture, transportation to distant colonies, and issuance of "tickets of leave."
- Today most felons leave prison and are supervised by parole officers for a period of time. They

may be returned to prison if they commit another crime or violate the conditions (rules) of their release.

3 Name and define the mechanisms for the release of felons to the community.

- There are four types of release: expiration release, mandatory release, other conditional release, and discretionary release.
- Expiration release occurs when inmates have completed their full sentence. They have "maxed out" and leave the prison without community supervision.
- Mandatory release is the required release of an inmate to the community upon the expiration of a certain period, as specified by a determinate-sentencing law or parole guidelines.
- Other conditional release is the placement of convicts in various community settings while under supervision; some states use this to avoid the rigidity of mandatory release.
- Discretionary release is based on a decision by the parole board within the boundaries set by the sentence and the penal law.
- Describe differences in the parole board process in different states.

4 **Describe how ex-offenders are supervised in the community.**

- Parole officers are assigned to supervise and assist ex-inmates making the transition to society and to ensure that they follow the conditions of their release.
- Parole officers' functions include roles as cops and as social workers.
- Parole may be revoked for commission of a crime or for violating the rules governing behavior while on parole (failing to appear for meetings with parole officers, using drugs or alcohol, and so forth).

5 **Identify the problems that parolees face during their reentry.**

- Upon release, offenders face many problems. For instance, they must find housing and employment and reestablish relationships with family and friends.
- Adjustment to life outside the prison is often difficult in that those released must move from the highly structured environment of an institution into a world with temptations and complicated problems.

Questions for Review

1. What are the basic assumptions of parole?
2. How do mandatory release, discretionary release, and unconditional release differ?

3. What roles does the parole officer play?
4. What problems confront parolees upon their release?

Key Terms

conditions of release (p. 466)

discretionary release (p. 460)

expiration release (p. 458)

furlough (p. 468)

halfway house (p. 468)

mandatory release (p. 458)

other conditional release (p. 458)

parole (p. 456)

work and educational release (p. 467)

AP Images/Daniel Brenner

14 Technology and Criminal Justice

LEARNING OBJECTIVES

1 Describe how adaptation and belief in science can affect the use of technology.

2 Identify the various aspects of cybercrime and counterfeiting.

3 Explain the role of communications, computers, and databases in policing.

4 Describe developments and problems in DNA testing and new weapons technologies.

5 Name the uses of technology in courts and corrections.

6 List some continuing questions about the effects of technology on civil liberties.

On January 21, 2015, a man wearing a motorcycle helmet and what appeared to be a vest wired with explosives robbed a bank in Salt Lake City, Utah, then fled the scene on foot. Police officers chased the man, and caught him. As they handcuffed him, they noticed wires sticking out of his vest. Suspecting explosives, they left him on the ground, backed away, and sealed off the nearby area. When the police bomb squad arrived, officers stayed at a distance away while they directed two robots to where the suspect was lying on the ground. A camera on a robot enabled officers to examine the vest; they used a microphone to speak to the suspect. Then tools on the robot's arm were used to remove the vest and move it 20 feet away. An officer in protective gear examined the vest, then stepped away before the robot used vibrations to see if the vest would detonate. As it turned out, the vest was a hoax; it contained no explosives (Alberty & Mims, 2015; Reavy, 2015).

Not so many years ago, officers would have needed to risk their own lives in order to remove the vest, examine it, and seek to detonate it. Today, however, technology developments have given police officers greater capacity to address certain situations while exposing officers to fewer risks. New technologies can provide useful tools for addressing various situations in criminal justice. They are not perfect, and they can never remove all risk from the situations officers face. Yet they can improve aspects of policing and other operations of criminal justice, albeit with the introduction of new issues and problems that inevitably accompany the introduction of new devices and techniques.

Contemporary Americans take for granted the availability and usefulness of technology. American television viewers are fascinated by the *CSI: Crime Scene Investigation* television shows and other programs that show the impressive ability of scientists to identify criminal suspects by examining microscopic bits of evidence. Because the United States is a relatively wealthy and technologically sophisticated country, it can fund and benefit from the development of new technologies that provide crucial assistance in various operations of the criminal justice system. As we learn about the role and impact of technology in criminal justice, we must also remember that existing technological resources are not necessarily available for use in all state and county criminal justice systems. Agencies must have enough money to acquire new technology, and their personnel must have expertise and resources for training in order to make effective use of it.

In this chapter, we examine the role of technology in criminal justice. Each year brings new inventions—as well as improvements to existing technologies—that affect crime and justice. As we shall see,

AP Images/Daniel Brenner

technological change affects the nature of crime even as it boosts the capacity of law enforcement officials to prevent criminal acts and apprehend criminal offenders. Technology also impacts the processing of criminal cases in courts and the monitoring and control of convicted offenders in correctional settings. The use of technology increases the capability of criminal justice officials to perform their vital functions effectively. Simultaneously, however, technology creates its own issues and problems, including concerns about the ways it may collide with citizens' expectations about their privacy and other constitutional rights.

Technological Development and Criminal Justice

Throughout history, humans have sought to invent tools to advance their goals. The invention of early tools and wheels, for example, promoted agriculture and transport. Over time, simple farming tools gave way to gigantic tractors and other farm machinery. The wheel has similarly been updated through advancing transportation mechanisms—from horse-drawn wagons to steam trains to jet planes' tires. The appreciation for the advantages of technology naturally leads to inventive developments affecting all areas of human experience, including criminal justice.

However, the use of technology in criminal justice differs from its use in many other areas of human activity. Technology in this case is not merely an effort to overcome the natural environment by increasing productivity, easing daily life, and expanding the range of travel. In criminal justice, as in military affairs, technology becomes an element in the interaction, competition, and conflict among human beings who have opposing objectives. In this case, the clash is between those who would seek to profit or cause harm by breaking society's laws (as in theft or murder) and those who seek to stop, identify, apprehend, process, and punish criminals. This observation highlights two important points about technological development in criminal justice. First, new developments that benefit one side in this competition, whether lawbreaker or law enforcer, will lead to adjustments and adaptations by the other. Second, the pressure to find new and better devices to combat crime can lead to excessive faith in the effectiveness of technology; this can lead to problems when people do not stop to examine all the consequences of new technology. After we briefly examine each of these points, keep them in mind to see how they relate to the topics discussed in the rest of this chapter.

Competition and Adaptation

Throughout history, the development of both weapons and protective devices has affected the preservation of persons and property, which is one of the fundamental goals of criminal justice. As weaponry advanced from daggers and swords to firearms and then later to multi-shot pistols that could be concealed inside pockets, the threats posed by robbers increased. Thus, when American policing expanded in the nineteenth century, law enforcement officers in the western frontier, and later throughout the country, armed themselves in a way that would help them deal with pistol-toting criminals. These developments continue. News reports have made contemporary Americans well aware that many police departments now struggle to match the firepower of the automatic weapons possessed by some criminal offenders and organized crime groups (A. Klein, 2008).

Similarly, the development of fortified walls, door locks, and safes led to criminals' adaptive strategies for overcoming these barriers. For example, the creation of locks spawned devices and techniques for picking locks. So, too, the creation of safes led to the birth of professional safecrackers. Later, the introduction of police radar to detect speeders led to a profitable industry selling radar detectors to motorists who wanted to drive at excessive speeds without paying fines. Today, criminals' efforts to overcome residential burglar alarms, as well as cybercriminals' creativity in overcoming security software, illustrate the interactions among technological development, criminals' adaptive behavior, and society's efforts to counteract new forms of criminality.

Fundamentally, these examples should remind us that technological developments do not always help criminal justice officials. New technologies can be developed and used by those who seek to violate criminal laws. Moreover, new devices designed specifically to protect property or to assist police officers will generate adaptive behavior by would-be lawbreakers who adjust their behavior, invent their own devices, or otherwise develop strategies to overcome new barriers to the attainment of their goals. James Byrne summarizes the overall impact of technology:

> Advances...in technology have resulted in new opportunities for crime (through the Internet), new forms of criminality (e.g., Internet scams...), new techniques for committing crimes (e.g., computer software programs,...the use of [T]asers as weapons in robberies), and new categories of offenders and victims (such as online predators and identity theft victims) (Byrne, 2008:10–11).

Science and the Presumption of Progress

From the mid-nineteenth century through today, Americans have benefited from industrialization, the development of electricity, the rise of the scientific method, and advances in various scientific fields, such as medicine and engineering. In light of the extraordinary advancements in human knowledge and the new inventions that have dramatically altered the nature of American society, it is not surprising that many people equate technological advancements with "progress." However, contemporary Americans are regularly reminded that new developments can produce consequences, such as side effects from new medicines, that are unexpected and undesirable. Thus, in the field of criminal justice, as in other fields, we need to guard against the assumption that new technologies will always be better than older techniques and devices. Similarly, even when the benefits of new technologies are clear, we need to consider the possibility of undesirable risks and consequences that have not yet been discovered.

In the late nineteenth century, the development of electricity brought with it efforts to apply this "miracle" resource to various societal needs. One idea applied to criminal justice was the invention of the electric chair as a modern method to produce an instantaneous and presumably humane execution for criminals

Many people presumed that the electric chair provided a quicker, more humane way to execute criminals, because the use of electricity was developed through experimentation and other methods of science. In fact, many such executions seemed to be far more painful and prolonged than the traditional execution by hanging. Are there any new technologies in criminal justice that are likely to have unexpected and undesirable consequences?

sentenced to death. At that time, most executions were carried out through hanging. This "old-fashioned" execution method had been used for centuries, with little change in its use of rope and a means to drop the condemned person's body so that the neck would break or the person would be strangled.

The first man condemned to execution by electric chair was William Kemmler, a convicted murderer in New York. Kemmler challenged his sentence through the court system, eventually presenting to the U.S. Supreme Court a claim that execution by electricity constituted "cruel and unusual punishment" in violation of Kemmler's constitutional rights. After all, what could be more "unusual" than to be the first person executed through the use of a newfangled invention?

In rejecting Kemmler's claim in 1890, the U.S. Supreme Court noted that the New York statute permitting execution by electric chair "was passed in the effort to devise a more humane method of reaching the result [of extinguishing life and] that courts were bound to presume that the legislature was possessed of the facts upon which it took action" (*In re Kemmler,* 1890). Thus, there was acceptance of the idea that this new scientific method would be more effective and humane than hanging. When Kemmler was actually executed, however, the first jolt of 1,000 volts did not kill him, and witnesses saw that he was still breathing despite the attending physician's initial declaration that he was dead (Moran, 2002). The wires were reattached to his head, and the chair was revved up to 2,000 volts for an extended period.

> Froth oozed out of Kemmler's strapped mouth. The small blood vessels under his skin began to rupture. Blood trickled down his face and arms.... The awful smell of burning flesh filled the death chamber. Kemmler's body first smoldered and then caught fire.... From the moment he first sat down on the chair until the electricity was shut off the second time, eight minutes had elapsed. (Moran, 2002:15–19)

Did the electric chair fulfill its presumed function of using science to provide instantaneous, humane executions? Although it was used in 2,000 executions in the century after Kemmler's death, highly publicized instances of other gruesome death-chamber scenes eventually led to a complete reconsideration of its use. In 2001, Georgia's Supreme Court declared that this method of execution imposed unconstitutional "cruel and unusual punishment" on condemned offenders in its state criminal justice system (H. Weinstein, 2001). By the time that the Nebraska Supreme Court made an identical ruling in 2008, all states had moved toward the use of lethal injection as the method of execution for new capital murder convictions. Clearly, the original presumptions about the humane scientific "progress" represented by the electric chair had been rejected nationwide (Mears, 2008). Interestingly, however, when European countries refused to sell some of the specific drugs required for use in executions, several states began to discuss the possibility of returning to "old-fashioned methods," such as hanging and the gas chamber (Salter, 2014).

The story of the electric chair provides a graphic example of slow reconsideration of the effects of particular technological and scientific developments. Today we see similar examples concerning the actual risks and consequences of certain technologies. For example, the National Academy of Sciences (2009)

CRIMINAL JUSTICE

Myth&Reality

COMMON BELIEF: As long as forensic scientists do not mishandle evidence, modern scientific methods ensure that reliable conclusions can be drawn after the laboratory testing of various forms of evidence, including fingerprints, hair, soil, handwriting, and bite marks.

REALITY

- In reality, a study of crime lab evidence analysis by the National Academy of Sciences concluded that "many forensic disciplines—including analysis of fingerprints, bite marks, and the striations and indentations left by a pry bar or a gun's firing mechanism—were not grounded in the kind of rigorous, peer-reviewed research that is the hallmark of classic science" (Fountain, 2009).
- Major scandals have emerged when experts purported to state definitive conclusions about bite marks, handwriting analysis, and other forms of evidence after scientific testing, only to discover later that these conclusions were incorrect and had led to the conviction of innocent people (F. Santos, 2007).
- DNA analysis is the only form of scientific evidence that has been subjected to rigorous testing through the methods of science.
- Although courts admit into evidence other forms of scientific testing, as well as conclusions drawn about such evidence by scientists, many of these other tests have not been validated through rigorous research. Thus, judges and attorneys should display caution in examining and accepting such evidence.

produced a report that questioned the validity and accuracy of many forensic science methods used by police and prosecutors. In one section, the report said that forensic science "analyses are often handled by poorly trained technicians who then exaggerate the accuracy of their methods in court" (S. Moore, 2009). Obviously, the effectiveness of technology is limited by the errors made by the human beings who use that technology. Despite the seeming infallibility of forensic techniques dramatized in *CSI: Crime Scene Investigation* and other popular shows, even the use of a simple photo from a surveillance camera can cause problems when people make mistakes. This point was experienced by Cornell University sociology professor Stephen Morgan in New York when he saw that his old driver's license photo was being mistakenly circulated on the Internet—instead of a photo of another Stephen Morgan who was being sought for a fatal shooting in Connecticut at Wesleyan University's student bookstore in 2009—as officials asked for the public's help in finding the shooter (M. Spencer, 2009). In addition, the technology itself, even when properly used, may also produce unanticipated risks and consequences. An accurate understanding of the role of technology in criminal justice requires recognition of the potential for undesirable results. Think about your own perceptions of the scientific testing of criminal evidence as you read "Criminal Justice: Myth & Reality."

▼ **CHECK POINT**

1. **What are two reasons to be cautious about assuming that new technological developments automatically provide benefits for the criminal justice system?**
   Lawbreakers can develop and use technology for the purpose of committing crimes; new technologies produce the risks of undesirable risks and unanticipated consequences.

STOP & ANALYZE

What steps do you take to avoid victimization by technology-based crimes? Which technology-based crimes do you fear most?

Crime and Technology

As new technologies emerge, so do people who take advantage of them for their own gain. One has only to think of how the invention of the automobile enhanced criminals' mobility to realize the extent to which computers and other new technologies will enhance existing criminal enterprises. For example, the acquisition of automatic weapons can make drug traffickers more dangerous in battling their rivals and threatening witnesses. Instantaneous transfers of funds between banks via computer networks can make it easier for criminals to move money in order to purchase weapons, drugs, and other contraband, as well as to hide assets from government agencies responsible for law enforcement and tax collection. Computers and other technologies also create opportunities to commit new kinds of crimes, such as cybercrime and counterfeiting. We should note, as well, that individual citizens can respond by using technology themselves to thwart crime through improved lighting and alarm systems in their homes, security software on their computers, and pepper-spray canisters and other weapons for personal protection.

Cybercrime

As we saw in Chapter 2, cybercrimes involve the use of computers and the Internet to commit acts against people, property, public order, or morality. Cybercriminals use computers to steal information, resources, or funds. These thefts can be aimed at simply stealing money, or they can involve the theft of companies' trade secrets, chemical formulas, and other valuable information. The scope of these thefts can be shocking when discovered and revealed to the public. In 2014, for example, the Target chain of stores revealed that hackers had obtained credit and debit card information on as many as 70 million of the stores' customers, putting those individuals at risk of identity theft (Yang & Jayakumar, 2014). Other criminals use computers for malicious, destructive acts, such as releasing Internet viruses and "worms" to harm computer systems. They may also use innocent victims' computers, via remote commands, to assist in crimes such as the dissemination of child pornography (Kravets, 2011). In 2012, the countries in the European Union announced that they would open a new anticrime center in the Netherlands dedicated to combatting cybercrimes, many of which are increasingly perpetrated by organized crime groups. The European Union has estimated that organized crime groups gained $388 billion annually from cybercrime, an amount greater than the total profits produced through global trade in marijuana, cocaine, and heroin (H. Morris, 2012).

Downloading copyrighted software, music, videos, and other materials is a federal crime. However, although millions of Americans perform illegal downloads every day, they are seldom prosecuted unless the government identifies individuals or organizations with substantial involvement in such activities (Hinduja, 2007). The government has acted to shut down large operations engaged in illegally disseminating movies and other copyrighted entertainment media. In 2012, for example, the FBI, in cooperation with officials in nearly a dozen countries, arrested three individuals in New Zealand and sought three other suspects abroad for gaining more than $175 million in illegal profits from posting movies and other copyrighted works online (U.S. Department of Justice, 2012).

identity theft The theft of social security numbers, credit card numbers, and other information in order to secure loans, withdraw bank funds, and purchase merchandise while posing as someone else—the unsuspecting victim who will eventually lose money in these transactions.

Identity theft has become a huge problem affecting many middle-class and affluent Americans who would otherwise seldom find themselves victimized by criminals. Perpetrators of identity theft use other people's credit card numbers and social security numbers to secure fraudulent loans and steal money and merchandise (Harrell, 2015). New reports about identity theft rings seem to emerge almost every week. During one week in April 2016, a man in New York City was charged with stealing credit card information and using it to purchase $400,000 worth of luxury goods that he intended to resell to others (Rosenberg, 2016). At the same time, a model in Miami was charged with helping her boyfriend steal the identities of senior citizens to steal $2 million worth of travel and merchandise (Jacobs & Annese, 2016). According to the National Crime Victimization Survey, millions of American households were victimized by identity theft in 2012, with losses totaling $24.7 billion (Harrell & Langton, 2013).

For many Americans, identity theft can occur without any financial loss if, for example, they are reimbursed by a bank or credit card company for their losses.

Law enforcement officers need up-to-date knowledge and equipment to have any hope of pursuing cybercriminals on the Internet. Local police officers often successfully pretend to be teenagers in chat rooms, drawing out people who would sexually abuse children. Local officials cannot usually maintain the expertise to counteract international cybercrime operations, so the FBI takes the lead in those efforts. Should computer science courses become a required component of every college criminal justice program?

AP Images/Mel Evans

TABLE 14.1 — Type of Identity Theft Experienced by Households and Total Financial Loss Attributed to Each Type of Identity Theft in 2014 (most recent victimization during year)

	Number of Victims	Percent of Victimizations	Average Total Out-of-Pocket Loss
All types	17.6 million	100%	—
Existing credit card	7.3 million	41.7%	$902
Existing bank account	6.7 million	38.3%	$943
Other existing account	980,000	5.6%	$2,376
Personal information	546,000	3.1%	$6,276
New account	683,000	3.9%	$6,467
Multiple types	1.3 million	7.4%	$5,800

Source: E. Harrell, "Victims of Identity Theft, 2014," *Bureau of Justice Statistics Bulletin*, September 2015, pp. 2, 16.

Yet they still suffer victimization from computer crime, since they may have to go through lengthy hassles in changing online financial records, getting new credit cards, or straightening out government records (Florencio & Herley, 2012).

As indicated by Table 14.1, the theft of existing credit card information is the most common form of identity theft, although other thefts involve existing bank accounts, PayPal accounts, and personal information used by thieves to set up fraudulent new accounts or file for fraudulent tax refunds. Credit card numbers can be stolen by dishonest restaurant servers and retail clerks who use electronic "skimmer" devices to quickly record the magnetic strip on the back of the card so that the information can be sold to organized crime gangs or used to purchase items and manufacture counterfeit credit cards (Conte, 2012).

Other offenders use the Internet to disseminate child pornography, to advertise sexual services, or to stalk the unsuspecting. Police departments have given special emphasis to stopping computer predators who establish online relationships with juveniles in order to manipulate those children into sexual victimization (Newton, 2016). Thus, officers often pose as juveniles in "chat rooms" to see if sexual predators will attempt to cultivate a relationship and set up a personal meeting (Bai, 2012; Eichenwald, 2006). However, local police departments face challenges in training and equipping officers to investigate online child pornography and other cybercrimes (Newton, 2016; Holt & Bossier, 2012).

In attacking these problems, the FBI's National Computer Crime Squad lists its responsibilities as covering the following:

- Intrusions of the public switched network (the telephone company)
- Major computer network intrusions
- Network integrity violations
- Privacy violations
- Industrial espionage
- Pirated computer software
- Other crimes where the computer is a major factor in committing the criminal offense

The global nature of the Internet presents new challenges to the criminal justice system. For example, in 2014, with the cooperation of foreign law enforcement officials, the U.S. Justice Department announced the arrest of individuals in Romania, India, and China, as well as several of their American customers, related to the sale of passwords that could be used to hack into thousands of e-mail accounts (U.S. Department of Justice, 2014).

Nigerian thieves have become well known for their "419 scams," named after a section of their country's criminal code, in which they send e-mail messages to

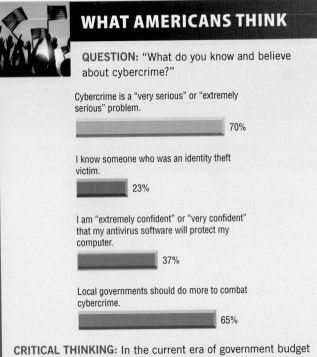
Americans and people in other countries offering large sums of money in exchange for payments that will enable the thieves to "unfreeze" nonexistent assets in banks and trust funds. For example, they falsely claim that if the individual will simply send $5,000 to cover an overdue fee owed to a bank, the bank will unfreeze an account containing a multi-million-dollar inheritance that will be split with the scam victim (Bjelopera & Finklea, 2012).

In another example of cybercrime, stolen credit card numbers are sold on the Internet, primarily by dealers based in states that were formerly part of the Soviet Union. Computer hackers steal thousands of credit card numbers from the computer systems of legitimate businesses and sell them in bulk to dealers who market them throughout the world via members-only websites. Credit card fraud costs online merchants more than $1 billion each year (Perlroth & Gelles, 2014; Segal, Ngugi, & Mana, 2011).

It is extremely difficult to know how many cybercrimes occur and how much money is lost through identity theft, auction fraud, investment fraud, and other forms of financial computer crime. Unfortunately for businesses, many harmful attacks and thefts carried out by computer are done by company employees. Moreover, many of these events are not reported to the police.

Efforts to create and enforce effective laws that will address such activities have been hampered by the international nature of cybercrime. Agencies in various countries are seeking to improve their ability to cooperate and share information. However, not all law enforcement officials throughout the world are equally committed to, nor capable of, catching cyber thieves and hackers. Criminals in some countries may have better computer equipment and expertise than do the officials trying to catch them. However, the FBI and other law enforcement agencies have made a concerted effort to improve their equipment, hire computer experts, and train their officers to investigate cybercrime. The FBI uses Cyber Action Teams, or CATs, to act quickly in addressing large-scale or very damaging cybercrimes. The FBI describes CATs as "small, highly trained teams of FBI agents, analysts, and computer forensics and malicious code experts who travel around the world on a moment's notice to respond to cyber intrusions" (FBI, 2006).

Since the events of September 11, 2001, many countries' law enforcement agencies have increased their communication and cooperation to thwart terrorist activities. As these countries cooperate in investigating and monitoring the financial transactions of groups that employ terror tactics, it seems likely that they will also improve their capacity to discover and pursue cybercriminals.

Law enforcement agencies cannot prevent cybercrimes from occurring. Generally, they react to such harmful activities in order to limit theft and damage. People cannot rely on law enforcement efforts to protect them from such harms. The first defense against some forms of cybercrime is citizen awareness and caution. Read "What Americans Think" to consider whether people know enough about cybercrime.

Counterfeiting

Traditional counterfeiting involves the creation of fake currency that can be used for illegal profit. Counterfeiting not only enables theft by permitting criminals to exchange fake bills for actual products and services but also harms the economy by placing into circulation bills that have no monetary value. Additional victims may receive the worthless paper as change in a purchase transaction or in payment for products and services. Historically, currency counterfeiters in the United States had difficulty matching the paper, ink, and intricate designs of real currency. While they could produce counterfeit bills that might fool individual clerks in stores, restaurants, and banks, criminals rarely avoided the eventual discovery that the bills were fakes. As image-reproduction technology developed, however, especially photocopiers and scanners, criminals found new ways of counterfeiting. Among the reasons that it is a crime to make any reproduction of U.S. currency is that counterfeiters initially found ways to photocopy currency images and feed those images into change machines. In went the fake paper currency and out came an equal amount of coins with real monetary value that the counterfeiters could then take to a bank and exchange for real paper money.

Continued improvements in computer and printing technology have permitted counterfeiters to produce fake currency of increasing quality (Lazarus, 2010). Thus, in 1996, the United States began to redesign American currency and employ new technological techniques in order to make imitation more difficult. Unfortunately, North Korea purchased the same currency-printing technology that a Swiss company had sold to the U.S. Department of Treasury. As a result, American officials have seized shipments of counterfeit currency that North Korea reportedly produced specifically to harm the American economy and gain income for itself (Mihm, 2006; Rose, 2009). The U.S. government began circulating a newly designed $100 bill in 2013 as an additional countermeasure against actions by the North Korean government and other counterfeiters (Eckel, 2013).

Currency is not the only product susceptible to counterfeiting through the use of available reproduction technologies. For example, legitimate businesses lose billions of dollars in potential sales each year when consumers purchase illegally copied, or "pirated," Hollywood DVDs, as well as counterfeit luxury products that purport to have authentic name brands. According to government estimates, the pirated American movies, music, computer software, and other intellectual property produced in China alone cost legitimate businesses more than $40 billion (Palmer, 2011). In 2014, for example, a man in Springfield, Massachusetts, was convicted of selling counterfeit products bearing the brand names of Gucci, Nike, Coach, Chanel, and Oakley (U.S. Department of Justice, 2014b). Although American law enforcement agencies can attempt—with limited success—to prevent the importation of counterfeit and pirated products, they can do little to prevent the manufacture of such products without the cooperation of authorities in the countries where the counterfeiters are located.

Although counterfeit consumer products impose significant costs on American businesses, far worse human costs result from the counterfeiting of another product: prescription drugs (McNiff, 2015; Toscano, 2011). Technological advancements produced a sharp increase in counterfeit medications during the first decade of the twenty-first century. The discovery of counterfeit versions of specific medications increased from 5 different prescription and over-the-counter drugs per year in the late 1990s to more than 20 new counterfeit drugs per year beginning in 2000 (Grady, 2003). The dangers of counterfeit drugs are obvious: they can cause the deaths or prevent the recoveries of patients who believe that they are taking genuine medications. In 2008, a counterfeit version of the blood-thinning drug heparin came to the United States from China and led to the deaths of 19 Americans as well as causing hundreds of serious allergic reactions (Bogdanich, 2008).

Imagine needing immediate medications to fight a dangerous illness but unknowingly receiving counterfeit drugs that will have no effect on the illness. This kind of illegal activity can easily kill vulnerable people. In 2012, a warning was issued that counterfeit vials of the best-selling cancer drug Avastin were turning up in hospital pharmacies (Associated Press, 2012b). These drugs represented exactly the type of worst-case situation in which a counterfeit product could lead to the deaths of people receiving medical treatments.

The U.S. Food and Drug Administration (FDA) and other government agencies face significant challenges in finding and seizing counterfeit drugs. New efforts to inspect and supervise pharmaceutical production facilities in the United States and abroad and to track individual medications as they move from factory to pharmacy have sought to reduce the risks for the American public (Harris, 2014). Unfortunately, profit-seeking criminals are working just as hard to defeat any new monitoring systems that are developed to intercept counterfeits. The proliferation of Internet pharmacies, which sell prescription medications online, has presented new challenges. Such enterprises may be located outside the borders of the United States. FDA officials have worked to warn Americans against purchasing medications from online sources other than the websites of established pharmacy retail chains.

In addition to counterfeit medications, there are numerous other kinds of counterfeit products that can harm people's health. Imagine if technicians unwittingly installed counterfeit and defective airbags, brakes, or other safety mechanisms in your car ("How Did Counterfeit Autoparts Become Such a Booming Business?" 2016). In addition, there have been problems with counterfeit building products, such as drywall and flooring, that contain dangerous chemicals. In 2015, Customs and Border Protections, an agency within the U.S. Department of Homeland Security, seized more than $1.35 billion worth of fake products that people were attempting to ship into the United States (Giaritelli, 2016). Many of these products violated intellectual property rights of American companies, such as patents and trademarks, and thereby harmed the economic interests of these companies that are legally entitled to control their own inventions and products. This represented a 10-percent increase over the seizures in the prior year, yet we know that thousands of fake products make it into the country (Giaritelli, 2016).

CHECK POINT

2. **What actions have been taken to combat counterfeit currency in the United States?**
Redesign of U.S. currency; seizure of counterfeit currency.

3. **What types of harm are caused by counterfeit products in the United States?**
Billions of dollars in losses for American businesses due to counterfeit and pirated products; deaths and other harmful health consequences due to counterfeit medications.

STOP & ANALYZE

If you were the director of the U.S. Food and Drug Administration, what steps would you recommend to diminish the likelihood that counterfeit prescription drugs would reach American patients?

Policing and New Technology

Policing has long made use of technological developments. Twentieth-century police departments adopted the use of automobiles and radios in order to increase the effectiveness of their patrols, including better response time to criminal events and emergencies. Over time, technological advances also helped to provide video evidence of events and better protection for police officers, including stronger, lighter bulletproof vests and protective features of patrol cars. See Table 14.2 for a summary of video technologies used by police departments in cities of various sizes. Technology has affected the investigation of crime as well. As early as 1911, fingerprint evidence was used to convict an offender. Police officers have collected fingerprints, blood, fibers, and other crime-scene materials to be analyzed through scientific methods in order to identify and convict criminal offenders.

Police officers also use polygraphs, the technical name for lie detectors, that measure people's heart rates and other physical responses as they answer questions.

TABLE 14.2	Use of Selected Video Technologies by Local Police Departments, by Size of Population Served, 2013			
	In-Car Video Cameras	Body-Worn Cameras	License Plate Readers	Unmanned Aerial Drones
All sizes	68%	32%	17%	—
1,000,000 or more	57	21	93	7%
500,000–999,999	73	30	77	3
250,000–499,999	63	20	87	2
100,000–249,999	70	19	77	1
50,000–99,999	63	26	55	1
25,000–49,999	76	22	50	0
10,000–24,999	71	26	24	0
2,500–9,999	71	34	10	0
2,499 or fewer	64	35	6	0

Source: B. Reaves, "Local Police Departments, 2013: Equipment and Technology," *Bureau of Justice Statistics Bulletin*, July 2015, p. 4.

Although polygraph results are typically not admissible as evidence, police officers have often used these examinations on willing suspects and witnesses as a basis for excluding some suspects or for pressuring others to confess.

Several issues arise as police adopt new technologies. First, questions about the accuracy and effectiveness of technological developments persist, even though the developments were originally embraced with great confidence. For example, despite the long and confident use of fingerprint evidence by police and prosecutors, its accuracy has been questioned. In 2002, a federal judge ruled that expert witnesses could compare crime-scene fingerprints with those of a defendant, but they could not testify that the prints definitely matched. The judge pointed out that fingerprint evidence processes have not been scientifically verified, the error rate for such identifications has never been measured, and there are no scientific standards for determining when fingerprint samples match (Loviglio, 2002). Prosecutors later persuaded the judge to reverse his original decision and admit the expert testimony about a fingerprint match, but the judge's first decision raises the possibility that other judges will scrutinize fingerprint evidence more closely.

Second, some worry that innovative technologies will create new collisions with citizens' constitutional rights. As police gain greater opportunities for sophisticated electronic surveillance, for example, new questions arise about what constitutes a search that violates citizens' reasonable expectations of privacy. In 2016, the public's attention was captured by a dispute between Apple computer company and the federal government over whether the company should provide law enforcement investigators with the means to unlock cell phones, amid concerns about people's privacy rights and the risk of excessive government access to private data from people who have done nothing wrong (Moyer, 2016).

As another example, a technology that allows law enforcement agencies to intercept e-mail messages raises questions about privacy that were not foreseeable in prior decades. Similarly, in several cities, police officers with DNA evidence from a rape have asked all the men in a particular community to submit a DNA sample from inside the cheek in order to find a match with DNA of the perpetrator. Many critics believe that innocent citizens who have done nothing suspicious should not be pressured to provide the government with a sample of their DNA. Yet in *Maryland v. King* (2013), the Supreme Court approved a state law mandating taking DNA samples from everyone arrested for certain serious crimes despite these suspects' legal status as "presumptively innocent" prior to being actually convicted of any crime.

Communications and Computer Technology

Communications and the exchange of information serve as central elements in effective law enforcement. Dispatchers receive calls for service and bear responsibility for communicating citizens' immediate needs to patrol officers. Police officers also rely on dispatchers to obtain and communicate essential information, such as whether a particular car was stolen or whether a particular individual is being sought under an arrest warrant. New computer technology has altered both citizens' communications with dispatchers and police officers' reliance on their central headquarters. In addition, the use of computers and databases has enhanced the ability of law enforcement officers to investigate many kinds of crimes (E. Sullivan, 2013).

Communications In many places, the number of calls to 911 emergency operators increased significantly as the spread of cell phones made it easier for people to call as incidents arose. In 1997, the Federal Communications Commission (FCC) set aside "311" as an option for cities to use as a nonemergency number. First Baltimore, then Detroit and New York implemented the 311 call system, but many cities have not done so. The FCC later dedicated "211" for social services information and "511" for traffic information, but relatively few cities have implemented call centers to use these numbers (Nam & Pardo, 2014; McMahon, 2002). Although 911 systems can automatically trace the location of calls made from landlines, many cities are struggling to upgrade their 911 systems so that they can trace wireless calls to the vicinity of the nearest cell-phone tower (Reaves, 2010; Dewan, 2007). Such efforts to upgrade equipment, procedures, and training become more visible in the aftermath of tragedies (Kelly & Keefe, 2015). One such example is the murder of a University of Wisconsin student in 2008 who dialed 911 from her cell phone, apparently when confronted by an intruder in her apartment; the operator did not know her precise location or the nature of the emergency (Arnold, 2008). Similar tragedies have occurred affecting callers with medical emergencies and urgent automobile situations, such as a driver calling with a cell phone while the car sinks in a lake or flooded road (Kelly & Keefe, 2015).

Computers The use of computers inside patrol cars has improved police efficiency and reduced officers' demands on central office dispatchers. Computers enable instant electronic communication that permits the radio airwaves to be reserved for emergency calls rather than being used for requests to check license numbers and other routine matters. Computer programs also permit officers to type information about traffic violations, crime suspects, and investigations directly into central computers without filling out numerous separate forms by hand. For example, new computers in the Lansing, Michigan, police department patrol cars permit officers to swipe the bar code on Michigan drivers' licenses to call up a driver's record instantly (M. Miller, 2009). Increasingly, police vehicles are equipped with automated license plate readers. These readers use high-speed cameras to scan, record, and send to a central computer the license plate numbers of passing vehicles and parked cars so that officials can identify stolen vehicles as well as those associated with unpaid tickets and expired insurance (Musgrave, 2013).

Databases exist to permit officers to use their computers to check vehicle records, driving records, outstanding warrants, protection orders, prior calls for service, and criminal histories (Reaves, 2015). However, not all departments have access to all of these categories of information; those in small towns are less likely to have the resources for complete access (Reaves, 2015). With more-advanced computers and software, some officers can even receive mug shots and fingerprint records on their computer screens. With separate mobile scanners, officers can potentially run a quick check of an individual's fingerprints against the millions of fingerprint records stored in the FBI's database.

New technology can reduce the time required for an officer to process a drunken-driving arrest from four hours to less than one hour and enable officers to ticket twice as many speeders. The computer-connected officers have been shown to make more felony and misdemeanor arrests, presumably because paperwork absorbs less of their time. In a recent example, the Wyoming Highway Patrol upgraded its in-car computer systems in 2014 to give troopers new nationwide access to drivers' license checks and vehicle registrations as well as to facilitate the elimination of verbal radio traffic by enabling two-way computer messaging with dispatchers (Wyoming Highway Patrol, 2014).

The increase in efficiency gained through the use of computers may give police administrators greater flexibility in deciding how to deploy officers on patrol. However, the new technology has its costs and consequences. Patrol-car computers can require increased time and money for training officers. They also raise safety issues, in that the computers become dangerous projectiles within the vehicles during high-speed pursuits or collisions. In addition, because local police departments are under the control of local governments that do not possess equal resources, some departments cannot afford to purchase computers for patrol cars. The availability of communications and information technology is expanding, yet it still varies depending on departmental resources.

As mentioned, patrol-car computers enhance police officers' investigative capabilities through quick access to databases and other sources of information that help identify suspects. Most people are familiar with the presence of dashboard cameras in many police vehicles. New developments with these systems include automatic downloads to a central computer server, so that officers do not have to worry about running out of recording tape during a questioning or filling the car's hard drive with photos. There can be a second camera pointed at the backseat so that, without turning around, the officer can see on a screen what arrested suspects are doing. In addition, these systems use Global Positioning Systems (GPS) to automatically record the vehicle's location, speed, and the use of sirens and other emergency equipment. Thus, the technology helps to keep officers safer and provides a basis for supervisors to evaluate aspects of the officers' performance on patrol ("UTC Police," 2014).

Police patrol vehicles now often carry a computer, license plate reader, radar speed detectors, and dashboard cameras, as well as handheld devices for recording fingerprints and alcohol on drivers' breath. As the devices assist officers in gathering information more effectively, do they also make officers' jobs more complex and demanding? How will small-town police departments find the money to keep their vehicles well-equipped during an era of budget cuts?

George Frey/Getty Images

Computers have become very important for investigating specific types of crimes, especially cybercrimes. Many police departments have begun to train and use personnel to investigate people who use computers to meet children online with the intention of luring them into exploitative relationships (Bundy, 2012). As we have seen, computer investigations also involve pursuing people who commit identity theft, steal credit card numbers, and engage in fraudulent financial transactions using computers. At the national level, federal officials must use computers to detect and prevent sophisticated efforts to hack into government and corporate computer systems in order to steal secrets or harm critical infrastructures, such as regional electrical systems and emergency warning systems (Edwards, 2014).

Computers are also essential for crime analysis and crime mapping, methods used with increasing frequency by local police departments. Through the use of **Geographic Information System (GIS)** technology and software, police departments can analyze hot spots, crime trends, and other crime patterns with a level of sophistication and precision that was previously unavailable (Ratcliffe, 2010). By analyzing the locations and frequency of specific crimes, such as burglary, or the nature of calls for service in various neighborhoods, police are better able to deploy their personnel effectively and plan targeted crime-prevention programs (Stroshine, 2005).

Geographic Information System (GIS) Computer technology and software used by law enforcement officials to map problem locations in order to understand calls for service and the nature and frequency of crimes and other issues within specific neighborhoods.

The use of GIS is one component of the rapidly expanding development of computer software programs that process various kinds of information that help guide decisions about where to deploy police resources. In 2013, police officials in Tempe, Arizona, credited information analysis and data sharing for significant decreases in crime. New software helped officers to analyze crime trends and update records databases immediately. Information on reported crimes, suspects, and other aspects of investigations is instantly added to national databases, from which it can be instantly accessed by officers in the field. Information sharing has led to greater cooperation with neighboring police departments as well as state and federal officials, and has contributed to solving a number of crimes (Coe, 2013).

Police officials in Santa Cruz, California, contacted researchers who had developed software to predict earthquakes and asked them to develop prediction software to anticipate when and where crimes such as burglary, bicycle thefts, and assaults were likely to take place. Based on existing crime data, officers were given reports at the start of each shift about the likeliest times and locations for specific crimes to occur. The city saw nearly a 20 percent reduction in burglaries over the course of a year, in spite of a decrease in police personnel due to budget cuts (Kelly, 2012). Other California cities followed the lead of Santa Cruz, and soon after, the Seattle police department also began to use prediction software to address its crime problems (deLeon, 2013).

Although these advances in the analysis of data make it possible for cities to employ evidence-based practices, certain risks can arise from the acquisition of new technology. An audit of the Oakland, California, police department in 2012 found that the department had purchased several expensive anticrime technology systems—yet did not end up using them. One system did not work as expected, and then the company that sold it went out of business, so no refund or repair was possible. The use of other systems can be affected by the need to periodically upgrade software or upgrade equipment at moments when budget cuts limit resources available for new technology purchases (Kanaracus, 2012).

Another promising computerized tool for police is a system for detecting gunshots, quickly analyzing their location, and instantly communicating the information to police without reliance on human witnesses to dial the phone and guess where a shooting took place. Read the "Close Up" feature to learn about this technological advancement that assists with public safety and crime investigation.

Databases Computer technology permits law enforcement officials to gather, store, and analyze data. In minutes, or even seconds, computers can sort through data with the effectiveness that spares a user from spending hours combing through papers stored in a filing cabinet. For example, New York City detectives solved an

Gunshot Detection Technology

In January 2013, the U.S. Secret Service, the agency assigned to protect the president's safety, announced that it was interested in information about gunshot detection systems, presumably for use in protecting the White House. The request called attention to a promising computerized tool that analyzes the location of gunshots and instantly communicates that information to police without reliance on human witnesses to dial the phone and guess where a shooting took place. These systems were originally developed for the military as a means to identify sniper locations. For police use, once the system is installed, it is supposed to electronically distinguish gunshots from other sounds and detect the location of the gunshots through the interaction between a series of sound sensors placed in a specific neighborhood. As a result, the system can enable police officers to drive straight to the spot of the shooting and avoid driving around a neighborhood trying to figure where a shooting occurred. The precision in pinpointing the location of the shooting can help to save the lives of shooting victims by allowing them to receive first aid more quickly as well as assist in catching whoever fired the shots.

The systems are expensive and thus difficult to acquire for many cities that are struggling with budget cuts. More than 70 cities, however, have decided that such systems are important enough for the expenditure of funds and the allocation of personnel to monitor the technology. Many cities have systems that rely on technicians at a corporate headquarters far away who use satellite maps to quickly communicate the location of gunfire to the police department in the affected city. It would be prohibitively expensive for most cities to install systems with enough sensors to provide coverage throughout an entire municipality; typically, the sensors are placed only in areas that have recurring crime problems involving gun violence.

Police officials generally express enthusiasm about the usefulness of the gunshot detection technology. It can provide a huge advantage over the prior practice of waiting to respond to a 911 call about gunshots without always knowing the exact location of the shooting. In addition, there is often a delay of five minutes or longer as residents decide whether or not to call the police at the sound of a gunshot. Indeed, use of gunshot detection systems has demonstrated that in certain neighborhoods, gunshots are so routine that residents do not even bother to call 911 when they hear shooting. The new technology can call police to the location even if no citizens are willing to report the gunfire. Enthusiasm for the systems is such that in Springfield, Massachusetts, a neighborhood group raised money to acquire a system for its residential area as a way to assist police at a moment of tight budgets.

As with any technology, there are questions about the accuracy of the system, particularly with respect to distinguishing gunshots from other sounds, such as firecrackers or car horns. In addition, sometimes the sensors pick up and record yelling or loud conversations, troubling many privacy experts about the prospect of this technology inadvertently becoming a government surveillance system that records the private verbal communications of citizens on the streets. In 2014, Wilmington, Delaware, concluded that the particular gunshot detection system the city had purchased with the assistance of $250,000 federal grant had failed to perform as expected. During a period in which 600 people called police about shootings and 175 people were shot, the system detected the sounds of gunshots only a half dozen times. This raised concerns that the range of the system's sensors was too limited to fulfill the city's purposes.

Researching the Internet

To read a government summary of research on gunshot detection technology, access http://www.crimesolutions.gov /ProgramDetails.aspx?ID=273.

For Critical Thinking and Analysis

If you were a mayor or police chief, how much would you be willing to spend to acquire a gunshot detection system? The systems can have annual costs of $40,000 to $60,000 per square mile of coverage. Would your answer depend on how many shootings your city typically experienced each year within a particular neighborhood? If you had to reduce any part of the police department's budget in order to acquire this technology, what cuts would you make? Describe how you would address these issues.

Sources: H. Gold, "ShotSpotter: Gunshot Detection System Raises Privacy Concerns on Campuses," *The Guardian*, July 17, 2015 (www.theguardian.com); E. Goode, "Shots Fired, Pinpointed and Argued Over," *New York Times*, May 28, 2012 (www .nytimes.com); M. McGuinness, "Secret Service Seeks Gunshot Detection Technology," January 22, 2013 (http://news.msn.com /science-technology/secret-service-seeks -gunshot-detection-technology); G. Toppo, "Gunshot Detection System in Delaware Comes Up Blank," *USA Today*, February 7 (www.usatoday.com); P. Tuthill, "Springfield Police Expand Use of Gunshot Detection Technology," WAMC.com, March 14, 2013 (www.wamc.org/post/springfield-police -expand-use-gunshot-detection-technology).

armed robbery case in 2005 by taking a witness's description of the robber's tattoo and running it through the police department's computerized tattoo database. Very quickly, the detectives identified a suspect, showed his mug shot to the robbery victim, and tracked him down to make the arrest. The New York Police Department's database contains records on criminal complaints, warrants, 911 calls,

MACON VALERIE/SIPA/Newscom/Sipa Press/LOS ANGELES CALIFORNIA USA

individuals' criminal and parole records, and other kinds of property and public records (Hays, 2006).

In the discussion that follows, keep in mind that the usefulness of any database depends on both the accurate input of correct information and the methods that permit the information to be accessed efficiently by police officers. Human errors in database development and management not only limit the usefulness of this technology but also wreak havoc in the lives of people whose information is misclassified. For example, since 9/11, many innocent people, including small children, have faced problems trying to board airplanes because their names were among the thousands on the Transportation Safety Agency's overly broad terrorist watch list. Even the late Senator Edward Kennedy of Massachusetts found himself denied plane tickets when the name "Edward Kennedy" appeared on the list (Sharkey, 2008; Swarns, 2004).

One of the largest and historically most important criminal justice databases is the fingerprint database. Police departments throughout the country can submit fingerprints from a crime scene in the hope of finding the criminal's identity from among the more than 47 million sets of fingerprints stored in the FBI computers. Local and federal law enforcement officials routinely submit the fingerprints of everyone arrested for a serious charge so that the prints can be added to the database. If a suspect is found not guilty, the prints are supposed to be removed from the system. These databases may also be used for background checks on people who work in regulated industries such as casinos and banks (Engber, 2005).

Matching fingerprints was initially time consuming, because fingerprints had to be sent to the FBI on cards. Since 1999, however, the Integrated Automated Fingerprint Identification System (IAFIS) has enabled police to send fingerprints electronically and have them matched against the millions of prints in the database. Upon request, the FBI can also provide electronic images of individuals' fingerprints to local law enforcement agencies (Byrum, 2015). Finally, the FBI provides training for state and local police on taking fingerprints and transmitting those prints to the IAFIS for evaluation.

The Department of Homeland Security has developed its own fingerprint database from two primary sources. New post-9/11 rules require the collection of fingerprints from every noncitizen entering the United States. This has created a database of more than 64 million fingerprints that can be linked to the FBI database containing an additional 40 million sets. Military and intelligence officials are also collecting unidentified **latent fingerprints** from cups, glasses, firearms, ammunition, doorknobs, and any other objects that they find overseas in abandoned al-Qaeda training camps, safe houses, and battle sites. These prints are the patterned residue of natural skin secretions or contaminating materials such as ink, blood, or dirt that were present on the fingertips at the time of their contact with the objects. The hope is that terrorists will be identified if their fingerprints match those of visitors to the United States (Richey, 2006). As we shall see later in this chapter, DNA databases present similar hopes for identifying perpetrators, especially in domestic criminal cases (Eligon & Kaplan, 2012).

New debates have emerged about whether there should be a comprehensive national database of ballistic evidence (King, Wells, Katz, et al., 2013). Advocates argue that every gun sold should undergo a firing test so that its ballistic fingerprint can be stored in the database, just in case the weapon is later used in a crime. Opponents claim that this is an undesirable step toward national gun registration and that such a database would be useless because the ballistic characteristics of a gun's fired bullets change as the gun is used over time (Chaddock, 2002). The usefulness of these databases depends on the accuracy of technology to match evidence with stored information and the accessibility of database information to police departments and individual officers (M. A. Johnson, 2010). In addition, as indicated by the debate about ballistic evidence, the nature and use of evidence databases rely in part on public policy regarding what information can be gathered and how it will be used.

latent fingerprints Impressions of the unique pattern of ridges on the fingertip that are left behind on objects; these impressions are the residue of natural skin secretions or contaminating materials such as ink, blood, or dirt that were present on the fingertips at the time of their contact with the objects.

▼ CHECK POINT

4. **How do computers in patrol cars aid officers in communication issues?**
   Officers do not need to tie up the radio airwaves and the attention of dispatchers to check on stolen cars, drivers' records, and other important information that can be accessed via computer.

5. **How can the use of Geographic Information Systems (GIS) assist criminal justice officials?**
   They can create sophisticated maps for the analyses of crime patterns and other problems in neighborhoods.

6. **What kinds of information can be collected in law enforcement databases?**
   Fingerprints, tattoos, DNA samples, gun/ballistics records.

STOP & ANALYZE

Are there other kinds of information that could be usefully stored in databases to help solve crimes? Are there any kinds of information that pose risks of error or risks to people's rights if kept in databases and used by the police?

DNA Analysis

In recent years, scientific advances have enabled police and prosecutors to place greater reliance on **DNA analysis**. This technique identifies people through their distinctive gene patterns (also called *genotypic features*). DNA, or deoxyribonucleic acid, is the basic component of all chromosomes; all the cells in an individual's body, including those in skin, blood, organs, and semen, contain the same unique DNA. The characteristics of certain segments of DNA vary from person to person and thus form a genetic fingerprint. Forensic labs can analyze DNA from, for example, samples of hair, and compare them with those of suspects. As described by several law enforcement officials, the increasing effectiveness of DNA testing as an investigative tool has stemmed from "improved technology, better sharing of DNA databases among states and a drop in crime...that allowed detectives more time to work on unsolved cases" (Yardley, 2006). Although fingerprint evidence is still used, advances in DNA technology have greatly reduced reliance on the less precise testing of blood and hair evidence as the sole means of identifying suspects (Hulette, 2014).

Forensic science laboratories perform many kinds of scientific tests. As indicated in Table 14.3, many of these labs examine narcotics, firearms, and fingerprints, as well as DNA. The information in Table 14.3 is from 2009, the last year for which the Bureau of Justice Statistics has data, so one might presume that the capacity of

DNA analysis A scientific technique that identifies people through their distinctive gene patterns (also called *genotypic features*). DNA, or deoxyribonucleic acid, is the basic component of all chromosomes; all the cells in an individual's body, including those in skin, blood, organs, and semen, contain the same unique DNA.

TABLE 14.3   Percentage of Labs Performing Each Function, by Jurisdiction Type

Forensic Function	Total*	State	County	Municipal
Controlled substances	82%	86%	85%	75%
Firearms/toolmarks	55	55	63	62
Biology screening/DNA	59	64	66	49
Latent prints	60	54	63	78
Trace evidence	50	50	55	44
Toxicology	42	50	43	35
Impressions	44	44	53	43
Crime scene	52	44	62	71
Questioned documents	16	13	13	24
Digital/computer evidence	19	10	21	32
Number of labs reporting	397	211	88	63

*Includes federal labs, not shown separately.

Source: M. R. Durose, K. A. Walsh, and A. M. Burch, "Census of Publicly Funded Forensic Crime Laboratories, 2009," *Bureau of Justice Statistics Bulletin*, August 2012, p. 2.

crime labs to do additional tests has expanded over time. However, the impact of government budget cuts has affected crime labs and led to reduced capability and longer delays in processing evidence for testing (M. A. Johnson, 2010). Alabama, for example, cut the annual funding for crime labs from $15 million to $9 million over the period of 2009 to 2012. Several crime labs were closed, and toxicology tests statewide were directed to a single lab, leading to 90-day waiting periods for police departments to obtain results (Malone, 2012). Budget cuts also affected forensic labs and police investigations in Virginia at the end of 2014 (McDonald, 2014).

Although many publicly funded labs are not equipped to do DNA testing, DNA analysis has become especially important in criminal justice. It is revolutionizing the use of science for the investigation of crimes. Because scientists are increasing their capacity to extract testable DNA samples from tiny samples of biological material, law enforcement officials are increasingly able to tie specific individuals to a location or piece of evidence. When the local government lab is not able to conduct DNA tests, agencies hire private labs to do the analysis.

DNA Databases   In spite of questions about which offenders should be required to submit DNA samples, many states and the federal government are building a national database of DNA records that is maintained by the FBI. Known as CODIS, which stands for Combined DNA Index System, the project began in 1990 as a pilot project serving a few state and local laboratories. CODIS has now grown to include 137 laboratories in 47 states and the District of Columbia. The federal Justice for All Act, enacted in October 2004, greatly expanded the number of offenders in the federal justice system who must submit DNA samples. Previously, samples were taken only from those who had committed specific violent crimes. Later, collection expanded to federal offenders convicted of any felony, violent act, or conspiracy. In 2009, collection of DNA samples expanded further to all people arrested for federal crimes and all noncitizens who are detained (Weiss, 2008).

The Federal Bureau of Prisons obtains DNA through blood samples from *all* incoming offenders. In addition, federal probation offices must now obtain samples under the newer law. Federal probation offices are scrambling to find qualified phlebotomists (people trained to draw blood samples), as well as to acquire enough test kits for thousands of additional offenders. Moreover, Congress mandated that the samples be collected but did not provide any funds for the probation offices within federal courts to collect these samples (Administrative Office of the U.S. Courts, 2005). Thus, the new requirement is causing budget problems in the justice system.

States throughout the country have their own laws mandating which people are required to submit DNA samples. Depending on a particular state's law, samples are taken from either convicted offenders or those arrested for specific crimes. In 2012, for example, New York officials began to collect samples from all convicted offenders; previously the state's law had mandated collection only for those convicted of specific offenses (Eligon & Kaplan, 2012). In 2008, Maryland joined a dozen other states in collecting samples from people arrested but not yet convicted for murder, rape, and assault (Arena & Bohn, 2008). California began taking samples from everyone arrested on felony charges in 2009, whether or not they are ultimately convicted of a crime (Felch & Dolan, 2008). Georgia instituted a new law in 2008 to permit investigators to compare DNA evidence with samples collected from unconvicted criminal suspects who were required by judge-issued search warrants to submit to DNA testing. Previously, DNA evidence in Georgia could only be compared with samples taken from convicted felons (Armstrong, 2008). One Southern California prosecutor regards DNA databases as such a useful resource for solving serious crimes that he began to dismiss some misdemeanor and drug charges against defendants if they would agree to provide a DNA sample. Skeptics questioned whether the so-called "spit and acquit" program was appropriate, because it permitted drug offenders to go free without any treatment (Weiss, 2009a).

Another proposal to expand the use of DNA testing and evidence concerns searches that look for relatives rather than the exact person whose DNA was left at the crime scene. Although only exact matches of crime-scene evidence and an individual's DNA are supposed to be used in court, it is possible to identify other suspects through wider comparisons. For example, DNA comparisons may indicate that a convicted felon whose sample is in the database is not the perpetrator of a rape, but that he is a relative of the rapist. Thus, police would have reason to undertake further investigations of the convicted felon's close male relatives. So-called "kinship-based DNA searching" is already used in Great Britain but is not used as widely in the United States (Wade, 2006).

By taking samples from people convicted of specific crimes in the state and federal systems, officials hope that CODIS will enable them to close unsolved crimes that involve DNA evidence. Unfortunately, problems and delays in collecting and processing the samples persist. Nonetheless, the use of DNA testing and databases has led to arrests in a growing number of unsolved cases.

Many examples illustrate the use of DNA identification to close cold cases. In March 2011, DNA tests on a discarded cigarette butt led to the arrest of a Connecticut man who was tied through DNA testing to 17 rapes in various eastern states from 1997 through 2009 (T. Moore, 2011). In April 2005, DNA tests linked a man in Georgia with 25 unsolved rapes in three states, including a rape committed in New York in 1973. The man had fled New York nearly 20 years earlier when facing different rape charges. He was eventually located as the result of a routine background check when the man attempted to purchase a gun in Georgia. At the time, officials did not know he was linked to the other unsolved rapes, but the matches emerged when his sample was run through the national database (Preston, 2005). The successful use of the DNA database to close an old case raised officials' optimism about solving other cold cases by testing evidence that had been saved from many years ago. Such was the case, for example, of an imprisoned man in Georgia whose DNA analysis in 2006 indicated that he was responsible for four unsolved murders in Connecticut in the late 1980s and early 1990s (Yardley, 2006) and a serial murderer-rapist in Buffalo, New York, whose unsolved crimes spanned two decades (Staba, 2007).

Issues and Problems with DNA Analysis Such examples illustrate the benefit of using DNA testing and databases, but other cases demonstrate problems that need to be addressed. In Truro, Massachusetts, a writer was raped and murdered in her home in 2002. When a friend came to check on her whereabouts, she found the writer's two-year-old daughter clinging to her mother's bloody corpse on the floor. The police sought DNA samples from all men in the small community. Their efforts to obtain these samples led to protests by civil liberties advocates who believed the rights of innocent men were threatened, especially when police said that they would look closely at men who refused to provide a sample. In April 2005, police arrested a man after his sample matched DNA from the crime scene. The suspect was the trash collector who went to the victim's house each week. Unfortunately, although the suspect had volunteered to provide a sample in April 2002, the police did not collect the sample until March 2004. Further, because of a backlog of DNA samples to be tested at the state crime lab, the sample was not evaluated until April 2005 (Belluck, 2005). The suspect could have committed additional crimes during the long delay.

In another example, it took police only five days to identify a man in Vermont as a murder suspect by his DNA sample. Unfortunately, the crime had been committed five years previously—five years had passed between the time when the man provided the DNA sample and the time when Vermont crime lab officials put the sample in the state's database (Ring, 2005). Thus, the long delay prevented quick identification and arrest. The lack of resources for prompt tests always raises the possibility that additional crimes could have been prevented if a suspect had been identified and arrested earlier in the process.

The most disheartening problem is the fact that there are tens of thousands of "rape kits"—biological evidence taken from rape victims that could potentially identify rapists—that remain untested in evidence storage rooms around the country ("What's Being Done," 2016). Some of the kits did not have sufficient material to be tested accurately by DNA tests that existed at the time of the crime. Other kits appear to have been set aside because police departments did not place a priority on solving these crimes quickly. Others languished because of a lack of resources for doing scientific tests. National publicity regarding thousands of untested kits forgotten and then discovered in Detroit led to the identification of untested evidence in other cities and increasing actions by legislatures to require timely testing and to provide funds for testing ("What's Being Done," 2016).

The problem of too few laboratories and inadequate staff and equipment plagues many states and the federal government. These issues can be compounded by contemporary budget cuts and expanded categories of individuals required to provide samples. The move from collecting samples of convicted felons to also testing arrestees in many states, as well as detained illegal immigrants, greatly expanded the number of samples to be processed and tested. Technological advances may eventually reduce this problem.

Another potential problem with DNA testing, along with other aspects of forensic science, concerns the ethics and competence of scientists and technicians. Such problems have emerged in the FBI crime labs as well as in various states (M. A. Johnson, 2010). For example, crime laboratories in Houston and Fort Worth, Texas, were investigated and shut down after improper handling and analyzing of DNA evidence led to the convictions of people who were actually innocent. Scandals involving improper lab procedures and erroneous testimony by forensic scientists have led states such as Oklahoma and Texas to enact laws requiring crime labs to meet national accreditation standards (Kimberly, 2003). Yet, the FBI itself admitted in 2015 that its own lab technicians gave flawed testimony about hair evidence that was slanted to favor prosecutors in hundreds of trials, including several dozen that resulted in death sentences (Hsu, 2015).

The federal government now requires crime labs to meet national accreditation standards to qualify for federal funds, but many labs have not yet gone through the credentialing process. Moreover, critics contend that accreditation will not prevent mistakes and erroneous testimony by scientists and technicians with questionable ethics, skills, or knowledge. This is especially true in the worst cases, such as that of a West Virginia forensic scientist who falsified test results and provided false testimony in order to help prosecutors gain convictions (Roane & Morrison, 2005). In Massachusetts, a lab scientist was sentenced to prison and caused hundreds of cases to be reopened after falsifying test results and testimony in drug cases (Bidgood, 2015d). Scientists have an obligation to present truthful and impartial analyses, so they must avoid seeing themselves as part of the law enforcement team that seeks to convict people of crimes.

The expansion of DNA databases is raising a new issue that ultimately may be viewed as related to ethics. Sometimes genetic material from an unsolved case deteriorates over the years. By the time it is tested against a database, forensic scientists may not be able to identify all 13 markers that are usually used to match DNA profiles. However, using fewer markers creates risks that an apparent match is incorrect. In one case in Britain, a man's DNA sample matched six markers from criminal evidence, but when officials identified and tested four more markers, his DNA no longer matched (Felch & Dolan, 2008). The reliance on incomplete marker comparisons can lead DNA testing to produce erroneous results.

DNA is an investigative tool for law enforcement, but it can also be used to correct grave errors by exonerating wrongly convicted people when old evidence is tested with new scientific techniques or when newly discovered evidence is tested. As of April 2016, there had been 337 postconviction DNA exonerations of people nationwide who had spent an average of 14 years in prison for crimes that they did not commit (Innocence Project, 2016). However, it can only serve this aspect of justice when evidence is properly preserved and available for later testing as DNA technology steadily improves. In the 1990s, states belatedly began to create laws concerning the preservation of evidence and opportunities for convicted offenders to obtain tests on old and on newly discovered evidence. However, errors by court clerks and lab technicians have led to the disposal of relevant evidence, even in states with laws that require preservation. In addition, many such laws impose strict time limits and other restrictions on opportunities for convicted offenders to have evidence tested. Most troubling to many critics is the tendency of prosecutors to fight against having tests conducted even when those tests might prove that an innocent person has wrongly spent many years in prison (Dewan, 2009). A more uniform and structured system of evidence preservation is necessary for DNA to benefit the justice system fully.

CHECK POINT

7. **From whom is DNA collected for submission to the national database?**
   Federal officials and some states collect samples from all arrestees. Other states collect samples from convicted felons. Very few states do not have laws mandating collection of DNA samples from offenders.

8. **What problems exist in the effective use of DNA analysis?**
   Inadequate resources to test the backlog of DNA samples; careless testing or unethical testimony from some labs; prosecutors' opposition to permitting convicted offenders to have DNA tests performed on old or new evidence.

STOP & ANALYZE

Should state governments increase funding for crime labs? Why or why not? If necessary, what aspects of criminal justice should receive reduced funding to allow for increased resources for crime labs?

Surveillance and Identification

Police have begun using surveillance cameras in many ways. American cities increasingly use surveillance cameras at intersections to monitor and ticket people who run red lights or exceed speed limits, although quality problems affecting the video and photographs can limit the effectiveness of these efforts (Hensley & Wynn, 2009). In Scotland, England, and Australia, law enforcement officials have adopted the use of surveillance cameras that permit police to monitor activities that occur in downtown commercial areas or other selected locations. Officials in a control room can watch everyone who passes within the cameras' fields. Advances in camera technology enable these officials to see clearly the license plate numbers of cars and other specific information. American cities, such as New York and Washington, have made moves toward experimenting with this approach to combat crime in specific areas.

Chicago has moved forward with plans for the widespread use of surveillance cameras in public places. Using a $5 million grant from the U.S. Department of

Homeland Security, Chicago's 2,000 cameras will rotate 360 degrees, possess night-vision capability, and use software designed to detect suspicious activity, such as someone leaving a suitcase or other potential bomb container in a busy public place. City officials hope that surveillance will help them fight crime as well as improve their ability to identify and prevent potential acts of terrorism. Thus, the increased use of surveillance cameras in cities may become one element of local police departments' increased emphasis on homeland security. Surveillance cameras frequently help local police solve crimes such as robberies and burglaries (Daley, 2016).

Critics complain that constant surveillance by the government intrudes on the privacy of innocent, unsuspecting citizens and that there is insufficient evidence that this surveillance leads to reduced crime rates (Peralta, 2011; Taifa, 2002). See "The Policy Debate" about the controversy over the potential use of aerial drones for law enforcement surveillance. There may be other problems with surveillance, as well. For example, there are allegations in some British cities that bored officers in the control booth spend their time engaged in close-up monitoring of attractive

THE POLICY DEBATE

Should Law Enforcement Agencies Use Drones within the United States?

Unmanned aircraft called "drones" were developed for use by the military. They can carry cameras to follow and record the movement of enemy forces or to spy on areas that are too dangerous to view from helicopters or planes. In addition, drones can carry missiles and be used to kill enemies by remote command. The Obama administration has drawn sharp criticism for using drones overseas to eliminate suspected terrorists, including Americans. Drone strikes in such places as Pakistan and Yemen are alleged to have killed people other than the intended targets. Moreover, there are questions about the proof that should be required before someone is assassinated by drone.

In 2011, the first use of a drone by local American law enforcement officials occurred in North Dakota. Drones had already been used for specific investigations by federal agencies such as the FBI and the Drug Enforcement Administration. A North Dakota county sheriff who was chased off a ranch by armed men asked for assistance from drones stationed at a nearby Air Force base. (U.S. Customs and Border Protection had begun using drones in 2005 to monitor the North Dakota–Canada border to prevent illegal immigrants and smuggling.) An unarmed drone flew over the ranch and helped local officials determine when the men had set down their guns

so that they could be arrested by sheriff's deputies. This operation was done without detailed consideration of important legal and ethical questions. For example, does the use of drones operated by military officers violate the legal and traditional limitations on activity within the United States by American armed forces? Does the use of drones threaten the privacy of individuals, since a drone can fly over a house or business for many hours while transmitting high-quality photos and video to those monitoring the activity on computer screens?

By 2013, two developments contributed to major debates about the use of drones. First, the price of drones decreased and their availability from manufacturers increased so that it became possible for police departments to acquire these devices. A small drone can cost as little as $3,000. Thus, businesses and non–law enforcement government agencies also sought to use drones to inspect pipelines and monitor highway traffic. Second, there were intensified debates about the use of drones to kill suspected terrorists and the fear that the federal government might claim the authority to make such assassination strikes within the United States. Eventually, the Obama administration provided reassurances about not using drones for

lethal domestic missions, yet controversy remained about the legality, ethics, and effects of raining death from the sky.

For Police Use of Drones:

- Drones can film or take photos of locations that are too difficult for law enforcement officials to reach (e.g., mountains) or too dangerous to enter (e.g., a ranch with armed people behind barricades).
- The use of drones reduces the risk of injury and death of law enforcement officers who would otherwise personally enter specific places.
- Drones are now inexpensive enough for local law enforcement agencies to purchase.
- Drones can cover a broad area quickly to follow a criminal suspect or search for a lost child.

Against Police Use of Drones

- Drones can be armed to shoot and kill people, thereby creating risks that operators of police drones will either intentionally or accidently shoot people without proper justification or authorization.
- Photographs and films taken from flying drones can invade the privacy of individuals, including innocent citizens. Small drones could hover almost unnoticed outside the

women and ignore or hide evidence of police misconduct that is caught on camera. Training, supervision, and the establishment of clear procedures will be necessary to avoid such problems. Despite these allegations, the 500,000 surveillance cameras in London proved especially valuable in the aftermath of the July 2005 subway and bus terrorist bombings, when officials used recorded images to identify the bombing suspects (Stecklow, Singer, & Patrick, 2005).

Cameras can also help protect rights and hold police accountable when used in different surveillance contexts. For example, some states now mandate the video recording of police interrogations for murder cases and other serious crimes. In theory, police are less likely to engage in questionable behavior that may violate suspects' rights when they know that their actions are being recorded (Taslitz, 2012). Nevertheless, video cameras in police cars and surveillance cameras on buildings have caught officers engaged in crimes or using excessive force. For example, a surveillance camera showed two police officers entering and exiting an apartment building multiples times—and trying to avoid the camera in the process—on a night that led

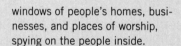

windows of people's homes, businesses, and places of worship, spying on the people inside.

- Drones could eventually be used for perpetual surveillance by the law enforcement officials of many public places; Americans would always feel that they were being watched.

- Police reliance on drones clashes with Americans' expectations about person-to-person contact with police officers who are visible, engaged participants in the community.

What Should the Policy Be?

In response to the growing debates, states and cities began to take action to define and limit the possibilities for the use of drones within the United States. No one denied that drones would be useful for such purposes as ensuring port security, conducting search and rescue, and finding missing persons. However, there were grave concerns about privacy and other aspects of overhead surveillance. For example, Virginia initially enacted legislation to ban unmanned aircraft in the state for two years, but later sought to change the law to permit specific uses by law enforcement agencies. Idaho's law required police to obtain warrants for most uses of drones. Proposals in North Carolina followed

Idaho's approach. The Seattle City Council required that any use of drones have prior approval by the Council, but created a controversial exception for police investigations and circumstances approved by a search warrant.

Clearly, inexpensive unmanned aircraft carrying cameras can have useful purposes for law enforcement agencies. However, the publicity and debates surrounding the military uses of drones overseas heightened sensitivity to the risks that might be posed if use of such aircraft in the United States is not carefully defined and controlled. It remains to be seen how law enforcement agencies will, under the watchful eye of state legislatures, develop proposals for clearly defining the uses of this new technology.

Researching the Internet

To see the concerns about police use of drones raised by civil liberties groups, see the American Civil Liberties Union's website https://www.aclu.org/issues /privacy-technology/surveillance -technologies/domestic-drones? redirect=blog/tag/domestic-drones.

Analyzing the Issue

Should local law enforcement agencies be able to use drones? If so, for what purposes? Should prior approval by a judge

or city council be required for each use? Are there any situations in which police could use an armed drone capable of firing at targets on the ground? Imagine that you and your classmates are divided into groups that will represent each side in a public debate. One group should make a list of arguments that might be presented by a police chief. The other group should present arguments from the perspective of a civil liberties group. Write down the arguments for both sides.

Sources: B. Bennett, "Police Employ Predator Drone Spy Planes on Home Front," *Los Angeles Times*, December 10, 2011 (www .latimes.com); E. Greenway, "Virginia Beach City Council Considering Use of Drones by Police, Other Departments," New Channel 3 WTKR, January 5, 2016 (http://wtkr.com); J. Hinton, "Legislation Would Restrict Use of Drones by Police and Deputies," *Winston-Salem Journal*, March 24, 2013 (www .journalnow.com); J. Koebler, "Virginia Governor on Drone Ban: Police Use OK," *U.S. News and World Report*, March 26, 2013 (www.usnews.com); "North Dakota Law Aims to Set Parameters for Police Use of Drones," National Public Radio, August 31, 2015 (www.npr.org); L. Thompson, "Except for Police, Use of Drones Would Need City's OK," *Seattle Times*, March 18, 2013 (www .seattletimes.com); L. Zuckerman, "Idaho Restricts Drone Use by Police Agencies Amid Privacy Concerns," Reuters News Service, April 11, 2013 (www.reuters.com).

a woman to file a rape complaint against an officer who had escorted her back to her building when she was drunk (Lee, 2009). In California, a camera in 2009 recorded an officer kicking a suspect in the head after a chase (Vives & Blankstein, 2009).

As discussed in Chapter 5, the use of individual body cameras by police officers is expanding rapidly. Many advocates of body cameras are focused on deterring police misconduct, especially the excessive use of force. However, cameras can also provide evidence of lawbreaking actions by individuals who confront police—and if citizens are aware that officers are wearing body cameras, they may try harder to keep their emotions under control when they disagree with a police officer. Read "A Question of Ethics" at the end of the chapter to consider the frequently reported problem of officers damaging or turning off body cameras and cameras in their cars under circumstances in which it appears that they wish to avoid accountability for their actions.

American law enforcement officials have experimented with other surveillance and detection technologies. The National Institute of Justice provides funding to help scientists develop devices that will assist the police. For example, scanners have been developed to permit officers to detect whether individuals are carrying weapons, bombs, or drugs. Some of these devices detect foreign masses hidden on the human body, while others detect trace particles and vapors that are differentiated from those associated with human bodies and clothing (U.S. Transportation Safety Administration, 2012; Business Wire, 2001b; PR Newswire, 2001). There are public debates about the use of backscatter X-rays at airports, both because of fears about radiation exposure for flyers every time they pass through airport security and because of privacy concerns about the near-naked image of each individual seen by the TSA officer on the monitor (Ravitz, 2009). There are also mobile versions of these scanners in vans and trucks. These models were originally designed for use by the military to detect car bombs, but they are available for broader use in border security to detect contraband in vehicles (Greenberg, 2010). They could also have applications for detection of weapons and contraband by police on America's streets.

The use of such technology is likely to expand as part of the government's efforts to identify suspected terrorists. The USA PATRIOT Act enhances federal law enforcement officials' authority to monitor electronic communications, including the use of "roving" surveillance aimed at particular individuals, without identifying or limiting specific facilities and devices to be monitored (Savage, 2011). In 2012, controversies emerged about cell-phone companies providing information to local police agencies that sought to monitor individuals without obtaining a court order (Lichtblau, 2012).

The U.S. Supreme Court has already given signs that it will look critically at some new police technologies. In *United States v. Jones* (2012), the justices decided that placing a GPS device on a car to follow a suspected drug trafficker's movements constituted a "search" and therefore required a warrant or a sufficient justification. Officers cannot freely place electronic monitoring devices on vehicles.

Kyllo v. United States (2001)
Law enforcement officials cannot examine a home with a thermal-imaging device unless they obtain a warrant.

In *Kyllo v. United States* (2001), the court looked at the use of thermal-imaging devices to detect unusual heat sources. Law enforcement officials had pointed such a device at a house, thinking that it might detect evidence of marijuana being cultivated under grow lights. Their efforts led to a search of the home and the discovery of 100 marijuana plants. In the majority opinion, Justice Antonin Scalia declared the use of the device in this manner to be an illegal search. According to Scalia, "Obtaining by sense-enhancing technology any information regarding the interior of the home that could not otherwise have been obtained without physical intrusion into a constitutionally protected area constitutes a search" and is therefore covered by the limitations of the Fourth Amendment, especially the warrant requirement (*Kyllo v. United States*, 2001:2043). It is clear that judges will continue to evaluate the constitutionally permissible uses of new technologies. More recently, the Supreme Court showed concern about privacy issues related to technology by forbidding police officers from scrolling through the contents of a driver's cell phone after the driver was arrested on an outstanding warrant (*Riley v. California*, 2014). The officers are required to seek a search warrant from a judge after taking possession of an arrestee's phone. Consider how you would decide emerging issues as a judge by reading "You Make the Decision."

Trial Judge

The U.S. Supreme Court has said that police officers with an *arrest warrant* can enter a home "when there is reason to believe that the suspect is within" (*Payton v. New York*, 1980). If they do not have reason to believe that the target of the arrest warrant is inside the home, then they would need a separate *search warrant* to enter a house or apartment. At a hearing to determine the admissibility of evidence, a defense attorney is asking you—the trial judge—to rule that police officers violated the Fourth Amendment prohibition on unreasonable searches because, while attempting to execute an arrest warrant, they used a handheld radar device to detect whether there were any people within the home. In other words, without a search warrant, they examined the inside of the home with the radar device—and used information from the radar device to decide to enter the quiet dwelling where they found the defendant, as well as guns that could be used to convict him of a federal firearms crime. The Fourth Amendment requires police to obtain search warrants from a judge in order to protect the "right of the people to be secure in their . . . houses, papers and effects, against unreasonable seizures."

In a previous case, the Supreme Court had said that it violates the Fourth Amendment when the police, without a search warrant, point a heat-detection device at a house to try to determine if there are hot lights for growing marijuana plants inside the house (*Kyllo v. United States*, 2001). The Supreme Court said such actions violate people's reasonable expectation of privacy concerning their homes and therefore police officers are required to obtain a search warrant from a judge before using such a device.

Does the warrantless use of the radar device to detect the presence of people inside a home similarly violate the Fourth Amendment and therefore require the exclusion of the guns from evidence? Give reasons for your decision. Then search the Internet and read the decision by the U.S. Court of Appeals in *United States v. Denson* (December 30, 2014).

---

9. **What issues have been raised concerning police surveillance technology, including scanners used to examine people boarding planes at airports?**
   There are concerns about government intrusions on people's privacy as well as concerns about other impacts of specific technologies, such as radiation exposure from X-ray devices.

What government surveillance activities, if directed at you, your computer, and your communications, would you consider to be going "too far" if officials did not have a basis to suspect you of any wrongdoing? Should police be required to seek a search warrant from a judge before monitoring any activities on computers and cell phones?

Weapons Technology

Police officers in the United States typically carry firearms. There are millions of guns available throughout American society that individuals can use to commit crimes or threaten police officers. Americans are accustomed to reading periodically throughout each year about tragic situations in which officers were killed when unexpectedly shot by someone while they conducted their patrol duties. For example, in 2016, a female police officer in Virginia was tragically shot and killed during her very first day on the job (Fandos & Hauser, 2016). Police officers face challenges in trying to protect themselves while maintaining order in society. Decisions about increasing the equipment and firepower available to police can raise controversies about the excessive use of force, needless deaths of citizens, and detrimental effects for police–community relations. Read the "Current Controversies in Criminal Justice" about police departments' acquisition of military equipment for use in dealing with citizens within their communities.

Police officers have been sued in many cases when they injured or killed people without proper justification. Some of these lawsuits have resulted in cities and counties paying millions of dollars to people who were injured when police used guns

Military Equipment and Local Police

Television news crews and newspaper photographers from around the nation gathered in Ferguson, Missouri, in November 2014 to cover the anticipated protests—or potential public celebrations—that would follow from the grand jury's decision on whether or not to bring criminal charges against Office Darren Wilson for the shooting death of unarmed teenager Michael Brown. The prosecutor's announcement that no indictment would be issued ignited protests that produced arson and property damage. Among the most striking images published from Ferguson were those of unarmed protesters holding their hands aloft, as if to emulate witnesses' statement that Michael Brown was surrendering when he was shot, standing face-to-face with helmeted police officers in military-style gear and holding high-powered military-style weapons. These images contributed to new national debates about the so-called militarization of American police and, especially, the transfer of millions of dollars' worth of military weapons and vehicles from the downsizing U.S. Department of Defense to local police departments.

As described by one news report, "Since President Obama took office, the Pentagon has transferred to police departments tens of thousands of machine guns; nearly 200,000 ammunition magazines; thousands of pieces of camouflage and night-vision equipment; and hundreds of silencers, armored cars, and aircraft" (Apuzzo, 2014). The draw-down of American military forces from the wars in Iraq and Afghanistan left the federal government with surplus equipment that local police departments eagerly requested. Law enforcement agencies in Florida alone received $266 million worth of equipment, including 45 mine-resistant ambush-protected (MRAP) armored vehicles designed to withstand blasts from roadside bombs.

Many police officials see military equipment as useful for several reasons. There may be hostage situations and standoffs with armed people for which the police need vehicles and equipment that can take officers close to buildings while providing protection from gunshots. Police officers may need to be able to have firepower equal to that of lawbreakers who are using high-powered semiautomatic weapons. In addition, one component of homeland security planning since 2001 has been the idea that police officers need to be ready to respond to any kind of terrorism attack in their local communities, including coordinated efforts by multiple attackers who might plant bombs and use military-style weapons against the police.

There are grave concerns, however, that the use of military equipment and tactics will alter the attitudes and behavior of police and have detrimental consequences for citizens' perception of and willingness to cooperate with the police. In countries governed by dictators, military forces are used to suppress freedom and control people. By contrast, policing in the American democracy is supposed to make police officers part of the community, working with the community, and under the control of mayors and other officials elected by the community. The birth of community policing in the 1970s was driven, in part, by heavy-handed police tactics. These police actions often occurred during civil rights protests, both peaceful and those that involved civil disorder. People in poor neighborhoods came to view the police as an occupying force opposed to their desires for racial equality and the freedom to go about their daily affairs without surveillance and suspicion. After the events in Ferguson, the presence of police clad and equipped as soldiers renewed concerns about police roles and relationships in the community. In May 2015, President Obama signed an executive order to tighten the rules and conditions for the transfer of military equipment to local police.

Does the use of military-style uniforms and equipment make citizens see the police as more impersonal, distant, and hostile? Do people feel less free to approach and interact in a friendly manner with officers in military-style dress and military vehicles than with officers in traditional uniforms on foot and driving squad cars? If so, are there also risks that a militarized self-image will affect how police officers treat people? Tom Nolan, a criminal justice scholar and former lieutenant in the Boston Police Department says, "When you equip domestic police officers in civilian law enforcement with military uniforms, military equipment, and military weapons—they'll conduct themselves as if they're waging war in our communities" (Ledbetter, 2014). Many police officials disagree with this viewpoint, but clearly there are widespread concerns about the impact of the militarization of American police.

For Critical Thinking and Analysis

Do military-style uniforms and equipment create risks that the public's view of and voluntary cooperation with police officers will change? What risks, if any, exist concerning potential changes in police officers' attitudes and actions? If you were a police chief, what three arguments would you give concerning your view of the risks—or benefits—of acquiring surplus military equipment?

Sources: M. Apuzzo, "What Military Gear Your Local Police Department Bought," *New York Times*, August 20, 2014 (www.nytimes.com); R. Balko, *Rise of the Warrior Cop*, New York: Public Affairs, 2013; M. Landler, "Obama Offers New Standards on Police Gear in Wake of Ferguson Protests," *New York Times*, December 1, 2014 (www.nytimes.com); S. Ledbetter, "Surplus Military Hardware Finds Way into Area Police Agencies," WPTZ-News Channel 5, November 11, 2014 (www.wptz.com); P. Shinkman, "Ferguson and the Militarization of Police," *U.S. News and World Report*, August 14, 2014 (www.usnews.com).

or nightsticks improperly or in an inappropriate situation. To avoid future lawsuits, departments have given greater attention to the training of officers. They have also sought nonlethal weapons that could be used to incapacitate or control people without causing serious injuries or deaths (Reaves, 2015). Traditional **less-lethal weapons**, such as nightsticks and pepper spray, can be used only when officers are in close contact with suspects, and they are not suitable for all situations that officers face.

Police officers need to have the ability to incapacitate agitated people who are threatening to harm themselves or others. This need arises when they confront someone suspected of committing a serious crime as well as when they are attempting to control a crowd causing civil disorder. They also seek to enhance their ability to stop criminal suspects from fleeing. A variety of less-lethal weapons have been developed to accomplish these goals. Police use some of them widely, while others are still undergoing testing and refinement.

Projectile weapons shoot objects at people whom the police wish to subdue. Some projectiles, such as rubber bullets, can travel a long distance. Others are employed only when suspects are within a few yards of the officers. Rubber bullets have been used for many years. Although they are generally nonlethal, they can cause serious injuries or death if they hit someone in the eye or elsewhere in the head. Many departments have turned to the use of beanbags, small canvas bags containing tiny lead beads, fired from a shotgun (C. Spencer, 2000). They are intended to stun people on impact without causing lasting injury. Several police departments in the Los Angeles area, however, abandoned the use of beanbags because of concerns about injuries and a few deaths caused by these projectiles as well as dissatisfaction with their accuracy when fired at a target (Leonard, 2002). Yet the weapons continue to be used elsewhere ("Officers Use Bean Bag Rounds," 2015; "Police Use Bean-Bag Ammo," 2015).

Other departments have used air guns that shoot pepper balls, small plastic pellets filled with a peppery powder that causes coughing and sneezing on release after the suspect is stunned by the impact of the pellet. Officers can also fill the pellets with green dye in order to mark and later arrest individuals in an out-of-control crowd (Randolph, 2001). Pellet weapons drew increased scrutiny after an Emerson College student died when she was hit in the eye by a pellet as police officers attempted to disperse a crowd of revelers who were celebrating a Boston Red Sox victory (CNN, 2004a). In 2015, an 88-year-old man in New Mexico who was distraught over the death of his wife reportedly waved a knife and asked officers to shoot him. Officers allegedly shot him with pepper balls and unleashed a police dog to incapacitate him. He suffered injuries and died a month later (Boetel, 2016). Such events cause police executives to constantly reevaluate which weapons their officers should carry.

Other weapons under development include one that shoots nets that wrap around

less-lethal weapons Weapons such as pepper spray, air-fired beanbags, or nets that are meant to incapacitate a suspect without inflicting serious injuries.

Conducted energy devices, such as Tasers, now give police officers the opportunity to subdue threatening people by using less-than-lethal force, when in prior years they might have used firearms. Because some people have died after being subjected to these alternative weapons, controversies exist about whether their use should be strictly limited to truly dangerous situations. Are there risks that new weapons technology will be used in the field without a fully understanding the harm that may be inflicted on people with specific medical conditions or other vulnerabilities?

individual suspects and another that sprays a fountain of foam that envelops the suspect in layers of paralyzing ooze. Law enforcement agencies may also eventually have versions of new weapons being developed for the military, such as devices that send out incapacitating blasts of heat or blinding flash explosions (Hambling, 2005). For example, a new military weapon called "Silent Guardian" shoots a focused beam of radiation that is tuned precisely to stimulate human pain nerves. It inflicts unbearable, incapacitating pain but, according to the inventors, does not cause injuries (Hanlon, 2007). A law enforcement version, if it worked as intended, could be an alternative to using lethal firearms in some situations.

For suspects who are close at hand, many police departments use conducted energy devices (CEDs), the most well-known of which is the Taser, a weapon with prongs that sends an incapacitating electric jolt of 50,000 volts into people on contact (Ith, 2001). More than 12,000 law enforcement agencies in the United States use these devices. As a result, there is great potential for the devices to be used frequently. However, a study by Amnesty International found that more than 330 people died in the United States between 2001 and 2008 after being shocked by Tasers (Ferretti & Feighan, 2009). Nearly all of them were unarmed. Some of those who received shocks for failing to obey police commands reportedly suffered from mental or physical disabilities that impeded their ability to cooperate. The manufacturer of Tasers as well as some researchers dispute whether the device actually caused the deaths.

Issues have also arisen about whether officers are too quick to use Tasers when they could use persuasion or other means to calm agitated or uncooperative people. The controversy reached a high point when Miami police officers used a Taser on a six-year-old child who was threatening to harm himself (CNN, 2004b). In late 2012 and early 2013, there were news reports of cities in Utah, Ohio, and North Carolina paying large sums to settle significant lawsuits based on deaths and permanent injuries that occurred after police officers' use of CED weapons (Callahan, 2013; Adams, 2012; T. Reaves, 2012). One man's death in Utah led that state's legislature to enact a resolution encouraging police departments to participate in specific training on how to handle uncooperative people affected by mental illnesses without resorting quickly to the use of force (Rogers, 2011).

The development of less-lethal weapons has undoubtedly saved officers from firing bullets in many situations in which they previously might have felt required to shoot threatening suspects. The use of CEDs may reduce overall injuries to officers and citizens (Bulman, 2010). However, these weapons do not magically solve the problem of incapacitating suspects safely. Mechanical problems or misuse by the officer may make the new weapons ineffectual or create risks of unnecessary injuries and deaths (Thompson & Berman, 2015). In addition, officers may act too quickly in firing a less-lethal weapon during inappropriate situations. In such circumstances, needless minor injuries may be inflicted, or the targeted person may become more enraged and thus more threatening to the officers who later must transport the person to jail. Moreover, an officer can carry only so many weapons in her or his arms. The existence of less-lethal weapons will not ensure that such weapons are actually handy when officers must make difficult, on-the-spot decisions about how to handle a threatening situation.

▼ **CHECK POINT**

STOP & ANALYZE

10. **What kinds of new weaponry have police employed?**
   Less-lethal weapons, including beanbag projectiles, CEDs, and pepper ball projectiles.

Should all police officers submit themselves during training to be the targets of any less-than-lethal weapons that they might be called upon to use? Why or why not?

Much of the investment in new technology has been directed toward surveillance equipment and investigation techniques, including DNA analysis, that will assist law enforcement officers in identifying and convicting criminal offenders. Although fewer resources have been directed toward technology in courts and corrections, both of these segments of the justice system face new issues and opportunities stemming from the use of technology.

Courts

Many local courthouses struggle to keep up with the processing of cases and the attendant consequences of case backlogs. One of the central issues for many busy courthouses is simply how to keep case files up to date and readily available for judges, prosecutors, and defense attorneys. The volume of files in many courthouses can create storage and accessibility problems. There are only so many rooms and filing cabinets available for storing files in any building. Thus, older files may be moved to remote locations where they are not easily accessible and must be retrieved if a case is reexamined on appeal or through later motions concerning the discovery of new evidence and other matters.

Technology provides a mechanism for reducing the problems of "too much paper" in courthouse files. Many courts have moved toward **electronic file management** systems in which records are digitized and made available as computer files. Such systems typically also use electronic filing systems in which attorneys file motions and other documents via e-mail rather than as traditional paper documents.

One example of a court moving toward a reduction in paper used for case processing is the state circuit court in Eaton County, Michigan. The prosecutors carry into the courtroom laptops that can wirelessly access police reports, 911 calls, court orders, and crime-scene photos. As noted by the county prosecutor, "We go to court with much more information than a prosecutor carrying a stack of files" (Grasha, 2009a). Gradually, other courts throughout the country are purchasing equipment and software to enable efficient access to information and to reduce the costs of producing and storing paper documents (Richter & Humke, 2011).

electronic file management
Computerization of court records done to reduce reliance on paper documents and make documents easily accessible to the judge and attorneys via computer.

Computers, projection screens, and other technologies permit attorneys to present evidence more effectively in the courtroom. Do these high-tech presentations necessarily advance the search for truth?

Don Hogan Charles/The New York Times/Redux Pictures

Computers can also help increase efficiency in judges' calculations of possible sentencing options. The development of sentencing guidelines has reduced judges' discretion for determining appropriate sentences. Instead, judges add up points, based on the offense and the prior record, to determine the sentence range mandated by the legislature. Private computer companies have developed software that will do sentencing calculations quickly for judges and for the probation officers who write presentence reports.

Does relying on computer calculations pose any risks? Obviously, if incorrect numbers are included in the calculations, an improper sentence will be produced. For defendants with complex records, such as numerous arrests and probation violations, the person inputting the data could easily miscount arrests and reported probation violations in the score, even though the sentence is supposed to be based on the number of actual criminal convictions. More importantly, does the software program diminish the image of justice, giving the impression that sentencing occurs by machine? State judges are supposed to represent the community, delivering messages about justice on the community's behalf as they make rulings.

The presentation of evidence in court is changing through the introduction of new technology. Previously, lawyers presenting documents and objects as evidence often needed to carry them in front of jurors or have jurors pass them through the jury box. This meant that jurors often got only a fleeting glimpse of specific pieces of evidence. Now, many courthouses are developing electronic courtrooms, using presentation technologies that have long been used in business meetings. These mechanisms include projection screens or multiple monitors that permit jurors to study documents and photographs simultaneously. Websites of U.S. district courts often list the equipment available in each courtroom and instruct attorneys on how to use the equipment. For example, a partial list of equipment presented on one district court's website includes the following:

- *Evidence presentation cart*, containing
  Evidence camera
  Annotation monitor
  Microphone
  VCR
  Auxiliary connections
- *Counsel table*, containing
  PC connection
  Internet access
  Real-time court reporting connection
- *Jury box/plasma screen*. A 50-inch retractable plasma screen over the jury box can be lowered when needed.
- *Gallery*. Two monitors located on the sides of the gallery allow spectators to see evidence being presented during a court proceeding.
- *Side camera*. A side camera located near the ceiling above the jury box can be used to display images of exhibits to the judge, the witness, the jury, all counsel, and those seated in the gallery at the same time.
- *Hearing assistance system*. Wireless headphones are available for use by the hearing impaired or for language interpretation.
- *Color video printer*. At the request of counsel, displayed images can be printed for admission into evidence.

Such technologies are obviously useful in communicating more effectively to everyone in the courtroom (Michael, 2013). There are risks, however, that some uses of technology may distort rather than clarify an accurate understanding of the evidence. For example, the use of computer simulations raises issues about the accurate presentation of evidence.

Attorneys have traditionally attempted to use their words to "paint a picture" for the jurors. In a criminal case, the prosecutor and defense each presents its own version of a chain of events or the circumstances under which a crime allegedly occurred. It is entirely possible that after hearing the same presentations, individual jurors will leave the courtroom with very different perceptions about what happened at the crime scene. Contemporary attorneys have attempted to use computer technology to advance a highly realistic-looking image of their version of events. (McCormick, 2000). The jury may see, for example, a computer-generated film of a person being struck from behind or falling in a manner consistent with the victim's injuries. Yet this film will be prepared in accordance with a particular version of events, the prosecutor's or the defendant's. There are risks that the realism of the recreated events on the screen will stick in the minds of jurors, even if the presentation is not an objective interpretation of the facts in the case (Schofield, 2011). Judges and attorneys must be wary about the use of such technologies if they distort perceptions rather than contribute to accurate fact finding.

Problems also arise through jurors' use of technology. Typically, a judge will tell jurors that they cannot investigate the facts of a case on their own. They are sometimes instructed not to read any articles in a newspaper about the case being presented before them. The widespread use of the Internet, however, makes seeking information about a case not only easy but also quite tempting for some jurors. Whereas a judge may hear if a juror attempted to visit a crime scene and thereby exclude the juror from the trial for misconduct, it is much more difficult to know whether jurors have sought information about a case through an Internet search. The use of such devices as iPhones has even enabled disobedient jurors to do their own research on a case during a lunch break in the middle of the attorneys' arguments. In one case in Florida, 8 out of 12 jurors eventually admitted that they had done their own Internet research on the case, including finding information that was excluded from presentation at trial through the rules of evidence. Thus, the judge had to declare a mistrial, and eight weeks of work by prosecutors and defense attorneys went to waste; the long, complex trial had to begin again after the selection of a new jury (Schwartz, 2009).

Problems have also arisen as jurors use blogs and social media sites to post announcements about the progress of a case or about jury deliberations. There is evidence that some jurors even send out messages by cell phone during breaks in the trial (Schwartz, 2009). Thus, judges have become more keenly aware of the need to bar jurors from bringing cell phones to court as well as the need to give thorough and stern warnings about the rule against jurors conducting their own investigations. Under the adversarial system, evidence is presented by the opposing attorneys who have been trained to respect the rules of evidence. Independent examinations of evidence by jurors acting as amateur detectives can enhance risks of inaccurate conclusions about facts. Because of media attention directed at the misbehavior of jurors in San Francisco, starting in 2012, California implemented a new law that authorized judges to impose jail sentences on jurors who used cell phones or other devices to either research a case or provide information to others about a case (Ward, 2011).

Another potential impact of technology on jury trials is embodied in fears of a so-called *CSI effect* that makes jurors unwilling to render "guilty" verdicts unless there is scientific evidence to link the defendant to the crime (Rath, 2011). Americans are fascinated by dramatized television programs that show the use of science for solving crimes and medical mysteries. According to a 2009 Harris Poll, the television show *CSI: Crime Scene Investigation* set in Las Vegas is Americans' all-time favorite television series (Harris Poll, 2009). The show was so popular that the CBS network created two *CSI* spin-off shows, set in Miami and New York, respectively. Another popular set of shows, *NCIS* and *NCIS: Los Angeles*, parallel dramas about the U.S. Navy's Criminal Investigative Service, also portray the use of forensic science, as do the shows *Bones* and *Rosewood* on the Fox network.

Because these popular programs portray specialists using science to make definitive conclusions, many judges and prosecutors believe jurors now erroneously think there should be DNA evidence, soil sample testing, and other scientific evidence in every criminal case (Toobin, 2007). In fact, the evidence in many cases consists of witness testimony, circumstantial evidence, and objects with no

CSI effect A hypothetical but unproven consequence of watching television dramas revolving around forensic science. Some prosecutors and judges believe that these dramas raise jurors' expectations about the use of scientific evidence in criminal cases and thereby reduce the likelihood of "guilty" verdicts in trials that rely solely on witness testimony and other forms of nonscientific evidence.

Many prosecutors and judges worry that the "*CSI* effect" may help guilty defendants go free if there is no DNA or other scientific evidence to use against them. Critics claim that the *CSI* effect is a myth that is perpetuated by prosecutors and the media. What evidence would you want to see in order to conclude whether or not the *CSI* effect exists?

CBS Photo Archive/Getty Images

fingerprints or DNA on them. Moreover, the television programs show fictional situations in which experts instantly make accurate and definitive conclusions about a "match" between hair samples, fiber samples, handwriting samples, or other materials. Real forensic scientists have grave doubts about anyone's ability to make definitive identifications of suspects based on such "matches."

Students of criminal justice should regard claims about the *CSI* effect with caution. The claims emerge from individual prosecutors' and judges' feelings of surprise or disappointment with the decisions and questions of juries in particular cases. Moreover, because news stories have presented the *CSI* effect as if it were a real phenomenon, prosecutors and judges may assume that it affects jurors' decisions when, in fact, it may not even exist.

Actual research on the *CSI* effect calls its existence into question (S. Stephens, 2007; Podlas, 2006). Surveys indicate that jurors may expect to see specific kinds of scientific evidence, but this expectation may be related to a more general "tech effect" of Americans using technology in their daily lives rather than watching specific television shows. Moreover, the increased expectation for scientific evidence does not necessarily mean that jurors will not vote to convict a defendant without it (Huey, 2010). The debate about the *CSI* effect illustrates the possibility that decision making within the criminal justice system can be affected by popular perceptions and assumptions about the role of technology and science in the investigation of criminal cases (Dysart, 2012).

CHECK POINT

11. How is technology employed in courthouses?
Electronic file management for records; presentation technology in courtrooms for displaying evidence.

12. How can technology disrupt jury trials?
Jurors using the Internet to investigate cases or using blogs and social media sites to reveal information about jury deliberations; jurors expecting more technological forensic evidence than is available (the so-called *CSI* effect).

STOP & ANALYZE

Should one side in a case be permitted to present computer simulations in the courtroom if the other side—such as a poor defendant represented by a public defender—cannot afford to hire consultants who are experts in using technology?

Corrections

Many of the technologies previously discussed for policing and courts also have applications in corrections. Computerized record keeping and statewide databases can reduce the burden of maintaining, storing, and transporting paper files on each prisoner. Instead, officials throughout the state can access records instantly via computer. In fact, many states have set up online records-retrieval systems that are accessible to the public. Often called OTIS (Offender Tracking Information Systems), these accessible databases permit crime victims to keep track of when specific offenders gain release on parole. They can also help employers to do background checks on job applicants. Separate public-access information systems often provide specific information on the residences of convicted sex offenders. Typically, members of the public can use the state correctional department's website to discover the identities and home addresses of sex offenders within a specific zip code. These databases are intended to warn people about the presence of a specific category of ex-convicts in their neighborhoods.

Public access to information about ex-offenders can cause serious problems. In separate incidents in Maine, Washington, and New Hampshire, individuals have looked up the names and addresses of released sex offenders on a state database, then hunted them down and shot them. As we saw in Chapter 13, one of the murder victims in Maine was on the sex offender registry for the "sex crime" of misdemeanor sexual abuse because, as a 19-year-old youth, he had had consensual sex with his girlfriend, who was two weeks shy of her sixteenth birthday, at which point the sexual contact would have been legal (Ellement & Smalley, 2006). These crimes led to debates about which offenders should actually be listed in databases and whether such databases should be open to the public.

In correctional institutions, technology enhances safety and security through the use of such developments as electronically controlled cell doors and locks, motion sensors, surveillance cameras, and small radios attached to the shirts of correctional officers. Note that surveillance cameras are not always popular with correctional officers, because cameras also reveal whether officers are doing their jobs conscientiously and properly. There is also a big push in many prisons to provide body armor for correctional officers. Although the stiff vests may be uncomfortable and make upper-body movements less free and easy, they can save lives by protecting officers against being stabbed by inmates' homemade knives (U.S. Government Accountability Office, 2011).

Because security is the top priority for correctional institutions, most technology resources are devoted to this goal rather than to prisoners' vocational training and rehabilitation. In a fast-changing world, prisoners who face the challenges of reentry are often like Rip Van Winkle, the character in the Washington Irving short story who awakens after sleeping for 20 years and discovers many changes in the world. For a contemporary inmate emerging from prison after serving a long sentence, basic facts of modern life, such as e-mail and cell phones, may be completely unknown or baffling. Released prisoners may also lack basic skills for modern employment, such as the rudimentary use of computers, word processing, and spreadsheet programs. Although new technologies change modern life, limited resources cause correctional officials to focus on improvements in security rather than on a fuller range of goals serving prisoners.

As in policing, technological developments increase the variety of less-lethal weapons that are available for correctional officers to use in subduing and controlling offenders who pose a threat to institutional safety or who attempt to escape. Corrections officers typically do not have weapons when they are working within the prison population; they are so outnumbered by the prisoners, they would be at a great disadvantage if a prisoner were to get hold of a weapon. In 2012, however, Michigan began issuing Tasers for corrections officers, enabling them to break up fights without putting themselves at risk by becoming physically involved in the conflict (Kloepfer, 2012). It remains to be seen if there are adverse consequences from the presence of less-lethal weapons within the yard and cellblocks that are numerically dominated by prisoners.

The transportation of prisoners presents a daily challenge for officials at courts, jails, and prisons. People in custody must be moved from jails and prisons to courts for hearings. They must be transferred from jails to prisons and moved between different prisons when they begin to serve their sentences. New technologies have been developed to prevent prisoners from attempting to escape or otherwise misbehaving while being transported. The most controversial device is the remote-controlled stun belt that prisoners may be required to wear while being transported. The deputy or bailiff in control of the belt can deliver an excruciating eight-second, 50,000-volt jolt of electricity to prisoners. Americans became aware of the belts when a California prisoner, who was zapped in a courtroom at the order of a judge, filed a $50 million lawsuit. The prisoner had not attempted to escape or threaten anyone; he had merely talked too much when the judge had told him to be silent (Canto, 1998). The international human rights organization Amnesty International mounted a campaign to have the devices banned as torture (Amnesty International, 1999). Although the New York Corrections Department canceled an order for the devices, 25 state correctional departments and 100 county jails reportedly still use them.

Such devices may reduce the number of officers required to escort a prisoner, and they deter prisoners from misbehaving. However, such a jolt of electricity may kill some people if their heart rhythm is susceptible to disruption or if they hit their heads when they fall during the electric shock. There are also issues about whether officers will limit their use to appropriate circumstances.

One particularly important and expanding use of technology is the electronic monitoring of offenders within the community. Offenders in home confinement or "on tether" in the community wear various electronic devices that help monitor whether they obey curfews, remain at home, or otherwise observe restrictions about where they are permitted to be. Increasingly, local jails are offering nonviolent offenders the choice of paying for electronic monitoring and home confinement rather than spending time in jail; this saves money for the county, as it is less expensive to monitor an offender than to provide food and supervision in jail (Grasha, 2009b). There is also expanded use of monitors with GPS capability to track the movements of criminal stalkers and perpetrators of domestic violence. Thus, law enforcement officials can be warned if individuals under restraining orders attempt to approach the homes of their victims (A. Green, 2009).

CHECK POINT	STOP & ANALYZE
13. Corrections has several goals. Which of these goals are advanced by the use of technology? Technology is used for security, control surveillance, and record keeping. It is less likely to be devoted to rehabilitation.	If you were a prison warden, would you require corrections officers to wear body armor? How would you respond to their complaints that the vests are too hot in the summer and interfere with their mobility if they need to run to another part of the prison to respond to an urgent situation?

Current Questions and Challenges for the Future

As we have just seen, technological changes have affected nearly every agency and process within the criminal justice system. Most of this chapter's discussion has focused on new technological devices designed to assist officials with specific tasks. James Byrne (2008) classifies these devices as "hard technology" and contrasts them with the development of "soft technology," such as computer software for crime mapping and sentencing calculations. Both categories of technology are important for criminal justice. In some respects, the soft technology may present especially significant possibilities for affecting the performance of criminal justice officials, as computer experts invent new ways to gather and evaluate information that can be used for training, classification of offenders, risk assessment, and other important purposes. Table 14.4 shows examples of various hard and soft technological innovations that have affected each institutional segment of the criminal justice system.

There is no doubt that the desire for efficiency and effectiveness will lead to continued efforts to create new technologies and refine existing technologies to assist the police in their tasks. One can easily envision increased access to information through computers, better surveillance cameras and body scanners, and expanded use of GPS devices. In addition, there will be continued development and experimentation with less-lethal weapons, some of which are likely to be borrowed from those being developed by the U.S. military, including devices that rely on heat or light or sound to incapacitate threatening individuals.

TABLE 14.4	**The Application of Hard and Soft Technology to Crime Prevention and Control**

	Hard Technology	Soft Technology
Crime prevention	• CCTV • Street lighting • Citizen-protection devices (e.g., Mace, Tasers) • Metal detectors • Ignition interlock systems (drunk drivers)	• Threat assessment instruments • Risk assessment instruments • Bullying ID protocol • Sex-offender registration • Risk assessment prior to involuntary civil commitment • Profiling
Police	• Improved police protection devices (helmets, vests, cars, buildings) • Improved/new weapons • Less-than-lethal force (mobile/riot control) • Computers in squad cars • Hands-free patrol-car control (Project 54) • Offender and citizen IDs via biometrics/fingerprints • Gunshot-location devices	• Crime mapping (hot spots) • Crime analysis (e.g., COMPSTAT) • Criminal-history data systems enhancement • Info sharing within CJS and private sector • New technologies to monitor communications (phone, mail, Internet) to/from targeted individuals • Amber alerts
Court	• The high-tech courtroom (computers, video, cameras, design features of buildings) • Weapon-detection devices • Video conferencing • Electronic court documents • Drug testing at pretrial stage	• Case-flow management systems • Radio frequency identification technology • Data warehousing • Automation of court records • Problem-oriented courts
Institutional corrections	• Contraband detection devices • Duress alarm systems • Language-translation devices • Remote monitoring • Perimeter screening • Less-than-lethal force in prison • Prison design (supermax) • Expanded use of segregation units	• Use of simulations as training tools (mock prison riots) • Facial-recognition software • New inmate classification systems (external/internal) • Within-prison crime analysis (hot spots; high-rate offenders) • Information sharing with police, community, victims, and community-based corrections (reentry)
Community corrections	• GPS for offender monitoring and location-restriction enforcement • New devices (breathalyzers, instant drug tests, language translators, plethysmographs) • Polygraph tests (improved) • Laptops/GPS for line staff • Reporting kiosks	• New classification devices for sex, drugs, and MI offenders [offenders with mental illnesses] • New workload software • New computer monitoring programs for sex offenders • Information with community police, treatment providers (for active offender supervision and for absconder location)

Source: James M. Byrne, "The Best Laid Plans: An Assessment of the Varied Consequences of New Technologies for Crime and Social Control," *Federal Probation* 72 (no. 3, 2008): 11.

In light of the financial problems affecting state and local correctional budgets, there will inevitably be efforts to refine and expand the use of surveillance and monitoring technology to reduce the costs associated with confining lesser offenders. For example, the future will likely see the expanded use of ignition interlock systems for convicted drunken drivers. In cars equipped with these devices, drivers blow into a "breathalyzer" tube, and the engine starts only if their breath meets the state's guidelines for alcohol consumption. This can help prevent drunken driving without relying so heavily on incarceration for first offenders. New and expanded use of surveillance and control mechanisms may also improve officials' ability to monitor probationers, parolees, and other offenders under correctional supervision in the community.

As noted, technological developments produce risks, questions, and consequences beyond increased efficiency in carrying out tasks. Technological devices are operated by human beings who can make errors that affect the lives of others. What happens when a forensic scientist makes an error in conducting a test? What happens when incorrect information about an individual is entered into a database? With a perception that new weapons will not cause serious injury or death, are police officers more inclined to use CEDs, pepper balls, and other less-lethal weapons in situations that might otherwise have been resolved through determined use of verbal warnings and other communications? These are important questions that arise with increasing frequency as we analyze events in which technology produces unintended and undesirable results.

Equally important are concerns about the impact of technology on the civil rights and liberties of individual Americans. In the post-9/11 era, there are already indications that some government officials will react to perceived threats by making use of available technology without necessarily planning for the protection of civil liberties or adherence to existing law. The administration of President George W. Bush, for example, secretly intercepted Americans' phone calls and emails without the court authorizations required under federal law (Sanger & Lichtblau, 2006). When Congress later granted limited authority to undertake such electronic surveillance of communications, the National Security Agency (NSA) violated the law by intercepting calls that did not fall within the scope of the law (Lichtblau & Risen, 2009).

Similar complaints arose concerning actions in the Obama administration as information became public about the NSA keeping records of Americans' phone calls (Gellman & Soltani, 2014). As with other technologies, the means available could be misused in ways that violate Fourth Amendment restrictions on unreasonable searches and other rights under the Constitution.

Another large question looms. Have new technologies been effective in preventing crime and catching criminals? See the "Evidence-Based Practice and Policy" feature to consider this issue. We know that certain technologies, such as DNA testing, have been highly effective in identifying individuals whose biological matter, such as blood or tissue, is found at a crime scene or on a weapon. It is less clear, however, that all of the surveillance, communications, and search technologies have produced entirely desirable benefits. For example, in pointing to declining clearance rates for homicide crimes, James Byrne concludes, "I would be hard pressed to offer an assessment of the positive effect of new technological innovations during this period given these data on police performance" (2008:14). The underlying point is that we know many new technologies expand the scope of social control by government through collecting information, watching and searching the citizenry, and providing new tools for police to use in coercing compliant behavior (as in CEDs). Are the costs of this social control justified? Can we use the benefits of technology without reducing the extent of Americans' freedom and privacy? These are questions that future criminal justice officials and policymakers must continually reexamine. They can do this by systematically studying the performance of police, courts, and corrections as well as by evaluating the consequences for Americans' civil liberties.

Putting Technology to the Test

Early in this chapter, we saw a long history of optimism that new technology would provide beneficial progress. Technology can be put into use when practitioners see benefits from its use, even if the consequences of using the technology have not yet been completely explored. The federal government's website displaying evidence-based practices and policies for criminal justice (www.crimesolutions.gov), itemizes a limited number of technology-based programs that have been certified as "effective" based on experimental research. These programs include keeping information on guns in a ballistics database, upgrading lighting on streets and public places, and using car ignition control devices as a means to prevent drunk driving and automobile theft. It is clear that much more research needs to be done to test whether various technologies used in the criminal justice system provide the hoped-for benefits without causing too many undesirable consequences.

At the same website, among the programs listed as "promising" for showing positive results were two that involved GPS monitoring of parolees and other offenders under community supervision. An examination of such uses of GPS monitoring reveals some of the challenges faced in the use of this technology to achieve desired objectives.

A number of different technologies have been used to track parolees, most frequently systems using GPS (global positioning systems). With this technology, parole officers can track the geographic location of parolees, to ensure that they avoid areas where they are forbidden to be and do show up where they are supposed to be—at work, school, or home.

Although useful, this technology is not perfect. Offenders have been able to remove their GPS "bracelets" and evade tracking. In one high-profile case, a California sex offender under surveillance named Philip Garrido kidnapped a teenager in 1991. Garrido held the victim hostage in his home for 18 years, fathering two children with her during her captivity. Even though Garrido had a history of prior sexual violence, he was classified in the "lower risk" monitoring system and frequently traveled farther than his parole allowed, with no follow-up from corrections officials.

In 2013, California ordered one company's GPS devices to be removed from all of its nearly 8,000 high-risk parolees, primarily sex offenders and gang members, and replaced with another company's GPS units. A study had found that with the old units, "batteries died early, cases cracked, reported locations were off by as much as three miles. Officials also found that tampering alerts failed and offenders were able to disappear by covering the devices with foil, deploying illegal GPS jammers, or ducking into cars or buildings" (St. John, 2013). Such problems with technology threaten public safety, especially in cases when officials have no idea that a device has been removed or stopped working. The California example demonstrates the need for officials to continually test devices and consider whether alternative devices would be more reliable or effective.

However, some states have determined that the use of GPS systems for high-risk sex offenders can both (1) reduce the recidivism of these offenders, and (2) help protect the public by allowing corrections officials to intercept offenders who violate conditions of parole. The state of New Jersey, for example, has determined that the recidivism rates for sex offenders in their GPS monitoring program is lower than the national rate. In other cases, parolees wearing GPS devices have been detected at the scene of a crime. Thanks to a GPS monitoring system, police were able to charge Saquan Evans of Syracuse, New York, with homicide in the shooting death of a 20-month-old infant.

North Carolina mandated for several years that certain repeat sex offenders must wear GPS technology for life. Torrey Grady had two convictions for sexual offenses, but argued that wearing a GPS monitor for life is in violation of the Fourth Amendment's ban on unreasonable searches and seizures. The U.S. Supreme Court decided that the use of the device constitutes a "search" under the Fourth Amendment but left it to future court decisions to decide whether such searches are "unreasonable" (*Grady v. North Carolina*, 2015).

Researching the Internet

Examine evidence-based programs publicized by the federal government, including those under the category Forensics and Technology, at the government website: www.crimesolutions.gov.

Implementing New Practices

It is possible that officials will be tempted to release higher-risk offenders on parole based on a belief that GPS technology will permit them to closely monitor these individuals. Does the opportunity to save money by using GPS technology instead of imprisonment outweigh the risks of placing serious offenders in the community? If you were responsible for parole supervision in a specific city, would you want additional evidence before deciding what to do? Should this evidence be regarding the technology itself or about the behavior of those subjected to the use of this technology? Briefly describe three concerns that would affect your decision about whether to expand the use of GPS monitoring.

Sources: P. J. Barnes, *Report on New Jersey's GPS Monitoring of Sex Offenders*, New Jersey State Parole Board, December 5, 2007 (www.state.nj.us/parole/docs/reports/gps.pdf); P. Bulman, "Sex Offenders Monitored by GPS Found to Commit Fewer Crimes," National Institute of Justice Journal, 271 (nij.gov/journals); M. B. Farrell, "Report: GPS Parole Monitoring of Phillip Garrido Failed," *Christian Science Monitor*, November 6, 2009 (www.csmonitor.com); L. Hurley, "U.S. Supreme Court Revives Sex Offender's Ankle Bracelet Case," Reuters, March 30, 2015 (www.reuters.com); J. O'Hara, "Accused Killer Linked to Child's Death by Eyewitness and Parole GPS," *Syracuse Post-Standard*, March 25, 2011 (www.syracuse.com); P. St. John, "Tests Found Major Flaws in Parolee GPS Monitoring Devices," *Los Angeles Times*, March 30, 2013 (www.latimes.com).

14. What questions about technology will bear watching in the future?

How will government budget problems affect the use of technology? How will the risk of human errors affect the use of technology? How will technology impact civil rights and liberties? Are new technologies actually effective in preventing crime and catching criminals?

If you were a governor or mayor struggling with difficult budget choices as tax revenues decline, what decisions would you make about technology affecting criminal justice? Would increasing the use of technology be a high priority for you? If so, what other aspects of the government budget would you cut to advance this priority? Among the various technologies currently available, which ones would you regard as especially worthy of additional expenditures from your budget? Why?

A QUESTION OF ETHICS

Think, Discuss, Write

In 2016, reports emerged that 80 percent of the videos taken from police patrol cars in Chicago lacked audio. The police department said that the problem stemmed from "officer error" and "intentional destruction." In other cities, officers have been seen on their patrol cameras returning to the car to turn off the camera just before a person was assaulted, allegedly by the officer. Reports of the same issues have emerged with respect to body cameras. If officers turn off or damage video equipment in order to hide their own misbehavior, they are obviously defeating the accountability and evidence-gathering purposes of video cameras.

Discussion/Writing Assignment

If you were a police chief, how would you address this problem? Is it a problem that can be solved through ethics training and shaping the culture of a police agency? Does it require changing technology so that officers are not able to turn cameras off? However, even removing the cameras from officers' control would not guarantee that officers would not break the equipment. Describe what you would do to address police behaviors that defeat the desired benefits of technology.

Source: R. Balko, "80 Percent of Chicago PD Dash-Cam Videos Are Missing Audio Due to 'Officer Error' or 'Intentional Destruction.'" *Washington Post*, January 29, 2016 (www.washington post.com).

SUMMARY

1 Describe how adaptation and belief in science can affect the use of technology.
- New technology can be employed by criminals as well as by criminal justice officials.
- Criminal justice officials and the public must be wary of automatically assuming that new scientific developments will achieve their intended goals or will produce only desirable consequences.

2 Identify the various aspects of cybercrime and counterfeiting.
- Cybercrime includes identity theft, Internet child pornography, hackers' theft of trade secrets, and destruction of computer networks.

- Counterfeiting extends beyond currency and consumer goods to include dangerous and worthless fake prescription drugs.

3 Explain the role of communications, computers, and databases in policing.
- Calls for service to police have expanded from 911 numbers to 311 and 211 for nonemergency purposes.
- Computers in patrol cars have expanded police officers' access to information.
- Police also use computers in crime mapping, gunshot detection systems, and investigation of cybercrimes.

- Databases permit the collection and matching of information concerning fingerprints, DNA, tattoos, criminal records, and other useful data.

4 Describe developments and problems in DNA testing and new weapons technologies.

- DNA testing permits scientists to identify the source of biological material with a high degree of certainty.
- Some crime labs have been careless and unethical in testifying about DNA results, and some prosecutors have opposed DNA testing that might benefit criminal defendants.
- New less-lethal weapons such as CEDs (e.g., Tasers), pepper balls, and other projectiles are used by police.
- Less-lethal weapons have been involved in incidents that led to the deaths of individuals against whom the police used these weapons.

5 Name the uses of technology in courts and corrections.

- Courts use technology in computerized record keeping and presentation of evidence.

- Technology underlies the presentation during trials of evidence based on forensic science testing. The misuse of technology by jurors, such as being distracted by smartphones or seeking information from online sources, can create problems.
- Correctional officials use technology for security purposes and for monitoring offenders in the community.

6 List some continuing questions about the effects of technology on civil liberties.

- The expanded use of technology by government raises questions about the protection of Americans' rights.
- There are questions about the extent to which many new technologies advance criminal justice goals and do not merely expand mechanisms for societal surveillance and control.

Questions for Review

1. How have criminals adapted to changes in technology?
2. How are computers used to investigate crimes?
3. What questions and problems arise from the development of new weapons for police?
4. What undesirable effects can science and technology have on jury trials?

5. How can GPS devices assist correctional officials?
6. How can the use of technology clash with Americans' expectations about rights, liberty, and privacy?

Key Terms and Cases

CSI effect (p. 509)

DNA analysis (p. 495)

electronic file management (p. 507)

Geographic Information System (GIS) (p. 492)

identity theft (p. 484)

latent fingerprints (p. 495)

less-lethal weapons (p. 505)

Kyllo v. United States (2001) (p. 502)

AP Images/Peter Pereira

15 Juvenile Justice

LEARNING OBJECTIVES

1 Describe the extent of youth crime in the United States.

2 Explain how the juvenile justice system developed and the assumptions on which it was based.

3 Identify what determines the jurisdiction of the juvenile justice system.

4 Describe how the juvenile justice system operates.

5 Name some of the issues facing the American system of juvenile justice.

On July 12, 2014, 18-year-old Conrad Roy III committed suicide in the parking lot of a KMart in Fairhaven, Massachusetts. He had purchased a portable generator, started it in the cab of his truck, and succumbed to carbon monoxide poisoning (Glaun, 2016). Roy had a history of depression and had attempted suicide at age 16 by taking painkillers (Lavoie, 2015).

Shortly after Roy's suicide, police investigators discovered a string of text messages from his girlfriend, 17-year-old Michelle Carter, which seemed to be encouraging him to commit suicide. Over the course of one week, Carter worked with Roy to devise a plan to carry out the suicide in the least painful way possible. When he expressed doubts that he could go through with it, telling Carter that he was "freaking out," she responded, "You're so hesitant because you keep overthinking it and pushing it off. You just need to do it, Conrad" (Bombard, 2015). In text messages recovered after Roy's death, Carter admitted to a friend that Roy had exited his truck in the middle of the attempt out of fear and called her; in response, she told him to get back in the vehicle. Hours later, she pretended to have no knowledge of the plan and texted his family, wondering where he was.

In February 2015, Carter was charged with involuntary manslaughter for urging Roy to commit suicide. This charge treats Carter as being responsible for the death of Roy despite her lack of *malice aforethought*—that is, the crime does not require the specific intentions associated with other homicide offenses. A spokesman for the juvenile court explained that Carter should have helped Roy by notifying his family or school officials that he was again contemplating suicide. In effect, the charge indicated that prosecutors believed her negligence—lack of due care—led to his death (Hand, 2015).

Carter's attorney argued that her speech could not be considered the cause of Roy's death; Roy caused his own death. Unlike some other states, Massachusetts has no law against assisting or encouraging suicide. Her attorney stated that in the weeks prior to the event, Carter had tried to talk him out of it several times before giving up and "supporting" his decision. In addition, her supporters pointed out that after Roy's death, she organized several charity events to raise money in his name for mental health awareness and the local hospital (Hand, 2015).

Another complication in this case was the fact that Carter was a juvenile at the time of the alleged crime. She was charged as a "youthful offender," which placed her in a status between juvenile and adult—a status used by the State of Massachusetts to allow harsher penalties than those available in the juvenile court. It also allowed the case documents to be viewed publicly (Glaun, 2016). The Massachusetts Supreme Judicial Court had to make a decision about whether to dismiss the charges against Carter, charge her with manslaughter as a juvenile, or charge her with manslaughter as an adult.

Carter was a juvenile at the time of the suicide, but had nearly reached the age of majority (18). If she had assisted Roy after her eighteenth birthday, she would have been automatically charged as an adult; however, her age gave the State of Massachusetts flexibility in deciding how to charge her with a crime. Juveniles aged 14–17 can be charged as adults in Massachusetts. The process of waiver—juveniles being charged as adults—gives judges options for imposing severe sentences. Research indicates that juveniles have different brain development than adults and may not fully understand the consequences of their actions. Does that help explain Carter's behavior in this incident?

AP Images/Peter Pereira

Although the juvenile justice system is separate from the adult criminal justice system, the key values of freedom, fairness, and justice undergird both systems. The formal processes of each differ mainly in emphasis, not in values. Although different, the systems are interrelated. One cannot separate the activities and concerns of policing, courts, and corrections from the problems of youth.

Youth Crime in the United States

Newspaper reports regularly remind Americans about juveniles' involvement in serious crimes. In Arkansas, a teenager faces counts of second-degree murder and theft in the killings of two people. In Chicago, a 16-year-old boy is charged with shooting a police officer with a pellet gun. A teenager in Pennsylvania is arrested after stealing a car, driving it under the influence, and fleeing arrest—eventually crashing the car and receiving non-life-threatening injuries. Such dramatic criminal acts make headlines. Are these only isolated incidents, or is the United States facing a major increase in youth crime?

The juvenile crime incidents just described are rare. In a nation with 74 million people under age 18, about 800,000 arrests of juveniles occur each year, 42,000 of which (just over 5 percent) are for violent crimes (FBI, 2015, Table 41). Murders committed by juveniles have decreased dramatically since 1993, when juveniles were responsible for 16 percent of all murder arrests; in 2012 this fell to 6.5 percent of all arrests for murder, which represents a record low for juvenile homicide (Snyder & Mulako-Wangota, 2016).

Youth crimes range from UCR Index Crimes (for example, murder, rape, robbery, assault, see Figure 15.1) to "youthful crimes" such as violating curfew, loitering, and being a runaway. Consistent with the trends discussed above, although about 1.1 million delinquency cases were handled in the juvenile court in 2013, the decline in caseloads since the mid-1990s is the largest since 1960. Most juvenile crimes are committed by young men, but young women make up an increasing

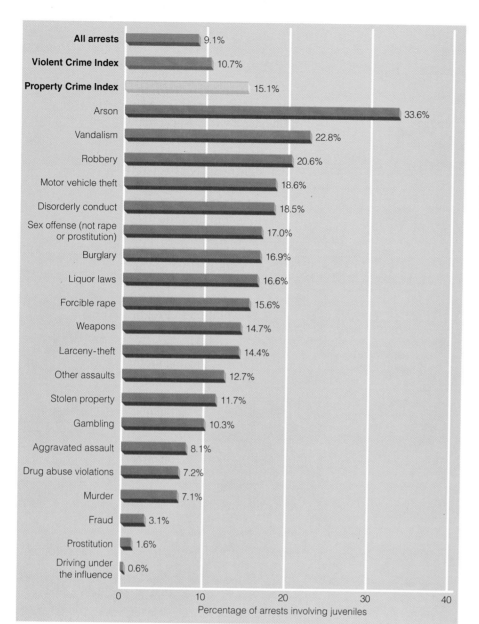

FIGURE 15.1

Percentage of Arrests of People under 18 Years Old (rounded) Juveniles are arrested for a wide range of offenses. For some offenses—such as arson, vandalism, motor-vehicle theft, and burglary—juveniles account for a larger proportion of arrests than the percentage of juveniles in the general population would suggest.

Source: Federal Bureau of Investigation, *Crime in the United States, 2014* (Washington, DC: U.S. Government Printing Office, 2015), Table 41.

percentage of juveniles appearing in court. Between 1985 and 2003, the percentage of young women appearing in juvenile courts increased from 19 percent to 27 percent of all cases heard, and has been stable at that level since (Sickmund, Sladky, & Kang, 2015).

Criminologists have tried to explain the "epidemic" of violent youth crime that erupted in the mid-1980s, reaching its peak in 1993. One of the first explanations used a "cohort" approach, arguing that during the 1980s, the increase in violence was due to an increase in the prevalence of exceptionally violent individuals—so-called "super predators." Critics of this approach, however, say that the birth cohort that peaked during the early 1990s was not at all exceptional with respect to violent behavior in their younger years (P. J. Cook & Laub, 2002). In addition, there was little evidence that "super predators" even existed, and much of the attention given to this explanation was blamed on media hype (Haberman, 2014).

A different explanation focuses on environmental factors that influenced the rise in violent youth crime. Scholars point to the impact of the drug trade, especially crack cocaine, and the related increase in gun use and possession by youths. Alfred Blumstein (2002) suggests that as more juveniles, particularly inner-city minorities, were recruited into the drug trade, they armed themselves with guns and used those firearms in battles over market turf. Other factors may have also played a role—violent crime by youth was most prevalent in neighborhoods with deteriorating social and economic conditions. These changes led to reductions in family stability and shared social expectations about behavior, particularly in minority neighborhoods (Strom & MacDonald, 2007). Exposure to environmental toxins may also play a role in delinquent activity, as discussed in Chapter 2 with respect to the Flint water crisis. Juveniles living in disadvantaged areas are more likely to be exposed to lead early in life, which can lead to future delinquency (Narag, Pizarro, & Gibbs, 2009).

Certainly, drug use by juveniles has significantly affected the juvenile justice system. From 1985 to 1997, the number of drug offense cases processed by juvenile courts increased from about 75,000 to about 191,000 per year. This number has recently decreased to 141,000—the lowest number of juvenile drug arrests since 1994 (Sickmund, Sladky, & Kang, 2015). In addition, drug use cases involving white juveniles have skyrocketed, increasing 341 percent from 1984 to 2004 (compared with a 32 percent increase for African American juveniles). Drug use has resulted in higher caseloads handled by juvenile courts in the past 20 years (Stahl, 2008).

Youth gangs are another factor explaining violent youth crime. Gangs such as the Black P. Stone Nation, CRIPS (Common Revolution in Progress), and Bloods first came to police attention in the 1970s. The National Youth Gang Survey estimates that there are now more than 30,000 gangs with 850,000 members in the United States and that the most significant factor related to gang violence is drug activity (National Gang Center, 2016).

Gangs are a primary source of fear and peril in many neighborhoods. A gang can destabilize neighborhood life, especially when gang members are armed. Youth gangs are not restricted to large cities—crackdowns on violence in cities sometimes force gangs into suburban areas (Sanchez & Giordano, 2008). Fear of being a crime victim can lead youths to seek protection through gang membership without realizing that as gang members, they are actually more likely than other juveniles to be victims of violence and property crimes (Melde, Taylor, & Esbensen, 2009).

Many cities have developed programs to help deal with gang problems. Some programs, such as the GRYD (Gang Reduction and Youth Development) program in Los Angeles, focus on preventing youths from joining gangs. Other programs focus on intervention—that is, identifying gang members and attempting to get them to leave the gang. Some researchers suggest that targeting the "core" gang members and limiting their involvement will result in the greatest decreases in gang violence (Maxson, 2011), while others argue that police agencies have had difficulty targeting the appropriate individuals for intervention (Melde, Gavassi, et al., 2011). Recent research indicates that a comprehensive approach to gang violence—addressing prevention and intervention as well as law enforcement—is promising. The Comprehensive Anti-Gang Initiative (CAGI) has reduced gun violence in several major cities in the United States (McGarrell et al., 2013).

Although juvenile delinquency, neglect, and dependency have been concerns since the nation's earliest years, not until the early twentieth century did a separate system to deal with these problems evolve. The contemporary juvenile justice system has gone through a major shift of emphasis as well. The rest of this chapter explores the history of juvenile justice, the process it follows today, and some of the problems associated with it.

▼ **CHECK POINT**

1. **How have criminologists attempted to explain the epidemic of violent crime committed by juveniles in the 1990s?**
   Large youth cohorts, gun use related to drug sales, and gangs.

STOP & ANALYZE

There appears to be a strong link between drug use and delinquency rates. What might you recommend to lawmakers to help reduce juvenile drug use so that delinquency rates can be decreased?

The Development of Juvenile Justice

The system and philosophy of juvenile justice that began in the United States during the social reform period of the late nineteenth century was based on the idea that the state should act as a parent would in the interest of the child. This view remained unchallenged until the 1960s, when the Supreme Court ushered in the juvenile rights period. With the rise in juvenile crime in the 1980s, the juvenile justice system shifted again to one focusing on the problem of controlling youth crime. Today people are again reexamining the philosophy and processes of the juvenile justice system.

The idea that children should be treated differently from adults originated in the common law and in the chancery courts of England. The common law had long prescribed that children under seven years of age were incapable of felonious intent and were therefore not criminally responsible. Children aged 7–14 could be held accountable only if it could be shown that they understood the consequences of their actions.

The English chancery courts, established during the Middle Ages, heard only civil cases, mainly concerning property. However, under the doctrine of **parens patriae**, which held the king to be the father of the realm, the chancery courts exercised protective jurisdiction over all children, particularly orphans and those involved in cases of neglect. At this time, the criminal courts, not a separate juvenile court, dealt with juvenile offenders. In legitimizing the actions of the state on behalf of the child, however, the concept of *parens patriae* laid the groundwork for the development of juvenile justice.

Table 15.1 outlines the shifts in how the United States has dealt with the problems of youth. These shifts fall into six periods of American juvenile justice history. Each was characterized by changes in juvenile justice that reflected the social, intellectual, and political currents of the time. During the past 200 years, population shifts from rural to urban areas, immigration, developments in the social sciences, political reform movements, and the continuing problem of youth crime have all influenced how Americans have treated juveniles.

> **parens patriae** The state as parent; the state as guardian and protector of all citizens (such as juveniles) who cannot protect themselves.

The Puritan Period (1646–1824)

The English procedures were maintained in the American colonies and continued into the nineteenth century. The earliest attempt by a colony to deal with problem children was the passage of the Massachusetts Stubborn Child Law in 1646. With this law, the Puritans of the Massachusetts Bay Colony imposed the view that the child was evil, and emphasized the duty of the family to discipline youths. Those children who would not obey their parents were dealt with by the law.

The Refuge Period (1824–1899)

As the population of American cities began to grow during the early 1800s, the problem of youth crime and neglect became a concern for reformers. Just as the Quakers of Philadelphia were instrumental in reforming correctional practices, other groups supported changes concerning the education and protection of youths. These reformers focused their efforts primarily on the urban immigrant poor, seeking to have parents

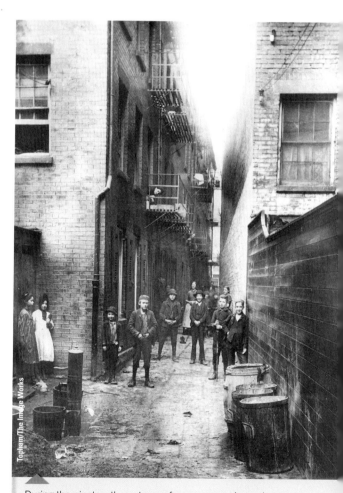

During the nineteenth century, reformers were alarmed by the living conditions of inner-city youths. Reformers in Chicago ushered in the juvenile justice system. Why should juveniles be treated differently than adults when they commit the same criminal acts?

TABLE 15.1   Juvenile Justice Developments in the United States

Period	Major Developments	Causes and Influences	Juvenile Justice System
Puritan 1646–1824	Massachusetts Stubborn Child Law (1646)	A. Puritan view of child as evil B. Economically marginal agrarian society	Law provides A. Symbolic standard of maturity B. Support for family as economic unit
Refuge 1824–1899	Institutionalization of deviants; House of Refuge in New York established (1825) for delinquent and dependent children	A. Enlightenment B. Immigration and industrialization	Child seen as helpless, in need of state intervention
Juvenile court 1899–1960	Establishment of separate legal system for juveniles; Illinois Juvenile Court Act (1899)	A. Reformism and rehabilitative ideology B. Increased immigration; urbanization; large-scale industrialization	Juvenile court institutionalized legal irresponsibility of child
Juvenile rights 1960–1980	Increased "legalization" of juvenile law; *Gault* decision (1967); Juvenile Justice and Delinquency Prevention Act (1974) calls for deinstitutionalization of status offenders	A. Criticism of juvenile justice system on humane grounds B. Civil rights movement by disadvantaged groups	Movement to define and protect rights as well as to provide services to children
Crime control 1980–2005	Concern for victims; punishment for serious offenders; transfer to adult court of serious offenders; protection of children from physical and sexual abuse	A. More-conservative public attitudes and policies B. Focus on serious crimes by repeat offenders	System more formal, restrictive, punitive; increased percentage of police referrals to court; incarcerated youths stay longer periods
"Kids are different" 2005–present	Elimination of death penalty for juveniles, focus on rehabilitation, states increasing age of transfer to adult court	A. *Roper v. Simmons* (2005) B. Scientific evidence on youth's biological, emotional, and psychological development	Recognition that juveniles are less culpable than adults

Sources: Portions adapted from Barry Krisberg, Ira M. Schwartz, Paul Litsky, and James Austin, "The Watershed of Juvenile Justice Reform," *Crime and Delinquency* 32 (January 1985): 5–38; U.S. Department of Justice, *A Preliminary National Assessment of the Status Offender and the Juvenile Justice System* (Washington, DC: U.S. Government Printing Office, 1980), 29.

declared "unfit" if their children roamed the streets and were apparently "out of control." Not all such children were engaged in criminal acts, but the reformers believed that children whose parents did not discipline and train them to abide by the rules of society would end up in prison. The state would therefore use its power to prevent delinquency. The solution was to create institutions where these children could learn good work and study habits, live in a disciplined and healthy environment, and develop "character."

The first of these institutions was the House of Refuge of New York, which opened in 1825. This half-prison, half-school housed destitute and orphaned children as well as those convicted of crimes (Friedman, 1993:164). Similar facilities followed in Boston, Philadelphia, and Baltimore. Children were placed in these homes by court order usually because of neglect or vagrancy. They often stayed until they were old enough to be legally regarded as adults. The houses were run according to a strict program of work, study, and discipline.

Some states created "reform schools" to provide discipline and education in a "homelike" atmosphere, usually in rural areas. The first, the Lyman School for Boys, opened in Westboro, Massachusetts, in 1848. A similar Massachusetts reform school for girls opened in 1855 for "the instruction . . . and reformation, of exposed, helpless, evil disposed and vicious girls" (Friedman, 1993:164). Institutional programs began in New York in 1849; in Ohio in 1850; and in Maine, Rhode Island, and Michigan in 1906.

Despite these reforms, children could still be arrested, detained, tried, and imprisoned. Even in states that had institutions for juveniles, the criminal justice process for children was the same as that for adults.

The Juvenile Court Period (1899–1960)

With most states providing services to neglected youth by the end of the nineteenth century, the problem of juvenile criminality became the focus of attention. Progressive reformers pushed for the state to provide individualized care and treatment to deviants of all kinds—adult criminals, the mentally ill, juvenile delinquents. They urged the adoption of probation, treatment, indeterminate sentences, and parole for adult offenders and succeeded in establishing similar programs for juveniles.

Referred to as "child savers," these upper-middle-class reformers sought to use the power of the state to save children from a life of crime (Platt, 1977). They shared a concern about the effect of environmental factors on behavior and a belief that benevolent state action could solve social problems. They also believed the claim of the new social sciences that they could treat the problems underlying deviance.

Reformers wanted a separate juvenile court system that could address the problems of individual youths by using flexible procedures that, as one reformer said, "banish entirely all thought of crime and punishment" (Rothman, 1980:213). They put their idea into action with the creation of the juvenile court.

Passage of the Juvenile Court Act by Illinois in 1899 established the first comprehensive system of juvenile justice. The act placed cases of dependency, neglect, and delinquency ("incorrigibles and children threatened by immoral associations as well as criminal lawbreakers") under one jurisdiction for children under 16. The act had four major elements:

1. A separate court for delinquent, dependent, and neglected children
2. Special legal procedures that were less adversarial than those in the adult system
3. Separation of children from adults in all portions of the justice system
4. Programs of probation to assist the courts in deciding what the best interest of the state and the child would entail

The juvenile court concept was successfully promoted by activists such as Jane Addams, Lucy Flower, and Julia Lathrop of the settlement-house movement; Henry Thurston, a social work educator; and the National Congress of Mothers. By 1904, ten states had implemented procedures similar to those of Illinois. By 1917, all but three states provided for a juvenile court.

The philosophy of the juvenile court derived from the idea that the state should deal with a child who broke the law much as a wise parent would deal with a wayward child. The doctrine of *parens patriae* again helped legitimize the system. Procedures would be informal and private, and records would be considered to be confidential. Children would be detained apart from adults, and probation and social workers would be appointed to help them. Even the vocabulary and physical setting of the juvenile system were changed to emphasize diagnosis and treatment instead of findings of guilt. The term *criminal behavior* was replaced with *delinquent behavior* when referring to the acts of children. The terminology reflected the underlying belief that these children could be "cured" and returned to society as law-abiding citizens.

Because procedures were not to be adversarial, lawyers were unnecessary. The main professionals attached to the system were psychologists and social workers, who could determine the juvenile's underlying behavioral problem. These reforms, however, took place in a system in which children lacked the due process rights held by adults.

While the creation of the juvenile court was a positive development for juveniles in general, some contemporary researchers criticize the tendency for these reformers to hold different standards for girls and boys. For example, girls found guilty of the status offense of "promiscuity" were frequently incarcerated until adulthood (age 18) for their own protection. Boys were rarely charged with this type of offense.

The Juvenile Rights Period (1960–1980)

Until the early 1960s, few questioned the sweeping powers of juvenile justice officials. When the U.S. Supreme Court expanded the rights of adult defendants, however, lawyers and scholars began to criticize the extensive discretion given to juvenile justice officials. In a series of decisions (see Figure 15.2), the U.S. Supreme Court expanded the rights of juveniles.

In the first of these cases, *Kent v. United States* (1966), the Supreme Court ruled that juveniles had the right to counsel at a hearing at which a juvenile judge could waive jurisdiction and pass the case to the adult court.

In re Gault (1967) extended due process rights to juveniles. Fifteen-year-old Gerald Gault had been sentenced to six years in a state training school for making a prank

In re Gault (1967)
Juveniles have the right to counsel, to confront and examine accusers, and to have adequate notice of charges when confinement is a possible punishment.

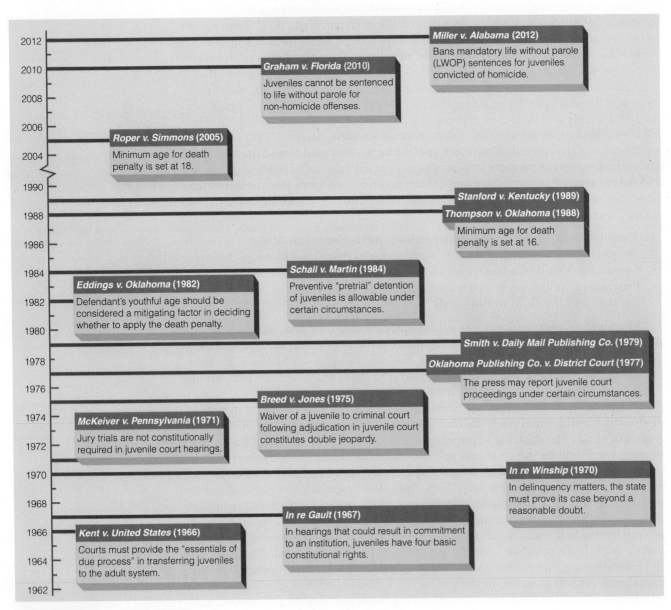

FIGURE 15.2

Major Decisions by the U.S. Supreme Court Regarding the Rights of Juveniles Since the mid-1960s, the Supreme Court has gradually expanded the rights of juveniles but has continued to recognize that the logic of the separate system for juvenile offenders justifies differences from some adult rights.

Note: For discussion of death penalty cases, see Chapter 9.

Sources: Office of Juvenile Justice and Delinquency Prevention, *1999 National Report* (Washington, DC: U.S. Government Printing Office, 1999), 90–91; *Roper v. Simmons*, 543 U.S. 551 (2005); *Graham v. Florida*, 130 S. Ct. 2011 (2010); *Miller v. Alabama*, 132 S. Ct. 2455 (2012).

phone call. Had he been an adult, the maximum punishment for making such a call would have been a fine of $5 to $50 or imprisonment for two months at most. Gault had been convicted and sentenced in an informal proceeding without being represented by counsel. The justices held that a child in a delinquency hearing must be given certain procedural rights, including notice of the charges, right to counsel, right to confront and cross-examine witnesses, and protection against self-incrimination. Writing for the majority, Justice Abe Fortas emphasized that due process rights and procedures have a place in juvenile justice: "Under our Constitution the condition of being a boy does not justify a kangaroo court."

The precedent-setting *Gault* decision was followed by a series of cases further defining the rights of juveniles. In the case of ***In re Winship*** **(1970)**, the Court held that proof must be established "beyond a reasonable doubt" and not on "a preponderance of the evidence" before a juvenile could be classified as a delinquent for committing an act that would be a crime if committed by an adult. The Court was not willing to give juveniles every due process right, however: it held in ***McKeiver v. Pennsylvania*** **(1971)** that "trial by jury in the juvenile court's adjudicative stage is not a constitutional requirement." But in ***Breed v. Jones*** **(1975)**, the Court extended the protection against double jeopardy to juveniles by requiring that before a case is adjudicated in juvenile court, a hearing must be held to determine if it should be transferred to the adult court.

Another area of change concerned **status offenses**—acts that are not illegal if committed by an adult; these include skipping school, running away from home, and living a "wayward, idle or dissolute life" (Feld, 1993:203). In 1974, Congress passed the Juvenile Justice and Delinquency Prevention Act, which included provisions for taking status offenders out of correctional institutions. Since then, people have worked on diverting such children out of the system, reducing the possibility of incarceration, and rewriting status offense laws.

As juvenile crime rates continued to rise during the 1970s, the public began calling for tougher approaches in dealing with delinquents. In the 1980s, at the same time that stricter sanctions were imposed on adult offenders, juvenile justice policies shifted to crime control.

Although the courts expanded the definition of rights for juveniles, consider the state of teenagers' rights today as you read "Criminal Justice: Myth & Reality."

The Crime Control Period (1980–2005)

The public demand to "crack down on crime" began in 1980. Legislators responded in part by changing the juvenile system. Greater attention began to be focused on repeat offenders, with policy makers calling for harsher punishment for juveniles who commit crimes.

In *Schall v. Martin* **(1984)**, the Supreme Court significantly departed from the trend toward increased juvenile rights. The Court confirmed that the general notion of *parens patriae* was a primary basis for the juvenile court, equal in importance to the Court's desire to protect the community from crime. Thus, juveniles may be held in preventive detention before trial if they are deemed a "risk" to the community.

CRIMINAL JUSTICE

Myth&Reality

COMMON BELIEF: With the exception of convicted criminal offenders, who have limited constitutional rights, all other Americans receive identical protections from the rights contained in the Constitution.

REALITY

- The recognition and expansion of rights for youths in the justice system did not lead to equal application of rights for juveniles and adults.
- Some of the most obvious differences concern protections against unreasonable searches and seizures, especially in the context of public schools.
- The U.S. Supreme Court has approved school policies that mandate random drug testing for student athletes (*Vernonia School District v. Acton*, 1995) and for all other students participating in extracurricular activities (*Board of Education v. Earls*, 2002).
- Schools can mandate drug tests, which are considered searches under the Fourth Amendment, even if there is no reason to suspect wrongdoing by a student. By contrast, the Supreme Court forbade the state of Georgia from requiring drug testing of adult candidates for political office (*Chandler v. Miller*, 1997).
- Students possess some protections in schools. In 2009, the Supreme Court declared that a teenage girl's constitutional rights were violated when school officials strip-searched her based on the false claim by another student that she was carrying prescription-strength painkillers (*Safford Unified School District #1 v. Redding*, 2009).

In re Winship **(1970)** The standard of proof "beyond a reasonable doubt" applies to juvenile delinquency proceedings.

McKeiver v. Pennsylvania **(1971)** Juveniles do not have a constitutional right to a trial by jury.

Breed v. Jones **(1975)** Juveniles cannot be found delinquent in juvenile court and then transferred to adult court without a hearing on the transfer; to do so violates the protection against double jeopardy.

status offense Any act committed by a juvenile that is considered unacceptable for a child, such as truancy or running away from home, but that would not be a crime if it were committed by an adult.

During the final decades of the twentieth century, the police and courts followed crime control policies in reacting to juvenile crime. Many legislators favor severe sentences for juveniles who commit serious crimes. Can the threat of long prison sentences deter juveniles from committing crimes?

AP Images/Sue Ogrocki

Schall v. Martin (1984)
Juveniles can be held in preventive detention if there is concern that they may commit additional crimes while awaiting court action.

The *Schall* decision reflects the ambivalence permeating the juvenile justice system. On one side are the liberal reformers, who call for increased procedural and substantive legal protections for juveniles accused of crime. On the other side are conservatives, who are devoted to crime control policies and alarmed by the rise in juvenile crime.

Crime control policies during this period resulted in many more juveniles being tried in adult courts. As noted by Alex Kotlowitz, "the crackdown on children has gone well beyond those accused of violent crimes" (1994:40). Data from the National Juvenile Court Data Archive show that delinquency cases waived to the adult criminal courts increased 121 percent from 1985 to 1994, demonstrating the "get tough" attitude during this period (Sickmund, Sladky, & Kang, 2015). In addition, some claim that increased penalties are more harmful in the long run to minority youths (Feld, 1999; 2003).

The "Kids Are Different" Period (2005–Present)

Some observers believe that a new period in juvenile justice may be developing. In *Roper v. Simmons* (2005), discussed in Chapter 9, the U.S. Supreme Court ruled that executions were unconstitutional for crimes committed by those younger than 18 years of age. This important ruling shepherded in a new era of juvenile justice. In *Roper,* the Court focused on the issue of culpability. The justices ruled that juveniles were less culpable than adults because of factors related to physical and emotional development that result from the growth and maturation process of the human brain (MacArthur Foundation, 2007c). Research indicates that intellectual maturity occurs at age 16, but that other factors (such as control over impulsiveness) are not fully developed until age 24–26. This growing recognition of teenage development provides a basis for new programs, and laws have been proposed to treat juveniles differently from adults in terms of treatment and punishment.

Emotional and intellectual development also play a role in how juveniles understand (or fail to understand) their rights according to the Constitution, particularly with regard to their rights during questioning by police. In 2011, a divided Court decided that police must take age into account when explaining *Miranda* rights to juveniles (*J. D. R. v. North Carolina*). As stated by Justice Sotomayor, "[t]he law has historically reflected the same assumption that children characteristically lack the capacity to exercise mature judgment and possess only an incomplete ability to understand the world around them."

Current program trends aim at helping juvenile offenders through rehabilitation and the prevention of delinquency. Such programs are not yet widespread or fully developed. For example, there are few free substance-abuse programs for juveniles outside correctional institutions. This means that a juvenile must be incarcerated to receive such assistance. Reducing drug use before it increases delinquency is important for limiting criminal behavior, so there is increasing interest in developing more programs that are accessible to youths in the community. Research is also focusing on the relationship between parents and children and how parenting programs may help to keep kids out of juvenile court (MacArthur Foundation, 2007b).

The use of judicial **waiver**, the process to waive juvenile court jurisdiction in order to move juveniles into adult court for prosecution and punishment, peaked in 1994, when 13,000 juveniles were waived to adult court. After that, the use of waiver decreased substantially, and reached an all-time low in 2013, with 4,000 juveniles waived (Sickmund, Sladky, & Kang, 2015). This decrease in waiver mirrors the decrease in violent juvenile crime since the mid-1990s (Adams & Addie, 2011). In recognition of the "Kids Are Different" philosophy, several states are considering the abolition of juvenile waiver by increasing the minimum age for adult trial to 18. Research on public attitudes also indicates that U.S. citizens are becoming less supportive of waiver and believe it should be used "sparingly and selectively" and only when the adult justice system is able to provide a rehabilitative component to punishment for juveniles (Applegate, Davis, & Cullen, 2009). However, the state of Florida has been criticized for its "direct file" law, which allows prosecutors to send juveniles directly to adult court without input from a judge (Human Rights Watch, 2014). Florida transfers more youth to adult courts than any other state and uses transfers disproportionately for black youth (Clark, 2014). As you read the "You Make the Decision" feature, consider how you would handle the challenge of determining when a juvenile should face trial as an adult.

Courts are beginning to focus on the use of life without parole, or LWOP, for juvenile offenders. In 2010, the Supreme Court decided in *Graham v. Florida* that the use of LWOP was unconstitutional for juveniles convicted of *non-homicide* offenses; however, only a small percentage of juveniles were then serving life sentences for non-homicide crimes (Graham himself was convicted of armed burglary and later violated the terms of his probation). Some legal scholars have argued that the "Kids Are Different" philosophy should apply to all juveniles, even those convicted of serious crimes (Berkheiser, 2011). In 2012, the Court placed another limitation on sentences. In *Miller v. Alabama,* the majority ruled that juveniles cannot be subject to a mandatory LWOP sentence for *homicide* offenses. States are beginning to change their policies as a result—for example, the Michigan Supreme Court recently ruled that any juveniles sentenced to LWOP must be resentenced (Shepard, 2016).

waiver Procedure by which the juvenile court waives its jurisdiction and transfers a juvenile case to the adult criminal court.

YOU MAKE THE DECISION

Prosecutor

When juveniles are accused of serious criminal offenses, decisions must be made about whether they should be prosecuted in juvenile court, which typically leads to sentences of limited length, or prosecuted as adults, which can lead to long sentences in adult prisons. Some states require juveniles accused of certain offenses, such as first-degree murder, to be charged as adults. For other offenses, the decision is made either by the prosecutor or by a judge, depending on the procedures specified in a state's laws. As prosecutor, you face a case in which three 16-year-olds and one 15-year-old are accused of hitting a man in the back of the head, rendering him unconscious, kicking him while he was on the ground so hard that he lost several teeth, and stealing his wallet. Should these youths be charged as adults? Explain what you would decide and the factors that guided your decision. Then search the Internet and read the New Jersey Supreme Court's decision in *State in the Interest of V. A.* (2012). (Note: "V. A." represents the initials of a defendant; states may seek to protect against identifying juveniles by name in the news media for certain cases).

In spite of the increasingly tough policies directed at juvenile offenders in the late twentieth century, changes that occurred during the juvenile rights period continue to affect the system profoundly. Lawyers are now routinely present at court hearings and other stages of the process, adding a note of formality that was not present 30 years ago. Status offenders seldom end up in secure punitive environments such as training schools. The juvenile justice system looks more like the adult justice system than it did, but it remains less formal. Its stated intention is also less harsh: to keep juveniles in the community whenever possible. The rulings in *Roper v. Simmons* and *Graham v. Florida* may indicate further changes away from tough policies.

The Juvenile Justice System

Juvenile justice operates through a variety of procedures in different states; even different counties within the same states vary. Because the offenses committed by juveniles are mostly violations of state laws, there is little federal involvement in the juvenile justice system. Despite internal differences, the juvenile justice system is characterized by two key factors: (1) the age of clients and (2) the categories of cases under juvenile instead of adult court jurisdiction.

Age of Clients

Age normally determines whether a person is processed through the juvenile or the adult justice system. The upper age limit for original juvenile court jurisdiction varies from 15 to 17. In 39 states and the District of Columbia, offenders can no longer be tried in juvenile court after their eighteenth birthday; in nine states, the seventeenth; and in the remaining two states, the sixteenth (Hockenberry & Puzzanchera, 2015). In 45 states, judges have the discretion to transfer juveniles to adult courts through a waiver hearing (Puzzanchera & Addie, 2014). Figure 15.3 shows the age at which juveniles can be transferred to adult court.

Categories of Cases under Juvenile Court Jurisdiction

Four types of cases fall under the jurisdiction of the juvenile justice system: delinquency, status offenses, neglect, and dependency. Mixing together young criminals and children who suffer from their parents' inadequacies dates from the earliest years of juvenile justice.

delinquent A child who has committed an act that if committed by an adult would be a criminal act.

   Delinquent children have committed acts that if committed by an adult would be criminal—for example, auto theft, robbery, or assault. In 2013, juvenile courts handled about 1.1 million delinquency cases each year. Males are most frequently in court, representing 72 percent of delinquency cases. Among the criminal charges brought before the juvenile court, 26 percent are for crimes against the person, 35 percent for property offenses, 13 percent for drug law violations, and 26 percent for public-order offenses (Hockenberry & Puzzanchera 2015).

FIGURE 15.3

The Youngest Age at Which Juveniles May Be Transferred to Adult Criminal Court by Discretionary Waiver of Juvenile Jurisdiction The waiver provisions of states vary greatly, and no clear regional or other factor explains the differences.

Map legend:
- No minimum age
- 10 years
- 12 years
- 13 years
- 14 years
- 15 years

Source: *OJJDP Statistical Briefing Book*. Online at http://www.ojjdp.gov/ojstatbb/structure_process/qa04110.asp?qaDate=2014. Released on October 1, 2015.

Recall that certain acts are illegal only when committed by a juvenile. Status offenders have not violated a penal code; instead, they are charged with being ungovernable or incorrigible: as runaways, truants, or **PINS** (persons in need of supervision). Status offenders make up about 10 percent of the juvenile court caseload. Although female offenders account for only 28 percent of delinquency cases, they make up 42 percent of the status offense cases. In addition, females are more likely than males to be referred for runaway and truancy status offenses (Hockenberry & Puzzanchera, 2015).

Some states do not distinguish between delinquent offenders and status offenders; they label both as juvenile delinquents. Thus, those judged to be ungovernable and those judged to be robbers may be sent to the same correctional institution. Beginning in the early 1960s, many state legislatures attempted to distinguish status offenders and to exempt them from a criminal record. In states that have decriminalized status offenses, juveniles who participate in these activities may now be classified as dependent children and placed in the care of child-protective agencies.

Juvenile justice also deals with problems of neglect and dependency. Some children are hurt through no fault of their own, because their parents have failed to provide a proper environment for them. People see the state's proper role as acting as a parent to a child whose own parents are unable or unwilling to provide proper care. Illinois, for example, defines a **neglected child** as one who is receiving inadequate care because of some action or inaction of his or her parents. This may include not being sent to school, not receiving medical care, being abandoned, living in an injurious environment, or not receiving some other care necessary for the child's well-being. A **dependent child** either has no parent or guardian or is receiving inadequate care because of the physical or mental disability of the parent. The law governing neglected and dependent children is broad and includes situations in which the child is viewed as a victim of adult behavior.

PINS Acronym for *person(s) in need of supervision,* a term that designates juveniles who are either status offenders or thought to be on the verge of trouble.

neglected child A child who is receiving inadequate care because of some action or inaction of his or her parents.

dependent child A child who has no parent or guardian or whose parents cannot give proper care.

Juvenile courts hear cases related to delinquency, status offenses, and dependency cases. The system, then, deals with both criminal and noncriminal cases. Often, juveniles who have done nothing wrong are categorized, either officially or in the public mind, as delinquents. In some states, little effort is made in pre-adjudication detention facilities or in social service agencies to separate the classes of juveniles.

▼ **CHECK POINT**

4. **What are the jurisdictional criteria for the juvenile court?**
   The age of the youth, usually under 16 or 18, and the type of case—delinquency, status offense, neglect, or dependency.

STOP & ANALYZE

Why do most state laws use 18 as the age of majority? Is there something special that occurs at age 18 that indicates a shift from "juvenile" to "adult"? Would you use a specific age, design some tests of knowledge and maturity, or devise some other basis for deciding whether to try an older teen as a juvenile or an adult? Give reasons for your choice.

The Juvenile Justice Process

Underlying the juvenile justice system is the philosophy that police, judges, and correctional officials should focus primarily on the interests of the child. Prevention of delinquency is the system's justification for intervening in the lives of juveniles who are involved in either status or criminal offenses.

In theory at least, juvenile proceedings are to be conducted in a nonadversarial environment. The juvenile court is to be a place where the judge, social workers, clinicians, and probation officers work together to diagnose the child's problem and select a treatment program to attack that problem.

Juvenile justice is a bureaucracy based on an ideology of social work. It is staffed primarily by people who think of themselves as members of the helping professions. Not even the recent emphasis on crime control and punishment has removed the treatment philosophy from most juvenile justice arenas. However, political pressures and limits on resources may stymie the implementation of this philosophy by focusing on the punishment of offenders rather than the prevention of delinquency. Politicians may view increased spending for rehabilitative programs as being "soft on crime," even though the public supports rehabilitation and believes that juvenile offenders can be reformed (Piquero et al., 2010).

Like the adult system, juvenile justice functions within a context of exchange relationships between officials of various government and private agencies that influence decisions. The juvenile court must deal not only with children and their parents but also with patrol officers, probation officers, welfare officials, social workers, psychologists, and the heads of treatment institutions, all of whom have their own goals, perceptions of delinquency, and concepts of treatment.

Figure 15.4 outlines the sequence of steps that are taken from police investigation to correctional disposition. As you examine this figure, compare the procedures with those of the criminal justice system for adults. Note the various options available to decision makers and the extensive discretion that they can exercise.

Police Interface

Many police departments, especially in cities, have special juvenile units. The juvenile officer is often selected and trained to relate to youths, knows much about relevant legal issues, and is sensitive to the special needs of young offenders. This officer also serves as an important link between the police and other community institutions, such as schools and other organizations serving young people. As discussed in Chapter 5, some communities hire *school resource officers* (SROs) to provide counseling and a security presence in school buildings. There is debate about whether SROs actually reduce crime in schools (Na & Gottfredson, 2011), but some studies report that

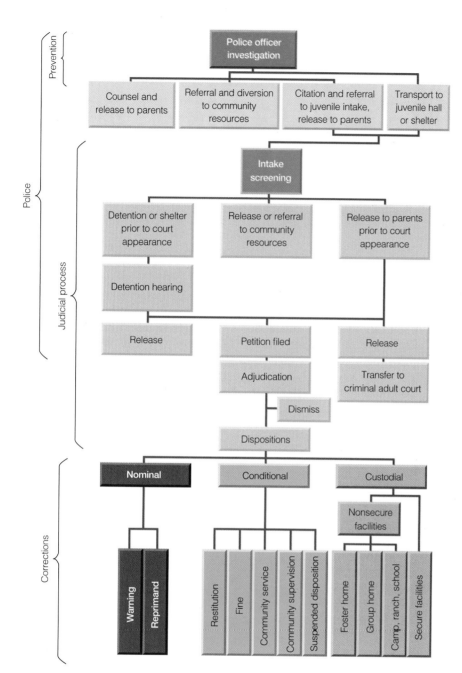

FIGURE 15.4

The Juvenile Justice System Decision makers have more options for the disposition of juvenile offenders, compared with options in the criminal justice system for adults.

Source: National Advisory Commission on Criminal Justice Standards and Goals, *Report of the Task Force on Juvenile Justice and Delinquency Prevention* (Washington, DC: Law Enforcement Assistance Administration, 1976).

SROs provide students with a positive image of police and increase the likelihood that students will report problems (Finn & McDevitt, 2005). Others find that perceptions of safety are heavily determined by race, with African Americans feeling less safe in the presence of school officers than white students (Theriot & Orme, 2014). There are also concerns that the presence of SROs leads to larger numbers of youths being sent into the juvenile court system for misbehavior that could otherwise be handled through a school's internal disciplinary procedures (Na & Gottfredson, 2014).

Most complaints against juveniles are brought by the police, although an injured party, school officials, and even the parents can initiate them, as well. The police must make three major decisions with regard to the processing of juveniles:

1. Whether to take the child into custody
2. Whether to request that the child be detained following apprehension
3. Whether to refer the child to court

The police exercise enormous discretion in these decisions. They do extensive screening and make informal adjustments in the street and at the station house.

FIGURE 15.5

Disposition of Juveniles Taken into Police Custody The police have discretion in the disposition of juvenile arrest cases. What factors can influence how a case is disposed?

Source: Federal Bureau of Investigation, *Uniform Crime Reports, 2014*, Table 68 (www.fbi.gov).

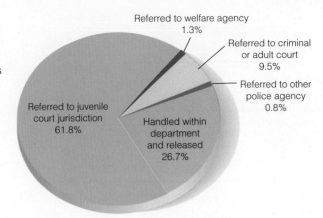

Referred to welfare agency
1.3%

Referred to criminal
or adult court
9.5%

Referred to other
police agency
0.8%

Referred to juvenile
court jurisdiction
61.8%

Handled within
department
and released
26.7%

In communities and neighborhoods where the police have developed close relationships with the residents or where policy dictates, the police may deal with violations by giving warnings to the juveniles and notifying their parents. Figure 15.5 shows the disposition of juveniles taken into police custody.

Initial decisions about what to do with a suspected offender are influenced by such factors as the predominant attitude of the community; the officer's attitude toward the juvenile, the juvenile's family, the offense, and the court; and the officer's conception of her or his own role. The disposition of juvenile cases at the arrest stage also relies on the seriousness of the offense, the child's prior record, and his or her demeanor. To summarize, several key factors influence how the police dispose of a case of juvenile delinquency:

1. The seriousness of the offense
2. The willingness of the parents to cooperate and to discipline the child
3. The child's behavioral history as reflected in school and police records
4. The extent to which the child and the parents insist on a formal court hearing
5. The local political and social norms concerning dispositions in such cases
6. The officer's beliefs and attitudes

Although young people commit many serious crimes, the juvenile function of police work is concerned largely with order maintenance. In most incidents of this sort, the law is ambiguous, and blame cannot easily be assigned. Many offenses committed by juveniles that involve physical or monetary damage are minor infractions: breaking windows, hanging around the business district, disturbing the peace, public sexual behavior, and shoplifting. Here the function of the investigating officer is not so much to solve crimes as to handle the often legally uncertain complaints involving juveniles. The officer seeks both to satisfy the complainant and to keep the youth from future trouble. Given this emphasis on settling cases within the community instead of strictly enforcing the law, the threat of arrest can be used as a weapon to deter juveniles from criminal activity and to encourage them to conform to the law.

Intake Screening at the Court

The juvenile court processing of delinquency cases begins with a referral in the form of a petition, not an arrest warrant as in the adult system. When a petition is filed, an intake hearing is held, over which a hearing officer presides. During this stage, the officer determines whether the alleged facts are sufficient for the juvenile court to take jurisdiction or whether some other action would be in the child's best interest.

Nationally, 45 percent of all referrals are disposed of at this stage, without formal processing by a judge (Puzzanchera, Adams, & Hockenberry, 2012). **Diversion** is the process of screening children out of the system without a decision by the court, thereby limiting their involvement in the formal juvenile justice system. In 42 percent of these cases, the charges are dismissed; another 24 percent are diverted to an informal probation, and 33 percent are dealt with through some agreed-on

diversion The process of screening children out of the juvenile justice system without a decision by the court.

The concept of restorative justice is applied to juveniles in some settings. Teen courts, for example, deal with less serious offenses, often before formal charges have been brought. Teens are judged by their peers, and typically the sentences include restitution, letters of apology, and community service. Is this an effective way to deal with youthful offenders?

The Washington Post/Getty Images

alternative sanction (Puzzanchera & Robson, 2014). Read the "Evidence-Based Practice and Policy" feature to learn more about diversion.

Pretrial Procedures

When a decision is made to refer the case to the court, the court holds an initial hearing. Here the juveniles are informed of their rights and told that if a plea is given, it must be voluntary.

If the juvenile is to be detained pending trial, most states require a **detention hearing,** which determines if the youth is to be released to a parent or guardian or to be held in a detention facility until adjudication. Some children are detained to keep them from committing other crimes while awaiting trial. Others are held to protect them from the possibility of harm from gang members or parents. Still others are held because, if released, they will likely not appear in court as required. Nationally, about 20 percent of all delinquency cases involve detention between referral to the juvenile court and disposition of the case (Sickmund, Sladky, & Kang, 2012).

The conditions in many detention facilities are poor; abuse is often reported. In some rural areas, juveniles continue to be detained in adult jails even though the federal government has pressed states to hold youths in separate facilities. In 2003, the city of Baltimore unveiled a new juvenile detention facility meant to expedite juvenile cases and centralize services to delinquent youth. After its opening, the facility was called a "monstrosity," with poor sight lines (officers cannot easily observe and supervise the juvenile detainees), overcrowding, and increasing rates of violence within its walls (Bykowicz, 2008). A 2010 evaluation determined that the high rate of violence in the facility had begun to decrease (Dedel, 2010), and the rate continued to drop from 2010 to 2012 (Moroney, 2014). Baltimore currently holds juveniles charged as adults in the same facility as adult offenders, which has been a source of controversy, as well. In 2013, officials determined that this facility was controlled by gang members and that guards had been sneaking in contraband (Toobin, 2014). After much debate, the state of Maryland decided in 2015 to renovate an existing facility to use for juvenile offenders (E. Cox, 2015).

Believing that detaining youths accelerates their delinquent behaviors, some jurisdictions have attempted to stem the tide of rising numbers of juveniles in detention. In Durham, North Carolina, a new program is being implemented to keep 16- and 17-year-olds who commit minor crimes out of the juvenile justice system.

detention hearing A hearing by the juvenile court to determine if a juvenile is to be detained or released prior to adjudication.

Evidence-Based Diversion Programs

The juvenile justice system has been increasingly relying on programs demonstrated to be effective through rigorous scientific testing. Many of these programs are designed to divert juveniles from the justice system to avoid the stigma and impact of being processed in the formal court system.

In Michigan, the Adolescent Diversion Project (ADP) was created by Michigan State University using the tenets of three theories of juvenile delinquency: social control, social learning, and labeling theories (see Chapter 2). Student volunteers at MSU are trained to work with juvenile offenders to determine their specific needs and help to strengthen their skills in areas in which they might be lacking. For example, some juveniles may benefit from strengthening their family relationships, while others may need help structuring their free-time activities. Evaluations of this program have indicated that youths who complete it have a lower recidivism rate than youths who are processed in the juvenile courts.

New York has implemented a similar program with the same name, in which 16- and 17-year-old offenders are diverted from adult court processing (in New York, offenders in these age groups are automatically tried as adults). This ADP project aims to divert juvenile offenders from the adult system in order to avoid the civil disabilities experienced by many adult offenders, including impediments to employment, financial credit, and participation in jury duty and elections. Judges who have received specific training in adolescent brain development, substance abuse, and other issues relevant to adolescent offenders determine the offender's suitability for the ADP program. Evaluations of this program indicate that the juvenile offenders who experience ADP have similar recidivism rates as those offenders who are processed in the adult system. The advantage of diversion is that it does not increase the rate of recidivism, and the offender who keeps a clean record after the first offense is spared the lifetime consequences of a criminal conviction.

The State of Texas has implemented the Front-End Diversion Initiative (FEDI), a diversion program specifically for juvenile offenders with mental health needs. Intake officers with special training determine whether a juvenile offender should be evaluated for mental health issues. If the offender qualifies, then prosecution is deferred for six months while the offender works with a probation officer. These specially trained officers work with the juvenile to set goals and create a plan to meet those goals. The educational, mental health, family, and community needs of the juvenile are all assessed and strengthened during the program. Evaluations of the program indicate that FEDI significantly reduced the rate of juveniles adjudicated. Many youths were able to successfully avoid prosecution by meeting the goals set by their probation officer.

Researching the Internet

For more on Michigan's Adolescent Diversion Project, go to the website of the MSU's Department of Psychology at http://psychology.msu.edu/MSUAP/Newsletter.aspx.

Implementing New Practices

Each of these programs was based on a foundation of criminological theory and then evaluated using valid research methodologies. Diversion of juveniles from formal processing may help reduce their recidivism rates as well as the stigma (and civil disabilities) faced by those with criminal convictions. Supporters point out that the programs are less expensive than incarceration, and more effective. However, critics are wary that troubled youths in these programs will be inadequately supervised and controlled, and thus will have opportunities for victimizing more people in the community. How would you convince critics that the juvenile justice system should spend funds on diversion rather than focus on policing and incarceration? What are the strongest arguments that you can present in favor of diversion?

Source: Adapted from the Office of Juvenile Justice and Delinquency Prevention "Model Programs Guide" (http://www.crimesolutions.gov).

The "Misdemeanor Diversion Program" allows juvenile offenders to complete community service requirements and avoid being charged as adults, as they would be under state law (Oleniacz, 2014).

Transfer (Waiver) to Adult Court

One of the first decisions to be made after a juvenile is referred is whether a case should be transferred to the criminal (adult) justice system. In 45 states, juvenile court judges may waive their jurisdiction. This means that after considering the seriousness of the charge, the age of the juvenile, and the prospects of rehabilitation, the judge can transfer the case to adult court. In 29 states, certain violent crimes, such as murder, rape, and armed robbery, are excluded by law from the jurisdiction of the juvenile courts. In 1970, only three states allowed prosecutors the authority to decide whether to file in adult or juvenile court. Today 15 states give prosecutors the authority to do so (P. Griffin, 2011). Critics question whether prosecutors will "make

The juvenile waiver process permits juveniles to be sent to adult court and receive the same punishments as adults for serious crimes—except for the death penalty and life without parole for non-homicide offenses. Here a juvenile suspect makes a court appearance after being charged with murder. What is the appropriate sentence for a juvenile who commits violent crimes such as murder or rape?

AP Images/Greg Lynch

better informed and more appropriate 'criminal adulthood' decisions than would judges in an adversarial waiver hearing" (Feld, 2004:599).

After a "tougher" approach to juvenile crime took hold in the 1970s, the number of cases transferred increased dramatically. Several states expanded their ability to transfer juveniles by excluding certain crimes from juvenile court jurisdiction or lowering the minimum age for transfer to adult court. The likelihood of waiver varies by seriousness of offense, offender age, and offender race. This disparity can be affected by offending patterns (that is, which offenses are more frequently committed by which youths) as well as by biased decision making. Even after controlling for seriousness of arrest and prior criminal record, African American and Hispanic juveniles are more likely to be waived than white juveniles, and boys are more likely to be waived than girls (Brown & Sorensen, 2013).

Between 1985 and 1997, one result of the increased use of the waiver was that more juveniles were being sent to adult state prisons; the number doubled from 3,400 to 7,400 (Austin, Johnson, & Gregoriou, 2000). As the use of waiver subsequently declined, so, too, did the number of juveniles sent to prison. From 1997 to 2002, there was a 45-percent decline in the number of new admissions of offenders under age 18 into state prisons (Snyder & Sickmund, 2006). Critics of the policies claim that waiver subverts the intent of the juvenile justice system and exposes juvenile offenders to harsh conditions in adult prisons—where they are susceptible to physical and sexual victimization (DeJong & Merrill, 2000). In addition, those juveniles tried in adult courts are more likely to reoffend after release (Johnson, Lanza-Kaduce, & Woolard, 2011). There is also evidence that increased use of waiver has had no effect on juvenile crime rates (Steiner, Hemmens, & Bell, 2006; Steiner & Wright, 2006). Transferring juveniles to be tried in the adult courts remains controversial, as outlined in "Close Up."

Adjudication

Juvenile courts deal with almost 1.5 million delinquency cases a year (Knoll & Sickmund, 2012). *Adjudication* is the trial stage of the juvenile justice process. If the child has not admitted to the charges and the case has not been transferred to the adult court, an adjudication hearing is held to determine the facts in the case and, if appropriate, to label the juvenile as a "delinquent."

Juveniles in Adult Correctional Facilities

In Massachusetts, children as young as 14 years old can be tried in adult court rather than juvenile court; however, there are policies in place that prevent juveniles from being placed in adult facilities if convicted. Not all states have such policies, however, and it is possible for juvenile offenders to be incarcerated in adult facilities. This is especially true in states such as New York and North Carolina, where offenders aged 16 and 17 are automatically tried as adults.

Teens serving time in adult prisons face greater risks of physical violence and sexual assault than their peers in juvenile facilities. To combat this problem, the U.S. government passed the Prison Rape Elimination Act (PREA). One provision of the PREA requires that juveniles be housed separately from adults in state prisons; however, not all states have changed their policies to comply with PREA requirements. While Arizona, Iowa, Maine, Mississippi, Missouri, New Hampshire, New Jersey, North Dakota, Oregon, Tennessee, and Washington have demonstrated they are in full compliance with PREA, another 40 states and territories have submitted "assurances" that they are working toward compliance. Only Alaska, Arkansas, and Utah have not agreed to abide by the requirements in PREA.

In the effort to protect younger inmates from others who might harm them, juvenile inmates in adult facilities are frequently placed in "protective custody"—typically, solitary confinement—for their own safety. Because of the risk of psychological harm from isolation, there is a great deal of debate over the use of solitary confinement, especially for juveniles (see "The Policy Debate" later in this chapter).

Teenagers held in adult prisons not only face increased risk of victimization, but they are also more likely to return to prison later in life, and more likely to commit suicide than those in juvenile facilities. Adult facilities are frequently unable to provide educational opportunities or adequate and appropriate mental health care to juveniles.

In response to these concerns, New York is renovating the Hudson Correctional Facility, a medium-security prison, into a facility specifically designed to house all juveniles currently held in adult prisons. This facility will also have a unit designed for short-term jail stays. Thus, after November 2016, teens who commit crimes in New York City will no longer be housed at Rikers Island—a jail for adult offenders.

Researching the Internet

The 2015 PREA certifications and assurances are listed online at https://www.bja.gov/Programs/15PREA-AssurancesCertifications.pdf. What is the status of your state with regard to PREA compliance?

For Critical Thinking and Analysis

New York has taken the step to create a special prison for teenage offenders, but what is the solution for states that have small numbers of teens placed in adult facilities? Not every state can afford to build a special prison for a handful of offenders. Should these offenders instead be placed in juvenile facilities? If so, what happens when they reach the age of 18? Should they automatically be moved to adult facilities, even if they are benefitting from placement in a juvenile center?

Sources: "Governor Cuomo Signs Executive Order to Separate Teens from Adult Prisoners," Office of the Governor of New York State, December 22, 2015 (www.governor.ny.gov); J. Lahey, "The Steep Costs of Keeping Juveniles in Adult Prisons," *The Atlantic*, January 8, 2016 (www.theatlantic.com); C. Lewis and A. Rap-Herel, "New York Teens Often Isolated in Adult Prisons," *Women's E-News*, September 21, 2015 (www.womensenews.org).

The Supreme Court's decision in *Gault* and other due process rulings mandated changes that have altered the philosophy and actions of the juvenile court. Contemporary juvenile proceedings are more formal than those of the past, although still more informal than those in adult courts. The parents and child must receive copies of petitions with specific charges; counsel may be present, and free counsel can be appointed if the juvenile cannot pay; witnesses can be cross-examined; and a transcript of the proceedings must be kept.

As with other Supreme Court decisions, local practice may differ sharply from the procedures spelled out in the high court's rulings. Juveniles and their parents often waive their rights in response to suggestions from the judge or probation officer. The lower social status of the offender's parents, the intimidating atmosphere of the court, and judicial hints that the outcome will be more favorable if a lawyer is not present are reasons the procedures outlined in *Gault* might not be followed. The litany of "getting treatment," "doing what's right for the child," and "working out a just solution" may sound enticing, especially to people who are unfamiliar with the intricacies of formal legal procedures. In practice, then, juveniles still lack many of the protections given to adult offenders. Some of the differences between the juvenile and adult criminal justice systems are listed in Table 15.2.

The increased concern about crime has given prosecuting attorneys a more prominent part in the system. In keeping with the traditional child-saver philosophy, prosecuting attorneys rarely appeared in juvenile court prior to the *Gault* decision. Now that a defense attorney is present, the state often uses legal counsel as well. In many jurisdictions, prosecutors are assigned to deal specifically with juvenile cases. Their functions are to advise the intake officer, administer diversion programs, negotiate pleas, and act as an advocate during judicial proceedings.

Juvenile proceedings and court records have traditionally remained closed to the public to protect the child's privacy and potential for rehabilitation. Thus, judges in the adult courts usually do not have access to juvenile records. This means that people who have already served time on juvenile probation or in institutions are erroneously perceived to be first offenders when they are processed for crimes as adults. Some people argue that adult courts should have access to juvenile records and that young criminals should be treated more severely than adults to deter them from future illegal activity.

TABLE 15.2	The Adult and Juvenile Criminal Justice Systems		
Compare the basic elements of the adult and juvenile systems. To what extent does a juvenile have the same rights as an adult? Are the different decision-making processes necessary because a juvenile is involved?			
	Adult System	**Juvenile System**	
Philosophical assumptions	Decisions made as a result of adversarial system in context of due process rights	Decisions made as a result of inquiry into needs of juvenile within context of some due process elements	
Jurisdiction	Violations of criminal law	Violations of criminal law, status offenses, neglect, dependency	
Primary sanctioning goals	Retribution, deterrence, rehabilitation	Retribution, rehabilitation	
Official discretion	Widespread	Widespread	
Entrance	Official action of arrest, summons, or citation	Official action, plus referral by school, parents, other sources	
Role of prosecuting and defense attorneys	Required and formalized	Sometimes required; less structured; poor role definition	
Adjudication	Procedural rules of evidence in public jury trial required	Less formal structure to rules of evidence and conduct of trial; no right to public trial or jury in most states	
Treatment programs	Run primarily by public agencies	Broad use of private and public agencies	
Terminology	Arrest Preliminary hearing Prosecution Sentencing Parole	Referral Intake Adjudication Disposition Aftercare	
Application of Bill of Rights amendments			
Fourth	Unreasonable searches and seizures	Applicable	Applicable
Fifth	Double jeopardy Self-incrimination	Applicable Applicable (*Miranda* warnings)	Applicable (re: waiver to adult court) Applicable
Sixth	Right to counsel Public trial Trial by jury	Applicable Applicable Applicable	Applicable Applicable in less than half of states Applicable in less than half of states
Fourteenth	Right to treatment	Not applicable	Applicable

Disposition

If the court makes a finding of delinquency, the judge will schedule a dispositional hearing to decide what action should be taken. Typically, before passing sentence, the judge receives a *predispositional report* prepared by a probation officer. Similar to a presentence report, it serves to assist the judge in deciding on a disposition that is in the best interests of the child and is consistent with the treatment plan developed by the probation officer.

The court finds most juveniles to be delinquent at trial, because the intake and pretrial processes normally filter out cases in which a law violation cannot be proved. Besides dismissal, four other choices are available: (1) probation, (2) intermediate sanctions, (3) custodial care, and (4) community treatment. Intermediate sanctions might include assigning the juvenile to a specific treatment program or suspending the judgment while monitoring the youth's behavior and performance in school with the possibility of later dismissing the charge.

Juvenile court advocates have traditionally believed that rehabilitation is the only goal of sanctions imposed on young people. For most of the twentieth century, judges sentenced juveniles to indeterminate sentences so that correctional administrators could decide when release was appropriate. As in the adult criminal justice system, indeterminate sentences and unbridled discretion in juvenile justice have faced attack during the last three decades. Several states have tightened the sentencing discretion of judges, especially with regard to serious offenses.

Corrections

Many aspects of juvenile corrections resemble those of adult corrections. Both systems, for example, mix rehabilitative and retributive sanctions. However, juvenile corrections differs in many respects from the adult system. Some of the differences flow from the *parens patriae* concept and the youthful, seemingly innocent people with whom the system deals. At times, the differences show up in formal operational policies, such as contracting for residential treatment. At other times, the differences appear only in the style and culture of an operation, as they do in juvenile probation.

One predominant aim of juvenile corrections is to avoid unnecessary incarceration. When children are removed from their homes, they are inevitably damaged emotionally, even when the home life is harsh and abusive, for they are forced to abandon the only environment they know. Further, placing children in institutions has labeling effects; the children may perceive themselves as bad because they have received punitive treatment, and children who see themselves as "bad" may actually behave that way. Finally, treatment is believed to be more effective when the child is living in a normal, supportive home environment. For these reasons, noninstitutional forms of corrections are seen as highly desirable in juvenile justice and have proliferated in recent years.

Probation In 60 percent of cases, the juvenile delinquent is placed on probation and released to the custody of a parent or guardian (Livsey, 2012). Often the judge orders that the delinquent undergo some form of education or counseling. The delinquent can also be required to pay a fine or make restitution while on probation.

Juvenile probation operates in much the same way that adult probation does, and sometimes the same agency carries it out. In two respects, however, juvenile probation can differ markedly from adult probation. First, juvenile probation officers have smaller caseloads. Second, the juvenile probation officer is often infused with the sense that the offender is worthwhile and can change and that the job is valuable and enjoyable. Such attitudes make for greater creativity than probation officers who work with adults usually express. For example, a young offender can be paired with a "big brother" or "big sister" from the community.

Intermediate Sanctions Although probation and commitment to an institution are the system's two main dispositional options, intermediate sanctions served in the community now account for 13 percent of adjudicated juvenile cases (Puzzanchera, Adams, & Hockenberry, 2012). Judges have wide discretion to warn, to fine, to arrange for restitution, to order community service, to refer a juvenile for treatment at either a public or a private community agency, or to withhold judgment.

Judges sometimes suspend judgment—that is, they continue a case without a finding when they wish to put a youth under supervision but are reluctant to apply the label "delinquent." The judge holds off on a definitive judgment, but can give one should a youth misbehave while under the informal supervision of a probation officer or parents.

Custodial Care Of those juveniles declared delinquent, 28 percent are placed in public or private facilities, with girls less likely to be placed (22%) than boys (30%). The placement rate of juveniles over time has decreased from about one in three adjudicated juveniles in 1985 to about one in four in 2010 (Sickmund, Sladky, & Kang, 2013). In 2010, the national incarceration rate per 100,000 juveniles aged 10–18 was 225—this includes juveniles held both prior to trial and as a sentence of incarceration. Like the adult incarceration rate, these rates vary widely among the states, with the highest rate (575) in South Dakota and the lowest (53) in Vermont.

The number of juveniles incarcerated in public and private facilities decreased steadily from 1997 through 2010, with only a few states exhibiting increased rates of incarceration of juvenile delinquents during that period (Arkansas, Idaho, Nebraska, North Dakota, Pennsylvania, South Dakota, and West Virginia) (Hockenberry, 2013).

Policy makers are concerned about the overrepresentation of incarcerated African American juveniles. Research has found that the disproportionate confinement of minority juveniles often stems from disparity at the early stages of case processing. Thus, if more African Americans are detained than others, more of them will likely be adjudicated in juvenile court and more placed in residential facilities. Some research suggests that juvenile court actors have biased perceptions of minority juveniles, and thus, these youths receive more-severe treatment at all levels of the juvenile justice system (Leiber & Mack, 2003). Other studies indicate the importance of examining both race and gender when analyzing court outcomes, as girls are generally treated more leniently than boys in the justice system (Guevara, Herz, & Spohn, 2006). See "What Americans Think" for a picture of attitudes toward punishment for juveniles.

Detention inside a juvenile facility can be an intimidating experience for many youths. They may be threatened, bullied, or assaulted by older or larger teens. The physical condition of the facilities and the limited number of educational and training programs may contribute to the difficult experience of living there. Are taxpayers willing to pay for the personnel and facilities necessary to provide a good environment for implementing effective treatment programs for juvenile offenders?

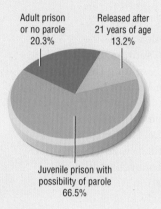

WHAT AMERICANS THINK

QUESTION: "Tell me which of the following punishments you think an adolescent convicted of committing a homicide should receive as punishment, offering three options—(a) the adolescent should be sentenced to a juvenile facility and should be released after 21 years of age, (b) the adolescent should be sentenced to a juvenile facility with the possibility of parole after 21 years of age, or (c) the adolescent should be sentenced to adult prison and no possibility of parole at the age of 21."

Adult prison or no parole 20.3%

Released after 21 years of age 13.2%

Juvenile prison with possibility of parole 66.5%

CRITICAL THINKING: Do the responses to this question indicate that most Americans disagree with the Supreme Court's decisions that treat juveniles differently from adults by prohibiting death sentences for juveniles and life without parole sentences for non-homicide offenses? Do you believe that the results would be different if the question asked specifically about applying the death penalty to juveniles? Why or why not?

Source: T. T. Allen, E. Trzcinski, and S. P. Kubiak, 2012, "Public Attitudes toward Juveniles Who Commit Crimes: The Relationship between Assessments of Adolescent Development and Attitudes toward Severity of Punishment," *Crime & Delinquency*, 58(1): 8–102.

Institutions for juvenile offenders are classified as either nonsecure or secure. *Nonsecure* placements (foster homes, group homes, camps, ranches, or schools) include a significant number of non-offenders—youths referred for abuse, neglect, or emotional disturbance. *Secure* facilities, such as reform schools and training schools, deal with juveniles who have committed crimes and have significant personal problems. Most secure juvenile facilities are small, designed to hold 40 or fewer residents. However, many states have at least one facility holding 200 or more hard-core delinquents who are allowed limited freedom. Because the residents are younger and somewhat more volatile than adults, behavioral control is often an everyday issue, and fights and aggression are common. Poor management practices can lead to difficult situations. Some custodial facilities have been taken to task recently for the use of solitary confinement for juveniles. Review "The Policy Debate" below to learn more about this issue.

Boot camps for juvenile offenders saw a growth spurt in the early 1990s. By 1997, more than 27,000 teenagers were passing through 54 camps in 34 states annually. However, as with boot camps for adults, the results have not been promising. A national study shows that recidivism among boot-camp attendees ranges from 64 percent to 75 percent, slightly higher than for youths sentenced to adult prisons (Blair, 2000). Additionally, reports of mistreatment of inmates at juvenile boot camps prompted the U.S. House of Representatives to develop standards of care for such inmates (J. Abrams, 2008). States are rethinking their policies, with many closing their programs.

The Survey of Youth in Residential Placement (SYRP), conducted in 2003, showed that 43 percent of juveniles were incarcerated for violent offenses, 44 percent were under the influence of alcohol or drugs at the time of their arrest, and 45 percent were living with only one parent when they were

THE POLICY DEBATE

Solitary Confinement for Juveniles

Kalief Browder was 16 years old when he was accused of stealing a backpack in New York City. While awaiting trial, he was held in the Rikers Island Jail—an adult facility—for three years, two of which were spent primarily in solitary confinement. Prosecutors eventually dropped the charges and released Browder, but some believe he suffered

severe damage to his mental health while incarcerated. Unable to cope with his experience, he committed suicide at the age of 22.

In the state of New York, juvenile offenders who are 16 or 17 years old are automatically tried as adults. If convicted and incarcerated, they are sent to adult facilities as punishment. Offenders convicted in New York City

who receive a jail sentence are sent to Rikers Island, one of the largest jails in the world. Prior to 2015, if these teens misbehaved or otherwise broke the rules, they faced time in solitary confinement—23 hours per day in a 6-by-8-foot concrete cell with no human companionship. New York City officially ended the use of solitary confinement for juvenile offenders on

January 1, 2015. However, the city continues to use Rikers Island to hold juveniles.

The American Civil Liberties Union (ACLU) has called for the end of solitary confinement for juvenile offenders, citing the risk of psychological harm and suicide. Pointing to research indicating that juveniles do not have the same emotional and psychological maturity as adults, the ACLU argues that this punishment will cause great physical, emotional, and developmental harm to juveniles—especially those with prior trauma or a disability. In 2016, President Obama banned the use of solitary confinement for juvenile offenders held in federal custody, but this order does not affect state policies regarding those accused or convicted of violating state laws (Eilperin, 2016).

Several lawsuits have been filed by juvenile offenders in an attempt to end this practice and gain remuneration for poor treatment. In 2014, the state of Ohio agreed to phase out the use of solitary confinement for juvenile offenders (*S.H. v. Reed*, 2008). Also in 2014, the state of Illinois agreed to improve conditions at juvenile facilities, including eliminating solitary confinement for disciplinary reasons, after the ACLU filed a court case on behalf of a juvenile detainee (*R.J. v. Jones*, 2012). A lawsuit brought by two juveniles against the State of New Jersey resulted in a $400,000 settlement for them after they were placed in solitary confinement for extended periods of time (*T.D. and O.S. v. Mickens et al.*, 2010).

Against Solitary Confinement

Opponents of solitary confinement claim that the mental health consequences of such punishment are cruel and unusual. Specifically:

- In many cases, solitary confinement means spending as many as 23 hours per day alone in a cell, with only an hour or two of daily "recreation" time. This out-of-cell time is often spent in an outdoor "cell" surrounded by fencing, and still without human interaction.
- Psychiatrists have spoken out about the use of solitary confinement, indicating that it can result in

depression, anxiety, and psychosis; and that juvenile offenders are at higher risk for these illnesses than adults due to their stage of emotional development.
- Research indicates that suicides in juvenile facilities are more often committed by individuals in solitary confinement.
- Solitary confinement does not provide any rehabilitative benefits for the prisoner experiencing the punishment.
- Prisoners kept in solitary confinement may not be allowed visitors; thus they have no access to family contact. They may also be kept from participating in other group activities, such as educational programs.

In Support of Solitary Confinement

While solitary confinement has been shown to damage mental health, some argue that it is justified in certain circumstances.

- Solitary confinement is the only way to protect inmates from others who would do them harm. This may be particularly true for inmates who are LGBT or at higher risk of victimization.
- Solitary confinement may be necessary for a prisoner who poses a danger to other prisoners, or to staff. There may be no other way to protect others than to isolate problem prisoners in solitary.
- Isolating a prisoner in solitary confinement may be the only way to punish violations of jail/prison policies.
- Some believe that solitary confinement aids in self-reflection and provides prisoners with a way to think about their crimes and the impact their crimes have had on others. Recall from Chapter 10 that this was the "penitentiary" model used in the Pennsylvania system at the dawn of the nineteenth century.

What Should U.S. Policy Be?

Incarceration in the United States is costly and designed to meet specific purposes of punishment. Solitary confinement seems to create conditions that are harmful to prisoners and fails

to meet the expected rehabilitation purposes of punishment. Yet prison officials face challenges in deciding how to reduce the risk of prisoner assaults and other harmful behavior while also providing humane conditions that advance correctional goals.

Researching the Internet

Human Rights Watch and the American Civil Liberties Union published a report in 2012 entitled "Growing Up Locked Down: Youth in Solitary Confinement and Prisons Across the United States" (https://www.aclu.org/files/assets /us1012webwcover.pdf). Review the alternatives provided by HRW and the ACLU—what might work best in terms of criminal justice policy?

Analyzing the Issue

If solitary confinement has been demonstrated to be harmful, especially to juveniles, why is it still imposed in juvenile and adult facilities on juvenile offenders? If it is outlawed, how can correctional administrators maintain order and punish juvenile offenders who are disruptive in the facility? Should solitary confinement be used to protect juvenile detainees from other inmates looking to cause them harm? Which is the greater harm faced by detainees—the consequences of solitary confinement or victimization by other prisoners?

Sources: "Solitary Confinement of Juvenile Offenders," American Academy of Child & Adolescent Psychiatry, April 2012 (www .aacap.org); "Alone & Afraid: Children Held in Solitary Confinement and Isolation in Juvenile Detention and Correctional Facilities," American Civil Liberties Union, June 2014 (aclu.org); J. Eilperin, "Obama Bans Solitary Confinement for Juveniles in Federal Prisons," *Washington Post*, January 26, 2016 (www.washingtonpost.com); L. Kirchner, "Why Solitary Confinement Hurts Juveniles More than Adults," *Pacific Standard Magazine*, October 9, 2014 (psmag.com); A. Morrison, "After Rikers Island Scandal, NYC Officials Push Juvenile Justice Reform; 'Raise the Age' Bill for Young Offenders," *International Business Times*, June 3, 2015 (ibtimes .com); M. Schwirtz and M. Winerip, "Kalief Browder, Held at Rikers Island for 3 Years without Trial, Commits Suicide," *New York Times*, June 8, 2015. (www.nytimes.com).

FIGURE 15.6

Juveniles in Correctional Facilities: Types of Offenses and Non-delinquent Reasons for Placement

Source: M. Sickmund and C. Puzzanchera, *Juvenile Offenders and Victims: 2014 National Report.* National Center for Juvenile Justice, 2014, 188.

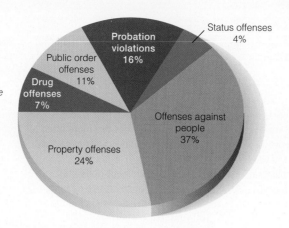

taken into custody. Also, 85 percent of the residents were male. The percentages of African Americans (32%) and Hispanics (24%) were greater than the percentages of those groups in the general population, and the majority (57%) had been suspended from school in the same year of their entry into the juvenile justice system (Snyder & Sickmund, 2006). Figure 15.6 shows the types of offenses of juveniles in public correctional facilities.

The 2008–2010 recession led to major funding cuts for state juvenile justice agencies around the United States. For example, the state of New York cut 371 juvenile justice workers from its payroll in 2011 (J. Campbell, 2011); New Hampshire cut the majority of funding for its CHINS (Children in Need of Services) program (Fahey, 2011); and Fresno County, California, considered the partial closure of a juvenile facility that was built in 2006 (K. Alexander, 2011). It is unclear how these cuts will impact the rate of juvenile delinquency in these areas, but the lack of treatment options for juveniles does not bode well for their ability to avoid criminal behavior as adults.

Institutional Programs   Because of the emphasis on rehabilitation that has dominated juvenile justice for much of the past 50 years, a wide variety of treatment programs have been used. Counseling, education, vocational training, and an assortment of psychotherapeutic methods have been incorporated into the juvenile correctional programs of most states. Unfortunately, research has raised many questions about the effectiveness of rehabilitation programs in juvenile corrections. For example, incarceration in a juvenile training institution primarily seems to prepare many offenders for entry into adult corrections. John Irwin's (1970) concept of the "state-raised youth" is a useful way of looking at children who come in contact with institutional life at an early age, lack family relationships and structure, become accustomed to living in a correctional facility, and cannot function in other environments. Current recommendations focus on the importance of prevention and keeping first-time juvenile offenders out of placement and in their homes, with family (Ryan, Abrams, & Huang, 2014).

aftercare Juvenile justice equivalent of parole, in which a delinquent is released from a custodial sentence and supervised in the community.

Aftercare   The juvenile equivalent of parole is known as **aftercare**. Upon release, the offender is placed under the supervision of a juvenile parole officer, who assists with educational, counseling, and treatment services. Quality aftercare is associated with lower rates of recidivism after release from incarceration, and many have blamed the failure of boot camps on poor aftercare (Kurlychek & Kempinen, 2006). As with the adult system, juveniles can be returned to custodial care should they violate the conditions of their parole.

Community Treatment   In the past decade, treatment in community-based facilities has become much more common. Today many private, nonprofit agencies contract with states to provide services for troubled youths. Community-based options include foster homes, in which juvenile offenders live with families,

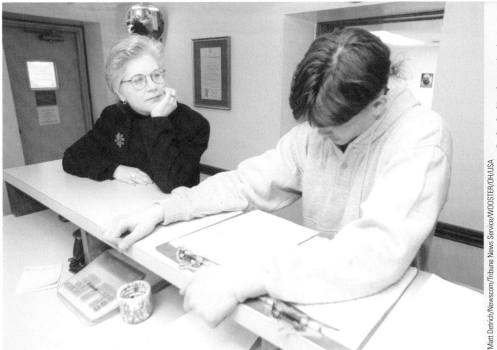

Many courts develop community programs in an effort to avoid confining youthful offenders in juvenile institutions. Here a juvenile offender meets with his attorney for monitoring, guidance, and support. What are the potential advantages and benefits of emphasizing community-based programs?

Matt Detrich/Newscom/Tribune News Service/WOOSTER/OH/USA

usually for a short period, and group homes, which are often privately run facilities for groups of 12–20 juvenile offenders. Each group home has several staff personnel who work as counselors or house parents during 8- or 24-hour shifts. Group-home placements provide individual and group counseling, allow juveniles to attend local schools, and offer a more structured life than most of the residents have received in their own homes. These programs must be adequately funded and staffed with trained professionals in order to be effective. However, critics suggest that group homes often are mismanaged and may do little more than "warehouse" youths.

Reforms developed to increase the use of community treatment can also have unintended effects elsewhere in the system. For example, a 2012 report on the Texas juvenile corrections system found that as more offenders were diverted to community programs, the secure institutional settings were left with higher concentrations of the most difficult offenders. In the wake of these changes, youth-on-youth assaults increased from 17 assaults per 100 detained youths in 2007 to 54 assaults per 100 in 2011. The institutions experienced a similar rise in assaults against staff by youths (Grissom, 2012). Criminal justice planners think very carefully about the impacts of new policies, yet it can be very difficult to anticipate what issues may arise. Read "A Question of Ethics" at the end of the chapter to consider what recommendations you would make to address behavioral problems in correctional settings for juveniles.

▼ CHECK POINT

5. **What three discretionary decisions do the police make with regard to processing juveniles?**
   Whether to take the child into custody, request that the child be detained, or refer the child to court.

6. **What is the purpose of diversion?**
   To avoid formal proceedings when the child's best interest can be served by treatment in the community.

7. **What sentencing dispositions are available to the judge?**
   Probation, intermediate sanctions, custodial care, community treatment.

STOP & ANALYZE

Juvenile records are sealed and generally cannot be used against adult offenders. Why would such a policy exist? Would it make more sense to allow juvenile records to be used routinely in adult criminal proceedings? State your view, and give two reasons to support your position.

Problems and Perspectives

Much of the criticism of juvenile justice has emphasized the disparity between the treatment ideal and the institutionalized practices of an ongoing bureaucratic system. Commentators have focused on how the language of social reformers has disguised the day-to-day operations that lack the elements of due process and in which custodial incarceration is all too frequent. Other criticisms claim that the juvenile justice system does not control juvenile crime.

The juvenile court, in both theory and practice, is a remarkably complex institution that must perform a wide range of functions. The juvenile justice system must play such a wide variety of roles that goals and values will inevitably collide.

In many states, the same judges, probation officers, and social workers are asked to deal with both neglected children and young criminals. Although departments of social services usually deal primarily with cases of neglect, the distinction between the criminal and the neglected child is often not maintained.

In addition to recognizing that the juvenile system has organizational problems, society must acknowledge that little is known about the causes of delinquency and its prevention or treatment. Over the years, people have advanced various social and behavioral theories to explain delinquency. One generation looked to slum conditions as the cause of juvenile crime, and another pointed to the affluence of the suburbs. Psychologists sometimes point to masculine insecurity in a matriarchal family structure, and some sociologists note the peer-group pressures of the gang. This array of theories has led to a variety of proposed and often contradictory treatments. In such confusion, those interested in the problems of youth may despair. What is clear is that we need additional research on the causes of delinquency and the treatment of juvenile offenders.

Youth gangs pose unique problems to those making decisions in the juvenile justice system. Gangs are responsible for a significant amount of delinquency in communities, and they also thrive in correctional institutions (particularly in adult institutions). How does the presence and behavior of youth gangs affect juvenile justice policy? Recent research has indicated that gang members are more likely than non–gang members to carry guns, which thereby increases the probability of severe or lethal violence among these groups. Gang members are also more likely to receive longer sentences, given that gang membership and weapon ownership can increase the severity of punishment for juveniles (Melde, Esbensen, & Taylor, 2009).

In recent years, juveniles have been engaging in delinquent behavior online. The phenomenon of "cyberbullying" involves the use of computers, cell phones, and other electronic devices by youths to mistreat and harm their peers. There have been cases of teens bullying others into suicide—does the case of Michelle Carter and Conrad Roy (discussed at the start of the chapter) fit this description? Some believe her relentless encouragement of his suicide constitutes cyberbullying, or at a minimum, harassment. Approximately 24 percent of adolescents have been bullied online, while approximately 16 percent of youth admit to cyberbullying others (Cyberbullying Research Center, 2014). While additional inquiry is necessary, cyberbullying has been correlated with traditional bullying and various forms of school violence (Hinduja & Patchin, 2007). Online delinquent behavior can also take the form of "sexting," in which juveniles share illicit sexual material. Several states have made cyberbullying and sexting criminal offenses—but should they really be crimes? These issues are discussed in the "Current Controversies" feature.

What trends foretell the future of juvenile justice? The conservative crime control policies that hit the adult criminal justice system with their emphasis on deterrence, retribution, and getting tough have also influenced juvenile justice in the past 20 years. One can point to growing levels of overcrowding in juvenile institutions, increased litigation challenging the abuse of children in training schools and detention centers, and higher rates of minority youth incarceration. All of these problems have emerged during a period of declining youth populations and fewer

Criminalizing Cyberbullying and Sexting

As the use of cell phones and mobile devices becomes more widespread, schools and parents must deal with more juveniles using technology to engage in harmful acts. Cyberbullying is a form of harassment in which victims are targeted and bullied online. This behavior can sometimes lead to devastating consequences. In perhaps the most infamous case of cyberbullying, a Canadian girl, 15-year-old Rehtaeh Parsons, committed suicide in 2013 after digital images of her rape were posted online, along with "slut shaming" comments about her.

In addition to cyberbullying, teens are increasingly "sexting," in which they engage in sexually explicit conversations and share explicit images via text messaging and cell phones. In 2015, a large number of football players and other students in Cañon City, Colorado, were accused of taking nude pictures of themselves and sharing them with other students—some as young as 12 years old. In the same year in Massachusetts, four middle-school girls, ages 12 and 13, sent nude photos of themselves to a group of their male classmates. Experts warn that sexting is on the rise, especially among middle-school students; and unfortunately, legislation on this issue is not being created fast enough to keep up with technology.

Actions to reduce the harm caused by cyberbullying and sexting have focused on both prevention and punishment. Preventive measures may include parents installing digital applications that can assist in reducing cyberbullying. For example the ReThink app pops up when phrases such as "I hate you" or "You suck" are typed on the phone, asking the writer to rethink the message they are sending. Canadian authorities are considering initiating a cyberbullying prevention program that monitors children's digital communications to stop cyberbullying before it can cause harm. However, experts believe that this will just decrease communication between children and parents/schools—a preferable strategy would be to target bullying, since that existed long before digital devices.

In terms of punishment, juveniles who engage in cyberbullying and sexting can face serious consequences in school, and potentially in court. Some states' laws allow schools to suspend students found guilty of cyberbullying and/or sexting, and other states have set criminal penalties. A middle school in Massachusetts discovered that one of its 14-year-old students had sent nude pictures of herself to a few classmates, who had circulated the pictures to others. Rather than contact the police, the school confiscated as many phones as possible to search for evidence. In some communities, the police and prosecutor may prefer to see school officials confiscate phones, delete images, and impose suspensions and other school discipline rather than use the scarce resources of the criminal justice system to pursue this form of teen misbehavior.

According to the Cyberbullying Research Center, all 50 states currently have laws on bullying, and all but two (Alaska and Wisconsin) include electronic harassment as a form of bullying. Eighteen states currently have criminal penalties for bullying. In Maryland, for example, cyberbullying is a misdemeanor punishable by a $500 fine or potentially up to one year in jail. Only 20 states currently have laws against sexting, so many states rely on child pornography laws to punish offenders. Prosecutions under these laws can result in harsh sentences.

For Critical Thinking and Analysis

The varying attitudes of police and prosecutors, as well as the limits of their budgets, may lead to different outcomes for youths who are caught sexting, depending on the community in which they live. The fates of individual juveniles, especially whether they are entered into the justice system instead of merely experiencing school discipline, may also depend on the extent to which victims' parents complain and insist on action by criminal justice officials. Rapid changes in

technology and behavior have made it difficult for the criminal justice system to keep up with the range of consequences resulting from this phenomenon.

All states currently have laws against bullying (and most for cyberbullying), but very few have laws specifically focused on sexting. To what extent should juveniles be punished for bullying someone else, especially if that action results in a suicide? Should juveniles who send sexually explicit pictures of themselves via cell phone be charged with a crime? Should other students who forward such pictures to others be charged with the crime of child pornography? Consider the purposes of laws against child pornography—are they designed to prosecute these types of behaviors? Imagine you are a school principal who has discovered that sexting is going on in your school—make a list of the pros and cons of handling the incident internally rather than calling the police.

Sources: A. Blake, "Australian High School Suspends 50-Plus Students for Cyberbullying," *Washington Times*, April 8, 2016 (washingtontimes.com); G. Botelho and M. Martinez, "DA: No Charges against Colorado Students in Sexting Scandal," *CNN*, December 9, 2015 (cnn.com); S. Hinduja and J. Patchin, *State Cyberbullying Laws: A Brief Review of State Cyberbullying Laws and Policies*, January 2016 (cyberbullying.org); E. Janney, "Kids Sexting Happens 'on a Daily Basis': Harford County Detective," *Bel Air Patch*, April 1, 2015 (patch.com); K. Jeffries, "ReThink App Trying to Help Cyberbullying," *First Coast News*, April 7, 2016 (firstcoastnews.com); "New Maryland Law Makes Cyber-Bullying a Misdemeanor," NBC Washington, May 3, 2013 (nbcwashington.com); P. Newton, "Canadian Teen Commits Suicide after Alleged Rape, Bullying," CNN, April 10, 2013 (www.cnn.com); J. Pearson, "Canada Is Considering Spying on Kids to Stop Cyberbullying," *Motherboard Magazine*, April 26, 2016 (motherboard.vice.com); V. Warren, "Everett Police Investigating Middle School Sexting," *WHDH News*, March 9, 2015 (wdhd.com).

arrests of juveniles. With a renewed focus on juvenile crime under the philosophy that "kids are different," the juvenile justice system may be embarking on a less severe path to dealing with juvenile offenders.

On the other hand, future developments and events might ultimately lead to a continuation of the crime control orientation in many states. We must wait to see if we are truly moving into a new era that recognizes and focuses on the vast developmental differences between juveniles and adults. For example, the Supreme Court's ban on the execution of offenders for crimes committed prior to the age of 18 is not necessarily permanent. *Roper v. Simmons* (2005) was decided on a five-to-four vote of the Supreme Court's justices. Similarly, the decision in *Miller v. Alabama* (2012) forbidding mandatory life-without-parole sentences for juvenile homicide offenders was also decided by a five-to-four vote. Thus, a change in the Court's composition may lead to the reinstatement of the death penalty or mandatory life-without-parole sentences for juveniles in some states if a newly appointed future justice replaces a supporter of the *Roper* or *Miller* majorities and votes to change the law when the issue arises in a new case.

CHECK POINT

8. **What contemporary issues pose special challenges for juvenile justice?**
Gangs, cyberbullying, sexting, and debates about whether to process and punish teens in the same manner as adults for serious offenses.

STOP & ANALYZE

If you were a state legislator, what laws, if any, would you write concerning teens' sexting and cyberbullying? Should these behaviors be treated as crimes?

A QUESTION OF ETHICS

Think, Discuss, Write

In 2015, the U.S. Department of Justice completed an investigation of the treatment of youthful offenders held in juvenile facilities in California. This investigation considered the same issues as an earlier newspaper investigation that revealed pepper spray was used in San Diego County juvenile detention facilities 461 times in 2011 and 414 times in 2012. By contrast, pepper spray was used only 91 times in Los Angeles County in 2011. Its use in San Diego was characterized as exceptionally high by experts who examined the detention facilities' records. Does the disparity in usage between large urban counties in the same state raise questions about why it is used so often in one county?

Thirty-six states do not use pepper spray in juvenile facilities, and 9 of the 14 states that do permit its use do not allow it to be carried routinely by officers. It is stored for use only in riot-type emergencies. By contrast, California permits detention officers to carry pepper spray, and it was used 60 times in 2012 in incidents that were unrelated to fights. One former detainee said pepper spray was used on him for talking back to an officer and for failing to fall into line properly when instructed to do so.

Many experts argue that pepper spray should not be used in juvenile detention facilities. They claim that appropriate training and policies can produce an atmosphere within detention facilities that make such less-than-lethal weapons unnecessary. In addition, exposure to the spray can be dangerous to juveniles with asthma or those who take

medications for psychiatric conditions. Other techniques for control can arguably avoid these serious risks. In light of these issues, Oklahoma is phasing out the use of pepper spray in juvenile detention centers.

Discussion/Writing Assignment

What ethical considerations arise when staff members of a juvenile corrections facility choose to pepper spray a teenager, especially if the application was for failing to obey an order rather than to stop acts of violence? Are there risks that staff will use such weapons too quickly without attempting to understand the nature and source of the problem? Does the use of such weapons communicate to the juvenile offenders that it is legitimate to use weapons and violence to solve conflicts? Might such weapons be used inconsistently or in discriminatory ways when deciding which juveniles to spray rather than restrain? Describe the policies and training that you would develop for instructing staff members on when to use pepper spray—if at all—and when to use physical restraint.

Sources: D. Maass, "The Sting of Juvenile Detention," *Crime Report* online, July 29, 2013 (http://www.thecrimereport.org/news/inside-criminal-justice/2013-07-the-sting-of-juvenile-detention); J. Palmer, "Oklahoma to Phase Out Pepper Spray in Juvenile Detention Centers," NewsOK, January 4, 2016 (newsok.com); A. Sewell, "Federal Monitoring of L.A. County Juvenile Probation Camps Ending," *Los Angeles Times*, April 3, 2015 (www.latimes.com).

SUMMARY

1 Describe the extent of youth crime in the United States.

- Crimes committed by juveniles remain a serious concern even though crimes of violence in general have decreased.

2 Explain how the juvenile justice system developed and the assumptions on which it was based.

- The history of juvenile justice comprises six periods: Puritan, refuge, juvenile court, juvenile rights, crime control, and "kids are different."
- Creation of the juvenile court in 1899 established a separate juvenile justice system.
- The *In re Gault* decision by the U.S. Supreme Court in 1967 brought due process to the juvenile justice system.

3 Identify what determines the jurisdiction of the juvenile justice system.

- The juvenile system handles cases based on the ages of youths.
- Juvenile cases fall into one of four categories: delinquency, status offenses, neglect, or dependency.

4 Describe how the juvenile justice system operates.

- Decisions by police officers and juvenile intake officers dispose of a large portion of the many cases that are never referred to the court.

- In juvenile court, most cases are settled through a plea agreement.
- After conviction or plea, a disposition hearing is held. Before passing sentence, the judge reviews the offense and the juvenile's social history.
- Possible dispositions of a juvenile case include probation, intermediate sanctions, custodial care, and community treatment.
- Juvenile court jurisdiction may be waived so that youths can be tried in the adult criminal justice system, but such waivers have decreased since the mid-1990s.

5 Name some of the issues facing the American system of juvenile justice.

- Juvenile justice faces issues of racial disparities in punishment; criminal activity by gangs; and new behavioral problems, such as cyberbullying, that involve computers and other electronic devices.
- It remains to be seen whether the current move toward increased rehabilitation will continue or whether crime control policies will remain a priority.

Questions for Review

1. What are the major historical periods of juvenile justice in the United States?
2. What is the jurisdiction of the juvenile court system?
3. What are the major processes in the juvenile justice system?
4. What are the sentencing and institutional alternatives for juveniles who are judged delinquent?
5. What due process rights do juveniles have?

Key Terms and Cases

aftercare (p. 544)

delinquent (p. 530)

dependent child (p. 531)

detention hearing (p. 535)

diversion (p. 534)

neglected child (p. 531)

parens patriae (p. 523)

PINS (p. 531)

status offense (p. 527)

waiver (p. 529)

Breed v. Jones (1975) (p. 527)

In re Gault (1967) (p. 526)

In re Winship (1970) (p. 527)

McKeiver v. Pennsylvania (1971) (p. 527)

Schall v. Martin (1984) (p. 528)

Glossary

accusatory process The series of events from the arrest of a suspect to the filing of a formal charge (through an indictment or information) with the court.

adjudication The process of determining whether the defendant is guilty.

adversarial process Court process, employed in the United States and other former British colonies, in which lawyers for each side represent their clients' best interests in presenting evidence and formulating arguments as a means to discover the truth and protect the rights of defendants.

affidavit Written statement of fact, supported by oath or affirmation, submitted to judicial officers to fulfill the requirements of probable cause for obtaining a warrant.

aftercare Juvenile justice equivalent of parole, in which a delinquent is released from a custodial sentence and supervised in the community.

aggressive patrol A patrol strategy designed to maximize the number of police interventions and observations in the community.

anomie A breakdown or disappearance of the rules of social behavior.

appeal A request to a higher court that it review actions taken in a trial court.

appellate courts Courts that do not try criminal cases, but hear appeals of decisions of lower courts.

arraignment The court appearance of an accused person in which the charges are read and the accused, advised by a lawyer, pleads guilty or not guilty.

arrest The physical taking of a person into custody on the grounds that there is reason to believe that he or she has committed a criminal offense. Police are limited to using only reasonable physical force in making an arrest. The purpose of the arrest is to hold the accused for a court proceeding.

assigned counsel An attorney in private practice assigned by a court to represent an indigent. The attorney's fee is paid by the government with jurisdiction over the case.

Atkins v. Virginia (2002) Execution of developmentally disabled offenders is unconstitutional.

bail An amount of money, specified by a judge, to be paid as a condition of pretrial release to ensure that the accused will appear in court as required.

Barron v. Baltimore (1833) Case deciding that the protections of the Bill of Rights apply only to actions of the federal government.

bench trials Trials conducted by a judge who acts as fact finder and determines issues of law. No jury participates.

Bill of Rights The first 10 amendments added to the U.S. Constitution to provide specific rights for individuals, including criminal justice rights concerning searches, trials, and punishments.

biological explanations Explanations of crime that emphasize physiological and neurological factors that may predispose a person to commit crimes.

boot camp A short-term institutional sentence, usually followed by probation, that puts the offender through a physical regimen designed to develop discipline and respect for authority. Also referred to as *shock incarceration*.

Bordenkircher v. Hayes (1978) A defendant's rights are not violated by a prosecutor who warns that refusing to enter a guilty plea may result in a harsher sentence.

Boykin v. Alabama (1969) Before a judge may accept a plea of guilty, defendants must state that they are making the plea voluntarily.

Breed v. Jones (1975) Juveniles cannot be found delinquent in juvenile court and then transferred to adult court without a hearing on the transfer; to do so violates the protection against double jeopardy.

chain of command Organizational structure based on a military model with clear definition of ranks to indicate authority over subordinates and obligations to obey orders from superiors.

challenge for cause Removal of a prospective juror by showing that he or she has some bias or some other legal disability. The number of such challenges available to attorneys is unlimited.

Chimel v. California (1969) Supreme Court decision that endorsed warrantless searches for weapons and evidence in the immediate vicinity of people who are lawfully arrested.

circumstantial evidence Evidence provided by a witness from which a jury must infer a fact.

citation A written order or summons, issued by a law enforcement officer, directing an alleged offender to appear in court at a specific time to answer a criminal charge.

civil infractions Minor offenses that are typically punishable by small fines and produce no criminal record for the offender.

civil law Law regulating the relationships between or among individuals, usually involving property, contracts, or business disputes.

civilian review board Citizens' committee formed to investigate complaints against the police.

classical criminology A school of criminology that views behavior as stemming from free will, demands responsibility and accountability of all perpetrators, and stresses the need for punishments severe enough to deter others.

classification The process of assigning an inmate to a category based on his or her risk to security, educational level, ability to work, and readiness for release.

clearance rate The percentage of crimes known to the police that they believe they have solved through an arrest; a statistic used to measure a police department's productivity.

Commission on Accreditation for Law Enforcement Agencies (CALEA) Nonprofit organization formed by major law enforcement executives' associations to develop standards for police policies and practice; on request, will review police agencies and award accreditation upon meeting those standards.

community corrections A model of corrections based on the goal of reintegrating the offender into the community.

community crime prevention Programs through which criminal justice officials cultivate relationships with and rely on assistance from citizens in preventing crime and apprehending offenders within neighborhoods.

community justice A model of justice that emphasizes reparation to the victim and the community, a problem-solving perspective with regard to crime, and citizen involvement in crime prevention.

community policing Approach to policing that emphasizes close personal contact between police and citizens and the inclusion of citizens in efforts to solve problems, including vandalism, disorder, youth misbehavior, and crime.

community service A sentence requiring the offender to perform a certain amount of unpaid labor in the community.

CompStat Approach to crime prevention and police productivity measurement pioneered in New York City and then adopted in other cities that involves frequent meetings among police supervisors to examine detailed crime statistics for each precinct and develop immediate approaches and goals for problem solving and crime prevention.

conditions of release Conduct restrictions that parolees must follow as a legally binding requirement of being released.

congregate system A penitentiary system, developed in Auburn, New York, in which each inmate was held in isolation during the night but worked and ate with other prisoners during the day under a rule of silence.

consent search A permissible warrant-less search of a person, vehicle, home, or other location based on a person with proper authority or the reasonable appearance of proper authority voluntarily granting permission for the search to take place.

continuance An adjournment of a scheduled case until a later date.

contract counsel An attorney in private practice who contracts with the government to represent all indigent defendants in a county during a set period of time and for a specified dollar amount.

contract labor system A system under which inmates' labor was sold on a contractual basis to private employers who provided the machinery and raw materials with which inmates made salable products in the institution.

control theories Theories holding that criminal behavior occurs when the bonds that tie an individual to society are broken or weakened.

Cooper v. Pate (1964) Prisoners are entitled to the protection of the Civil Rights Act of 1871 and may challenge in federal courts the conditions of their confinement.

corrections The variety of programs, services, facilities, and organizations responsible for the management of people who have been accused or convicted of criminal offenses.

count Each separate offense of which a person is accused in an indictment or an information.

crime control model A model of the criminal justice system that assumes freedom for the public to live without fear is so important that every effort must be made to repress crime; it emphasizes efficiency, speed, finality, and the capacity to apprehend, try, convict, and dispose of a high proportion of offenders.

crime control model of corrections A model of corrections based on the assumption that criminal behavior can be controlled by more use of incarceration and other forms of strict supervision.

crimes Actions that violate laws defining which socially harmful behaviors will be subject to the government's power to impose punishments.

criminogenic Having factors thought to bring about criminal behavior in an individual.

critical criminology Theories that assume criminal law and the criminal justice system are primarily a means of controlling the lower classes, women, and minorities.

CSI **effect** A hypothetical but unproven consequence of watching television dramas revolving around forensic science. Some prosecutors and judges believe that these dramas raise jurors' expectations about the use of scientific evidence in criminal cases and thereby reduce the likelihood of "guilty" verdicts in trials that rely solely on witness testimony and other forms of nonscientific evidence.

custodial model A model of incarceration that emphasizes security, discipline, and order.

cybercrimes Offenses that involve the use of one or more computers.

dark figure of crime A metaphor that emphasizes the dangerous dimension of crimes that are never reported to the police.

day reporting center A community correctional center where an offender reports each day to comply with elements of a sentence.

defense attorney The lawyer who represents accused offenders and convicted offenders in their dealings with criminal justice.

delinquent A child who has committed an act that if committed by an adult would be a criminal act.

demonstrative evidence Evidence that is not based on witness testimony but that demonstrates information relevant to the crime, such as maps, X-rays, and photographs; includes real evidence involved in the crime.

dependent child A child who has no parent or guardian or whose parents cannot give proper care.

detectives Police officers, typically working in plain clothes, who investigate crimes that have occurred by questioning witnesses and gathering evidence.

detention hearing A hearing by the juvenile court to determine if a juvenile is to be detained or released prior to adjudication.

determinate sentence A sentence that fixes the term of imprisonment at a specific period.

differential response A patrol strategy that assigns priorities to calls for service and chooses the appropriate response.

direct evidence Eyewitness accounts.

directed patrol A proactive form of patrolling that directs resources to known high-crime areas.

discovery A prosecutor's pretrial disclosure to the defense of facts and evidence to be introduced at trial.

discretion The authority to make decisions without reference to specific rules or facts, using instead one's own judgment; allows for individualization and informality in the administration of justice.

discretionary release The release of an inmate from prison to conditional supervision at the discretion of the parole board, within the boundaries set by the sentence and the penal law.

discrimination Differential treatment of individuals or groups based on race, ethnicity, gender, sexual orientation, or economic status, instead of on their behavior or qualifications.

disparity A difference between groups that may be explained either by legitimate factors or by discrimination.

diversion The process of screening children out of the juvenile justice system without a decision by the court.

DNA analysis A scientific technique that identifies people through their distinctive gene patterns (also called *genotypic features*). DNA, or deoxyribonucleic acid, is the basic component of all chromosomes; all the cells in an individual's body, including those in skin, blood, organs, and semen, contain the same unique DNA.

domestic violence The term commonly used to refer to intimate partner violence or violent victimizations between spouses, boyfriends, and girlfriends or those formerly in intimate relationships. Such actions account for a significant percentage of the violent victimizations experienced by women.

double jeopardy The subjecting of a person to prosecution more than once in the same jurisdiction for the same offense; prohibited by the Fifth Amendment.

dual court system A system consisting of a separate judicial system for each state in addition to a national system. Each case is tried in a court of the same jurisdiction as that of the law or laws broken.

due process model A model of the criminal justice system that assumes freedom for individuals who are wrongly accused and risk unjust punishment is so important that every effort must be made to ensure that criminal justice decisions are based on reliable information; it emphasizes the adversarial process, the rights of defendants, and formal decision-making procedures.

earned time Reduction in a prisoner's sentence as a reward for participation in educational or other rehabilitation programs and for work assignments such as disaster relief and conservation projects.

electronic file management Computerization of court records done to reduce reliance on paper documents and make documents easily accessible to the judge and attorneys via computer.

Enlightenment A movement during the eighteenth century in England and France in which concepts of liberalism, rationalism, equality, and individualism dominated social and political thinking.

entrapment The defense that the individual was induced by the police to commit the criminal act.

evidence-based policing Police strategies and deployment of resources developed through examination of research on crime, social problems, and previously used strategies.

evidence-based practices Policies developed through guidance from research studies that demonstrate which approaches are most useful and cost-effective for advancing desired goals.

excessive use of force Applications of force against individuals by police officers that violate either departmental policies or constitutional rights by exceeding the level of force permissible and necessary in a given situation.

exchange A mutual transfer of resources; a balance of benefits and deficits that flow from behavior based on decisions about the values and costs of alternative courses of action.

exclusionary rule The principle that illegally obtained evidence must be excluded from trial.

exigent circumstances When there is an immediate threat to public safety or the risk that evidence will be destroyed, officers may search, arrest, or question suspects without obtaining a warrant or following other usual rules of criminal procedure.

expiration release The release of an inmate from incarceration, without further correctional supervision; the inmate cannot be returned to prison for any remaining portion of the sentence for the current offense.

FBI special agents The sworn law enforcement officers in the FBI who conduct investigations and make arrests.

federalism A system of government in which power is divided between a central (national) government and regional (state) governments.

felonies Serious crimes usually carrying a penalty of death or of incarceration for more than one year.

feminist theories Theories that criticize existing theories for ignoring or undervaluing women's experiences as offenders, victims, and people subjected to decision making by criminal justice officials. These theories seek to incorporate an understanding of differences between the experiences and treatment of men and women while also integrating consideration of other factors, such as race and social class.

filtering process A screening operation; a process by which criminal justice officials screen out some cases while advancing others to the next level of decision making.

fine A sum of money to be paid to the state by a convicted person, as punishment for an offense.

forfeiture Government seizure of property and other assets derived from or used in criminal activity.

frankpledge A system in old English law in which members of a tithing (a group of 10 families) pledged to be responsible for keeping order and bringing violators of the law to court.

fundamental fairness A legal doctrine supporting the idea that so long as a state's conduct maintains basic standards of fairness, the Constitution has not been violated.

furlough The temporary release of an inmate from a correctional institution for a brief period, usually one to three days, for a visit home. Such programs help maintain family ties and prepare inmates for release on parole.

Furman v. Georgia (1972) The death penalty, as administered, constitutes cruel and unusual punishment.

fusion centers Centers run by states and large cities that analyze and facilitate sharing of information to assist law enforcement and homeland security agencies in preventing and responding to crime and terrorism threats.

Gagnon v. Scarpelli **(1973)** Before probation can be revoked, a two-stage hearing must be held and the offender must be provided with specific elements of due process. Requested counsel will be allowed on a case-by-case basis.

general deterrence Punishment of criminals that is intended to be an example to the general public and to discourage the commission of offenses.

Geographic Information System (GIS) Computer technology and software used by law enforcement officials to map problem locations in order to understand calls for service and the nature and frequency of crimes and other issues within specific neighborhoods.

Gideon v. Wainwright **(1963)** Case deciding that indigent defendants have a right to counsel when charged with serious crimes for which they could face six or more months of incarceration.

going rate Local court officials' shared view of the appropriate sentence for a given offense, the defendant's prior record, and other case characteristics.

"good faith" exception Exception to the exclusionary rule that permits the use of improperly obtained evidence when police officers acted in honest reliance on a defective statute, a warrant improperly issued by a magistrate, or a consent to search by someone who lacked authority to give such permission.

good time A reduction of an inmate's prison sentence, at the discretion of the prison administrator, for good behavior or participation in vocational, educational, or treatment programs.

grand jury Body of citizens drawn from the community to hear evidence presented by the prosecutor in order to decide whether enough evidence exists to file charges against a defendant.

Gregg v. Georgia **(1976)** Death penalty laws are constitutional if they require the judge and jury to consider certain mitigating and aggravating circumstances in deciding which convicted murderers should be sentenced to death. Proceedings must also be divided into a trial phase and a punishment phase, and there must be opportunities for appeal.

habeas corpus A writ or judicial order requesting the release of a person being detained in a jail, prison, or mental hospital. If a judge finds the person is being held improperly, the writ may be granted and the person released.

halfway house A correctional facility housing convicted felons who spend a portion of their day at work in the community but reside in the halfway house during nonworking hours.

hands-off policy Judges should not interfere with the administration of correctional institutions.

home confinement A sentence requiring the offender to remain inside his or her home during specified periods.

Hudson v. Palmer **(1984)** Prison officials have the authority to search cells and confiscate any materials found.

identity theft The theft of social security numbers, credit card numbers, and other information in order to secure loans, withdraw bank funds, and purchase merchandise while posing as someone else—the unsuspecting victim who will eventually lose money in these transactions.

Illinois v. Gates **(1983)** U.S. Supreme Court decision that established the flexible "totality of circumstances" test for determining the existence of the probable cause needed for obtaining a search warrant.

In re Gault **(1967)** Juveniles have the right to counsel, to confront and examine accusers, and to have adequate notice of charges when confinement is a possible punishment.

In re Winship **(1970)** The standard of proof "beyond a reasonable doubt" applies to juvenile delinquency proceedings.

incapacitation Depriving an offender of the ability to commit crimes against society, usually by detaining the offender in prison.

inchoate or incomplete offenses Conduct that is criminal even though the harm that the law seeks to prevent has not been done, but merely planned or attempted.

incident-driven policing Policing in which calls for service are the primary instigators of action.

incorporation The extension of the due process clause of the Fourteenth Amendment to make binding on state governments many of the rights guaranteed in the first 10 amendments to the U.S. Constitution (the Bill of Rights).

indeterminate sentence A period set by a judge that specifies a minimum and a maximum time to be served in prison. Sometime after the minimum, the offender may be eligible for parole.

indictment A document returned by a grand jury as a "true bill" charging an individual with a specific crime on the basis of a determination of probable cause as presented by a prosecuting attorney.

"inevitable discovery" rule Supreme Court ruling that improperly obtained evidence can be used if it would inevitably have been discovered by the police.

information A document charging an individual with a specific crime. It is prepared by a prosecuting attorney and presented to a court at a preliminary hearing.

inmate code The values and norms of the prison social system that define the inmates' idea of the model prisoner.

inquisitorial process Court process, employed in most countries of the world, in which the judge takes an active role in investigating the case and examining evidence by, for example, questioning witnesses.

integrated theories Theories that combine differing theoretical perspectives into a larger model.

intelligence-led policing An approach to policing, in conjunction with concerns about homeland security, that emphasizes gathering and analyzing information to be shared among agencies in order to develop cooperative efforts to identify, prevent, and solve problems.

intensive supervision probation (ISP) Probation granted under conditions of strict reporting to a probation officer with a limited caseload.

intermediate sanctions A variety of punishments that are more restrictive than traditional probation but less severe and less costly than incarceration.

internal affairs unit A branch of a police department that receives and investigates complaints alleging violation of rules and policies on the part of officers.

Interpol The International Criminal Police Organization formed in 1946 and based in France with the mission of facilitating international cooperation in investigating transnational criminal activities and security threats.

inventory search Permissible warrantless search of a vehicle that has been "impounded"—meaning that it is in police custody—so that police can make a record of the items contained in the vehicle.

jail An institution authorized to hold pretrial detainees and sentenced misdemeanants for periods longer than 48 hours.

jurisdiction The geographic territory or legal boundaries within which control may be exercised; the range of a court's authority.

jury A panel of citizens selected according to law and sworn to determine matters of fact in a criminal case and to deliver a verdict of guilty or not guilty.

Kyllo v. United States (2001) Law enforcement officials cannot examine a home with a thermal-imaging device unless they obtain a warrant.

labeling theories Theories emphasizing that the causes of criminal behavior are found not in the individual but in the social process that labels certain acts as deviant or criminal.

latent fingerprints Impressions of the unique pattern of ridges on the fingertip that are left behind on objects; these impressions are the residue of natural skin secretions or contaminating materials such as ink, blood, or dirt that were present on the fingertips at the time of their contact with the objects.

law enforcement The police function of controlling crime by intervening in situations in which the law has clearly been violated and the police need to identify and apprehend the guilty person.

law enforcement certification Preservice training required for sworn officers in many states, which includes coursework on law, psychology, police procedures, and the use of weapons. Police departments for state and large cities often run training programs called *police academies* for their own recruits.

law enforcement intelligence Information, collected and analyzed by law enforcement officials, concerning criminal activities and organizations such as gangs, drug traffickers, and organized crime.

learning theories Theories that see criminal behavior as learned, just as legal behavior is learned.

lease system A system under which inmates were leased to contractors who provided prisoners with food and clothing in exchange for their labor.

legal responsibility The accountability of an individual for a crime because of the perpetrator's characteristics and the circumstances of the illegal act.

legalistic style Style of policing that emphasizes strict enforcement of laws and reduces officers' authority to handle matters informally.

less-lethal weapons Weapons such as pepper spray, air-fired beanbags, or nets that are meant to incapacitate a suspect without inflicting serious injuries.

life course theories Theories that identify factors affecting the start, duration, nature, and end of criminal behavior over the life of an offender.

local legal culture Norms shared by members of a court community as to how cases should be handled and how a participant should behave in the judicial process.

mala in se Offenses that are wrong by their very nature.

mala prohibita Offenses prohibited by law but not necessarily wrong in themselves.

mandatory release The required release of an inmate from incarceration to community supervision upon the expiration of a certain period, as specified by a determinate sentencing law or parole guidelines.

mandatory sentence A sentence determined by statutes and requiring that a certain penalty be imposed and carried out for convicted offenders who meet certain criteria.

Mapp v. Ohio (1961) Supreme Court decision that applied the exclusionary rule as the remedy for improper searches by state and local officials.

mark system A point system in which prisoners can reduce their term of imprisonment and gain release by earning "marks," or points, through labor, good behavior, and educational achievement.

McCleskey v. Kemp (1987) The Supreme Court rejected a challenge of Georgia's death penalty on grounds of racial discrimination.

McKeiver v. Pennsylvania (1971) Juveniles do not have a constitutional right to a trial by jury.

medical model A model of corrections based on the assumption that criminal behavior is caused by biological or psychological conditions that require treatment.

mens rea "Guilty mind," or blameworthy state of mind, necessary for legal responsibility for a criminal offense; criminal intent, as distinguished from innocent intent.

merit selection A reform plan by which judges are nominated by a committee and appointed by the governor for a given period. When the term expires, the voters approve or disapprove the judge for a succeeding term. If the judge is disapproved, the committee nominates a successor for the governor's appointment.

Miranda v. Arizona (1966) U.S. Supreme Court decision declaring that suspects in custody must be informed of their rights to remain silent and to be represented during questioning.

misdemeanors Offenses less serious than felonies and usually punishable by incarceration of no more than one year in jail, or by probation or intermediate sanctions.

Missouri v. Frye (2012) Criminal defendants' Sixth Amendment right to counsel includes protection against ineffective assistance of counsel in the plea bargaining process, such as defense attorneys' failures to inform their clients about plea bargain offers.

money laundering Moving the proceeds of criminal activities through a maze of businesses, banks, and brokerage accounts so as to disguise their origin.

Morrissey v. Brewer (1972) Due process rights require a prompt, informal, two-stage inquiry handled by an impartial hearing officer before parole may be revoked. The parolee may present relevant information and confront witnesses.

motion An application to a court requesting that an order be issued to bring about a specific action.

National Crime Victimization Surveys (NCVS) Interviews of samples of the U.S. population conducted by the Bureau of Justice Statistics to determine the number and types of criminal victimizations and thus the extent of unreported as well as reported crime.

National Incident-Based Reporting System (NIBRS) A reporting system in which the police describe each offense in a crime incident, together with data describing the offender, victim, and property.

neglected child A child who is receiving inadequate care because of some action or inaction of his or her parents.

net widening Process in which new sentencing options increase rather than reduce control over offenders' lives.

Nix v. Williams (1984) Legal decision in which the Supreme Court created the "inevitable discovery" exception to the exclusionary rule.

nolle prosequi An entry, made by a prosecutor on the record of a case and announced in court, indicating that the charges specified will not be prosecuted. In effect, the charges are thereby dismissed.

nonpartisan election An election in which candidates' party affiliations are not listed on the ballot.

North Carolina v. Alford (1970) A plea of guilty by a defendant who maintains his or her innocence may be accepted for the purpose of a lesser sentence.

occupational crimes Criminal offenses committed through opportunities created in a legal business or occupation.

order maintenance The police function of preventing behavior that disturbs or threatens to disturb the public peace or that involves face-to-face conflict between two or more people. In such situations, the police exercise discretion in deciding whether a law has been broken.

organized crime A framework for the perpetration of criminal acts—usually in fields such as gambling, drugs, and prostitution—providing illegal services that are in great demand.

other conditional release A term used in some states to avoid the rigidity of mandatory release by placing convicts in various community settings, under supervision.

parens patriae The state as parent; the state as guardian.

parole The conditional release of an inmate from incarceration, under supervision, after part of the prison sentence has been served.

partisan election An election in which candidates openly affiliated with political parties are presented to voters for selection.

patrol units The core operational units of local police departments that deploy uniformed officers to handle the full array of police functions for service, order maintenance, and law enforcement.

penitentiary An institution intended to punish criminals by isolating them from society and from one another so they can reflect on their past misdeeds, repent, and reform.

percentage bail Defendants may deposit a percentage (usually 10 percent) of the full bail with the court. The full amount of the bail is required if the defendant fails to appear. The percentage of bail is returned after disposition of the case, although the court often retains 1 percent for administrative costs.

peremptory challenge Removal of a prospective juror without giving a reason. Attorneys are allowed a limited number of such challenges.

PINS Acronym for *person(s) in need of supervision*, a term that designates juveniles who are either status offenders or thought to be on the verge of trouble.

plain view doctrine Officers may examine and use as evidence, without a warrant, contraband or evidence that is in open view at a location where they are legally permitted to be.

plea bargain A defendant's plea of guilty to a criminal charge with the reasonable expectation of receiving some consideration from the state for doing so, usually a reduction of the charge. The defendant's ultimate goal is a penalty lighter than the one formally warranted by the charged offense.

police bureaucracy The organizational description of police departments' design and operations that seek to achieve efficiency through division of labor, chain of command, and rules to guide staff.

police corruption Police officers' violations of law and departmental policy for personal gain or to help their families and friends.

political crime An act, usually done for ideological purposes, that constitutes a threat against the state (such as treason, sedition, or espionage); or a criminal act by the state.

positivist criminology A school of criminology that views behavior as stemming from social, biological, and psychological factors. It argues that

punishment should be tailored to the individual needs of the offender.

Powell v. Alabama (1932) Case deciding that an attorney must be provided to a poor defendant facing the death penalty.

presentence report A report, prepared by a probation officer, that presents a convicted offender's background and is used by the judge in selecting an appropriate sentence.

presumptive sentence A sentence for which the legislature or a commission sets a minimum and a maximum range of months or years. Judges are to fix the length of the sentence within that range, allowing for special circumstances.

preventive detention Holding a defendant for trial, based on a judge's finding that if the defendant were released on bail, he or she would endanger the safety of any other person and the community or would flee.

preventive patrol Making the police presence known, to deter crime and to enable officers to respond quickly to calls.

prison An institution for the incarceration of people convicted of serious crimes, usually felonies.

proactive Acting in anticipation; actively searching for potential offenders without waiting for a crime to be reported. Arrests for victimless crimes are usually proactive.

probable cause Reliable information indicating that it is more likely than not that evidence will be found in a specific location or that a specific person is guilty of a crime.

probation A sentence that the offender is allowed to serve under supervision in the community.

problem-oriented policing Community policing strategy that emphasizes solving problems of disorder in a neighborhood that may contribute to fear of crime and to crime itself.

problem-solving courts Lower-level local courts dedicated to addressing particular social problems or troubled populations. Examples of such courts include drug courts, domestic violence courts, and mental health courts.

procedural criminal law Law defining the procedures that criminal justice officials must follow in enforcement, adjudication, and corrections.

prosecuting attorney A legal representative of the state with sole responsibility for bringing criminal charges. Depending on the state, this person is referred to as the district attorney, state's attorney, commonwealth attorney, or county attorney.

psychological explanations Explanations of crime that emphasize mental processes and behavior.

public defender An attorney employed on a full-time, salaried basis by a public or private nonprofit organization.

"public safety" exception Exception to *Miranda* requirements that permits police to immediately question a suspect in custody without providing any warnings, if public safety would be jeopardized by their taking the time to supply the warnings.

reactive Acting in response to a notification about suspicious activity, a crime, a medical emergency, or other service need.

real evidence Physical evidence—such as a weapon, records, fingerprints, and stolen property—involved in the crime.

reasonable doubt The standard used by a jury to decide if the prosecution has provided enough evidence for a conviction.

reasonable expectation of privacy The objective standard developed by courts for determining whether a government intrusion into an individual's person or property constitutes a search because it interferes with the individual's interests that are normally protected from government examination.

reasonable suspicion A police officer's belief, based on articulable facts that would be recognized by others in a similar situation, that criminal activity is afoot and necessitates further investigation that will intrude on an individual's reasonable expectation of privacy.

recidivism A return to criminal behavior.

reformatory An institution that emphasizes training, a mark system of classification, indeterminate sentences, and parole.

rehabilitation The goal of restoring a convicted offender to a constructive place in society through some form of vocational or educational training or therapy.

rehabilitation model A model of incarceration that emphasizes treatment programs to help prisoners address the personal problems and issues that led them to commit crimes.

reintegration model A correctional model that emphasizes maintaining the offender's ties to family and community as a method of reform, recognizing that the offender will be returning to society.

release on recognizance (ROR) Pretrial release granted on the defendant's promise to appear in court because the judge believes that the defendant's ties to the community guarantee that she or he will appear.

restitution Repayment—in the form of money or service—by an offender to a victim who has suffered some loss from the offense.

restorative justice Punishment designed to repair the damage done to the victim and community by an offender's criminal act.

retribution Punishment inflicted on a person who has harmed others and so deserves to be penalized.

Ricketts v. Adamson **(1987)** Defendants must uphold the plea agreement or suffer the consequences.

Roper v. Simmons **(2005)** Execution of offenders for crimes committed while under the age of 18 is unconstitutional.

Santobello v. New York **(1971)** When a guilty plea rests on a promise of a prosecutor, the promise must be fulfilled.

Schall v. Martin **(1984)** Juveniles can be held in preventive detention if there is concern that they may commit additional crimes while awaiting court action.

school resource officers (SROs) Police officers assigned for duty in schools to assist in order maintenance while also developing positive relationships with students, which may assist in delinquency prevention.

search Government officials' examination of and hunt for evidence on a person or in a place in a manner that intrudes on reasonable expectations of privacy.

Section 1983 lawsuits Civil lawsuits authorized by a federal statute against state and local officials and local agencies when citizens have evidence that these officials or agencies have violated their federal constitutional rights.

seizures Situations in which police officers use their authority to deprive people of their liberty or property and that must not be "unreasonable" according to the Fourth Amendment.

selective incapacitation Making the best use of expensive and limited prison space by targeting for incarceration those individuals whose incapacitation will do the most to reduce crime in society.

self-incrimination The act of exposing oneself to prosecution by being pressured to respond to questions when the answers may reveal that one has committed a crime. The Fifth Amendment protects defendants against compelled self-incrimination.

sentencing guideline A mechanism to indicate to judges the expected sanction for certain offenses, in order to reduce disparities in sentencing.

separate confinement A penitentiary system, developed in Pennsylvania, in which each inmate was held in isolation from other inmates. All activities, including craftwork, took place in the cells.

service The police function of providing assistance to the public for many matters unrelated to crime as well as for crime prevention education.

service style Style of policing in which officers cater to citizens' desire for favorable treatment and sensitivity to individual situations by using discretion to handle minor matters in ways that seek to avoid embarrassment or punishment.

sheriff Top law enforcement official in county government who was an exceptionally important police official during the country's westward expansion and continues to bear primary responsibility for many local jails.

shock probation A sentence in which the offender is released after a short incarceration and resentenced to probation.

slave patrols Distinctively American form of law enforcement in Southern states that sought to catch and control slaves through patrol groups that stopped and questioned African Americans on the roads and elsewhere in public places.

social conflict theories Theories that view crime as the result of conflict in society, such as conflict between economic classes caused by elites using law as a means to maintain power.

social process theories Theories that see criminality as normal behavior. Everyone has the potential to become a criminal, depending on (1) the influences that impel one toward or away from crime and (2) how one is regarded by others.

social structure theories Theories that blame crime on the existence of a powerless lower class that lives with poverty and deprivation and often turns to crime in response.

socialization The process by which the rules, symbols, and values of a group or subculture are learned by its members.

sociological explanations Explanations of crime that emphasize as causes of criminal behavior the social conditions that bear on the individual.

special units Units within local police departments that deploy officers, often in plain clothes if not assigned to the traffic unit, who are dedicated to a specific task, such as investigation, or type of crime, such as narcotics enforcement.

specific deterrence Punishment inflicted on criminals to discourage them from committing future crimes.

state attorney general Chief legal officer of a state, responsible for both civil and criminal matters.

status offense Any act committed by a juvenile that is considered unacceptable for a child, such as truancy or running away from home, but that would not be a crime if it were committed by an adult.

stop Government officials' interference with an individual's freedom of movement for a duration that typically lasts less than one hour and only rarely extends for as long as several hours.

stop-and-frisk search Limited search approved by the Supreme Court in *Terry v. Ohio*, which permits police officers to pat down the clothing of people on the street if there is reasonable suspicion of dangerous criminal activity.

subculture The symbols, beliefs, values, and attitudes shared by members of a subgroup of the larger society.

substantive criminal law Law that defines acts that are subject to punishment and specifies the punishments for such offenses.

sworn officers Police employees who have taken an oath and been given powers by the state to make arrests and to use necessary force in accordance with their duties.

system A complex whole consisting of interdependent parts whose actions are directed toward goals and are influenced by the environment in which they function.

technical violation The probationer's failure to abide by the rules and conditions of probation (specified by the judge), resulting in revocation of probation.

Tennessee v. Garner (1985) Deadly force may not be used against an unarmed and fleeing suspect unless necessary to prevent the escape and unless the officer has probable cause to believe that the suspect poses a significant threat of death or serious injury to the officers or others.

Terry v. Ohio (1968) Supreme Court decision endorsing police officers' authority to stop and frisk suspects on the streets when there is reasonable suspicion that they are armed and involved in criminal activity.

testimony Oral evidence provided by a legally competent witness.

theory of differential association The theory that people become criminals because they encounter more influences that view criminal behavior as normal and acceptable than they do influences that are hostile to criminal behavior.

totality of circumstances Flexible test established by the Supreme Court for identifying whether probable cause exists that permits the judge to determine whether the available evidence is both sufficient and reliable enough to issue a warrant.

transnational crime Profit-seeking criminal activities that involve planning or execution across national borders.

trial courts of general jurisdiction Criminal courts with jurisdiction over all offenses, including felonies. In some states, these courts also hear appeals.

trial courts of limited jurisdiction Criminal courts with trial jurisdiction over misdemeanor cases and preliminary matters in felony cases. Sometimes these courts hold felony trials that may result in penalties below a specific limit.

Uniform Crime Reports (UCR) An annually published statistical summary of crimes reported to the police, based on voluntary reports to the FBI by local, state, and federal law enforcement agencies.

United States attorneys Officials responsible for the prosecution of crimes that violate the laws of the United States. Appointed by the president and assigned to a U.S. district court jurisdiction.

United States v. Drayton (2002) Judicial decision declaring that police officers are not required to inform people of their right to decline to be searched when police ask for consent to search.

United States v. Leon (1984) Supreme Court decision announcing the "good faith" exception to the exclusionary rule.

United States v. Salerno and Cafero (1987) Preventive detention provisions of the Bail Reform Act of 1984 are upheld as a legitimate use of government power designed to prevent people from committing crimes while on bail.

U.S. Border Patrol Federal law enforcement agency with responsibility for border security by patrolling national land borders and coastal waters to prevent smuggling, drug trafficking, and illegal entry, including entry by potential terrorists.

U.S. marshals Federal law enforcement officials originally appointed to handle duties in western territories; today they bear responsibility for providing federal court security and apprehending fugitives.

USA PATRIOT Act A federal statute passed in the aftermath of the terrorist attacks of September 11, 2001, that broadens government authority to conduct searches and wiretaps and expands the definitions of crimes involving terrorism.

victimless crimes Offenses involving a willing and private exchange of illegal goods or services that are in strong demand. Participants do not feel they are being harmed, but these crimes are prosecuted on the grounds that society as a whole is being injured.

victimology A field of criminology that examines the role the victim plays in precipitating a criminal incident and also examines the impact of crimes on victims.

visible crime An offense against persons or property, committed primarily by members of the lower class. Often referred to as "street crime" or "ordinary crime," this type of offense is the one most upsetting to the public.

voir dire A questioning of prospective jurors to screen out people the attorneys think might be biased or otherwise incapable of delivering a fair verdict.

waiver Procedure by which the juvenile court waives its jurisdiction and transfers a juvenile case to the adult criminal court.

warrant A court order authorizing police officers to take certain actions—for example, to arrest suspects or to search premises.

watch system Practice of assigning individuals to night observation duty to warn the public of fires and crime; first introduced to the American colonies in Boston and later evolved into a system of paid, uniformed police.

watchman style Style of policing that emphasizes order maintenance and tolerates minor violations of law as officers use discretion to handle small infractions informally but make arrests for major violations.

Weeks v. United States (1914) Supreme Court decision applying the exclusionary rule as the remedy for improper searches by federal law enforcement officials.

Williams v. Florida (1970) Juries of fewer than 12 members are constitutional.

Witherspoon v. Illinois (1968) Potential jurors who object to the death penalty cannot be automatically excluded from service; however, during voir dire, those who feel so strongly about capital punishment that they could not give an impartial verdict may be excluded.

Wolf v. Colorado (1949) Supreme Court decision in which the Fourth Amendment was applied against searches by state and local police officers, but the exclusionary rule was not imposed as the remedy for violations of the Fourth Amendment by these officials.

Wolff v. McDonnell (1974) Basic elements of procedural due process must be present when decisions are made about imposing significant punishments on prisoners for violating institutional rules.

work and educational release The daytime release of inmates from correctional institutions so they can work or attend school.

work group A collection of individuals who interact in the workplace on a continuing basis, share goals, develop norms regarding how activities should be carried out, and eventually establish a network of roles, all of which differentiate the group from others and facilitate cooperation.

working personality A set of emotional and behavioral characteristics developed by members of an occupational group in response to the work situation and environmental influences.

References

"Aaron Hernandez Trial: Prosecutors Continue to Detail Police Evidence Tying Him to Murder." 2015. ABC News online, February 20. http://abcnews.go.com.

Abbe, O. G., and P. S. Herrnson. 2002. "How Judicial Election Campaigns Have Changed." *Judicature* 85:286–95.

Abdilla, K., and M. Kranz. 2014. "Livingston County Judge Gives I-96 Shooter up to 44 Years in Prison for Terrorism, Assault." *State News,* March 3. http://statenews.com/article/2014/03/casteelsentence2-web.

Abid, A. 2012. "Restorative Justice in the Gilded Age: Shard Principles Underlying Two Movements in Criminal Justice." *Criminal Law Brief* 8:29–42.

Abrams, J. 2008. "House Sets Standards for Juvenile Boot Camps." Associated Press, June 25. http://www.ap.org.

Abwender, D. A., and K. Hough. 2001. "Interactive Effects of Characteristics of Defendant and Mock Juror on U.S. Participants' Judgment and Sentencing Recommendations." *Journal of Social Psychology* 141:603–16.

Acker, J. R. 2007. "Impose an Immediate Moratorium on Executions." *Criminology & Public Policy* 6:641–50.

Acoca, L. 1997. "Hearts on the Ground: Violent Victimization and Other Themes in the Lives of Women Prisoners." *Corrections Management Quarterly* 1:44–55.

Adams, B. 2012. "Utah's Cardall Family Settles Lawsuit over Taser Death." *Salt Lake City Tribune,* December 29. http://www.sltrib.com.

Adams, B., and S. Addie. 2011. "Delinquency Cases Waived to Criminal Court, 2008." Office of Juvenile Justice and Delinquency Programs. Washington, DC: U.S. Government Printing Office.

Adams, G. 2006. "Sex Offenders' Killer Studied States' Lists." http://www.boston.com.

Adams, K. 1992. "Adjusting to Prison Life." In *Crime and Justice: A Review of Research*, vol. 16, ed. M. Tonry. Chicago: University of Chicago Press, 275–359.

Adams, S. 2013. "The Most Stressful Jobs of 2013." *Forbes Magazine* website, January 3. www.forbes.com.

Adang, O. M. J., and J. Mensink. 2004. "Pepper Spray: An Unreasonable Response to Suspect Verbal Resistance." *Policing* 27:206–19.

Aden, H., and C. Koper. 2011. "The Challenges of Hot Spots Policing." *Translational Criminology* (Summer):6–7.

Adler, S. J. 1994. *The Jury: Disorder in the Court.* New York: Doubleday.

Administrative Office of the U.S. Courts. 2005. "Need for DNA Testing Taxes Courts." *The Third Branch* 37 (February):3.

Agnes, K. 2016. "Ridgefield Park Teen Arrested over Social Media Threat." NorthJersey.com, January 28. http://northjersey.com.

Ahmadi, S. 2011. "The Erosion of Civil Rights: Exploring the Effects of the Patriot Act on Muslims in America." *Rutgers Race and the Law Journal* 12:1–55.

Alarcon, A. L. 2007. "Remedies for California's Death Row Gridlock." *Southern California Law Review* 80:697–52.

Alarid, L., and C. Montemayor. 2010. "Legal and Extralegal Factors in Attorney Recommendations of Pretrial Diversion." *Criminal Justice Studies* 23:239–52.

Albanese, J. 2010. *Organized Crime in Our Times.* Burlington, MA: Elsevier.

———. 2011. *Transnational Crime and the 21st Century.* New York: Oxford University Press.

Alberty, E., and B. Mims. 2015. "Police Arrest Alleged Utah Bank Robber Who Wore Suspected Explosive Vest." *Salt Lake Tribune,* January 23. www.sltrib.com.

Alexander, K. 2011. "Fresno Co. Juvenile Justice Campus Hit by Budget Woes." *Fresno Bee,* April 25. http://www.fresnobee.com.

Alexander, M. 2011. "The New Jim Crow." *Ohio State Journal of Criminal Law* 9:7–26.

———. 2012. *The New Jim Crow: Mass Incarceration in the Age of Colorblindness.* New York: New Press.

Ali, F. 2013. "Multilingual Prospective Jurors: Assessing California Standards Twenty Years after *Hernandez v. New York.*" *Northwestern Journal of Law and Social Policy* 8:236–72.

Alpert, G. 2007. "Eliminate Race as the Only Reason for Police–Citizen Encounters." *Criminology & Public Policy* 6:671–78.

Amar, A. R. 1997. *The Constitution and Criminal Procedure: First Principles.* New Haven, CT: Yale University Press.

Amar, V. 2008. "An Enigmatic Court? Examining the Roberts Court as It Begins Year Three: Criminal Justice." *Pepperdine Law Review* 35:523–31.

Amnesty International. 1999. "Annual General Meeting Highlights USA Campaign." *Amnesty Action,* Summer, 10.

Anderson, G., R. Litzenberger, and D. Plecas. 2002. "Physical Evidence of Police Officer Stress." *Policing* 25:399–420.

Anderson, R. 2016. "Deadly Shooting at Seattle's 'Jungle' Homeless Camp Spurs Soul-Searching in the City." *Los Angeles Times,* January 13, http://latimes.com.

Anderson, T. L. 2003. "Issues in the Availability of Healthcare for Women in Prison." In *The Incarcerated Woman: Rehabilitative Programming in Women's Prisons*, eds. S. F. Sharp and R. Muraskin. Upper Saddle River, NJ: Prentice Hall, 49–60.

Andrews, D. A., and J. Bonta. 1994. *The Psychology of Criminal Behavior.* Cincinnati, OH: Anderson.

Andrews, D. A., I. Zinger, R. D. Hoge, J. Bonta, P. Gendreau, and F. T. Cullen. 1990. "Does Correctional Treatment Work? A Clinically Relevant and Psychologically Informed Meta-Analysis." *Criminology* 28:369–404.

Anglen, R. 2008. "Judge Rules for Taser in Cause-of-Death Decisions." *Arizona Republic,* May 2. http://www.azcentral.com.

Antonuccio, R. 2008. "Prisons for Profit: Do the Social and Political Problems Have a Legal Solution?" *Journal of Corporation Law* 33:577–92.

Appelbaum, P. 2013. "Law and Psychiatry: Does the Constitution Require an Insanity Defense?" *Psychiatric Services* 64:943–45.

Applebome, P. 2012. "Death Penalty Repeal Goes to Connecticut Governor." *New York Times,* April 12. www.nytimes.com.

Applegate, B. K., R. K. Davis, and F. T. Cullen. 2009. "Reconsidering Child Saving: The Extent and Correlates of Public Support for Excluding Youths from the Juvenile Court." *Crime & Delinquency* 55(1):51–77.

Apuzzo, M., and S. Cohen. 2015. "Police Chiefs, Looking to Diversify Forces, Face Structural Hurdles." *New York Times,* November 7. www.nytimes.com.

Archbold, C., and Hassell, K. 2009. "Paying a Marriage Tax: An Examination of the Barriers to the Promotion of Female Police Officers. *Policing: An International Journal of Police Strategies and Management* 32:56–74.

Arditti, J. A., and T. Parkman. 2011. "Young Men's Reentry after Incarceration: A Development Paradox. *Family Relations* 60:205–20.

Arena, K., and K. Bohn. 2008. "Rape Victim Pushes for Expanded DNA Database." CNN.com, May 12. http://www.cnn.com.

Armour, M. 2008. "Dazed and Confused: The Need for a Legislative Solution to the Constitutional Problem of Juror Comprehension." *Temple Political and Civil Rights Law Review* 17:641–73.

Armstrong, G. S., and D. L. MacKenzie. 2003. "Private versus Public Juvenile Facilities: Do Differences in Environmental Quality Exist?" *Crime & Delinquency* 49 (October):542–63.

Armstrong, J. 2008. "Perdue Signs DNA Bill, Expanding Use in Crimes; It Allows Comparisons from Suspects, Not Just Those Already Convicted." *Florida Times Union*, May 8. http://jacksonville.com.

Armstrong, K. 2014. "Lethal Mix: Lawyers' Mistakes, Unforgiving Law." *Washington Post*, November 15. www.washingtonpost.com.

———. 2015. "In Aaron Hernandez Trial, Judge and Prosecutor Argue over Text Messages." *New York Daily News*, February 20. www.nydailynews.com.

Armstrong, K., and S. Mills. 1999. "Death Row Justice Derailed." *Chicago Tribune*, November 14 and 15, p. 1.

Arnold, H. 2016. "The Prison Officer," In *Handbook on Prisons*, eds. Y. Jewkes, J. Bennett, and B. Crewe. New York: Routledge.

Arterton, J.B. 2008. "Unconscious Bias and the Impartial Jury." *Connecticut Law Review* 40:1023–33.

Arthur, M., J. D. Hawkins, E. Brown, J. Briney, S. Oesterle, and R. Abbott. 2010. "Implementation of the Communities That Care Prevention System by Coalitions in the Community Youth Development Study." *Journal of Community Psychology* 38:245–58.

Associated Press. 2012. "Roche Warns of Counterfeit Avastin in U.S." *USA Today*, February 14. www.usatoday.com.

———. 2013. "Maryland House Gives Initial Approval to Medical Marijuana Proposal with Little Discussion." *Washington Post*, March 23, www.washingtonpost.com.

———. 2014a. "Police Body Cameras Raise Privacy Concerns." *New York Daily News*, March 15.

———. 2014b. "Questions That Arise When Placing Cameras on Cops." *New York Times*, March 15. www.nytimes.com.

———. 2014c. "New Jersey Charges 11 with Mob Loansharking Scheme." CBS News, October 21. http://www.cbsnews.com.

———. 2016. "'Saved by the Bell' Actor Screech Booked in Wisconsin Jail." WMTV, January 15. www.nbc15.com.

Auerhahn, K. 1999. "Selective Incapacitation and the Problem of Prediction." *Criminology* 37:703–34.

Austin, J., T. Fabelo, A. Gunter, and K. McGinnis. 2006. Sexual Violence in the Texas Prison System. Washington, DC: The JFA Institute.

Austin, J., K. D. Johnson, and M. Gregoriou. 2000. Juveniles in Adult Prisons and Jails. Bureau of Justice Assistance Monograph. Washington, DC: U.S. Department of Justice.

Austin, P. 2011. "Seal Beach Man Sentenced in Corrupt Bail Bond Scheme." *Los Alamitos–Seal Beach Patch*. January 28. http://losalamitos.patch.com/articles/seal-beach-man-sentenced-in-corrupt-bail-bond-scheme.

Axtman, K. 2005. "A New Motion to Make Jury Service More Attractive." *Christian Science Monitor*, May 23, pp. 2–3.

Bagnato, C. F. 2010. "Change Is Needed: How Latinos Are Affected by the Process of Jury Selection." *Chicana/o-Latina/o Law Review* 29:59–67.

Bai, M. 2012. "Scott Ritter's Other War." *New York Times*, October 27. www.nytimes.com.

Baker, A. 2008a. "11 Years of Police Gunfire, in Painstaking Detail." *New York Times*, May 8. www.nytimes.com.

———. 2008b. "Police Data Shows Increase in Street Stops." *New York Times*, May 6. www.nytimes.com.

——— 2016. "Police Leaders Unveil Principles Intended to Shift Policing Practices Nationwide." *New York Times*, January 29. www.nytimes.com.

Baker, P. 2010. "Obama Signs Law Narrowing Cocaine Sentencing Disparities." *New York Times*, August 3. www.nytimes.com.

Baldus, D. C., G. Woodworth, and C. A. Pulaski. 1994. *Equal Justice and the Death Penalty: A Legal and Empirical Analysis*. Boston: Northeastern University Press.

Bandy, D. 1991. "$1.2 Million to Be Paid in Stray-Bullet Death." *Akron Beacon Journal*, December 3, p. B6.

Bartels, L., and A. Gaffney. 2011. Good Practices in Women's Prisons: A Literature Review. Canberra, Australia: Australian Institute of Criminology.

Bass, P. 2012. "CompStat Ramps Up." *New Haven Independent*, January 31. www.newhavenindependent.org.

Battson, H. 2012. "Parole Granted More Often, Revoked Less." Press release, August 13. Texas Board of Pardons and Paroles. http://www.tdcj.state.tx.us/bpp/parole_increase.pdf.

Baumgartner, B., S. Linn, and A. Boydstun. 2010. "The Decline of the Death Penalty: How Media Framing Changed Capital Punishment in America." In *Winning with Words: The Origins and Impact of Framing*, eds. B. Schaffner and P. Sellers. New York: Routledge, 159–84.

BBC News, 2016. "El Chapo Guzman: Extradition to US Could Take 'At Least Year,'" January 11. www.bbc.com.

Beck, A. J., M. Berzofsky, R. Caspar, and C. Krebs. 2013. *Sexual Victimization in Prisons and Jails Reported by Inmates, 2011–2012*. Washington, DC: Bureau of Justice Statistics.

Beck, A. J., and P. M. Harrison. 2001. "Prisoners in 2000." Bureau of Justice Statistics *Bulletin*. Washington, DC: U.S. Department of Justice.

Beck, A. J., J. C. Karberg, and P. M. Harrison. 2002. "Prison and Jail Inmates at Mid-Year 2001." Bureau of Justice Statistics *Bulletin*, April.

Beckett, K., K. Nyrop, and L. Pfingst. 2006. "Race, Drugs, and Policing: Understanding Disparities in Drug Delivery Arrests." *Criminology* 44:105–37.

Beichner, D., and C. Spohn. 2012. "Modeling the Effects of Victim Behavior and Moral Character on Prosecutors' Charging Decisions in Sexual Assault Cases." *Violence and Victims* 27:3–24.

Bell, D. 1967. *The End of Ideology*. 2nd rev. ed. New York: Collier.

Belluck, P. 2001. "Desperate for Prison Guards, Some States Even Rob Cradles." *New York Times*, April 21, p. A1.

Belson, K., and V. Mather. 2015. "Aaron Hernandez Found Guilty of First-Degree Murder." *New York Times*, April 15. www.nytimes.com.

Bender, K., J. Cobbina, and E. McGarrell. 2016. "Reentry Programming for High-Risk Offenders: Insights from Participants." *International Journal of Offender Therapy and Comparative Criminology* (forthcoming).

Bennion, E. 2011. "Death Is Different No Longer: Abolishing the Insanity Defense Is Cruel and Unusual under *Graham v. Florida*." *DePaul Law Review* 61:1–56.

Berestein, L. 2008. "Lawsuits Raise Questions about Private Prisons. *San Diego Union-Tribune*, May 4. http://www.signonsandiego.com/uniontrib/20080504/news_1n4detain.html.

Berkheiser, M. 2011. "Death Is Not So Different after All: *Graham v. Florida* and the Court's 'Kids Are Different' Eighth Amendment Jurisprudence." *Vermont Law Review* 36(1):1–62.

Bersin, A. D. 2012. "Lines and Flows: The Beginning and End of Borders." *Brooklyn Journal of International Law* 37:389–406.

Betts, S. 2014. "Court Gives Former Camden Charity President Extension in Embezzlement Lawsuit." *Bangor Daily News*, December 24. http://bangordailynews.com.

———. 2015. "Rusty Brace Sentenced to Four Years for Stealing from the Needy." *Bangor Daily News*, October 9. www.bangordailynews.com.

Bever, L. 2014. "Oklahoma Court Postpones Executions Because State Can't Get Drugs in Time." *Washington Post*, March 19. www.washingtonpost.com.

Bidgood, J. 2015a. "In Girl's Account, Rite at St. Paul's Boarding School Turned into Rape." *New York Times*, August 19. http://www.nytimes.com/2015/08/20 /us/in-st-pauls-rape-trial-girl-vividly -recounts-night-of-school-ritual.html.

———. 2015b. Owen Labrie Gets Year in Jail for St. Paul's School Assault." *New York Times*, October 29. www .nytimes.com.

———. 2015c. "Owen Labrie of St. Paul's School Is Found Not Guilty of Main Rape Charge." *New York Times*, August 28. http://www.nytimes.com/2015/08 /29/us/st-pauls-school-rape-trial-owen -labrie.html.

———. 2015d. "Massachusetts Justices Clear Way for New Trials in Cases Chemist May Have Tainted." *New York Times*, May 18. www.nytimes.com.

Bisbee, J. 2010. "Oklahoma Indigent Defense System Struggles to Survive Cuts." *Oklahoman*, April 14. http:// newsok.com.

Bjelopera, J., and K. Finklea. 2012. *Organized Crime: An Evolving Challenge for U.S. Law Enforcement*. Congressional Research Service Report to Congress, January 6. http://www.fas.org/sgp/crs /misc/R41547.pdf.

BJS (Bureau of Justice Statistics). 2008. "Survey Methodology for Criminal Victimization in the United States." Washington, DC: U.S. Department of Justice.

———. 2011. Sourcebook of Criminal Justice Statistics. http://www.albany.edu /sourcebook/.

———. 2014. *Sourcebook of Criminal Justice Statistics*. Washington, DC: U.S. Department of Justice.

———. 2015a. "Estimated Sentenced State and Federal Prisoners per 100,000 U.S. Residents, by Sex, Race, Hispanic Origin, and Age, December 31, 2014." Generated using the Corrections Statistical Analysis Tool at www.bjs.gov.

———. 2015b. "Number of Violent Victimizations by Sex and Victim-Offender Relationship, 2014." NCVS Victimization Analysis Tool (NVAT) at www .bjs.gov.

———. 2015c. "Rates of Violent Victimizations by Weapon Category and Location of Residence, 2014." NCVS Victimization Analysis Tool (NVAT) at www .bjs.gov.

———. 2016. *Sourcebook of Criminal Justice Statistics*. Washington, DC: U.S. Bureau of Justice Statistics. http://www .albany.edu/sourcebook/.

Blackman, J. 2014. "Documents: Former St. Paul's Student Negotiating Plea Deal." *Valley News* (VT), November 3. http://www.vnews.com/news/14155861 -95/st-pauls-suspect-possibly-nearing -plea-deal.

———. 2015. "St. Paul's Rape Suspect Remains Free on Bail, Hires Former Bulger Attorney." *Valley News* (VT), March 12. http://www.vnews.com /news/16059230-95/st-pauls-rape -suspect-remains-free-on-bail-hires -former-bulger-attorney.

Blackmon, D. 2008. *Slavery by Another Name: The Re-Enslavement of Black Americans from the Civil War to World War II*. New York: Anchor Books.

Blair, J. 2000. "Ideas and Trends; Boot Camps: An Idea Whose Time Came and Went." *New York Times*, January 2. http://nytimes.com.

Blasko, B., P. Friedmann, A. Rhodes, and F. Taxman. 2015. "The Parolee-Parole Officer Relationship as a Mediator of Criminal Justice Outcomes." *Criminal Justice and Behavior* 42:722–40.

Blitz, C. L., N. Wolff, and J. Shi. 2008. "Physical Victimization in Prison: The Role of Mental Illness." *International Journal of Law and Psychiatry* 31(5):385–93.

Bluestein, G. 2011. "State Budget Cuts Clog Criminal Justice System." *Seattle Post Intelligencer*, October 26. www .seattlepi.com.

Blumstein, A. 2002. "Youth, Guns, and Violent Crime." The Future of Children, Volume 12 (Number 2). Los Altos, CA: The David and Lucille Packard Foundation.

Blumstein, A., and A. Beck. 2005. "Reentry as a Transient State between Liberty and Recommitment" (with Allen J. Beck). In *Prisoner Reentry and Crime in America*, eds. Jeremy Travis and Christy Visher. New York: Cambridge University Press, 55–79.

Blumstein, J. F., M. A. Cohen, and S. Seth. 2008. "Do Government Agencies Respond to Market Pressures? Evidence from Private Prisons." *Virginia Journal of Social Policy and Law* 15:446–69.

Boetel, R. 2016. "BCSO Used Pepperballs and K-9 on 88-Year-Old Man." *Albuquerque Journal*, February 4. www .abqjournal.com.

Bogdanich, W. 2008. "Heparin Find May Point to Chinese Counterfeiting." *New York Times*, March 20. http://www .nytimes.com.

Bohmert, M. B., and G. Duwe. 2011. "Minnesota's Affordable Homes Program: Evaluating the Effects of a Prison Work Program on Recidivism, Employment and Cost Avoidance." Criminal Justice Policy Review (online).

Boland, B., E. Brady, H. Tyson, and J. Bassler. 1983. *The Prosecution of Felony Arrests*. Washington, DC: Bureau of Justice Statistics, U.S. Government Printing Office.

Bombard, N.R. 2015. "Texts Show Michelle Carter Encouraged Boyfriend to Commit Suicide: 'You Just Need To Do It.'" *Mass Live*, September 9. http:// masslive.com.

Bonczar, T. 2011. "Table 10: First Releases from State Prison, 2009: Sentence Length, Time Served in Prison, by Offense, and Sex." *National Corrections Reporting Program*. Washington DC: Bureau of Justice Statistics.

Bontrager, S., W. Bales, and T. Chiricos. 2005. "Race, Ethnicity, Threat and the Labeling of Convicted. Felons." *Criminology* 43:589–622.

Bornstein, B., and E. Green. 2011. "Jury Decision Making: Implications For and From Psychology." *Current Directions in Psychological Science* 20:63–67.

Bosman, J. 2015. "Nebraska Bans Death Penalty, Defying a Veto." *New York Times*, May 27. www.nytimes.com.

Bourgon, G., L. Guitierrez, and J. Ashton. 2012. "The Evolution of Community Supervision Practice: The Transformation from Case Manager to Change Agent." *Federal Probation* (September):27–35.

Bousquet, S. 2012a. "Plan to Close Prison Re-Entry Centers Angers Lawmakers." *Tampa Bay Times*, March 2. www .tampabay.com.

———. 2012b. "Prison System Will Keep Re-Entry Centers Open." *Tampa Bay Times*, March 7. www.tampabay.com.

Bowen, D. M. 2009. "Calling Your Bluff: How Prosecutors and Defense Attorneys Adapt Plea Bargaining Strategies to Increased Formalization." *Justice Quarterly* 26:2–29.

Bowers, J. 2008. "Punishing the Innocent." *University of Pennsylvania Law Review* 156:1117–79.

———. 2010. "Legal Guilt, Normative Innocence, and the Equitable Decision Not to Prosecute." *Columbia Law Review* 110:1655–726.

Bowker, L. H. 1982. "Victimizers and Victims in American Correctional Institutions." In *Pains of Imprisonment*, eds. R. Johnson and H. Toch. Beverly Hills, CA: Sage.

Boyd, T. 2011. "Domestic Violence Court— 55th District Court." *Michigan Bar Journal* 90:42–43.

Bradley, C. 1992. "Reforming the Criminal Trial." *Indiana Law Journal* 68:659–64.

Bradley, C. M. 2010. "Reconceiving the Fourth Amendment and the Exclusionary Rule." *Law and Contemporary Problems* 73:211–38.

Braithwaite, J. 2007. "Encourage Restorative Justice." *Criminology & Public Policy* 6:689–96.

Braithwaite, L., H. M. Treadwell, and K. R. J. Arriola. 2005. "Health Disparities and Incarcerated Women: A Population Ignored." *American Journal of Public Health* 95:1679–81.

Branan, B. 2013. "Sacramento County Probation Officers Have Highest Caseload in the State." *Sacramento Bee*, April 10. http://www.sacbee.com.

Brandenburg, B., and M. Berg. 2012. "The New Storm of Money and Politics around Judicial Retention Elections." *Drake Law Review* 60:703–13.

Bray, K. 1992. "Reaching the Final Chapter in the Story of Peremptory Challenges." *U.C.L.A. Law Review* 40:517–55.

Breslin, D. M. 2010. "Judicial Merit Retention Elections in Pennsylvania." *Duquesne Law Review* 48:891–907.

Brezosky, L. 2012. "Bail Bondsman Sentenced in Corrupt Judge Case." MySanAntonio.Com. February 14. http://www.mysanantonio.com/news/article/Bail-bondsman-sentenced-in-corrupt-judge-case-3323702.php.

Brink, B. 2014. "Paul Lee, Seattle Pacific University Shooting Victim, Was a 'Brother to Everybody,' Family Says." *Oregon Live*, June 12. http://www.oregonlive.com.

Britt, C. 2000. "Social Context and Racial Disparities in Punishment Decisions." *Justice Quarterly* 17:707–32.

Bronsteen, J. 2010. "Retribution's Role." *Indiana Law Journal* 84:1129–56.

Brown, D. M. 2009. "Calling Your Bluff: How Prosecutors and Defense Attorneys Adapt Plea Bargaining Strategies to Increased Formalization." *Justice Quarterly* 26:2–29.

Brown, F. 2015. "Lawyer Says Justin Bieber Is Making Progress on Probation Terms." CBS News, February 10. www.cbsnews.com.

Brown, J. M., and J. R. Sorensen. 2013. "Race, Ethnicity, Gender, and Waiver to Adult Court." *Journal of Ethnicity in Criminal Justice* 11:181–95.

Brown, K. 2013. "Somebody Poisoned the Jury Pool: Social Media's Effect on Jury Impartiality." *Texas Wesleyan Law Review* 19:809–35.

Brown, P., and M. Ryan. 2016. "'Staggering Corruption': 46 Correctional Officers Charged in Years-Long Drug Trafficking Sting." CNN.com, February 12. www.cnn.com.

Browne, A., A. Cambier, and S. Agha. 2011. "Prisons within Prisons: The Use of Segregation in the United States." *Federal Sentencing Reporter* 24:46–49.

Bruce, M. 2003. "Contextual Complexity and Violent Delinquency among Black and White Males." *Journal of Black Studies* 35:65–98.

Brunson, R. 2007. " 'Police Don't Like Black People': African American Young Men's Accumulated Police Experiences." *Criminology & Public Policy* 6:71–102.

Bueermann, J. 2012. "Being Smart on Crime with Evidence-Based Policing." *National Institute of Justice Journal* 269 (March):12–15.

Bulman, P. 2010. "Police Use of Force: The Impact of Less-Lethal Weapons and Tactics." *National Institute of Justice Journal* 267:4–10.

Bundy, T. 2011. "At Critical Time, Budget Ax Falls on Parole Courts." *Bay Citizen*, October 8. www.baycitizen.org.

———. 2012. "Trying to Prepare for the Toughest of Jobs." *New York Times*, March 29. www.nytimes.com.

Bureau of Justice Statistics. *See* BJS (Bureau of Justice Statistics).

Bureau of Labor Statistics. 2014a. "Correctional Officers." In *Occupational Outlook Handbook.* www.bls.gov.

———. 2014b. "Employment Situation Summary." *Economic News Release*, February 7. Table A-2. www.bls.gov.

———. 2015. *U.S. Department of Labor, Occupational Outlook Handbook, 2016-17 Edition, Correctional Officers and Bailiffs.* www.bls.gov/ooh/protective-service/correctional-officers.htm.

———. 2016. "Employment Situation Summary." *Economic News Release*, January 8. Table A-2. www.bls.gov.

Bureau of Prisons. 2014. "BOP Statistics: Staff." U.S. Bureau of Prisons website.

Burgess-Proctor, A. 2006. "Intersections of Race, Class, Gender, and Crime: Future Directions for Feminist Criminology." *Feminist Criminology* 1:27–47.

———. 2012. Pathways of Victimization and Resistance: Toward a Feminist Theory of Battered Women's Help-Seeking. *Justice Quarterly*, 29(3).

Burriss, A. 2015. "Funding Pressure Leads to Cuts at Public Defender Office." *Shreveport Times*, July 10. www.shreveporttimes.com.

Burns, A. C. 2007. "*Beard v. Banks*: Restricted Reading, Rehabilitation, and Prisoners' First Amendment Rights." *Journal of Law and Policy* 15:1225–70.

Burns, S. 2010. "The Role of Problem-Solving Courts: Inside the Courts and Beyond." *University of Maryland Journal of Race, Religion, Gender, and Class* 10:73–87.

Buruma, I. 2005. "What Teaching a College-Level Class at a Maximum Security Correctional Facility Did for the Inmates—and for Me." *New York Times Magazine*, February 20, pp. 36–41.

Business Wire. 2001. "WorldNet Technologies, Creators of a State of the Art Weapons Detection System, Signs Consulting Deal with NuQuest."

November 27. http://findarticles.com/p/articles/mi_m0EIN/is_2001_Nov_27/ai_80345651/.

Butler, P. 2010. "One Hundred Years of Race and Crime." *Journal of Criminal Law and Criminology* 100:1043–60.

Butterfield, F. 2004. "Repaving the Long Road out of Prison." *New York Times*, May 4. http://www.nytimes.com.

Buzawa, E. S., and A. D. Buzawa. 2013. "Evidence Based Prosecution: Is It Worth the Cost?" *Criminology and Public Policy* 12:491–506.

Bykowicz, J. 2008. "Juvenile Center Home to Despair." *Baltimore Sun*, May 25. http://baltimoresun.com.

Bynum, T., and S. Varano. 2002. "The AntiGang Initiative in Detroit: An Aggressive Enforcement Approach to Gangs." In *Policing Gangs and Youth Violence*, eds. S. H. Decker. Belmont, CA: Wadsworth, 214–38.

Byrne, J. M. 2008. "The Best Laid Plans: An Assessment of the Varied Consequences of New Technologies for Crime and Social Control." *Federal Probation* 72 (3):10–21.

Byrne, J. M., and D. Hummer. 2007. "Myths and Realities of Prison Violence: A Review of the Evidence." *Victims and Offenders* 2:77–90.

Byrum, J. 2015. "Fingerprint Technician Helps Solve Case, Wins Award." GoUpstate.com (South Carolina news), October 4. www.goupstate.com.

Cadigan, T. 2009. "Implementing Evidence-Based Practices in Federal Pretrial Services." *Federal Probation* 73:30–32.

Cadigan, T. P., J. L. Johnson, and C. T. Lowenkamp. 2012. "The Re-validation of the Federal Pretrial Services Risk Assessment (PTRA)." *Federal Probation* (September):3–9.

Cady, M.S., and J. R. Phelps. 2008. "Preserving the Delicate Balance between Judicial Accountability and Independence: Merit Selection in the Post-White World." *Cornell Journal of Law and Public Policy* 17:343–81.

Cahill, M. T. 2007a. "Attempt, Reckless Homicide, and the Design of Criminal Law." *University of Colorado Law Review* 78:879–956.

———. 2007b. "Retributive Justice in the Real World." *Washington University Law Quarterly* 85:815–70.

California Department of Corrections and Rehabilitation. 2014. "Career Opportunities." California Department of Corrections and Rehabilitation website. www.cdcr.ca.gov_opportunities/por/documents.html.

———. 2016a. "Board of Parole Hearings." California Department of Corrections and Rehabilitation website. www.cdcr.ca.gov.

———. 2016b. *Pay and Benefits.* www .cdcr.ca.gov/Career_Opportunities/POR /Pay.html.

———. 2016c. *Training Schedule and Course Information,* March 25. www .cdcr.ca.gov/employee_resources/training _and_professional_development/docs /TrainingScheduleLinks.pdf.

"California to Redesign Prison Education Programs." 2011. *Correctional News,* March 16. www.correctionalnews.com.

Callahan, D. G. 2013. "Oxford Settles Taser Lawsuit." *Dayton Daily News,* March 7. http://www.daytondailynews.com.

Callahan, L. A., M. A. McGreevy, C. Cirincione, and H. J. Steadman. 1992. "Measure the Effects of the Guilty but Mentally Ill (GBMI) Verdict." *Law and Human Behavior* 16:447–62.

Cammack, M. 2010. "The Exclusionary Rule: The Rise and Fall of the Constitutional Exclusionary Rule in the United States." *American Journal of Comparative Law* 58:631–58.

Camp, C. G. 2003. *Corrections Yearbook, 2002.* Middletown, CT: Criminal Justice Institute.

Camp, S. D., and G. G. Gales. 2002. "Growth and Quality of U.S. Private Prisons: Evidence from a National Survey." *Criminology & Public Policy* 1:427–50.

Campbell, B. 2015. "Guest Commentary: Denver Sobriety Court Celebrates Fourth Anniversary." *Denver Post,* June 3. www.denverpost.com.

Campbell, C., J. Moore, W. Maier, and M. Gaffney. 2015. "Unnoticed, Untapped, and Underappreciated: Clients' Perceptions of Their Public Defenders." *Behavioral Sciences & the Law* 33:751–70.

Campbell, J. 2011. "State Unions Brace for Impact of Layoffs." *Press & Sun Bulletin,* May 22. http://www .pressconnects.com.

———. 2012. "Budget Cuts Could Gut Probation Officers." Fox 13 News online, March 2. www.myfoxtampabay.com.

Cancino, J. M., and R. Enriquez. 2004. "A Qualitative Analysis of Officer Peer Retaliation: Preserving the Police Culture." *Policing: International Journal of Police Strategies and Management* 27:320–40.

Candiotti, S. 2015. "Aaron Hernandez's Fiancée Granted Immunity in Murder Trial." CNN.con, February 10. www .cnn.com.

Canes-Wrone, B., T. Clark, and J. Park. 2012. "Judicial Independence and Retention Elections." *Journal of Law, Economics, and Organization* 28:211–34.

Canto, M. 1998. "Federal Government Investigates Use of Stun Belt." *Lansing* (MI) *State Journal,* August 7, p. 4A.

Caputo, M., and C. M. Miller. 2006. "In Wake of Death, Juvenile Boot Camp System Is Scrapped." *Miami Herald,* April 27. http://www.miami.com /miamiherald/14438114.htm.

Cardona, F. 2010. Clark Gets Life Plus More than 1,000 Years in Broncos' Death." *Denver Post,* April 30. www.denverpost .com.

Carlon, A. 2007. "Entrapment, Punishment, and the Sadistic State." *Virginia Law Review* 93:1081–1134.

Carodine, M. 2010. "Keeping It Real: Reform of the 'Untried Conviction' Impeachment Rule." *Maryland Law Review* 69:501–86.

Carr, P. J., L. Napolitano, and J. Keating. 2007. "We Never Call the Cops and Here's Why: A Qualitative Examination of Legal Cyncism in Three Philadelphia Neighborhoods." *Criminology* 45:445–80.

Carroll-Ferrary, N. L. 2006. "Incarcerated Men and Women, the Equal Protection Clause, and the Requirement of 'Similarly Situated.'" *New York Law School Law Review* 51:594–617.

Carroll, L. 1974. *Hacks, Blacks, and Cons: Race Relations in a Maximum Security Prison.* Lexington, MA: Lexington Books.

Carson, E. A. 2015. "Prisoners in 2014." *Bureau of Justice Statistics Bulletin,* September. NCJ 248955.

Carson, E. A., and D. Golinelli. 2013a. "Prisoners in 2012—Advance Counts." *Bureau of Justice Statistics Bulletin,* July. NCJ 242467.

———. 2013b. "Prisoners in 2012: Trends in Admissions and Releases, 1991–2012." *Bureau of Justice Statistics Bulletin,* December. NCJ 243920.

Carson, E. A. and J. Mulako-Wangota. 2016. "Count of Total Jurisdiction Population." March 28. Generated Using the *Corrections Statistical Analysis Tool (CSAT)–Prisoners* at www.bjs.gov Washington, DC: Bureau of Justice Statistics.

Carson, E. A., and W. J. Sabol. "Prisoners in 2011." *Bureau of Justice Statistics Bulletin,* December. NCJ 239808.

Carter, J. G., S. W. Phillips, and S. M. Gayadeen. 2014. "Implementing Intelligence-Led Policing: An Application of Loose-Coupling Theory." *Journal of Criminal Justice* 42: 433–42.

Cave, B., C. Telep, and J. Grieco. 2015. "Rigorous Evaluation Research among U.S. Police Departments: Special Cases or a Representative Sample?" *Police Practice and Research* 16: 254–68.

CBS News. 2016. "Crimesider's Biggest Crime Stories of 2015," January 14. www.cbsnews.com.

Chacon, J. M. 2010. "Border Exceptionalism in the Era of Moving Borders." *Fordham Urban Law Journal* 38:129–52.

Chaddock, G. R. 2002. "Sniper Revives Prospects for Gun-Tracking Moves." *Christian Science Monitor,* October 17, p. 1.

Champion, D. J. 1989. "Private Counsels and Public Defenders: A Look at Weak Cases, Prior Records, and Leniency in Plea Bargaining." *Journal of Criminal Justice* 17:253–63.

Chanen, D. 2014. "Hennepin County No Longer Will Honor 'ICE Hold' Requests." *Minneapolis Star Tribune,* June 12. www.startribune.com.

Chapman, S. G. 1970. *Police Patrol Readings.* 2nd ed. Springfield, IL: Thomas.

Chappell, B. 2015. "Number of Police Officers Killed by Gunfire Fell 14 Percent in 2015, Study Says." National Public Radio, December 30. www.npr.org.

Chapper, J. A., and R. A. Hanson. 1989. *Understanding Reversible Error in Criminal Appeals.* Williamsburg, VA: National Center for State Courts.

Chavez, P. 2005. "Shooting Raises Racial Tension in L.A." *Sacramento Union,* February 21. http://www.sacunion.com.

Cheeseman, K.A., and R. A. Downey. 2012. "'Talking 'bout My Generation': The Effect of 'Generation' on Correctional Employee Perceptions of Work Stress and Job Satisfaction." *Prison Journal* 92:24–44.

Chen, C., and D. Wilbur. 2014. "Heroin Resurgence in U.S. Sparked by Cheap Cost, Access." *Business Week,* February 4. www.businessweek.com.

Cheng, E. 2005. "Mitochondrial DNA: Emerging Legal Issues." *Journal of Law and Policy* 13:99–118.

Chermak, S., and E. McGarrell. 2004. "Problem-Solving Approaches to Homicide: An Evaluation of Indianapolis Violence Reduction Partnership." *Criminal Justice Policy Review* 15:161–92.

Chertoff, M., and D. Robinson. 2012. "Check One and the Accountability Is Done: The Harmful Impact of Straight-Ticket Voting on Judicial Elections." *Albany Law Review* 75:1773–97.

"Chicago Council Approves $5 Million Settlement in Police Shooting." 2015. Channel 5 NBC Chicago website, April 15. www.nbcchicago.com.

Chidress, S. 2015. "After Riot, Feds End Contract for Private Texas Prison." Public Broadcasting System website, March 17. www.pbs.org.

Childress, S. 2013. "Why ICE Released Those 2,000 Immigrant Detainees." Public Broadcasting System website, March 19. www.pbs.org.

Cho, S., A. Dreher, and E. Naumayer. 2013. "Does Legalized Prostitution Increase Human Trafficking?" *World Development, 41,* 67–82.

Christopher, R. L. 1994. "Mistake of Fact in the Objective Theory of Justification." *Journal of Criminal Law and Criminology* 85:295–332.

Church, T. W. 1985. "Examining Local Legal Culture." *American Bar Foundation Research Journal* 1985 (Summer): 449.

City of Seattle. 2016. "Sworn Salary Schedule." Seattle Police Department website. www.seattle.gov.

City of Westminster, CO. 2014. "Volunteers in Probation." City of Westminster website. http://www.ci.westminster.co.us /GetInvolved/VolunteerWestminster /VolunteersinProbation.aspx.

Clark, M. 2011. "States Beginning to Rethink Indigent Defense Systems: Stateline: State Politics & Policy website (Pew Center on the States), December 1. http://stateline.org.

———. 2014. "Report: Florida Leads the National on Charging Kids as Adults." MSNBC, April 11th. http://www.msnbc.com.

Clear, T., G. Cole, and M. Reisig. 2012. *American Corrections.* 10th ed. Belmont, CA: Cengage Wadsworth.

Clear, T. R. 1994. *Harm in American Penology.* Albany: State University of New York Press.

Clear, T. R., and D. R. Karp. 1999. *Community Justice: Preventing Crime and Achieving Justice.* New York: Westview Press.

Clisura, A. 2010. "None of Their Business: The Need for Another Alternative to New York's Bail Bond Business." *Journal of Law and Policy* 19:307–51.

CNN. 2004a. "Boston Police Accept 'Full Responsibility' in Death of Red Sox Fan." October 22. http://www.cnn.com.

———. 2004b. "Police Review Policy after Tasers Used on Kids." November 14. http://www.cnn.com.

Cochran, J. C., and P. Y. Warren. 2012. "Racial, Ethnic, and Gender Differences in Perceptions of the Police: The Salience of Officer Race within the Context of Racial Profiling." *Journal of Contemporary Criminal Justice* 28(2):206–27.

Coe, J., 2013. "Police: Technology Helped with Drop in Tempe Crime." *Arizona Republic,* March 13. www .azcentral.com.

Coffin, K. G. 2010. "Double Take: Evaluating Double Jeopardy Reform." *Notre Dame Law Review* 85:771–808.

Cohen. A. 2014. "Freedom after 30 Years on Death Row." *The Atlantic,* March 11. www.theatlantic.com.

Cohen, L. E., and M. Felson. 1979. "Social Change and Crime Rate Trends: A Routine Activity Approach." *American Sociological Review,* 44:588–608.

Cohen, T. H., and T. Kyckelhahn. 2010. "Felony Defendants in Large Urban Counties, 2006." Bureau of Justice Statistics *Bulletin,* May. NCJ 228944.

Coleman, K. 2011. "The Mob Goes Green." National Public Radio. http://www .npr.org/blogs/thetwo-way/2011/12/07 /143271128/the-mob-goes-green -organizedcrime-profits-with-new -jersey-recycling.

Coleman, T., and D. Cotton. 2010. "Reducing Risk and Improving Outcomes of Police Interactions with People with Mental Illness." *Journal of Police Crisis Negotiations* 10:39–57.

Collins, D. 2016. "AP News Break: Racial Disparities Seen in Police Stun Gun Use." Associated Press website, January 27. bigstory.ap.org.

Collins, J. 2005. *Preventing Identity Theft in Your Business: How to Protect Your Business, Customers, and Employees.* New York: Wiley.

Comey, J. B. 2015. "Statement before the Senate Judiciary Committee." Washington, DC. December 9. www.fbi.gov.

"Connecticut Mourns after Newtown Massacre; 27 Dead, Including 20 Children." *New Haven Register,* December 14. http://www.nhregister.com.

Constantin, L. 2016. "Hyatt Hackers Snagged Credit Card Numbers from 250 Locations." *Computerworld,* January 15. www.computerworld.com.

Conte, M. 2012. "Former Belleville Man Charged As Member of Credit Card Forgery Ring." *Jersey Journal,* February 23. www.nj.com.

Cook, J. 2013. "Plea Bargaining, Sentence Modification, and the Real World." *Wake Forest Law Review* 48:65–94.

Cook, N. 2010. "How the Recession Hurts Private Prisons." *Newsweek,* June 29. http://www.thedailybeast.com /newsweek/2010/06/30/how-the -recession-hurts-private-prisons.html.

Cook, P. J. 2013. "The Great American Gun War: Notes from Four Decades in the Trenches." *Crime and Justice* 42:19–63.

Cook, P. J., and J. Laub. 2002. "After the Epidemic: Recent Trends in Youth Violence in the United States." *Crime and Justice: A Review of Research* 29:1–37.

Cooney, M. 1994. "Evidence as Partisanship." *Law & Society Review* 28:833–58.

Cooper, C. 2009. "Yes Virginia, There Is a Police Code of Silence: Prosecuting Police Officers and the Police Subculture." *Criminal Law Bulletin* 45:277–82.

Cooper, M. 2015. "How A '90s Internet Law Determined a 2014 Rape Case." *Time,* December 18. www.time.com.

Copes, H., F. Brookman, and A. Brown. 2013. "Accounting for Violations of the Convict Code." *Deviant Behavior,* 34:841–58.

Copes, H., G. E. Higgins, R. Tewksbury, and D. Dabney. 2010. "Participation in the Prison Economy and Likelihood of Physical Victimization." *Victims & Offenders* 6(1):1–18.

COPS (Community Oriented Policing Services, U.S. Department of Justice). 2014. COPS website. Accessed March 3. http://www.cops.usdoj.gov/.

Cordner, G., and E. P. Biebel. 2005. "Problem-Oriented Policing in Practice." *Criminology & Public Policy* 4:155–80.

Cornwell, E., and V. Hans. 2011. "Representation through Participation: A Multilevel Analysis of Jury Deliberations." *Law & Society Review* 45:667–98.

Corsaro, N., R. Brunson, and E. McGarrell. 2012. "Problem-Oriented Policing and Open-Air Drug Markets: Examining the Rockford Pulling Levers Deterrence Strategy." *Crime and Delinquency* (forthcoming).

Costanzo, M. 1997. *Just Revenge.* New York: St. Martin's Press.

Costinett, A. H. 2011. "'In a Puff of Smoke': Drug Crime and the Perils of Subjective Entrapment." *American Criminal Law Review* 48:1757–87.

Cotton, M. 2015. "The Necessity Defense and the Moral Limits of Law." *New Criminal Law Review* 18:35–70.

Coughlin, M. 2012. "Prison Reform Bill to Help Fund Probation and Parole." PhillyBurbs.com website, July 15. www .phillyburbs.com.

Covey, R. 2013. "Police Misconduct as a Cause of Wrongful Conviction." *Washington University Law Review* 90:1133–89.

Covey, R. D. 2011. "Longitudinal Guilt: Repeat Offenders, Plea Bargaining, and the Variable Standard of Proof." *Florida Law Review* 63:431–55.

———. 2013. "Plea Bargaining after *Laflar* and *Frye.*" *Duquesne Law Review* 51:595–623.

Cox, A. 2015. "Does It Stay, or Does It Go? Application of the Good-Faith Exception When the Warrant Relied Upon Is Fruit of the Poisonous Tree." *Washington & Lee Law Review* 72:1505–48.

Coyle, M. 2009. "New Report Shows Sharp Rise in Prison Time for Federal Offenders." *National Law Journal,* February 12. www.law.com.

Crandall, S. 2013. "Teacher Who Had Sex with Students Sentenced to 20 Years. Fox4 News online, November 13. www .fox4news.com.

Crawford, C., T. Chiricos, and G. Kleck. 1998. "Race, Racial Threat, and Sentencing of Habitual Offenders." *Criminology* 36 (August):481–512.

Cristani, A. S., and B. C. Frueh. 2011. "Risk of Trauma Exposure among Persons with Mental Illness in Jails and Prisons: What Do We Really Know?" *Current Opinion in Psychiatry* 24(5):431–35.

Crummy, K. 2009. "Colorado Criminals Owe State's Victims Nearly $778 Million." *Denver Post,* September 24. www .denverpost.com.

Cruz, C. 2014. "Ybarra Chose SPU for Shootings Because He Was Unfamiliar with It, Journal Says." *Seattle Times,* July 22. www.seattletimes.com.

Cruz, C., and M. Baker. 2014. "SPU Shooting Suspect Raised in Home of Tumult." *Seattle Times,* July 19. www .seattletimes.com.

Cullen, F. T., T. Leming, B. Link, and J. Wozniak. 1985. "The Impact of Social Supports in Police Stress." *Criminology* 23:503–22.

Cunningham, W. C., J. J. Strauchs, and C. W. Van Meter. 1990. *Private Security Trends, 1970 to the Year 2000.* Boston: Butterworth-Heinemann.

Cyberbullying Research Center. 2014. "Cyberbullying Facts." http://cyberbullying.us/research/facts/.

D'Alessio, S., J. Flexon, and L. Stolzenberg. 2013. "The Effect of Conjugal Visitation on Sexual Violence in Prison." *American Journal of Criminal Justice* 38:13–26.

D'Zurilla, C. 2013a. "Stephen Baldwin Avoids Jail with Guilty Plea in Tax Case." *Los Angeles Times*, March 29. http://www.latimes.com.

———. 2013b. "Wesley Snipes Released from Prison, Still under House Arrest." *Los Angeles Times.* April 5. http://www.latimes.com.

Dabney, D. A., H. Copes, R. Tewksbury, and S. R. Hawk-Tourtelot. 2013. "A Qualitative Assessment of Stress Perceptions among Members of a Homicide Unit." *Justice Quarterly* 30:811–36.

Daftary-Kapur, T., R. Dumas, and S. D. Penrod. 2010. "Jury Decision-Making Biases and Methods to Counter Them." *Legal and Criminological Psychology* 15:133–54.

Daley, W. 2016. "Crime Watch: Chicago Needs More Surveillance Cameras." *Chicago Tribune*, January 22. www.chicagotribune.com.

Damron, G., E. Anderson, and J. Wisely. 2013. "Wayne County Prosecutor Kym Worth Cuts Start to Affect Suburbs." *Detroit Free Press,* April 1. www.freep.com.

Dansky, K. 2008. "Understanding California Sentencing." *University of San Francisco Law Review* 43:45–86.

Dantzker, M. and J. McCoy. 2006. "Psychological Screening of Police Recruits: A Texas Perspective." *Journal of Police and Criminal Psychology* 21:23–32

Davey, J. D. 1998. *The Politics of Prison Expansion: Winning Elections by Waging War on Crime.* Westport, CT: Praeger.

Davey, M., and J. Bosman. 2014. "Protests Flare after Ferguson Police Officer Is Not Indicted." *New York Times,* November 24. www.nytimes.com.

Davis, A. 2008. *Arbitrary Justice: The Power of the American Prosecutor.* New York: Oxford University Press.

Davis, L. M., R. Bozick, J. L. Steele, J. Saunders, and J. N. V. Miles (2013). *Evaluating the Effectiveness of Correctional Education: A Meta-Analysis of Programs That Provide Education to Incarcerated Adults.* Pittsburgh, PA: Rand Corporation.

Davis, M., R. Lundman, and R. Martinez Jr. 1991. "Private Corporate Justice: Store Police, Shoplifters, and Civil Recovery." *Social Problems* 38:395–408.

Davis, R. C., C. S. O'Sullivan, D. J. Farole, and M. Rempel. 2008. "A Comparison of Two Prosecution Policies in Cases of Intimate Partner Violence: Mandatory Case Filing versus Following the Victim's Lead." *Criminology & Public Policy* 7:633–62.

Davis, S. 2012. "Ionia Site Targeted in Budget Proposal." *Lansing State Journal*, April 7. www.lsj.com.

Davitz, T. 1998. "The Gangs behind Bars." *Insight on the News*, September 28.

Dawson, M., and R. Dinovitzer. 2001. "Victim Cooperation and the Prosecution of Domestic Violence in a Specialized Court." *Justice Quarterly* 18:593–622.

De Leon, 2013. "Seattle Police Turn to Computer Software to Predict, Fight Crime." *Seattle Times,* February 27. www.seattletimes.com.

Death Penalty Information Center. 2014. *Facts about the Death Penalty,* March 21.

Dedel, K. 2010. "Fifth Monitor's Report for the Baltimore City Juvenile Justice Center (BCJJC) for the Period of July 1, 2009 through December 31, 2009." http://www.djs.state.md.us.

DeFrances, C. J., and J. Litras. 2000. "Indigent Defense Services in Large Counties, 1999." Bureau of Justice Statistics *Bulletin*, November.

DeJohn, I. 2014. "'Loud Music' Case: Jury Was Deadlocked Two Days into Trial Due to Stand Your Ground Law: Juror." *New York Daily News,* February 19. www.nydailynews.com.

DeJong, C. 2012. "Policing Styles, Officer Gender and Decision Making." In *The Routledge International Handbook of Gender and Crime Studies*, eds. C. M. Renzetti, S. L. Miller, and A. R. Gover. New York: Routledge.

DeJong, C., S. Mastrofski, and R. Parks. 2001. "Patrol Officers and Problem Solving: An Application of Expectancy Theory." *Justice Quarterly* 18:31–61.

DeJong, C., and E. S. Merrill, 2000. "Getting 'Tough on Crime': Juvenile Waiver and the Criminal Court." *Ohio Northern University Law Review* 27:175–96.

Deng, X. 2012. "Prison Population Continues to Drop." *Daily Tribune*, April 1. www.dailytribune.com.

Dery, G. 2011. "Do You Believe in *Miranda*? The Supreme Court Reveals Its Doubts in *Berghuis v. Thompkins* by Paradoxically Ruling That Suspects Can Only Invoke Their Right to Remain Silent by Speaking." *George Mason University Civil Rights Law Journal* 21:407–40.

Devaney, T. 2015. "Feds Training Police to Respond to Mass Shootings, Bombs." *The Hill*, June 8. http://thehill.com.

Devers, L. 2011. *Plea and Charge Bargaining: Research Summary.* Washington, DC: U.S. Bureau of Justice Assistance.

Dewan, S. 2007. "An SOS for 911 Systems in Age of High-Tech." *New York Times,* April 6. http://www.nytimes.com.

———. 2009. "Prosecutors Block Access to DNA Testing for Inmates." *New York Times*, May 18. http://www.nytimes.com.

———. 2015. "Court by Court, Lawyers Fight Policies That Fall Heavily on the Poor." *New York Times*, October 23. www.nytimes.com.

Diamond, S., D. Peery, F. Dolan, and E. Dolan. 2009. "Achieving Diversity on the Jury: Jury Size and the Peremptory Challenge." *Journal of Empirical Legal Studies* 6:425–49.

Dickerson, B.E. 2008. "Hard Lemonade, Hard Price." *Detroit Free Press,* April 28. http://www.freep.com.

Diedrich, J. 2014. "Florida Jury Rules Man with Low IQ Not Guilty in Set-Ups." *Milwaukee Journal Sentinel*, August 2. www.jsonline.com.

———. 2016. "Man Gets Prison, Deportation for Defrauding Kohl's Cash Program." *Milwaukee-Wisconsin Journal Sentinel,* January 21. www.jsonline.com.

Diedrich, J., and G. Barton. 2013. "New Milwaukee Police Procedures Address Racial Profiling, Crime Data." *Milwaukee Journal Sentinel*, February 7. www.jsonline.com.

DiIulio, J. J., Jr. 1987. *Governing Prisons.* New York: Free Press.

———. 1991. *No Escape: The Future of American Corrections.* New York: Basic Books.

———. 1993. "Rethinking the Criminal Justice System: Toward a New Paradigm." In *Performance Measures for the Criminal Justice System.* Washington, DC: Bureau of Justice Statistics, U.S. Government Printing Office.

Dirks-Linhorst, P. A., D. Kondrat, D. M. Linhorst, and N. Morani. 2013. "Factors Associated with Mental Health Court Nonparticipation and Negative Termination." *Justice Quarterly* 30:681–710.

Doerner, J. K., and S. Demuth. 2010. "The Independent and Joint Effects of Race/Ethnicity, Gender, and Age on Sentencing Outcomes in U.S. Federal Courts." *Justice Quarterly* 27:1–27.

Donziger, S. R., ed. 1996. *The Real War on Crime: The Report of the National Criminal Justice Commission.* New York: HarperCollins.

Dority, B. 2005. "The USA Patriot Act Has Decimated Many Civil Liberties." In *Homeland Security: Current Controversies*, ed. A. Nakaya. Detroit: Thomson /Gale, 130–36.

———. 2014a. "Affidavit Details Alleged St. Paul's Sexual Assault." *Concord*

Monitor, July 26. http://www
.concordmonitor.com/community
/town-by-town/concord/12893570-95
/affidavit-details-alleged-st-pauls
-sexual-assault.

———. 2014b. "Tunbridge Teen Charged with Sexual Assault." *Valley News* (VT), July 17. http://www.vnews.com /news/12784585-95/tunbridge-teen -charged-with-sexual-assault.

Dripps, D. 2010. "The 'New' Exclusionary Rule Debate: From 'Still Preoccupied with 1985' to 'Virtual Deterrence,'" *Fordham Urban Law Journal* 37:743–801.

Dubail, J. 2009. "Cuyahoga County Jury Pay Cut to Save Money." May 14. www .cleveland.com.

Duke, A. 2013. "Lindsay Lohan Goes to Jail on Probation Violation." CNN.com, September. www.cnn.com.

Duncan, I. 2013. "Lawmakers Call for Replacement of Baltimore Jail." *Baltimore Sun*, December 11th. http:// baltimoresun.com.

Durose, M. R., E. L. Schmitt, and P. Langan. 2005. *Contacts between Police and Public: Findings from the 2002 National Survey*. Washington, DC: Bureau of Justice Statistics, U.S. Government Printing Office, April.

Dyer, B. 2012. "Mayors' Courts Should Be Nuked." *Akron Beacon Journal*, January 24. www.ohio.com.

Dysart, K. 2012. "Managing the *CSI* Effect in Jurors." American Bar Association website, May 28. www.americanbar.org.

Dzur, A. 2011. "Restorative Justice and Democracy: Fostering Public Accountability for Criminal Justice." *Contemporary Justice Review*, 14:367–81.

Earley, P. 1992. *The Hot House: Life inside Leavenworth Prison*. New York: Bantam Books.

Eaton, L., and L. Kaufman. 2005. "In Problem-Solving Court, Judges Turn Therapist." *New York Times*, April 26. www .nytimes.com.

Eckholm, E. 2008a. "Citing Workload, Public Lawyers Reject New Cases." *New York Times*, November 9. http://www .nytimes.com.

———. 2008b. "New Tack on Straying Parolees Offers a Hand Instead of Cuffs." *New York Times*, May 17. www .nytimes.com.

———. 2008c. "U.S. Shifting Prison Focus to Re-entry Into Society." *New York Times*, April 8. http://www.nytimes .com.

———. 2010. "Congress Moves to Narrow Cocaine Sentencing Disparities." *New York Times*, July 28. www.nytimes.com.

———. 2013. "With Police in Schools, More Children in Court." *New York Times*, April 12. www.nytimes.com.

"Economics of CJA Representations Costly to Attorneys." 2008. *The Third Branch*

(April) http://www.uscourts.gov/news /TheThirdBranch/08-04-01/Economics _of_CJA_Representations_Costly_to _Attorneys.aspx.

Edgemon, E. 2013. "10 Minutes per Month: Alabama Probation, Parole Officers Get Little Time with 67,410 They Oversee." *Birmingham News*. May 20. http:// blog.al.com.

Edkins, V. 2011. "Defense Attorney Plea Recommendations and Client Race: Does Zealous Representation Apply Equally to All?" *Law and Human Behavior* 35:413–25.

Edwards, B. 2014. "Cyber-Crime Becoming Top Priority for Federal Law Enforcement." CBS Chicago online, Feburary 18. http://chicago.cbslocal.com/2014 /02/18/cyber-crime-becoming-top -priority-for-federal-law-enforcement/.

Egan, P. 2014. "Michigan Urged to Reject $145M Prison Food Contract over Safety Concerns." *Detroit Free Press*, March 19. www.freep.com.

———. 2015. "MSP [Michigan State Police] Aiming to Diversify in '16." *Lansing* (MI) *State Journal*, July 25, p. 1.

Egelko, B. 2014. "2 San Francisco Police Officers Convicted of Corruption." SFGATE.com, December 5. www.sfgate .com.

Egley, A. and J. C. Howell. 2013. *Highlights of the 2011 National Youth Gang Survey* (NCJ 242884). Washington, DC: U.S. Department of Justice.

Eichenwald, K. 2006. "On the Web, Pedophiles Extend Their Reach." *New York Times*, August 21. http://www.nytimes .com.

Eigenberg, H. 2000. "Correctional Officers and Their Perceptions of Homosexuality, Rape, and Prostitution in Male Prisons." *Prison Journal* 80 (December): 415–33.

Eisenberg, T., P. Hannaford-Agor, V. P. Hans, N. L. Mott, G. T. Munsterman, S. J. Schwab, and M. T. Wells. 2005. "Judge-Jury Agreement in Criminal Cases: A Partial Replication of Kalven and Zeisel's *The American Jury*." *Journal of Empirical Legal Studies* 2:171–206.

Eisenstein, J., R. B. Flemming, and P. F. Nardulli. 1988. *The Contours of Justice: Communities and Their Courts*. Boston: Little, Brown.

Eith, C., and M. R. Durose. 2011. "Contacts between Police and the Public, 2008." *BJS Special Report*. October. NCJ234599.

Eligon, J., and T. Kaplan. 2012. "New York State Set to Add All Convict DNA to Its Database." *New York Times*, March 13. www.nytimes.com.

Ellement, J. R., and S. Smalley. 2006. "Six Crime Disclosure Questioned." *Boston Globe*, April 18. http://www .boston.com.

Elliot, D., B. Garg, K. Kuehl, C. DeFrancesco, and A. Sleigh. 2015. "Why Are Women Law Enforcement Officers More Burned Out and What Might Help Them?" *Occupational Medicine & Health Affairs*. 3:204.

Emmelman, D. S. 1996. "Trial by Plea Bargain: Case Settlement as a Product of Recursive Decisionmaking." *Law & Society Review* 30:335–60.

Engber, D. 2005. "Does the FBI Have Your Fingerprints?" *Slate*, April 22. http:// www.slate.msn.com/id/2117226.

Engel, R. S., and J. M. Calnon. 2004. "Examining the Influence of Drivers' Characteristics during Traffic Stops with Police: Results from a National Survey." *Justice Quarterly* 21:49–90.

Engel, R. S., J. M. Calnon, and T. J. Bernard. 2002. "Theory and Racial Profiling: Shortcomings and Future Directions in Research." *Justice Quarterly* 19:249–73.

Engen, R. 2009. "Assessing Determinate and Presumptive Sentencing—Making Research Relevant." *Criminology & Public Policy* 8:323–36.

Enion, M.R. 2009. "Constitutional Limits on Private Policing and the State's Allocation of Force." *Duke Law Journal* 59:519–51.

Enriquez, R., and J. W. Clark. 2007. "The Social Psychology of Peremptory Challenges: An Examination of Latino Jurors." *Texas Hispanic Journal of Law and Policy* 13:25–38.

Epp, C., and S. Maynard-Moody. 2014. "Driving while Black." *Washington Monthly*, January/February. www .washingtonmonthly.com.

Epp, C. R. 2009. *Making Rights Real: Activists, Bureaucrats, and the Creation of the Legalistic State*. Chicago: University of Chicago Press.

Erhard, S. 2008. "Plea Bargaining and the Death Penalty: An Exploratory Study." *Justice System Journal* 29:313–27.

Estep, D. 2009. "Wyoming Mom Says Michigan Youth Challenge Academy Pays Off, Deserves State Funding." *Grand Rapids Press*, August 29. www .mlive.com.

Fahey, T. 2011. "Tough Decisions Remain Regarding State Budget." *Union Leader*, May 20. http://www.unionleader.com.

Fak, M. 2013. "Musical Chairs Complete with Dwight Women Transferred to Logan County Correctional Center." *Logan County Herald*, March 30. http://www .logancountyherald.com.

Fandos, N., and C. Hauser. 2016. "Thousands Honor Virginia Officer Killed on Her First Day on the Job." *New York Times*, March 1. www.nytimes.com.

Fantz, A. 2013. "Ariel Castro Agrees to Plea to Avoid Death Penalty." CNN.com, July 28. www.cnn.com.

Farole, D. J., and L. Langton. 2010. "County-Based and Local Public

Defender Offices, 2007." Bureau of Justice Statistics *Special Report*, September. NCJ 231175.

Fathi, D. C. 2010. "The Challenge of Prison Oversight." *American Criminal Law Review* 47:1453–62.

Faturechi, R. 2011. "Report Details Misconduct by L.A. County Sheriff's Deputies." *Los Angeles Times*, August 5. www.latimes.com.

Fausset, R. 2015. "Walter Scott Family Reaches a $6.5 Million Settlement for South Carolina Police Shooting Case." *New York Times*, October 8. www.nytimes.com.

Fausset, R., R. Perez-Pena, and A. Blinder. 2015. "Race and Discipline in Spotlight after South Carolina Officer Drags Student." *New York Times*, October 27. www.nytimes.com.

Favate, S. 2012. "Shrinking State Court Budgets: Not Just A New York Thing." *Wall Street Journal*, January 12. www.wsj.com.

FBI (Federal Bureau of Investigation). 2006. "FBI Cyber Action Teams: Traveling the World to Catch Cyber Criminals." March 6. http://www.fbi.gov.

———. 2008. "Cyber Solidarity: Five Nations, One Mission." March 18. http://www.fbi.gov.

———. 2011. *Hate Crime Statistics*, 2010. Washington, DC.

———. 2012. "Special Agent FAQs." FBI website. https://www.fbijobs.gov/114.asp.

———. 2013a. *Crime in the United States, 2012* (Uniform Crime Reports). www.fbi.gov.

———. 2013b. *Crime in the United States, 2013 (Preliminary Semiannual Uniform Crime Report)*. http://www.fbi.gov.

———. 2013c. "NIBRS Participation by State." *National Incident Based Reporting System, 2012* (Uniform Crime Reports). http://www.fbi.gov.

———. 2013d. *Today's FBI: Facts and Figures, 2013–14*. Washington, DC: U.S. Department of Justice.

———. 2013e. NIBRS Participation by State. *National Incident-Based Reporting System*. www.fbi.gov.

———. 2014. "Special Agent Frequently Asked Questions." www.fbi.gov.

———. 2014b. *Today's FBI: Facts and Figures, 2013–2014*. www.fbi.gov.

———. 2015a. *Crime in the United States, 2014*. Uniform Crime Reports. www.fbi.gov.

———. 2015b. "Human Trafficking Report." *Crime in the United States, 2014*. www.fbi.gov.

———. 2016. "Quick Facts." FBI website *About Us* tab. www.fbi.gov.

FBI Press Release. 2012. "Portsmouth Bail Bondsman Sentenced to 30 Months in Prison for Bribing Public Officials." November 2. http://www.fbi.gov.

Federal Bureau of Prisons. 2016. "Staff Gender." *Statistics*. www.bop.gov/about/statistics/statistics_staff_gender.jsp.

Feehan, J. 2014. "Teacher Sentenced to 17 Months for Sexual Relations with Students." *Toledo Blade*, August 5. www.toledoblade.com.

Feeley, M., and E. Rubin. 1998. *Judicial Policy Making and the Modern State*. New York: Cambridge University Press.

Feingold, D.A. 2005. "Human Trafficking." *Foreign Policy* 150:26–30.

Felch, J. 2003. "How a 'Calm but Aggravated' Teenager Died on East Thrill Place." *Denver Post*, July 11. http://www.denverpost.com.

Felch, J., and M. Dolan. 2008. "DNA Matches Aren't Always a Lock." *Los Angeles Times*, May 4. http://www.latimes.com.

Feld, B. 1999. *Bad Kids: Race and the Transformation of the Juvenile Court*. New York: Oxford University Press.

———. 2004. "Editorial Introduction: Juvenile Transfers." *Criminology & Public Policy* 3 (November):599–603.

Feld, B. C. 1993. "Criminalizing the American Juvenile Court." In *Crime and Justice: A Review of Research*, vol. 17, ed. M. Tonry. Chicago: University of Chicago Press, 197–280.

Fenton, J. 2011. "More than 30 Baltimore Police Officers Charged, Suspended in Towing Scheme." *Baltimore Sun*, February 23. www.baltimoresun.com.

Ferguson, D. 2015. "Screech Convicted of Misdemeanors in Stabbing." *USA Today*, May 30. www.usatoday.com.

Ferguson, J. 2009. "Professional Discretion and the Use of Restorative Justice Programs in Appropriate Domestic Violence Cases: An Effective Innovation. *Criminal Law Brief* 4:3–17.

Fernandez, M. 2014. "Despite Chaos, Police in Ferguson React with Restraint Not Shown after August Killing." *New York Times*, November 25. www.nytimes.com.

Ferner, M. 2015. "These Programs Are Helping Prisoners to Live Again on the Outside." Huffington Post, July 28. www.huffingtonpost.com.

Ferretti, C. and M. Feighan. 2009. "Teen Dies after Warren Police Use Taser." *Detroit News*, April 11. http://www.detnews.com.

Feuer, A. 2006. "For Ex-F.B.I. Agent Accused in Murders, a Case of What Might Have Been." *New York Times*, April 15. http://www.nytimes.com.

Fields, G., and J. R. Emshwiller. 2012. "Federal Guilty Pleas Soar as Bargains Trump Trials." *Wall Street Journal*, September 23. http://online.wsj.com.

Fields, J., and K. Peveto. 2008. "Local Cop Cars Going Hi-Tech." *Abilene* (TX) *Reporter News*, December 4. http://www.reporternews.com.

Finley, A. 2011. "California Prison Academy: Better Than a Harvard Degree." *Wall Street Journal*, April 30. http://online.wsj.com.

Finn, B., M. Shively, J. McDevitt, W. Lassiter, and T. Rich. 2005. *Comparison of Activities and Lessons Learned among 19 School Resource Officer (SRO) Programs*. Boston: Abt Associates.

Finn, M. 2013. "Evidence-Based and Victim-Centered Prosecutorial Policies: Examination of Deterrent and Therapeutic Jurisprudence Effects on Domestic Violence." *Criminology and Public Policy* 12:443–72.

Finn, P., and J. McDevitt. 2005. National Assessment of School Resource Officer Programs. Report to the National Institute of Justice. Unpublished.

Firozi, P. 2014. "Police Ticket Quotas Get Warning." *USA Today*, August 19. www.usatoday.com.

Fischman, J., and M. Schanzenbach. 2011. "Do Standards of Review Matter? The Case of Federal Criminal Sentencing." *Journal of Legal Studies* 40:405–37.

Fisher, B. S., L. E. Daigle, and F. T. Cullen. 2010. "What Distinguishes Single from Recurrent Sexual Victims? The Role of Lifestyle-Routine Activities and First-Incident Characteristics," *Justice Quarterly*, 27(1):102–29.

Fisher, D. M. 2007. "Striking a Balance: The Need to Temper Judicial Discretion against a Background of Legislative Interest in Federal Sentencing." *Duquesne Law Review* 46:65–97.

Flanagan, F. 2015. "Peremptory Challenges and Jury Selection." *Journal of Law and Economics* 58:385–416.

Flanagan, T. J., ed. 1995. *Long-Term Imprisonment*. Thousand Oaks, CA: Sage.

Flango, V. E. 1994. *Habeas Corpus in State and Federal Courts*. Williamsburg, VA: National Center for State Courts.

Fleisher, M. S., and J. L. Krienert. 2006. The Culture of Prison Sexual Violence. Unpublished.

Flock, E. 2012. "California School Protests: 5 Reasons Students Are Demonstrating." *Washington Post*, March 6. www.washingtonpost.com.

Florencio, D., and C. Herley. 2012. "The Cybercrime Wave That Wasn't." *New York Times*, April 14. www.nytimes.com.

Flores, A. 2014. "Indigent Defense System Debated: Other Texas Counties Take Judges out of the Process." *El Paso Times*, April 20. www.elpasotimes.com.

Florey, K. 2013. "Beyond Uniqueness: Reimagining Tribal Courts' Jurisdiction." *California Law Review* 101:1499–1564.

Florida Office of Program Policy Analysis and Government Accountability. 2010. *Intermediate Sanctions for Non-Violent*

Offenders Could Produce Savings, Report No. 10–27 (March).

Florida Tax Watch, 2014. "Florida's Aging Prisoner Problem." September. www .floridataxwatch.org/resources/pdf /ElderlyParoleFinal.pdf.

Flowers, R. 2010. "The Role of the Defense Attorney: Not Just An Advocate." *Ohio State Journal of Criminal Law* 7:647–52.

Foley, S. 2013. "The Newly Murky World of Searches Incident to Lawful Arrest: Why the *Gant* Restrictions Should Apply to All Searches Incident to Arrest." *University of Kansas Law Review* 61:753–83.

"For Federal Courts, Shutdown Caused Broad Disruptions." 2013. *The Third Branch News*, October 25. http://news .uscourts.gov/federal-courts-shutdown -caused-broad-disruptions.

Ford, D., M. Martinez, and J. Sterling. 2013. "Not Guilty Plea for Suspect in Alleged Decade-Long Ohio Kidnapping." CNN. com, June 12. www.cnn.com.

Fortier, M. 2016. "Dzhokhar Tsarnaev Ordered to Pay $101 Million in Restitution to Boston Marathon Bombing Victims." New England Cable News, January 15. www.necn.com.

Fountain, H. 2009. "Plugging Holes in the Science of Forensics." *New York Times*, May 12. http://www.nytimes.com.

Fox, J. G. 1982. *Organizational and Racial Conflict in Maximum Security Prisons.* Lexington, MA: Lexington Books.

Frantz, S., and R. Borum. 2011. "Crisis Intervention Teams May Prevent Arrests of People with Mental Illnesses." *Police Practice and Research: An International Journal* 12:265–72.

Freskos, B. 2011. "Education in N.C. Prisons Is Top of the Class." *Wilmington Star News*, May 20. www.starnewsonline.com.

Fridell, L. 1990. "Decision Making of the District Attorney: Diverting or Prosecuting Intrafamilial Child Sexual Abuse Offenders." *Criminal Justice Policy Review* 4:249–67.

Friedersdorf, C. 2014. "California Can't Police Its Own Cops Stealing Nude Photos of Women." *The Atlantic*, October 29. www.theatlantic.com.

Friedman, L. M. 1993. *Crime and Punishment in American History*. New York: Basic Books.

Friedrichs, D. O. 2010. *Trusted Criminals: White Collar Crime in Contemporary Society.* 4th ed. Belmont, CA: Cengage.

Frohmann, L. 1997. "Convictability and Discordant Locales: Reproducing Race, Class, and Gender Ideologies in Prosecutorial Decisionmaking." *Law & Society Review* 31:531–56.

Frosch, D., and K. Johnson. 2012. "Gunman Kills 12 in Colorado, Reviving Gun Law Debate." *New York Times*, July 20. www.nytimes.com.

Gabbidon, S., and G. Higgins. 2009. "The Role of Race/Ethnicity and Race Relations on Public Opinion Related to the Treatment of Blacks by the Police." *Police Quarterly* 12:102–15.

Gabbidon, S., G. Higgins, and H. Potter. 2011. "Race, Gender, and the Perception of Recently Experiencing Unfair Treatment by the Police: Exploratory Results from an All-Black Sample." *Criminal Justice Review* 36:5–21.

Gaines, D., and W. Wells. 2016. "Investigators' and Prosecutors' Perceptions of Collaborating with Victim Advocates on Sexual Assault Casework." *Criminal Justice Policy Review* (forthcoming 2016).

Galanek, J. 2013. "The Cultural Construction of Mental Illness in Prison: A Perfect Storm of Pathology." *Culture, Medicine, and Psychiatry* 37:195–225.

Garcia, M. 2005. "N.Y. Using Terrorism Law to Prosecute Street Gang." *Washington Post*, February 1, p. A3.

Garner, J. H., C. D. Maxwell, and C. G. Heraux. 2002. "Characteristics Associated with the Prevalence and Severity of Force Used by the Police." *Justice Quarterly* 19:705–46.

Gass, H. 2015. "Get Out of Jail Free: U.S. Cities Eye Bail Reform, Other Efforts to Help Poor." *Christian Science Monitor*, July 31. www.csmonitor.com.

Gau, J. 2016. "A Jury of Whose Peers? The Impact of Selection Procedures on Racial Composition and the Prevalence of Majority-White Juries." *Journal of Criminal Justice* 39:75–87.

Gau. J., and R. Brunson. 2010. "Procedural Justice and Order Maintenance Policing: A Study of Inner-City Young Men's Perceptions of Police Legitimacy." *Justice Quarterly* 27: 255–79.

Gearty, R., and C. Siemaszko. 2013. "Stop-and-Frisk Trial: Cop's Secret Tape Reveals Boss Ordered Him to Target Black Males Ages 14 to 21." *New York Daily News*, March 21. www.nydailynews.com.

Gebo, E., N. Stracuzzi, and V. Hurst. 2006. "Juvenile Justice Reform and the Courtroom Workgroup: Issues of Perception and Workload." *Journal of Criminal Justice* 34:425–33.

Gelman, A., J. Fagan, and A. Kiss. 2007. "An Analysis of the New York City Police Department's 'Stop-and-Frisk' Policy in the Context of Claims of Racial Bias." *Journal of the American Statistical Society* 102:813–23.

Genter, S., G. Hooks, and C. Mosher. 2013. "Prisons, Jobs, and Privatization: The Impact of Prisons on Employment Growth in Rural U.S. Counties, 1997–2004." *Social Science Research* 42:596–610.

Georgiady, B. N. 2008. "An Exceedingly Painful Encounter: The Reasonableness of Pain and De Minimis Injuries for Fourth Amendment Excessive Force Claims." *Syracuse Law Review* 59:123–64.

Gershon, R. R. M., B. Barocas, A. N. Canton, X. Li, and D. Vlahov. 2009. Health Outcomes Associated with Perceived Work Stress in Police Officers. *Journal of Criminal Justice and Behavior* 36:275–89.

Gerstein, C. 2013. "Plea Bargaining and the Right to Counsel at Bail Hearings." *Michigan Law Review* 111:1513–34.

Gest, T. 2013. "Juvenile Justice Programs Face Sharp New Cuts in Federal $$." *Crime Report*, July 12. www .thecrimereport.org.

Geyh, C. 2012. "Can the Rule of Law Survive Judicial Politics?" *Cornell Law Review* 97:191–253.

Gezari, V. M. 2008. "Cracking Open." *Washington Post*, June 1. http://www .washingtonpost.com.

Giaritelli, A. 2016. "$1.35B of Counterfeit Goods Seized in 2015." *Washington Examiner*, April 15. www .washingtonexaminer.com.

Giblin, M. J., G. W. Burruss, and J. A. Schafer. 2014. "A Stone's Throw from the Metropolis: Re-Examining Small-Agency Homeland Security Practices." *Justice Quarterly* 31:368–93.

Gill, J., and M. Pasquale-Styles. 2009. "Firearm Deaths by Law Enforcement." *Journal of Forensic Sciences* 54:185–88.

Girshick, L. B. 1999. *No Safe Haven: Stories of Women in Prison*. Boston: Northeastern University Press.

Gladstone, R. 2016. "Research Doesn't Back a Link between Migrants and Crime in the U.S." *New York Times*, January 13. www.nytimes.com.

Glaun, D. 2016. "Supreme Judicial Court to Hear Case of Michelle Carter, Teenager Accused of Encouraging Boyfriend to Kill Himself." *Mass Live*, February 3. http://masslive.com.

Glaze, L. 2011. "Correctional Population in the United States, 2010." Bureau of Justice Statistics *Bulletin*, December. NCJ236319.

Glaze, L., and E. J. Herberman. 2013. "Correctional Populations in the United States, 2012." *Bureau of Justice Statistics Bulletin*, December. NCJ 243936.

Glaze, L. E., and T. P. Bonczar. 2009. "Probation and Parole in the United States, 2007 Statistical Tables." *Bureau of Justice Statistics Bulletin*, August. NCJ 224707.

———. 2010. "Probation and Parole in the United States, 2009." Bureau of Justice Statistics *Bulletin*, December. NCJ 231674.

Glaze, L. E., and L. M. Maruschak. 2008. Parents in Prison and Their Minor Children. Bureau of Justice Statistics *Special Report*. Washington, DC: U.S. Department of Justice.

Goldfarb, R. L. 1965. *Ransom: A Critique of the American Bail System.* New York: Harper & Row.

Goldkamp, J. S., and E. R. Vilcica. 2008. "Targeted Enforcement and Adverse System Side Effects: The Generation of Fugitives in Philadelphia." *Criminology* 46:371–409.

———. 1990. *Problem-Oriented Policing.* New York: McGraw-Hill.

Goldman, R. 2013. "Gang Leader Impregnates Four Female Prison Guards." ABC News online, April 24. http://abcnews.go.com.

Goldman, S., E. Slotnick, and S. Schiavoni. 2013. "Obama's First Term Judiciary." *Judicature* 97: 7–47.

Goldschmidt, D., and C. E. Shoichet. 2013. "Former Guards Accused of Smuggling Cell Phones into Texas Prison." CNN.com, February 28. http://www.cnn.com.

Goldstein, J. 2013. "Judge Tells Ex-Chief of Police Not to Turn Testimony into a Speech." *New York Times*, April 9. http://www.nytimes.com.

Goldstein, S. 2014. "Both Sides of the Michael Dunn Trial Speak Out against Jury's Ruling." *New York Daily News*, February 17. www.nydailynews.com.

Goode, E. 2012. "Stronger Hand for Judges in the 'Bazaar' of Plea Deals." *New York Times*, March 22. www.nytimes.com.

Goodman, J. 1994. *Stories of Scottsboro.* New York: Random House.

———. 2015. "Officer in James Blake Arrest Used Excessive Force, Panel Says." *New York Times*, October 7. www.nytimes.com.

———. 2015b. "Police Leaders' Competing Claims Draw Focus to How New York Counts Crime." *New York Times*, December 30. www.nytimes.com.

———. 2016. "New York City Is Set to Adopt New Approach on Policing Minor Offenses." *New York Times*, January 20. www.nytimes.com.

Goodman, J. D. 2013. "Report Documents a Rise in Fatal Shootings by New York City's Police Officers." *New York Times*, November 19. www.nytimes.com.

Gordon, J. 2005. "In Patriots' Cradle, the Patriot Act Faces Scrutiny." *New York Times*, April 24. http://www.nytimes.com.

Gordon, J. A., B. Proulx, and P. H. Grant. 2013. "Trepidation among the "Keepers": Gendered Perceptions of Fear and Risk of Victimization among Corrections Officers." *American Journal of Criminal Justice* 38:245–65.

Gordon, S. 2013. "Through the Eyes of Jurors: The Use of Schemas in the Application of 'Plain Language' Jury Instructions." *Hastings Law Journal* 64:643–67.

Gover, A. R., J. M. MacDonald, and G. P. Alpert. 2003. "Combating Domestic Violence: Findings from an Evaluation of a Local Domestic Violence Court." *Criminology & Public Policy* 3: 109–31.

Governing Magazine Special Report, 2015. "Diversity on the Force: Where Police Don't Mirror Communities." *Governing* magazine, September. www.governing.com.

Governor's Office on Drug Control Policy. 2006. *Iowa's Drug Control Strategy, 2006.* http://www.iowa.gov/odcp/images/pdf/Strategy_06.pdf.

Grady, D. 2003. "F.D.A. Outlines Plans to Counter Growing Trade in Counterfeit Pharmaceuticals." *New York Times*, October 3. http://www.nytimes.com.

Grasha, K. 2009a. "Going Paperless." *Lansing (MI) State Journal*, February 9, pp. 1A, 4A.

———. 2009b. "Ingham Co. Jail Inmates May Opt for House Arrest." *Lansing (MI) State Journal*, March 11, p. 1A–2A.

Grattet, R., J. Lin, and J. Petersilia. 2011. "Supervision Regimes, Risk, and Official Reactions to Parolees Deviance." *Criminology* 49:371–400.

Gray, D. 2013. "A Spectacular Non Sequitur: The Supreme Court's Contemporary Fourth Amendment Exclusionary Rule Jurisprudence." *American Criminal Law Review* 50:1–57.

Green, A. 2009. "More States Use GPS to Track Abusers." *New York Times*, May 9. http://www.nytimes.com.

Green, F. 2011. "System Allows Federal Prisoners to Send E-Mail." *Richmond Times-Dispatch*, September 6. www2.timesdispatch.com.

Green, R. 2011. "State Puts Gingerich in Facility for Youths." *Ft. Wayne Journal Gazette*, January 15. www.journalgazette.com.

Greenberg, A. 2010. "Full-Body Scan Technology Deployed in Street-Roving Vans." *Forbes*, August 24. www.forbes.com.

Greene, J. A. 1999. "Zero Tolerance: A Case Study of Police Policies and Practices in New York City." *Crime and Delinquency* 45 (April):171–87.

Greene, J. R. 2014. "New Directions in Policing: Balancing Prediction and Meaning in Police Research." *Justice Quarterly* 31:193–228.

Greenwood, T., and H. Fournier. 2015. "Police: Parolee Arrested after 1 Adult, 2 Kids Stabbed." *Detroit News*, March 11. www.detroitnews.com.

Greer, K. R. 2000. "The Changing Nature of Interpersonal Relationships in a Women's Prison." *Prison Journal* 80 (December):442–68.

Griffin, K. 2009. "Criminal Lying, Prosecutorial Power, and Social Meaning." *California Law Review* 97:1515–68.

Griffin, L. 2010. "Untangling Double Jeopardy in Mixed Verdict Cases. *Southern Methodist University Law Review* 63:1033–68.

Griffin, M. L., and J. R. Hepburn. 2013. "Inmate Misconduct and the Institutional Capacity for Control." *Criminal Justice and Behavior* 40:270–88.

Griffin, P. 2011. "National Overviews." State Juvenile Justice Profiles. Pittsburgh: National Center for Juvenile Justice. http://www.ncjj.org/stateprofiles.

Grissom, B. 2011. "Proposals Could Make It Harder to Leave Prison." *New York Times*, March 12. www.nytimes.com.

Gross, J. 2013. "Rationing Justice: The Underfunding of Assigned Counsel Systems." Gideon *at 50, Part 1: A Three-Part Examination of Criminal Defense in America.* Washington, DC: National Association of Criminal Defense Lawyers, pp. 7–32.

Gross-Shader, C. 2011. "Partnerships in Evidence-Based Policing." *Translational Criminology* (Summer) 8–9.

Grubman, S. 2011. "Bark with No Bite: How the Inevitable Discovery Rule Is Undermining the Supreme Court's Decision in *Arizona v. Gant.*" *Journal of Criminal Law and Criminology* 101:119–70.

Guajardo, S. 2015. "New York City Police Department Downsizing and Its Impact on Female Officer Employment." *Journal of Ethnicity in Criminal Justice* 13:255–82.

Guerino, P., and A. J. Beck. 2011. *Sexual Victimization Reported by Adult Correctional Authorities, 2007–2008.* Bureau of Justice Statistics *Special Report.* Washington, DC: U.S. Department of Justice.

Guerino, P., P. M. Harrison, and W. J. Sabol. 2011. "Prisoners in 2010." Bureau of Justice Statistics *Bulletin*, December. NCJ 236096.

Guevara, L., D. Herz, and C. Spohn. 2006. "Gender and Juvenile Justice Decision-Making: What Role Does Race Play?" *Feminist Criminology* 1(4):258–82.

Gunnell, J. J., and S. J. Ceci. 2010. "When Emotionality Trumps Reason: A Study of Individual Processing Style and Juror Bias." *Behavioral Sciences and the Law* 28:850–77.

Haarr, R. N., and M. Morash. 1999. "Gender, Race and Strategies of Coping with Occupational Stress in Policing." *Justice Quarterly* 16:303–36.

Haba, C. W., R. A. Sarver III, R. R. Dobbs, and M. B. Sarver. 2009. "Attitudes of College Students towards Women in Policing." *Women & Criminal Justice* 19: 235–250.

Haberman, C. 2014. "When Youth Violence Spurred 'Superpredator' Fear." *New York Times*, April 6.

Habes, H. 2011. "Paying for the Graying: How California Can More Effectively Manage Its Growing Elderly Inmate Population." *Southern California Interdisciplinary Law Journal* 20:395–424.

Hackett, D. P., and J. M. Violanti, eds. 2003. *Police Suicide: Tactics for Prevention.* Springfield, IL: Thomas.

Hagan, F. E. 1997. *Political Crime: Ideology and Criminality.* Needham Heights, MA: Allyn & Bacon.

Hails, J., and R. Borum. 2003. "Police Training and Specialized Approaches to Respond to People with Mental Illness." *Crime and Delinquency* 49:52–61.

Hall, J. 1947. *General Principles of Criminal Law.* 2nd ed. Indianapolis: Bobbs-Merrill.

Hall, M., and C. Bonneau. 2013. "Attack Advertising, the *White* Decision, and Voter Participation in State Supreme Court Elections." *Political Research Quarterly* 66:115–26.

Hallinan, J. T. 2001. *Going Up the River: Travels in a Prison Nation.* New York: Random House.

Hambling, D. 2005. "Police Toy with 'Less Lethal' Weapons." *New Scientist*, April 30. http://www.newscientist.com.

Hamilton, Z. 2010. Do Reentry Courts Reduce Recidivism? Results from the Harlem Parole Reentry Court. New York: Center for Court Innovation. http://www.courtinnovation.org.

Hand, J. 2015. "KP Student Charged with Manslaughter in Fairhaven Friend's Death: Authorities Say She Encouraged Him to Commit Suicide. *Sun Chronicle*, February 27. http://thesunchronicle.com.

Hanlon, M. 2007. "Run Away the Ray-Gun Is Coming: We Test U.S. Army's New Secret Weapon." *Daily Mail*, September 18. http://www.dailymail.co.uk.

Hanna, L. "3 Connecticut High School Students Charged Following Sexting Scandal that Involved 50 Teens," *New York Daily News*, January 29. www.nydailynews.com.

Hannaford-Agor, P. 2011. "Systematic Negligence in Jury Operations: Why the Definition of Systematic Exclusion in Fair Cross Section Claims Must Be Expanded." *Drake Law Review* 59:762–98.

Hans, V., and N. Vidmar. 2008. "The Verdict on Juries." *Judicature* 91:226–30.

Hanson, R. A., and J. Chapper. 1991. *Indigent Defense Systems.* Williamsburg, VA: National Center for State Courts.

Harcourt, B. E., and J. Ludwig. 2006. "Broken Windows: New Evidence from New York City and a Five-City Social Experiment." *University of Chicago Law Review* 73:271–320.

Harkin, T. 2005. "Confronting the Meth Crisis." Press release, February 7. http://www.harkin.senate.gov.

Harlow, C. 2000. "Defense Counsel in Criminal Cases." Bureau of Justice Statistics *Bulletin*, November.

Harrell, E., and L. Langton. 2013. "Victims of Identity Theft, 2012." *Bureau of Justice Statistics Bulletin,* December. NCJ 243779.

Harrell, E., L. Langton, M. Berzofsky, L. Couzens, and H. Smiley-McDonald. 2014. Household Poverty and Nonfatal Violent Victimization, 2008–12. *Bureau of Justice Statistics Bulletin.* NCJ248384.

Harris, D. 2013. "Across the Hudson: Taking the Stop and Frisk Debate beyond New York City." *NYU Journal of Legislation and Public Policy* 16:853–82.

Harris, G. 2014. "Medicines Made in India Set Off Safety Worries." *New York Times*, February 14. www.nytimes.com.

Harris, J., and P. Jesilow. 2000. "It's Not the Old Ball Game: Three Strikes and the Courtroom Workgroup." *Justice Quarterly* 17:185–204.

Harris Poll. 2009. "Who Are You? *CSI* Answers that Question Each Week and Is America's Favorite TV Show." *Harris Interactive*, April 21. http://www.harrisinteractive.com.

Harris, R. 2011. "Shootings by Police Continue to Decline." *New York Times*, November 22. www.nytimes.com.

Harrison, C. 2011. "Ten Rules for Great Jury Selection: With Some Lessons from Texas Case Law." *Defense Counsel Journal* 78:29–54.

Harrison, M. T. 2006. "True Grit: An Innovative Program for Elderly Inmates." *Corrections Today* 68(7):46–49.

Hartley, R., S. Maddan, and C. Spohn. 2007. "Prosecutorial Discretion: An Examination of Substantial Assistance Departures in Federal Crack Cocaine and Powder Cocaine Cases." *Justice Quarterly* 24:382–407.

Hassell, K. D., and S. G. Brandl. 2009. "An Examination of the Workplace Experiences of Police Patrol Officers: The Role of Race, Sex, and Sexual Orientation." *Police Quarterly* 12:408–30.

Hastie, R., S. Penrod, and N. Pennington. 1983. *Inside the Jury.* Cambridge, MA: Harvard University Press.

Hayden, J. 2011. "Stretching Police Dollars—How Badly Are Budget Cuts Putting Citizens' Safety in Jeopardy?" *Holland* (MI) *Sentinel*, November 13. www.hollandsentinel.com.

Hayes, M., and M. Giblin. 2014. "Homeland Security Risk and Preparedness in Police Agencies: The Insignificance of Actual Risk Factors." *Police Quarterly* 17: 30–53.

Hays, T. 2006. "NYC Real Time Crime Center Tracks Suspects." *Washington Post*, May 10. http://www.washingtonpost.com.

Healy, J. 2014. "Colorado Expects to Reap Tax Bonanza from Legal Marijuana Sales." *New York Times*, February 20. http://www.nytimes.com.

Heaphy, W. 2010. "Wayne County's Mental Health Court." *Michigan Bar Journal* 89:36–38.

Heath, B., and K. McCoy. 2013. "Arrest Raises Questions on Rights of Terror Suspects." *USA Today*, April 21. www.usatoday.com.

Heffernan, E. 1972. *Making It in Prison.* New York: Wiley.

Heil, E. 2014. "Sen. Mark Udall's Son Charged with Trespassing, Heroin Possession." *Washington Post*, January 30. www.washingtonpost.com.

Heise, M. 2009. "Federal Criminal Appeals: A Brief Empirical Perspective." *Marquette Law Review* 93:825–43.

Henning, K. 2013. "Criminalizing Normal Adolescent Behavior in Communities of Color: The Role of Prosecutors in Juvenile Justice Reform." *Cornell Law Review* 98:383–461.

Henrichson, C., and R. Delaney. 2012. *The Price of Prisons: What Incarceration Costs Taxpayers.* New York: Vera Institute of Justice, 2012.

Hensley, J. J., and M. Wynn. 2009. "Close to Two-Thirds of Photos Taken by Speed Cameras Tossed." *Arizona Republic*, May 15. http://www.azcentral.com.

Herbert, S. 1996. "Morality in Law Enforcement: Chasing "Bad Guys" with the Los Angeles Police Department." *Law and Society Review* 30:799–818.

Hermann, P. 2014. "Air Force Major Charged in Child Pornography Case." *Washington Post*, January 31. www.washingtonpost.com.

"Hernandez Jurors See Police Video." 2015. ESPN News online, February 17. http://espn.go.com.

Hickman, M., and B. Reaves. 2006. *Local Police Departments, 2003* (NCJ210118). Washington, DC: U.S. Department of Justice, Bureau of Justice Statistics.

Hinduja, S., 2007. "Neutralization Theory and Online Software Piracy: An Empirical Analysis." *Ethics and Information Technology* 9 (3):187–204.

Hinduja, S., and J. W. Patchin. 2007. "Offline Consequences of Online Victimization: School Violence and Delinquency." *Journal of School Violence* 6(3):89–112.

Hirsch, A. J. 1992. *The Rise of the Penitentiary.* New Haven, CT: Yale University Press.

Hirsch, M. 2007. "Midnight Run Re-Run: Bail Bondsmen, Bounty Hunters, and the Uniform Criminal Extradition Act." *University of Miami Law Review* 62:59–94.

Hirschel, D., and I. Hutchinson. 2003. "The Voices of Domestic Violence Victims: Predictors of Victim Preference for Arrest and the Relationship between Preference for Arrest and

Revictimization." *Crime and Delinquency* 49:313–36.

Hirschkorn, P. 2011. "WH OKs Military Detention of Terrorism Suspects." CBS News.com, December 14. www .cbsnews.com.

Hockenberry, S. 2013. *Juveniles in Residential Placement, 2010* (NCJ 241060). Washington, DC: U.S. Department of Justice.

Hockenberry, S., and C. Puzzanchera. 2015. *Juvenile Court Statistics 2013*. Pittsburgh, PA: National Center for Juvenile Justice.

Hoctor, M. 1997. "Domestic Violence as a Crime against the State." *California Law Review* 85 (May):643–700.

Hoffman, M. 1999. "Abolish Peremptory Challenges." *Judicature* 82:202–4.

Holder, E. 2013. Speech at National Association of Counties Legislative Conference, March 4, Washington, DC. http://www.justice.gov.

Holleran, D., D. Beichner, and C. Spohn. 2010. "Examining Charging Agreement between Police and Prosecutors in Rape Cases." *Crime and Delinquency* 56:385–413.

Holt, T., and A. Bossler. 2012. "Predictors of Patrol Officer Interest in Cybercrime Training and Investigation in Selected United States Police Departments." *Cyberpsychology, Behavior, and Social Networking*. 15:464-72.

Holtfreter, K., and M. Morash. 2003. "The Needs of Women Offenders." *Women & Criminal Justice* 14, 137–60.

Holvast, N., and N. Doornbos. 2015. "Exit, Voice, and Loyalty within the Judiciary: Judges' Responses to New Managerialism in the Netherlands." *Utrecht Law Review* 11: 49–63.

Homan, C. 2010. "Michigan Lawmakers to Debate Bringing Good Time Back for Prisoners." *Holland Sentinel,* February 15. www.hollandsentinel.com.

Horne, P. 2006. "Policewomen: Their First Century and the New Era." *Police Chief*, 73 (9), September. policechiefmagazine .org.

Horwitz, S. 2013. "New FBI Director James B. Comey Stunned Impact of Sequestration on Agents in the Field." *Washington Post*, September 27. www .washingtonpost.com.

"How Did Counterfeit Auto Parts Become Such a Booming Business?" 2016. Thompson Reuters, February 3. www .thomsonreuters.com.

Howlett, D. 2004. "Chicago Plans Advanced Surveillance." *USA Today*, September 9. http://www.usatoday.com .http://www.albany.edu/sourcebook/.

Hsu, S. 2015. "FBI Admits Flaws in Hair Analysis over Decades." *Washington Post*, April 18. www.washingtonpost.com.

Hubert, C. 2010. "Placerville Shooting Fuels Debate about Use of Deadly Force

against Mentally Ill." *Sacramento Bee*, April 4. www.sacbee.com.

Hudson, J. 2012. "Contemporary Origins of Restorative Justice Programming: The Minnesota Restitution Center." *Federal Probation* (September):49–55.

Huebner, B. M., and R. Gustafson. 2007. "The Effect of Maternal Incarceration on Adult Offspring Involvement in the Criminal Justice System." *Journal of Criminal Justice* 35:283–96.

Huey, L. 2010. "'I've Seen This on *CSI*': Criminal Investigators Perceptions about the Management of Public Expectations in the Field." *Crime, Media, Culture* 6:49–68.

Huff, C. R. 2002. "Wrongful Conviction and Public Policy: The American Society of Criminology, 2001 Presidential Address." *Criminology* 40:1–18.

Huisman, W., and E. R. Kleemans. 2014. "The Challenges of Fighting Sex Trafficking in the Legalized Prostitution Market of the Netherlands." *Crime Law and Social Change* 61(2), 215–28.

Hulette, E. 2014. "DNA Testing Advances Help Beach Police Solve Rapes." *Virginian-Pilot*, September 29. http://pilotonline.com.

Human Rights Watch. 2014. *Branded for Life: Florida's Prosecution of Children as Adults under its "Direct File" Statute*. New York: Human Rights Watch.

Humes, K. R., N. A. Jones, and R. R. Ramirez. 2011. "Overview of Race and Hispanic Origin: 2010." *2010 Census Briefs* (March). Washington, DC: U.S. Census Bureau.

Hunt, K. 2010. "GOP Rips Holder on *Miranda* Rights." January 27. www .politico.com.

Hurdle, J. 2008. "Police Beating of Suspects Is Taped by TV Station in Philadelphia." *New York Times*, May 8. www .nytimes.com.

Hutchinson, D. 2015. "There's Never Been a Better Time for Bail Reform." *Washington Post*, July 20. www .washingtonpost.com.

Indiana Department of Corrections. 2009. "Press Release: Plainfield Educational Facility Relocates to Indianapolis." December 16. http://www.in.gov/idoc/files /PREF_Relocation_Press_Release.pdf.

"Indiana's Answer to Prison Costs." 2011. *New York Times*, January 17. www .nytimes.com.

Ingold, J. 2011. "Prison Black Market a Steal: Correctional Officers Get Drawn into Contraband Smuggling." *Denver Post*, December 18. www.denverpost .com.

Ingraham, C. 2015. "The Justice Department Just Shut Down a Huge Asset Forfeiture Program." *Washington Post*, December 23. www.washingtonpost .com.

Innocence Project. 2016. "The Cases: DNA Exoneree Profiles." www .innocenceproject.org.

Internet Crime Complaint Center. 2015. *2014 IC3 Annual Report*. Washington, DC: Federal Bureau of Investigation.

Irwin, J. 1970. *The Felon*. Englewood Cliffs, NJ: Prentice-Hall.

———. 1980. *Prisons in Turmoil*. Boston: Little, Brown.

Irwin, J., and D. Cressey. 1962. "Thieves, Convicts, and the Inmate Culture." *Social Problems* 10:142–55.

Israelsen, R. G. 2013. "Applying the Fourth Amendment's National-Security Exception to Airport Security and the TSA." *Journal of Air Law and Commerce* 78:501–39.

Ith, I. 2001. "Taser Fails to Halt Man with Knife; Seattle Officer Kills 23-Year-Old." *Seattle Times*, November 28, p. A1.

Jacob, H. 1973. *Urban Justice*. Boston: Little, Brown.

Jacobs, C., and C. Smith. 2011. "The Influence of Justice John Paul Stevens: Opinion Assignments by the Senior Associate Justice." *Santa Clara Law Review* 51: 743–74.

Jacobs, S., and J. Annese. 2016. "Bikini Model, 26, Accused of Being Part of $2M Identity Theft Ring." *New York Daily News*, April 6. www .nydailynews.com.

Jaksic, V. 2007. "Public Defenders, Prosecutors Face Crisis in Funding." *National Law Journal*, March 27. http://www .law.com.

Jalbert, S. K., and W. Rhodes. 2012. "Reduced Caseloads Improve Probation Outcomes." *Journal of Crime and Justice* 35:221–38.

"January Trial Set for Man Accused of SPU Shooting Rampage." 2015. *Seattle Times*, June 17. www.seattletimes.com.

Joh, E. 2015. "The Myth of Arrestee DNA Expungement." *University of Pennsylvania Law Review Online* 164:51–60. www.pennlawreview.com.

Johansen, L. 2015. "Guilty but Mentally Ill: The Ethical Dilemma of Mental Illness as a Tool of the Prosecution." *Alaska Law Review* 32:1–29.

Johnson, A. 2011. "Sentencing Overhaul Would Save State $78 Million." *Columbus Dispatch*, May 5. www .dispatchpolitics.com.

Johnson, B. D. 2006. "The Multilevel Context of Criminal Sentencing: Integrating Judge- and County-Level Influences." *Criminology* 44:259–98.

———. 2011. "Some States Rethink Felony Property Crimes." *USA Today*, October 30. www.usatoday.com.

Johnson, C. 2013. "Some Public Defenders Warn: 'We Have Nothing Left to Cut.'" National Public Radio, April 10. www .npr.org.

Johnson, K. 2010. "How Racial Profiling in America Became the Law of the Land." *Georgetown Law Journal* 98:1005–77.

Johnson, K. 2015. "Big Problems for Small Police Departments." *USA Today*, June 24. www.usatoday.com.

Johnson, K., and R. Chebium. 2013. "Justice Dept. Won't Challenge State Marijuana Laws." *USA Today*, August 29. http://www.usatoday.com.

Johnson, K., L. Lanza-Kaduce, and J. Woolard. 2011. "Disregarding Graduated Treatment: Why Transfer Aggravates Recidivism." *Crime & Delinquency* 57:756–77.

Johnson, M. A. 2010. "Already under Fire, Crime Labs Cut to the Bone." MSNBC.com, February 23. www.msnbc.com.

Johnson, M., and L. A. Johnson. 2012. "Bail: Reforming Policies to Address Overcrowded Jails, the Impact of Race on Detention, and Community Revival in Harris County, Texas." *Northwestern Journal of Law and Social Policy* 7:42–87.

Jones, J. 2013. "U.S. Death Penalty Support Lowest in More than 40 Years." Gallup Poll, October 29. www.gallup.com.

Jordan, J. 2002. "Will Any Woman Do? Police, Gender and Rape Victims." *Policing* 25:319–44.

Jordan, W. T., L. Fridell, D. Faggiani, and B. Kubu. 2009. "Attracting Females and Racial/Ethnic Minorities to Law Enforcement." *Journal of Criminal Justice*, 37:333–41.

Justice Policy Institute. 2010. "How to Safely Reduce Prison Populations and Support People Returning to Their Communities." Press release, June. http://www.justicepolicy.org/images/upload/10-06_fac_forimmediaterelease_ps-ac.pdf.

Kaeble, D., L. Glaze, A. Tsoutis, and T. Minton. 2015. "Correctional Populations in the United States, 2014." *Bureau of Justice Statistics Bulletin*, December. NCJ249513.

Kaeble, D., L. Maruschak, and T. Bonczar, "Probation and Parole in the United States, 2014," *Bureau of Justice Statistics Bulletin*, November 2015. NCJ 249057.

Kainen, J. L. 2013. "Shields, Swords, and Fulfilling the Exclusionary Rule's Deterrent Function." *American Criminal Law Review* 50:59–108.

Kaiser, K., and K. Holtfreter. 2016. "An Integrated Theory of Specialized Court Programs." *Criminal Justice and Behavior* 43:45–62.

Kanaracus, C. 2012. "Audit: Police Wasted Millions on Software, Crime-Fighting Tech They Never Used." *Computer World*, August 1. www.computerworld.com.

Kang, M., and K. Stokes. 2014. "After 2 Deadly Shootings in a Week, Seattle Mayor Says, 'We Must Find a Solution.'" *KPLU News*, June 6. www.kplu.org.

"Kansas City Police Officer Convicted of Corruption." 2014. KSDK News, April 5. www.ksdk.com.

Karmen, A. 2001. *Crime Victims*. 4th ed. Belmont, CA: Wadsworth.

Karnow, C. E. A. 2008. "Setting Bail for Public Safety." *Berkeley Journal of Criminal Law* 13:1–30.

Karnowski, S. 2008. "City's I-35W Bridge Response Generally Praised." Associated Press, April 22. www.twincities.com.

Kaste, M. 2016. "California Cops Frustrated with 'Catch-and-Release' Crime-Fighting." National Public Radio, January 22. www.npr.org.

KATC-TV. 2010. "New Prison 'Good Time' Law Frees 463." KATC.com, October 27. www.katc.com.

Keller, B. 2014. "Americans on Probation." *New York Times*, January 26. www.nytimes.com.

Kelley, M. 2013. "GUILTY: Verdict Handed Down in Steubenville High School Rape Case." Business Insider, March 17. www.businessinsider.com.

Kelling, G., and C. Coles. 1996. *Fixing Broken Windows: Restoring and Reducing Crime in Our Communities*. New York: Free Press.

Kelling, G. L., and M. Moore. 1988. "The Evolving Strategy of Policing." In *Perspective on Policing, no. 13*. Washington, DC: National Institute of Justice.

Kelling, G. L., T. Pate, D. Dieckman, and C. E. Brown. 1974. *The Kansas City Preventive Patrol Experiments: A Summary Report*. Washington, DC: Police Foundation.

Kelly, H. 2012. "Police Embracing Tech That Predicts Crime." CNN.com, July 9. www.cnn.com.

Kelly, J., and B. Keefe. 2015. "911's Deadly Flaw: Lack of Location Data." *USA Today*, February 22. www.usatoday.com.

Kenney, D. J., and J. O. Finckenauer. 1995. *Organized Crime in America*. Belmont, CA: Wadsworth.

Kenny, K. 2009. "When Cultural Tradition and Criminal Law Collide: Prosecutorial Discretion in Cross-Cultural Cases." *Judicature* 92:216–19.

Kentucky Department of Corrections. 2014. *2014 Division of Corrections Training Program Catalog*. http://corrections.ky.gov.

Kerley, K. R., A. Hochstetler, and H. Copes. 2009. "Self-Control, Prison Victimization, and Prison Infractions." *Criminal Justice Review*, 34:553–68.

Kerlikowske, R. 2004. "The End of Community Policing: Remembering the Lessons Learned," *FBI Law Enforcement Bulletin* 73 (April): 6–11.

Keyes, S. 2015. "Colorado's Marijuana Tax Revenues Nearly Double Last Year's Figures." *Guardian*, September 21. www.theguardian.com.

Killman, C., and B. Hoberock. 2013. "Lawmakers Benefit from Private Prison Donations." *Tulsa World*, May 19. http://www.tulsaworld.com.

Kim, B., C. Spohn, and E. Hedberg. 2015. "Federal Sentencing as a Complex Collaborative Process: Judges, Prosecutors, Judge-Prosecutor Dyads, and Disparity in Sentencing." *Criminology* 53:597–623.

Kim, K., and M. Denver. 2011. *A Case Study on the Practices of Pretrial Services and Risk Assessment in Three Cities*. Washington, DC: District of Columbia Policy Institute.

Kimber, K. 2008. "Mental Health Courts—Idaho's Best Kept Secret." *Idaho Law Review* 45:249–81.

Kimberly, J. 2003. "House Passes Crime Lab Bill." *Houston Chronicle*, May 2. http://www.houstonchronicle.com.

King, N., F. Cheesman, and B. Ostrom. 2007. *Habeas Litigation in the U.S. District Courts: An Empirical Study of Habeas Corpus Cases Filed by State Prisoners under the Antiterrorism and Effective Death Penalty Act of 1996*. Williamsburg, VA: National Center for State Courts.

King, N., and J. Hoffmann. 2011. *Habeas for the 21st Century*. Chicago: University of Chicago Press.

King, N. J., and S. Sherry. 2008. "Habeas Corpus and Sentencing Reform: A Story of Unintended Consequences." *Duke Law Journal* 58:1–67.

King, W., W. Wells, C. Katz, E. Maguire, and J. Frank. 2013. *Opening the Black Box of NIBIN: A Descriptive Process and Outcome Evaluation of the Use of NIBIN and Its Effects on Criminal Investigations*. Report to the National Institute of Justice (October). www.ncjrs.gov.

Kingkade, T. 2015. "124 Colleges, 40 School Districts under Investigation for Handling of Sexual Assault." Huffington Post, July 24. www.huffingtonpost.com.

Kingsnorth, R., R. MacIntosh, and S. Sutherland. 2002. "Criminal Charge or Probation Violation? Prosecutorial Discretion and Implications for Research in Criminal Court Processing." *Criminology* 40:553–77.

Kinports, K. 2011. "The Supreme Court's Love-Hate Relationship with *Miranda*." *Journal of Criminal Law and Criminology* 101:375–440.

Kirby, S., A. Quinn, and S. Keay. 2010. "Intelligence-Led and Traditional Policing Approaches to Open Drug Markets—A Comparison of Offenders." *Drugs and Alcohol Today* 10:13–19.

Kish, R. J., and A. F. Lipton. 2013. "Do Private Prisons Really Offer Savings

Compared with Their Public Counterparts?" *Economic Affairs* 33:93–107.

Klahm, C., and R. Tillyer. 2010. "Understanding Police Use of Force: A Review of the Evidence." *Southwest Journal of Criminal Justice* 7:214–39.

Klain, E. 2012. "President Obama Signed the National Defense Authorization Act—Now What?" *Forbes*, January 2. www.forbes.com.

Kleck, G., B. Sever, S. Li, and M. Gertz. 2005. "The Missing Link in General Deterrence Research." *Criminology* 43 (3):623–59.

Klein, A. 2008. "D.C. Police to Carry Semi-automatic Rifles on Patrol." *Washington Post*, May 17, p. B1.

Kleymeyer, C. 2010. Division of Corrections Training 2010 Annual Report. Kentucky Department of Corrections.

Klingler, D. 2012. "On the Problems and Promise of Research on Legal Police Violence." *Homicide Studies* 16:78–96.

Kloepfer, C. 2012. "Prison Guards Now Equipped with Tasers." WLNS.com, March 2. www.wlns.com.

Klofas, J., and J. Yandrasits. 1989. "'Guilty but Mentally Ill' and the Jury Trial: A Case Study." *Criminal Law Bulletin* 24:423–43.

Knoll, C., and M. Sickmund. 2012. *Delinquency Cases in Juvenile Court, 2009* (NCJ 239081). Washington, DC: U.S. Department of Justice.

Kotch, S., and R. Mosteller. 2010. "The Racial Justice Act and the Long Struggle with Race and the Death Penalty in North Carolina." *North Carolina Law Review* 88:2031–128.

Kotlowitz, A. 1994. "Their Crimes Don't Make Them Adults." *New York Times Magazine*, February 13, p. 40.

Kovaleski, S. 2014. "U.S. Issues Marijuana Guidelines for Banks," *New York Times*. February 14. www.nytimes.com.

Kramer, G. P., and D. M. Koenig. 1990. "Do Jurors Understand Criminal Justice Instructions? Analyzing the Results of the Michigan Juror Comprehension Project." *University of Michigan Journal of Law Reform* 23:401–37.

Krautt, P. 2002. "Location, Location, Location: Interdistrict and Intercircuit Variation in Sentencing Outputs for Federal Drug-Trafficking Offenses." *Justice Quarterly* 19 (December):633–71.

Kravets, D. 2011. "Wi-Fi-Hacking Neighbor from Hell Sentenced to 18 Years in Prison." wired.com, July 12. http://www.wired.com/threatlevel/2011/07/hacking-neighbor-from-hell/.

Kris, D. 2011. "Law Enforcement as a Counterterrorism Tool." *Journal of National Security Law and Policy* 5:1–79.

Krischke, S. 2010. "Absent Accountability: How Prosecutorial Impunity Hinders the Fair Administration of Justice in America." *Journal of Law and Policy* 19:395–434.

Kruger, K. 2007. "Pregnancy and Policing: Are They Compatible? Pushing the Legal Limits on Behalf of Equal Employment Opportunities." *Wisconsin Women's Law Journal* 22:61–89.

Kruttschnitt, C. 2010. "The Paradox of Women's Imprisonment." *Daedelus*, 139(3):32–42.

Kruttschnitt, K. 2013. "Gender and Crime."*Annual Review of Sociology* 39(1):291–308.

KTKA-TV. 2011. "Shawnee Co. Looks to Cost Cuts with Early Retirement, Jury Pay Cuts." KTKA.com, February 10. www.ktka.com.

Kurlychek, M. 2010. "Transforming Attitudinal Change into Behavioral Change: The Missing link." *Criminology & Public Policy*. 9:119–26.

Kurlychek, M., and C. Kempinen. 2006. "Beyond Boot Camp: The Impact of Aftercare on Offender Re-Entry." *Criminology & Public Policy* 5:363–88.

Kuruvilla, C. 2014. "Juror Claims 'Race Was Never a Factor' over Deliberations in Michael Dunn's Shooting of Jordan Davis." *New York Daily News*, February 21. www.nydailynews.com.

Kyckelhahn, T. 2015. *Justice Expenditure and Employment Extracts, 2012–Preliminary*. U.S. Bureau of Justice Statistics, February 26. NCJ 248628. www.bjs.gov.

Kyckelhahn, T., and T. Cohen. 2008. *Felony Defendants in Large Urban Counties, 2004—Statistical Tables*. Washington, DC: Bureau of Justice Statistics.

Kyckelhahn T., and T. Martin, 2013. "Justice Expenditure and Employment Extracts, 2010—Preliminary." *Bureau of Justice Statistics Bulletin*, July. NCJ 242544. www.bjs.gov.

LaFraniere, S. 2009. "Facing Counterfeiting Crackdown, Beijing Vendors Fight Back." *New York Times*, March 2. http://www.nytimes.com.

LaFraniere, S., and A. Lehren. 2015. "The Disproportionate Risks of Driving while Black." *New York Times*, October 24. www.nytimes.com.

Lagos, M. 2015. "Cutbacks Still Felt Deeply in California's Civil Courts." KQED News, March 11. http://ww2.kqed.org/news/2015/03/12/court-budget-cuts-delay-justice.

Lambert, L. 2011. "States Seek to Escape Rising Prison Costs." Reuters News Service, May 20. www.reuters.com.

Langan, P., and D. Levin. 2002. "Recidivism of Released Prisoners Released in 1994. Bureau of Justice Statistics *Special Report*, June. NCJ 193427.

Langton, L. 2010. "Women in Law Enforcement, 1987–2008," *Bureau of Justice Statistics Crime Data Brief*. NCJ230521. www.bjs.gov.

Langton, L., and D. Farole. 2010. "State Public Defender Programs, 2007." Bureau of Justice Statistics *Special Report*, September. NCJ 228229.

Larson, A. 2015. "30 Calif. Bond Agents Arrests in 'Operation Bail Out.'" KSBW-Action News 8, September 1. www.ksbw.com.

Lattman, P. 2011. "Galleon Chief Sentenced to 11-Year Term in Insider Case." *New York Times*, October 13. www.nytimes.com.

Lave, T. R. 1998. "Equal before the Law." *Newsweek*, July 13, p. 14.

LaVigne, N., S. Bieler, L. Cramer, H. Ho, C. Kontonias, D. Mayer, D. McClure, L. Pacifici, E. Parks, B. Peterson, and J. Samuels. 2014. *Justice Reinvestment Initiative State Assessment Report*, January. Washington, DC.: Urban Institute and U.S. Bureau of Justice Assistance.

Lavoie, D. 2015. "Plainville Teen Charged in Boyfriend's Suicide Cites Free Speech." *CBS Boston*, September 9. http://boston.cbslocal.com.

Lawrence, A. 2009. *Cutting Corrections Costs: Earned Time Policies for State Prisoners*. Denver, CO: National Conference of State Legislatures.

Lazarus, D. 2010. "Customer Stuck with Counterfeit Money from Post Office." *Los Angeles Times*, May 25. www.latimes.com.

LeDuff, C. 2011. "Riding along with the Cops in Murdertown, U.S.A." *New York Times*, April 15. www.nytimes.com.

Lee, H., and M. Vaughn. 2010. "Organizational Factors that Contribute to Police Deadly Force Liability." *Journal of Criminal Justice* 38:193–206.

Lee, J. 2009. "Study Questions whether Cameras Cut Crime." *New York Times*, March 3. http://www.nytimes.com.

Lehti, M., and K. Aromaa. 2006. "Trafficking for Sexual Exploitation." *Crime and Justice* 34:133–227.

Leiber, M. J., and K. Y. Mack. 2003. "The Individual and Joint Effects of Race, Gender, and Family Status on Juvenile Decision-Making." *Journal of Research in Crime & Delinquency* 40(1):34–70.

Leland, J. 2014. "Drug-Selling Charges Dropped against Man Arrested in Hoffman Case." *New York Times*, August 28. www.nytimes.com.

Leo, R. A. 1996. "*Miranda*'s Revenge: Police Interrogation as a Confidence Game." *Law & Society Review* 30:259–88.

Leonard, J. 2002. "Dropping 'Nonlethal' Beanbags as Too Dangerous." *Los Angeles Times*, June 3, p. 1.

Levy, M. 2011. "The Mechanics of Federal Appeals: Uniformity and Case Management in Circuit Courts." *Duke Law Journal* 61:315–91.

Lewis, N. A., 2009. "Stimulus Plan Has $1 Billion to Hire More Local Police." *New York Times*, February 6. www.nytimes.com.

Lichtblau, E. 2008. "Senate Approves Bill to Broaden Wiretap Powers." *New York Times*, July 10. www.nytimes.com.

———. 2012. "Police Are Using Tracking as Routine Tool." *New York Times*, March 31. www.nytimes.com.

Lichtblau, E., and J. Risen. 2009. "Officials Say U.S. Wiretaps Exceeded Law." *New York Times*, April 16. http://www.nytimes.com.

Lim, C., and J. Snyder. 2015. "Is More Information Always Better? Party Cues and Candidate Quality in U.S. Judicial Elections." *Journal of Public Economics* 128:107–23.

Lineberger, K. 2011. "The United States–El Salvador Extradition Treaty: A Dated Obstacle in the Transnational War against Mara Salvatrucha (MS-13)." *Vanderbilt Journal of Transnational Law* 44:187–216.

Linke, L., and P. Ritchie. 2004. *Releasing Inmates from Prison: Profiles of State Practices.* Washington, DC: National Institute of Corrections.

Liptak, A. 2003. "County Says It's Too Poor to Defend the Poor." *New York Times*, April 15. http://www.nytimes.com.

———. 2008a. "Electrocution Is Banned in Last State to Rely on It." *New York Times*, February 9. http://www.nytimes.com.

———. 2008c. "U.S. Prison Population Dwarfs That of Other Nations." *New York Times*, April 23. www.nytimes.com.

———. 2009. "Supreme Court Steps Closer to Repeal of Evidence Ruling." *New York Times*, January 31. www.nytimes.com.

———. 2011. "Justices, 5–4, Tell California to Cut Prisoner Population." *New York Times*, May 23. www.nytimes.com.

———. 2012. "Justices' Ruling Expands Rights of Accused in Plea Bargains." *New York Times*, March 21. www.nytimes.com.

Listwan, S. J., M. Colvin, D. Hanley, and D. Flanner. 2010. "Victimization, Social Support, and Psychological Well-Being: A Study of Recently Released Prisoners." *Criminal Justice and Behavior* 37:1140–59.

Lithwick, D., and J. Turner. 2003. "A Guide to the Patriot Act, Part 4." *Slate*, September 11. http://www.slate.msn.com.

Livsey, S. 2012. *Juvenile Delinquency Probation Caseload, 2009.* Washington, DC: Office of Juvenile Justice and Delinquency Programs.

Loewy, A. 2011. "Rethinking Search and Seizure in a Post-9/11 World." *Mississippi Law Journal* 80:1507–21.

Logan, C. 1993. "Criminal Justice Performance Measures in Prisons." In *Performance Measures for the Criminal Justice System.* Washington, DC: Bureau of Justice Statistics, U.S. Government Printing Office, 19–60.

Lord, V., and P. Friday, 2003. "Choosing a Career in Police Work: A Comparative Study between Applicants for Employment with a Large Police Department and Public High School Students." *Police Practice and Research: An International Journal* 4:63–78.

Lord, V. B., and M. Sloop. 2010. "Suicide by Cop: Police Shooting as a Method of Self-Harming." *Journal of Criminal Justice* 38:889–95.

Lowenkamp, C. T., J. L. Johnson, A. M. Holsinger, S. W. VanBenschoten, and C. R. Robinson. 2012. "The Federal Post Conviction Risk Assessment (PCRA): A Construction and Validation Study." *Psychological Services.* http://www.apadivisions.org/division-18/publications/journals/index.aspx

Luginbuhl, J., and M. Burkhead. 1994. "Sources of Bias and Arbitrariness in the Capital Trial." *Journal of Social Issues* 7:103–12.

Lum, C., P. Crafton, R. Parson, D. Beech, T. Smarr, and M. Connors. 2015. "Discretion and Fairness in Airport Security Screening." *Security Journal* 28:353–73.

Lum, C., C. Koper, and C. Telep. 2011. "The Evidence-Based Policing Matrix." *Journal of Experimental Criminology* 7:3–26.

Lum, C., and D. Nagin. 2015. "Reinventing American Policing." *Crime Report*, June 24. www.thecrimereport.org.

Lum, C., C. Telep, C. Koper, and J. Grieco. 2012. "Receptivity to Research in Policing." *Justice Research and Policy* 14:61–95.

Lumb, R., and R. Breazeale. 2002. "Police Officer Attitudes and Community Policing Implementation: Developing Strategies for Durable Organizational Change." *Policing and Society: An International Journal of Research and Policy* 13:91–106.

Lundman, R., and R. Kaufman. 2003. "Driving while Black: Effects of Race, Ethnicity, and Gender on Citizen Self-Reports of Traffic Stops and Police Actions." *Criminology* 41:195–220.

Lunney, L. A. 2009. "Has the Fourth Amendment Gone to the Dogs?: Unreasonable Expansion of Canine Sniff Doctrine to Include Sniffs of the Home." *Oregon Law Review* 88:829–903.

Lynch, J. P., and L. A. Addington. 2009. *Understanding Crime Statistics: Revisiting the Divergence of the NCVS and UCR.* New York: Cambridge University Press.

Lynch, L. 2016. "National Reentry Week: An Essential Part of Our Mission." Huffington Post, March 21. www.huffingtonpost.com.

Lynem, J. N. 2002. "Guards Call for Higher Wages, More Training: Industry Faces Annual Staff Turnover Rate of up to 300%." *San Francisco Chronicle*, August 22, p. B3.

Maag, C. 2008. "Police Shooting of Mother and Infant Exposes a City's Racial Tension." *New York Times*, January 30. http://www.nytimes.com.

MacArthur Foundation. 2007b. "Creating Turning Points for Serious Adolescent Offenders: Research on Pathways to Desistance." MacArthur Foundation Research Network on Adolescent Development and Juvenile Justice, *Issue Brief 2.* http://www.aadj.org/content.

———. 2007c. "Less Guilty by Reason of Adolescence." MacArthur Foundation Research Network on Adolescent Development and Juvenile Justice, *Issue Brief 3.* http://www.aadj.org/content.

MacCormack, J. 2011. "Border Issues Not Confined to the Border." *San Antonio Express-News*, June 8. www.mysanantonio.com.

Madhani, A. 2016. "Family Mourns Chicago Police Shooting Victim as Questions Persist." *USA Today,* January 6. www.usatoday.com.

Magda, L., A. Canton, and R. Gershon. 2010. "Web-Based Weapons of Mass Destruction Training for Transit Police." *Journal of Public Transportation* 13:63–78.

Maguire, E., C. Uchida, and K. Hassell. 2012. "Problem-Oriented Policing in Colorado Springs: A Content Analysis of 753 Cases." *Crime and Delinquency* 61:71–95.

Maitland, A. S., and R. D. Sluder. 1998. "Victimization and Youthful Prison Inmates: An Empirical Analysis." *Prison Journal* 78:55–73.

Maki, A. 2012. "Crimes Lurk in Memphis Police Department Memos." *Memphis Commercial Appeal*, January 25. www.commercialappeal.com.

Males, M. 2015. *Realignment and Crime in 2014: California's Violent Crime in Decline.* Center on Juvenile and Criminal Justice (August). www.cjcj.org.

Malone, P. 2012. "Crime Labs Fear Budget Cuts." Fox 10 TV, January 12. www.fox10tv.com.

"Man Acquitted of Concealed Weapon Charge on 'Necessity' Defense." *San Francisco Examiner*, July 10. www.sfexaminer.com.

"Man Found Not Guilty in Father's Death." 2014. *Des Moines Register*, August 7. www.desmoinesresgister.com.

Mann, D. 2011. "Why the Willingham Case Matters." *Texas Observer*, September 8. www.texasobserver.org.

Mann, J. 2014. "Webster Groves Ballet Teacher Sentenced to 10 Years for Sex with Student." *St. Louis Post Dispatch*, July 7. www.stltoday.com.

Mannheimer, M. 2011. "Not the Crime but the Cover-Up: A Deterrence-Based Rationale for the Premeditation-Deliberation Formula." *Indiana Law Journal* 86:879–37.

Manning, A. 2012. "Local Officials Look to State to Pay Indigent-Defense Bills."

Columbus Dispatch, February 26. www.dispatch.com.

Marceau, J. F. 2008. "Un-Incorporating the Bill of Rights: The Tension between the Fourteenth Amendment and the Federalism Concerns of Modern Criminal Procedure Reforms." *Journal of Criminal Law and Criminology* 98:1231–302.

Marchocki, K. 2016. "Nashua, Manchester Narcotics Units Threatened by Cut in Funds." *Nashua* (NH) *Telegraph*, January 28. www.nashuatelegraph.com.

Marcos, C. 2015. "Bill Would Clarify 'Good Time Credit' for Prisoners." *The Hill*, March 5. http://thehill.com.

Mardar, N. 2010. Answering Jurors' Questions: Next Steps in Illinois." *Loyola University Chicago Law Journal* 41:727–52.

Marimow, A. E. 2013. "John Hinckley Case Attorneys Debate Plans for Unsupervised Visits." *Washington Post*, January 24. www.washingtonpost.com.

Marso, A. 2014. "Corrections Secretary: Funding Cuts Drive Recidivism." *Topeka Capital-Journal*, January 14. http://cjonline.com/news/2014-01-14/corrections-secretary-funding-cuts-drive-recidivism.

"Martial Arts Teacher Sentenced for Sex with Teen." 2014. CBS Baltimore News online, August 13. http://Baltimore.cbslocal.com.

Martin, B., and R. Grattet. 2015. *Alternatives to Incarceration in California*. Public Policy Institute of California. www.ppic.org.

Martin, L. 2011. "Debt to Society: Asset Poverty and Prisoner Reentry." *Review of Black Political Economy* 38:131–43.

Martindale, M. 2012. "Audit: Michigan's Prisoner Re-Entry Initiative Harms Public Safety, Fails to Track ExConvicts." *Detroit News*, February 8. www.detroitnews.com.

Martinez, M. 2013. "Stephen Baldwin Pleads Guilty to Tax Charge, Will Pay $300,000." CNN.com, March 30. http://www.cnn.com.

Martinez, M., and R. Young. 2015. "Protesters Disrupt Holiday Shopping Again on Chicago's Michigan Avenue." CNN.com, December 24. www.cnn.com.

Martinson, R. 1974. "What Works? Questions and Answers about Prison Reform." *Public Interest*, Spring, p. 25.

Mastrofski, S. D., M. D. Reisig, and J. D. McCluskey. 2002. "Police Disrespect toward the Public: An Encounter-Based Analysis." *Criminology* 40:519–52.

Maruschak, L., and T. Bonczar. 2013. "Probation and Parole in the United States, 2012." *Bureau of Justice Statistics Bulletin,* December. NCJ 243826.

Maruschak, L. M. 2009. "HIV in Prisons, 2007–2008." Bureau of Justice Statistics *Bulletin.* Washington, DC: U.S. Department of Justice.

———. 2012. "HIV in Prisons, 2001–2010." *Bureau of Justice Statistics Bulletin*, September. NCJ 238877.

Mascaro, L. 2011. "Patriot Act Provisions Extended Just in Time." *Los Angeles Times*, May 27. www.latimes.com.

Maschke, K. J. 1995. "Prosecutors as Crime Creators: The Case of Prenatal Drug Use." *Criminal Justice Review* 20:21–33.

Mauer, M. 2011. "Opposing View: Reduce Prison Populations." *USA Today*, May 24. www.usatoday.com.

Mauer, M., and M. Chesney-Lind, eds. 2002. *Invisible Punishment: The Collateral Consequences of Mass Imprisonment*. New York: New Press.

Maxson, C. 2011. *Street Gangs. In Crime and Public Policy*, eds. J. Q. Wilson and J. Petersilia. New York: Oxford University Press.

Maxwell, S. R. 1999. "Examining the Congruence between Predictors of ROR and Failures to Appear." *Journal of Criminal Justice* 27:127–41.

May, J. D., R. Duke, and S. Gueco. 2013. "Pretext Searches and Seizures: In Search of Solid Ground." *Alaska Law Review* 30:151–88.

Mayrack, B. 2008. "The Implications of *State ex rel. Thomas v. Schwarz* on Wisconsin Sentencing Policy after Truth-in-Sentencing II." *Wisconsin Law Review* 2008:181–223.

McAuliff, B., and T. Duckworth. 2010. "I Spy with My Little Eye: Jurors' Detection of Internal Validity Threats in Expert Evidence." *Law and Human Behavior* 34:489–500.

McCall, M. A., M. M. McCall, and C. E. Smith. 2008. "Criminal Justice and the U.S. Supreme Court 2007–2008 Term." *Southern University Law Review* 36:33–87.

McCall, M. M., M. A. McCall, and C. Smith. 2011. "Criminal Justice and the 2010–2011 United States Supreme Court Term." *South Texas Law Review* 53:307–43.

McCall, M. M., M. A. McCall, and C. Smith. 2013. "Criminal Justice and the 2011–2012 United States Supreme Court Term." *Florida Coastal Law Review* 14:239–84.

McCampbell, S. W. 2005. *Gender-Responsive Strategies for Women Offenders*. Washington, DC: National Institute of Corrections.

McCarthy, B. 2012. "Marlon Defillo Is Still Coordinating Police Details for Movie Sets." *New Orleans Times-Picayune*, February 6. www.nola.com.

McCartney, A. 2011. "Mel Gibson Pleads Guilty to Battery Charge of Ex-Girlfriend." *Chicago Sun Times*, March 12. www.suntimes.com.

McCormick, J. 2000. "Scene of the Crime." *Newsweek*, February 28, p. 60.

McCoy, C. 1993. *Politics and Plea Bargaining: Victims' Rights in California*. Philadelphia: University of Pennsylvania Press.

———. 2007. "Caleb Was Right: Pretrial Detention Mostly Determines Everything." *Berkeley Journal of Criminal Law* 12:135–48.

McDonald, B. 2014. "Cuts to Forensic Lab Evidence Analysis." NBC12 News, December 2. www.nbc12.com.

McFarlane, L. 2009. "Ending Prisoner Rape in Michigan." *Free Press*, July 21.

McGarrell, E., S. Chermak, A. Weiss, and J. Wilson. 2001. "Reducing Firearms Violence through Directed Patrol." *Criminology & Public Policy* 1:119–48.

McGarrell, E. F., N. Corsaro, C. Melde, N. K. Hipple, T. Bynum, and J. Cobbina. 2013. "Attempting to Reduce Firearms Violence through a Comprehensive Anti-Gang Initiative (CAGI): An Evaluation of Process and Impact." *Journal of Criminal Justice* 41(1): 33–43.

McGreevy, P., and C. Megerian. 2013. "California Lawmakers OK a Dozen Gun Control Measures." *Los Angeles Times,* May 29. www.latimes.com.

McKee, K. 2015. "Neighbors Say 'Not In My Neighborhood' to Amelia Island Halfway House." *Action News Jacksonville*, March 18. www.actionnewsjax.com.

McKee, T. A. 2007. "Judges as Umpires." *Hofstra Law Review* 35:1709–24.

McKelvey, B. 1977. *American Prisons*. Montclair, NJ: Patterson Smith.

McKinley, J., and J. C. McKinley. 2016. "Cuomo Proposes Higher-Education Initiative in New York Prisons." *New York Times*, January 10. www.nytimes.com.

McKinley, J. C. 2013. "Lauryn Hill Sentenced to 3 Months in Tax Case." *New York Times.* May 6. http://www.nytimes.com.

McLaughlin, E. C., and P. Brown. 2013. "Judge Sentences Cleveland Kidnapper Ariel Castro to Life, Plus 1,000 Years." CNN.com, August 1. www.cnn.com.

McLaughlin, M. 2014. "Seattle Pacific University Shooting Leaves at Least 1 Dead." Huffington Post, June 5. www.huffingtonpost.com.

McMahon, P. 2002. "311 Lightens Load for Swamped 911 Centers." *USA Today*, March 5. http://www.usatoday.com.

McNiff, E. 2015. "ABC News Investigation into Counterfeit Prescription Drug Operations in the U.S." ABC News, May 15. http://abcnews.go.com.

McNulty, T. L., and P. E. Bellair. 2003. "Explaining Racial and Ethnic Differences in Adolescent Violence: Structural Disadvantage, Family, Well-Being, and Social Capital." *Justice Quarterly* 20:1–31.

McVicker, S. 2005. "Officer Downloads Driver's Nude Photos Off Phone." *Houston Chronicle*, March 25. www.chron.com.

Meade, B., and B. Steiner. 2010. "The Total Effects of Boot Camps that House Juveniles: A Systematic Review of the Evidence." *Journal of Criminal Justice* 38:841–53.

Mears, B. 2008. "Nebraska Court Bans the Electric Chair." CNN, February 8. http://www.cnn.com.

Meier, R. F., and T. D. Miethe. 1993. "Understanding Theories of Criminal Victimization." In *Crime and Justice: A Review of Research*, ed. M. Tonry. Chicago: University of Chicago Press.

Michael, P. 2013. "Technology in the Courtroom." *Law Technology Today*, July 9. www.lawtechnologytoday.org.

Meisner, J. 2011. "What Happened to the Elite Officers Charged." *Chicago Tribune*, September 9. www.chicagotribune.com.

Melde, C. 2009. "Lifestyle, Rational Choice, and Adolescent Fear: A Test of a Risk-Assessment Framework." *Criminology* 47:781–812.

Melde, C., S. Gavassi, E. McGarrell, and T. Bynum. 2011. "On the Efficacy of Targeted Gang Interventions: Can We Identify Those Most at Risk?" *Youth Violence and Juvenile Justice* 9:279–94.

Melde, C., F.-A. Esbensen, and T. J. Taylor. 2009. "May Piece Be with You: A Typological Examination of the Fear and Victimization Hypothesis of Adolescent Weapon Carrying." *Justice Quarterly* 26:348–76.

Melendez, L. 2011. "BART's Citizen Review Board Questions SFPD Investigation." KGO-TV website, September 19. http://abclocal.go.com/kgo.

———. 2014. "SF Celebrates First Year of Vet Court." KGO-TV website, March 5. http://abclocal.go.com/kgo/story?section=news/local/san_francisco&id=9456255.

Menard, S. 2000. 'The Normality' of Repeat Victimization from Adolescence through Early Adulthood." *Justice Quarterly* 17:543–74.

Messner, S. F., S. Galea, K. J. Tardiff, and M. Tracy. 2007. "Policing, Drugs, and the Homicide Decline in New York City in the 1990s." *Criminology* 45:385–413.

Michigan Department of Corrections. 2015. "Detroit Reentry Center (DRC)." www.michigan.gov/corrections.

Mihm, S. 2006. "No Ordinary Counterfeit." *New York Times*, July 23. http://www.nytimes.com.

Milhizer, E. 2004. "Justification and Excuse: What They Were, What They Are, and What They Ought to Be." *St. Johns Law Review* 78:725–895.

Miller, M. 2009. "LPD Cars Receive $24K Upgrade." *Lansing* (MI) *State Journal*, May 14, p. 4B.

———. 2014. "Court Backs Firing of State Prison Guard Who Repeatedly Kicked Inmate." PennLive website, February 11. www.pennlive.com.

———. 2015. "Woman Who Shot at Shoplifters Vows to 'Never Help Anybody Again' after Conviction." *Chicago Tribune*, December 11. www.chicagotribune.com.

Miller, S. L., K. Zielaskowski, and E. A. Plant. 2012. "The Basis of Shooter Biases: Beyond Cultural Stereotypes." *Personality and Social Psychology Bulletin* 38:1358–66.

Miller, T. 2015. "Digital Border Searches after *Riley v. California*." *Washington Law Review* 90:1943–96.

Minnesota Department of Corrections. 2014. "Adult Facilities." Department of Corrections website. www.doc.state.mn.us.

Minton, T., 2013. "Jail Inmates at Midyear 2012—Statistical Tables." *Bureau of Justice Statistics Bulletin,* May. NCJ 241264.

Minton, T., and Z. Zeng. 2015. "Jail Inmates at Midyear 2014." *Bureau of Justice Statistics Bulletin,* May. NCJ 248629.

Miroff, N. 2008. "Detainee Program Strains Va. Jail." *Washington Post*, April 8, p. A01.

Misjak, L. 2013. "Police Interview Tossed in Child Death Case." *Lansing State Journal*, March 1, p. 3A.

Mongrain, S., and J. Roberts. 2009. "Plea Bargaining with Budgetary Constraints." *International Review of Law and Economics* 29:8–12.

Monkkonen, E. 1981 *Police in Urban America: 1869–1920*. Cambridge: Cambridge University Press.

Moore, M. 1992. "Problem-Solving and Community Policing." In *Modern Policing*, eds. M. Tonry and N. Morris. Chicago: University of Chicago Press, 99–158.

Moore, S. 2009. "Number of Life Terms Hits Record." *New York Times*, July 22. www.nytimes.com.

Moore, T. 2011. " 'East Coast Rapist' Caught, Officials Say after Man's DNA Linked to Spree of Sex Assaults." *New York Daily News*, March 5. www.dailynews.com.

Moran, R. 2002. *Executioner's Current: Thomas Edison, George Westinghouse, and the Invention of the Electric Chair.* New York: Knopf.

Morash, M., and R. Haarr. 2012. "Doing, Redoing, and Undoing Gender: Variation in Gender Identities of Women Working as Police Officers." *Feminist Criminology* 7:3–23.

Morash, M., J. K. Ford, J. P. White, and J. G. Boles. 2002. "Directing the Future of Community-Policing Initiatives." In *The Move to Community Policing: Making Change Happen*, eds. M. Morash and J. Ford. Thousand Oaks, CA: Sage, 277–88.

Morash, M., R. N. Haarr, and L. Rucker. 1994. "A Comparison of Programming for Women and Men in the U.S. Prisons in the 1980s." *Crime and Delinquency* 40 (April):197–221.

Morash, M., D. Kashy, S. Smith, and J. Cobbina. 2015. "The Effects of Probation or Parole Agent Relationship Style and Women Offenders' Criminogenic Needs on Offenders' Responses to Supervision Interactions." *Criminal Justice and Behavior* 42: 412–34.

Morgan, D. 2013. "Impressed by Fairfield Police Crisis Intervention Team." *Connecticut Post,* February 20. http://www.ctpost.com/opinion/article/Impressed-by-Fairfield-Police-Crisis-Intervention-4294457.php.

Moroney, N. 2014. *Juvenile Justice Monitoring Unit, 2013 Annual Report.* Baltimore, MD: Office of the Attorney General.

Morris, H. 2012. "Europe Cracks Down on Cybercrime." *New York Times*, March 29. www.nytimes.com.

Morris, N., and M. Tonry. 1990. *Between Prison and Probation: Intermediate Punishments in a Rational Sentencing System.* New York: Oxford University Press.

Morris, R. G., and J. L. Worrall. 2014. "Prison Architecture and Inmate Misconduct: A Multilevel Assessment." *Crime & Delinquency*, 60(7):1083–1109.

Moses, P. 2005. "Corruption? It Figures: NY Police Department's Crime Stats and the Art of Manipulation." *Village Voice*, March 29. http://www.villagevoice.com.

Mosher, C., T. Miethe, and D. Phillips. 2002. *The Mismeasure of Crime.* Thousand Oaks, CA: Sage.

———. 2011b. "Statement before Senate Committee on Homeland Security and Governmental Affairs." Washington, DC, September 13.

Moyer, J. 2016. "FBI Director Makes Personal, Passionate Plea on Apple–San Bernardino Controversy." *Washington Post*, February 22. www.washingtonpost.com.

Mullainathan, S. 2015. "Police Killings of Blacks: What the Data Says." *New York Times*, October 16. www.nytimes.com.

Mumola, C. 2005. "Suicide and Homicide in State Prisons and Local Jails." *Bureau of Justice Statistics Special Report,* August. NCJ 210036.

Murphy, P. V. 1992. "Organizing for Community Policing." In *Issues in Policing: New Perspectives*, ed. J. W. Bizzack. Lexington, KY: Autumn Press, 113–28.

Musgrave, S. 2013. "Boston Police Halt License Scanning Program." *Boston Globe*, December 14. www.boston.com.

Muskal, M., and M. Pearce. 2013. "Ariel Castro Commits Suicide, Hangs Himself with Bedsheet, Officials Say." *Los Angeles Times*, September 4. www.latimes.com.

Na, C., and D. Gottfredson. 2013. "Police Officers in Schools: Effects on School Crime and the Processing of Offending Behaviors." *Justice Quarterly* 30:619–50.

Na, C., and D. C. Gottfredson. 2011. "Police Officers in Schools: Effects on School Crime and the Processing of Offending Behaviors." *Justice Quarterly*, 1–32.

Nagin, D., and D. Weisburd. 2013. "Evidence and Public Policy: The Example of Evaluation Research in Policing." *Criminology & Public Policy* 12:651–79.

Nakamura, D. 2012. "Obama Signs Defense Bill, Pledges to Maintain Legal Rights of U.S. Citizens." *Washington Post*, December 31. www.washingtonpost.com.

Nakashima, E., and A. Marimow. 2013. "Judge: NSA's Collecting of Phone Records Is Probably Unconstitutional." *Washington Post*, December 16. www.washingtonpost.com.

Nalla, M. 2002. "Common Practices and Functions of Corporate Security: A Comparison of Chemical, Financial, Manufacturing, Service, and Utility Industries." *Journal of Security Administration* 25:33–46.

Nam, T., and T. Pardo. 2014. "The Changing Face of City Government: A Case Study of Philly 311." *Government Information Quarterly* (supplement 1). 31:S1–S9.

Narag, R., J. Pizarro, and C. Gibbs. 2009. "Lead Exposure and Its Implications for Criminological Theory." *Criminal Justice and Behavior* 39(9):954–73.

National Academy of Sciences. 2009. *Strengthening Forensic Sciences in the United States*. Washington, DC: National Academy of Sciences.

National Association of Women Judges. 2016. "2016 Representation of United States State Court Women Judges." http://www.nawj.org/us_state_court_statistics_2016.asp.

National Gang Center. 2016. "National Youth Gang Survey Analysis." http://www.nationalgangcenter.gov/Survey-Analysis.

National Guard Youth Foundation. 2016. "About Youth Challenge." www.ngyf.org.

National Public Radio (NPR). 2011. "Nation's Jails Struggle with Mentally Ill Prisoners." *All Things Considered* show website, September 4. www.npr.org.

Natoli, M. 2013. "Au Revoir, Voir Dire and Other Costly and Socioeconomically Unjust Judicial Practices." *New England Law Review* 47:605–29.

Nava, M. 2008. "The Servant of All: Humility, Humanity, and Judicial Diversity." *Golden Gate University Law Review* 38:175–94.

Nelson, A. J. 2014. "Judge Commits Teen to Psych Unit." *Omaha World-Herald*, December 9. www.omaha.com.

Nelson, S. 2013. "Marijuana Business Rules Debated in Colorado, Washington." *U.S. News and World Report*, March 22, 2013. www.usnews.com.

Nesper, L. 2015. "Ordering Legal Plurality: Allocating Jurisdiction in State and Tribal Courts in Wisconsin." *Political and Legal Anthropology Review* 38:30–52.

New York Police Department. 2016. "Frequently Asked Questions." NYPD website. www.nyc.gov.

New York State Division of Criminal Justice Services. 2008. *New York State Probation Population: 2007 Profile*. (June).

Newport, F. 2010. "In U.S., 64% Support Death Penalty in Cases of Murder. Gallup Poll, November 8. www.gallup.com.

———. 2012. "Americans Want Fed Gov't out of State Marijuana Laws." Gallup Poll, December 10. www.gallup.com.

Newton, J. 2016. "Police Team Up against Child Porn on the 'Dark Web.'" *Chicago Tribune*, January 18. www.chicagotribune.com.

Nicholson, K. 2015. "Hector Diaz Sentence Continued after Request to Go to Colombia Denied." *Denver Post*, May 29. www.denverpost.com.

Nir, S. 2011. "Indictment of 55 in Cybercrime Ring Expected Friday." *New York Times*, December 15. www.nytimes.com.

Noblet, A., J. Rodwell, and A. Allisey. 2009. "Job Stress in the Law Enforcement Sector: Comparing the Linear, Non-linear, and Interaction Effects of Working Conditions." *Stress and Health* 25:111–20.

Nolasco, C., R. delCarmen, and M. Vaughn. 2011. "What *Herring* Hath Wrought: An Analysis of Post-*Herring* Cases in the Federal Courts." *American Journal of Criminal Law* 38:221–61.

Norman, J. 2015. "In U.S., Women, Poor, Urbanites Most Fearful of Walking Alone." Gallup Poll, November 10. www.gallup.com.

Nowlin, J. W. 2012. "The Warren Court's House Built on Sand: From Security in Persons, Houses, Papers, and Effects to Mere Reasonableness in Fourth Amendment Doctrine." *Mississippi Law Journal* 81:1017–82.

O'Brien, B. 2009. "A Recipe for Bias: An Empirical Look at the Interplay between Institutional Incentives and Bounded Reality in Prosecutorial Decision Making." *Missouri Law Review* 74:999–1048.

O'Harrow, R. 2008. "Centers Tap into Personal Databases." *Washington Post*, April 2. www.washingtonpost.com.

O'Hear, M. 2014. "Good Conduct Time for Prisoners: Why (and How) Wisconsin Should Provide Credits toward Early Release." *Marquette Law Review* 98:487–553.

O'Hear, M. M. 2006. "The End of *Bordenkircher*: Extending the Logic of *Apprendi* to Plea Bargaining." *Washington University Law Review* 84:835–49.

O'Keefe, K. 2010. "Two Wrongs Make a Wrong: A Challenge to Plea Bargaining and Collateral Consequence Statutes through Their Integration." *Journal of Criminal Law and Criminology* 100:243–77.

O'Neal, E., K. Tellis, and C. Spohn. 2015. "Prosecuting Intimate Partner Sexual Assault: Legal and Extra-Legal Factors That Influence Charging Decisions." *Violence against Women* 21:1237–58.

Oberfield, Z. W. 2012. "Socialization and Self-Selection: How Police Develop Their Views about Using Force." *Administration and Society* 44:702–30.

Office of Juvenile Justice and Delinquency Prevention (OJJDP). 2012. *OJJDP Statistical Briefing Book*. http://www.ojjdp.gov/ojstatbb/structure_process/qa04101.asp?qaDate=2011.

"Officers Use Bean Bag Rounds to Subdue Suicidal Man after Assault." 2015. KWTX News, August 10. www.kwtx.com.

Ohio Department of Rehabilitation and Correction (2016). *Ohio Department of Rehabilitation and Correction Corrections Training Academy*. www.drc.ohio.gov/web/cta.htm

Oleniacz, L. 2014. "Durham Minor Misdemeanor Diversion Program Launches for 16, 17-Year-Olds." *Herald Sun,* April 4. http://www.heraldsun.com.

Oppel, R. A. 2011. "Private Prisons Found to Offer Little in Savings." *New York Times*, May 18. www.nytimes.com.

Oram, S., H. Stocki, J. Busza, L. M. Howard, and C. Zimmerman. 2013. "Prevalence and Risk of Violence and the Physical, Mental, and Sexual Health Problems Associated with Human Trafficking: Systematic Review. *PLoS Med* 9(5), online.

Osborne, J. 2011. "Union Faults Camden County Jail's Elevators." *Philadelphia Inquirer*, April 18. www.philly.com.

Ostermann, M. 2009. "An Analysis of New Jersey's Day Reporting Center and Halfway Back Program: Embracing the Rehabilitative Ideal through Evidence-Based Practices." *Journal of Offender Rehabilitation* 48:139–53.

"Our View: Don't Just Cut Prisoners Loose" [Editorial]. 2011. *USA Today*, May 24. www.usatoday.com.

Outlook Handbook online. www.bls.gov/ooh/protective-service/correctional-officers.htm.

Owen, B. 1998. *"In the Mix": Struggle and Survival in a Woman's Prison*. Albany: State University of New York Press.

Owen, B., J. Wells, J. Pollock, B. Muscat, and S. Torres. 2008. "Gendered Violence and Safety: A Contextual Approach to Improving Security in Women's Facilities" (Final Report). Unpublished.

Owens, S., E. Accetta, J. Charles, and S. Shoemaker. 2015. "Indigent Defense Services in the United States, FY 2008–2012, Updated." *Bureau of Justice Statistics Technical Report*, April 21. NCJ 246683.

Packer, H. L. 1968. *The Limits of the Criminal Sanction*. Stanford, CA: Stanford University Press.

Palmer, B. 2011. "Oklahoma's Female Inmate Population Skyrockets." *Oklahoman*, January 30. http://newsok.com.

Palmer, D. 2011. "China Piracy Cost U.S. Firms $48 Billion in 2009: Report." Reuters News Service, May 18. www.reuters.com.

Palmer, J. 2015. "Private Prisons Prove Costly to Oklahoma." *Oklahoma City Oklahoman*, October 8. www.oklahoman.com.

Paoline, Eugene A., III. 2003. "Taking Stock: Toward a Richer Understanding of Police Culture." *Journal of Criminal Justice*. 31:199–214.

Parascandola, R., and C. Lestch. 2013. "NYPD Sergeant First to Be Fired, Lose Pension in Massive Police Ticket-Fixing Scandal." *New York Daily News*, December 10. www.nydailynews.com.

Parent, D. 2003. *Correctional Boot Camps: Lessons from a Decade of Research*. Washington, DC: National Institute of Justice.

"Parolee Arrested Again on Drug Trafficking Charges." 2015. *Central Kentucky News*, March 25. www.centralkynews.com.

"Parolee Arrested for Attempted Murder of Acquaintance Made while in Prison." 2013. *Salt Lake Tribune*, March 13. www.sltrib.com.

Patchin, J. W., and S. Hinduja. 2012. *Cyberbullying Prevention and Response: Expert Perspectives*. New York: Routledge.

Paynter, B. 2011. "Prison Economics: How Fish and Coffee Became Cash." *Wired Magazine*, January 31. www.wired.com.

Pearson, M. 2015. "'Wish Me Luck': Chris Rock Posts Selfies of Police Stops." CNN.com, April 2. www.cnn.com.

Perlroth, N., and D. Gelles. 2014. "Russian Hackers Amass over a Billion Internet Passwords." *New York Times*, August 5. www.nytimes.com.

Peart, N. 2011. "Why Is the N.Y.P.D. after Me?" *New York Times*, December 17. www.nytimes.com.

Pennsylvania Department of Corrections. 2014. "About Us—Department of Corrections." Department of Corrections website. www.cor.state.pa.us.

Peralta, E. 2011. "In Report, ACLU Claims Chicago's Surveillance Cameras Violate Privacy." National Public Radio, February 8. www.npr.org.

Perez, D. M., A. R. Gover, K. M. Tennyson, and S. Santos. 2009. "Individual and Institutional Characteristics Related to Inmate Victimization." *International Journal of Offender Therapy and Comparative Criminology* 54:378–94.

Perin, M. 2009. "Hazswat Changed?: Combining Hazmat and SWAT Training for Tactical Operations." *Law Enforcement Technology* 36:20–25.

Perrine, J., V. Speirs, and J. Horwitz. 2010. "Fusion Centers and the Fourth Amendment." *Capital University Law Review* 38:721–87.

Petersilia, J. 1990. "When Probation Becomes More Dreaded Than Prison." *Federal Probation*, March, p. 24.

———. 2003. *When Prisoners Come Home: Parole and Prisoner Reentry*. New York: Oxford University Press.

———. 2009. *When Prisoners Come Home: Parole and Prisoner Reentry*. 2nd ed. New York: Oxford University Press.

Peterson, J. L., and M. J. Hickman. 2005. "Census of Publicly Funded Forensic Crime Laboratories, 2002." Bureau of Justice Statistics *Bulletin*, February, p. 1.

Peterson, M. 2005. *Intelligence-Led Policing: The Intelligence Architecture*. Washington, DC: U.S. Bureau of Justice Assistance.

Petteruti, A. 2011. *Education under Arrest: The Case against Police in Schools*. Washington, DC: Justice Policy Institute.

Petteruti, A., and N. Walsh. 2008. *Jailing Communities: The Impact of Jail Expansion and Effective Public Safety Strategies*. Washington, DC: Justice Policy Institute.

Pew Center on the States. 2007. "What Works in Community Corrections: An Interview with Dr. Joan Petersilia." *Public Safety Performance Project*, No. 2. November.

———. 2008. One in 100: Behind Bars in America 2008. Washington, DC: Pew Center on the States.

———. 2009. *One in 31: The Long Reach of American Corrections*. Washington, DC: Pew Charitable Trusts.

———. 2011. *State of Recidivism: The Revolving Door of America's Prisons*. Washington, DC: Pew Charitable Trusts

———. 2012. *Time Served: The High Cost, Low Return of Longer Prison Terms*, June. Washington, DC: Pew Center on the States.

Pew Charitable Trusts. 2012. Public Opinion on Sentencing and Corrections Policy in America (March). http://www.pewstates.org/research/analysis/public-opinion-on-sentencing-and-corrections-policy-in-america-85899380361.

———. 2013. *Managing Prison Health Care Spending*. Washington, DC: Pew Charitable Trusts. http://www.pewstates.org.

Phelps, M. S. 2011. "Rehabilitation in the Punitive Era: The Gap between Rhetoric and Reality in U.S. Prison Programs." *Law & Society Review* 45, 33–68.

Phillips, M. 2011. *Commercial Bail Bonds in New York City: Characteristics and Implications*. New York: New York City Criminal Justice Agency.

Phillips, S. 1977. *No Heroes, No Villains*. New York: Random House.

Piel, J. 2015. "The Defense of Involuntary Intoxication by Prescribed Medications: An Appellate Case Review." *Journal of the American Academy of Psychiatry and Law* 43:321–28.

Pinto, N. 2015. "The Bail Trap." *New York Times Magazine*, August 16. pp. 38–45.

Piquero, A. R., F. T. Cullen, J. D. Unnever, N. L. Piquero, and J. A. Gordon. 2010. "Never Too Late: Public Optimism about Juvenile Rehabilitation." *Punishment & Society* 12:187–207.

Pisciotta, A. W. 1994. *Benevolent Repression: Social Control and the American Reformatory-Prison Movement*. New York: New York University Press.

Place, T. 2013. "Closing Direct Appeal to Ineffectiveness Claims: The Supreme Court of Pennsylvania's Denial of State Constitutional Rights." *Widener Law Journal* 22:687–719.

Platt, A. 1977. *The Child Savers*. 2nd ed. Chicago: University of Chicago Press.

Pochna, P. 2002. "N.J. Police Linking with National Data Network." *Baltimore Sun*, April 2. http://articles.baltimoresun.com/2002-04-02/news/0204020041_1_jersey-state-police-bergen-county-computer-center.

Podgor, E. 2010. "The Tainted Federal Prosecutor in an Overcriminalized Justice System." *Washington and Lee Law Review* 67:1569–85.

Podlas, K. 2006. "The '*CSI* Effect' and Other Forensic Fictions." *Loyola of Los Angeles Entertainment Law Review* 27:87–125.

Police Executive Research Forum. 2016. "Use of Force: Taking Police to a Higher Standard," *Critical Issues in Policing Series*, January 29. http://www.policeforum.org/assets/30%20guiding%20principles.pdf.

"Police Use Bean-Bag Ammo to Subdue Downtown L.A. Bank Robbery Suspect." 2015. *Los Angeles Daily News*, October 26. www.dailynews.com.

Porter, R. 2011. *Choosing Performance Indicators for Your Community Prosecution Initiative*. Washington, DC: Association of Prosecuting Attorneys.

Porter, R., S. Lee, and M. Lutz. 2002. *Balancing Punishment and Treatment: Alternatives to Incarceration in New York City*. New York: Vera Institute of Justice.

Post, L. 2004. "ABA Wants to Transform Way Jurors Do Their Jobs." *New Jersey Law Journal,* August 16:1.

Poston, B. 2011. "Racial Gap Found in Traffic Stops in Milwaukee." *Milwaukee Journal Sentinel*, December 3. www.jsonline.com.

———. 2016. "L.A. Crime Hits Highest Level since 2009 Amid More Gang Violence and Homelessness." *Los Angeles Times*, January 13. www.latimes.com.

PR Newswire. 2001. "Ion Track Instruments Unveils New Technology to Aid in Fight against Terrorism and Drug Trafficking." March 22 (available on Lexis-Nexis).

Pransky, N. 2014. "Officers Bend Rules to Boost Sex Sting Arrest Totals." WTSP-TV. August 9. www.wtsp.com.

Pratt, J. 2011. "Are We Being Fair to Our Judges and the Perception of Justice in Alabama by Having Partisan Elections for Judicial Office?" *Alabama Lawyer* 72:443–44.

Pratt, T. 2015. "Former County Corrections Officer Pleads Guilty in Contraband Smuggling Operation." *Annapolis Capital Gazette,* December 15. www.capitalgazette.com.

Preston, J. 2005. "Rape Victims' Eyes Were Covered, but a Key Clue Survived." *New York Times*, April 28. http://www.nytimes.com.

Price, M. 2009. "Performing Discretion or Performing Discrimination: Race, Ritual, and Peremptory Challenges in Capital Jury Selection." *Michigan Journal of Race and Law* 15:57–107.

"Private Jails: Locking in the Best Price." 2007. *Economist*, January 25. http://www.economist.com/node/8599146.

Propper, A. 1982. "Make Believe Families and Homosexuality among Imprisoned Girls." *Criminology* 20:127–39.

Provine, D. M. 1996. "Courts in the Political Process in France." In *Courts, Law, and Politics in Comparative Perspective*, eds. H. Jacob, E. Blankenburg, H. Kritzer, D. M. Provine, and J. Sanders. New Haven, CT: Yale University Press, 177–248.

Prussel, D., and K. Lonsway. 2001. "Recruiting Women Police Officers." *Law and Order* 49 (July):91–96.

Public Opinion Strategies. 2010. *National Research of Public Attitudes on Crime and Punishment* (September). Washington, DC: Pew Center on the States.

Puzzanchera, C., B. Adams, and S. Hockenberry. 2012. *Juvenile Court Statistics, 2009*. Pittsburgh: National Center for Juvenile Justice.

Puzzanchera, C., and W. Kang. 2011. "Easy Access to the FBI's Supplementary Homicide Reports: 1980–2009." http://www.ojjdp.gov/ojstatbb/ezashr/.

Puzzanchera, C., and C. Robson. 2014. *Delinquency Cases in Juvenile Court, 2010* (NCJ 243041). Washington, DC: U.S. Department of Justice.

Puzzanchera, D., and S. Addie. 2014. *Delinquency Cases Waived to Criminal Court, 2010* (NCJ 243042). Washington, DC: U.S. Department of Justice.

Rabe-Hemp, C. 2008. "Female Officers and the Ethic of Care: Does Officer Gender Impact Police Behaviors?" *Journal of Criminal Justice* 36:426–34.

Radelet, M. L. 2004. "Post-*Furman* Botched Executions." http://www.deathpenaltyinfor.org/article.php?scid=8&did=478.

Rafter, N. H. 1983. "Prisons for Women, 1790–1980." In *Crime and Justice*, 5th ed., eds. M. Tonry and N. Morris. Chicago: University of Chicago Press.

Raganella, A. J., and M. D. White. 2004. "Race, Gender, and Motivation for Becoming a Police Officer: Implications for Building a Representative Police Department." *Journal of Criminal Justice* 32:501–13.

Rainville, G., and S. Smith. 2003. "Juvenile Felony Defendants in Criminal Courts." Bureau of Justice Statistics *Special Report*, May. NCJ 197961.

Ramos, N. (2014). "Maine Philanthropist Accused of Embezzling $3.8m." *Boston Globe*, November 16. www.bostonglobe.com.

Rand, M., and J. Robinson. 2011. "*Criminal Victimization in the United States, 2008—Statistical Tables*. Bureau of Justice Statistics (May). NCJ 231137.

Randolph, E. D. 2001. "Inland Police Like New Weaponry." *Riverside* (CA) *PressEnterprise,* November 24, p. B4.

Ratcliffe, J. 2010. "Crime Mapping: Spatial and Temporal Challenges." *Handbook of Quantitative Criminology* 1:5–24.

Ratcliffe, J., T. Taniguchi, E. Groff, and J. Wood. 2011. "The Philadelphia Foot Patrol Experiment: A Randomized Controlled Trial of Police Patrol Effectiveness in Violent Crime Hotspots." *Criminology* 49:795–831.

Rath, A. 2011. "Is the 'CSI Effect' Influencing Courtrooms?" National Public Radio, February 5. www.npr.org.

Ravitz, J. 2009. "Scanners Take 'Naked' Pics, Groups Says." CNN.com, May 18. www.cnn.com.

Reaves, B. 2006. "Violent Felons in Large Urban Counties." Bureau of Justice Statistics *Special Report*, July. NCJ 205289.

———. 2010. *Local Police Departments, 2007*. Washington, DC: U.S. Bureau of Justice Statistics.

———. 2011. "Census of State and Local Law Enforcement Agencies, 2008." Bureau of Justice Statistics *Bulletin*, July. NCJ233982.

———. 2012. "Federal Law Enforcement Officers, 2008." *Bureau of Justice Statistics*.

———. 2013. "Felony Defendants in Large Urban Counties, 2009—Statistical Tables." *Bureau of Justice Statistics Bulletin*, December. NCJ 243777.

———. 2015. "Local Police Departments, 2013: Equipment and Technology," *Bureau of Justice Statistics Bulletin*, July. NCJ 248767.

Reavy, P. 2015. "Police Use Robot to Remove Wired Vest from Bank Robbery Suspect." *Deseret News*, January 22. www.deseretnews.com.

Redlich, A., S. Liu, H. Steadman, L. Callahan, and P. Robbins. "Is Diversion Swift? Comparing Mental Health Court and Traditional Criminal Justice Processing." *Criminal Justice and Behavior* 39:420–33.

"Re-entry Services Center to Open on Macdonald Avenue." 2015. *Richmond Standard*, October 8. http://richmond-standard.com.

Regoli, R., J. Crank, and R. Culbertson. 1987. "Rejonder—Police Cynicism: Theory Development and Reconstruction." *Justice Quarterly* 4:281–86.

Reid, T. R. 2004. "Rape Case against Bryant Is Dropped." *Washington Post*, September 2. http://www.washingtonpost.com.

Reisenwitz, H. (2014). "Why It's Time to Legalize Prostitution." *Daily Beast*, August 15. www.thedailybeast.com.

Reisig, M. D. 2010. "Community and Problem-Oriented Policing." *Crime and Justice* 39:2–53.

Reiss, A. 1992. "Police Organization in the Twentieth Century." In *Crime and Justice: A Review of Research*, vol. 15., eds. M. Tonry and N. Morris. Chicago: University of Chicago Press, 51–97.

Reiter, K. A. 2012. "Parole, Snitch, or Die: California's Supermax Prisons and Prisoners, 1997–2007." *Punishment and Society* 14:530–63.

Rempel, M., J. Zweig, C. Lindquist, J. Roman, S. Rossman, and D. Krastein. 2012. "Multi-Site Evaluation Demonstrates Effectiveness of Adult Drug Courts." *Judicature* 95:154–57.

Renzema, M., and E. Mayo-Wilson. 2005. "Can Electronic Monitoring Reduce Crime for Moderate to High-Risk Offenders?" *Journal of Experimental Criminology* 1:215–37.

Reuland, M. 2010. "Tailoring the Police Response to People with Mental Illness to Community Characteristics in the USA." *Police Practice and Research: An International Journal* 11:315–29.

Reuters. 2014. "Justin Bieber Gets Two Years Probation for Egging Incident." Huffington Post "Entertainment," July 9. www.huffingtonpost.com.

Reyes, J. W. (2015). "Lead Exposure and Behavior: Effects on Antisocial and Risky Behavior among Children and Adolescents." *Economic Inquiry* 53(3):1580–1605.

Riccardi, N. 2009. "Cash-Strapped States Revise Laws to Get Inmates Out." *Los Angeles Times*, September 5. www.latimes.com.

Rich, J., S. E. Wakeman, and S. L. Dickman. 2011. "Medicine and the Epidemic of Incarceration in the United States." *New England Journal of Medicine* 364:2081–83.

Richey, W. 2006. "US Creates Terrorist Fingerprint Database." *Christian Science Monitor*, December 27, pp. 1, 4.

Richmond, K. M. 2012. "The Impact of Federal Prison Industries Employment on the Recidivism Outcomes of Female Inmates." *Justice Quarterly* 31:719–45.

Richtel, M. 2002. "Credit Card Theft Thrives Online as Global Market." *New York Times*, May 13. http://www.nytimes.com.

Richter, E., and A. Humke. 2011. "Demonstrative Evidence: Evidence and Technology in the Courtroom." In *Handbook of Trial Consulting*, eds. Richard L. Wiener and B. H. Bornstein. New York: Springer, 187–201.

Riddell, K. 2014. "Hoffman's Death Highlights U.S. Spike in Heroin Use." *Washington Times*, February 3. www.washingtontimes.com.

Riely, K. 2014. "Study: New Probation Day Reporting Centers Are Reducing Relapses." *Pittsburgh Post-Gazette*, February 23. www.post-gazette.com.

Ring, W. 2005. "Backlogs in Labs Undercut DNA's Crime-Solving Value." *Lansing (MI) State Journal*, April 28, p. A3.

Rivard, R. 2014. "Prison U." *Inside Higher Education*, February 28. www.inside-highereducation.com.

Roane, K. R., and D. Morrison. 2005. "The CSI Effect." *U.S. News and World Report*, April 25. http://www.usnews.com.

Robbins, L. 2011. "A Fateful Stop for Candy for a Helper to So Many." *New York Times*, November 1. www.nytimes.com.

Robbins, T. 2015. "A Brutal Beating Wakes Attica's Ghosts." *New York Times*, February 28. www.nytimes.com.

Robbins, T., and L. D'Avolio. 2015. "3 Attica Guards Resign in Deal to Avoid Jail." *New York Times*, March 2. www.nytimes.com.

Roberts, C. 2012. "T.J. Holmes, Former CNN Anchor, Pulled over in Atlanta, Tweets: 'Driving while Black Ain't No Joke.'" *New York Daily News*, July 30. www.nydailynews.com.

Roberts, D. E. 2004. "The Social and Moral Costs of Mass Incarceration in African-American Communities." *Stanford Law Review* 56 1271–1305.

Roberts, S. 2013. "Police Surveillance May Earn Money for City." *New York Times*, April 3. www.nytimes.com.

Robertson, C. 2014. "In a Mississippi Jail, Convictions and Counsel Appear Optional." *New York Times*, September 24. www.nytimes.com.

———. 2015. "A City Where Policing, Discrimination and Raising Revenue Went Hand in Hand," *New York Times,* March 4. www.nytimes.com.

Robinson, P. H., and M. D. Dubber. 2007. "The American Model Penal Code: A Brief Overview." *New Criminal Law Review* 10:319–41.

Robinson, P., M. Kussmaul, C. Stoddard, I. Rudyak, and A. Kuersten. 2015. "The American Criminal Code: General Defenses." *Journal of Legal Analysis* 7:37–150.

Roche, P. R., J. T. Pickett, and M. Gertz. 2015. The Scary World of Online News? Internet News Exposure and Public Attitudes toward Crime and Justice. *Journal of Quantitative Criminology* (online), 1–22.

Rockwell, F. G. 2008. "The Chesterfield /Colonial Heights Drug Court: A Partnership between the Criminal Justice System and the Treatment Community." *University of Richmond Law Review* 43:5–17.

Rogers, B. 2014. "Reports: Sentence Doubled for Teacher in Sex Case." *Houston Chronicle*, January 14. www.chron.com.

Rogers, M. 2011. "Cardell's Taser Death Inspires Utah Police Training." *Salt Lake City Tribune*, May 12. http://www.sltrib.com.

Rogers, R., J. Rogstad, J. Steadham, and E. Drogin. 2011. "In Plain English: Avoiding Recognized Problems with *Miranda* Miscomprehension." *Psychology, Public Policy, and Law* 17:264–85.

Rojek, J., G. Alpert, and S. Decker. 2012. "The Racial Stratification of Searches in Police Traffic Stops." *Criminology* 50:993–1024.

Rojek, J., R. Rosenfeld, and S. Decker. 2012. "Policing Race: The Racial Stratification of Searches in Police Traffic Stops." *Criminologyy* 50:993–1024.

Romney, L. 2012. "Task Force Seeks to Change California's Mental Health Commitment Law." *Los Angeles Times*, April 8. http://articles.latimes.com/2012/apr/08/local/la-me-mental-health-task-force-20120409.

Rose, D. 2009. "North Korea's Dollar Store." *Vanity Fair*, August 5. www.vanityfair.com.

Rosen, L. 1995. "The Creation of the Uniform Crime Report: The Role of Social Science." *Social Science History* 19:215–38.

Rosenberg, R. 2016. "Aspiring Rapper Busted in Massive Identity Theft Scam." *New York Post*, April 13. http://nypost.com.

Rosenberg, T. 2012. "Out of Jail, and into a Job." *New York Times*, March 28. www.nytimes.com.

Rosenfeld, R., R. Fornango, and E. Baumer. 2005. "Did *Ceasefire, Compstat,* and *Exile* Reduce Homicide?" *Criminology & Public Policy* 4:419–50.

Rosenfeld, R., R. Fornango, and A. F. Rengifo. 2007. "The Impact of Order-Maintenance Policing on New York City Homicide and Robbery Rates: 1988–2001. *Criminology* 45:355–83.

Rosenmerkel, S., M. Durose, and D. Farole. 2009. "Felony Sentences in State Courts, 2006—Statistical Tables." Bureau of Justice Statistics *Statistical Tables* (December). http://bjs.ojp.usdoj.gov/.

Rossi, P. H., and R. A. Berk. 1997. *Just Punishments: Federal Guidelines and Public Views Compared.* New York: Aldine DeGruyter.

Rothman, D. 1980. *Conscience and Convenience: The Asylum and Its Alternatives in Progressive America.* New York: Aldine de Gruyter.

Rothman, D. J. 1971. *The Discovery of the Asylum: Social Order and Disorder in the New Republic.* Boston: Little, Brown.

Rotman, E. 1995. "The Failure of Reform." In *Oxford History of the Prison*, eds. N. Morris and D. J. Rothman. New York: Oxford University Press.

Rousey, D. 1984. "Cops and Guns: Police Use of Deadly Force in Nineteenth-Century New Orleans." *American Journal of Legal History* 28:41–66.

Rowe, B. 2016. "Predictors of Texas Police Chiefs' Satisfaction with Police–Prosecutor Relationships." *American Journal of Criminal Justice* (forthcoming).

Rudolph, J. 2012. "Police Layoffs Ripple through Key Swing State of Florida." Huffington Post, January 31. http://www.huffingtonpost.com/2012/01/31/police-layoffs-florida_n_1244364.html.

Ruiter, G. 2014. "Prison Cuts Force Grand Rapids to Scale Back Prison Reentry Services." *Calvin College Chimes*, March 20. http://www.calvin.edu/chimes/2014/03/20/prison-cuts-force-grand-rapids-to-scale-back-prison-reen-try-services/.

Ryan, J. P., L. S. Abrams, and H. Huang. 2014. "First-Time Violent Juvenile Offenders: Probation, Placement, and Recidivism." *Social Work Research* 38:7–18.

Ryley, S., and D. Gregorian. 2014. "NYPD's Most Sued Cop Also among Top Overtime Earners for Past Two Years." *New York Daily News*, February 17. www.nydailynews.com.

Saad, L. 2015. "Americans' Faith in the Honesty and Ethics of Police Rebounds." Gallup Poll, December 21. www.gallup.org.

Sabo, D., T. A. Kupers, and W. London. 2001. "Gender and the Politics of Punishment." In *Prison Masculinities*, eds. D. Sabo, T. A. Kupers, and W. London. Philadelphia: Temple University Press.

Sack, K. 2011. "Executions in Doubt in Fallout over Drug." *New York Times*, March 16. www.nytimes.com.

Sacks, E. 2014. "Dustin Diamond, 'Saved by the Bell' Star, Arrested on Weapon Charges after Allegedly Stabbing Man in a Bar Fight," *New York Daily News*, December 26. www.nydailynews.com.

Sadler, M., J. Correll, B. Park, and C. Judd. 2012. "The World Is Not Black and White: Racial Bias in the Decision to

Shoot in a Multiethnic Context." *Journal of Social Issues* 68:286–313.

Salter, J. 2014. "States Consider Reviving Old-Fashioned Executions." *Lansing State Journal*, February 2. www .lansingstatejournal.com.

Samaha, J. 2011. *Criminal Law*. 10th ed. Belmont, CA: Cengage.

Sanchez, C. E., and M. Giordano. 2008. "Gang Activity in Suburbs Acknowledged." *Nashville Tennessean*, April 28. http://tennessean.com.

Sands, W. L. 2013. "Plea Bargaining after *Frye* and *Lafler*: A Real Problem in Search of a Reasonable and Practical Solution." *Duquesne Law Review* 51:537–49.

Sanger, D. E., and E. Lichtblau. 2006. "Administration Starts Weeklong Blitz in Defense of Eavesdropping Program." *New York Times*, January 24. http:// www.nytimes.com.

Santos, F. 2007. "'CSI Effect'; Evidence From Bite Marks, It Turns Out, Is Not So Elementary." *New York Times*, January 28. http://www.nytimes.com.

———. 2008. "Plan to Close Prisons Stirs Anxiety in Rural Towns." *New York Times*, January 27. www.nytimes.com.

Santos, M. 2004. *About Prison*. Belmont, CA: Wadsworth.

———. 2013. "California's Realignment: Real Prison Reform or Shell Game?" Huffington Post, March 11. http://www .huffingtonpost.com.

Sarche, J. 2005. "Kobe Case Settled." *Pasadena Star-News*, March 2. http://www .pasadenastarnews.com.

Savage, C. 2011. "Trend to Lighten Harsh Sentences Catches on in Conservative States." *New York Times*, August 12. www.nytimes.com.

Scalia, J. 2002. "Prisoners Petitions Filed in U.S. District Courts, 2000, with Trends 1980–2000." Bureau of Justice Statistics *Special Report*, January.

Schaible, L., and V. Gecas. 2010. "The Impact of Emotional Labor and Value Dissonance on Burnout among Police Officers." *Police Quarterly* 13:316–41.

Schinella, T. 2015. "65 Inmates Apply for Earned Time." *Concord Patch*, January 23. http://patch.com/new-hampshire/.

Schlanger, M. 2008. "Jail Strip-Search Cases: Patterns and Participants." *Law and Contemporary Problems* 71:65–88.

Schlesinger, T. 2011. "The Failure of Race Neutral Policies: How Mandatory Terms and Sentencing Enhancements Contribute to Mass Incarceration." *Crime and Delinquency* 57:56–81.

———. 2013. "Racial Disparities in Pretrial Diversion: An Analysis of Outcomes Among Men Charged with Felonies and Processed in State Courts." *Race and Justice* 3:210–38.

Schlosser, L. Z., D. A. Safran, and C. A. Sbaratta. 2010. "Reasons for Choosing a Correction Officer Career." *Psychological Services* 7(1):34–43.

Schmidt, M. 2014. "In Policy Change, Justice Dept. to Require Recording of Interrogations." *New York Times*, May 22. www.nytimes.com.

Schofield, D. 2011. "Playing with Evidence: Using Video Games in the Courtroom." *Entertainment Computing* 2:47–58.

Schultz, D. 2000. "No Joy in Mudville Tonight: The Impact of Three Strikes' Laws on State and Federal Corrections Policy, Resources, and Crime Control." *Cornell Journal of Law and Public Policy* 9:557–83.

Schwartz, J. 2009. "Mistrial by iPhone: Juries' Web Research Upends Trials." *New York Times*, March 18. http://www .nytimes.com.

Schwartz, J., and E. G. Fitzsimmons. 2011. "Illinois Governor Signs Capital Punishment Ban." *New York Times*, March 9. www.nytimes.com.

Secret, M. 2010. "N.Y.C. Misdemeanor Defendants Lack Bail Money." *New York Times*, December 2. www.nytimes.com.

Seelye, K. 2015. "In Heroin Crisis, White Families Seek Gentler War on Drugs." *New York Times*, October 30. www .nytimes.com.

Segal, D. 2009. "Financial Fraud Is Focus of Attack by Prosecutors." *New York Times*, March 12. http://www .nytimes.com.

Segal, L., B. Ngugi, and J. Mana. 2011. "Credit Card Fraud: A New Perspective on Tackling an Intransigent Problem." *Fordham Journal of Corporate and Financial Law* 16:743–81.

Senzarino, P. 2013a. "Closing Arguments Presented in Crooks Trial." *Mason City* (Iowa) *Globe Gazette*, May 10. globegazette.com

———. 2013b. "Noah Crooks Convicted of Second-Degree Murder in Mom's Slaying." *Mason City* (IA) *Globe Gazette*, May 13. globegazette.com.

———. 2014a. "Barlas Found Not Guilty by Reason of Insanity in Father's Death." *Mason City* (IA) *Globe Gazette*, December 31. www.globegazette.com.

———. 2014b. "Insanity Defense: Rarely Used, Rarely Effective." *Mason City* (IA) *Globe Gazette*, September 20. globegazette.com.

Sevigny, E. L., B. K. Fuliehan, and Ferdik. 2013. "Do Drug Courts Reduce the Use of Incarceration? A Meta-Analysis. *Journal of Criminal Justice* 41:416–25.

Shamir, H. 2012. "A Labor Paradigm for Human Trafficking." *UCLA Law Review* 60:76–136.

Shane, J. 2010. "Organizational Stressors and Police Performance." *Journal of Criminal Justice* 38:807–18.

Shapiro, B. 1997. "Sleeping Lawyer Syndrome." *Nation*, April 7, pp. 27–29.

Shapiro, E., and G. Benitez. 2015. "Owen Labrie Found Not Guilty of Felony Sexual Assault in Prep School Trial." ABC News online, August 28. http://abcnews.go.com.

Sharkey, J. 2008. "Mistakes on Terrorist Watch List Affect Even Children." *New York Times*, September 9. http://www .nytimes.com.

Shay, G. 2009. "What We Can Learn about Appeals from Mr. Tillman's Case: More Lessons from Another DNA Exoneration." *University of Cincinnati Law Review* 77:1499–553.

———. 2013. "The New State Postconviction." *Akron Law Review* 46:473–88.

Shea, K. 2016. "Mercer County Plans to Move 600 Inmates, Layoff Jail Employees." NJ.com, February 11. www .nj.com.

Sheeler, A. 2015. "Girl Injured When Firecracker Thrown into Car." *Bismarck* (ND) *Tribune*, August 3. bismarcktribune.com.

"Shells Near Ex-NFL Star's Alleged Victim, in Car, from Same Gun: Witness." 2015. *New York Times*, February 25. www .nytimes.com.

Shepard, L. 2016. "Mich. Supreme Court: Youth Lifers Must Be Resentenced." *Detroit Free Press*, April 26. http:// freep.com.

Sherman, L. 2015. "A Tipping Point for 'Totally Evidenced Policing': Ten Ideas for Building an Evidence-Based Police Agency." *International Criminal Justice Review* 25:11–29.

Sherman, L. W. 1998. "Police." In *Handbook of Crime and Punishment*, ed. M. Tonry. New York: Oxford University Press, 429–56.

Sherman, L. W., and D. A. Weisburd. 1995. "General Deterrent Effects of Police Patrol in Crime 'Hot Spots': A Randomized Controlled Trial." *Justice Quarterly* 12 (December):625–48.

Shermer, L., and B. D. Johnson. 2010. "Criminal Prosecutions: Examining Prosecutorial Discretion and Charging Decisions in U.S. Federal District Courts" *Justice Quarterly* 27:394–430.

Shoichet, C., and M. Cuevas. 2015. "Walter Scott Shooting Case: Court Documents Reveal New Details." CNN.com, September 10. www.cnn.com.

Sickmund, M., A. Sladky, and W. Kang. 2013. "Easy Access to Juvenile Court Statistics: 1985–2010." Pittsburgh: National Center for Juvenile Justice. www.ojjdp.gov/ojstatbb/ezajcs/.

Sickmund, M., A. Sladky, and W. Kang. 2015. "Easy Access to Juvenile Court Statistics: 1985–2013." *National Juvenile Court Data Archive: Juvenile Court Case Records 1985–2013*. Pittsburgh: National Center for Juvenile Justice. http://www.ojjdp.gov/ojstatbb /ezajcs/.

Silverman, E. 1999. *NYPD Battles Crime.* Boston: Northeastern University Press.

Simmons, A., and B. Rankin. 2010. "Gwinnett Cuts Pay Rate for Defending Indigent." *Atlanta Journal Constitution*, February 1. www.ajc.com.

Simonoff, J., C. Restropo, R. Zimmerman, Z. Naphtali, and H. Willis. 2011. "Resource Allocation, Emergency Response Capability, and Infrastructure Concentration around Vulnerable Sites." *Journal of Risk Research* 5:597–613.

Simons, K. W. 2008. "Self-Defense: Reasonable Belief or Reasonable Self-Control?" *New Criminal Law Review* 11:51–90.

Simons, M. 2010. "Prosecutorial Discretion in the Shadow of Advisory Guidelines and Mandatory Minimums." *Temple Political and Civil Rights Law Review* 19:377–87.

Simpson, N. 2015. "Norfolk DA Cuts Four Prosecutors." *Patriot Ledger* (MA), May 26. www.patriotledger.com.

Singer, N. 2008. "Budget Cuts Force King County Charging Process to Change." *Seattle Times*, September 25. http://seattletimes.nwsource.com.

Skogan, W. G. 1995. "Crime and Racial Fears of White Americans." *Annals of the American Academy of Political and Social Science* 539 (May):59–71.

Skogan, W. G., S. M. Hartnett, N. Bump, and J. Dubois. 2008. Evaluation of CeaseFire-Chicago. Unpublished Report (March 20).

Skolnick, J. H., and D. H. Bayley. 1986. *The New Blue Line.* New York: Free Press.

Skolnick, J. H., and J. J. Fyfe. 1993. *Above the Law: Police and Excessive Use of Force.* New York: Free Press.

Skorton, D., and G. Altschuler. 2013. "College behind Bars: How Educating Prisoners Pays Off." *Forbes*, March 25. http://www.forbes.com.

Skutch, J. 2015. "Former Savannah-Chatham Police Chief Willie Lovett Sentenced to 7.5 Years in Prison." *Savannah Morning News*, February 6. http://savannahnow.com.

Slabaugh, S. 2011. "Inmate Education Programs Facing Major Budget Cuts." *Muncie Star Press*, May 21. www.thestarpress.com.

Smalarz, L., and G. Wells. 2015. "Contamination of Eyewitness Self-Reports and the Mistaken-Identification Problem." *Current Directions in Psychological Science* 24:120–124.

Smith, C. E. 1990. *United States Magistrates in the Federal Courts: Subordinate Judges.* New York: Praeger.

———. 1995. "Federal Habeas Corpus Reform: The State's Perspective." *Justice System Journal* 18:1–11.

———. 1997. *Courts, Politics, and the Judicial Process.* 2nd ed. Belmont, CA: Wadsworth.

———. 1999. "Criminal Justice and the 1997–98 U.S. Supreme Court Term." *Southern Illinois University Law Review* 23:443–67.

———. 2000a. "The Governance of Corrections: Implications of the Changing Interface of Courts and Corrections." In *Boundary Changes in Criminal Justice Organizations.* Vol. 2 of *Criminal Justice 2000.* Washington, DC: National Institute of Justice, 113–66.

———. 2000b. *Law and Contemporary Corrections.* Belmont, CA: Wadsworth.

———. 2004. *Constitutional Rights: Myths and Realities.* Belmont, CA: Wadsworth.

———. 2007. "Prisoners' Rights and the Rehnquist Court Era." *Prison Journal* 87:457–76.

———. 2010a. "Justice John Paul Stevens and Capital Punishment." *Berkeley Journal of Criminal Law* 15:205–60.

———. 2010b. "Justice John Paul Stevens: Staunch Defender of *Miranda* Rights." *DePaul Law Review* 60:99–140.

———. 2011. "The Changing Supreme Court and Prisoners' Rights." *Indiana Law Review* 44:853–88.

———. 2013. "*Brown v. Plata*, the Roberts Court, and the Future of Conservative Perspectives on Rights behind Bars." *Akron Law Review* 46:519–50.

———. 2014. "What I Learned about Stop-and-Frisk from Watching My Black Son." *The Atlantic*, April 1. www.theatlantic.com.

Smith, C. E., C. DeJong, and M. McCall. 2011. *The Rehnquist Court and Criminal Justice.* Lanham, MD: Lexington Books.

Smith, C. E., and H. Feldman. 2001. "Burdens of the Bench: State Supreme Courts' Non-Judicial Tasks." *Judicature* 84:304–9.

Smith, C. E., M. A. McCall, and M. M. McCall. 2009. "The Roberts Court and Criminal Justice at the Dawn of the 2008 Term." *Charleston Law Review* 3:265–87.

Smith, C. E., M. McCall, and C. Perez McCluskey. 2005. *Law and Criminal Justice: Emerging Issues in the Twenty-First Century.* New York: Peter Lang.

Smith, C. E., and R. Ochoa. 1996. "The Peremptory Challenge in the Eyes of the Trial Judge." *Judicature* 79:185–89.

Smith, E. 2015. "Oregon Witness Jailed for 905 Days Goes Free with Check for $5,750." *Portland Oregonian*, March 19. www.oregonlive.com.

Smith, K., D. Chanen, and J. Reinan. 2015. "Black Lives Matter Protests Spill Over to Light Rail, Airport." *Minneapolis Star Tribune*, December 24. www.startribune.com.

Smith, L. 2012. "Wyoming City Council Adopts Zoning Limits on Where Parolees May Live." Michigan Public Radio. January 16. http://michiganradio.org.

Snyder, H. N. 2012. *Arrest in the United States, 1980–2010.* Washington, DC: U.S. Department of Justice.

Snyder, H. N., and J. Mulako-Wangota. 2016. "Arrests by Age in the U.S., 2012." *Arrest Data Analysis Tool.* Washington, DC: Bureau of Justice Statistics. www.bjs.gov.

Snyder, H. N., and M. Sickmund. 2006. *Juvenile Offenders and Victims: 2006 National Report.* Washington, DC: U.S. Office of Juvenile Justice and Delinquency Prevention.

Sommers, S. 2009. "On the Obstacles to Jury Diversity." *Jury Expert* 21:1–10.

Soree, N. B. 2013. "Show and Tell, Seek and Find: A Balanced Approach to Defining a Fourth Amendment Search and the Lessons of Rape Reform." *Seton Hall Law Review* 43:127–227.

Sorensen, J. R., and D. H. Wallace. 1999. "Prosecutorial Discretion in Seeking Death: An Analysis of Racial Disparity in the Pretrial Stages of Case Processing in a Midwestern County." *Justice Quarterly* 16:561–78.

Spangenberg, R. L., and M. L. Beeman. 1995. "Indigent Defense Systems in the United States." *Law and Contemporary Problems* 58:31–49.

Spears, J. W., and C. C. Spohn. 1997. "The Effect of Evidence Factors and Victim Characteristics on Prosecutors' Charging Decisions in Sexual Assault Cases." *Justice Quarterly* 14:501–24.

Spencer, C. 2000. "Nonlethal Weapons Aid Lawmen: Police Turn to Beanbag Guns, Pepper Spray to Save Lives of Defiant Suspects." *Arkansas Democrat-Gazette*, November 6, p. B1.

Spencer, M. 2009. "The Wrong Stephen Morgan's Photo Posted Online in Wesleyan Student's Death." *Hartford Courant*, May 8. http://www.courant.com.

Spohn, C. 2011. "Unwarranted Disparity in the Wake of the *Booker/Fanfan* Decision: Implications for Research and Policy." *Criminology & Public Policy* 10(4):1119–27.

Spohn, C., and D. Holleran. 2001. "The Imprisonment Penalty Paid by Young, Unemployed Black and Hispanic Male Offenders." *Criminology* 38:281–306.

St. Clair, S. 2008. "R. Kelly Verdict: Not Guilty." *Chicago Tribune*, June 13. http://www.chicagotribune.com.

St. Clair, S., and K. Ataiyero. 2008. "R. Kelly Defense Rests Case after 2 Days of Testimony." *Chicago Tribune*, June 10. http://articles.chicagotribune.com.

St. Clair, S., and J. Gorner. 2013. "City Plans $4.1 Million Settlement in Fatal Police Shooting." *Chicago Tribune*, February 8. http://articles.tribune.com.

Staba, D. 2007. "Killer of 3 Women in Buffalo Area Is Given a Life Term." *New York Times*, August 15. http://www.nytimes.com.

Stafford, M. C., and M. Warr. 1993. "A Reconceptualization of General and Specific Deterrence." *Journal of Research in Crime and Delinquency* 30 (May):123–35.

Stahl, A. 2008. "Drug Offense Cases in Juvenile Courts." 1985–2004. Washington, DC: U.S. Department of Justice.

Stahlkopf, C., M. Males, and D. Macallair. 2010. "Testing Incapacitation Theory: Youth Crime and Incarceration in California." *Crime and Delinquency* 56:253–68.

Stanko, E. 1988. "The Impact of Victim Assessment on Prosecutors' Screening Decisions: The Case of the New York District Attorney's Office." In *Criminal Justice: Law and Politics*, 5th ed., ed. G. F. Cole. Pacific Grove, CA: Brooks /Cole.

Stanley, K. 2011. "Florida Crime Keeps Falling, and Experts and Law Enforcement Search for Why." *St. Petersburg Times*, November 17. http://www .tampabay.com/news/publicsafety /crime/article1203703.ece.

Staples, B. 2012. "California Horror Stories and the 3-Strikes Law." *New York Times*, November 24. www .nytimes.com.

Starr, S., and M. Rehavi. 2013. "Mandatory Sentencing and Racial Disparity: Assessing the Roles of Prosecutors and the Effects of *Booker*." *Yale Law Journal* 123:2–79.

State of Florida Correctional Medical Authority. 2014. *2013–2014 Annual Report and Report on Elderly Offenders* (December). Tallahassee, FL: Correctional Medical Authority (CMA).

Staton, M., and A. Lurigio. 2015. "Mental Health Courts in Illinois: Comparing and Contrasting Program Models, Sanction Applications, Information Sharing, and Professional Roles." *Federal Probation* (June): 21–26.

Stecklow, S., J. Singer, and A. O. Patrick. 2005. "Watch on the Thames." *Wall Street Journal*, July 8. http://www .wsj.com.

Steden, R., and R. Sarre. 2007. "The Growth of Private Security: Trends in the European Union." *Security Journal* 20:222–35.

Stedman, A. 2016. "'Power Rangers' Star Ricardo Medina Charged with Murder." *Variety*, January 14. http://variety. com/2016/tv/news/ricardo-medina -arrested-power-rangers-murder -1201680254/.

Steen, S., R. Engen, and R. Gainey. 2005. "Images of Danger and Culpability: Racial Stereotyping, Case Processing, and Criminal Sentencing." *Criminology* 43:435–68.

Steffen, J. 2014. "July Court Date Set for Broncos' T. J. Ward in Strip Club Case." *Denver Post*, June 23. www.denverpost.com.

Steffensmeier, D., and S. Demuth. 2010. "Ethnicity and Judges' Sentencing Decisions: Hispanic-Black-White Comparisons." *Criminology* 39:145–78.

Steffensmeier, D., B. Feldmeyer, C. T. Harris, and J. T. Ulmer. 2011. "Reassessing Trends in Black Violent Crime 1980–2008: Sorting out the 'Hispanic Effect' in Uniform Crime Reports Arrests, National Crime Victimization Survey Offender Estimates, and U.S. Prisoner Counts." *Criminology* 49:197–252.

Steffensmeier, D., J. Kramer, and C. Streifel. 1993. "Gender and Imprisonment Decisions." *Criminology* 31:411–46.

Steffensmeier, D., J. Ulmer, and J. Kramer. 1998. "The Interaction of Race, Gender, and Age in Criminal Sentencing: The Punishment Cost of Being Young, Black, and Male." *Criminology* 36:763–97.

Stein, R., and C. Griffith. 2016. "Resident and Police Perceptions of the Neighborhood: Implications for Community Policing." *Criminal Justice Policy Review* (forthcoming).

Steinberg, J. 1999. "The Coming Crime Wave Is Washed Up." *New York Times*, January 3, p. 4WK.

Steiner, B., and E. Wright. 2006. "Assessing the Relative Effects of State Direct File Waiver Laws on Violent Juvenile Crime: Deterrence or Irrelevance?" *Journal of Criminal Law and Criminology* 96:1451–77.

Steiner, B., C. Hemmens, and V. Bell. 2006. "Legislative Waiver Reconsidered: General Deterrent Effects of Statutory Exclusion Laws Enacted Post-1979." *Justice Quarterly* 23(1):34–59.

Steiner, B., M. Makarios, L. Travis, and B. Meade. 2012. "Examining the Effects of Community-Based Sanctions on Offender Recidivism." *Justice Quarterly* 29:229–55.

Stensland, J. 2011. "Island County Sheriff, Prosecutor Struggle with Cuts." *Whidbey* (WA) *News Times*, January 25. www.whidbeynewstimes.com.

Stephan, J. 2008. *Census of State and Federal Correctional Facilities, 2005*, October. NCJ 222182.

Stephan, J., and J. Karberg. 2003. *Census of State and Federal Correctional Facilities, 2000*. (August) Washington, DC: Bureau of Justice Statistics.

Stephens, M. 2008. "Ignoring Justice: Prosecutorial Discretion and the Ethics of Charging." *Northern Kentucky Law Review* 35:53–65.

Stephens, S. 2007. "The True Effect of Crime Scene Television on the Justice System: The "CSI Effect" on Real Crime Labs." *New England Law Review* 41:591–607.

Stevens, C. 2015. "A Diverse Judiciary?" *Michigan Bar Journal* (May): 26–40.

Stevens, G. 2014. "East Liverpool Police Chief Unhappy with Drug Dealer Sentence." WFMJ-TV, November 24. www.wfmj.com.

Steward, D., and M. Totman. 2005. *Racial Profiling: Don't Mind If I Take a Look, Do Ya? An Examination of Consent Searches and Contraband Hits at Texas Traffic Stops*. Austin: Texas Justice Coalition.

Stewart, D., and W. Oliver. 2016. "The Adoption of Homeland Security Initiatives in Texas Police Departments: A Contextual Perspective." *Criminal Justice Review* (forthcoming).

Stewart, E., E. Baumer, R. Brunson, and R. Simons. 2009. "Neighborhood Racial Context and Perceptions of Police-Based Racial Discrimination among Black Youth." *Criminology* 47:847–87.

Stickels, J. W., B. J. Michelsen, and A. Del Carmen. 2007. "Elected Texas District and County Attorneys' Perceptions of Crime Victim Involvement in Prosecution." *Texas Wesleyan Law Review* 14:1–25.

Stoddard, E. R. 1968. "The Informal 'Code' of Police Deviancy: A Group Approach to Blue-Coat Crime." *Journal of Criminal Law, Criminology, and Police Science* 59:204–11.

Stojkovic, S. 1990. "Accounts of Prison Work: Corrections Officers' Portrayals of Their Work Worlds." *Perspectives on Social Problems* 2:211–30.

Stolzenberg, L., and S. J. D'Alessio. 1994. "Sentencing and Unwarranted Disparity: An Empirical Assessment of the Long-Term Impact of Sentencing Guidelines in Minnesota." *Criminology* 32:301–10.

Streib, V. 2010. "Innocence: Intentional Wrongful Conviction of Children." *Chicago-Kent Law Review* 85:163–77.

Streitfeld, D. 2008. R. Kelly Is Acquitted in Child Pornography Case." *New York Times*, June 14. www.nytimes.com.

Strickland, C. 2011. "Regulation without Agency: A Practical Response to Private Policing in *United States v. Day*." *North Carolina Law Review* 89:1338–62.

Strodtbeck, F., R. James, and G. Hawkins. 1957. "Social Status in Jury Deliberations." *American Sociological Review* 22:713–19.

Strom, K., M. Berzofsky, B. Shook-Sa, K. Barrick, C. Daye, N. Horstmann, and S. Kinsey. 2010. "The Private Security Industry: A Review of the Definitions, Available Data Sources, and Paths Moving Forward." Report prepared for U.S. Bureau of Justice Statistics (December), https://www.ncjrs.gov/pdffiles1/bjs /grants/232781.pdf.

Strom, K. J., and J. M. MacDonald 2007. "The Influence of Social and Economic Disadvantage on Racial Patterns in Youth Homicide over Time." *Homicide Studies* 11(1):50–69.

Stroshine, M. S. 2005. "Information Technology Innovations in Policing." In *Critical Issues in Policing*, 5th ed., eds. R. G. Dunham and G. P. Alpert. Long Grove, IL: Waveland Press, 172–83.

Struckman-Johnson, C., and D. Struckman-Johnson. 2013. "Stopping Prison Rape: The Evolution of Standards Recommended PREA's National Prison Rape Elimination Commission. *Prison Journal* 93:335–54.

Sullivan, C. 2014. "Legislature Looks at Softening Illegal Drug Punishments." MyNorthwest.com, January 15. http://mynorthwest.com/11/2433407/Legislature-looks-at-softening-illegal-drug-punishments.

Sullivan, E. 2013. "Local Police Grapple with Response to Cybercrimes." *Lexington Herald Leader*. April 13. http://www.kentucky.com.

Sullivan, J. 2009. "New Statewide Database Tracks Sex Offenders." *Seattle Times*, March 10. www.seattletimes.com.

Sullivan, K. M. 2003. "Under a Watchful Eye: Incursions on Personal Privacy." In *The War on Our Freedoms: Civil Liberties in an Age of Terrorism*, eds. R. C. Leone and G. Anrig Jr. New York: Public Affairs, 128–46.

Sullo, M. 2016. "State Prosecutors Say Budget Cuts Could Mean 50 Layoffs." *Connecticut Law Tribune*, February 12. www.ctlawtribune.com.

Summers, A., R. D. Hayward, and M. Miller. 2010. "Death Qualification as Systematic Exclusion of Jurors with Certain Religious and Other Characteristics." *Journal of Applied Social Psychology* 40:3218–34.

Sundby, S. 2010. "War and Peace in the Jury Room: How Capital Juries Reach Unanimity." *Hastings Law Journal* 62:103–54.

Sung, C. 2014. "Chris Brown Loses Effort to Toss D.C. Assault Charge." CNN.com, April 7. www.cnn.com.

Sung, H., A. M. Mahoney, and J. Mellow. 2011. "Substance Abuse Treatment Gap among Adult Parolees: Prevalence, Correlates, and Barriers." *Criminal Justice Review* 36:40–77.

Swaine, J., B. Jacobs, and P. Lewis. 2015. "Baltimore Protests Turn into Riots as Mayor Declares State of Emergency." *Guardian,* April 28. www.theguardian.com.

Swaine, J., O. Laughland, and J. Larty. 2015. "Black Americans Killed by the Police Twice as Likely to be Unarmed as White People." *Guardian,* June 1. www.theguardian.com.

Swarns, R. L. 2004. "Senator? Terrorist? A Watch List Stops Kennedy at Airport." *New York Times*, August 20. http://www.nytimes.com.

Swarz, J. 2004. "Inmates vs. Outsourcing." *USA Today*, July 6, p. 1.

Swift. A. 2013. "For First Times, Americans Favor Legalizing Marijuana." Gallup Poll, October 22. www.gallup.com.

Sykes, G. M. 1958. *The Society of Captives*. Princeton, NJ: Princeton University Press.

Taifa, N. 2002. Testimony on Behalf of American Civil Liberties Union of the National Capital Area Concerning Proposed Use of Surveillance Cameras, before the Joint Public Oversight Hearing Committee on the Judiciary, Council of the District of Columbia, June 13. http://www.dcwatch.com.

Talbot, M. 2015. "The Case against Cash Bail." *New Yorker*, August 25. www.newyorker.com.

Tashima, A. W. 2008. "The War on Terror and the Rule of Law." *Asian American Law Journal* 15:245–65.

Taslitz, A. E. 2010. "Fourth Amendment Federalism and the Silencing of the American Poor." *Chicago-Kent Law Review* 85:277–312.

———. 2012. "High Expectations and Some Wounded Hopes: The Policy and Politics of a Uniform Statute on Videotaping Custodial Interrogations." *Northwestern Journal of Law and Social Policy* 7:400–54.

Taxman, F. S., and S. Belenko, 2013. *Implementing Evidence-Based Practices in Community Corrections and Addiction Treatment*. New York: Springer.

Taylor, B., C. Koper, and D. J. Woods. 2010. "A Randomized Controlled Trial of Different Policing Strategies at Hot Spots of Violent Crime." *Journal of Experimental Criminology* 7:149–81.

Taylor, M. 2009. *Achieving Better Outcomes for Adult Probation*. Sacramento: Legislative Analyst's Office (May).

Teeters, N. K., and J. D. Shearer. 1957. *The Prison at Philadelphia's Cherry Hill*. New York: Columbia University Press.

Telep, C., and D. Weisburd. 2012. "What Is Known about the Effectiveness of Police Practices in Reducing Crime and Disorder?" *Police Quarterly* 15:331–57.

Tepfer, D. 2013. "Towns to Pay $3.5M in Deadly Raid." *Connecticut Post,* February 20. http://www.ctpost.com.

Terrill, W. 2005. "Police Use of Force: A Transactional Approach." *Justice Quarterly* 22:107–38.

Terrill, W., and E. Paoline. 2012. "Conducted Energy Devices (CEDs) and Citizen Injuries: The Shocking Empirical Reality." *Justice Quarterly* 29:153–82.

Texas Board of Pardons and Paroles. 2014. "Hearing Process." Texas Board of Pardons and Paroles website. http://www.tdcj.state.tx.us/bpp/publications/Hearings.pdf.

———. 2015. *Annual Statistical Report: Fiscal Year 2014*. Austin, TX: Texas Board of Pardons and Paroles.

Texas Department of Criminal Justice. 2015. *Correctional Officer Salary*. www.tdcj.state.tx.us/divisions/hr/coinfo/cosalary.html.

Theriot, M. T., and J. G. Orme. 2014. "School Resource Officers and Students' Feelings of Safety at School." *Youth Violence and Juvenile Justice*, 14(2):130–46.

Third Branch. 2008a. "Economics of CJA Regulations Costly to Attorneys." Administrative Office of the U.S. Courts. Vol. 40 (4), April. http://www.uscourts.gov.

———. 2008b. "National Summits Help Federal Courts Prepare for Sentence Reduction Requests." Administrative Office of the U.S. Courts. Vol. 40 (2), February, pp. 1–3, 6. http://www.uscourts.gov.

Thompson, C., and M. Berman. 2015. "Improper Techniques, Increased Risks." *Washington Post*, November 26. www.washingtonpost.com.

Thompson, G. 2009. "Couple's Capital Ties Said to Veil Spying for Cuba." *New York Times*, June 18. http://www.nytimes.com.

Thornhill, T. 2015. "Finnish Man Given 40,000 [pounds sterling] for Going 14 mph over Limit." *Daily Mail*, March 15. http://dailymail.co.uk.

"Thumb on the Scale." 2013. *Economist*. January 26. http://www.economist.com.

Thurman, Q., J. Zhao, and A. Giacomazzi. 2001. *Community Policing in a Community Era*. Los Angeles: Roxbury.

Tillman, Z. 2012. "D.C. Judicial Applicants, Complaints up in 2011." *The Blog of the Legal Times*, February 24. http://legaltimes.typepad.com/blt/2012/02/dc-judicial-applicants-complaints-up-in-2011.html.

Toch, H. 1976. *Peacekeeping: Police, Prisons, and Violence*. Lexington, MA: Lexington Books.

Tonry, M. 1993. "Sentencing Commissions and Their Guidelines." In *Crime and Justice*, vol. 17, ed. M. Tonry. Chicago: University of Chicago Press.

———. 1995. *Malign Neglect: Race, Crime, and Punishment in America*. New York: Oxford University Press.

———. 2008. "Learning from the Limitations of Deterrence Research." *Crime and Justice* 37:279–307.

Tonry, M., and M. Lynch. 1996. "Intermediate Sanctions." In *Crime and Justice*, vol. 20, ed. M. Tonry. Chicago: University of Chicago Press, 99–144.

Toobin, J. 2007. "The CSI Effect." *New Yorker*, May 7. http://www.newyorker.com.

———. 2014. "'This Is My Jail': Where Gang Members and Female Guards Set the Rules." *New Yorker*, April 14th.

Toscano, P. 2011. "The Dangerous World of Counterfeit Prescription Drugs." *USA Today*. October 7. www.usatoday.com.

Travis, J. 2002. "Invisible Punishment: An Instrument of Social Exclusion." In *Invisible Punishment: The Collateral Consequences of Mass Imprisonment*, eds. M. Bauer and M. Chesney-Lind. New York: New Press, 15–36.

Travis, J., and J. Petersilia. 2001. "Reentry Reconsidered: A New Look at an Old Question." *Crime and Delinquency* 47 (July):291–313.

Truman, J., and L. Langton, 2015. "Criminal Victimization, 2014." *Bureau of Justice Statistics Bulletin*, August. NCJ 248973.

Truman, J., and M. Rand. 2010. "Criminal Victimization 2009." Bureau of Justice Statistics *Bulletin*, October. NCJ 231327.

Truman, J. L., and Planty, M. 2002. "Criminal Victimization, 2011." *Bureau of Justice Statistics Bulletin*, October. NCJ239437.

Tuohy, L. 2014. "New Hampshire House Votes to Repeal Death Penalty." *Boston Globe*, March 12. www.boston.com.

———. 2015. "Vt.'s Labrie Turned Down Plea Deals." *Valley News* (VT), October 31. http://www.vnews.com /news/state/region/19239192-95 /vts-labrie-turned-down-plea-deals.

Turk, J. 2016. "Clarkston Brandon Community Credit Union CFO Charged with 14 Counts of Embezzlement after Confessing to Taking $20M from Branch." *Oakland* (MI) *Press*, January 18. http://www.theoaklandpress .com/article/OP/20160108 /NEWS/160109584.

Tyler, K. A., and M. R. Beal. 2010. "The High-Risk Environment of Homeless Young Adults: Consequences for Physical and Sexual Victimization." *Violence and Victims* 25:101–15.

Uchida, C. 2005. "The Development of the American Police: An Historical Overview." In *Critical Issues in Policing*, eds. R. Dunham and G. Alpert. Long Grove, IL: Waveland Press, 20–40.

Uchida, C., and T. Bynum. 1991. "Search Warrants, Motions to Suppress and 'Lost Cases': The Effects of the Exclusionary Rule in Seven Jurisdictions." *Journal of Criminal Law and Criminology* 81:1034–66.

Ullman, S. 2007. "A 10-Year Update of 'Review and Critique of Empirical Studies of Rape Avoidance.'" *Criminal Justice and Behavior* 34:411–29.

Ulmer, J. T., J. Eisenstein, and B. Johnson. 2010. "Trial Penalties in Federal Sentencing: Extra-Guidelines Factors and District Variation." *Justice Quarterly* 27:560–92.

Ulmer, J. T., M. T. Light, and J. H. Kramer. 2011. "Racial Disparity in the Wake of the *Booker/Fanfan* Decision." *Criminology & Public Policy* 10(4):1077–118.

Unah, I. 2010. "Choosing Who Will Die: The Effect of Race, Gender, and Law in Prosecutorial Decisions to Seek the Death Penalty in Durham County, North Carolina." *Michigan Journal of Race and Law* 15:135–79.

"Under the Dome: Today Is February 1, the 20th Day of 60-Day Legislative Session." *Olympian* (Olympia, WA), February 1, 2014 www.theolympian .com/2014/02/01/2960527/news-brief -01domes.html.

United Nations Office on Drugs and Crime (UNODC). 2011. *Research Report: Estimating Illicit Financial Flows Resulting from Drug Trafficking and Other Transnational Organized Crimes*. October. Vienna: UNODC.

Unnever, J. D. 2008. "Two Worlds Far Apart: Black-White Differences in Beliefs about Why African-American Men Are Disproportionately Imprisoned." *Criminology* 46:511–38.

Urbina, I. 2009. "Citing Cost, States Consider End to Death Penalty." *New York Times*, February 25. http://www .nytimes.com.

Urbina, I., and S. D. Hamill. 2009. "Judges Plead Guilty in Scheme to Jail Youths for Profit." *New York Times*, February 13, p. A1.

U.S. Bureau of Prisons. 2016. "About Us." Federal Bureau of Prisons website. www.bop.gov.

U.S. Courts. 2013. "Supervision Costs Significantly Less than Incarceration in Federal System." July 18. http:// uscourts.gov.

U.S. Department of Education. 2014. "U.S. Department of Education Releases List of Higher Education Institutions with Open Title IX Sexual Violence Investigations." Press release, May 1. www.ed.gov.

———. 2015. "U.S. Department of Education Launches Second Chance Pell Pilot Program for Incarcerated Individuals." Press release, July 31.

U.S. Department of Health and Human Services. 2007. "Illicit Drug Use, by Race/ Ethnicity, in Metropolitan and Non-Metropolitan Counties: 2004 and 2005." *NSDUH Report* (National Survey on Drug Use and Health), June 21.

———. 2013. "Information on Poverty and Income Statistics: A Summary of 2013 Current Population Survey Data." *ASPE Issue Brief*, September 17. http://aspe .hhs.gov/hsp/13/PovertyAndIncomeEst /ib_poverty2013.pdf.

U.S. Department of Health and Human Services. 2014. "Results from the 2013 National Survey on Drug Use and Health: Summary of National Findings." Rockville, MD: Substance Abuse and Mental Health Services Administration.

U.S. Department of Health and Human Services. 2015. "Income and Poverty in the United States, 2014." http://www .census.gov.

U.S. Department of Justice, 2011. "Department of Justice Disrupts International Cyber Crime Rings Distributing Scareware." *FBI National Press Releases*, June 22. www.fbi.gov.

———. 2012. "Justice Department Charges Leaders of Megaupload with Widespread Online Copyright Infringement." *FBI National Press Releases*, January 19. www.fbi.gov.

———. 2014. "Springfield Man Pleads Guilty to Trafficking Counterfeit Goods." Press release, March 6. www .justice.gov.

U.S. Department of Justice. 2015. "Justice Department Announces $53 Million in Grant Awards to Reduce Recidivism among Adults and Youth" Press release, October. www.justice.gov.

U.S. Government Accountability Office. 2000. *U.S. Customs Service: Better Targeting of Airline Passengers for Personal Searches Could Produce Better Results*. Washington, DC: U.S. Government Printing Office.

———. 2011. "Bureau of Prisons: Evaluating the Impact of Protective Equipment Could Help Enhance Officer Safety." April. GAO-11–410.

U.S. Marshals Service. 2016. "Facts and Figures, 2015." www.usmarshals.gov.

U.S. President's Commission on Law Enforcement and Administration of Justice. 1967. *The Challenge of Crime in a Free Society*. Washington, DC: U.S. Government Printing Office.

U.S. Sentencing Commission. 2006. *Final Report on the Impact of* United States v. Booker *on Federal Sentencing* (Washington, DC: U.S. Sentencing Commission).

U.S. Transportation Safety Administration. 2012. "TSA Awards Contracts for Additional Explosives Detection Systems." TSA Press release, February 10. www .tsa.gov.

Utz, P. 1978. *Settling the Facts*. Lexington, MA: Lexington Books.

Valley, J. 2012. "Re-entry Programs Give Former Prisoners Hope in the Real World." *Las Vegas Sun*, August 23. www.lasvegassun.com.

Van Stelle, K., and J. Goodrich. 2009. *The 2008/2009 Study of Probation and Parole Revocation*. Madison: University of Wisconsin Population Health Institute (June).

Vaughn, M. S. 2001. "Assessing the Legal Liabilities in Law Enforcement: Chiefs' Views." *Crime and Delinquency* 47:3–27.

Vermont Department of Corrections. 2015. *Vermont Parole Board Manual*. www .doc.state.vt.us.

Vickovic, S., and M. L. Griffin. 2013. "A Comparison of Line and Supervisory Officers and the Impact of Support on Commitment to the Prison

Organization." *Criminal Justice Policy Review* online edition, October 3.

Vidmar, N., and V. P. Hans. 2007. *American Juries: The Verdict*. New York: Prometheus Books.

Vielmetti, B. 2015. "Trial Ordered for Dustin Diamond—Screech on 'Saved by the Bell—in Bar Fight." *Milwaukee Journal Sentinel*, January 6. www.jsonline.com.

Vila, B., and D. J. Kenney. 2002. "Tired Cops: The Prevalence and Potential Consequences of Police Fatigue." *National Institute of Justice Journal* 248:16–21.

Virtanen, M. 2014. "Report Details NY Indigent Defense Caseloads." *Wall Street Journal*, September 24. www.wsj.com.

Viser, M. 2013. "Tensions Emerge over Lack of Tsarnaev Information Shared between FBI, Local Authorities." *Boston Globe*, May 9. www.boston.com.

Visher, C., S. Debus-Sherrill, and J. Yahner. 2011. "Employment after Prison: A Longitudinal Study of Former Prisoners." *Justice Quarterly* 28:698–718.

Vitiello, M. 2008. "Punishing Sex Offenders: When Good Intentions Go Bad." *Arizona State Law Journal* 40:651–90.

Vives, R., and A. Blankstein. 2009. "A Mixed Reaction to a Use of Force." *Los Angeles Times*, May 15. http://www.latimes.com.

Vogel, E. 2014. "Inmate Is Their Name, True Grit Is Their Gain," *Las Vegas Review-Journal*, January 12. reviewjournal.com.

Volunteers in Probation. 2016. San Diego County Probation Department. www.volunteersinprobation.org.

von Hirsch, A. 1976. *Doing Justice*. New York: Hill and Wang.

Wade, N. 2006. "Wider Use of DNA Lists Is Urged in Fighting Crime." *New York Times*, May 12. http://www.nytimes.com.

Wagner, J. 2014. "Md. Gubernatorial Hopeful Mizeur Introduces Bill that Would Decriminalize Marijuana." *Washington Post*, February 7. www.washingtonpost.com.

Waldman, E. 2007. "Restorative Justice and the Pre-Condition for Grace: Taking Victims' Needs Seriously." *Cardozo Journal of Conflict Resolution* 9:91–108.

Walker, R. N. 2006. "How the Malfunctioning Death Penalty Challenges the Criminal Justice System." *Judicature* 89 (5):265–69.

———. 1999. *The Police in America*. 3rd ed. New York: McGraw-Hill.

———. 2001. *Sense and Nonsense about Crime and Drugs: A Policy Guide*. 5th ed. Belmont, CA: Wadsworth.

Walker, S., and B. Wright. 1995. "Citizen Review of the Police, 1994: A National Survey." In *Fresh Perspectives*. Washington, DC: Police Executive Research Forum.

Walker, S., C. Spohn, and M. DeLeone. 2012. *The Color of Justice: Race, Ethnicity and Crime in America*. 5th ed. Belmont, CA: Cengage Learning.

Walsh, D. 2013. "The Dangers of Eyewitness Identification: A Call for Greater State Involvement to Ensure Fundamental Fairness." *Boston College International and Comparative Law Review* 36:1415–1453.

Ward, M. 2012. "Parole Rates Surge to Avoid Unsupervised Cases." *Austin American-Statesman,* May 15. www.statesman.com.

Ward, S. 2011. "Tweeting Jurors to Face Jail Time with New California Law." *American Bar Association Journal*, August 8. www.abajournal.com.

Warren, J. 2008. *One in 100: Behind Bars in America 2008*. Washington, DC: Pew Center on the States.

———. 2011. "What Blagojevich's Sentence Says about Corruption and Greed." *New York Times*, December 8. www.nytimes.com.

Warren, P., D. Tomaskovic-Devey, W. Smith, M. Zingraff, and M. Mason. 2006. "Driving while Black: Bias Processes and Racial Disparity in Police Stops." *Criminology* 44:709–38.

Warren, R. 2007. "Evidence-Based Practices and State Sentencing Policy: Ten Policy Initiatives to Reduce Recidivism." *Indiana Law Journal* 82:1307–17.

Washburn, K. K. 2008. "Restoring the Grand Jury." *Fordham Law Review* 76:2333–88.

Washington County Sheriff's Office (OR). 2016. "Electronic Home Detention." Sheriff's Office website. www.co.washington.or.us.

Wasserman, D. T. 1990. *A Sword for the Convicted: Representing Indigent Defendants on Appeal*. New York: Greenwood Press.

Weiner, J. 2013a. "Monitoring Programs Have History of Trouble." *Orlando Sentinel*, May 25. http://www.orlandosentinel.com.

———. 2013b. "Review of Home Confinement Program Finds Lost Defendants, New Crime." *Orlando Sentinel*. March 23. http://www.orlandosentinel.com.

Weinstein, H. 2001. "Georgia High Court Relegates Electric Chair to History." *Los Angeles Times*, October 6. http://www.latimes.com.

Weisberg, R. 2010. "The Not-So-Golden State of Sentencing and Corrections: Calfornia's Lessons for the Nation." *Justice Research and Policy* 12:133–68.

Weisburd, D. 2011. "The Evidence for Place-Based Policing." *Translational Criminology* (Summer), 10–11, 16.

Weisburd, D., J. Hinkle, A. Braga, and A. Wooditch. 2015. "Understanding the Mechanisms Underlying Broken Windows Policing: The Need for Evaluation Evidence." *Journal of Research in Crime and Delinquency* 52:589–608.

Weisburd, D., S. D. Mastrofski, A. M. McNally, R. Greenspan, and J. J. Willis. 2003. "Reforming to Preserve: Compstat and Strategic Problem Solving in American Policing." *Criminology & Public Policy* 2:421–56.

Weisburd, D., C. Telep, J. Hinkle, and J. Eck. 2010. "Is Problem-Oriented Policing Effective in Reducing Crime and Disorder?" *Criminology & Public Policy* 9:139–72.

Weiser, B. 2008. "Police in Gun Searches Face Disbelief in Court." *New York Times*, May 12, p. 1.

———. 2011. "A New York Prosecutor with Worldwide Reach." *New York Times*, March 27. www.nytimes.com.

Weiser, B., and J. Goldstein. 2014. "Mayor Says New York City Will Settle Suits on Stop-and-Frisk Tactics." *New York Times,* January 30. www.nytimes.com.

Weiser, B., and M. Schwirtz. 2014. "U.S. Inquiry Finds a 'Culture of Violence' against Teenage Inmates at Rikers Island." *New York Times*, August 4. www.nytimes.com.

Weiss, D. C. 2008. "New DOJ Rule Expands FBI Database to Include Arrestee DNA." *American Bar Association Journal*, December 12. http://abajournal.com.

———. 2009a. "Calif. DA Dismisses Misdemeanor and Drug Charges in Exchange for DNA." *American Bar Association Journal*, April 15. http://abajournal.com.

———. 2009b. "Fear of Financial Ruin Has More Potential Jurors Claiming Hardship." *American Bar Association Journal*, September 2. www.abajournal.com.

Weisselberg, C. 2011. "Selected Criminal Law Cases in the United States Supreme Court and a Look Ahead." *Court Review* 47:52–62.

Weisselberg, C. D. 2008. "Mourning *Miranda*." *California Law Review* 96:1519–600.

Weitzer, R. 2002. "Incidents of Police Misconduct and Public Opinion." *Journal of Criminal Justice* 30:397–408.

Welch, M. 1994. "Jail Overcrowding: Social Sanitation and the Warehousing of the Urban Underclass." In *Critical Issues in Crime and Justice*, ed. A. Roberts. Thousand Oaks, CA: Sage, 249–74.

Wells, J., and M. Keasler. 2011. "Criminal Procedure: Confessions, Searches, and Seizures." *Southern Methodist University Law Review* 64:199–220.

Welna, D. 2016. "GOP Presidential Candidates Bring Torture Back into the Spotlight." National Public Radio, February 9. www.npr.org.

Wert, J. 2011. *Habeas Corpus in America*. Lawrence, KS: University of Kansas Press.

Westergaard, R., A. Spaulding, and T. Flanigan. 2013. "HIV among Persons Incarcerated in the U.S.: A Review of Evolving Concepts in Testing, Treatment, and Linkage to Community Care." *Current Opinion in Infectious Diseases* 26:10–16.

Wexler, C. 2015. *Re-engineering Training on Police Use of Force.* Washington, DC: Police Executive Research Forum.

"What's Being Done to Address the Country's Backlog of Untested Rape Kits." 2016. National Public Radio, January 17. www.npr.org.

Whetzel, J., M. Paparozzi, M. Alexander, and C. T. Lowenkamp. 2011. "Goodbye to a Worn-Out Dichotomy: Law Enforcement, Social Work, and a Balanced Approach (A Survey of Federal Probation Officer Attitudes)." *Federal Probation* 75:7–12.

White, J. 2004. *Defending the Homeland.* Belmont, CA: Thomson/Wadsworth.

White, M. D., J. Cooper, J. Saunders, and A. J. Raganella. 2010. "Motivations for Becoming a Police Officer: Re-assessing Officer Attitudes and Job Satisfaction after Six Years on the Street. *Journal of Criminal Justice* 38:520–30.

White, M. D., J. Fyfe, S. Campbell, and J. Goldkamp. 2003. "The Police Role in Preventing Homicide: Considering the Impact of Problem-Oriented Policing on the Prevalence of Murder." *Journal of Research in Crime and Delinquency* 40:194–225.

White, M. S. 1995. "The Nonverbal Behaviors in Jury Selection." *Criminal Law Bulletin* 31:414–45.

White, T., and E. Baik. 2010. "Venire Reform: Assessing the State and Federal Efforts to Attain Fair, Cross-Sectional Representation in Jury Pools." *Journal of Social Sciences* 6:113–18.

Williams, C. J. 2010. "Weighed Down by Recession Woes, Jurors Are Becoming Disgruntled." *Los Angeles Times*, February 15. www.latimes.com.

Williams, M. R., S. Demuth, and J. E. Holcomb. 2007. "Understanding the Influence of Victim Gender in Death Penalty Cases: The Importance of Victim Race, Sex-Related Victimization, and Jury Decision Making." *Criminology* 45:865–91.

Williams, T. 2015. "Chicago Rarely Penalizes Officers for Complaints, Data Shows." *New York Times*, November 18. www.nytimes.com.

Williams, V., and M. Fish. 1974. *Convicts, Codes, and Contraband.* Cambridge, MA: Ballinger.

Willis, J., S. Mastrofski, and T. Kochel. 2010. "Recommendations for Integrating Compstat and Community Policing." *Policing: A Journal of Policy and Practice* 4:182–93.

Willis, J. J., S. D. Mastrofski, and D. Weibrud. 2004. "Compstat and Bureaucracy: A Case Study of Challenges and Opportunities for Change." *Justice Quarterly* 21:463–96.

Wilson, J. Q. 1968. *Varieties of Police Behavior.* Cambridge, MA: Harvard University Press.

Wilson, P. 2010. "Norfolk Police May Try 12-Hour Shifts to Offset Budget Cuts." *Virginian-Pilot*, June 13. http:// pilotonline.com.

Winerip. M. 2015. "Rikers Officers Who Hogtied and Beat an Inmate in 2012 Are Fired." *New York Times*, January 21. www.nytimes.com.

Winerip, M., and M. Schwirtz. 2015. "Even as Many Eyes Watch, Brutality at Rikers Island Persists." *New York Times*, February 21. www.nytimes.com

Winkeljohn, M. 2002. "A Random Act of Hate: Duckett's Attack Linked to Racism." *Atlanta Journal and Constitution*, August 4, p. E1.

Winterdyk, J., and R. Ruddell. 2010. "Managing Prison Gangs: Results from a Survey of U.S. Prison Systems." *Journal of Criminal Justice* 38:730–36.

Wiseman, S. 2009. "Discrimination, Coercion, and the Bail Reform Act of 1984." *Fordham Urban Law Journal* 26:121–57.

Witt, H. 2009. "Highway Robbery? Texas Police Seize Black Motorists' Cash, Cars." *Chicago Tribune*, March 10. www.chicagotribune.com.

Witte, B. 2013. "Maryland Death Penalty Repeal Signed into Law by Martin O'Malley." Huffington Post, May 2. http://www.huffingtonpost.com.

WKYC. 2014. "Steubenville Rape Case Defendant/Coach Found Guilty." WKYC News, April 22. http://www.wkyc.com.

Wodahl, E. J., B. Garland, S. E. Culhane, and William P. McCarty. 2011. "Utilizing Behavioral Interventions to Improve Supervision Outcomes in Community-Based Corrections." *Criminal Justice and Behavior* 38:386–405.

Wolcott, R. J. 2015. "Former Northern Michigan Teacher Sentenced to up to 10 Years behind Bars in Student Sex Case." MLIVE.com, January 21. www .mlive.com.

Wolf, A., B. E. Bloom, and B. A. Krisberg. 2008. "The Incarceration of Women in California." *University of San Francisco Law Review* 43:139–70.

Wood, R. W. 2013. "Lauryn Hill Jail Time— What's a Fair Tax Sentence?" *Forbes.* May 7. http://www.forbes.com.

Wooldredge, J. 2012. "Distinguishing Race Effects in Pre-Trial Release and Sentencing Decisions." *Justice Quarterly* 29:41–75.

Worden, A. P. 1993. "The Attitudes of Women and Men in Policing: Testing Conventional and Contemporary Wisdom." *Criminology* 31 (May):203–24.

———. 1995. "The Judge's Role in Plea Bargaining: An Analysis of Judges' Agreement with Prosecutors' Sentencing Recommendations." *Justice Quarterly* 12:257–78.

Worth, R. F. 2001. "73 Tied to Genovese Family Are Indicted, Officials Say." *New York Times*, December 6, p. A27.

Wright, J. 2013. "Applying *Miranda*'s Public Safety Exception to Dzhokhar Tsarnaev: Restricting Criminal Procedure Rights by Expanding Judicial Exceptions." *Columbia Law Review Sidebar* 113:136–55.

Wright, K., and J. Rosky, 2011. "Too Early Is Too Soon: Lessons from the Montana Department of Corrections Early Release Program." *Criminology & Public Policy* 10:881–908.

Wu, J. 2016. "Racial/Ethnic Discrimination and Prosecution: A Meta-Analysis." *Criminal Justice and Behavior* (forthcoming).

Wu, J., and C. Spohn. 2010. "Interdistrict Disparity in Sentencing in Three U.S. District Courts." *Crime and Delinquency* 56:290–322.

Wu, Y. 2014. "Race/Ethnicity and Perceptions of Police: A Comparison of White, Black, Asian, and Hispanic Americans." *Policing and Society* 24: 135–57.

Wyoming Board of Parole. 2016. "Frequently Asked Questions." Wyoming Board of Parole website. http://wyo .gov/bop/home.

Wyoming Highway Patrol. 2014. "WHP Advances to In-Car Computer Aided Dispatch and Reporting." Press release, January 17. www.whp.dot.state.wy.us.

Yang, J. L, and A. Jayakumar. 2014. "Target Says up to 70 Million More Customers Were Hit by December Data Breach." *Washington Post*, January 10, 2014. www.washingtonpost.com.

Yardley, W. 2006. "DNA Samples Link 4 Murders in Connecticut." *New York Times*, June 8. http://www.nytimes.com.

Yu, H. 2015. "An Examination of Women in Federal Law Enforcement: An Exploratory Analysis of the Challenges They Face in the Work Environment." *Feminist Criminology* 10: 259–78.

Zagaris, B. 1998. "U.S. International Cooperation against Transnational Organized Crime." *Wayne Law Review* 44 (Fall):1401–64.

Zaitz, L. 2011. "Oregon Taxpayers Pay Spiraling Cost of Prison Health Care with No Solution in Sight." June 18, 2011. http://oregonlive.com.

Zalman, M., and B. W. Smith. 2007. "The Attitudes of Police Executives toward *Miranda* and Interrogation Policies." *Journal of Criminal Law and Criminology* 97:873–942.

Zedlewski, E. 2010. "Alternatives to Custodial Supervision: The Day Fine."

National Institute of Justice Discussion Paper, April. NCJ 230401. https:// www.ncjrs.gov/pdffiles1/nij/grants /230401.pdf.

Zedner, L. 1995. "Wayward Sisters." In *The Oxford History of Prisons*, eds. N. Morris and D. J. Rothman. New York: Oxford University Press, 329–61.

Zeidman, S. 2012. "Whither the Criminal Court: Confronting Stops-and-Frisks." *Albany Law Review* 76:1187–9.

Zhang, Y., L. Zhang, and M. Vaughn. 2014. "Indeterminate and Determinate Sentencing Models: A State-Specific Analysis of Their Effects on Recidivism." *Crime and Delinquency* 60:693–715.

Zhao, J., C. Gibson, N. Lovrich, and M. Gaffney. 2002. "Participation in Community Crime Prevention: Are Volunteers More or Less Fearful of Crime?" *Journal of Crime & Justice* 25:41–61.

Zhao, J. S., N. P. He, N. Loverich, and J. Cancino. 2003. "Marital Status and Police Occupational Stress." *Journal of Crime & Justice* 26:23–46.

Zimmerman, E. 2011. "The Federal Sentencing Guidelines: A Misplaced Trust." *University of Michigan Journal of Law Reform* 43:841–70.

Zimring, F. E. 2007. *The Great American Crime Decline*. New York: Oxford University Press.

Name Index

Subject Index

Accelerated release of offenders, 458, 459
Accusatory process, 259
Active electronic monitoring equipment, 441
Actus reus, 94
Adams v. Williams, 216, 222
Adjudication, 22
Administrative Office of the U.S. Courts, 357, 435, 497
Adolescent Diversion Project (ADP), 536
ADP. *See* Adolescent Diversion Project (ADP)
Adversarial process, 239
Affidavit, 211
African Americans. *See also* Race and ethnicity
 "Black Lives Matter," 30, 210, 284
 crack cocaine, 320, 341, 342
 deaths of blacks at hands of white police, 30
 Ferguson, Missouri, grand jury (2014), 256–257
 improperly running justice system to make money for city, 335–336
 racial disparities, 33
 Scottsboro boys, 108
 stop-and-frisk search, 38–40
Aftercare, 544
Age
 crime, 63–56
 crime victimization, 67
 juveniles. *See* Juvenile justice
 police, 136
 police discretion, 165
 prison inmates, 399
 violence in prison, 418
Age Discrimination in Employment Act, 375
Aggravated assault, 92
Aggressive patrol, 183, 185
AIDS, prisoners with, 400–401
Air guns, 505
Americans with Disabilities Act, 375
Anti-Contract Law of 1887, 353
Antisocial personality, 77
Antiterrorism and Effective Death Penalty Act, 306
Antiterrorism task force, 181
Appeal, 26, 305–307
Appellate courts, 240–241
Apprehension process, 180, 181
Aramark Corporation, 410
Argersinger v. Hamlin, 264
Arizona v. Gant, 217, 229
Arraignment, 25–26, 277–278
Arrest, 24–25, 210
Arrest warrant, 277, 503
Arson, 92
Asset forfeiture, 439–441
Assigned counsel, 265–267
ATF. *See* Bureau of Alcohol, Tobacco, Firearms, and Explosives (ATF)
Atkins v. Virginia, 327
Attorney effectiveness and competence, 267–268, 329
Austin v. United States, 114
Automobile searches, 218–222
Avastin, 487

Backscatter X-rays (airports), 502
Bail, 280. *See also* Bail system
Bail agents, 282–283
Bail bondsman, 282–283
Bail fund, 285
Bail guidelines, 285–286
Bail Reform Act, 114, 286
Bail system, 113–114, 280–286
 bail, defined, 280
 bail agents, 282–283
 bail fund, 285
 bail guidelines, 285–286
 consequences of failing to make bail, 281
 excessive bail, 280
 median bail amounts, 282
 percentage bail, 285
 reforming the system, 284
 setting bail, 283–284
 ten percent cash bail, 285
Bailey v. United States, 212
Ballistic evidence, 495
Ban on plea bargaining, 290
"Ban the box," 472
Barron v. Baltimore, 108
BART. *See* Bay Area Regional Transit (BART)
Batson v. Kentucky, 298, 299
Bay Area Regional Transit (BART), 172
Baze v. Rees, 327

Beanbag projectile weapons, 505
Beard v. Banks, 367
Bell v. Wolfish, 371
Bench trial, 26, 294
Berhuis v. Thompkins, 225
Bicycle patrol, 184
Big house, 386
Bill of Rights, 103–108, 212
Biological explanations, 74–75, 82
"Black Lives Matter," 30, 210, 284
Blackledge v. Allison, 288
Blakely v. Washington, 339
Blue-coat crime, 170
Board of Education v. Earls, 526
"Bobbies," 123
Body cameras, 174–175, 489, 502
Bones (TV), 300, 509
Booking, 25, 277
Boot camp, 331, 445–446, 542
Bordenkircher v. Hayes, 292
Border and Transportation Security (DHS), 14
Bow Street Runners, 123
Boykin v. Alabama, 292
Brady v. Maryland, 252
Breaking and entering (burglary), 92
Breed v. Jones, 526
Brewer v. Williams, 231
Brigham City, Utah v. Stuart, 217
Brink's, 200
"Broken Windows: The Police and Neighborhood Safety" (Wilson/Kelling), 127
Broken windows theory, 185
Bronx Freedom Fund, 285
Brown v. Mississippi, 223
Brown v. Plata, 371, 373, 416, 460
Budget cuts
 accelerated release of offenders, 458
 closing of reentry facilities (Florida), 455
 courts, 242
 crime labs, 496
 defense attorney, 266
 effect of, 15
 incarceration, 321
 juvenile justice, 544
 nonviolent felonies, 91
 policing, 130, 150, 188
 prerelease facilities and programs, 469
 probation, 430, 434
 reentry into the community, 454, 469, 474
 resource scarcity, 279
 violence in prison, 421
Bumper v. North Carolina, 218, 222
Burch v. Louisiana, 295
Bureau of Alcohol, Tobacco, Firearms, and Explosives (ATF), 132, 136, 226
Bureau of Prisons, 357, 415, 445, 496
Burger Court era, 112
Burglary, 92, 94
Burns International Security Services, 200

CAGI. *See* Comprehensive Anti-Gang Initiative (CAGI)
CALEA. *See* Commission on Accreditation for Law Enforcement Agencies (CALEA)
California v. Acevedo, 221, 222
Capital punishment. *See* Death penalty
Carroll v. United States, 218, 222
Catching a suspect, 180, 181
CATs. *See* Cyber action teams (CATs)
Causation, 94
CCA. *See* Corrections Corporation of America (CCA)
CCE. *See* Continuing Criminal Enterprise Act (CCE)
CED. *See* Conducted energy device (CED)
Celebrity tax offenders (Close Up box), 338
Chain of command, 151–152
Challenge for cause, 297
ChalleNGe programs, 446
Challenges, 297–299
Chandler v. Miller, 526
Charging, 25
Child pornography, 485
Child savers, 525
Chimel v. California, 216, 222
CHINS (Children in Need of Services) program, 544
Cincinnati Declaration of Principles, 353, 354
Circuit court, 241
Circumstantial evidence, 299
CIT. *See* Crisis intervention training (CIT)
Citation, 284
Citizen crime-watch groups, 191

City of Indianapolis v. Edmond, 215, 222
Civic accountability, 171–175, 375
Civil forfeiture laws, 440
Civil infractions, 90
Civil law, 89
Civil liability lawsuits, 174, 375, 503–505
Civil Rights Act of 1871, 366
Civil Rights Act of 1964, 375
Civil service laws, 375
Civilian review board, 172
Clark v. Arizona, 100
Classical criminology, 73
Classification, 412–413
Classified documents, releasing, 55
Clearance rate, 178
Close Up boxes
 automobile searches, 219–221
 criminal intent and appropriateness of punishment, 97
 Flint, Michigan water crisis, 75–76
 gunshot detection technology, 493
 Heien v. North Carolina, 219–221
 Holt v. Hobbs, 369
 life in prison, 388–389
 PERF's 2016 proposed principles on use of force, 168–169
 police training, 140
 private probation, 432–433
 problem-solving courts, 246
 scientific evidence and "CSI effect," 300
 sentencing disparities (celebrity tax offenders), 338
 stop-and-frisk search (African American), 38–40
 survival tips for prison first-timers, 403
Closing arguments, 302
CNN.com/CRIME, 113
Coast Guard, 14
Cocaine, 320, 341, 342
CODIS, 496
Coercion (duress), 98
College campuses, sexual assaults, 69
Colonial era and early republic, 124, 349
Commission on Accreditation for Law Enforcement Agencies (CALEA), 172
Commissioners, 123
Community-based outreach teams, 169
Community-based residential correctional facilities, 469
Community corrections, 355–356
 assumptions, 426–427
 defined, 355
 future of, 448
 least restrictive alternative, 427
 legal issues, 374–375
 parole. *See also* Parole
 placement of community corrections centers, 444
 probation, 377. *See also* Probation
 state-by-state variability, 357
 technological advancements, 513
Community crime prevention, 191
Community justice, 429
Community model of corrections, 349, 355–356
Community policing, 128, 130, 185–187
Community policing era (1970-present), 127–129
Community prosecution, 258
Community service, 331, 442–443
Comprehensive Anti-Gang Initiative (CAGI), 522
Comprehensive Crime Control Act, 102
Compstat, 177
Computer crime, 35, 485. *See also* Cybercrime
Computers, 490–492
Concurrence, 95
Conditions of release, 466
Conducted energy device (CED), 506
Congregated system, 352
Connick v. Thompson, 252, 253
Consent search, 218, 222
Constitution of the United States. *See* U.S. Constitution
Constitutional rights of prisoners, 366–372
 cruel and unusual punishment, 371
 due process. *See* Procedural criminal law
 Eighth Amendment, 371
 equal protection, 372
 First Amendment, 367–368
 Fourteenth Amendment, 371–372
 Fourth Amendment, 368–371
 freedom of speech and religion, 367–368, 369
 Myth & Reality, 367
 prison discipline, 372

Constitutional rights of prisoners (*Continued*)
  prisoners' rights movement, 372
  search and seizure, 368–371
Continuance, 269
Continuing Criminal Enterprise Act (CCE), 439
Contract counsel, 265, 266–267
Contract labor system, 352
Contractual security services, 200–201
Control theories, 78
Controversies. *See* Current Controversies in Criminal Justice
Coolidge v. New Hampshire, 207
Cooper v. Pate, 366, 375
Copping a plea (copping out), 286. *See also* Plea bargaining
COPS Hiring Program, 129
COPS Office, 129
Correctional costs, 375–376
Correctional officers
  civil service laws, 375
  discretion, 17
  female officers, 396
  liability, 375
  minority officers, 396
  Myth & Reality, 392
  preservice training, 396–397
  recruitment, 395–397
  role, 395
  salaries, 396
  Section 1983 lawsuits, 174, 375
  sexually assaulting female prisoners, 409
  use of force, 397
  violence in prison, 420
Corrections, 22, 26
  correctional populations (1992-2012), 375
  costs of, 375–376
  federal system, 357
  historical overview, 348–356
  jail. *See* Jail
  juvenile justice, 540–545
  prison. *See* Prison
  private prisons, 360–361
  specific correctional eras, 349
  state systems, 357–360
  technological advancements, 511–512, 513
Corrections Corporation of America (CCA), 360
Costs of crime, 70
Count, 255
Counterfeit building products, 488
Counterfeit medications, 487–488
Counterfeiting, 486–488
Counterterrorism, 13
County law enforcement agencies, 133
Court of appeal, 240–241
Court of last resort, 240
COURT-TV, 113
Courtroom work group, 269–270, 288
Courts and adjudication, 237–273
  adversarial process, 239
  appellate courts, 240–241
  budget cuts, 242
  decentralization, 242
  defense attorney. *See* Defense attorney
  dual court system, 21–22, 242
  federal court system, 241, 242
  felony courts, 337
  functions of courts, 239–240
  judge. *See* Judge
  local legal culture, 268–269
  misdemeanor courts, 335
  norm enforcement function, 239–240
  policy making, 240
  problem-solving courts, 241, 246
  prosecutor. *See* Prosecutorial system
  state court system, 242
  structure of court, 240–242
  Supreme Court. *See* Supreme Court
  technological advancements, 507–510, 513
  trial courts, 240
  tribal courts, 239
  work groups, 269–270
Crack cocaine, 320, 341, 342
Creaming, 447
Credit card companies, 197
Crime
  blue-coat, 170
  causes. *See* Theories of crime
  costs of, 70
  cyber, 56–58, 483–486
  defined, 6
  elements of, 93–94
  fear of, 71
  how much is there?. *See* Crime statistics
  occupational, 52
  organized, 52–53, 54
  political, 55–56
  rate of, 378

routine activity explanations, 66
  transnational, 53–54
  trends, 63–65
  types, 51–58
  victimless, 54–55
  victims. *See* Crime victimization
  visible, 51–52
Crime and Human Nature (Wilson/Herrnstein), 74
Crime control model
  corrections (correctional era), 349, 356
  criminal justice system, 28, 29
Crime control period (1980-2005), 524, 527–528
Crime labs. *See* Technology and criminal justice
Crime rate, 378
Crime statistics
  dark figure of crime, 59
  discrepancies between various measures, 63
  NCVS, 61–62
  NIBRS, 61
  UCR. *See* Uniform Crime Reports (UCR)
  violent and property victimizations (2014), 59
Crime Stoppers, 191
Crime victimization, 65–72
  acquaintances and strangers, 69–70
  experience of victims in justice system, 71–72
  low-income city dwellers, 68
  parole, 462–463
  role of victims, 72
  sexual assaults on college campuses, 69
  violent crime, 67
  who is victimized?, 66–68
  women, youths, nonwhites, 67–68
Criminal defense. *See* Defense attorney
Criminal homicide, 91, 92
Criminal justice process
  appeal, 305–307
  arraignment, 25–26, 277–278
  bail. *See* Bail system
  booking, 25, 277
  felony case. *See* Felony case
  flowchart, 24
  habeas corpus, 306
  initial appearance, 25, 277
  jury trial. *See* Jury trial
  Michigan vs. Jones, 44–47
  overview, 23–27
  plea bargaining. *See* Plea bargaining
  sentencing. *See* Sentencing
Criminal justice system
  controversies. *See* Current Controversies in Criminal Justice
  decision-making process, 23–27
  discretion, 17
  employees, 14
  filtering, 19–20, 278
  goals, 6–8
  police bureaucracy, 152–153
  process. *See* Criminal justice process
  racial bias, 36–41
  resource dependence, 18
  sequential tasks, 19
  social system, 15–16
  wedding cake model, 27–28
Criminal justice wedding cake, 27–28
Criminal law
  foundations, 89–90
  procedural. *See* Procedural criminal law
  seven principles, 94–95
  substantive law. *See* Substantive criminal law
Criminal sanction, 318. *See also* Punishment
Criminogenic, 74
Crisis intervention training (CIT), 145
Critical criminology, 79, 82
Critical Decision-Making Model, 169
Cross-examination, 301
Cruel and unusual punishment, 114–115, 371
CSI: Crime Scene Investigation (TV), 180, 300, 479, 483, 510
CSI effect, 300, 301, 509
Cupp v. Murphy, 217
Current Controversies in Criminal Justice
  asset forfeiture, 440
  criticism of police officers, 31–32
  cyberbullying, 547
  Ferguson, Missouri, grand jury (2014), 256–257
  improperly running justice system to make money for city, 335–336
  mandating corporations' technological assistance (Apple case), 208
  military equipment and local police, 504
  police "code of silence," 173
  President's Task Force on 21st Century Policing, 145
  prison inmates' phone calls, 362
  privatization of services in prison and risk of miscon- duct, 410
  racial disparities and aggressive policing, 107–108

sexting, 547
  terrorism, 56–57
  voucher system for criminal defense?, 291
Custodial model, 387
Customs and Border Protection, 133, 488
Cyber action teams (CATs), 486
Cyberbullying, 546, 547
Cybercrime, 56–58, 483–486

Dark figure of crime, 59
Data analysis techniques, 130, 492
Databases, 492–495
Day fine, 438
Day reporting center, 443
De-escalation, 169
DEA. *See* Drug Enforcement Administration (DEA)
Deadlocked jury, 304
Deadly force, 209. *See also* Use of force
Death penalty, 323–332
  abolishment?, 332
  constitutionality, 326–328
  death-qualified juries, 329–330
  death row census (2016), 324
  effectiveness of counsel, 329
  legal issues, 328
  mentally ill inmates, 329
  new death sentences and executions (1980-2013), 325
  What Americans Think, 329
Death-qualified juries, 329–330
Decision-making process, 23–27. *See also* Criminal justice process
Declaration of Independence, 30
Defense attorney, 260–268
  assigned counsel, 266, 267
  attorney effectiveness and competence, 267–268, 329
  budget cuts, 266
  contract system, 266–267
  defined, 260
  environment of criminal practice, 263
  felony case (typical actions), 261–262
  indigent defendants, 263–266
  plea bargaining, 288
  pretrial proceedings, 278
  public defender, 262, 265, 267
  realities of the job, 262
  role, 261–262
  specialists in criminal defense, 262
  state-run/county-run systems, 265
  voucher system, 291
Defenses against criminal charges
  duress (coercion), 98
  entrapment, 98–99
  excuse defenses, 98–102
  infancy, 99
  insanity, 100–102
  intoxication, 100
  justification defenses, 96–98
  mistake of fact, 99–100
  necessity, 98
  self-defense, 96–98
Definitions (glossary), 550–558
Delaware v. Prouse, 215
Delinquent, 530
Demonstrative evidence, 299
Deoxyribonucleic acid (DNA), 495
Department contract model, 198
Department of Homeland Security (DHS), 13, 14, 192, 494. *See also* Homeland security
Department of Justice, 132
Dependent child, 531
Deserved punishment, 314
Detectives, 150, 180
Detention hearing, 535
Determinate sentence, 319–320
Deterrence, 314–315, 318
Detroit Reentry Center, 455
DHS. *See* Department of Homeland Security (DHS)
Dickerson v. United States, 225
Differential response, 177
Direct evidence, 299
Directed patrol, 184
Discovery, 255
Discretion, 17
  police, 164–166
  prosecutor, 17, 254–255
Discretionary release, 460
Discrimination, 34
Disorganized criminal, 404
Disparity, 34
Dispatchers, 490
District Attorney's Office v. Osborne, 342
District of Columbia v. Heller, 104–105
Diversion, 534, 536
DNA. *See* Deoxyribonucleic acid (DNA)
DNA analysis, 495–499
DNA databases, 496–497

R. J. v. Jones, 543
Race and ethnicity, 189–190
    African Americans. See African Americans
    aggressive policing practices, 107–108, 185
    biased criminal justice system, 36–41
    correctional officers, 396
    crime victimization, 67, 68
    explaining the disparities, 34–41
    implicit bias, 143
    jail inmates, 364
    juvenile justice, 541
    low-income city dwellers, 68
    minority judges, 244
    multiracial feminism, 81
    Native American Tribal Police, 133–134
    organized crime, 53
    parolees, 467
    people of color commit more crimes, 34–36
    police discretion, 165
    police officers, 138
    poverty, 36
    preemptory challenge, 297–299
    prison gangs, 418
    prison inmates, 399
    racial disparities, 33
    racially biased society, 41
    sentencing, 340–341
    tribal courts, 239
    unemployment, 36
    violence in prison, 418
    What Americans Think, 34, 190
Racial profiling, 36, 37
Racketeer Influence and Corrupt Organizations Act
    (RICO), 439
Rape kits, 498
Reactive, 176
Real evidence, 299
Reasonable doubt, 302
Reasonable expectation of privacy, 207
Rebuttal witnesses, 302
Recidivism, 398–399, 413, 427
Reentry courts, 474
Reentry into the community, 451–477
    adjustment to life outside prison, 471–473
    "ban the box," 472
    budget cuts, 454, 469, 474
    community programs following release, 467–469
    discretionary release, 460
    employment of ex-prisoners, 472
    evidence-based practices, 475
    expiration release, 458
    future of prisoner reentry, 474–475
    institutional reentry preparation programs, 454–455
    invisible punishment, 471
    mandatory release, 458
    NIMBY ("not in my backyard") attitude, 469
    other conditional release, 458–460
    parole. See Parole
    prerelease facilities and programs, 455
    reentry courts, 474
    reentry preparation programs, 454–455
    reentry problem, 453, 467, 471, 511
    release mechanisms, 457–466
    requirements of successful reentry, 453–454
    Rip Van Winkle effect, 511
    sexual offender notification laws, 471–472
Reentry preparation programs, 454–455
Reentry problem, 453, 467, 471, 511
Reform school, 524
Reformatory, 353
Reformatory movement, 349, 353–354
Refuge period (1824-1899), 523–525
Rehabilitation, 316–317, 318
Rehabilitation model, 349, 354–355, 387–388
Reintegration model, 388
Release, 27
Release mechanisms, 457–466
Release on recognizance (ROR), 25, 285
Releasing classified documents, 55
Religious freedom, 367–368, 369
Religious Freedom Restoration Act (RFRA), 368
Religious Land Use and Institutionalized Persons Act
    (RLUIPA), 368
Remote-controlled stun belt, 512
Resource dependence, 18
Resource scarcity, 279
Restitution, 331, 438–439
Restorative justice, 317
Retribution, 313–314, 318
RFRA. See Religious Freedom Restoration Act (RFRA)
Ricketts v. Adamson, 292
RICO. See Racketeer Influence and Corrupt Organizations
    Act (RICO)
Right to bear arms, 241
Right to counsel, 112, 263, 264
Right to impartial jury, 113
Right to speedy and public trial, 112–113

Riley v. California, 206, 212, 216, 502
Rip Van Winkle effect, 511
RLUIPA. See Religious Land Use and Institutionalized
    Persons Act (RLUIPA)
Robbery, 92
Robinson v. California, 94
Rodriguez v. United States, 110, 209
Roper v. Simmons, 327, 526, 528, 548
ROR. See Release on own recognizance (ROR)
Rosewood (TV), 300, 509
Ross v. Moffitt, 112, 264
Rothgery v. Gillespie County, Texas, 264
Routine activity explanations of crime, 66
"Roving" surveillance, 502
Rubber bullets, 505

S. H. v. Reed, 543
Safford Unified School District #1 v. Redding, 526
Samson v. California, 374
Santobello v. New York, 288, 292
Schall v. Martin, 526, 527, 528
Schedule I narcotic, 58
School resource officer (SRO), 181–182, 532–533
Science and Technology (DHS), 14
Scientific evidence, 300
Scott v. Illinois, 112
Scottsboro boys, 108
Search and seizure, 109–111
    definitions, 207, 208
    drug-sniffing dog, 208
    GPS, 208
    mere suspicion, 211
    Myth & Reality, 221
    objective reasonableness, 210
    plain view doctrine, 207
    prisoners, 368–371
    probable cause, 210–212
    reasonable expectation of privacy, 207
    search warrant, 210–212
    stop, 209
    technology-based issues, 514
    totality of circumstances test, 212
    use of force, 209–210
    warrantless search. See Warrantless searches
Search by consent, 218, 222
Search incident to lawful arrest, 216–217, 222
Search warrant, 210–212, 502, 503
Second Amendment, 103, 241
Secret Service, 14, 133, 136, 180
Section 1983 lawsuits, 174, 366, 375
Secure juvenile facilities, 542
Security at borders, 192
Security management and private policing, 196–201
    contractual security services, 200–201
    functions, 197
    growth, 196
    homeland security, 197
    licensing requirements, 200
    private employment of public police, 197–198
    proprietary security personnel, 201
    public-private interface, 198–199
    recruitment and training, 199–201
    wages/salaries, 200
Security threat groups, 418
Seizure, 208. See also Search and seizure
Selective incapacitation, 316
Self-defense, 96–98
Self-incrimination, 111, 222, 301
Sentencing, 26, 40, 333–341. See also Incarceration
    blameworthiness, 337
    celebrity tax offenders (Close Up box), 338
    costs to correctional system, 338
    evidence-based sentencing (EBS), 334
    felony courts, 337
    going rate, 269
    guidelines, 339–341
    Minnesota Sentencing Guidelines Grid, 340
    misdemeanor courts, 335
    Myth & Reality, 315
    practical implications of sentence, 337
    presentence report, 338–339
    protection of the community, 337
    racial disparities, 340–341
    tougher sentencing practices, 377, 379
    wrongful convictions, 341
Sentencing guidelines, 339–341
Separate confinement, 351
Sequestration of jury, 304
Service, 149
Service style, 156
Seven principles of criminal law, 94–95
Sex offenders, 471–472, 511, 515
Sex trafficking, 54
Sexting, 547
Sexual assault, 69
Sexual offender notification laws, 471–472
Sheriff, 125

Shire reeve, 125
Shock incarceration, 331, 445
Shock probation, 323
Showup, 228
"Silent Guardian" (weapon), 506
Sisters in Crime (Adler), 81
Sixth Amendment, 106, 112–113
Skinner v. Oklahoma, 74
Slave patrols, 124
Slavery by Another Name: The Re-Enslavement of Black
    Americans from the Civil War to World War II
    (Blackmon), 353
Smith v. Daily Mail Publishing Co., 526
Snyder v. Louisiana, 298
Social conflict theories, 79
Social process theories, 78–79, 82
Social sanitation, 287
Social structure theories, 77–78, 82
Socialization, 141
Sociological explanations, 77–79
Sociopath, 77
Soft technology, 512, 513
Solitary confinement, 542–543
South Dakota v. Opperman, 221
Special jurisdiction agencies, 134
Special operations, 180–182
Special Operations Bureau, 151
Special populations, 189
Special units, 152
Specific deterrence, 314
Split probation, 323
SRO. See School resource officer (SRO)
Standards and accreditation, 172–173
Stanford v. Kentucky, 526
STARR program, 435
START. See Study of Terrorism and Responses to
    Terrorism (START)
State attorney general, 250
State corrections systems, 357–360
State court system, 242
State law enforcement agencies, 133
State of Prisons in England and Wales, The
    (Howard), 350
State of Recidivism: The Revolving Door of
    America's Prisons (Pew Center), 455
State politics, 380–381
State-raised youth, 544
State supreme court, 240
Status offenses, 527, 531, 544
Statute of Winchester, 123
Stop, 209
Stop-and-frisk search
    African Americans, 38–40
    defined, 215
    exclusionary rule, 215
    New York City, 107
    requirements for legal stop and frisk, 215
    Supreme Court cases, 222
    Terry v. Ohio, 215
Stranger-in-the-bushes stereotype of rape, 69
Street crime, 51
Stress, 146–147
Strickland v. Washington, 264, 329
Strict liability offenses, 95
Study of Terrorism and Responses to Terrorism
    (START), 57
Styles of policing, 155–156
Subculture, 141
Substantial capacity test, 101–102
Substantive criminal law, 90–102
    defenses. See Defenses against criminal charges
    defined, 89
    definitions of offenses, 91–93
    elements of a crime, 93–94
    federal vs. state penal codes, 91
    felonies/misdemeanors, 90, 91
    seven principles of criminal law, 94–95
    statute law, 103
Summary (bench) trial, 26
Summer Night Lights, 83
Super predators, 521
Supermax prison, 358
Supreme Court
    bias in favor of police action, 116
    caseload, 241
    court of last resort, 241
    exclusionary rule, 232
    justices, 116–117, 241
    juvenile justice, 526
    right to counsel, 264
    warrantless searches, 222
Surveillance cameras, 499–502
Survey of Youth in Residential Placement (SYRP), 542
Sworn officers, 179
SYRP. See Survey of Youth in Residential
    Placement (SYRP)
System, 15